ONE WORLD OF LITERATURE

 Houghton Mifflin Company

College Division

Marybeth Chapman
Sales Representative

University Square
101 Campus Drive
Princeton, N.J. 08540

(609) 452-0200
(800) 445-6575

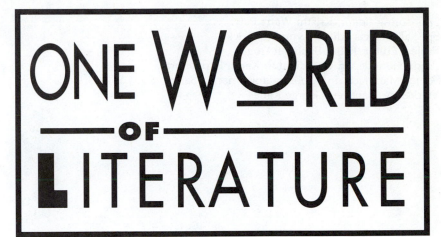

ONE WORLD OF LITERATURE

Shirley Geok-lin Lim

University of California at Santa Barbara

Norman A. Spencer

Nassau Community College, State University of New York

As part of Houghton Mifflin's ongoing commitment to the environment, this text has been printed on recycled paper.

Houghton Mifflin Company   Boston   Toronto
Dallas   Geneva, Illinois   Palo Alto   Princeton, New Jersey

Sponsoring Editor: Kristin Watts Perri
Special Projects Editor: Lynn Walterick
Project Editor: Robin Bushnell Hogan
Production/Design Coordinator: Karen Rappaport
Senior Manufacturing Coordinator: Priscilla Bailey
Marketing Manager: George Kane

Cover and interior design by Catherine Hawkes

Printed in the USA.

Library of Congress Catalog Card Number: 91-71975
ISBN: 0-395-58880-4

123456789-AH-96 95 94 93 92

TABLE OF CONTENTS

ASIA   191

AUSTRALIA AND OCEANIA   373

EUROPE   477

LATIN AMERICA AND
THE CARIBBEAN   753

NORTH AMERICA 905

PREFACE

One World of Literature is intended for instructors who want a collection that significantly enlarges the repertoire of standard anthologies. What distinguishes this book is its insistence on reading literature as an international phenomenon and, even within nations such as the United States, as multicultural texts. Our twofold purpose may at first seem paradoxical, but ultimately it is not: to introduce the rich diversity of national literatures and, through this experience, to arrive at an understanding of the global nature of that very human endeavor, writing.

Several major premises underlie the creation of *One World:*

- **We live in an age in which an understanding of global cultures is more critical than ever.** National borders are only temporary and frail fences that do not isolate the lives within them. We are all affected by individuals, events, and ideas from other cultures and countries, a truth the late twentieth century has brought home to almost everyone. *One World* seeks to counter suppositions of homogeneity, universalism, and ethnocentrism that may arise from reading parochially—reading only one type of literature, for example, or literature written in only one language. We have collected 165 selections from 52 countries on all 6 inhabited continents; the text is organized geographically, grouping selections by country within each continent unit. The number of works in English from such English-speaking countries as the United States, Canada, Australia, New Zealand, Britain, and Ireland is balanced by the number of works in translation from such languages as Bahasa Indonesian, Chinese, Japanese, French, Spanish, German, Russian, and others. We have paid careful attention to works by women and diverse ethnic, racial and class groups within continents.
- **A contemporary focus offers particular relevance and accessibility to students.** We have chosen to focus on twentieth-century and contemporary writing for several important reasons. The twentieth century has seen the collapse of empires East and West; it has seen the retreat of imperialism and colonialism and the shift from feudal agrarian societies to industrial and metropolitan ones. As technological advances such as air travel and telecommunications have broken down physical and cultural isolationism, more and more people have sought empowerment and protection through the ideology of a national identity, and ancient and new ethnicities have often led to communal pride and hostile con-

frontations. The literature written in every country in this century has reflected, expressed, and embodied these international forces and events. Not so paradoxically, therefore, we can find in the most local of contexts the echo, trace, or imprint of global cause and effect.

Yet technology—although it has made physical contact with other cultures easier—has not enhanced our ability to comprehend and absorb the massive amounts of information about the world we receive daily. Stories, poems, and plays—among the most traditional forms of human communication—have the power to work on our imagination. Literature is a master guide that enables us to enter, through imagination, both ordinary and strange worlds and to cross borders of race, ethnicity, class, and culture.

- **An anthology should collect selections that have not only significant literary quality but also strong social content that interests students.** We have chosen works that possess high qualities of imagination, literary power, and beauty, and that give students an entry to understanding human experience in our own and other cultural domains. Students will be able to see global commonalities—as reflected, for example, in the omnipresence of such themes as gender construction, relations between the sexes, the rights of women. They will also observe some of the ways that the sociopolitical experiences of nations and regions cause certain issues to be foregrounded in the literatures of those places. Indeed, many of the selections from places that have experienced colonialism or great social conflict, such as Latin America, South Africa, and Eastern Europe, are often marked by more overtly political themes than those from other places.
- **Strong contextualizing materials enhance readers' understanding and appreciation of literature.** We have provided what we believe are thorough and thoughtful instructional materials to accompany the selections in *One World*.

  - *Introductory essays to each continental unit* provide sociohistorical, geographic, cultural, and literary background. Each introduction includes a *map* of the continent; a map of the world appears in the front of the text.
  - Each selection is prefaced by a *headnote* giving biographical information about the author and contextualizing the selection.
  - *Study questions,* designed to help students think and write about their reading, follow each selection.
  - Appearing at the end of the text are brief *essays about genres*—fiction, poetry, and drama—as well as a *discussion of translation,* a *brief guide to researching and documenting literature papers,* a *glossary of literary terms and movements,* and a selected *bibliography of secondary sources* for individual countries and writers.

For the instructor, we have written an *Instructor's Resource Manual* that discusses themes among the selections, offers suggestions for teaching a thematic table of contents, and provides workups for each selection in the anthology. It includes two alternate tables of contents, one thematic and one organized by genre.

But, strongly as we believe in the importance of contextualizing materials, we want to stress that in no way do we see our editorial interventions as an end unto themselves. The end they do share is this: to lead the reader back to the stories, poems, and plays that help us see the one world in so many divergent worlds.

Many people contributed generously to this text. We thank our assistant editors, Phyllis Fahrie Edelson of Pace University and Gundega Kazaks of the Convent of the Sacred Heart, for the introductions, headnotes, and study questions for the section on Australia and the unit on Europe. Thanks also to George Kane, Carolyn Potts, and Lynn Walterick at Houghton Mifflin for helping us shape this anthology. We are grateful to our families and our institutions for their support and our colleagues Kitty Dean, Julie Marzàn Aishah Rahman, and Jill Levine for their advice. We owe a special debt to Walter Sullivan of the State University of New York, who invited us to participate in a seminar on internationalizing the English curriculum, funded by the National Endowment for the Humanities. And we thank our colleagues around the country who reviewed our work and offered meaningful recommendations:

Peter Baker, Towson State University
John Bellue, West Virginia Institute of Technology
Rebecca Bushnell, University of Pennsylvania
William T. Cotton, Loyola University (LA)
Lisa Gerrard, University of California, Los Angeles
Donald Gray, Indiana University, Bloomington
David S. Gross, University of Oklahoma
Barbara Harlow, University of Texas at Austin
Marina Heung, Bernard M. Baruch College
David Lenson, University of Massachusetts at Amherst
John Pekins, Tallahassee Community College
Raquel Halty Pfaff, Simmons College
Melita Schaum, University of Michigan, Dearborn
Joseph Skerrett, Jr., University of Massachusetts at Amherst
Eric Solomon, San Francisco State University
Gregory L. Ulmer, University of Florida
Michael Vivion, University of Missouri, Kansas City
Maria Elena Yepes, East Los Angeles College

Shirley Geok-lin Lim
Norman A. Spencer

THEMATIC TABLE

OF CONTENTS

ONE WORLD
OF
LITERATURE

AFRICA AND THE MIDDLE EAST

AFRICA AND THE MIDDLE EAST

Introduction

B ounded by the Atlantic and Indian oceans and the Mediterranean and Red seas, the continent of Africa is exceeded in size by Asia alone. Marked by diversity, its population of three hundred million is organized in over fifty countries and speaks hundreds of local languages and dialects as well as French, English, Portuguese, Arabic, and Swahili. Although Africa lies astride the equator, areas with tropical rain forests are few. More typical of the environment are regions with savanna grasslands and deserts. Most of the population is concentrated along the coasts or in close proximity to river basins. The majority of Africans are small-scale traditional farmers. The more skilled and educated people are found in urban centers, which have the highest standard of living. Overall the continent is well endowed with mineral resources such as coal, iron, petroleum, uranium, gold, and diamonds. The distribution of these resources, however, is uneven. Except for South Africa, this wealth of mineral deposits has not led to large-scale industrialization.

Topographically, Africa has few major impediments to travel and migration. The great mountain ranges and deserts have not provided insurmountable obstacles to population movement. Hence, Africa has never been cut off from the crosscurrents of world history. For centuries great communication lines have existed between Africa and other parts of the world. The continent was linked to Asia through its participation in the Indian Ocean trading system while caravan routes across the Sahara

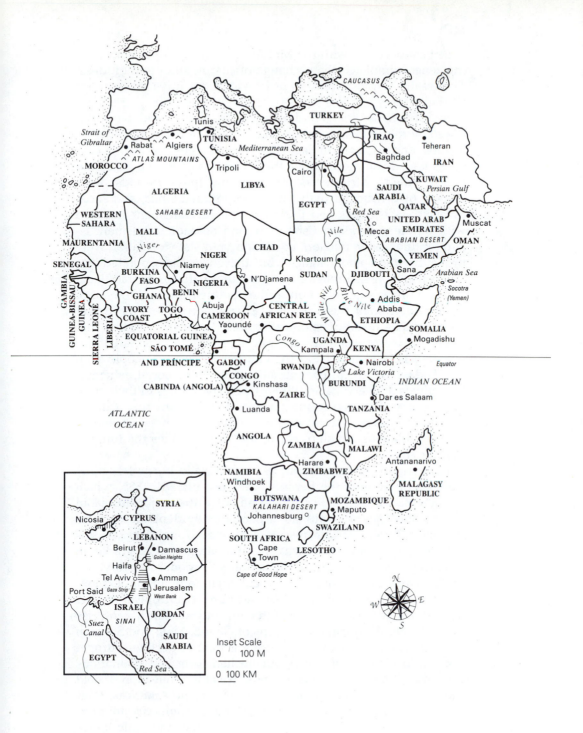

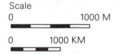

desert connected it with the Middle East and Europe. Both trading zones stimulated the exchange of commodities and of ideas. The wealth derived from them provided the financial basis for the building of empires and city-states. In West Africa, the kingdoms of Ghana, Mali, and Songhai flourished and were followed by the successive states and empires of the Hausa, Benin, Yoruba, and Ashanti. In East Africa, there were the Swahili city-states and in southern Africa the kingdoms of Kongo and Zimbabwe ruled. African societies during these periods were marked by artistic creativity, strong communal ethos, and social diversity. Aristocrats and the most refined craftsmen coexisted with simple cultivators, fishermen, and nomadic herdsmen. Islamic influences in religion, education, and state formation were pronounced in some instances, but these were incorporated into the well-established religious and cultural patterns of traditional Africa. Europe's intervention in the continent through the slave trade undermined this way of life. Traditional life was further modified as a result of colonization and Africa's integration into a modern world economy. Despite these disruptions, a continuum can be said to exist in the cultures of African people even to this day. In Africa, communal values define social behavior. Individuals at every stage of their lives have duties to their community as well as rights and reciprocal obligations they can expect from others. This communal ethos, which is reinforced through religious worship, ritual, and art, provides the foundation for cohesion.

Modern African history can be said to begin in the late nineteenth century with the Berlin Conference in 1884–1885, which officially partitioned the continent amongst the major European nations and tried to legitimate a permanently dependent global status for Africa. African response to and struggle against this European conquest, colonization, and attempted degradation comprises the framework of the continent's modern history.

The Berlin Conference was the culmination of a long, exploitative relationship between Africa and Europe. European contact with Africa first came in the fifteenth and sixteenth centuries when the great African civilizations of Ghana, Mali, and Songhai either had declined or were entering a state of decline. Europeans, equipped with firearms, established forts and plantations along the coasts. Their initial purpose was the acquisition of gold and spices. With the demand for labor from the Americas, their purpose became the slave trade. Working through African intermediaries, using violence, coercion, diplomacy, and guile, Europeans reaped immense profits from enslaving Africans and transporting them to the Americas. The results for Africa were catastrophic. Over a period of four centuries, from the 1500s to the mid-1800s, close to ten million people were enslaved. Entire communities were annihilated. Local economies were disrupted. The very fiber of African society was undermined, though by no means destroyed.

In the latter half of the nineteenth century, with the onset of active European colonization, Africa was vulnerable to territorial conquest. The political states were in no position to withstand successfully the superior military technology of an industrializing Europe. Although primarily motivated by competition for markets and raw materials, the European nations rationalized their colonial conquests with moral and intellectual arguments based upon a racist ideology. Proclaiming the superiority of Western civilization, Europeans propounded a "civilizing mission" to bring enlightenment and progress to backward regions of the world. Despite its moral claims, European colonization was brutal and oppressive. Once in control, Europeans devised complex strategies of divide and rule in order to dominate the indigenous populations.

Although the colonial powers varied in the ways that they implemented their policies, their goals were ultimately similar. They aimed to control Africa for their own economic development. Hence, they converted Africa's diversified economies to the production of cash crops, they expropriated communal lands, and they transformed African farmers into an impoverished, landless laboring force. The effects of colonialism in social and political terms were debilitating as well. The loss of sovereignty resulted in the cooption of indigenous social and political institutions and the formation of a ruling class open only to those of European ancestry. Similarly, the Eurocentric policies of Christian missionaries and of the colonial educational system undermined traditional African cultures and religions. They also had the unforeseeable result of creating an African intelligentsia which spearheaded the struggle for independence.

The colonial regimes remained relatively secure until 1945. Although there had been revolts and acts of resistance throughout the colonial era, it was not until after the Second World War that national independence movements came into direct confrontation with European imperialism. By 1945, Europe was vulnerable. It had been ravaged by war and was no longer perceived by its colonial subjects as invincible. A mood of self-determination pervaded the continent. Militant leaders such as Kwame Nkrumah and Jomo Kenyatta gave voice to the rising expectations of the broad masses and launched campaigns to end colonial rule. Beginning with the independence of Ghana in

1957, over the next three decades, Europe's African colonies gained their freedom.[1]

Independence ushered in an exciting period of African history. Drawing on all segments of society, the independence movements had united the politicians and the general population in a common struggle and vision. Independence was to raise the quality of life and restore dignity and glory to the African people. The democratic and communal values that at one time had been the cornerstone of traditional life were now to provide the ethos for a new modern society. It was not long before the initial hope and optimism began to fade. Increasingly, African elites followed the example set by their European predecessors and appropriated economic surpluses for themselves. Even those governments that remained true to the egalitarian principles of the independence movements floundered. The economies of these nations continued to be entrapped in the same import/export pattern that prevailed during the colonial period. The challenge today is for African nations to inaugurate autonomous strategies for economic development. To accomplish this goal, many governments are attempting to cooperate regionally. Simultaneously, political and social movements have arisen to challenge the sterility of existing regimes. They are calling for popular participation in government, unity among ethnic groups, and more equitable relations between their countries and the industrialized nations of the world.

Equally important to the future of the continent is the fate of South Africa, the richest, most developed, and most powerful nation in the region. With its gold and diamond mines, strategic minerals, and modern industry, South Africa has the capacity to generate economic growth and development throughout Africa. As long as it is governed by a white minority regime that oppresses and exploits the black majority through its racist policies of apartheid this possibility will remain unrealized. Today there is hope for the downfall of apartheid. Resistance movements within South Africa, most notably the African National Congress (ANC) and the Pan-African Congress (PAC) have waged and continue to wage antiapartheid struggles that have an international dimension. In the face of continual resistance within its borders and of worldwide condemnation, the South African government has recently responded by releasing political prisoners such as Nelson Mandela, has opened dialogue with the ANC, and has accepted

---

1. *The manner in which the various colonies won independence varied. In those colonies where there was an entrenched white settler class—British Kenya and the Portuguese colonies, for example— armed struggle was necessary.*

in principle the idea of multiracial democracy. It is too soon to tell whether or not these developments will lead to a peaceful end to apartheid. It does seem certain that it is only a matter of time before the black majority will be in a position to emancipate itself and to forge a new political order.

LITERATURE

The struggle for national independence and the search for an authentic cultural identity often coincide. In the case of Africa, cultural assertion and the revival of indigenous social traditions have gone hand in hand with the political struggle for freedom from foreign domination. Modern African literature, which is primarily the expression of a nationalist intelligentsia, is deeply rooted in this twofold discourse. Its antecedents go back to the turn of the nineteenth century to the historical and ethnological treatises of Edward Blyden and Casely-Hayford, who labored to dispel the European myth of Africa's cultural inferiority. Later, the "negritude" writers of the 1930s and 1940s, most notably Léopold Sédar Senghor and subsequently Camara Laye, turned with pride to traditional culture for inspiration. In their writings they sought to celebrate a vibrant way of life that had remained uncontaminated by imperialism. In a similar vein, the "independence" writers of the late 1950s found inspiration in the anti-colonial struggle. Writers such as Ferdinand Oyono, Ousmane Sembène, Chinua Achebe, and Ngugi wa Thiong'o, sharing the hopes and aspirations of the broad masses, used their creativity to expose the destructive nature of imperialism, to document the mental anguish that resulted from colonial racialist policies, and to rehabilitate Africa's cultural integrity.

By the late 1960s, a new direction in modern African literature emerged. It represents an important departure. There is still the self-conscious attempt to recapture the authenticity of traditional African culture and to portray the injustices of foreign rule, but much of the literature over the next two decades also contains a critique and exposé of African independence. Disillusionment, betrayal, and outrage pervade the novels of Kofi Awoonor and Ayi Kwei Armah, who are among the first to confront the failings of independence. With time Sembène, Achebe, Soyinka, and Ngugi will come to shift their focus to evoking the socioeconomic, political, and cultural contradictions of independent Africa. Ama Ata Aidoo, Buchi Emecheta, and Bessie Head bring a feminist perspective to bear. Utilizing themes and motifs drawn from diverse cultural sources, these writers portray the ambiguities and contradictions of the postindependence period. Their discourse is of an Africa where the traditional and the modern, the precapitalist and the capitalist, the individual and the collective coincide and compete with each other for ascendancy.

In some ways the literary situation in South Africa is very different from the rest of the continent. The social and political divisions between races there have led to the development of several South African literatures, each with its own traditions. There is a white South African literature in English and one in Afrikaans. There are oral and written literatures in the indigenous African languages, and there is a black literature in English. Although these literatures can be traced back to nineteenth-century roots, in the twentieth century they all do have an underlying framework. Twentieth-century South African writing, whether black or white, is situated within the racial divisions of that society. The common motif of living in a segregated society can be seen in the work of Peter Abrahams, the first black author to gain international prominence, and in the novels of Alan Paton, the first widely acclaimed white writer.

Abrahams and Paton were important predecessors of the literary outburst that came with the 1950s. A generation of black writers and intellectuals began their careers as journalists covering both the vibrant life of black townships and the mounting political challenge to the government's racial policies. Nat Nakasa and Can Themba inaugurated a hard-boiled style of writing that relied on wit and irony to convey the pathos and resilience of the oppressed black majority. Later Bloke Modisane, Alfred Hutchinson, Ezekiel Mphahlele, Todd Matshikiza, and Lewis Nkosi incorporated this style into their remarkable autobiographies and personal reminiscences. Similarly, Alex La Guma, the most politically conscious novelist of his generation, made use of this provocative urban style. The 1950s was an important time for white South African writing as well. South Africa's most famous novelist and playwright began their careers during this period. Athol Fugard attempted to confront the cultural contradictions of apartheid through township theater, while Nadine Gordimer documented the dilemma of white liberals in an illiberal society. In the decades that followed, these writers won international recognition and influenced the development of South African literature. Significantly, the Afrikaans writers Breyten Breytenbach, André Brink, and J. M. Coetzee now openly challenge in their works the totalitarian nature of white minority rule.

In the 1970s, a new generation of black South African writers emerged. Politicized by the Sharpeville massacre (1960) and the Soweto uprising (1976), these writers aligned themselves with the

Black Consciousness Movement with the aim of fostering national unity and resistance among the black masses. Mongane Serote, Sipho Sepamla, and numerous others turned from a literature of protest to a populist literature of combat. Now, poets draw on the oral traditions and perform at concerts, funerals, and mass rallies. Novelists and short story writers depict political struggle. Playwrights and theater directors seek actively to engage their audiences in a militant consciousness raising to challenge the government. This populist tradition continues to this day and forms the catalyst for an ongoing culture of resistance.

THE REGION KNOWN as the Middle East/Maghrib (North Africa) is inhabited by diverse ethnic groups of which Arabic people are the most numerous. Hence, this area is often referred to as the Arab World. Islam is the dominant religion, and its culture is prominent throughout the region. Located along the Mediterranean at the crossroads where Europe, Asia, and Africa meet, the Middle East/Maghrib comprises northern Africa and the area of southwest Asia that includes the Arabian peninsula. Historically, the region is the birthplace of the world's three great monotheistic religions, Judaism, Christianity, and Islam, and is the site of the two oldest civilizations, Mesopotamia and Egypt. It was, at different times, a part of the Greek, Roman, and Ottoman empires. In the nineteenth century, it came to be dominated by Europe, especially England and France. Today it includes politically significant nations such as Egypt, Algeria, Iran, Iraq, and Israel as well as countries with some of the richest oil fields in the world, for example, Saudi Arabia, Kuwait, and the United Arab Emirates. Because of its vast petroleum deposits and strategic location, foreign nations continue to take great interest in the area.

Geology and climate have had an enormous effect on the region. From the earliest millennium, water—or the lack of it—has been a key factor in people's lives. The many mountain ranges prevent adequate rainfall so that much of the region consists of deserts. Indeed, sand seas cover one third of the Arabian peninsula and North Africa. In contrast, the coasts and river valleys contain some of the world's most fertile soil and so became homes to the first civilizations. On the whole, however, fresh water and fertile land are limited. Historically, control of the region's water resources has been an important political issue and the cause of much rivalry. These geographic factors as well as the region's fortuitous location at the crossroads of continents have shaped the indigenous societies' bent toward trade. Historically, most of the area's great civilizations have been commercial and urban.

The religion of Islam, which was founded in the seventh century, became an extremely important unifying force throughout the Middle East and North Africa. Through its conquests, it consolidated and expanded the economic base of the area. Just as significantly, it brought together the nomadic people of the deserts, the peasant farmers, and the town dwellers in a common worldview in which religious teaching informed the moral code of the community. On the other hand, Islam's spirit of tolerance allowed it to coexist with local customs and traditions. Equally, it allowed Islam to incorporate the multitudinous intellectual heritage of the various civilizations into a cosmopolitan Muslim culture. Islam today continues to provide moral and social cohesion to the majority of the peoples in the region.

The modern period in the Middle East/Maghrib begins in the late nineteenth century when the region became integrated into the European imperialist system either directly through colonial rule or indirectly through economic and military alliances. The situation was similar to that of Asia, sub-Saharan Africa, and Latin America. This was the age when Europe dominated the world. Industrialization, technological advances, and an increase in military power resulted in the expansion of European economies. As a result, the Middle East/Maghrib was forced into a subordinate position and was restricted to providing raw materials for Europe's factories and new markets for its manufactured goods. A by-product of this arrangement was that the Arab world was denied opportunities to industrialize and the social groups (landlords, merchants, bureaucrats) who benefited from the unequal exchange between the two regions saw it in their interests to preserve the status quo. Europe's penetration of the region had a number of other consequences. It had a profound effect on the intellectual climate of the time. Through education and travel, the Arab elite was introduced to European social and political ideas as well as scientific discoveries. This exposure led to a drive for modernization. Islam likewise incorporated some of the new knowledge and used it to stand up to the challenge of foreign intervention. European domination also provoked an antiimperialist response by those sectors of the middle and working classes who were disadvantaged by imperialist dependency.

Arab nationalism was fueled by this discontent and emerged as a reaction to European domination. As early as the 1880s, there were attempts in Egypt and Tunisia to limit or end British and French occupation. With the collapse of the Ottoman Empire at the end of World War I and the assumption by European powers of "mandates" to rule the area, Arab nationalism became an effective political force. Espousing an ideology of regeneration, it mobilized a broad section of the population to liberate the region from foreign exploitation and to restore to the Arab people the glory and autonomy of the past.

As a result of the efforts of well-organized antiimperialist movements, most Arab countries achieved national independence in the post–World War II era. Like their counterparts in Asia, Africa, and the Caribbean, these nationalist movements forced Europe to dismantle its empires. Although the nature of independence and the terms under which it was achieved varied, in most countries it was won peacefully after economic and political concessions by the liberation movements. In Algeria, where there was a well-established and powerful French settler community, nationalists had to wage war (1954–1962). In the wake of formal independence, there was a resurgence of pan-Arab nationalism. The emergence of the United States and the Soviet Union as powers interested in the region and the continuing influence of France and Britain prompted efforts toward creating Arab unity.

Throughout the 1950s and 1960s, Arab nationalism was closely associated with Nasserism. The term is derived from the policies of Gamal Abdel Nasser, the charismatic Egyptian leader who became an important spokesman for the nonaligned movement that tried to chart an independent course for emerging Third World nations. Severing ties with European imperialist nations, Nasser, like other Arab leaders who followed his example, nationalized strategic sectors of the economy for the purpose of achieving autonomous growth. Initially promising, Nasserism eventually bogged down in autocracy, religious neoorthodoxy, and myriad regional rivalries of which Arab antagonism to Israel and Israel's denial of Palestinian rights stand out.

For much of the post–World War II period the Palestinian/ Israeli conflict has been central to tensions in the region. The origin of the conflict lies in the European Zionist movement, which designated Palestine, the ancient Hebrew kingdom, as the territory for a national Jewish homeland. Reflecting deep-seated secular and religious aspirations, Zionism was a response to the rise of anti-Semitism in Europe. It was distinctive in the history of nationalism in that it emerged outside the area of the future homeland. While Palestine was a British mandate (1920–1948), the British government officially sanctioned Zionism's home policy and facilitated both Jewish immigration and the transfer of land to Zionist settlers. From the onset, Arab Palestinians contested the Zionist settlements, viewing them as an extension of Europe's imperialist policies. As the Jewish community increased and gained in power, much of the Arab population was displaced and lost the means of self-government and the capacity to safeguard its future. After the 1948 war between Israel and five Arab states, in which Israel increased its territory, Palestine ceased to exist as a political and administrative entity. To a large degree, Arab Palestine became Jewish Israel. The majority of the Arab population was transformed into stateless refugees out of whose ranks emerged Palestinian liberation movements. By the 1960s, these movements were taking direct action within Israel. Since 1948, other Arabs also have viewed Israel with animosity, so tensions have been rife and several armed conflicts have resulted. At present, the issues of a Palestinian homeland and Palestinian rights within Israel still remain unresolved. For Arab nations the fate of Palestine carries with it the legacy of foreign domination and a continued threat to regional sovereignty. Ironically, the struggle for Palestinian self-determination poses a dangerous precedent for autocratic Arab regimes, which deny their own populations full civil and political rights. For Israel the crisis has resulted in internal dissent, an undermining of its claims to democracy, and the loss of international support. The Palestinian situation also overshadows Israel's own historical legacy as a haven for an oppressed minority.

The decline of Arab unity is another significant concern in the region. Following the Arab defeat by Israel in the Six-Day War in 1967 and the death of Nasser in 1970, Egypt abandoned its nonaligned stance and took a strongly pro-Western one. Economically, it moved away from state socialism and encouraged private enterprise and foreign investment. Egypt's shift in policy was a reflection of the growing division in the Arab world between governments aligned with the United States and ones with close ties to the U.S.S.R., between oil-producing countries and those with limited economic surpluses, between secular states and states governed by religious orthodoxy, between nations following a capitalist road to development and others committed to socialist experiments. These divisions, in turn, have left the Arab world vulnerable to regional conflicts and foreign intervention as exemplified by the Gulf war.

Equally important to the region are internal pressures for change. Increased wealth through economic growth and oil revenues has been unevenly distributed and in many instances generated a wider gap between social classes. Where this has occurred, the disadvantaged have called into question the justice of the social order and the legitimacy of their governments. In Iran, this led to an Islamic revolution. In other countries, women and minority ethnic and religious groups have become important catalysts for challenging society through their demands for equality. Finally, the growing economic interdependency between Arab states has generated a need for further cooperation while a just resolution of the Palestinian/Israeli conflict is crucial to the well-being and prosperity of the region.

LITERATURE

The Middle East and North Africa have rich and ancient literary traditions. Classical Arabic literature dates back to the seventh century and was influenced by earlier forms. Poetry, folk tales, prose epics, and intellectual treatises are all a part of this literary heritage, for the aim of literature was broad. Its function was not merely aesthetic. Literature was seen as the receptacle of human values. It was the means for expressing the moral, political, and religious concerns of the community.

Modern Arabic literature draws upon this literary tradition with its broad interpretation of the purpose of writing. It likewise has been influenced by the West and has taken from it two major literary forms, the novel and short story. Like other Western art forms, these came to the Arab world as a consequence of European imperialism. First serving as cultural accoutrements of colonialism, the novel and short story were adopted during the interwar period by local intellectuals as a means of articulating the concerns and aspirations of the Arab people. They came to reflect as well the growing nationalist sentiments of the times and implicitly challenged European domination and cultural hegemony.

In the postwar period, the novel and short story have continued to develop both realism and stream-of-consciousness techniques. They remain important genres for exploring the social and cultural changes that are taking place in the region. Modern Arabic poetry also has undergone transformations. Drawing on traditional styles, it has been influenced by Western artistic currents such as romanticism, symbolism, and free verse. Like the novel and short story, it, too, has served as a tool for the awakening of national consciousness. Recently poetry has become an important medium for confronting social issues and questioning outmoded values. Similar patterns of development exist in Persian and Turkish literature. Modern literature in Hebrew, however, has a very different history. It originated in Jewish communities in Europe. During the early twentieth century, its primary themes were the breakdown of traditional life and the corresponding rootlessness experienced by European Jews. Originally, Berlin and Odessa were the centers for this literature. After the rise of Nazism, Israel became the home of Hebrew writing.

There it has retained its European influences as Israeli writers attempt to forge a new national identity.

Until recently, the literature of the region was relatively unknown to the general public in Europe and North America. Israeli writing, perceived as an adjunct to Western literature, has been translated, and authors such as S. Y. Agnon, Yehuda Amichai, and Amos Oz have been well received and acquired a following. A school of North African writers from Algeria and Morocco, including Mohammed Dib and Driss Chraibi, achieved recognition in France during the 1950s for confronting the cultural and political contradictions of Arab life under colonialism. As writing from Latin America and Asia won international recognition and an audience in the West, Arab writers were discovered and published. Through the novels and short stories of Naguib Mahfouz and Yussef Idriss, particularly after Mahfouz received the Nobel Prize in 1988, readers were introduced to a wide panorama of life in Egypt that ranged from the predicament of educated Arabs torn between their own inherited culture and that of Europe to the condition of the urban and rural poor. Similarly, they were confronted with the situation of Arab women in the feminist writing of Nawal El Saadawi, and through the work of Ghassan Kanafani, Mahmoud Darwish, and Tawfiq Awwad, Westerners became familiar with the plight of Palestinians and the concerns of Arab nationalism. This body of literature challenges Eurocentric distortions of Arab culture and society and is illustrative of the artistic ferment in the Middle East and North Africa.

Norman A. Spencer

ALGERIA

 MOHAMMED DIB

Mohammed Dib was born in 1920 in Tlemcen, Algeria, near the Moroccan frontier. He was raised a Muslim and educated in Algeria and Morocco. After leaving college, he found difficulty earning a living. He was a primary school teacher, carpet weaver, and railway worker before becoming a journalist for a local newspaper. During this period, he began contributing articles and short stories to French-language Algerian magazines. In 1959 he left Algeria and settled in France, where he has been awarded a number of prestigious literary prizes for his novels and short stories. Several of his books have been translated into English, including Omneros *(1978) and* Who Remembers the Sea *(1985).*

Dib's work can be divided into three categories: first, the naturalism and social commentary of his early efforts; second, the experimentation with styles inspired by psychoanalysis and surrealism; and third, the exploration of human conflict in wartime and postindependence Algeria. "Naema— Whereabouts Unknown" is an example of the third category. It documents with vivid detail the ravages of the Algerian War for Independence, and in so doing poses important moral questions about the effects of war on the human personality.

Naema—Whereabouts Unknown

Five weeks have gone by, and still no news of Naema. Nothing at all. 1
Some people think she's imprisoned in the Bedeau barracks. The Bedeau barracks . . . the prisoners held there are considered to be hostages; dreadful things are said about what happens to them.

How to be sure? It's impossible to get any definite news, no one has ever 2
returned home from that place. Wait, that's all—for some news to trickle through, for Naema, by some miracle, to be brought to trial. Wait—that's all that's left to us.

I take the children out, often to the public gardens that we call 'the little 3
garden', where we spend a short time in the afternoons. Autumn is tinging the foliage, and its russets and yellows mingle with the blue of the sky. We cannot stay long. Everyone leaves the gardens early in the evening and it is dangerous to linger on. Still, the children enjoy being there. And I, too, find there the only moments of relief that I ever have now. It will happen to all of us, in this war.

But if some do come through safely, they will have learnt a lot. Rahim, 4
who is only seven, has already lived through three years of war, and he looks at me so seriously and with mute questioning that I am upset and feel guilty.

A few days ago I asked him why he was staring at me in that manner. 5

'You mustn't dawdle, Daddy, must you, when you throw a grenade?' 6
he said.

Sadness overwhelmed me. What could I say to him? Pitch him a tale? 7
That doesn't work any more, not even with Rahim. Killings, attacks, ambushes . . . there's an echo of it all in his words and thoughts. I don't try to teach him to be careful, for he wouldn't understand. There's already this rent between us.

Another day, all unsuspecting, I laughingly asked him: 'What do you 8
think ought to be done?'

'Kill the lot. Keep throwing bombs.' 9

He had answered without a moment's hesitation and still gazing at me 10
with his innocent look.

'You'd do that, would you?' 11

'Yes. Wouldn't you?' 12

'No,' I said. 13

I can still see the incredulous look he gave me. 14

The other tenants rarely mention Naema now. I do my best to be a 15
mother to the children while she's in prison. The women from the other flats do most of the household chores for me, sweeping out, cooking the meals, washing up, doing the laundry. It was they who took over; on no account would they have allowed a man to do such tasks. Sometimes they even give Benali, Zahya and Rahim their meal while I'm away. A veiled woman regularly brings a sum of money—the allowance from the Liberation Front—which they hand over to me. This woman has never shown them her face, and they have never managed to find out who she is. Besides, they take good care not to ask too many questions.

The tenement is in a state of perpetual commotion. It was still dark this 16
morning, a cool and sweet-smelling day was dawning, when raised voices and terrified whisperings ran through the building. Fortunately, it was only a false alarm. These spasms of nervous tension are frequent and reach their highest pitch after bomb-explosions. On those occasions, some of the tenants come hurrying back with news, shout it to the others, and everyone rushes down into the courtyard to add his or her comment. Nothing like that happened this morning, but the day had only just begun.

In the midst of all these upheavals, my thoughts turn to Naema. Not to 17
know where she is, what they have done to her, is a torment. In the town,
disappearances, deaths and funerals have become so numerous that no
one counts them any more, and those of today cause yesterday's to be
forgotten.

There are posters everywhere showing men being shot. Every day, the 18
courts pass sentences of death. Summary executions increase, and every
dawn discloses mutilated corpses. Most of my neighbours think that
Naema will not return; they do not dare tell me so, but I can see it on their
faces.
　　Yesterday, two strangers stopped me in the street and made me keep 19
watch outside a tailor's workshop. When they had gone, the tailor said to
me in a most natural way, 'Yes, they left some things here.'
　　'What do you mean?' 20
　　'Well!' he said. 21
　　I understood. 22
　　And it came to me then, that my only reaction to danger now is one of 23
defiance.

This afternoon, as I was crossing the street leading to Soc-el-Ghezel Square, 24
which is always teeming with people, it happened. First, the crowd wa-
vered and fell back, and there were some shrieks. Two shots had just rung
out, followed by an explosion. People pushed and trod on one another; in
a twinkling, the square emptied. Only the body of a man was left lying
there, face down. I made off, in order not to be nabbed by the police,
whose whistles were already piercing the air.
　　I took refuge in a shoemaker's shop in a near-by narrow street. 25
　　'Well, what is it? What's going on? Something new?' asked the cobbler, 26
surprised at my hurried entry.
　　'All that's new is that someone's been killed in Soc-el-Ghezel,' I said, 27
and stopped for breath.
　　'Ah!' was his only comment. 28
　　A smile lit up the pallor of his long, delicate face. 'I'd have wagered it 29
was peace, I'd have wagered that you were bringing peace.'
　　'Peace?' I said. 'That's something no one's ever heard of.' 30
　　That moment and his words still stand out very clearly in my memory. 31
All the more clearly as I had barely finished speaking and was laughing
rather nervously at my fright, when two more explosions shook the street.
We heard wild yells from close at hand, frenzied shooting broke out and
quickly developed into a concentrated hail of fire. Figures suddenly bent
double and collapsed before our eyes.
　　The stuttering of sub-machine-guns drew nearer. I suggested to the 32
cobbler that he should shut his shop door. Without a word he went and
bolted it and we both dropped to the floor.
　　I listened to the din which was now sweeping into the street. I don't 33

remember being afraid. I was calm and collected; just curious to know what would happen next. The seconds passed sluggishly.

Then there came a hammering on the door, as though someone was trying to break it down. The cobbler wanted to open it; he looked inquiringly at me. I signed to him not to move. The blows increased in violence, became more imperative, more furious. Finally the door gave way, and a soldier stepped inside. He didn't look far; grabbing my companion by the scruff of the neck, he dragged him outside. On the threshold, he gave him such a violent blow on the chest with the butt of his gun that the cobbler vomited blood and fell to the ground, where he remained face uppermost. I noticed a loft above my head, climbed up and crouched there. But the soldier did not come back. 34

I waited, lying there in the gloom amongst the rolls of leather. Through a gap in the floorboards I could make out a stretch of the street. Dusk crept into the shop. I lay still, watching, breathing in the smell of leather, and the minutes went by. 35

The turmoil had passed on; all that could be heard were dull rumblings in the distance. I got to my feet and brushed myself down. As I went out, past the broken door, I had to step over the cobbler's body. The streets I went through were strangely quiet and deserted. 36

We are prepared to die, but we have not yet learnt to depart this life. That night, everything was silent—my thoughts, the town, the war. I sat up and looked around; it all seemed so absurd to me. The children were asleep. Why these children? What were they doing there? I had a sudden desire to dress and hurry out to the old town, despite the curfew. It took me a long time to get to sleep again, and when I did my head seemed to be rolling in an ever-mounting tide. 37

As soon as dawn streaked the sky, I went out. People were already hurrying about their business, cyclists were weaving through the crowds, ringing their bells, and street vendors were cluttering the pavements. In Soc-el-Ghezel Square the only shops still shut were those whose owners had been killed. The walls were scarred by bullets and the shop shutters had jagged tears in them still; I had not dreamt it. Broken glass and splintered brick were strewn about the roadway. 38

I arrived at the shoemaker's shop. 39

Shut. I had left it open yesterday. This morning there was a padlock on the street door. I stood there looking at it. What had been done about the shoemaker? I went to see the near-by shopkeepers in the hope of finding out a little more than I already knew. But not a word could I get from them, except that there would be no funeral. All the dead had been collected during the night, taken to the cemetery and buried by the authorities without their relatives being informed. 40

I walked away and roamed aimlessly about. I felt detached from this 41 clear day. I had to think. But the yawning sky, the balmy air and the flavour of things prevented thought.

I wandered round for a long time. Everything, I soon realized, had the smell and taste of blood. 42

It was night again, and again I was snatched from sleep. I listened. Shouts and yells were coming from houses in the distance. Then more uproars, just as fearful, spread from place to place. Shots were whipping through the air, broken by bursts from sub-machine-guns. I lay still, holding my breath. The cries of pain and terror were coming from men and women. Then silence fell. I closed my eyes. The beasts of the Apocalypse were roaming the land. 43

Only the distant purring of motors could be heard; then that, too, faded away. 44

Morning came. A light-blue sky and a dazzling light. And there was no one who did not leave home without a pang of impatience in his heart. 45

Mutilated bodies have been found, dropped at the gates of the town. A dozen, three of them women. 46

The war goes on; it may last for years yet. No one can now imagine what life is like without continual bursts of firing and explosions. News of horrible things is whispered around. I hardly ever walk along the streets without often glancing back, without being ready to throw myself flat if a grenade is thrown or a bomb goes off. The glimpse of any suspicious gesture puts me on my guard; I never wait to see what might happen. Once you leave home, you cannot be sure of returning alive. 47

There are some squares and market-places and intersections, especially those patrolled by the Riot Squad, that I always avoid now, as I do streets and alleys with barbed-wire barriers. It's not wise to take refuge in one of them when an outrage occurs; you find yourself caught in a trap. 48

While we remain at the mercy of these butchers, bound hand and foot, the real war is taking place elsewhere. So we find our only defence against this daily terror is in disturbances and the breakdown of law and order. We have paid too dearly already, to hesitate or draw back. Something has got under way which is even worse than war. 49

There are times when I should like to meet my death in one of the numerous outrages committed every day; this blood that splashes us, this stench as from a slaughter-house, makes me heave and fills me with horror. Then I suddenly feel such a hunger for life, such a thirst to know what it will all be like *after*, that I am ready to face all the armies and police forces in the world. 50

How will those who survive the war adapt themselves to life? What will the return to peace mean to them? For us, the world has lost its savour and its colour. How will they manage to give it a human face again? 51

*   *   *

I had no sooner sat down at the Tizaoui café, a short time ago, than a patrol   52
descended on us; and with all the other customers at the terrace tables I
was pushed inside with my hands above my head. We stood packed tightly
together, each waiting his turn to be searched and have his identity
checked. The black muzzles of automatic weapons promised death to anyone foolish enough to move. We stood without flinching and in silence, a
silence over which a strange calm reigned. I said to myself, 'They won't,
they won't get the better of us.'

The checking lasted an hour, an hour in which each man had to put his   53
self-control to the test. Then we were released into an afternoon laden with
menace. My throat was sore from the insults I had swallowed. Curfew,
which was at half-past four, would soon be emptying the streets. I left the
café, but instead of going straight home I decided to walk round for a bit.
The fronts of houses were set in deathly expectation. People were going
about in silence, walking carefully. The town was hunched up in itself and
had its look of evil days.

At the end of the boulevard the blue Mansourah hills were standing out   54
against a pale sky, and cast an unfailing promise of happiness into my face.
I would have walked round the ramparts, gone through the gates and . . .
If it had still been possible!

The aim of my stroll was merely the newspaper-kiosk in the Place de   55
l'Hôtel de Ville; as I knew the paper-seller slightly I should be able to glance
at all the papers without being obliged to buy any. I read the news, which
was much like the previous day's, and went on my way again. I was
walking past the museum railings and had just reached the corner, when
it happened. The blast shook the walls around me so violently that I was
brought up against a rush of air, which scorched my face. At the same
moment, there came a deafening avalanche of glass and cries rose from all
sides. People were scattering in every direction across the tree-lined square.
I plunged down the nearest street. That, too, was noisy with cries, shouts,
orders.

A burst of small-arms fire swept the street. A man fell just in front of me,   56
and then a woman, who got entangled in her long veil.

The street froze.   57

Sirens wailing loudly, some army trucks arrived, braked violently, and   58
armed paratroops swarmed down. One of them, with icy blue eyes, motioned that I could go. I made off. But at the corner of the next street some
Arab Territorials[1] shouted to me to stop.

I halted. Then, looking straight at them, I made the decision to walk   59
towards them. At every moment I expected them to open fire on me. I was
quite cool and calm, and filled with disdain. 'They shan't have the satisfaction of seeing the man they shoot cringe before them,' I was thinking as

---

1. Arab Territorials: *Local Arab police employed by the colonial French government.*

I forced myself to go forward. Among them were some whose faces I knew by sight; a few had been at school with me.

'Don't move!' shouted one of the group. 60

I took a few more steps, then a sick feeling came over me. I don't 61 remember just what happened after that. I was led back to the square, having received a blow on the back of the neck. I found myself standing with a number of other Algerian Arabs being held at gun-point. There were dead and dying bodies sprawled on the roadway. Just in front of us one of the dying was moaning feebly, 'Help me, help . . .'

No one made the slightest move to go to his aid. In the square and the 62 streets leading off it, the man-hunt was continuing. Uniformed figures, bent forward over their pointed weapons, were chasing other running figures. One or the other of these would suddenly throw up his arms and fall forward, to merge with the grey of the ground.

Just then, a man coming out of a bar spotted someone in a corner and 63 started to gesticulate and shout. 'That's him! That's the man who left the bomb! I saw him do it!'

The other looked at him in bewilderment and clutched a rubbishy basket 64 to his shabby black jacket. A few of the Territorials ran across and grasped him by the arms. The man made no resistance. They dragged him to the middle of the square, then shot him several times in the chest and stomach. He sank to the ground, still clutching his worthless basket.

The man who had denounced him, a bookseller, shouted, 'Hurrah for 65 justice!'

It was undoubtedly he, that poor little man, who saved us all; a builder's 66 labourer by the look of him, smaller still in death, lying there in the middle of the square, rigid, but seeming to challenge the whole world now. I could not tear my eyes away from him or rid my mind of his muteness.

Soon afterwards, in fact, we were allowed to go. The military cordons 67 were withdrawn, and people again moved about freely; cyclists darted along, customers went into shops and others came out, a rag-and-bone man uttered his plaintive cry and a street-trader came along pushing his barrow. The fright was over. Only a faint smell of blood still lingered, but it lay over everything, weighing down heart and mind. I went on my way, up the street that led back home.

There is still the same suspense, the same lunacy. Still the same gaping 68 abyss which engulfs our lives.

This morning, twenty bodies were found laid out on the square in the 69 old town. I hurried there, as did lots of other people; faces with burning eyes were staring out of windows.

Soldiers were holding back the crowds from the approaches to the 70 square and erecting barriers at all the entrances. It was impossible to go any farther. I dodged from one place to another.

Suddenly there appeared the most astounding procession ever seen in 71 the town. It consisted entirely of children and Arab women without their veils, and this impulsive torrent was sweeping forward shrieking out the Liberation Anthem. Violence, rage, suffering or defiance. It was impossible to tell which was the dominant force driving these women and barefoot children towards the machine-gun carriers. A white and green flag made from old clothing and tied to a stick fluttered above their heads. The paratroops formed up round the square, and as the women went past they knocked off their berets.

All at once, automatic weapons began to stutter. Everything swam before my eyes. And we others, we who were watching them, listening to their harsh voices rising to the sky, we seemed to merge into the same melting-pot of blood and death. I wanted to run across to them, to bellow that anthem with them and be exposed to that fire.   72

The hail of bullets was turned on us. Everyone scattered, trampled on others amid cries and screams, dropped to their knees.   73

Two o'clock in the morning.   74

An explosion shatters the silence. A rumbling can be heard in the distance. Then the darkness is punctuated by shots, which provoke spasmodic bursts of firing. Half-tracks shake the houses as they clatter past. And that is all. Nothing more is heard. The silence makes another wall in the night.   75

Dawn rises in creamy freshness, and oceans of light pour forth; even the cicadas are affected by it and break into song. Children swarm out of the houses and take over the street.   76

A wild hope buoys me up today. Does it spring from a desire to survive the general collapse, in spite of everything? I'm ready to swear, believe it or not, that tomorrow will bring safety, peace and victory! I draw myself up, radiating strength, and I hold out—no, give—courage to others.   77

Nevertheless, refugees are beginning to flock in from the countryside. Hungry and exhausted, they bring the smell of the earth with them, a breath of death and a speechless violence. I think of the peace of the fields around the town, and of the menace concealed in that peace. Even the trees, quite still, their fawn foliage licked by unseen flames, seem on the watch for something.   78

But seeing the women at their doors or gathered in the courtyard, hearing their voluble chatter, gives me the peculiar impression that nothing has changed, that nothing will ever change. Like this continuous lovely weather. Neither fog nor rain will ever spoil it. What sheer folly it is, this weather!   79

I am still at liberty and still alive, but every day I wonder what I have done to deserve this and what good it is. There are constant bursts of firing, my thoughts go immediately to Naema, then revert to the dangers that every moment brings. I think of her at night, when I lie awake staring into the   80 darkness and listening to the slightest noise in the town, but especially when morning comes and the children wake up, and we have most need of her presence. These bright, blue mornings, almost like winter mornings, are what would most likely reconcile me to the world were it not that I get up as I had gone to bed—with anguish lodged in my heart.

Life is a benumbing nightmare, although this waiting slowly brings 81 acceptance of the inevitable. I am gradually beginning to think that I shall never see Naema again, that she will not come back, will never walk about this room again. However, I go on living, I still listen for the sounds and voices in the building and lend an ear to the tales of the neighbours.

We have had several very windy days. The glories of autumn were swept 82 away and grey weather at last set in. The trees braced themselves, while above their withered branches dark clouds crowded the sky. Even in my despair and indifference, I was glad of this change. The last days of autumn had become unbearable, with all their brilliance, light and purity.

Then it started to rain—a real deliverance. The rain continued for a long 83 time, incessant, pervading, stifling, sliding slowly over the dried-up land. Street warfare was in abeyance.

As I turn the pages of this diary, it is still raining, seems never to have 84 stopped raining since that time. I wasted still more days and weeks going round the sodden, streaming town making inquiries, begging for news, knocking at innumerable doors in my efforts to find my wife. It was yesterday, but it seems like today. All was in vain. The rain is still falling from a murky sky on bare trees and houses darkened by the wet. I look out at this lowering sky, the same overcast sky as then, and the same steamy, misty streets, the same passing phantoms appear before my eyes. I was then still sustained by some kind of hope, but hope so enclosed in inaccessible places that I now hesitate to call it hope. A stone had been dropped into an abyss and I listened to its interminable fall. I was that stone, and the hope I clung to was that it would never reach the bottom.

From time to time, when a bright interval cast a dull light over the town, 85 I would go out and wander about the streets. I tried to take an interest in other people's lives, for want of interest in my own; in this way, I didn't think about myself. Then one morning, quite early, someone came to the tenement and asked to see me.

I knew the man waiting at the door only slightly. He drew me aside, 86 then began talking in a low voice. He explained that since the death of a certain shoemaker, they had been in some difficulty; his shop was in a very useful position and its role had not been discovered by the police, in spite of what had happened. So it could be used again.

'You must have been a friend of his,' the man added, 'as you went to ask 87 his neighbours what had become of him, the morning after the massacre. Since then, we haven't been able to find anyone to replace him and open up the shop. Especially someone who's known in the neighbourhood. And it's absolutely essential to make use of those premises again. Perhaps you would like to. . . . Oh, you've time to think it over, we won't hurry you! You needn't give an answer at all, if you don't care to.'

I let him deliver his little speech, giving me time to sum him up. 88

'Have you the keys?' I said when he had finished. 89

He produced a ring with two keys from his trouser pocket. I took it, and 90
he went off.

I am closing this diary now. It was thinking of my wife, the shoemaker 91
and the others, which sustained me and helped me to carry on until now. They knew why they died, they did.

Translated from the Arabic by Len Ortzen

STUDY QUESTIONS

1. The story is set during the Algerian War for Independence, when Arab nationalists fought against French colonialists and their supporters. How is this conflict portrayed? What are some examples in the story of the effect of the war on the local population?
2. What does the narrator mean when he says, "Something has got under way which is even worse than war"?
3. Discuss the narrator's experience in the story. What is his reaction to his wife's internment? How does he respond to the atrocities committed against his people? Is he inspired by the patriotic resistance to oppression? Does he find solace in working for the Liberation Front at the end of the story?
4. Is the diary form an effective means of documenting the psychological impact of historical events on people's lives? Why or why not?

BOTSWANA

 **BESSIE HEAD**

*Bessie Head (1937–1986) was born in Pietermaritzburg, South Africa.
Brought up in a foster home, she had a difficult childhood and adolescence.
After completing her education, she worked as a journalist and teacher, but the
oppressive policies of apartheid forced her into exile. She and her son settled in
neighboring Botswana in 1963. Desiring to live simply and calmly, she chose
to work as a teacher and gardener in a local village.*

*Head's fiction reflects her personal experience of alienation and her interest
in village life. Her first novel,* When Rain Clouds Gather *(1968), celebrates
the struggle of a village to survive the devastation of a drought. In her next
two novels,* Maru *(1971) and* A Question of Power *(1973), she portrays
women protagonists who struggle to overcome their disabilities.* The Collector
of Treasures *(1977) depicts village life and reiterates a persecution theme.
The powerful title story is a compelling portrait of a woman's unhappiness due
to her status and position in society.*

The Collector of Treasures

The long-term central state prison in the south was a whole day's jour-   1
ney away from the villages of the northern part of the country. They
had left the village of Puleng at about nine that morning and all day long
the police truck droned as it sped southwards on the wide, dusty cross-
country track-road. The everyday world of ploughed fields, grazing cattle,
and vast expanses of bush and forest seemed indifferent to the hungry eyes
of the prisoner who gazed out at them through the wire mesh grating at the
back of the police truck. At some point during the journey, the prisoner
seemed to strike at some ultimate source of pain and loneliness within her
being and, overcome by it, she slowly crumpled forward in a wasted heap,
oblivious to everything but her pain. Sunset swept by, then dusk, then
dark and still the truck droned on, impersonally, uncaring.

At first, faintly on the horizon, the orange glow of the city lights of the new independence town of Gaborone, appeared like an astonishing phantom in the overwhelming darkness of the bush, until the truck struck tarred roads, neon lights, shops and cinemas, and made the bush a phantom amidst a blaze of light. All this passed untimed, unwatched by the crumpled prisoner; she did not stir as the truck finally droned to a halt outside the prison gates. The torchlight struck the side of her face like an agonising blow. Thinking she was asleep, the policeman called out briskly: 2

'You must awaken now. We have arrived.' 3

He struggled with the lock in the dark and pulled open the grating. She crawled painfully forward, in silence. 4

Together, they walked up a short flight of stairs and waited a while as the man tapped lightly, several times, on the heavy iron prison door. The night-duty attendant opened the door a crack, peered out and then opened the door a little wider for them to enter. He quietly and casually led the way to a small office, looked at his colleague and asked: 'What do we have here?' 5

'It's the husband murder case from Puleng village,' the other replied, handing over a file. 6

The attendant took the file and sat down at a table on which lay open a large record book. In a big, bold scrawl he recorded the details: Dikeledi Mokopi. Charge: Man-slaughter. Sentence: Life. A night-duty wardress appeared and led the prisoner away to a side cubicle, where she was asked to undress. 7

'Have you any money on you?' the wardress queried, handing her a plain, green cotton dress which was the prison uniform. The prisoner silently shook her head. 8

'So, you have killed your husband, have you?' the wardress remarked, with a flicker of humour. 'You'll be in good company. We have four other women here for the same crime. It's becoming the fashion these days. Come with me,' and she led the way along a corridor, turned left and stopped at an iron gate which she opened with a key, waited for the prisoner to walk in ahead of her and then locked it with the key again. They entered a small, immensely high-walled courtyard. On one side were toilets, showers, and a cupboard. On the other, an empty concrete quadrangle. The wardress walked to the cupboard, unlocked it and took out a thick roll of clean-smelling blankets which she handed to the prisoner. At the lower end of the walled courtyard was a heavy iron door which led to the cell. The wardress walked up to this door, banged on it loudly and called out: 'I say, will you women in there light your candle?' 9

A voice within called out: 'All right,' and they could hear the scratch-scratch of a match. The wardress again inserted a key, opened the door and watched for a while as the prisoner spread out her blankets on the floor. The four women prisoners already confined in the cell sat up briefly, and stared silently at their new companion. As the door was locked, they all 10 greeted her quietly and one of the women asked: 'Where do you come from?'

'Puleng,' the newcomer replied, and seemingly satisfied with that, the light was blown out and the women lay down to continue their interrupted sleep. And as though she had reached the end of her destination, the new prisoner too fell into a deep sleep as soon as she had pulled her blankets about her.

The breakfast gong sounded at six the next morning. The women stirred themselves for their daily routine. They stood up, shook out their blankets and rolled them up into neat bundles. The day-duty wardress rattled the key in the lock and let them out into the small concrete courtyard so that they could perform their morning toilet. Then, with a loud clatter of pails and plates, two male prisoners appeared at the gate with breakfast. The men handed each woman a plate of porridge and a mug of black tea and they settled themselves on the concrete floor to eat. They turned and looked at their new companion and one of the women, a spokesman for the group said kindly:

'You should take care. The tea has no sugar in it. What we usually do is scoop the sugar off the porridge and put it into the tea.'

The woman, Dikeledi, looked up and smiled. She had experienced such terror during the awaiting-trial period that she looked more like a skeleton than a human being. The skin creaked tautly over her cheeks. The other woman smiled, but after her own fashion. Her face permanently wore a look of cynical, whimsical humour. She had a full, plump figure. She introduced herself and her companions: 'My name is Kebonye. Then that's Otsetswe, Galeboe, and Monwana. What may your name be?'

'Dikeledi Mokopi.'

'How is it that you have such a tragic name,' Kebonye observed. 'Why did your parents have to name you *tears*?'

'My father passed away at that time and it is my mother's tears that I am named after,' Dikeledi said, then added: 'She herself passed away six years later and I was brought up by my uncle.'

Kebonye shook her head sympathetically, slowly raising a spoonful of porridge to her mouth. That swallowed, she asked next:

'And what may your crime be?'

'I have killed my husband.'

'We are all here for the same crime,' Kebonye said, then with her cynical smile asked: 'Do you feel any sorrow about the crime?'

'Not really,' the other woman replied.

'How did you kill him?'

'I cut off all his special parts with a knife,' Dikeledi said.

'I did it with a razor,' Kebonye said. She sighed and added: 'I have had a troubled life.'

A little silence followed while they all busied themselves with their food, then Kebonye continued musingly:

'Our men do not think that we need tenderness and care. You know, my husband used to kick me between the legs when he wanted that. I once aborted with a child, due to this treatment. I could see that there was no way to appeal to him if I felt ill, so I once said to him that if he liked he could keep some other woman as well because I couldn't manage to satisfy all his needs. Well, he was an education-officer and each year he used to suspend about seventeen male teachers for making school girls pregnant, but he used to do the same. The last time it happened the parents of the girl were very angry and came to report the matter to me. I told them: "You leave it to me. I have seen enough." And so I killed him.' 27

They sat in silence and completed their meal, then they took their plates and cups to rinse them in the wash-room. The wardress produced some pails and a broom. Their sleeping quarters had to be flushed out with water; there was not a speck of dirt anywhere, but that was prison routine. All that was left was an inspection by the director of the prison. Here again Kebonye turned to the newcomer and warned: 28

'You must be careful when the chief comes to inspect. He is mad about one thing—attention! Stand up straight! Hands at your sides! If this is not done you should see how he stands here and curses. He does not mind anything but that. He is mad about that.' 29

Inspection over, the women were taken through a number of gates to an open, sunny yard, fenced in by high, barbed-wire where they did their daily work. The prison was a rehabilitation centre where the prisoners produced goods which were sold in the prison store; the women produced garments of cloth and wool; the men did carpentry, shoe-making, brick-making, and vegetable production. 30

Dikeledi had a number of skills—she could knit, sew, and weave baskets. All the women at present were busy knitting woollen garments; some were learners and did their work slowly and painstakingly. They looked at Dikeledi with interest as she took a ball of wool and a pair of knitting needles and rapidly cast on stitches. She had soft, caressing, almost boneless hands of strange power—work of a beautiful design grew from those hands. By mid-morning she had completed the front part of a jersey and they all stopped to admire the pattern she had invented in her own head. 31

'You are a gifted person,' Kebonye remarked, admiringly. 32

'All my friends say so,' Dikeledi replied smiling. 'You know, I am the woman whose thatch does not leak. Whenever my friends wanted to thatch their huts, I was there. They would never do it without me. I was always busy and employed because it was with these hands that I fed and reared my children. My husband left me after four years of marriage but I managed well enough to feed those mouths. If people did not pay me in money for my work, they paid me with gifts of food.' 33

'It's not so bad here,' Kebonye said. 'We get a little money saved for us out of the sale of our work, and if you work like that you can still produce money for your children. How many children do you have?' 34

'I have three sons.'   35
'Are they in good care?'   36
'Yes.'   37
'I like lunch,' Kebonye said, oddly turning the conversation. 'It is the   38
best meal of the day. We get samp and meat and vegetables.'
So the day passed pleasantly enough with chatter and work and at   39
sunset the women were once more taken back to the cell for lock-up time.
They unrolled their blankets and prepared their beds, and with the candle
lit continued to talk a while longer. Just as they were about to retire for the
night, Dikeledi nodded to her new-found friend, Kebonye:
'Thank you for all your kindness to me,' she said, softly.   40
'We must help each other,' Kebonye replied, with her amused, cynical   41
smile. 'This is a terrible world. There is only misery here.'
And so the woman Dikeledi began phase three of a life that had been   42
ashen in its loneliness and unhappiness. And yet she had always found
gold amidst the ash, deep loves that had joined her heart to the hearts of
others. She smiled tenderly at Kebonye because she knew already that she
had found another such love. She was the collector of such treasures.

There were really only two kinds of men in the society. The one kind   43
created such misery and chaos that he could be broadly damned as evil. If
one watched the village dogs chasing a bitch on heat, they usually moved
around in packs of four or five. As the mating progressed one dog would
attempt to gain dominance over the festivities and oust all the others from
the bitch's vulva. The rest of the hapless dogs would stand around yapping
and snapping in its face while the top dog indulged in a continuous spurt
of orgasms, day and night until he was exhausted. No doubt, during that
Herculean feat, the dog imagined he was the only penis in the world and
that there had to be a scramble for it. That kind of man lived near the
animal level and behaved just the same. Like the dogs and bulls and
donkeys, he also accepted no responsibility for the young he procreated
and like the dogs and bulls and donkeys, he also made females abort. Since
that kind of man was in the majority in the society, he needed a little
analysing as he was responsible for the complete breakdown of family life.
He could be analysed over three time-spans. In the old days, before the
colonial invasion of Africa, he was a man who lived by the traditions and
taboos outlined for all the people by the forefathers of the tribe. He had
little individual freedom to assess whether these traditions were compassionate or not—they demanded that he comply and obey the rules, without
thought. But when the laws of the ancestors are examined, they appear on
the whole to have been vast, external disciplines for the good of the society
as a whole, with little attention given to individual preferences and needs.
The ancestors made so many errors and one of the most bitter-making
things was that they relegated to men a superior position in the tribe, while

women were regarded, in a congenital sense, as being an inferior form of human life. To this day, women still suffered from all the calamities that befall an inferior form of human life. The colonial era and the period of migratory mining labour to South Africa was a further affliction visited on this man. It broke the hold of the ancestors. It broke the old, traditional form of family life and for long periods a man was separated from his wife and children while he worked for a pittance in another land in order to raise the money to pay his British Colonial poll-tax. British Colonialism scarcely enriched his life. He then became 'the boy' of the white man and a machine-tool of the South African mines. African independence seemed merely one more affliction on top of the afflictions that had visited this man's life. Independence suddenly and dramatically changed the pattern of colonial subservience. More jobs became available under the new government's localization programme and salaries sky-rocketed at the same time. It provided the first occasion for family life of a new order, above the childlike discipline of custom, the degradation of colonialism. Men and women, in order to survive, had to turn inwards to their own resources. It was the man who arrived at this turning point, a broken wreck with no inner resources at all. It was as though he was hideous to himself and in an effort to flee his own inner emptiness, he spun away from himself in a dizzy kind of death dance of wild destruction and dissipation.

One such man was Garesego Mokopi, the husband of Dikeledi. For four   44 years prior to independence, he had worked as a clerk in the district administration service, at a steady salary of R50.00[1] a month. Soon after independence his salary shot up to R200.00 a month. Even during his lean days he had had a taste for womanising and drink; now he had the resources for a real spree. He was not seen at home again and lived and slept around the village, from woman to woman. He left his wife and three sons—Banabothe, the eldest, aged four; Inalame, aged three; and the youngest, Motsomi, aged one—to their own resources. Perhaps he did so because she was the boring, semi-literate traditional sort, and there were a lot of exciting new women around. Independence produced marvels indeed.

There was another kind of man in the society with the power to create   45 himself anew. He turned all his resources, both emotional and material, towards his family life and he went on and on with his own quiet rhythm, like a river. He was a poem of tenderness.

One such man was Paul Thebolo and he and his wife, Kenalepe, and   46 their three children, came to live in the village of Puleng in 1966, the year of independence. Paul Thebolo had been offered the principalship of a

---

1. R50.00: *An abbreviation of "50 rand." The rand is South Africa's basic unit of currency.*

primary school in the village. They were allocated an empty field beside the yard of Dikeledi Mokopi for their new home.

Neighbours are the centre of the universe to each other. They help each other at all times and mutually loan each other's goods. Dikeledi Mokopi kept an interested eye on the yard of her new neighbours. At first, only the man appeared with some workmen to erect the fence, which was set up with incredible speed and efficiency. The man impressed her immediately when she went around to introduce herself and find out a little about the newcomers. He was tall, large-boned, slow-moving. He was so peaceful as a person that the sunlight and shadow played all kinds of tricks with his eyes, making it difficult to determine their exact colour. When he stood still and looked reflective, the sunlight liked to creep into his eyes and nestle there; so sometimes his eyes were the colour of shade, and sometimes light brown. 47

He turned and smiled at her in a friendly way when she introduced herself and explained that he and his wife were on transfer from the village of Bobonong. His wife and children were living with relatives in the village until the yard was prepared. He was in a hurry to settle down as the school term would start in a month's time. They were, he said, going to erect two mud huts first and later he intended setting up a small house of bricks. His wife would be coming around in a few days with some women to erect the mud walls of the huts. 48

'I would like to offer my help too,' Dikeledi said. 'If work always starts early in the morning and there are about six of us, we can get both walls erected in a week. If you want one of the huts done in woman's thatch, all my friends know that I am the woman whose thatch does not leak.' 49

The man smilingly replied that he would impart all this information to his wife, then he added charmingly that he thought she would like his wife when they met. His wife was a very friendly person; everyone liked her. 50

Dikeledi walked back to her own yard with a high heart. She had few callers. None of her relatives called for fear that since her husband had left her she would become dependent on them for many things. The people who called did business with her; they wanted her to make dresses for their children or knit jerseys for the winter time and at times when she had no orders at all, she made baskets which she sold. In these ways she supported herself and the three children but she was lonely for true friends. 51

All turned out as the husband had said—he had a lovely wife. She was fairly tall and thin with a bright, vivacious manner. She made no effort to conceal that normally, and every day, she was a very happy person. And all turned out as Dikeledi had said. The work-party of six women erected the mud walls of the huts in one week; two weeks later, the thatch was complete. The Thebolo family moved into their new abode and Dikeledi Mokopi moved into one of the most prosperous and happy periods of her life. Her life took a big, wide upward curve. Her relationship with the 52

Thebolo family was more than the usual friendly exchange of neighbours. It was rich and creative.

It was not long before the two women had going one of those deep, affectionate, sharing-everything kind of friendships that only women know how to have. It seemed that Kenalepe wanted endless amounts of dresses made for herself and her three little girls. Since Dikeledi would not accept cash for these services—she protested about the many benefits she received from her good neighbours—Paul Thebolo arranged that she be paid in household goods for these services so that for some years Dikeledi was always assured of her basic household needs—the full bag of corn, sugar, tea, powdered milk, and cooking oil. Kenalepe was also the kind of woman who made the whole world spin around her; her attractive personality attracted a whole range of women to her yard and also a whole range of customers for her dressmaking friend, Dikeledi. Eventually, Dikeledi became swamped with work, was forced to buy a second sewing-machine and employ a helper. The two women did everything together—they were forever together at weddings, funerals, and parties in the village. In their leisure hours they freely discussed all their intimate affairs with each other, so that each knew thoroughly the details of the other's life.

'You are a lucky someone,' Dikeledi remarked one day, wistfully. 'Not everyone has the gift of a husband like Paul.'

'Oh yes,' Kenalepe said happily. 'He is an honest somebody.' She knew a little of Dikeledi's list of woes and queried: 'But why did you marry a man like Garesego? I looked carefully at him when you pointed him out to me near the shops the other day and I could see at one glance that he is a butterfly.'

'I think I mostly wanted to get out of my uncle's yard,' Dikeledi replied. 'I never liked my uncle. Rich as he was, he was a hard man and very selfish. I was only a servant there and pushed about. I went there when I was six years old when my mother died, and it was not a happy life. All his children despised me because I was their servant. Uncle paid for my education for six years, then he said I must leave school. I longed for more because as you know, education opens up the world for one. Garesego was a friend of my uncle and he was the only man who proposed for me. They discussed it between themselves and then my uncle said: "You'd better marry Garesego because you're just hanging around here like a chain on my neck." I agreed, just to get away from that terrible man. Garesego said at that time that he'd rather be married to my sort than the educated kind because those women were stubborn and wanted to lay down the rules for men. Really, I did not ever protest when he started running about. You know what the other women do. They chase after the man from one hut to another and beat up the girlfriends. The man just runs into another hut, that's all. So you don't really win. I wasn't going to do anything like that. I am satisfied I have children. They are a blessing to me.'

'Oh, it isn't enough,' her friend said, shaking her head in deep sympathy. 'I am amazed at how life imparts its gifts. Some people get too much. Others get nothing at all. I have always been lucky in life. One day my parents will visit—they live in the south—and you'll see the fuss they make over me. Paul is just the same. He takes care of everything so that I never have a day of worry . . .'

The man Paul attracted as wide a range of male friends as his wife. They 58 had guests every evening; illiterate men who wanted him to fill in tax forms or write letters for them, or his own colleagues who wanted to debate the political issues of the day—there was always something new happening every day now that the country had independence. The two women sat on the edge of these debates and listened with fascinated ears, but they never participated. The following day they would chew over the debates with wise, earnest expressions.

'Men's minds travel widely and boldly,' Kenalepe would comment. 'It 59 makes me shiver the way they freely criticise our new government. Did you hear what Petros said last night? He said he knew all those bastards and they were just a lot of crooks who would pull a lot of dirty tricks. Oh dear! I shivered so much when he said that. The way they talk about the government makes you feel in your bones that this is not a safe world to be in, not like the old days when we didn't have governments. And Lentswe said that ten per cent of the population in England really control all the wealth of the country, while the rest live at starvation level. And he said communism would sort all this out. I gathered from the way they discussed this matter that our government is not in favour of communism. I trembled so much when this became clear to me . . .' She paused and laughed proudly, 'I've heard Paul say this several times: "The British only ruled us for eighty years." I wonder why Paul is so fond of saying that?'

And so a completely new world opened up for Dikeledi. It was so 60 impossibly rich and happy that, as the days went by, she immersed herself more deeply in it and quite overlooked the barrenness of her own life. But it hung there like a nagging ache in the mind of her friend, Kenalepe.

'You ought to find another man,' she urged one day, when they had one 61 of their personal discussions. 'It's not good for a woman to live alone.'

'And who would that be?' Dikeledi asked disillusioned. 'I'd only be 62 bringing trouble into my life whereas now it is all in order. I have my eldest son at school and I can manage to pay the school fees. That's all I really care about.'

'I mean,' said Kenalepe, 'we are also here to make love and enjoy it.' 63

'Oh I never really cared for it,' the other replied. 'When you experience 64 the worst of it, it just puts you off altogether.'

'What do you mean by that?' Kenalepe asked, wide-eyed. 65

'I mean it was just jump on and jump off and I used to wonder what it 66 was all about. I developed a dislike for it.'

'You mean Garesego was like that!' Kenalepe said, flabbergasted. 'Why, 67 that's just like a cock hopping from hen to hen. I wonder what he is doing with all those women. I'm sure they are just after his money and so they flatter him . . .' She paused and then added earnestly: 'That's really all the more reason you should find another man. Oh, if you knew what it was really like, you would long for it, I can tell you! I sometimes think I enjoy that side of life far too much. Paul knows a lot about all that. And he always has some new trick with which to surprise me. He has a certain way of smiling when he has thought up something new and I shiver a little and say to myself: "Ha, what is Paul going to do tonight!" '

Kenalepe paused and smiled at her friend, slyly.   68

'I can loan Paul to you if you like,' she said, then raised one hand to   69
block the protest on her friend's face. 'I would do it because I have never
had a friend like you in my life before whom I trust so much. Paul had
other girls you know, before he married me, so it's not such an uncommon
thing to him. Besides, we used to make love long before we got married
and I never got pregnant. He takes care of that side too. I wouldn't mind
loaning him because I am expecting another child and I don't feel so well
these days . . .'

Dikeledi stared at the ground for a long moment, then she looked up at   70
her friend with tears in her eyes.

'I cannot accept such a gift from you,' she said, deeply moved. 'But if   71
you are ill I will wash for you and cook for you.'

Not put off by her friend's refusal of her generous offer, Kenalepe men-   72
tioned the discussion to her husband that very night. He was so taken
off-guard by the unexpectedness of the subject that at first he looked
slightly astonished, and burst out into loud laughter and for such a lengthy
time that he seemed unable to stop.

'Why are you laughing like that?' Kenalepe asked, surprised.   73

He laughed a bit more, then suddenly turned very serious and thought-   74
ful and was lost in his own thoughts for some time. When she asked him
what he was thinking he merely replied: 'I don't want to tell you everything. I want to keep some of my secrets to myself.'

The next day Kenalepe reported this to her friend.   75

'Now whatever does he mean by that? I want to keep some of my secrets   76
to myself?'

'I think,' Dikeledi said smiling, 'I think he has a conceit about being a   77
good man. Also, when someone loves someone too much, it hurts them to
say so. They'd rather keep silent.'

Shortly after this Kenalepe had a miscarriage and had to be admitted to   78
hospital for a minor operation. Dikeledi kept her promise 'to wash and
cook' for her friend. She ran both their homes, fed the children and kept
everything in order. Also, people complained about the poorness of the
hospital diet and each day she scoured the village for eggs and chicken,
cooked them, and took them to Kenalepe every day at the lunch-hour.

One evening Dikeledi ran into a snag with her routine. She had just   79
dished up supper for the Thebolo children when a customer came around

with an urgent request for an alteration on a wedding dress. The wedding was to take place the next day. She left the children seated around the fire eating and returned to her own home. An hour later, her own children asleep and settled, she thought she would check the Thebolo yard to see if all was well there. She entered the children's hut and noted that they had put themselves to bed and were fast asleep. Their supper plates lay scattered and unwashed around the fire. The hut which Paul and Kenalepe shared was in darkness. It meant that Paul had not yet returned from his usual evening visit to his wife. Dikeledi collected the plates and washed them, then poured the dirty dishwater on the still-glowing embers of the outdoor fire. She piled the plates one on top of the other and carried them to the third additional hut which was used as a kitchen. Just then Paul Thebolo entered the yard, noted the lamp and movement in the kitchen hut and walked over to it. He paused at the open door.

'What are you doing now, Mma-Banabothe?' he asked, addressing her   80
affectionately in the customary way by the name of her eldest son, Banabothe.

'I know quite well what I am doing,' Dikeledi replied happily. She   81
turned around to say that it was not a good thing to leave dirty dishes standing overnight but her mouth flew open with surprise. Two soft pools of cool liquid light were in his eyes and something infinitely sweet passed between them; it was too beautiful to be love.

'You are a very good woman, Mma-Banabothe,' he said softly.   82

It was the truth and the gift was offered like a nugget of gold. Only men   83
like Paul Thebolo could offer such gifts. She took it and stored another treasure in her heart. She bowed her knee in the traditional curtsey and walked quietly away to her own home.

Eight years passed for Dikeledi in a quiet rhythm of work and friendship   84
with the Thebolos. The crisis came with the eldest son, Banabothe. He had to take his primary school leaving examination at the end of the year. This serious event sobered him up considerably as like all boys he was very fond of playtime. He brought his books home and told his mother that he would like to study in the evenings. He would like to pass with a 'Grade A' to please her. With a flushed and proud face Dikeledi mentioned this to her friend, Kenalepe.

'Banabothe is studying every night now,' she said. 'He never really   85
cared for studies. I am so pleased about this that I bought him a spare lamp and removed him from the children's hut to my own hut where things will be peaceful for him. We both sit up late at night now. I sew on buttons and fix hems and he does his studies . . .'

She also opened a savings account at the post office in order to have   86
some standby money to pay the fees for his secondary education. They were rather high—R85.00. But in spite of all her hoarding of odd cents,

towards the end of the year, she was short on R20.00 to cover the fees. Midway during the Christmas school holidays the results were announced. Banabothe passed with a 'Grade A.' His mother was almost hysterical in her joy at his achievement. But what to do? The two youngest sons had already started primary school and she would never manage to cover all their fees from her resources. She decided to remind Garesego Mokopi that he was the father of the children. She had not seen him in eight years except as a passer-by in the village. Sometimes he waved but he had never talked to her or enquired about her life or that of the children. It did not matter. She was a lower form of human life. Then this unpleasant something turned up at his office one day, just as he was about to leave for lunch. She had heard from village gossip, that he had eventually settled down with a married woman who had a brood of children of her own. He had ousted her husband, in a typical village sensation of brawls, curses, and abuse. Most probably the husband did not care because there were always arms outstretched towards a man, as long as he looked like a man. The attraction of this particular woman for Garesego Mokopi, so her former lovers said with a snicker, was that she went in for heady forms of love-making like biting and scratching.

Garesego Mokopi walked out of his office and looked irritably at the   87
ghost from his past, his wife. She obviously wanted to talk to him and he walked towards her, looking at his watch all the while. Like all the new, 'success men', he had developed a paunch, his eyes were blood-shot, his face was bloated, and the odour of the beer and sex from the previous night clung faintly around him. He indicated with his eyes that they should move around to the back of the office block where they could talk in privacy.

'You must hurry with whatever you want to say,' he said impatiently.   88
'The lunch-hour is very short and I have to be back at the office by two.'

Not to him could she talk of the pride she felt in Banabothe's achieve-   89
ment, so she said simply and quietly: 'Garesego, I beg you to help me pay Banabothe's fees for secondary school. He has passed with a "Grade A" and as you know, the school fees must be produced on the first day of school or else he will be turned away. I have struggled to save money the whole year but I am short by R20.00.'

She handed him her post office savings book, which he took, glanced at   90
and handed back to her. Then he smiled, a smirky know-all smile, and thought he was delivering her a blow in the face.

'Why don't you ask Paul Thebolo for the money?' he said. 'Everyone   91
knows he's keeping two homes and that you are his spare. Everyone knows about that full bag of corn he delivers to your home every six months so why can't he pay the school fees as well?'

She neither denied this, nor confirmed it. The blow glanced off her face   92
which she raised slightly, in pride. Then she walked away.

As was their habit, the two women got together that afternoon and   93
Dikeledi reported this conversation with her husband to Kenalepe who

tossed back her head in anger and said fiercely: 'The filthy pig himself! He thinks every man is like him, does he? I shall report this matter to Paul, then he'll see something.'

And indeed Garesego did see something but it was just up his alley. He was a female prostitute in his innermost being and like all professional prostitues, he enjoyed publicity and sensation—it promoted his cause. He smiled genially and expansively when a madly angry Paul Thebolo came up to the door of his house where he lived with *his* concubine. Garesego had been through a lot of these dramas over those eight years and he almost knew by rote the dialogue that would follow.

'You bastard!' Paul Thebolo spat out. 'Your wife isn't my concubine, do you hear?'

'Then why are you keeping her in food?' Garesego drawled. 'Men only do that for women they fuck! They never do it for nothing.'

Paul Thebolo rested one hand against the wall, half dizzy with anger, and he said tensely: 'You defile life, Garesego Mokopi. There's nothing else in your world but defilement. Mma-Banabothe makes clothes for my wife and children and she will never accept money from me so how else must I pay her?'

'It only proves the story both ways,' the other replied, vilely. 'Women do that for men who fuck them.'

Paul Thebolo shot out the other hand, punched him soundly in one grinning eye and walked away: Who could hide a livid, swollen eye? To every surprised enquiry, he replied with an injured air:

'It was done by my wife's lover, Paul Thebolo.'

It certainly brought the attention of the whole village upon him, which was all he really wanted. Those kinds of men were the bottom rung of government. They secretly hungered to be the President with all eyes on them. He worked up the sensation a little further. He announced that he would pay the school fees of the child of his concubine, who was also to enter secondary school, but not the school fees of his own child, Bana-bothe. People half liked the smear on Paul Thebolo; he was too good to be true. They delighted in making him a part of the general dirt of the village, so they turned on Garesego and scolded: 'Your wife might be getting things from Paul Thebolo but it's beyond the purse of any man to pay the school fees of his own children as well as the school fees of another man's children. Banabothe wouldn't be there had you not procreated him, Gare-sego, so it is your duty to care for him. Besides, it's your fault if your wife takes another man. You left her alone all these years.'

So that story was lived with for two weeks, mostly because people wanted to say that Paul Thebolo was a part of life too and as uncertain of his morals as they were. But the story took such a dramatic turn that it made all the men shudder with horror. It was some weeks before they could find the courage to go to bed with women; they preferred to do something else.

Garesego's obscene thought processes were his own undoing. He really believed that another man had a stake in his hen-pen and like any cock, his hair was up about it. He thought he'd walk in and re-establish his own claim to it and so, after two weeks, once the swelling in his eye had died down, he espied Banabothe in the village and asked him to take a note to his mother. He said the child should bring a reply. The noted read: 'Dear Mother, I am coming home again so that we may settle our differences. Will you prepare a meal for me and some hot water that I might take a bath. Gare.'

Dikeledi took the note, read it and shook with rage. All its overtones were clear to her. He was coming home for some sex. They had had no differences. They had not even talked to each other. 104

'Banabothe,' she said. 'Will you play nearby? I want to think a bit then I will send you to your father with the reply.' 105

Her thought processes were not very clear to her. There was something she could not immediately touch upon. Her life had become holy to her during all those years she had struggled to maintain herself and the children. She had filled her life with treasures of kindness and love she had gathered from others and it was all this that she wanted to protect from defilement by an evil man. Her first panic-striken thought was to gather up the children and flee the village. But where to go? Garesego did not want a divorce, she had left him to approach her about the matter, she had desisted from taking any other man. She turned her thoughts this way and that and could find no way out except to face him. If she wrote back, don't you dare put foot in the yard I don't want to see you, he would ignore it. Black women didn't have that kind of power. A thoughtful, brooding look came over her face. At last, at peace with herself, she went into her hut and wrote a reply: 'Sir, I shall prepare everything as you have said. Dikeledi.' 106

It was about midday when Banabothe sped back with the reply to his father. All afternoon Dikeledi busied herself making preparations for the appearance of her husband at sunset. At one point Kenalepe approached the yard and looked around in amazement at the massive preparations, the large iron water pot full of water with a fire burning under it, the extra cooking pots on the fire. Only later Kenalepe brought the knife into focus. But it was only a vague blur, a large kitchen knife used to cut meat and Dikeledi knelt at a grinding-stone and sharpened it slowly and methodically. What was in focus then was the final and tragic expression on the upturned face of her friend. It threw her into confusion and blocked their usual free and easy feminine chatter. When Dikeledi said: 'I am making some preparations for Garesego. He is coming home tonight,' Kenalepe beat a hasty retreat to her own home terrified. They knew they were involved because when she mentioned this to Paul he was distracted and uneasy for the rest of the day. He kept on doing upside-down sorts of things, not replying to questions, absent-mindedly leaving a cup of tea until it got quite cold, and every now and again he stood up and paced about, lost in his own thoughts. So deep was their sense of disturbance 107 that towards evening they no longer made a pretence of talking. They just sat in silence in their hut. Then, at about nine o'clock, they heard those wild and agonized bellows. They both rushed out together to the yard of Dikeledi Mokopi.

He came home at sunset and found everything ready for him as he had 108 requested, and he settled himself down to enjoy a man's life. He had brought a pack of beer along and sat outdoors slowly savouring it while every now and then his eye swept over the Thebolo yard. Only the woman and children moved about the yard. The man was out of sight. Garesego smiled to himself, pleased that he could crow as loud as he liked with no answering challenge.

A basin of warm water was placed before him to wash his hands and 109 then Dikeledi served him his meal. At a separate distance she also served the children and then instructed them to wash and prepare for bed. She noted that Garesego displayed no interest in the children whatsoever. He was entirely wrapped up in himself and thought only of himself and his own comfort. Any tenderness he offered the children might have broken her and swerved her mind away from the deed she had carefully planned all that afternoon. She was beneath his regard and notice too for when she eventually brought her own plate of food and sat near him, he never once glanced at her face. He drank his beer and cast his glance every now and again at the Thebolo yard. Not once did the man of the yard appear until it became too dark to distinguish anything any more. He was completely satisfied with that. He could repeat the performance every day until he broke the mettle of the other cock and forced him into angry abuse. He liked that sort of thing.

'Garesego, do you think you could help me with Banabothe's school 110 fees?' Dikeledi asked at one point.

'Oh, I'll think about it,' he replied casually. 111

She stood up and carried buckets of water into the hut, which she 112 poured into a large tin bath that he might bathe himself, then while he took his bath she busied herself tidying up and completing the last of the household chores. Those done, she entered the children's hut. They played hard during the day and they had already fallen asleep with exhaustion. She knelt down near their sleeping mats and stared at them for a long while, with an extremely tender expression. Then she blew out their lamp and walked to her own hut. Garesego lay sprawled across the bed in such a manner that indicated he only thought of himself and did not intend sharing the bed with anyone else. Satiated with food and drink, he had fallen into a deep, heavy sleep the moment his head touched the pillow. His concubine had no doubt taught him that the correct way for a man to go to bed, was naked. So he lay, unguarded and defenceless, sprawled across the bed on his back.

The bath made a loud clatter as Dikeledi removed it from the room, but still he slept on, lost to the world. She re-entered the hut and closed the door. Then she bent down and reached for the knife under the bed which she had merely concealed with a cloth. With the precision and skill of her hard-working hands, she grasped hold of his genitals and cut them off with one stroke. In doing so, she slit the main artery which ran on the inside of the groin. A massive spurt of blood arched its way across the bed. And Garesego bellowed. He bellowed his anguish. Then all was silent. She stood and watched his death anguish with an intent and brooding look, missing not one detail of it. A knock on the door stirred her out of her reverie. It was the boy, Banabothe. She opened the door and stared at him, speechless. He was trembling violently. 113

'Mother,' he said, in a terrified whisper. 'Didn't I hear father cry?' 114

'I have killed him,' she said, waving her hand in the air with a gesture that said—well, that's that. Then she added sharply: 'Banabothe, go and call the police.' 115

He turned and fled into the night. A second pair of footsteps followed hard on his heels. It was Kenalepe running back to her own yard, half out of her mind with fear. Out of the dark Paul Thebolo stepped towards the hut and entered it. He took in every detail and then he turned and looked at Dikeledi with such a tortured expression that for a time words failed him. At last he said: 'You don't have to worry about the children, Mma-Banabothe. I'll take them as my own and give them all a secondary school education.' 116

STUDY QUESTIONS

1. Why is the main character, Dikeledi, referred to as a collector of treasures?
2. Is Garesego's murder justified? What is the author's point of view?
3. Why are Paul Thebolo and Kenalepe important characters?
4. What are the similarities between the story and a folktale or morality play?
5. In what ways is the story a feminist critique of African society?

E G Y P T

🔷 YUSSEF IDRISS

Yussef Idriss (b. 1927) is a short story writer, dramatist, and novelist. As a young man, he left his home town of al-Bayrum, in Egypt's Nile delta, to study medicine at the University of Cairo. There he became involved in leftist politics and began to write stories about the living conditions of the poor. After achieving literary fame, he gave up his medical career and has since worked full-time as a journalist, theater director, and creative writer. Idriss's early fiction was influenced by social realism, but in the 1960s he began to write symbolic and surreal tales that explore human psychology. His most recent writing is primarily concerned with sexuality. The influences of Maxim Gorki, Franz Kafka, and D. H. Lawrence coexist in his work along with elements drawn from the oral literary traditions of the village. "A House of Flesh" is an example of the author's ability to combine the social, psychological, and erotic in one story.

A House of Flesh

The ring beside the lamp . . . silence hangs heavy, ears grow blind. Fingers move stealthily, in silence grasp the ring and put out the light. Darkness reigns and in darkness eyes grow blind. The woman, her three daughters, and their house, a mere room.

The beginning is silence. The widow is tall, fair-skinned, willowy, about   1
thirty-five. Her daughters are also tall and full-bodied. They continue to
wear their long black mourning dresses. The youngest is sixteen, the eldest
in her twenties, all three unattractive, having inherited the father's dark,
badly proportioned body, corpulent and flabby; retaining their mother's
build. The room, in spite of its size, holds them during the daytime. Despite
its extreme poverty, the room is neatly arranged in an intimate, cozy atmosphere which reflects a feminine touch. When night falls, their bodies are

scattered all over the room. Huge piles of warm throbbing flesh, sprawled on the single bed or on the couch: breathing, heaving, deeply insomniac.

Silence has hovered over the home since the man's death two years ago   2
after a long illness. The mourning period was over, but the habits of those in mourning remained, most predominantly the habit of silence. It was in fact a silence of waiting, for the girls were growing older and the period of waiting was weighing upon them. No suitors were knocking on their doors. What man would dare to knock on the door of poor unattractive girls, particularly if they happened to be fatherless? But hope still lived of course (wine can remain in the barrels until the right buyer comes along), and each girl believed her luck would change. (No matter how poor one may be, there will always be someone else yet poorer, and if ugliness prevails there will always be someone even uglier . . . and dreams are fulfilled if one has enough patience. . . .)

That silence was occasionally interrupted by the sound of a voice recit-   3
ing the Koran, a voice rising monotonously, emotionless. A recitation by a muqri.[1] The muqri is blind, but the prayers are for the soul of the deceased, always delivered at the same time. Every Friday afternoon, he comes poking his stick at their door. He abandons himself to the extended hand that leads him inside. There he sits cross-legged on the mat and recites. When it is over, he gropes for his sandals and pronounces a greeting that no one bothers to reciprocate, and then leaves. Out of habit he comes, out of habit he recites, and out of habit he leaves. No one notices him any more.

Forever this silence . . . even when the Friday afternoon recitation dis-   4
turbs it. It is as if silence is broken only with silence. Waiting is forever, like hope, little hope but constant hope, for there is hope for every insignificant being, there is somewhere one who is even more insignificant. And they do not aspire to much, no, they do not aspire.

Silence persisted until something happened, until one Friday when the   5
muqri did not show up. Every agreement comes to an end, no matter how long it has lasted, and it seemed this agreement had come to its end. Only then did the widow and her daughters realize that not only was he the sole male voice that broke their silence once a week, but also that he was the only man who ever knocked at their door. Other things began to dawn upon them. True, he was as poor as they were, but his outfits were always clean, his sandals always shone, his headdress was wrapped meticulously (putting to shame any man with eyes), and above all, his voice was strong, deep, and melodious. The proposition hovered in the air: why not renew the agreement, and why not summon him immediately? Could he be busy elsewhere? They could wait, for waiting was an old game they were very good at.

Evening was drawing to its end, and he recited as if for the first time.   6

---

1. Muqri: *One who reads verses of the Koran (the Islamic holy book).*

Then the proposition came up: why shouldn't one of them marry a man whose voice would fill the house?

He was a bachelor with a sprouting moustache, a young man. Words [7] generate words, and he too was looking for the right woman. The girls confer about the matter and the mother scans their faces trying to figure who the lucky one would be. But their faces evade her searching looks and seem to say: Is this how we are to be rewarded for our long wait? Shall we break our fast with a blind man? For they still dreamt of suitors, and suitors are usually young men with eyes. Poor things, they have yet to know the world of men. Impossible for them to perceive at this stage in their lives that a man is not to be judged by sight alone.

"Mother, you marry him . . . marry him." [8]

"Me? What shame, what will people say?" [9]

"Let them say what they will, no matter what. It will be better than [10] living in a house without a man, the resounding voice of a man."

"Do you want me to marry before you? Never . . ." [11]

"Wouldn't it be better if you marry before us, so that our house becomes [12] a treading ground for men? Then we can marry after you."

"Marry him, mother. O marry him . . ." [13]

And she married him . . . and one more breath was added to the air and [14] their income grew just a little bit more, and a much greater problem arose. True, they survived their first night, but they didn't dare come close to each other, even inadvertently. The girls were sleeping, or pretending to do so, but the mother could feel pairs of searching beams inspecting the space that lay between them, searching lights of human eyes, prospecting antennas. The girls are old enough to understand, and the room is suddenly transformed into sentient throbbing presences, vibrating in the light of day.

One by one, each left the house when morning set in, only to return by [15] sunset, hesitant, embarrassed. Dragging their feet, they came back to a house filled with laughter, occasionally interrupted by faint noises of a woman. It must be the mother laughing, and the dignified *muqri* they had known was now laughing too. Their mother greeted them, bareheaded, hair wet and with a comb in hand, still laughing. They looked at her face and realized that it had been for all those years like an unlit lamp in whose corners spiders and cobwebs had taken refuge. Now suddenly that face had burst into light, electrified, glistening tearful eyes, with laughter lodged there instead. The silence dissipated completely. Suppertime bustled with loud voices, jokes, highlighted by the *muqri*'s imitation of Umm Kulthum[1] and Abd al-Wahab[2] in his gushing, whining, beautiful voice.

Well done, mother. Soon this gaiety and laughter will draw more men [16] to the house, for the presence of men attracts other men.

---

1. *The third of four daughters born to Muhammad.*

2. *Islamic teacher and reformer (1703–1792) who advocated the return to pure Islam.*

Be confident, girls. Soon men will be coming and suitors will make their calls. But in fact what was preoccupying her was that young man, not the suitors. True, he was blind, but how often are we blinded ourselves from seeing others, just because they happen to be blind? Yes, she was seeing this healthy young man. His overflowing vitality had made up for those years of sickness, impotence, and early old age.   17

The silence was gone, never to return, and the beat of life was there to stay. The man is her legal husband; she married him according to the law of God and his Prophet,[1] and according to his Sunna.[2] No, nothing will make her feel ashamed, for all that she does is legitimate, even when she makes no effort to hide or keep the secret, or when night creeps up and they are all huddled together, and the power of the body and soul takes over, even with the girls there aware and awake in their observation posts, fighting to control sighs and groans.   18

Her mornings were spent washing clothes in rich people's homes, and his days were whiled away by reciting the Quran[3] in homes of the poor.   19

At the beginning, he didn't return home for a break during the day, but as his nights grew longer, he started coming home to rest his exhausted body, to regain strength for the night to come.   20

And once, after they had had their fill of the night, and the night had had its fill of them, he suddenly asked her what had been the matter with her during the lunch hour. Why was it that she was now so voluble and eager to talk, but then had adopted total silence? Why was she now wearing his cherished ring, the ring that was all he had given her in form of dowry, gift, wedding band? Why hadn't she been wearing it during the lunch hour?   21

She could have torn herself away distraught, screaming. She could have lost her senses. He could have gotten himself killed. For there could be but one meaning to what he was saying, a horrible, atrocious meaning. A choking sob kept everything back. She held her breath and kept her peace. With her ears, which she transformed into noses, eyes, and other organs of sense, she strained her every fibre to find out who the culprit was. For some reason she was positive it was the middle one, because in her eyes had grown a certain daring look that only a bullet could check. But she listened. The breathing of the three grew louder, deeper and feverish, flaming hot, hesitant and intermittent, growling in youthful dreams which would be sinful to interrupt!   22

Heavings turn into burning flames, into lava vomited by thirsty lands. The knots in her throat deepen and choke her. There are hungry breaths. With all her straining she cannot differentiate between one vibrant, hot pile   23

---

1. *Muhammad (570–632), Arab prophet and founder of Islam.*

2. *Traditional doctrine of Islam based on the life and teachings of Muhammad.*

3. *Koran.*

of flesh and another. All are hungry. All groan and scream. And the groans are not just groans. They are pleas, supplications perhaps, perhaps something more.

She has totally immersed herself in her second legitimate right, and forgotten all about her first legitimate duty, her girls. Patience has become myrrh. Even the mirage of suitors is no more. Suddenly, as if bitten, as though awakened to a secret call, the girls are hungry. The food is forbidden, but hunger is yet more sinful. There exists nothing more sinful than this hunger. How well she has known it. And how well it has known her, freed her spirit, searched her bones. She has known it. Now that she has had her fill, it is impossible for her to forget. 24

Hungry ones! She who took the bread from her own mouth to feed them, she whose only preoccupation was to feed them even if she were to go hungry, she the mother—has she forgotten? 25

And no matter how insistent his demands, her pain was changed into silence. The mother became silent, and from that moment onwards, silence never left her. At breakfast, just as she had thought, the middle girl was silent and was to remain silent from then onwards. At suppertime, the young man was gay and jovial, blind and happy, singing and laughing, with only the youngest and eldest tuning in. 26

Patience is tried and its bitterness becomes a sickness and no one comes knocking on their door. One day the eldest looks at the mother's ring and expresses her admiration, and the mother's heart sinks; and its beating grows louder when the daughter begs to wear the ring just for the day. In silence the mother takes it off her finger, and in silence the girl slips it onto her own. 27

And that evening the eldest girl keeps silent, refusing to utter a word. 28

And the blind man is singing and laughing boisterously with only the youngest tuning in. 29

With unrewarded patience, and luck that has never turned with her worrying, the youngest grows older, and asks for her turn in the ring game, and in silence her turn comes. 30

The ring lies beside the lamp and silence sets in and ears become blind, and in silence the finger whose turn comes gropes stealthily for the ring and turns off the light. 31

Darkness prevails, and in darkness eyes grow blind. Only the blind young man remains happy. Yet behind his loudness and happiness he is tormented by this silence, he is tortured by uncertainty. At the beginning he would say to himself, it must be a woman's nature to be ever-changing. One time she is fresh as the morning dew, at another time she is worn out, exhausted like swampy waters. At times satiny like rose leaves, at others prickly like cacti. True, the ring is always there, but each time the finger it encircles seems to be different. He was almost positive that they knew for 32 sure. So why doesn't silence speak, why doesn't it speak? The mere thought made him choke on his bread. And from that moment on, he never uttered a word. He lived in fear of the violation of that collapse. This time the silence was different, respected by all. A conscious silence, not caused by poverty, nor patience, nor despair, but the most profound kind of silence, the most binding of all, a silence implemented without formal agreement. The widow and her three daughters, and the house which was a room. This was a new kind of silence. The blind reciter brought along this silence, with silence convincing himself that his companion in bed was always his legitimate wife, bearer of his ring, ever changing, unpredictable. Young and old, silken soft or callous and scaly, sometimes fat, at other times thin, whatever, this really was her business. Actually, all this was the business of those with sight and their sole responsibility.

For *they* alone possess the grace of certainty; *they* are capable of discernment; but the most *he* can know is doubt, doubt that can be removed only through the blessing of sight. So long as he is deprived of it, he will be denied certainty, for he is the one who is blind and there is no shame for the blind.

Or is there shame for the blind?

33

34

Translated from the Arabic by Mona Mikhail

STUDY QUESTIONS

1. What is the situation of the widow and her daughters at the beginning of the story?
2. How does the blind *muqri* alter the balance of the household?
3. What accounts for the sexual deviation? Who must be held morally responsible? What is the meaning of the final sentence, "Or is there shame for the blind?"
4. In what ways does this story resemble a fairy tale or parable?

NAGUIB MAHFOUZ

Naguib Mahfouz is the Arab world's most prolific and famous novelist. His work has been translated into numerous foreign languages, and in 1988 he won the Nobel Prize for Literature. Born in Cairo in 1911, Mahfouz has spent his entire life in Egypt. He graduated from Cairo University with a degree in philosophy, then worked as a civil servant for most of his career. Mahfouz is an avid reader, and his work has been influenced by literary developments in Europe and North America, though it is uniquely Egyptian and highly original. In style it ranges from realism to experiments with allegory and stream of consciousness. Most of Mahfouz's writing focuses on the condition and state of mind of the Egyptian middle classes and reflects their conformity and disinclination to challenge authority. More recently, it documents the crisis of identity and conscience suffered by Egyptian intellectuals during periods of social turmoil and political dissatisfaction. Mahfouz's best-known work is Cairo Trilogy *(1956–1957), which portrays the experiences of three generations of a Cairo merchant family during the turbulent first half of the twentieth century. It is a remarkable study of the social, political, and religious life of Egyptians during a period of rapid political and cultural change. He has also written numerous short stories which are frequently concerned—as is "The Happy Man"—with philosophic questions about what it means to be human.*

The Happy Man

When he woke up, he found himself happy. That was most strange compared with his habitual state of mind in the early morning. For he usually got up with a terrible headache from working late hours in his office at the newspaper, or with a hangover from too much eating and drinking at some wild party. The worries of the day before and the problems of the present day usually assailed him then, so that he dragged himself out of bed with great difficulty, trying to muster all his energy and face the troubles of life. But today he was unquestionably happy, overflowing with happiness. The feeling was so clear and intense that it imposed itself on his mind and senses. Yes, he was happy. If this was not happiness, what was it then? He felt all his organs were functioning in perfect harmony with each other and with the whole world around him. Inside him there was infinite energy and a tremendous capacity to achieve anything with great skill and confidence. And his heart was brimming with love for people, animals and things, with an overwhelming feeling of optimism, as if he had finally defeated fear, anxiety, sickness and death. Above all, there was the incomprehensible sensation which penetrated his body and soul, playing a delightful tune of joy, contentment and peace. 1

Intoxicated with this ecstasy, he savored it slowly and with a deep sense of wonder about its mysterious source. There was nothing in his past to explain it or in his future to justify it. How did it come? How long would it last? Oh no, this must be just a fleeting mood which could never be permanent. For if it lasted forever, man would become an angel and reach the world beyond. Let him enjoy it now, live with it, treasure it, before it became a vague memory in the distant horizon. 2

He ate his breakfast with great appetite, looking from time to time with 3 a bright, smiling face at Am Beshir who was serving the food. The old man became increasingly surprised and anxious, because his master did not normally look in his direction except to give orders or ask questions. Then he said to him:

"Tell me, Am Beshir, am I a happy man?" 4

The man was embarrassed, since the master was for the first time ad- 5 dressing him as a companion or friend. After moments of uneasy silence, he replied:

"My master is happy with God's gifts and blessings." 6

"Do you mean that I must be happy with my excellent position, beau- 7 tiful apartment and good health? Is this what you mean? But do you really think I am a happy man?"

"My master exerts himself beyond human endurance and often gets 8 angry in heated discussions with other people."

He interrupted him with a loud laugh and asked: 9

"What about you? Don't you have any worries?" 10

"Of course. Nobody lives without worries." 11

"Do you mean that perfect happiness is impossible?" 12

"Well, this is the nature of life." 13

How could Beshir, or anybody else, imagine his wonderful state of 14 happiness? It was something strange and unique, as if it were his own private secret of all people on earth.

In the conference room at the newspaper, he saw his greatest rival in 15 this world turning the pages of a magazine. The man heard his footsteps but did not raise his eyes. No doubt he somehow glanced quickly but tried to ignore him for his own peace of mind. In regular meetings they often disagreed violently and exchanged the harshest words until they were on the verge of fighting. And only last week he was shamefully defeated by his rival in the union elections, which was a terrible blow to his pride that filled him with bitterness and darkened his vision. But here he was now approaching his enemy with a pure and carefree heart, intoxicated with that wonderful happiness, overflowing with tolerance and forgiveness, as if he were another man who conveyed the promise of a new friendship. And without feeling awkward, he smilingly greeted him. Taken by surprise, the man raised his eyes in wonder and for moments remained silent until he could collect himself and answer the greeting briefly, as if he did not believe his eyes and ears. He sat close to him, saying:

"The weather is gorgeous today." 16

"Oh yes." 17

"It's the kind of weather that fills the heart with deep happiness." 18

The man looked at him cautiously and intently, then mumbled: 19

"I am glad that you're happy." 20

He said laughingly: 21

"It's happiness beyond comprehension." 22

The other replied hesitantly: 23

"I hope that I will not spoil your mood at the meeting of the editorial 24
board today."

"Oh, never. My opinion is well known to everybody. But I don't mind 25
if the members accept your view. This will not spoil my happiness at
all."

"You have changed considerably overnight." 26

"In fact, I am happy beyond comprehension." 27

"I bet your son has changed his mind about staying in Canada for 28
good."

He chuckled and said: 29

"No, my friend, he has not changed his decision." 30

"But that was your greatest source of grief." 31

"Oh, yes. I have pleaded with him again and again to come back in 32
order to relieve my loneliness and serve his country. But he told me that he
intended to start an engineering business with a Canadian partner, and
even invited me to join him there. Let him live where he likes. But here I
am—as you see—happy, unbelievably happy."

"This is unique courage on your part." 33

"I don't know what it is, but I am happy in the full sense of the word." 34

Yes, this was happiness, rich and touchable, firm like absolute power, 35
free as the air, violent as a flame, fascinating as the scent of flowers. Yet this
unnatural feeling could not last forever.

The other man, attracted by his friendliness, said amicably: 36

"In fact, I always regarded you as a man with a violent nature that 37
caused you a good deal of suffering."

"Really?" 38

"You don't know the meaning of compromise. You live intensely with 39
your nerves, with your whole being, fighting fiercely as if any problem
were a matter of life or death."

"Yes, that's true." 40

He accepted this criticism tolerantly, as though it were a little wave in 41
his infinite ocean of happiness, and with a bright smile on his face, asked:

"Then, you believe that there should be some balance in my approach to 42
events?"

"Certainly. Take, for example, our discussion yesterday about racism. 43
We share the same opinion, and the issue is worthy of enthusiasm to the
point of anger. But what kind of anger? It should, in a sense, be intellectual, abstract anger. Not the anger that would fray the nerves, cause indi-
gestion and raise blood pressure. Right?"

"That is very clear to me now." 44

His heart would not release a single drop of its joys. Racism, Vietnam, 45
Angola, Palestine . . . no problem could invade the fortress of happiness
which surrounded his heart. Whenever he remembered a problem, his
heart chuckled joyfully. It was, so to speak, a gigantic happiness, indiffer-

ent to any misery, always smiling in the face of suffering. He wished to laugh, to dance, to sing, spreading his infinite mirth over problems of the world.

Suddenly he felt that the office was too small for him; he had no desire 46 to work. The mere thought of his daily work was treated with absolute indifference and contempt, and he failed completely to bring his mind down from the heaven of bliss. How could he write about the trolley bus which sank in the Nile, when he was intoxicated with all this terrifying happiness? Yes, it was terrifying, coming as it did from nowhere, violent to the point of exhaustion and paralyzing his will. Besides, it was now midday and the feeling still possessed him without any sign of diminishing at all. He left his papers blank on the desk and started pacing his room, laughing and snapping his fingers.

He had a moment of anxiety which did not sink deeply inside him, but 47 floated as an abstract thought on the surface of the mind. It occurred to him to recall deliberately the tragedies of his life in order to test their effect on his present mood, hoping they might help him regain some equanimity or at least reassure him that this happiness might eventually fade away. He recreated in his memory, for example, the death of his wife with all its tragic circumstances. But the event seemed to him as a series of movements without meaning or effect, as if it happened to another woman, the wife of another man, in a remote age of ancient history. The recollection even had a pleasant effect on him so that he smiled and could not help laughing loudly.

The same thing happened when he remembered the first letter he re- 48 ceived from his son, declaring his intention to emigrate to Canada. And when he started to review mentally the bloody tragedies of the world, his chuckles became so loud they might have been heard in the other offices or even in the street. Nothing could touch his happiness. The memories of grief floated softly like gentle waves touching the sands of the shore. Then he left his office and the whole building, without a note of apology for not attending the editorial meeting. After lunch, he went to bed for the usual nap, but felt that sleep was impossible. There was no sign of its approach in this bright, boisterous world of joy that kept him wide awake. He must have some rest and tranquillity, some inertia, some numbness in his senses. But how? Finally he left his bed and started humming a tune while pacing his apartment back and forth. And he said to himself that if this state of mind and feeling lasted longer, he would become totally incapable of sleep or work or grief. It was time to go to the club, but he did not feel like meeting any of his friends. There was no sense in these endless talks about public affairs or private worries. And what would his friends think of him if they found him laughing at the most serious matters? No, he did not need anybody; he had no desire for conversation. It was essential for him to sit by himself or walk for miles to release some of this tremendous energy. He must think deeply of what happened to him. How did this fabulous happiness assault him? For how long could he carry this intolerable burden? Will this feeling deprive him forever of his work and friends, of his sleep and peace of mind? Should he yield to it and drift with the current? Or should he seek an outlet, through mental effort, strenuous work or professional advice?

He felt a little awkward when he was called to the examination room in the   49
office of his friend, the eminent doctor. The physician looked at him smilingly and said:

"You don't seem to have any sickness."   50

"I didn't come to you because I am ill but because I am happy. Yes, I am   51
extremely happy," he replied hesitantly.

There was a moment of silence charged with anxiety and surprise.   52

"It's a very strange sensation which I cannot define in words. But it's   53
quite serious."

The doctor laughed and said jokingly: 54

"I wish your disease would be infectious."   55

"Oh, don't take the matter lightly. As I told you, it's very serious."   56

Then he started to tell the story of his happiness from the moment he   57
got up in the morning until this visit for advice.

"Did you take any liquor or drugs or tranquilizers?"   58

"No, nothing of this sort at all."   59

"Maybe you have achieved something valuable in terms of work, love or   60
money?"

"No, nothing of this sort either. Actually, in my life there is much more   61
cause for sadness than happiness."

The doctor examined him very carefully, then said, shrugging his shoul-   62
ders in wonder:

"You are in perfect health. I can give you some sleeping pills, but you   63
must consult a neurologist."

The same thorough examination was carried out by the other specialist,   64
who then said to him:

"Your nerves are in perfect shape."   65

"Don't you have any convincing explanation for my condition?"   66

"I'm sorry, there is absolutely nothing wrong with your nerves."   67

Whenever he heard the same reply from other specialists, he laughed,   68
then apologized laughingly for his laughter, as if that was his way to express anxiety and despair. He felt very lonely in the company of this overwhelming happiness, without a friend or guide to help him. Suddenly he remembered there was the office of a psychiatrist across the street. But he did not trust these psychiatrists, in spite of his knowledge of the nature of psychoanalysis. Besides, he knew quite well that their treatment extended over long periods of time, so that they became almost constant companions of their patients. And he laughed when he remembered their

method of treatment by free association to reveal the neuroses buried in the subconscious mind. While his feet were leading him to the doctor's office, he was still laughing, especially as he visualized the man listening to his strange complaint of happiness, when he usually listened to people complaining of hysteria, depression, anxiety or schizophrenia.

"To tell you the truth, doctor, I came to you because I am happy beyond comprehension." 69

And he looked at his face to see the effect of his words, but the doctor kept his calm. Hardly had he started to tell his story when the man stopped him with a gesture of his hand, and asked quietly: 70

"It is an overwhelming, strange, exhausting sort of happiness?" 71

He looked at him in amazement and was about to say something when the doctor resumed: 72

"It's happiness that would make you incapable of work, tired of friends and unable to sleep. And whenever you face any suffering you burst out laughing." 73

"You must be a mind reader." 74

"Oh no, nothing of this sort, but I see similar cases at least once a week." 75

"Is it an epidemic?" 76

"I didn't say that. I don't even claim that I have been able, so far, to trace a single case to its original cause." 77

"But it's a disease?" 78

"All the cases are still under treatment." 79

"But you are undoubtedly convinced they are all abnormal?" 80

"Well, in our field this is a necessary hypothesis." 81

"Did you observe a sign of insanity or emotional disturbance in any of them?" he asked anxiously. And he pointed to his head in fear, but the doctor said with certainty: 82

"No. I assure you they are all sane in the proper sense of the word. But you will need two sessions every week. You shouldn't worry or grieve . . ." 83

Worry, grief? He smiled and the smile widened on his face until he burst out laughing. Then his resistance collapsed completely and he could not control his tears. 84

Translated from the Arabic by Saad El-Gabalawy

STUDY QUESTIONS

1. What is the main character's condition when he wakes up? What is unusual about his experience?
2. What happens when the main character goes to work? How does his

frame of mind differ from his normal disposition? How does he test his experience? What does he learn from the physician, neurologist, and psychiatrist?

3. What is the meaning of the end of the story? What philosophical issues does the story raise about human experience?

4. Why is the main character unnamed? Is the allegorical style appropriate? Why or why not?

 ## Alifa Rifaat

Alifa Rifaat (b. 1930) is considered an important new voice in Egyptian literature. She is in her early sixties and lives in Cairo with her family. The widow of a police officer, she spent most of her married life in the Egyptian countryside, an experience that provides the basis for much of her writing. To date, she has published two collections of stories in Arabic and a selection of her work has appeared in English under the title Distant View of a Minaret *(1983). Her stories have been included in several recent anthologies. "Another Evening at the Club" explores male/female relations in a modern postcolonial setting.*

Another Evening at the Club

In a state of tension, she awaited the return of her husband. At a loss to   1
predict what would happen between them, she moved herself back and forth in the rocking chair on the wide wooden verandah that ran along the bank and occupied part of the river itself, its supports being fixed in the river bed, while around it grew grasses and reeds. As though to banish her apprehension, she passed her fingers across her hair. The spectres of the eucalyptus trees ranged along the garden fence rocked before her gaze, with white egrets slumbering on their high branches like huge white flowers among the thin leaves.

The crescent moon rose from behind the eastern mountains and the   2
peaks of the gently stirring waves glistened in its feeble rays, intermingled with threads of light leaking from the houses of Manfalout scattered along the opposite bank. The coloured bulbs fixed to the trees in the garden of the club at the far end of the town stood out against the surrounding darkness. Somewhere over there her husband now sat, most likely engrossed in a game of chess.

It was only a few years ago that she had first laid eyes on him at her   3 father's house, meeting his gaze that weighed up her beauty and priced it before offering the dowry. She had noted his eyes ranging over her as she presented him with the coffee in the Japanese cups that were kept safely locked away in the cupboard for important guests. Her mother had herself laid them out on the silver-plated tray with its elaborately embroidered spread. When the two men had taken their coffee, her father had looked up at her with a smile and had told her to sit down, and she had seated herself on the sofa facing them, drawing the end of her dress over her knees and looking through lowered lids at the man who might choose her as his wife. She had been glad to see that he was tall, well-built and clean-shaven except for a thin greying moustache. In particular she noticed the well-cut coat of English tweed and the silk shirt with gold links. She had felt herself blushing as she saw him returning her gaze. Then the man turned to her father and took out a gold case and offered him a cigarette.

"You really shouldn't, my dear sir," said her father, patting his chest   4
with his left hand and extracting a cigarette with trembling fingers. Before he could bring out his box of matches Abboud Bey had produced his lighter.

"No, after you, my dear sir," said her father in embarrassment. Mingled   5
with her sense of excitement at this man who gave out such an air of worldly self-confidence was a guilty shame at her father's inadequacy.

After lighting her father's cigarette Abboud Bey sat back, crossing his   6
legs, and took out a cigarette for himself. He tapped it against the case before putting it in the corner of his mouth and lighting it, then blew out circles of smoke that followed each other across the room.

"It's a great honour for us, my son," said her father, smiling first at   7
Abboud Bey, then at his daughter, at which Abboud Bey looked across at her and asked:

"And the beautiful little girl's still at secondary school?"   8

She lowered her head modestly and her father had answered: 9

"As from today she'll be staying at home in readiness for your happy life   10
together, Allah permitting," and at a glance from her father she had hurried off to join her mother in the kitchen.

"You're a lucky girl," her mother had told her. "He's a real find. Any   11
girl would be happy to have him. He's an Inspector of Irrigation though he's not yet forty. He earns a big salary and gets a fully furnished government house wherever he's posted, which will save us the expense of setting up a house—and I don't have to tell you what our situation is—and that's besides the house he owns in Alexandria where you'll be spending your holidays."

Samia had wondered to herself how such a splendid suitor had found   12
his way to her door. Who had told him that Mr. Mahmoud Barakat, a mere clerk at the Court of Appeal, had a beautiful daughter of good reputation?

The days were then taken up with going the rounds of Cairo's shops   13
and choosing clothes for the new grand life she would be living. This was made possible by her father borrowing on the security of his government

pension. Abboud Bey, on his part, never visited her without bringing a present. For her birthday, just before they were married, he bought her an emerald ring that came in a plush box bearing the name of a well-known jeweller in Kasr el-Nil Street. On her wedding night, as he put a diamond bracelet round her wrist, he had reminded her that she was marrying someone with a brilliant career in front of him and that one of the most important things in life was the opinion of others, particularly one's equals and seniors. Though she was still only a young girl she must try to act with suitable dignity.

"Tell people you're from the well-known Barakat family and that your   14
father was a judge," and he went up to her and gently patted her cheeks in a fatherly, reassuring gesture that he was often to repeat during their times together.

Then, yesterday evening, she had returned from the club somewhat   15
light-headed from the bottle of beer she had been required to drink on the occasion of someone's birthday. Her husband, noting the state she was in, hurriedly took her back home. She had undressed and put on her nightgown, leaving her jewellery on the dressing-table, and was fast asleep seconds after getting into bed. The following morning, fully re-covered, she slept late, then rang the bell as usual and had breakfast brought to her. It was only as she was putting her jewellery away in the wooden and mother-of-pearl box that she realized her emerald ring was missing.

Could it have dropped from her finger at the club? In the car on the way   16
back? No, she distinctly remembered it last thing at night, remembered the usual difficulty she had in getting it off her finger. She stripped the bed of its sheets, turned over the mattress, looked inside the pillow cases, crawled on hands and knees under the bed. The tray of breakfast lying on the small bedside table caught her eye and she remembered the young servant com-ing in that morning with it, remembered the noise of the tray being put down, the curtains being drawn, the tray then being lifted up again and placed on the bedside table. No one but the servant had entered the room. Should she call her and question her?

Eventually, having taken two aspirins, she decided to do nothing and   17
await the return of her husband from work.

Directly he arrived she told him what had happened and he took her by   18
the arm and seated her down beside him:

"Let's just calm down and go over what happened."   19

She repeated, this time with further details, the whole story.   20

"And you've looked for it?"   21

"Everywhere. Every possible and impossible place in the bedroom and   22
the bathroom. You see, I remember distinctly taking it off last night."

He grimaced at the thought of last night, then said: 23

"Anybody been in the room since Gazia when she brought in the break-   24
fast?"

"Not a soul. I've even told Gazia not to do the room today."   25

"And you've not mentioned anything to her?" 26

"I thought I'd better leave it to you." 27

"Fine, go and tell her I want to speak to her. There's no point in your 28
saying anything but I think it would be as well if you were present when
I talk to her."

Five minutes later Gazia, the young servant girl they had recently em- 29
ployed, entered behind her mistress. Samia took herself to a far corner of
the room while Gazia stood in front of Abboud Bey, her hands folded
across her chest, her eyes lowered.

"Yes, sir?" 30

"Where's the ring?" 31

"What ring are you talking about, sir?" 32

"Now don't make out you don't know. The one with the green stone. It 33
would be better for you if you hand it over and then nothing more need be
said."

"May Allah blind me if I've set eyes on it." 34

He stood up and gave her a sudden slap on the face. The girl reeled 35
back, put one hand to her cheek, then lowered it again to her chest and
made no answer to any of Abboud's questions. Finally he said to her:

"You've got just fifteen seconds to say where you've hidden the ring or 36
else, I swear to you, you're not going to have a good time of it."

As he lifted up his arm to look at his watch the girl flinched slightly but 37
continued in her silence. When he went to the telephone Samia raised her
head and saw that the girl's cheeks were wet with tears. Abboud Bey got
through to the Superintendent of Police and told him briefly what had
occurred.

"Of course I haven't got any actual proof but seeing that no one else 38
entered the room, it's obvious she's pinched it. Anyway I'll leave the
matter in your capable hands—I know your people have their ways and
means."

He gave a short laugh, then listened for a while and said: "I'm really 39
most grateful to you."

He put down the receiver and turned round to Samia: 40

"That's it, my dear. There's nothing more to worry about. The Super- 41
intendent has promised me we'll get it back. The patrol car's on the way."

The following day, in the late afternoon, she'd been sitting in front of her 42
dressing-table rearranging her jewellery in its box when an earring slipped
from her grasp and fell to the floor. As she bent to pick it up she saw the
emerald ring stuck between the leg of the table and the wall. Since that
moment she had sat in a state of panic awaiting her husband's return from
the club. She even felt tempted to walk down to the water's edge and
throw it into the river so as to be rid of the unpleasantness that lay ahead.

At the sound of the screech of tyres rounding the house to the garage, 43
she slipped the ring onto her finger. As he entered she stood up and raised

her hand to show him the ring. Quickly, trying to choose her words but knowing that she was expressing herself clumsily, she explained what an extraordinary thing it was that it should have lodged itself between the dressing-table and the wall, what an extraordinary coincidence she should have dropped the earring and so seen it, how she'd thought of ringing him at the club to tell him the good news but . . .

She stopped in mid-sentence when she saw his frown and added 44 weakly: "I'm sorry. I can't think how it could have happened. What do we do now?"

He shrugged his shoulders as though in surprise. 45

"Are you asking me, my dear lady? Nothing of course." 46

"But they've been beating up the girl—you yourself said they'd not let 47 her be till she confessed."

Unhurriedly, he sat himself down as though to consider this new aspect 48 of the matter. Taking out his case, he tapped a cigarette against it in his accustomed manner, then moistened his lips, put the cigarette in place and lit it. The smoke rings hovered in the still air as he looked at his watch and said:

"In any case she's not got all that long before they let her go. They can't 49 keep her for more than forty-eight hours without getting any evidence or a confession. It won't kill her to put up with things for a while longer. By now the whole town knows the servant stole the ring—or would you like me to tell everyone: "Look, folks, the fact is that the wife got a bit tiddly on a couple of sips of beer and the ring took off on its own and hid itself behind the dressing-table."? What do you think?"

"I know the situation's a bit awkward . . ." 50

"Awkward? It's downright ludicrous. Listen, there's nothing to be done 51 but to give it to me and the next time I go down to Cairo I'll sell it and get something else in its place. We'd be the laughing-stock of the town."

He stretched out his hand and she found herself taking off the ring and 52 placing it in the outstretched palm. She was careful that their eyes should not meet. For a moment she was on the point of protesting and in fact uttered a few words:

"I'd just like to say we could . . ." 53

Putting the ring away in his pocket, he bent over her and with both 54 hands gently patted her on the cheeks. It was a gesture she had long become used to, a gesture that promised her continued security, that told her that this man who was her husband and the father of her child had also taken the place of her father who, as though assured that he had found her a suitable substitute, had followed up her marriage with his own funeral. The gesture told her more eloquently than any words that he was the man, she the woman, he the one who carried the responsibilities, made the decisions, she the one whose role it was to be beautiful, happy, carefree. Now, though, for the first time in their life together the gesture came like a slap in the face.

Directly he removed his hands her whole body was seized with an 55
uncontrollable trembling. Frightened he would notice, she rose to her feet
and walked with deliberate steps towards the large window. She leaned
her forehead against the comforting cold surface and closed her eyes tightly
for several seconds. When she opened them she noticed that the café lights
strung between the trees on the opposite shore had been turned on and
that there were men seated under them and a waiter moving among the
tables. The dark shape of a boat momentarily blocked out the café scene; in
the light from the hurricane lamp hanging from its bow she saw it cutting
through several of those floating islands of Nile waterlilies that, rootless,
are swept along with the current.

Suddenly she became aware of his presence alongside her. 56

"Why don't you go and change quickly while I take the car out? It's hot 57
and it would be nice to have supper at the club."

"As you like. Why not?" 58

By the time she had turned round from the window she was smiling. 59

Translated from the Arabic by Denys Johnson-Davies

STUDY QUESTIONS

1. What does the story tell you about gender and class relations in Egypt?
2. To what extent is the story an exploration of the way middle-class Egyptians combine traditional and foreign beliefs and behavior?
3. How would you characterize Samia and Abboud Bey and their relationship? What is the basis for their marriage?
4. What is the significance of the ring?
5. Discuss the ending. Why is Samia smiling?

◈ NAWAL EL SAADAWI

Nawal El Saadawi (b. 1930) is an internationally acclaimed Egyptian feminist writer and intellectual. Born in Cairo, she completed her secondary and college education in Egypt and later studied at Columbia University in New York. She has worked as a physician and a psychiatrist in Cairo and in the rural areas of Egypt. She is the author of seven novels, four collections of short stories, and five nonfiction books. Much of her work is deemed controversial because it openly challenges the traditional role of women in Arab society, and in this "A Modern Love Letter" is typical. She lost her position as Director of

Education in the Ministry of Health because of her outspoken views, and the publication of her book Women and Sex *(1972). She was later imprisoned for several months. Since her release in 1982, she has been active in pan-Arab women's organizations.*

A Modern Love Letter

I am writing this letter to you, my friend, so that you may perhaps understand me or that I may perhaps understand myself. The attempt may come to nothing, for who is able to understand himself or the other? Who is able to break the shell? Just as attempting to break it merely confirms that it is not broken, so attempting to understand only increases the feeling of not understanding. And yet I try. I realize for certain that the attempt is futile but that does not stop me trying, just as I do not give up living my life, knowing that death is inevitable.

You may or may not be surprised that I call this a love letter, since in our relationship we have never mentioned the word love. We may have used other words, like affection or friendship or esteem. But these words are meaningless, imprecise. What is the meaning of the word 'affection' which we once used to describe our relationship? It doesn't mean a thing. It means neither love nor lack of love, but is a halfway feeling between love and no love, a halfway position between something and nothing, when a person loves and doesn't love, is angry and is not angry, hates and doesn't hate, speaks and doesn't speak, and always holds the rope in the centre. It is that fluid moderate position in everything which psychologists praise and to which they give the name mental health. Such health, in their view, consists of moderation in all things—in intelligence, in enthusiasm, in love, in hate, in ambition, in honesty.

And because honesty knows no moderation, so a person must lie to a certain extent to win the stamp of mental health from psychologists. And since love, like honesty, knows no moderation, so the word 'affection' means nothing in a relationship.

What is the relationship between us? How did it develop? Did it have a starting point? Did it, in other words, begin at the first meeting or at the last meeting or in the middle? I try now to gather the threads of my memory, to recall when the first meeting was, how your features appeared to me. The attempt seems to me now to be impossible, like trying to remember the first time I saw my face in the mirror. Or my mother's face. Or that of my father. There are some features which, the moment we set eyes on them, appear as though we have known them all along, as though they were part of us or within us and not external to us. Do you remember the first time you saw me? When was it? In your office? In my office? In your house? In my house? In a field or at one of those gatherings where intellectuals always meet? Those faces tense when both smiling and frowning, cheeks distended both in speech and silence, stomach muscles slack when inhaling and exhaling, glances always fixed upwards, whatever that upwards is, red or green, valuable or cheap.

When I look into your eyes, I do not feel that you belong to this class. I 5 see a different expression in your eyes which makes things different, less contradictory. Your smile is a smile, your frown a frown. Your features move with the muscles of your face in a spontaneous natural movement. I neither see it nor feel it and yet I know it exists, like the movement of time or of the earth or of an aeroplane which, although I do not feel it when I am inside it, I know to be there.

Sometimes that expression appears when I am sleeping or walking in 6 the street or sitting or driving my car or engrossed in work. It remains before me, strangely compelling, taking me out of the state I was in, willing me to look at it, to understand the reason for its urgency. I push it away gently at first, then forcefully, then harshly, then with an anger resembling madness.

Once it pestered me with such insistence that I asked myself whether it 7 was really a feeling of loneliness. My office is crowded, my house is crowded, Cairo is crowded. But, as in all such large cities, we live with crowdedness and loneliness at one and the same time. Between one person and another, despite close bodily contact, there is a thick wall which gets higher as people rise up the social ladder. And at night, when the city is immersed in sleep, I look around me like an orphan. I open my address book and flick through the names and telephone numbers, many numbers and many names, all set out in alphabetical order. And yet there is no one who can dispel the loneliness. This sprawling city stretched out before me is devoid of men. And yet it is crammed with males, not one of whom can meet a woman alone without thinking of jumping on her. Life in our world is made for men and nothing in it can amuse a woman other than that sort of amusement which neither amuses nor gratifies me and which only shows life in its ugliness and man in his baseness.

From time to time my phone rings and from time to time I accept some 8 man's invitation out of my desire to find out the truth and to learn about life and people. It is also an attempt to dispel loneliness. I realize the impossibility of living inside myself, of remaining without others. If I wrote for myself alone, I would choke on my words. If I spoke to myself alone, my voice would fail. If I looked at my own face all the time, I would lose my mind.

And yet I always run from others. I love to disappear far away from 9 them but I do so in order to remain in their thoughts. It is distance for the sake of closeness, separation for the sake of contact. And that's my dilemma. I want to be a separate entity and at the same time I want to be an inseparable part of others. This contradiction tears me apart, splitting me into two, one part inside myself far from others, the other part outside myself in the heart of others. One part is quiet and immobile and observes the movement of the other. Is it I who observes the other or is it the other which observes me? Which of us is motionless in time and place and which of us moves within time and on earth?

I am preoccupied with the answer to these questions, whilst the man 10 who has invited me sits silently before me, looking at me now and again to catch some movement or a glance from me which could encourage him to invite me to bed. When he finds nothing, he is surprised. He may wonder if I am affected by twentieth-century complexes or if I am like a cave woman and still like rape and pain.

I cannot deny that the idea of rape, like the idea of suicide, holds some 11 attraction for me and has been with me since time immemorial, no matter how I wrestle with its vestiges or seeds. But I do not commit suicide and nobody can rape me. No matter how difficult my life becomes, however much I suffocate, I do not commit suicide. However much a man desires me, he cannot overpower me. It is not, as you once told me, that I kill or castrate men, but I am always able to stare a man in the eyes and can always see the muscle around his mouth or his fingers quiver. It may only be quick and last no longer than a moment or two, but it is always enough for me to see it and to bend his will to mine. His muscular power, even the power of all the men in the world, is incapable of making the muscles of my hand yield under his.

You told me once that I was a strong woman. The truth is that I'm not 12 always strong. Sometimes I let my hand yield. Sometimes I feel as lost as a tiny speck in the grip of a wild surge or in the grasp of some vast creature as predatory as fate and I feel unable to do anything of my own will or choice, incapable of holding on to truth and reality. You once asked me about my dreams. In truth, most of the time I live in my dreams for I can choose and change them, whereas it is reality which changes me without my choosing. I no longer see reality as real unless it is rooted in my dreams. I admit to you that my unconscious is stronger than my conscious mind and most of the time I obey it.

I saw you in one of my dreams. You were sitting with me somewhere far 13 from the world, a place enclosing us alone, something that has never happened in reality. I was sitting beside you. Deep inside me there was a violent movement, stillness and quiet on the surface. I had a feeling of some sort of sad and mysterious happiness, a silent pulse in the body, an intense elation and a desire so strong it went beyond desire. I don't know what it was exactly that I wanted. That your eyes should remain on mine for ever? That you should raise your arms and encircle me and hide me inside yourself for ever? I awoke from sleep but you remained where you were beside me. I closed my eyes to rid myself of you, but you stayed, near to me, almost but not quite touching me, almost but not quite leaving me. Why? Why didn't you leave me? Is there something obligatory between us? Does anyone obligate you? Does anyone obligate me? I know there is no one, no one at all. And yet, I cannot say that I go to you from choice or will or that our relationship is not as vital to me as the air that enters and leaves my chest or the blood that flows in my veins.

This involuntary side of my relationship with you arouses rebellion in me, for I value my freedom. That's why I rebel against you. At times I tell you I won't see you again. Or I try to pile up your mistakes or slips of the tongue and may accuse you of things of which I accuse other men. But it is always a failed revolution, at times resembling my revolution against myself, at times making me want to throw my body from the window and rid myself of it for ever. The result is always the same. My body remains attached to me and you remain in your place before my eyes, near to me, almost but not quite touching me. Why? Why do you never touch me? Are you simply a ghost? Do you exist in reality? 14

Sometimes, when you used to see me to the door, I would feel as though you briefly touched my hand or put your arm around my waist, a light rapid touch which no sooner happened than was gone. It may not even have been a touch since there was always a distance between your hand and my body, a hair's breadth, but always enough to separate us and for my moment of certainty to vanish. Again I ask myself whether it was real or a dream? Why does this distance always remain? Is it my fear of you? Is it your fear of me? Is there really anything to fear? 15

Once I wanted to dispel the dream, to reach out and touch certainty. I invited you to my house. Do you remember the date? In your voice I heard an unusual tremor of surprise or hesitation or fear or uncertainty. You did not come. I did not ask you why. I knew that, like me, you always want to waver between certainty and doubt. 16

Is there anything to dispel doubt? Is there proof of anything? There is nothing definite between me and you that I can cling to, no appropriate word, no language, no movement, no touch, nothing at all between us to confirm anything. But there is one thing of which I'm sure (and which also cannot be proved), and that is that you feel towards me what I feel for you, to the same extent, in the same way and at the same time. Am I mistaken? I may or may not be. 17

That's how I am, my friend. I draw near to you and then draw back. I appear and disappear. I step forward and then I retreat. I decide on confrontation and then I run away. Day after day, month after month, twenty months or more. You once told me that our lives are passing, that a day that has gone will not return, that I'm wasting my life searching for the impossible or the absolute, that no one except God can satisfy me. One day I was hiding my eyes behind a pair of large sunglasses and you asked me to take them off, which I did. When you looked into my eyes, I nearly confessed to you that you are the only certainty and truth in my life. But the telephone or the doorbell rang or something happened or perhaps one of your children appeared or maybe you looked away or moved your head or arm. It seems to me that you glanced at the clock, deliberately or not. It 18 lasted no longer than a second but it was enough to tear the fine silken hair on which was balanced the feeling of certainty.

You told me once that I run away from life, that I am incapable of loving, that I suffer from the sickness of the age, that I need pills or medicine or something of the sort. I was surprised and not surprised, sad for myself and not sad. I was on the verge of feeling ill and of swallowing the pills of the twentieth-century. You asked me more than once why I did not take pills, like all intellectuals. But, my friend, I do not belong to this age, neither am I one of those intellectuals. I don't read the newspapers as they do. My eyes close in spite of themselves when they look at the papers and my ears shut when they hear the news being read. When I walk in the street I do not see faces and I appear to people to be blind and deaf. But, my friend, I am neither blind nor deaf. I see every face that passes in front of me and I read every letter written on the face of the earth and I hear every sound, even the patter of an ant or the beat of an orphan heart in the breast of a child. Do you think I'm talking nonsense? Do you really think I don't see? I saw you once when I was walking along Tahrir Street. Your car was moving fast, like all the other cars. Your face was tired, like all the other faces and your eyes were sad, like all the other eyes. It was very crowded, bodies crammed together, vehicles crammed together. The air was stagnant and sticky. Everyone was panting in a sea of sweat, practically suffocating, shouting for help, begging to be saved. But nobody saw anyone else. Nobody heard anyone else. Nobody saved anyone else. 19

Despite the speed of your car, I managed to study your face for a brief moment. Your features were not your features, your eyes were not your eyes. I wondered whether it was you or not. I quickly turned around. Your car had almost vanished in the crowd but I managed to catch the number. I stood still for a moment, wondering where you had come from and where you were going and why you were going so fast. I knew that you were coming from your office and were on your way home or going to an appointment with someone big or small, someone sick or well. I knew all that and yet I stood looking around in surprise as though I knew nothing. 20

Then I continued on my way again, my head and heart heavy with a cold creeping depression and a question with no answer: Why all this? What's it all for? Is it the pursuit of money? Or the attempt to gain power? Or is it the search for fame? But you have a great deal of all these things. What is it then? Can it be love? But does love make a face tired and the eyes sad? 21

I felt I hated this city, those faces, those eyes, the hands of the clock, everything. The hatred was so intense that I tried to close my eyes and ears and all the pores of my body. I had a violent desire to run as fast as possible and get away from everything, a violent desire to separate myself from the world, to the point of dying. 22

But one thing I did not want—to lose your face in the crowd, that in time 23 you should vanish from before my eyes. You know, my friend, that I don't want anything from you. I eat and drink and sleep and have sex and drive a car like yours. But I don't want to lose you in this crowd. Life without you is like a silent black-and-white movie. But with you, everything changes. Colours return and all things are luminous.

At this moment I wish that I could hold your hand in mine, that my 24 whole life would become delicate tender fingers to touch your face, that my whole body would split into millions of tiny fingers to wipe the tiredness from your eyes. After all this, can you still accuse me of being incapable of loving? Can you again tell me that I don't understand, that I don't have natural intelligence? Can you now understand me a little? And do I understand you a little? I hope so. It must be so!

Translated from the Arabic by Shirley Eber

STUDY QUESTIONS

1. Why is the story called "A Modern Love Letter"?
2. Discuss the narrator's problematic feelings toward her friend.
3. What accounts for the narrator's indecision, isolation, and sense of loneliness?
4. In what ways does the young woman's state of mind reflect her rebellion against the norms of society?

GHANA

 KOFI AWOONOR

*Kofi Awoonor was born in 1935 at Wheta in the Volta region of Ghana. He
received his primary school education at various missionary schools, and went
on to attend University College of Ghana. After graduating, he became a
research fellow at the Institute of African Studies and was director of the
Ghana Film and Television Corporation in Kwame Nkrumah's government.
After Nkrumah's government was overthrown in 1966, he left Ghana to study
at the University of London. Subsequently, he became a professor of
comparative literature at the State University of New York at Stony Brook.
Shortly after he returned to Ghana in 1975, he was arrested and imprisoned
for a year during a period of political crisis. Released the next year, he
accepted an appointment in Ghana's diplomatic corps. He has served as
Ghana's ambassador to Brazil and Cuba and is now head of Ghana's mission
to the United Nations.*

*Awoonor is considered one of Africa's leading poets. He is also the
author of a highly acclaimed novel,* This Earth My Brother *(1971), and
several radio and television plays. In poetry, fiction, and drama, he draws
on the traditional culture and oral literary traditions of his region. "Night
of My Blood" is a good example of the author's ability to synthesize
Western and non-Western influences. It is also representative of the poet's
commitment to preserving and making available to a wider audience the
cultural life of his society. Here the focus is a traditional initiation rite in
which the young men symbolically relive and endure the historical experience
of their community.*

Night of My Blood

Did they whisper to us the miracle of time
Telling us over the dark waters
Where we came from? Did they
Call us unto themselves
With the story of time and beginning?   5

We sat in the shadow of our ancient trees
While the waters of the land washed
Washed against our hearts,
Cleansing, cleansing.
The purifier sat among us   10
In sackcloth and ashes,
Bearing on himself the burdens
of these people. He touched our
foreheads with the wine of sour corn
and sprinkled our feet   15
with the blood of the sacred ram
Whilst the baobab rained dew on our heads.
Comforter, where is your comforting?
With all our woes and our sins,

We walked from the beginning   20
towards the land of sunset.
We were a band of malefactors
And saints.
The purifier walked in our shadow
bearing the fly-wisk of his ancestors   25
for his task is not finished.
We stumbled through the briar bush
Consoling us, moved against the
passion of rest forever.
The touchstone of our journey   30
was the silent prayers of the purifier.
Then they asked whether the harvest
should be gathered. Who sowed the crops?
We do not know: the harvesters
We know them,   35
Them that howl all night in the lanes
returning every night from funerals
officiating at a million wakes
Comforter, where is your comfort?

Gather us, gather us unto yourself our fathers   40
That we may bear the terror of this journey.
Through the briar we stumble
bearing the million crucifixes of time.
Save us the terror of our burden
Cleanse us,   45
The desert trees howl with wind blows
for the waters had washed
The sand which tossed in eyes

that opened wide in night's darkness
and there was no light   50
save the silent prayers of the purifier
As we bore the million crosses
across the vastness of time.
Then they appeared, the owners of the land
Among them were the silent lovers   55
of night's long harmattans; questioners
at the father's weary court.
The girls bearing the flowers of the desert
Cinnamon and smeared with yellow pollen of the palm
Swaying through the earth beaten path fingers   60
pointed
singing songs we could not hear,
Tearing down the glories of a thousand shrines
and dancing.
Muddying the paved paths of the fathers   65
anointed, and the offering
they bore on the wooden plates
eyes glued on the offering plates
asking for the glory of the fathers' rebirth,
Their penance-prayer voicing   70
unto the fathers
Not asking for forgiveness.
We sat among the thistles of the desert
chewing the cactus freshened
by the tear-drops of long-ago.   75
Revelling howlers in time's garden
entering the forbidden grounds
stirring us from that sleep of time,
the bearers' head turned to sunset
trampling through desert sand   80
sang a song we could not
hear the music of.
It was the season of dry wind.

We are the sons of the land
bearing the terror of this journey   85
carrying the million crucifixes of time
Then we arrived by the river Mono.[1]

---

1. Mono is a river in Dahomey: marks an important stage in the migratory journeys of the Ewes to
   their present homes from the upper regions of the Niger River. The Ewes as a people cover the
   territory that stretches between the Volta River in Ghana and the Mono in Dahomey.

There we planted our bean plants
not to wait for the season of rain

We then were the harvesters   90
As we filled our barns
With the crops of the land
the strange land that gave no food to eat.
We opened wide our hearts
washed by the desert wind   95
for cleansing in the sacred river
Our dreams were of a homeland
forever;
of a happier world.

Then we moved one day at dawn   100
carrying with us the remnants
of the feast of the passover
stumbling through dusk dawn faded
daylight making for the forests of the south.
We marched through marsh and marsh   105
retrieving acres of white sand
inhabitants sea-crabs and the
nocturnal wail of the bull frog.
One day at noon[1] we arrived;

my people, we arrived.   110
The shiny shingles washed white
glistening like the sacred ram
sacrifice awaiting; the dart of surf thrusts
into the sides of the glistening ram
the foam topping the crest of the ram   115
The drums beat that day and many days
and still beat for the deliverance
from the terror of the burden of that journey.

STUDY QUESTIONS

1. How is the narrator's initiation described? What are the ritual elements? How is the experience of the community reenacted? What hur-

---

1. *"One day at noon": refers to the arrival of Togbui Wenya and the Anlo wing of the Ewes at their
   present home at Anloga on the sea coast in the south-eastern corner of Ghana around the
   thirteenth century, or maybe earlier.*

dles and obstacles must the narrator overcome to achieve knowledge?
2. Compare the narrator's initiation with other initiation rites such as bar mitzvahs, confirmations, and graduations you may be familiar with.

◈ AMA ATA AIDOO

Ama Ata Aidoo was born in Abeadzi Kyiakor in the central region of Ghana in 1942. She was educated at the University of Ghana, and she was later a writer in residence at Stanford and Harvard universities in the United States during the 1960s. In Ghana she was a research fellow at the Institute of African Studies, and for a number of years Aidoo was a member of the English faculty at the University of Cape Coast. During the late 1970s she served as the minister for education in the government. For the last few years, she has been living in Zimbabwe and lecturing at universities in the United States and Great Britain. She also has traveled abroad to participate in international conferences in Eastern Europe and the Soviet Union.

Aidoo is known primarily as a playwright and short story writer, although she has published poetry and written an autobiographical novel. Her most acclaimed works are the plays The Dilemma of a Ghost *(1965) and* Anowa *(1970) and the collection of stories* No Sweetness Here *(1972). Her subject matter ranges from a concern with the social, political, and cultural problems of emergent elites in modern Africa to an exploration of the changing role of women in traditional society. Her artistic strength lies in her use of dialogue and monologue to create atmosphere and dramatic situation. "In the Cutting of a Drink" dramatizes the conflict between the country and the city.*

In the Cutting of a Drink

I say, my uncles, if you are going to Accra and anyone tells you that the best place for you to drop down is at the Circle, then he has done you good, but . . . Hm . . . I even do not know how to describe it. . . .

'Are all these beings that are passing this way and that way human? Did men buy all these cars with money . . . ?'

But my elders, I do not want to waste your time. I looked round and did not find my bag. I just fixed my eyes on the ground and walked on. . . . Do not ask me why. Each time I tried to raise my eyes, I was dizzy from the number of cars which were passing. And I could not stand still. If I did, I felt as if the whole world was made up of cars in motion. There is something somewhere, my uncles. Not desiring to deafen you with too long a story . . .

I stopped walking just before I stepped into the Circle itself. I stood there for a long time. Then a lorry came along and I beckoned to the driver to stop. Not that it really stopped.   4

'Where are you going?' he asked me.   5

'I am going to Mamprobi,' I replied. 'Jump in,' he said, and he started todrive away. Hm . . . I nearly fell down climbing in. As we went round the thing which was like a big bowl on a very huge stump of wood, I had it in mind to have a good look at it, and later Duayaw told me that it shoots water in the air . . . but the driver was talking to me, so I could not look at it properly. He told me he himself was not going to Mamprobi but he was going to the station where I could take a lorry which would be going there. . . .   6

Yes, my uncle, he did not deceive me. Immediately we arrived at the station I found the driver of a lorry shouting 'Mamprobi, Mamprobi'. Finally when the clock struck about two-thirty, I was knocking on the door of Duayaw. I did not knock for long when the door opened. Ah, I say, he was fast asleep, fast asleep I say, on a Saturday afternoon.   7

'How can folks find time to sleep on Saturday afternoons?' I asked myself. We hailed each other heartily. My uncles, Duayaw has done well for himself. His mother Nsedua is a very lucky woman.   8

'How is it some people are lucky with school and others are not? Did not Mansa go to school with Duayaw here in this very school which I can see for myself? What have we done that Mansa should have wanted to stop going to school?'   9

But I must continue with my tale. . . . Yes, Duayaw has done well for himself. His room has fine furniture. Only it is too small. I asked him why and he told me he was even lucky to have got that narrow place that looks like a box. It is very hard to find a place to sleep in the city. . . .   10

He asked me about the purpose of my journey. I told him everything. How, as he himself knew, my sister Mansa had refused to go to school after 'Klase Tri' and how my mother had tried to persuade her to go . . .   11

My mother, do not interrupt me, everyone present here knows you tried to do what you could by your daughter.   12

Yes, I told him how, after she had refused to go, we finally took her to this woman who promised to teach her to keep house and to work with the sewing machine . . . and how she came home the first Christmas after the woman took her but has never been home again, these twelve years.   13

Duayaw asked me whether it was my intention then to look for my sister in the city. I told him yes. He laughed saying, 'You are funny. Do you think you can find a woman in this place? You do not know where she is staying. You do not even know whether she is married or not. Where can we find her if someone big has married her and she is now living in one of those big bungalows which are some ten miles from the city?'   14

Do you cry 'My Lord', mother? You are surprised about what I said 15 about the marriage? Do not be. I was surprised too, when he talked that way. I too cried 'My Lord' . . . Yes, I too did, mother. But you and I have forgotten that Mansa was born a girl and girls do not take much time to 5 grow. We are thinking of her as we last saw her when she was ten years old. But mother, that is twelve years ago. . . .

Yes, Duayaw told me that she is by now old enough to marry and to do 16 something more than merely marry. I asked him whether he knew where she was and if he knew whether she had any children—'Children?' he cried, and he started laughing, a certain laugh. . . .

I was looking at him all the time he was talking. He told me he was not 17 just discouraging me but he wanted me to see how big and difficult it was, what I proposed to do. I replied that it did not matter. What was necessary was that even if Mansa was dead, her ghost would know that we had not forgotten her entirely. That we had not let her wander in other people's towns and that we had tried to bring her home. . . .

These are useless tears you have started to weep, my mother. Have I 18 said anything to show that she was dead?

Duayaw and I decided on the little things we would do the following 19 day as the beginning of our search. Then he gave me water for my bath and brought me food. He sat by me while I ate and asked me for news of home. I told him that his father has married another woman and of how last year the *akatse* spoiled all our cocoa. We know about that already. When I finished eating, Duayaw asked me to stretch out my bones on the bed and I did. I think I slept fine because when I opened my eyes it was dark. He had switched on his light and there was a woman in the room. He showed me her as a friend but I think she is the girl he wants to marry against the wishes of his people. She is as beautiful as sunrise, but she is not of our tribe. . . .

When Duayaw saw that I was properly awake, he told me it had struck 20 eight o'clock in the evening and his friend had brought some food. The three of us ate together.

Do not say 'Ei', Uncle, it seems as if people do this thing in the city. A 21 woman prepares a meal for a man and eats it with him. Yes, they do so often.

My mouth could not manage the food. It was prepared from cassava and 22 corn dough, but it was strange food all the same. I tried to do my best. After the meal Duayaw told me we were going for a night out. It was then I remembered my bag. I told him that as matters stood, I could not change my cloth and I could not go out with them. He would not hear of it. 'It would certainly be a crime to come to this city and not go out on a Saturday night.' He warned me though that there might not be many people, or anybody at all, where we were going who would also be in cloth but I should not worry about that.

Cut me a drink, for my throat is very dry, my Uncle. . . . 23

When we were on the street I could not believe my eyes. The whole place was as clear as the sky. Some of these lights are very beautiful indeed. Everyone should see them . . . and there are so many of them! 'Who is paying for all these lights?' I asked myself. I could not say that aloud for fear Duayaw would laugh.

We walked through many streets until we came to a big building where a band was playing. Duayaw went to buy tickets for the three of us.

You all know that I had not been to anywhere like that before. You must allow me to say that I was amazed. 'Ei, are all these people children of human beings? And where are they going? And what do they want?'

Before I went in, I thought the building was big, but when I went in, I realised the crowd in it was bigger. Some were in front of a counter buying drinks, others were dancing . . .

Yes, that was the case, Uncle, we had gone to a place where they had given a dance, but I did not know.

Some people were sitting on iron chairs around iron tables. Duayaw told some people to bring us a table and chairs and they did. As soon as we sat down, Duayaw asked us what we would drink. As for me, I told him *lamlale* but his woman asked for 'Beer' . . .

Do not be surprised, Uncles.

Yes, I remember very well, she asked for beer. It was not long before Duayaw brought them. I was too surprised to drink mine. I sat with my mouth open and watched the daughter of a woman cut beer like a man. The band had stopped playing for some time and soon they started again. Duayaw and his woman went to dance. I sat there and drank my *lamlale*. I cannot describe how they danced.

After some time, the band stopped playing and Duayaw and his woman came to sit down. I was feeling cold and I told Duayaw. He said, 'And this is no wonder, have you not been drinking this women's drink all the time?'

'Does it make one cold?' I asked him.

'Yes,' he replied. 'Did you not know that? You must drink beer.'

'Yes,' I replied. So he bought me beer. When I was drinking the beer, he told me I would be warm if I danced.

'You know I cannot dance the way you people dance,' I told him.

'And how do we dance?' he asked me.

'I think you all dance like white men and as I do not know how that is done, people would laugh at me,' I said. Duayaw started laughing. He could not contain himself. He laughed so much his woman asked him what it was all about. He said something in the white man's language and they started laughing again. Duayaw then told me that if people were dancing, they would be so busy that they would not have time to watch others dance. And also, in the city, no one cares if you dance well or not . . .

Yes, I danced too, my Uncles. I did not know anyone, that is true. My Uncle, do not say that instead of concerning myself with the business for which I had gone to the city, I went dancing. Oh, if you only knew what happened at this place, you would not be saying this. I would not like to stop somewhere and tell you the end . . . I would rather like to put a rod under the story, as it were, clear off every little creeper in the bush . . .

But as we were talking about the dancing, something made Duayaw 40 turn to look behind him where four women were sitting by the table. . . . Oh! he turned his eyes quickly, screwed his face into something queer which I could not understand and told me that if I wanted to dance, I could ask one of those women to dance with me.

My Uncles, I too was very surprised when I heard that. I asked Duayaw 41 if people who did not know me would dance with me. He said 'Yes.' I lifted my eyes, my Uncles, and looked at those four young women sitting round a table alone. They were sitting all alone, I say. I got up.

I hope I am making myself clear, my Uncles, but I was trembling like 42 water in a brass bowl.

Immediately one of them saw me, she jumped up and said something in 43 that kind of white man's language which everyone, even those who have not gone to school, speak in the city. I shook my head. She said something else in the language of the people of the place. I shook my head again. Then I heard her ask me in Fante whether I wanted to dance with her. I replied 'Yes.'

Ei! my little sister, are you asking me a question? Oh! you want to know 44 whether I found Mansa? I do not know. . . . Our Uncles have asked me to tell everything that happened there, and you too! I am cooking the whole meal for you, why do you want to lick the ladle now?

Yes, I went to dance with her. I kept looking at her so much I think I was 45 all the time stepping on her feet. I say, she was as black as you and I, but her hair was very long and fell on her shoulders like that of a white woman. I did not touch it but I saw it was very soft. Her lips with that red paint looked like a fresh wound. There was no space between her skin and her dress. Yes, I danced with her. When the music ended, I went back to where I was sitting. I do not know what she told her companions about me, but I heard them laugh.

It was this time that something made me realise that they were all bad 46 women of the city. Duayaw had told me I would feel warm if I danced, yet after I had danced, I was colder than before. You would think someone had poured water on me. I was unhappy thinking about these women. 'Have they no homes?' I asked myself. 'Do not their mothers like them? God, we are all toiling for our threepence to buy something to eat . . . but oh! this is no work.'

When I thought of my own sister, who was lost, I became a little happy 47 because I felt that although I had not found her, she was nevertheless married to a man and all was well with her.

When they started to play the band again, I went to the women's table 48 to ask the one with whom I had danced to dance again. But someone had gone with her already. I got one of the two who were still sitting there. She went with me. When we were dancing she asked me whether it was true that I was a Fante. I replied, 'Yes.' We did not speak again. When the band stopped playing, she told me to take her to where they sold things to buy her beer and cigarettes. I was wondering whether I had the money. When we were where the lights were shining brightly, something told me to look at her face. Something pulled at my heart.

'Young woman, is this the work you do?' I asked her. 49

'Young man, what work do you mean?' she too asked me. I laughed. 50

'Do you not know what work?' I asked again. 51

'And who are you to ask me such questions? I say, who are you? Let me 52 tell you that any kind of work is work. You villager, you villager, who are you?' she screamed.

I was afraid. People around were looking at us. I laid my hands on her 53 shoulders to calm her down and she hit them away.

'Mansa, Mansa,' I said. 'Do you not know me?' She looked at me for a 54 long time and started laughing. She laughed, laughed as if the laughter did not come from her stomach. Yes, as if she was hungry.

'I think you are my brother,' she said. 'Hm.' 55

Oh, my mother and my aunt, oh, little sister, are you all weeping? As for 56 you women!

What is there to weep about? I was sent to find a lost child. I found her 57 a woman.

Cut me a drink . . . 58

Any kind of work is work. . . . This is what Mansa told me with a mouth 59 that looked like clotted blood. Any kind of work is work . . . so do not weep. She will come home this Christmas.

My brother, cut me another drink. Any form of work is work . . . is 60 work . . . is work!

STUDY QUESTIONS

1. What does the narrator find unusual about life in the city? How has there been a breakdown in social values?
2. What motivates the narrator to seek Mansa?
3. Who is responsible for Mansa's downfall?
4. Discuss the similarities between the organization of the story and traditional storytelling techniques.

ISRAEL

YEHUDA AMICHAI

Yehuda Amichai is recognized as one of the most important poets writing in Israel today. He was born in Würzburg, Germany, in 1924, but the brutal treatment of Jews after the Nazis came to power prompted Amichai's family to flee Germany. They emigrated to Palestine and settled in Jerusalem in 1936. He received a religious education and later graduated from Hebrew University. When World War II broke out, he fought for the British army, and during the Israeli war of independence in 1948, he served in the Jewish armed forces. Since then, he has divided his time between teaching and traveling abroad to give lectures and poetry readings. Much of Amichai's poetry is concerned with exploring inner consciousness and experimenting with language. In his writing, he strives to intertwine seemingly conflicting levels of meaning and arrive at a unified vision. Like many other writers of his generation, Amichai is skeptical about the Israeli government's policies, and he views the Palestinian–Israeli conflict as tragic. His humanist concerns over these issues are reflected in "Jerusalem" and "Sort of an Apocalypse."

Jerusalem

On a roof in the Old City
laundry hanging in the late afternoon sunlight:
the white sheet of a woman who is my enemy,
the towel of a man who is my enemy,
to wipe off the sweat of his brow.   5

In the sky of the Old City
a kite.
At the other end of the string,
a child

I can't see   10
because of the wall.

We have put up many flags,
they have put up many flags.
To make us think that they're happy.
To make them think that we're happy.   15

Translated from the Hebrew by Chana Bloch
and Stephen Mitchell

Sort of an Apocalypse

The man under his fig tree telephoned the man under his vine:
"Tonight they definitely might come. Assign
positions, armor-plate the leaves, secure the tree,
tell the dead to report home immediately."

The white lamb leaned over, said to the wolf: 5
"Humans are bleating and my heart aches with grief.
I'm afraid they'll get to gunpoint, to bayonets in the dust.
At our next meeting this matter will be discussed."

All the nations (united) will flow to Jerusalem
to see if the Torah has gone out. And then,   10
inasmuch as it's spring, they'll come down
and pick flowers from all around.

And they'll beat swords into plowshares and plowshares into
    swords,
and so on and so on, and back and forth.   15

Perhaps from being beaten thinner and thinner,
the iron of hatred will vanish, forever.

Translated from the Hebrew by Chana Bloch
and Stephen Mitchell

STUDY QUESTIONS

1. How does the poet define the division between Arabs and Jews in
   "Jerusalem"?

2. How is imagery used in "Jerusalem" to convey a human predicament?
3. How does the humor and incongruity in "Sort of an Apocalypse" help convey the message?
4. What does the author mean by the title "Sort of an Apocalypse"?

◈ Amos Oz

Amos Oz was born in Jerusalem in 1939. As a teenager, he rebelled against his conservative Zionist family by joining a kibbutz and changing his name from Khausner to Oz. He left the kibbutz to pursue his education, first at Hebrew University and later at Oxford. Except for traveling and lecturing abroad, he continues to live on a kibbutz, to which, according to custom, he signs over all outside income. As a reserve soldier, Oz has seen military service in two armed conflicts—in the Sinai in 1967 and in the Golan Heights in 1973. He has published four novels and several collections of stories, novellas, and essays. His first novel, Elsewhere, Perhaps *(1973), is considered the best fictional account of kibbutz life to come out of Israel.*

A central concern of Oz's fiction is the conflict between the ideals of Zionism and the realities of Israeli life. The author takes the myths associated with Israel—the reclamation of the soil, the noble experiments of the kibbutz, the transformation of the Jewish spirit, the wars against the Arabs—and examines their hidden truth. Like many Israeli writers and intellectuals, he is disturbed by the policies of the Israeli government toward the Palestinians. Another theme in his work is the conflict between the will of the individual and the demands of the community. In "Nomad and Viper," the Arab-Israeli conflict is at center stage, with life on the kibbutz reflecting the experience of a broader Jewish community.

Nomad and Viper

1

The famine brought them. 1

They fled north from the horrors of famine, together with their dusty 2 flocks. From September to April the desert had not known a moment's relief from drought. The loess was pounded to dust. Famine had spread through the nomads' encampments and wrought havoc among their flocks.

The military authorities gave the situation their urgent attention. De- 3 spite certain hesitations, they decided to open the roads leading north to the Bedouins. A whole population—men, women, and children—could not simply be abandoned to the horrors of starvation.

Dark, sinuous, and wiry, the desert tribesmen trickled along the dirt   4
paths, and with them came their emaciated flocks. They meandered along
gullies hidden from town dwellers' eyes. A persistent stream pressed
northward, circling the scattered settlements, staring wide-eyed at the
sights of the settled land. The dark flocks spread into the fields of golden
stubble, tearing and chewing with strong, vengeful teeth. The nomads'
bearing was stealthy and subdued; they shrank from watchful eyes. They
took pains to avoid encounters. Tried to conceal their presence.

If you passed them on a noisy tractor and set billows of dust loose on   5
them, they would courteously gather their scattered flocks and give you a
wide passage, wider by far than was necessary. They stared at you from a
distance, frozen like statues. The scorching atmosphere blurred their appearance and gave a uniform look to their features: a shepherd with his
staff, a woman with her babes, an old man with his eyes sunk deep in their
sockets. Some were half-blind, or perhaps feigned half-blindness from
some vague alms-gathering motive. Inscrutable to the likes of you.

How unlike our well-tended sheep were their miserable specimens: 6
knots of small, skinny beasts huddling into a dark, seething mass, silent
and subdued, humble as their dumb keepers.

The camels alone spurn meekness. From atop tall necks they fix you   7
with tired eyes brimming with scornful sorrow. The wisdom of age seems
to lurk in their eyes, and a nameless tremor runs often through their skin.

Sometimes you manage to catch them unawares. Crossing a field on   8
foot, you may suddenly happen on an indolent flock standing motionless,
noon-struck, their feet apparently rooted in the parched soil. Among them
lies the shepherd, fast asleep, dark as a block of basalt. You approach and
cover him with a harsh shadow. You are startled to find his eyes wide
open. He bares most of his teeth in a placatory smile. Some of them are
gleaming, others decayed. His smell hits you. You grimace. Your grimace
hits him like a punch in the face. Daintily he picks himself up, trunk erect,
shoulders hunched. You fix him with a cold blue eye. He broadens his
smile and utters a guttural syllable. His garb is a compromise: a short,
patched European jacket over a white desert robe. He cocks his head to one
side. An appeased gleam crosses his face. If you do not upbraid him, he
suddenly extends his left hand and asks for a cigarette in rapid Hebrew.
His voice has a silken quality, like that of a shy woman. If your mood is
generous, you put a cigarette to your lips and toss another into his wrinkled palm. To your surprise, he snatches a gilt lighter from the recesses of
his robe and offers a furtive flame. The smile never leaves his lips. His
smile lasts too long, is unconvincing. A flash of sunlight darts off the thick
gold ring adorning his finger and pierces your squinting eyes.

Eventually you turn your back on the nomad and continue on your way.   9
After a hundred, two hundred paces, you may turn your head and see him
standing just as he was, his gaze stabbing your back. You could swear that
he is still smiling, that he will go on smiling for a long while to come.

And then, their singing in the night. A long-drawn-out, dolorous wail   10
drifts on the night air from sunset until the early hours. The voices penetrate to the gardens and pathways of the kibbutz and charge our nights
with an uneasy heaviness. No sooner have you settled down to sleep than
a distant drumbeat sets the rhythm of your slumber like the pounding of
an obdurate heart. Hot are the nights, and vapor-laden. Stray clouds caress
the moon like a train of gentle camels, camels without any bells.

The nomads' tents are made up of dark drapes. Stray women drift   11
around at night, barefoot and noiseless. Lean, vicious nomad hounds dart
out of the camp to challenge the moon all night long. Their barking drives
our kibbutz dogs insane. Our finest dog went mad one night, broke into
the henhouse, and massacred the young chicks. It was not out of savagery
that the watchmen shot him. There was no alternative. Any reasonable
man would justify their action.

2

You might imagine that the nomad incursion enriched our heat-prostrated   12
nights with a dimension of poetry. This may have been the case for some
of our unattached girls. But we cannot refrain from mentioning a whole
string of prosaic, indeed unaesthetic disturbances, such as foot-and-mouth
disease, crop damage, and an epidemic of petty thefts.

The foot-and-mouth disease came out of the desert, carried by their   13
livestock, which had never been subjected to any proper medical inspection. Although we took various early precautions, the virus infected our
sheep and cattle, severely reducing the milk yield and killing off a number
of animals.

As for the damage to the crops, we had to admit that we had never   14
managed to catch one of the nomads in the act. All we ever found were the
tracks of men and animals among the rows of vegetables, in the hayfields,
and deep inside the carefully fenced orchards. And wrecked irrigation
pipes, plot markers, farming implements left out in the fields, and other
objects.

We are not the kind to take such things lying down. We are no believers   15
in forbearance or vegetarianism. This is especially true of our younger
men. Among the veteran founders there are a few adherents of Tolstoyan
ideas and such like. Decency constrains me not to dwell in detail on certain
isolated and exceptional acts of reprisal conducted by some of the youngsters whose patience had expired, such as cattle rustling, stoning a nomad
boy, or beating one of the shepherds senseless. In defense of the perpetrators of the last-mentioned act of retaliation I must state clearly that the
shepherd in question had an infuriatingly sly face. He was blind in one
eye, broken-nosed, drooling; and his mouth—on this the men responsible

were unanimous—was set with long, curved fangs like a fox's. A man with such an appearance was capable of anything. And the Bedouins would certainly not forget this lesson.

The pilfering was the most worrisome aspect of all. They laid hands on the unripe fruit in our orchards, pocketed the faucets, whittled away piles of empty sacks in the fields, stole into the henhouses, and even made away with the modest valuables from our little houses. 16

The very darkness was their accomplice. Elusive as the wind, they passed through the settlement, evading both the guards we had posted and the extra guards we had added. Sometimes you would set out on a tractor or a battered jeep toward midnight to turn off the irrigation faucets in an outlying field and your headlights would trap fleeting shadows, a man or a night beast. An irritable guard decided one night to open fire, and in the dark he managed to kill a stray jackal. 17

Needless to say, the kibbutz secretariat did not remain silent. Several times Etkin, the secretary, called in the police, but their tracking dogs betrayed or failed them. Having led their handlers a few paces outside the kibbutz fence, they raised their black noses, uttered a savage howl, and stared foolishly ahead. 18

Spot raids on the tattered tents revealed nothing. It was as if the very earth had decided to cover up the plunder and brazenly outstare the victims. Eventually the elder of the tribe was brought to the kibbutz office, flanked by a pair of inscrutable nomads. The short-tempered policemen pushed them forward with repeated cries of "Yallah, yallah." 19

We, the members of the secretariat, received the elder and his men politely and respectfully. We invited them to sit down on the bench, smiled at them, and offered them steaming coffee prepared by Geula at Etkin's special request. The old man responded with elaborate courtesies, favoring us with a smile which he kept up from the beginning of the interview till its conclusion. He phrased his remarks in careful, formal Hebrew. 20

It was true that some of the youngsters of his tribe had laid hands on our property. Why should he deny it. Boys would be boys, and the world was getting steadily worse. He had the honor of begging our pardon and restoring the stolen property. Stolen property fastens its teeth in the flesh of the thief, as the proverb says. That was the way of it. What could one do about the hotheadedness of youth? He deeply regretted the trouble and distress we had been caused. 21

So saying, he put his hand into the folds of his robe and drew out a few screws, some gleaming, some rusty, a pair of pruning hooks, a stray knife-blade, a pocket flashlight, a broken hammer, and three grubby bank notes, as a recompense for our loss and worry. 22

Etkin spread his hands in embarrassment. For reasons best known to himself, he chose to ignore our guest's Hebrew and to reply in broken 23

Arabic, the residue of his studies during the time of the riots and the siege. He opened his remarks with a frank and clear statement about the brotherhood of nations—the cornerstone of our ideology—and about the quality of neighborliness of which the peoples of the East had long been justly proud, and never more so than in these days of bloodshed and groundless hatred.

To Etkin's credit, let it be said that he did not shrink in the slightest from reciting a full and detailed list of the acts of theft, damage, and sabotage that our guest—as the result of oversight, no doubt—had refrained from mentioning in his apology. If all the stolen property were returned and the vandalism stopped once and for all, we would be wholeheartedly willing to open a new page in the relations of our two neighboring communities. Our children would doubtless enjoy and profit from an educational courtesy visit to the Bedouin encampment, the kind of visit that broadens horizons. And it went without saying that the tribe's children would pay a return visit to our kibbutz home, in the interest of deepening mutual understanding. 24

The old man neither relaxed nor broadened his smile, but kept it sternly at its former level as he remarked with an abundance of polite phrases that the gentlemen of the kibbutz would be able to prove no further thefts beyond those he had already admitted and for which he had sought our forgiveness. 25

He concluded with elaborate benedictions, wished us health and long life, posterity and plenty, then took his leave and departed, accompanied by his two barefooted companions wrapped in their dark robes. They were soon swallowed up by the wadi that lay outside the kibbutz fence. 26

Since the police had proved ineffectual—and had indeed abandoned the investigation—some of our young men suggested making an excursion one night to teach the savages a lesson in a language they would really understand. 27

Etkin rejected their suggestion with disgust and with reasonable arguments. The young men, in turn, applied to Etkin a number of epithets that decency obliges me to pass over in silence. Strangely enough, Etkin ignored their insults and reluctantly agreed to put their suggestion before the kibbutz secretariat. Perhaps he was afraid that they might take matters into their own hands. 28

Toward evening, Etkin went around from room to room and invited the committee to an urgent meeting at eight-thirty. When he came to Geula, he told her about the young men's ideas and the undemocratic pressure to which he was being subjected, and asked her to bring along to the meeting a pot of black coffee and a lot of good will. Geula responded with an acid smile. Her eyes were bleary because Etkin had awakened her from a troubled sleep. As she changed her clothes, the night fell, damp and hot and close. 29

3

Damp and close and hot the night fell on the kibbutz, tangled in the dust-laden cypresses, oppressed the lawns and ornamental shrubs. Sprinklers scattered water onto the thirsty lawn, but it was swallowed up at once: perhaps it evaporated even before it touched the grass. An irritable phone rang vainly in the locked office. The walls of the houses gave out a damp vapor. From the kitchen chimney a stiff column of smoke rose like an arrow into the heart of the sky, because there was no breeze. From the greasy sinks came a shout. A dish had been broken and somebody was bleeding. A fat house-cat had killed a lizard or a snake and dragged its prey onto the baking concrete path to toy with it lazily in the dense evening sunlight. An ancient tractor started to rumble in one of the sheds, choked, belched a stench of oil, roared, spluttered, and finally managed to set out to deliver an evening meal to the second shift, who were toiling in an outlying field. Near the Persian lilac Geula saw a bottle dirty with the remnants of a greasy liquid. She kicked at it repeatedly, but instead of shattering, the bottle rolled heavily among the rosebushes. She picked up a big stone. She tried to hit the bottle. She longed to smash it. The stone missed. The girl began to whistle a vague tune. [30]

Geula was a short, energetic girl of twenty-nine or so. Although she had not yet found a husband, none of us would deny her good qualities, such as the dedication she lavished on local social and cultural activities. Her face was pale and thin. No one could rival her in brewing strong coffee—coffee to raise the dead, we called it. A pair of bitter lines were etched at the corners of her mouth. [31]

On summer evenings, when the rest of us would lounge in a group on a rug spread on one of the lawns and launch jokes and bursts of cheerful song heavenward, accompanied by clouds of cigarette smoke, Geula would shut herself up in her room and not join us until she had prepared the pot of scalding, strong coffee. She it was, too, who always took pains to ensure that there was no shortage of biscuits. [32]

What had passed between Geula and me is not relevant here, and I shall make do with a hint or two. Long ago we used to stroll together to the orchards in the evening and talk. It was all a long time ago, and it is a long time since it ended. We would exchange unconventional political ideas or argue about the latest books. Geula was a stern and sometimes merciless critic: I was covered in confusion. She did not like my stories, because of the extreme polarity of situations, scenery, and characters, with no intermediate shades between black and white. I would utter an apology or a denial, but Geula always had ready proofs and she was a very methodical thinker. Sometimes I would dare to rest a conciliatory hand on her neck, and wait for her to calm down. But she never relaxed completely. If once or twice she leaned against me, she always blamed her broken sandal or [33] her aching head. And so we drifted apart. To this day she still cuts my stories out of the periodicals, and arranges them in a cardboard box kept in a special drawer devoted to them alone.

I always buy her a new book of poems for her birthday. I creep into her room when she is out and leave the book on her table, without any inscription or dedication. Sometimes we happen to sit together in the dining hall. I avoid her glance, so as not to have to face her mocking sadness. On hot days, when faces are covered in sweat, the acne on her cheeks reddens and she seems to have no hope. When the cool of autumn comes, I sometimes find her pretty and attractive from a distance. On such days Geula likes to walk to the orchards in the early evening. She goes alone and comes back alone. Some of the youngsters come and ask me what she is looking for there, and they have a malicious snicker on their faces. I tell them that I don't know. And I really don't. 34

4

Viciously Geula picked up another stone to hurl at the bottle. This time she did not miss, but she still failed to hear the shattering sound she craved. The stone grazed the bottle, which tinkled faintly and disappeared under one of the bushes. A third stone, bigger and heavier than the other two, was launched from ridiculously close range: the girl trampled on the loose soil of the flower bed and stood right over the bottle. This time there was a harsh, dry explosion, which brought no relief. Must get out. 35

Damp and close and hot the night fell, its heat prickling the skin like broken glass. Geula retraced her steps, passed the balcony of her room, tossed her sandals inside, and walked down barefoot onto the dirt path. 36

The clods of earth tickled the soles of her feet. There was a rough friction, and her nerve endings quivered with flickers of vague excitement. Beyond the rocky hill the shadows were waiting for her: the orchard in the last of the light. With determined hands she widened the gap in the fence and slipped through. At that moment a slight evening breeze began to stir. It was a warmish summer breeze with no definite direction. An old sun rolled westward, trying to be sucked up by the dusty horizon. A last tractor climbed back to the depot, panting along the dirt road from the outlying plots. No doubt it was the tractor that had taken the second-shift workers their supper. It seemed shrouded in smoke or summer haze. 37

Geula bent down and picked some pebbles out of the dust. Absently she began to throw them back again, one by one. There were lines of poetry on her lips, some by the young poets she was fond of, others her own. By the irrigation pipe she paused, bent down, and drank as though kissing the faucet. But the faucet was rusty, the pipe was still hot, and the water was tepid and foul. Nevertheless she bent her head and let the water pour over her face and neck and into her shirt. A sharp taste of rust and wet dust 38 filled her throat. She closed her eyes and stood in silence. No relief. Perhaps a cup of coffee. But only after the orchard. Must go now.

5

The orchards were heavily laden and fragrant. The branches intertwined, converging above the rows of trunks to form a shadowy dome. Underfoot the irrigated soil retained a hidden dampness. Shadows upon shadows at the foot of those gnarled trunks. Geula picked a plum, sniffed and crushed it. Sticky juice dripped from it. The sight made her feel dizzy. And the smell. She crushed a second plum. She picked another and rubbed it on her cheek till she was spattered with juice. Then, on her knees, she picked up a dry stick and scratched shapes in the dust. Aimless lines and curves. Sharp angles. Domes. A distant bleating invaded the orchard. Dimly she became aware of a sound of bells. She was far away. The nomad stopped behind Geula's back, as silent as a phantom. He dug at the dust with his big toe, and his shadow fell in front of him. But the girl was blinded by a flood of sounds. She saw and heard nothing. For a long time she continued to kneel on the ground and draw shapes in the dust with her twig. The nomad waited patiently in total silence. From time to time he closed his good eye and stared ahead of him with the other, the blind one. Finally he reached out and bestowed a long caress on the air. His obedient shadow moved in the dust. Geula stared, leapt to her feet, and leaned against the nearest tree, letting out a low sound. The nomad let his shoulders drop and put on a faint smile. Geula raised her arm and stabbed the air with her twig. The nomad continued to smile. His gaze dropped to her bare feet. His voice was hushed, and the Hebrew he spoke exuded a rare gentleness: 39

"What time is it?" 40

Geula inhaled to her lungs' full capacity. Her features grew sharp, her glance cold. Clearly and dryly she replied: 41

"It is half past six. Precisely." 42

The Arab broadened his smile and bowed slightly, as if to acknowledge a great kindness. 43

"Thank you very much, miss." 44

His bare toe had dug deep into the damp soil, and the clods of earth crawled at his feet as if there were a startled mole burrowing underneath them. 45

Geula fastened the top button of her blouse. There were large perspiration stains on her shirt, drawing attention to her armpits. She could smell the sweat on her body, and her nostrils widened. The nomad closed his blind eye and looked up. His good eye blinked. His skin was very dark; it was alive and warm. Creases were etched in his cheeks. He was unlike any man Geula had ever known, and his smell and color and breathing were also strange. His nose was long and narrow, and a shadow of a mustache 46 showed beneath it. His cheeks seemed to be sunk into his mouth cavity. His lips were thin and fine, much finer than her own. But the chin was strong, almost expressing contempt or rebellion.

The man was repulsively handsome, Geula decided to herself. Uncon- 47 sciously she responded with a mocking half-smile to the nomad's persistent grin. The Bedouin drew two crumpled cigarettes from a hidden pocket in his belt, laid them on his dark, outstretched palm, and held them out to her as though proffering crumbs to a sparrow. Geula dropped her smile, nodded twice, and accepted one. She ran the cigarette through her fingers, slowly, dreamily, ironing out the creases, straightening it, and only then did she put it to her lips. Quick as lightning, before she realized the purpose of the man's sudden movement, a tiny flame was dancing in front of her. Geula shielded the lighter with her hand even though there was no breeze in the orchard, sucked in the flame, closed her eyes. The nomad lit his own cigarette and bowed politely.

"Thank you very much," he said in his velvety voice. 48

"Thanks," Geula replied. "Thank you." 49

"You from the kibbutz?" 50

Geula nodded. 51

"Goo-d." An elongated syllable escaped from between his gleaming 52 teeth. "That's goo-d."

The girl eyed his desert robe. 53

"Aren't you hot in that thing?" 54

The man gave an embarrassed, guilty smile, as if he had been caught 55 red-handed. He took a slight step backward.

"Heaven forbid, it's not hot. Really not. Why? There's air, there's wa- 56 ter. . . ." And he fell silent.

The treetops were already growing darker. A first jackal sniffed the 57 oncoming night and let out a tired howl. The orchard filled with a scurry of small, busy feet. All of a sudden Geula became aware of the throngs of black goats intruding in search of their master. They swirled silently in and out of the fruit trees. Geula pursed her lips and let out a short whistle of surprise.

"What are you doing here, anyway? Stealing?" 58

The nomad cowered as though a stone had been thrown at him. His 59 hand beat a hollow tattoo on his chest.

"No, not stealing, heaven forbid, really not." He added a lengthy oath 60 in his own language and resumed his silent smile. His blind eye winked nervously. Meanwhile an emaciated goat darted forward and rubbed against his leg. He kicked it away and continued to swear with passion:

"Not steal, truly, by Allah not steal. Forbidden to steal." 61

"Forbidden in the Bible," Geula replied with a dry, cruel smile. "For- 62 bidden to steal, forbidden to kill, forbidden to covet, and forbidden to commit adultery. The righteous are above suspicion."

The Arab cowered before the onslaught of words and looked down at 63 the ground. Shamefaced. Guilty. His foot continued to kick restlessly at the loose earth. He was trying to ingratiate himself. His blind eye narrowed. Geula was momentarily alarmed: surely it was a wink. The smile left his lips. He spoke in a soft, drawn-out whisper, as though uttering a prayer.

"Beautiful girl, truly very beautiful girl. Me, I got no girl yet. Me still 64 young. No girl yet. Yaaa," he concluded with a guttural yell directed at an impudent goat that had rested its forelegs against a tree trunk and was munching hungrily at the foliage. The animal cast a pensive, skeptical glance at its master, shook its beard, and solemnly resumed its munching.

Without warning, and with amazing agility, the shepherd leapt through 65 the air and seized the beast by the hindquarters, lifted it above his head, let out a terrifying, savage screech, and flung it ruthlessly to the ground. Then he spat and turned to the girl.

"Beast," he apologized. "Beast. What to do. No brains. No manners." 66

The girl let go of the tree trunk against which she had been resting and 67 leaned toward the nomad. A sweet shudder ran down her back. Her voice was still firm and cool.

"Another cigarette?" she asked. "Have you got another cigarette?" 68

The Bedouin replied with a look of anguish, almost of despair. He apol- 69 ogized. He explained at length that he had no more cigarettes, not even one, not even a little one. No more. All gone. What a pity. He would gladly, very gladly, have given her one. None left. All gone.

The beaten goat was getting shakily to its feet. Treading circumspectly, 70 it returned to the tree trunk, disingenuously observing its master out of the corner of its eye. The shepherd watched it without moving. The goat reached up, rested its front hoofs on the tree, and calmly continued munching. The Arab picked up a heavy stone and swung his arm wildly. Geula seized his arm and restrained him.

"Leave it. Why. Let it be. It doesn't understand. It's only a beast. No 71 brains, no manners."

The nomad obeyed. In total submission he let the stone drop. Then 72 Geula let go of his arm. Once again the man drew the lighter out of his belt. With thin, pensive fingers he toyed with it. He accidentally lit a small flame, and hastily blew at it. The flame widened slightly, slanted, and died. Nearby a jackal broke into a loud, piercing wail. The rest of the goats, meanwhile, had followed the example of the first and were absorbed in rapid, almost angry munching.

A vague wail came from the nomad encampment away to the south, the 73 dim drum beating time to its languorous call. The dusky men were sitting around their campfires, sending skyward their single-noted song. The night took up the strain and answered with dismal cricket-chirp. Last glimmers of light were dying away in the far west. The orchard stood in darkness. Sounds gathered all around, the wind's whispering, the goats' sniffing, the rustle of ravished leaves. Geula pursed her lips and whistled an old tune. The nomad listened to her with rapt attention, his head cocked to one side in surprise, his mouth hanging slightly open. She glanced at her watch. The hands winked back at her with a malign, phosphorescent glint, but said nothing. Night.

The Arab turned his back on Geula, dropped to his knees, touched his 74 forehead on the ground, and began mumbling fervently.

"You've got no girl yet," Geula broke into his prayer. "You're still too 75 young." Her voice was loud and strange. Her hands were on her lips, her breathing still even. The man stopped praying, turned his dark face toward her, and muttered a phrase in Arabic. He was still crouched on all fours, but his pose suggested a certain suppressed joy.

"You're still young," Geula repeated, "very young. Perhaps twenty. 76 Perhaps thirty. Young. No girl for you. Too young."

The man replied with a very long and solemn remark in his own lan- 77 guage. She laughed nervously, her hands embracing her hips.

"What's the matter with you?" she inquired, laughing still. "Why are 78 you talking to me in Arabic all of a sudden? What do you think I am? What do you want here, anyway?"

Again the nomad replied in his own language. Now a note of terror 79 filled his voice. With soft, silent steps he recoiled and withdrew as though from a dying creature. She was breathing heavily now, panting, trembling. A single wild syllable escaped from the shepherd's mouth: a sign between him and his goats. The goats responded and thronged around him, their feet pattering on the carpet of dead leaves like cloth ripping. The crickets fell silent. The goats huddled in the dark, a terrified, quivering mass, and disappeared into the darkness, the shepherd vanishing in their midst.

Afterward, alone and trembling, she watched an airplane passing in the 80 dark sky above the treetops, rumbling dully, its lights blinking alternately with a rhythm as precise as that of the drums: red, green, red, green, red. The night covered over the traces. There was a smell of bonfires on the air and a smell of dust borne on the breeze. Only a slight breeze among the fruit trees. Then panic struck her and her blood froze. Her mouth opened to scream but she did not scream, she started to run and she ran barefoot with all her strength for home and stumbled and rose and ran as though pursued, but only the sawing of the crickets chased after her.

6

She returned to her room and made coffee for all the members of the 81 secretariat, because she remembered her promise to Etkin. Outside the cool of evening had set in, but inside her room the walls were hot and her body was also on fire. Her clothes stuck to her body because she had been running, and her armpits disgusted her. The spots on her face were glowing. She stood and counted the number of times the coffee boiled—seven successive boilings, as she had learned to do it from her brother Ehud before he was killed in a reprisal raid in the desert. With pursed lips she counted as the black liquid rose and subsided, rose and subsided, bubbling fiercely as it reached its climax.

That's enough, now. Take clean clothes for the evening. Go to the show- 82 ers.

What can that Etkin understand about savages. A great socialist. What 83 does he know about Bedouins. A nomad sniffs out weakness from a distance. Give him a kind word, or a smile, and he pounces on you like a wild beast and tries to rape you. It was just as well I ran away from him.

In the showers the drain was clogged and the bench was greasy. Geula 84 put her clean clothes on the stone ledge. I'm not shivering because the water's cold. I'm shivering with disgust. Those black fingers, and how he went straight for my throat. And his teeth. And the goats. Small and skinny like a child, but so strong. It was only by biting and kicking that I managed to escape. Soap my belly and everything, soap it again and again. Yes, let the boys go right away tonight to their camp and smash their black bones because of what they did to me. Now I must get outside.

7

She left the shower and started back toward her room, to pick up the coffee 85 and take it to the secretariat. But on the way she heard crickets and laughter, and she remembered him bent down on all fours, and she was alarmed and stood still in the dark. Suddenly she vomited among the flowering shrubs. And she began to cry. Then her knees gave way. She sat down to rest on the dark earth. She stopped crying. But her teeth continued to chatter, from the cold or from pity. Suddenly she was not in a hurry any more, even the coffee no longer seemed important, and she thought to herself: There's still time. There's still time.

Those planes sweeping the sky tonight were probably on a night- 86 bombing exercise. Repeatedly they roared among the stars, keeping up a constant flashing, red, green, red, green, red. In counterpoint came the singing of the nomads and their drums, a persistent heartbeat in the distance: One, one, two. One, one, two. And silence.

8

From eight-thirty until nearly nine o'clock we waited for Geula. At five to 87 nine Etkin said that he could not imagine what had happened; he could not recall her ever having missed a meeting or been late before; at all events, we must now begin the meeting and turn to the business on the agenda.

He began with a summary of the facts. He gave details of the damage 88 that had apparently been caused by the Bedouins, although there was no formal proof, and enumerated the steps that had been taken on the committee's initiative. The appeal to good will. Calling in the police. Strengthening the guard around the settlement. Tracking dogs. The meeting with the elder of the tribe. He had to admit, Etkin said, that we had now reached an impasse. Nevertheless, he believed that we had to maintain a sense of balance and not give way to extremism, because hatred always gave rise to further hatred. It was essential to break the vicious circle of hostility. He therefore opposed with all the moral force at his disposal the approach—and particularly the intentions—of certain of the younger members. He wished to remind us, by way of conclusion, that the conflict between herdsmen and tillers of the soil was as old as human civilization, as seemed to be evidenced by the story of Cain, who rose up against Abel, his brother. It was fitting, in view of the social gospel we had adopted, that we should put an end to this ancient feud, too, just as we had put an end to other ugly phenomena. It was up to us, and everything depended on our moral strength.

The room was full of tension, even unpleasantness. Rami twice interrupted Etkin and on one occasion went so far as to use the ugly word "rubbish." Etkin took offense, accused the younger members of planning terrorist activities, and said in conclusion, "We're not going to have that sort of thing here."

Geula had not arrived, and that was why there was no one to cool down the temper of the meeting. And no coffee. A heated exchange broke out between me and Rami. Although in age I belonged with the younger men, I did not agree with their proposals. Like Etkin, I was absolutely opposed to answering the nomads with violence—for two reasons, and when I was given permission to speak I mentioned them both. In the first place, nothing really serious had happened so far. A little stealing perhaps, but even that was not certain: every faucet or pair of pliers that a tractor driver left in a field or lost in the garage or took home with him was immediately blamed on the Bedouins. Secondly, there had been no rape or murder. Hereupon Rami broke in excitedly and asked what I was waiting for. Was I perhaps waiting for some small incident of rape that Geula could write poems about and I could make into a short story? I flushed and cast around in my mind for a telling retort.

But Etkin, upset by our rudeness, immediately deprived us both of the right to speak and began to explain his position all over again. He asked us how it would look if the papers reported that a kibbutz had sent out a lynch mob to settle scores with its Arab neighbors. As Etkin uttered the phrase "lynch mob," Rami made a gesture to his young friends that is commonly used by basketball players. At this signal they rose in a body and walked out in disgust, leaving Etkin to lecture to his heart's content to three elderly women and a long-retired member of Parliament.

After a moment's hesitation I rose and followed them. True, I did not share their views, but I, too, had been deprived of the right to speak in an arbitrary and insulting manner.

9

If only Geula had come to the meeting and brought her famous coffee with   93
her, it is possible that tempers might have been soothed. Perhaps, too, her
understanding might have achieved some sort of compromise between the
conflicting points of view. But the coffee was standing, cold by now, on the
table in her room. And Geula herself was lying among the bushes behind
the Memorial Hall, watching the lights of the planes and listening to the
sounds of the night. How she longed to make her peace and to forgive. Not
to hate him and wish him dead. Perhaps to get up and go to him, to find
him among the wadis and forgive him and never come back. Even to sing
to him. The sharp slivers piercing her skin and drawing blood were the
fragments of the bottle she had smashed here with a big stone at the
beginning of the evening. And the living thing slithering among the slivers
of glass among the clods of earth was a snake, perhaps a venomous snake,
perhaps a viper. It stuck out a forked tongue, and its triangular head was
cold and erect. Its eyes were dark glass. It could never close them, because
it had no eyelids. A thorn in her flesh, perhaps a sliver of glass. She was
very tired. And the pain was vague, almost pleasant. A distant ringing in
her ears. To sleep now. Wearily, through the thickening film, she watched
the gang of youngsters crossing the lawn on their way to the fields and the
wadi to even the score with the nomads. We were carrying short, thick
sticks. Excitement was dilating our pupils. And the blood was drumming
in our temples.

Far away in the darkened orchards stood somber, dust-laden cypresses,   94
swaying to and fro with a gentle, religious fervor. She felt tired, and that
was why she did not come to see us off. But her fingers caressed the dust,
and her face was very calm and almost beautiful.

Translated from the Hebrew by the author

STUDY   QUESTIONS

1. How does the theme of the scapegoat apply to the story?
2. What are the sources and the evidence of conflict between the Israeli
   settlers and the nomads?
3. Discuss the confrontation between Etkin and the young members of
   the kibbutz.
4. What are Geula's feelings toward the Arab intruder? What evidence is
   there that her rape is imaginary? How does her brother's death and the
   airplanes flying bombing exercises contribute to her state of mind at
   the end?
5. Why is the title appropriate?

KENYA

◈ NGUGI WA THIONG'O

Ngugi wa Thiong'o (b. 1938) is one of Africa's most original and outspoken writers. Born at Limuru in the Kikuyu Highlands in Kenya, he attended missionary schools and the Kikuyu independent schools that were founded in opposition to the prevailing colonial education policies denigrating traditional customs and rationalizing imperialist domination. His education and the experience of living through the Mau Mau war of resistance influenced his intellectual development. Ngugi completed his higher education at Makerere College, in Kampala, Uganda, and at Leeds University, England. On returning to Kenya, he worked briefly as a journalist before accepting a teaching appointment at Nairobi University. Subsequently, he became an outspoken critic of postcolonial regimes. Much of his work reflects his indignation over the betrayal of the independence movement. In 1978, Ngugi was imprisoned and held in solitary confinement for a year. Since then, he has lived in exile in Zimbabwe and England. Recently he was a visiting professor at Yale University.

Ngugi's significance as a writer lies in his attempt to confront the historical and political contradictions of his times. Artistically, his novels have become increasingly complex and ambitious. In A Grain of Wheat (1967), Petals of Blood (1977), and Devil on the Cross (1982), he successfully incorporates myth, legend, and traditional storytelling techniques. Ngugi now writes in Kikuyu instead of English. "The Return" reflects Ngugi's concern with the impact of history on the lives of ordinary people.

The Return

The road was long. Whenever he took a step forward, little clouds of dust rose, whirled angrily behind him, and then slowly settled again. But a thin train of dust was left in the air, moving like smoke. He walked on, however, unmindful of the dust and ground under his feet. Yet with

1

every step he seemed more and more conscious of the hardness and apparent animosity of the road. Not that he looked down; on the contrary, he looked straight ahead as if he would, any time now, see a familiar object that would hail him as a friend and tell him that he was near home. But the road stretched on.

He made quick, springing steps, his left hand dangling freely by the side 2 of his once white coat, now torn and worn out. His right hand, bent at the elbow, held onto a string tied to a small bundle on his slightly drooping back. The bundle, well wrapped with a cotton cloth that had once been printed with red flowers now faded out, swung from side to side in harmony with the rhythm of his steps. The bundle held the bitterness and hardships of the years spent in detention camps. Now and then he looked at the sun on its homeward journey. Sometimes he darted quick sideglances at the small hedged strips of land which, with their sickly-looking crops, maize, beans, and peas, appeared much as everything else did— unfriendly. The whole country was dull and seemed weary. To Kamau, this was nothing new. He remembered that, even before the Mau Mau[1] emergency, the overtilled Gikuyu holdings wore haggard looks in contrast to the sprawling green fields in the settled area.

A path branched to the left. He hesitated for a moment and then made 3 up his mind. For the first time, his eyes brightened a little as he went along the path that would take him down the valley and then to the village. At last home was near and, with that realization, the faraway look of a weary traveller seemed to desert him for a while. The valley and the vegetation along it were in deep contrast to the surrounding country. For here green bush and trees thrived. This could only mean one thing: Honia river still flowed. He quickened his steps as if he could scarcely believe this to be true till he had actually set his eyes on the river. It was there; it still flowed. Honia, where so often he had taken a bathe, plunging stark naked into its cool living water, warmed his heart as he watched its serpentine movement round the rocks and heard its slight murmurs. A painful exhilaration passed all over him, and for a moment he longed for those days. He sighed. Perhaps the river would not recognize in his hardened features that same boy to whom the riverside world had meant everything. Yet as he approached Honia, he felt more akin to it than he had felt to anything else since his release.

A group of women were drawing water. He was excited, for he could 4 recognize one or two from his ridge. There was the middle-aged Wanjiku, whose deaf son had been killed by the Security Forces just before he

---

1. Mau Mau: *The name given to the black nationalist uprising in Kenya against British rule in the 1950s. The organization, consisting of Gikuyu (or Kikuyu) tribespeople, sought to reclaim richer agricultural land which British settlers had taken over. The uprising was suppressed, and most of the Mau Mau were killed or captured.*

himself was arrested. She had always been a darling of the village, having a smile for everyone and food for all. Would they receive him? Would they give him a 'hero's welcome'? He thought so. Had he not always been a favourite all along the Ridge? And had he not fought for the land? He wanted to run and shout: 'Here I am. I have come back to you.' But he desisted. He was a man.

'Is it well with you?' A few voices responded. The other women, with tired and worn features, looked at him mutely as if his greeting was of no consequence. Why! Had he been so long in the camp? His spirits were damped as he feebly asked: 'Do you not remember me?' Again they looked at him. They stared at him with cold, hard looks; like everything else, they seemed to be deliberately refusing to know or own him. It was Wanjiku who at last recognized him. But there was neither warmth nor enthusiasm in her voice as she said, 'Oh, is it you, Kamau? We thought you—' She did not continue. Only now he noticed something else—surprise? fear? He could not tell. He saw their quick glances dart at him and he knew for certain that a secret from which he was excluded bound them together. 5

'Perhaps I am no longer one of them!' he bitterly reflected. But they told him of the new village. The old village of scattered huts spread thinly over the Ridge was no more. 6

He left them, feeling embittered and cheated. The old village had not even waited for him. And suddenly he felt a strong nostalgia for his old home, friends and surroundings. He thought of his father, mother, and—and—he dared not think about her. But for all that, Muthoni, just as she had been in the old days, came back to his mind. His heart beat faster. He felt desire and a warmth thrilled through him. He quickened his step. He forgot the village women as he remembered his wife. He had stayed with her for a mere two weeks; then he had been swept away by the Colonial Forces. Like many others, he had been hurriedly screened and then taken to detention without trial. And all that time he had thought of nothing but the village and his beautiful woman. 7

The others had been like him. They had talked of nothing but their homes. One day he was working next to another detainee from Muranga. Suddenly the detainee, Njoroge, stopped breaking stones. He sighed heavily. His worn-out eyes had a faraway look. 8

'What's wrong, man? What's the matter with you?' Kamau asked. 9

'It is my wife. I left her expecting a baby. I have no idea what has happened to her.' 10

Another detainee put in: 'For me, I left my woman with a baby. She had just been delivered. We were all happy. But on the same day, I was arrested . . .' 11

And so they went on. All of them longed for one day—the day of their return home. Then life would begin anew. 12

Kamau himself had left his wife without a child. He had not even finished paying the bride-price. But now he would go, seek work in Nairobi, 13 and pay off the remainder to Muthoni's parents. Life would indeed begin anew. They would have a son and bring him up in their own home. With these prospects before his eyes, he quickened his steps. He wanted to run—no, fly to hasten his return. He was now nearing the top of the hill. He wished he could suddenly meet his brothers and sisters. Would they ask him questions? He would, at any rate, not tell them all: the beating, the screening and the work on roads and in quarries with an askari[1] always nearby ready to kick him if he relaxed. Yes. He had suffered many humiliations, and he had not resisted. Was there any need? But his soul and all the vigour of his manhood had rebelled and bled with rage and bitterness.

One day these wazungu[2] would go!   14

One day his people would be free! Then, then—he did not know what   15
he would do. However, he bitterly assured himself no one would ever flout his manhood again.

He mounted the hill and then stopped. The whole plain lay below. The   16
new village was before him—rows and rows of compact mud huts, crouching on the plain under the fast-vanishing sun. Dark blue smoke curled upwards from various huts, to form a dark mist that hovered over the village. Beyond, the deep, blood-red sinking sun sent out finger-like streaks of light that thinned outwards and mingled with the grey mist shrouding the distant hills.

In the village, he moved from street to street, meeting new faces. He   17
inquired. He found his home. He stopped at the entrance to the yard and breathed hard and full. This was the moment of his return home. His father sat huddled up on a three-legged stool. He was now very aged and Kamau pitied the old man. But he had been spared—yes, spared to see his son's return—

'Father!'   18

The old man did not answer. He just looked at Kamau with strange   19
vacant eyes. Kamau was impatient. He felt annoyed and irritated. Did he not see him? Would he behave like the women Kamau had met at the river?

In the street, naked and half-naked children were playing, throwing   20
dust at one another. The sun had already set and it looked as if there would be moonlight.

'Father, don't you remember me?' Hope was sinking in him. He felt   21
tired. Then he saw his father suddenly start and tremble like a leaf. He saw him stare with unbelieving eyes. Fear was discernible in those eyes. His mother came, and his brothers too. They crowded around him. His aged mother clung to him and sobbed hard.

'I knew my son would come. I knew he was not dead.'   22

'Why, who told you I was dead?'   23

---

1. Askari: *A guard or soldier.*
2. Wazungu: *White people or Europeans.*

'That Karanja, son of Njogu.'   24

And then Kamau understood. He understood his trembling father. He   25
understood the women at the river. But one thing puzzled him: he had
never been in the same detention camp with Karanja. Anyway he had
come back. He wanted now to see Muthoni. Why had she not come out?
He wanted to shout, 'I have come, Muthoni; I am here.' He looked around.
His mother understood him. She quickly darted a glance at her man and
then simply said:

'Muthoni went away.'   26

Kamau felt something cold settle in his stomach. He looked at the village   27
huts and the dullness of the land. He wanted to ask many questions but he
dared not. He could not yet believe that Muthoni had gone. But he knew
by the look of the women at the river, by the look of his parents, that she
was gone.

'She was a good daughter to us,' his mother was explaining. 'She waited   28
for you and patiently bore all the ills of the land. Then Karanja came and
said that you were dead. Your father believed him. She believed him too
and keened for a month. Karanja constantly paid us visits. He was of your
Rika, you know. Then she got a child. We could have kept her. But where
is the land? Where is the food? Ever since land consolidation, our last
security was taken away. We let Karanja go with her. Other women have
done worse—gone to town. Only the infirm and the old have been left
here.'

He was not listening; the coldness in his stomach slowly changed to   29
bitterness. He felt bitter against all, all the people including his father and
mother. They had betrayed him. They had leagued against him, and
Karanja had always been his rival. Five years was admittedly not a short
time. But why did she go? Why did they allow her to go? He wanted to
speak. Yes, speak and denounce everything—the women at the river, the
village and the people who dwelt there. But he could not. This bitter thing
was choking him.

'You—you gave my own away?' he whispered.   30
'Listen, child, child—'   31
The big yellow moon dominated the horizon. He hurried away bitter   32
and blind, and only stopped when he came to the Honia river.

And standing at the bank, he saw not the river, but his hopes dashed on   33
the ground instead. The river moved swiftly, making ceaseless monotonous murmurs. In the forest the crickets and other insects kept up an
incessant buzz. And above, the moon shone bright. He tried to remove his
coat, and the small bundle he had held on to so firmly fell. It rolled down
the bank and before Kamau knew what was happening, it was floating
swiftly down the river. For a time he was shocked and wanted to retrieve
it. What would he show his—Oh, had he forgotten so soon? His wife had
gone. And the little things that had so strangely reminded him of her and
that he had guarded all those years, had gone! He did not know why, but

somehow he felt relieved. Thoughts of drowning himself dispersed. He began to put on his coat, murmuring to himself, 'Why should she have waited for me? Why should all the changes have waited for my return?'

.

STUDY QUESTIONS

1. What is the role of nature in "The Return"?
2. What are the expectations of the central character, Kamau, on his return from detention?
3. What details serve to build suspense in the story?
4. How does Kamau resolve the betrayal of his family and community? Should they be held accountable?

M A L I

OUOLOGUEM YAMBO

Ouologuem Yambo, novelist and poet, was born in Bandiagara in the region of Mopti in the Republic of Mali. The son of a civil servant and a member of a traditional Dogon ruling-class family, he speaks several African and European languages. Ouologuem was educated in Bamako in Mali and Paris and has university degrees in literature, sociology, and philosophy. His first novel, Bound to Violence, *won the coveted Prix Renaudot in France in 1968 and was translated into many foreign languages. Written in the griot, or village storytelling tradition, it is a scathing exposé of African history. This novel was followed by a collection of letters that denounced the hypocrisy of Europeans and Africans alike. Ouologuem's poetry has appeared in journals and anthologies, but has not as yet been collected into a single volume. "When Black Men's Teeth Speak Out" is a good example of the author's mocking sense of humor and moral outrage.*

When Black Men's Teeth Speak Out

People think I'm a cannibal
But you know how people talk

People see that I have red gums but then who has
White ones
Hurrah for tomatoes   5

People say that there aren't as many tourists coming
Nowadays
But you know

We aren't in America and nobody
Has much cash   10

People think it's all my fault and that they're afraid of my teeth
But look
My teeth are white not red
I've never eaten anybody

People are pretty nasty and they say I gobble up   15
Tourists boiled alive
Or maybe grilled
So I said which is it grilled or boiled
Then they shut up and took an uneasy look at my gums
Hurrah for tomatoes   20

Everyone knows that they grow things in a farming country
Hurrah for vegetables

Everyone says that no farmer
Can live off his vegetables
And that I'm a pretty husky guy for someone so   25
    under-developed
A no good lowlife who lives on tourists
Down with my teeth

So all of a sudden I was surrounded
Tied up   30
Thrown to the ground
At the feet of justice

Cannibal or not a cannibal
Yes or no
Ha ha you think you're pretty clever   35
Playing high and mighty

Well we'll see about that I'll settle your hash
You're sentenced to death poor thing
What are your last words

I yelled hurrah for tomatoes   40

People are no good and women are a pretty inquisitive bunch
There happened to be one in the curious crowd
Who yapped
With a voice like a leper's rattle and the gurgle

Of a leaky pot   45
Open his stomach
I'm sure that daddy is still inside

With no knives around
Which is understandable for vegetarians
Of the Western world   50
Somebody grabbed a Gillette blade
And very patiently
Slishhh
Slashhh
Plonkkk   55
They opened my belly

And there they found a tomato field in bloom
Washed by streams flowing with palm-tree wine
Hurrah for tomatoes

Translated from the French by Gerald Moore

STUDY QUESTIONS

1. What is the purpose of exaggeration in "When Black Men's Teeth
   Speak Out"?
2. How does the poem expose and counteract racial stereotypes?

N I G E R I A

 WOLE SOYINKA

*Wole Soyinka (b. 1934) is one of the most prolific of modern African writers
and the most versatile in his accomplishments. Playwright, novelist, poet,
and critic, he has been awarded major literary prizes in Africa and Europe.
In 1986, he won the Nobel Prize for Literature. Soyinka was born in
Abeokuta, Nigeria, and was educated at University College, Ibadan, and at
Leeds University, England. Upon graduation, he worked for the Royal Court
theatre in London, where his plays were first produced. Returning to Nigeria,
he founded the Orisun Players, a theatre group, became coeditor of the
literary journal* Black Orpheus, *and taught drama and comparative literature
at the Universities of Ibadan, Lagos, and Ife. During the Nigerian Civil War,
he was imprisoned for two years. Although Soyinka continues to reside in
Nigeria, in recent years he has held visiting appointments at universities in
England and the United States. His plays are performed around the world.
His major works include the play* The Road *(1965), the novels* The
Interpreters *(1965) and* Season of Anomy *(1973), and the recent
autobiography,* Isara *(1989).*

*Soyinka's range as a dramatist is wide, encompassing tragedy, comedy,
and farce. Often these elements mingle and coexist in the same play. Like
other African writers, he has been influenced by Western artistic and
intellectual traditions, but his work remains deeply rooted in the Yoruba
culture of Nigeria. He draws on the myths, religion, and history of his region
to reveal ideal ethical and social paradigms that could help Africa maintain its
integrity and forge its own course of development. According to Soyinka's
vision, Africa still remains a victim of its colonized and exploited past. In his
work, visionary and creative individuals challenge their fate and reveal the
need to alter societal patterns.* The Swamp Dwellers *(1964), one of
Soyinka's early plays, is an examination of a society in a state of transition. In
this work, there is the conflict between the city and the countryside, the theme
of corruption and spiritual death, and the example of a blind beggar who
transcends the restraints of his environment.*

The Swamp Dwellers

CHARACTERS

ALU, an old woman
MAKURI, her husband
A BEGGAR
KADIYE, priest
IGWEZU, son to Alu
A DRUMMER
ATTENDANTS TO KADIYE

A village in the swamps.
Frogs, rain and other swamp noises.

> The scene is a hut on stilts, built on one of the scattered semi-firm islands
> in the swamps. Two doors on the left lead into other rooms, and the one
> on the right leads outside. The walls are marsh stakes plaited with hemp
> ropes.
>
> The room is fairly large, and is used both as the family workshop and
> as the 'parlour' for guests. About the middle of the right half of the stage
> is a barber's swivel chair, a very ancient one. On a small table against the
> right wall is a meagre row of hairdressing equipment—a pair of clippers,
> scissors, local combs, lather basin and brush, razor—not much else. A
> dirty white voluminous agbada[1] serves for the usual customer's sheet.
>
> MAKURI, an old man of about sixty, stands by the window, looking
> out. Near the left down-stage are the baskets he makes from the rushes
> which are strewn in front of him. Up-stage left, his equally aged wife,
> ALU, sits on a mat, busy at her work, unravelling the patterns in dyed
> 'adire' cloths. ALU appears to suffer more than the normal viciousness of
> the swamp flies. She has a flick by her side which she uses frequently,
> yelling whenever a bite has caught her unawares.
>
> It is near dusk, and there is a gentle wash of rain outside.

ALU: Can you see him?
MAKURI: See who?
ALU: My son Igwezu. Who else?
MAKURI: I did not come to look for him. Came only to see if the rain looks
like stopping.   5

---

1. Agbada: *A full-length cotton robe worn by the Yoruba people of Nigeria.*

ALU: Well, does it?

MAKURI: [grunts.]

ALU: [goes back to her work. Then—] It is time he was back. He went hours and hours ago.

MAKURI: He knows the way. He's a grown-up man, with a wife.   10

ALU: [flaring up with aged lack of heat.] If you had any good at all in you, you'd go and look for him.

MAKURI: And catch my death of cramp? Not likely . . . And anyway, [getting warmer] what's preventing you from going?

ALU: I want to be here when he gives me the news. I don't want to fall   15
down dead out in the open.

MAKURI: The older you get, the more of a fraud you become. Every day for the past ten years, you've done nothing but swear that your son was dead in the marshes. And now you sit there like a crow and tell me that you're waiting for news about him.   20

ALU: [stubbornly.] I know he's dead.

MAKURI: Then what do you want Igwezu to tell you?

ALU: I only want to know if . . . I only want to ask him . . . I . . . I . . . He shouldn't have rushed off like that . . . dashing off like a madman before anyone could ask him a thing.   25

MAKURI: [insistently.] Before anyone could ask him WHAT?

ALU: [flares up again.] You're always trying to make me a liar.

MAKURI: I don't have to make you one.

ALU: Bah! Frog-face! [Resumes her work.] . . . Dropped his bundle and rushed off before I could ask him a thing . . . And to think he   30
could have found him after all. To think he could have found him in the city . . .

MAKURI: Dead men don't go to the city. They go to hell.

ALU: I know one dead man who is sitting right here instead of going quietly to hell.   35

MAKURI: Now see who is calling who . . .

ALU: You're so useless now that it takes you nearly a whole week to make one basket . . . and to think you don't even cut your own rushes!

MAKURI: If you had to get up so often to shave the heads of the whole   40
village . . . and most of them crusted with kraw-kraw so that a man has to scrape and scrape until . . .

ALU: [yells suddenly and slaps herself on the arm.]

MAKURI: [looks at her for a moment.] Ha! Don't tell me now that a fly has been trying to suck blood from your dried-up veins.   45

ALU: If you had enough blood to hold you up, you'd prove it by going to look for your own son, and bring him home to supper.

MAKURI: He'll come home when he's hungry.

ALU: Suppose he's lost his way? Suppose he went walking in the swamps and couldn't find his way back?   50

MAKURI: [*in bewilderment.*] Him? Get lost? Woman, isn't it your son we're speaking of? The one who was born here, and has lived here all his life?

ALU: But he has been away now for some time. You cannot expect him to find his way about so quickly. 55

MAKURI: No, no. Of course not. The poor child has been away for eight . . . whole . . . months . . . ! Tch, tch. You'd drive a man to drown himself in the swamps—just to get away from your fussing.

ALU: [*puts aside her work and rises.*] I'm going after him. I don't want to 60 lose him too. I don't want him missing his foothold and vanishing without a cry, without a chance for anyone to save him.

MAKURI: Stay where you are.

[ALU *crosses to doorpost and looks out.*]

ALU: I'm going out to shout his name until he hears me. I had another 65 son before the mire drew him into the depths. I don't want Igwezu going the same way.

MAKURI: [*follows her.*] You haven't lost a son yet in the slough, but you will soon if you don't stop calling down calamities on their heads.

ALU: It's not what I say. The worst has happened already. Awuchike 70 was drowned.

MAKURI: You're a blood-thirsty woman. Awuchike got sick of this place and went into the city. That's where you'll find him, fadding it out with the gentlemen. But you'll be satisfied with nothing less than a festering corpse beneath the mire . . . 75

ALU: It's the truth.

MAKURI: It's a lie. All the young men go into the big town to try their hand at making money . . . only some of them remember their folk and send word once in a while.

ALU: You'll see. When Igwezu returns, you'll find that he never saw a 80 trace of him.

MAKURI: And if he didn't? The city is a large place. You could live there all your life and never meet half the people in it.

ALU: They are twins. Their close birth would have drawn them together even if they were living at the opposite ends of the town. 85

MAKURI: Bah!

ALU: Bah to yourself. Nobody has ever seen him. Nobody has ever heard of him, and yet you say to me . . .

MAKURI: Nobody? Did you say nobody?

ALU: No one that really knew him. No one that could swear it was he. 90

MAKURI: [*despairingly.*] No one. No one that could swear . . . Ah, what a woman you are for deceiving yourself.

ALU: No one knows. Only the Serpent can tell. Only the Serpent of the swamps, the Snake that lurks beneath the slough.

MAKURI: The serpent be . . . ! Bah! You'll make me voice a sacrilege before   95
I can stop my tongue. The traders came. They came one year, and
they came the next. They looked at Igwezu and asked, Has he a
twin? Has he a twin brother who lives in the town?

ALU: There are many people who look alike.

MAKURI: [*sits down and takes up his work.*] Well, I'll not perform the death   100
rites for a son I know to be living.

ALU: If you felt for him like a true father, you'd know he was dead. But
you haven't any feelings at all. Anyone would think they weren't
your own flesh and blood.

MAKURI: Well, I have only your own word for that.   105

ALU: Ugh! You always did have a dirty tongue.

MAKURI: [*slyly.*] The land is big and wide, Alu, and you were often out by
yourself, digging for crabs. And there were all those shifty-eyed
traders who came to hunt for crocodile skins . . . Are you sure
they didn't take your own skin with them . . . you old crocodile!   110

ALU: And if they did?

MAKURI: Poor luck to them. They couldn't have minded much which crocodile they took.

ALU: You're asking . . . Ayi! [*Slaps off a fly and continues more furiously.*]
You're asking to have your head split and the wind let out.   115

MAKURI: And to think . . .

ALU: [*makes a move to rise.*] And I'll do it for you if you carry on the
same . . .

MAKURI: Now, now, Alu. You know I didn't mean a word of that.

[ALU *tightens her lips and resumes her work.*]   120

[*In a hurriedly placating tone.*] There wasn't a woman anywhere
more faithful than you, Alu; I never had a moment of worry in the
whole of my life . . . [*His tone grows more sincere.*] Not every man
can look his wife in the face and make that boast, Alu. Not every
man can do it.

[ALU *remains inflexible.*]   125

And the chances you could have taken. Those traders—everyone
of them wanted you to go back with him; promised he'd make
you live like a lady, clothe you in silks and have servants to wait
on your smallest wants . . . You don't belong here, they used to
tell you. Come back with us to the city where men know the value
of women . . . No, there was no doubt about it. You could have   130
had your choice of them. You turned their heads like a pot of cane
brew.

[ALU *begins to smile in spite of herself.*]

MAKURI: And the way I would go walking with you, and I could hear their heads turning round, and one tongue hanging out and saying to the other, Now I wonder what she sees in him . . . Poor fools . . . if only they knew. If only they could see me take you out into the mangrove, and I so strong that I could make you gripe and sweat and sink your teeth into my cheeks. 135

ALU: You were always one for boasting. 140

MAKURI: And you with your eyes shut so tight that I thought the skin would tear itself. Your eyes always shut, so that up till this day, you cannot tell what I looked like when the spirit took me, and I waxed as hot as the devil himself.

ALU: Be quiet. 145

MAKURI: You never feared the swamp then. You could walk across it day and night and go to sleep in the middle of it . . . Alu, do you remember our wedding night?

ALU: [pleased just the same.] We're past that kind of talk now. Have you no shame? 150

MAKURI: Come on, my own Alu. Tell old Makuri what you did on the night of our wedding.

ALU: No.

MAKURI: You're a stubborn old hen . . . Won't you even tell how you dragged me from the house and we went across the swamps, 155 though it was so dark that I could not see the whites of your eyes?

ALU: [stubbornly.] I do not remember.

MAKURI: And you took me to the point where the streams meet, and there you said . . . [Pauses.]

ALU: [shyly.] Well, it was my mother who used to say it. 160

MAKURI: Tell me just the same . . . just as you said it that night when I thought they were your own words.

ALU: My memory is not so good . . . but . . .

MAKURI: It will come. Think slowly.

ALU: [with a shy smile.] She said I had to say it on my bridal bed. 165

MAKURI: Just where we stood. Go on, say it again.

ALU: 'Where the rivers meet, there the marriage must begin. And the river bed itself is the perfect bridal bed.'

MAKURI: [thoughtfully.] Ay-ii . . . The bed of the river itself . . . the bed of the river . . . [Bursts suddenly into what appears to be illogical laugh- 170 ter.]

ALU: Eh? Why? What are you laughing at now?

MAKURI: [futile effort to control himself.] Ay—ya-ya! The river bed . . . [Bursts out laughing again.]

ALU: Are you well, Makuri? 175

MAKURI: Ay—ii! You must be really old, Alu. If you don't remember this, you're too old to lie on another river-bed.

ALU: I don't . . . What are you . . . ?

MAKURI: Think hard, woman. Do you not remember? We did not know that the swamp came up as far as that part of the stream . . . The ground . . . gave . . . way beneath us! 180

ALU: [*beginning to laugh.*] It is all beginning to come back . . . yes, yes, so it did. So it did!

MAKURI: And can you remember that you were left kicking in the mire . . . ha ha! 185

ALU: [*no longer amused.*] I was? I suppose you never even got your fingers muddy?

MAKURI: Well, I jumped up in time, didn't I? But you went down just as you were, flat on your back. And there I stood looking at you . . .

ALU: Ay. Gawking and yelling your head off with laughter. I can re- 190 member now.

MAKURI: You'd have laughed too if you had stood where I did and seen what could be seen of you.

ALU: Call yourself a man? And all my ribs bruised because you stood on me trying to get me out. 195

MAKURI: If you hadn't been thrashing about so much, I'd have got you out much quicker . . .

[ALU *has tightened her lips again. Bends rigidly over her work. Pause.*]

MAKURI: The whole village said that the twins were the very colour of the swamp . . . eh . . . Alu? 200

[ALU *remains deaf to him.*]

MAKURI: Ah well . . . Those were the days . . . those days were really good. Even when times were harsh and the swamp overran the land, we were able to laugh with the Serpent . . . [*Continues to work.*] . . . but these young people . . . They are no sooner born 205 than they want to get out of the village as if it carried a plague . . . [*Looks up suddenly.*] I bet none of them has ever taken his woman into the swamps.

ALU: They have more sense than that. [*She says this with an effort and immediately resumes her frigidity.*] 210

MAKURI: It is not sense they have . . . not sense at all. Igwezu was hardly joined to his wife before he took her off into the city. What would a girl like Desala do in a place like that, I ask you. What would she find to do in the city?

ALU: [*primly.*] If you'd kept your eyes about you, you would have 215 known that she made him promise to take her there before she would wed him.

MAKURI: It ruins them. The city ruins them. What do they seek there except money? They talk to the traders, and then they cannot sit still . . . There was Gonushi's son for one . . . left his wife and 220 children . . . not a word to anyone.

ALU: [almost between her teeth.] It was the swamp . . . He went the same
way as my son . . .
MAKURI: [throwing down his basket.] Woman . . . !

[He is interrupted by the sound of footsteps on the planks outside.]   225

MAKURI: That must be Igwezu now.
ALU: Thank heavens. It will soon be dark.
MAKURI: You'd better make the most of him. He might be going back
tomorrow.
ALU: Why should he?   230
MAKURI: He came for his crops. Now that he knows they've been ruined
by the floods, he'll be running back to the city.
ALU: He will stay a few days at least.
MAKURI: [licking his lips.] With a full-bosomed woman like Desala waiting
for him in the city . . . ? You must be getting old.   235
ALU: It's a let-down for him—coming all the way back and finding no
harvest.
MAKURI: Now don't you start. We've had worse years before this.
ALU: [flaring.] But you haven't journeyed three days only to be cheated
of your crops . . .   240

[The footsteps are right at the door. There is a knock on the wall.]

ALU: That's a queer mood he's in. Why is he knocking?
MAKURI: It's not Igwezu . . . I didn't think they were his footsteps. [Goes
towards the door and pulls aside the door matting.] A good evening to
you, stranger.   245
VOICE OFF-STAGE: Allah protect you.
MAKURI: Were you sent to me? Come in. Come into the house.

[The caller enters, feeling his way with a staff.]

MAKURI: [picks up the bundle from the floor.] Alu, take this bundle out of here
. . . And bring some light. It is too dark in here.   250
BEGGAR: No, no. Not on my account. It makes no difference whatever to
me.
MAKURI: [in a bewildered manner.] Oh . . . oh . . . I understand. [Takes hold
of the other end of the staff and leads him to the swivel chair.] Sit here
. . . Ah. [Touches the stranger's forehead, and then his, saying   255
devoutly—] Blessed be the afflicted of the gods.
BEGGAR: Allah grant everlasting peace to this house.

[The blind man is tall and straight. It is obvious from his dress that he is a stranger
to these parts. He wears a long, tubular gown, white, which comes below his calf,
and a little skull cap. Down one ear hangs a fairly large ear-ring, and he wears a   260
thick ring on one of his fingers. He has a small beard, which, with the skull cap,
accentuates the length of his face and emphasizes its ebony-carving nature.

His feet are muddy above the ankles. The rest of him is lightly wet. His bearing is of quiet dignity.]

MAKURI: You have journeyed far?   265
BEGGAR: Very far. I came all the way down the river.
MAKURI: Walking?
BEGGAR: Most of the way. Wherever it was possible, I walked. But some-
times, I was forced to accept a lift from the ferries.
MAKURI: [*looks rapidly down his legs.*] Alu! Some water for the man to wash   270
his feet.
ALU: [*coming in with the taper.*] Give me time. I can't do everything at
once, can I? [*Lights the oil lamps which are hanging from the rafters.
Goes back again.*]
MAKURI: Have you met anyone in the village? Were you directed here?   275
BEGGAR: No. This happened to be the first house on my way . . . Are you
the head of this house?
MAKURI: Y-yes, yes I am.
BEGGAR: Then it is with you I must speak.
MAKURI: We haven't much, but you can have shelter for the night, and   280
food for . . .
BEGGAR: I have not come to beg for alms.
MAKURI: Oh? Do you know anyone here?
BEGGAR: No. I come from far away in the North. Have you ever heard of
Bukanji?   285
MAKURI: Bukanji? Bukan . . . ? Ah, is that not the village of beggars?
BEGGAR: So it is known by the rest of the world . . . the village of beggars
. . . but I have not come to beg.
MAKURI: Bukanji! That is a march of several weeks!
BEGGAR: I have been journeying for longer than that. I resolved to follow   290
the river as far as it went, and never turn back. If I leave here, it
will be to continue in the same direction.
MAKURI: But this is the end—this is where the river ends!
BEGGAR: No, friend. There are many more miles left of this river.
MAKURI: Yes, yes . . . But the rest is all swamp. Between here and the sea,   295
you'll not find a human soul.
BEGGAR: I must stay here or walk on. I have sworn to tread only where the
soil is moist.
MAKURI: You'll not get far in that direction. This is the end. This is as far as
human beings can go, even those who have the use of their sight.   300
BEGGAR: Then I must stay here.
MAKURI: What do you want?
BEGGAR: Work.
MAKURI: Work?
BEGGAR: Yes, work. I wish to work on the soil. I wish to knead it between   305
my fingers.

MAKURI: But you're blind. Why don't you beg like others? There is no true worshipper who would deny you his charity.

BEGGAR: I want a home, and I wish to work with my hands.

MAKURI: [*in utter bewilderment.*] You . . . the afflicted of the gods! Do you 310 really desire to work, when even the least devout lives under the strict injunction of hospitality towards you?

BEGGAR: [*getting up.*] No more, no more. All the way down the river the natives read me the code of the afflicted, according to their various faiths. Some fed and clothed me. Others put money in my 315 hands, food and drink in my bag. With some, it was the children and their stones, and sometimes the dogs followed me and whetted their teeth on my ankles . . . Good-bye. I shall follow the river to the end.

MAKURI: Wait. You are very hasty. Did you never learn that the blind man 320 does not hurry for fear he out-walks his guide? Sit down again . . . Alu! Alu! When is that supper coming?

ALU: [*from inside.*] What supper? The last time it was water for washing his feet.

MAKURI: Well, hurry . . . [*Helps the blind man back into the chair.*] There . . . 325 Now tell me all about your journey . . . Did you come through any of the big cities?

BEGGAR: One or two, but I did not stop there. I walked right through them without a halt.

MAKURI: And you have been on the road for . . . how long did you say? 330

BEGGAR: I have lost all count of time. To me, one day is just like another . . . ever since my sight became useless.

MAKURI: It must be strange . . . living in perpetual dark.

BEGGAR: I did not have many years to enjoy the benefit of the eyes. Four or five years at the most, and then . . . You have heard of the fly 335 sickness?

MAKURI: [*shaking his head.*] Who hasn't? Who hasn't?

BEGGAR: It is fatal to cattle. The human beings fall ill and suffer agonies. When the sickness is over, the darkness begins . . . At first, it is mystifying and then . . . [*smiles.*] When it happened to me, I 340 thought I was dead and that I had gone to a paradise where my earthly eyes were unsufficing.

MAKURI: You did? If it had been Old Makuri, he would have thought that he was in the darkest corner of hell.

BEGGAR: [*smiling still.*] But I was only a child, and I knew that I had com- 345 mitted no sins. Moreover, my faith promises paradise for all true believers—paradise in the company of Muhammad and all the prophets . . . [*Becoming serious.*] Those few moments were the happiest in my life. Any moment, I thought, and my eyes would be opened to the wonders around me. I heard familiar voices, and 350 I rejoiced, because I thought that they were dead also, and were in paradise with me . . . And then slowly, the truth came to me, and I knew that I was living—but blind.

MAKURI: The gods be merciful.

BEGGAR: Even before anyone told me, I knew exactly what I had to do to live. A staff, a bowl, and I was out on the roads begging for alms from travellers, singing my prayers, pouring out blessings upon them which were not mine to give . . . 355

MAKURI: No, my friend. The blessings were yours. My faith teaches me that every god shakes a beggar by the hand, and his gifts are passed into his heart so that every man he blesses . . . 360

BEGGAR: Ah, but did I bless them from the heart? Were they not so many that I blessed without thought, and took from whatever hand was willing, however vile it was? Did I know if the alms came from a pure heart or from a robber and taker of lives, from the devout, or the profane . . . ? I thanked and blessed them equally, even before I had the time to discover the size of their bounty . . . [Begins to nod his head in time to his chanting.] 365

[His chanting is tonal. No clear words.

Faint drumming can now be heard off-stage. The BEGGAR hears it and stops abruptly, listening hard for the sound.] 370

BEGGAR: Have you a festivity in the village tonight?

MAKURI: No. Why?

BEGGAR: I can hear drumming.

MAKURI: [after listening for a moment.] It must be the frogs. There is a whole city of them in the marshes. 375

BEGGAR: No, this is drumming. And it is coming this way . . . yes, it is drawing nearer.

MAKURI: Y—yes . . . I think I can hear it now . . . Alu!

ALU: [from inside] What now? 380

MAKURI: Can you hear the drumming?

ALU: What drumming?

MAKURI: That means you can't. [Confidentially.] She was deaf the day she was born. [Goes to the door and looks out.] They are not within sight yet, whoever it is . . . Ah, I know who it must be . . . My son. 385

BEGGAR: You have a son?

MAKURI: Yes. He only came back today. He has been in the city making money.

BEGGAR: So he is wealthy?

MAKURI: We don't know yet. He hardly said a word to anyone before he rushed off again to see what the floods had done to his farm . . . The man is a fool. I told him there wasn't a thing to see except the swamp water, but he rushed out like a madman, dropping his bundle on the floor. He said he had to see for himself before he would believe it. 390

  395

BEGGAR: Was there much damage to the farm?

MAKURI: Much damage? Not a grain was saved, not one tuber in the soil . . . And what the flood left behind was poisoned by the oil in the swamp water. [*Shakes his head.*] . . . It is hard for him, coming back for a harvest that isn't there.   400

BEGGAR: But it is possible then. It is possible to plant on this land in spite of the swamp?

MAKURI: [*straining his eyes into the dark outside.*] Oh yes. There are little bits of land here and there where a man can sow enough to keep his family, and even take to the market . . . Not much, but . . . I can't 405 see them . . . But I'm sure it is he. He must have run into one of the drummers and been merry-making all afternoon. You can trust Luyaka to drum him back to his own house in welcome.

BEGGAR: Is there land here which a man can till? Is there any land to spare for a man who is willing to give his soul to the soil?   410

MAKURI: [*shakes his head.*] No, friend. All the land that can take the weight of a hoe is owned by someone in the village. Even the few sheep and goats haven't any land on which to graze. They have to be fed on cassava and other roots.

BEGGAR: But if a man is willing to take a piece of the ground and redeem 415 it from the swamp—will they let him? If a man is willing to drain the filth away and make the land yield coco-yams and lettuce— will they let him?

MAKURI: [*stares wildly.*] Mind what you are saying, son. Mind what pro- fanities you utter in this house.   420

BEGGAR: [*surprised.*] I merely ask to be given a little of what land is useless to the people.

MAKURI: You wish to rob the Serpent of the Swamps? You wish to take the food out of his mouth?

BEGGAR: The Serpent? The Serpent of the Swamps?   425

MAKURI: The land that we till and live on has been ours from the beginning of time. The bounds are marked by ageless iroko trees that have lived since the birth of the Serpent, since the birth of the world, since the start of time itself. What is ours is ours. But what be- longs to the Serpent may never be taken away from him.   430

BEGGAR: I beg your forgiveness. [*Rises.*] I have not come to question your faith. Allah reward you for your hospitality . . . I must continue my journey . . .

MAKURI: Wait. [*He listens for a moment to the drumming which is now nearly just outside the door.*] That is the drummer of the priest . . . [*Enter* 435 ALU *running.*] Alu, is that not the priest's salutations coming from the drums?

ALU: Yes. It must be the Kadiye.

MAKURI: It is. It is . . . Well, don't stand there. Get the place fit to receive him . . . Clear away all the litter . . .   440

[ALU *begins to tidy the room hastily. She takes away* MAKURI's *baskets and rushes, returns to fetch her own things and takes them out of the room. She trims the lamp wicks and takes away any oddments lying around.*]

MAKURI: And see if there is any brew in the attic. The Kadiye might like
some.   445

   ALU: [*grumbling.*] Take this away . . . Prepare supper . . . See if there is
any brew in the . . . Why don't you try and do something to
help . . . !

MAKURI: Do you want me to be so ill-mannered as to leave my guest by
himself? . . . [*Takes the blind man by the arm and leads him towards his*   450
stool.] . . . You mustn't pay any attention to that ill-tempered hen
. . . She always gets in a flutter when the Kadiye honours our
house. [*Picks up his stool and moves off towards* ALU's *corner.*] . . .
He's probably come to offer prayers of thanks for the safe return
of our son . . . He's our holy man, the Servant and Priest of the   455
Serpent of the Swamp . . . [*Puts down the stool.*] Here. Sit down
here. We must continue our talk when he is gone.

[*The drummer is now at the door, and footsteps come up the gangway.*

The drummer is the first to enter. He bows in backwards, drumming praises of the
KADIYE. *Next comes the* KADIYE *himself, a big, voluminous creature of about fifty,*   460
smooth-faced except for little tufts of beard around his chin. His head is shaved
clean. He wears a kind of loin-cloth, white, which comes down to below his knees
and a flap of which hangs over his left arm. He is bare above the waist. At least half
of the KADIYE's *fingers are ringed. He is followed by a servant, who brushes the*
flies off him with a horse-tail flick.]   465

MAKURI: [*places his arm across his chest and bows.*] My house is open to you,
Kadiye. You are very welcome.

[*The* KADIYE *places a hand on his head.*]
[ALU *hurries into the room and kneels. The* KADIYE *blesses her also.*]

KADIYE: [*looks at the* BEGGAR *who remains sitting. Signs to the drummer to*   470
stop.] Did Igwezu bring a friend with him?

MAKURI: No, Kadiye. This is a stranger who called at my house for charity.
He is blind.

KADIYE: The gods protect you, friend.

BEGGAR: Allah shield you from all evil.   475

KADIYE: [*startled.*] Allah? is he from the North?

MAKURI: He is. He journeyed all the way from Bukanji.

KADIYE: Ah, from Bukanji. [*To the servant.*] Kundigu, give the man something.

[*The servant brings out a purse and approaches the* BEGGAR. *When he is about a* 480
foot away, the BEGGAR, *without a change of expression turns his bowl upside down.*

The servant stands puzzled and looks to his master for further instructions. KADIYE looks quickly away, and the servant tries to turn the bowl inside up. But the BEGGAR keeps it firmly downwards. The servant looks backwards at the KADIYE—who by now has hemmed and begun to talk to MAKURI—slips the money into his own pocket, pulls the strings shut and returns to his place.] 485

KADIYE: Ahem . . . Where is your son? I hear he has returned.

MAKURI: Yes he has. He went out in the afternoon to see his . . . He must have been detained by old friends and their sympathizing.

KADIYE: Yes, it is a pity. But then, he is not the only one. Others lost even more than he did . . . And anyway, he has probably made himself a fortune in the city . . . Hasn't he? 490

MAKURI: I don't know. He hasn't told us . . . Won't you sit here . . . ?

KADIYE: [*sits on the swivel chair.*] They all do. They all make money.

MAKURI: Well, I only hope he has. He'll need something on which he can fall back. 495

KADIYE: [*patting the arm of the chair.*] Didn't he send you this chair within a few weeks of his arriving in the city?

MAKURI: Yes, he did. He's a man for keeping his word. Before he left, he said to me, With the first money I make, I am going to buy you one of those chairs which spin like a top. And you can put your customers in it and spin them until they are giddy. 500

KADIYE: [*pushing his toes into the ground to turn the chair.*] Ay—It is comfortable.

MAKURI: It is. When I have no customers, I sit in it myself. It is much better than a rocking chair . . . Alu! 505

ALU: Coming.

MAKURI: When are we having something to drink? Are you going to keep us waiting all night . . . ? [*Back to the KADIYE*—] And when they were bringing it over the water, it knocked a hole in the bottom of the canoe and nearly sank it . . . But that wasn't all. The carrier got stuck in the swamps and they had to dig him out . . . Alu! 510

ALU: [*comes out with a gourd and a number of calabash-cups.*] Here it is . . . There is no need to split your guts with shouting. 515

MAKURI: [*takes the gourd from her and serves the drinks. ALU takes it round. She curtseys to the KADIYE when she hands him his cup. MAKURI takes a smell at the liquor before he begins to pour it out.*] A-a-ah! You'll find this good, Kadiye . . .

KADIYE: Has it been long fermenting? 520

MAKURI: Months and months. I pulped the canes nearly . . .

ALU: *You* did?

MAKURI: If you'd only give me a chance, woman! . . . I was going to say that my son pulped the canes before he left for the city.

ALU: [*looking out of the door in between serving the drinks.*] I wish he'd 525 come. I wish he'd hurry up and come home. It is so dark and the swamps are . . .

MAKURI: [*impatiently*.] Here, here, take this to the drummer and stop your cackling. It will be his own fault if he doesn't come and we finish the lot. Pah! He's probably used to drinking bottled beer by now, instead of thriving on good wholesome cane brew, fermented in the froth of the swamp itself. 530

[*Everyone now has a drink, except the* BEGGAR, *who, in spite of a dumb persuasive attempt by* ALU, *refuses a cup. The* KADIYE *waits for* MAKURI *to come and taste his drink.*] 535

MAKURI: [*taking the cup from the* KADIYE.] If my face belies my thoughts, may the venom grip at once. [*Drinks a mouthful and hands it back.*]

KADIYE: The protection of the heavens be on us all. [*Drinks and smacks his lips. Then he looks round the room and announces gravely—*] The rains have stopped. 540

MAKURI: [*shakes his head in distrust.*] They have stopped too often Kadiye. It is only a lull.

KADIYE: No. They have stopped finally. My soothsayers have confirmed it. The skies are beginning to open: what few clouds there are, are being blown along the river. 545

MAKURI: [*shrugs, without much enthusiasm.*] The gods be praised.

KADIYE: The floods are over . . . The river will recede and we can plant again . . . I am now released of my vow.

MAKURI: Your vow, Kadiye?

KADIYE: Yes. When the floods began and the swamps overran the land, I vowed to the Serpent that I would neither shave nor wash until the rains ceased altogether . . . 550

MAKURI: [*drops his cup.*] I had no idea . . . is that the reason for your visit?

KADIYE: Yes, of course. Did you not guess?

MAKURI: [*getting out the lather.*] I will only be a moment . . . 555

KADIYE: No, old man, I shall wait for your son.

MAKURI: For Igwezu? . . . As you please, Kadiye . . . I hope he still remembers his trade. It must be a long time since he last wielded a razor.

KADIYE: Be it as it may, his hand is steadier than yours. 560

MAKURI: [*replacing the lather.*] True. True . . . We must all get old some time.

KADIYE: Has he been out long?

MAKURI: All day . . . But he should be back any moment now. He must be drinking with his friends . . . they haven't seen him for a whole season, and they won't let him go in a hurry . . . 565

ALU: He ought to be back by now. Who of his friends could have kept him so long?

KADIYE: Did he bring his wife?

ALU: No. He wouldn't want to expose her to the flooded roads and 570
other discomforts of the journey.

MAKURI: [*disgustedly.*] Ah! They're soft. This younger generation is as soft
as . . .

ALU: Aw, shut up in a while. Igwezu himself was lucky to get here at
all. He would have had to turn back at the river if it wasn't for old 575
Wazuri who is still ferrying travellers across the swollen stream.
All the other fishermen have hung up their boats with their nets.
[*Goes into the house.*]

MAKURI: And isn't that what I am telling you? As soon as the floods came,
the younger men ran home to their wives. But not Wazuri! He's 580
as old as the tortoise himself, but he keeps the paddle in his hand.

[*The servant comes up and whispers in* KADIYE'S *ear.*]

KADIYE: Ah yes . . . I nearly forgot. [*Drains his cup and gives it to* MAKURI.]
I must go first to Daruga. His son is going to be circumcised
tonight and he wants me to say the usual prayers . . . I'll call 585
again on my way back. [*Rises, the servant helping him.*]

MAKURI: Just as you please, Kadiye. And if Igwezu returns I shall tell him
to prepare for you.

KADIYE: I shall send a man to find him out . . . [*Rubs his chin.*] This nest is
beginning to attract the swamp flies. I must get it off tonight. 590

[*Goes out, preceded by his drummer who drums him out as before, bowing backwards.*]

MAKURI: [*who has held the matting aside for them. Looks after them as the drumming dies away. Sighs.*] What a day! What a day! The whole world
seems to have picked the same day to drop into my house . . . 595
[*Stops suddenly as he is smitten by a recollection . . .*] The pot-bellied
pig! So I am too old to shave him now, am I? Too old! Why he's
nearly as old as the Serpent himself . . . Bah! I hope Igwezu has
been celebrating with his friends and comes home drunk. He-he!
We'll see who has the steady hand then. We'll see who goes from 600
here with his chin all slashed and bleeding . . . He-he . . . [*Stops
again, thinking hard . . .*] Now where was I before . . . ? Alu!

ALU: [*enters simultaneously with a bowl of warm water.*] If you want to
bellow, go out into the swamp and talk to the frogs.

MAKURI: Aha, is that the water? No, no, bring it over here . . . Come on, 605
my friend . . . come over here. It will be easier to wash your feet
sitting in this chair . . . [*Leads him to the swivel chair . . .*] Do you
realize it? You've brought good luck with you.

BEGGAR: Have I?

MAKURI: Well, didn't you hear what the Kadiye said? The rains have 610
stopped . . . the floods are over. You must carry luck with your
staff.

BEGGAR: Yes, I could feel the air growing lighter, and the clouds clearing over my head. I think the worst of your season is over.

MAKURI: I hope so. Only once or twice in my whole lifetime have we had it so bad.

BEGGAR: How thankful we would have been for the excess that you had here. If we had had the hundredth part of the fall you had, I would not be sitting under your roof this moment.

MAKURI: Is it really dry up country?

BEGGAR: [Smiles indulgently.] A little worse than that.

MAKURI: Drought? Did you have a drought?

[While the BEGGAR is speaking, ALU squats down and washes his feet. When this is finished, she wipes them dry, takes a small jar from one of the shelves, and rubs his feet with some form of ointment.]

BEGGAR: We are used to droughts. Our season is one long continuous drought . . . But we are used to it. Even when it rained, the soil lets the water run through it and join some stream in the womb of the earth. All that we knew, and were content to live on alms . . . Until one day, about a year or more ago . . .

[There is only the gentle lapping of the water in the bowl. MAKURI has brought his stool and is sitting on the left side of the chair, looking up at the BEGGAR.]

. . . then we had more rain than I had ever known in my life. And the soil not only held the water, but it began to show off a leaf here and there . . . even on kola trees which had been stunted from birth. Wild millet pushed its way through the soil, and little tufts of elephant grass appeared from seeds which had lain forgotten season upon season . . . Best of all, hope began to spring in the heart of everyone . . . It was true that the land had lain barren for generations, that the fields had yielded no grain for the lifetime of the eldest in the village. We had known nothing but the dryness of the earth. Dry soil. Dry crumbs of dust. Clouds of dust even when there was no wind, but only a vulture flying low and flapping its wings over the earth . . . But now . . . we could smell the sweetness of lemon leaves, and the feel of the fronds of desert palm was a happiness which we had never known . . . The thought was no sooner born than we set to work before the soil changed its mind and released its moisture. We deserted the highways and marched on this land, hoes and mattocks in hand— and how few of these there were! The village had been long unused to farming, and there was no more than a handful of hoes. But we took our staffs and drove them into the earth. We sharpened stakes and pricked the sand and the pebble until they bled . . . And it seemed as if the heavens rejoiced in our labour, for their blessings were liberal, and their goodwill on our side.

The rains came when we wanted. And the sun shone and the 655
seeds began to ripen.

[IGWEZU *enters quietly, and remains by the door, unobserved.*]

Nothing could keep us from the farms from the moment that the
shoots came through the surface, and all through the months of
waiting. We went round the plantains and rubbed our skins
against them, lightly, so that the tenderest bud could not be hurt. 660
This was the closest that we had ever felt to one another. This was
the moment that the village became a clan, and the clan a household, and even that was taken by Allah in one of his large hands
and kneaded together with the clay of the earth. We loved the
sound of a man's passing footsteps as if the rustle of his breath it 665
was that gave life to the sprouting wonder around us. We even
forgot to beg, and lived on the marvel of this new birth of the
land, and the rich smell of its goodness . . . But it turned out to
have been an act of spite. The feast was not meant for us,—but for
the locusts. 670
MAKURI: [*involuntarily.*] Locusts!
BEGGAR: They came in hordes, and squatted on the land. It only took an
hour or two, and the village returned to normal.
ALU: [*moaning.*] Ay-ii, Ay-ii . . .

[MAKURI *buries his head in his hands.*] 675

BEGGAR: I headed away from my home, and set my face towards the river.
When I said to the passing stranger, Friend, set my face towards
the river, he replied, which river? But I only said to him, Towards
any river, towards any stream; set my face towards the sea itself.
But let there be water, because I am sick of the dryness. 680
MAKURI: Ay-ii, the hands of the gods are unequal. Their gifts become the
burden of . . .

[ALU, *who has now finished her task, takes the bowl and rises. She is startled by
suddenly seeing* IGWEZU, *and she drops the bowl in her fright.*]

ALU: My son! 685
MAKURI: Hm? Oh, he's back at last . . . [*Wakes suddenly to the dropped bowl,
shouts—*] But was that a reason for you to be drowning the whole
house? Now go and wipe it up instead of gawking at the man . . .
Come on here, Igwezu. Come and sit down.
BEGGAR: [*rising.*] Your son? Is that the son you spoke of? 690
MAKURI: Yes . . . Now hurry up. Hurry up and dry the place.

[*The* BEGGAR *feels for his staff and moves out of the chair.* IGWEZU *sits down. He
appears indifferent to his surroundings.*]

MAKURI: What held you? Have you been carousing?

IGWEZU: No. I went for a walk by myself.   695
MAKURI: All afternoon?

[IGWEZU *nods*.]

Do you mean to tell me . . . ? [*anxiously*.] Son, are you feeling
well?
ALU: [*coming into the room with a piece of rag, overhears the last question*.] Is
he unwell? What is the matter with him?   700
MAKURI: He is not unwell. I merely asked him how he felt.
ALU: [*on her knees, begins to wipe the floor*.] Well, how does he feel?
IGWEZU: [*without any kind of feeling*.] Glad to be home. Glad to be once again
with my own people . . . Is that not what every home-coming son
should feel?   705
MAKURI: [*after watching him for a moment*.] Have you seen the farm?

[IGWEZU *is silent*.]

Son, you mustn't take it so hard. There is nothing that . . . [*Shakes
his head in energetic despair and sees* ALU *still wiping the floor*.] Hurry
up, woman! Is the man not to get any supper after walking around
by himself all day?   710

[ALU *gasps*.]

IGWEZU: No, don't give yourself the trouble. I want no supper.
MAKURI: But you've eaten nothing all day.
IGWEZU: I have had my feast of welcome. I found it on the farm where the
beans and the corn had made an everlasting pottage with the   715
mud.
BEGGAR: [*coming forward*.] Master, it will thrive again.
IGWEZU: [*He looks up at the* BEGGAR, *as if seeing him for the first time*.] Who are
you? And why do you call me master?
BEGGAR: I am a wanderer, a beggar by birth and fortunes. But you own a   720
farm. I have stood where your soil is good and cleaves to the toes
like the clay of bricks in the mixing; but it needs the fingers of
drought whose skin is parchment. I shall be your bondsman. I
shall give myself to you and work the land for your good. I feel I
can make it yield in my hands like an obedient child.   725
IGWEZU: [*looks from* ALU *to* MAKURI, *who only shrugs his shoulders*.] Where do
you come from?
BEGGAR: Bukanji.
IGWEZU: [*relapsing into his former manner*.] Bukanji. Yes, I have heard of it,
I have heard of it . . .   730

[*The* KADIYE'S *drum has begun again to sound off stage*.]

MAKURI: The Kadiye! I had forgotten. Son, the Kadiye has been here. I think I can hear him returning now. He wants you to shave him tonight.

IGWEZU: Does he? 735

MAKURI: Yes. Now that the rains have ceased, his vow is come to an end. He wanted me to do it, but I said, No, Kadiye; I am still strong and healthy, but my fingers shake a little now and then, and your skin is tender.

IGWEZU: Yes. Is it not strange that his skin is tender? Is it not strange that 740 he is smooth and well-preserved?

BEGGAR: [*eagerly.*] Is he fat, master? When he spoke, I detected a certain bulk in his voice.

IGWEZU: Ay, he is fat. He rolls himself like a fat and greasy porpoise.

ALU: Son, you must speak better of the holy man. 745

MAKURI: [*tut-tutting.*] The city has done him no good. No good at all.

BEGGAR: Master, is it true what they say? Do you speak ill of the holy man because your heart is in the city?

IGWEZU: Why? What does it matter to you?

BEGGAR: The bondsman must know the heart of the master; then he may 750 serve him well.

[IGWEZU *continues to stare at the* BEGGAR, *puzzled.*]

BEGGAR: Do you serve the Serpent, master? Do you believe with the old man—that the land may not be redeemed? That the rotting swamps may not be purified? 755

IGWEZU: You make a strange slave with your questioning. What is all this to you?

BEGGAR: Even a slave may know the bounds of his master's kingdom.

IGWEZU: You know that already.

BEGGAR: Perhaps. I know that the Serpent has his share, but not who sets 760 the boundaries . . . Is it the priest, or is it the master?

IGWEZU: What does it matter?

BEGGAR: I am a free bondsman. I give myself willingly. I gave without the asking. But I must know whom I serve, for then I will not stint my labour. 765

IGWEZU: Serve whom you please. It does not matter to Igwezu.

BEGGAR: Does the priest live well? Is the Serpent well kept and nourished?

IGWEZU: You may see for yourself. His thighs are like skinfuls of palm oil . . .

[*The* BEGGAR *throws back his head and laughs. It is the first time he has done so,* 770 *and the effect is immediate on* MAKURI *and* ALU, *who stare at him in wonder.* IGWEZU *looks up ordinarily.*]

IGWEZU: It is a careless bondsman who laughs before his master.

BEGGAR: How does the Serpent fare in times of dearth? Does he thrive on the poisonous crabs? Does he drink the ooze of the mire? 775

MAKURI: [*trembling with anger.*] Beware. That borders upon sacrilege. That trespasses on the hospitality of this house.

BEGGAR: [*with dignity.*] I beg your forgiveness. It is for the master to question, not the slave. [*He feels his way to the far corner, and remains there, standing.*] 780

IGWEZU: [*thoughtfully.*] Ay. So it is . . . So it is . . . And yet, I saw him come into this house; but I turned and went away again, back to the Serpent with whom I'd talked all afternoon.

MAKURI: You did what? Who are you talking about?

IGWEZU: The Kadiye. I saw him when he entered this house, but I went 785 away and continued my walk in the swamps.

MAKURI: You did?

IGWEZU: Yes, I did not trust myself.

MAKURI: You did not trust yourself. Why? What has the Kadiye ever done to you? 790

IGWEZU: I do not know. At this moment, I do not know. So perhaps it is as well that he comes. Perhaps he can explain. Perhaps he can give meaning to what seems dark and sour . . . When I met with harshness in the city, I did not complain. When I felt the nakedness of its hostility, I accepted it. When I saw its knife sever the 795 ties and the love of kinship, and turn brother against brother . . .

ALU: [*quickly.*] You met him then. You found your brother in the city.

IGWEZU: Did I?

ALU: Your silence has deceived no one, Igwezu. Do you think I did not know all the time? 800

IGWEZU: He is dead. You've said so yourself. You have said it often enough.

ALU: Which death did he die—that is all I want to know. Surely a mother may say that much, and be forgiven the sin of lying to herself—even at the moment of the asking. And he is still my son, 805 Igwezu; he is still your own twin.

[IGWEZU *remains silent.*]

ALU: I am too old to be pilgrim to his grave. I am too weak to seek to bring him back to life . . . I only seek to know . . . Igwezu, did you find my son? 810

[*After a moment,* IGWEZU *nods slowly.*]

ALU: Let me hear it through your lips, and then I will know it is no trick of my eyes. Does my son live?

IGWEZU: [*wearily.*] He lives.

ALU: [*nodding.*] He lives. What does it matter that he breathes a foreign 815 air. Perhaps there is something in the place that makes men forget. [*Going.*] What if he lives sufficient only to himself. He lives. One cannot ask too much. [*Goes into the house.*]

MAKURI: [*ordinarily.*] Was he well?

[IGWEZU *nods.*]   820

MAKURI: [*obviously uncertain how to proceed. He keeps his eyes on the ground, from where he spies on* IGWEZU. *Slowly, and with hesitation . . .*] Did you . . . did you often . . . meet?

IGWEZU: I lived under his roof—for a while.

MAKURI: [*shouting at the departed* ALU.] Did you hear that? Did you hear that   825 you stubborn old crow? . . . Was he . . . Did . . . er . . . ? You did say he was in good health?

IGWEZU: Healthier than you or I. And a thousand times as wealthy.

MAKURI: There! [*shouting out again.*] Did you hear? Did I not always say so? [*more confidently now.*] How did he make his money?   830

IGWEZU: In timber. He felled it and floated it over the seas . . . He is wealthy, and he is big.

MAKURI: Did he ever talk of his father? Does he remember his own home?

IGWEZU: Awuchike is dead to you and to his house. Let us not raise his ghost.   835

MAKURI: [*stands bewildered for a moment. Then, with a sudden explosiveness . . .*] What did he do, son? What happened in the city?

IGWEZU: Nothing but what happens to a newcomer to the race. The city reared itself in the air, and with the strength of its legs of brass kicked the adventurer in the small of his back.   840

MAKURI: And Awuchike? Was he on the horse that kicked?

[IGWEZU *is silent.*]

MAKURI: Did your own brother ride you down, Igwezu? . . . Son, talk to me. What took place between you two?

[IGWEZU *is silent again, and then*]   845

IGWEZU: The wound heals quicker if it is left unopened. What took place is not worth the memory . . . Does it not suffice that in the end I said to myself . . . I have a place, a home, and though it lies in the middle of the slough, I will go back to it. And I have a little plot of land which has rebelled against the waste that surrounds it,   850 and yields a little fruit for the asking. I sowed this land before I went away. Now is the time for harvesting, and the cocoa-pods must be bursting with fullness . . . I came back with hope, with consolation in my heart. I came back with the assurance of one who has lived with his land and tilled it faithfully . . .   855

MAKURI: It is the will of the heavens . . .

IGWEZU: It was never in my mind . . . the thought that the farm could betray me so totally, that it could drive the final wedge into this growing loss of touch . . .

[*The* KADIYE'S *drum has become more audible.*] 860

BEGGAR: Master, I think the Serpent approaches.
IGWEZU: I can hear him, bondsman. I can hear him.

[*The* KADIYE'S *party arrive at the door.* MAKURI *runs to hold the matting aside, and the party enters as before.* ALU *comes out again and curtseys.*]

KADIYE: Is he back? Ah, Igwezu, it is good to see you again. [IGWEZU *rises* 865 *unhurriedly. The* KADIYE *tries to bless him but* IGWEZU *avoids this, as if by accident.*] I am glad to see you safe and well . . . [*Seats himself in the chair.*] Ah, what an affair that was. The child was crying loud enough to drown all the frogs in the swamp . . .
MAKURI: [*leaning down to him. With fiendishness on his face—*] Did it happen, 870 Kadiye? Did the child take his revenge?
KADIYE: Oh yes, he did. He drenched the healer with a sudden gush!

[MAKURI *dances delightedly, laughing in his ghoulish manner.*]

KADIYE: And that wasn't all. The foolish mother! She heard the cries and tried to get to her son from where she has been locked. 875
MAKURI: And pollute her own son!
KADIYE: Amazing, is it not? The mothers can never be trusted . . . And to think that she did succeed in the end!
MAKURI: [*snapping his fingers over his head.*] The gods forbid it!
KADIYE: She did. I had to purify the boy and absolve him from the crime 880 of contamination. That is the fourth circumcision where I have known it to happen.
MAKURI: The best thing is to send the mother out of the house.
KADIYE: Do you think that hasn't been tried? It is harder to shift them than to get the child to stay still. 885
MAKURI: Ay. That is true enough. All women are a blood-thirsty lot. They love to hear the child wailing and crying out in pain. Then they can hug themselves and say, Serve you right, you little brat. Now you'll know what pains I went through, giving birth to you.
KADIYE: Ah, that is the truth of it . . . Anyway, it is all over now . . . all 890 over and done with . . . [*Hems with pomposity and turns to* IGWEZU.] And how is the city, gentleman? Have you been making a lot of money, Igwezu?
IGWEZU: None . . . where must I shave, Kadiye?
KADIYE: [*puzzled.*] Where? 895
IGWEZU: Is it the head or the chin?
MAKURI: [*gasps. Then tries to force a casualness in his tone.*] Pay no attention, Kadiye. It is only the humour of the townsmen.
KADIYE: A-ah . . . The chin, Igwezu. Shave off the beard.

IGWEZU: [begins to prepare the instruments.] Did you make other vows, 900
Kadiye? Were there other pleasures from which you abstained
until the rains abated?

KADIYE: Oh, yes. Oh, yes indeed. I vowed that my body would remain
unwashed.

IGWEZU: Ah. Did you keep within doors? 905

KADIYE: No. I had my duties . . . People still die, you know. And mothers
give birth to children.

IGWEZU: And it rained throughout? Almost without a stop?

KADIYE: Yes, it did.

IGWEZU: Then perhaps once or twice you were out in the rain . . . ? 910

MAKURI: [quickly.] Igwezu you . . . you . . . you were going to tell Kadiye
about the big town.

IGWEZU: Was I?

KADIYE: Ah, yes. Tell me about the place. Was business as good as they
say? 915

IGWEZU: For some people.

KADIYE: And you? Did your business thrive?

IGWEZU: No more than my farming has done.

KADIYE: Come now, Igwezu. I am not trying to obtain the promise of an
ox for sacrifice . . . You did make some money? 920

IGWEZU: No.

KADIYE: I see he must be coaxed . . . Admit you've made enough to buy
this village—men, livestock and all.

IGWEZU: [slips the agbada over the KADIYE's head.] No, Kadiye. I made none
at all. 925

KADIYE: A-ah, they are all modest . . . Did you make a little then?

IGWEZU: No I made none at all.

KADIYE: [looks hard at him. He is obviously disturbed by IGWEZU's manner.
Speaks nervously.] Well, never mind, never mind. To some it comes
quickly; to others a little more slowly. But your own turn will 930
come soon, Igwezu; it will come before long.

IGWEZU: I'm afraid I have had my turn already. I lost everything; my
savings, even my standing as a man. I went into debt.

KADIYE: Impossible!

IGWEZU: Shall I tell you what I offered as security? Would you like to 935
know, Kadiye?

KADIYE: Not your pretty wife, I hope. [guffawing.] I notice you had to come
without her.

IGWEZU: No, holy one. It was not my wife. But what I offered had a lot in
common with her. I put down the harvest from my farm. 940

MAKURI: Ha?

ALU: Igwezu. My poor Igwezu.

KADIYE: [laughing.] Now what do you take us for? As if anyone in the city
would lend money on a farm which he had never even seen. Are
they such fools—these business men of yours? 945

IGWEZU: No. They are not fools; my brother least of all. He is anything but a fool.

ALU: Awuchike!

MAKURI: My own son? Your own flesh and blood?

[ALU *remains staring at* IGWEZU *for several moments. Then, shaking her head in*   950
*complete and utter bewilderment, she turns round slowly and goes into the house,
more slouched than ever before.*]

IGWEZU: [*in the same calm relentlessness.*] Wait, mother . . . I have not told you all. [*He begins to lather the* KADIYE's *face.*]

ALU: I know enough. [*She has stopped but does not turn round.*] But I no   955
longer understand. I feel tired, son. I think I'll go to sleep.

IGWEZU: Don't you want news of my wife? Have you no interest in the simple and unspoilt child whom you wooed on my behalf?

[ALU *goes slowly out of the room.*

IGWEZU *begins to shave the* KADIYE. *There is silence.*]   960

IGWEZU: [*without stopping.*] Father. Tell me, father, is my brother a better man than I?

MAKURI: No, son. His heart is only more suited to the city.

IGWEZU: And yet we are twins. And in spite of that, he looked at my wife, and she went to him of her own accord . . . Tell me, father, are   965
women so easily swayed by wealth? Are all women the same?

MAKURI: Alu was different. She turned their heads but she kept her own.

IGWEZU: Thank you, father. Now where is the stranger who would be my bondsman?

BEGGAR: Here, master.   970

IGWEZU: You sightless ones are known to be gifted with more than human wisdom. You detected from the Kadiye's voice that he was fat . . . Keep still, priest of the swamps; this razor is keen and my hand is unsettled . . . Have I still your attention, bondsman? You have listened to me. Is there anything in my voice which tells you what   975
is lacking? Does something in my voice tell you why the bride of less than a season deserts her husband's side?

BEGGAR: I must seek that answer in the voice of the bride.

IGWEZU: That was wisely spoken. You have all the makings of a true bonds-man.   980

MAKURI: You talk strangely, Igwezu. What is running in your head?

IGWEZU: It is only a game of children, father. Only a game of riddles and you have answered yours. So has my bondsman. Now it is the turn of the Kadiye.

KADIYE: I am prepared.   985

IGWEZU: With you, holy one, my questions must be roundabout. But you will unravel them, because you speak with the voice of gods . . . ?

KADIYE: As I said before, I am ready.

IGWEZU: Who must appease the Serpent of the Swamps?

KADIYE: The Kadiye.   990

IGWEZU: Who takes the gifts of the people, in order that the beast may be
gorged and made sleepy-eyed with the feast of sacrifice?

KADIYE: The Kadiye.

IGWEZU: [His speech is increasing in speed and intensity.] On whom does the
land depend for the benevolence of the reptile? Tell me that,   995
priest. Answer in one word.

KADIYE: Kadiye.

IGWEZU: Can you see my mask, priest? Is it of this village?

KADIYE: Yes.

IGWEZU: Was the wood grown in this village?   1000

KADIYE: Yes.

IGWEZU: Does it sing with the rest? Cry with the rest? Does it till the
swamps with the rest of the tribe?

KADIYE: Yes.

IGWEZU: And so that the Serpent might not vomit at the wrong season and   1005
drown the land, so that He might not swallow at the wrong
moment and gulp down the unwary traveller, do I not offer my
goats to the priest?

KADIYE: Yes.

MAKURI: Igwezu, sometimes the guardians of the air are hard to please . . . 1010

IGWEZU: Be quiet, father! . . . And did he offer them in turn to the Serpent?

KADIYE: He did.

IGWEZU: Everything which he received, from the grain to the bull?

KADIYE: Everything.

IGWEZU: The goat and the white cockerel which I gave before I left?   1015

KADIYE: Every hair and feather of them.

IGWEZU: And he made it clear—that the offering was from me? That I
demanded the protection of the heavens on me and my house, on
my father and my mother, on my wife, land and chattels?

KADIYE: All the prayers were repeated.   1020

IGWEZU: And ever since I began to till the soil, did I not give the soil his
due? Did I not bring the first of the lentils to the shrine, and pour
the first oil upon the altar?

KADIYE: Regularly.

IGWEZU: And when the Kadiye blessed my marriage, and tied the heaven-   1025
made knot, did he not promise a long life? Did he not promise
children? Did he not promise happiness?

[IGWEZU has shaved off all except a last smear of lather. He remains standing with
one hand around the KADIYE's jowl, the other retaining an indifferent hold on the
razor, on the other side of his face.]   1030

KADIYE: [Does not reply this time.]

IGWEZU: [*slowly and disgustedly.*] Why are you so fat, Kadiye?

[*The drummer stares, hesitates, and runs out. The servant moves nearer the door.*]

MAKURI: [*snapping his fingers round his head.*] May heaven forgive what has been uttered here tonight. May earth reject the folly spoken by   1035
my son.

IGWEZU: You lie upon the land, Kadiye, and choke it in the folds of a serpent.

MAKURI: Son, listen to me . . .

IGWEZU: If I slew the fatted calf, Kadiye, do you think the land might   1040
breathe again? If I slew all the cattle in the land and sacrificed every measure of goodness, would it make any difference to our lives, Kadiye? Would it make any difference to our fates?

[*The servant runs out also.*]

KADIYE: [*in a choking voice.*] Makuri, speak to your son. . . .   1045
BEGGAR: Master . . . master . . .

[IGWEZU *suddenly shaves off the final smear of lather with a rapid stroke which makes the* KADIYE *flinch. Releases him and throws the razor on the table.*

KADIYE *scrambles up at once, tearing the cloth from his neck. Makes for the door.*]

KADIYE: [*panting.*] You shall pay for this . . . I swear I shall make you pay   1050
for this . . . Do you think that you can make an ass of the Kadiye?
. . . Do you think that you can pour your sacrilege into my ears with impunity?

IGWEZU: Go quickly, Kadiye. [*Sinks into the chair.*] And the next time that you wish to celebrate the stopping of the rains, do not choose a   1055
barber whose harvest rots beneath the mire.

KADIYE: You will pay, I swear . . . You will pay for this.

[*Flings off the sheet and goes out.*]

MAKURI: Son, what have you done?
IGWEZU: I know that the floods can come again. That the swamp will   1060
continue to laugh at our endeavours. I know that we can feed the Serpent of the Swamp and kiss the Kadiye's feet—but the vapours will still rise and corrupt the tassels of the corn.

MAKURI: I must go after him or he'll stir up the village against us. [*Stops at the door.*] This is your home, Igwezu, and I would not drive you   1065
from it for all the world. But it might be best for you if you went back to the city until this is forgotten.

[*Exit.*]

[*Pause.*]

BEGGAR: [*softly.*] Master . . . master . . . slayer of serpents.   1070

IGWEZU: [*in a tired voice.*] I wonder what drove me on.

BEGGAR: What, master?

IGWEZU: Do you think that my only strength was that of despair? Or was there something of a desire to prove myself?

[*The* BEGGAR *remains silent.*] 1075

IGWEZU: Your fat friend is gone. But will he stay away?

BEGGAR: I think that the old man was right. You should go back to the city.

IGWEZU: Is it of any earthly use to change one slough for another?

BEGGAR: I will come and keep you company. If necessary, I will beg for you. 1080

IGWEZU: [*stares at him, slowly shaking his head.*] What manner of man are you? How have I deserved so much of you that you would beg for me?

BEGGAR: I made myself your bondsman. This means that I must share your hardships. 1085

IGWEZU: I am too tired to see it all. I think we all ought to go to bed. Have they given you a place to sleep?

BEGGAR: Will I return with you to the city?

IGWEZU: No, friend. You like this soil. You love to scoop it up in your hands. You dream of cleaving ridges under the flood and making 1090 little balls of mud in which to wrap your seeds. Is that not so?

BEGGAR: Yes, master.

IGWEZU: And you have faith, have you not? Do you not still believe in what you sow? That it will sprout and see the harvest sun?

BEGGAR: It must. In my wanderings, I think that I have grown a healer's 1095 hand.

IGWEZU: Then stay. Stay here and take care of the farm. I must go away.

[*He crosses the room as if to go into the house.*

Hesitates at the door, then turns round and walks slowly away.]

Tell my people I could not stop to say good-bye.

BEGGAR: You are not going now, master? 1100

IGWEZU: I must not be here when the people call for blood.

BEGGAR: But the water is high. You should wait until the floods subside.

IGWEZU: No. I want to paddle as I go.

BEGGAR: Is it not night? Is it not dark outside?

IGWEZU: It is. 1105

BEGGAR: Then I shall come with you. I know the dark. Let me come with you over the swamp, as far as the river's edge.

IGWEZU: Two blind men groping in the dark? No.

BEGGAR: And how would you cross the river? There is no ferryman to be found after dark. 1110

IGWEZU: [*still looking out of the window. Pauses. He walks away, picks up the old man's work in absent movements. He drops it and looks up.*] Only the children and the old stay here, bondsman. Only the innocent and the dotards. [*Walks slowly off.*]

BEGGAR: But you will return, master? 1115

[IGWEZU *checks briefly, but does not stop.*]

BEGGAR: The swallows find their nest again when the cold is over. Even the bats desert dark holes in the trees and flap wet leaves with wings of leather. There were wings everywhere as I wiped my feet against your threshold. I heard the cricket scratch himself 1120 beneath the armpit as the old man said to me . . .

[*The door swings to. The* BEGGAR *sighs, gestures a blessing and says.*] I shall be here to give account.

[*The oil lamps go out slowly and completely. The* BEGGAR *remains on the same spot, the moonlight falling on him through the window.*] 1125

STUDY QUESTIONS

1. Compare the twins Awuchike and Igwezu. How do their attitudes toward society differ?
2. Contrast Kadiye, the Priest of the Serpent, with the blind Beggar from the North. How does the Beggar challenge religious authority?
3. To what extent does the Beggar provide Igwezu with a paradigm for moral and spiritual transcendence?
4. Discuss the plight of the Swamp Dwellers. How does Soyinka convey it artistically?
5. Is Soyinka's vision in this play bleak? What is his message?

◈ CHINUA ACHEBE

Chinua Achebe (b. 1930) is the most widely read of contemporary African writers. Born in Ogidi, Nigeria, Achebe was brought up in a Christian household but felt at home with the Ibo religious and social customs of his community. He was one of the first graduates of University College, Ibadan. Until the outbreak of the Nigerian Civil War in 1967, Achebe worked as a producer and director of the Nigerian Broadcasting Service. During the war, he actively supported the Biafran struggle for independence. With the defeat of the Republic of Biafra, Achebe joined the University of Nigeria, Nsukka, as a senior research fellow and edited Okike, a journal devoted to African literature. Since then, Achebe has traveled and lectured extensively.

Achebe is known primarily as a novelist, though he has also published essays, poetry, short stories, and children's literature. His widely acclaimed first novel, Things Fall Apart (1958), and Arrow of God (1964) are considered classics of African literature. Through them, Achebe portrays with artistic subtlety and sophistication the great depth, value, and beauty of a traditional African society that was being undermined by British colonial rule. In No Longer at Ease (1960), A Man of the People (1966), and Anthills of the Savannah (1988), he confronts the concerns of contemporary Africa. Throughout his career, Achebe has insisted that African writers have the responsibility for providing society with a moral vision. In the moving story "Civil Peace," from the collection Girls at War and Other Stories (1973), Achebe portrays the struggle and endurance of a family that has survived the destruction of war and must cope in its aftermath.

Civil Peace

Jonathan Iwegbu counted himself extra-ordinarily lucky. 'Happy survival!' 1
meant so much more to him than just a current fashion of greeting old friends in the first hazy days of peace. It went deep to his heart. He had come out of the war with five inestimable blessings—his head, his wife Maria's head and the heads of three out of their four children. As a bonus he also had his old bicycle—a miracle too but naturally not to be compared to the safety of five human heads.

The bicycle had a little history of its own. One day at the height of the 2
war it was commandeered 'for urgent military action'. Hard as its loss would have been to him he would still have let it go without a thought had he not had some doubts about the genuineness of the officer. It wasn't his disreputable rags, nor the toes peeping out of one blue and one brown canvas shoes, nor yet the two stars of his rank done obviously in a hurry in biro, that troubled Jonathan; many good and heroic soldiers looked the same or worse. It was rather a certain lack of grip and firmness in his manner. So Jonathan, suspecting he might be amenable to influence, rum-maged in his raffia bag and produced the two pounds with which he had been going to buy firewood which his wife, Maria, retailed to camp officials for extra stock-fish and corn meal, and got his bicycle back. That night he buried it in the little clearing in the bush where the dead of the camp, including his own youngest son, were buried. When he dug it up again a year later after the surrender all it needed was a little palm-oil greasing. 'Nothing puzzles God,' he said in wonder.

He put it to immediate use as a taxi and accumulated a small pile of 3

Biafran money ferrying camp officials and their families across the four-mile stretch to the nearest tarred road. His standard charge per trip was six pounds and those who had the money were only glad to be rid of some of it in this way. At the end of a fortnight he had made a small fortune of one hundred and fifteen pounds.

Then he made the journey to Enugu and found another miracle waiting for him. It was unbelievable. He rubbed his eyes and looked again and it was still standing there before him. But, needless to say, even that monumental blessing must be accounted also totally inferior to the five heads in the family. This newest miracle was his little house in Ogui Overside. Indeed nothing puzzles God! Only two houses away a huge concrete edifice some wealthy contractor had put up just before the war was a mountain of rubble. And here was Jonathan's little zinc house of no regrets built with mud blocks quite intact! Of course the doors and windows were missing and five sheets off the roof. But what was that? And anyhow he had returned to Enugu early enough to pick up bits of old zinc and wood and soggy sheets of cardboard lying around the neighbourhood before thousands more came out of their forest holes looking for the same things. He got a destitute carpenter with one old hammer, a blunt plane and a few bent and rusty nails in his tool bag to turn this assortment of wood, paper and metal into door and window shutters for five Nigerian shillings or fifty Biafran pounds. He paid the pounds, and moved in with his overjoyed family carrying five heads on their shoulders. 4

His children picked mangoes near the military cemetery and sold them to soldiers' wives for a few pennies—real pennies this time—and his wife started making breakfast akara balls[1] for neighbours in a hurry to start life again. With his family earnings he took his bicycle to the villages around and bought fresh palm-wine which he mixed generously in his rooms with the water which had recently started running again in the public tap down the road, and opened up a bar for soldiers and other lucky people with good money. 5

At first he went daily, then every other day and finally once a week, to the offices of the Coal Corporation where he used to be a miner, to find out what was what. The only thing he did find out in the end was that that little house of his was even a greater blessing than he had thought. Some of his fellow ex-miners who had nowhere to return at the end of the day's waiting just slept outside the doors of the offices and cooked what meal they could scrounge together in Bournvita tins. As the weeks lengthened and still nobody could say what was what Jonathan discontinued his weekly visits altogether and faced his palm-wine bar. 6

But nothing puzzles God. Came the day of the windfall when after five days of endless scuffles in queues and counter-queues in the sun outside 7

---

1. Akara balls: *A spicy mixture of mashed beans and onions, crisply deep-fried.*

the Treasury he had twenty pounds counted into his palms as ex gratia award for the rebel money he had turned in. It was like Christmas for him and for many others like him when the payments began. They called it (since few could manage its proper official name) *egg-rasher*.

As soon as the pound notes were placed in his palm Jonathan simply closed it tight over them and buried fist and money inside his trouser pocket. He had to be extra careful because he had seen a man a couple of days earlier collapse into near-madness in an instant before that oceanic crowd because no sooner had he got his twenty pounds than some heartless ruffian picked it off him. Though it was not right that a man in such an extremity of agony should be blamed yet many in the queues that day were able to remark quietly on the victim's carelessness, especially after he pulled out the innards of his pocket and revealed a hole in it big enough to pass a thief's head. But of course he had insisted that the money had been in the other pocket, pulling it out too to show its comparative wholeness. So one had to be careful. 8

Jonathan soon transferred the money to his left hand and pocket so as to leave his right free for shaking hands should the need arise, though by fixing his gaze at such an elevation as to miss all approaching human faces he made sure that the need did not arise, until he got home. 9

He was normally a heavy sleeper but that night he heard all the neighbourhood noises die down one after another. Even the night watchman who knocked the hour on some metal somewhere in the distance had fallen silent after knocking one o'clock. That must have been the last thought in Jonathan's mind before he was finally carried away himself. He couldn't have been gone for long, though, when he was violently awakened again. 10

'Who is knocking?' whispered his wife lying beside him on the floor. 11

'I don't know,' he whispered back breathlessly. 12

The second time the knocking came it was so loud and imperious that the rickety old door could have fallen down. 13

'Who is knocking?' he asked then, his voice parched and trembling. 14

'Na tief-man and him people,' came the cool reply. 'Make you hopen de door.' This was followed by the heaviest knocking of all. 15

Maria was the first to raise the alarm, then he followed and all their children. 16

'Police-o! Thieves-o! Neighbours-o! Police-o! We are lost! We are dead! Neighbours, are you asleep? Wake up! Police-o!' 17

This went on for a long time and then stopped suddenly. Perhaps they had scared the thief away. There was total silence. But only for a short while. 18

'You done finish?' asked the voice outside. 'Make we help you small. Oya, everybody!' 19

'Police-o! Tief-man-o! Neighbours-o! we done loss-o! Police-o! . . .' 20

There were at least five other voices besides the leader's. 21

Jonathan and his family were now completely paralysed by terror. Maria 22
and the children sobbed inaudibly like lost souls. Jonathan groaned continuously.

The silence that followed the thieves' alarm vibrated horribly. Jonathan 23
all but begged their leader to speak again and be done with it.

'My frien,' said he at long last, 'we don try our best for call dem but I tink 24
say dem all done sleep-o . . . So wetin we go do now? Sometaim you wan
call soja? Or you wan make we call dem for you? Soja better pass police. No
be so?'

'Na so!' replied his men. Jonathan thought he heard even more voices 25
now than before and groaned heavily. His legs were sagging under him
and his throat felt like sand-paper.

'My frien, why you no de talk again. I de ask you say you wan make we 26
call soja?'

'No'. 27

'Awrighto. Now make we talk business. We no be bad tief. We no like 28
for make trouble. Trouble done finish. War done finish and all the katakata
wey de for inside. No Civil War again. This time na Civil Peace. No be so?'

'Na so!' answered the horrible chorus. 29

'What do you want from me? I am a poor man. Everything I had went 30
with this war. Why do you come to me? You know people who have
money. We . . .'

'Awright! We know say you no get plenty money. But we sef no get 31
even anini. So derefore make you open dis window and give us one hundred pound and we go commot. Orderwise we de come for inside now to
show you guitar-boy like dis . . .'

A volley of automatic fire rang through the sky. Maria and the children 32
began to weep aloud again.

'Ah, missisi de cry again. No need for dat. We done talk say we na good 33
tief. We just take our small money and go nwayorly. No molest. Abi we de
molest?'

'At all!' sang the chorus. 34

'My friends,' began Jonathan hoarsely. 'I hear what you say and I thank 35
you. If I had one hundred pounds . . .'

'Lookia my frien, no be play we come play for your house. If we make 36
mistake and step for inside you no go like am-o. So derefore . . .'

'To God who made me; if you come inside and find one hundred 37
pounds, take it and shoot me and shoot my wife and children. I swear to
God. The only money I have in this life is this twenty-pounds *egg-rasher*
they gave me today . . .'

'OK. Time de go. Make you open dis window and bring the twenty 38
pound. We go manage am like dat.'

There were now loud murmurs of dissent among the chorus: 'Na lie de 39
man de lie; e get plenty money . . . Make we go inside and search properly
well . . . Wetin be twenty pound? . . .'

'Shurrup!' rang the leader's voice like a lone shot in the sky and silenced 40
the murmuring at once. 'Are you dere? Bring the money quick!'

'I am coming,' said Jonathan fumbling in the darkness with the key of 41
the small wooden box he kept by his side on the mat.

At the first sign of light as neighbours and others assembled to commis- 42
erate with him he was already strapping his five-gallon demijohn to his
bicycle carrier and his wife, sweating in the open fire, was turning over
akara balls in a wide clay bowl of boiling oil. In the corner his eldest son
was rinsing out dregs of yesterday's palm wine from old beer bottles.

'I count it as nothing,' he told his sympathizers, his eyes on the rope he 43
was tying. 'What is *egg-rasher*? Did I depend on it last week? Or is it greater
than other things that went with the war? I say, let *egg-rasher* perish in the
flames! Let it go where everything else has gone. Nothing puzzles God.'

STUDY QUESTIONS

1. What does Jonathan Iwegbu mean by "Nothing puzzles God"?
2. What is ironic about the thief's comment "No Civil War again. This
   time na Civil Peace. No be so"? Why is the title of the story appropriate?
3. What accounts for Jonathan's survival?
4. What is Achebe's view of his characters? How does he convey his
   feelings?

PALESTINE

Mahmoud Darwish

Mahmoud Darwish (b. 1941) was born in al-Barwa, a village east of Acre in what was then Palestine. When the state of Israel was established in 1948, Darwish's family, unlike many other Palestinians, chose to stay. He grew up in Haifa, where he was a member of Rakah, a pro-Arab faction of the Communist Party of Israel. Because of his political activities, he was imprisoned and subjected to house arrest by the Israeli authorities. He left Israel in 1971 and settled in Beirut, Lebanon. He later moved to Damascus, Syria, where he now works as a journalist and is president of the Union of Arab Poets. He remains active in Palestinian liberation organizations.

Darwish is a well-known Palestinian writer and intellectual. He has published several volumes of poems and has been included in a number of important anthologies. In 1969, he was awarded the Lotus Prize by Indira Gandhi at the Fourth Afro-Asian Writers Conference held in New Delhi. Like other Palestinian writers who live in exile, in refugee camps, or under Israeli control, he is opposed to the Zionist displacement of Palestinians and is committed fervently to the national aspirations of his people. These sentiments are the subject of "Identity Card."

Identity Card

Put it on record.
    I am an Arab.
And the number of my card is fifty thousand
I have eight children
And the ninth is due after summer.   5
What's there to be angry about?

Put it on record.
    I am an Arab.

Working with comrades of toil in a quarry.
I have eight children   10
For them I wrest the loaf of bread,
The clothes and exercise books
From the rocks
And beg for no alms at your door,
    Lower not myself at your doorstep.   15
    What's there to be angry about?

Put it on record.
    I am an Arab.
I am a name without a title,[1]
Patient in a country where everything   20
Lives in a whirlpool of anger.
    My roots
    Took hold before the birth of time
    Before the burgeoning of the ages,
    Before cypress and olive trees,   25
    Before the proliferation of weeds.

My father is from the family of the plough
    Not from highborn nobles.
And my grandfather was a peasant
    Without line or genealogy.   30
My house is a watchman's hut
    Made of sticks and reeds.
Does my status satisfy you?
    I am a name without a surname.

Put it on record.   35
    I am an Arab.
Colour of hair: jet black.
Colour of eyes: brown.
My distinguishing features:
    On my head the *'iqal* cords over a *keffiyeh*[2]   40
    Scratching him who touches it.
My address:
    I'm from a village, remote, forgotten,
    Its streets without name
    And all its men in the fields and quarry.   45

---

1. 'I am a name without a title': *Titles such as Bey and Pasha, introduced by the Turks, are commonly employed in the Arab world.*

2. 'Iqal *and* keffiyeh: *traditional Arab headgear consisting of a headscarf (keffiyeh) kept in place by a double row of rope, generally black, made of camel hair ('iqal).*

What's there to be angry about?

Put it on record.
    I am an Arab.
You stole my forefathers' vineyards
    And land I used to till,   50
    I and all my children,
    And you left us and all my grandchildren
    Nothing but these rocks.
    Will your government be taking them too
    As is being said?   55

So!
    Put it on record at the top of page one:
    I don't hate people,
    I trespass on no one's property.
And yet, if I were to become hungry   60
    I shall eat the flesh of my usurper.
    Beware, beware of my hunger
    And of my anger!

Translated from the Arabic by Denys Johnson-Davies

STUDY QUESTIONS

1. Who is the narrator of the poem? For whom does he speak?
2. How does the poem define the plight of Palestinians? What examples
   are used?
3. What are the claims of the final stanza? How do they reinforce assertions made elsewhere in the poem?

⬧ GHASSAN KANAFANI

Ghassan Kanafani (1936–1972) was born in Palestine. After the establishment of the State of Israel, he fled with his family to Syria, where he was educated and worked as a teacher and journalist. Later he moved to Kuwait and finally settled in Beirut, Lebanon, where he wrote for newspapers and founded and edited Al-Hadof (The Aim), *the weekly magazine of the Popular Front for the Liberation of Palestine. Like many Palestinians of his generation, Kanafani's political views were influenced by Arab nationalism and Marxism. He believed that the solution to the Palestinian problem could be achieved only if there were a social revolution throughout the Arab world. He was assassinated by a car bomb in 1972.*

Kanafani is one of the best-known Palestinian writers. The author of five novels, five collections of short stories, and two plays, his novel Men in the Sun *(1962) was also made into a film. As a writer, Kanafani wanted to fashion a literature that would appeal to a broad audience and provoke it into confronting the social and political issues of the region. His success as an artist lies in his ability to achieve these goals indirectly. This is especially true of "The Land of Sad Oranges," in which Kanafani conveys the anguish and destitution of the Palestinian people through the themes of banishment and exile.*

The Land of Sad Oranges

When we set out from Jaffa for Acre there was nothing tragic about our departure. We were just like anybody who goes to spend the festival season every year in another city. Our time in Acre passed as usual, with nothing untoward. I was young then, and so I probably enjoyed those days because they kept me from going to school. But whatever the fact of the matter, the picture gradually became clearer on the night of the great attack on Acre. That night passed, cruel and bitter, amidst the despondency of the men and the prayers of the women. You and I and the others of our age were too young to understand what the story meant from beginning to end, but that night the threads began to grow clearer. In the morning, when the Jews withdrew, threatening and fuming, a big lorry was standing at the door of our house. A simple collection of bedding was being thrown into it, from here and there, quickly and feverishly. I was standing leaning against the ancient wall of the house when I saw your mother climb into the lorry, followed by your aunt and the children. Your father started tossing you and your brothers and sisters into the lorry, and on top of the belongings, and then he seized me from my corner and lifted me over his head into the iron rack on the roof of the driver's cab, where I found my brother Riyad sitting quietly. The lorry was already moving off before I had

1

settled myself into a comfortable position. Beloved Acre was already disappearing behind the bends in the road going up to Ras Naqoura.

It was rather cloudy, and a chilly feeling invaded my body. Riyad was 2 sitting quite quietly, with his legs hanging over the edge of the rack, leaning his back against the luggage, as he stared into the sky. I sat silently, with my chin between my knees and my arms wrapped round them. The groves of orange trees followed each other in succession along the side of the road. We were all eaten up with fear. The lorry panted over the damp earth, and the sound of distant shots rang out like a farewell.

When Ras Naqoura came into sight in the distance, cloudy on the blue 3 horizon, the lorry stopped. The women climbed down over the luggage and made for a peasant sitting cross-legged with a basket of oranges just in front of him. They picked up the oranges, and the sound of their weeping reached our ears. I thought then that the oranges were something dear and these big, clean fruits were beloved objects in our eyes. When the women had bought some oranges, they brought them over to the lorry and your father climbed down from the driver's side and stretched out his hand to take one. He began to gaze at it in silence, and then burst into tears like a despairing child.

In Ras Naqoura our lorry stopped beside many others. The men began 4 handing their weapons to the policeman stationed there for the purpose, and as our turn came and I saw the rifles and machine-guns lying on the table and looked towards the long line of lorries entering Lebanon, rounding the bends in the roads and putting more and more distance between themselves and the land of the oranges, I too burst into a storm of weeping. Your mother was still looking silently at the orange. And all the orange trees which your father had abandoned to the Jews shone in his eyes, all the well-tended orange trees which he had bought one by one were printed on his face and reflected in the tears which he could not control in front of the officer at the police post.

In the afternoon, when we reached Sidon, we had become refugees. 5

We were among those swallowed up by the road. Your father looked as 6 though it was a long time since he had slept. He was standing in the street in front of the belongings heaped on the ground, and I quite imagined that if I ran over to say something to him he would explode in my face: 'Damn your father! Damn . . . !' Those two oaths were clearly etched on his face. I myself, a child educated in a strict religious school, at that moment doubted whether this God really wanted to make men happy. I also doubted whether this God could hear and see everything. The coloured pictures which were handed out to us in the school chapel showing the Lord having compassion on children and smiling in their faces seemed like another of the lies made up by people who open strict schools in order to get higher fees. I was sure that the God we had known in Palestine had left it too, and was a refugee in some place which I did not know, unable to find a solution to his own problems. And we, human refugees, sitting on

the pavement waiting for a new Fate to bring some solution, were responsible for providing a roof under which to spend the night. Pain had begun
to undermine the child's simple mind.

Night is a fearful thing. The darkness which gradually came down over 7
us cast terror into my heart. The mere thought that I would spend the night
on the pavement aroused all kinds of fears within me. They were cruel and
harsh. No one was prepared to have pity on me. I could not find anyone
to console me. Your father's silent glance cast fresh terror into my breast.
The orange which your mother held in her hand set my head on fire.
Everyone was silent, staring at the black road, keen for Fate to appear
round the corner and hand out solutions to our difficulties, so that we
could follow him to some shelter. Suddenly Fate did come; your uncle had
reached the town before us, and he was our fate.

Your uncle never had great faith in ethics, and when he found himself 8
on the pavement like us he lost it entirely. He made for a house occupied by
a Jewish family, opened the door, threw his belongings inside and jerked
his round face at them, saying very distinctly: 'Go to Palestine!' It is certain
that they did not go, but they were frightened by his desperation, and they
went into the next room, leaving him to enjoy the roof and tiled floor.

Your uncle led us to that shelter of his and pitched us into it with his 9
belongings and family. During the night we slept on the floor, and it was
completely taken up with our small bodies. We used the men's coats for
coverings, and when we got up in the morning we found that the men had
passed the night sitting up. The tragedy had begun to eat into our very
souls.

We did not stay long in Sidon. Your uncle's room was not large enough 10
for half of us, but it held us for three nights. Then your mother asked your
father to look for some job, or let us return to the orange trees. Your father
shouted in her face, the rancour trembling in his voice, and she fell silent.
Our family problems had begun. The happy, united family we had left
behind, with the land, the house, and the martyrs killed defending them.

I don't know where your father got the money from. I know that he sold 11
the gold he had bought for your mother when he wanted to make her
happy and proud that she was his wife. But the gold did not bring in a sum
large enough to solve our problems. There must have been another source.
Did he borrow at all? Did he sell something else he had brought away
without us noticing? I don't know. But I do remember that we moved to a
village on the outskirts of Sidon, and there your father sat on the high
stone balcony, smiling for the first time and waiting for the fifteenth of May
in order to return in the wake of the victorious armies.

The fifteenth of May came, after a bitter period of waiting. At exactly 12
midnight your father poked me with his foot as I lay asleep and said in a
voice vibrant with hope: 'Get up and see for yourself as the Arab armies
enter Palestine.' I was up like a shot, and we clambered down barefoot
over the hills to the main road, which lay a full kilometre from the village.

All of us, young and old, panted as we ran like madmen. The lights of the lorries climbing to Ras Naqoura shone in the distance. When we got to the road we felt cold but your father's shout drove everything else from our minds. He had begun to race after the lorries like a small boy. He was calling out to them. He was giving hoarse shouts and gasping for breath, but still he raced along after the string of lorries like a little boy. We ran along beside him, shouting in unison with him. The friendly soldiers were looking at us from under their helmets, silent and motionless. We were gasping for breath. Meanwhile your father, racing along despite his fifty years, pulled cigarettes out of his pocket to throw to the soldiers and went on shouting to them. We were still running along beside him, like a little flock of goats.

Suddenly the lorries were at an end. We went back to the house ex- 13
hausted, our breathing coming with a low whistle as we gasped for air. Your father was absolutely silent, and we too were incapable of speech. When the lights of a passing car fell on your father's face his cheeks were wet with tears.

Things dragged past extremely slowly after that. The communiqués de- 14
ceived us, and then the truth in all its bitterness cheated us. Despondency found its way back to people's faces. Your father began to find enormous difficulty in mentioning Palestine and talking of the happy past spent in his plantations and houses. And we were the ones who formed the massive walls of the tragedy which dominated his new life, as well as being the wretches who discovered, without any difficulty at all, that the idea behind climbing the hills in the early morning, as your father ordered, was to distract us from demanding breakfast.

Complications set in. In some extraordinary way the simplest thing was 15
enough to rouse your father. I remember perfectly the time when someone asked him for something—I neither know nor recall what. He shuddered, and then began trembling as though he had received an electric shock. His eyes glittered as they roamed over our faces. A diabolical thought had implanted itself in his brain, and he jumped up like a man who has found a satisfactory conclusion. Overwhelmed by his awareness that he was able to put an end to his difficulties, and by the dread of someone who is about to undertake a momentous action, he began to mutter to himself as he turned round and round, looking for something we could not see. Then he pounced on a chest which had accompanied us from Acre and started to scatter its contents with terrible nervous movements. Your mother had understood everything in an instant and, caught up in the agitation which mothers feel when their children are exposed to danger, she set about pushing us out of the room and telling us to run away to the mountain. But we stayed by the window. We plastered our little ears to its shutters, and heard your father's voice: 'I want to kill them. I want to kill myself. I want to be done with . . . I want . . .'

Your father fell silent. When we looked into the room again, through the 16 cracks in the door, we saw him lying on the ground, gasping for breath and grinding his teeth as he wept, while your mother sat at one side watching him anxiously.

We did not understand. But I remember that when I saw the black   17
revolver lying on the floor beside him I understood everything. Driven by the mortal terror of a child who has suddenly caught sight of an ogre, I ran off towards the mountain, fleeing from the house.

As I left the house behind, I left my childhood behind too. I realized that   18
our life had ceased to be pleasant, and it was no longer easy for us to live in peace. Things had reached the point where the only solution was a bullet in the head of each one of us. So we must take care to behave suitably in all that we did, not asking for something to eat even when we were hungry, keeping silent when your father spoke of his difficulties and nodding and smiling when he said to us: 'Go and climb the mountain, and don't come back till midday.'

I returned home in the evening, when dusk had fallen. Your father   19
was still ill and your mother was sitting beside him. Your eyes all had a cat-like glitter and your lips were sealed as though they had never been opened, as though they were the scars left by an old wound not properly healed.

You were huddled there, as far from your childhood as you were from   20
the land of the oranges—the oranges which, according to a peasant who used to cultivate them until he left, would shrivel up if a change occurred and they were watered by a strange hand.

Your father was still ill in bed. Your mother was choking back the tears   21
of a tragedy which has not left her eyes till now. I slipped into the room like a pariah. When my glance fell on your father's face which was twitching with impotent fury I saw at the same moment the black revolver lying on the low table, and beside it an orange.

The orange was dried-up and shrivelled.   22

Translated from the Arabic by Hilary Kilpatrick

STUDY QUESTIONS

1. How does the title of the story reflect the theme of exile?
2. Chart the mood shifts of the narrator's uncle. What are the events that are responsible for the changes in his personality?
3. Discuss the consequences of exile on the family. At what point do the children lose their innocence? Cite examples of their disillusionment.
4. Who is the narrator addressing? What is the purpose of his tale?
5. How is the story an effective vehicle for conveying the plight of Palestinians?

SAUDI ARABIA

Fawziyya Abu-Khalid

Fawziyya Abu-Khalid was born in Riyadh, Saudi Arabia, in 1955 to a Westernized upper-middle-class family. She was educated in Saudi Arabia but went on to study sociology at the American University in Beirut and at Lewis and Clark College in the United States. She began writing poetry as a young girl, and some of her early poems appeared in local newspapers. Her first collection, Until When Will They Go on Raping You on Your Wedding Night?, *was published in Lebanon but was banned in Saudi Arabia. Her latest collection is entitled* Reading the Secret of the History of Arab Silence. *"Mother's Inheritance" is from Abu-Khalid's first volume of poetry and is indicative of her provocative style.*

Mother's Inheritance

Mother,
You did not leave me an inheritance of necklaces for a wedding
but a neck
      that towers above the guillotine
Not an embroidered veil for my face   5
but the eyes of a falcon
      that glitter like the daggers
      in the belts of our men.
Not a piece of land large enough
      to plant a single date palm   10
but the primal fruit of The Fertile Crescent:[1]
My Womb.

---

1. *The Middle East, flanked by the Nile and the Tigris and Euphrates Rivers; historically and symbolically the cradle of civilization.*

You let me sleep with all the children
          of our neighborhood
that my agony may give birth   15
          to new rebels

In the bundle of your will
I thought I could find
          a seed from The Garden of Eden
          that I may plant in my heart   20
          forsaken by the seasons
Instead
You left me with a sheathless sword
          the name of an obscure child carved on its blade
Every pore in me   25
          every crack
          opened up:

A sheath.

I plunged the sword into my heart
          but the wall could not contain it   30
I thrust it into my lungs
          but the window could not box it
I dipped it into my waist
          but the house was too small for it
It lengthened into the streets   35
          defoliating the decorations
          of official holidays
Tilling asphalt
Announcing the season of
The Coming Feast.   40

Mother,
Today, they came to confiscate the inheritance
          you left me.
They could not decipher the children's fingerprints
They could not walk the road that stretches   45
          between the arteries of my heart
          and the cord that feeds the babe
          in every mother's womb.
They seized the children of the neighborhood
          for interrogation   50
They could not convict the innocence in their eyes.
They searched my pockets
          took off my clothes
          peeled my skin

But they failed to reach
   the glistening silk that nestles
   the twin doves
   in my breast.

Translated from the Arabic by Kamal Boullata

STUDY QUESTIONS

1. In what ways is "Mother's Inheritance" a scathing attack on Arab society and an exposé of its effect on women?
2. How does the poet use imagery to convey the psychological state of mind of the narrator?

55

SENEGAL

◈ LÉOPOLD SÉDAR SENGHOR

Léopold Sédar Senghor, poet, politician, polemicist, and intellectual, was born in 1906 in Joal, a small coastal town in Senegal. The son of a prosperous Catholic family, he attended local missionary schools but remained in touch with the ancient customs of his community through contact with peasants and fishermen. A brilliant student, he attended secondary school in Dakar and later graduated from the prestigious Lycée Louis le-Grand in Paris. Subsequently, he earned advanced degrees from the Sorbonne. As a student in Paris, Senghor, along with Aimé Césaire of Martinique and Leon Damas of French Guiana, inaugurated the intellectual and artistic movement known as "negritude." The aim of negritude was to redeem and restore pride in Africa's culture and history. Until the outbreak of World War II, Senghor taught in a French lycée. During the war, he served as an officer in the French army and was captured and interned in a German prison camp. Upon his release, Senghor co-founded the black cultural journal Présence Africaine. *Senghor became a leading political figure in the nationalist movement for independence in French Colonial Africa, and from 1960 until 1980 he served as the elected president of Senegal.*

Senghor's achievement as an artist lies in implementing the ideals of negritude. With strong verbal rhythms, a wealth of African allusions, and an exaltation of traditional communal values, he delved beneath the layers of colonial history to rediscover Africa's own cultural legacy. Many of his books have been translated into English, among them Nocturnes (1969) *and* Poems of a Black Orpheus (1981). *"Prayer to Masks" and "New York" are examples of Senghor's search for the truth and beauty of the black experience.*

Prayer to Masks

Masks! Masks!
Black mask red mask, you white-and-black masks
Masks of the four points from which the Spirit blows

In silence I salute you!
Nor you the least, Lion-headed Ancestor   5
You guard this place forbidden to all laughter of women, to all
    smiles that fade
You distill this air of eternity in which I breathe the air of my
    Fathers.
Masks of unmasked faces, stripped of the marks of illness and   10
    the lines of age
You who have fashioned this portrait, this my face bent over
    the altar of white paper
In your own image, hear me!
The Africa of the empires is dying: see the agony of a pitiful   15
    princess
And Europe too where we are joined by the navel.
Fix your unchanging eyes upon your children, who are given
    orders
Who give away their lives like the poor their last clothes.   20
Let us report present at the rebirth of the World
Like the yeast which white flour needs.
For who would teach rhythm to a dead world of machines and
    guns?
Who would give the cry of joy to wake the dead and the   25
    bereaved at dawn?
Say, who would give back the memory of life to the man
    whose hopes are smashed?
They call us men of coffee cotton oil
They call us men of death.   30
We are the men of the dance, whose feet draw new strength
    pounding the hardened earth.

Translated from the French by John Reed and Clive Wake

New York

Jazz orchestra: solo trumpet

1

New York! At first your beauty confused me, and your great
    longlegged golden girls.
I was so timid at first under your blue metallic eyes, your
    frosty smile
So timid. And the disquiet in the depth of your skyscraper   5
    streets

Lifting up owl eyes in the sun's eclipse.
Your sulphurous light and the livid shafts (their heads
    dumbfounding the sky)
Skyscrapers defying cyclones on their muscles of steel and their   10
    weathered stone skins.
But a fortnight on the bald sidewalks of Manhattan
—At the end of the third week the fever takes you with the
    pounce of a jaguar
A fortnight with no well or pasture, all the birds of the air   15
Fall suddenly dead below the high ashes of the terraces.
No child's laughter blossoms, his hand in my fresh hand
No mother's breast. Legs in nylon. Legs and breasts with no
    sweat and no smell.
No tender word for mouths are lipless. Hard cash buys   20
    artificial hearts.
No book where wisdom is read. The painter's palette flowers
    with crystals of coral.
Insomniac nights O nights of Manhattan, tormented by fatuous
    fires, while the klaxons cry through the empty hours   25
And dark waters bear away hygienic loves, like the bodies of
    children on a river in flood.

     2

It is the time of signs and reckonings
New York! It is the time of manna and hyssop.
Only listen to God's trombones, your heart beating to the   30
    rhythm of blood your blood.
I have seen Harlem humming with sounds and solemn colour
    and flamboyant smells
—(It is tea-time for the man who delivers pharmaceutical
    products)   35
I have seen them preparing at flight of day, the festival of the
    Night. I proclaim there is more truth in the Night than in
    the day.
It is the pure hour when God sets the life before memory
    germinating in the streets   40
All the amphibious elements shining like suns.
Harlem Harlem! I have seen Harlem Harlem! A breeze green
    with corn springing from the pavements ploughed by the
    bare feet of dancers in
Crests and waves of silk and breasts of spearheads, ballets of   45
    lilies and fabulous masks
The mangoes of love roll from the low houses under the police
    horses' hooves.

I have seen down the sidewalks streams of white rum and
    streams of black milk in the blue haze of cigars.   50
I have seen the sky at evening snowing cotton flowers and
    wings of seraphim and wizard's plumes.
Listen, New York, listen to your brazen male voice your
    vibrant oboe voice, the muted anguish of your tears falling
    in great clots of blood   55
Listen to the far beating of your nocturnal heart, rhythm and
    blood of the drum, drum and blood and drum.

3

New York! I say to New York, let the black blood flow into
    your blood
Cleaning the rust from your steel articulations, like an oil of life   60
Giving your bridges the curve of the hills, the liana's
    suppleness.
See, the ancient times come again, unity is rediscovered the
    reconciliation of the Lion the Bull and the Tree
The idea is linked to the act the ear to the heart the sign to the   65
    sense.
See your rivers murmuring with musky caymans, manatees
    with eyes of mirage. There is no need to invent the
    Mermaids.
It is enough to open your eyes to the April rainbow   70
And the ears, above all the ears to God who with a burst of
    saxophone laughter created the heavens and the earth in six
    days.
And on the seventh day, he slept his great negro sleep.

Translated from the French by John Reed and Clive Wake

STUDY QUESTIONS

1. Why is the speaker in "Prayer to Masks" paying homage to the masks?
2. Who is responsible for the world's rebirth? What is meant by "a dead world of machines and guns" (lines 23–24)?
3. Contrast the first two sections of "New York." What is the difference between Manhattan in the first section and Harlem in the second?
4. What is the poet proclaiming in "New York" when he writes, "the ancient times come again, unity is rediscovered . . ." (line 63)?
5. How does the author use imagery in "New York"? What are some examples?

SOUTH AFRICA

 NADINE GORDIMER

Nadine Gordimer was born in 1923 in Springs, Transvaal, South Africa. The daughter of a Jewish father who had immigrated from Europe and a mother born in England, she was educated in local schools and attended the University of Witwatersrand. She began writing at a young age and quickly won international acclaim. To date she has published nine novels and nine collections of short stories and her work has been widely translated. She is recognized as a leading critic of apartheid, and as a result, several of her books have been banned by the South African government. For most of her life she has lived in Johannesburg, but she has traveled extensively and taught at Harvard, Northwestern, Michigan, and Columbia universities in the United States.

Gordimer claims D. H. Lawrence, Henry James, Ernest Hemingway, and Albert Camus as literary influences. The themes of alienation and exile dominate much of her work, as does a concern with the problematic nature of race relations. What is most remarkable about her work is the shifting political vision. At the beginning of her career, she confronted race relations from a liberal humanist perspective. In the novels A World of Strangers *(1958) and* Occasion for Loving *(1963), a simple human commitment to justice and equality is offered as a solution for overcoming the social barriers of apartheid. As the political crisis in South Africa intensified and the black population demonstrated through its struggle that change could occur only through direct collective action, her work increasingly embraced a radical viewpoint. In the novels* The Late Bourgeois World *(1966),* Burger's Daughter *(1979), and* July's People *(1981), she aligns herself with the revolutionary aims of the liberation movement. "A Soldier's Embrace," from a short story collection of the same title published in 1980, explores the nature of interracial relations after a liberation movement achieves power.*

A Soldier's Embrace

The day the cease-fire was signed she was caught in a crowd. Peasant   1
boys from Europe who had made up the colonial army and freedom
fighters whose column had marched into town were staggering about together outside the barracks, not three blocks from her house in whose
rooms, for ten years, she had heard the blurred parade-ground bellow of
colonial troops being trained to kill and be killed.

The men weren't drunk. They linked and swayed across the street;   2
because all that had come to a stop, everything *had* to come to a stop: they
surrounded cars, bicycles, vans, nannies with children, women with loaves
of bread or basins of mangoes on their heads, a road gang with picks and
shovels, a Coca-Cola truck, an old man with a barrow who bought bottles
and bones. They were grinning and laughing amazement. That it could be:
there they were, bumping into each other's bodies in joy, looking into each
other's rough faces, all eyes crescent-shaped, brimming greeting. The
words were in languages not mutually comprehensible, but the cries were
new, a whooping and crowing all understood. She was bumped and jostled and she let go, stopped trying to move in any self-determined direction. There were two soldiers in front of her, blocking her off by their
clumsy embrace (how do you do it, how do you do what you've never
done before) and the embrace opened like a door and took her in—a pink
hand with bitten nails grasping her right arm, a black hand with a big-
dialled watch and thong bracelet pulling at her left elbow. Their three
heads collided gaily, musk of sweat and tang of strong sweet soap clapped
a mask to her nose and mouth. They all gasped with delicious shock. They
were saying things to each other. She put up an arm round each neck, the
rough pile of an army haircut on one side, the soft negro hair on the other,
and kissed them both on the cheek. The embrace broke. The crowd wove
her away behind backs, arms, jogging heads; she was returned to and took
up the will of her direction again—she was walking home from the post
office, where she had just sent a telegram to relatives abroad: ALL CALM
DON'T WORRY.

The lawyer came back early from his offices because the courts were not   3
sitting although the official celebration holiday was not until next day. He
described to his wife the rally before the Town Hall, which he had watched
from the office-building balcony. One of the guerilla leaders (not the most
important; he on whose head the biggest price had been laid would not
venture so soon and deep into the territory so newly won) had spoken for
two hours from the balcony of the Town Hall. 'Brilliant. Their jaws
dropped. Brilliant. They've never heard anything on that level: precise,
reasoned—none of them would ever have believed it possible, out of the
bush. You should have seen de Poorteer's face. He'd like to be able to get
up and open his mouth like that. And be listened to like that . . .' The

Governor's handicap did not even bring the sympathy accorded to a stammerer; he paused and gulped between words. The blacks had always used a portmanteau name for him that meant the-crane-who-is-trying-to-swallow-the-bullfrog.

One of the members of the black underground organization that could now come out in brass-band support of the freedom fighters had recognized the lawyer across from the official balcony and given him the freedom fighters' salute. The lawyer joked about it, miming, full of pride. 'You should have been there—should have seen him, up there in the official party. I told you—really—you ought to have come to town with me this morning.' 4

'And what did you do?' She wanted to assemble all details. 5

'Oh I gave the salute in return, chaps in the street saluted *me* . . . everybody was doing it. *It was marvellous.* And the police standing by; just to think, last month—only last week—you'd have been arrested.' 6

'Like thumbing your nose at them,' she said, smiling. 7

'Did anything go on around here?' 8

'Muchanga was afraid to go out all day. He wouldn't even run up to the post office for me!' Their servant had come to them many years ago, from service in the house of her father, a colonial official in the Treasury. 9

'But there was no excitement?' 10

She told him: 'The soldiers and some freedom fighters mingled outside the barracks. I got caught for a minute or two. They were dancing about; you couldn't get through. All very good-natured.—Oh, I sent the cable.' 11

An accolade, one side a white cheek, the other a black. The white one she kissed on the left cheek, the black one on the right cheek, as if these were two sides of one face. 12

That vision, version, was like a poster; the sort of thing that was soon peeling off dirty shopfronts and bus shelters while the months of wrangling talks preliminary to the take-over by the black government went by. 13

To begin with, the cheek was not white but pale or rather sallow, the poor boy's pallor of winter in Europe (that draft must have only just arrived and not yet seen service) with homesick pimples sliced off by the discipline of an army razor. And the cheek was not black but opaque peat-dark, waxed with sweat round the plump contours of the nostril. As if she could return to the moment again, she saw what she had not consciously noted: there had been a narrow pink strip in the darkness near the ear, the sort of tender stripe of healed flesh revealed when a scab is nicked off a little before it is ripe. The scab must have come away that morning: the young man picked at it in the troop carrier or truck (whatever it was the freedom fighters had; the colony had been told for years that they were supplied by the Chinese and Russians indiscriminately) on the way to enter the capital in triumph. 14

According to newspaper reports, the day would have ended for the two young soldiers in drunkenness and whoring. She was, apparently, not yet 15 too old to belong to the soldier's embrace of all that a land-mine in the bush might have exploded for ever. That was one version of the incident. Another: the opportunity taken by a woman not young enough to be clasped in the arms of the one who (same newspaper, while the war was on, expressing the fears of the colonists for their women) would be expected to rape her.

She considered this version. 16

She had not kissed on the mouth, she had not sought anonymous lips 17 and tongues in the licence of festival. Yet she had kissed. Watching herself again, she knew that. She had—god knows why—kissed them on either cheek, his left, his right. It was deliberate, if a swift impulse: she had distinctly made the move.

She did not tell what happened not because her husband would suspect 18 licence in her, but because he would see her—born and brought up in the country as the daughter of an enlightened white colonial officer, married to a white liberal lawyer well known for his defence of blacks in political trials—as giving free expression to liberal principles.

She had not told, she did not know what had happened. 19

She thought of a time long ago when a school camp had gone to the sea 20 and immediately on arrival everyone had run down to the beach from the train, tripping and tearing over sand dunes of wild fig, aghast with ecstatic shock at the meeting with the water.

De Poorteer was recalled and the lawyer remarked to one of their black 21 friends, 'The crane has choked on the bullfrog. I hear that's what they're saying in the Quarter.'

The priest who came from the black slum that had always been known 22 simply by that anonymous term did not respond with any sort of glee. His reserve implied it was easy to celebrate; there were people who 'shouted freedom too loud all of a sudden'.

The lawyer and his wife understood: Father Mulumbua was one who 23 had shouted freedom when it was dangerous to do so, and gone to prison several times for it, while certain people, now on the Interim Council set up to run the country until the new government took over, had kept silent. He named a few, but reluctantly. Enough to confirm their own suspicions— men who perhaps had made some deal with the colonial power to place its interests first, no matter what sort of government might emerge from the new constitution? Yet when the couple plunged into discussion their friend left them talking to each other while he drank his beer and gazed, frowning as if at a headache or because the sunset hurt his eyes behind his spectacles, round her huge-leaved tropical plants that bowered the terrace in cool humidity.

They had always been rather proud of their friendship with him, this 24 man in a cassock who wore a clenched fist carved of local ebony as well as a silver cross round his neck. His black face was habitually stern—a high seriousness balanced by sudden splurting laughter when they used to tease him over the fist—but never inattentively ill-at-ease.

'What was the matter?' She answered herself; 'I had the feeling he didn't   25
want to come here.' She was using a paper handkerchief dipped in gin to
wipe greenfly off the back of a pale new leaf that had shaken itself from its
folds like a cut-out paper lantern.

'Good lord, he's been here hundreds of times.'   26

'—Before, yes.'   27

What things were they saying?   28

   With the shouting in the street and the swaying of the crowd, the sweet   29
powerful presence that confused the senses so that sound, sight, stink
(sweat, cheap soap) ran into one tremendous sensation, she could not
make out words that came so easily.

Not even what she herself must have said.   30

A few wealthy white men who had been boastful in their support of the   31
colonial war and knew they would be marked down by the blacks as arch
exploiters, left at once. Good riddance, as the lawyer and his wife remarked. Many ordinary white people who had lived contentedly, without
questioning its actions, under the colonial government, now expressed an
enthusiastic intention to help build a nation, as the newspapers put it. The
lawyer's wife's neighbourhood butcher was one. 'I don't mind blacks.' He
was expansive with her, in his shop that he had occupied for twelve years
on a licence available only to white people. 'Makes no difference to me who
you are so long as you're honest.' Next to a chart showing a beast mapped
according to the cuts of meat it provided, he had hung a picture of the most
important leader of the freedom fighters, expected to be first President.
People like the butcher turned out with their babies clutching pennants
when the leader drove through the town from the airport.

   There were incidents (newspaper euphemism again) in the Quarter. It   32
was to be expected. Political factions, tribally based, who had not fought
the war, wanted to share power with the freedom fighters' Party.
Muchanga no longer went down to the Quarter on his day off. His friends
came to see him and sat privately on their hunkers near the garden com-
post heap. The ugly mansions of the rich who had fled stood empty on the
bluff above the sea, but it was said they would make money out of them
yet—they would be bought as ambassadorial residences when independence came, and with it many black and yellow diplomats. Zealots who
claimed they belonged to the Party burned shops and houses of the poorer
whites who lived, as the lawyer said, 'in the inevitable echelon of colonial
society', closest to the Quarter. A house in the lawyer's street was noticed
by his wife to be accommodating what was certainly one of those families,
in the outhouses; green nylon curtains had appeared at the garage window, she reported. The suburb was pleasantly overgrown and well-to-do;

no one rich, just white professional people and professors from the university. The barracks was empty now, except for an old man with a stump and a police uniform stripped of insignia, a friend of Muchanga, it turned out, who sat on a beer-crate at the gates. He had lost his job as nightwatchman when one of the rich people went away, and was glad to have work.

The street had been perfectly quiet; except for that first day. 33

The fingernails she sometimes still saw clearly were bitten down until 34 embedded in a thin line of dirt all round, in the pink blunt fingers. The thumb and thick fingertips were turned back coarsely even while grasping her. Such hands had never been allowed to take possession. They were permanently raw, so young, from unloading coal, digging potatoes from the frozen Northern Hemisphere, washing hotel dishes. He had not been killed, and now that day of the cease-fire was over he would be delivered back across the sea to the docks, the stony farm, the scullery of the grand hotel. He would have to do anything he could get. There was unemployment in Europe where he had returned, the army didn't need all the young men any more.

A great friend of the lawyer and his wife, Chipande, was coming home 35 from exile. They heard over the radio he was expected, accompanying the future President as confidential secretary, and they waited to hear from him.

The lawyer put up his feet on the empty chair where the priest had sat, 36 shifting it to a comfortable position by hooking his toes, free in sandals, through the slats. 'Imagine, Chipande!' Chipande had been almost a protégé—but they didn't like the term, it smacked of patronage. Tall, cocky, casual Chipande, a boy from the slummiest part of the Quarter, was recommended by the White Fathers' Mission (was it by Father Mulumbua himself?—the lawyer thought so, his wife was not sure they remembered correctly) as a bright kid who wanted to be articled to a lawyer. That was asking a lot, in those days—nine years ago. He never finished his apprenticeship because while he and his employer were soon close friends, and the kid picked up political theories from the books in the house he made free of, he became so involved in politics that he had to skip the country one jump ahead of a detention order signed by the crane-who-was-trying-to-swallow-the-bullfrog.

After two weeks, the lawyer phoned the offices the guerilla-movement- 37 become-Party had set up openly in the town but apparently Chipande had an office in the former colonial secretariat. There he had a secretary of his own; he wasn't easy to reach. The lawyer left a message. The lawyer and his wife saw from the newspaper pictures he hadn't changed much: he had a beard and had adopted the Muslim cap favoured by political circles in exile on the East Coast.

He did come to the house eventually. He had the distracted, insistent 38 friendliness of one who has no time to re-establish intimacy; it must be taken as read. And it must not be displayed. When he remarked on a shortage of accommodation for exiles now become officials, and the lawyer said the house was far too big for two people, he was welcome to move in and regard a self-contained part of it as his private living quarters, he did not answer but went on talking generalities. The lawyer's wife mentioned Father Mulumbua, whom they had not seen since just after the cease-fire. The lawyer added, 'There's obviously some sort of big struggle going on, he's fighting for his political life there in the Quarter.' 'Again,' she said, drawing them into a reminder of what had only just become their past.

But Chipande was restlessly following with his gaze the movements of 39 old Muchanga, dragging the hose from plant to plant, careless of the spray; 'You remember who this is, Muchanga?' she had said when the visitor arrived, yet although the old man had given, in their own language, the sort of respectful greeting even an elder gives a young man whose clothes and bearing denote rank and authority, he was not in any way overwhelmed nor enthusiastic—perhaps he secretly supported one of the rival factions?

The lawyer spoke of the latest whites to leave the country—people who 40 had got themselves quickly involved in the sort of currency swindle that draws more outrage than any other kind of crime, in a new state fearing the flight of capital; 'Let them go, let them go. Good riddance.' And he turned to talk of other things—there were so many more important questions to occupy the attention of the three old friends.

But Chipande couldn't stay. Chipande could not stay for supper; his 41 beautiful long velvety black hands with their pale lining (as she thought of the palms) hung impatiently between his knees while he sat forward in the chair, explaining, adamant against persuasion. He should not have been there, even now; he had official business waiting, sometimes he drafted correspondence until one or two in the morning. The lawyer remarked how there hadn't been a proper chance to talk; he wanted to discuss those fellows in the Interim Council Mulumbua was so warily distrustful of— what did Chipande know?

Chipande, already on his feet, said something dismissing and very 42 slightly disparaging, not about the Council members but of Mulumbua—a reference to his connection with the Jesuit missionaries as an influence that 'comes through'. 'But I must make a note to see him sometime.'

It seemed that even black men who presented a threat to the Party could 43 be discussed only among black men themselves, now. Chipande put an arm round each of his friends as for the brief official moment of a photograph, left them; he who used to sprawl on the couch arguing half the night before dossing down in the lawyer's pyjamas. 'As soon as I'm settled I'll contact you. You'll be around, ay?'

'Oh we'll be around.' The lawyer laughed, referring, for his part, to 44 those who were no longer. 'Glad to see you're not driving a Mercedes!' he called with reassured affection at the sight of Chipande getting into a modest car. How many times, in the old days, had they agreed on the necessity for African leaders to live simply when they came to power!

On the terrace to which he turned back, Muchanga was doing some- 45
thing extraordinary—wetting a dirty rag with Gilbey's. It was supposed to be his day off, anyway; why was he messing about with the plants when one wanted peace to talk undisturbed?

'Is those thing again, those thing is killing the leaves.' 46

'For heaven's sake, he could use methylated for that! Any kind of alco- 47
hol will do! Why don't you get him some?'

There were shortages of one kind and another in the country, and gin 48
happened to be something in short supply.

Whatever the hand had done in the bush had not coarsened it. It, too, was 49
suède-black, and elegant. The pale lining was hidden against her own skin where the hand grasped her left elbow. Strangely, black does not show toil—she remarked this as one remarks the quality of a fabric. The hand was not as long but as distinguished by beauty as Chipande's. The watch a fine piece of equipment for a fighter. There was something next to it, in fact looped over the strap by the angle of the wrist as the hand grasped. A bit of thong with a few beads knotted where it was joined as a bracelet. Or amulet. Their babies wore such things; often their first and only garment. Grandmothers or mothers attached it as protection. It had worked; he was alive at cease-fire. Some had been too deep in the bush to know, and had been killed after the fighting was over. He had pumped his head wildly and laughingly at whatever it was she—they—had been babbling.

The lawyer had more free time than he'd ever remembered. So many of his 50
clients had left; he was deputed to collect their rents and pay their taxes for them, in the hope that their property wasn't going to be confiscated—there had been alarmist rumours among such people since the day of the cease-fire. But without the rich white there was little litigation over possessions, whether in the form of the children of dissolved marriages or the houses and cars claimed by divorced wives. The Africans had their own ways of resolving such redistribution of goods. And a gathering of elders under a tree was sufficient to settle a dispute over boundaries or argue for and against the guilt of a woman accused of adultery. He had had a message, in a round-about way, that he might be asked to be consultant on consti-tutional law to the Party, but nothing seemed to come of it. He took home with him the proposals for the draft constitution he had managed to get hold of. He spent whole afternoons in his study making notes for counter or improved proposals he thought he would send to Chipande or one of the other people he knew in high positions: every time he glanced up, there through his open windows was Muchanga's little company at the

bottom of the garden. Once, when he saw they had straggled off, he wandered down himself to clear his head (he got drowsy, as he never did when he used to work twelve hours a day at the office). They ate dried shrimps, from the market: that's what they are doing! The ground was full of bitten-off heads and black eyes on stalks. His wife smiled. 'They bring them. Muchanga won't go near the market since the riot.' 'It's ridiculous. Who's going to harm him?'

There was even a suggestion that the lawyer might apply for a profes-   51 sorship at the university. The chair of the Faculty of Law was vacant, since the students had demanded the expulsion of certain professors engaged during the colonial regime—in particular of the fuddy-duddy (good riddance) who had gathered dust in the Law chair, and the quite decent young man (pity about him) who had had Political Science. But what professor of Political Science could expect to survive both a colonial regime and the revolutionary regime that defeated it? The lawyer and his wife decided that since he might still be appointed in some consultative capacity to the new government it would be better to keep out of the university context, where the students were shouting for Africanization, and even an appointee with his credentials as a fighter of legal battles for blacks against the colonial regime in the past might not escape their ire.

Newspapers sent by friends from over the border gave statistics for the   52 number of what they termed 'refugees' who were entering the neighbouring country. The papers from outside also featured sensationally the inevitable mistakes and misunderstandings, in a new administration, that led to several foreign businessmen being held for investigation by the new regime. For the last fifteen years of colonial rule, Gulf had been drilling for oil in the territory, and just as inevitably it was certain that all sorts of questionable people, from the point of view of the regime's determination not to be exploited preferentially, below the open market for the highest bidder in ideological as well as economic terms, would try to gain concessions.

His wife said, 'The butcher's gone.'   53

He was home, reading at his desk; he could spend the day more usefully   54 there than at the office, most of the time. She had left after breakfast with her fisherman's basket that she liked to use for shopping, she wasn't away twenty minutes. 'You mean the shop's closed?' There was nothing in the basket. She must have turned and come straight home.

'Gone. It's empty. He's cleared out over the weekend.'   55

She sat down suddenly on the edge of the desk; and after a moment of   56 silence, both laughed shortly, a strange, secret, complicit laugh. 'Why, do you think?' 'Can't say. He certainly charged, if you wanted a decent cut. But meat's so hard to get, now; I thought it was worth it—justified.'

The lawyer raised his eyebrows and pulled down his mouth: 'Exactly.'   57 They understood; the man probably knew he was marked to run into trouble for profiteering—he must have been paying through the nose for his supplies on the black market, anyway, didn't have much choice.

Shops were being looted by the unemployed and loafers (there had   58
always been a lot of unemployed hanging around for the pickings of the
town) who felt the new regime should entitle them to take what they dared
not before. Radio and television shops were the most favoured objective for
gangs who adopted the freedom fighters' slogans. Transistor radios were
the portable luxuries of street life; the new regime issued solemn warnings,
over those same radios, that looting and violence would be firmly dealt with
but it was difficult for the police to be everywhere at once. Sometimes their
actions became sweet battles, since the struggle with the looters changed
character as supporters of the Party's rival political factions joined in with
the thieves against the police. It was necessary to be ready to reverse direction, quickly turning down a side street in detour if one encountered such
disturbances while driving around town. There were bodies sometimes;
both husband and wife had been fortunate enough not to see any close up,
so far. A company of the freedom fighters' army was brought down from
the north and installed in the barracks to supplement the police force; they
patrolled the Quarter, mainly. Muchanga's friend kept his job as gatekeeper although there were armed sentries on guard: the lawyer's wife
found that a light touch to mention in letters to relatives in Europe.

'Where'll you go now?'   59

She slid off the desk and picked up her basket. 'Supermarket, I suppose.   60
Or turn vegetarian.' He knew that she left the room quickly, smiling,
because she didn't want him to suggest Muchanga ought to be sent to look
for fish in the markets along the wharf in the Quarter. Muchanga was
being allowed to indulge in all manner of eccentric refusals; for no reason,
unless out of some curious sentiment about her father?

She avoided walking past the barracks because of the machine guns the   61
young sentries had in place of rifles. Rifles pointed into the air but machine
guns pointed to the street at the level of different parts of people's bodies,
short and tall, the backsides of babies slung on mothers' backs, the round
heads of children, her fisherman's basket—she knew she was getting like
the others; what she felt was afraid. She wondered what the butcher and
his wife had said to each other. Because he was at least one whom she had
known. He had sold the meat she had bought that these women and their
babies passing her in the street didn't have the money to buy.

It was something quite unexpected and outside their own efforts that de-   62
cided it. A friend over the border telephoned and offered a place in a
lawyers' firm of highest repute there, and some prestige in the world at
large, since the team had defended individuals fighting for freedom of the
press and militant churchmen upholding freedom of conscience on political issues. A telephone call; as simple as that. The friend said (and the
lawyer did not repeat this even to his wife) they would be proud to have
a man of his courage and convictions in the firm. He could be satisfied he
would be able to uphold the liberal principles everyone knew he had

always stood for; there were many whites, in that country still ruled by a white minority, who deplored the injustices under which their black population suffered etc. and believed you couldn't ignore the need for peaceful change etc.

His offices presented no problem; something called Africa Seabeds (For- 63 mosan Chinese who had gained a concession to ship seaweed and dried shrimps in exchange for rice) took over the lease and the typists. The senior clerks and the current articled clerk (the lawyer had always given a chance to young blacks, long before other people had come round to it—it wasn't only the secretary to the President who owed his start to him) he managed to get employed by the new Trades Union Council; he still knew a few blacks who remembered the times he had acted for black workers in disputes with the colonial government. The house would just have to stand empty, for the time being. It wasn't imposing enough to attract an embassy but maybe it would do for a Chargé d'Affaires—it was left in the hands of a half-caste letting agent who was likely to stay put: only whites were allowed in, at the country over the border. Getting money out was going to be much more difficult than disposing of the house. The lawyer would have to keep coming back, so long as this remained practicable, hoping to find a loophole in exchange control regulations.

She was deputed to engage the movers. In their innocence, they had 64 thought it as easy as that! Every large vehicle, let alone a pantechnicon, was commandeered for months ahead. She had no choice but to grease a palm, although it went against her principles, it was condoning a practice they believed a young black state must stamp out before corruption took hold. He would take his entire legal library, for a start; that was the most important possession, to him. Neither was particularly attached to furniture. She did not know what there was she felt she really could not do without. Except the plants. And that was out of the question. She could not even mention it. She did not want to leave her towering plants, mostly natives of South America and not Africa, she supposed, whose aerial tubes pushed along the terrace brick erect tips extending hourly in the growth of the rainy season, whose great leaves turned shields to the spatter of Muchanga's hose glancing off in a shower of harmless arrows, whose two-hand-span trunks were smooth and grooved in one sculptural sweep down their length, or carved by the drop of each dead leaf-stem with concave medallions marking the place and building a pattern at once bold and exquisite. Such things would not travel; they were too big to give away.

The evening she was beginning to pack the books, the telephone rang 65 in the study. Chipande—and he called her by her name, urgently, commandingly—'What is this all about? Is it true, what I hear? Let me just talk to him—'

'Our friend,' she said, making a long arm, receiver at the end of it, 66 towards her husband.

'But you can't leave!' Chipande shouted down the phone. '*You* can't go! 67 I'm coming round. *Now*.'

She went on packing the legal books while Chipande and her husband 68
were shut up together in the living-room.

'He cried. You know, he actually cried.' Her husband stood in the door- 69
way, alone.

'I know—that's what I've always liked so much about them, whatever 70
they do. They feel.'

The lawyer made a face: there it is, it happened; hard to believe. 71

'Rushing in here, after nearly a year! I said, but we haven't seen you, all 72
this time . . . he took no notice. Suddenly he starts pressing me to take the
university job, raising all sorts of objections, why not this . . . that. And
then he really wept, for a moment.'

They got on with packing books like builder and mate deftly handling 73
and catching bricks.

And the morning they were to leave it was all done; twenty-one years of 74
life in that house gone quite easily into one pantechnicon. They were quiet
with each other, perhaps out of apprehension of the tedious search of their
possessions that would take place at the border; it was said that if you
struck over-conscientious or officious freedom fighter patrols they would
even make you unload a piano, a refrigerator or washing machine. She had
bought Muchanga a hawker's licence, a hand-cart, and stocks of small
commodities. Now that many small shops owned by white shopkeepers
had disappeared, there was an opportunity for humble itinerant black
traders. Muchanga had lost his fear of the town. He was proud of what she
had done for him and she knew he saw himself as a rich merchant; this was
the only sort of freedom he understood, after so many years as a servant.
But she also knew, and the lawyer sitting beside her in the car knew she
knew, that the shortages of the goods Muchanga could sell from his cart,
the sugar and soap and matches and pomade and sunglasses, would soon
put him out of business. He promised to come back to the house and look
after the plants every week; and he stood waving, as he had done every
year when they set off on holiday. She did not know what to call out to him
as they drove away. The right words would not come again; whatever they
were, she left them behind.

STUDY QUESTIONS

1. What is the setting of the story? Why is the tone nostalgic?
2. How do the relationships between the white and black characters change?
3. What is the meaning of the soldier's embrace at the beginning of the story? By the time the story ends, does the embrace appear ironic?
4. The story focuses on the role of white liberals in Africa in a period of political transformation. How does Gordimer define this role and convey its problematic nature?

 ## AHMED ESSOP

Ahmed Essop was born in 1931 in India but grew up in Fordsburg, a large, mostly Indian suburb of Johannesburg. He graduated from the University of South Africa and has taught in various secondary schools. In 1979 he was awarded the Olive Schreiner Prize by the English Academy of Southern Africa for his collection The Hajji and Other Stories *(1988). He has also published two novels:* The Visitation *(1980) and* The Emperor *(1984). With humor and sensitivity, Essop portrays the diverse religious, political, cultural, and economic preoccupations of Johannesburg's Indian community. When he confronts the harsh social realities of apartheid, he is gentle and compassionate in his depiction of the lives affected. "The Hajji" is a good example of the emotional richness of Essop's stories.*

The Hajji

W hen the telephone rang several times one evening and his wife did   1
not attend to it as she usually did, Hajji Hassen, seated on a settee in the lounge, cross-legged and sipping tea, shouted: "Salima, are you deaf?" And when he received no response from his wife and the jarring bell went on ringing, he shouted again: "Salima, what's happened to you?"

The telephone stopped ringing. Hajji Hassen frowned in a contempla-   2
tive manner, wondering where his wife was now. Since his return from Mecca after the pilgrimage, he had discovered novel inadequacies in her, or perhaps saw the old ones in a more revealing light. One of her salient inadequacies was never to be around when he wanted her. She was either across the road confabulating with her sister, or gossiping with the neighbours, or away on a shopping spree. And now, when the telephone had gone on assaulting his ears, she was not in the house. He took another sip of the strongly spiced tea to stifle the irritation within him.

When he heard the kitchen door open he knew that Salima had entered.   3
The telephone burst out again in a metallic shrill and the Hajji shouted for his wife. She hurried to the phone.

"Hullo . . . Yes . . . Hassen . . . Speak to him? . . . Who speaking? . . .   4
Caterine? . . . Who Caterine? . . . Au-right . . . I call him."

She put the receiver down gingerly and informed her husband in Gu-   5
jarati that a woman named "Caterine" wanted to speak to him. The name evoked no immediate association in his memory. He descended from the settee and squeezing his feet into a pair of crimson sandals, went to the telephone.

"Hullo . . . Who? . . . Catherine? . . . No, I don't know you . . . Yes . . .   6
Yes . . . Oh . . . now I remember . . . Yes . . ."

He listened intently to the voice, urgent, supplicating. Then he gave his answer: 7

"I am afraid I can't help him. Let the Christians bury him. His last wish 8 means nothing to me . . . Madam, it's impossible . . . No . . . Let him die . . . Brother? Pig! Pig! Bastard!" He banged the receiver onto the telephone in explosive annoyance.

"O Allah!" Salima exclaimed. "What words! What is this all about?" 9

He did not answer but returned to the settee, and she quietly went to the bedroom. 10

Salima went to bed and it was almost midnight when her husband came 11 into the room. His earlier vexation had now given place to gloom. He told her of his brother Karim who lay dying in Hillbrow. Karim had cut himself off from his family and friends ten years ago; he had crossed the colour line (his fair complexion and grey eyes serving as passports) and gone to co-habit with a white woman. And now that he was on the verge of death he wished to return to the world he had forsaken and to be buried with Muslim funeral rites and in a Muslim cemetery.

Hajji Hassen had, of course, rejected the plea, and for a good reason. 12 When his brother had crossed the colour line, he had severed his family ties. The Hajji at that time had felt excoriating humiliation. By going over to the white Herrenvolk, his brother had trampled on something that was a vital part of him, his dignity and self-respect. But the rejection of his brother's plea involved a straining of the heartstrings and the Hajji did not feel happy. He had recently sought God's pardon for his sins in Mecca, and now this business of his brother's final earthly wish and his own intran-sigence was in some way staining his spirit.

The next day Hassen rose at five to go to the mosque. When he stepped 13 out of his house in Newtown the street lights were beginning to pale and clusters of houses to assume definition. The atmosphere was fresh and heady, and he took a few deep breaths. The first trams were beginning to pass through Bree Street and were clanging along like decrepit yet burning spectres towards the Johannesburg City Hall. Here and there a figure moved along hurriedly. The Hindu fruit and vegetable hawkers were start-ing up their old trucks in the yards, preparing to go out for the day to sell to suburban housewives.

When he reached the mosque the Somali muezzin in the ivory-domed 14 minaret began to intone the call for prayers. After prayers, he remained behind to read the Koran in the company of two other men. When he had done the sun was shining brilliantly in the courtyard onto the flowers and the fountain with its goldfish.

Outside the house he saw a car. Salima opened the door and whispered, 15 "Caterine." For a moment he felt irritated, but realising that he might as well face her he stepped boldly into the lounge.

Catherine was a small woman with firm fleshly legs. She was seated 16 cross-legged on the settee, smoking a cigarette. Her face was almost boyish, a look that partly originated in her auburn hair which was cut very short, and partly in the smallness of her head. Her eye-brows, firmly pencilled, accentuated the grey-green glitter of her eyes. She was dressed in a dark grey costume.

He nodded his head at her to signify that he knew who she was. Over the telephone he had spoken with aggressive authority. Now, in the presence of the woman herself, he felt a weakening of his masculine fibre.   17

"You must, Mr Hassen, come to see your brother."   18

"I am afraid I am unable to help," he said in a tentative tone. He felt uncomfortable; there was something so positive and intrepid about her appearance.   19

"He wants to see you. It's his final wish."   20

"I have not seen him for ten years."   21

"Time can't wipe out the fact that he's your brother."   22

"He is white. We live in different worlds."   23

"But you must see him."   24

There was a moment of strained silence.   25

"Please understand that he's not to blame for having broken with you. I am to blame. I got him to break with you. Really you must blame me, not Karim."   26

Hassen found himself unable to say anything. The thought that she could in some way have been responsible for his brother's rejection of him had never occurred to him. He looked at his feet in awkward silence. He could only state in a lazily recalcitrant tone: "It is not easy for me to see him."   27

"Please come, Mr Hassen, for my sake, please. I'll never be able to bear it if Karim dies unhappily. Can't you find it in your heart to forgive him, and to forgive me?"   28

He could not look at her. A sob escaped from her, and he heard her opening her handbag for a handkerchief.   29

"He's dying. He wants to see you for the last time."   30

Hassen softened. He was overcome by the argument that she had been responsible for taking Karim away. He could hardly look on her responsibility as being in any way culpable. She was a woman.   31

"If you remember the days of your youth, the time you spent together with Karim before I came to separate him from you, it will be easier for you to pardon him."   32

Hassen was silent.   33

"Please understand that I am not a racialist. You know the conditions in this country."   34

He thought for a moment and then said: "I will go with you."   35

He excused himself and went to his room to change. After a while they set off for Hillbrow in her car.   36

He sat beside her. The closeness of her presence, the perfume she exuded stirred currents of feeling within him. He glanced at her several   37 times, watching the deft movements of her hands and legs as she controlled the car. Her powdered profile, the outline taut with a resolute quality, aroused his imagination. There was something so businesslike in her attitude and bearing, so involved in reality (at the back of his mind there was Salima, flaccid, cowlike and inadequate) that he could hardly refrain from expressing his admiration.

"You must understand that I'm only going to see my brother because you have come to me. For no one else would I have changed my mind." 38

"Yes, I understand. I'm very grateful." 39

"My friends and relatives are going to accuse me of softness, of weakness." 40

"Don't think of them now. You have decided to be kind to me." 41

The realism and the commonsense of the woman's words! He was overwhelmed by her. 42

The car stopped at the entrance of a building in Hillbrow. They took the lift. On the second floor three white youths entered and were surprised at seeing Hassen. There was a separate lift for non-whites. They squeezed themselves into a corner, one actually turning his head away with a grunt of disgust. The lift reached the fifth floor too soon for Hassen to give a thought to the attitude of the three white boys. Catherine led him to apartment 65. 43

He stepped into the lounge. Everything seemed to be carefully arranged. There was her personal touch about the furniture, the ornaments, the paintings. She went to the bedroom, then returned and asked him in. 44

Karim lay in bed, pale, emaciated, his eyes closed. For a moment Hassen failed to recognize him: ten years divided them. Catherine placed a chair next to the bed for him. He looked at his brother and again saw, through ravages of illness, the familiar features. She sat on the bed and rubbed Karim's hands to wake him. After a while he began to show signs of consciousness. She called him tenderly by his name. When he opened his eyes he did not recognize the man beside him, but by degrees, after she had repeated Hassen's name several times, he seemed to understand. He stretched out a hand and Hassen took it, moist and repellent. Nausea swept over him, but he could not withdraw his hand as his brother clutched it firmly. 45

"Brother Hassen, please take me away from here." 46

Hassen's agreement brought a smile to his lips. 47

Catherine suggested that she drive Hassen back to Newtown where he could make preparations to transfer Karim to his home. 48

"No, you stay here. I will take a taxi." And he left the apartment. 49

In the corridor he pressed the button for the lift. He watched the indicator numbers succeed each other rapidly, then stop at five. The doors opened— and there they were again, the three white youths. He hesitated. The boys looked at him tauntingly. Then suddenly they burst into deliberately brutish laughter. 50

"Come into the parlour," one of them said. 51

"Come into the Indian parlour," another said in a cloyingly mocking 52
voice.

Hassen stood there, transfixed. They laughed at him in a raucous chorus 53
as the lift doors shut. He remained immobile, his dignity clawed. Was
there anything so vile in him that the youths found it necessary to maul the
last recess of his self-respect? "They are white," he said to himself in bitter
justification of their attitude.

He would take the stairs and walk down the five floors. As he de- 54
scended he thought of Karim. Because of him he had come there and
because of him he had been insulted. The enormity of the insult bridged
the gap of ten years since Karim had spurned him, and diminished his
being. Now he was diminished again.

He was hardly aware that he had gone down five floors when he reached 55
ground level. He stood still, expecting to see the three youths again. But
the foyer was empty and he could see the reassuring activity of street life
through the glass panels. He quickly walked out as though he would
regain in the hubbub of the street something of his assaulted dignity.

He walked on, structures of concrete and glass on either side of him, 56
and it did not even occur to him to take a taxi. It was in Hillbrow that Karim
had lived with the white woman and forgotten the existence of his brother;
and now that he was dying he had sent for him. For ten years Karim had
lived without him. O Karim! The thought of the youth he had loved so
much during the days they had been together at the Islamic Institute, a
religious seminary though it was governed like a penitentiary, brought the
tears to his eyes and he stopped against a shop window and wept. A few
pedestrians looked at him. When the shopkeeper came outside to see the
weeping man, Hassen, ashamed of himself, wiped his eyes and walked on.

He regretted his pliability in the presence of the white woman. She had 57
come unexpectedly and had disarmed him with her presence and subtle
talk. A painful lump rose in his throat as he set his heart against forgiving
Karim. If his brother had had no personal dignity in sheltering behind his
white skin, trying to be what he was not, he was not going to allow his own
moral worth to be depreciated in any way.

When he reached central Johannesburg he went to the station and took 58
the train. In the coach with the blacks he felt at ease and regained his
self-possession. He was among familiar faces, among people who respected him. He felt as though he had been spirited away by a perfumed,
well-made wax doll, but had managed with a prodigious effort to shake her
off.

When he reached home Salima asked him what had been decided and 59
he answered curtly, "Nothing." But feeling elated after his escape from
Hillbrow he added condescendingly, "Karim left of his own accord. We
should have nothing to do with him."

Salima was puzzled, but she went on preparing the supper. 60

* * *

Catherine received no word from Hassen and she phoned him. She was 61
stunned when he said: "I'm sorry but I am unable to offer any help."

"But . . ." 62

"I regret it. I made a mistake. Please make some other arrangements. 63
Goodbye."

With an effort of will he banished Karim from his mind. Finding his 64
composure again he enjoyed his evening meal, read the paper and then
retired to bed. Next morning he went to mosque as usual, but when he
returned home he found Catherine there again. Angry that she should
have come, he blurted out: "Listen to me, Catherine. I can't forgive him.
For ten years he didn't care about me, whether I was alive or dead. Karim
means nothing to me now."

"Why have you changed your mind? Do you find it so difficult to forgive 65
him?"

"Don't talk to me about forgiveness. What forgiveness, when he threw 66
me aside and chose to go with you? Let his white friends see to him, let
Hillbrow see to him."

"Please, please, Mr Hassen, I beg you . . ." 67

"No, don't come here with your begging. Please go away." 68

He opened the door and went out. Catherine burst into tears. Salima 69
comforted her as best she could.

"Don't cry, Caterine. All men hard. Dey don't understand." 70

"What shall I do now?" Catherine said in a defeated tone. She was an 71
alien in the world of the non-whites. "Is there no one who can help me?"

"Yes, Mr Mia help you," replied Salima. 72

In her eagerness to find some help, she hastily moved to the door. 73
Salima followed her and from the porch of her home directed her to Mr
Mia's. He lived in a flat on the first floor of an old building. She knocked
and waited in trepidation.

Mr Mia opened the door, smiled affably and asked her in. 74

"Come inside, lady; sit down . . . Fatima," he called to his daughter, 75
"bring some tea."

Mr Mia was a man in his fifties, his bronze complexion partly covered by 76
a neatly trimmed beard. He was a well-known figure in the Indian com-
munity. Catherine told him of Karim and her abortive appeal to his brother.
Mr Mia asked one or two questions, pondered for a while and then said:
"Don't worry, my good woman. I'll speak to Hassen. I'll never allow a
Muslim brother to be abandoned."

Catherine began to weep. 77

"Here, drink some tea and you'll feel better." He poured tea. Before 78
Catherine left he promised that he would phone her that evening and told
her to get in touch with him immediately should Karim's condition deteriorate.

Mr Mia, in the company of the priest of the Newtown mosque, went to 79
Hassen's house that evening. They found several relatives of Hassen's

seated in the lounge (Salima had spread the word of Karim's illness). But Hassen refused to listen to their pleas that Karim should be brought to Newtown.

"Listen to me, Hajji," Mr Mia said. "Your brother can't be allowed to die among the Christians." 80

"For ten years he has been among them." 81

"That means nothing. He's still a Muslim." 82

The priest now gave his opinion. Although Karim had left the community, he was still a Muslim. He had never rejected the religion and espoused Christianity, and in the absence of any evidence to the contrary it had to be accepted that he was a Muslim brother. 83

"But for ten years he has lived in sin in Hillbrow." 84

"If he has lived in sin that is not for us to judge." 85

"Hajji, what sort of a man are you? Have you no feeling for your brother?" Mr Mia asked. 86

"Don't talk to me about feeling. What feeling had he for me when he went to live among the whites, when he turned his back on me?" 87

"Hajji, can't you forgive him? You were recently in Mecca." 88

This hurt Hassen and he winced. Salima came to his rescue with refreshments for the guests. 89

This ritual of tea-drinking established a mood of conviviality and Karim was forgotten for a while. After tea they tried to press Hassen into forgiving his brother, but he remained adamant. He could not now face Catherine without looking ridiculous. Besides, he felt integrated now; he would resist anything that negated him. 90

Mr Mia and the priest departed. They decided to raise the matter with the congregation in the mosque. But they failed to move Hassen. Actually, his resistance grew in inverse ratio as more people came to learn of the dying Karim and Hassen's refusal to forgive him. By giving in he would be displaying mental dithering of the worst kind, as though he were a man without an inner fibre, decision and firmness of will. 91

Mr Mia next summoned a meeting of various religious dignitaries and received their mandate to transfer Karim to Newtown without his brother's consent. Karim's relatives would be asked to care for him, but if they refused Mr Mia would take charge. 92

The relatives, not wanting to offend Hassen and also feeling that Karim was not their responsibility, refused. 93

Mr Mia phoned Catherine and informed her of what had been decided. She agreed that it was best for Karim to be amongst his people during his last days. So Karim was brought to Newtown in an ambulance hired from a private nursing home and housed in a little room in a quiet yard behind the mosque. 94

The arrival of Karim placed Hassen in a difficult situation and he bitterly regretted his decision not to accept him into his own home. He first heard of his brother's arrival during the morning prayers when the priest offered 95 a special prayer for the recovery of the sick man. Hassen found himself in the curious position of being forced to pray for his brother. After prayers several people went to see the sick man; others went up to Mr Mia to offer help. Hassen felt out of place and as soon as the opportunity presented itself he slipped out of the mosque.

In a mood of intense bitterness, scorn for himself, hatred of those who had decided to become his brother's keepers, infinite hatred for Karim, Hassen went home. Salima sensed her husband's mood and did not say a word to him.

In his room he debated with himself. In what way should he conduct himself so that his dignity remained intact? How was he to face the congregation, the people in the streets, his neighbours? Everyone would soon know of Karim and smile at him half sadly, half ironically, for having placed himself in such a ridiculous position. Should he now forgive the dying man and transfer him to his home? People would laugh at him, snigger at his cowardice, and Mr Mia perhaps even deny him the privilege: Karim was now *his* responsibility. And what would Catherine think of him? Should he go away (on the pretext of a holiday) to Cape Town, to Durban? But no, there was the stigma of being called a renegade. And besides, Karim might take months to die, he might not die at all.

"O Karim, why did you have to do this to me?" he said, moving towards the window and drumming the pane nervously. It galled him that a weak, dying man could bring such pain to him. An adversary could be faced, one could either vanquish him or be vanquished, with one's dignity unravished, but with Karim what could he do?

He paced his room. He looked at his watch; the time for afternoon prayers was approaching. Should he expose himself to the congregation? "O Karim! Karim!" he cried, holding on to the burglar-proof bar of his bedroom window. Was it for this that he had made the pilgrimage—to cleanse his soul in order to return into the penumbra of sin? If only Karim would die he would be relieved of his agony. But what if he lingered on? What if he recovered? Were not prayers being said for him? He went to the door and shouted in a raucous voice: "Salima!"

But Salima was not in the house. He shouted again and again, and his voice echoed hollowly in the rooms. He rushed into the lounge, into the kitchen, he flung the door open and looked into the yard.

He drew the curtains and lay on his bed in the dark. Then he heard the patter of feet in the house. He jumped up and shouted for his wife. She came hurriedly.

"Salima, Salima, go to Karim, he is in a room in the mosque yard. See how he is, see if he is getting better. Quickly!"

Salima went out. But instead of going to the mosque, she entered her neighbour's house. She had already spent several hours sitting beside Karim. Mr Mia had been there as well as Catherine—who had wept.

After a while she returned from her neighbour. When she opened the 104
door her husband ran to her. "How is he? Is he very ill? Tell me quickly!"

"He is very ill. Why don't you go and see him?" 105

Suddenly, involuntarily, Hassen struck his wife in the face. 106

"Tell me, is he dead? Is he dead?" he screamed. 107

Salima cowered in fear. She had never seen her husband in this raging 108
temper. What had taken possession of the man? She retired quickly to the
kitchen. Hassen locked himself in the bedroom.

During the evening he heard voices. Salima came to tell him that several 109
people, led by Mr Mia, wanted to speak to him urgently. His first impulse
was to tell them to leave immediately; he was not prepared to meet them.
But he had been wrestling with himself for so many hours that he welcomed a moment when he could be in the company of others. He stepped
boldly into the lounge.

"Hajji Hassen," Mr Mia began, "please listen to us. Your brother has 110
not long to live. The doctor has seen him. He may not outlive the night."

"I can do nothing about that," Hassen replied, in an audacious, matter- 111
of-fact tone that surprised him and shocked the group of people.

"That is in Allah's hand," said the merchant Gardee. "In our hands lie 112
forgiveness and love. Come with us now and see him for the last time."

"I cannot see him." 113

"And what will it cost you?" asked the priest who wore a long black 114
cloak that fell about his sandalled feet.

"It will cost me my dignity and my manhood." 115

"My dear Hajji, what dignity and what manhood? What can you lose by 116
speaking a few kind words to him on his death-bed? He was only a young
man when he left."

"I will do anything, but going to Karim is impossible." 117

"But Allah is pleased by forgiveness," said the merchant. 118

"I am sorry, but in my case the circumstances are different. I am indif- 119
ferent to him and therefore there is no necessity for me to forgive him."

"Hajji," said Mr Mia, "you are only indulging in glib talk and you know 120
it. Karim is your responsibility, whatever his crime."

"Gentlemen, please leave me alone." 121

And they left. Hassen locked himself in his bedroom and began to pace 122
the narrow space between bed, cupboard and wall. Suddenly, uncontrollably, a surge of grief for his dying brother welled up within him.

"Brother! Brother!" he cried, kneeling on the carpet beside his bed and 123
smothering his face in the quilt. His memory unfolded a time when Karim
had been ill at the Islamic Institute and he had cared for him and nursed
him back to health. How much he had loved the handsome youth!

At about four in the morning he heard an urgent rapping. He left his 124
room to open the front door.

"Brother Karim dead," said Mustapha, the Somali muezzin of the 125
mosque, and he cupped his hands and said a prayer in Arabic. He wore a

black cloak and a white skull-cap. When he had done he turned and walked away.

Hassen closed the door and went out into the street. For a moment his release into the street gave him a sinister jubilation, and he laughed hysterically as he turned the corner and stood next to Jamal's fruitshop. Then he walked on. He wanted to get away as far as he could from Mr Mia and the priest who would be calling upon him to prepare for the funeral. That was no business of his. They had brought Karim to Newtown and they should see to him. 126

He went up Lovers' Walk and at the entrance of Orient House he saw the night-watchman sitting beside a brazier. He hastened up to him and warmed his hands by the fire, but he did this more as a gesture of fraternization as it was not cold, and he said a few words facetiously. Then he walked on. 127

His morbid joy was ephemeral, for the problem of facing the congregation at the mosque began to trouble him. What opinion would they have of him when he returned? Would they not say: he hated his brother so much that he forsook his prayers, but now that his brother is no longer alive he returns. What a man! What a Muslim! 128

When he reached Vinod's Photographic Studio he pressed his forehead against the neon-lit glass showcase and began to weep. 129

A car passed by filling the air with nauseous gas. He wiped his eyes, and looked for a moment at the photographs in the showcase; the relaxed, happy, anonymous faces stared at him, faces whose momentary expressions were trapped in film. Then he walked on. He passed a few shops and then reached Broadway Cinema where he stopped to look at the lurid posters. There were heroes, lusty, intrepid, blasting it out with guns; women in various stages of undress; horrid monsters from another planet plundering a city; Dracula. 130

Then he was among the quiet houses and an avenue of trees rustled softly. He stopped under a tree and leaned against the trunk. He envied the slumbering people in the houses around him, their freedom from the emotions that jarred him. He would not return home until the funeral of his brother was over. 131

When he reached the Main Reef Road the east was brightening. The lights along the road seemed to be part of the general haze. The buildings on either side of him were beginning to thin and on his left he saw the ghostly mountains of mine sand. Dawn broke over the city and when he looked back he saw the silhouettes of tall buildings bruising the sky. Cars and trucks were now rushing past him. 132

He walked for several miles and then branched off onto a gravel road and continued for a mile. When he reached a clump of blue-gum trees he sat down on a rock in the shade of the trees. From where he sat he could see a constant stream of traffic flowing along the highway. He had a stick in his hand which he had picked up along the road, and with it he prodded 133 a crevice in the rock. The action, subtly, touched a chord in his memory and he was sitting on a rock with Karim beside him. The rock was near a river that flowed a mile away from the Islamic Institute. It was a Sunday. He had a stick in his hand and he prodded at a crevice and the weather-worn rock flaked off and Karim was gathering the flakes.

"Karim! Karim!" he cried, prostrating himself on the rock, pushing his 134 fingers into the hard roughness, unable to bear the death of that beautiful youth.

He jumped off the rock and began to run. He would return to Karim. A 135 fervent longing to embrace his brother came over him, to touch that dear form before the soil claimed him. He ran until he was tired, then walked at a rapid pace. His whole existence precipitated itself into one motive, one desire, to embrace his brother in a final act of love.

His heart beating wildly, his hair dishevelled, he reached the highway 136 and walked on as fast as he could. He longed to ask for a lift from a passing motorist but could not find the courage to look back and signal. Cars flashed past him, trucks roared in pain.

When he reached the outskirts of Johannesburg it was nearing ten 137 o'clock. He hurried along, now and then breaking into a run. Once he tripped over a cable and fell. He tore his trousers in the fall and found his hands were bleeding. But he was hardly conscious of himself, wrapped up in his one purpose.

He reached Lovers' Walk, where cars growled around him angrily; he 138 passed Broadway Cinema, rushed towards Orient House, turned the corner at Jamal's fruitshop. And stopped.

The green hearse, with the crescent moon and stars emblem, passed by; 139 then several cars with mourners followed, bearded men, men with white skull-caps on their heads, looking rigidly ahead, like a procession of puppets, indifferent to his fate. No one saw him.

STUDY QUESTIONS

1. Discuss the moral conflict of the story. Why is Hassen unable to comply with his brother's deathbed request? How does the Muslim community respond to Hassen's predicament? What accounts for Hassen's change of heart?
2. How does the ending complicate the story?
3. To what extent is the story a comment on South Africa's system of racial injustice?

SIPHO SEPAMLA

Sipho Sepamla, poet and novelist, was born in Krugersdorp, a South African mining town, in 1932. He was trained as a teacher but has worked at various jobs. Apart from publishing prize-winning volumes of poetry and two acclaimed novels, Sepamla has served as a promoter of the arts in his capacity as editor of journals and organizer of poetry readings, conferences, and workshops. He is now the full-time director of the Federated Union of Black Arts.

Sepamla is one of the most respected South African writers in international circles. He is a "township poet" who confronts the teeming ghetto life of urban South Africa. His work has been subjected to censorship; a collection of poems, The Soweto I Love *(1977), and the novel* A Ride on the Whirlwind *(1984) were banned by the South African government because they openly challenge the status quo. Both books record the growing assertiveness and collective will of the black masses. In "To Whom It May Concern," Sepamla depicts the oppressive nature of the pass laws.*

To Whom It May Concern

Bearer
Bare of everything but particulars
Is a Bantu
The language of a people in Southern Africa
He seeks to proceed from here to there   5
Please pass him on
Subject to these particulars
He lives subject to the provisions
Of the Urban Natives Act of 1925
Amended often   10
To update it to his sophistication
Subject to the provisions of the said Act
He may roam freely within a prescribed area
Free only from the anxiety of conscription
In terms of the Abolition of Passes Act   15
A latter-day amendment
In keeping with moon-age naming
Bearer's destination is Reference number 417181
And (he) acquires a niche in the said area
As a temporary sojourner   20
To which he must betake himself
At all times
When his services are dispensed with for the day
As a permanent measure of law and order
Please note   25

The remains of R/N 417181
Will be laid to rest in peace
On a plot
Set aside for Methodist Xhosas[1]
A measure also adopted   30
At the express request of the Bantu
In anticipation of any faction fight
Before the Day of Judgement

STUDY QUESTIONS

1. What do you learn about the pass system from "To Whom It May Concern"? How does the system restrict the lives of black South Africans?
2. Does the poem's documentary style effectively convey the nature of apartheid?

 ALFRED TEMBA QABULA

Alfred Temba Qabula was born in 1942 in Flagstaff, Transkei, South Africa. His father and uncles worked in the mines and in the sugarcane fields. As a result, his family's life was governed by migrancy and the apartheid laws regulating employment. Qabula grew up under harsh conditions. He was orphaned and brought up by relatives. As a young man he lived through the Pondoland rebellion against government rural policies. He became a migrant worker in the mines, forced to leave his wife and children behind on the land. Later he worked in a factory in Durban and joined the Metal and Allied Workers Union.

Qabula is known to thousands of workers in Natal Province because of his poetry performances, plays, and songs. He is part of a growing trade union cultural movement that is reviving indigenous oral literary traditions in support of the ongoing struggle against apartheid. His poems and plays are composed for performance at mass meetings, trade union and community gatherings, and weddings and funerals. He voices the concerns and struggles of ordinary black workers.

Migrant's Lament—A Song

If I have wronged you Lord forgive me
All my cattle were dead

---

1. Xhosas: *One of a Bantu people of Cape of Good Hope Province, South Africa.*

My goats and sheep were dead
And
I did not know what to do   5
Oh Creator forgive me
If I had done wrong to you
My children: out of school
Out of uniforms and books
My wife and I were naked—naked . . .   10
Short of clothing

If I have wronged you Lord forgive me
I went to WENELA[1]
To get recruited for the mines
I went to SILO[2]   15
To work at sugarcane
Oh creator forgive me
If I had done wrong to you
But they chased me away
They needed those with experience   20
With long service tickets and no one more

If I have wronged you Lord
Forgive me
I left my wife and children
To look for work alone   25
I had to find a job
Oh Creator forgive me
If I had done wrong to you
I was despairing in Egoli
After months searching for this job   30
And when I found one
I lost it
For I didn't have a "SPECIAL"[3]

If I have wronged you Lord
Forgive me   35
I found a casual job
I felt that my children would be happy

---

1. WENELA: *The Employment Bureau of Africa, the mine-labor recruiting organization of the Chamber of Mines.*
2. SILO: *Sugar Industry Labour Organisation, a labor-recruiting organization for the sugar plantations.*
3. SPECIAL: *Migrant workers for the mines and plantations get a "special" after long service.*

With my earnings
Oh how happy I was!
Oh creator forgive me   40
If I had done wrong to you
Yes, as my children were happy
And as I was working
The blackjacks arrived to arrest me
So again I lost my job   45

If I have wronged you Lord
Forgive me
When out of jail I searched again—
Another casual job, happy again
The boss was happy too   50
And he gave me a letter
To fetch a permit from back home
Oh creator forgive me
If I had done wrong to you
But the clerk said: "I can't see the paper"   55
And added: "You must go in peace my man"
So I had to buy him beer, meat and brandy
For him to "learn" to read my piece of paper

If I have wronged you Lord
Forgive me   60
I was working again
But I realized so far for nothing
Oh Creator forgive me
If I had done wrong to you
So I joined the union to fight my boss   65
For I realized: there was no other way Lord
But to fight with the employer
There was no other way
Now go troublemaker go.

STUDY QUESTIONS

1. What is the purpose of the refrain "If I have wronged you Lord forgive me"?
2. What examples does Qabula offer to document the oppressive living and working conditions in South Africa? What is his solution?
3. How might this poem be performed?

JEREMY CRONIN

Jeremy Cronin was born in 1949 in Cape Town, South Africa. The son of an officer in the South African navy, he spent most of his childhood in various naval bases. He attended the University of Cape Town and the Sorbonne in Paris, then taught in the philosophy and politics departments of the University of Cape Town. In 1976, he was arrested under the Terrorism Act for having carried out ANC (African National Congress) activities for a number of years. He spent seven years in various prisons, including three years among the death-row prisoners in the notorious Pretoria Maximum jail. He was released from prison in 1983 and now serves as the Western Cape executive of the United Democratic Front, a broad-based antiapartheid coalition. To date, Cronin has published one volume of poems, Inside (1983), which received much critical attention. "A Person Is a Person Because of Other People" is typical of these poems, which document the author's prison experience.

A Person Is a Person Because of Other People

By holding my mirror out of the window I see
Clear to the end of the passage.
There's a person down there.
A prisoner polishing a doorhandle.
In the mirror I see him see   5
My face in the mirror,
I see the fingertips of his free hand
Bunch together, as if to make
An object the size of a badge
Which travels up to his forehead   10
The place of an imaginary cap.
    (This means: A *warder*.)
Two fingers are extended in a vee
And wiggle like two antennae.
    (He's being watched.)   15
A finger of his free hand makes a watch-hand's arc
On the wrist of his polishing arm without
Disrupting the slow-slow rhythm of his work.
    (*Later.* Maybe, later we can speak.)
Hey! Wat maak jy daar?[1]   20

---

1. *"What are you doing?"*

—a voice from around the corner.
No. Just polishing baas.[1]
He turns his back to me, now watch
His free hand, the talkative one,
Slips quietly behind   25
    —*Strength brother*, it says,
In my mirror,
    A black fist.

S T U D Y   Q U E S T I O N S

1. What does the title of the poem mean?
2. In what ways is the poem a challenge to South Africa's system of apartheid?

 MTUTUZELI MATSHOBA

Mtutuzeli Matshoba was born in 1950 in Orlando East, South Africa. He was brought up (and still lives) in Soweto, an enormous urban ghetto near Johannesburg. He began his education at a Salvation Army school but later attended boarding schools at Lovedale in the Cape province and at Vryheid in Natal. Until the 1976 Soweto uprising, he attended Fort Hare, the oldest black college in South Africa, founded in 1916 and now the University College for the Xhosa. At various times, he has been under police surveillance.

Matshoba began publishing his stories in Straffrider, *the first magazine to provide a forum for the literary and artistic work of the oppressed communities of South Africa. His fiction reflects the urgency and stridency of the generation of black South Africans who were influenced by the Black Consciousness Movement and the Soweto uprising. Matshoba's subtly crafted stories reach a broad audience. He often inserts into his stories characters who bear witness to human travail and voice the conscience of the community. In 1981, he won the Thomas Pringle Award given by the English Academy of Southern Africa for his short story collection* Call Me Not a Man *(1979). Ironically, despite the prize, the book was banned by the South African government.*

---

1. Baas: *Boss.*

Call Me Not a Man

For neither am I a man in the eyes of the law,
Nor am I a man in the eyes of my fellow man.

B y dodging, lying, resisting where it is possible, bolting when I'm al-   1
ready cornered, parting with invaluable money, sometimes calling my
sisters into the game to get amorous with my captors, allowing myself to
be slapped on the mouth in front of my womenfolk and getting sworn at
with my mother's private parts, that component of me which is man has
died countless times in one lifetime. Only a shell of me remains to tell you
of the other man's plight, which is in fact my own. For what is suffered by
another man in view of my eyes is suffered also by me. The grief he knows
is a grief that I know. Out of the same bitter cup do we drink. To the same
chain-gang do we belong.

Friday has always been their chosen day to go plundering, although now-   2
adays they come only occasionally, maybe once in a month. Perhaps they
have found better pastures elsewhere, where their prey is more predictable
than at Mzimhlope, the place which has seen the tragic demise of three of
their accomplices who had taken the game a bit too far by entering the hostel
on the northern side of our location and fleecing the people right in the midst
of their disgusting labour camps. Immediately after this there was a notable
abatement in the frequency of their visits to both the location and the ad-
jacent hostel. However the lull was short-lived, lasting only until the storm
had died down, because the memory tarnishes quickly in the locations, especially the memory of death. We were beginning to emit sighs of relief and
to mutter 'good riddance' when they suddenly reappeared and made their
presence in our lives felt once again. June, 'seventy-six had put them out of
the picture for the next year, during which they were scarcely seen. Like a
recurring pestilence they refuse to vanish absolutely from the scene.

A person who has spent some time in Soweto will doubtless have   3
guessed by now that the characters I am referring to are none other than
some of the so-called police reservists who roam our dirty streets at weekends, robbing every timid, unsuspecting person, while masquerading as
peace officers to maintain law and order in the community. There are no
greater thieves than these men of the law, men of justice, peace officers
and volunteer public protectors in the whole of the slum complex because,
unlike others in the same trade of living off the sweat of their victims, they
steal out in the open, in front of everybody's eyes. Of course nothing can
be done about it because they go out on their pillaging exploits under the
banners of the law, and to rise in protest against them is analogous to
defiance of the powers that be.

So, on this Friday too we were standing on top of the station bridge at   4

Mzimhlope. It was about five in the afternoon and the sun hung over the western horizon of spectacularly identical coalsmoke-puffing rooftops like a gigantic, glowing red ball which dyed the foamy clouds with the crimson sheen of its rays. The commuter trains coming in from the city paused below us every two or three minutes to regurgitate their infinite human cargo, the greater part of whom were hostel-dwellers who hurried up Mohale Street to cook their meagre suppers on primus stoves. The last train we had seen would now be leaving Phefeni, the third station from Mzimhlope. The next train had just emerged from the bridge this side of New Canada, junction to East and West Soweto. The last group of the hostel people from the train now leaving Phefeni had just turned the bend at Mohale Street where it intersects with Elliot. The two hundred metre stretch to Elliot was therefore relatively empty, and people coming towards the station could be clearly made out.

As the wheels of the train from New Canada squealed on the iron tracks and it came to a jerking stop, four men, two in overalls and the others in dustcoats, materialised around the Mohale Street bend. There was no doubt who they were, from the way they filled the whole width of the street and walked as if they owned everything and everybody in their sight. When they came to the grannies selling vegetables, fruit and fried mealies along the ragged, unpaved sides of the street, they grabbed what they fancied and munched gluttonously the rest of the way towards us. Again nothing could be done about it, because the poverty-stricken vendors were not licensed to scrape together some crumbs to ease the gnawing stomachs of their fatherless grandchildren at home, which left them wide open for plunder by the indifferent 'reserves'.

'*Awu!* The Hellions,' remarked Mandla next to me. 'Let's get away from here, my friend.'

He was right. They reminded one of the old western film; but I was not moving from where I was simply because the reservists were coming down the street like a bunch of villains. One other thing I knew was that the railway constable who was on guard duty that Friday at the station did not allow the persecution of the people on his premises. I wanted to have my laugh when they were chased off the station.

'Don't worry about them. Just wait and see how they're going to be chased away by this copper. He won't allow them on the station,' I answered.

They split into twos when they arrived below us. Two of them, a tall chap with a face corroded by skin-lightening cream and wearing a yellow golf cap on his shaven head, and another stubby, shabbily dressed, middle-aged man with a bald frontal lobe and a drunk face, chewing at a cooked sheep's foot that he had taken from one of the grannies, climbed the stairs on our right hand side. The younger man took the flight in fours. The other two chose to waylay their unsuspecting victims on the street corner at the base of the left hand staircase. The first wave of the people who had alighted from the train was in the middle of the bridge when the second man reached the top of the stairs.

Maybe they knew the two reservists by sight, maybe they just smelt cop 10 in the smoggy air, or it being a Friday, they were alert for such possibilities. Three to four of the approaching human wall turned suddenly in their tracks and ran for their dear freedom into the mass behind them. The others were caught unawares by this unexpected movement and they staggered in all directions trying to regain balance. In a split second there was commotion on the station, as if a wild cat had found its way into a fowlrun. Two of those who had not been quick enough were grabbed by their sleeves, and their passes demanded. While they were producing their books the wolves went over their pockets, supposedly feeling for dangerous weapons, dagga and other illegal possessions that might be concealed in the clothes, but really to ascertain whether they had caught the right people for their iniquitous purposes. They were paging through the booklets when the Railway policeman appeared.

'Wha . . . ? Don't you fools know that you're not supposed to do that 11 shit here? Get off! Get off and do that away from Railway property. Fuck off!' He screamed at the two reservists so furiously that the veins threatened to burst in his neck.

'Arrest the dogs, *baba*! Give them a chance also to taste jail!' Mandla 12 shouted.

'Ja,' I said to Mandla, 'you bet, they've never been where they are so 13 prepared to send others.'

The other people joined in and we jeered the cowards off the station. 14 They descended the stairs with their tails tucked between their legs and joined their companions below the station. Some of the commuters who had been alerted by the uproar returned to the platform to wait there until the reservists had gone before they would dare venture out of the station.

We remained where we had been and watched the persecution from 15 above. I doubted if they even read the passes (if they could), or whether the victims knew if their books were right or out of order. Most likely the poor hunted men believed what they were told by the licensed thieves. The latter demanded the books, after first judging their prey to be weak propositions, flicked through the pages, put the passes into their own pockets, without which the owners could not continue on their way, and told the dumbfounded hostel men to stand aside while they accosted other victims. Within a very short while there was a group of confused men to one side of the street, screaming at their hostel mates to go to room so and so and tell so and so that they had been arrested at the station, and to bring money quickly to release them. Few of those who were being sent heard the messages since they were only too eager to leave the danger zone. Those who had money shook hands with their captors, received their books back and ran up Mohale Street. If they were unlucky they came upon another 'roadblock' three hundred metres up the street where the process was repeated. Woe unto them who had paid their last money to the first extortionists, for this did not matter. The police station was their next stopover before the Bantu Commissioners, and thence their final destination, Modderbee Prison, where they provided the farmers with ready cheap labour until they had served their terms for breaking the law. The terms vary from a few days to two years for *loaferskap*, which is in fact mere unemployment, for which the unfortunate men are not to blame. The whole arrangement stinks of forced labour.

The large *kwela-kwela*[1] swayed down Mohale Street at breakneck speed. 16
The multitudes scattered out of its way and hung onto the sagging fences until it had passed. To be out of sight of the people on the station bridge, it skidded and swerved into the second side street from the station. More reservists poured out of it and went immediately to their dirty job with great zeal. The chain-gang which had been lined up along the fence of the house nearest the station was kicked and shoved to the *kwela-kwela* into which the victims were bundled under a rain of fists and boots, all of them scrambling to go in at the same time through the small door. The driver of the *kwela-kwela*, the only uniformed constable among the group, clanged the door shut and secured it with the locking lever. He went to stand authoritatively near one of the vendors, took a small avocado pear, peeled it and put it whole into a gargantuan mouth, spitting out the large stone later. He did not have to take the trouble of accosting anyone himself. His gangsters would all give him a lion's share of whatever they made, and moreover buy him some beers and brandy. He kept adjusting his polished belt over his potbelly as the .38 police special in its leather holster kept tugging it down. He probably preferred to wear his gun unconventionally, cowboy style.

A boy of about seventeen was caught with a knife in his pocket, a dan- 17
gerous weapon. They slapped him a few times and let him stand handcuffed against the concrete wall of the station. Ten minutes later his wellrounded sister alighted from the train to find her younger brother among the prisoners. As she was inquiring from him why he had been arrested, and reprimanding him for carrying a knife, one of the younger reservists came to stand next to her and started pawing her. She let him carry on, and three minutes later her brother was free. The reservist was beaming all over his face, glad to have won himself a beautiful woman in the course of his duties and little knowing that he had been given the wrong address. Some of our black sisters are at times compelled to go all the way to save their menfolk, and as always, nothing can be done about it.

There was a man coming down Mohale Street, conspicuous amidst the 18
crowd because of the bag and baggage that was loaded on his overall-clad frame. On his right shoulder was a large suitcase with a grey blanket

---

1. Kwela-kwela: *Vehicle used to transport a group of police or prisoners.*

strapped to it with flaxen strings. From his left hand hung a bulging card-board box, only a few inches from the ground, and tilting him to that side. He walked with the bounce of someone used to walking in gumboots or on uneven ground. There was the urgency of someone who had a long way to travel in his gait. It was doubtless a *goduka* on his way home to his family after many months of work in the city. It might even have been years since he had visited the countryside.

He did not see the hidden *kwela-kwela*, which might have forewarned   19
him of the danger that was lurking at the station. Only when he had stumbled into two reservists, who stepped into his way and ordered him to put down his baggage, did he perhaps remember that it was Friday and raid-day. A baffled expression sprang into his face as he realised what he had walked into. He frantically went through the pockets of his overalls. The worried countenance deepened on his dark face. He tried again to make sure, but he did not find what he was looking for. The men who had stopped him pulled him to one side, each holding him tightly by the sleeve of his overall. He obeyed meekly like a tame animal. They let him lift his arms while they searched him all over the body. Finding nothing hidden on him, they demanded the inevitable book, although they had seen that he did not have it. He gesticulated with his hands as he explained what had caused him not to be carrying his pass with him. A few feet above them, I could hear what was said.

'Strue, *madoda*,' he said imploringly, 'I made a mistake. I luggaged the   20
pass with my trunk. It was in a jacket that I forgot to search before I packed it into the trunk.'

'How do we know that you're not lying?' asked one of the reservists in   21
a querulous voice.

'I'm not lying, *mfowethu*. I swear by my mother, that's what happened,'   22
explained the frightened man.

The second reservist had a more evil and uncompromising attitude.   23
'That was your own stupidity, mister. Because of it you're going to jail now; no more to your wife.'

'Oh, my brother. Put yourself in my shoes. I've not been home to my   24
people for two years now. It's the first chance I have to go and see my twin daughters who were born while I've been here. Feel for another poor black man, please, my good brother. Forgive me only for this once.'

'What? Forgive you? And don't give us that slush about your children.   25
We've also got our own families, for whom we are at work right now, at this very moment,' the obstinate one replied roughly.

'But, *mfo*. Wouldn't you make a mistake too?'   26

That was a question the cornered man should not have asked. The reply   27
this time was a resounding slap on the face. 'You think I'm stupid like you, huh? Bind this man, Mazibuko, put the bloody irons on the dog.'

'No, man. Let me talk to the poor bloke. Perhaps he can do something   28
for us in exchange for the favour of letting him proceed on his way home,'

the less volatile man suggested, and pulled the hostel man away from the rest of the arrested people.

'*Ja*. Speak to him yourself, Mazibuko. I can't bear talking to rural fools like him. I'll kill him with my bare hands if he thinks that I've come to play here at Johannesburg!' The anger in the man's voice was faked, the fury of a coward trying to instil fear in a person who happened to be at his mercy. I doubted if he could face up to a mouse. He accosted two boys and ran his hands over their sides, but he did not ask for their passes.

'You see, my friend, you're really in trouble. I'm the only one who can help you. This man who arrested you is not in his best mood today. How much have you got on you? Maybe if you give something he'll let you go. You know what wonders money can do for you. I'll plead for you; but only if I show him something he can understand.' The reservist explained the only way out of the predicament for the trapped man, in a smooth voice that sounded rotten through and through with corruption, the sole purpose for which he had joined the 'force'.

'I haven't got a cent in my pocket. I bought provisions, presents for the people at home and the ticket with all the money they gave me at work. Look, *nkosi*, I have only the ticket and the papers with which I'm going to draw my money when I arrive at home.' He took out his papers, pulled the overall off his shoulders and lowered it to his thighs so that the brown trousers he wore underneath were out in the open. He turned the dirty pockets inside out. 'There's nothing else in my pockets except these, mister, honestly.'

'Man!'

'Yessir?'

'You want to go home to your wife and children?'

'Yes, *please*, good man of my people. Give me a break.'

'Then why do you show me these damn papers? They will feed your own children, but not mine. When you get to your home you're going to draw money and your kids will be scratching their tummies and dozing after a hectic meal, while I lose my job for letting you go and my own children join the dogs to scavenge the trashbins. You're mad, *mos*.' He turned to his mate. 'Hey, Baloyi. Your man says he hasn't got anything, but he's going to his family which he hasn't seen for two years.'

'I told you to put the irons on him. He's probably carrying a little fortune in his underpants. Maybe he's shy to take it out in front of the people. It'll come out at the police station, either at the charge office or in the cells when the small boys shake him down.'

'Come on, you. Your hands, maan!'

The other man pulled his arms away from the manacles. His voice rose desperately. '*Awu* my people. You mean you're really arresting me? Forgive me! I pray do.'

A struggle ensued between the two men.

'You're resisting arrest? You—' and a stream of foul vitriolic words concerning the anatomy of the hostel man's mother gushed out of the reservist's mouth.

'I'm not, I'm not! But please listen!' The hostel man heaved and broke   42
loose from the reservist's grip. The latter was only a lump of fat with
nothing underneath. He staggered three steps back and flopped on his
rump. When he bounced back to his feet, unexpectedly fast for his bulk,
his eyes were blazing murder. His companions came running from their
own posts and swarmed upon the defenceless man like a pack of hyenas
upon a carcass. The other people who had been marooned on the bridge
saw a chance to go past while the wolves were still preoccupied. They ran
down the stairs and up Mohale like racehorses. Two other young men who
were handcuffed together took advantage of the diversion and bolted down
the first street in tandem, taking their bracelets with them. They ran awkwardly with their arms bound together, but both were young and fit and
they did their best in the circumstances.

We could not stand the sickening beating that the other man was receiving   43
anymore.

'Hey! Hey. *Sies,* maan. Stop beating the man like that. Arrest him if you   44
want to arrest him. You're killing him, dogs!' we protested loudly from the
station. An angry crowd was gathering.

'Stop it or we'll stop you from doing anything else forever!' someone   45
shouted.

The psychopaths broke their rugger scrum and allowed us to see their   46
gruesome handiwork. The man was groaning at the base of the fence,
across the street where the dirt had gathered. He twisted painfully to a
sitting position. His face was covered with dirt and blood from where the
manacles that were slipped over the knuckles had found their marks, and
his features were grotesquely distorted. In spite of that, the fat man was
not satisfied. He bent and gathered the whimpering man's wrists with the
intention of fastening them to the fence with the handcuffs.

'Hey, hey, hey, Satan! Let him go. Can't you see that you've hurt that   47
man enough?'

The tension was building up to explosion point and the uniformed po-   48
liceman sensed it.

'Let him go, boys. Forgive him. Let him go,' he said, shooting nervous   49
glances in all directions.

Then the beaten-up man did the most unexpected and heartrending   50
thing. He knelt before the one ordering his release and held his dust-
covered hands with the palms together in the prayer position, and still
kneeling he said, 'Thank you very much, my lord. God bless you. Now I
can go and see my twins and my people at home.'

He would have done it. Only it never occurred in his mind at that   51
moment of thanksgiving to kiss the red gleaming boots of the policeman.

The miserable man beat the dust off his clothes as best he could, gath-   52 ered his two parcels and clambered up the stairs, trying to grin his thanks to the crowd that had raised its voice of protest on his behalf. The policemen decided to call it a day. The other unfortunates were shepherded to the waiting *kwela-kwela*.

I tried to imagine how the man would explain his lumps to his wife. In the eye of my mind I saw him throwing his twins into the air and gathering them again and again as he played with them.   53

'There's still a long way to cover, my friend,' I heard Mandla saying into my ear.   54

'Before?' I asked.   55

'Before we reach hell. Ha, ha, ha! Maybe there we'll be men.'   56

'Ha, we've long been there. We've long been in hell.'   57

'Before we get out, then.'   58

STUDY QUESTIONS

1. What are some examples in the story that confirm the opening quotation?
2. What evidence is there in the story that illustrates the black community's resistance to oppression?
3. Why is the story's style appropriate to its subject matter?
4. Are the concluding comments of the narrator and his friend cynical? What is their role in the story?

TURKEY

NAZIM HIKMET

Nazim Hikmet (1902–1963) is considered Turkey's national poet. As a young man, he attended secondary schools in Istanbul. Later, he studied economics and sociology at the Oriental University in Moscow and became involved in the avant garde movements in the arts, which were flourishing in the wake of the Russian Revolution. When he returned to Turkey in 1928, he was a member of the Turkish Communist Party and became a dominant force in the literary scene, publishing poems, producing plays, and writing articles for local newspapers. In 1938, he was arrested on charges of sedition and sentenced to twenty-eight years in prison. After extensive pressure from intellectuals in Turkey and abroad, he was released in 1950. He then returned to the Soviet Union, where he lived until his death.

Hikmet's published work is considerable, and encompasses volumes of poetry, drama, stories, newspaper columns, letters, and novels. Things I Didn't Know I Loved: Selected Poems of Nazim Hikmet *appeared in English in 1975. Internationally, he is known as a socially engaged poet who, under the influence of Vladimir Mayakovsky, wrote free verse that reflected a deep-seated respect and concern for the lives of ordinary people. "About Your Hands and Lies" is typical of his style and subject matter.*

About Your Hands and Lies

Your hands grave like all stones,
sad like all songs sung in prison,
clumsy and heavy like all beasts of burden,
your hands that are like the sullen faces of hungry children.
Your hands nimble and light like bees,
full like breasts with milk,
brave like nature,
your hands that hide their friendly softness under their rough
                                                              skin.

5

This world doesn't rest on the horns of a bull, 10
        this world rests on your hands.
People, oh my people,
they feed you with lies.
But you're hungry,
you need to be fed with meat and bread. 15
And never once eating a full meal at a white table,
you leave this world where every branch is loaded with fruit.
Oh my people,
especially those in Asia, Africa,
    the Near East, Middle East, Pacific islands 20
    and my countrymen—
I mean, more than seventy percent of all people—
you are old and absent-minded like your hands,
you are curious, amazed, and young like your hands.
Oh my people, 25
my European, my American,
you are awake, bold, and forgetful like your hands,
like your hands you're quick to seduce,
    easy to deceive. . .

People, oh my people, 30
if the antennas are lying,
if the presses are lying,
if the books lie,
if the poster on the wall and the ad in the column lie,
if the naked thighs of girls on the white screen lie, 35
if the prayer lies,
if the lullaby lies,
if the dream is lying,
if the violin player at the tavern is lying,
if the moonlight on the nights of hopeless days lies, 40
if the voice lies,
if the word lies,
if everything but your hands,
if everyone, is lying,
it's so your hands will be obedient like clay, 45
blind like darkness,
stupid like sheep dogs, it's so your hands won't rebel.
And it's so that in this mortal, this livable world
    —where we are guests so briefly anyway—
    this merchant's empire, this cruelty, won't end. 50

Translated from the Turkish by Randy Blasing and
Mutlu Konuk

STUDY QUESTIONS

1. What are some examples of the images associated with hands and lies? What is the relationship between the two categories?
2. What is the author's vision of humanity? Does the poem offer an alternative to the status quo?

THEMATIC QUESTIONS

1. Traditional society provides the background for some of the literature in this section. Select examples and discuss each author's attitude toward indigenous culture.
2. Women's oppression is a subject of concern in African and Middle Eastern literature. Based on your reading, discuss how this topic has been approached. How differently do female writers present the subject from their male counterparts?
3. Race is an important theme in South African writing. Explain how it operates in the stories of Matshoba, Essop, and Gordimer.
4. The stories by Dib (Algeria) and Ngugi (Kenya) are set in Africa and the Maghrib during the periods of anticolonial revolt. Discuss how they reflect the changes that are taking place in these societies.
5. The Palestinian/Israeli conflict is an important theme in literature from the Middle East. Discuss how it is treated in the selections by Kanafani, Amichai, Oz, and Darwish.
6. The central characters in Achebe's "Civil Peace" and Mahfouz's "The Happy Man" discover important truths about the human condition. Discuss how they arrive at a new understanding of their circumstances.
7. Nawal El Saadawi and Bessie Head are feminist writers who write about women who struggle to liberate themselves from the restraints of society. Discuss how this process operates in "A Modern Love Story" and "The Collector of Treasures."

ASIA

A S I A

Introduction

Asia, the largest and most populous continent, contains more than half of the world's population; total population was estimated in 1985 at 2,896,165,000. The People's Republic of China alone has 1.13 billion people, India 844 million.

In speaking about Asia, one must ask, Which Asia? The continent is bound on the north by the Arctic Ocean; northern Asia includes Siberia in the former Soviet Union, Mongolia, North Korea, and the ethnic territories of the People's Republic of China. Asia is bound on the south by the Indian Ocean and encompasses the vast subcontinent of India, with its fourteen official languages and hundreds of native and tribal languages, Nepal, Pakistan, Bangladesh, and Sri Lanka. Southeast Asia includes the thousands of islands of Indonesia and the Philippines and nations such as Brunei, Burma, Singapore, Thailand, Malaysia, Vietnam, and Cambodia. To the east, Asia is bound by the Pacific Ocean and includes the nations of Japan, Hong Kong, South Korea, and the People's Republic of China. And to the west, it is separated from Europe by the north-south-running Ural Mountains and includes the Turkic- and Arabic-speaking nations of southwest Asia.

Because Asia's heterogeneous vastness cannot be dealt with comprehensively in a few pages, this introduction and the literary selections that follow will focus chiefly on China (including the separate Chinese nation of Taiwan), Japan, and India. The countries of the Middle East are also geographically part of the Asian landmass, but because of the cultural and linguistic links between the Middle East and North Africa, those countries are covered in the unit on Africa and the Middle East.

192

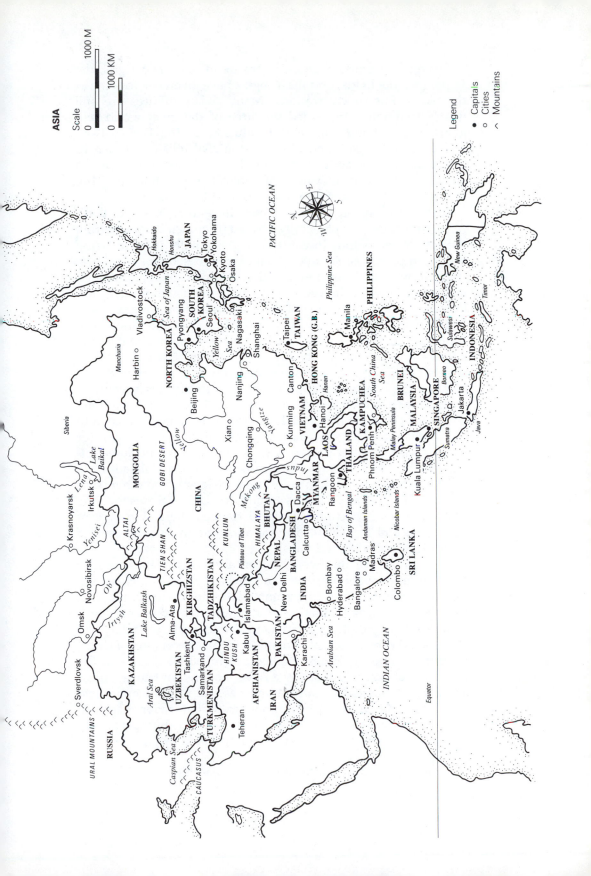

Some of the world's largest rivers are in Asia. The Tigris, the Euphrates, the Indus, and the Yangtze have given rise to some of the oldest known civilizations. Many Asian cultures are still deeply traditional, grounded on three of the great world religions: Islam, Buddhism, and Hinduism. In the Far East—in China, Korea, Japan, and Taiwan—the civil religion known as Confucianism has led to shared social values. Neo-Confucianism encourages the secular values of benevolence, familial and bureaucratic stability, agrarian interests, and learning.

Right up to the end of the nineteenth century, many of these Asian countries were physically isolated from each other and from the rest of the world. In contrast to the rapidly industrializing European countries, Asian economies were based on agriculture. Aside from a small court elite and urban mercantile population, most of Asia was composed chiefly of peasants whose lives followed the ancient rhythms of the seasons and planting.

The twentieth century was marked by rapid and almost uncontrolled change in these societies, chiefly brought about by the aggressive economic, military, and colonizing activities of Western countries. Beginning in the nineteenth century, seeking markets for their factory-produced goods, primary resources and wealth for their own people, and new lands for their expanding civil authorities, countries such as Britain, Holland, France, and the United States forced Asian peoples to accept unjust terms for trade. These Western powers later set up their own colonial offices in the place of Asian governments. Britain claimed all of India, Ceylon (now Sri Lanka), Burma, Malaysia, and other parts of Southeast Asia as part of its empire; the United States took the Philippines as its territory; Holland claimed the archipelago of Indonesia; and France ruled over Indochina (now composed of Vietnam, Cambodia, and Laos).

The first half of the twentieth century saw the expansion of Western (and Japanese) power and the accompanying change in the colonized countries to accommodate the economic plans of the Western rulers. Plantation economies replaced peasant agriculture in Southeast Asia, Sri Lanka, and parts of India, and widespread exploitation of minerals and the importation of cheap labor from other countries resulted in irrevocable change in the landscape and societies of these Asian nations. In China, India, and other Asian states, native dynasties and ruling families lost their positions. In their place, more egalitarian leaders began to mount a resistance against Western aggression. European military and economic expansion was finally halted by Japanese military power in World War II.

Japan had been forced to accept European trade in 1854 when

Commodore Matthew Perry sat in Tokyo Bay with his fleet. The Japanese quickly understood the necessity to adapt their societies to compete with European interests. Borrowing their educational system from the Germans, their railroads from the British, and their naval armaments from the Americans, the Japanese defeated China in 1895 and Russia in 1904. As an imperial power, they took over Taiwan, Korea, and Manchuria and, in 1941, went on to invade the Western colonies of Burma, Indochina, Malaysia, the Philippines, and Indonesia. The destruction of the U.S. Navy at Pearl Harbor in 1941 and the invasion of British and American bases in the Pacific destroyed forever the myth of Western superiority. The Pacific war affected every Asian country. It brought misery and suffering to millions of Asians, but the defeat of the Japanese also resulted in an upsurge of nationalism that countered Western colonialism and liberated countries such as China and Korea from Japanese incursions.

The second half of the twentieth century saw a gradual assertion of independence among Asians and a remarkable progress in their economic strength and national formation. After 1945, the colonized countries fought for and received independence: the Philippines in 1946, India and Pakistan in 1947, Ceylon and Burma in 1948, Indonesia in 1949, Vietnam in 1954, Malaysia in 1957, Singapore in 1959.

The independence movements were often occasions of organized insurrection against colonial authority that developed into internal civil war and partition of the region along ethnic, religious, linguistic, or ideological lines. In China, the Communist forces of Mao Zedong defeated Chiang Kai-shek's Kuomintang (Nationalist) Army and established the People's Republic in 1949. Chiang's forces withdrew to the island of Taiwan and set up a separate Chinese territory officially recognized in the United Nations as the Republic of China until it was ousted in 1971. In the subcontinent of India, Muslims and Hindus massacred each other in the thousands before the British-ruled territory was partitioned into predominantly Hindu India and Muslim Pakistan and political stability was restored. Similar power struggles between Sikhs or hill tribes and Indian Hindus threaten to further fragment India today. Many other Asian societies, as in Sri Lanka, under pressure of Western influence, population growth, increased inequities between the masses of poor people and the few wealthy families, are also affected by other factors of fragmentation: linguistic, religious, racial and ethnic rivalries, and rapid urbanization, for example.

In the second half of the century, the United States was increasingly drawn into armed conflicts in Korea and Vietnam. The Korean War (1950–1953) divided the country into a Communist

North Korea and a U.S.-style capitalist South Korea. The parallel partition of Vietnam into Communist North and U.S.-protected South Vietnam in 1954 resulted in an escalation of military conflict, ending with U.S. withdrawal from Vietnam in 1973, and reunification under Communist rule in 1976.

Today, Japan, Taiwan, South Korea, and parts of Southeast Asia have become significant trading partners with the West. Extensive land reform in Taiwan, China, North and South Korea, and Japan after 1945 was accompanied by rapid industrialization in East Asia. Some Asian economies, for example, Indonesia and the Philippines, have not become fully industrialized and exhibit unevenly distributed incomes leading to political tensions and instabilities. Generally, however, the economies of Asian nations are expected to continue to grow much faster than those of the United States and other Western nations. For instance, Japan's astonishing reconstruction after World War II led to a trade dominance in the 1970s that currently rivals U.S. economic power. In exploiting free trade opportunities, Japan has now succeeded in dominating Asian and world economies, a goal that its Pacific war failed to achieve.

The nationalist movement and socioeconomic changes have been accompanied by increased cultural vitality and literary production. Together with improved printing technology, access to education, higher rates of literacy, and increased cultural confidence, the numbers of books published in Asian countries rose dramatically in the second half of the twentieth century. Many Asian literatures, both in the national and native languages and the language of the colonial administration, grew in size and complexity, reflecting the influence of Western genres such as short fiction, the novel, and experimental free verse.

Social problems and ills are often reflected in the content and themes of Asian literature. Many Asian writers consciously adopt a political position, protesting the feudalistic forces of their societies and championing the poor and the underclass; Pramoedya Ananta Toer of Indonesia, for example, was imprisoned for many years because of his novels of social protest. The Japanese novelist Yukio Mishima committed hara-kiri in 1970 as a protest against the loss of Japanese military and imperial values.

The extraordinary changes in the economies and social functions of these countries must be set side by side with the fact that many of these societies value and preserve their traditional folkways, whether it is shown in their reverence for their monarchist system, as in Japan, Thailand, Brunei, and Malaysia, or in their continued religious practices, as in the Islamic states of southwest Asia. The literatures of these Asian countries therefore exhibit the stresses of revolutionary content in contestation with the conservative forces of tradition and religion. Twentieth-century literature in China, Japan, and India, for example, is heir to centuries of classical and religious writing, including the ancient classics of the *Tao te ching*, the *Bhagavad Gita*, and the *Manyōshū*.

In the People's Republic of China, twentieth-century literature can be read in three stages, each inverting the terms of the previous stage. The first modern Chinese piece can be said to have been written by Lu Xün in 1918. Humiliated by a series of defeats, e.g., in the Sino-Japanese War of 1894–1895, Chinese writers and intellectuals issued a manifesto in 1919 as part of the larger May Fourth Movement that attacked dead traditions and Chinese inferiority to Western and Japanese power and claimed autonomy for literary expression. Attacking neo-Confucianist social hierarchy, writers were influenced by the spirit of science and of democracy and equality. Lu Xun, for instance, translated passages by Friedrich Nietzche and Aldous Huxley in his radical break with Chinese tradition.

Ravaged by the Japanese invasion and internal civil strife, China was taken over by Mao Zedong's Communist forces in 1949. Even before the Communist victory, the talks at the Yenan Forum on Literature and Art in May 1942 abandoned the writers' claims of autonomy and subsumed them to a larger political context. Socialist realism, first prescribed by Andrey Zhdanov at the First Soviet Writers' Congress in 1932, decreed that writers should produce "the representation of reality not as it is but as it ought to be." Literature should portray themes and attitudes provided by Marxism and the Communist Party national planners and should exhibit positive portraits of the Party through socialist heroes, adopting forms and styles that conform to peasant and national culture. Intellectuals, made to feel guilty over their separation from the masses of proletariat in their society, and with no supporting economic conditions, could not withstand the attack of the state on their position.

In 1966, Mao began the Cultural Revolution (1966–1976), which effectively paralyzed the nation's intellectual life. Schools were closed for two years while the junior and high school and university students joined the Red Guards. While there is a current revulsion against the excesses of the Cultural Revolution, the literature from China is still actively engaged in politics even in its very attempt to get away from politics.

In Japan, the Meiji Restoration in 1868 led to rapid modernization. Translations of major European works encouraged writers to abandon traditional forms and to attempt realistic prose. At the same time, many writers were influenced by German idealism and romanticism and subscribed to a notion of aestheticism in their work. Among the strongest development was the tendency toward confessional and semiautobiographical writing—the *watakushi shōsetsu* (or the "novel") tradition—and naturalistic style, perhaps reflecting the increasing break between the individual writers and their society.

Japan's growing confidence after its victory over Russia in the Russo-Japanese War (1904–1905) was reflected in the proliferation of writers after 1910. Numerous schools of writing flourished. The First World War resulted in more socialist writing sympathetic to the working class. Many of the proletarian writers were politically involved and asserted the importance of portraying social reality over literary style. During the 1930s, however, and up to the end of World War II, an extremist militarist government persecuted these left-wing intellectuals. Japan's defeat in 1945 resulted in liberating writers who were finally able to criticize the military and imperial aspects of their society.

Currently, literary activity is burgeoning in Japan. A great deal of commercial and popular writing exists, but serious literary writers remain, including many who are socially committed. Japan now has its own canon of modern writers and is not as heavily influenced by Western writers as it was in the earlier part of the twentieth century. Younger Japanese writers are as likely to be influenced by twentieth-century masters such as Yasunari Kawabata and Mishima as by European and American writers like Charles Baudelaire, Walt Whitman, and William Faulkner. Nonetheless, the modern short story tradition owes more to Western forms, especially to Guy de Maupassant's realistic short fiction, than to Japanese classical literature.

India, with its rich store of languages (at least 106 different mother tongues and fourteen officially recognized languages), offers a challenging and diverse literature. India is also as diverse culturally as it is linguistically. It is home to many religious groups, including Hindus, Moslems, Buddhists, Christians, Sikhs, and Jains. Each language and religious group works out of its own traditions. Hindus claim an impressive body of classical Sanskrit writing and myths, as, for example, those in the *Mahabharata* and *Ramayana* epics. Muslims refer to the Koran and to a tradition of Urdu poetry, particularly the *ghazel*, which is derived from earlier Persian love poetry.

But whether written in Bengali, Tamil, or English, these literatures share sociopolitical experiences and a common history of Hindu-Islamic culture, British colonialism, and nationalistic aspirations. And, despite their enormous differences, Indian writers share common themes and concerns. Most of the writing documented prior to World War II was of a religious or political nature. Indians in their struggle for autonomy and self-rule wrote many political essays and tracts. The early English-language writers, using the language of their colonial rulers, also imitated the forms of English literature.

Gradually, however, as Indians liberated themselves from the cultural dominance of the British, they found their own themes and styles. The concerns of Indian writers after Indian independence in 1947 included a critique of specific social problems, such as poverty and the almost feudalistic oppression of peasants by landowners and priests or the patriarchal structures that exploit and devalue women. As with literature from other colonized areas, some Indian writers also attack the attitudes of inferiority that many Indians suffer from, as well as the insensitive and racist views of Indians held by many Westerners. A: European-born writer like Ruth Prawer Jhabvala, who is married to an Indian architect and has lived in the country for many years, writes simultaneously from inside Indian culture and outside it. She is able to observe satirically and closely the particular foibles of caste and gender divisions that distinguish Indian society from other cultural groups. Many Indian writers, particularly those writing in English, such as R. K. Narayan and Nissim Ezekiel, show the influence of British literary traditions in their style and forms. But many other less exposed to Western education, such as Mahasweta Devi, express their themes and create characters within their native histories and traditions, traditions that are able to affect us forcefully even in English translation.

Many other Asian countries have a strong and growing body of literature, often categorized and legitimated as a national canon. In multilingual countries such as Indonesia and the Philippines, the national canon is inclusive and extends to works in all of the languages written by the peoples of that nation, including the language of the former colonizers. Other countries such as Vietnam and Malaysia resist the threat to their country language and strive for a canon wholly in the tongue of the dominant ethnic group.

Regardless of language choices and nationally based literary criteria, Asian literatures come under common social influences, among them the pressure to modernize and compete globally, the pressure to preserve communal identity in the face of change and external economic forces, and the pressure to correct inherent injustices. The challenge of modernization is evident in the push to experimentation, moving away from traditional forms to incorporate Western genres and styles, such as the novel and free verse. The issues of communal identity and social justice are clearly manifest in the question of women's rights, which forms a major theme throughout Asian literatures. As seen in the work of the Chinese writer Ding Ling in the 1920s, the Japanese writer Hayashi Fumiko in the 1940s, and Mahasweta Devi in the 1970s, the voices of Asian women redressing their positions of economic and social inferiority form some of the strongest writings from that continent.

Shirley Geok-Lin Lim

C H I N A

Lu Xün

Lu Xün (1881–1936), or Lu Hsun, was born into a landowning family. He went to Japan in 1902 and studied Western medicine before turning to writing. He returned to China in 1909 and worked for the Ministry of Education in Beijing. His first story for New Youth, *"The Diary of a Madman" (1918), a critique of Chinese society, influenced his generation of writers to think more critically of their society. His disillusionment with the Nationalist government caused him to turn to Marxist thought in the 1930s. His essays, letters, short stories, translations, and diaries expressed the political and social consciousness of a generation in continuous crisis. Lu Xün's stories have been published in English in* Dawn Blossoms Plucked at Dusk *(1976) and* Selected Stories of Lu Xün *(1979).*

My Old Home

B raving the bitter cold, I traveled more than seven hundred miles back to the old home I had left over twenty years before. 1

It was late winter. As we drew near my former home the day became overcast and a cold wind blew into the cabin of our boat, while all one could see through the chinks in our bamboo awning were a few desolate villages, void of any sign of life, scattered far and near under the somber yellow sky. I could not help feeling depressed. 2

Ah! Surely this was not the old home I had remembered for the past twenty years? 3

The old home I remembered was not in the least like this. My old home was much better. But if you asked me to recall its peculiar charm or describe its beauties, I had no clear impression, no words to describe it. And now it seemed this was all there was to it. Then I rationalized the matter to myself, saying: Home was always like this, and although it has not im- 4 proved, still it is not so depressing as I imagine; it is only my mood that has changed, because I am coming back to the country this time without any illusions.

This time I had come with the sole object of saying goodbye. This old house our clan had lived in for so many years had already been sold to another family, and was to change hands before the end of the year. I had to hurry there before New Year's Day to say goodbye forever to the familiar old compound, and to move my family far from the old home town they knew to the other place where I was making a living.

At dawn on the second day I reached the gateway of my home. Broken stems of withered grass on the roof, trembling in the wind, made it very clear why this old house would inevitably change hands. Several branches of our clan had probably already moved away, so it was unusually quiet. By the time I reached our own house my mother was already at the door to welcome me, and my eight-year-old nephew, Hung-erh, rushed out after her.

Though Mother was delighted, she was also trying to hide a certain feeling of sadness. She told me to sit down, rest, have some tea, and not discuss the business of moving just yet. Hung-erh, who had never seen me before, stood watching me at a distance.

But finally we had to talk about moving. I said that I had already rented a place elsewhere, and I had bought a little furniture; in addition it would be necessary to sell all the furniture in the house in order to buy more things. Mother agreed, saying that the luggage was nearly all packed, and about half the furniture that could not easily be moved had already been sold. Only it was difficult to collect the money for it.

"You must rest for a day or two, and call on our relatives to pay your respects. Then we can go," said Mother.

"That's fine."

"Then there is Jun-t'u. Each time he comes here he asks about you, and wants very much to see you again. I told him the probable date of your return home, and he may be coming any time."

At this point a strange picture suddenly flashed into my mind: a golden moon suspended in a deep blue sky and beneath it the seashore, planted as far as the eye could see with jade-green watermelons. In their midst a boy of eleven or twelve, wearing a silver necklet and grasping a steel pitchfork in his hand, was thrusting with all his might at a *zha*[1] which dodged the blow and escaped between his legs.

This boy was Jun-t'u. When I first met him he was just over ten—that was thirty years ago. At that time my father was still alive and the family well off, so I was really a "young master." That year it was our family's turn to take charge of a big ancestral sacrifice, which came around only

1. *Zha:* A word invented by Lu Xün for a kind of animal, probably a badger.

once in thirty years or more, and so was an important one. In the first month the ancestral images were presented and offerings made, and since the sacrificial vessels were very fine and there was such a crowd of worshippers, it was necessary to guard against theft. Our family had only one part-time laborer. (In our district we divide laborers into three classes. Those who are hired by the day are called dailies; and those who farm their own land and only work for one family at New Year, during festivals, or when rents are being collected are called part-timers.) And since there was so much to be done, he told my father that he would send for his son Jun-t'u to look after the sacrificial vessels.

When my father gave his consent I was overjoyed, because I had long since heard of Jun-t'u and knew that he was about my own age, born in the intercalary month.[1] When his horoscope was told it was found that of the five elements, the earth element was lacking, so his father called him Jun-t'u, "Intercalary Earth." He could set traps and catch small birds.

I looked forward every day to New Year, for New Year would bring Jun-t'u. At last, one day when the end of the year came, Mother told me that Jun-t'u had come, and I flew to see him. He was standing in the kitchen. He had a round, ruddy face and wore a small felt cap on his head and a gleaming silver necklet around his neck. From this it was obvious that his father doted on him and, fearing he might die, had made a pledge with the gods and Buddhas, using the necklet as a talisman. He was very shy, and I was the only person he was not afraid of. When there was no one else there, he would talk with me, so in a few hours we were close friends.

I don't know what we talked of then, but I remember that Jun-t'u was in high spirits, saying that since he had come to town he had seen many new things.

The next day I wanted him to catch birds.

"I can't do it," he said. "It's only possible after a heavy snowfall. On our sands, after it snows, I sweep clear a patch of ground, prop up a big threshing basket with a short stick, and scatter husks of grain beneath. When the birds come there to eat, I tug on a long, long string tied to the stick, and the birds are caught in the basket. There are all kinds: wild pheasants, woodcocks, wood-pigeons, 'blue-backs' . . ."

Accordingly I really hoped it would snow.

"Just now it's too cold," said Jun-t'u another time, "but you must come to our place in summer. In the daytime we'll go to the seashore to look for shells and 'Buddah hands.' In the evening when dad and I go to see the watermelons, you'll come along too."

---

1. The Chinese lunar calendar reckons three hundred and sixty days to a year, and each month comprises twenty-nine or thirty days, never thirty-one. Hence every few years a thirteenth, or intercalary, month is inserted in the calendar.

"Is it to look out for thieves?" 21

"No. If passersby are thirsty and pick a watermelon, folk down our way 22
don't consider it stealing. What we have to look out for are badgers, hedge-
hogs, and *zha*. When under the moonlight you hear the crunching sound
made by the *zha* when it bites the melons, then you take your pitchfork and
creep stealthily over . . ."

I had no idea then what this thing called *zha* was—and I am not much 23
clearer now for that matter—but somehow I felt it was something like a
small dog, and very fierce.

"Don't they bite people?" 24

"You have a pitchfork. You go across, and when you see it you strike. 25
It's a very cunning creature and will rush toward you and get away between your legs. Its fur is as slippery as oil . . ."

I had never known that all these fresh and exciting things existed: at the 26
seashore there were shells all colors of the rainbow; watermelons were
exposed to such danger, yet all I had known of them before was that they
were sold in the fruit and vegetable shop.

"On our shore, when the tide comes in, there are lots of jumping fish, 27
each has two legs like a frog . . ."

Jun-t'u's mind was a treasure house of such strange lore, all of it un- 28
known to my other friends. They were ignorant of all these things and,
while Jun-t'u lived by the sea, they like me could see only the four corners
of the sky above the high courtyard wall.

Unfortunately, a month after New Year Jun-t'u had to go home. I was so 29
upset I burst into tears and he hid in the kitchen, crying and refusing to
come out, until finally his father carried him off. Later he had his father
bring me a packet of shells and a few very beautiful feathers, and I sent him
presents once or twice, but we never saw each other again.

Now that my mother mentioned him, this childhood memory sprang 30
into life like a flash of lightning, and I seemed to see my beautiful old
home. So I answered:

"Fine! And he—how is he?" 31

"He? Things aren't going very well for him," said Mother. And then, 32
looking out of the door: "Here come those people again. They say they
want to buy our furniture; but actually they'll casually walk off with something. I must go and watch them."

Mother stood up and went out. The voices of several women could be 33
heard outside. I called Hung-erh to me and started talking to him, asking
him whether he could write, and whether he would be glad to leave.

"Are we going to take the train?" 34

"Yes, we're going to take the train." 35

"And a boat?" 36

"First we'll take a boat." 37

A strange shrill voice suddenly rang out: 38

"Looking like this! With such a long moustache!"   39

I looked up with a start, and saw a woman of about fifty with prominent   40
cheekbones and thin lips standing in front of me. With her hands on her
hips, not wearing a skirt but with her trousered legs apart, she seemed just
like a thin, spindly-legged compass in a box of geometrical instruments.

I was really startled.   41

"Don't you know me? Why, I have held you in my arms!"   42

I was even more taken aback. Fortunately my mother came in just then   43
and broke in:

"He's been away so long, you must excuse his forgetting. You should   44
remember," she said to me, "this is Mrs. Yang from across the road. She
has a beancurd shop."

Then, of course, I remembered. When I was a child there was a Mrs.   45
Yang who used to sit nearly all day long in a beancurd shop across the
road, and everybody used to call her Beancurd Beauty. She used to powder
herself, and her cheekbones were not so prominent then nor her lips so
thin; besides, she sat there the whole day, so that I had never noticed this
resemblance to a compass. In those days people said that, thanks to her,
that beancurd shop did a very good business. But, probably on account of
my age, she had made no impression on me, so that later I forgot her
entirely. However, the Compass was extremely indignant and looked at
me contemptuously, just as one might look at a Frenchman who had never
heard of Napoleon or an American who had never heard of Washington.
Smiling sarcastically she said:

"You had forgotten? Naturally I am beneath your notice."   46

"Certainly not . . . I . . ." I answered nervously, getting to my feet.   47

"Then you listen to me, Master Xün. You have grown rich, and they are   48
too heavy to move, so you can't possibly want these worn-out pieces of
furniture anymore. You had better let me take them away. Poor people like
us can make use of them."

"I haven't grown rich. I must sell these in order to buy—"   49

"Oh, come now, you have been made the intendant of a circuit; how can   50
you still say you're not rich? Hah! You can't hide anything from me."

I knew there was nothing I could say, so I kept quiet and just stood still   51
there.

"Come now, really, the more money people have the more miserly they   52
get, and the more miserly they are the more money they get," jabbered the
Compass, as she turned away indignantly and walked slowly off, casually
picking up a pair of my mother's gloves and stuffing them into her pocket
as she left.

After this a number of relatives in the neighborhood came to call. In the   53
intervals between entertaining them I did some packing, and so three or
four days passed.

One very cold afternoon, I sat drinking tea after lunch when I was aware   54 of someone coming in, and turned my head to see who it was. At the first glance I gave an involuntary start, hastily stood up, and went over to welcome him.

The newcomer was Jun-t'u. But although I knew at a glance that this was Jun-t'u, it was not the Jun-t'u I remembered. He had grown to twice his former size. His round face, once ruddy, had become sallow and now had deep lines and wrinkles; his eyes too were like his father's, the rims swollen and red. I knew that most peasants who work by the sea and are exposed all day to the wind from the ocean were like this. He wore a shabby felt cap and just a very thin padded jacket, and was shivering from head to foot. He carried a package wrapped in paper and a long pipe. His hands were not the plump red hands I remembered, but coarse and clumsy and chapped, like the bark of a pine tree.   55

I was delighted, but I didn't know what words to use, so I only said: 56
"Oh! Jun-t'u—so it's you? . . ."   57

There were so many things then to talk about that I wanted to spew   58
them out like a string of beads: woodcocks, jumping fish, shells, *zha* . . .
But something seemed to hold me back. Everything just swirled around in my head and I couldn't get the words out.

He stood there, joy and sadness both showing on his face. His lips   59
moved, but not a sound did he utter. Finally, assuming a respectful attitude, he said clearly:

"Master!"   60

I felt a shiver run through me, for I knew then what a lamentably thick   61
wall had grown up between us. Yet I could not say anything.

He turned his head to call: 62

"Shui-sheng, bow to the master." Then he pulled forward a boy who   63
had been hiding behind his back, and this was just the Jun-t'u of twenty years before, only a little paler and thinner, and he had no silver necklet.

"This is my fifth," he said. "He hasn't had any experience with social   64
occasions, so he's shy and awkward."

Mother came downstairs with Hung-erh, probably after hearing our   65
voices.

"I got your letter some time ago, madam," said Jun-t'u. "I was really so   66
pleased to know the master was coming back."

"Now, why are you so polite? Didn't you consider yourselves brothers   67
in the past?" said Mother gaily. "Why don't you still call him Brother Xün as you used to?"

"Oh, you are really too . . . What bad manners that would be. I was a   68
child then and didn't understand." As he was speaking Jun-t'u motioned Shui-sheng to come and bow, but the child was shy, and stood stock still behind his father.

"So he is Shui-Sheng? Your fifth?" asked Mother. "We are all strangers,   69
you can't blame him for feeling shy. Hung-erh had better take him out to play."

When Hung-erh heard this he went over to Shui-sheng, and Shui-sheng   70
went out with him, entirely at his ease. Mother asked Jun-t'u to sit down,
and after a little hesitation he did so; then, leaning his long pipe against the
table, he handed over the paper package, saying:

"In winter there is nothing worth bringing; but these few green beans   71
we dried ourselves, if you will excuse the liberty, sir."

When I asked him how things were with him, he just shook his head.   72

"In a very bad way. Even my sixth can do a little work, but still we   73
haven't enough to eat . . . and there is no security . . . all sorts of people want money, there is no fixed rule . . . and the harvests are bad. You
grow things, and when you take them to sell you always have to pay
several taxes and lose money, while if you don't try to sell the things will
only spoil . . ."

He kept shaking his head; yet, although his face was lined with wrin-   74
kles, not one of them moved, just as if he were a stone statue. No doubt he
felt intensely bitter, but could not openly express himself. After a pause he
took up his pipe and began to smoke in silence.

From her chat with him, Mother learned that he was busy at home and   75
had to go back the next day; and since he had had no lunch, she told him
to go to the kitchen and fry some rice for himself.

After he had gone out, Mother and I both shook our heads over his hard   76
life: many children, famines, taxes, soldiers, bandits, officials, and landed
gentry, all had been so hard on him that he seemed a wooden image of a
man. Mother said that we should offer him all the things we didn't need to
take with us, letting him choose for himself.

That afternoon he picked out a number of things: two long tables, four   77
chairs, an incense burner and candlesticks, and a balance. He also asked
for all the ashes from the stove (in our region we cook over straw, and the
ashes can be used to fertilize sandy soil), saying that when we left he
would come to take them away by boat.

That night we talked again, but not of anything serious; and the next   78
morning he went away with Shui-sheng.

After another nine days it was time for us to leave. Jun-t'u came in the   79
morning. Shui-sheng did not come with him—he had just brought a little
girl of five to watch the boat. We were very busy all day, and had no time
to talk. We also had quite a number of visitors, some to see us off, some to
fetch things, and some to do both. It was nearly evening when we left by
boat, and by that time everything in the house, however old or shabby,
large or small, fine or coarse, had been cleared out.

As we set off, in the dusk, the green mountains on either side of the   80
river became deep blue, receding toward the stern of the boat.

Hung-erh and I, leaning against the cabin window, were both watching   81
the indistinct scene outside, when suddenly he asked:

"Uncle, when shall we go back?"   82

"Go back? Do you mean that before you've left you want to go back?"   83

"Well, Shui-sheng has invited me to his home . . ." He opened wide his   84
black eyes, engrossed in thought.

Mother and I both felt rather sad, and so Jun-t'u's name came up again.   85
Mother said that ever since our family started packing up, Mrs. Yang from
the beancurd shop had come over every day, and the day before in the
ash-heap she had unearthed a dozen bowls and plates, which after some
discussion she insisted must have been buried there by Jun-t'u, so that
when he came to remove the ashes he could take them home at the same
time. After making this discovery Mrs. Yang was very pleased with herself,
and flew off taking the dog-teaser with her. (The dog-teaser is used by
poultry keepers in our parts. It is a wooden cage inside which food is put,
so that hens can stretch their necks in to eat but dogs can only look on
furiously.) And it was a marvel, considering the thick-soled shoes on her
bound feet, how fast she could run.

I was leaving the old house farther and farther behind, while the hills   86
and rivers of my old home were also receding gradually ever farther in the
distance. But I felt no regret. I only felt that all around me was an invisible
high wall, cutting me off from others, and this depressed me thoroughly.
The vision of that small hero with the silver necklet among the watermelons had formerly been as clear as day, but now it suddenly blurred, adding
to my depression.

Mother and Hung-erh fell asleep.   87

I lay down, listening to the water rippling beneath the boat, and knew   88
that I was going my own way. I thought: although there is such a barrier
between Jun-t'u and myself, the children still have much in common, for
wasn't Hung-erh thinking of Shui-sheng just now? I hope they will not be
like us, that they will not allow a barrier to grow up between them. Then
again, I wouldn't want them, because they want to be alike, to have a
treadmill existence like mine nor to suffer like Jun-t'u until they become
stupefied, nor yet, like others, to lead a cruel life of dissipation. They
should have a new life, a life we never experienced.

The thought of hope made me suddenly afraid. When Jun-t'u asked for   89
the incense burner and candlesticks I had laughed at him to myself, to
think that he still worshipped idols and could not put them out of his
mind. Yet what I now called hope, wasn't it nothing more than an idol I
had created myself? The only difference was that what he desired was close
at hand, while what I desired was less easily realized.

As I dozed, a stretch of jade-green seashore spread itself before my eyes,   90
and above a round golden moon hung in a deep blue sky. I thought: hope
cannot be said to exist, nor can it be said not to exist. It is just like pathways
over the land. For actually there were no paths originally, but when many
people traveled one way, a road was made.

Translated from the Chinese by Yang Hsien-yi
and Gladys Yang

A Small Incident

Six years have slipped by since I came from the country to the capital. During that time the number of so-called affairs of state I have witnessed or heard about is far from small, but none of them made much impression. If asked to define their influence on me, I can only say they made my bad temper worse. Frankly speaking, they taught me to take a poorer view of people every day.

One small incident, however, which struck me as significant and jolted me out of my irritability, remains fixed even now in my memory.

It was the winter of 1917, a strong north wind was blustering, but the exigencies of earning my living forced me to be up and out early. I met scarcely a soul on the road, but eventually managed to hire a rickshaw to take me to S— Gate. Presently the wind dropped a little, having blown away the drifts of dust on the road to leave a clean broad highway, and the rickshaw man quickened his pace. We were just approaching S— Gate when we knocked into someone who slowly toppled over.

It was a grey-haired woman in ragged clothes. She had stepped out abruptly from the roadside in front of us, and although the rickshaw man had swerved, her tattered padded waistcoat, unbuttoned and billowing in the wind, had caught on the shaft. Luckily the rickshaw man had slowed down, otherwise she would certainly have had a bad fall and it might have been a serious accident.

She huddled there on the ground, and the rickshaw man stopped. As I did not believe the old woman was hurt and as no one else had seen us, I thought this halt of his uncalled for, liable to land him in trouble and hold me up.

"It's all right," I said. "Go on."

He paid no attention—he may not have heard—but set down the shafts, took the old woman's arm and gently helped her up.

"Are you all right?" he asked.

"I hurt myself falling."

I thought: I saw how slowly you fell, how could you be hurt? Putting on an act like this is simply disgusting. The rickshaw man asked for trouble, and now he's got it. He'll have to find his own way out.

But the rickshaw man did not hesitate for a minute after hearing the old woman's answer. Still holding her arm, he helped her slowly forward. Rather puzzled by this I looked ahead and saw a police-station. Because of the high wind, there was no one outside. It was there that the rickshaw man was taking the old woman.

Suddenly I had the strange sensation that his dusty retreating figure had in that instant grown larger. Indeed, the further he walked the larger he loomed, until I had to look up to him. At the same time he seemed gradually to be exerting a pressure on me which threatened to overpower the small self hidden under my fur-lined gown.

Almost paralyzed at that juncture I sat there motionless, my mind a 13 blank, until a policeman came out. Then I got down from the rickshaw.

The policeman came up to me and said, "Get another rickshaw. He can't 14 take you any further."

On the spur of the moment I pulled a handful of coppers from my coat 15 pocket and handed them to the policeman. "Please give him this," I said.

The wind had dropped completely, but the road was still quiet. As I 16 walked along thinking, I hardly dared to think about myself. Quite apart from what had happened earlier, what had I meant by that handful of coppers? Was it a reward? Who was I to judge the rickshaw man? I could give myself no answer.

Even now, this incident keeps coming back to me. It keeps distressing 17 me and makes me try to think about myself. The politics and the fighting of those years have slipped my mind as completely as the classics I read as a child. Yet this small incident keeps coming back to me, often more vivid than in actual life, teaching me shame, spurring me on to reform, and imbuing me with fresh courage and fresh hope.

*Translated from the Chinese by Yang Hsien-yi
and Gladys Yang*

STUDY QUESTIONS

1. Why is the narrator returning to his old home? What are his feelings during this trip?
2. What are some specific memories that are raised on this visit? What kinds of inferences can you make of the narrator's earlier life and of his position in society from these memories?
3. What is the relationship between Jun-t'u and the narrator? What does their relationship reveal of the way that Chinese society was structured then?
4. Does the story suggest an impression of stagnation and/or change? What are some of the details that support one or the other impression? Discuss the effects of such impressions in the construction of the story's theme.
5. If we take the narrator to represent the intellectual and Jun-t'u the peasant class, how does "My Old Home" portray the relationship between the intellectuals and the peasants in China at the beginning of the twentieth century? What kind of future does the intellectual wish for?

6. What is the narrator's mood at the beginning of "A Small Incident" and how does he account for it?
7. Describe the differences between the narrator's response to the incident and the rickshaw man's.
8. What is happening to the speaker in the paragraph that begins, "Suddenly I had the strange sensation . . . ." (par. 12).
9. How does this incident change the narrator's view of himself and of his society? Why does this incident leave more of an impression on him than do the political events of his time?

 DING LING

Ding Ling (1907–1988) studied in Shanghai, then lived in Beijing, where she married Hu Yeh-p'in, also a writer. Her early stories, which examined the effects of modernization on China's youth, made her famous. Her husband was executed for his Communist affiliation in 1931, and Ding Ling lived on parole in Nanking for three years before regaining her freedom and joining the Communist forces in Yenan. In 1957, during the Anti-Rightist Movement, she came under attack and was exiled to Manchuria. Ding Ling was rehabilitated a few years before her death. Several of her books have appeared in English, including her prize-winning novel on land reform, The Sun Shines Over the Sanggan River *(1984),* Miss Sophie's Diary *(1985), and* I Myself Am a Woman *(1989).*

When I Was in Xia Village

Because of the turmoil in the Political Department, Comrade Mo Yü decided to send me to stay temporarily in a neighboring village. Actually, I was already completely well, but the opportunity to rest for a while in a quiet environment and arrange my notes from the past three months did have its attractions. So I agreed to spend two weeks in Xia Village, a place about ten miles from the Political Department.

A female comrade from the Propaganda Department, who was apparently on a work assignment, went with me. Since she wasn't a person who enjoyed conversation, however, the journey was rather lonely. Also because her feet had once been bound and my own spirits were low, we traveled slowly. We set out in the morning, but it was nearly sunset by the time we reached our destination.

The village looked much like any other from a distance, but I knew it contained a very beautiful Catholic church that had escaped destruction and a small grove of pine trees. The place where I would be staying was in the midst of these trees, which clung to the hillside. From that spot it would be possible to look straight across to the church. By now I could see orderly rows of cave dwellings and the green trees above them. I felt content with the village.

My traveling companion had given me the impression that the village was very busy, but when we entered it, not even a single child or dog was to be seen. The only movement was dry leaves twirling about lightly in the wind. They would fly a short distance, then drop to earth again.

"This used to be an elementary school, but last year the Jap devils destroyed it. Look at those steps over there. That used to be a big class-room," my companion, Agui, told me. She was somewhat excited now, not so reserved as she had been during the day. Pointing to a large empty courtyard, she continued: "A year and a half ago, this area was full of life. Every evening after supper, the comrades gathered here to play soccer or basketball." Becoming more agitated, she asked, "Why isn't anyone here? Should we go to the assembly hall or head up the hill? We don't know where they've taken our luggage either. We have to straighten that out first."

On the wall next to the gate of the village assembly hall, many white paper slips had been pasted. They read "Office of the [Communist] Association," "Xia Village Branch of the [Communist] Association," and so on. But when we went inside, we couldn't find a soul. It was completely quiet, with only a few tables set about. We were both standing there dumbly when suddenly a man rushed in. He looked at us for a moment, seemed about to ask us something, but swallowed his words and prepared to dash away. We called to him to stop, however, and made him answer our questions.

"The people of the village? They've all gone to the west door. Baggage? Hmm. Yes, there was baggage. It was carried up the hill some time ago to Liu Erma's home." As he talked, he sized us up.

Learning that he was a member of the Peasant's Salvation Association, we asked him to accompany us up the hill and also asked him to deliver a note to one of the local comrades. He agreed to take the note, but he wouldn't go with us. He seemed impatient and ran off by himself.

The street too was very quiet. The doors of several shops were closed. Others were still open, exposing pitch-black interiors. We still couldn't find anyone. Fortunately, Agui was familiar with the village and led me up the hill. It was already dark. The winter sun sets very quickly.

The hill was not high, and a large number of stone cave dwellings were scattered here and there from the bottom to the top. In a few places, people were standing out in front peering into the distance. Agui knew very well that we had not yet reached our destination, but whenever we met someone she asked, "Is this the way to Liu Erma's house?" "How far is it to Liu Erma's house?" "Could you please tell me the way to Liu Erma's house?" Or, she would ask, "Did you notice any baggage being sent to Liu Erma's house? Is Liu Erma home?"

The answers we received always satisfied us, and this continued right up to the most distant and highest house, which was the Liu family's. Two small dogs were the first to greet us. Then a woman came out and asked who we were. As soon as they heard it was me, two more women came out. Holding a lantern, they escorted us into the courtyard and then into a cave on the side toward the east. The cave was virtually empty. On the *kang* under the window were piled my bedroll, my small leather carrying case, and Agui's quilt. 11

Some of the people there knew Agui. They took her hand and asked her many questions, and after a while they led her out, leaving me alone in the room. I arranged my bed and was about to lie down when suddenly they all crowded back in again. One of Liu Erma's daughters-in-law was carrying a bowl of noodles. Agui, Liu Erma, and a young girl were holding bowls, chopsticks, and a dish of onions and pepper. The young girl also brought in a brazier of burning coal. 12

Attentively, they urged me to eat some noodles and touched my hands and arms. Liu Erma and her daughter-in-law also sat down on the *kang*. There was an air of mystery about them as they continued the conversation interrupted by their entry into the room. 13

At first I thought I had caused their amazement, but gradually I realized that this wasn't the case. They were interested in only one thing—the topic of their conversation. Since all I heard were a few fragmentary sentences, I couldn't understand what they were talking about. This was especially true of what Liu Erma said because she frequently lowered her voice, as if afraid that someone might overhear her. Agui had changed completely. She now appeared quite capable and was very talkative. She listened closely to what the others were saying and seemed able to grasp the essence of their words. The daughter-in-law and the young girl said little. At times they added a word or two, but for the most part they just listened intently to what Agui and Liu Erma were saying. They seemed afraid to miss a single word. 14

Suddenly the courtyard was filled with noise. A large number of people had rushed in, and they all seemed to be talking at once. Liu Erma and the others climbed nervously off the *kang* and hurried outside. Without thinking, I followed along behind them to see what was happening. 15

By this time the courtyard was in compete darkness. Two red paper lanterns bobbed and weaved above the crowd. I worked my way into the throng and looked around. I couldn't see anything. The others also were squeezing in for no apparent reason. They seemed to want to say more, but they did not. I heard only simple exchanges that confused me even more. 16

"Yüwa, are you here too?" 17

"Have you seen her yet?"   18

"Yes, I've seen her. I was a little afraid."   19

"What is there to be afraid of? She's just a human being, and prettier   20
than ever too."

At first I was sure that they were talking about a new bride, but peo-   21
ple said that wasn't so. Then I thought there was a prisoner present, but
that was wrong too. I followed the crowd to the doorway of the central
cave, but all there was to see was more people packed tightly together.
Thick smoke obscured my vision, so I had no choice but to back away.
Others were also leaving by now, and the courtyard was much less
crowded.

Since I couldn't sleep, I set about rearranging my carrying case by the   22
lantern light. I paged through several notebooks, looked at photographs,
and sharpened some pencils. I was obviously tired, but I also felt the kind
of excitement that comes just before a new life begins. I prepared a time
schedule for myself and was determined to adhere to it, beginning the very
next day.

At that moment there was a man's voice at the door. "Are you asleep,   23
comrade?" Before I could reply, the fellow entered the room. He was about
twenty years old, a rather refined-looking country youth. "I received Director Mo's letter some time ago," he said. "This area is relatively quiet.
Don't worry about a thing. That's my job. If you need something, don't
hesitate to ask Liu Erma. Director Mo said you wanted to stay here for two
weeks. Fine. If you enjoy your visit, we'd be happy to have you stay
longer. I live in a neighboring cave, just below these. If you need me, just
send someone to find me."

He declined to come up on the *kang*, and since there was no bench on the   24
floor to sit on, I jumped down and said, "Ah! You must be Comrade Ma. Did
you receive the note I sent you? Please sit down and talk for a while."

I knew that he held a position of some responsibility in the village. As   25
a student he had not yet finished junior high school.

"They tell me you've written a lot of books," he responded. "It's too bad   26
we haven't seen a single one." As he spoke he looked at my open carrying
case that was lying on the *kang*. Our conversation turned to the subject of
the local level of study. Then he said, "After you've rested for a few days,
we'll definitely invite you to give a talk. It can be to a mass meeting or a
training class. In any case, you'll certainly be able to help us. Our most
difficult task here is 'cultural recreation.' "

I had seen many young men like him at the Front. When I first met   27
them, I was always amazed. I felt that these youth, who were somewhat
remote from me, were really changing fast. Changing the subject, I asked
him, "What was going on just now?"

"Zhenzhen, the daughter of Liu Dama, has returned," he answered. "I   28
never thought she could be so great." I immediately sensed a joyful, ra-

diant twinkle in his eyes. As I was about to ask another question, he added, "She's come back from the Japanese area. She's been working there for over a year."

"Oh my!" I gasped. 29

He was about to tell me more when someone outside called for him. All 30 he could say was that he'd be sure to have Zhenzhen call on me the next day. As if to provoke my interest further, he added that Zhenzhen must certainly have a lot of material for stories.

It was very late when Agui came back. She lay down on the *kang* but could 31 not sleep. She tossed and turned and sighed continuously. I was very tired, but I still wished that she would tell me something about the events of the evening.

"No, comrade," she said. "I can't talk about it now. I'm too upset. I'll 32 tell you tomorrow. Ahh . . . How miserable it is to be a woman." After this she covered her head with her quilt and lay completely still, no longer sighing. I didn't know when she finally fell asleep.

Early the next morning I stepped outside for a stroll, and before I knew 33 it I had walked down to the village. I went into a general store to rest and buy red dates for Liu Erma to put in the rice porridge. As soon as the owner learned that I was living with Liu Erma, his small eyes narrowed and he asked me in a low, excited voice, "Did you get a look at her niece? I hear her disease has even taken her nose. That's because she was abused by the Jap devils." Turning his head, he called to his wife, who was standing in the inner doorway, "She has nerve, coming home! It's revenge against her father, Liu Fusheng."

"That girl was always frivolous. You saw the way she used to roam 34 around the streets. Wasn't she Xia Dabao's old flame? If he hadn't been poor, wouldn't she have married him a long time ago?" As she finished speaking, the old woman lifted her skirts and came into the store.

The owner turned his face back toward me and said, "There are so many 35 rumors." His eyes stopped blinking and his expression became very serious. "It's said that she has slept with at least a hundred men. Humph! I've heard that she even became the wife of a Japanese officer. Such a shameful woman should not be allowed to return."

Not wanting to argue with him, I held back my anger and left. I didn't 36 look back, but I felt that he had again narrowed his small eyes and was feeling smug as he watched me walk away. As I neared the corner by the Catholic church, I overheard a conversation by two women who were drawing water at the well. One said, "She sought out Father Lu and told him she definitely wanted to be a nun. When Father Lu asked her for a reason, she didn't say a word, just cried. Who knows what she did there? Now she's worse than a prostitute . . ."

"Yesterday they told me she walks with a limp. Achh! How can she face people?"   37

"Someone said she's even wearing a gold ring that a Jap devil gave her!"   38

"I understand she's been as far away as Datong and has seen many things. She can even speak Japanese."   39

My walk was making me unhappy, so I returned home. Since Agui had already gone out, I sat alone in my room and read a small pamphlet. After a while, I raised my eyes and noticed two large baskets for storing grain sitting near the wall. They must have had a long history, because they were as black as the wall itself. Opening the moveable portion of the paper window, I peered out at the gray sky. The weather had changed completely from what it had been when I arrived the day before. The hard ground of the courtyard had been swept clean, and at the far edge a tree with a few withered branches stood out starkly against the leaden sky. There wasn't a single person to be seen.   40

I opened my carrying case, took out pen and paper, and wrote two letters. I wondered why Agui had not yet returned. I had forgotten that she had work to do. I was somehow thinking that she had come to be my companion. The days of winter are very short, but right then I was feeling that they were even longer than summer days.   41

Some time later, the young girl who had been in my room the night before came out into the courtyard. I immediately jumped down off the *kang*, stepped out the door, and called to her, but she just looked at me and smiled before rushing into another cave. I walked around the courtyard twice and then stopped to watch a hawk fly into the grove of trees by the church. The courtyard there had many large trees. I started walking again and, on the right side of the courtyard, picked up the sound of a woman crying. She was trying to stop, frequently blowing her nose.   42

I tried hard to control myself. I thought about why I was here and about all my plans. I had to rest and live according to the time schedule I had made. I returned to my room, but I couldn't sleep and had no interest in writing in my notebook.   43

Fortunately, a short while later Liu Erma came to see me. The young girl was with her, and her daughter-in-law arrived soon after. The three of them climbed up on the *kang* and took seats around the small brazier. The young girl looked closely at my things, which were laid out on the little square *kang* table.   44

"At that time no one could take care of anyone else," Liu Erma said, talking about the Japanese attack on Xia Village a year and a half before. "Those of us who lived on the hilltop were luckier. We could run away quickly. Many who lived in the village could not escape. Apparently it was all fate. Just then, on that day, our family's Zhenzhen had run over to the Catholic church. Only later did we learn that her unhappiness about what was happening had caused her to go to talk to the foreign priest about becoming a nun. Her father was in the midst of negotiating a marriage for   45 her with the young proprietor of a rice store in Xiliu Village. He was almost thirty, a widower, and his family was well respected. We all said he would be a good match, but Zhenzhen said no and broke into tears before her father. In other matters, her father had always deferred to her wishes, but in this case the old man was adamant. He had no son and had always wanted to betroth his daughter to a good man. Who would have thought that Zhenzhen would turn around in anger and run off to the Catholic church. It was at that moment that the Japs caught her. How could her mother and father help grieving?"

"Was that her mother crying?"   46

"Yes."   47

"And your niece?"   48

"Well, she's really just a child. When she came back yesterday, she cried   49
for a long time, but today she went to the assembly in high spirits. She's
only eighteen."

"I heard she was the wife of a Japanese. Is that true?"   50

"It's hard to say. We haven't been able to find out for sure. There are   51
many rumors, of course. She contracted a disease, but how could anyone
keep clean in such a place? The possibility of her marrying the merchant
seems to be over. Who would want a woman who was abused by the Jap
devils? She definitely has the disease. Last night she said so herself. This
time she's changed a lot. When she talks about those devils, she shows no
more emotion than if she were talking about an ordinary meal at home.
She's only eighteen, but she has no sense of embarrassment at all."

"Xia Dabao came again today," the daughter-in-law said quietly, her   52
questioning eyes fixed on Erma.

"Who is Xia Dabao?" I asked.   53

"He's a young man who works in the village flour mill," replied Liu   54
Erma. "When he was young, he and Zhenzhen were classmates for a year.
They liked each other very much, but his family was poor, even poorer
than ours. He didn't dare do anything, but our Zhenzhen was head over
heels in love with him and kept clinging to him. Then she was upset when
he didn't respond. Isn't it because of him that she wanted to be a nun?
After Zhenzhen fell into the hands of the Jap devils, he often came to see
her parents. At first just the sight of him made Zhenzhen's father angry. At
times he cursed him, but Xia Dabao would say nothing. After a scolding he
would leave and then come back another day. Dabao is really a good boy.
Now he's even a squad leader in the self-defense corps. Today he came
once again, apparently to talk with Zhenzhen's mother about marrying
Zhenzhen. All I could hear was her crying. Later he left in tears himself."

"Does he know about your niece's situation?"   55

"How could he help knowing? There is no one in this village who   56
doesn't know everything. They all know more than we do ourselves."

"Mother, everyone says that Xia Dabao is foolish," the young girl in-   57
terjected.

"Humph! The boy has a good conscience. I approve of this match. Since   58
the Jap devils came, who has any money? Judging from the words of Zhenzhen's parents, I think they approve too. If not him, who? Even without
mentioning her disease, her reputation is enough to deter anyone."

"He was the one wearing the dark blue jacket and the copper-colored felt   59
hat with the turned-up brim," the young girl said. Her eyes were sparkling
with curiosity, and she seemed to understand this matter very well.

His figure began to take shape in my memory. When I went out for my   60
walk earlier that morning, I had seen an alert, honest-looking young man
who fit this description. He had been standing outside my courtyard, but
had not shown any intention of coming in. On my way home, I had seen
him again, this time emerging from the pine woods beyond the cave dwellings. I had thought he was someone from my courtyard or from a neighboring one and hadn't paid much attention to him. As I recalled him now,
I felt that he was a rather capable man, not a bad young man at all.

I now feared that my plan for rest and recuperation could not be real-   61
ized. Why were my thoughts so confused? I wasn't particularly anxious to
meet anybody, and yet my mind still couldn't rest. Agui had come in
during the conversation, and now she seemed to sense my feelings. As she
went out with the others, she gave me a knowing smile. I understood her
meaning and busied myself with arranging the *kang*. My bedroll, the lamp,
and the fire all seemed much brighter. I had just placed the tea kettle on the
fire when Agui returned. Behind her I heard another person.

"We have a guest, comrade!" Agui called. Even before she finished   62
speaking, I heard someone giggling.

Standing in the doorway, I grasped the hands of this person whom I had   63
not seen before. They were burning hot, and I couldn't help being a bit
startled. She followed Agui up onto the *kang* and sat down. A single long
braid hung down her back.

In the eyes of the new arrival, the cave that depressed me seemed to be   64
something new and fresh. She looked around at everything with an excited
glint in her eyes. She sat opposite me, her body tilted back slightly and her
two hands spread apart on the bedroll for support. She didn't seem to want
to say anything. Her eyes finally came to rest on my face.

The shadows lengthened her eyes and made her chin quite pointed. But   65
even though her eyes were in deep shadow, her pupils shown brightly in
the light of the lamp and the fire. They were like two open windows in a
summer home in the country, clear and clean.

I didn't know how to begin a conversation without touching an open   66
wound and hurting her self-respect. So my first move was to pour her a
cup of hot tea.

It was Zhenzhen who spoke first: "Are you a Southerner? I think so.   67
You aren't like the people from this province."

"Have you seen many Southerners?" I asked, thinking it best to talk   68
about what she wanted to talk about.

"No," she said, shaking her head. Her eyes still fixed on me, she added, "I've only seen a few. They always seem a little different. I like you people from the South. Southern women, unlike us, can all read many, many books. I want to study with you. Will you teach me?" 69

I expressed my willingness to do so, and she quickly continued, "Japanese women also can read a lot of books. All those devil soldiers carried a few well-written letters, some from wives, some from girlfriends. Some were written by girls they didn't even know. They would include a photograph and use syrupy language. I don't know if those girls were sincere or not, but they always made the devils hold their letters to their hearts like precious treasures." 70

"I understand that you can speak Japanese," I said. "Is that true?" 71

Her face flushed slightly before she replied, in a very open manner, "I was there for such a long time. I went around and around for over a year. I can speak a fair amount. Being able to understand their language had many advantages." 72

"Did you go to a lot of different places with them?" 73

"I wasn't always with the same unit. People think that because I was the wife of a Jap officer I enjoyed luxury. Actually, I came back here twice before. Altogether, this is my third time. I was ordered to go on this last mission. There was no choice. I was familiar with the area, the work was important, and it was impossible to find anyone else in a short time. I won't be sent back anymore. They're going to treat my disease. That's fine with me because I've missed my dad and mom, and I'm glad to be able to come back to see them. My mother, though, is really hopeless. When I'm not home, she cries. When I'm here, she still cries." 74

"You must have known many hardships." 75

"She has endured unthinkable suffering," Agui interrupted, her face twisted in a pained expression. In a voice breaking with emotion, she added, "It's a real tragedy to be a woman, isn't it, Zhenzhen?" She slid over to be next to her. 76

"Suffering?" Zhenzhen asked, her thoughts apparently far, far away. "Right now I can't say for certain. Some things were hard to endure at the time, but when I recall them now they don't seem like much. Other things were no problem to do when I did them, but when I think about them now I'm very sad. More than a year . . . It's all past. Since I came back this time, a great many people have looked at me strangely. As far as the people of this village are concerned, I'm an outsider. Some are very friendly to me. Others avoid me. The members of my family are just the same. They all like to steal looks at me. Nobody treats me the way they used to. Have I changed? I've thought about this a great deal, and I don't think I've changed at all. If I have changed, maybe it's that my heart has become somewhat harder. But could anyone spend time in such a place and not become hardhearted? People have no choice. They're forced to be like that!" 77

There was no outward sign of her disease. Her complexion was ruddy. 78

Her voice was clear. She showed no signs of inhibition or rudeness. She did not exaggerate. She gave the impression that she had never had any complaints or sad thoughts. Finally, I could restrain myself no longer and asked her about her disease.

"People are always like that, even if they find themselves in worse situations. They brace themselves and see it through. Can you just give up and die? Later, after I made contact with our own people, I became less afraid. As I watched the Jap devils suffer defeat in battle and the guerrillas take action on all sides as a result of the tricks I was playing, I felt better by the day. I felt that even though my life was hard, I could still manage. Somehow I had to find a way to survive, and if at all possible, to live a life that was meaningful. That's why I'm pleased that they intend to treat my disease. It will be better to be cured. Actually, these past few days I haven't felt too bad. On the way home, I stayed in Zhangjiayi for two days and was given two shots and some medicine to take orally. The worst time was in the fall. I was told that my insides were rotting away, and then, because of some important information and the fact that no one could be found to take my place, I had to go back. That night I walked alone in the dark for ten miles. Every single step was painful. My mind was filled with the desire to sit down and rest. If the work hadn't been so important, I definitely wouldn't have gone back. But I had to. Ahh! I was afraid I might be recognized by the Jap devils, and I was also worried about missing my rendezvous. After it was over, I slept for a full week before I could pull myself together. It really isn't all that easy to die, is it?"

Without waiting for me to respond, she continued on with her story. At times she stopped talking and looked at us. Perhaps she was searching for reactions on our faces. Or maybe she was only thinking of something else. I could see that Agui was more troubled than Zhenzhen. For the most part she sat in silence, and when she did speak, it was only for a sentence or two. Her words gave voice to a limitless sympathy for Zhenzhen, but her expression when silent revealed even more clearly how moved she was by what Zhenzhen was saying. Her soul was being crushed. She herself was feeling the suffering that Zhenzhen had known before.

It was my impression that Zhenzhen had no intention whatever of trying to elicit sympathy from others. Even as others took upon themselves part of the misfortune that she had suffered, she seemed unaware of it. But that very fact made others feel even more sympathetic. It would have been better if, instead of listening to her recount the events of this period with a calmness that almost made you think she was talking about someone else, you could have heard her cry. Probably you would have cried with her, but you would have felt better.

After a while Agui began to cry, and Zhenzhen turned to comfort her. There were many things that I had wanted to discuss with Zhenzhen, but I couldn't bring myself to say anything. I wished to remain silent. After

Zhenzhen left, I forced myself to read by the lamp for an hour. Not once did I look at Agui or ask her a question, even though she was lying very close to me, even though she tossed and turned and sighed all the time, unable to fall asleep.

After this Zhenzhen came to talk with me every day. She did not talk about herself alone. She very often showed great curiosity about many aspects of my life that were beyond her own experiences. At times, when my words were far removed from her life, it was obvious that she was struggling to understand, but nevertheless she listened intently. The two of us also took walks together down to the village. The youth were very good to her. Naturally, they were all activists. People like the owner of the general store, however, always gave us cold, steely stares. They disliked and despised Zhenzhen. They even treated me as someone not of their kind. This was especially true of the women, who, all because of Zhenzhen, became extremely self-righteous, perceiving themselves as saintly and pure. They were proud about never having been raped. 83

After Agui left the village, I grew even closer to Zhenzhen. It seemed that neither of us could be without the other. As soon as we were apart, we thought of each other. I like people who are enthusiastic and lively, who can be really happy or sad, and at the same time are straightforward and candid. Zhenzhen was just such a person. Our conversations took up a great deal of time, but I always felt that they were beneficial to my studies and to my personal growth. As the days went by, however, I discovered that Zhenzhen was not being completely open about something. I did not resent this. Moreover, I was determined not to touch upon this secret of hers. All people have things buried deeply in their hearts that they don't want to tell others. This secret was a matter of private emotions. It had nothing to do with other people or with Zhenzhen's own morality. 84

A few days before my departure, Zhenzhen suddenly began to appear very agitated. Nothing special seemed to have happened, and she showed no desire to talk to me about anything new. Yet she frequently came to my room looking disturbed and restless, and after sitting for a few minutes, she would get up and leave. I knew she had not eaten well for several days and was often passing up meals. I had asked her about her disease and knew that the cause of her uneasiness was not simply physical. Sometimes, after coming to my room, she would make a few disjointed remarks. At other times, she put on an attentive expression, as if asking me to talk. But I could see that her thoughts were elsewhere, on things that she didn't want others to know. She was trying to conceal her emotions by acting as if nothing was wrong. 85

Twice I saw that capable young man come out of Zhenzhen's home. I had already compared my impression of him with Zhenzhen, and I sympathized with him deeply. Zhenzhen had been abused by many men, and had contracted a stigmatized, hard-to-cure disease, but he still patiently 86 came to see her and still sought the approval of her parents to marry her. He didn't look down on her. He did not fear the derision or the rebukes of others. He must have felt she needed him more than ever. He understood what kind of attitude a man should have toward the woman of his choice at such a time and what his responsibilities were.

But what of Zhenzhen? Although naturally there were many aspects of her emotions and her sorrows that I had not learned during this short period, she had never expressed any hope that a man would marry her or, if you will, comfort her. I thought she had become so hard because she had been hurt so badly. She seemed not to want anything from anyone. It would be good if love, some extraordinarily sympathetic commiseration, could warm her soul. I wanted her to find a place where she could cry this out. I was hoping for a chance to attend a wedding in this family. At the very least, I wanted to hear of an agreement to marry before I left. 87

"What is Zhenzhen thinking of?" I asked myself. "This can't be delayed indefinitely, and it shouldn't be turned into a big problem." 88

One day Liu Erma, her daughter-in-law, and her young daughter all came to see me. I was sure they intended to give me a report on something, but when they started to speak, I didn't allow them the opportunity to tell me anything. If my friend wouldn't confide in me, and I wouldn't ask her about it directly, then I felt it would be harmful to her, to myself, and to our friendship to ask others about it. 89

That same evening at dusk, the courtyard was again filled with people milling about. All the neighbors were there, whispering to one another. Some looked sad, but there were also those who appeared to find it all exciting. The weather was frigid, but curiosity warmed their hearts. In the severe cold, they drew in their shoulders, hunched their backs, thrust their hands into their sleeves, puffed out their breath, and looked at each other as if they were investigating something very interesting. 90

At first all I heard was the sound of quarreling coming from Liu Dama's dwelling. Then I heard Liu Dama crying. This was followed by the sound of a man crying. As far as I could tell, it was Zhenzhen's father. Next came a crash of dishes breaking. Unable to bear it any longer, I pushed my way thought the curious onlookers and rushed inside. 91

"You've come at just the right time," Liu Erma said as she pulled me inside. "You talk to our Zhenzhen." 92

Zhenzhen's face was hidden by her long disheveled hair, but two wild eyes could still be seen peering out at the people gathered there. I walked over to her and stood beside her, but she seemed completely oblivious to my presence. Perhaps she took me as one of the enemy and not worth a moment's concern. Her appearance had changed so completely that I could hardly remember the liveliness, the bright pleasantness I had found in her before. She was like a cornered animal. She was like an evening goddess. Whom did she hate? Why was her expression so fierce? 93

"You're so heartless. You don't think about your mother and father at 94

all. You don't care how much I've suffered because of you in the last year."
Liu Dama pounded on the *kang* as she scolded her daughter, tears like
raindrops dropping to the *kang* or the floor and flowing down the contours
of her face. Several women had surrounded her and were preventing her
from coming down off the *kang*. It was frightening to see a person lose her
self-respect and allow all her feelings to come out in a blind rage. I thought
of telling her that such crying was useless, but at the same time, I realized
that nothing I could say now would make any difference.

Zhenzhen's father looked very weak and old. His hands hung down   95
limply. He was sighing deeply. Xia Dabao was seated beside him. There
was a helpless look in his eyes as he stared at the old couple.

"You must say something. Don't you feel sorry for your mother?"   96

"When the end of a road is reached, one must turn. After water has   97
flowed as far as it can, it must change direction. Aren't you going to change
at all? Why make yourself suffer?" The women were trying to persuade
Zhenzhen with such words.

I could see that this affair could not turn out the way that everyone was   98
hoping. Zhenzhen had shown me much earlier that she didn't want anyone's sympathy. She, in turn, had no sympathy for anyone else. She had
made her decision long ago and would not change. If people wanted to call
her stubborn, then so be it. With teeth tightly clenched, she looked ready
to stand up to all of them.

At last the others agreed to listen to me, and I asked Zhenzhen to come   99
to my room and rest. I told them that everything could be discussed later
that night. But when I led Zhenzhen out of the house, she did not follow
me to my room. Instead, she ran off up the hillside.

"That girl has big ideas."   100

"Humph! She looks down on us country folk."   101

"She's such a cheap little hussy and yet she puts on such airs. Xia Dabao   102
deserves it . . ."

These were some of the comments being made by the crowd in the   103
courtyard. Then, when they realized that there was no longer anything of
interest to see, the crowd drifted away.

I hesitated for a while in the courtyard before deciding to go up the   104
hillside myself. On the top of the hill were numerous graves set among the
pine trees. Broken stone tablets stood before them. No one was there. Not
even the sound of a falling leaf broke the stillness. I ran back and forth
calling Zhenzhen's name. What sounded like a response temporarily comforted my loneliness, but in an instant the vast silence of the hills became
even deeper. The colors of sunset had completely faded. All around me a
thin, smokelike mist rose silently and spread out to the middle slopes of
the hills, both nearby and in the distance. I was worried and sat down
weakly on a tombstone. Over and over I asked myself, "Should I go on up
the hill or wait for her here?" I was hoping that I could relieve Zhenzhen
of some of her distress.

At that moment I saw a shadow moving toward me from below. I 105 quickly saw that it was Xia Dabao. I remained silent, hoping that he wouldn't see me and would continue on up the hill, but he came straight at me. At last I felt that I had to greet him and called, "Have you found her? I still haven't seen her."

He walked over to me and sat down on the dry grass. He said nothing, 106 only stared into the distance. I felt a little uneasy. He really was very young. His eyebrows were long and thin. His eyes were quite large, but now they looked dull and lifeless. His small mouth was tightly drawn. Perhaps before it had been appealing, but now it was full of anguish, as if trying to hold in his pain. He had an honest-looking nose, but of what use was it to him now?

"Don't be sad," I said. "Maybe tomorrow everything will be all right. I'll 107 talk to her this evening."

"Tomorrow, tomorrow—she'll always hate me. I know that she hates 108 me." He spoke in a sad low voice that was slightly hoarse.

"No," I replied, searching my memory. "She has never shown me that 109 she hates anyone." This was not a lie.

"She wouldn't tell you. She wouldn't tell anyone. She won't forgive me 110 as long as she lives."

"Why should she hate you?" 111

"Of course—" he began. Suddenly he turned his face toward me and 112 looked at me intently. "Tell me," he said, "at that time I had nothing. Should I have encouraged her to run away with me? Is all of this my fault? Is it?"

He didn't wait for my answer. As if speaking to himself, he went on, "It 113 is my fault. Could anyone say that I did the right thing? Didn't I bring this harm to her? If I had been as brave as she, she never would have—I know her character. She'll always hate me. Tell me, what should I do? What would she want me to do? How can I make her happy? My life is worthless. Am I of even the slightest use to her? Can you tell me? I simply don't know what I should do. Ahhh! How miserable things are! This is worse than being captured by the Jap devils." Without a break, he continued to mumble on and on.

When I asked him to go back home with me, he stood up and we took 114 several steps together. Then he stopped and said that he had heard a sound coming from the very top of the hill. There was nothing to do but encourage him to go on up, and I watched until he had disappeared into the thick pines. Then I started back. By now it was almost completely dark. It was very late when I went to bed that night, but I still hadn't received any news. I didn't know what had happened to them.

Even before I ate breakfast the next morning, I finished packing my 115 suitcase. Comrade Ma had promised that he would be coming this day to help me move, and I was all prepared to return to the Political Department and then go on to [my next assignment]. The enemy was about to start another "mopping-up campaign," and my health would not permit me to remain in this area. Director Mo had said that the ill definitely had to be moved out first, but I felt uneasy. Should I try to stay? If I did, I could be a burden to others. What about leaving? If I went, would I ever be able to return? As I was sitting on my bedroll pondering these questions, I sensed someone slipping quietly into my room.

With a single thrust of her body, Zhenzhen jumped up onto the *kang* 116 and took a seat opposite me. I could see that her face was slightly swollen, and when I grasped her hands as she spread them over the fire, the heat that had made such an impression on me before once again distressed me. Then and there I realized how serious her disease was.

"Zhenzhen," I said, "I'm about to leave. I don't know when we'll meet 117 again. I hope you'll listen to your mother—"

"I have come to tell you," she interrupted, "that I'll be leaving tomorrow 118 too. I want to leave home as soon as possible."

"Really?" I asked. 119

"Yes," she said, her face again revealing that special vibrancy. "They've 120 told me to go in for medical treatment."

"Ah," I sighed, thinking that perhaps we could travel together. "Does 121 your mother know?"

"No, she doesn't know yet. But if I say that I'm going for medical 122 treatment and that after my disease is cured I'll come back, she'll be sure to let me go. Just staying at home doesn't have anything to offer, does it?"

At this moment I felt that she had a rare serenity about her. I recalled the 123 words that Xia Dabao had spoken to me the previous evening and asked her directly, "Has the problem of your marriage been resolved?"

"Resolved? Oh, well, it's all the same." 124

"Did you heed your mother's advice?" I still didn't dare express my 125 hopes for her. I didn't want to think of the image left in my mind by that young man. I was hoping that someday he would be happy.

"Why should I listen to what they say? Did they ever listen to me?" 126

"Well, are you really angry with them?" 127

There was no response. 128

"Well, then, do you really hate Xia Dabao?" 129

For a long time she did not reply. Then, in a very calm voice, she said, 130 "I can't say that I hate him. I just feel now that I'm someone who's diseased. It's a fact that I was abused by a large number of Jap devils. I don't remember the exact number. In any case, I'm unclean, and with such a black mark I don't expect any good fortune to come my way. I feel that living among strangers and keeping busy would be better than living at home where people know me. Now that they've approved sending me to [Yan'an] for treatment, I've been thinking about staying there and doing some studying. I hear it's a big place with lots of schools and that anyone can attend. It's better for each of us to go our own separate ways than it is to have everyone stay together in one place. I'm doing this for myself, but

I'm also doing it for the others. I don't feel that I owe anyone an apology. Neither do I feel especially happy. What I do feel is that after I go to [Yan'an], I'll be in a new situation, I will be able to start life fresh. A person's life is not just for one's father and mother, or even for oneself. Some have called me young, inexperienced, and bad-tempered. I don't dispute it. There are some things that I just have to keep to myself."

I was amazed. Something new was coming out of her. I felt that what she had said was really worth examining. There was nothing for me to do but express approval of her plan.   131

When I took my departure, Zhenzhen's family was there to see me off. She, however, had gone to the village office. I didn't see Xia Dabao before I left either.   132

I wasn't sad as I went away. I seemed to see the bright future that Zhenzhen had before her. The next day I would be seeing her again. That had been decided. And we would still be together for some time. As soon as Comrade Ma and I walked out the door of Zhenzhen's home, he told me of her decision and confirmed that what she had told me that morning would quickly come to pass.   133

Translated from the Chinese by Gary J. Bjorge

STUDY QUESTIONS

1. From the descriptions provided, what do you know about the character of the first-person narrator?
2. In her visit to Xia Village, the narrator comes upon an unexpected mystery. How does the use of the first-person narrator allow you to understand and be sympathetic to this mysterious woman, Zhenzhen?
3. What can we tell about the villagers from the way they respond to Zhenzhen's return?
4. "It's a real tragedy to be a woman." Explain how Zhenzhen's situation illustrates or controverts this position.

🌀 AI QING

Ai Qing (b. 1910) studied painting before he left his native Shanghai for Paris in 1929. He began writing poetry in Paris, joined the Association of Chinese Left-Wing Artists in Shanghai in 1932, and was imprisoned for his political beliefs. He wrote "Dayanhe—My Wet-Nurse" in prison. He became a leading figure in the Communist government of the People's Republic of China but was exiled to northeast China in 1958 for ideological disagreements. He was rehabilitated after seventeen years. Influenced by the French Symbolists, his fourteen books of poetry exhibit the turn away from classical Chinese forms to greater use of sensuous imagery and social address.

Dayanhe—My Wet-Nurse

Dayanhe, my wet-nurse:
Her name was the name of the village which gave her birth;
She was a child-bride:
My wet-nurse, Dayanhe.

I am the son of a landlord,   5
But I have been brought up on Dayanhe's milk:
The son of Dayanhe.
Raising me Dayanhe raised her own family;
I am one who was raised on your milk,
Oh Dayanhe, my wet-nurse.   10

Dayanhe, today, looking at the snow falling makes me think of
    you:
Your grass-covered, snow-laden grave,
The withered weeds on the tiled eaves of your shut-up house,
Your garden-plot, ten-foot square, and mortgaged,   15
Your stone seat just outside the gate, overgrown with moss,
Dayanhe, today, looking at the snow falling makes me think of
    you.

With your great big hands, you cradled me to your breast,
    soothing me;   20
After you had stoked the fire in the oven,
After you had brushed off the coal-ashes from your apron,
After you had tasted for yourself whether the rice was cooked,
After you had set the bowls of black soybeans on the black table,
After you had mended your sons' clothes, torn by thorns on   25
    the mountain ridge,
After you had bandaged the hand of your little son, nicked
    with a cleaver,
After you had squeezed to death, one by one, the lice on your
    children's shirts,   30
After you had collected the first egg of the day,
With your great big hands, you cradled me to your breast,
    soothing me.

I am the son of a landlord,
After I had taken all the milk you had to offer,   35
I was taken back to my home by the parents who gave me birth.
Ah, Dayanhe, why are you crying?

I was a newcomer to the parents who gave me birth!
I touched the red-lacquered, floral-carved furniture,
I touched the ornate brocade on my parents' bed,   40
I looked dumbly at the "Bless This House" sign above the
    door—which I couldn't read,
I touched the buttons on my new clothes, made of silk and
    mother-of-pearl,
I saw in my mother's arms a sister whom I scarcely knew,   45
I sat on a lacquered stool with a small brazier set underneath,
I ate white rice which had been milled three times.
Still, I was bashful and shy! Because I,
I was a newcomer to the parents who gave me birth.
Dayanhe, in order to survive,   50
After her milk had run dry,
She began to put those arms, arms that had cradled me, to
    work,
Smiling, she washed our clothes,
Smiling, she carried the vegetables, and rinsed them in the icy   55
    pond by the village,
Smiling, she sliced the turnips frozen through and through,
Smiling, she stirred the swill in the pigs' trough,
Smiling, she fanned the flames under the stove with the
    broiling meat,   60
Smiling, she carried the bailing baskets of beans and grain to
    the open square where they baked in the sun,
Dayanhe, in order to survive,
After the milk in her had run dry,
She put those arms, arms that had cradled me, to work.   65

Dayanhe was so devoted to her foster-child, whom she
    suckled;
At New Year's, she'd busy herself cutting winter-rice candy for
    him,
For him, who would steal off to her house by the village,   70
For him, who would walk up to her and call her "Mama",
Dayanhe, she would stick his drawing of Guan Yu, the war
    god, bright green and bright red, on the wall by the stove,
Dayanhe, how she would boast and brag to her neighbors
    about her foster-child.   75
Dayanhe, once she dreamt a dream she could tell no one,

In her dream, she was drinking a wedding toast to her
    foster-child,
Sitting in a resplendent hall bedecked with silk,
And the beautiful young bride called her affectionately,   80
    "Mother."
. . . .
Dayanhe, she was so devoted to her foster-child!

Dayanhe, in a dream from which she has not awakened, has
    died.   85
When she died, her foster-child was not at her side,
When she died, the husband who often beat her shed tears for
    her.
Her five sons each cried bitter tears,
When she died, feebly, she called out the name of her   90
    foster-child,
Dayanhe is dead:
When she died, her foster-child was not at her side.

Dayanhe, she went with tears in her eyes!
Along with forty-nine years, a lifetime of humiliation at the   95
    hands of the world,
Along with the innumerable sufferings of a slave,
Along with a two-bit casket and some bundles of rice-straw,
Along with a plot of ground to bury a casket in a few square
    feet,   100
Along with a handful of ashes, from paper money burned,
Dayanhe, she went with tears in her eyes.

But these are the things that Dayanhe did not know:
That her drunkard husband is dead,
That her eldest son became a bandit,   105
That her second died in the smoke of war,
That her third, her fourth, her fifth,
Live on, vilified by their teachers and their landlords,
And I—I write condemnations of this unjust world.
When I, after drifting about for a long time, went home   110
On the mountain ridge, in the wilds,
When I saw my brothers, we were closer than we were 6 or 7
    years ago,
This, this is what you, Dayanhe, calmly sleeping in repose,
This is what you do not know!   115

Dayanhe, today, your foster-child is in jail,
Writing a poem of praise, dedicated to you,

Dedicated to your spirit, purple shade under the brown soil,
Dedicated to your outstretched arms that embraced me,
Dedicated to your lips that kissed me,   120
Dedicated to your face, warm and soft, the color of earth,
Dedicated to your breasts that suckled me,
Dedicated to your sons, my brothers,
Dedicated to all of them on earth,
The wet-nurses like my Dayanhe, and all their sons,   125
Dedicated to Dayanhe, who loved me as she loved her own
    sons.

Dayanhe,
I am one who grew up suckling at your breasts,
Your son.   130
I pay tribute to you,
With all my love.

On a snowy morning, January 14, 1933
Translated from the Chinese by Eugene Chen Eoyang

STUDY QUESTIONS

1. In traditional China, wealthy women sometimes hired a new mother as
   a nurse for their children. Part of the duties of these "wet-nurses" was
   to provide milk for their employers' babies. In this poem, the speaker
   identifies himself as "the son of a landlord." He notes, however, that
   he had been "brought up" on the milk of a peasant woman. Is the
   relationship between the poet and Dayanhe presented as strictly economic? If not, what else is it?
2. What contrasts does the poem draw between the poet's parental home
   and the setting for Dayanhe's life? What can you infer from the speaker's attitudes toward each of them?
3. Is Dayanhe's life presented as futile and defeated or as purposeful and
   heroic? What place and value does work have in such a life?
4. "Dayanhe—My Wet-Nurse" suggests some of the philosophical and
   cultural transformations that Chinese intellectuals undertook in response to China's modernization from a feudalistic society to a more
   egalitarian nation. Discuss how this poem articulates this particular
   historical moment in Chinese history.

Bei Dao

Bei Dao, born in Beijing in 1949, is a graduate of a senior middle school.
During the Cultural Revolution, which began in the mid-1960s and had begun
to dissipate by the end of the decade, he was a member of the Red Guards, the
young activists who engaged in the sociopolitical upheavals. He worked as a
forger of iron tools and began writing poetry in 1970. He helped set up the
magazine Jintian (Today) *and became a voice for the disillusionment and*
personal pain that followed the Cultural Revolution's collapse. His poetry,
criticized by cultural officials as being obscure and too private, uses strategies
of juxtaposition and indeterminacy to open up questions on social issues.
"Notes from the City of the Sun" comes from the book of the same name,
published in English in 1983.

Notes from the City of the Sun

    Life
The sun has risen too

    Love
Tranquillity. The wild geese have flown
over the virgin wasteland   5
the old tree has toppled, with a crash
acrid, salty rain drifts through the air

    Freedom
Torn scraps of paper
fluttering   10

    Child
A picture holding the whole ocean
is folded into a white crane

    Girl
A shimmering rainbow   15
gathers brightly colored birds' feathers

    Youth
Red waves
soak a solitary oar

        Art
A million scintillating suns
appear in a shattered mirror

        People
The moon is torn into gleaming grains of wheat
and sown in the honest sky and earth   25

        Labor
A pair of hands, encircling the earth

        Fate
A child strikes at random at a railing
The railing strikes at random at the night   30

        Faith
A flock of sheep spills into a green ditch
the shepherd boy pipes his monotonous tune

        Peace
In the land where the king is dead   35
the old rifle sprouts branches and new shoots
and becomes a cripple's cane

        Motherland
Cast on a shield of bronze
she leans against a darkening museum wall   40

        Living
A net

Translated from the Chinese by Bonnie S. McDougall

STUDY QUESTIONS

1. "Notes from the City of the Sun" is composed of a series of images
   attached to a number of common but large abstractions such as life,
   love, and freedom. Some of these images appear straightforward and
   simple: "Life / The sun has risen too" and "Labor / A pair of hands,
   encircling the earth." Some are more complex and suggest ambivalent
   or ambiguous attitudes. What are the possible meanings in the images
   associated with Freedom, Fate, and Motherland?
2. The images for child and girl appeal to the romantic senses. In Chinese
   mythology, the white crane is a symbol of long life. How is a child like

a picture holding the whole ocean, and how does this image relate to
the origami of a white crane?
3. How does the last image relate to the romantic and optimistic elements
of the poem's other images?
4. Examine the poem as a post–Cultural Revolution expression and point
out and discuss its various images that suggest oblique social and
political commentary.

 CAN XUE

*Can Xue, also known as Deng Xiao-hua (b. 1953), was born in Hunan
Province. In 1957, her parents were condemned as ultra-Rightists. In 1959,
the family of nine was moved to a tiny hut at the foot of Yueyusban
Mountain. Can Xue graduated from grade school in 1966, early in the
Cultural Revolution, and went to work in a factory for ten years. After her
marriage in 1978, she and her husband established themselves as tailors. "Hut
on the Mountain" is from her first collection of short stories in English
translation,* Dialogues in Paradise *(1989). It falls in the tradition of
allegorical treatments that express a criticism of China's social and political
failures.*

Hut on the Mountain

On the bleak and barren mountain behind our house stood a wooden 1
hut.

Day after day I busied myself by tidying up my desk drawers. When I 2
wasn't doing that I would sit in the armchair, my hands on my knees,
listening to the tumultuous sounds of the north wind whipping against the
fir-bark roof of the hut, and the howling of the wolves echoing in the
valleys.

"Huh, you'll never get done with those drawers," said Mother, forcing 3
a smile. "Not in your lifetime."

"There's something wrong with everyone's ears," I said with sup- 4
pressed annoyance. "There are so many thieves wandering about our
house in the moonlight, when I turn on the light I can see countless tiny
holes poked by fingers in the windowscreens. In the next room, Father and
you snore terribly, rattling the utensils in the kitchen cabinet. Then I kick
about in my bed, turn my swollen head on the pillow and hear the man

locked up in the hut banging furiously against the door. This goes on till daybreak."

"You give me a terrible start," Mother said, "every time you come into 5 my room looking for things." She fixed her eyes on me as she backed toward the door. I saw the flesh of one of her cheeks contort ridiculously.

One day I decided to go up to the mountain to find out what on earth 6 was the trouble. As soon as the wind let up, I began to climb. I climbed and climbed for a long time. The sunshine made me dizzy. Tiny white flames were flickering among the pebbles. I wandered about, coughing all the time. The salty sweat from my forehead was streaming into my eyes. I couldn't see or hear anything. When I reached home, I stood outside the door for a while and saw that the person reflected in the mirror had mud on her shoes and dark purple pouches under her eyes.

"It's some disease," I heard them snickering in the dark. 7

When my eyes became adapted to the darkness inside, they'd hidden 8 themselves—laughing in their hiding places. I discovered they had made a mess of my desk drawers while I was out. A few dead moths and dragonflies were scattered on the floor—they knew only too well that these were treasures to me.

"They sorted the things in the drawers for you," little sister told me, 9 "when you were out." She stared at me, her left eye turning green.

"I hear wolves howling," I deliberately tried to scare her. "They keep 10 running around the house. Sometimes they poke their heads in through the cracks in the door. These things always happen after dusk. You get so scared in your dreams that cold sweat drips from the soles of your feet. Everyone in this house sweats this way in his sleep. You have only to see how damp the quilts are."

I felt upset because some of the things in my desk drawers were miss- 11 ing. Keeping her eyes on the floor, Mother pretended she knew nothing about it. But I had a feeling she was glaring ferociously at the back of my head since the spot would become numb and swollen whenever she did that. I also knew they had buried a box with my chess set by the well behind the house. They had done it many times, but each time I would drag the chess set out. When I dug for it, they would turn on the light and poke their heads out the window. In the face of my defiance they always tried to remain calm.

"Up there on the mountain," I told them at mealtime, "there is a hut." 12

They all lowered their heads, drinking soup noisily. Probably no one 13 heard me.

"Lots of big rats were running wildly in the wind," I raised my voice and 14 put down the chopsticks. "Rocks were rolling down the mountain and crashing into the back of our house. And you were so scared cold sweat dripped from your soles. Don't you remember? You only have to look at your quilts. Whenever the weather's fine, you're airing the quilts; the clothesline out there is always strung with them."

Father stole a glance at me with one eye, which, I noticed, was the   15
all-too-familiar eye of a wolf. So that was it! At night he became one of the
wolves running around the house, howling and wailing mournfully.

"White lights are swaying back and forth everywhere." I clutched Moth-   16
er's shoulder with one hand. "Everything is so glaring that my eyes blear
from the pain. You simply can't see a thing. But as soon as I return to my
room, sit down in my armchair, and put my hands on my knees, I can see
the fir-bark roof clearly. The image seems very close. In fact, every one of
us must have seen it. Really, there's somebody squatting inside. He's got
two big purple pouches under his eyes, too, because he stays up all night."

Father said, "Every time you dig up the well and hit stone with a screech-   17
ing sound, you make Mother and me feel as if we were hanging in midair.
We shudder at the sound and kick with bare feet but can't reach the
ground." To avoid my eyes, he turned his face toward the window, the
panes of which were thickly specked with fly droppings.

"At the bottom of the well," he went on, "there's a pair of scissors   18
which I dropped some time ago. In my dreams I always make up my mind
to fish them out. But as soon as I wake, I realize I've made a mistake. In
fact, no scissors have ever fallen into the well. Your mother says positively
that I've made a mistake. But I will not give up. It always steals into my
mind again. Sometimes while I'm in bed, I am suddenly seized with regret:
the scissors lie rusting at the bottom of the well, why shouldn't I go fish
them out? I've been troubled by this for dozens of years. See my wrinkles?
My face seems to have been furrowed. Once I actually went to the well and
tried to lower a bucket into it. But the rope was thick and slippery. Suddenly my hands lost their grip and the bucket flopped with a loud boom,
breaking into pieces in the well. I rushed back to the house, looked into the
mirror, and saw the hair on my left temple had turned completely white."

"How that north wind pierces!" I hunched my shoulders. My face   19
turned black and blue with cold. "Bits of ice are forming in my stomach.
When I sit down in my armchair I can hear them clinking away."

I had been intending to give my desk drawers a cleaning, but Mother   20
was always stealthily making trouble. She'd walk to and fro in the next
room, stamping, stamping, to my great distraction. I tried to ignore it, so
I got a pack of cards and played, murmuring "one, two, three, four,
five. . . ."

The pacing stopped all of a sudden and Mother poked her small dark   21
green face into the room and mumbled, "I had a very obscene dream. Even
now my back is dripping cold sweat."

"And your soles, too," I added. "Everyone's soles drip cold sweat. You   22
aired your quilt again yesterday. It's usual enough."

Little sister sneaked in and told me that Mother had been thinking of   23
breaking my arms because I was driving her crazy by opening and shutting
the drawers. She was so tortured by the sound that every time she heard
it, she'd soak her head in cold water until she caught a bad cold.

"This didn't happen by chance." Sister's stares were always so pointed 24
that tiny pink measles broke out on my neck. "For example, I've heard
Father talking about the scissors for perhaps twenty years. Everything has
its own cause from way back. Everything."

So I oiled the sides of the drawers. And by opening and shutting them 25
carefully, I managed to make no noise at all. I repeated this experiment for
many days and the pacing in the next room ceased. She was fooled. This
proves you can get away with anything as long as you take a little precaution. I was very excited over my success and worked hard all night. I was
about to finish tidying up my drawers when the light suddenly went out.
I heard Mother's sneering laugh in the next room.

"That light from your room glares so that it makes all my blood vessels 26
throb and throb, as though some drums were beating inside. Look," she
said, pointing to her temple, where the blood vessels bulged like fat earth-
worms. "I'd rather get scurvy. There are throbbings throughout my body
day and night. You have no idea how I'm suffering. Because of this ailment, your father once thought of committing suicide." She put her fat
hand on my shoulder, an icy hand dripping with water.

Someone was making trouble by the well. I heard him letting the bucket 27
down and drawing it up, again and again; the bucket hit against the wall
of the well—boom, boom, boom. At dawn, he dropped the bucket with a
loud bang and ran away. I opened the door of the next room and saw
Father sleeping with his vein-ridged hand clutching the bedside, groaning
in agony. Mother was beating the floor here and there with a broom; her
hair was disheveled. At the moment of daybreak, she told me, a huge
swarm of hideous beetles flew in through the window. They bumped
against the walls and flopped onto the floor, which now was scattered with
their remains. She got up to tidy the room, and as she was putting her feet
into her slippers, a hidden bug bit her toe. Now her whole leg was swollen
like a thick lead pipe.

"He," Mother pointed to Father, who was sleeping stuporously, "is 28
dreaming it is he who is bitten."

"In the little hut on the mountain, someone is groaning, too. The black 29
wind is blowing, carrying grape leaves along with it."

"Do you hear?" In the faint light of morning, Mother put her ear against 30
the floor, listening with attention. "These bugs hurt themselves in their fall
and passed out. They charged into the room earlier, at the moment of
daybreak."

I did go up to the mountain that day, I remember. At first I was sitting 31
in the cane chair, my hands on my knees. Then I opened the door and
walked into the white light. I climbed up the mountain, seeing nothing but
the white pebbles glowing with flames.

There were no grapevines, nor any hut. 32

Translated from the Chinese by Ronald R. Janssen
and Jian Zhang

1. Describe the narrator's relations with her family members. How are her relationships different from the idealized constructions of the family in your society?
2. The father has an obsessive dream of retrieving a pair of scissors from the bottom of the well. What criticism of the older generation, the generation that participated in the Communist Revolution, can you read into this passage?
3. What is the mother's response to the daughter's actions, that is, to her intellectual activism? Does the story present the mother's character in a realistic way? Explain your answer.
4. How is the narrator different from her parents and sister? What criticisms of Chinese society are expressed through her thoughts, actions, and point of view?
5. What is the symbolic function of the hut on the mountain? Discuss the significance of the story's conclusion.

 WANG XIAONI

The literary career of Wang Xiaoni (b. 1955) illustrates the politically charged nature of writing in late-twentieth-century China. A graduate of Jilin University in northern China, she is a member of the Chinese Writers Association of Jilin. Because of ideological differences with the state authorities, she and her husband, the poet and critic Xu Jingya, were unable to find jobs in Jilin. As a result, they are now living in Guangdong Province in southern China.

Dark Night on a Southbound Train

On this night
dark as pitch
countless black wheels
pump through
invisible space.   5

I stretch
out all
my fingers
yet can't feel
any familiar breath.   10
Without that pair of hands
even a burning match
seems quite dark.
Nothing here
but my all-black valise   15
and the long
night.

Closing my eyes
I salute
the blue door   20
with my imagination.
A greeting from anyone
kind enough to penetrate
this dark night
would make the mountains, rivers   25
and roads all glisten.

Translated from the Chinese by Fang Dai, Dennis Ding,
and Edward Morin

STUDY QUESTIONS

1. "Dark Night on a Southbound Train" expresses some of the emotions
   of a political refugee. What emotions accompany the speaker on her
   journey south?
2. What is suggested in the image of the "blue door"? How does the color
   blue work in this poem?
3. What does the speaker hope for in requesting "a greeting from anyone"?

I N D I A

R. K. NARAYAN

R(asipuram) K(rishnaswami) Narayan (b. 1906) is the author of many novels and short stories. Most of his writing is set in the fictional town of Malgudi in his native state of Mysore. Narayan writes in English, and his short stories, most of which were first published in the Madras Hindu, *are intended for Indians who read English. He is often praised for his lucid, informal use of English and for his depiction of characters whose idiosyncratic illusions show up a richly peopled and distinctively Hindu world.*

Gateman's Gift

When a dozen persons question openly or slyly a man's sanity, he begins to entertain serious doubts himself. This is what happened to ex-gateman Govind Singh. And you could not blame the public either. What could you do with a man who carried about in his hand a registered postal envelope and asked, "Please tell me what there is inside"? The obvious answer was: "Open it and see. . . ." He seemed horrified at this suggestion. "Oh, no, no, can't do it," he declared, and moved off to another friend and acquaintance. Everywhere the suggestion was the same, till he thought everyone had turned mad. And then somebody said, "If you don't like to open it and yet want to know what is inside you must take it to the X-ray Institute." This was suggested by an ex-compounder who lived in the next street.

"What is it?" asked Govind Singh. It was explained to him. "Where is it?" He was directed to the City X-ray Institute.

But before saying anything further about his progress, it would be useful to go back to an earlier chapter in his history. After war service in 1914–18, he came to be recommended for a gatekeeper's post at Engladia's. He liked the job very much. He was given a khaki uniform, a resplendent band across his shoulder and a short stick. He gripped the stick and sat down on a stool at the entrance to the office. And when his chief's car pulled up at the gate he stood at attention and gave a military salute. The office consisted of a staff numbering over a hundred, and as they trooped in and out every day he kept an eye on them. At the end of the day he awaited the footsteps of the General Manager coming down the stairs, and rose stiffly and stood at attention, and after he left, the hundreds of staff poured out. The doors were shut; Singh carried his stool in, placed it under the staircase and placed his stick across it. Then he came out and the main door was locked and sealed. In this way he had spent twenty-five years of service, and then he begged to be pensioned off. He would not have thought of retirement yet, but for the fact that he found his sight and hearing playing tricks on him; he could not catch the Manager's footsteps on the stairs, and it was hard to recognize him even at ten yards. He was ushered into the presence of the chief, who looked up for a moment from his papers and muttered, "We are very pleased with your work for us, and the company will give you a pension of twelve rupees for life. . . ." Singh clicked his heels, saluted, turned on his heel and went out of the room, his heart brimming with gratitude and pride. This was the second occasion when the great man had spoken to him, the first being on the first day of his service. As he had stood at his post, the chief, entering the office just then, looked up for a moment and asked, "Who are you?"

"I'm the new gatekeeper, master," he had answered. And he spoke 4 again only on this day. Though so little was said, Singh felt electrified on both occasions by the words of his master. In Singh's eyes the chief had acquired a sort of godhood, and it would be quite adequate if a god spoke to one only once or twice in a lifetime. In moments of contemplation Singh's mind dwelt on the words of his master, and on his personality.

His life moved on smoothly. The pension together with what his wife 5 earned by washing and sweeping in a couple of houses was quite sufficient for him. He ate his food, went out and met a few friends, slept and spent some evenings sitting at a cigarette shop which his cousin owned. This tenor of life was disturbed on the first of every month when he donned his old khaki suit, walked to his old office and salaamed the accountant at the counter and received his pension. Sometimes if it was closing he waited on the roadside for the General Manager to come down, and saluted him as he got into his car.

There was a lot of time all around him, an immense sea of leisure. In this 6 state he made a new discovery about himself, that he could make fascinating models out of clay and wood dust. The discovery came suddenly, when one day a child in the neighbourhood brought to him its little doll for repair. He not only repaired it but made a new thing of it. This discovery pleased him so much that he very soon became absorbed in it. His back yard gave him a plentiful supply of pliant clay, and the carpenter's shop next to his cousin's cigarette shop sawdust. He purchased paint for a few annas.[1] And lo! he found his hours gliding. He sat there in the front part of his home, bent over his clay, and brought into existence a miniature universe; all the colours of life were there, all the forms and creatures, but of the size of his middle finger; whole villages and towns were there, all the persons he had seen passing before his office when he was sentry there— that beggar woman coming at midday, and that cucumber vendor; he had the eye of a cartoonist for human faces. Everything went down into clay. It was a wonderful miniature reflection of the world; and he mounted them neatly on thin wooden slices, which enhanced their attractiveness. He kept these in his cousin's shop and they attracted huge crowds every day and sold very briskly. More than from the sales Singh felt an ecstasy when he saw admiring crowds clustering around his handiwork.

On his next pension day he carried to his office a street scene (which he ranked as his best), and handed it over the counter to the accountant with the request: "Give this to the Sahib, please!" 7

"All right," said the accountant with a smile. It created a sensation in the office and disturbed the routine of office working for nearly half an hour. On the next pension day he carried another model (children at play) and handed it over the counter. 8

"Did the Sahib like the last one?" 9

"Yes, he liked it." 10

"Please give this one to him—" and he passed it over the counter. He made it a convention to carry on every pension day an offering for his master, and each time his greatest reward was the accountant's stock reply to his question: "What did the Sahib say?" 11

"He said it was very good." 12

At last he made his masterpiece. A model of his office frontage with himself at his post, a car at the entrance and the chief getting down: this composite model was so realistic that while he sat looking at it, he seemed to be carried back to his office days. He passed it over the counter on his pension day and it created a very great sensation in the office. "Fellow, you have not left yourself out, either!" people cried, and looked admiringly at Singh. A sudden fear seized Singh and he asked, "The master won't be angry, I hope?" 13

"No, no, why should he be?" said the accountant, and Singh received his pension and went home. 14

A week later when he was sitting on the *pyol* kneading clay, the postman came and said, "A registered letter for you. . . ." 15

"For me!" Any letter would have upset Singh; he had received less than three letters in his lifetime, and each time it was a torture for him till the contents were read out. Now a registered letter! This was his first registered letter. "Only lawyers send registered letters, isn't it so?" 16

---

1. *An anna is roughly equivalent to a penny.*

"Usually," said the postman.   17

"Please take it back. I don't want it," said Singh.   18

"Shall I say 'Refused'?" asked the postman. "No, no," said Singh. "Just   19
take it back and say you have not found me. . . ."

"That I can't do. . . ." said the postman, looking serious.   20

Singh seemed to have no option but to scrawl his signature and receive   21
the packet. He sat gloomily—gazing at the floor. His wife who had gone
out and just returned saw him in this condition and asked, "What is it?"
His voice choked as he replied, "It has come." He flung at her the registered letter. "What is it?" she asked. He said, "How should I know. Perhaps our ruin . . ." He broke down. His wife watched him for a moment,
went in to attend to some domestic duty and returned, still found him in
the same condition and asked, "Why not open it and see, ask someone to
read it?" He threw up his arms in horror. "Woman, you don't know what
you are saying. It cannot be opened. They have perhaps written that my
pension is stopped, and God knows what else the Sahib has said. . . ."

"Why not go to the office and find out from them?"   22

"Not I! I will never show my face there again," said Singh. "I have lived   23
without a single remark being made against me, all my life. Now!" He
shuddered at the thought of it. "I knew I was getting into trouble when I
made that office model. . . ." After deeper reflection he said, "Every time
I took something there, people crowded round, stopped all work for nearly
an hour. . . . That must also have reached the Sahib's ears."

He wandered about saying the same thing, with the letter in his pocket.   24
He lost his taste for food, wandered about unkempt, with his hair standing
up like a halo—an unaccustomed sight, his years in military service having
given him a habitual tidiness. His wife lost all peace of mind and became
miserable about him. He stood at crossroads, clutching the letter in his
hand. He kept asking everyone he came across, "Tell me, what is there in
this?" but he would not brook the suggestion to open it and see its contents.

So forthwith Singh found his way to the City X-ray Institute at Race   25
Course Road. As he entered the gate he observed dozens of cars parked
along the drive, and a Gurkha watchman at the gate. Some people were
sitting on sofas reading books and journals. They turned and threw a brief
look at him and resumed their studies. As Singh stood uncertainly at the
doorway, an assistant came up and asked, "What do you want?" Singh
gave a salute, held up the letter uncertainly and muttered, "Can I know
what is inside this?" The assistant made the obvious suggestion. But Singh
replied, "They said you could tell me what's inside without opening it—"
The assistant asked, "Where do you come from?" Singh explained his life,
work and outlook, and concluded, "I've lived without remark all my life.
I knew trouble was coming—" There were tears on his cheeks. The assistant looked at him curiously as scores of others had done before, smiled
and said, "Go home and rest. You are not all right. . . . Go, go home."

"Can't you say what is in this?" Singh asked pathetically. The assistant   26 took it in his hand, examined it and said, "Shall I open it?" "No, no, no," Singh cried, and snatched it back. There was a look of terror in his eyes. The assembly looked up from their pages and watched him with mild amusement in their eyes. The assistant kindly put his arms on his shoulder and let him out. "You get well first, and then come back. I tell you—you are not all right."

Walking back home, he pondered over it. "Why are they all behaving   27 like this, as if I were a madman?" When this word came to his mind, he stopped abruptly in the middle of the road and cried, "Oh! That's it, is that it?—Mad! Mad!" He shook his head gleefully as if the full truth had just dawned upon him. He now understood the looks that people threw at him. "Oh! oh!" he cried aloud. He laughed. He felt a curious relief at this realization. "I have been mad and didn't know it. . . ." He cast his mind back. Every little action of his for the last so many days seemed mad; particularly the doll-making. "What sane man would make clay dolls after twenty-five years of respectable service in an office?" He felt a tremendous freedom of limbs, and didn't feel it possible to walk at an ordinary pace. He wanted to fly. He swung his arms up and down and ran on with a whoop. He ran through the Market Road. When people stood about and watched he cried, "Hey, don't laugh at a madman, for who knows, you will also be mad when you come to make clay dolls," and charged into their midst with a war cry. When he saw children coming out of school, he felt it would be nice to amuse their young hearts by behaving like a tiger. So he fell on his hands and knees and crawled up to them with a growl.

He went home in a terrifying condition. His wife, who was grinding chilli   28 in the back yard, looked up and asked, "What is this?" His hair was covered with street dust; his body was splashed with mud. He could not answer because he choked with mirth as he said, "Fancy what has happened!"

"What is it?"   29

"I'm mad, mad." He looked at his work-basket in the corner, scooped   30 out the clay and made a helmet of it and put it on his head. Ranged on the floor was his latest handiwork. After his last visit to the office he had been engaged in making a model village. It was a resplendent group: a dun road, red tiles, green coconut trees swaying, and the colour of the saris of the village women carrying water pots. He derived the inspiration for it from a memory of his own village days. It was the most enjoyable piece of work that he had so far undertaken. He lived in a kind of ecstasy while doing it. "I am going to keep this for myself. A memento of my father's village," he declared. "I will show it at an exhibition, where they will give me a medal." He guarded it like a treasure: when it was wet he never allowed his wife to walk within ten yards of it. "Keep off, we don't want your foot dust for this village. . . ."

Now, in his madness, he looked down on it. He raised his foot and   31 stamped everything down into a multicoloured jam. They were still half-wet. He saw a donkey grazing in the street. He gathered up the jam and flung it at the donkey with the remark: "Eat this if you like. It is a nice village. . . ." And he went out on a second round. This was a quieter outing. He strode on at an even pace, breathing deeply, with the clay helmet on, out of which peeped his grey hair, his arms locked behind, his fingers clutching the fateful letter, his face tilted towards the sky. He walked down the Market Road, with a feeling that he was the sole occupant of this globe: his madness had given him a sense of limitless freedom, strength and buoyancy. The remarks and jeers of the crowds gaping at him did not in the least touch him.

While he walked thus, his eye fell on the bulb of a tall street lamp. "Bulb of the size of a papaya fruit!" he muttered and chuckled. It had been a long cherished desire in him to fling a stone at it; now he felt, in his joyous and free condition, that he was free from the trammels of conventions and need not push back any inclination. He picked up a pebble and threw it with good aim. The shattering noise of glass was as music to his ears. A policeman put his hand on his shoulder. "Why did you do it?" Singh looked indignant. "I like to crack glass papaya fruit, that is all," was the reply. The constable said, "Come to the station." 32

"Oh, yes, when I was in Mesopotamia they put me on half-ration once," he said, and walked on to the station. He paused, tilted his head to the side and remarked, "This road is not straight. . . ." A few carriages and cycles were coming up to him. He found that everything was wrong about them. They seemed to need some advice in the matter. He stopped in the middle of the road, stretched out his arms and shouted, "Halt!" The carriages stopped, the cyclists jumped off and Singh began a lecture: "When I was in Mesopotamia—I will tell you fellows who don't know anything about anything." The policeman dragged him away to the side and waved to the traffic to resume. One of the cyclists who resumed jumped off the saddle again and came towards him with, "Why! It is Singh. Singh, what fancy dress is this? What is the matter?" Even through the haze of his insane vision Singh could recognize the voice and the person—the accountant at the office. Singh clicked his heels and gave a salute. "Excuse me, sir, didn't intend to stop you. You may pass. . . ." He pointed the way generously, and the accountant saw the letter in his hand. He recognized it although it was mud-stained and crumpled. 33

"Singh, you got our letter?" 34

"Yes, sir—Pass. Do not speak of it. . . ." 35

"What is the matter?" He snatched it from his hand. "Why haven't you opened it!" He tore open the envelope and took out of it a letter and read aloud: "The General Manager greatly appreciates the very artistic models you have sent, and he is pleased to sanction a reward of 100 rupees and hopes it will be an encouragement for you to keep up this interesting hobby." 36

It was translated to him word for word, and the enclosure, a cheque for one hundred rupees, was handed to him. A big crowd gathered to watch this scene. Singh pressed the letter to his eyes. He beat his brow and wailed, "Tell me, sir, am I mad or not?" 37

"You look quite well, you aren't mad," said the accountant. Singh fell at his feet and said with tears choking his voice, "You are a god, sir, to say that I am not mad. I am so happy to hear it." 38

On the next pension day he turned up spruce as ever at the office counter. As they handed him the envelope they asked, "What toys are you making now?" 39

"Nothing, sir. Never again. It is no occupation for a sane man. . . ." he said, received his pension and walked stiffly out of the office. 40

STUDY QUESTIONS

1. Describe the life that Govind Singh led up to the time of his retirement. What can you infer about his personality from this portrayal?
2. How is Singh's "play" with clay and wood dust different from his previous work?
3. Why would Singh be intimidated by a registered letter? How does his fear affect him?
4. Singh abandons his avocation of making models after he discovers that the registered letter contains a reward from the General Manager for his last model. What criticism of Indian social and economic conservatism is the story voicing through Singh's "madness" and return to "sanity"?

 AMRITA PRITAM

Amrita Pritam (b. 1919) is an acclaimed writer who has published over sixty books of poetry and prose, including The Revenue Stamps: An Autobiography *(1983). She has received numerous national prizes, and her work has been widely translated from the Panjabi. Born in what is now Pakistan, Pritam is also a political figure. In her own life and work, Pritam exhibits the paradigm of the woman coming to her own subject condition through her struggle for independent creation and self-expression.*

Amrita Pritam

There was a pain
I inhaled it
Silently,

Like a cigarette.
There are a few songs
I've flicked off
Like ashes
From the cigarette.

Translator unknown

STUDY QUESTIONS

1. The poem constructs a portrait of the speaker through the symbol of
   the cigarette. In traditional India, a woman smoking a cigarette is still
   a strikingly modern image. How are the separate notions of pain and
   songs related through this symbol?
2. The poem has an air of casualness, yet it asserts indirectly a condition
   of being. Discuss the attitudes and experiences suggested in the narrator's actions of inhaling and flicking.

 NISSIM EZEKIEL

*Nissim Ezekiel was born in Bombay in 1924, and except for brief visits to
countries outside India, has lived there all his life. He has published over ten
books of poetry, including* Selected Poems 1965–75 *(1976). Ezekiel is an
Indian Jew who calls himself "a natural outsider [whose] circumstances and
decisions relate me to India." His poems possess a strong sense of form, a keen
intelligence, great sensuality, and, increasingly, a return to Judaic mysticism.*

Goodbye Party for
Miss Pushpa T. S.

Friends,
our dear sister
is departing for foreign
in two three days,
and   5

we are meeting today
to wish her bon voyage.

You are all knowing, friends,
what sweetness is in Miss Pushpa.
I don't mean only external sweetness   10
but internal sweetness.
Miss Pushpa is smiling and smiling
even for no reason
but simply because she is feeling.

Miss Pushpa is coming   15
from very high family.
Her father was renowned advocate
in Bulsar or Surat,
I am not remembering now which place.

Surat? Ah, yes,   20
once only I stayed in Surat
with family members
of my uncle's very old friend—
his wife was cooking nicely . . .
that was long time ago.   25

Coming back to Miss Pushpa
she is most popular lady
with men also and ladies also.

Whenever I asked her to do anything,
she was saying, 'Just now only   30
I will do it.' That is showing
good spirit. I am always
appreciating the good spirit.

Pushpa Miss is never saying no.
Whatever I or anybody is asking   35
she is always saying yes,
and today she is going
to improve her prospects
and we are wishing her bon voyage.

Now I ask other speakers to speak   40
and afterwards Miss Pushpa
will do the summing up.

1. What are some instances of the poem's use of Indian constructions of the English language? What is the effect of using such local idioms?
2. "Goodbye Party for Miss Pushpa T. S." is an address on the occasion of Miss Pushpa's departure from India. What inferences can be made from the address as to what kind of character the speaker is?
3. The speaker presents Miss Pushpa as "most popular lady." What kinds of qualities does the speaker impute to her, and what values would inform a society in which such qualities are esteemed?
4. Do you read the poem as a mild or a harsh critique of one class of Indian society? What evidence can you provide to support your reading?

 # Ruth Prawer Jhabvala

Ruth Prawer Jhabvala, born in Germany in 1927, married a Parsi and has lived in India since 1951. She also resides part of the time in the United States. Jhabvala is best known for her novels on contemporary India, but some people wonder if she is truly an Indian novelist. Her ironic, comic, and incisive examinations of Indian social relations (although from a Western sensibility), however, are generally accepted as among the best of Anglo-Indian writings. Her work constructs the details of a Westernized Indian culture and in the process fills in the nuances of a moral world that is distinctly her own vision of India. Her books include How I Became a Holy Mother and Other Stories *(1976) and* Out of India: Selected Stories.

The Interview

I am always very careful of my appearance, so you could not say that I spent much more time than usual over myself that morning. It is true, I trimmed and oiled my moustache, but then I often do that; I always like it to look very neat, like Raj Kapoor's, the film star's. But I knew my sister-in-law and my wife were watching me. My sister-in-law was smiling, and she had one hand on her hip; my wife only looked anxious. I knew she was anxious. All night she had been whispering to me. She had whispered, "Get this job and take me away to live somewhere alone, only you and I and our children." I had answered, "Yes," because I wanted to go to sleep. I don't know where and why she has taken this notion that we should go and live alone.

When I had finished combing my hair, I sat on the floor and my sister-in-law brought me my food on a tray. It may sound strange that my sister-in-law should serve me, and not my wife, but it is so in our house. It used to be my mother who brought me my food, even after I was married; she would never allow my wife to do this for me, though my wife wanted to very much. Then, when my mother got so old, my sister-in-law began to serve me. I know that my wife feels deeply hurt by this, but she doesn't dare to say anything. My mother doesn't notice many things anymore, otherwise she certainly would not allow my sister-in-law to bring me my food; she has always been very jealous of this privilege herself, though she never cared who served my brother. Now she has become so old that she can hardly see anything, and most of the time she sits in the corner by the family trunks and folds and strokes her pieces of cloth. For years now she has been collecting pieces of cloth. Some of them are very old and dirty, but she doesn't care, she loves them all equally. Nobody is allowed to touch them. Once there was a great quarrel, because my wife had taken one of them to make a dress for our child. My mother shouted at her—it was terrible to hear her: but then, she has never liked my wife—and my wife was very much afraid and cried and tried to excuse herself. I hit her across the face, not very hard and not because I wanted to, but only to satisfy my mother. The old woman kept quiet then and went back to folding and stroking her pieces of cloth.

All the time I was eating, I could feel my sister-in-law looking at me and smiling. It made me uncomfortable. I thought she might be smiling because she knew I wouldn't get the job for which I had to go and be interviewed. I also knew I wouldn't get it, but I didn't like her to smile like that. It was as if she were saying, "You see, you will always have to be dependent on us." It is clearly my brother's duty to keep me and my family until I can get work and contribute my own earnings to the family household. There is no need for her to smile about it. But it is true that I am more dependent on her now than on anyone else. Since my mother has got so old, my sister-in-law has become more and more the most important person in the house, so that she even keeps the keys and the household stores. At first I didn't like this. As long as my mother managed the household, I was sure of getting many extra tidbits. But now I find that my sister-in-law is also very kind to me—much more kind than she is to her husband. It is not for him that she saves the tidbits, nor for her children, but for me; and when she gives them to me, she never says anything and I never say anything, but she smiles and then I feel confused and rather embarrassed. My wife has noticed what she does for me.

I have found that women are usually kind to me. I think they realize that I am a rather sensitive person and that therefore I must be treated very gently. My mother has always treated me very gently. I am her youngest child, and I am fifteen years younger than my brother who is next to me (she did have several children in between us, but they all died). Right from the time when I was a tiny baby, she understood that I needed greater care and tenderness than other children. She always made me sleep close beside her in the night, and in the day I usually sat with her and my grandmother and my widowed aunt, who were also very fond of me. When I got bigger, my father sometimes wanted to take me to help in his stall (he had a little grocer's stall, where he sold lentils and rice and cheap cigarettes and colored drinks in bottles) but my mother and grandmother and aunt never liked to let me go. Once he did take me with him, and he made me pour some lentils out of paper bags into a tin. I rather liked pouring the lentils— they made such a nice noise as they landed in the tin—but suddenly my mother came and was very angry with my father for making me do this work. She took me home at once, and when she told my grandmother and aunt what had happened, they stroked me and kissed me and then they gave me a hot fritter to eat. The fact is, right from childhood I have been a person who needs a lot of peace and rest, and my food too has to be rather more delicate than that of other people. I have often tried to explain this to my wife, but as she is not very intelligent, she doesn't seem to understand.

Now my wife was watching me while I ate. She was squatting on the 5 floor, washing our youngest baby; the baby's head was in her lap, and all one could see of it was the back of its legs and its naked bottom. My wife did not watch me as openly as my sister-in-law did; only from time to time she raised her eyes to me, I could feel it, and they were very worried and troubled. She too was thinking about the job for which I was going to be interviewed, but she was anxious that I should get it. "We will go and live somewhere alone," she had said. Why did she say it? When she knows that it is not possible and never will be.

And even if it were possible, I would not like it. I can't live away from 6 my mother; and I don't think I would like to live away from my sister-in-law. I often look at her and it makes me happy. Even though she is not young anymore, she is still beautiful. She is tall, with big hips and big breasts and eyes that flash; she often gets angry, and when she is angry, she is the most beautiful of all. Then her eyes are like fire and she shows all her teeth, which are very strong and white, and her head is proud with the black hair flying loose. My wife is not beautiful at all. I was very disappointed in her when they first married me to her. Now I have got used to her and I even like her, because she is so good and quiet and never troubles me at all. I don't think anybody else in our house likes her. My sister-in-law always calls her "that beauty," but she does not mean it; and she makes her do all the most difficult household tasks, and often she shouts at her and even beats her. This is not right; my wife has never done anything to her—on the contrary, she always treats her with respect. But I cannot interfere in their quarrels.

Then I was ready to go, though I didn't want to go. I knew only too well   7
what would happen at the interview. My mother blessed me, and my
sister-in-law looked at me over her shoulder and her great eyes flashed
with laughter. I didn't look at my wife, who still sat squatting on the floor,
but I knew she was pleading with me to get the job like she had pleaded
in the night. As I walked down the stairs, the daughter of the carpenter,
who lives in one of the rooms on the lower floor, came out of her door and
she walked up the stairs as I walked down, and she passed very close
beside me, with her eyes lowered but her arm just touching my sleeve. She
always waits for me to come out and then she passes me on the stairs. We
have never spoken together. She is a very young girl, her breasts are only
just forming; her blouse has short sleeves and her arms are beautiful, long
and slender. I think soon she is to be married, I have heard my sister-in-law
say so. My sister-in-law laughed when she told me, she said, "It is high
time" and then she said something coarse. Perhaps she has noticed that
the girl waits for me to pass on the stairs.

No, I did not want to go to the interview. I had been to so many   8
during the last few months, and always the same things happened. I
know I have to work, in order to earn money and give it to my mother
or my sister-in-law for the household, but there is no pleasure for me in
the work. Last time I had work, it was in an insurance office and all day
they made me sit at a desk and write figures. What pleasure could there
be for me in that? I am a very thoughtful person, and I like always to sit
and think my own thoughts; but while I thought my own thoughts in the
office, I sometimes made mistakes over the figures and then my superiors were very angry with me. I was always afraid of their anger, and I
begged their forgiveness and admitted that I was much at fault. When
they forgave me, I was no longer afraid and I continued doing my work
and thinking my thoughts. But the last time they would not forgive me
again, though I begged and begged and cried what a faulty, bad man I
was and what good men they were, and how they were my mother and
my father and how I looked only to them for my life and the lives of my
children. But when they still said I must go, I saw that the work there
was really finished and I stopped crying. I went into the washroom and
combed my hair and folded my soap in my towel, and then I took my
money from the accountant without a word and I left the office with my
eyes lowered. But I was no longer afraid, because what is finished is
finished, and my brother still had work and probably one day I would
get another job.

Ever since then my brother has been trying to get me into government   9
service. He himself is a clerk in government service and enjoys many
advantages: every five years he gets an increase of ten rupees[1] in his salary

---

1. Rupees: *The rupee is the main unit of currency in India.*

and he has ten days sick leave in the year and when he retires he will get a pension. It would be good for me also to have such a job; but it is difficult to get, because first there is an interview at which important people sit at a desk and ask many questions. I am afraid of them, and I cannot understand properly what they are saying, so I answer what I think they want me to answer. But it seems that my answers are not after all the right ones, because up till now they have not given me a job.

On my way to this interview, I thought how much nicer it would be to go to the cinema instead. If I had had ten annas,[1] perhaps I would have gone; it was just time for the morning show. The young clerks and the students would be collecting in a queue outside the cinema now. They would be standing and not talking much, holding their ten annas and waiting for the box office to open. I enjoy these morning shows, perhaps because the people who come to them are all young men like myself, all silent and rather sad. I am often sad; it would even be right to say that I am sad most of the time. But when the film begins, I am happy. I love to see the beautiful women, dressed in golden clothes with heavy earrings and necklaces and bracelets covering their arms, and their handsome lovers who are all the things I would like to be. And when they sing their love songs, so full of deep feelings, the tears sometimes come into my eyes; but not because I am sad, no, on the contrary, because I am so happy. After the film is over, I never go home straightaway, but I walk around the streets and think about how wonderful life could be.

When I arrived at the place where the interview was, I had to walk down many corridors and ask directions from many peons before I could find the right room. The peons were all rude to me, because they knew what I had come for. They lounged on benches outside the offices, and when I asked them, they looked me up and down before answering, and sometimes they made jokes about me with one another. I was very polite to them, for even though they were only peons, they had uniforms and jobs and belonged here, and they knew the right way whereas I did not. At last I came to the room where I had to wait. Many others were already sitting there, on chairs that were drawn up all around the room against the wall. No one was talking. I also sat on a chair, and after a while an official came in with a list and he asked if anyone else had come. I got up and he asked my name, and then he looked down the list and made a tick with a pencil. He said to me very sternly, "Why are you late?" I begged pardon and told him the bus in which I had come had an accident. He said, "When you are called for interview, you have to be here exactly on time, otherwise your name is crossed off the list." I begged pardon again and asked him very humbly please not to cross me off this time. I knew that all the others were

10

11

---

1. Annas: *Copper coins equal to ¹⁄₁₆ of a rupee.*

listening, though none of them looked at us. He was very stern with me and even scornful, but in the end he said, "Wait here, and when your name is called, you must go in at once."

I did not count the number of people waiting in the room, but there were many. Perhaps there was one job free, perhaps two or three. I knew that all the others were very worried and anxious to get the job, so I became worried and anxious too. The walls of the room were painted green half-way up and white above that and were quite bare. There was a fan turning from the ceiling, but it was not turning fast enough to give much breeze. Behind the big door the interview was going on; one by one we would all be called in behind this closed door.

I began to worry desperately. It always happens like this. When I come to an interview, I don't want the job at all, but when I see all the others waiting and worrying, I want it terribly. Yet at the same time I know that I don't want it. It would only be the same thing over again: writing figures and making mistakes and then being afraid when they found out. And there would be a superior officer to whom I would have to be very defer-ential, and every time I saw him or heard his voice I would begin to be afraid that he had found out something against me. For weeks and months I would sit and write figures, getting wearier of it and wearier, so that more and more I would be thinking my own thoughts. Then the mistakes would come, and my superior officer would be angry and I afraid.

My brother never makes mistakes. For years he has been sitting in the same office, writing figures and being deferential to his superior officer; he concentrates very hard on his work, and so he doesn't make mistakes. But all the same he is afraid; that is why he concentrates so hard—because he is afraid that he will make a mistake and they will be angry with him and take away his job. He is afraid of this all the time. And he is right: what would become of us all if he also lost his job? It is not the same with me. I think I am afraid to lose my job only because that is a thing of which one is expected to be afraid. When I have actually lost it, I am really relieved. But I am very different from my brother; even in appearance I am very different. It is true, he is fifteen years older than I am, but even when he was my age, he never looked like I do. My appearance has always attracted others, and up to the time I was married, my mother used to stroke my hair and my face and say many tender things to me. Once, when I was walking on my way to school through the bazaar, a man called to me, very softly, and when I came he gave me a ripe mango, and then he took me into a dark passage that led to a disused mosque, and he touched me under my clothes and he said, "You are so nice, so nice." He was very kind to me. I love wearing fine clothes, very thin white muslin kurtas that have been freshly washed and starched and are embroidered at the shoulders. Some-times I also use scent, a fine khas smell; my hair oil also smells of khas. Some years ago, when the carpenter's daughter was still a small child and did not yet wait for me on the stairs, there was a girl living in the tailor's

12

13

14

shop opposite our house and she used to follow me when I went out. But it is my brother who is married to a beautiful wife, and my wife is not beautiful at all. He is not happy with his wife; when she talks to him, she talks in a hard scornful way; and it is not for him that she saves the best food, but for me, even though I have not brought money home for many months.

The big closed door opened and the man who had been in there for interview came out. We all looked at him, but he walked out in a great hurry, with a preoccupied expression on his face; probably he was going over in his mind all that had been said at the interview. I could feel the anxiety in the other men getting stronger, so mine got stronger too. The official with the list came and we all looked at him. He read out another name and the man whose name was called jumped up from his chair; he did not notice that his dhoti[1] had got caught on a nail in the chair and he wondered why he could not go farther. When he realized what had happened, he tried to disentangle himself, but his fingers shook so much that he could not get the dhoti off the nail. The official watched him and said, "Hurry, now, do you think the gentlemen will wait for you for as long as you please?" Then the man also dropped the umbrella he was carrying and now he was trying both to disentangle the dhoti and to pick up the umbrella. When he could not get the dhoti loose, he became so desperate that he tore at the cloth and ripped it free. It was a pity to see the dhoti torn because it was a new one, which he was probably wearing for the first time and had put on specially for the interview. He clasped his umbrella to his chest and walked in a great hurry to the interviewing room, with his dhoti hanging about his legs and his face swollen with embarrassment and confusion. 15

We all sat and waited. The fan, which seemed to be a very old one, made a creaking noise. One man kept cracking his finger joints—*tik*, we heard, *tik* (it made my own finger joints long to be cracked too). All the rest of us kept very still. From time to time the official with the list came in, he walked around the room very slowly, tapping his list, and then we all looked down at our feet and the man who had been cracking his finger joints stopped doing it. A faint and muffled sound of voices came from behind the closed door. Sometimes a voice was raised, but even then I could not make out what was being said, though I strained very hard. 16

The last time I had an interview, it was very unpleasant for me. One of the people who was interviewing took a dislike to me and shouted at me very loudly. He was a large fat man and he wore an English suit; his teeth were quite yellow, and when he became angry and shouted, he showed them all, and even though I was very upset, I couldn't help looking at them and wondering how they had become so yellow. I don't know why he was angry. He shouted: "Good God, man, can't you understand what's said to 17

---

1. Dhoti: *A loincloth worn by Hindu men.*

you?" It was true, I could not understand, but I had been trying so hard to answer well. What more did he expect of me? Probably there was something in my appearance that he did not like. It happens that way sometimes—they take a dislike to you, and then of course there is nothing you can do.

When I thought of the man with the yellow teeth, I became more anx- 18 ious than ever. I need great calm in my life. Whenever anything worries me too much, I have to cast the thought of it off immediately, otherwise there is a danger that I may become very ill. All my limbs were itching so that it was difficult for me to sit still, and I could feel blood rushing into my brain. It was this room that was doing me so much harm: all the other men waiting, anxious and silent, and the noise from the fan and the official with the list walking around, tapping his list or striking it against his thigh, and the big closed door behind which the interview was going on. I felt great need to get up and go away. I didn't *want* the job. I wasn't even thinking about it anymore—I was thinking only about how to avoid having to sit here and wait.

Now the door opened again and the man with the torn new dhoti came 19 out. He was biting his lip and scratching the back of his neck, and he too walked straight out without looking at us at all. The big door was left slightly open for a moment, and I could see a man's arm in a white shirtsleeve and part of the back of his head. His shirt was very white and of good material, and his ears stood away from his head so that one could see how his spectacles fitted into the backs of his ears. I realized at once that this man would be my enemy and that he would make things very difficult for me and perhaps even shout at me. Then I knew it was no use for me to stay there. The official with the list came back and great panic seized me that he would read out my name. I got up quickly, murmuring, "Please excuse me—bathroom," and went out. The official with the list called after me, "Hey mister, where are you going?" so I lowered my head and walked faster. I would have started to run, but that might have caused suspicion, so I just walked as fast as I could, down the long corridors and right out of the building. There at last I was able to stop and take a deep breath, and I felt much better.

I stood still for only a little while, then I moved on, though not in any 20 particular direction. There were many clerks and peons moving around in the street, hurrying from one office building to another and carrying files and papers. Everyone seemed to have something to do. I was glad when I had moved out of this block and on to the open space where people like myself, who had nothing to do, sat under the trees or in any other patch of shade they could find. But I couldn't sit there; it was too close to the office blocks, and any moment someone might come and say to me, "Why did you go away?" So I walked farther. I was feeling quite light-hearted; it was such a relief for me not to have to be interviewed.

I came to a row of eating stalls, and I sat down on a wooden bench 21
outside one of them, which was called the Paris Hotel, and asked for tea.
I felt badly in need of tea, and since I intended to walk part of the way
home, I was in a position to pay for it. There were two Sikhs sitting at the
end of my bench who were eating with great appetite, dipping their hands
very rapidly into brass bowls. In between eating they exchanged remarks
with the proprietor of the Paris Hotel, who sat high up inside his stall,
stirring in a big brass pot in which he was cooking the day's food. He was
chewing a betel leaf, and from time to time he spat out the red betel juice
far over the cooking pot and on to the ground between the wooden benches
and tables.

I sat quietly at my end of the bench and drank my tea. The food smelled 22
very good, and it made me realize that I was hungry. I decided that if I
walked all the way home, I could afford a little cake (I am very fond of
sweet things). The cake was not new, but it had a beautiful piece of bright-
green peel inside it. On reaching home I would lie down at once to sleep
and not wake up again till tomorrow morning. That way no one would be
able to ask me any questions. I would not look at my wife at all, so I would
be able to avoid her eyes. I would not look at my sister-in-law either; but
she would be smiling, that I knew already—leaning against the wall with
her hand on her hip, looking at me and smiling. She would know that I had
run away, but she would not say anything.

Let her know! What does it matter? It is true I have no job and no 23
immediate prospect of getting one. It is true that I am dependent on my
brother. Everyone knows that. There is no shame in it: there are many
people without jobs. And she has been so kind to me up till now, there is
no reason why she should not continue to be kind to me. Though I know
she is not by nature a kind woman; she speaks mostly with a very harsh
tongue and her actions also are harsh. Only to me she has been kind.

The Sikhs at the end of the bench had finished eating. They licked their 24
fingers and belched deeply, the way one does after a good meal. They
started to laugh and joke with the proprietor. I sat quiet and alone at the
end of the bench. Of course they did not laugh and joke with me. They
knew that I was superior to them, for whereas they work with their hands,
I am a lettered man who does not have to sweat for a living but sits on a
chair in an office and writes figures and can speak in English. My brother
is very proud of his superiority, and he has great contempt for carpenters
and mechanics and such people who work with their hands. I am also
proud of being a lettered man, but when I listened to the Sikhs laughing
and joking, the thought came to me that perhaps their life was happier
than mine. It was a thought that had come to me before. There is the
carpenter who lives downstairs in our house, the one whose daughter
waits for me on the stairs, and though he is poor, there is always great
eating in his house and many people come and I hear them laughing and
singing and even dancing. The carpenter is a big strong man and he always

looks happy, never anxious and sick with worry the way my brother does. He doesn't wear shoes and clean white clothes like my brother and I do, nor does he speak any English, but all the same he is happy. Even though his work is inferior, I don't think he gets as weary of it as I do of mine, and he has no superior officer to make him afraid.

Then I thought again about my sister-in-law and I thought that if I were kind to her, she would continue to be kind to me. I became quite excited when I thought of being kind to her. I would know then how her big breasts felt under the blouse, how warm they were and how soft. And I would know about the inside of her mouth with the big strong teeth. Her tongue and palate are very pink, like the pink satin blouse she wears on festive occasions, and I had often wondered whether they felt as soft as the blouse too. Her eyes would be shut and perhaps there would be tears on the lashes; and she would be making warm animal sounds and her big body too would be warm like an animal's. I became very excited when I thought of it; but when the excitement had passed, I was sad. Because then I thought of my wife, who is thin and not beautiful and there is no excitement in her body. But she does whatever I want and always tries to please me. I remembered her whispering to me in the night, "Take me away, let us go and live somewhere alone, only you and I and our children." That can never be, and so always she will have to be unhappy. 25

I was very sad when I thought of her being unhappy; because it is not only she who is unhappy but I also and many others. Everywhere there is unhappiness. I thought of the man whose new dhoti had been torn and who would now have to go home and sew it carefully so that the tear would not be seen. I thought of all the other men sitting and waiting to be interviewed, all but one or two of whom would not get the job for which they had come to be interviewed, and so again they would have to go to another interview and another and another, to sit and wait and be anxious. And my brother who has a job, but is frightened that he will lose it; and my mother so old that she can only sit on the floor and stroke her pieces of cloth; and my sister-in-law who does not care for her husband; and the carpenter's daughter who is to be married and perhaps she also will not be happy. Yet life could be so different. When I go to the cinema and hear the beautiful songs they sing, I know how different it could be; and also sometimes when I sit alone and think my thoughts, then I have a feeling that everything could be so beautiful. But now my tea was finished and also my cake, and I wished I had not bought them, because it was a long way to walk home and I was tired. 26

STUDY QUESTIONS

1. The main character in "The Interview" is also the story's narrator. Describe his relationship with the various women in his household.

2. Based on the way these women treat the narrator, what kinds of inferences can you make about a woman's position in this society?
3. What kinds of classes are portrayed in the short story, and what is the narrator's relation to these classes?
4. "Everywhere there is unhappiness. . . . Yet life could be so different" (last paragraph). What are the various forces that give rise to unhappiness in this society? Does the story suggest ways in which life can be different?

 # AMBAI

Ambai, also known as C. S. Lakshmi, was born in 1918 and began publishing at age eighteen. She writes in the Tamil language, spoken in India's south and in neighboring Sri Lanka. Some of her writing was included in The Face Behind the Mask: Women in Tamil Literature *(1983). Ambai's short stories focus largely on domestic themes, presenting women's experiences and views on marriage and family. She often uses humor to put across a feminist consciousness.*

Fall, My Mother

When I think of Mother, some incidents, vividly recalled, tug at my heart.   1

My older sister Kalyani used to have fainting fits. I was not old enough to understand. I was four.   2

I wake up early one morning I hear a drum. I go to the door to look. Kalyani has been seated on a plank. A man stands before her with a bunch of leaves in his hand. My laughing, gurgling baby brother of a few months is in his crib in the same room with me.   3

Someone says, "Niranjakshi, go and bring it."   4

I looked at my mother.   5

I remember the dark blue sari. She has tied her hair in a knot. She goes into the small room next to mine. She removes the *pallav*[1] of her sari, squeezes out some milk from her breasts into a small cup. Tears pour from her eyes.   6

---

1. Pallav: *The part of a sari that is drawn across the breasts and thrown over the shoulder.*

Mother rises every day in the dark before dawn to light the fire under   7
the big cauldron in the bathroom.

One morning I see her. The knot of her hair has come undone and it   8
hangs loose. She is squatting, her hair over her cheeks and ears. When the
fire is lit and the flames rise, her bent face glows red. That day she is clad
in a red sari. Even as I stare, she gets up briskly. Her hair hangs to her
knees. Her *pallav* has slid to one side and the hooks of her blouse have
come undone to reveal her white breasts, green-veined. She seems to me
the daughter of the Fire God, flown in from somewhere. Is she Mother? My
own mother?

Why do these lines of the *sloka*[1] come to mind: *Kālī Kālī Mahakālī*   9
Bhadrakālī namostu te?[2]

"Amma. . . ."   10

Mother turns her head and sees me.   11

"What are you doing here?"   12

I cannot speak. The sweat beads up.   13

They are having a *homa*[3] in the house. Maybe it is the scarlet of her lips   14
or the shining red of her *kumkum*[4]—the flaring flame-shapes appear to be
Mother herself. They pour ghee into the fire intoning in elongated, stressed
syllables: "*Agnaye Swāhā*. . . ."[5] At the *swāhā* my eyes dart from the fire to
her face.

Mother is giving me an oil bath. She has tucked up her sari, showing   15
her smooth white thigh. The green veins show up as she bends and
straightens up.

"Amma, why are you so fair? And I am so dark?"   16

A chuckle.   17

"Silly, who can be as pretty as you are?"   18

The events are disjointed. But Mother is the queen in all of them. She is   19
the Fire which purifies, burning up all that is ugly or dirty. At her laughter
myriad beauties gather up in a festoon across my mind. She is the Creator.
When I lie with my head in her lap, she would stroke me with her long cool
fingers and say, "I shall give you dance lessons. You have the right build,"
or "What lovely thick hair you have," or some such ordinary remark. But
something inside me would blossom.

I do not know if it was her design or my own fancies which were re-   20
sponsible for the way I felt about Mother. Nor what it was that she con-

---

1. Sloka: *Sanskrit couplet or stanza.*
2. Kālī Kālī Mahakālī Bhadrakālī namostu te: *Kālī is the black goddess. This* sloka *is an invocation to her, literally translated Kālī, Great Kālī, Gracious Kālī. Bhadrakālī is also an epithet of Durga, the Devi, or goddess in her fierce aspect.*
3. Homa: *A sacred fire; traditionally a sacrificial fire.*
4. Kumkum: *The red powder traditionally used by a married woman on her forehead.*
5. Agnaye Swāhā: *An offering to the Fire-God; part of the chant at a Homā.*

firmed or created for herself while she planted all these glad blooms in me.

I am 13. My skirts are becoming too short for me. Mother lets out the 21
hem to lengthen them.

Lying with my head in her lap of an evening, I am reminded of some- 22
thing I had read somewhere and I ask her:

"Amma, what is 'coming of age'?" 23

Silence. 24

A prolonged silence. 25

Suddenly she says: "I want you to be just as you are now—romping 26
around in your swirling skirts . . ."

Mother has gone away to my aunt's. Some people are coming to "see" 27
my cousin Radhu. Mother is not home on that eventful day.

It is Kalyani who gives me an oil bath that *Diwali*[1] day. As she rinses my 28
hair, I look out of the window at the still dark sky and say, "Kalloos, you
got me up too early. I do not hear any firecrackers yet."

"I have to have my own bath after finishing with you. You are all of 13 29
but you cannot manage by yourself. Bend down."

Kalyani is not the patient sort. She rubs my scalp so hard that it hurts. 30

Mother has made me a skirt in lavender satin for Diwali. My heart had 31
throbbed with excitement as it slithered along on the sewing machine.
Mother had to measure me for the skirt.

"Come here. I have to measure you. You have grown." She straightens 32
up and says, "This girl is two inches taller now."

My lavender satin skirt will not be short like the others. It will flow to the 33
floor.

Kalyani pulls me up brusquely and dries my hair. I slip on my chemise 34
and run to the *pūja*[2] room.

Father gives me my new clothes from the pile on a plank at the altar. 35

"Here, dark one!" That is the way he calls me. 36

Sometimes when Father says that, I go to the big mirror hanging in the 37
hall and stand looking at myself. I would hear Mother whispering in my
ear: "How beautiful you are!"

My satin skirt slithers around me like the fish in Sarala's fish bowl. I 38
put on the velvet blouse and then with *bindi*[3] on my forehead I go to my
father.

"Mm. . . . Not bad at all!" he says in mock surprise. 39

I fetch my crackers but leave them in the front room and run to the 40
champa tree. It is my job every morning to gather flowers from the tree.
When I fill a basket and bring it to Mother, she would exclaim, wide-eyed,

---

1. Diwali: *A festival of lights and crackers.*

2. Pūja: *A ritual of worship; the pūja room is the special room in the house, usually near the kitchen, where the images of the gods are kept and worshiped each morning.*

3. Bindi: *The dot placed on the forehead.*

"How much there is!" and dip her fingers in. One could not tell the fingers from the flowers.

My satin skirt hinders my climbing and I cannot get to the top branch.   41
It is still dark. As I climb down a cracker suddenly explodes somewhere and I jump down the last bit, trembling. I rush into the house, panting.

I calm myself, get my crackers and start lighting them. I remember the   42
flowers only after all the crackers are gone.

It is light now.   43

Holding up the hem of my skirt I pick up the basket lying under the tree.   44
Some flowers have scattered. As I squat to pick them up my skirt spreads out and I notice it has stains on it here and there. Is it from the tree?

I go in calling to my sister. "Kalloos, I have spoilt my new skirt. Will   45
Amma scold me?" I stand there before her holding out the basket of flowers.

Kalyani stares at me for a minute and calling out "Appa" goes out.   46

Her look and her abrupt departure without even taking the basket from   47
me—a caterpillar wriggles inside of me. I look at my skirt and feel my velvet blouse.

Has anything happened to me?   48

Please god, nothing has happened to me, has it? Even as I ask myself I   49
know that something has happened. Crackers are going off everywhere. Baskets still in hand I stand there shaking, shaking, breath coming fast, lips trembling.

A mighty sob bursts forth.   50

I want to be with Mother. I want to put my head on her shoulder. Tell   51
her "I am afraid" and cry shamelessly. My mother will stroke my head. Something frightful has happened . . .

Kalyani returns bringing with her Murukku-Patti, the old widow who   52
sometimes comes to help Mother make *murukkū*.[1]

Patti comes near.   53

"What is all the tears and fuss about, girl! Is it anything unheard of in   54
the world?"

I understand nothing that she says. My instinct tells me something that   55
makes me shiver. I don't know what to think. From the depths of my being rises a wail of desperate need . . . Amma . . .

I think of the time I had got lost when I was five. I am in a big park,   56
walking away from the others, unaware of the darkening evening. Suddenly it is dark. The looming shapes of trees, the quiet, and the noises frighten. It is my father who finds me. But the sobs burst forth only when I see Mother.

Mother holds me close. She strokes me. Murmurs softly, "Nothing hap-   57

---

1. Murukkū: *A crisp South Indian snack made of rice and lentil flour, delicately spiced, piped into concentric circles and deep fried.*

pened at all. See, everything is all right now." Her scarlet lips like glowing lines of fire, she puts her face against mine.

I tremble the same way now, feeling lost and frightened.   58

I sit down, put my head on my knees, and I cry. Something seems to   59
have come to an end. It is like going away leaving something behind, like leaving the theater when they show "The End" on the screen. I feel I am the only one in the whole history of the world who has been so struck down. All the sorrows of my being weighing on my slender, velvet-clad shoulders, I cry.

Why has mother never told me about this on any of those evenings   60
when we were together?

Fear is all I am conscious of. Not the fear you feel of strangers or strange   61
places. It is the tongue-paralyzing fear of coming upon a snake suddenly. It hangs like cobwebs from every cranny of my mind.

I think of the prone figure I had once seen, its blanched lips split. The   62
skull had cracked against a stone. A moment earlier it had been walking ahead of me, a pink, slightly bald head. Now it lay like a cavern, a deep red stream of blood gushing out of its mouth. The blood spattered on the ground and I had stood staring at it. The red spread everywhere, it was in my eyes. Inwardly I screamed again and again, "Oh, the blood! so much of it!" But my tongue uttered no sound. Now I see it all again—the bed of blood, the open mouth, the staring eyes.

How terrifying is blood . . . blanching lips . . . paralyzing limbs . . .   63

I need my mother. I need her now to be freed of this fear just as I needed   64
her to hold me close and croon to me when I was frightened of the dark. If only mother were here to put her cool hand on my shoulder and say, "This is something beautiful too."

Kalyani has been sitting next to me and having a cry too. Now she begs,   65
"How long are you going to be at this? Get up now. Please."

"Amma . . ."   66

"You know Mother will be back next week. I have just written to her   67
about this. She will be back after they have seen Radhu and talked things over. Now you just get up from there." She was beginning to lose patience. "What a nuisance you are!"

"Tell me what has happened to me."   68

"There you go again. How many times do you want me to tell you?"   69

"I should not climb trees any more?"   70

Kalyani raps her knuckles sharply on my head.   71

"Mule-head! Here I am begging you the last half hour to get up and let   72
me change your clothes and you start asking me this and that."

She calls out to Father. "Appa, this girl is being so difficult!"   73

Father comes. "You mustn't be silly. You must listen to your sister."   74

When his back is turned, Murukku-Patti adds, "What tantrums! The   75
wretched thing happens to everybody!"

Seven days. Seven days before Mother will be back. Radhu has to be   76
"seen" first.

Seven days of groping in the dark. 77

One day the ladies from next door and the house opposite call. 78

"Haven't you given her a *dāvani*[1] to wear, Kalyani?" 79

"Only after Mother returns, Auntie. This tigress will only listen to her." 80

"She will begin to behave better now. She will calm down." 81

Why? What is going to be different from now on? 82

Why should I have to wear a dāvani? Mother had said that day: "Do not 83
change. Be just as you are swirling your skirts . . ." Why must I change?

Nobody explains anything to me. 84

They sit around me and talk as though I were a doll. When Father comes 85
they cover themselves and lower their voices.

The fifth day Kalyani hands me a cup of warm oil and says: "Go on, go 86
and have your oil bath."

After a tearful battle in the bathroom with my waist-length hair, I emerge 87
in my chemise to stand before the mirror in the hall.

"You must dress fully in the bathroom hereafter, all right?" says Father. 88

I close the door after him. I slip off my chemise. The mirror shows me 89
my dark body. Shoulders, arms, chest, waist and soft thighs, somewhat
darker than my face. I feel them with my hands. I am not the same girl
now? What is Mother going to say?

I put on my school uniform. 90

When I open the door Kalyani comes. "What will you say when they ask 91
you at school about your staying away?"

I stare at her. My spirits which had picked up at the prospect of going 92
to school, sag again.

"Don't say anything. Just keep mum." 93

That evening I do not go to the games field. Instead I hide myself behind 94
a thick tree. I had skipped games like this once before. The next day in class
Miss Menon had asked, "Who are the fools who did not play last evening?"
I had not got up.

"Why didn't you stand up?" she had asked. 95

"But I am not a fool, Miss," I had answered. She wrote "Impertinent" 96
on my report card.

But today even the thought of Miss Menon's scolding does not bother 97
me. Nothing can bother me now but this dreadful thing that has happened
to me.

I do not sit there reading Enid Blyton.[2] I ask of the dried leaves falling 98
around me:

"What oh what is it that has happened to me?" 99

---

1. Dāvani: *A half saree or piece of cloth, about three yards long, worn with a skirt and blouse meant to cover the growing breasts. A girl usually begins wearing it when she first menstruates.*
2. Enid Blyton: *A prolific British writer of children's stories, still very popular among young Indian children.*

Like the prisoner in the dock with eyes only for the judge's lips, I wait 100
only for what my mother will tell me.

Will she lower her eyes to mine and say, "This that has happened to you 101
is also a beautiful thing?" With a single spark of her smile, she will blow
away Murukku-Patti and Kalyani and their frightening insinuations.
Mother is different. Where she is, all ugliness is destroyed and only beauty
remains. To her beauty is all there is.

I need Mother badly. Something has to be explained. Why I break into 102
a sweat and tremble when I even think of my lavender satin skirt, my
tongue turning wooden and immobile, a sudden darkness descends and
before one can turn, there is the sound of something hitting against a
stone and in the darkness appear a stream of blood and a long stiff
body—someone has to explain all this to me in soft, understanding
words.

I feel lost, abandoned. 103

I get up when the gardener calls out and slowly make my way home. 104

"Why are you so late? Where have you been?" 105

"Nowhere. Just sat under the tree." 106

"Alone?" 107

"Yes." 108

"You! Are you still a little girl? What if something happens?" 109

I fling my school bag away. My face flushes. I shut my ears with my 110
hands and scream:

"I will sit there alone, I will! Nothing has happened to me!" 111

I scream passionately, stressing and stretching each word. 112

Father and Kalyani stare, shocked. 113

I go up to the terrace nursing my huff. It will be nice to be alone here 114
with the fragrance from the champa tree. Father and Kalyani must not
come here. Just myself and this fragrance. It does not speak and does not
touch but feels closer to me than the people in the house. If only they will
stop saying things! If only I could see Mother's wide-eyed smile!

When Mother looks at one like that, a warmth spreads inside one. One 115
wants to laugh aloud. Or sing. Mother is Creator. A turn of her head—and
the magic of her smile would summon forth all that was joyful, exciting,
beautiful.

Kalyani comes up. 116

"Come and have your dinner, your highness! Amma has spoilt you 117
altogether."

I pout my lips at her and get up. 118

Mother is back the next morning. The taxi door opens, and my mother, 119
her dark green sari crumpled, comes into the house.

"What is the outcome?" asks father. 120

"The fellow declined. Said the girl was dark." 121

"How does your sister feel?" 122

"She is very disappointed, poor woman." 123

"We have a dark-skinned daughter too."   124

Abruptly I go and stand before my mother.   125

I want to tell her everything myself, more than what Kalyani must   126
have written in her letter. I want to put my lips close to her neck and
pour out everything in soft whispers . . . Tell her of this crawling fear in
my heart.

She will explain to me this strange mystery—this choking feeling every   127
night when I go to bed, this alienation from my own body. I look up at her
face in hope. She is going to gather me close in her long slender arms. And
I am going to bawl out aloud. I shall put my fingers in her hair and cry out
loud.

Mother looks at me.   128

I do not know if she sees me as Radhu for a moment.   129

"What is your hurry about this wretched thing, girl? We have one more   130
problem on our hands now."

A whiplash of a question.   131

Whom is she accusing?   132

Sobs surge soundlessly against my breast.   133

Mother's lips and nose, her bindi and nose-screw, and her eyes—all   134
appear to spew blood-red tongues of flame.

In the blaze, the cloak of divinity I had clothed her in falls off her, I   135
behold her naked, a mere human mother. The cruel words rise up as
sharpened blades and hack blindly at the glad sprouts planted before.
Never-to-be-forgotten fears cling to the mind like dark shrouds.

"*Agnaye swaa. . . . haa. . . .*" It was not just the dirt that was burnt away.   136
Buds and blossoms were also scorched.

Translated from the Tamil by Kamala Ramji

STUDY QUESTIONS

1. The story opens with the young narrator's impressions of her
   mother. In what ways are these impressions woven in with religious
   images?
2. What happens to the narrator when she is thirteen? Why does she
   react to this incident so violently?
3. What is the significance of the narrator's dark skin and its association
   with her cousin Radhu?
4. In India, one of the family's major financial responsibilities is paying a
   dowry for a daughter's marriage. Hence, the mother's response to the
   daughter's "coming of age" is to see it in economic terms, as "one
   more problem." Discuss how the mother's image changes for the
   daughter as a consequence of this response.

MAHASWETA DEVI

Mahasweta Devi (b. 1926), a fiction writer and journalist, has published over fifty works in her native Bengali language. Born to a middle-class family, she received an M.A. in English, then went on to teach at a college for working-class women—both rare accomplishments for Indian women. Her writing is marked by the centrality of her political concerns and by her carefully researched use of history in her novels. Her work, as seen in her short story collection Agnigarbha (Womb of Fire, 1978), exhibits multiple stylistic levels, using colloquial language, slang, and literary and formal elements to focus on traditionally dispossessed individuals and groups.

Breast-Giver

My aunties they lived in the woods, in the forest their home they did make. Never did Aunt say here's a sweet dear, eat, sweetie, here's a piece of cake.

Jashoda doesn't remember if her aunt was kind or unkind. It is as if she were Kangalicharan's wife from birth, the mother of twenty children, living or dead, counted on her fingers. Jashoda doesn't remember at all when there was no child in her womb, when she didn't feel faint in the morning, when Kangali's body didn't *drill* her body like a geologist in a darkness lit only by an oil-lamp. She never had the time to calculate if she could or could not bear motherhood. Motherhood was always her way of living and keeping alive her world of countless beings. Jashoda was a mother by profession, *professional mother*. Jashoda was not an *amateur* mama like the daughters and wives of the master's house. The world belongs to the professional. In this city, this kingdom, the amateur beggar-pickpocket-hooker has no place. Even the mongrel on the path or sidewalk, the greedy crow at the garbage don't make room for the upstart *amateur*. Jashoda had taken motherhood as her profession.

The responsibility was Mr. Haldar's new son-in-law's Studebaker and the sudden desire of the youngest son of the Haldar-house to be a driver. When the boy suddenly got a whim in mind or body, he could not rest unless he had satisfied it instantly. These sudden whims reared up in the loneliness of the afternoon and kept him at slave labor like the khalifa of Bagdad. What he had done so far on that account did not oblige Jashoda to choose motherhood as a profession.

One afternoon the boy, driven by lust, attacked the cook and the cook, since her body was heavy with rice, stolen fishheads, and turnip greens, and her body languid with sloth, lay back, saying, "Yah, do what you like." Thus did the incubus of Bagdad get off the boy's shoulders and he wept repentant tears, mumbling, "Auntie, don't tell." The cook—saying, "What's there to tell?"—went quickly to sleep. She never told anything. She was sufficiently proud that her body had attracted the boy. But the thief thinks of the loot. The boy got worried at the improper supply of fish and fries in his dish. He considered that he'd be fucked if the cook gave him away. Therefore on another afternoon, driven by the Bagdad djinn, he stole his mother's ring, slipped it into the cook's pillowcase, raised a hue and cry, and got the cook kicked out. Another afternoon he lifted the radio set from his father's room and sold it. It was difficult for his parents to find the connection between the hour of the afternoon and the boy's behavior, since his father had created him in the deepest night by the astrological calendar and the tradition of the Haldars of Harisal. In fact you enter the sixteenth century as you enter the gates of this house. To this day you take your wife by the astrological almanac. But these matters are mere blind alleys. Motherhood did not become Jashoda's profession for these afternoon-whims.

One afternoon, leaving the owner of the shop, Kangalicharan was re- 4 turning home with a handful of stolen samosas and sweets under his dhoti. Thus he returns daily. He and Jashoda eat rice. Their three offspring return before dark and eat stale samosas and sweets. Kangalicharan stirs the seething vat of milk in the sweet shop and cooks and feeds "food cooked by a good Brahmin" to those pilgrims at the Lionseated goddess's temple who are proud that they are not themselves "fake Brahmins by sleight of hand." Daily he lifts a bit of flour and such and makes life easier. When he puts food in his belly in the afternoon he feels a filial inclination toward Jashoda, and he goes to sleep after handling her capacious bosom. Coming home in the afternoon, Kangalicharan was thinking of his immi- nent pleasure and tasting paradise at the thought of his wife's large round breasts. He was picturing himself as a farsighted son of man as he thought that marrying a fresh young thing, not working her overmuch, and feeding her well led to pleasure in the afternoon. At such a moment the Haldar son, complete with Studebaker, swerving by Kangalicharan, ran over his feet and shins.

Instantly a crowd gathered. It was an accident in front of the house after 5 all, "otherwise I'd have drawn blood," screamed Nabin, the pilgrim-guide. He guides the pilgrims to the Mother goddess of Shakti-power, his temper is hot in the afternoon sun. Hearing him roar, all the Haldars who were at home came out. The Haldar chief started thrashing his son, roaring, "You'll kill a Brahmin, you bastard, you unthinking bull?" The youngest son-in- law breathed relief as he saw that his Studebaker was not much damaged and, to prove that he was better human material than the money rich, culture-poor in-laws, he said in a voice as fine as the finest muslin, "Shall we let the man die? Shouldn't we take him to the hospital?"—Kangali's boss was also in the crowd at the temple and, seeing the samosas and sweets flung on the roadway was about to say, "Eh Brahmin!! Stealing food?" Now he held his tongue and said, "Do that sir." The youngest son-in-law and the Haldar-chief took Kangalicharan quickly to the hospital. The master felt deeply grieved. During the Second War, when he helped the anti-Fascist struggle of the Allies by buying and selling scrap iron— then Kangali was a mere lad. Reverence for Brahmins crawled in Mr. Haldar's veins. If he couldn't get chatterjeebabu in the morning he would touch the feet of Kangali, young enough to be his son, and put a pinch of dust from his chapped feet on his own tongue. Kangali and Jashoda came to his house on feast days and Jashoda was sent a gift of cloth and ver-million when his daughters-in-law were pregnant. Now he said to Kangali—"Kangali! don't worry son. You won't suffer as long as I'm around." Now it was that he thought that Kangali's feet, being turned to ground meat, he would not be able to taste their dust. He was most un-happy at the thought and he started weeping as he said, "What has the son of a bitch done." He said to the doctor at the hospital, "Do what you can! Don't worry about cash."

But the doctors could not bring the feet back. Kangali returned as a lame   6
Brahmin. Haldarbabu had a pair of crutches made. The very day Kangali returned home on crutches, he learned that food had come to Jashoda from the Haldar house every day. Nabin was third in rank among the pilgrim-guides. He could only claim thirteen percent of the goddess's food and so had an inferiority complex. Inspired by seeing Rama-Krishna in the movies a couple of times, he called the goddess "my crazy one" and by the book of the Kali-worshippers kept his consciousness immersed in local spirits. He said to Kangali, "I put flowers on the crazy one's feet in your name. She said I have a share in Kangali's house, he will get out of the hospital by that fact." Speaking of this to Jashoda, Kangali said, "What? When I wasn't there, you were getting it off with Nabin?" Jashoda then grabbed Kangali's suspicious head between the two hemispheres of the globe and said, "Two maid servants from the big house slept here every day to guard me. Would I look at Nabin? Am I not your faithful wife?"

In fact Kangali heard of his wife's flaming devotion at the big house as   7
well. Jashoda had fasted at the mother's temple, had gone through a fe-male ritual, and had travelled to the outskirts to pray at the feet of the local guru. Finally the Lionseated came to her in a dream as a midwife carrying a *bag* and said, "Don't worry. Your man will return." Kangali was most overwhelmed by this. Haldarbabu said, "See, Kangali? The bastard unbe-lievers say, the Mother gives a dream, why togged as a midwife? I say, she creates as mother, and preserves as midwife."

Then Kangali said, "Sir! How shall I work at the sweetshop any   8
longer. I can't stir the vat with my kerutches.[1] You are god. You are feed-

---

1. Kerutches: *Underclass Bengali pronunciation for "crutches."*

ing so many people in so many ways. I am not begging. Find me a job."

Haldarbabu said, "Yes Kangali! I've kept you a spot. I'll make you a 9
shop in the corner of my porch. The Lionseated is across the way! Pilgrims
come and go. Put up a shop of dry sweets. Now there's a wedding in the
house. It's my bastard seventh son's wedding. As long as there's no shop,
I'll send you food."

Hearing this, Kangali's mind took wing like a rainbug in the rainy sea- 10
son. He came home and told Jashoda, "Remember Kalidasa's pome? You
eat because there isn't, wouldn't have got if there was? That's my lot,
chuck. Master says he'll put up a shop after his son's wedding. Until then
he'll send us food. Would this have happened if I had legs? All is Mother's
will, dear!"

Everyone is properly amazed that in this fallen age the wishes and wills 11
of the Lionseated, herself found by a dream-command a hundred and fifty
years ago, are circulating around Kangalicharan Patitundo. Haldarbabu's
change of heart is also Mother's will. He lives in independent India, the
India that makes no distinctions among people, kingdoms, languages,
varieties of Brahmins, varieties of Kayasthas and so on. But he made his
cash in the British era, when *Divide and Rule* was the policy. Haldarbabu's
mentality was constructed then. Therefore he doesn't trust anyone—not a
Panjabi-Oriya-Bihari-Gujarati-Marathi-Muslim. At the sight of an unfortunate Bihari child or a starvation-ridden Oriya beggar his flab-protected
heart, located under a forty-two inch Gopal brand vest, does not itch with
the rash of kindness. He is a successful son of Harisal. When he sees a
West Bengali fly he says, "Tchah! at home even the flies were fat—in the
bloody West everything is pinched-skinny." All the temple people are
struck that such a man is filling with the milk of humankindness toward
the West Bengali Kangalicharan. For some time this news is the general
talk. Haldarbabu is such a patriot that, if his nephews or grandsons read
the lives of the nation's leaders in their schoolbook, he says to his employees, "Nonsense! why do they make 'em read the lives of characters
from Dhaka, Mymansingh, Jashore? Harisal is made of the bone of the
martyr god. One day it will emerge that the *Veda*s and the *Upanishad*s
were also written in Harisal." Now his employees tell him, "You have
had a *change of heart*, so much kindness for a West Bengali, you'll see
there is divine *purpose* behind this." The Boss is delighted. He laughs
loudly and says, "There's no East or West for a Brahmin. If there's a
sacred thread around his neck you have to give him respect even when
he's taking a shit."

Thus all around blow the sweet winds of sympathy-compassion- 12
kindness. For a few days, whenever Nabin tries to think of the Lionseated,
the heavy-breasted, languid-hipped body of Jashoda floats in his mind's
eye. A slow rise spreads in his body at the thought that perhaps she is
appearing in his dream as Jashoda just as she appeared in Jashoda's as a
midwife. The fifty percent pilgrim-guide says to him, "Male and female

both get this disease. Bind the root of a white forget-me-not in your ear when you take a piss."

Nabin doesn't agree. One day he tells Kangali, "As the Mother's son I won't make a racket with Shakti-power. But I've thought of a plan. There's no problem with making a Hare Krishna racket. I tell you, get a Gopal in your dream. My Aunt brought a stony Gopal from Puri. I give it to you. You announce that you got it in a dream. You'll see there'll be a to-do in no time, money will roll in. Start for money, later you'll get devoted to Gopal." 13

Kangali says, "Shame, brother! Should one joke with gods?" 14

"Ah get lost," Nabin scolds. Later it appears that Kangali would have done well to listen to Nabin. For Haldarbabu suddenly dies of heart failure. Shakespeare's *welkin*[1] breaks on Kangali and Jashoda's head. 15

2

Haldarbabu truly left Kangali in the lurch. Those wishes of the Lionseated that were manifesting themselves around Kangali *via-media* Haldarbabu disappeared into the blue like the burning promises given by a political party before the elections and became magically invisible like the heroine of a fantasy. A European witch's *bodkin*[2] pricks the colored balloon of Kangali and Jashoda's dreams and the pair falls in deep trouble. At home, Gopal, Nepal, and Radharani whine interminably for food and abuse their mother. It is very natural for children to cry so for grub. Ever since Kangalicharan's loss of feet they'd eaten the fancy food of the Haldar household. Kangali also longs for food and is shouted at for trying to put his head in Jashoda's chest in the way of Gopal, the Divine Son. Jashoda is fully an Indian woman, whose unreasonable, unreasoning, and unintelligent devotion to her husband and love for her children, whose unnatural renunciation and forgiveness had been kept alive in the popular consciousness by all Indian women from Sati-Savitri-Sita through Nirupa Roy and Chand Osmani. The creeps of the world understand by seeing such women that the old Indian tradition is still flowing free—they understand that it was with such women in mind that the following aphorisms have been composed—"a female's life hangs on like a turtle's"—"her heart breaks but no word is uttered"—"the woman will burn, her ashes will fly / Only then will we sing her / praise on high." Frankly, Jashoda never once wants to blame her husband for the present misfortune. Her mother-love wells up for Kangali as much as for the children. She wants to become the earth and feed her crippled husband and helpless children with a fulsome harvest. 16

---

1. Welkin: *The vault of the sky, the heavens.*
2. Bodkin: *A dagger.*

Sages did not write of this motherly feeling of Jashoda's for her husband. They explained female and male as Nature and the Human Principle. But this they did in the days of yore—when they entered this *peninsula* from another land. Such is the power of the Indian soil that all women turn into mothers here and all men remain immersed in the spirit of holy childhood. Each man the Holy Child and each woman the Divine Mother. Even those who deny this and wish to slap *current posters* to the effect of the *"eternal she"*—"Mona Lisa"—"La passionaria"—"Simone de Beauvoir," et cetera, over the old ones and look at women that way are, after all, Indian cubs. It is notable that the educated Babus desire all this from women outside the home. When they cross the threshold they want the Divine Mother in the words and conduct of the revolutionary ladies. The *process* is most complicated. Because he understood this the heroines of Saratchandra always fed the hero an extra mouthful of rice. The apparent simplicity of Saratchandra's and other similar writers' writings is actually very complex and to be thought of in the evening, peacefully after a glass of wood-apple juice. There is too much influence of fun and games in the lives of the people who traffic in studies and intellectualism in West Bengal and therefore they should stress the wood-apple correspondingly. We have no idea of the loss we are sustaining because we do not stress the wood-apple-type-herbal remedies correspondingly.

However, it's incorrect to cultivate the habit of repeated incursions into 17 *bye-lanes* as we tell Jashoda's life story. The reader's patience, unlike the cracks in Calcutta streets, will not widen by the decade. The real thing is that Jashoda was in a cleft stick. Of course they ate their fill during the Master's funeral days, but after everything was over Jashoda clasped Radharani to her bosom and went over to the big house. Her aim was to speak to the Mistress and ask for the cook's job in the vegetarian kitchen.

The Mistress really grieved for the Master. But the lawyer let her know 18 that the Master had left her the proprietorship of this house and the right to the rice warehouse. Girding herself with those assurances, she has once again taken the rudder of the family empire. She had really felt the loss of fish and fish-head.[1] Now she sees that the best butter, the best milk sweets from the best shops, heavy cream, and the best variety of bananas can also keep the body going somehow. The Mistress lights up her easychair. A six-months' babe in her lap, her grandson. So far six sons have married. Since the almanac approves of the taking of a wife almost every month of the year, the birth rooms in a row on the ground floor of the Mistress's house are hardly ever empty. The *lady doctor* and Sarala the midwife never leave the house. The Mistress has six daughters. They too breed every year and a half. So there is a constant *epidemic* of blanket-quilt-feeding spoon-bottle-oilcloth-*Johnson's baby powder*-bathing basin.

---

1. *In West Bengal, Hindu widows signal their lifelong mourning by becoming vegetarians.*

The Mistress was out of her mind trying to feed the boy. As if relieved 19
to see Jashoda she said, "You come like a god! Give her some milk, dear,
I beg you. His mother's sick—such a brat, he won't touch a bottle." Jashoda immediately suckled the boy and pacified him. At the Mistress's special request Jashoda stayed in the house until nine P.M. and suckled the
Mistress's grandson again and again. The Cook filled a big bowl of rice and
curry for her own household. Jashoda said as she suckled the boy, "Mother! The Master said many things. He is gone, so I don't think of them. But
Mother! Your Brahmin-son does not have his two feet. I don't think for
myself. But thinking of my husband and sons I say, give me any kind of
job. Perhaps you'll let me cook in your household?"

"Let me see dear! Let me think and see." The Mistress is not as sold on 20
Brahmins as the Master was. She does not accept fully that Kangali lost his
feet because of her son's afternoon whims. It was written for Kangali as
well, otherwise why was he walking down the road in the blazing sun
grinning from ear to ear? She looks in charmed envy at Jashoda's *mammal
projections* and says, "The good lord sent you down as the legendary Cow
of Fulfillment. Pull the teat and milk flows! The ones I've brought to my
house, haven't a quarter of this milk in their nipples!"

Jashoda says, "How true Mother! Gopal was weaned when he was 21
three. This one hadn't come to my belly yet. Still it was like a flood of milk.
Where does it come from, Mother? I have no good food, no pampering!"

This produced a lot of talk among the women at night and the menfolk 22
got to hear it too at night. The second son, whose wife was sick and whose
son drank Jashoda's milk, was particularly uxorious. The difference between him and his brothers was that the brothers created progeny as soon
as the almanac gave a good day, with love or lack of love, with irritation or
thinking of the accounts at the works. The second son impregnates his wife
at the same *frequency*, but behind it lies deep love. The wife is often pregnant, that is an act of God. But the second son is also interested in that the
wife remains beautiful at the same time. He thinks a lot about how to
combine multiple pregnancies and beauty, but he cannot fathom it. But
today, hearing from his wife about Jashoda's surplus milk, the second son
said all of a sudden, "Way found."

"Way to what?" 23

"Uh, the way to save you pain." 24

"How? I'll be out of pain when you burn me. Can a year-breeder's 25
health mend?"

"It will, it will, I've got a divine engine in my hands! You'll breed yearly 26
and keep your body."

The couple discussed. The husband entered his Mother's room in the 27
morning and spoke in heavy whispers. At first the Mistress hemmed and
hawed, but then she thought to herself and realized that the proposal was
worth a million rupees. Daughters-in-law *will* be mothers. When they are
mothers, they will suckle their children. Since they will be mothers as long

as it's possible—progressive suckling will ruin their shape. Then if the sons look outside, or harass the maidservants, she won't have a voice to object. Going out because they can't get it at home—this is just. If Jashoda becomes the infants' suckling-mother, her daily meals, clothes on feast days, and some monthly pay will be enough. The Mistress is constantly occupied with women's rituals. There Jashoda can act as the fruitful Brahmin wife. Since Jashoda's misfortune is due to her son, that sin too will be lightened.

Jashoda received a portfolio when she heard her proposal. She thought   28
of her breasts as most precious objects. At night when Kangalicharan started to give her a feel she said, "Look. I'm going to pull our weight with these. Take good care how you use them." Kangalicharan hemmed and hawed that night, of course, but his Gopal frame of mind disappeared instantly when he saw the amounts of grains—oil—vegetables coming from the big house. He was illuminated by the spirit of Brahma the Creator and explained to Jashoda, "You'll have milk in your breasts only if you have a child in your belly. Now you'll have to think of that and suffer. You are a faithful wife, a goddess. You will yourself be pregnant, be filled with a child, rear it at your breast, isn't this why Mother came to you as a midwife?"

Jashoda realized the justice of these words and said, with tears in her   29
eyes, "You are husband, you are guru. If I forget and say no, correct me. Where after all is the pain? Didn't Mistress-Mother breed thirteen? Does it hurt a tree to bear fruit?"

So this rule held. Kangalicharan became a professional father. Jashoda   30
was by *profession* Mother. In fact to look at Jashoda now even the skeptic is convinced of the profundity of that song of the path of devotion. The song is as follows:

> Is a Mother so cheaply made?
> Not just by dropping a babe!

Around the paved courtyard on the ground floor of the Haldar house   31
over a dozen auspicious milch cows live in some state in large rooms. Two Biharis look after them as Mother Cows. There are mountains of rind-bran-hay-grass-molasses. Mrs. Haldar believes that the more the cow eats, the more milk she gives. Jashoda's place in the house is now above the Mother Cows. The Mistress's sons become incarnate Brahma and create progeny. Jashoda preserves the progeny.

Mrs. Haldar kept a strict watch on the free flow of her supply of milk.   32
She called Kangalicharan to her presence and said, "Now then, my Brahmin son? You used to stir the vat at the shop, now take up the cooking at home and give her a rest. Two of her own, three here, how can she cook at day's end after suckling five?"

Kangalicharan's intellectual eye was thus opened. Downstairs the two   33
Biharis gave him a bit of chewing tobacco and said, "Mistress Mother said right. We serve the Cow Mother as well—your woman is the Mother of the World."

From now on Kangalicharan took charge of the cooking at home. Made   34
the children his assistants. Gradually he became an expert in cooking plantain curry, lentil soup, and pickled fish, and by constantly feeding Nabin
a head-curry with the head of the goat dedicated to the Lionseated he
tamed that ferocious canabis-artist and drunkard. As a result Nabin inserted Kangali into the temple of Shiva the King. Jashoda, eating well-
prepared rice and curry every day, became as inflated as the *bank account* of
a Public Works Department *officer*. In addition, Mistress-Mother gave her
milk gratis. When Jashoda became pregnant, she would send her preserves, conserves, hot and sweet balls.

Thus even the skeptics were persuaded that the Lionseated had ap-   35
peared to Jashoda as a midwife for this very reason. Otherwise who has
ever heard or seen such things as constant pregnancies, giving birth, giving milk like a cow, without a thought, to others' children? Nabin too lost
his bad thoughts. Devotional feelings came to him by themselves. Whenever he saw Jashoda he called out "Mother! Mother! Dear Mother!" Faith
in the greatness of the Lionseated was rekindled in the area and in the air
of the neighborhood blew the *electrifying* influence of goddess-glory.

Everyone's devotion to Jashoda became so strong that at weddings,   36
showers, namings, and sacred-threadings they invited her and gave her
the position of chief fruitful woman. They looked with a comparable eye on
Nepal-Gopal-Neno-Boncha-Patal etc. because they were Jashoda's children, and as each grew up, he got a sacred thread and started catching
pilgrims for the temple. Kangali did not have to find husbands for Radharani, Altarani, Padmarani and such daughters. Nabin found them husbands with exemplary dispatch and the faithful mother's faithful daughters
went off each to run the household of her own Shiva! Jashoda's worth went
up in the Haldar house. The husbands are pleased because the wives'
knees no longer knock when they riffle the almanac. Since their children
are being reared on Jashoda's milk, they can be the Holy Child in bed at
will. The wives no longer have an excuse to say "no." The wives are
happy. They can keep their figures. They can wear blouses and bras of
"European cut." After keeping the fast of Shiva's night by watching all-
night picture shows they are no longer obliged to breast-feed their babies.
All this was possible because of Jashoda. As a result Jashoda became vocal
and, constantly suckling the infants, she opined as she sat in the Mistress's
room, "A woman breeds, so here medicine, there bloodpeshur,[1] here doctor's visits. Showoffs! Look at me! I've become a year-breeder! So is my
body failing, or is my milk drying? Make your skin crawl? I hear they are
drying their milk with injishuns.[2] Never heard of such things!"

The fathers and uncles of the current young men of the Haldar house   37

---

1. Bloodpeshur: *Underclass Bengali pronunciation for "blood pressure."*
2. Injishuns: *Underclass Bengali pronunciation for "injections."*

used to whistle at the maidservants as soon as hair grew on their upper lips. The young ones were reared by the Milk-Mother's milk, so they looked upon the maid and the cook, their Milk-Mother's friends, as mothers too and started walking around the girls' school. The maids said, "Joshi! You came as The Goddess! You made the air of this house change!" So one day as the youngest son was squatting to watch Jashoda's milking, she said, "There dear, my Lucky! All this because you swiped him in the leg! Whose wish was it then?" "The Lionseated's," said Haldar junior.

He wanted to know how Kangalicharan could be Brahma without feet? 38
This encroached on divine area, and he forgot the question.

All is the Lionseated's will! 39

3

Kangali's shins were cut in the fifties, and our narrative has reached the 40
present. In twenty-five years, sorry in thirty, Jashoda has been confined twenty times. The maternities toward the end were profitless, for a new wind entered the Haldar house somehow. Let's finish the business of the twenty-five or thirty years. At the beginning of the narrative Jashoda was the mother of three sons. Then she became gravid seventeen times. Mrs. Haldar died. She dearly wished that one of her daughters-in-law should have the same good fortune as her mother-in-law. In the family the custom was to have a second wedding if a couple could produce twenty children. But the daughters-in-law called a halt at twelve-thirteen-fourteen. By evil counsel they were able to explain to their husbands and make arrangements at the hospital. All this was the bad result of the new wind. Wise men have never allowed a new wind to enter the house. I've heard from my grandmother that a certain gentleman would come to her house to read the liberal journal *Saturday Letter*. He would never let the tome enter his home. "The moment wife, or mother, or sister reads that paper," he would say, "she'll say 'I'm a woman! Not a mother, not a sister, not a wife.'" If asked what the result would be, he'd say, "They would wear shoes while they cooked." It is a perennial rule that the power of the new wind disturbs the peace of the women's quarter.

It was always the sixteenth century in the Haldar household. But at the 41
sudden significant rise in the *membership* of the house the sons started building new houses and splitting. The most objectionable thing was that in the matter of motherhood, the old lady's granddaughters-in-law had breathed a completely different air before they crossed her threshold. In vain did the Mistress say that there was plenty of money, plenty to eat. The old man had dreamed of filling half Calcutta with Haldars. The granddaughters-in-law were unwilling. Defying the old lady's tongue, they took off to their husbands' places of work. At about this time, the pilgrim-guides of the Lionseated had a tremendous fight and some unknown per-

son or persons turned the image of the goddess around. The Mistress's heart broke at the thought that the Mother had turned her back. In pain she ate an unreasonable quantity of jackfruit in full summer and died shitting and vomiting.

4

Death liberated the Mistress, but the sting of staying alive is worse than 42
death. Jashoda was genuinely sorry at the Mistress's death. When an elderly person dies in the neighborhood, it's Basini who can weep most elaborately. She is an old maidservant of the house. But Jashoda's meal ticket was offered up with the Mistress. She astounded everyone by weeping even more elaborately.

"Oh blessed Mother!," Basini wept. "Widowed, when you lost your 43
crown you became the Master and protected everyone! Whose sins sent you away Mother! Ma, when I said, don't eat so much jackfruit, you didn't listen to me at all Mother!"

Jashoda let Basini get her breath and lamented in that pause, "Why 44
should you stay, Mother! You are blessed, why should you stay in this sinful world. The daughters-in-law have moved the throne! When the tree says I won't bear, alas it's a sin! Could you bear so much sin, Mother! Then did the Lionseated turn her back, Mother! You knew the abode of good works had become the abode of sin, it was not for you Mother! Your heart left when the Master left Mother! You held your body only because you thought of the family. O mistresses, o daughters-in-law! take a vermillion print of her footstep! Fortune will be tied to the door if you keep that print! If you touch your forehead to it every morning, pain and disease will stay out!"

Jashoda walked weeping behind the corpse to the burning ghat and said 45
on return, "I saw with my own eyes a chariot descend from heaven, take Mistress Mother from the pyre, and go on up."

After the funeral days were over, the eldest daughter-in-law said to 46
Jashoda, "Brahmin sister! the family is breaking up. Second and Third are moving to the house in Beleghata. Fourth and Fifth are departing to Maniktala-Bagman. Youngest will depart to our Dakshireswar house."

"Who stays here?" 47

"I will. But I'll let the downstairs. Now must the family be folded up. 48
You reared everyone on your milk, food was sent every day. The last child was weaned, still Mother sent you food for eight years. She did what pleased her. Her children said nothing. But it's no longer possible."

"What'll happen to me, elder daughter-in-law-sister?" 49

"If you cook for my household, your board is taken care of. But what'll 50
you do with yours?"

"What?" 51

"It's for you to say. You are the mother of twelve living children! The 52
daughters are married. I hear the sons call pilgrims, eat temple food, stretch
out in the courtyard. Your Brahmin-husband has set himself up in the
Shiva temple I hear. What do you need?"

Jashoda wiped her eyes. "Well! Let me speak to the Brahmin." 53

Kangalicharan's temple had really caught on. "What will you do in my 54
temple?" he asked.

"What does Naren's niece do?" 55

"She looks after the temple household and cooks. You haven't been 56
cooking at home for a long time. Will you be able to push the temple
traffic?"

"No meals from the big house. Did that enter your thieving head? 57
What'll you eat?"

"You don't have to worry," said Nabin. 58

"Why did I have to worry for so long? You're bringing it in at the 59
temple, aren't you? You've saved everything and eaten the food that
sucked my body."

"Who sat and cooked?" 60

"The man brings, the woman cooks and serves. My lot is inside out. 61
Then you ate my food, now you'll give me food. Fair's fair."

Kangali said on the beat, "Where did you bring in the food? Could you 62
have gotten the Haldar house? Their door opened for *you* because *my* legs
were cut off. The Master had wanted to set *me* up in business. Forgotten
everything, you cunt?"

"Who's the cunt, you or me? Living off a wife's carcass, you call that a 63
man?"

The two fought tooth and nail and cursed each other to the death. 64
Finally Kangali said, "I don't want to see your face again. Buzz off!"

"All right." 65

Jashoda too left angry. In the meantime the various pilgrim-guide fac- 66
tions conspired to turn the image's face forward, otherwise disaster was
imminent. As a result, penance rituals were being celebrated with great
ceremony at the temple. Jashoda went to throw herself at the goddess's
feet. Her aging, milkless, capacious breasts are breaking in pain. Let the
Lionseated understand her pain and tell her the way.

Jashoda lay three days in the courtyard. Perhaps the Lionseated has also 67
breathed the new wind. She did not appear in a dream. Moreover, when,
after her three days' fast, Jashoda went back shaking to her place, her
youngest came by. "Dad will stay at the temple. He's told Naba and I to
ring the bells. We'll get money and holy food every day."

"I see! Where's dad?" 68

"Lying down. Golapi-auntie is scratching the prickly heat on his back. 69
Asked us to buy candy with some money. So we came to tell you."

Jashoda understood that her usefulness had ended not only in the Hal- 70
dar house but also for Kangali. She broke her fast in name and went to

Nabin to complain. It was Nabin who had dragged the Lionseated's image the other way. After he had settled the dispute with the other pilgrim-guides re the overhead income from the goddess Basanti ritual, the goddess Jagaddhatri ritual, and the autumn Durgapuja, it was he who had once again pushed and pulled the image the right way. He'd poured some liquor into his aching throat, had smoked a bit of cannabis, and was now addressing the local electoral candidate: "No offerings for the Mother from you! Her glory is back. Now we'll see how you win!"

Nabin is the proof of all the miracles that can happen if, even in this   71
decade, one stays under the temple's power. He had turned the goddess's head himself and had himself believed that the Mother was averse because the pilgrim-guides were not organizing like all the want-votes groups. Now, after he had turned the goddess's head he had the idea that the Mother had turned on her own.

Jashoda said, "What are you babbling?"   72

Nabin said, "I'm speaking of Mother's glory."   73

Jashoda said, "You think I don't know that you turned the image's head   74
yourself?"

Nabin said, "Shut up, Joshi. God gave me ability, and intelligence, and   75
only then could the thing be done through me."

"Mother's glory has disappeared when you put your hands on her."   76

"Glory disappeared! If so, how come, the fan is turning, and you are   77
sitting under the fan? Was there ever an elettiri[1] fan on the porch ceiling?"

"I accept. But tell me, why did you burn my luck? What did I ever do to   78
you?"

"Why? Kangali isn't dead."   79

"Why wait for death? He's more than dead to me."   80

"What's up?"   81

Jashoda wiped her eyes and said in a heavy voice, "I've carried so many,   82
I was the regular milk-mother at the Master's house. You know everything. I've never left the straight and narrow."

"But of course. You are a portion of the Mother."   83

"But Mother remains in divine fulfillment. Her 'portion' is about to die   84
for want of food. Haldar-house has lifted its hand from me."

"Why did you have to fight with Kangali? Can a man bear to be insulted   85
on grounds of being supported?"

"Why did you have to plant your niece there?"   86

"That was divine play. Gopali used to throw herself in the temple. Little   87
by little Kangali came to understand that he was the god's companion-incarnate and she *his* companion."

"Companion indeed! I can get my husband from her clutches with one   88
blow of a broom!"

---

1. Elettiri: *Underclass Bengali pronunciation for "electric."*

Nabin said, "No! that can't be any more. Kangali is a man in his prime, how can he be pleased with you any more? Besides, Gopali's brother is a real hoodlum, and he is guarding her. Asked *me* to *get out.* If I smoke ten pipes, he smokes twenty. Kicked me in the midriff. I went to speak for you. Kangali said, don't talk to me about her. Doesn't know her man, knows her master's house. The master's house is her household god, let her go there." 89

"I will." 90

Then Jashoda returned home, half-crazed by the injustice of the world. 91 But her heart couldn't abide the empty room. Whether it suckled or not, it's hard to sleep without a child at the breast. Motherhood is a great addiction. The addiction doesn't break even when the milk is dry. Forlorn Jashoda went to the Haldaress. She said, "I'll cook and serve, if you want to pay me, if not, not. You must let me stay here. That sonofabitch is living at the temple. What disloyal sons! They are stuck there too. For whom shall I hold my room?"

"So stay. You suckled the children, *and* you're a Brahmin. So stay. But 92 sister, it'll be hard for you. You'll stay in Basini's room with the others. You mustn't fight with anyone. The master is not in a good mood. His temper is rotten because his third son went to Bombay and married a local girl. He'll be angry if there's noise."

Jashoda's good fortune was her ability to bear children. All this misfor- 93 tune happened to her as soon as that vanished. Now is the downward time for Jashoda, the milk-filled faithful wife who was the object of the rever- ence of the local houses devoted to the Holy Mother. It is human nature to feel an inappropriate vanity as one rises, yet not to feel the *surrender* of "let me learn to bite the dust since I'm down" as one falls. As a result one makes demands for worthless things in the old way and gets kicked by the weak.

The same thing happened to Jashoda. Basini's crowd used to wash her 94 feet and drink the water. Now Basini said easily, "You'll wash your own dishes. Are you my master, that I'll wash your dishes. You are the master's servant as much as I am."

As Jashoda roared, "Do you know who I am?" she heard the eldest 95 daughter-in-law scold, "This is what I feared. Mother gave her a swelled head. Look here, Brahmin sister! I didn't call you, you begged to stay, don't break the peace."

Jashoda understood that now no one would attend to a word she said. 96 She cooked and served in silence and in the late afternoon she went to the temple porch and started to weep. She couldn't even have a good cry. She heard the music for the evening worship at the temple of Shiva. She wiped her eyes and got up. She said to herself, "Now save me, Mother! Must I finally sit by the roadside with a tin cup? Is that what you want?"

The days would have passed in cooking at the Haldar-house and com- 97 plaining to the Mother. But that was not enough for Jashoda. Jashoda's body seemed to keel over. Jashoda doesn't understand why nothing pleases her. Everything seems confused inside her head. When she sits down to cook she thinks she's the milk-mother of this house. She is going home in a showy sari with a free meal in her hand. Her breasts feel empty, as if wasted. She had never thought she wouldn't have a child's mouth at her nipple.

Joshi became bemused. She serves nearly all the rice and curry, but forgets to eat. Sometimes she speaks to Shiva the King, "If Mother can't do it, you take me away. I can't pull any more." 98

Finally it was the sons of the eldest daughter-in-law who said, "Mother! Is the milk-mother sick? She acts strange." 99

The eldest daughter-in-law said, "Let's see." 100

The eldest son said, "Look here? She's a Brahmin's daughter, if anything happens to her, it'll be a sin for us." 101

The eldest daughter-in-law went to ask. Jashoda had started the rice and then lain down in the kitchen on the spread edge of her sari. The eldest daughter-in-law, looking at her bare body, said, "Brahmin sister! Why does the top of your left tit look so red? God! flaming red!" 102

"Who knows? It's like a stone pushing inside. Very hard, like a rock." 103
"What is it?" 104
"Who knows? I suckled so many, perhaps that's why?" 105
"Nonsense! One gets breast-stones or pus-in-the-tit if there's milk. Your youngest is ten." 106
"That one is gone. The one before survived. That one died at birth. Just as well. This sinful world!" 107
"Well the doctor comes tomorrow to look at my grandson. I'll ask. Doesn't look good to me." 108

Jashoda said with her eyes closed, "Like a stone tit, with a stone inside. At first the hard ball moved about, now it doesn't move, doesn't budge." 109
"Let's show the doctor." 110
"No, sister daughter-in-law, I can't show my body to a male doctor." 111

At night when the doctor came the eldest daughter-in-law asked him in her son's presence. She said, "No pain, no burning, but she is keeling over." 112

The doctor said, "Go ask if the *nipple* has shrunk, if the armpit is swollen like a seed." 113

Hearing "swollen like a seed," the eldest daughter-in-law thought, "How crude!" Then she did her field investigations and said, "She says all that you've said has been happening for some time." 114
"How old?" 115
"If you take the eldest son's age she'll be about fifty-five." 116
The doctor said, "I'll give medicine." 117

Going out, he said to the eldest son, "I hear your *Cook* has a problem with her *breast*. I think you should take her to the *cancer hospital*. I didn't see her. But from what I heard it could be *cancer* of the *mammary gland*." 118

Only the other day the eldest son lived in the sixteenth century. He has 119 arrived at the twentieth century very recently. Of his thirteen offspring he has arranged the marriages of the daughters, and the sons have grown up and are growing up at their own speed and in their own way. But even now his grey cells are covered in the darkness of the eighteenth- and the pre-Bengal-Renaissance nineteenth centuries. He still does not take smallpox vaccination and says, "Only the lower classes get smallpox. I don't need to be vaccinated. An upper-class family, respectful of gods and Brahmins, does not contract that disease."

He pooh-poohed the idea of cancer and said, "Yah! Cancer indeed! That easy. You misheard, all she needs is an ointment. I can't send a Brahmin's daughter to a hospital just on your word." 120

Jashoda herself also said, "I can't go to hospital. Ask me to croak instead. I didn't go to hospital to breed, and I'll go now? That corpse-burning devil turned a cripple because he went to hospital!" 121

The elder daughter-in-law said, "I'll get you a herbal ointment. This ointment will surely soothe. The hidden boil will show its tip and burst." 122

The herbal ointment was a complete failure. Slowly Jashoda gave up eating and lost her strength. She couldn't keep her sari on the left side. Sometimes she felt burning, sometimes pain. Finally the skin broke in many places and sores appeared. Jashoda took to her bed. 123

Seeing the hang of it, the eldest son was afraid, if at his house a Brahmin died! He called Jashoda's sons and spoke to them harshly, "It's your mother, she fed you so long, and now she is about to die! Take her with you! She had everyone and she should die in a Kayastha[1] household?" 124

Kangali cried a lot when he heard this story. He came to Jashoda's almost dark room and said, "Wife! You are a blessed auspicious faithful woman! After I spurned you, within two years the temple dishes were stolen, I suffered from boils in my back, and that snake Gopali tricked Napla, broke the safe, stole everything and opened a shop in Tarakeswar. Come, I'll keep you in state." 125

Jashoda said, "Light the lamp." 126
Kangali lit the lamp. 127
Jashoda showed him her bare left breast, thick with running sores and said, "See these sores? Do you know how these sores smell? What will you do with me now? Why did you come to take me?" 128

"The Master called." 129
"Then the Master doesn't want to keep me."—Jashoda sighed and said, "There is no solution about me. What can you do with me?" 130

"Whatever, I'll take you tomorrow. Today I clean the room. Tomorrow for sure." 131

"Are the boys well? Noblay and Gaur used to come, they too have stopped." 132

---

1. *Second caste.*

"All the bastards are selfish. Sons of my spunk after all. As inhuman   133
as I."

"You'll come tomorrow?"   134

"Yes—yes—yes."   135

Jashoda smiled suddenly. A heart-splitting nostalgia-provoking smile.   136

Jashoda said, "Dear, remember?"   137

"What, wife?"   138

"How you played with these tits? You couldn't sleep otherwise? My lap   139
was never empty, if this one left my nipple, there was that one, and then
the boys of the Master's house. How I could, I wonder now!"

"I remember everything, wife!"   140

In this instant Kangali's words are true. Seeing Jashoda's broken, thin,   141
suffering form even Kangali's selfish body and instincts and belly-centered
consciousness remembered the past and suffered some empathy. He held
Jashoda's hand and said, "You have fever?"

"I get feverish all the time. I think by the strength of the sores."   142

"Where does this rotten stink come from?"   143

"From these sores."   144

Jashoda spoke with her eyes closed. Then she said, "Bring the holy   145
doctor. He cured Gopal's *typhoid* with *homeopathy.*"

"I'll call him. I'll take you tomorrow."   146

Kangali left. That he went out, the tapping of his crutches, Jashoda   147
couldn't hear. With her eyes shut, with the idea that Kangali was in the
room, she said spiritlessly, "If you suckle you're a mother, all lies! Nepal
and Gopal don't look at me, and the Master's boys don't spare a peek to
ask how I'm doing." The sores on her breast kept mocking her with a
hundred mouths, a hundred eyes. Jashoda opened her eyes and said, "Do
you hear?"

Then she realized that Kangali had left.   148

In the night she sent Basini for *Lifebuoy* soap and at dawn she went to   149
take a bath with the soap. Stink, what a stink! If the body of a dead cat or
dog rots in the garbage can you get a smell like this. Jashoda had forever
scrubbed her breasts carefully with soap and oil, for the master's sons had
put the nipples in their mouth. Why did those breasts betray her in the
end? Her skin burns with the sting of soap. Still Jashoda washed herself
with soap. Her head was ringing, everything seemed dark. There was fire
in Jashoda's body, in her head. The black floor was very cool. Jashoda
spread her sari and lay down. She could not bear the weight of her breast
standing up.

As Jashoda lay down, she lost sense and consciousness with fever.   150
Kangali came at the proper time: but seeing Jashoda he lost his grip. Finally
Nabin came and rasped, "Are these people human? She reared all the boys
with her milk and they don't call a doctor? I'll call Hari the doctor."

Haribabu took one look at her and said, "Hospital."   151

Hospitals don't admit people who are so sick. At the efforts and recom-   152
mendations of the eldest son, Jashoda was admitted.

"What's the matter? O Doctorbabu, what's the problem?"—Kangali 153
asked, weeping like a boy.

"Cancer." 154

"You can get cancer in a tit?" 155

"Otherwise how did she get it?" 156

"Her own twenty, thirty boys at the Master's house—she had a lot of 157
milk—"

"What did you say? How many did she *feed*?" 158

"About fifty for sure." 159

"Fif-ty!" 160

"Yes sir." 161

"She had twenty children?" 162

"Yes sir." 163

"*God!*" 164

"Sir!" 165

"What?" 166

"Is it because she suckled so many—?" 167

"One can't say why someone gets cancer, one can't say. But when 168
people breast-feed too much—didn't you realize earlier? It didn't get to this
in a day?"

"She wasn't with me, sir. We quarreled—" 169

"I see." 170

"How do you see her? Will she get well?" 171

"Get well! See how long she lasts. You've brought her in the last stages. 172
No one survives this stage."

Kangali left weeping. In the late afternoon, harassed by Kangali's lam- 173
entations, the eldest son's second son went to the doctor. He was mini-
mally anxious about Jashoda—but his father nagged him and he was
financially dependent on his father.

The doctor explained everything to him. It happened not in a day, but 174
over a long time. Why? No one could tell. How does one perceive breast
cancer? A hard lump inside the breast toward the top can be removed.
Then gradually the lump inside becomes large, hard, and like a congealed
pressure. The skin is expected to turn orange, as is expected a shrinking of
the nipple. The gland in the armpit can be inflamed. When there is *ulcer-
ation*, that is to say sores, one can call it the final stages. Fever? From the
point of view of seriousness it falls in the second or third category. If there
is something like a sore in the body, there can be fever. That is *secondary*.

The second son was confused with all this specialist talk. He said, "Will 175
she live?"

"No." 176

"How long will she suffer?" 177

"I don't think too long." 178

"When there's nothing to be done, how will you treat her?" 179

"*Painkiller, sedative, antibiotic* for the fever. Her body is very, very *down*." 180

"She stopped eating." 181

"You didn't take her to a doctor?"   182
"Yes."   183
"Didn't he tell you?"   184
"Yes."   185
"What did he say?"   186
"That it might be cancer. Asked us to take her to the hospital. She didn't   187
agree."
"Why would she? She'd die!"   188
The second son came home and said, "When Arun-doctor said she had   189
cancer, she might have survived if treated then."
His mother said, "If you know that much then why didn't you take her?   190
Did I stop you?"
Somewhere in the minds of the second son and his mother an unknown   191
sense of guilt and remorse came up like bubbles in dirty and stagnant water
and vanished instantly.
Guilt said—she lived with us, we never took a look at her, when did the   192
disease catch her, we didn't take it seriously at all. She was a silly person,
reared so many of us, we didn't look after her. Now, with everyone around
her she's dying in hospital, so many children, husband living, when she
clung to us, then we had ——! What an alive body she had, milk leaped out
of her, we never thought she would have this disease.
The disappearance of guilt said—who can undo Fate? It was written that   193
she'd die of *cancer*—who'd stop it? It would have been wrong if she had
died here—her husband and sons would have asked, how did she die? We
have been saved from that wrongdoing. No one can say anything.
The eldest son assured them, "Now Arun-doctor says no one survives   194
cancer. The cancer that Brahmin-sister has can lead to cutting of the tit,
removing the uterus, even after that people die of *cancer*. See, Father gave
us a lot of reverence toward Brahmins—we are alive by father's grace. If
Brahmin-sister had died in our house, we would have had to perform the
penance-ritual."
Patients much less sick than Jashoda die much sooner. Jashoda aston-   195
ished the doctors by hanging on for about a month in hospital. At first
Kangali, Nabin, and the boys did indeed come and go, but Jashoda remained the same, comatose, cooking with fever, spellbound. The sores on
her breast gaped more and more and the breast now looks like an open
wound. It is covered by a piece of thin *gauze* soaked in *antiseptic lotion*, but
the sharp smell of putrefying flesh is circulating silently in the room's air
like incense-smoke. This brought an ebb in the enthusiasm of Kangali and
the other visitors. The doctor said as well, "Is she not responding? All for
the better. It's hard to bear without consciousness, can anyone bear such
death-throes consciously?"
"Does she know that we come and go?"   196
"Hard to say."   197
"Does she eat?"   198

"Through tubes." 199

"Do people live this way?" 200

"Now you're very ——" 201

The doctor understood that he was unreasonably angry because Jashoda 202
was in this condition. He was angry with Jashoda, with Kangali, with
women who don't take the signs of breast-cancer *seriously* enough and
finally die in this dreadful and hellish pain. Cancer constantly defeats
patient and doctor. One patient's cancer means the patient's death and the
defeat of science, and of course of the doctor. One can medicate against the
secondary symptom, if eating stops one can *drip glucose* and feed the body,
if the lungs become incapable of breathing there is *oxygen*—but the advance
of *cancer*, its expansion, spread, and killing, remained unchecked. The
word *cancer* is a general signifier, by which in the different parts of the body
is meant different *malignant growths*. Its characteristic properties are to destroy the infected area of the body, to spread by *metastasis*, to return after
removal, to create *toximeia*.

Kangali came out without a proper answer to his question. Returning to 203
the temple, he said to Nabin and his sons, "There's no use going any more.
She doesn't know us, doesn't open her eyes, doesn't realize anything. The
doctor is doing what he can."

Nabin said, "If she dies?" 204

"They have the *telephone number* of the old Master's eldest son, they'll 205
call."

"Suppose she wants to see you. Kangali, your wife is a blessed auspi- 206
cious faithful woman! Who would say the mother of so many. To see her
body—but she didn't bend, didn't look elsewhere."

Talking thus, Nabin became gloomily silent. In fact, since he'd seen 207
Jashoda's infested breasts, many a philosophic thought and sexological
argument have been slowly circling Nabin's drug-and-booze-addled dim
head like great rutting snakes emptied of venom. For example, I lusted
after her? This is the end of that intoxicating bosom? Ho! Man's body's a
zero. To be crazy for that is to be crazy.

Kangali didn't like all this talk. His mind had already *rejected* Jashoda. 208
When he saw Jashoda in the Haldar-house he was truly affected and even
after her admission into hospital he was passionately anxious. But now
that feeling is growing cold. The moment the doctor said Jashoda wouldn't
last, he put her out of mind almost painlessly. His sons are his sons. Their
mother had become a distant person for a long time. Mother meant hair in
a huge topknot, blindingly white clothes, a strong personality. The person
lying in the hospital is someone else, not Mother.

Breast *cancer* makes the *brain comatose*, this was a solution for Jashoda. 209

Jashoda understood that she had come to hospital, she was in the hos- 210
pital, and that this desensitizing sleep was a medicated sleep. In her weak,
infected, dazed brain she thought, has some son of the Haldar-house become a doctor? No doubt he sucked her milk and is now repaying the

milk-debt? But those boys entered the family business as soon as they left high school! However, why don't the people who are helping her so much free her from the stinking presence of her chest? What a smell, what treachery? Knowing these breasts to be the rice-winner, she had constantly conceived to keep them filled with milk. The breast's job is to hold milk. She kept her breast clean with perfumed soap, she never wore a top, even in youth, because her breasts were so heavy.

When the *sedation* lessens, Jashoda screams, "Ah! Ah! Ah!"—and looks for the *nurse* and the doctor with passionate bloodshot eyes. When the doctor comes, she mutters with hurt feelings, "You grew so big on my milk, and now you're hurting me so?" 211

The doctor says, "She sees her milk-sons all over the world." 212

After injection and sleepy numbness. Pain, tremendous pain, the cancer is spreading *at the expense of the human host*. Gradually Jashoda's left breast bursts and becomes like the *crater* of a volcano. The smell of putrefaction makes approach difficult. 213

Finally one night, Jashoda understood that her feet and hands were getting cold. She understood that death was coming. Jashoda couldn't open her eyes, but she understood that some people were looking at her hand. A needle pricked her arm. Painful breathing inside. Has to be. Who is looking? Are these her own people? The people whom she suckled because she carried them, or those she suckled for a living? Jashoda thought, after all, she had suckled the world, could she then die alone? The doctor who sees her every day, the person who will cover her face with a sheet, will put her on a cart, will lower her at the burning ghat, the untouchable who will put her in the furnace, are all her milk-sons. One must become Jashoda[1] if one suckles the world. One has to die friendless, with no one left to put a bit of water in the mouth. Yet someone was supposed to be there at the end. Who was it? It was who? Who was it? 214

Jashoda died at 11 P.M. 215

The Haldar-house was called on the phone. The phone didn't ring. The Haldars *disconnected* their phone at night. 216

Jashoda Devi, Hindu female, lay in the hospital morgue in the usual way, went to the burning ghat in a van, and was burnt. She was cremated by an untouchable. 217

Jashoda was God manifest, others do and did whatever she thought. Jashoda's death was also the death of God. When a mortal masquerades as God here below, she is forsaken by all and she must always die alone. 218

Translated from the Bengali by Gayatri Chakravorty Spivak

---

1. Jashoda: *The mythic mother of the god Kirshna, and in that sense the suckler of the world.*

STUDY QUESTIONS

1. Although Kangalicharan is a Brahmin (the highest caste in Indian Hindu society), he is poor and belongs to the struggling working class. Mr. Haldar (Haldarbabu) is a wealthy businessman but belongs to the lower caste of merchants. How does this explain Mr. Haldar's actions toward Kangalicharan after the accident?

2. What is meant by the statement "Jashoda is fully an Indian woman"? According to the story, how does "the old Indian tradition" represent the ideal woman? Do you read the appeal to Indian tradition here as straightforward or ironic?

3. What motivates the Haldar household to hire Jashoda as a wet nurse (a woman who is paid to breast-feed the child of another woman)? How do Jashoda and her husband respond to this offer? Trace Jashoda's consequent success as a *professional mother*.

4. Jashoda becomes the mother of twenty children. The Haldars' daughters-in-law "called a halt at twelve-thirteen-fourteen," but the granddaughters-in-law leave the home and join their husbands in the workplace. How does Jashoda's treatment by the Haldar family and by her own family once her economic productivity as a wet nurse ends function as a criticism of Indian culture?

5. What is symbolized by Jashoda's illness and death? Is hers the death of an oppressed individual or an ironic critique of Indian culture?

INDONESIA

 ## PRAMOEDYA ANANTA TOER

Pramoedya Ananta Toer (b. 1925), a short story writer and novelist, was active in the Indonesian Nationalist Movement in the 1940s. He was imprisoned by the Dutch from 1947 to 1949, then later by the Indonesian government from 1965 to 1979 for his revolutionary ideals. His novels, many of which he wrote in prison, demonstrate a strong mystical element and a style distinctly his own. He is best known for his historical novel Bumi Manusia (This Earth of Mankind, 1980) *and its sequels.* Bumi Manusia *was banned in Indonesia because of its alleged Marxist elements and led to Toer's house arrest in 1981.*

Inem

Inem was one of the girls I knew. She was eight years old—two years older than me. She was no different from the others. And if there was a difference, it was that she was one of the prettier little girls in our neighborhood. People liked to look at her. She was polite, unspoiled, deft, and hard-working—qualities which quickly spread her fame even into other neighborhoods as a girl who would make a good daughter-in-law. 1

And once when she was heating water in the kitchen, she said to me, "Gus[1] Muk, I'm going to be married." 2

"You're fooling!" I said. 3

"No, the proposal came a week ago. Mama and Papa and all the relatives have accepted the proposal." 4

"What fun to be a bride!" I exclaimed happily. 5

---

1. Gus: *A title of respect which Inem, as a servant, uses toward the son of the family for whom she works.*

"Yes, it'll be fun, I know it will! They'll buy me all sorts of nice clothes. 6
I'll be dressed up in a bride's outfit, with flowers in my hair, and they'll
make me up with powder and mascara. Oh, I'll like that!"

And it was true. One afternoon her mother called on mine. At that time 7
Inem was living with us as a servant. Her daily tasks were to help with the
cooking and to watch over me and my younger brothers and sisters as we
played.

Inem's mother made a living by doing batik work. That was what the 8
women in our neighborhood did when they were not working in the rice
fields. Some put batik designs on sarongs, while others worked on head
cloths. The poorer ones preferred to do head cloths; since it did not take
so long to finish a head cloth, they received payment for it sooner. And
Inem's mother supported her family by putting batik designs on head
cloths. She got the cloth and the wax from her employer, the Idjo Store.
For every two head cloths that she finished, she was paid one and a half
cents. On the average, a woman could do eight to eleven head cloths a
day.

Inem's father kept gamecocks. All he did, day after day, was to wager 9
his bird in cockfights. If he lost, the victor would take his cock. And in
addition he would have to pay two and a half rupiahs, or at the very least
seventy-five cents. When he was not gambling on cockfights, he would
play cards with his neighbors for a cent a hand.

Sometimes Inem's father would be away from home for a month or half 10
a month, wandering around on foot. His return would signify that he was
bringing home some money.

Mother once told me that Inem's father's main occupation had been 11
robbing people in the teak forest between our town, Blora, and the coastal
town of Rembang. I was then in the first grade, and heard many stories of
robbers, bandits, thieves, and murderers. As a result of those stories and
what Mother told me, I came to be terrified of Inem's father.

Everybody knew that Inem's father was a criminal, but no one could 12
prove it and no one dared complain to the police. Consequently he was
never arrested by the police. Furthermore, almost all of Inem's mother's
relatives were policemen. There was even one with the rank of agent first
class. Inem's father himself had once been a policeman but had been dis-
charged for taking bribes.

Mother also told me that in the old days Inem's father had been an 13
important criminal. As a way of countering an outbreak of crime that was
getting out of hand, the Netherlands Indies government had appointed
him a policeman, so that he could round up his former associates. He never
robbed any more after that, but in our area he continued to be a focus of
suspicion.

When Inem's mother called on my mother, Inem was heating water in 14
the kitchen. I tagged along after Inem's mother. The visitor, Mother, and
I sat on a low, red couch.

"Ma'am," said Inem's mother, "I've come to ask for Inem to come back 15
home."

"Why do you want Inem back? Isn't it better for her to be here? You 16
don't have any of her expenses, and here she can learn how to cook."

"Yes, ma'am, but I plan for her to get married after the coming harvest." 17

"What?" exclaimed Mother, startled. "She's going to be married?" 18

"Yes, ma'am. She's old enough to be married now—she's eight years 19
old," said Inem's mother.

At this my mother laughed. And her visitor was surprised to see Mother 20
laugh.

"Why, a girl of eight is still a child!" said Mother. 21

"We're not upper-class people, ma'am. I think she's already a year too 22
old. You know Asih? She married her daughter when she was two years
younger than mine."

Mother tried to dissuade the woman. But Inem's mother had another 23
argument. Finally the visitor spoke again: "I feel lucky that someone wants
her. If we let a proposal go by this time, maybe there will never be another
one. And how humiliating it would be to have a daughter turn into an old
maid! And it just might be that if she gets married she'll be able to help out
with the household expenses."

Mother did not reply. Then she looked at me and said; "Go get the betel[1] 24
set and the spittoon."

So I went to fetch the box of betel-chewing ingredients and the brass 25
spittoon.

"And what does your husband say?" 26

"Oh, he agrees. What's more, Markaban is the son of a well-to-do man— 27
his only child. Markaban has already begun to help his father trade cattle
in Rembang, Tjepu, Medang, Pati, Ngawen, and also here in Blora," said
Inem's mother.

This information seemed to cheer Mother up, although I could not 28
understand why. Then she called Inem, who was at work in the kitchen. Inem came in. And Mother asked, "Inem, do you want to get
married?"

Inem bowed her head. She was very respectful toward Mother. I never 29
once heard her oppose her. Indeed, it is rare to find people who are
powerless opposing anything that others say to them.

I saw then that Inem was beaming. She often looked like that; give her 30
something that pleased her even a little and she would beam. But she was
not accustomed to saying "thank you." In the society of the simple people
of our neighborhood, the words "thank you" were still unfamiliar. It was
only through the glow radiating from their faces that gratitude found expression.

---

1. Betel: *A plant whose leaves are chewed by many Asians.*

"Yes, ma'am," said Inem so softly as to be almost inaudible.   31

Then Inem's mother and mine chewed some betel. Mother herself did   32
not like to chew betel all the time. She did it only when she had a woman
visitor. Every few moments she would spit into the brass spittoon.

When Inem had gone back to the kitchen Mother said, "It's not right to   33
make children marry."

These words surprised Inem's mother. But she did not say anything nor   34
did her eyes show any interest.

"I was eighteen when I got married," said Mother.   35

Inem's mother's surprise vanished. She was no longer surprised now,   36
but she still did not say anything.

"It's not right to make children marry," repeated Mother.   37

And Inem's mother was surprised again.   38

"Their children will be stunted."   39

Inem's mother's surprise vanished once more.   40

"Yes, ma'am." Then she said placidly, "My mother was also eight when   41
she got married."

Mother paid no attention and continued, "Not only will they be stunted,   42
but their health will be affected too."

"Yes, ma'am, but ours is a long-lived family. My mother is still alive,   43
though she's over fifty-nine. And my grandmother is still alive too. I think
she must be seventy-four. She's still vigorous and strong enough to pound
corn in the mortar."

Still ignoring her, Mother went on, "Especially if the husband is also a   44
child."

"Yes, ma'am, but Markaban is seventeen."   45

"Seventeen! My husband was thirty when he married me."   46

Inem's mother was silent. She never stopped shifting the wad of tobacco   47
leaves that was stuck between her lips. One moment she would move the
tobacco to the right, a moment later to the left, and the next moment she
would roll it up and scrub her coal-black teeth with it.

Now Mother had no more arguments with which to oppose her visitor's   48
intention. She said, "Well, if you've made up your mind to marry Inem off,
I only hope that she gets a good husband who can take care of her. And I
hope she gets someone who is compatible."

Inem's mother left, still shifting the tobacco about in her mouth.   49

"I hope nothing bad happens to that child."   50

"Why would anything bad happen to her?" I asked.   51

"Never mind, Muk, it's nothing." Then Mother changed the subject. "If   52
the situation of their family improves, we won't lose any more of our
chickens."

"Is somebody stealing our chickens, Mama?" I asked.   53

"No, Muk, never mind," Mother said slowly. "Such a little child! Only   54
eight years old. What a pity it is. But they need money. And the only way
to get it is to marry off their daughter."

Then Mother went to the garden behind the house to get some string 55
beans for supper.

Fifteen days after this visit, Inem's mother came again to fetch her 56
daughter. She seemed greatly pleased that Inem made no objection to
being taken away. And when Inem was about to leave our house, never to
be a member of our family again, she spoke to me in the kitchen doorway,
"Well, good bye, Gus Muk. I'm going home, Gus Muk," she said very
softly.

She always spoke softly. Speaking softly was one of the customary ways 57
of showing politeness in our small-town society. She went off as joyfully as
a child who expects to be given a new blouse.

From that moment, Inem no longer lived in our house. I felt very deeply 58
the loss of my constant companion. From that moment also, it was no
longer Inem who took me to the bathing cubicle at night to wash my feet
before going to bed, but my adoptive older sister.

Sometime I felt an intense longing to see Inem. Not infrequently, when 59
I had got into bed, I would recall the moment when her mother drew her
by the hand and the two of them left our house. Inem's house was in back
of ours, separated only by a wooden fence.

She had been gone a month. I often went to her house to play with her, 60
and Mother always got angry when she found out that I had been there.
She would always say, "What can you learn at Inem's house that's of any
use?"

And I would never reply. Mother always had a good reason for scolding 61
me. Everything she said built a thick wall that was impenetrable to excuses.
Therefore my best course was to be silent. And as the clinching argument
in her lecture, she was almost certain to repeat the sentences that she
uttered so often: "What's the point to your playing with her? Aren't there
lots of other children you can ask to play with you? What's more, she's a
woman who's going to be married soon."

But I kept on sneaking over to her house anyway. It is really surprising 62
sometimes how a prohibition seems to exist solely in order to be violated.
And when I disobeyed I felt that what I did was pleasurable. For children
such as I at that time—oh, how many prohibitions and restrictions were
heaped on our heads! Yes, it was as though the whole world was watching
us, bent on forbidding whatever we did and whatever we wanted. Inevitably we children felt that this world was really intended only for adults.

Then the day of the wedding arrived. 63

For five days before the ceremony, Inem's family was busy in the 64
kitchen, cooking food and preparing various delicacies. This made me visit
her house all the more frequently.

The day before the wedding, Inem was dressed in all her finery. Mother 65
sent me there with five kilos of rice and twenty-five cents as a neighborly

contribution. And that afternoon we children crowded around and stared at her in admiration. The hair over her forehead and temples and her eyebrows had been carefully trimmed with a razor and thickened with mascara. Her little bun of hair had been built up with a switch and adorned with the paper flowers with springs for stalks that we call *sunduk mentul*. Her clothes were made of satin. Her sarong was an expensive one made in Solo. These things had all been rented from a Chinaman in the Chinese quarter near the town square. The gold rings and bracelets were all rented too.

The house was decorated with constructions of banyan leaves and young coconut fronds. On each wall there were crossed tricolor flags encircled by palm leaves. All the house pillars were similarly decorated with tricolor bunting. 66

Mother herself went and helped with the preparations. But not for long. Mother rarely did this sort of thing except for her closest neighbors. She stayed less than an hour. And it was then too that the things sent by Inem's husband-to-be arrived: a load of cakes and candies, a male goat, a quantity of rice, a packet of salt, a sack of husked coconuts, and half a sack of granulated sugar. 67

It was just after the harvest. Rice was cheap. And when rice was cheap all other foodstuffs were cheap too. That was why the period after the harvest was a favorite time for celebrations. And for that reason Inem's family had found it impossible to contract for a puppet performance. The puppet masters had already been engaged by other families in various neighborhoods. The puppet theater was the most popular form of entertainment in our area. In our town there were three types of puppet performance: the *wajan purwa* or shadow play, which recounted stories from the *Mahabharata* and the *Ramayana*, as well as other stories similar in theme; the *wajang krutjil*, in which wooden puppets in human shape acted out stories of Arabia, Persia, India, and China, as well as tales of Madjapahit times; and the *wajang golek*, which employed wooden dolls. But this last was not very popular. 68

Because there were no puppet masters available, Inem's family engaged a troupe of dancing girls. At first this created a dispute. Inem's relatives on her mother's side were religious scholars and teachers. But Inem's father would not back down. The dance troupe came, with its *gamelan* orchestra, and put on a *tajuban*. 69

Usually, in our area, a *tajuban* was attended by the men who wanted to dance with the girls and by little children who only wanted to watch—little children whose knowledge of sexual matters did not go beyond kissing. The grown boys did not like to watch; it embarrassed them. This was even more the case with the women—none of them attended at all. And a *tajuban* in our area—in order to inflame sexual passions—was always accompanied by alcoholic beverages: arrack, beer, whisky, or gin. 70

The *tajuban* lasted for two days and nights. We children took great 71 delight in the spectacle of men and women dancing and kissing one another and every now and then clinking their glasses and drinking liquor as they danced and shouted, *"Huse!"*

And though Mother forbade me to watch, I went anyway on the sly.   72

"Why do you insist on going where those wicked people are? Look at   73 your religious teacher: he doesn't go to watch, even though he is Inem's father's brother-in-law. You must have noticed that yourself."

Our religious teacher also had a house in back of ours, to the right of   74 Inem's house. Subsequently the teacher's failure to attend became a topic that was sure to enliven a conversation. From it there arose two remarks that itched on the tip of everyone's tongue: that the teacher was certainly a pious man, and that Inem's father was undoubtedly a reprobate.

Mother reinforced her scolding with words that I did not understand at   75 the time: "Do you know something? They are people who have no respect for women," she said in a piercing voice.

And when the bridegroom came to be formally presented to the bride,   76 Inem, who had been sitting on the nuptial seat, was led forth. The bridegroom had reached the veranda. Inem squatted and made obeisance to her future husband, and then washed his feet with flower water from a brass pot. Then the couple were tied together and conducted side by side to the nuptial seat. At that time the onlookers could be heard saying, "One child becomes two. One child becomes two. One child becomes two."

And the women who were watching beamed as though they were to be   77 the recipients of the happiness to come.

At that very moment I noticed that Inem was crying so much that her   78 make-up was spoiled, and tears were trickling down her pretty face. At home I asked Mother, "Why was the bride crying, Mama?"

"When a bride cries, it's because she is thinking of her long-departed   79 ancestors. Their spirits also attend the ceremony. And they are happy that their descendant has been safely married," replied Mother.

I never gave any thought to those words of hers. Later I found out why   80 Inem had been crying. She had to urinate, but was afraid to tell anyone.

The celebration ended uneventfully. There were no more guests coming   81 with contributions. The house resumed its everyday appearance, and by the time the moneylenders came to collect, Inem's father had left Blora. After the wedding, Inem's mother and Inem herself went on doing batik work—day and night. And if someone went to their house at three o'clock in the morning, he would be likely to find them still working. Puffs of smoke would be rising between them from the crucible in which the wax was melted. In addition to that, quarreling was often heard in that house.

And once, when I was sleeping with Mother in her bed, a loud scream   82 awakened me: "I won't! I won't!"

It was still night then. The screams were repeated again and again,   83 accompanied by the sound of blows and pounding on a door. I knew that the screams came from Inem's mouth. I recognized her voice.

"Mama, why is Inem screaming?" I asked. 84

"They're fighting. I hope nothing bad happens to that little girl," she 85
said. But she gave no explanation.

"Why would anything bad happen to her, mama?" I asked insistently. 86

Mother did not reply to my question. And then, when the screaming 87
and shouting were over, we went back to sleep. Such screams were almost
sure to be heard every night. Screams and screams. And every time I heard
them, I would ask my mother about them. Mother would never give a
satisfactory answer. Sometimes she merely sighed, "What a pitty, such a
little child!"

One day Inem came to our house. She went straight in to find my 88
mother. Her face was pale bloodless. Before saying anything, she set the
tone of the occasion by crying—crying in a respectful way.

"Why are you crying, Inem? Have you been fighting again?" Mother 89
asked.

"Ma'am," said Inem between her sobs, "I hope that you will be willing 90
to take me back here as before."

"But you're married, aren't you, Inem?" 91

And Inem cried some more. Through her tears she said, "I can't stand 92
it ma'am."

"Why, Inem? Don't you like your husband?" asked Mother. 93

"Ma'am, please take pity on me. Every night all he wants to do is 94
wrestle, ma'am."

"Can't you say to him, 'Please, dear, don't be like that'?" 95

"I'm afraid, ma'am. I'm afraid of him. He's so big. And when he wres- 96
tles he squeezes me so hard that I can't breathe. You'll take me back, won't
you, ma'am?" she pleaded.

"If you didn't have a husband, Inem, of course I'd take you back. But 97
you have a husband . . ."

And Inem cried again when she heard what Mother said. "Ma'am, I 98
don't want to have a husband."

"You may not want to, but the fact is that you do, Inem. Maybe even- 99
tually your husband will change for the better, and the two of you will be
able to live happily. You wanted to get married, didn't you?" said Mother.

"Yes, ma'am . . . but, but . . ." 100

"Inem, regardless of anything else, a woman must serve her husband 101
faithfully. If you aren't a good wife to your husband, your ancestors will
curse you," said Mother.

Inem began crying harder. And because of her crying she was unable to 102
say anything.

"Now, Inem, promise me that you will always prepare your husband's 103
meals. When you have an idle moment, you should pray to God to keep
him safe. You must promise to wash his clothes, and you must massage

him when he is tired from his work. You must rub his back vigorously when he catches cold."

Inem still made no reply. Only her tears continued to fall. 104

"Well now, you go home, and from this moment on be a good wife to 105
him. No matter whether he is good or bad, you must serve him faithfully, because after all he *is* your husband."

Inem, who was sitting on the floor, did not stir. 106

"Get up and go home to your husband. You . . . if you just up and quit 107
your husband the consequences will not be good for you, either now or in the future," Mother added.

"Yes, ma'am," Inem said submissively. Slowly she rose and walked 108
home.

"How sad, she's so little," said Mother. 109

"Mama, does daddy ever wrestle you?" I asked. 110

Mother looked searchingly into my eyes. Then her scrutiny relaxed. She 111
smiled. "No," she said. "Your father is the best person in the whole world, Muk."

Then Mother went to the kitchen to get the hoe, and she worked in the 112
garden with me.

A year passed imperceptibly. On a certain occasion Inem came again. In 113
the course of a year she had grown much bigger. It was quite apparent that she was mature, although only nine years old. As usual, she went directly to where Mother was and sat on the floor with her head bowed. She said, "Ma'am, now I don't have a husband any more."

"What?" 114

"Now I don't have a husband any more." 115

"You're divorced?" asked Mother. 116

"Yes, ma'am." 117

"Why did you separate from him?" 118

She did not reply. 119

"Did you fail to be a good wife to him?" 120

"I think I was always a good wife to him, ma'am." 121

"Did you massage him when he came home tired from work?" asked 122
Mother probingly.

"Yes, ma'am, I did everything you advised me to." 123

"Well then, why did you separate?" 124

"Ma'am, he often beat me." 125

"Beat you? He beat a little child like you?" 126

"I did everything I could to be a good wife, ma'am. And when he beat 127
me and I was in pain—was that part of being a good wife, ma'am?" she asked, in genuine perplexity.

Mother was silent. Her eyes scrutinized Inem. "He beat you," Mother 128
whispered then.

"Yes, ma'am—he beat me just the way Mama and Papa do." 129

"Maybe you failed in some way after all in your duty to him. A husband   130
would never have the heart to beat a wife who was really and truly a good
wife to him."

Inem did not reply. She changed the subject: "Would you be willing to   131
take me back, ma'am?"

There was no hesitation in Mother's reply. She said firmly, "Inem,   132
you're a divorced woman now. There are lots of grown boys here. It
wouldn't look right to people, would it?"

"But they wouldn't beat me," said the divorcee.   133

"No. That isn't what I mean. It just doesn't look right for a divorced   134
woman as young as you to be in a place where there are lots of men."

"Is that because there's something wrong with me, ma'am?"   135

"No, Inem, it's a question of propriety."   136

"Propriety, ma'am? It's for the sake of propriety that I can't stay here?"   137

"Yes, that's the way it is, Inem."   138

The divorcee did not say anything more. She remained sitting on the   139
floor, and seemed to have no intention of leaving the place where she was
sitting. Mother went up to her and patted her shoulder consolingly. "Now,
Inem . . . the best thing is for you to help your parents earn a living. I really
regret that I can't take you back here."

Two tears formed in the corners of the little woman's eyes. She got up.   140
Listlessly she moved her feet, leaving our house to return to her parents'
house. And from then on she was seldom seen outside her house.

And thereafter, the nine-year-old divorcee—since she was nothing but a   141
burden to her family—could be beaten by anyone who wanted to: her
mother, her brothers, her uncles, her neighbors, her aunts. Yet Inem never
again came to our house.

Her screams of pain were often heard. When she moaned, I covered my   142
ears with my hands. And Mother continued to uphold the respectability of
her home.

Translated from the Indonesian by Rufus S. Hendron

STUDY QUESTIONS

1. How is Inem at eight different from the narrator, who is six years old?
2. Analyze the function of class background as a motivating force in
   Inem's fate.
3. What is the function of the narrator's mother? Explain the mother's use
   of the world "propriety" in the story's conclusion.
4. Discuss the use of point-of-view (that of a young and innocent child)
   in constructing a criticism of traditional Indonesian attitudes toward
   poor and working-class girls.

JAPAN

HAYASHI FUMIKO

Hayashi Fumiko (1904–1951) had an impoverished nomadic childhood, an experience that is reflected in her work. Indeed, her first book bore the title Journal of a Vagabond *(1930). As an adult, she worked as a waitress, a domestic, a street peddler, and a clerk. Her fiction uses the strategies of the I-novel, treating autobiographical materials to express strong and resistant female consciousness. A pioneer feminist piece, "Late Chrysanthemum" received the Women's Prize for Literature in 1948. The story is an early yet still startlingly topical and vivid critique of women's roles of dependency on male approval. It sets forward the grounds of difference between male and female desire and the need for women to find a separate and independent economic base.*

Late Chrysanthemum

"I'll be round this evening, about five," the voice on the telephone had said. Well, it certainly was a surprise, after a whole year of silence. But then, one never knew. . . . Kin looked at her watch; there were still some two hours to go before five. First and foremost, then, a bath: she gave the maid instructions to prepare an early meal, and hurried off to the bathroom. She must look younger than ever, younger than when they had last said good-bye; one suggestion of her age, and all was up. So thinking, she allowed herself a leisurely soak.

Back from the bath, she got out some ice from the icebox, crushed it finely, wrapped it in a double layer of gauze and spent ten minutes with it before the mirror, massaging her face all over. Her face grew red and numb. Somewhere at her woman's breast there gnawed the realisation of her fifty-six years but, determined that her years of experience should help her to cover up mere age, she took out her long-treasured jar of imported

1

2

cream and smeared it over her cold face. In the mirror an elderly woman's face, with a deathly, bluish pallor, stared wide-eyed back at her.

For a moment as she worked she was seized with a sudden disgust for   3
her own face; across her mind floated a vision of the bewitching beauty that had been hers, that beauty once celebrated on the picture postcards of the day. She pulled up her clothes, and gazed intently at her thighs. Their former ripe plumpness was gone, and a network of tiny blue veins stood out over the skin. And, yet, she was not skinny—that was one thing to be thankful for—and her thighs when closed still met each other firmly and squarely. Whenever she had a bath, she would seat herself on her heels in formal fashion, knees together, and pour water into the hollow of her thighs. The water remained, forming a pool in the groove between her legs. At this, she would feel a comforting sense of relief, and her age no longer seemed to matter so much. She could still attract a man: while that was true, Kin felt, life still had some meaning. She spread her thighs apart, and furtively, almost as though shy of herself, stroked the skin on the inner side. It was smooth and soft, as doeskin becomes after long treatment with oil.

Kin had once read a novel by the eighteenth-century writer Saikaku, an   4
account of a journey through Japan. In it were described, among the attractions of Ise at the time, two beautiful girls who played the samisen, one named Osugi and the other Tama. Around them as they played were stretched ropes of vivid scarlet, and people would play a kind of game, throwing money through the ropes in an attempt to hit the girls' faces. This scene, with the two girls inside the red ropes, came to Kin's mind with the beauty of some old colour print. Beauty like that was for her, she felt, long since a thing of the past.

In her youth she had been consumed with the lust for money, blind to   5
all else. But now she was getting old; she had lived, moreover, through the fearful ravages of war, and life without men seemed somehow blank and forlorn. Her beauty, too, had altered by imperceptible degrees with age, and the advance of the years had wrought a change in its very character. The older she became, the more careful she was to avoid the gaudy in her dress. She despised the strange wiles resorted to by some women over fifty who ought to know better—the necklace above the sunken breasts, the check skirt in a red more suitable for an undergarment, the too-full white satin blouse, the broad-brimmed hat hiding the wrinkled forehead. Equally did she dislike the woman in Japanese dress who affected a little scarlet peeping out around the neck in the manner of prostitutes.

Kin had never once worn Western dress. Her kimono was of a dark blue   6
silk, freshened with a neckband of purest white crepe. Her sash was of pale cream silk with raised flecks of white; the belt beneath it was pale blue, but she never, as some did, let it show above her sash in front. Her bosom she made to look full and round, her hips narrow; next to her skin, a girdle drawn as tightly as possible, and at her buttocks a pad lightly stuffed with

silk-wadding. Her hair had always been lighter than average and, taken with her fair complexion, never suggested a woman of over fifty. Perhaps because her height made her wear her kimono rather short, the hemline at the bottom was always neat and trim, and had an air of freshness.

Before a meeting with a man, Kin would always dress, as today, with a restraint which betrayed years of experience. Then, seated before the mirror, she would gulp down a cup of cold rice wine, never forgetting afterwards to clean her teeth to remove the smell. The merest sip of alcohol, she found, did things for her physically which no cosmetics could ever do. The slight intoxication it produced gave a flush to the cheekbones and the right misty look to the eyes. Her face, smoothed over with face lotion and cream, took on a fresh glow as if new life had been breathed into it. The best-quality lipstick, and that in a dark shade, was the only touch of red she allowed herself. Not once in her life had she painted her nails, and she had even less intention of doing so now that she was old: on an old woman's hands it only contrived to look grasping, undignified and quite incongruous. She confined herself, therefore, to patting lotion into the back of her hands, keeping her nails almost morbidly short and polishing them with a piece of cloth. The colours that peeped out from inside the sleeve of her under-kimono were all pastel shades. Her perfume—a sweetish brand— she rubbed on her shoulders and her plump arms; nothing would induce her to put it behind her ears.

Kin refused to forget her femininity. Death itself was preferable to the blowsiness of the average old woman. There was a poem—composed, they said, by some famous woman of the past—

> Never could human form
> Aspire, I know,
> To beauty ripe as that now bends
> This rose. Yet, somewhere here,
> I see myself.

A life bereft of men was too dreadful to bear thinking of: Kin gazed into the pale pink petals of the roses Itaya had brought her, their splendour conjuring images from her past. Times had changed since those far-off days; her own tastes, the things that gave her pleasure—these too, little by little, had changed; and yet she was glad. Sometimes, when she slept alone, she would wake in the night and amuse herself by secretly counting over on her fingers the number of men in her life since she had been a girl. There was that one, and that one, and him, and oh yes, I'd forgotten him! But perhaps he came before? Or was it after, now . . . ? And as she reeled them off the memories whirled up in her breast and clutched at her throat. Some of them made the tears flow when she remembered how they had parted, so she preferred to think only of the first meetings. "There was once a man . . ." She always remembered the beginning of the old romance. Her own mind was piled high with men who, as in the story, had "once been," and for this reason, perhaps, it gave her pleasure on her nights alone to drowse in bed over the men of the past.

The call from Tabe had come as a surprise to Kin, like a rare and ex- 10 pensive present out of the blue. He was coming, of course, for old times' sake—coming, as it were, to inspect the burnt-out ruins of love, in the sentimental hope of finding some relic from the past. But she would not let it be enough, this standing and sighing among the weeds and rubble. Nor must any suggestion of the wretchedness of age or poverty be allowed to intrude. Her manner towards him must above all be dignified, the atmosphere that of a discreet tête-à-tête. When he left, he must carry away with him an indelible impression of the unchanging beauty of the woman who had been his.

At last her toilet was successfully completed and Kin, like an actress 11 waiting for her cue, stood before the mirror anxiously surveying the result for possible omissions. She went into the living room. The evening meal was already on the table and, seating herself opposite the maid, she ate the frugal meal of thin *miso* soup and substitute rice with pickles. The meal finished, she broke an egg and swallowed the yolk.

Kin had never been in the habit of giving her men visitors a meal. She 12 had not the slightest wish to be the kind of woman who prepared meals carefully and laid them proudly before a man in the hope of winning his heart with her cooking. Domesticity had no appeal for her. What need had she, who had not the faintest intention of getting married, to put on a show of domesticity for men? Such was her nature, yet the men who came to Kin brought with them presents of every kind. She found nothing strange in this. Kin would have nothing to do with a man without money; nothing held less charm for her. The man who made love in an unbrushed suit, the man who did nothing about the missing buttons on his underwear—such men were damned at once in Kin's eyes. Love in itself, she felt, should be like the creation of a succession of works of art.

When she was a girl, people had claimed that she bore a likeness to the 13 famous geisha Manryū. She had once seen Manryū after her marriage. Her beauty was as dazzling as ever; it had produced an unforgettable impression on Kin, who realised then that the one thing indispensable to a woman who wished to keep her beauty indefinitely was money.

Kin had first become a geisha when she was nineteen; her beauty alone 14 had won her acceptance, for she had little training in the necessary arts of the trade. Soon after she started, she had been summoned to entertain a Frenchman—no longer young—who happened to be in Japan in the course of a sightseeing tour of Asia. He took a fancy to her, dubbing her a Japanese Marguerite Gautier, and at one period, indeed, Kin had seen herself as a kind of Dame aux Camélias. Though he had proved surprisingly inadequate as a lover, something about him had made him stay in Kin's mind ever after. His name had been Michel, and judging from his age at the time he doubtless already lay at rest somewhere in the north of France.

On his return home, he had sent Kin a present—a bracelet studded with opals and tiny diamonds. During the war, even when things were at their worst, she had resolutely refused to part with this particular possession, whatever else had to go.

All the men whose mistress Kin had been had ended by making names 15 for themselves in their own particular fields, but she had lost touch with most of them during the war and did not even know their whereabouts. Some people claimed that Kin had acquired in her time no small amount of property. True or not, she resisted any temptation to follow in the footsteps of other former geisha and start a tea-house or a restaurant of her own. She was not, in fact, as rich as rumour had it; her only property consisted of the house—spared in the war—in which she lived, and a villa by the sea in Atami. The villa she got rid of, seizing the opportunity afforded by the postwar housing shortage.

She did no work, living entirely from day to day. She had a maid, 16 Okinu, who had been found for her by her foster-sister. Okinu was deaf and dumb. The outsider would have been surprised at the austerity of the life Kin led. For her, neither the cinema nor the theatre held any attractions, nor did she care for pointless outings. She shrank from the light of day, for it exposed her age to the gaze of all and sundry. No costly clothes, she knew, were of any avail beneath the pitiless glare of the sun.

She asked no more than to live the life of the kept woman, and she had 17 a passion for reading novels. Occasionally, people would suggest that she adopt a daughter to comfort her in her old age. To Kin's mind, however, the thought of old age and all it entailed was repugnant. All her life, moreover, she had never been used to attachments of such a kind.

Hers, indeed, was a special case. She had no parents; all that she knew 18 of her origins was that she had been born in Akita Prefecture, in a village called Osagawa. When she was about five, a Tokyo family had adopted her. She had taken their name, and lived with them as their daughter. Her adoptive father had been a civil engineer, and one year his business had taken him to work in Manchuria. He never returned; letters ceased to arrive from him while Kin was still in primary school, and no more was heard of him from that time on. His wife Ritsu was, fortunately, no mean business woman. She dabbled in shares, and built houses which she let. As a result, the family acquired, even in the well-to-do area in which they lived, the reputation of being quite wealthy.

About the time that Kin reached nineteen, a man called Torigoe started 19 to frequent her home, and from that time on the fortunes of the family began almost imperceptibly to decline. Then Kin's foster-mother Ritsu took to drink, and would storm and rage in her cups. Before long Kin led a new life of hardship. The climax came when Torigoe, whose habit it was to flirt with Kin, one day became violent and assaulted her. Kin, past caring what happened, fled the house and eventually took refuge in a tea-house in Akasaka, where she was taken on as a geisha. She made her debut under the name of Kinya, and in no time her photo was appearing in popular story books and on the picture-postcards which were the rage at the time.

Though all these things, for Kin, were now part of the dim and distant 20 past she still found it difficult to accept herself as a woman on the wrong side of fifty. At times the years weighed heavily on her, but she was also smitten occasionally by a sense of the shortness of her youth. On the death of her foster-mother, the dwindled remains of the family fortune had gone to a daughter, Sumiko, born after Kin's adoption. Kin was freed thus from all further sense of obligation to the family.

She had first met Tabe about the time of the outbreak of the Pacific War, 21 during a period when Sumiko and her husband were running a boarding-house for students in Totsuka. She had broken with her patron of the past three years, and was now living a life of leisure in a room she had rented in the house. Tabe was one of the students she saw from time to time in the living room. She struck up an acquaintance with him, and though he was young enough to be her son their friendship had developed before they realised it into a full-blown clandestine affair. Kin's beauty was still that of a woman of a mere thirty-seven or so rather than the fifty she really was, and there was enchantment in her thick black brows. On graduating, Tabe was whisked into the army as a sub-lieutenant. His unit, however, instead of going straight to the front, was stationed for a while in Hiroshima, and twice Kin went there to see him.

On each occasion, no sooner was she installed in her hotel than the 22 uniformed Tabe put in his appearance. She shrank from the odour of leather that clung to his body, but spent the two nights with him at the hotel nevertheless. She had come far to see him and her utter weariness left her like a scrap of paper tossed in the storm of his masculinity; as she confessed later, she had felt as if her end were near. She went to Hiroshima twice, but refused to go to again despite repeated telegrams from Tabe. In 1942 he was sent to Burma, and came back demobilized in May of the year following the war's end. He at once came up to Tokyo and called on Kin in her house at Numabukuro. He had aged terribly, and his front teeth were missing; seeing him Kin felt let down, her dreams shattered.

Tabe came originally from Hiroshima, but with the aid of his eldest 23 brother he started an automobile company and within the year was back in Tokyo. He came to see Kin, who scarcely recognised him, so grand was his appearance now, and announced that he was soon to take a wife. Since then more than a year had passed, during which time she had not even seen him.

Kin had bought her present house in Numabukuro, complete with 24 telephone, for a mere song during the worst of the air raids, and had evacuated herself thither from Totsuka. The two houses were little more than a stone's throw apart, but while Sumiko's house had been burnt down Kin's had come through unscathed. Sumiko and her family took shelter in Kin's house, but when the war ended she promptly turned them out again. By now, however, Sumiko actually seemed to feel grateful to Kin for this, for she had had to build a new house on the site of the old without further ado; this was just after the war, and, as things had turned out, she had managed it more cheaply then than she could have done at any time since.

Kin now sold the villa at Atami. With the proceeds she bought old and dilapidated houses, had them refurnished, and sold them again at three or four times the original price. Where money matters were concerned, she was never known to lose her head. Money, long years of experience had taught her, brought its own returns, growing steadily like a snowball provided only one kept one's wits about one. She took to lending money also, preferring low rates of interest with reliable securities to higher rates without them. Since the war, she had lost her faith in banks, and kept her money circulating as far as possible, not being so foolish as to keep it stored in the house as a peasant might do. To carry out these transactions, she employed Sumiko's husband Hiroyoshi. It was also part of her knowledge that people would work to one's heart's content so long as one paid them a percentage of the profits by way of commission. 25

She lived alone with her maid. Though the four-roomed house looked lonely from the outside, yet Kin was by no means lonely. Nor, thanks to her dislike of going out, was it at all inconvenient that the two should live alone. Where burglars were concerned, Kin had more trust in firmly-fastened doors than in any watchdog, and no house could have been better locked at night than hers. Whatever men came to the house she had no fear of gossip, for the maid was deaf and dumb. 26

Despite all this, there were times when she visualised herself meeting some horrible death. Even she was not immune to that disquieting feeling of suspense that hangs over a perfectly silent house, and she invariably kept the radio turned on from morning to night. 27

Kin's affair of the moment was with a man called Itaya, who grew flowers at a place just outside Tokyo; they had met through his brother, the man who had bought Kin's villa in Atami. During the war, Itaya had started a trading company in Hanoi, but had been repatriated when peace came and had launched into horticulture with capital supplied by his brother. Though only forty or thereabouts, he was almost completely bald, which made him look old for his age. He had visited Kin two or three times on business connected with the villa, and these visits had somehow or other become regular weekly affairs. 28

From that time on, Kin's house was gay with the flowers he brought her. Today was no exception: into a vase in the alcove had been thrust a mass of yellow roses. Somehow, they reminded her of the beauty of a mature woman, and their scent brought back the past in all its poignancy. Now that Tabe had telephoned, she realised that his youth gave him an appeal that Itaya did not possess. She had suffered at Hiroshima, true, but then he had been a soldier, and the very violence of his youth seemed now in 29 retrospect only natural, somehow touching and a memory to be treasured. For some reason, she thought, it was always the most tempestuous times that made one feel most nostalgic later.

It was well past five when Tabe arrived. 30

From within the bundle he carried he produced whisky, ham, cheese 31 and other things, then plumped himself down by the charcoal brazier. He had lost every trace of his former youthfulness, and his grey check jacket and dark green trousers were typical of the mechanical engineer of today at his leisure.

"Beautiful as ever, I see," Tabe said once they had settled down. 32

"Really? Thank you for saying so. But I've had my day, you know," Kin 33 replied.

"Not a bit of it. You've still got more of what it takes than my wife." 34

"She's young, I expect?" Kin asked. 35

"Oh, she may be young, but she's only a country girl." 36

Kin took a cigarette from Tabe's silver case. He lit it for her. The maid 37 brought whisky glasses and a plate on which slices of the ham and cheese had been arranged. Tabe looked at the maid with a leer.

"Nice girl you've got there," he said. 38

"Mm. But she's deaf and dumb." 39

"Is she, now?" Tabe raised his eyebrows and fixed the maid with a look 40 of new interest; she bowed her head deferentially. Kin, her attention drawn for the first time to the maid's youthfulness, suddenly found it irritating.

"You get on well together, I suppose?" Kin asked. Tabe recalled himself 41 with a start and puffed out a cloud of smoke.

"We've got a kid due next month," he replied. 42

Her face registering due surprise at this announcement, Kin got up and 43 fetched the whisky. She gave a glass to Tabe, who drained it at a gulp and poured out a glass for Kin in her turn.

"How I envy your life here," he continued. 44

"Why, for goodness sake?" 45

"Well, however rough the going is outside you seem to stay the same as 46 ever. . . . I can't make it out. Of course, though, when a woman's got all you have she's sure to have a good patron. Lucky devils, women."

"Are you getting at me? I've never done anything to you to make you 47 say that kind of thing, have I?"

"Don't get angry, now. You didn't understand me." His tone was pac- 48 ifying. "I just meant that you were lucky. You made me feel what a hard time men have, having to work. A man just can't afford to take it easy these days. Either you do someone else down or he does you down. Take me, for instance—life's a sort of continual gamble for me, you know."

"But business is good, isn't it?" Kin asked. 49

"That's what you think! You feel you're walking on a tightrope all the 50 time. Money's so tight it hurts."

Kin sipped at her whisky without replying. A cricket chirped dismally in   51
the wall. Tabe drank a second glass of whisky and suddenly, without
warning, reached out across the brazier and seized Kin's hand roughly in
his. The softness of her ringless hand was insubstantial as a silk handkerchief. Kin remained still, scarcely breathing. Her hand, which rested in his
with deliberate passivity, was terribly cold and limp.

Through the drunken fumes in Tabe's mind came crowding and whirl-   52
ing a host of pictures from the past. There she still sat, her remembered
beauty untouched. He felt a sense of wonder: time rolled by relentlessly,
one gained experience bit by bit, one had one's ups, one had one's downs—
and all the time this woman from one's past sat there as large as life,
changeless and unchanging. He peered intently at Kin's eyes. Yes, even
the little wrinkles around them were as they had always been. Her face,
too, retained its firmness of outline. He wished he knew more about the
way she lived. For all he knew, the social upheavals of the past years had
left her untouched. There she still sat and smiled, secure among her
possessions—the chest of drawers, the brazier, the magnificence of the
roses heaped in the vase. Tabe did not know her real age, but she must
have passed fifty by now. Into his mind there came a picture of his wife at
work in their apartment home, already tired and haggard though barely
twenty-five.

Kin opened the drawer in the brazier and took out a slender pipe of   53
beaten silver. Thrusting in the end of her cigarette, she lit it. Something in
the way Tabe's knees twitched nervously from time to time made her feel
uneasy. Could it be that he was in financial straits? She scrutinized his face
carefully. No longer, now, could she feel the all-absorbing love she had felt
in Hiroshima. Now that they were actually together again, the long silence
seemed to have created a barrier between them, a barrier which made Kin
feel impatient and desolate at once. Somehow, the old emotions refused to
be kindled. Was it, she wondered, overfamiliarity with him physically that
had robbed him of his old appeal for her? Why, she thought with something approaching panic, why, when everything in the setting was right,
did the heart remain so cold?

Tabe spoke. "I suppose you couldn't find someone willing to lend me   54
about four hundred thousand, could you?"

Kin started. "Money? Four hundred thousand's an awful lot, isn't it?"   55

"It is, but I've just got to get it somehow. Now. No idea of anybody?"   56

"None at all. But why talk to me about such things, when you know I   57
don't even have any income to begin with?"

"That's as may be. Look here, I'd give you a very good rate of interest.   58
How about it?"

"It's no good, I tell you! Whatever you say."   59

A cold chill crept over Kin, and the even tenor of her relationship with   60
Itaya seemed suddenly eminently desirable. Despair in her heart, she

reached for the kettle that had begun to sing on the brazier and filled the teapot.

"Couldn't twenty thousand be managed somehow? I'd be eternally grateful. . . ."   61

"I don't understand you at all. Why talk to me about money when you know very well I don't have any. . . . I could do with it myself, I can tell you. Did you come to talk about money then, and not to see me?"   62

"No, I came to see you, of course. Well, I admit it, I did think at the same time that you being the one person I could talk to about anything. . . ."   63

"Why not speak to your brother about it?" Kin asked.   64

"He's no good in this case."   65

Kin was silent. Another year or two, she thought, and she would be old. She could see now that for all its intensity that love of theirs had passed, and left them both untouched. Perhaps, then, it had not been love at all, but only the relationship of two animals drawn together by lust. A fragile tie between man and woman, to be blown away like a dead leaf in the winds of time, leaving Tabe and herself sitting here now, bound only by a trivial bond of acquaintance. A cold ache filled Kin's breast. She picked up her tea and started to drink.   66

"Mind if I stay the night?" Tabe asked with a leer. His voice had dropped and its tone was casual. Kin looked up from her tea in feigned surprise.   67

"Yes, I do. You shouldn't poke fun at me like that at my age." She smiled, deliberately emphasizing as she did so the crow's-feet round her eyes. Her false teeth flashed brilliantly white.   68

"Don't be so horribly cold and hard," Tabe said. "I'll stop talking about money. Must have got carried away, thinking I was talking to the same old Kin I used to know. But . . . that's all done with now, isn't it?" He paused. "You have the devil's own luck, don't you? Come through smiling whatever happens. Don't know how you do it. None of these young girls nowadays could do it. I say, go in for dancing at all?"   69

"What do you take me for! And you?"   70

"A bit," he replied.   71

"Aha, I expect there's someone special you take, isn't there? Is that what you want the money for, then?"   72

"Don't be a fool. Do you think I earn enough to waste it on keeping a woman?"   73

"I don't know about that, but look at the way you're got up. You couldn't put up a show like that without quite a profitable job."   74

"This is only so much show. Look in the pockets and what do you find—nothing! Everybody has their ups and downs, but things lately have been getting just a bit too fast and furious."   75

Kin was laughing quietly to herself, her eyes riveted on Tabe's shock of black hair. It still showed little sign of thinning, and it came forward over his forehead. He had lost the youthful freshness she had found so charming in his student days, but something in the line of his cheek had the   76 mature appeal of middle age and, while his bearing lacked refinement, he still retained a certain brute strength. Kin poured Tabe a cup of tea, her eye on him the while in the way one animal scents another in the distance.

"They say money's going to be devaluated soon," she said, half in joke. 77 "Is it true?"

"Oh, so you've got enough to get worried, have you?" Tabe enquired. 78

"How you do jump to conclusions! You certainly have changed, haven't 79 you! I just asked because I'd heard rumours and was interested."

"I don't know, but I shouldn't think Japan could afford to do anything 80 like that just now. At any rate, people who don't have any money don't have to worry, do they?"

"That's true," Kin replied, and with a cheerful air poured Tabe another 81 whisky.

"How I'd like to go to Hakone or somewhere else quiet," he said. "I 82 think it would do me good to do nothing but sleep and sleep for two or three days in a place like that."

"Tired?" 83

"Yes. All this worry about money, you know." 84

"But it suits you to be worried about money. It's not a woman's worry, 85 at least."

The smug correctness of Kin's manner irritated Tabe intensely, but at 86 the same time her likeness to a rather refined piece of antique ware amused him. To spend a night with her, he thought, would only be like giving alms to a beggar. His eyes strayed to Kin's chin: the firm line of the jawbone betrayed the strength of will that lay behind it. Suddenly, a vision of the dumb maid—of her freshness and her youth—seemed to impose itself before his eyes; she was not beautiful, the maid, but she was young, and youth was like a breath of fresh air to a connoisseur of women such as Tabe. Probably, he thought, if this were his first meeting with Kin, he would not have this sense of fretful impatience. The tiredness in Kin's face had come nearer the surface now, and she suddenly seemed old in his eyes.

As if sensing his feeling, Kin got up abruptly and went into the next 87 room. Going to the dressing-table, she picked up a syringe full of hormone and jabbed it into her arm, then, while she was scrubbing at the place with a piece of cotton wool, peered at herself in the mirror. She picked up a powder-puff and dabbed at her nose with it. A wave of mortification swept over her at the pointlessness of such a meeting between a man and woman who were physically dead to each other, and the unbidden tears stood for a moment in her eyes. If it had been Itaya, she could have wept on his lap, wheedled him even. But the Tabe who now sat by the fire in there—she had no idea what she felt for him. One moment she wished to see him gone, the next she had the desperate feeling that he must not go till she had moved him to some further recognition of her. There had been many other women in Tabe's life since they had parted. . . .

She went to the toilet; on her way back, she peeped into the maid's 88
room. Kinu was absorbed in practising her dressmaking, cutting patterns
out of newspaper. Her large buttocks were planted firmly on the mat, her
body crouched over the scissors she was plying. The nape of her neck
beneath the tightly-bound hair gleamed white in the light, and her whole
body had a striking buxomness.

Kin left her working and went back to the brazier. Tabe was sprawled 89
asleep on the floor. She turned on the radio. Music blared out with a
startling volume. Tabe sat up with a start and raised the whisky glass to his
lips again.

"Remember the time we went to that hotel at Shibamata together?" he 90
asked. "There was a terrific downpour and the rain came in, and we ate the
eels by themselves because there wasn't any rice."

"So we did. Food was terribly scarce then, wasn't it. Before you went in 91
the army, that was. Do you remember, there was a red lily in the alcove
and the two of us knocked the vase over?"

"So we did, didn't we." Kin's face seemed suddenly to fill out, and her 92
expression became younger.

"How about going again some day?" Tabe asked. 93

"That's a nice idea, but, you know, I'm too lazy these days. And I expect 94
you can get anything you like to eat there now—it wouldn't seem the
same."

Fearful lest the sentimental mood that had overtaken her a while back 95
should disappear, she tried gently to coax back the past once more. In vain
though, for it was not Tabe but another man who came at her summons.
On one later occasion, just after the war, she had gone to Shibamata with
a man called Yamazaki. He had died only a day or two ago, after a stomach
operation. They had gone to the hotel on the banks of the Edo River one
muggy day the previous summer, and the atmosphere of that dusty room
came back to her vividly now . . . the clanking of the motor pump drawing
water outside, the incessant song of the cicadas and the silver flashing from
the wheels of the bicycles pacing along the embankment. It had been her
second meeting with Yamazaki, whose youthful naivety where women
were concerned seemed, to Kin, almost sacred. There had been plenty to
eat, and now that the war was over the wearied world had seemed
strangely quiet, as if one were living in a vacuum. They had come back to
Tokyo in the evening, and the bus by which they had returned to the
station had run along a wide road once built for army use.

"Come across anybody who took your fancy since I last saw you?" Tabe 96
asked.

"Me?" 97

"Yes." 98

"Took my fancy? There isn't anybody but you." 99

"Liar!" 100

"Why? It's true! Who's likely to be interested in me any longer?" 101

"I don't trust you!"   102

"You don't? . . . . Well at any rate, I'm going to blossom out and enjoy   103
life from now on. I'm alive like anybody else."

"Got a long time to go yet, eh?"   104

"That's right. I shall go on and on, till I get too old and decrepit for   105
anything."

"And just as fickle as ever?"   106

"My God, how you've changed! You used to be such a decent boy.   107
What's happened to you, to make you say such nasty things? You were so
nice, once."

Tabe took the silver pipe from Kin and tried a puff at it. A jet of thick   108
bitter liquid struck his tongue. He took out a handkerchief and spat into it.

"It's blocked, it needs cleaning." Kin took it from him with a smile and   109
shook it with short, vigorous movements onto a piece of paper.

Tabe was mystified by the way Kin lived, by the way the cruel world   110
outside had, it appeared, left life in this house completely untouched. One
would think she could manage two or three thousand somehow, judging
from her present circumstances. Her body no longer awoke any response
in him, but he sensed beneath the surface of her daily life an abundance
which seemed to Tabe to offer a straw at which he might clutch. Back from
the wars, he had gone into business more for the fun of it than anything
else; the capital his brother had given him had vanished in less than six
months. He was having an affair with another woman outside his marriage, and she was to have a child by him shortly. He had remembered Kin
again, and had visited her just on the chance that she might be able to help.
Kin's old simplicity, however, had been replaced by a dismaying degree of
worldly wisdom. She remained utterly unmoved, even at meeting Tabe
again after so long. The stiffness of her posture, the correctness of her
manner kept him helplessly at a distance.

He took her hand again and gave it a tentative squeeze, but Kin showed   111
no sign of response. Perhaps he had hoped she would come round the
brazier to his side; instead, she carried on cleaning the pipe with her free
hand.

Exposure to the years had engraved a complex and different pattern of   112
emotions on both their hearts. They had gradually grown older, he in his
way, she in hers, and the old fondness was gone beyond recall. Plunged in
a sense of disillusion, they took silent stock of each other as they were now.
They were weary with a host of different emotions. Nothing could be less
like the storybook meeting with its charming fictions than this reality. It
would all, without doubt, have been made much prettier in a novel—the
truth about life was too subtle. To reject each other—this had been the only
purpose of their coming together today.

The idea of killing Kin drifted through Tabe's head. Yet—and the idea   113
seemed somehow strange—to kill even this woman would be murder.
Why should it be wrong to kill a woman or two who meant nothing to

anybody? Even as he thought this, he realized what it would mean. It was fantastic. This old woman's existence was as unimportant as that of the lowest insect, and yet she must be allowed to go on living her placid life in this house. The two chests of drawers must be crammed with all the clothes she had made herself in the past fifty years. That bracelet from a Frenchman she had shown him once—she must have that and other jewels too somewhere or other. The house must be hers, too. She was a lone woman, with a maid who was deaf and dumb: to kill her should be easy enough.

His fancy led him on and on. And yet, at the same time, the memory of 114 his student days when she had been all to him, the memory of their secret meetings, came back with a painful freshness and vividness. He was drunk. Perhaps this was why the past and present seemed to become blurred, and the image of Kin as she sat before him seemed to take possession of his body. He did not desire her now, but their past together pressed heavily on his heart.

Kin got up. Going to a cupboard, she got out a photograph of Tabe taken 115 when he was a student and brought it to show him. Tabe stared at it in surprise.

"Good Lord, fancy your keeping a thing like that!" he exclaimed. 116

"I found it at Sumiko's, and got her to let me have it. Taken before I 117 knew you, wasn't it? You know, you were a proper young gentleman when this was taken. Look at that kimono you were wearing—don't you think it suited you? Here—you have it, I'm sure your wife would like to see it." She paused. "You know, you were so nice-looking in those days—not the kind of man you'd think could say such unpleasant things."

"So I was really like this once, was I?" he asked, studying the photo- 118 graph.

"You were. I should know. If only you'd gone on in the same way, 119 you'd really have been something, you know."

"By which you mean that I didn't go on in the same way, I suppose?" 120 he asked.

"Yes I do." 121

"Well, no wonder, what with you, and all those years of war." 122

"Don't try to get out of it! Things like that have nothing to do with it. 123 You've just got coarser somehow . . . awfully so."

"I have, have I? Coarser, eh? But aren't all people the same?" 124

"What about me?" Kin replied. "Haven't I kept this photograph by me 125 all these years? Doesn't that show people can sometimes keep their finer feelings?"

"I suppose it just gave you something to look back on. You didn't give 126 me one of you, did you?"

"A photo? Of me?" 127

"Yes." 128

"Photographs give me the creeps." She reflected. "But didn't I send you 129 one of me as a geisha, though—while you were in the army over there?"

"Believe you did, but it must have got lost somewhere, I . . ."   130

"There, that shows you!"   131

Still the brazier remained between them, an apparently impenetrable   132
barrier. By now Tabe was quite drunk, but Kin's first glass remained hardly
touched before her. Tabe picked up his tea and drained the now cold liquid
at a gulp. The photograph of himself he laid to one side with an apparent
complete lack of interest.

"How are you for trains?" Kin asked.   133

"Trains? I can't possibly go home. You wouldn't turn me out drunk like   134
this, would you?"

"Yes, I would. Out, like that." She gestured with her hands. "There are   135
no men in this house, and I don't want the neighbours talking."

"The neighbours? Come off it. Since when have you started worrying   136
about things like that?"

"Well, I do worry."   137

"Got a gentleman friend coming, have you?"   138

"Oh, what a beastly mind you've got! Oh, really. . . . ! I hate you when   139
you say things like that!"

"Go on, hate me then. But if I don't get the money, I just can't go home   140
for a day or two. Thought you might put me up here for. . . ."

Kin, chin cupped in hands, gazed with fixed, wide-open eyes at Tabe's   141
bluish lips. So this was how it all ended, that love one swore would last for
ever. . . . Silently, she took in every detail of the man slumped before her.
Gone, quite gone, was the romantic excitement they had once felt. No trace
now of the young man's bashfulness he had once had. . . .

For a moment she was tempted to offer him a bribe to go and leave her   142
in peace, yet something forbade her giving a single penny to this man now
sprawled so drunkenly before her. Far rather would she give it to some
man of the unsophisticated type; nothing disgusted her so much as a man
like Tabe with no self-respect. She was attracted by a lack of sophistication
in men—she had found it time and again among those who had fallen
victim to her charms—and even found something noble in it. Her only
interest lay in choosing the right men for herself. She despised Tabe in her
heart for the way he had let himself go to seed. Why should he have come
back from the wars when others had not? But then, Fate was like that. . . .
She had done her duty by Tabe in going to Hiroshima after him, and she
should have had the sense to ring down the curtain on their relationship at
that time.

"Why are you staring at a man like that?"   143

"I thought it was you who'd been staring at me. What were you   144
thinking—looking so pleased with yourself?"

"Just looking and thinking how you never seemed to change. Beautiful   145
as ever."

"Really? Me too. I was thinking what a fine man you'd turned out."   146

"Coincidence, eh," Tabe said. It was on the tip of his tongue to say that 147
he had been toying with the idea of murder, but he checked himself in time.

"You're lucky, you know," Kin said. "You've got the prime of life still 148
to come."

"What about you? You've got a long time to go yet, surely," Tabe re- 149
plied.

"Me? I've had my day. I shall just go on gradually withering. I'm think- 150
ing of going to live in the country in two or three years' time."

"Then you didn't mean it when you talked about going on as fickle as 151
ever till you were old and decrepit?"

"I said no such thing! I'm a woman living on her memories. That's 152
all. . . . Can't we be good friends?"

"You're only running away from the question. Why don't you stop 153
talking like a schoolgirl? Memories can take care of themselves."

"I wonder. . . . You know, it was you who brought up our trip to 154
Shibamata."

Tabe had started twitching his knees again. He must get money. Mon- 155
ey. . . . Kin must lend it to him somehow. Even fifty thousand would be
better than nothing.

"So you really can't manage it? Not even if I put up the business as a 156
security?" He appealed to her.

"What, are you on about money again? It's no good, I tell you, whatever 157
you say I don't have a penny, and I don't know anybody who does. I'd like
to borrow some myself, let alone lend it to other people."

"Don't worry about that. If only things go well with me, I'll see you're 158
more than provided for. You're not the kind of person I'd be likely to
forget. . . ."

"Oh, stop that flattery! I've had enough of it. I thought you promised 159
not to mention money again?"

A chill wind like that of autumn nights seemed suddenly to howl 160
through the room and into Tabe's heart. He grasped the tongs on the
brazier. A spasm of violent rage darkened his face. Drawn irresistibly by
the image that floated sphinx-like before his eyes, he tightened his grip on
the tongs. A thunderous roaring pulsed in his veins. Go on, go on, it
seemed to say. Kin's eyes, riveted on his hand, were vaguely apprehensive. The feeling that somewhere, sometime, this had all happened before
mingled with the reality in her mind.

"You're drunk, you know. Why not stay the night?" she said. 161

Why not stay the night. The tongs fell from Tabe's hand. He pulled 162
himself tipsily to his feet and staggered off in the direction of the toilet.
Watching him go, Kin suddenly sensed what had been in his mind, and
felt a stir of contempt. The war had done something to people, she thought.

She took the philopon from the cupboard and hastily swallowed a tab- 163
let. She looked at the whisky bottle; it was still one-third full. He should
drink it all, sleep the sleep of the dead drunk and the next morning she

would show him the door. Sleep was not for her that night. Picking up the photograph of the young Tabe, she fed it to the blue flames that leapt from the charcoal in the brazier. Smoke rose in clouds, and a smell of burning filled the room. Kinu the maid peeped in through the sliding doors that Tabe had left partly open. With a smile, Kin signed to her to put out quilts for the night in the guest room. To cover up the smell of burning paper, she laid a thin slice of cheese on the fire.

"Hey, what are you burning?" It was Tabe, back from the toilet. He peered through the sliding doors, his hands on the maid's ample shoulders. 164

"Thought I'd toast some cheese to see what it tasted like, but I went and dropped it out of the tongs." 165

A column of black smoke rose up through the white, and the bright disc of the lamp-shade was now a moon floating in the clouds. A smell of burnt fat assailed the nostrils. Coughing and spluttering, Kin got up and hurried round the room flinging open the sliding doors. 166

Translated from the Japanese by John Bester

STUDY QUESTIONS

1. How are Kin's attitudes toward aging dramatized in the early part of "Late Chrysanthemum"? What are the values that support these attitudes?
2. Kin's life follows a dual yet reverse track: as she loses her beauty (and her ability to attract men), her success as a businesswoman increases. How does Kin's material success function as an element in the plot?
3. What are the different expectations Kin and Tabe bring to their meeting? How is each one disappointed?
4. What do their different expectations and desires tell you about the constructions of male and female identity in the story?

 ISHIGAKI RIN

Ishigaki Rin (b. 1920) began working in a bank at age fourteen. She published short stories and poems during World War II, but established her reputation only after the war. Her first collection of poems, The Pan, the Pot, the Fire I Have Before Me, *appeared in 1959 to critical acclaim. Winner of many prizes, her poetry underlines the inequities and shortcomings in women's lives while insisting on the social value of women's experiences and roles.*

The Pan, the Pot, the Fire I Have Before Me

For a long time
these things have always been placed
before us women:
the pan of a reasonable size
suited to the user's strength,   5
the pot in which it's convenient for rice
to begin to swell and shine, grain by grain,
the heat of the fire inherited from time immemorial—
before these there have always been
mothers, grandmothers, and their mothers.   10

What measures of love and sincerity
these persons must have poured
into these utensils—
now red carrots,
now black seaweed,   15
now crushed fish

in the kitchen, always accurately
for morning, noon, and evening, preparations have been made
and before the preparations, in a row, there have always been
some pairs of warm knees and hands.   20

Ah without those persons waiting
how could women have gone on
cooking so happily?
their unflagging care,
so daily a service they became unconscious of it.   25

Cooking was mysteriously assigned
to women, as a role,
but I don't think that was unfortunate;
because of that, their knowledge and positions in society
may have lagged behind the times   30
but it isn't too late:
the things we have before us,

the pan and the pot, and the burning fire,
before these familiar things,

let us study government, economy, literature   35
as sincerely
as we cook potatoes and meat.

not for vanity and promotion
but so everyone
may serve all   40
so everyone may work for love.

Translated from the Japanese by Hiroaki Sato

STUDY QUESTIONS

1. This poem uses the setting of the kitchen to place a history of "mothers, grandmothers, and their mothers." What kinds of social and emotional attitudes are associated with this domestic setting?
2. The poem attempts to balance women's traditional role as nurturer with the new roles implied in the study of "government, economics, literature." Do you find its assertion of balance persuasive? Explain your answer with close reference to the poem.
3. Do you agree that the assignment of daily domestic services to women was not "unfortunate"? What experiences or opinions of your own can you offer as support?

 YUKIO MISHIMA

Yukio Mishima (1925–1970) was a man of many interests. He was a writer of prodigious talent whose work is still read throughout the world, yet he was also a gifted swordsman, singer, actor, and director. He was also a complex man, a married homosexual who believed in the mystic militarism of imperial Japan and who committed seppuku (ritual suicide by self-disemboweling) publicly to protest the loss of the Japanese Emperor's power. He established his reputation with his first novel, Confessions of a Mask *(1949), experimented with writing modern No plays, and published prolifically in many forms. "Patriotism," Mishima's best known short story, appeared in English in the collection* Death in Midsummer and Other Stories *(1966).*

Patriotism

1

O n the twenty-eighth of February, 1936 (on the third day, that is, of the February 26 Incident), Lieutenant Shinji Takeyama of the Konoe Transport Battalion—profoundly disturbed by the knowledge that his closest colleagues had been with the mutineers from the beginning, and indignant at the imminent prospect of Imperial troops attacking Imperial troops—took his officer's sword and ceremonially disemboweled himself in the eight-mat room of his private residence in the sixth block of Aoba-chō, in Yotsuya Ward. His wife, Reiko, followed him, stabbing herself to death. The lieutenant's farewell note consisted of one sentence: "Long live the Imperial Forces." His wife's, after apologies for her unfilial conduct in thus preceding her parents to the grave, concluded: "The day which, for a soldier's wife, had to come, has come. . . ." The last moments of this heroic and dedicated couple were such as to make the gods themselves weep. The lieutenant's age, it should be noted, was thirty-one, his wife's twenty-three; and it was not half a year since the celebration of their marriage.

2

Those who saw the bride and bridegroom in the commemorative photograph—perhaps no less than those actually present at the lieutenant's wedding—had exclaimed in wonder at the bearing of this handsome couple. The lieutenant, majestic in military uniform, stood protectively beside his bride, his right hand resting upon his sword, his officer's cap held at his left side. His expression was severe, and his dark brows and wide-gazing eyes well conveyed the clear integrity of youth. For the beauty of the bride in her white over-robe no comparisons were adequate. In the eyes, round beneath soft brows, in the slender, finely shaped nose, and in the full lips, there was both sensuousness and refinement. One hand, emerging shyly from a sleeve of the over-robe, held a fan, and the tips of the fingers, clustering delicately, were like the bud of a moon-flower.

After the suicide, people would take out this photograph and examine it, and sadly reflect that too often there was a curse on these seemingly flawless unions. Perhaps it was no more than imagination, but looking at the picture after the tragedy it almost seemed as if the two young people before the gold-lacquered screen were gazing, each with equal clarity, at the deaths which lay before them.

Thanks to the good offices of their go-between, Lieutenant General Ozeki, they had been able to set themselves up in a new home at Aoba-chō in Yotsuya. "New home" is perhaps misleading. It was an old three-room rented house backing onto a small garden. As neither the six- nor the four-and-a-half-mat room downstairs was favored by the sun, they used the upstairs eight-mat room as both bedroom and guest room. There was no maid, so Reiko was left alone to guard the house in her husband's absence.

The honeymoon trip was dispensed with on the grounds that these 5 were times of national emergency. The two of them had spent the first night of their marriage at this house. Before going to bed, Shinji, sitting erect on the floor with his sword laid before him, had bestowed upon his wife a soldierly lecture. A woman who had become the wife of a soldier should know and resolutely accept that her husband's death might come at any moment. It could be tomorrow. It could be the day after. But, no matter when it came—he asked—was she steadfast in her resolve to accept it? Reiko rose to her feet, pulled open a drawer of the cabinet, and took out what was the most prized of her new possessions, the dagger her mother had given her. Returning to her place, she laid the dagger without a word on the mat before her, just as her husband had laid his sword. A silent understanding was achieved at once, and the lieutenant never again sought to test his wife's resolve.

In the first few months of her marriage Reiko's beauty grew daily more 6 radiant, shining serene like the moon after rain.

As both were possessed of young, vigorous bodies, their relationship 7 was passionate. Nor was this merely a matter of the night. On more than one occasion, returning home straight from maneuvers, and begrudging even the time it took to remove his mud-splashed uniform, the lieutenant had pushed his wife to the floor almost as soon as he had entered the house. Reiko was equally ardent in her response. For a little more or a little less than a month, from the first night of their marriage Reiko knew happiness, and the lieutenant, seeing this, was happy too.

Reiko's body was white and pure, and her swelling breasts conveyed a 8 firm and chaste refusal; but, upon consent, those breasts were lavish with their intimate, welcoming warmth. Even in bed these two were frighteningly and awesomely serious. In the very midst of wild, intoxicating passions, their hearts were sober and serious.

By day the lieutenant would think of his wife in the brief rest periods 9 between training; and all day long, at home, Reiko would recall the image of her husband. Even when apart, however, they had only to look at the wedding photograph for their happiness to be once more confirmed. Reiko felt not the slightest surprise that a man who had been a complete stranger until a few months ago should now have become the sun about which her whole world revolved.

All these things had a moral basis, and were in accordance with the 10 Education Rescript's injunction that "husband and wife should be harmonious." Not once did Reiko contradict her husband, nor did the lieutenant ever find reason to scold his wife. On the god shelf below the stairway, alongside the tablet from the Great Ise Shrine, were set photographs of their Imperial Majesties, and regularly every morning, before leaving for duty, the lieutenant would stand with his wife at this hallowed place and together they would bow their heads low. The offering water was renewed each morning, and the sacred sprig of *sasaki* was always green and fresh. Their lives were lived beneath the solemn protection of the gods and were filled with an intense happiness which set every fiber in their bodies trembling.

3

Although Lord Privy Seal Saitō's house was in their neighborhood, neither   11
of them heard any noise of gunfire on the morning of February 26. It was a bugle, sounding muster in the dim, snowy dawn, when the ten-minute tragedy had already ended, which first disrupted the lieutenant's slumbers. Leaping at once from his bed, and without speaking a word, the lieutenant donned his uniform, buckled on the sword held ready for him by his wife, and hurried swiftly out into the snow-covered streets of the still darkened morning. He did not return until the evening of the twenty-eighth.

Later, from the radio news, Reiko learned the full extent of this sudden   12
eruption of violence. Her life throughout the subsequent two days was lived alone, in complete tranquility, and behind locked doors.

In the lieutenant's face, as he hurried silently out into the snowy morn-   13
ing, Reiko had read the determination to die. If her husband did not return, her own decision was made: she too would die. Quietly she attended to the disposition of her personal possessions. She chose her sets of visiting kimonos as keepsakes for friends of her schooldays, and she wrote a name and address on the stiff paper wrapping in which each was folded. Constantly admonished by her husband never to think of the morrow, Reiko had not even kept a diary and was now denied the pleasure of assiduously rereading her record of the happiness of the past few months and consigning each page to the fire as she did so. Ranged across the top of the radio were a small china dog, a rabbit, a squirrel, a bear, and a fox. There were also a small vase and a water pitcher. These comprised Reiko's one and only collection. But it would hardly do, she imagined, to give such things as keepsakes. Nor again would it be quite proper to ask specifically for them to be included in the coffin. It seemed to Reiko, as these thoughts passed through her mind, that the expressions on the small animals' faces grew even more lost and forlorn.

Reiko took the squirrel in her hand and looked at it. And then, her   14
thoughts turning to a realm far beyond these childlike affections, she gazed

up into the distance at the great sunlike principle which her husband embodied. She was ready, and happy, to be hurtled along to her destruction in that gleaming sun chariot—but now, for these few moments of solitude, she allowed herself to luxuriate in this innocent attachment to trifles. The time when she had genuinely loved these things, however, was long past. Now she merely loved the memory of having once loved them, and their place in her heart had been filled by more intense passions, by a more frenzied happiness. . . . For Reiko had never, even to herself, thought of those soaring joys of the flesh as a mere pleasure. The February cold, and the icy touch of the china squirrel, had numbed Reiko's slender fingers; yet, even so, in her lower limbs, beneath the ordered repetition of the pattern which crossed the skirt of her trim *meisen* kimono, she could feel now, as she thought of the lieutenant's powerful arms reaching out toward her, a hot moistness of the flesh which defied the snows.

She was not in the least afraid of the death hovering in her mind. 15 Waiting alone at home, Reiko firmly believed that everything her husband was feeling or thinking now, his anguish and distress, was leading her— just as surely as the power in his flesh—to a welcome death. She felt as if her body could melt away with ease and be transformed to the merest fraction of her husband's thought.

Listening to the frequent announcements on the radio, she heard the 16 names of several of her husband's colleagues mentioned among those of the insurgents. This was news of death. She followed the developments closely, wondering anxiously, as the situation became daily more irrevocable, why no Imperial ordinance was sent down, and watching what had at first been taken as a movement to restore the nation's honor come gradually to be branded with the infamous name of mutiny. There was no communication from the regiment. At any moment, it seemed, fighting might commence in the city streets, where the remains of the snow still lay.

Toward sundown on the twenty-eighth Reiko was startled by a furious 17 pounding on the front door. She hurried downstairs. As she pulled with fumbling fingers at the bolt, the shape dimly outlined beyond the frosted-glass panel made no sound, but she knew it was her husband. Reiko had never known the bolt on the sliding door to be so stiff. Still it resisted. The door just would not open.

In a moment, almost before she knew she had succeeded, the lieutenant 18 was standing before her on the cement floor inside the porch, muffled in a khaki greatcoat, his top boots heavy with slush from the street. Closing the door behind him, he returned the bolt once more to its socket. With what significance, Reiko did not understand.

"Welcome home." 19

Reiko bowed deeply, but her husband made no response. As he had 20 already unfastened his sword and was about to remove his greatcoat, Reiko moved around behind to assist. The coat, which was cold and damp and had lost the odor of horse dung it normally exuded when exposed to the sun, weighed heavily upon her arm. Draping it across a hanger, and cradling the sword and leather belt in her sleeves, she waited while her husband removed his top boots and then followed behind him into the "living room." This was the six-mat room downstairs.

Seen in the clear light from the lamp, her husband's face, covered with   21
a heavy growth of bristle, was almost unrecognizably wasted and thin. The cheeks were hollow, their luster and resilience gone. In his normal good spirits he would have changed into old clothes as soon as he was home and have pressed her to get supper at once, but now he sat before the table still in his uniform, his head dropping dejectedly. Reiko refrained from asking whether she should prepare the supper.

After an interval the lieutenant spoke.   22

"I knew nothing. They hadn't asked me to join. Perhaps out of consid-   23
eration, because I was newly married. Kanō, and Homma too, and Ya-maguchi."

Reiko recalled momentarily the faces of high-spirited young officers,   24
friends of her husband, who had come to the house occasionally as guests.

"There may be an Imperial ordinance sent down tomorrow. They'll be   25
posted as rebels, I imagine. I shall be in command of a unit with orders to attack them. . . . I can't do it. It's impossible to do a thing like that."

He spoke again.   26

"They've taken me off guard duty, and I have permission to return   27
home for one night. Tomorrow morning, without question, I must leave to join the attack. I can't do it, Reiko."

Reiko sat erect with lowered eyes. She understood clearly that her hus-   28
band had spoken of his death. The lieutenant was resolved. Each word, being rooted in death, emerged sharply and with powerful significance against this dark, unmovable background. Although the lieutenant was speaking of his dilemma, already there was no room in his mind for vac-illation.

However, there was a clarity, like the clarity of a stream fed from melt-   29
ing snows, in the silence which rested between them. Sitting in his own home after the long two-day ordeal, and looking across at the face of his beautiful wife, the lieutenant was for the first time experiencing true peace of mind. For he had at once known, though she said nothing, that his wife divined the resolve which lay beneath his words.

"Well, then . . ." The lieutenant's eyes opened wide. Despite his ex-   30
haustion they were strong and clear, and now for the first time they looked straight into the eyes of his wife. "Tonight I shall cut my stomach."

Reiko did not flinch.   31

Her round eyes showed tension, as taut as the clang of a bell.   32

"I am ready," she said. "I ask permission to accompany you."   33

The lieutenant felt almost mesmerized by the strength in those eyes. His   34
words flowed swiftly and easily, like the utterances of a man in delirium,

and it was beyond his understanding how permission in a matter of such weight could be expressed so casually.

"Good. We'll go together. But I want you as a witness, first, for my own suicide. Agreed?" 35

When this was said a sudden release of abundant happiness welled up in both their hearts. Reiko was deeply affected by the greatness of her husband's trust in her. It was vital for the lieutenant, whatever else might happen, that there should be no irregularity in his death. For that reason there had to be a witness. The fact that he had chosen his wife for this was the first mark of his trust. The second, and even greater, mark was that though he had pledged that they should die together he did not intend to kill his wife first—he had deferred her death to a time when he would no longer be there to verify it. If the lieutenant had been a suspicious husband, he would doubtless, as in the usual suicide pact, have chosen to kill his wife first. 36

When Reiko said, "I ask permission to accompany you," the lieutenant felt these words to be the final fruit of the education which he had himself given his wife, starting on the first night of their marriage, and which had schooled her, when the moment came, to say what had to be said without a shadow of hesitation. This flattered the lieutenant's opinion of himself as a self-reliant man. He was not so romantic or conceited as to imagine that the words were spoken spontaneously, out of love for her husband. 37

With happiness welling almost too abundantly in their hearts, they could not help smiling at each other. Reiko felt as if she had return to her wedding night. 38

Before her eyes was neither pain nor death. She seemed to see only a free and limitless expanse opening out into vast distances. 39

"The water is hot. Will you take your bath now?" 40

"Ah yes, of course." 41

"And supper . . . ?" 42

The words were delivered in such level, domestic tones that the lieutenant came near to thinking, for the fraction of a second, that everything had been a hallucination. 43

"I don't think we'll need supper. But perhaps you could warm some sake?" 44

"As you wish." 45

As Reiko rose and took a *tanzen* gown from the cabinet for after the bath, she purposely directed her husband's attention to the opened drawer. The lieutenant rose, crossed to the cabinet, and looked inside. From the ordered array of paper wrappings he read, one by one, the addresses of the keepsakes. There was no grief in the lieutenant's response to this demonstration of heroic resolve. His heart was filled with tenderness. Like a husband who is proudly shown the childish purchases of a young wife, the lieutenant, overwhelmed by affection, lovingly embraced his wife from behind and implanted a kiss upon her neck. 46

Reiko felt the roughness of the lieutenant's unshaven skin against her 47
neck. This sensation, more than being just a thing of this world, was for
Reiko almost the world itself, but now—with the feeling that it was soon to
be lost forever—it had freshness beyond all her experience. Each moment
had its own vital strength, and the senses in every corner of her body were
reawakened. Accepting her husband's caresses from behind, Reiko raised
herself on the tips of her toes, letting the vitality seep through her entire
body.

"First the bath, and then, after some sake . . . lay out the bedding 48
upstairs, will you?"

The lieutenant whispered the words into his wife's ear. Reiko silently 49
nodded.

Flinging off his uniform, the lieutenant went to the bath. To faint back- 50
ground noises of slopping water Reiko tended the charcoal brazier in the
living room and began the preparations for warming the sake.

Taking the *tanzen*, a sash, and some underclothes, she went to the 51
bathroom to ask how the water was. In the midst of a coiling cloud of steam
the lieutenant was sitting cross-legged on the floor, shaving, and she could
dimly discern the rippling movements of the muscles on his damp, powerful back as they responded to the movement of his arms.

There was nothing to suggest a time of any special significance. Reiko, 52
going busily about her tasks, was preparing side dishes from odds and
ends in stock. Her hands did not tremble. If anything, she managed even
more efficiently and smoothly than usual. From time to time, it is true,
there was a strange throbbing deep within her breast. Like distant lightning, it had a moment of sharp intensity and then vanished without trace.
Apart from that, nothing was in any way out of the ordinary.

The lieutenant, shaving in the bathroom, felt his warmed body mirac- 53
ulously healed at last of the desperate tiredness of the days of indecision
and filled—in spite of the death which lay ahead—with pleasurable anticipation. The sound of his wife going about her work came to him faintly.
A healthy physical craving, submerged for two days, reasserted itself.

The lieutenant was confident there had been no impurity in that joy they 54
had experienced when resolving upon death. They had both sensed at that
moment—though not, of course, in any clear and conscious way—that
those permissible pleasures which they shared in private were once more
beneath the protection of Righteousness and Divine Power, and of a complete and unassailable morality. On looking into each other's eyes and
discovering there an honorable death, they had felt themselves safe once
more behind steel walls which none could destroy, encased in an impenetrable armor of Beauty and Truth. Thus, so far from seeing any inconsistency or conflict between the urges of his flesh and the sincerity of his
patriotism, the lieutenant was even able to regard the two as parts of the
same thing.

Thrusting his face close to the dark, cracked, misted wall mirror, the 55 lieutenant shaved himself with great care. This would be his death face. There must be no unsightly blemishes. The clean-shaven face gleamed once more with a youthful luster, seeming to brighten the darkness of the mirror. There was a certain elegance, he even felt, in the association of death with his radiantly healthy face.

Just as it looked now, this would become his death face! Already, in fact, 56 it had half departed from the lieutenant's personal possession and had become the bust above a dead soldier's memorial. As an experiment he closed his eyes tight. Everything was wrapped in blackness, and he was no longer a living, seeing creature.

Returning from the bath, the traces of the shave glowing faintly blue 57 beneath his smooth cheeks, he seated himself beside the now well-kindled charcoal brazier. Busy though Reiko was, he noticed, she had found time lightly to touch up her face. Her cheeks were gay and her lips moist. There was no shadow of sadness to be seen. Truly, the lieutenant felt, as he saw this mark of his young wife's passionate nature, he had chosen the wife he ought to have chosen.

As soon as the lieutenant had drained his sake cup he offered it to Reiko. 58 Reiko had never before tasted sake, but she accepted without hesitation and sipped timidly.

"Come here," the lieutenant said. 59

Reiko moved to her husband's side and was embraced as she leaned 60 backward across his lap. Her breast was in violent commotion, as if sadness, joy, and the potent sake were mingling and reacting within her. The lieutenant looked down into his wife's face. It was the last face he would see in this world, the last face he would see of his wife. The lieutenant scrutinized the face minutely, with the eyes of a traveler bidding farewell to splendid vistas which he will never revisit. It was a face he could not tire of looking at—the features regular yet not cold, the lips lightly closed with a soft strength. The lieutenant kissed those lips, unthinkingly. And suddenly, though there was not the slightest distortion of the face into the unsightliness of sobbing, he noticed that tears were welling slowly from beneath the long lashes of the closed eyes and brimming over into a glistening stream.

When, a little later, the lieutenant urged that they should move to the 61 upstairs bedroom, his wife replied that she would follow after taking a bath. Climbing the stairs alone to the bedroom, where the air was already warmed by the gas heater, the lieutenant lay down on the bedding with arms outstretched and legs apart. Even the time at which he lay waiting for his wife to join him was no later and no earlier than usual.

He folded his hands beneath his head and gazed at the dark boards of 62 the ceiling in the dimness beyond the range of the standard lamp. Was it death he was now waiting for? Or a wild ecstasy of the senses? The two seemed to overlap, almost as if the object of this bodily desire was death itself. But, however that might be, it was certain that never before had the lieutenant tasted such total freedom.

There was the sound of a car outside the window. He could hear the 63 screech of its tires skidding in the snow piled at the side of the street. The sound of its horn re-echoed from near-by walls. . . . Listening to these noises he had the feeling that this house rose like a solitary island in the ocean of a society going as restlessly about its business as ever. All around, vastly and untidily, stretched the country for which he grieved. He was to give his life for it. But would that great country, with which he was prepared to remonstrate to the extent of destroying himself, take the slightest heed of his death? He did not know; and it did not matter. His was a battlefield without glory, a battlefield where none could display deeds of valor: it was the front line of the spirit.

Reiko's footsteps sounded on the stairway. The steep stairs in this old 64 house creaked badly. There were fond memories in that creaking, and many a time, while waiting in bed, the lieutenant had listened to its welcome sound. At the thought that he would hear it no more he listened with intense concentration, striving for every corner of every moment of this precious time to be filled with the sound of those soft footfalls on the creaking stairway. The moments seemed transformed to jewels, sparkling with inner light.

Reiko wore a Nagoya sash about the waist of her *yukata*, but as the 65 lieutenant reached toward it, its redness sobered by the dimness of the light, Reiko's hand moved to his assistance and the sash fell away, slithering swiftly to the floor. As she stood before him, still in her *yukata*, the lieutenant inserted his hands through the side slits beneath each sleeve, intending to embrace her as she was; but at the touch of his finger tips upon the warm naked flesh, and as the armpits closed gently about his hands, his whole body was suddenly aflame.

In a few moments the two lay naked before the glowing gas heater. 66

Neither spoke the thought, but their hearts, their bodies, and their 67 pounding breasts blazed with the knowledge that this was the very last time. It was as if the words "The Last Time" were spelled out, in invisible brushstrokes, across every inch of their bodies.

The lieutenant drew his wife close and kissed her vehemently. As their 68 tongues explored each other's mouths, reaching out into the smooth, moist interior, they felt as if the still-unknown agonies of death had tempered their senses to the keenness of red-hot steel. The agonies they could not yet feel, the distant pains of death, had refined their awareness of pleasure.

"This is the last time I shall see your body," said the lieutenant. "Let me 69 look at it closely." And, tilting the shade of the lampstand to one side, he directed the rays along the full length of Reiko's outstretched form.

Reiko lay still with her eyes closed. The light from the low lamp clearly 70 revealed the majestic sweep of her white flesh. The lieutenant, not without a touch of egocentricity, rejoiced that he would never see this beauty crumble in death.

At his leisure, the lieutenant allowed the unforgettable spectacle to en- 71
grave itself upon his mind. With one hand he fondled the hair, with the other he softly stroked the magnificent face, implanting kisses here and there where his eyes lingered. The quiet coldness of the high, tapering forehead, the closed eyes with their long lashes beneath faintly etched brows, the set of the finely shaped nose, the gleam of teeth glimpsed between full, regular lips, the soft cheeks and the small, wise chin . . . these things conjured up in the lieutenant's mind the vision of a truly radiant death face, and again and again he pressed his lips tight against the white throat—where Reiko's own hand was soon to strike—and the throat reddened faintly beneath his kisses. Returning to the mouth he laid his lips against it with the gentlest of pressures, and moved them rhythmically over Reiko's with the light rolling motion of a small boat. If he closed his eyes, the world became a rocking cradle.

Wherever the lieutenant's eyes moved his lips faithfully followed. The 72
high, swelling breasts, surmounted by nipples like the buds of a wild cherry, hardened as the lieutenant's lips closed about them. The arms flowed smoothly downward from each side of the breast, tapering toward the wrists, yet losing nothing of their roundness or symmetry, and at their tips were those delicate fingers which had held the fan at the wedding ceremony. One by one, as the lieutenant kissed them, the fingers withdrew behind their neighbor as if in shame. . . . The natural hollow curving between the bosom and the stomach carried in its lines a suggestion not only of softness but of resilient strength, and while it gave forewarning of the rich curves spreading outward from here to the hips it had, in itself, an appearance only of restraint and proper discipline. The whiteness and richness of the stomach and hips was like milk brimming in a great bowl, and the sharply shadowed dip of the navel could have been the fresh impress of a raindrop, fallen there that very moment. Where the shadows gathered more thickly, hair clustered, gentle and sensitive, and as the agitation mounted in the now no longer passive body there hung over this region a scent like the smoldering of fragrant blossoms, growing steadily more pervasive.

At length, in a tremulous voice, Reiko spoke. 73

"Show me. . . . Let me look too, for the last time." 74

Never before had he heard from his wife's lips so strong and unequiv- 75
ocal a request. It was as if something which her modesty had wished to keep hidden to the end had suddenly burst its bonds of constraint. The lieutenant obediently lay back and surrendered himself to his wife. Lithely she raised her white, trembling body, and—burning with an innocent desire to return to her husband what he had done for her—placed two white fingers on the lieutenant's eyes, which gazed fixedly up at her, and gently stroked them shut.

Suddenly overwhelmed by tenderness, her cheeks flushed by a dizzying   76
uprush of emotion, Reiko threw her arms about the lieutenant's close-
cropped head. The bristly hairs rubbed painfully against her breast, the
prominent nose was cold as it dug into her flesh, and his breath was hot.
Relaxing her embrace, she gazed down at her husband's masculine face.
The severe brows, the closed eyes, the splendid bridge of the nose, the
shapely lips drawn firmly together . . . the blue, clean-shaven cheeks reflecting the light and gleaming smoothly. Reiko kissed each of these. She
kissed the broad nape of the neck, the strong, erect shoulders, the powerful chest with its twin circles like shields and its russet nipples. In the
armpits, deeply shadowed by the ample flesh of the shoulders and chest,
a sweet and melancholy odor emanated from the growth of hair, and in the
sweetness of this odor was contained, somehow, the essence of young
death. The lieutenant's naked skin glowed like a field of barley, and everywhere the muscles showed in sharp relief, converging on the lower
abdomen about the small, unassuming navel. Gazing at the youthful, firm
stomach, modestly covered by a vigorous growth of hair, Reiko thought of
it as it was soon to be, cruelly cut by the sword, and she laid her head upon
it, sobbing in pity, and bathed it with kisses.

At the touch of his wife's tears upon his stomach the lieutenant felt   77
ready to endure with courage the cruelest agonies of his suicide.

What ecstasies they experienced after these tender exchanges may well   78
be imagined. The lieutenant raised himself and enfolded his wife in a
powerful embrace, her body now limp with exhaustion after her grief and
tears. Passionately they held their faces close, rubbing cheek against cheek.
Reiko's body was trembling. Their breasts, moist with sweat, were tightly
joined, and every inch of the young and beautiful bodies had become so
much one with the other that it seemed impossible there should ever again
be a separation. Reiko cried out. From the heights they plunged into the
abyss, and from the abyss they took wing and soared once more to dizzying heights. The lieutenant panted like the regimental standard-bearer on
a route march. . . . As one cycle ended, almost immediately a new wave of
passion would be generated, and together—with no trace of fatigue—they
would climb again in a single breathless movement to the very summit.

4

When the lieutenant at last turned away, it was not from weariness. For   79
one thing, he was anxious not to undermine the considerable strength he
would need in carrying out his suicide. For another, he would have been
sorry to mar the sweetness of these last memories by overindulgence.

Since the lieutenant had clearly desisted, Reiko too, with her usual   80
compliance, followed his example. The two lay naked on their backs, with
fingers interlaced, staring fixedly at the dark ceiling. The room was warm

from the heater, and even when the sweat had ceased to pour from their bodies they felt no cold. Outside, in the hushed night, the sounds of passing traffic had ceased. Even the noises of the trains and streetcars around Yotsuya station did not penetrate this far. After echoing through the region bounded by the moat, they were lost in the heavily wooded park fronting the broad driveway before Akasaka Palace. It was hard to believe in the tension gripping this whole quarter, where the two factions of the bitterly divided Imperial Army now confronted each other, poised for battle.

Savoring the warmth glowing within themselves, they lay still and re- 81
called the ecstasies they had just known. Each moment of the experience was relived. They remembered the taste of kisses which had never wearied, the touch of naked flesh, episode after episode of dizzying bliss. But already, from the dark boards of the ceiling, the face of death was peering down. These joys had been final, and their bodies would never know them again. Not that joy of this intensity—and the same thought had occurred to them both—was ever likely to be reexperienced, even if they should live on to old age.

The feel of their fingers intertwined—this too would soon be lost. Even 82
the wood-grain patterns they now gazed at on the dark ceiling boards would be taken from them. They could feel death edging in, nearer and nearer. There could be no hesitation now. They must have the courage to reach out to death themselves, and to seize it.

"Well, let's make our preparations," said the lieutenant. The note of 83
determination in the words was unmistakable, but at the same time Reiko had never heard her husband's voice so warm and tender.

After they had risen, a variety of tasks awaited them. 84

The lieutenant, who had never once before helped with the bedding, 85
now cheerfully slid back the door of the closet, lifted the mattress across the room by himself, and stowed it away inside.

Reiko turned off the gas heater and put away the lamp standard. During 86
the lieutenant's absence she had arranged this room carefully, sweeping and dusting it to a fresh cleanness, and now—if one overlooked the rosewood table drawn into one corner—the eight-mat room gave all the appearance of a reception room ready to welcome an important guest.

"We've seen some drinking here, haven't we? With Kanō and Homma 87
and Noguchi . . ."

"Yes, they were great drinkers, all of them." 88

"We'll be meeting them before long, in the other world. They'll tease us, 89
I imagine, when they find I've brought you with me."

Descending the stairs, the lieutenant turned to look back into this calm, 90
clean room, now brightly illuminated by the ceiling lamp. There floated across his mind the faces of the young officers who had drunk there, and laughed, and innocently bragged. He had never dreamed then that he would one day cut open his stomach in this room.

In the two rooms downstairs husband and wife busied themselves 91 smoothly and serenely with their respective preparations. The lieutenant went to the toilet, and then to the bathroom to wash. Meanwhile Reiko folded away her husband's padded robe, placed his uniform tunic, his trousers, and a newly cut bleached loincloth in the bathroom, and set out sheets of paper on the living-room table for the farewell notes. Then she removed the lid from the writing box and began rubbing ink from the ink tablet. She had already decided upon the wording of her own note.

Reiko's fingers pressed hard upon the cold gilt letters of the ink tablet, 92 and the water in the shallow well at once darkened, as if a black cloud had spread across it. She stopped thinking that this repeated action, this pressure from her fingers, this rise and fall of faint sound, was all and solely for death. It was a routine domestic task, a simple paring away of time until death should finally stand before her. But somehow, in the increasingly smooth motion of the tablet rubbing on the stone, and in the scent from the thickening ink, there was unspeakable darkness.

Neat in his uniform, which he now wore next to his skin, the lieutenant 93 emerged from the bathroom. Without a word he seated himself at the table, bolt upright, took a brush in his hand, and stared undecidedly at the paper before him.

Reiko took a white silk kimono with her and entered the bathroom. 94 When she reappeared in the living room, clad in the white kimono and with her face lightly made up, the farewell note lay completely on the table beneath the lamp. The thick black brushstrokes said simply:

"Long Live the Imperial Forces—Army Lieutenant Takeyama Shinji." 95

While Reiko sat opposite him writing her own note, the lieutenant gazed 96 in silence, intensely serious, at the controlled movement of his wife's pale fingers as they manipulated the brush.

With their respective notes in their hands—the lieutenant's sword 97 strapped to his side, Reiko's small dagger thrust into the sash of her white kimono—the two of them stood before the god shelf and silently prayed. Then they put out all the downstairs lights. As he mounted the stairs the lieutenant turned his head and gazed back at the striking, white-clad figure of his wife, climbing behind him, with lowered eyes, from the darkness beneath.

The farewell notes were laid side by side in the alcove of the upstairs 98 room. They wondered whether they ought not to remove the hanging scroll, but since it had been written by their go-between, Lieutenant General Ozeki, and consisted, moreover, of two Chinese characters signifying "Sincerity," they left it where it was. Even if it were to become stained with splashes of blood, they felt that the lieutenant general would understand.

The lieutenant, sitting erect with his back to the alcove, laid his sword 99 on the floor before him.

Reiko sat facing him, a mat's width away. With the rest of her so se- 100 verely white the touch of rouge on her lips seemed remarkably seductive.

Across the dividing mat they gazed intently into each other's eyes. The 101
lieutenant's sword lay before his knees. Seeing it, Reiko recalled their first
night and was overwhelmed with sadness. The lieutenant spoke, in a
hoarse voice:

"As I have no second to help me I shall cut deep. It may look unpleas- 102
ant, but please do not panic. Death of any sort is a fearful thing to watch.
You must not be discouraged by what you see. Is that all right?"

"Yes." 103

Reiko nodded deeply. 104

Looking at the slender white figure of his wife the lieutenant experi- 105
enced a bizarre excitement. What he was about to perform was an act in his
public capacity as a soldier, something he had never previously shown his
wife. It called for a resolution equal to the courage to enter battle; it was a
death of no less degree and quality than death in the front line. It was his
conduct on the battlefield that he was now to display.

Momentarily the thought led the lieutenant to a strange fantasy. A lonely 106
death on the battlefield, a death beneath the eyes of his beautiful wife . . .
in the sensation that he was now to die in these two dimensions, realizing
an impossible union of them both, there was sweetness beyond words.
This must be the very pinnacle of good fortune, he thought. To have every
moment of his death observed by those beautiful eyes—it was like being
borne to death on a gentle, fragrant breeze. There was some special favor
here. He did not understand precisely what it was, but it was a domain
unknown to others; a dispensation granted to no one else had been permitted to himself. In the radiant, bridelike figure of his white-robed wife
the lieutenant seemed to see a vision of all those things he had loved and
for which he was to lay down his life—the Imperial Household, the Nation,
the Army Flag. All these, no less than the wife who sat before him, were
presences observing him closely with clear and never-faltering eyes.

Reiko too was gazing intently at her husband, so soon to die, and she 107
thought that never in this world had she seen anything so beautiful. The
lieutenant always looked well in uniform, but now, as he contemplated
death with severe brows and firmly closed lips, he revealed what was
perhaps masculine beauty at its most superb.

"It's time to go," the lieutenant said at last. 108

Reiko bent her body low to the mat in a deep bow. She could not raise 109
her face. She did not wish to spoil her make-up with tears, but the tears
could not be held back.

When at length she looked up she saw hazily through the tears that her 110
husband had wound a white bandage around the blade of his now un-
sheathed sword, leaving five or six inches of naked steel showing at the
point.

Resting the sword in its cloth wrapping on the mat before him, the 111
lieutenant rose from his knees, resettled himself cross-legged, and unfastened the hooks of his uniform collar. His eyes no longer saw his wife.

Slowly, one by one, he undid the flat brass buttons. The dusky brown chest was revealed, and then the stomach. He unclasped his belt and undid the buttons of his trousers. The pure whiteness of the thickly coiled loincloth showed itself. The lieutenant pushed the cloth down with both hands, further to ease his stomach, and then reached for the white-bandaged blade of his sword. With his left hand he massaged his abdomen, glancing downward as he did so.

To reassure himself on the sharpness of his sword's cutting edge the 112 lieutenant folded back the left trouser flap, exposing a little of his thigh, and lightly drew the blade across the skin. Blood welled up in the wound at once, and several streaks of red trickled downward, glistening in the strong light.

It was the first time Reiko had ever seen her husband's blood, and she 113 felt a violent throbbing in her chest. She looked at her husband's face. The lieutenant was looking at the blood with calm appraisal. For a moment—though thinking at the same time that it was hollow comfort—Reiko experienced a sense of relief.

The lieutenant's eyes fixed his wife with an intense, hawk-like stare. 114 Moving the sword around to his front, he raised himself slightly on his hips and let the upper half of his body lean over the sword point. That he was mustering his whole strength was apparent from the angry tension of the uniform at his shoulders. The lieutenant aimed to strike deep into the left of his stomach. His sharp cry pierced the silence of the room.

Despite the effort he had himself put into the blow, the lieutenant had 115 the impression that someone else had struck the side of his stomach agonizingly with a thick rod of iron. For a second or so his head reeled and he had no idea what had happened. The five or six inches of naked point had vanished completely into his flesh, and the white bandage, gripped in his clenched fist, pressed directly against his stomach.

He returned to consciousness. The blade had certainly pierced the wall 116 of the stomach, he thought. His breathing was difficult, his chest thumped violently, and in some far deep region, which he could hardly believe was a part of himself, a fearful and excruciating pain came welling up as if the ground had split open to disgorge a boiling stream of molten rock. The pain came suddenly nearer, with terrifying speed. The lieutenant bit his lower lip and stifled an instinctive moan.

With this *seppuku*?—he was thinking. It was a sensation of utter chaos, 117 as if the sky had fallen on his head and the world was reeling drunkenly. His will power and courage, which had seemed so robust before he made the incision, had now dwindled to something like a single hairlike thread of steel, and he was assailed by the uneasy feeling that he must advance along this thread, clinging to it with desperation. His clenched fist had grown moist. Looking down, he saw that both his hand and the cloth about the blade were drenched in blood. His loincloth too was dyed a deep red. It struck him as incredible that, amidst this terrible agony, things which could be seen could still be seen, and existing things existed still.

The moment the lieutenant thrust the sword into his left side and she 118
saw the deathly pallor fall across his face, like an abruptly lowered curtain,
Reiko had to struggle to prevent herself from rushing to his side. Whatever
happened, she must watch. She must be a witness. That was the duty her
husband had laid upon her. Opposite her, a mat's space away, she could
clearly see her husband biting his lip to stifle the pain. The pain was there,
with absolute certainty, before her eyes. And Reiko had no means of res-
cuing him from it.

The sweat glistened on her husband's forehead. The lieutenant closed 119
his eyes, and then opened them again, as if experimenting. The eyes had
lost their luster, and seemed innocent and empty like the eyes of a small
animal.

The agony before Reiko's eyes burned as strong as the summer sun, 120
utterly remote from the grief which seemed to be tearing herself apart
within. The pain grew steadily in stature, stretching upward. Reiko felt
that her husband had already become a man in a separate world, a man
whose whole being had been resolved into pain, a prisoner in a cage of
pain where no hand could reach out to him. But Reiko felt no pain at all.
Her grief was not pain. As she thought about this, Reiko began to feel as
if someone had raised a cruel wall of glass high between herself and her
husband.

Ever since her marriage her husband's existence had been her own 121
existence, and every breath of his had been a breath drawn by herself. But
now, while her husband's existence in pain was a vivid reality, Reiko could
find in this grief of hers no certain proof at all of her own existence.

With only his right hand on the sword the lieutenant began to cut 122
sideways across his stomach. But as the blade became entangled with the
entrails it was pushed constantly outward by their soft resilience; and the
lieutenant realized that it would be necessary, as he cut, to use both hands
to keep the point pressed deep into his stomach. He pulled the blade
across. It did not cut as easily as he had expected. He directed the strength
of his whole body into his right hand and pulled again. There was a cut of
three or four inches.

The pain spread slowly outward from the inner depths until the whole 123
stomach reverberated. It was like the wild clanging of a bell. Or like a
thousand bells which jangled simultaneously at every breath he breathed
and every throb of his pulse, rocking his whole being. The lieutenant could
no longer stop himself from moaning. But by now the blade had cut its way
through to below the navel, and when he noticed this he felt a sense of
satisfaction, and a renewal of courage.

The volume of blood had steadily increased, and now it spurted from 124
the wound as if propelled by the beat of the pulse. The mat before the
lieutenant was drenched red with splattered blood, and more blood overflowed onto it from pools which gathered in the folds of the lieutenant's

khaki trousers. A spot, like a bird, came flying across to Reiko and settled on the lap of her white silk kimono.

By the time the lieutenant had at last drawn the sword across to the right side of his stomach, the blade was already cutting shallow and had revealed its naked tip, slippery with blood and grease. But, suddenly stricken by a fit of vomiting, the lieutenant cried out hoarsely. The vomiting made the fierce pain fiercer still, and the stomach, which had thus far remained firm and compact, now abruptly heaved, opening wide its wound, and the entrails burst through, as if the wound too were vomiting. Seemingly ignorant of their master's suffering, the entrails gave an impression of robust health and almost disagreeable vitality as they slipped smoothly out and spilled over into the crotch. The lieutenant's head drooped, his shoulders heaved, his eyes opened to narrow slits, and a thin trickle of saliva dribbled from his mouth. The gold markings on his epaulettes caught the light and glinted.

Blood was scattered everywhere. The lieutenant was soaked in it to his knees, and he sat now in a crumpled and listless posture, one hand on the floor. A raw smell filled the room. The lieutenant, his head drooping, retched repeatedly, and the movement showed vividly in his shoulders. The blade of the sword, now pushed back by the entrails and exposed to its tip, was still in the lieutenant's right hand.

It would be difficult to imagine a more heroic sight than that of the lieutenant at this moment, as he mustered his strength and flung back his head. The movement was performed with sudden violence, and the back of his head struck with a sharp crack against the alcove pillar. Reiko had been sitting until now with her face lowered, gazing in fascination at the tide of blood advancing toward her knees, but the sound took her by surprise and she looked up.

The lieutenant's face was not the face of a living man. The eyes were hollow, the skin parched, the once so lustrous cheeks and lips the color of dried mud. The right hand alone was moving. Laboriously gripping the sword, it hovered shakily in the air like the hand of a marionette and strove to direct the point at the base of the lieutenant's throat. Reiko watched her husband make this last, most heart-rending, futile exertion. Glistening with blood and grease, the point was thrust at the throat again and again. And each time it missed its aim. The strength to guide it was no longer there. The straying point struck the collar and the collar badges. Although its hooks had been unfastened, the stiff military collar had closed together again and was protecting the throat.

Reiko could bear the sight no longer. She tried to go to her husband's help, but she could not stand. She moved through the blood on her knees, and her white skirts grew deep red. Moving to the rear of her husband, she helped no more than by loosening the collar. The quivering blade at last contacted the naked flesh of the throat. At that moment Reiko's impression was that she herself had propelled her husband forward; but that was not the case. It was a movement planned by the lieutenant himself, his last exertion of strength. Abruptly he threw his body at the blade, and the blade pierced his neck, emerging at the nape. There was a tremendous spurt of blood and the lieutenant lay still, cold blue-tinged steel protruding from his neck at the back.

5

Slowly, her socks slippery with blood, Reiko descended the stairway. The upstairs room was now completely still. 130

Switching on the ground-floor lights, she checked the gas jet and the main gas plug and poured water over the smoldering, half-buried charcoal in the brazier. She stood before the upright mirror in the four-and-a-half-mat room and held up her skirts. The bloodstains made it seem as if a bold, vivid pattern was printed across the lower half of her white kimono. When she sat down before the mirror, she was conscious of the dampness and coldness of her husband's blood in the region of her thighs, and she shivered. Then, for a long while, she lingered over her toilet preparations. She applied the rouge generously to her cheeks, and her lips too she painted heavily. This was no longer make-up to please her husband. It was make-up for the world which she would leave behind, and there was a touch of the magnificent and the spectacular in her brushwork. When she rose, the mat before the mirror was wet with blood. Reiko was not concerned about this. 131

Returning from the toilet, Reiko stood finally on the cement floor of the porchway. When her husband had bolted the door here last night it had been in preparation for death. For a while she stood in the consideration of a simple problem. Should she now leave the bolt drawn? If she were to lock the door, it could be that the neighbors might not notice their suicide for several days. Reiko did not relish the thought of their two corpses putrifying before discovery. After all, it seemed, it would be best to leave it open. . . . She released the bolt, and also drew open the frosted-glass door a fraction. . . . At once a chill wind blew in. There was no sign of anyone in the midnight streets, and stars glittered ice-cold through the trees in the large house opposite. 132

Leaving the door as it was, Reiko mounted the stairs. She had walked here and there for some time and her socks were no longer slippery. About halfway up, her nostrils were already assailed by a peculiar smell. 133

The lieutenant was lying on his face in a sea of blood. The point protruding from his neck seemed to have grown even more prominent than before. Reiko walked heedlessly across the blood. Sitting beside the lieutenant's corpse, she stared intently at the face, which lay on one cheek on the mat. The eyes were opened wide, as if the lieutenant's attention had been attracted by something. She raised the head, folding it in her sleeve, wiped the blood from the lips, and bestowed a last kiss. 134

Then she rose and took from the closet a new white blanket and a waist 135
cord. To prevent any derangement of her skirts, she wrapped the blanket
about her waist and bound it there firmly with the cord.

Reiko sat herself on a spot about one foot distant from the lieutenant's 136
body. Drawing the dagger from her sash, she examined its dully gleaming
blade intently, and held it to her tongue. The taste of the polished steel was
slightly sweet.

Reiko did not linger. When she thought how the pain which had pre- 137
viously opened such a gulf between herself and her dying husband was
now to become a part of her own experience, she saw before her only the
joy of herself entering a realm her husband had already made his own. In
her husband's agonized face there had been something inexplicable which
she was seeing for the first time. Now she would solve that riddle. Reiko
sensed that at last she too would be able to taste the true bitterness and
sweetness of that great moral principle in which her husband believed.
What had until now been tasted only faintly through her husband's example she was about to savor directly with her own tongue.

Reiko rested the point of the blade against the base of her throat. She 138
thrust hard. The wound was only shallow. Her head blazed, and her hands
shook uncontrollably. She gave the blade a strong pull sideways. A warm
substance flooded into her mouth, and everything before her eyes reddened, in a vision of spouting blood. She gathered her strength and
plunged the point of the blade deep into her throat.

Translated from the Japanese by Geoffrey W. Sargent

STUDY QUESTIONS

1. "Patriotism" begins with a summary of the married couple's deaths.
   As these deaths are never in doubt, what becomes the central focus of
   the narrative?
2. Do you believe the graphic descriptions of violence are necessary in the
   narrative? What is their purpose and what do they achieve?
3. Although the story is extremely violent, it offers certain ideals of erotic
   beauty and heroism. How does the relationship between Reiko and her
   husband exemplify these ideals?
4. "Patriotism" revolves around a suicide pact between a passionate married couple and presents that act as highly moral. Analyze the moral
   code that underlies this representation. Explain why you are sympathetic or unsympathetic to this code.

MIKI TAKU

Miki Taku was born in Tokyo in 1935, but spent his childhood in Manchuria. A graduate of one of Japan's most prestigious universities, Waseda University, he majored in Russian literature. A writer of children's literature, he worked as an editor in a literary publishing house. "Genealogy" is from his first book of poems, 3 a.m. Tokyo (1966).

Genealogy

The night I turned up in this world
Mama was incoherent with joy.
Papa, in a flurry, ran to the pawn shop,
and then to wake up the *sake* shop keeper.
After guzzling the wine,
he tied his sweat band really tight
and began working himself to death. In fact, he died.
After his death Mama worked hard,
grinding her widow's teeth.
Keep going! I entered a university in Tokyo
and finally, she made me graduate.
Mama, born in the year of the fire-horse, the pretty girl
who captivated Papa, at sixty is fat
but still full of energy.
Well now, I just had a daughter
and my wife was incoherent with joy.
In a flurry, I ran to the pawn shop,
and then to wake up the *sake* shop keeper.

Translated from the Japanese by Whang Insu

STUDY QUESTIONS

1. What associations are suggested by the pawn shop and the *sake* shop in "Genealogy"? What do these associations tell us about the father's response to the birth of the child?
2. "Genealogy" refers to the line of descent in a family. What vision of his father's life does the poet present?
3. What does the poem suggest about the poet's own life and therefore about families in general?

 ## MORI YŌKO

Mori Yōko (b. 1940) began writing at age thirty-five. She says that she "is a complete devotee of things Western who, even as a child, never went to see a Japanese movie." Her fiction reflects the intermixing of Western and Japanese cultures, the ferment of hybridity, that is a major feature of postmodernism and late-twentieth-century Japan.

Spring Storm

The small orange light on the lobby wall showed the elevator was still at the seventh floor. Natsuo's eyes were fixed on it. 1

From time to time her heart pounded furiously, so furiously that it seemed to begin skipping beats. For some time now she had been wild with excitement. 2

Intense joy is somewhat like pain, she thought. Or like a dizzy spell. Strangely, it was not unlike grief. The suffocating feeling in her chest was almost unbearable. 3

The elevator still had not moved from the seventh floor. 4

The emergency stairway was located alongside the outer walls of the building, completely exposed to the elements. Unfortunately for Natsuo, it was raining outside. There was a wind, too. 5

A spring storm. The words, perhaps romantic, well described the heavy, slanting rain, driven by a wind that had retained the rawness of winter. If Natsuo were to climb the stairs to the sixth floor, she would be soaked to the skin. 6

She took a cigarette from her handbag and lit it. 7

This is unusual for me, she thought. She had never smoked while waiting for the elevator. Indeed, she had not smoked anywhere while standing up. 8

Exhaling the smoke from the depths of her throat, she fell to thinking. I'll be experiencing all kinds of new things from now on, I've just come a big step up the ladder. No, not just one, I've jumped as many as ten steps in one leap. There were thirty-four rivals, and I beat them all. 9

All thirty-four people were well-experienced performers. There was a dancer with considerably more skill than she. Physically also the odds were against her: there were a sizable number of women with long, stylish legs and tight, shapely waists. One Eurasian woman had such alluring looks that everyone admired her. There were professional actresses currently active on the stage, too. 10

In spite of everything, Natsuo was the one selected for the role. 11

When the agency called to tell her the news, she at first thought she was being teased. 12

"You must be kidding me," she said, a little irritated. She had indeed taken it for a bad joke. "You can't trick me like this. I don't believe you." 13

"Let me ask you a question, then," responded the man who had been acting as her manager. In a teasing voice, he continued, "Were you just kidding when you auditioned for that musical?" 14

"Of course not!" she retorted. She had been quite serious and, although she would not admit it, she had wanted the role desperately. At the audition, she had done her very best. 15

"But I'm sure I didn't make it," she said to her manager. "At the interview, I blushed terribly." 16

Whenever she tried to express herself in front of other people, blood would rush to her face, turning it scarlet. 17

"You're a bashful person, aren't you?" one of her examiners had commented to her at the interview. His tone carried an objective observation rather than sympathetic inquiry. 18

"Do you think you're an introvert?" another examiner asked. 19

"I'm probably on the shy side," Natsuo answered, painfully aware that her earlobes had turned embarrassingly red and her palms were moist. 20

"The heroine of this drama," added the third examiner, "is a spirited woman with strong willpower. Do you know that?" 21

Natsuo had sensed the skepticism that was running through the panel of examiners. Without doubt she was going to fail the test, unless she did something right now. She looked up. 22

"It's true that I'm not very good at expressing myself, or speaking up for myself, in front of other people. But playing a dramatic role is something different. It's very different." She was getting desperate. "I'm very bashful about myself. But I'm perfectly all right when I play someone else." 23

If I am to express someone else's emotion, I have no reason to be shy, she confirmed to herself. I can calmly go about doing the job. 24

"Well, then, would you please play someone else?" the chief examiner said, with a nod toward the stage. 25

Natsuo retired to the wings of the stage and tried to calm herself. When she trotted out onto the stage and confidently faced them, she was no longer a timid, blushing woman. 26

It was impossible to guess, though, how the examiners appraised her performance. They showed little, if any, emotion. When the test was over there was a chorus of murmured "Thank yous." That was all. 27

Her manager was still speaking on the phone. "I don't know about the third-raters. But I can tell you that most good actors and actresses are introverted, naive, and always feeling nervous inside." 28

He then added ,"If you don't believe me, why don't you go to the office of that production company and find out for yourself?" 29

Natsuo decided to do just that. 30

At the end of a dimly lit hallway, a small group of men and women were   31
looking at a large blackboard. Most of the board was powdered with half-
obliterated previous scribblings, but at the top was written the cast of the
new musical, with the names of the actors and actresses selected for the
roles.

Natsuo's name was second from the top. It was scrawled in a large,   32
carefree hand. The name at the top was her co-star, a well-known actor in
musicals.

Natsuo stood immobile for ten seconds or so, staring at her name on the   33
blackboard. It was her own name, but she felt as if it belonged to someone
else. Her eyes still fixed on the name, she moved a few steps backwards.
Then she turned around and hurried out of the building. It never occurred
to her to stop by the office and thank the staff.

Sheer joy hit her a little later.   34

It was raining, and there was wind, too. She had an umbrella with her,   35
but she walked without opening it. Finally realizing the fact, she stopped
to unfold the umbrella.

"I did it!" she cried aloud. That was the moment. An incomparable joy   36
began to rise up inside her, like the bubbles crowding to exit from a champagne bottle; and not just joy, pain as well, accompanied by the flow and
ebb of some new irritation. That was how she experienced her moment of
victory.

When she came to, she found herself standing in the lobby of her apart-   37
ment building. The first person she wanted to tell the news to was, naturally, her husband, Yūsuke.

The elevator seemed to be out of order. It was not moving at all. How   38
long had she been waiting there? Ten minutes? A couple of minutes?
Natsuo had no idea. Her senses had been numbed. A round clock on the
wall showed 9:25. Natsuo gave up and walked away.

The emergency stairway that zigzagged upwards was quite steep and   39
barely wide enough for one person, so Natsuo could not open her umbrella. She climbed up the stairs at a dash.

By the time she reached the sixth floor, her hair was dripping wet and,   40
with no raincoat on, her dress, too, was heavy with rain.

But Natsuo was smiling. Drenched and panting, she was still beaming   41
with an excess of happiness when she pushed the intercom buzzer of their
apartment.

"Why are you grinning? You make me nervous," Yūsuke said as he let   42
her in. "You're soaking wet, too."

"The elevator never came."   43

"Who would have considered using the emergency stairs in this rain!"   44

"This apartment is no good, with a stairway like that," Natsuo said with   45
a grin. "Let's move to a better place."

"You talk as if that were something very simple." Yūsuke laughed wryly   46
and tossed a terry robe to her.

"But it is simple." 47

"Where would we find the money?" 48

"Just be patient. We'll get the money very soon," Natsuo said cheer- 49
fully, taking off her wet clothes.

"You passed the audition, didn't you?" Yūsuke asked, staring intently 50
at her face. "Didn't you?"

Natsuo stared back at him. He looked nervous, holding his breath and 51
waiting for her answer.

"Natsuo, did you pass the audition?" As he asked again, his face col- 52
lapsed, his shoulders fell. He looked utterly forlorn.

"How . . . ," she answered impulsively, "how could I have passed? I 53
was just kidding."

Yūsuke frowned. "You failed?" 54

"I was competing with professionals, you know—actresses with real 55
stage experience. How could I have beaten them?" Natsuo named several
contending actresses.

"You didn't pass?" Yūsuke repeated, his frown deepening. "Answer 56
me clearly, please. You still haven't told me whether you passed."

"What a mean person you are!" Natsuo stuttered. "You must have 57
guessed by now, but you're forcing me to spell it out." Her eyes met his for
a moment. "I didn't make it," she said, averting her eyes. "I failed with
flying colors."

There was silence. Wiping her wet hair with a towel, Natsuo was aghast 58
and mystified at her lie.

"No kidding?" said Yūsuke, starting to walk toward the kitchen. "I was 59
in a state of shock for a minute, really."

"How come? Were you so sure I wouldn't make it?" Natsuo spoke to 60
him from behind, her tone a test of his sincerity.

"You were competing with professionals." There was not a trace of 61
consolation in his voice. "It couldn't be helped. You'll have another
chance."

Although Yūsuke was showing sympathy, happiness hung in the air 62
about him.

"You sound as if you were pleased to see me fail and lose my chance." 63

Combing her hair, Natsuo inspected her facial expression in the small 64
mirror on the wall. You're a liar, she told her image. How are you going to
unravel this mess you've got yourself into?

"How could I be happy to see you fail?" Yūsuke responded, placing a 65
kettle on the gas range. His words carried with them the tarnish of guilt.
"But, you know, it's not that great for you to get chosen for a major role all
of a sudden."

"Why not?" 66

"Because you'd be a star. A big new star." 67

"You are being a bit too dramatic." Natsuo's voice sank low. 68

"When that happens, your husband would become like a Mr. Judy   69
Garland. Asai Yūsuke would disappear completely, and in his place there
would be just the husband of Midori Natsuo. I wouldn't like that."

"You're inventing problems for yourself," she said. "You are what you   70
are. You are a script writer named Asai Yūsuke."

"A script writer who might soon be forced to write a musical."   71

"But hasn't that been your dream, to write a musical?" Natsuo's voice   72
was tender. "Suppose, just suppose, that I make a successful debut as an
actress in a musical. As soon as I become influential enough and people
begin to listen to what I say, I'll let you write a script for a musical."

"Let you write, huh?" Yūsuke picked on Natsuo's phrasing. "If you talk   73
like that even when you're making it up, I wonder how it'd be for real."

The kettle began to erupt steam. Yūsuke flicked off the flame, dropped   74
instant coffee into two cups, and splashed in the hot water.

"Did you hear that story about Ingrid Bergman?" Yūsuke asked, his   75
eyes looking into the distance. "Her third husband was a famous theatrical
producer. A talented producer, too." Passing one of the cups to Natsuo, he
continued. "One day Bergman asked her producer-husband, 'Why don't
you ever try to get me a good play to act in?' He answered, 'Because you're
a goose that lays golden eggs. Any play that features you is going to be a
success. It will be a sellout for sure. For me, that's too easy.' " Yūsuke
sipped the coffee slowly. Then, across the rising steam, he added, "I perfectly understand how he felt."

"Does this mean that I'll have to be a minor actress all my life?" Natsuo   76
mused.

"Who knows? I may become famous one of these days," Yūsuke sighed.   77
"Or maybe you first."

"And what would you do in the latter case?"   78

"Well," Yūsuke stared at the coffee. "If that happens, we'll get a di-   79
vorce. That will be the best solution. Then, neither of us will be bothered
by all the petty problems."

Natsuo walked toward the window. "Are you serious?" she asked.   80

"Yes." Yūsuke came and stood next to her. "That's the only way to   81
handle the situation. That way, I'll be able to feel happy for you from the
bottom of my heart."

"Can't a husband be happy for his wife's success?"   82

"Ingrid Bergman's second husband was Roberto Rossellini. Do you   83
know the last words he said to her? He said, 'I'm tired of living as Mr.
Ingrid Bergman.' Even Rossellini felt that way."

"You are not a Rossellini, nor I a Bergman."   84

"Our situation would be even worse."   85

From time to time, gusts of rain slapped at the window.   86

"When this spring storm is over, I expect the cherry blossoms will sud-   87
denly be bursting out," Yūsuke whispered.

"There'll be another storm in no time. The blossoms will be gone, and   88
summer will be here." Brushing back her still-moist hair with her fingers,
Natsuo turned and looked over the apartment she knew so well.

"You've been standing all this time. Aren't you getting tired?" her hus-   89
band asked in a gentle voice. She shook her head.

"You're looking over the apartment as though it were for the first time."   90
Yūsuke said, gazing at his wife's profile. "Or, is it for the last time?"

Startled by his last words, Natsuo impulsively reached into her handbag   91
for a cigarette and put it in her mouth. Yūsuke produced a lighter from his
pocket and lit it for her.

"Aren't you going to continue with your work this evening?" she asked.   92

"No. No more work tonight."   93

"What's the matter?"   94

"I can't concentrate when someone else is in the apartment. You know   95
that, don't you?"

Natsuo nodded.   96

"Won't you sit down?" Yūsuke said.   97

"Why?"   98

"I have an uneasy feeling when you stand there and smoke like that."   99

Natsuo cast her eyes on the cigarette held between her fingers. "This is   100
the second time today I've been smoking without sitting down." The words
seemed to flow from her mouth at their own volition. His back towards
her, Yūsuke was collecting some sheets of writing paper scattered on his
desk.

"You passed the audition. Right?" he said. His voice was so low that the   101
last word was almost inaudible.

"How did you know?"   102

"I knew it from the beginning."   103

"From the beginning?"   104

"From the moment you came in. You were shouting with your whole   105
body—'I've made it, I'm the winner!' You were trembling like a drenched
cat, but your face was lit up like a Christmas tree."

Natsuo did not respond.   106

"The clearest evidence is the way you're smoking right now."   107

"Did you notice it?"   108

"Yes."   109

"Me, too. It first happened when I was waiting for the elevator down in   110
the lobby. I was so impatient, I smoked a cigarette while standing. I've got
the strangest feeling about myself."

"You feel like a celebrity?"   111

"I feel I've outreached myself."   112

"But the way you look now, it's not you."   113

"No, it's not me."   114

"You'd better not smoke standing up."   115

"Right. I won't do it again."   116

There was silence.   117

"You don't at all feel like congratulating me?" Natsuo asked.   118

Yūsuke did not answer.   119

"Somehow I knew it might be like this," Yūsuke continued. "I knew this   120
moment was coming."

Now she knew why her joy had felt like pain, a pain almost indistin-   121
guishable from grief. Now she knew the source of the suffocating presence
in her chest.

"That Rossellini, you know . . ." Yūsuke began again.   122

"Can't we drop the topic?"   123

"Please listen to me, dear. Rossellini was a jealous person and didn't   124
want to see his wife working for any director other than himself. He would
say to her, 'Don't get yourself involved in that play. It'll be a disaster.' One
time, Bergman ignored the warning and took a part in a play. It was a big
success. Rossellini was watching the stage from the wings. At the curtain
call, Bergman glanced at him while bowing to the audience. Their eyes
met. That instant, they both knew their love was over, with the thundering
applause of the audience ringing in their ears . . ." Yūsuke paused, and
then added, "I'll go and see your musical on the opening day."

Natsuo contemplated her husband's face from the wings of the room.   125
He looked across.

Their eyes met.   126

Translated from the Japanese by Makoto Ueda

STUDY QUESTIONS

1. What are Natsuo's feelings when she learns that she has just landed
   her first major acting role?
2. Natsuo is "mystified" at her lie to her husband, Yūsuke, about the
   result of her audition. Analyze her ambivalence and motivations for
   lying.
3. Why does Yūsuke bring up the Bergman-Rossellini story? What parallels are suggested in the relations between Natsuo and Yūsuke and
   those between Ingrid Bergman and Roberto Rossellini?
4. Discuss the possible symbolic significance of the nonworking elevator,
   Natsuo's smoking, and the spring storm. What effect do these elements have on the story's thematic and emotional meanings?

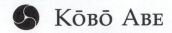

KŌBŌ ABE

Kōbō Abe (b. 1924), a prolific novelist, short story writer, and dramatist, grew up in Manchuria, then a colony of Japan. Influenced by his early exposure to Japanese militarism, Abe's works reject the concerns with cultural nationalism and history that pervade much contemporary Japanese literature. Instead, Abe writes from a metropolitan vantage that focuses on issues of alienation, urban loneliness, and annihilable tensions. The film adaptation (1964) of his novel The Woman in the Dunes *led to its publication in English and to his international reputation. His novels and plays combine elements of the bizarre with realism and philosophical content. Although they have been criticized for being obscure and difficult, they have also attracted praise and attention for their satirical treatment of the position of the individual vis-à-vis social institutions and state governments.*

The Man Who Turned into a Stick (death)

CHARACTERS

MAN FROM HELL, A supervisor
WOMAN FROM HELL, Recently appointed to the Earth Duty Squad
THE MAN WHO TURNED INTO A STICK
HIPPIE BOY
HIPPIE GIRL
VOICE FROM HELL

A hot, sticky Sunday afternoon in June. A main thoroughfare with the Terminal Department Store in the background. Crowds of people passing back and forth. (It is best not to attempt to represent this realistically.) A young man and a young woman sit on the sidewalk curb at stage center front about three yards apart. They are hippies. They stare vacantly ahead, completely indifferent to their surroundings, with withdrawn expressions. (If desired, they   5
can be shown sniffing glue.)

All of a sudden a stick comes hurtling down from the sky. A very ordinary stick, about four feet long. (It can be manipulated, perhaps in the manner of Grand Guignol, by the actor playing the part of the man before he turned into a stick.)

The stick rolls over and over, first striking against the edge of the sidewalk, then bounc-   10
ing back with a clatter, and finally coming to rest horizontally in the gutter near the curbstone, less than a yard from the two hippies. Reflex action makes them look at where the stick has fallen, then upward, frowning, to see where it came from. But considering the danger to which they have been exposed, their reactions are somewhat lacking in ur-
gency.   15

HIPPIE BOY: *(Still looking up.)* Goddamned dangerous.

MAN FROM HELL: In the twilight a white crescent moon, A fruit knife
    peeling the skin of fate.   20

WOMAN FROM HELL: Today, once again, a man
    Has changed his shape and become a stick.

HIPPIE BOY: *(Turns his gaze back to the stick and picks it up.)* Just a couple of
    feet closer and it would have finished me.

HIPPIE GIRL: *(Looks at the stick and touches it.)* Which do you suppose is the 25
    accident—when something hits you or when it misses?

HIPPIE BOY: How should I know? *(Bangs the stick on the pavement, making a
    rhythm.)*

MAN FROM HELL: The moon, the color of dirty
    chromium plate,   30
    Looks down and the streets
    are swirling.

WOMAN FROM HELL: Today, once again, a man
    Turned into a stick and vanished.

HIPPIE GIRL: Hey, what's that rhythm you're tapping?   35

HIPPIE BOY: Try and guess.

HIPPIE GIRL: *(Glancing up.)* Look! I'm sure that kid was the culprit!

HIPPIE BOY: *(Intrigued, looks up.)*

HIPPIE GIRL: Isn't he cute? I'll bet he's still in grade school. He must've
    been playing on the roof.   40

HIPPIE BOY: *(Looks into the distance, as before.)* Damned brats. I hate them
    all.

HIPPIE GIRL: Ohh—it's dangerous, the way he's leaning over the
    edge. . . . I'm sure he's ashamed now he threw it. . . . He seems
    to be trying to say something, but I can't hear him.   45

HIPPIE BOY: He's probably disappointed nobody got hurt, so now he's
    cursing us instead.

STICK: *(To himself.)* No, that's not so. He's calling me. The child saw me fall.

HIPPIE GIRL: *(Abruptly changing the subject.)* I know what it is, that rhythm.
    This is the song, isn't it? *(She hums some tune or other.)*   50

HIPPIE BOY: Hmmm.

HIPPIE GIRL: Was I wrong?

HIPPIE BOY: It's always been my principle to respect other people's tastes.

HIPPIE GIRL: *(Unfazed by this, she wiggles her body to the rhythm and goes on
    humming.)*   55

(In the meantime, THE MAN WHO TURNED INTO A STICK *is coordinating the movements
of his body with those of the stick in* HIPPIE BOY's *hand, all the while keeping his eyes
fastened on a point somewhere in the sky.)*

MAN FROM HELL: *(Walks slowly toward stage center.)*
    The moon is forgotten   60
    In a sky the color of cement,
    And the stick lies forgotten
    Down in the gutter.
WOMAN FROM HELL: *(Also walks in the same deliberate fashion toward stage*
    center.)   65
    The stick lies forgotten in the gutter,
    The streets from above form a whirlpool.
    A boy is searching for his vanished father.

(MAN and WOMAN FROM HELL meet at stage center, several feet behind HIPPIE BOY and
GIRL, just as they finish this recitation.)   70

MAN FROM HELL: *(In extremely matter-of-fact tones.)* You know, it wouldn't
    surprise me if this time we happened to have arrived exactly
    where we intended.
WOMAN FROM HELL: *(Opens a large notebook.)* The time is precisely twenty-
    two minutes and ten seconds before—   75
MAN FROM HELL: *(Looks at his wristwatch.)* On the button. . . .
WOMAN FROM HELL: *(Suddenly notices the stick in HIPPIE BOY's hand.)* I won-
    der, could that be the stick?
MAN FROM HELL: *(Rather perplexed.)* If it is, we've got a most peculiar ob-
    stacle in our path. . . . *(Walks up to HIPPIE BOY and addresses him* 80
    from behind, over his shoulder.) Say, pal, where did you get that stick?
HIPPIE BOY: *(Throws him a sharp glance but does not answer.)*
WOMAN FROM HELL: Lying in the gutter, wasn't it?
HIPPIE GIRL: It fell from the roof. We had a hairbreadth escape.
WOMAN FROM HELL: *(Delighted to have her theory confirmed.)* I knew it! *(To* 85
    MAN FROM HELL.) Sir, it was this stick, as I suspected.
MAN FROM HELL: *(To HIPPIE BOY.)* Sorry to bother you, but would you
    mind handing me that stick?
WOMAN FROM HELL: I'm sure you don't need it especially.
HIPPIE BOY: I don't know about that. . . .   90
MAN FROM HELL: We're making a survey. A little investigation.
HIPPIE GIRL: You from the police?
WOMAN FROM HELL: No, not exactly. . . .
MAN FROM HELL: *(Interrupting.)* But you're not too far off. . . .
HIPPIE BOY: Liars! You're the ones who threw the stick at us. And now 95
    you're trying to suppress the evidence. You think I'm going to
    play your game? Fat chance!

(Beating out a rhythm with the stick, he starts to hum the melody HIPPIE GIRL was singing.)

MAN FROM HELL: *(In mollifying tones.)* If you really suspect us, I'd be glad
    to go with you to the police station.   100
HIPPIE BOY: Don't try to wheedle your way around me.

HIPPIE GIRL: *(Looks up.)* You know, I think it was that kid we saw a while ago . . . He's not there anymore.

HIPPIE BOY: You shut up.

WOMAN FROM HELL: *(Animatedly.)* That's right, there was a child watching   105
everything, wasn't there? From the railing up there on the
roof. . . . And didn't you hear him calling his father? In a frightened, numb little voice. . . .

HIPPIE GIRL: *(Trying not to annoy HIPPIE BOY.)* How could I possibly hear
him? The average noise level in this part of town is supposed to   110
be over 120 decibels, on an average. *(Shaking her body to a go-go
rhythm.)*

WOMAN FROM HELL: *(To MAN FROM HELL.)* Sir, shall I verify the circumstances at the scene?

MAN FROM HELL: Yes, I suppose so. *(Hesitates a second.)* . . . But don't   115
waste too much time over it.

(WOMAN FROM HELL hurries off to stage left.)

STICK: *(To himself. His voice is filled with anguish.)* There's no need for
it. . . . I can hear everything. . . . In the grimy little office behind
the staircase marked "For store employees only" . . . my son,   120
scared to death, surrounded by scabby-looking, mean security
guards. . . .

MAN FROM HELL: *(To HIPPIE BOY.)* It's kind of hard to explain, but the fact
is, we have been entrusted, for the time being, with the custodi-
anship of that stick. . . . I wish you'd try somehow to understand.   125

HIPPIE BOY: I don't understand nothing.

HIPPIE GIRL: *(With a wise look.)* This is the age of the generation gap. We're
alienated.

STICK: *(To himself. In tones of unshakable grief.)* The child is lodging a complaint. . . . He says I turned into a stick and dropped from the   130
roof. . . .

MAN FROM HELL: *(To HIPPIE BOY.)* Well, let me ask you a simple question.
What do you intend to use the stick for? I'm sure you haven't any
particular aim in mind.

HIPPIE BOY: I'm not interested in aims.   135

HIPPIE GIRL: That's right. Aims are out-of-date.

MAN FROM HELL: Exactly. Aims don't amount to a hill of beans. So why
can't you let me have it? It isn't doing you any good. All it is is a
stick of wood. But, as far as we're concerned, it is a valuable item
of evidence relating to a certain person . . .   140

HIPPIE GIRL: *(Dreamily.)* But one should have a few. People don't have
enough. . . .

MAN FROM HELL: Enough what?

HIPPIE GIRL: Aims!

MAN FROM HELL: You're making too much of nothing. It's bad for your   145 health to want something that doesn't really exist. The uncertainty you feel at the thought you haven't got any aims, your mental anguish at the thought you have lost track of whatever aims you once had—they're a lot better proof that you are there, in that particular spot, than any aim I can think of. That's true, isn't it?   150

HIPPIE GIRL: *(To* HIPPIE BOY.*)* How about a kiss, huh?

HIPPIE BOY: *(Gives her a cold sidelong glance.)* I don't feel like it.

HIPPIE GIRL: You don't have to put on such airs with me.

HIPPIE BOY: I don't want to.   155

HIPPIE GIRL: Come on!

HIPPIE BOY: I told you, lay off the euphoria.

HIPPIE GIRL: Then scratch my back.

HIPPIE BOY: Your back?

*(*HIPPIE GIRL *bends over in* HIPPIE BOY's *direction, and lifts the back of her collar.* HIPPIE   160
BOY, *with an air of great reluctance, thrusts the stick down into her collar and moves the stick around inside her dress, scratching her back.)*

HIPPIE GIRL: More to the left. . . . That's right, there. . . .

HIPPIE BOY: *(Pulls out the stick and hands it to* HIPPIE GIRL.*)* Now you scratch me. *(Bends over toward* HIPPIE GIRL.*)*   165

HIPPIE GIRL: You don't mean it from the heart. . . . *(All the same, she immediately gives way and thrusts the stick down the back of* HIPPIE BOY's *collar.)* Is this the place?

HIPPIE BOY: Yes, there. And everywhere else.

HIPPIE GIRL: Everywhere?   170

HIPPIE BOY: *(Twisting his body and emitting strange noises.)* Uhhh . . . uhhh . . . uhhh . . . It feels like I haven't had a bath in quite some time. . . .

HIPPIE GIRL: *(Throwing down the stick.)* You egoist!

*(*MAN FROM HELL *nimbly jumps between the two of them and attempts to grab the stick. But*   175
HIPPIE BOY *brushes his hand away and picks up the stick again.)*

MAN FROM HELL: Look, my friend. I'm willing to make a deal with you. How much will you charge for letting me have this stick?

HIPPIE GIRL: *(Instantly full of life.)* One dollar.

MAN FROM HELL: A dollar? For a stick of wood like this?   180

HIPPIE BOY: Forget it. Not even for two dollars.

HIPPIE GIRL: *(To* HIPPIE BOY *in a low voice, reproachfully.)* You can find any number of sticks just like this one, if you really want it.

MAN FROM HELL: A dollar will keep you in cigarettes for a while.

HIPPIE BOY: Me and this stick, we understand each other. . . . Don't know   185
why. . . . *(Strikes a pose, holding the end of the stick in his hand.)*

HIPPIE GIRL: *(With scorn in her voice.)* You look alike. A remarkable resemblance.

HIPPIE BOY: *(Staring at the stick.)* So we look alike, do we? Me and this stick? *(Reflects awhile, then suddenly turns to* HIPPIE GIRL.*)* You got any 190
    brothers and sisters?
HIPPIE GIRL: A younger sister.
HIPPIE BOY: What was her name for you? *(*HIPPIE GIRL *hesitates.)* You must
    have been known as *something*. A nickname, maybe.
HIPPIE GIRL: You mean, the way she called me. 195
HIPPIE BOY: Precisely.
HIPPIE GIRL: Gaa-gaa.
HIPPIE BOY: Gaa-gaa?
HIPPIE GIRL: No, that's what my brother called me. My sister was differ-
    ent. She called me Mosquito. 200
HIPPIE BOY: What does Gaa-gaa mean?
HIPPIE GIRL: Mosquito—that's what my sister called me.
HIPPIE BOY: I'm asking what Gaa-gaa is.
HIPPIE GIRL: You don't know what Gaa-gaa is?
HIPPIE BOY: Has it got something to do with mosquitoes? 205
HIPPIE GIRL: Yes, but it's very complicated to explain.
MAN FROM HELL: Excuse me, but would you . . .
HIPPIE BOY: Yesterday there was a funeral at that haberdashery across the
    street.
HIPPIE GIRL: *(Looking around at the crowd.)* But it had nothing to do with any 210
    of these people, had it?
HIPPIE BOY: But what about Gaa-gaa and Mosquito?
MAN FROM HELL: Wasn't it Gar-Gar rather than Gaa-gaa?
HIPPIE GIRL: She died.
MAN FROM HELL: Who died? 215
HIPPIE GIRL: My sister.
MAN FROM HELL: What happened to her?
HIPPIE BOY: She became a corpse, naturally.
MAN FROM HELL: Of course. That's not surprising.
HIPPIE GIRL: That's why I don't understand anything anymore. Every- 220
    thing is wrapped in riddles.
HIPPIE BOY: What, for instance?
HIPPIE GIRL: Was it Gaa-gaa or Gar-gar?
HIPPIE BOY: You're just plain stupid.
MAN FROM HELL: By the way, in reference to that stick—she says you look 225
    like it. Let's suppose for the moment you do look like the stick—
    the meaning is not what you think it is.
HIPPIE GIRL: Tomorrow people will be calling tomorrow today.
MAN FROM HELL: To begin with, your conceptual framework with respect
    to the stick is basically— 230
HIPPIE BOY: I see. Once a human hand grabs something there's no telling
    what it can do.
HIPPIE GIRL: I missed grabbing it. It's too awful to think that the day after

tomorrow will always be tomorrow even hundreds of years from
now.   235

(WOMAN FROM HELL *returns, walking quickly.*)

WOMAN FROM HELL: (*She stops at some distance from the others.*) Sir . . .
MAN FROM HELL: (*Goes up to* WOMAN.) Well, what happened?
WOMAN FROM HELL: We've got to hurry . . .
MAN FROM HELL: (*Turns toward* HIPPIES.) This crazy bunch—I offered them   240
    a dollar for the stick, but they refuse to part with it.
WOMAN FROM HELL: The child is coming.
MAN FROM HELL: What for?
WOMAN FROM HELL: Just as I got into the department store I heard them
    making an announcement about a lost child. The child was ap-   245
    parently raising quite a rumpus. He claimed he saw his father
    turn into a stick and fall off the roof. But nobody seemed to
    believe him.
MAN FROM HELL: Of course not.
WOMAN FROM HELL: Then the child gave the matron the slip and ran out   250
    of the store, looking for his father.

(MAN *and* WOMAN FROM HELL *look uneasily off to stage left.*)

STICK: (*Talking brokenly to himself.*) The child saw it. I know he did. I was
    leaning against the railing at the time, the one that runs between
    the air ducts and the staircase, on a lower level. I was looking   255
    down at the crowds below, with nothing particular on my mind.
    A whirlpool . . . Look—it's just like one big whirlpool. . . .

(*Actual noises of city traffic gradually swell in volume, sounding something like a monster
howling into a tunnel. Suddenly* HIPPIE BOY *lets the stick drop in alarm.*)

HIPPIE GIRL: What happened?   260
STICK: (*Continuing his monologue.*) I stood there, feeling dizzy, as if the
    noises of the city were a waterfall roaring over me, clutching
    tightly to the railing, when my boy called me. He was pestering
    me for a dime, so he could look through the telescope for three
    minutes. . . . And that second my body sailed out into mid-   265
    air. . . . I had not the least intention of running away from the
    child or anything like that. . . . But I turned into a stick. . . . Why
    did it happen? Why should such a thing have happened to me?
HIPPIE GIRL: What's the matter, anyway?
HIPPIE BOY: (*Stares at the stick lying at his feet with a bewildered expression.*) It   270
    twitched, like a dying fish. . . .
HIPPIE GIRL: It couldn't have . . . You're imagining things.
WOMAN FROM HELL: (*Stands on tiptoes and stares off into the distance at stage
    left.*) Look! Sir, look! Do you see that child? The little boy with the

short neck, prowling around, looking with his big glasses over   275
the ground?

MAN FROM HELL: He seems to be gradually coming closer.

STICK: *(To himself.)* I can hear the child's footsteps . . . bouncing like a little
rubber ball, the sound threading its way through the rumblings of
the earth shaking under the weight of a million people. . . .   280

HIPPIE GIRL: *(Steals a glance in the direction of the* MAN *and* WOMAN FROM
HELL.) *Somehow those guys give me the creeps. . . . Why don't you
make some sort of deal with him?*

*(*HIPPIE BOY, *who has kept his eyes glued on the stick at his feet, snaps out of his daze and
stands up.* GIRL *also stands.)*   285

HIPPIE BOY: *(With irritation.)* I can't figure it out, but I don't like it. That
stick looks too much like me.

HIPPIE GIRL: *(Her expression is consoling.)* It doesn't really look all that much
like you. Just a little.

HIPPIE BOY: *(Calls to* MAN FROM HELL, *who has just that moment turned toward*   290
him, as if anticipating something.) Five dollars. What do you say?
(He keeps his foot on the stick.)

MAN FROM HELL: Five dollars?

STICK: *(To himself.)* He doesn't have to stand on me. . . . I'm soaked from
lying in the gutter. . . . I'll be lucky if I don't catch a cold.   295

HIPPIE BOY: I'm not going to force you, if you don't want it.

WOMAN FROM HELL: *(Nervously glancing off to stage left.)* Sir, he's almost
here.

*(*THE MAN WHO TURNED INTO A STICK *shows a subtle, complex reaction, a mixture of see
and rejection.)*   300

HIPPIE BOY: I'm selling it because I don't want to sell it. That's a contradiction of circumstances. Do you follow me?

HIPPIE GIRL: That's right. He's selling it because he doesn't want to. Can
you understand that?

MAN FROM HELL: *(Annoyed.)* All right, I guess . . . *(He pulls some bills from*   305
his pocket and selects from them a five-dollar bill.) Here you are. . . .
But I'll tell you one thing, my friend, you may imagine you've
struck a clever bargain, but one of these days you'll find out. It
wasn't just a stick you sold, but yourself.

(But HIPPIE BOY, *without waiting for* MAN *to finish his words, snatches away the dollar bill*   310
and quickly exits to stage right. HIPPIE GIRL *follows after him, smiling innocently. She
waves her hand.)*

HIPPIE GIRL: It's the generation gap. *(She exits with these words.)*

*(*MAN *and* WOMAN FROM HELL, *leaping into action, rush to the gutter where the stick is
laying. Just then the sun suddenly goes behind a cloud, and the street noises gradually fade.*   315

At the very end, for just a second, a burst of riveting is heard from a construction site somewhere off in the distance.)

MAN FROM HELL: *(Gingerly picks up the dirty stick with his fingertips. With his other hand he takes the newspaper that can be seen protruding from his pocket, spreads it open, and uses it to wipe the stick.)* Well, that was a   320
close one. . . .
WOMAN FROM HELL: Earth duty isn't easy, is it?
MAN FROM HELL: It was a good experience on your first day of on-the-job training.
WOMAN FROM HELL: I was on tenterhooks, I can tell you.   325

(THE MAN WHO TURNED INTO A STICK suddenly exhibits a strong reaction to something. MAN and WOMAN FROM HELL alertly respond to his reaction.)

WOMAN FROM HELL: There's the child!

*(MAN FROM HELL, greatly alarmed, at once hides the stick behind his back. On a sudden thought, he pushes the stick under his jacket, and finally down into his trousers. He stands   330
ramrod stiff for several seconds. Then, all at once, the excitement melts from the face of THE MAN WHO TURNED INTO A STICK. MAN and WOMAN FROM HELL, relieved, also relax their postures.)*

STICK: *(To himself.)* It doesn't matter. . . . There was nothing I could have
done, anyway, was there?   335
MAN FROM HELL: *(Pulling out the stick.)* Wow! That was a close shave. . . .
WOMAN FROM HELL: But you know, I kind of feel sorry for him.
MAN FROM HELL: Sympathy has no place in our profession. Well, let's get cracking. *(Holds out the stick.)* That crazy interruption has certainly
played havoc with our schedule.   340
WOMAN FROM HELL: *(Accepts the stick and holds it in both hands, as if to make a ceremonial offering.)* I didn't realize how light it was.
MAN FROM HELL: It couldn't be better for a first tryout. Now, make your report, in exactly the order you learned. . . .
WOMAN FROM HELL: Yes, sir. *(Examines the stick from every angle, with the   345
earnestness of a young intern.)* The first thing I notice is that a distinction may be observed between the top and bottom of this stick. The top is fairly deeply encrusted with dirt and grease from human hands. Note, on the other hand, how rubbed and scraped the bottom is. . . . I interpret this as meaning that the stick has   350
not always been lying in a ditch, without performing any useful function, but that during its lifetime it was employed by people for some particular purpose.
STICK: *(To himself. Angrily.)* That's obvious, isn't it? It's true of everybody.
WOMAN FROM HELL: But it seems to have suffered rather harsh treatment.   355
The poor thing has scars all over it. . . .
MAN FROM HELL: *(Laughs.)* Excellent! But what do you mean by calling it a

poor thing? I'm afraid you've been somewhat infected by human ideas.

WOMAN FROM HELL: Infected by human ideas? 360

MAN FROM HELL: We in hell have a different approach. To our way of thinking, this stick, which has put up with every kind of abuse, until its whole body is covered with scars, never running away and never being discarded, should be called a capable and faithful stick.

WOMAN FROM HELL: Still, it's only a stick. Even a monkey can make a stick 365 do what he wants. A human being with the same qualities would be simple-minded.

MAN FROM HELL: (Emphatically.) That's precisely what I meant when I said it was capable and faithful. A stick can lead a blind man, and it can also train a dog. As a lever it can move heavy objects, and it 370 can be used to thrash an enemy. In short, the stick is the root and source of all tools.

WOMAN FROM HELL: But with the same stick you can beat me and I can beat you back.

MAN FROM HELL: Isn't that what faithfulness means? A stick remains a 375 stick, no matter how it is used. You might almost say that the etymology of the word faithful is a stick.

WOMAN FROM HELL: (Unconvinced.) But what you're saying is too— miserable.

MAN FROM HELL: All it boils down to is, a living stick has turned into a 380 dead stick—right? Sentimentality is forbidden to Earth Duty personnel. Well, continue with your analysis. (WOMAN remains silent.) What's the matter now? I want the main points of your report!

WOMAN FROM HELL: (Pulling herself together.) Yes, sir. Next I will telephone 385 headquarters and inform them of the exact time and place of the disappearance of the person in question, and verify the certification number. Then I decide the punishment and register the variety and the disposition.

MAN FROM HELL: And what decision have you made on the punishment? 390 (WOMAN does not reply.) Surely there can be no doubt in your mind. A simple case like this . . .

WOMAN FROM HELL: You know, I rather enjoy wandering around the specimen room, but I just don't seem to recall any specimens of a stick. (Shakes her head dubiously.) 395

MAN FROM HELL: There aren't any, of course.

WOMAN FROM HELL: (Relieved.) So it is a special case, isn't it?

MAN FROM HELL: Now calm yourself, and just think . . . I realize this is your first taste of on-the-job training, but it's disturbing to hear anything quite so wide of the mark. . . . The fact that something 400 isn't in the specimen room doesn't necessarily mean it's so rare. On the contrary . . .

WOMAN FROM HELL: *(Catching on at last.)* You mean, it's because sticks are so common!

MAN FROM HELL: Exactly. During the last twenty or thirty years the per- 405
centage of sticks has steadily gone up. Why, I understand that in extreme cases, 98.4 percent of all those who die in a given month turn into sticks.

WOMAN FROM HELL: Yes, I remember now. . . . Probably it'll be all right if I leave the stick as it was during its lifetime, without any special 410
punishment.

MAN FROM HELL: Now you're on the right track!

WOMAN FROM HELL: The only thing I have to do is verify the certification number. It won't be necessary to register the punishment.

MAN FROM HELL: Do you remember what it says in our textbook? "They 415
who came up for judgment, but were not judged, have turned into sticks and filled the earth. The Master has departed, and the earth has become a grave of rotten sticks. . . ." That's why the shortage of help in hell has never become especially acute.

WOMAN FROM HELL: *(Takes out a walkie-talkie.)* Shall I call headquarters? 420

MAN FROM HELL: *(Takes the walkie-talkie from her.)* I'll show you how it's done, just the first time. *(Switches it on.)* Hello, headquarters? This is MC training squad on earth duty.

VOICE FROM HELL: Roger. Headquarters here.

MAN FROM HELL: Request verification of a certification number. MC 425
621. . . . I repeat, MC 621. . . .

VOICE FROM HELL: MC 621. Roger.

MAN FROM HELL: The time was twenty-two minutes ten seconds before the hour . . . The place was Ward B, thirty-two stroke four on the grid. Stick fell from the roof of Terminal Department Store. . . . 430

VOICE FROM HELL: Roger. Go ahead.

MAN FROM HELL: No punishment. Registration unnecessary. Over.

VOICE FROM HELL: Roger. Registration unnecessary.

MAN FROM HELL: Request information on next assignment.

VOICE FROM HELL: Six minutes twenty-four seconds from now, in Ward B, 435
thirty-two stroke eight on the grid. Over.

WOMAN FROM HELL: *(Opens her notebook and jots down a memo.)* That would make it somewhere behind the station . . .

MAN FROM HELL: Roger. Thirty-two stroke eight.

VOICE FROM HELL: Good luck on your mission. Over. 440

MAN FROM HELL: Roger. Thanks a lot. *(Suddenly changing his tone.)* I'm sorry to bother you, but if my wife comes over, would you mind telling her I forgot to leave the key to my locker?

VOICE FROM HELL: *(With a click of the tongue.)* You're hopeless. Well, this is the last time. Over. 445

MAN FROM HELL: *(Laughs.)* Roger. So long. *(Turns off walkie-talkie.)* That, in general, is how to do it.

WOMAN FROM HELL: Thank you. I think I understand now.
MAN FROM HELL: What's the matter? You look kind of down in the mouth. *(Returns walkie-talkie to WOMAN)* 450
WOMAN FROM HELL: *(Barely manages a smile.)* It's nothing, really . . .
MAN FROM HELL: Well, shall we say good-bye to our stick somewhere around here?
WOMAN FROM HELL: You mean you're going to throw it away, just like that? 455
MAN FROM HELL: Of course. That's the regulation. *(Looks around, discovers a hole in the gutter, and stands the stick in it.)* If I leave it standing this way it'll attract attention and somebody is sure to pick it up before long. *(Takes a step back and examines it again.)* It's a handy size and, as sticks go, it's a pretty good specimen. It could be used for the 460 handle of a placard. . . .

(WOMAN suddenly takes hold of the stick and pulls it from the hole.)

MAN FROM HELL: What do you think you're doing?
WOMAN FROM HELL: It's too cruel!
MAN FROM HELL: Cruel? *(He is too dumbfounded to continue.)* 465
WOMAN FROM HELL: We should give it to the child. Don't you think that's the least we can do? As long as we're going to get rid of it, anyway . . .
MAN FROM HELL: Don't talk nonsense. A stick is nothing more than a stick, no matter who has it. 470
WOMAN FROM HELL: But it's something special to that child.
MAN FROM HELL: Why?
WOMAN FROM HELL: At least it ought to serve as a kind of mirror. He can examine himself and make sure he won't become a stick like his father. 475
MAN FROM HELL: *(Bursts out laughing.)* Examine himself! Why should anyone who's satisfied with himself do that?
WOMAN FROM HELL: Was this stick satisfied with himself?
MAN FROM HELL: Don't you see, it was precisely because he was so satisfied that he turned into a stick? 480
WOMAN FROM HELL: *(Stares at stick. A short pause.)* Just supposing this stick could hear what we have been saying. . . .
STICK: *(To himself. Weakly.)* Of course I can hear. Every last word.
MAN FROM HELL: I have no specific information myself, since it's quite outside my own specialty, but scholars in the field have advanced 485 the theory that they can in fact hear what we are saying.
WOMAN FROM HELL: How do you suppose he feels to hear us talk this way?
MAN FROM HELL: Exactly as a stick would feel, naturally. Assuming, of course, that sticks have feelings. . . . 490
WOMAN FROM HELL: Satisfied?

MAN FROM HELL: *(With emphasis.)* There's no room for arguments. A stick is a stick. That simple fact takes precedence over problems of logic. Come, now, put the stick back where it was. Our next assignment is waiting for us. 495

(WOMAN FROM HELL, with a compassionate expression, gently returns STICK to the hole in the gutter. THE MAN WHO TURNED INTO A STICK up until this point has been registering various shades of reaction to the conversation of MAN and WOMAN, but from now on his emotions are petrified into an immobile state between fury and despair.)

STICK: *(To himself.)* Satisfied . . . 500
WOMAN FROM HELL: But why must we go through the motions of whipping a dead man this way?
MAN FROM HELL: We are not particularly concerned with the dead. Our job is to record their lives accurately. *(Lowering his voice.)* To tell the truth, it is extremely dubious whether or not we in fact exist. 505
WOMAN FROM HELL: What do you mean by that?
MAN FROM HELL: There is a theory that we are no more than the dreams that people have when they are on the point of death.
WOMAN FROM HELL: If those are dreams, they are horrible nightmares.
MAN FROM HELL: That's right. 510
WOMAN FROM HELL: Then there's no likelihood that they're satisfied. To have nightmares even though you're satisfied—that's a terrible contradiction, isn't it?
MAN FROM HELL: Perhaps it might be described as the moment of doubt that follows satisfaction. In any case, what's done is done. . . . *(In* 515 *tones meant to cheer* WOMAN.*)* We'll have to hurry. We have exactly three minutes. If we're late there'll be all hell to pay later on. . . . *(Starts walking, leading the way.)* Don't worry. You'll get used to it, before you know it. I was the same way myself. Sometimes you get confused by the false fronts people put on. But once you 520 realize that a stick was a stick, even while it was alive . . .
WOMAN FROM HELL: *(Still turns to look back at* STICK, *but somewhat more cheerful now.)* Is the next person going to be a stick, too?
MAN FROM HELL: Mmm. It would be nice if we got something more unusual this time. 525
WOMAN FROM HELL: What do you suppose those kids who tried to keep us from getting the stick will turn into?
MAN FROM HELL: Those hippies?
WOMAN FROM HELL: They didn't seem much like sticks, did they?
MAN FROM HELL: If they don't turn into sticks maybe they'll become rub- 530 ber hoses.

(MAN and WOMAN FROM HELL exit to stage right.)

STICK: *(To himself.)* Satisfied? Me? Stupid fools. Would a satisfied man run away from his own child and jump off a roof?

(In another section of the stage MAN *and* WOMAN FROM HELL *reappear as silhouettes.)*   535

MAN FROM HELL: The sky is the color of a swamp, cloudy with disinfec-
    tant.
    On the cold, wet ground
    Another man has changed into a stick.
WOMAN FROM HELL: He has been verified but not registered.   540
    He is shut up inside the shape of a stick.
    He is not unlucky, so he must be happy.
STICK: *(To himself.)* I've never once felt satisfied. But I wonder what it
    would be better to turn into, rather than a stick. The one thing
    somebody in the world is sure to pick up is a stick.   545
MAN FROM HELL: He has been verified but not registered.
    The man's been shut up inside the shape of a stick.
    He can't so much as budge anymore, and that's a problem.
WOMAN FROM HELL: Supposing he begins to itch somewhere—
    What'll he do? How will he fare?   550
MAN FROM HELL: I'm afraid a stick would probably lack
    The talent needed to scratch his own back.
WOMAN FROM HELL: But anyway, you mustn't mind,
    You're not the only one of your kind.
MAN FROM HELL: *(Steps forward and points his finger around the audience.)*   555
    Look—there's a whole forest of sticks around you. All those in-
    nocent people, each one determined to turn into a stick slightly
    different from everybody else, but nobody once thinking of turn-
    ing into anything besides a stick. . . . All those sticks. You may
    never be judged, but at least you don't have to worry about being   560
    punished. *(Abruptly changes his tone and leans farther out toward the
    audience.)* You know, I wouldn't want you to think I'm saying
    these things just to annoy you. Surely, you don't suppose I would
    be capable of such rudeness. . . . Heaven forbid. . . . *(Forces a
    smile.)* It's just the simple truth, the truth as I see it. . . .   565
WOMAN FROM HELL: *(Goes up to* THE MAN WHO TURNED INTO A STICK *and
    speaks in pleading, rather jerky phrases.)* Yes, that's right. You're not
    alone. You've lots of friends . . . men who turned into sticks.

Curtain.

Translated from the Japanese by Donald Keene

STUDY QUESTIONS

1. In this one-act play, every detail contributes to the major themes.
   Analyze the setting and discuss what aspects of twentieth-century life
   are being criticized through it.

2. Discuss how the central character, the Man Stick—who is mostly silent and inactive—is "developed" in the play. What do we learn about his previous life and his feelings?
3. Examine how the Hippie Boy and Girl function as a paired polarity to the characters of the Man from Hell and the Woman from Hell. In what ways are the male figures similar? In what ways do the female figures resemble each other?
4. Discuss the significance of the "absent" character, the little boy. What do references to this character contribute to the emotional texture of the play?
5. Analyze the multiple ways in which the stick is deployed in the play, for example, as a musical instrument, to relieve an itch. Discuss the accumulative meanings that accrue to the figure and relate these meanings to the title in which the central theme of metamorphosis from life to death is underlined.
6. What criticism of modern society is suggested in the play's self-reflexivity, that is, when it makes references to its own constructions; for example, "There is a theory that we are no more than the dreams that people have when they are on the point of death"?

SHIRLEY GEOK-LIN LIM

*Shirley Geok-lin Lim (b. 1944), a Malaysian of Chinese origin, received the
Commonwealth Poetry Prize for her first collection of poems,* Crossing the
Peninsula *(1980). Despite national policies that disenfranchise English-language
writing, she continues to write poetry and fiction in English from her present
residence in the United States. Her three books of poetry and one short story
collection construct the world and experiences of the minority Chinese Malaysians
(or Peranakans) and explore the situation of the transnational migrant.*

Modern Secrets

Last night I dreamt in Chinese.
Eating Yankee shredded wheat
I said it in English
To a friend who answered
In monosyllables: 5
All of which I understood.

The dream shrank to its fiction.
I had understood its end
Many years ago. The sallow child
Ate rice from its ricebowl   10
And hides still in the cupboard
With the china and tea-leaves.

STUDY QUESTIONS

1. Discuss what kind of linguistic community and history is being suggested in the first stanza. Are there parallels to your own experiences
   or experiences of people you know?

2. Referring to the second stanza, analyze how a language can "shrink" to its fiction. In what ways is Chinese a dream language? A fictional language?
3. What is the "secret" the poem is referring to? How is this secret related to the image of the child?

SINGAPORE

LEE, TZU PHENG

Lee, Tzu Pheng (b. 1943) grew up at a time when Singapore was still ruled as a British colony. Her two collections of poetry, Prospects of a Drowning *(1980) and* Against the Next Wave *(1988), have received national and regional prizes. Living through Singapore's independence in 1959, she writes poems that voice the wrenching changes that accompany decolonization. While many of her poems observe the uncertainties of a postcolonial, rapidly industrializing society, they also celebrate the mixed cultural identities that form the new nation-states of the late twentieth century.*

My Country and My People

My country and my people
are neither here nor there, nor
in the comfort of my preferences,
if I could even choose.
At any rate, to fancy is to cheat;   5
and, worse than being alien or
subversive without cause,
is being a patriot
of the will.

I came in the boom of babies, not guns,   10
a 'daughter of a better age';
I held a pencil in a school
while the 'age' was quelling riots
in the street, or cutting down
those foreign 'devils',   15
(whose books I was being taught to read).

Thus privileged I entered early
the Lion City's jaws.
But they sent me back as fast
to my shy, forbearing family.   20

So I stayed in my parents' house,
and had only household cares.
The city remained a distant way,
but I had no land to till;
only a duck that would not lay,   25
and a runt of a papaya tree,
which also turned out to be male.

Then I learnt to drive instead
and praise the highways till
I saw them chop the great trees down,   30
and plant the little ones;
impound the hungry buffalo
(the big ones and the little ones)
because the cars could not be curbed.

Nor could the population.   35
They built multi-mini-flats
for a multi-mini-society.
The chiselled profile in the sky
took on a lofty attitude,
but modestly, at any rate,   40
it made the tourist feel 'at home'.

My country and my people
I never understood.
I grew up in China's mighty shadow,
with my gentle, brown-skinned neighbours;   45
but I keep diaries in English.
I sought to grow
in humanity's rich soil,
and started digging on the banks, then saw
life carrying my friends downstream.   50

Yet, careful tending of the human heart
may make a hundred flowers bloom;
and perhaps, fence-sitting neighbour,
I claim citizenship in your recognition
of our kind.   55
My people, and my country,
are you, and you my home.

STUDY QUESTIONS

1. The first stanza presents three political positions: being an alien or outsider, being a subversive or rebel, and being "a patriot of the will." What does the last position signify? In what ways can this "willed patriotism" be said to be worse than the other two positions? Do you agree that having "willed patriotism" is worse than being an outsider or a rebel?

2. Discuss the situation suggested in the lines in the second stanza, "cutting down / those foreign 'devils', / (whose books I was being taught to read)." How do these lines relate to other postcolonial stories and poems you have read so far?

3. Stanzas 2, 3, and 4 present a certain view of the city. What attitudes toward the increasing urbanization of the environment does the poem articulate?

4. The last stanza revises the speaker's position toward her country, moving from "My country and my people / are neither here nor there" in the first stanza to "My people, and my country / are you, and you my home." Analyze what is suggested in the rearrangement of the sentence and in the placement of the noun "people" before "country." Through what means does the poem finally "claim citizenship"?

VIETNAM

Võ Phiên

Võ Phiên—also known as Doan The Nhon—was born in Binh Dinh, Vietnam, and came to the United States in 1975 as a refugee. A noted writer, journalist, and professor of literature in Vietnam, he continues to write and publish in California, where he founded and edits Van Hoc Nghe Thuat, *a Vietnamese-language literary journal.*

The Key

To say that the first picture in the memories of the wanderings of an unfortunate man who has lost his country and left everything behind is a shower seems ridiculous. What a strange recollection. Perhaps I should say something sorrowful, more poetic. But how can I? None could take refuge the way he wished.

We came to U.S. territory at night. Despite our excited state, darkness prohibited a clear view of part of a country we were going to spend the rest of our life in. At that late hour the island of Guam seemed to consist of thousands of lights.

Our ship dropped anchor about 3 A.M., July 5, 1975. We, nine thousand people, gathered on deck, confused at first. Then, one by one, we climbed down the rope ladder. One man led his son by the hand, another carried his old father; one carried his briefcase, another wrapped his property in a blanket and another loosely held a water container in his hand. One was really naked, wearing only underwear. These poor people were warmly received. Not only were U.S. military officers waiting at the port, there were also Red Cross workers, local authorities and some church leaders.

I watched the beginning of the exodus into the foreign land from the deck of the American Challenger. The refugees proceeded slowly into the well-dressed crowd. Everyone, whether Christian or not, was deeply moved by the presence of an old bishop on the deck in the early morning hours.

My fellow countrymen passed by the important persons cautiously. 5 Carrying sleeping mats and blankets, fathers and sons walked together quietly for nearly fifty feet and then they caught sight of the signs to . . . the showers! Yes, there were the Showers.

The first showers we saw in America stood there in open air. So from the 6 deck I watched people, old and young, quickly undress, rub off the dirt and splash under the showers. Taking a bath so hurriedly at that hour, close to such a solemn setting! I felt lost. "Yes, even in this country, sanitary measures went along with the warmest feelings. Good."

In my country, there is an expression, "rubbing off the dirt." In honor 7 of a friend or relative who just returned from a trip, we might have a party or a dinner "to rub the dirt off from the long journey." The word "dirt" is, of course, used figuratively. And so, I compared the rubbing-off-the-dirt feast in my country with the way people rub off the dirt with soap and water here and could not help but worry for the vast differences between the two cultures.

During our stay in tents on Orote Points, the baths at those open air 8 showers became an important part of our daily activities. From early morning until late afternoon, in the hot sun, people lined up to get to the showers. The gatherings around the showers were quite interesting. With 5, 6 or 7 persons in a small wooden room,—four rooms standing next to each other—, we could look at the sky above, watch the slowly drifting clouds and make conversation with new friends. We discussed many things: the ceremony of lowering the Vietnamese flag on a warship before entering the Subic Bay; the flavor of the ham we'd just eaten; the last days of the nation; getting milk for the babies, etc. Valuable experiences were exchanged, unexpected stories of the fates of friends and relatives were shared under the showers at Orote Points.

In contrast, we had another kind of bathroom at the Fort Indiantown 9 Gap, Pennsylvania, refugee camp. There, each section had about 100 people with only a small shower, a pitch dark, stifling shower with no window. There was no door either; just a curtain. In that small room, there were three showers so that three people of the same sex could take baths at the same time. There was a cardboard hanging on a curtain with one side reading "Men" and the other "Women." To avoid serious mistakes, one has to check and put out the appropriate side before using the shower.

As the shower was airtight, some people used it as a fumigator. If one 10 caught a cold, he came into the room, then turned on the shower and stepped aside to avoid the hot water. The steam would rise, the man would be soaked with perspiration and eventually would feel much better.

The shower was also used for recording. The refugees were thirsty for 11 musical tapes. Each family tried to get some familiar songs and favorite voices before they left the camp. Some thought of the shower. About midnight, when most of us had fallen asleep, when all the noises had quieted, one could bring two cassette recorders into the showers. Yes, this was the place for tape recording. With a few borrowed tapes, two recorders together, one as a transmitter, the other as a receiver, the country music lover could continue his work until the next morning.

And it was in the bathroom that I had the chance to listen to the con-   12
fessions of a man in his mid-fifties.

He was an extremely shy, cautious man. Ordinarily, he seldom talked to   13
anyone in an open manner. Nearly all of us had suffered many heart-breaking losses. Everyday, we moaned, talked on and on while the ladies often cried. Being together for a while, we came to understand the circumstances of others pretty soon, at least in a general way: This lady, wife of a colonel, could get out but her husband and sons got stuck in Vietnam; that fellow, student of the School of Agriculture, ran for his life from B. to N. province, then from N. to Saigon and met a rescue ship there and now his parents won't know what happened to him; or the family of that wealthy businessman hurriedly climbed on an American ship, leaving behind gold and dollars which could be worth millions of piasters; and so on . . .

However, I didn't know exactly what had happened to the family of that   14
old man.

His was a complete family of husband and wife, a daughter and two   15
sons. It was good enough, for who could expect to have brothers and sisters, aunts and uncles to go with? Yet, there was grief and apprehension on the couple's faces. That concern overruled their surroundings and even spoiled the liveliness of their young sons.

I'd wanted to ask him many times. But at the same time I found that it   16
was not an easy thing to do. I wondered if it might be too curious or crude, especially to a man like him. Besides, he didn't need us; he seemed to be trying to avoid our friendliness.

In fact, I had hardly ever met such a shy man. He was as shy as a girl   17
who just reached maturity. He spoke good English, and it was rumored that he'd been an English teacher for many years. At the refugee camp's main office, he was sometimes asked to do translation for other people. On such occasions he was even more bashful. If someone said something, he listened and remained quiet for a while. He would look at us questioningly as though it was too bold to say. And perhaps, for him, everything was too bold. He'd hesitate again until someone reminded, "Please translate it for me." And again, his attitude was the same.

Would it be too daring to ask anything from such a man?   18

And then, one night about 11 o'clock, I went to the shower. As I stood   19
in front of the curtain, I read the sign: "Men" and could hear the sound of splashing water inside. I asked, "Who's in there? May I come in?"

A cheerful voice replied, "Sure. Please come in."   20

Raising the curtain, I recognized the shy man immediately. He was   21
unusually kind to me.

"Hello! Feel free, please. More people, more fun. Ha, ha." 22

He was "feeling free" in the shower, indeed. He was naked and covered 23
with soapsuds. Vietnamese laws do not require a person to cover a particular part of his body in front of someone else, but we don't, however, get
accustomed to being nude at public baths as the Japanese do. His attitude
really encouraged me. I then started "feeling free."

While I was taking off my clothes, my new friend continued to talk, 24
asking question after question: "When did you leave Saigon? Oh, really?
April 29? Half a day earlier than us, then. Which street did you live on? H.
Street? We had an uncle who lived on that very street. We used to visit him
quite frequently . . . Might have passed by your house, who knows? Ha,
Ha. When did you come here? Applied for a sponsor yet? Which one? . . ."

I was amazed and delighted. It seemed to me this man was completely 25
different from the one I had known before. From one topic to another,
my friend talked and talked in a cheerful mood while rubbing his body.
We treated each other like long time old friends. I soon realized that
sometimes displaying human bodies eventually led to displaying human
hearts. Once getting rid of all the clumsy clothes, of all artificial relationships, suddenly feeling free, man in the shower would no longer be
afraid of any daring act.

Finally, he talked about his own trip: 26

"My father is 93 years old now. My wife and I had thought about it over 27
and over since N. province was lost. Surely it was time to run away, but
what about my father? He's too old and weak to bear any hazard we might
encounter during evacuation. As for us, we ran for our lives, not for any
trip, didn't we? On the other hand, we wouldn't have peace of mind
leaving him alone! I have a younger sister who lived in D. province. Since
the loss of that province, I haven't heard anything from her; she's dead or
alive, or where is she living now? I don't know. Oh yes, I still have a few
cousins, a few nephews and nieces, but they all planned to go. It's hard to
find someone to take care of him. To tell you the truth, it's been six years
that my father has become more and more senile. He's absent minded and
sometimes behaves like a child. Poor father. Whenever he thought about
his own age, he asked me to buy a coffin for him."

"A coffin?" 28

"Yes. A coffin. Traditionally, old men asked for a coffin ready at any 29
time. But that usually happened more in rural areas. Who dares to put a
coffin in his home if he lives in the city? It would look terrible, especially
since our children cannot accept old customs and habits. That's why we
had to keep promising him a coffin, a real good one for when he passed
away. Yet people said that if anyone died during the evacuation, the body
would be thrown into the sea. As you can see, how could we urge him to
throw himself in danger?

"Finally, our relatives met to solve the problem. We concluded that it 30
was almost certain that not all of us would be able to get out. Therefore,

anyone who stayed would take care of my father. On the other hand, if we could all get out, the friends and neighbors would be asked for help. All the money and valuable things would belong to those who stayed with my father.

"And then, on April 29, with him seated in a big chair in the living room, all of us, one by one, bowed and thanked him, saying goodbye. We knew this would be goodbye forever. 31

"What the military situation is, what is happening in the country, what his descendants are trying to do, and so on, I'm sure my father is not clear-sighted enough to understand. But, strangely enough, he could feel that something extraordinary, something tragic, was going on. Yes sir, he sat in the chair with tears flowing gently down his cheeks. We tried to comfort him, but he didn't say anything. 32

"Later, we packed our luggage. We hid all the money and valuables in a wardrobe and locked it up. An ounce of gold was set aside for buying his coffin. Anybody, friend or neighbor, who decides to take care of him, was entitled to all we left. We couldn't put it all in his pockets as it would be too hazardous for him. 33

"When we had prepared everything, around 8 P.M., he was still sleeping. It was painful to watch him sleep in the bed, his body all curled up like a small child. We hesitated for a while and then walked away. Waking him up at that time would be a heart-breaking thing to do. 34

"At that time, enemy forces had advanced into some areas of the city, and the situation was critical. We didn't even know if we could make it out." 35

"A friend of ours organized the evacuation program which would take place at the port of H. The small boat was so overcrowded that many times, I thought we would not survive. After three days of struggling for survival, on May 2 we were rescued by an American ship in the international territorial waters. We knew then we'd escaped death. 36

"But sir, it was right at that moment that I was shocked. As I was checking my luggage, I put my hand into my pocket and found that in my hurry I had forgotten to leave the key to the wardrobe for him. My God, I put all the money along with gold and jewelry in the wardrobe, then locked it up! 37

"I remained silent awhile. Then, gradually, various things appeared in my mind: my father's confusion when he woke up, finding himself alone in the empty house; the scene of our relatives and friends coming in, asking for money we had left; questions about the "hidden key" would be raised; the scene of smashing the wardrobe would frighten him. And thieves and robbers might come in and assault or beat him up. What made me so stupid, so absent minded like that . . . hic!" 38

The man stopped. He was choking on water maybe. I could hear just the sound of running water. Then he continued: 39

"My friend, since then I have been obsessed by those terrible pictures. 40

From day to day, month to month, I never feel relieved. God has punished us, you see. I'm so stupid. Hic. I brought the key with me. Hic."

The man stopped again. The water stopped running simultaneously. He 41 had finished his shower. His hands were searching for the towel. Having accustomed my eyes to the dark, I could see his shoulders tremble gently. The man wiped the water from his body and the tears from his eyes.

When did he cry? When I thought he had choked on water? But he was 42 dressing hurriedly as though he was trying to run away. As he stretched his hands out to put his shirt on, I saw a key hanging on a string. There, my old friend carried his key where a Christian typically wears a picture of his God.

Remaining alone in the bathroom, I stood motionless for a while. Then I 43 turned off the water, dressed, raised the curtain and left. Most people had gone back to their rooms and were asleep.

It was a quiet night. The moon was bright in a clear sky. I looked at the 44 shiny moon, touching lightly the key in my hand. Yes, I had a key, kept in my pocket, from a situation similar to that of the old man. (In fact, isn't it true that most of the refugees brought a key along? I mean, who did not feel sorry for a certain mistake, a certain shortcoming he had made to his relatives and close friends who were left behind, something he would feel sorry for the rest of his wandering life?)

Later, a few times, I tried to tell my own story to that man, but it was not 45 easy as he had returned to the attitude he had had before, extremely quiet and shy. Sometimes, I thought he avoided me as though he was avoiding the same mistake or seeing a bad moment in his life again.

I didn't have a chance to meet him again in the shower. 46

Translated from the Vietnamese by Phan Phan

STUDY QUESTIONS

"The Key" is actually a story within a story. The framing narrative is that of the unnamed narrator's refugee experiences from Guam to Indiantown Gap, Pennsylvania. The "interior" narrative belongs to the man with the key, also an unnamed narrator.

1. The showers—presented as an introduction or welcome to American culture—reminds the narrator of the Vietnamese welcoming party for returning friends and relatives. Both are constructed as "rubbing-off-the-dirt" rituals. How do these two activities reveal "the vast differences between the two cultures"?

2. The showers at Orote Points become a valuable place for community interchange. Describe how the refugees convert the less attractive showers at Indiantown Gap for community use.
3. Discuss the narrative of the shy man in its broader significance as representing the trauma and guilt of a refugee generation.
4. Analyze the ironic and symbolic significance of the key in the multiple refugee stories in this narrative.

THEMATIC QUESTIONS

Asia

1. Discuss the notion of "home" in Lu Xün's "My Old Home" and Can Xue's "Hut on the Mountain." If Lu Xün's story both privileges the gentry class by its nostalgia and criticizes its class privilege through the character of Jun-t'u, what kind of class and social criticism is being offered in "Hut on the Mountain"?
2. Different types of patriotism are appealed to in Ai Qing's "Dayanhe—My Wet Nurse" and Yukio Mishima's "Patriotism." Both, however, use the male's relationship with a woman as a metaphor for love of one's country. Discuss the strategies that Ai Qing and Mishima use to construct their notion of Chinese and Japanese nationhood.
3. Working-class characters play a significant role in Lu Xün's "A Small Incident," Ruth Prawer Jhabvala's "The Interview," and R. K. Narayan's "Gateman's Gift," yet the three stories have very different themes and construct different visions of society. Discuss how the strategies of social realism and satire function in each story to represent different social intentions.
4. In Ambai's "Fall, My Mother" and Pramoedya Ananta Toer's "Inem," preadolescent girls are seen as already precociously involved in marriage systems. Although a patriarchal organization can be said to undergird the social pressures that condemn these girls to restricted, unhappy lives, these stories present mothers as complicit agents in their daughters' fate. Discuss the implications of such representations to your understanding of mother-daughter relationships and of women's positions in patriarchal societies.
5. The twentieth century has been called the century of women's rights. The "women's question" was and continues to be one of the most urgent in nations undergoing social restructuring, as in China of the

1940s. Compare Zhenzhen's situation as a nationalist patriot suffering from venereal disease contracted as a spy among the invading Japanese forces in Ding Ling's "When I Was in Xia Village" with Kin's, the aging courtesan, in Hayashi Fumiko's "Late Chrysanthemum." In what ways are their characters and situations similar?

6. Many writers represent relations between men and women as sexually problematic. Conflicting ideals of male aggression and female nurturance result in depictions of male-female relations as power relations. Discuss how these ideals are represented, reversed, undermined, or even rejected in works such as Ai Qing's "Dayanhe—My Wet Nurse," Ishigaki Rin's "The Pan, the Pot, the Fire I Have Before Me," Mori Yoko's "Spring Storm," and Ruth Prawer Jhabvala's "The Interview."

7. The theme of exile recurs in contemporary literature, reflecting the enormous dislocations that accompanied wars and social upheavals in large regions of the world. Discuss how this theme is developed in works such as Wang Xiaoni's "Dark Night on a Southbound Train," Shirley Geok-lin Lim's "Modern Secrets," and Võ Phiên's "The Key," with particular attention to how images function as motifs for mental and emotional associations.

8. Under pressures of modernization and urbanization, many Asian writers represent the problems of their societies as that of the individual's alienation, loneliness, and loss in mass society. Discuss this theme in relation to Kōbō Abe's "The Man Who Turned into A Stick," Can Xue's "Hut on the Mountain," and Lee, Tzu Pheng's "My Country and My People."

AUSTRALIA AND OCEANIA

AUSTRALIA AND OCEANIA

Introduction

The smallest continent, Australia, is the only one that forms a single nation. As part of a geographical region identified as the Antipodes, Australia is increasingly included with New Zealand and the Pacific nations of Papua New Guinea, Fiji, Samoa, and certain smaller islands. The continent separated from other continents millions of years ago, and many species, such as the kangaroo, platypus, wombat, emu, and kookaburra (the largest of the kingfishers, which has a recognizable cackle), that are unknown elsewhere evolved there. Australia and Oceania, therefore, are distinct in nature and geography from the other continents, emphasizing and enlarging their sense of remoteness from the rest of the world.

Australian flora and fauna were new to the Europeans who settled in Australia. The European settlement (1788) came at a period of high interest in classifying and organizing knowledge about botany and zoology. Australia's "difference" fascinated the settlers; early European accounts took note of the "solitude," the "vacancy," of vast uninhabited distances of *Terra Australis Incognito* (unknown southern land), as the continent was named in European maps.

Adjusting to the difference has been one of the great themes of Australian literature. The land emerges as a character in major works such as Patrick White's *Voss* (1957), Randolph Stow's *Tourmaline* (1963), and David Malouf's *An Imaginary Life* (1978). Nature—its power and significance—is a reiterated motif corre-

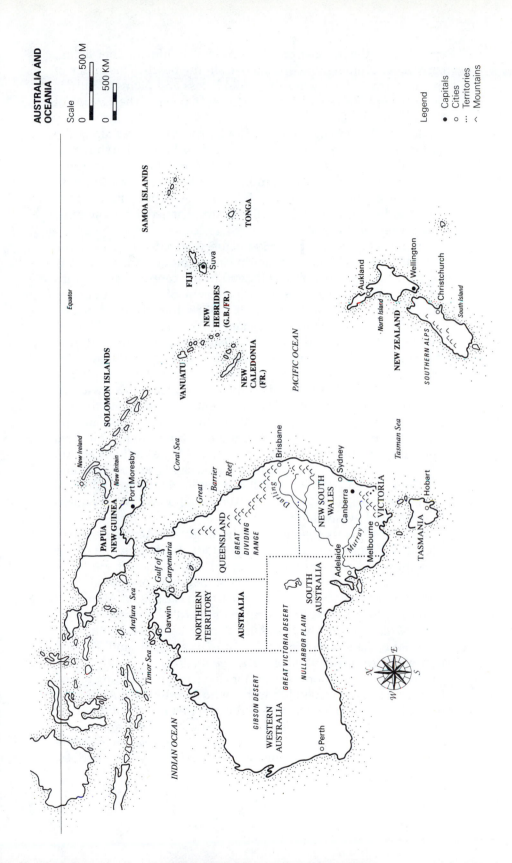

AUSTRALIA AND OCEANIA

Scale

0   500 M

0   500 KM

Legend

● Capitals
○ Cities
⋯ Territories
∧ Mountains

SAMOA ISLANDS

TONGA

FIJI

Suva

NEW HEBRIDES (G.B./FR.)

VANUATU

NEW CALEDONIA (FR.)

PACIFIC OCEAN

Equator

Aukland

Wellington

Christchurch

North Island

South Island

NEW ZEALAND

SOUTHERN ALPS

SOLOMON ISLANDS

New Ireland

New Britain

Port Moresby

PAPUA NEW GUINEA

Coral Sea

Great

Barrier

Reef

Brisbane

QUEENSLAND

GREAT DIVIDING RANGE

Darling

NEW SOUTH WALES

Sydney

Canberra

VICTORIA

Melbourne

Murray

Adelaide

SOUTH AUSTRALIA

Tasman Sea

TASMANIA

Hobart

NORTHERN TERRITORY

AUSTRALIA

Gulf of Carpentaria

Darwin

Arafura Sea

Timor Sea

INDIAN OCEAN

GIBSON DESERT

GREAT VICTORIA DESERT

NULLARBOR PLAIN

WESTERN AUSTRALIA

Perth

N
W E
S

sponding to the popular profile of Australian life: outdoor living, barbecues, camping out, and, above all, the beach. This image of the unrestrained, easy life with rural access and plenty of sun, is perfectly epitomized in Les A. Murray's poem "The Dream of Wearing Shorts Forever."

Most of the population of Australia, however, lives along the eastern and southern coasts because the outback, a harsh region with little rain and hot desert sun, lies not far beyond these coastal regions. Australia is, in fact, an urbanized country, with its thriving cities (Melbourne, Brisbane, Adelaide, Perth, Sydney, Canberra) located in fertile basins, circled by mountains and connected by plateaus.

In contrast, Ayers Rock, a 600-million-year-old ironstone monolith 1,100 feet high and six miles in circumference, the sacred site for the Aboriginal peoples, is located in the central plains southwest of Alice Springs, the principal town of central Australia. When the British annexed Australia in 1788, they did not consider the Aboriginal population, estimated at 300,000 to one million, as a nation. The Aborigines, who had learned to live with and from the land, revered and celebrated the sacred places of their mythic dreamtime. But to many of the colonials, they were an inferior race. As they settled Australia, English colonialists dispossessed its Aboriginal inhabitants. Misguided efforts to integrate the Aborigines into white society through schools, missions, and reserves failed, and alcoholism ravaged the communities. The civil rights movement of the 1960s in the United States influenced Aboriginal political agitation for a treaty, land rights, and reforms and was complemented by the production of literature by Aboriginal writers. Ayers Rock, symbolizing Aboriginal power, was restored to Aboriginal ownership in 1985.

White writers sympathetic to the plight of Aborigines have provided insights. "Bora Ring," by Judith Wright, is one of the best-known poems on the Aboriginal theme. Xavier Herbert's *Capricornia* (1939) chronicles the unjust treatment of Aborigines in northern Australia. Other white Australian classics on Aboriginal themes include Katharine Susannah Prichard's *Coonardoo, the Well in the Shadow* (1929), the first Australian novel to deal with interracial love; Randolph Stow's *To the Islands* (1958); and Thomas Keneally's *The Chant of Jimmie Blacksmith* (1972).

More recently, Aboriginal authors have begun speaking of and for their condition. Colin Johnson—who now uses his Aboriginal name, Mudrooroo Nyoongah—wrote the first novel published by an Aborigine, *Wild Cat Falling* (1965). Another of his novels, *Dr. Wooreddy's Prescription for Enduring the Ending of the World* (1983), re-creates early Aboriginal history through the eyes of a tribesman living the last days of his people and knowing himself powerless to stop the slaughter.

A significant tradition of Australian literature is "the legacy of the convict past." English-speaking Australia was founded as a penal colony for convicts whose crimes ranged from political protest to murder. Botany Bay, a harbor near Sydney, was sometimes used as the name for the entire penal colony established at Port Jackson. The British poet Samuel Taylor Coleridge called the enterprise "the colonization of despair."

A Commonwealth separate from British rule was proclaimed on January 1, 1901. The movement from colony to commonwealth is manifested in the increasing egalitarianism expressed in the literature, with the Australian bush (wild lands) and mateship (male bonding) as recurring motifs. Henry Lawson, often thought of as the father of the Australian short story, illustrates the theme of responsibility to one's mate in many of his stories. Katharine Susannah Prichard's "The Cooboo" presents a more terrifying picture of bush life as seen through a woman's eyes.

Australian autonomy, however, was accompanied by class and racial prejudice, particularly against would-be Asian immigrants. *The Bulletin*, the same newspaper that served as impetus and outlet for the vigorous Australian literature at the turn of the century, was anti-Semitic and virulently anti-Chinese. This newspaper propagated fears of miscegenation and the extinction of the white race. Australia followed a "White Australia" policy until 1966, when the law was substantially changed.

Australia fought as an ally of Britain in both World Wars I and II. More than 30,000 Australians were taken as prisoners of war by the Japanese. Recently, Australia has moved closer economically, politically, and culturally to the United States and sent troops to serve with the United States in the Korean War and the Vietnam War.

Much twentieth-century Australian writing reveals a strong social-realist sensibility. A central feature of Australian literature has been direct narrative rather than sophisticated techniques of presentation, a feature that suits the realistic subjects and social concerns of the writers.

Patrick White put Australia on the international literary map when he received the Nobel Prize for Literature in 1973. White's visionary characters, some heroic, some humble, are generally misfits in their communities, driven to reach for heights that others cannot even imagine. Familiar Australian motifs appear in White's novel *Voss*: the exploration of the forbidding interior, the encounter between Aborigine and convict, and the contrast between life in the untamed bush and the urban province. But

White's exploration is spiritual as well as physical, and his motifs are shaped by modernist, surrealist methods directed toward metaphysical ends.

Contemporary Australian literature demonstrates a dynamism in response to national and international forces. Women's writing, deliberately engaged in presenting a female viewpoint, is strong, as in the work of Thea Astley, Elizabeth Jolley, Jessica Anderson, and Helen Garner. Immigrant experience is also yielding ethnic authors who extend the range of Australian literature. Bruce Dawe's poem "Migrants" is a comment on the desired integration of new and old Australians. Novels set in Southeast Asia in the 1970s and '80s have foreshadowed Australia's geographic position.

Australian poetry also displays the resistance to modernist techniques noted in Australian fiction. Kenneth Slessor is often seen as the first significant modern poet. His contemporary A. D. Hope is a traditionalist who reworks myths to address contemporary concerns. Close in age to these poets, Judith Wright is a visionary in the tradition of William Blake and draws significance from natural subjects. Equally concerned with the land, Les A. Murray and David Malouf write close to central Australian literary traditions. These poets demonstrate the changing response in Australian literature to ecological and national cultural concerns and to increasing international influence.

The scattered islands of the central and south Pacific are often collectively called Oceania. New Zealand and the other nations of Oceania such as Fiji, Samoa, and Papua New Guinea, are island states. These islands are usually divided into three groups. Melanesia refers to the almost continental islands like New Guinea, northeast of Australia. New Guinea is the second largest island in the world (after Greenland). The western half of the island, known as Irian Jaya, is administered by Indonesia; the eastern half, once under Australian rule, forms the independent nation of Papua New Guinea. Micronesia, an island region of small coral atolls, is partly U.S. territory (Guam) and partly United Nations Trust Territory, administered by the U.S. Samoa, made up of eight islands in the central Pacific Ocean, was colonized at various times by the United Kingdom, Germany, and the United States. The German part was taken over by New Zealand in 1914. Polynesia is composed of a large stretch of the central Pacific and includes New Zealand and Easter Island.

While New Zealand, like Australia, was settled by the British, these lands of the Pacific have their own native populations. The earliest peoples were Malay-Polynesian; the Maoris, a Polynesian people, are said to have reached New Zealand about A.D. 900.

Captain Cook's landing in New Zealand in 1769 opened it to British settlement, and the Treaty of Waitangi (1840) ceded sovereignty to Great Britain while allowing the Maoris to keep their land ownership. New Zealand's biculturality is underlined by the widespread use of the Maori language.

The themes of island isolation, natural beauty, social pressures of conformity and individual deviance, rejection of provincial mores, biculturality, and Maori national identity are sounded repeatedly in New Zealand literature. Katherine Mansfield, New Zealand's most famous writer, left the island to make her career in Britain, but later returned to her childhood experiences for some of her strongest work. Similarly, many New Zealand writers such as Fleur Adcock follow the pattern of voluntary exile to Europe and now especially to the United States.

Other writers, such as Allen Curnow, C. K. Stead, and Bill Manhire, who have chosen to stay on in New Zealand, frequently write of the country's physical beauty and geographical isolation with irony and with tender defense. Curnow's "The Skeleton of the Great Moa in the Canterbury Museum, Christchurch" is a model of the ambivalence that writers express toward New Zealand's unique physical features.

The same isolation that ensures New Zealand's palpable sense of community also leads to cultural provincialism and narrowness. Many writers criticize the destructive complacency and prejudice fostered in a small, closed society. Janet Frame's autobiographical books and stories paint a rather terrifying portrait of psychologically dysfunctional characters and relationships. (Frame's troubled life and ultimately successful literary career were the subject of the 1991 film *Angel at My Table*.)

A younger Maori writer like Patricia Grace indicts racist policies against her proud Maori community. Witi Ihimaera, another Maori writer, however, asserts New Zealand's distinctive biculturality more positively in his allusion to Mansfield in the title of his collection of short stories, *Dear Miss Mansfield* (1990).

Even in countries with a native majority population and rule, the history of colonialism has led to writers whose work reflects a political consciousness of unequal power and express grievances against the European colonizers. Even after gaining political autonomy, native populations continue to react to the impact of other cultures through their adoption of Christianity and of economic capitalist systems that are alien to their early communal nonindustrial base. Fiji, for example, has recently seen a native Fijian repression of the immigrant East Indian population.

Representative of the postcolonial writer, Albert Wendt, the best-known Samoan author, is the son of a German father and a native mother. In his fiction, he invents a literary pidgin, a local dialect of English, to convey the islanders' colonized world of hybrid native and Western cultures. As seen in the works of Papuan New Guinean writers such as Kama Kerpi, these islanders must struggle with the subversion of their original societies by intrusive cultures whose values of individual rights and private property run counter to traditional native ideals. These writers from Oceania, usually educated in Western or Western-style universities, portray the ambiguities, conflicts, and complexities of communities in which rapid economic and social transformation in many cases threaten the viability and stability of traditional ways of life.

Phyllis Fahrie Edelson
Shirley Geok-lin Lim

AUSTRALIA

KATHARINE SUSANNAH PRICHARD

Katharine Prichard (1883–1969) was committed to writing and to social reform. From her early work as a governess, she moved to journalism and then to fiction, winning fame as a novelist but also writing plays, essays, and poems. "The Cooboo," her best known story, is from the collection Kiss on the Lips *(1932). She was born in Fiji, but spent most of her childhood in Tasmania and Victoria. After attending South Melbourne College, she lived for a time in Melbourne, then moved to Perth, western Australia, after her marriage to Hugh Throssell. She was a founding member of the Communist Party of Australia. She often explores controversial issues—sexual, political, and racial. Her writing constitutes a substantial chronicle of Australian life.*

The Cooboo

They had been mustering all day on the wide plains of Murndoo station. Over the red earth, black with ironstone pebbles, through mulga[1] and curari bush, across the ridges which make a blue wall along the horizon. The rosy, garish light of sunset was on plains, hills, moving cattle, men and horses. 1

Through red dust the bullocks mooched, restless and scary still, a wild mob from the hills: John Gray, in the rear with Arra, the boy who was his shadow: Wongana, on the right with his gin, Rose: Frank, the half-caste, on the left with Minni. 2

A steer breaking from the mob before Rose, she wheeled and went after him. Faint and wailing, a cry followed her, as though her horse had stepped on and crushed some small creature. But the steer was getting away. Arra 3

---

1. Mulga: *A variety of acacia found on the edges of deserts.*

went after him, stretched along his horse's neck, rounded the beast and rode him back to the mob, sulky and blethering. The mob swayed. It had broken three times that day.

John Gray called: "You damn fool, Rosey. Finish!"   4

The gin, on her slight, rough-haired horse, pulled up scowling.   5

"Tell Meetchie, Thirty Mile, tomorrow," John Gray said. "Miah, new   6
moon."

Rose slewed her horse away from the mob of men and cattle. That   7
wailing, thin and hard as hair-string, moved with her.

"Minni!"   8

John Gray jerked his head towards Rose. Minni's bare heels struck her   9
horse's belly. With a turn of the wrist she swung her horse off from the
mob, turned, leaned forward, rising in her stirrups, and came up with
Rose. But the glitter and tumult of Rose's eyes, Minni looked away from
them.

Thin, dark figures on their wiry station-bred horses, the gins[1] rode into   10
the haze of sunset towards the hills. The dull, dirty blue of the trousers
wrapped round their legs was torn; their short, fairish hair tousled by the
wind.

At a little distance, when men and cattle were a moving cloud of red   11
dust, Rose's anger gushed after them.

"Koo!"   12

Fierce as the cry of a hawk flew her last note of derision and defiance.   13

A far-away rattle of the men's laughter drifted back across country.   14

Alone the gins would have been afraid, as darkness coming up behind   15
was hovering near them, secreting itself among the low, writhen trees and
bushes: afraid of the evil spirits who wander over the plains and stony
ridges when the light of day is withdrawn. But together they were not so
afraid. Twenty miles away over there, below that dent in the hills where
Nyedee Creek made a sandy bed for itself among white-bodied gums, was
Murndoo homestead and the uloo of their people.

There was no track; and in the first darkness, thick as wool after the   16
glow of sunset faded, only their instinct would keep them moving in the
direction of the homestead and their own low, round huts of bagging,
rusty tin and dead boughs.

Both were Wongana's women: Rose, tall, gaunt and masterful; Minni,   17
younger, fat and jolly. Rose had been a good stockman in her day: one of
the best. Minni did not ride or track nearly as well as Rose.

And yet, as they rode along, Minni pattered complacently of how well   18
she had worked that day: of how she had flashed, this way and that,
heading-off breakaways, dashing after them, turning them back to the mob
so smartly that John had said: "Good man, Minni!" There was the white

---

1. Gins: *Aboriginal girls or women.*

bullock—he had rushed near the yards. Had Rose seen the chestnut mare stumble in a crab-hole and send Arra flying? Minni had chased the white bullock, chased him for a couple of miles, and brought him back to the yards. No doubt there would be nammery for her and a new gina-gina when the men came in from the muster.

She pulled a pipe from her belt, shook the ashes out, and with reins looped over one arm stuffed the bowl with tobacco from a tin tied to her belt. Stooping down, she struck a match on her stirrup-iron, guarded the flame to the pipe between her short, white teeth, and smoked contentedly. 19

The scowl of Rose's face deepened, darkened. That thin, fretted wailing came from her breast. 20

She unslung from her neck the rag rope by which the baby had been held against her body, and gave him a sagging breast to suck. Holding him with one arm, she rode slowly, her horse picking his way over the rough, stony earth. 21

It had been a hard day. The gins were mustering with the men at sunrise. Camped at Nyedee Well the night before, in order to get a good start, they had been riding through the timbered ridges all the morning, rounding up wild cows, calves and young bullocks, and driving them down to the yards at Nyedee, where John Gray cut out the fats, left old Jimmy and a couple of boys to brand calves, turn the cows and calves back to the ridge again while he took on the mob for trucking at Meekatharra. The bullocks were as wild as birds: needed watching all day. And all the time that small, whimpering bundle against her breast had hampered Rose's movements. 22

There was nothing the gins liked better than a muster, riding after cattle. They were quicker in their movements, more alert than the men, sharper at picking up tracks, but they did not go mustering very often nowadays. 23

Since John Gray had married, and there was a woman on Murndoo, she found plenty of washing, scrubbing and sweeping for the gins to do: would not spare them often to go after cattle. But John was short-handed. He had said he must have Rose and Minni to muster Nyedee. And all day her baby's crying had irritated Rose. The cooboo had wailed and wailed as she rode with him tied to her body. 24

The cooboo was responsible for the wrong things she had done all day. Stupid things. Rose was furious. The men had yelled at her. Wongana, her man, blackguarding her before everybody, had called her "a hen who did not know where she laid her eggs". And John Gray, with his "You damn fool, Rosey. Finish!" had sent her home like a naughty child. 25

Now there was Minni jabbering of the tobacco she would get and the new gina-gina. How pleased Wongana would be with her! And the cooboo, wailing, wailing. He wailed as he chewed Rose's empty breast, squirming against her: wailed and gnawed. 26

She cried out with hurt and impatience. Rage, irritated to madness, rushed like waters coming down the dry creek-beds after heavy rain. Rose 27 wrenched the cooboo from her breast and flung him from her to the ground. There was a crack as of twigs breaking.

Minni glanced aside. "Wiah!" she gasped, with widening eyes. But Rose 28
rode on, gazing ahead over the rosy, garish plains and wall of the hills,
darkening from blue to purple and indigo.

When the women came into the station kitchen, earth, hills and trees 29
were dark: the sky heavy with stars. Minni gave John's wife his message:
that he would be home with the new moon, in about a fortnight.

Meetchie, as the blacks called Mrs John Gray, could not make out why 30
the gins were so stiff and quiet: why Rose stalked, scowling and sulky-
fellow, sombre eyes just meeting hers, and moving away again. Meetchie
wanted to ask about the muster: what sort of condition the bullocks had
been in; how many were on the road; if many calves had been branded at
Nyedee. But she knew the women too well to ask questions when they
looked like that.

Only when she had given them bread and a tin of jam, cut off hunks of 31
corned beef for them, filled their billies with strong black tea, put sugar in
their empty tins, and the gins were going off to the uloo, she realised that
Rose was not carrying her baby as usual.

"Why, Rose," she exclaimed, "where's the cooboo?" 32

Rose stalked off into the night. Minni glanced back with scared eyes and 33
followed Rose.

In the dawn, when a cry, remote and anguished flew through the clear 34
air, Meetchie wondered who was dead in the camp by the creek. She
remembered how Rose had looked the night before, when she asked about
the cooboo.

Now, she knew the cooboo had died; Rose was wailing for him in the 35
dawn, cutting herself with stones until her body bled, and screaming in the
fury of her grief.

STUDY QUESTIONS

1. How do Rose and Minni feel about mustering?
2. Why was Rose so angry when she left work? What was upsetting her?
3. How was the cooboo responsible, in Rose's view, for what happened
   at the muster?
4. What did she do to the cooboo and how did she feel about it afterward?
5. In what sense can we say that Rose was caught between two sets of
   expectations: that she perform well in a male role and that she perform
   as would be traditionally expected of a female? Is there any connection
   between Rose's predicament and that of women in other cultures?
6. Can the cooboo's murder be seen as the result of Rose's conflict and
   desperation? What relationship do you see, if any, between Rose's act
   of murder and the current issue of child abuse?

XAVIER HERBERT

Born in northwest Australia to unmarried, somewhat unconventional parents,
Herbert (1901–1984) grew up in close contact with Aborigines. Educated to be
a pharmacist, he abandoned that field, worked as a pearl diver, drover, railway
worker, and prison guard before he wrote Capricornia. *This powerful novel,*
his second, won the Sesquicentennial Prize. Set in the northern region of
Australia, it recounts a tale of mistreatment of both Aborigines and the land.
Charged with Herbert's impassioned commitment to both, it makes up in energy
and vision for some flaws in design. Herbert's Poor Fellow My Country
(1975), a bitter but compelling poetic work, contains many of the same themes
treated in Capricornia. *Both works have become modern Australian classics.*

   In this excerpt, Oscar Shillingsworth, cattle owner of the Red Ochre
Station in the Northern Territory, early 1900's, tries unsuccessfully to rid
himself of responsibility for his illegitimate nephew, a half-caste child, son of
his brother Mark (White) and an Aboriginal woman.

Clothes Make a Man

Excerpt from *Capricornia*

Oscar held dominion over six hundred square miles of country, which   1
extended east and west from the railway to the summit of the Lonely
Ranges, and north and south from the horizons, it might be said, since
there was nothing to show where the boundaries lay in those directions.

Jasmine had said that he worshipped property. It was true. But he did   2
not value Red Ochre simply as a grazing-lease. At times it was to him six
hundred square miles where grazing grew and brolgas[1] danced in the
painted sunset and emus[2] ran to the silver dawn—square miles of jungle
where cool deep billabongs[3] made watering for stock and nests for shouting nuttagul geese—of grassy valleys and stony hills, useless for grazing,
but good to think about as haunts of great goannas[4] and rock-pythons—of
swamps where cattle bogged and died, but wild hog and buffalo wallowed
in happiness—of virgin forests where poison weed lay in wait for stock,
but where possums and kangaroos and multitudes of gorgeous birds dwelt
as from time immemorial. At times he loved Red Ochre.

---

1. Brolga: *A kind of crane native to Australia and New Guinea.*
2. Emu: *A large, flightless bird native to Australia.*
3. Billabong: *A creek, pool, or lagoon.*
4. Goanna: *Australian monitor lizard.*

At times he loved it best in Wet Season—when the creeks were running 3
and the swamps were full—when the multicoloured schisty rocks split
golden waterfalls—when the scarlet plains were under water, green with
wild rice, swarming with Siberian snipe—when the billabongs were brimming and the water-lilies blooming and the nuttaguls shouting loudest—
when bull-grass towered ten feet high, clothing hills and choking gullies—
when every tree was flowering and most were draped with crimson
mistletoe and droning with humming-birds and native bees—when cattle
wandered a land of plenty, fat and sleek, till the buffalo-flies and marsh-
flies came and drove them mad, so that they ran and ran to leanness, often
to their death—when mosquitoes and a hundred other breeds of madden-
ing insects were there to test a man's endurance—when from hour to hour
luke-warm showers drenched the steaming earth, till one was sodden to
the bone and mildewed to the marrow and moved to pray, as Oscar always
was when he had had enough of it, for that which formerly he had cursed—
the Dry! the good old Dry—when the grasses yellowed, browned, dried to
tinder, burst into spontaneous flame—when harsh winds rioted with choking dust and the billabongs became mere muddy holes where cattle pawed
for water—when gaunt drought loafed about a desert and exhausted cattle
staggered searching dust for food and drink, till they fell down and died
and became neat piles of bones for the wind to whistle through and the
gaunt-ribbed dingo[1] to mourn—then one prayed for the Wet again, or if
one's heart was small, packed up and left this Capricornia that fools down
South called the Land of Opportunity, and went back and said that nothing
was done by halves up there except the works of puny man.

Red Ochre was so named because an abundance of red ochre was to be 4
found in the locality. Not far from the homestead was a cleft hillock of
which the face was composed entirely of red ochre that was scored by the
implements of men of the Mullanmullak Tribe who had gathered the pig-
ment there for ages. From the hillock a score of red paths diverged as black
ones do from a colliery, one of them leading to the homestead itself, trodden, so it was said, by Tobias Batty, founder of the Station, who went mad
and took to painting his body after the fashion of the blacks.

Red Ochre was founded twenty years or more before Oscar settled 5
there. His predecessor, who succeeded the mad Batty, was a man named
Wellington Boots, formerly a Cockney grocer, who had a young wife whom
he worked like a horse and five young children whom he kept perpetually
in a state of virtual imprisonment. It was said that he used to weigh out the
rations of his native riders in niggardly quantities on loaded scales. He was
killed by a bull on the plain to the south and eaten by ants and crows and
kites till buried in a sack by his wife.

The homestead stood in these days just as Batty had built it. It was of 6

---

1. Dingo: *A type of wild dog native to Australia.*

corrugated iron on an angle-iron frame. In the dwelling the materials even of the doors were such as could not be destroyed by termites. The windows had been sheet-iron shutters till Oscar glazed them. But in spite of the materials, the house was airy and cool; for the walls stopped short of meeting the sprawling roof by a foot or two, leaving a wide well-ventilated space between the iron itself and the ceiling of paper-bark, the entry of possums and snakes and other pests being prevented by wire netting. The walls were lined with paper-bark, pipe-clayed and panelled with polished bloodwood. The floor was of ant-bed, the stuff of the termites' or white-ants' nests, which when crushed and wetted and beaten hard makes serviceable cement. Mrs. Boots was responsible for most of the interior fittings. Oscar had improved on them. Carpets and marsupial skins lay about the floors; bright pictures and hunting trophies such as tusks of boars and horns of buffaloes adorned the walls. Broad verandas surrounded the house, each screened with iron lattice covered with potato-creeper, and decorated with palms and ferns and furnished with punkahs[1] and rustic furniture made by Oscar.

The homestead was about twenty miles from the railway. It stood on the brow of a hill about which the Caroline River, hidden from view by a belt of scrub and giant trees, flowed in a semi-circle. It was the northern side of the house that faced the river, a side that was raised on a high stone foundation because of the rapid slope. The veranda on that side was the part of the house most used in dry weather. On the eastern veranda were the snowy mosquito-netted beds of the family, which now unhappily numbered only two. Peter Differ and his halfcaste daughter Constance lived in a little house of their own at the rear. Differ worked on the run as foreman. Constance, who was aged about eleven, worked in the house as a sort of maid. The eastern veranda was sheltered by two great mangoes, part of a grove that led down to the river. On the opposite side were poinciana trees and cassias and frangi-panis and many other tropical growths that made the place very brilliant and fragrant in Wet Season. 7

One afternoon a few days after that of the incidents at the Siding, Oscar was sitting on the front veranda with his daughter Marigold, watching an approaching storm, when the child pointed to the scrub by the river and said, "Look, Daddy—dere's a niggah wit sumpin on his back." 8

Oscar looked and saw a blackfellow in a red naga toiling up the flood-bank with a strangely clad halfcaste child on his back. The man came to the veranda steps, panting and sweating profusely, and set his burden down. "What name you want?" asked Oscar. For answer the blackfellow stooped and took from the waist-band of the spotted blue breeches of his burden 9

---

1. Punkah: *A portable fan.*

what proved to be a crumpled letter. He gave it to Oscar, who opened it and read:

DEAR OSCAR:

Herewith my nigger Muttonhead. I sent him acrost you with little ½ carst boy belong to your brother Mark his names No Name and belongs to Jock Driver of the Melisande Ma McLash reckons you knows all about it he got lef here in a truck we found him and trid keep for Jock nex train but carnt do it because hees too much damn trouble here Oscar hees gone bush 3 times allready and wats kwonskwence we friten for sponsibility to lose him plese you keep him there for Jock I will tell him if I heres from him hees good kid No Name and got good sense for yeler feler[1] but too damn cunin like a dingo be a long way corse if hees look after I reckon heel be O.K. corse you see we gotter go out to work and Ma McLash wont have no truck with him and no good of putin him with nigers seen hees your nefew and seen as how hees one for goan bush like he does. Plese you give my niger Muttonhead a feed and a stick of tobaco or he wont do nuthen more hees cheeky swine thet Muttonhead belt him if he givs you trouble excuse pensl and hast hoppen to find you as it leves me at present. I remain

Your obediant servent
JOE BALLEST
Ganger 80–Mile

Oscar raised a flushed face and looked at Nawnim, who was standing with hands clasped behind him and dirty yellow-brown face elevated and black eyes staring intently at Marigold. In a moment Nawnim became aware of Oscar's gaze and lowered his face slightly and regarded him slant-wise, assuming an expression almost baleful that reminded Oscar of Ballest's reference to a dingo.   10

Then a stream of white lightning poured from the heavens. The dead air stirred. Nawnim started, looked at Muttonhead. Thunder crashed, and monster echoes pealed through valleys and caverns of the mountainous clouds. Nawnim thrust his head into Muttonhead's belly. Again the white lightning poured; the thunder crashed; a blast of cool wind struck the trees and whisked a few leaves on to the veranda. Then rain came rushing across the river—humming drumming rain—and up the hill and over the house—hissing roaring rain.   11

"Round the back," yelled Oscar, pointing. Muttonhead took Nawnim's hand and ran.   12

Oscar and Marigold went into the house and through and out to the back veranda, from which through the teeming rain they saw Muttonhead and Nawnim crouched under the eaves by the wall of the detached kitchen.   13

---

1. Yeler feler: *Of mixed Aboriginal and white parentage.*

In spite of what Ballest had said about Muttonhead, he was evidently too well aware of his humbleness to enter a whiteman's shelter uninvited. Oscar had meant that they should go to the back veranda. Seeing that they were fairly well sheltered where they were, he let them stay.

Oscar bent to Marigold when he heard her reedy voice. 14

"Is dat a lil boy, Daddy?" she cried in his ear. 15

He nodded and smiled weakly, and, because the wind had changed and 16 was blowing the rain in on them, he led her inside to the dining-room, where he sat and held her between his knees.

"Dat not a lil niggah boy, Daddy?" she asked. 17

"No." 18

"What kind lil boy is he den, Daddy?" 19

"Little halfcaste." 20

"Like Conny Differ?" 21

He nodded, began to roll a cigarette. 22

"Is dat Mister Differ's lil boy, Daddy?" 23

Unpleasant subject. He frowned and said, "Now don't start asking silly 24 questions."

She fell silent, and gazing through the back door at the rain, turned over 25 in her mind a mass of thoughts about this boy, who, since he did not look like one of those prohibited Dirty Little Niggahs, might make a playmate. She was allowed to play with Constance, which was very pleasant, although Constance was more than twice her age and evidently not as eager to play as she herself. Carried away by her thoughts she asked, "Daddy— who dat lil boy's farver?"

The question came as a shock, because it interrupted thoughts of Mark. 26 He looked at her almost suspiciously, then said, "Go and play with your toys and don't worry me."

He went outside and lounged about, occupying himself alternately with 27 looking for leaks in the roof and studying his crouching nephew, till the rain stopped; then he went into the yard. After looking at Nawnim for a while as best he could—Nawnim slunk behind Muttonhead at his approach—he said to the blackfellow, "You takim piccanin back longa you boss."

"Wha' name?" asked Muttonhead, shaking Nawnim from a leg. 28

"Takim back longa Mister Ballest. Me no wantim. Him no-more belong 29 me."

Muttonhead gaped for a moment, then said, "Carn do it." 30

Oscar frowned and snapped, "Don't be cheeky or I'll crack you." 31

Muttonhead cringed and said, "Mist Ballest him say, 'Takim dat one pic 32 longa Boss Chilnsik—him belong him brudder.' "

"I don't give a damn what he said. Takim back. Here's some baccy— 33 now then—what say?"

"Tahng you very mush, Boss," said Muttonhead, placing a stick of 34 tobacco behind each ear. Two sticks of tobacco valued at tuppence each were perhaps small reward for a forty-mile walk with a child on his back, but no more than he expected. But he continued to protest, saying, "Carn do it, Boss. Me no-more go back longa railer line lo—ng time. Me go foot-walk longa Lonely River country for lookim up Ol' People." He jerked his thick lips in the opposite direction to that in which he had come.

"Then take the brat with you," snapped Oscar, and walked off. 35

Muttonhead turned out to be quite as bad as Ballest said. Oscar found 36 that out some hours after dismissing him. He was superintending a job in the smithy when he heard a commotion in the kitchen and went to investigate and found Nawnim being belaboured by the lubra[1] cook. The lubra turned an angry face when he entered the kitchen. Nawnim's howls died in his gaping mouth.

"What's the matter?" demanded Oscar. 37

"Him come sinikin longa brett," cried the lubra, pointing to bread-tins 38 that stood on the table ready for the oven. Nawnim tried to get behind her. She seized him, flung him back into exposure. He yelled.

"Shut up!" shouted Oscar. 39

There was dough on Nawnim's face and hands, and on a leg of the 40 table. Oscar stepped up and grabbed one of his skinny arms and demanded, "What name you no-more go away all-same me talk?" Nawnim blubbered and shrank away. "Which way Muttonhead?" demanded Oscar of the cook.

"Him go longa Lonely River, Boss." 41

"Blast him!" cried Oscar. "Left me with the brat after all!" He looked at 42 his captive, stared at him sourly for a while, then sighed and said, "Well, I don't know what I'm going to do with you, poor hungry little devil. God help you! Oh, give him some tucker, Princess, and don't hurt him. Get someone to wash him—he stinks."

Nawnim spent his first night at Red Ochre in the quarters of the native 43 servants. It was not the servants' choice, nor a particularly good one of their master's, since the place was not so far away from the house as to leave the occupants unaware of what was going on there when the going-on was as loud as Nawnim's. He wailed all night, set the dogs barking in the camp on the river and the dingoes howling in the bush and the pigs squealing in the sty and the horses snorting in the yards. The servants could pinch and punch and smother him into periods of silence but could not still the external racket he had raised, which seemed to be worse when he was silent and to his ears quite devilish, so that before long he would be moved to start again. The red day dawned on a red-eyed household and on a halfcaste brat who was covered with red wales and regarded with general malignity.

Oscar gave him into the care of Constance Differ. All went well through- 44

---

1. Lubra: *An Aboriginal female.*

out the day, because he slept. When he woke at sundown he set up a worse wailing than ever, and tried to escape, so that Constance had to lock him in. He would neither sit nor lie, but stood in a corner with hands clasped behind, watching Constance and venting his incessant tearless grief. Constance was gentle and patient as no one he had ever known but Anna. But she looked rather too much like Yeller Jewty. Differ tried his hand with him, first with food, then with dancing and singing and playing tricks, finally with a strap. At last Oscar rushed in and spanked by hand, and because the matter had become much worse, took Nawnim by the scruff of the neck and threw him at a blackfellow for removal to the camp. There was some peace in the homestead that night, but none on the river.

Three days passed, during which the people of Red Ochre adapted themselves to broken sleep and kept away from the native camp. Oscar sent a message to the Siding to learn whether Jock had inquired after his uncoveted property, and learnt that he had not. He settled down to wait for word, hoping that Jock might not be drinking at Copper Creek and that he might not go on his way forgetting his responsibilities. 45

On the afternoon of the fourth day Oscar was wakened from his siesta on the front veranda by sound of cat-like moaning in the yard below, and, rising to investigate, saw little Nawnim standing in the reddish shadow of a poinciana near the steps. Nawnim stopped moaning for about five seconds when Oscar's head appeared, then resumed. Oscar stared in astonishment. It was obvious from the way in which the child was studying him that the moaning did not interfere with his ability to take an interest in things about him. In fact he was not so much weeping as expressing a vague sense of misery he had felt ever since parting with Fat Anna. He stood in his usual attitude of hands behind back and eyes glancing sideways. When Oscar came to the head of the steps the moaning rose a note higher, but the moaner did not move. Oscar saw Marigold peeping from the hall and told her to go inside, then went down the steps, muttering. Nawnim did not move till Oscar reached the ground, when he retired slowly, walking sideways, watching with one eye and gouging the other with a grubby fist. 46

"Come here," said Oscar. 47

The moan rose by another note. Nawnim continued to retire. Oscar hurried. Nawnim yelled and ran. Oscar stopped. So did Nawnim, and dropped his voice to the moan. 48

"Blast you!" cried Oscar. "Shut up!" 49

Steady moan. 50

"Shut up!" roared Oscar, and moved. Nawnim moved. Oscar snatched up a stick and rushed. Nawnim fled howling, to fall shrieking when Oscar caught him a sound whack on the seat of the spotted blue pants. Oscar pounced on him shouting, "Shut up—shut up—shut up!" 51

Gritting his teeth with rage, Oscar picked him up and carried him down to the camp, prepared to ease his feelings on those he considered he could 52 flog without stooping to cowardice, the delinquent natives. But they were not there. Nawnim had worn their patience to rags. They had taken their belongings and gone bush. He had been driven to the homestead by hunger and loneliness.

As Oscar's precepts would not allow him to copy the wisdom of the 53 natives, he had to carry Nawnim back to the house. He dumped him under the scarlet tree where he had found him, and left him bawling, to go find Constance. Constance was away on the run with her father. Oscar came back fuming, to find to his surprise that Nawnim was as quiet as a mouse, standing in his usual attitude, staring at Marigold. When he saw Oscar he prepared for flight. Oscar was too wise to go near him. He crept back to his chair.

"Can I play with the lil boy, Daddy?" asked Marigold.   54
"No—stay where you are."   55
"But I wanna play."   56
"Stay where you are."   57
"But Daddy—" she said, coming towards him.   58
The instant she passed out of Nawnim's sight was announced by a   59
long-drawn moan. Realising at once what was the cause of the good behavior, Oscar said quickly, "Go back to the edge and stay there."
"But can't I play?"   60
"No—go back—for heaven's sake, go back!"   61
The moaning stopped. But Marigold did not stop entreating. "Why can't   62
I play wid him, Daddy?" she begged. "He's not a lil niggah."
"He is. Now be quiet. Throw him that doll—anything—everything if   63
you like—but stay where he can see you. Let me have a moment's peace, for heaven's sake. There's been no peace in the place since that brat came near it."

There was peace that night and thenceforth. Nawnim went to sleep on   64
a lounge on the back veranda within sound of the last sleepy words of Marigold. Next day he spent under the poinciana tree, playing with a doll and watching Marigold, seeing her not merely as a desirable playmate, as she saw him, but, since she was so different from any creature he had seen and clad in garments that amazed him, rather as a human monstrosity like Anna's Japs an' Chows.[1]

After a while he lost his distrust of Constance and could be placed in 65
Differ's house. He slept there in the cot that had been bought for his cousin Roger. Constance taught him to use a knife and fork and spoon, discouraged him from the practice of voiding urine indiscriminately, and made him a laughable suit of clothes.

But Oscar's troubles were far from done. The child was still his nephew. 66

---

1. Chows: *Derogatory term for Chinese people, especially immigrants or descendants of immigrants.*

He believed that in his heart though he would not admit it. The sight of him was a constant reminder of terrible disgrace. And Marigold made matters worse by pestering him for permission to play with the child, taking advantage of a situation he had created by frequent sentimental talks about Dear Mumma and the loneliness to which that faithless one had left them both, backing up her petitions with such heart-rending statements as, "Oh dear, I am such a lonely lil girl, Daddy—no mumma an' no nobody even to play wiv— Oh, oh, I am so lonely lonely!"

When Oscar and Marigold next went to meet the mail-train, Nawnim   67
went with them, not for a treat as he and she supposed, but for the purpose of being disposed of should a chance occur. Oscar had lately learnt that Jock had left Copper Creek for home, not by the usual route that would take him past the Melisande telegraph-station, but by one that lay far to westward, being forced to go out of his way because the Melisande River was in flood. And according to the report the fellow had gone on his way blind drunk. Oscar's hope was that there might be someone on the train going out Jock's way to whom he could give Nawnim. It turned out to be a vain one.

At the Siding he left Nawnim in the buckboard with a black boy and well   68
out of sight of the house, and studiously avoided any form of conversation with the people there that might lead to questions concerning him. He felt sure that they were laughing at him. When Mrs. McLash told him that some unknown person had sent her a box of unwanted kittens up from town last train he frowned and left her.

It happened that the people at the Siding had no need to ask questions   69
about Nawnim. Differ had been in a couple of times for grog since the child's arrival at Red Ochre and had talked, and Frank McLash had been out there for beef when the rioting was at its height. As a matter of fact, the story of Nawnim's doings since his coming into the district was known to nearly everyone on the one hundred and fifty-seven miles of railway.

STUDY QUESTIONS

1. What is the racial hierarchy in Capricornia? How many different races and racial mixes are mentioned? Which is the group at the top of the social ladder? Where does Nawnim fit in?
2. Although Oscar's reluctant adoption of Nawnim is often treated humorously, the author's anger at racial bigotry comes through. What are some of the instances of prejudice that you find, and how does the author's indignation show?
3. Nawnim is the aboriginal name for a dog that the tribe does not want but does not want to kill. How does this name fit the child?
4. Analyze Oscar Shillingsworth's attitudes toward Red Ochre Station. Are his attitudes consistent?

5. Paying close attention to the diction used throughout the excerpt, discuss Herbert's underlying theme of white settlement of natural or native wilderness. What values are attacked? What values are upheld?
6. Attitudes toward Nawnim change in the course of this excerpt. What kinds of relationships seem to be developing between Marigold, Oscar's daughter, and Nawnim? Between Oscar and Nawnim? What do these relationships suggest about the potential for closeness between races? What is the connection between the title and the idea of interracial acceptance?

◎ JUDITH WRIGHT

"Bora Ring," an early poem by Judith Wright (b. 1915), is indicative of her interest in the fate of the Australian Aboriginal community. She maintains this interest throughout her writing, as she does her concern for the Australian environment. Wright spent her childhood in the countryside of New South Wales and has lived in the forest areas there and in Queensland. She started publishing poetry in magazines at age ten. In 1946 she published her first collection, The Moving Image, *from which "Bora Ring" is taken. In addition to her poems, many of which are about love, she has written literary criticism, children's books, short stories, plays, and a memoir,* The Generations of Men *(1959), which describes her pioneer family. She is one of Australia's most significant women poets.*

Bora Ring[1]

The song is gone; the dance
is secret with the dancers in the earth,
the ritual useless, and the tribal story
lost in an alien tale.

Only the grass stands up
to mark the dancing-ring: the apple-gums[2]   5

---

1. Bora Ring: *Grounds where secret initiation rites for male Aboriginals are held.*
2. Apple gums: *A kind of gum tree (Australian Eucalyptus).*

posture and mime a past corroboree,[1]
murmur a broken chant.

The hunter is gone: the spear
is splintered underground; the painted bodies 10
a dream the world breathed sleeping and forgot.
The nomad feet are still.

Only the rider's heart
halts at a sightless shadow, an unsaid word
that fastens in the blood the ancient curse, 15
the fear as old as Cain.

STUDY QUESTIONS

1. The poem laments the destruction of the Aboriginal community in Australia. What are some aspects of the communal/cultural life that are mentioned as being lost?
2. How much interest did the world take in this community when it was alive? What lines support your answer, and how?
3. What is the connection between nature and some of the now lost rituals mentioned in the poem (see stanza two).
4. The last stanza shifts the focus from the vanished past world to the present. Who is the rider, what does he or she represent, and what is his or her attitude toward the loss?
5. How does the biblical story of Cain and Abel apply to the last three lines of the poem?

BRUCE DAWE

Bruce Dawe (b. 1930) is from Geelong, Victoria. He worked on farms, in the mills, in gardening, and in the postal service before he joined the Royal Australian Air Force. After completing his degree, he became a teacher in the Darling Downs Institute of Advanced Education in Toowoomba, Queensland.

---

1. Corroboree: *Aboriginal dance ceremony with song and music, sometimes a part of sacred ritual, sometimes secular.*

Migrants

In the fourth week the sea dropped clear away
And they were there . . .
                         At first the people's slurred
Indifference surprised them (was there a word
For love in this wry tongue, or did they say   5
All things with similar lack of emphasis?)
But still the skies stayed friendly, even if
They found themselves being shouted at like deaf
-Mutes whom one naturally hates the more for this.
But that, too, passed. Their children now less often   10
Came red-eyed home from school.
                               Dour neighbours bent
Slowly like hazel twigs towards that sound,
Guttural, labial, but beginning to soften,
In which both earth and water were being blent   15
As it pulsed up in rich wells from underground.

STUDY QUESTIONS

1. Australia has experienced heavy immigration in recent years. Dawe traces a profile of initial experiences that immigrants have in their new country. What does he say is the immigrants' reaction to the Australian way of speaking? Why were the migrants shouted at?
2. Why does the line "still the skies stayed friendly" tell us about Australian intentions toward the newcomers?
3. What does the double-edged line "Their children now less often / Came red-eyed home from school" say about the migrant children's initial and later experience at school?
4. Why does Dawe specifically mention "hazel twigs"? Why not "oak twigs"? Explain the extended simile in the lines surrounding "hazel twigs." What is the connection?
5. The final lines describe the blending of earth and water. What does this image have to do with the migrants' migration and their new country?

LES A. MURRAY

*Les Murray (b. 1938) spent his childhood on a dairy farm at Bunyan on the
north coast of New South Wales, a farming and forest region. Murray
envisions Australia as a nation in which rural and family life are important
and emphasizes the country's historical roots. A strong narrative line, humor,
and refreshing originality of language are characteristic of his work. The
tension between city life and country life, which he has experienced since his
education at the University of Sydney and subsequent residence in cities, is
one of his prominent themes. "The Dream of Wearing Shorts Forever" appears
in Murray's* Selected Poems *(1986).*

The Dream of Wearing Shorts Forever

To go home and wear shorts forever
in the enormous paddocks, in that warm climate,
adding a sweater when winter soaks the grass,

to camp out along the river bends
for good, wearing shorts, with a pocketknife,   5
a fishing line and matches,

or there where the hills are all down, below the plain,
to sit around in shorts at evening
on the plank verandah—

If the cardinal points of costume   10
are Robes, Tato, Rig and Scunge,[1]
where are shorts in this compass?

They are never Robes
as other bareleg outfits have been:
the toga, the kilt, the lava-lava,   15
the Mahatma's cotton dhoti;

---

1. Scunge: *Shorts worn by surfers.*

archbishops and field marshals
at their ceremonies never wear shorts.
The very word
means underpants in North America.   20

Shorts can be Tat,
Land-Rovering, bush-environmental tat,
socio-political ripped-and-metal-stapled tat,
solidarity-with-the-Third World tat tvam asi,

likewise track-and-field shorts worn to parties   25
and the further humid, modelling negligée
of the Kingdom of Flaunt,
that unchallenged aristocracy.

More plainly climatic, shorts
are farmers' rig, leathery with salt and bonemeal,   30
are sailors' and branch bankers' rig,
the crisp golfing style
of our youngest male National Costume.

Most loosely, they are Scunge,
ancient Bengal bloomers or moth-eaten hot pants   35
worn with a former shirt,
feet, beach sand, hair
and a paucity of signals.

Scunge, which is real negligée,
housework in a swimsuit, pyjamas worn all day,   40
is holiday, is freedom from ambition.
Scunge makes you invisible
to the world and yourself.

The entropy of costume,
scunge can get you conquered by more vigorous cultures   45
and help you to notice it less.

To be or to become
is a serious question posed by a work-shorts counter
with its pressed stacks, bulk khaki and blue,
reading Yakka or King Gee, crisp with steely warehouse odour.   50

Satisfied ambition, defeat, true unconcern,
the wish and the knack for self-forgetfulness
all fall within the scunge ambit

wearing board shorts or similar;
it is a kind of weightlessness.   55

Unlike public nakedness, which in Westerners
is deeply circumstantial, relaxed as exam time,
artless and equal as the corsetry of a hussar regiment,
shorts and their plain like
are an angelic nudity,   60
spirituality with pockets!
A double updraft as you drop from branch to pool!

Ideal for getting served last
in shops of the temperate zone
they are also ideal for going home, into space,   65
into time, to farm the mind's Sabine acres
for product or subsistence.

—Now that everyone who yearned to wear long pants
has essentially achieved them,
long pants, which have themselves been underwear   70
repeatedly, and underground more than once,
it is time perhaps to cherish the culture of shorts,

to moderate grim vigour
with the knobble of bare knees,
to cool bareknuckle feet in inland water,   75
slapping flies with a book on solar wind
or a patient bare hand, beneath the cadjiput trees,

to be walking meditatively
among green timber, through the grassy forest
towards a calm sea   80
and looking across to more of that great island
and the further tropics.

STUDY QUESTIONS

1. From a rhetorical point of view, this poem may be seen as an attempt
   at definition. Discuss the various definitions of wearing shorts. How
   many different meanings does Murray assign to them?
2. How does the "angelic nudity" (line 60) involved in wearing shorts
   differ from just plain nudity as it is viewed in Western culture?
3. What is the connection between the final stanza and the dream to
   which the title of the poem directs us?

COLIN JOHNSON

Colin Johnson (b. 1938) recently changed his name to Mudrooroo Nyoongah. He was born in Narogin, western Australia, and is part Aboriginal of the Bibbulmun people. Part of his childhood was spent in a Catholic orphanage. He worked in the Victorian public service, and in 1959 he wrote a play called The Delinks, *which won a contest sponsored by the journal* Westerly. *In 1965 he wrote his first novel, the first by an Aboriginal to be published in Australia:* Wild Cat Falling. *Then he left Australia to travel and was a Buddhist monk for seven years. Among his works are* Long Live Sandawarra *(1979) and* Dr. Wooreddy's Prescription for Enduring the Ending of the World *(1983). Johnson's poetry was published in* The Song Circle of Jacky and Selected Poems *(1986).*

In his novel, Colin Johnson tells the story of the British invasion of the Aboriginal homeland of Australia. Such stories are usually told by historians from the point of view of the invaders. Johnson, however, offers us the experience of invasion and finally genocide through the eyes of the native Aborigines. Based on historical fact, such as the appointment of George Augustus Robinson (Mr. Robinson) as Protector of the Aborigines, Johnson's novel recreates for us the destruction of a culture. In the text excerpt, Wooreddy meditates on what has happened to his people since the coming of the "num" or white man and attributes the devastation to the evil spirit, "Ria Warrawah," which he identifies with the ocean.

Dr. Wooreddy's Prescription for Enduring the Ending of the World

1

The island and the people continued to suffer. The darkness of the night-hidden land allied itself with the hidden, green, deep fears of the ocean. Wooreddy could feel it lapping about his middle and touching him with chilly fingers, cold as the white wetness he had once felt in the inland mountains. What had that been called? *turrana.* Now always he could taste salt on his lips and deep down his throat. The sea had invaded his body! This knowledge hit him one day as he was about to step on a snake which had no right to be on the snake-free island. His foot hit the ground a metre from the coiled black body in a rush of fear imagining a hissing death. *Ria Warrawah* had extended the boundary of his domain to include Bruny Island. He knew this for certain as he watched the coughing demon attack the few remaining people. *Ria Warrawah* sucked up souls and amid the vast sighing danger what could he do but chant the old protection spells, gash into his body extra-potent strength marks, carry about relics of the long dead, and hope—hope and watch the sun rise on another cloudy day of hopelessness? Day fell into day, and his numbness became a kangaroo-skin bag to hold his ever-growing panic. He told himself over and over again that he was destined to be a survivor—but, as he cast a glazed eye over the half-dozen people still alive and suffering, even his survival came into question. To survive, yes—but into what future? It lay ahead of him as dead as a fish tossed from the ocean. Automatically, he stared at the sea as he tried to imagine that his life—though not the old traditions giving it shape and meaning—would continue on aimlessly. He sighed and stared bleakly at the *num* crawling like insects on the very body of the devil. Behind him he heard the coughing demon acknowledge the sigh of the ocean. The demon hacked at his wife's chest and he could do nothing. She might eject the demon, but the odds were against it. For some reason he thought of the female, Trugernanna and this caused his mood to lift a little. She would never come to a quick end. The boat pointed in their direction. Its wooden legs swayed the body from side to side. She was every bit a survivor as he himself was. The *num* were coming to them. She would go on and on, just as he would go on, until the end.

In the bow of the boat a *num* stood and, although his body swayed   2 unsteadily, he still managed to impart to it an attitude of eagerness and readiness for action. Wooreddy watched uncaringly. Most *num* sat in their boats, this one did not—so what! Still, as the boat entered the surf, he felt an urge to flee into the safety of the bush. He stayed where he was examining the crew. He saw no killing sticks. This relieved him enough to wait to see what the boat would bring.

The bottom of the boat touched the ground. This was instantly followed   3 by a shouted order from the now-sprawling *num* at the grey-clad crew who grinned as they shipped their oars. At last, obeying the order, they slipped into the surf and manhandled the craft to dry sand. The head ghost scrambled up, assumed his dignity and shouted again: 'Harder, you ruffians, pull harder there.' The watching Wooreddy repeated the sounds *sotto voce* and wondered what they meant. If he had the energy, he might learn the language. The main *num* jumped dryshod onto the beach, saw the Aborigine and stamped toward him with hand outstretched.

The Aborigine waited for the strange intruder to reach him. The *num*   4 was short with a soft body plump from many days of good eating without hunting. Short, stubby legs marched that potbellied trunk over the sand with dainty, precise steps lacking the finesse of the hunter. Still there was something of the stamp of a sacred dance in the steps and this gave Wooreddy an interest in the visitor. His eyes brightened as his numbness lessened. The ghost's face, round like the moon, though unscarred, shone pink like the shoulder skin of the early morning sun. Sharp, sea-coloured eyes sought to bridge the gap between them. The ghostly eyes showed such an avid interest in him that he evaded those eyes by staring at the strange skin on the ghost's head. From under it, his hair showed rust-coloured like a vein of red ochre in grey rock.

The *num* grabbed, and succeeded in capturing Wooreddy's hand. It lay 5 limply in the grasp, while the pink-petalled lips began fluttering out sounds which were gibberish to the man. 'Such a poor, poor creature! Such a wretched being bereft of everything we civilised people hold dear. How right I was not to listen to my wife and friends who sought to dissuade me from this charitable and necessary task. No matter what hazard, it is truly the Lord's work and I will persevere.'

Behind his back, the convict crew twisted their faces in mockery. Some 6 of them had endured a visit from him in prison and were familiar with the style of his deliverance. They described it, in their colourful way, as a 'load of shit'. Perhaps it was their felt contempt which had driven George Augustus Robinson to the greener pastures of Aboriginal welfare.

Wooreddy's mouth hesitated on the way to a smile, then he saw the 7 faces the convicts were pulling and grinned for the first time in months. The ghost still clung to his hand. Now he fluted: 'Me, me Mr. Robinson.'

Wooreddy's agile mind discarded the pronouns and he repeated: 8 'Meeter Ro-bin-un.'

While behind him the convicts mouthed the words and even went into 9 a little dance, Robinson pushed his left index finger against Wooreddy's greasy chest and, pronouncing each word slowly and distinctly, asked: 'You, you, your, name, what?' Loud snickers from the boat crew caused him to whirl around and shout: 'Don't stand around. Get that boat up on the beach'—then he turned back to the Aborigine and repeated the words in the same fluting tone, though now edged with anger.

Wooreddy politely answered: *'Narrah warrah* (yes)' 10

'Pleased to make your acquaintance, I'm sure, Narrah Warrah,' the *num* 11 burbled enthusiastically, not caring if he was understood by the poor matted-haired apparition which stood before him with its nakedness partially covered by a dirty blanket. He had come to save such creatures and they would understand this intuitively. Already, this *Narrah Warrah* knew that he was their friend.

'I am your friend,' he said slowly, his voice dropping to a silky soft- 12 ness which oozed. 'Have no fear, Narrah Warrah'—a snigger from the convicts whipped a snarl into his tone. 'I have come to protect you from such scum as these ruffians behind me—' and he jerked a thumb over his shoulder. Wooreddy intuitively grasped what the gesture meant. He suddenly realised that here was an ally. The self-assured, pompous little ghost before him could be used to help him survive until the end of the world.

He accepted Meeter Ro-bin-un as his very own *num* with the same 13 readiness with which Robinson had accepted the fact that he was destined to save these poor, benighted people. Such a *modus vivendi*, lacking all the essentials of a properly understood relationship, held infinite possibilities from rich comedy to equally rich tragedy. At first, Wooreddy was over-joyed. He had found a protector and also a subject of study. He tested out the relationship by making a gesture and then walking off into the bush. He was happy to find the ghost following, but his happiness disappeared when the ghost marched past him and took the lead. Robinson was defining their relationship from the beginning.

In the camp Wooreddy's wife, Lunna, sat naked and uncaring on a piece 14 of blanket. The coughing demon hacked at her lungs. She didn't even lift her head when the *num* bent over her, his face filled with solicitude. A short distance away, one of her sons sat chewing on a tough piece of kangaroo meat while the other sat waiting his turn. They glanced up; their eyes filled with the image of the ghost, and with a united single shriek they were away into the scrub as fast as their little legs could carry them. The father called out, ordering them to return, but the sound of their feet diminished into the distance. Now and not for the first time, he wondered how he had fathered such boys. He remembered when he was their age and the sudden deep thoughts that had slowed his feet so that he more often found himself facing danger rather than fleeing from it. They had none of the qualities he cherished. It was the fault of their foreign mother. Wooreddy refused to acknowledge that his own stuffiness and indifference might have had something to do with their behavior patterns. He hardly ever spoke to them and often ignored his wife as well.

'Meridee bidai lidinee loomerai,' he said explaining the sickness of his wife, 15 but not his lack of concern—a concern which was expressed on the face of the ghost. But even that concern vanished when Trugernanna walked into the clearing clutching in each small fist an arm of the boys. Wooreddy had not been the only one observing the *num*. Trugernanna, hidden in the scrub, had studied him and decided that he was unlike the ones at the whaling station on the other side of the island. There, all that they wanted to do was take her off somewhere. At first she had found it flattering, but now it was just one of those things.

Away from the *num* the girl often went naked, but now she wore a 16 kangaroo skin wrapped about her full hips. This was a new style which the women had adopted. The old fashion of draping the skin over the shoulders was gone for ever. Now demure in her rough skirt she shot a glance at the ghost and caught his look of approval. They liked females to be covered below the waist for most of the time.

George Augustus Robinson, destined by God to make the Aborigines 17 the most interesting and profitable part of his life, leered at the forbidden fruits of the bare-breasted maiden who conjured up romantic visions of beautiful South Sea islands where missionaries laboured for the salvation of delightful souls. On this island and on the larger one of Van Diemen's Land, he too would be such a missionary. He went into his 'Me, Mr Robinson' routine and this time received a better response. The girl had been around the whalers and sawyers long enough to pick up quite a few words of the ghost language. She replied that her name was Trugernanna and set Robinson right in regard to the name of Wooreddy. In return Robinson smiled an expression which held more than that of the good shepherd at long last finding an intelligent sheep.

She spoke to Wooreddy and enlightened him about the *num*. Finally he 18 had the proof that the ghost was indeed an ally. As Robinson quaintly informed Trugernanna: 'Me look after you, give you food, clothing—bad white man no longer hurt you.' And as the girl just as quaintly echoed: 'Bad *num* no longer hurt us' as she took the protector's hand and gazed up into his face with all the adoration of a child—though the fullness of her breasts belied the pose. Wooreddy found himself ignored. It annoyed him that the woman had captured all the ghost's attention. After all Meeter Ro-bin-un was his ally too!

Wooreddy and Trugernanna helped Lunna and the two children to shift 19 along the coast to where Meeter Ro-bin-un had erected a ghost shelter. It was right on the channel and at night they could see, gleaming across the water, the lights of the main *num* settlement. Robinson wished to acquire a working knowledge of the Bruny language and took every opportunity to learn from the people. He did not offer to teach them his language in return. This would come later. But the Aborigines had realised that they needed to know the ghost language and they too took every opportunity to learn new words and sentences. They found that the main difficulty was in the pronunciation, unlike Robinson who floundered in the complicated grammar structuring Bruny. He never did advance beyond a form of creole, though by this time so few people were left who spoke the language that it did not matter.

The Aborigines soon discovered that their ally considered himself superior 20 to them. They were to be 'children' to his 'father'. The girl fell easily into the role expected and the word 'fader' constantly fell from her lips when Robinson was within hearing. But Wooreddy felt insulted. After all he was a full citizen, not only of his own nation, but of the South West too, and had he not collected, debated and even on one occasion refined a point of law regarding a custom of his people! He was a prominent citizen and a biological father to boot. What was this Ro-bin-un? . . . Then he saw and felt the sickness all around him and surrendered. It seemed a small price to pay for survival.

STUDY QUESTIONS

1. What are the various injuries, dangers, and changes in Aboriginal culture that the British settlement has brought to Wooreddy's land?
2. The author gives us multiple perspectives on "Mister Robinson" and

his mission to rescue the Aborigines who have been all but wiped out by invading Europeans. What is Mister Robinson's perspective on his mission?

3. What seems to be the author's view of Robinson? Which lines show the author questioning, qualifying, and casting doubt on the motives of Mister Robinson?

4. How does Dr. Wooreddy see Robinson? What does Wooreddy hope for from him? What does Mr. Robinson's walking off in front of Wooreddy suggest about the way Mr. Robinson sees their relationship?

5. Mr. Robinson is a re-imagined Robinson Crusoe, whose colonialist adoption of the native Man Friday was presented as a civilizing act in Daniel Defoe's well-known novel, *Robinson Crusoe*. Analyze the description of Mr. Robinson's meeting with the young aboriginal woman, Trugernanna, as an ironic commentary on race, sex, and colonial relations. If you are familiar with Defoe's novel, explain how this description revises Defoe's eighteenth-century European view of paternalistic colonialism.

◎ ELIZABETH JOLLEY

Elizabeth Jolley (b. 1923) was born in England and immigrated to Australia in 1959. Living in Western Australia, Jolley worked at various jobs as a nurse, domestic, and saleswoman before settling into a writing career. Although Jolley had a difficult time getting published (her first novel, Palomino, *appeared only in 1980), her many novels and collections of short stories are now internationally acclaimed for their comic strain, bizarre characters, and absurd quality that suggest profound conditions of loneliness and dislocations.*

Mr Parker's Valentine

After only a few weeks Pearson and Eleanor Page were tired of living in the rented house. The rooms were small and stuffy, and the repetitive floral carpet depressed them every time they stepped into the dark hall. Pearson felt his wife would be less homesick if they had a house and garden of their own.

'House hunting will do you the world of good,' he said to her. Friends of theirs, just as recently arrived from England, were happily settled already, busy with paving stones, garden catalogues and plans for attractive additions to their new homes.

So Eleanor looked at houses and quite soon she found exactly what she 3
had always wanted. In the evening they went together to see it. It was old
and had an iron roof. Wide wooden verandahs went all round the house,
and faced the sun, or were shaded at just the right times.

On either side of the street were old peppermint trees, and there was an 4
atmosphere of quiet dignity in the decaying remains of a once well-to-do
residential area.

There was, however, a difficulty about the house. They stood together 5
with the land agent out in the back garden, surrounded by the wilderness
of full-skirted red-splashed hibiscus and flower-laden oleanders. All round
them tall trees in a ring, sighing now and protesting, tossed their branches
in the afternoon sea breeze. Cape lilacs, jacarandas, flame trees and Nor-
folk pines, green, light green upon dark. And, nearly as big as the house
itself, a gnarled and thickly-leaved mulberry tree, with early ripened fruit
dropping, replenished the earth.

They stood in the noise of the wind, as if at the edge of waves, and were 6
submerged in the swaying green, as if in water of unknown depths, to
ponder over their problem.

At the end of the garden was a tall shed, stone-built with a patched 7
corrugated iron roof. The door of the shed opened to the western sun and,
in a little plot edged with stones and shells, herbs were growing and wild
tobacco flowers. A short clothes line stretched between the door post and
the fence. An old man lived in the shed.

'The trouble is,' the land agent said, 'he's lived here for years. The 8
owners hope that whoever buys the house will let him stay on. He has no
other home.'

'I'm afraid it's out of the question if we buy the house,' Pearson Page 9
said, shouting a little to increase his authority and determination. He was
a short man, fresh faced, looking younger than he was.

'Oh! I do so want the house,' Eleanor said. They stood remembering the 10
recent pleasure of large fireplaces and polished jarrah floor boards, of high
ceilings still with their graceful mouldings and, of course, the windows.
Tall windows, each one framed and filled from outside with green leaves
and woven patterns of stems and roses, jasmine and honeysuckle. And all
the rooms so fragrant just now with the scent of Chinese pivot.

'I never had a house with such a spacious kitchen,' Eleanor said, adding 11
to their thoughts. She wanted the house very much and felt the old man
being there could make so little difference.

They all moved down to peer into the shed. 12

A great deal was crammed inside the shed, an old man's lifetime of 13
experience and possessions. Boxes were stacked and his lumpy bed was
smoothed and tucked up in a black and grey plaid. Some matting covered
the floor and there was a plain wood table and three scrubbed chairs. Over
the wood stove were shelves piled with pans and crockery, and a toasting
fork hung on a nail. Ivy, growing in under the roof at the far end, hung

down in a dark curtain catching and concealing the full sun as it flooded in through the open double doors.

'Place would make a good biscuit factory,' Pearson tried a joke, as he 14 saw disaster in the corrugated iron and an old man's clothes hung out to dry in the sun.

The character and possibilities of the house were overwhelming; 15 Beethoven in the evenings and perhaps the writing of poetry. Eleanor longed for such evenings on the verandah. She stepped into the shed.

'Pity to turn the old man out,' she said. 'But it would make a marvellous 16 rumpus room for the boys.' She used the word 'rumpus' with the self-conscious effort of fitting in to the phrases of a new country.

'Ah, you have sons?' the house agent asked gently. 17

'Yes, two,' Eleanor explained. 'They are just finishing off the year at 18 boarding school in England and will be joining us later.'

'Mr Parker's out shopping just now,' the house agent continued in his 19 soft voice, his knowledge suggesting years of experience of Mr Parker's habits. 'He does not trouble the house at all,' he said.

The wind tossed the tumult of branches to and fro. 'Think it over,' the 20 house agent said.

The Pages had always enjoyed a single-minded, smooth partnership in 21 their marriage and now, for the first time, they were unable to come to some kind of agreement about the old man and whether he should be allowed to stay.

'I can't think why all this fuss,' Pearson said, his face very red because 22 of the sun; he scooped out the fragrant flesh of a rock melon. Juice stayed on his lips. 'We can buy the house if we want it. There's nothing about the old man to stop us buying the house. It can be ours tomorrow. All we have to do is to say we don't want him there. And he'll have to go. It's as simple as that. I can't think why you're so worried.'

'But Pearson, where would he go? We can't just turn him out. I couldn't 23 live there if we did that.'

Neither of them slept. 24

In the end Pearson agreed to the old man remaining. 'Any trouble,' he 25 shouted, 'and out he goes!' He did not want to disappoint Eleanor and, in any case, he wanted the house too.

On the day they moved in they were too pleased and excited at being 26 able to unpack their own things at last to think of the old man.

Pearson strutted in and out of the empty rooms giving instructions. He 27 was a sandy man and his face was fresh and rosy coloured, contrasting with the tired grey cheeks of the two men who were carrying in the furniture and the countless boxes; for Pearson and Eleanor had many books and pictures and other treasures.

In the evening the old man came up to the back door and introduced 28 himself. He was small and clean and had the faraway voice of a deaf person.

'I've roasted a half leg of lamb, the shank end, I thought you'd like a bit   29
of dinner. Six-thirty sharp, down at my place,' he said. 'Plenty of gravy.'

Eleanor in her dirty removal dress was embarrassed. 'Oh, no thank you.   30
We couldn't possibly spare the time . . .' she began, smiling kindly at his
best clothes. But he could not hear her.

'Don't be late! Six-thirty sharp; hotting up a roast spoils it,' he said, and   31
went off down the garden.

So there was nothing to do but leave their unpacking and arranging,   32
tidy themselves up and go in an awkward little procession of two down to
the shed.

Inside the shed it was surprisingly bright and cosy; it was the wood   33
stove and the smell of the hot meat. The old man told them about his life
when he travelled round Australia at the turn of the century. He was just
explaining about the quarantine camps of those far-off days, when he
suddenly stopped, and said, 'Yo' know what day it is?' Eleanor, smiling,
shook her head.

'Valentine's Day!' he said, and he climbed up on the boxes and fetched   34
down a grimy envelope from behind a rafter.

'Fifty years ago that was sent to me,' he said proudly. And he showed   35
them the dusty paper pillowed heart, stuck all over with faded daisies.

'Who sent it?' Eleanor asked. She had to shout the question three times,   36
self-consciously, trying to hide Pearson's boredom.

'Ah! You're not supposed to know who sends a Valentine,' the old man   37
creaked with the far-away reedy laughter of the deaf.

Late in the night, they made their way up the dark garden. The house,   38
neglected, was hostile with nothing done. Confusion in every room.

'Not even the bed made,' Pearson's voice was disagreeable with the   39
wasted evening. He had wanted to put up pictures and arrange their
Venetian glass.

'Oh Mr Parker's delightful.' Eleanor hurriedly found the sheets. Really   .40
Pearson's sulky ways made her very uncomfortable, especially as the old
man was so friendly.

In the next few weeks there were some things to trouble them. Old Mr   41
Parker, early one morning, painted all the verandah posts blue, spoiling
the appearance of the house.

'Protection against the weather,' he explained. He chopped down the   42
passion vine, his thin stumpy arms whirling the axe as if he had unlimited
strength.

'Too old,' he pointed at the gnarled twisted growth of the vine.   43

Every time Pearson started to do some gardening, Mr Parker was at his   44
elbow.

'Wrong time of the year to prune them lemon trees,' he said. And 'Yo'll   45
not pull up all them bricks in that path, I hope.' The reedy voice irritated
Pearson; he longed to work without interference. He sought for something
to heal himself in the garden. He had come to a new post, his first uni-

versity appointment, thinking to pour the culture and refinement of his mind over his new colleagues. It had been a surprise to him to find thoughts wider and greater than his own, and a wider establishment of learning than he had thought possible in the far-away place he had come to. Every day he had to adjust to some new discovery of his own ignorance. The garden could have been a place for a quiet renewal of his spirit and energy, but it was not so with the presence of the old man.

Eleanor too was strange, she seemed to like Mr Parker so much. Pearson wasted hours waiting for Eleanor, who had slipped down to the shed for two minutes. Sometimes she was there in that biscuit factory, with the stupid old goat, for a whole evening. Really, the old man would have to go. Pearson felt he could not wait to get him away, together with all the rubbish there was down there. 46

Eleanor said the old man meant well, but Pearson was not so sure of this. He could not understand her attitude, and she was unable to accept what she suddenly saw as a cruel side in his nature. 47

In the night Eleanor thought she heard a tiny shout. She sat up. Again, a tiny far-away shout in the night. 48

'It's the old man! Mr Parker's calling us.' She roused Pearson. 49

'Oh don't fuss,' yawned her husband. 'He's used to being alone. He can look after himself!' He turned over and went on sleeping. 50

Eleanor went down, in the dark, to the shed. The night was fragrant with the sweet scent of the datura, the long white bells trembled, swinging without noise, and the east wind snored in the restless tree tops. Fantastic fire-light danced in the shed and the old man called to her from his dishevelled bed. 51

'I've got the shivers,' he said. 'There's a good girl! Make up the stove for me and squeeze me some lemons and boil up the kettle.' He gave his orders and his teeth chattered. 52

'Just a chill,' he comforted Eleanor. 'Get me warm,' he said, 'an' tomorrer I'll be right you'll see.' 53

Eleanor did as she was told. 54

The old man slept a little and Eleanor sat there beside him. In the small light he looked ill and frail. She thought he might die. She thought it would be much easier if he did die. It was not that she wanted him to die, only that if this was the end of his life, and he had lived a long time, it would solve all their difficulties. Lately she had been so unhappy. 55

'Shall I get the doctor?' she shouted to him when he opened his eyes. But he laughed at her. 56

'Put some more wood on the stove, my dear. I got the shivers that's all, it's nothing.' 57

A bit later he opened his eyes. 58

'Yor husband's a quiet man,' he said. 'Still waters run deep they say.' He gave a little far-away laugh, and then he said, 'Thank you, my dear. I'm much obliged to you,' and he slept. 59

Eleanor went back up the dark garden, the moon rode on the restless 60
fragrance and she felt grateful for the old man's call.

'I think I should sit with him.' She woke Pearson. 61

'Whatever for, if we weren't here he would be alone.' 62

'But we are here.' Eleanor stood uneasily by their bed. 63

'I don't see that that comes into it. We bought the house it's true, and we 64
live in it, but that does not mean we are responsible for the old fool, and
his so-called illness.'

'But Pearson, he's really ill.' 65

'That's his lookout. We can't look after all the old men who are ill. If he 66
doesn't want to be alone, he shouldn't live there. You'll only wear yourself
out.' Pearson added his warning.

They seemed to face a wall in their marriage, and they tried to sleep and 67
could not.

By the next weekend Mr Parker was quite recovered. 68

Pearson was disappointed and angry to see him emerge from the shed 69
as if nothing had been wrong with him. Ignoring advice, 'It's not the best
time for it,' Pearson cut dead wood out of the hibiscus. 'Yo'll not touch
them roses I hope,' the reedy voice followed Pearson, so he turned his
attention to the flame tree. One great bough, he could see, was a danger to
the house.

Collecting necessary materials, he set to work. He sat in among the 70
thicket of leaves, straddling a branch near the trunk, and began with his
well-cared-for saw to cut the offending limb. Slowly and methodically the
saw went to and fro. Pearson was surprised the wood was so soft. He was
surprised too at the sharp thorns the tree had all over the branches; from
the ground the bark looked quite smooth.

Mr Parker stood under the tree. 71

'Yo' want to take that branch bit by bit,' he shouted, cupping his mouth 72
with one hand, though Pearson was only a few feet above his head.

'If yo' cut it there it'll tear,'' the old man warned. 'Them trees is best cut 73
when the leaves is off.'

'Too heavy,' he explained to Eleanor. 'Too heavy!' he shouted up to 74
Pearson.

'Oh mind your own business you old fool,' Pearson said, but of course 75
Mr Parker was so deaf it didn't matter what anyone said.

Eleanor, standing by, wished Pearson would not look so irritable. There 76
was no pleasure in anything they did now. She smiled at the old man.

'Mr Parker says the branch will tear,' she called up timidly. 77

'I heard,' Pearson replied grimly, the saw was stuck and he could see he 78
needed something to pull on the branch.

'Throw me the rope,' he called down. Eleanor could pull at the branch 79
from below.

'Yo'll rip right down the trunk,' Mr Parker called. 'He's new to our 80
trees,' he explained to Eleanor.

'Yes, yes, of course,' and she smiled at him. 81

'Pull! Haul!' Pearson called to Eleanor when the rope was secure. 82

'What if the branch falls on me?' she cried. 83

'I'll shout and you run for it,' Pearson called back. 84

'Pull! Haul!' He saw her straining, but nothing happened. The white 85
smile of wood remained tightly clenched on the saw.

'Yo' need to work at it bit by bit,' Mr Parker said to Eleanor. 'I'm a comin' 86
up!' he called to Pearson. And the next moment he was up the ladder with
Pearson's new pruning saw, and off onto the swaying branch along to the
end of it, cutting twigs and little branches. Leaf-laden tufts fell to the
ground below as he cut this side and that.

'Yo' want to lighten the branch and cut further out to start with,' he 87
explained to Pearson who, red-faced with anger, still sat straddling his
branch.

Pearson, before becoming a university professor, had a short but bril- 88
liant army career behind him, and he was not going to be ordered about by
old men.

'Go down this instant!' he shouted at the old man. His voice was so loud 89
Mr Parker heard it. He stopped his prancing on the branch and stared at
Pearson as if unable to understand the reason for the anger.

In that moment Pearson seemed to see the old man as something more 90
than a nuisance; he saw in him something tenacious and evil. And the
thought came to him that perhaps many people had taken the house and
been forced by reasons, unknown to the land agent, to leave.

'I must be ill,' Pearson thought to himself, 'to have such stupid ideas.' 91
But as he saw Mr Parker coming slowly along the swaying branch he felt
he would fight this thing, whatever it was, and he would keep the
house; he would fight with all his strength. Mr Parker advanced slowly,
in his hand he held the pruning saw and on his face was a strange expression.

From the ground, Eleanor thought he was going to cry, but the awk- 92
wardly pointing little saw, with its curve of sharp teeth, frightened her.

'Pearson!' she cried out. 93

'Go down this instant!' Pearson's voice was deep and loud. And still 94
seated astride the branch, his back against the trunk, he pointed down
towards the ground with authority.

'Yo' go down then,' Mr Parker said. In his reedy little voice there was no 95
anger. 'You've more weight nor me. Yo' pull on the rope, an' I'll get her
out.' He indicated the saw.

Pearson recognized this as commonsense, but he was not going to be 96
told what to do by this old fool.

'Go down. This instant!' he shouted, still pointing down. 97

'Well, orl right. I'll have a go on the rope with 'er then.' Mr Parker 98
scrambled down the ladder.

'Come on Missus,' he said to Eleanor, and together they took the rope. 99

Pearson watched the pantomime below. Eleanor, in her unfashionably 100
long skirt, pulling on the rope with the little old man dangling behind her.
The morning had become ridiculous.

'Pull! Haul! Heave! Haul!' he bellowed. 101

And then, to his amazement, the cut in the branch suddenly widened 102
and, with a roar, the great leaf-laden bough fell away, grazing his thigh as
it tore down the side of the trunk. He caught the saw before it fell.

'Timbah!' he yelled. 'Run for it!' 103

Of course Mr Parker heard nothing of the warning. And Eleanor, leap- 104
ing clear of the heavy falling foliage, tried to grab his shoulder to pull him
away, but a forked branch came sharply and painfully between them, and
Mr Parker was left there under the heavy fallen mass.

'Oh my God!' Pearson sprang from the tree and pushed through the 105
leaves and branches.

It was an action accompanied by feelings he was never able to forget 106
afterwards.

Eleanor could only stand and watch. She saw her husband's bare feet, 107
competent and clean in rubber thongs. She thought his feet looked cruel,
and she realised they must have always been like that.

Pearson toiled like a sick man to clear out the shed. He cleared and de- 108
stroyed as if cleaning himself of an infection. The whole place would be
different by the time his boys arrived from England.

As he worked he found himself thinking all the time of the old man. He 109
kept expecting to see the washed-out shirt between leaves and bushes, and
he missed the persistent reedy voice at his elbow. The garden, so much the
old man's place, seemed deserted.

He tried to discipline his mind. He thought about his boys and longed 110
for the time when they would come. He longed for their voices and the
noise of their healthy bodies about the house. He wanted to be concerned
again with examination results, sports training and dogs and bicycles and
the choosing of birthday presents.

The envelope, treasured up all the years, fluttered and fell with the dust 111
being brushed from the beams and rafters. The old man again.

'Who wins a fight anyway,' Pearson muttered to himself. He had to put 112
aside too, the thought that his boys were hardly boys now and would not
want the same things from him.

'It's Mr Parker's Valentine.' Eleanor picked it up. 'And he never knew 113
who sent it to him.' She experienced curiosity sadly. Beyond the double
doors of the shed, doves laughed softly in the silky morning.

'Put it on the fire,' Pearson ordered. 114

He thought, as he dragged boxes and tore down ivy, that everything 115
would have been different if the old man had found out all those years ago
who had sent him the Valentine.

Eleanor, carrying the dirty envelope up to the house, was thinking the 116 same thing. She had been fondly patient with Mr Parker and knew she was without blame, yet she felt the burden of Pearson's anger and resentment. He had shown how he felt, while she hid her feelings, so giving him full responsibility. She knew they would never speak of any of this now, and she could not reach Pearson in his grim remorse. All day they worked, separately.

'Pearson.' Eleanor called from the house.   117

'Coming.' He went slowly up the garden.   118

Some time earlier they had arranged to have a party, a kind of house   119
warming. Neither of them had suggested putting it off. It was time to start preparing for the evening and they tried to smile in readiness for their visitors.

STUDY QUESTIONS

1. Analyze the differences between Mr Parker's life, as symbolized by the shed and its furnishings, and the kind of life Pearson and Eleanor Page were looking forward to in buying the house.

2. How does Mr Parker's presence affect Pearson and Eleanor's marriage? What does Eleanor learn about her husband?

3. In what ways does Eleanor respond differently from Pearson to Mr Parker? Does the story absolve her of blame? Analyze the multiple meanings in the statement "[Pearson] had shown how he had felt, while she hid her feelings, so giving him full responsibility."

4. In representing Mr Parker's death, what is the story suggesting about the relationship between the pioneering settlers of Australia and the new immigrants from Britain?

◎ DAVID MALOUF

An internationally published novelist and essayist, David Malouf (b. 1934) was first known as a poet. He has published five collections of poetry and the libretto of an opera based on Patrick White's novel Voss. *Born in Brisbane, Queensland, he attended Brisbane Grammar School and the University of Queensland. He re-created his Brisbane childhood in an autobiographical memoir,* 12 Edmonstone Street *(1985). His first novel* Johnno *(1975), a story of youth, is also set in Brisbane and has been adopted as a text in many Australian secondary schools. Malouf left Australia for ten years, traveling and teaching school in England. He now divides his time between Australia and a village in Tuscany. Critics note the poetic use of language in his novels.*

Off the Map

All night headlamps dazzle
the leaves. Truck-drivers
throbbing on pills
climb out of the sleep

of farmtowns prim   5
behind moonlit lace, bronze Anzacs[1]
dozing, leaden-headed,
at ease between wars,

and out into a dream
of apple-orchards, paddocks   10
tumbling with mice,
bridges that slog the air,

black piers, bright water, silos
moonstruck, pointing nowhere
like saints practising stillness   15
in a ripple of grain.

They thunder across country
like the daredevil boys
of the 'Fifties who flourished
a pistol in banks,   20

and rode off into headlines
and hills or into legends
that hang, grey-ghostly, over
campfires in the rain.

Now kids, barefooted, wade   25
in the warm, hatched tyre-marks
of country dust, the print
of monsters; cattle stare.

All night through the upland silence
and ranges of our skull   30
in low gear shifting skyward
they climb towards dawn.

---

1. Anzac: *A World War II soldier from Australia or New Zealand.*

A lit butt glows, a beercan
clatters. Strung out
on the hills, new streets that glow   35
in the eyes of farmboys, cities

alive only at nightfall
that span a continent.
Nameless, not to be found
by day on any map.   40

STUDY QUESTIONS

1. Malouf threads together many details and images of the countryside as
   he follows the travels of the truck drivers. Trace and describe three of
   these images. What kind of surroundings does Malouf create?
2. Explain exactly what you would see if you were looking at
   1. "farmtowns prim
        behind moonlit lace" (stanza 2)
                    and
   2. "silos / moonstruck . . .
        like saints practising stillness" (stanza 4)
   What associations and mood do these images provoke?
3. Discuss how the drivers are like "the daredevil boys" mentioned in
   stanza 5? What contrast does the poet suggest between them and the
   countryside?
4. In what way can the "hatched tyre-marks" of stanza 7 be considered
   "the print of monsters"? Who are the monsters?
5. What dreams or yearnings can be found in the "glow in the eyes of the
   farmboys?"
6. Why are the cities not found on a map?

 # KENNETH SLESSOR

*Kenneth Slessor (1901–1971) worked as a journalist and editor in Sydney. His
poetry exhibits a stylistic development that ranges from works devoted to
Australian themes of the wilderness and identity to more philosophical and
individualistic statements. Although he stopped writing poetry after publishing
Five Bells (1939), the poems that appear in his selected collection, One
Hundred Poems, 1913–1939 (1944), are usually accepted as among the first
poems to compose an Australian national canon.*

South Country

After the whey-faced anonymity
    Of river-gums and scribbly-gums and bush,
After the rubbing and the hit of brush,
You come to the South Country

As if the argument of trees were done,   5
The doubts and quarrelling, the plots and pains,
All ended by these clear and gliding planes
Like an abrupt solution.

And over the flat earth of empty farms
The monstrous continent of air floats back   10
Coloured with rotting sunlight and the black,
Bruised flesh of thunderstorms:

Air arched, enormous, pounding the bony ridge,
Ditches and hutches, with a drench of light,
So huge, from such infinities of height,   15
You walk on the sky's beach

While even the dwindled hills are small and bare,
As if, rebellious, buried, pitiful,
Something below pushed up a knob of skull,
Feeling its way to air.   20

STUDY QUESTIONS

1. "South Country" can be described as a "landscape poem." Analyze the poem's use of contrasting personification to characterize the different parts of the country.
2. What sentiments toward the South Country are suggested in the image of the "abrupt solution" in the second stanza? Support your answer by examining the metaphorical extensions of this image in the subsequent stanzas.
3. What can you infer, from the kinds of images offered, of the relation of the observer to the land being observed? How is this relation explained by the history of Australian settlement?

PATRICK WHITE

Patrick White (1912–1990), Australia's leading novelist and a major figure in contemporary literature, was educated at a public school in England, though he came from a fourth-generation Australian family. During the war he was an RAF intelligence officer serving in the Middle East and Greece. After the war, he settled in Sydney with his life companion, Manoly Lascaris. From the publication of The Aunt's Story *(1948), the first of his mature works, until his death, he wrote a series of powerful novels, short stories, and plays. In 1973, he won the Nobel Prize for Literature for his novel* The Eye of the Storm. *His works, which combine the strengths of traditional narrative with modernist techniques, turned world attention to Australian writing. His short-story collections include* Overland *(1963), from which "Clay" is taken;* The Burnt Ones *(1964); and* The Cockatoos *(1974).*

Clay

When he was about five years old some kids asked Clay why his 1
mother had called him that. And he did not know. But began to wonder. He did, in fact, wonder a great deal, particularly while picking the bark off trees, or stripping a flower down to its core of mystery. He, too, would ask questions, but more often than not failed to receive the answer because his mother could not bring herself to leave her own train of thought.

Mrs Skerritt said: "If only your father hadn't died he'd still be putting 2
out the garbage the bin is too much for me the stooping not to mention the weight in anyone short of breath but you Clay I know will be good to your Mum and help when you are older stronger only that is still a long way off."

So that it was Clay's turn not to answer. What could you say, anyway? 3

Mrs Skerritt said: "I wouldn't ask anything of anyone but there are 4
certain things of course I wouldn't expect a gentleman to stand up for me in the tram while I have my own two legs only it's the sort of thing a gentleman ought to do and ladies take Mrs Pearl for instance what she expects of her husband and him with the sugar diabetes too."

Clay mooned about the house listening to his mother's voice boring 5
additional holes in the fretwork, for fretwork had been Dadda's hobby: there was fretwork just about everywhere, brackets and things, even a lace of fretwork hanging from tabletop and doorway. Stiff. Sometimes while his mother's voice bored and sawed further Clay would break off pieces of the brown fretwork and hide it away under the house. Under the house was full of fretwork finally.

Or he would moon about the terraces of garden, amongst the collaps- 6
ing lattices, flowerpot shards crackling underfoot, legs slapped by the
straps of dark, leathery plants, lungs filled with suffocating bursts of asparagus fern. He would dawdle down to the harbour, with its green
smell of sea-lettuce, and the stone wall, scribbled with white droppings
of gulls. The house itself leaned rather far towards the harbour, but had
not fallen, because some men had come and shored it up. There it hung,
however.

So Clay mooned. And would return often to the photograph. It was as 7
though his childhood were riveted to the wedding group. There was his
father, those thick thighs, rather tight about the serge crutch (unlike the
dadda he remembered lying Incurable in bed), and the influential Mr
Stutchbury, and Auntie Ada, and Nellie Watson (who died), and someone
else who was killed in action. But it was to his mum that Clay was drawn,
before and after all, into the torrential satin of the lap, by the face which
had just begun to move out of its fixture of fretted lace. And the shoe. He
was fascinated by the white shoe. Sometimes its great boat would float out
from the shore of frozen time, into the waters of his imagination, rocking
his cargo of almost transparent thoughts.

Once Mrs Skerritt came into the room and caught him at it though she 8
did not exactly see Clay for looking at herself.

"Ah dear," she said, "in the end things is sad." 9

She would often half cry, and at such moments her hair would look 10
more than ever like so many lengths of grey string, or on windy days, a tizz
of frayed dishcloth.

On the particular day when she caught Clay looking at the photograph, 11
his throat swelled, and he dared to ask:

"Why is my name Clay, Mum?" 12

Because by that time he was seven, and the kids were asking worse than 13
ever, and bashing him up (they were afraid that he was different).

"Why," she said, "let me think your father wanted Percival that is after 14
Mr Stutchbury but I could not bring myself I said there are so many things
you don't do but want take a name a name is yours take pottery I said I've
half a mind to try my hand if I can find some feller or lady you never know
I may be artistic but didn't because well there isn't the time always so much
to do the people who have to be told and who have to be told and then
Dadda's incurable illness so I did not do that only thought and thought
about it and that I believe is why you was called Clay."

Then she went out the back to empty the teapot on a bed of maidenhair 15
which tingled perpetually with moisture.

So the kids continued to bash Clay up, and ask why he was called that, 16
and he couldn't tell them, because how could you even when you knew.

There were times when it got extra bad, and once they chased him with 17
a woman's old cast-off shoe. He ran like a green streak, but not fast enough

in the end—they caught him at the corner of Plant Street, where he had been born and always lived, and the heel of their old shoe bored for ever into his mind.

Later, when he had let himself in, into the garden of the leaning house, lost amongst collapsing lattices and the yellow fuzz of asparagus fern, he cried a bit for the difference to which he had been born. But smeared his eyes dry at last, and his nose. The light was rising from the bay in all green peacefulness, as if the world of pointed objects did not exist alongside that of the dreamy bridal shoe.

But he did not embark. Not then. His ribs had not subsided yet.

Once Clay dreamed a dream, and came down into the kitchen. He had meant to keep the dream to himself. Then it was too late, he heard, he was telling it to his mum. Even though his mouth was frozen stiff he had to keep on, to tell.

"In this dream," he said, "the steps led on down."

His mum was pushing the rashers around, which went on buckling up in the pan.

"Under the sea," said Clay. "It was beautiful."

He was sorry, but he could not help it.

"Everything drawn out. Hair and things. And weeds. The knotted ones. And the lettucey kind. Some of the fish had beards, Mum, and barked, well, like dogs."

His mum had put the fried bread on a plate to one side, where the little squares were already stiffening.

"And shells, Mum," he said, "all bubbles and echoes as I went on down. It felt good. It felt soft. I didn't have to try. But just floated. Down."

He could see his mother's behind, how it had begun to quiver, and he dreaded what might happen when he told. There was no avoiding it, though, and his mum went on prodding the bacon in the pan.

"When I got to the bottom," he said, "and the steps ended, you should have seen how the sea stretched, over the sand and broken bottles. Everything sort of silvery. I don't remember much else. Except that I found, Mum," he said.

"What?" she asked.

He dreaded it.

"A cloud, Mum," he said, "and it was dead."

Then Mrs Skerritt turned round, it was dreadful, how she looked. She opened her mouth, but nothing came out at first, only Clay saw the little thing at the back. Raised. When suddenly it began to act like a clapper. She began to cry, she began to create.

"Whatever are you gunna do to me?" she cried, as she pummelled and kneaded the moist grey dough of her cheeks.

"On top of everything else I never ever thought I'd have a freak!"

But Clay could only stand, and receive the blows her voice dealt. It was 36
as though someone had taken a stick and drawn a circle round him. Him
at the centre. There was no furniture any more.

The bacon was burning in the pan. 37

When Mrs Skerritt had thought it over, and used a little eau-de-Cologne, 38
she took him up to McGillivray's. It was late by then, on a Saturday morning too. All the way Clay listened to her breathing, and sometimes the
sound of her corset. McGillivray was already closing, but agreed to do Mrs
Skerritt's lad. McGillivray was kind.

"We want it short short Mr McGillivray please," Mrs Skerritt said. 39

As the barber snipped Clay could hear his mum breathing, from where 40
she sat, behind his back, under the coloured picture of the King.

Mr McGillivray did his usual nice job, and was preparing to design the 41
little quiff when Mrs Skerritt choked.

"That is not short Mr McGillivray not what I mean oh no oh dear but it 42
is difficult to explain there is too much involved and I left school when I
turned fourteen."

McGillivray laughed, and said: "Short is not shorn!" 43

"I don't care," she said. 44

Clay could only look at the glass, and suck his cheeks in. 45

"Short is what I said and mean," Mrs Skerritt confirmed. "I was never 46
one for not coming to the point."

McGillivray was a gentle man, but he too began to breathe; he took the 47
clippers, and shore a path through his subject's hair. He shore, and shore.
Till there Clay was. Exposed.

"That suit you?" McGillivray asked. 48

"Thank you," she said. 49

So meek. 50

Then they went home. They crunched over the asphalt. They were that 51
heavy, both of them.

As they went down the hill towards the turn where the milko's cart had 52
plunged over, Mrs Skerritt said:

"There Clay a person is sometimes driven to things in defence of what 53
we know and love I would not of done this otherwise if not to protect you
from yourself because love you will suffer in life if you start talking queer
remember it doesn't pay to be different and no one is different without they
have something wrong with them."

Clay touched his prickly hair. 54

"Let it remind you," she said, "that your mum loves you that is why." 55

But Clay could no longer believe in love, and the kids bashed him up 56
worse than ever, because his no-hair made him a sort of different different.

"Wot was you in for?" the kids asked, and did windmills on his stubble. 57
"Old Broad Arrer!" they shouted, and punched.

Actually Clay grew up narrow. He was all knuckle, all wrist. He had 58 those drawn-out arms. He had a greenish skin from living under too many plants. He was long. And his eyes overflowed at dusk, merged with the street lights, and the oil patches on lapping water.

"Are you lonely, Clay?" Mrs Skerritt asked.   59

"No," he said. "Why?"   60

"I thought perhaps you was lonely you should get out and meet other   61
young people of your own age you should get to know nice girls otherwise
it is not normal."

Then she drew in her chin, and waited.   62

But Clay stroked his prickly hair. For he went to McGillivray's every so   63
often since it was ordained. When his voice broke the others no longer
bashed him up, having problems of their own. The blackheads came, the
pimples and moustaches.

Sometimes Mrs Skerritt would cry, sitting on the rotten veranda over-   64
looking the little bay in which cats so often drowned.

"Oh dear Clay," she cried, "I am your mother and have a responsibility   65
a double one since Dadda went I will ask Mr Stutchbury but cannot rely
totally do you know what you want to do?"

Clay said: "No."   66

"Oh dear," she moaned worse than ever, "how did I deserve a silent   67
boy who loves what I would like to know himself perhaps himself."

In fact Clay did not know what he loved. He would have liked to   68
think it was his mother, though it could have been Dadda. So he would
try to remember, but it was only cold yellow skin, and the smell of sick
sheets. When he had been forced to approach his father, lying Incurable
in the bed, his heart could have tumbled down out of the belfry of his
body.

Once his mother, it was evening, clutched his head against her apron,   69
so that she must have pricked her hands.

"You are not my son," she clanged, "otherwise you would act differ-   70
ent."

But he could not, did not want to. Sometimes, anyway, at that age, he   71
felt too dizzy from growing.

"How?" his voice asked, or croaked.   72

But she did not explain. She flung his long body away.   73

"It's not a matter," she said, "that anybody can discuss I will ask Mr   74
Stutchbury to see what we must do and how."

Mr Stutchbury was so influential, as well as having been a mate of Herb   75
Skerritt's all his life. Mr Stutchbury was something, Mrs Skerritt believed,
in the Department of Education, but if she did not clear the matter up, it
was because she considered there was not all that necessity.

She bought a T-bone steak, and asked him round.   76

"What," she asked, "should we do with Clay I am a widow as you know   77
and you was his father's friend."

Mr Stutchbury drew his moustache.   78
"We will see," he said, "when the time comes."   79
Then he folded his moist lips over a piece of yellow fat from the not- 80
so-tender T-bone steak.
When it was time, Mr Stutchbury thought up a letter to some fellow at   81
the Customs and Excise.

> Dear Archie (he composed),
>   This is to recommend the son of an old friend, Herb Skerritt, for many
> years in the Tramways, died in tragical circumstances—of cancer to be pre-
> cise . . .

(Clay, who of course opened the letter to see, got quite a shock from a   82
word his mother never on any account allowed to be used in the home.)

> . . . It is my duty and wish to further the interests of the above-mentioned
> boy. In brief, I would esteem it a favour if you could see your way taking him
> "under your wing". I do not predict wonders of young Skerritt, but am of
> the opinion, rather, that he is a decent, average lad. In any event wonders are
> not all that desirable, not in the Service anyway. It is the steady hand which
> pushes the pen a lifetime.
>   I will not expatiate further, but sent you my
>   Salaams!

The young lady whom Mr Stutchbury had persuaded to type the letter   83
had barely left the room, when his superior called, with the result that he
forgot to add as he intended: "Kindest regards to Mrs Archbold." Even
persons of influence have to consider the ground they tread on.

But Clay Skerritt started at the Customs, because Mr Archbold was not the   84
sort to refuse Mr Stutchbury the favour he asked. So Clay took the ferry,
mornings, in the stiff dark suit his mother had chosen. His long thin fingers
learned to deal in forms. He carried the papers from tray to tray. In time he
grew used to triplicate, and moistened the indelible before writing in his
long thin hand the details, and the details.
Clay Skerritt did not complain, and if he was ignored he had known   85
worse. For he was most certainly ignored, by the gentlemen who sat
amongst the trays of papers, by the young ladies of the Customs and
Excise, who kept their nails so beautifully, who took their personal towels
to the toilet, and giggled over private matters and cups of milky tea. If they
ever laughed at the junior in particular, at his tricky frame, his pimples,
and his stubble of hair, Clay Skerritt was not conscious of it. Why should
he be? He was born with inward-looking eyes.
That all was not quite in order, though, he began to gather from his   86
mother.

"When I am gone Clay," she said—it was the evening the sink got 87
blocked up, "you will remember how your mother was a messer but found
she only scraped the dishes into the sink because her mind was otherwise
engaged with you Clay your interests always some practical young lady
will rectify anything your mother ever did by good intention I would not
force you but only advise time is not to be ignored."

But on days when the wind blew black across the grey water Mrs Sker- 88
ritt might remark, peering out from the arbours of asparagus fern:

"Some young woman clever with her needle lighter-handed at the 89
pastry-board will make you forget your poor mum well it is the way."

Her son was bound to ignore what he could not be expected to believe. 90
He would take a look at the wedding group. All so solidly alive, the figures
appeared to announce a truth of which he alone could be the arbiter, just
as the great white shoe would still put out, into the distance, for destina-
tions of his choice.

His mother, however, continued in her mistaken attempts to celebrate 91
the passing of reality. There was the day she called, her voice intruding
amongst the objects which surrounded him:

"Take my grey costume dear up to the dry cleaner at the Junction tomato 92
sauce is fatal when a person is on the stoutish side."

Clay acted as he had been told. Or the streets were acting round him, 93
and the trams. It was a bright day. Metal sang. The brick homes were no
longer surreptitious, but opened up to disclose lives. In one window a
woman was looking into her armpit. It made Clay laugh.

At the cleaner's a lady finished a yarn with the young girl. The lady said 94
from alongside her cigarette:

"I'll leave you to it, Marj. I'm gunna make tracks for home and whip me 95
shoes off. My feet are hurting like hell."

Then the bell. 96

Clay was still laughing. 97

The young girl was looking down at the sheets of fresh brown paper, 98
through the smell of cleaning. She herself had a cleaned, pallid skin, with
pores.

"What's up," she asked, as the client continued laughing. 99

She spoke so very flat and polite. 100

"Nothing," he said, but added: "I think perhaps you are like my moth- 101
er."

Which was untrue, in a sense, because the girl was flat, still, and co- 102
lourless, whereas his mother was rotund, voluble, and at least several
tones of grey. But Clay had been compelled to say it.

The girl did not reply. She looked down at first, as though he had 103
overstepped the mark. Then she took the costume, and examined the spots
of tomato sauce.

"Ready tomorrow," she said. 104

"Go on!" 105

"Why not?" the girl replied. "We are a One-day." 106

But flat and absent she sounded. 107

Then Clay did not know why, but asked: "You've got something on your mind." 108

She said: "It's only that the sink got blocked yesterday evening." 109

It sounded so terribly grey, and she looking out with that expression of permanence. Then at once he knew he had been right, and that the girl at the dry cleaner's had something of his mother: it was the core of permanence. Then Clay got excited. For he did not believe in impermanence, not even when he watched the clods of earth tumble down on the coffin lid. Not while he was he. 110

So he said: "Tomorrow." 111

It sounded so firm, it was almost today. 112

Clay got used to Marj just as he had got used to his mum, only differently. They swung hands together, walking over the dead grass of several parks, or staring at animals in cages. They were already living together, that is, their silences intermingled. Each had a somewhat clammy palm. And if Marj spoke there was no necessity to answer, it was so flat, her remarks had the colour of masonite. 113

Marj said: "When I have a home of my own, I will turn out the lounge Fridays. I mean, there is a time and place for everything. There are the bedrooms too." 114

She said: "I do like things to be nice." 115

And: "Marriage should be serious." 116

How serious, Clay began to see, who had not told his mum. 117

When at last he did she was drying the apostle spoons, one of which she dropped, and he let her pick it up, on seeing that it was necessary for her to perform some therapeutic act. 118

"I am so glad Clay," she said, rather purple, after a pause, "I cannot wait to see this nice girl we must arrange some we must come to an agree there is no reason why a young couple should not hit it off with the mother-in-law if the home is large it is not so much temperament as the size of the home that causes friction." 119

Mrs Skerritt had always known herself to be reasonable. 120

"And Marj is so like you, Mum." 121

"Eh?" Mrs Skerritt said. 122

He could not explain that what was necessary for him, for what he had to do, was a continuum. He could not have explained what he had to do, because he did not know, not yet. 123

All Mrs Skerritt could say was: "The sooner we see the better we shall know." 124

So Clay brought Marj. Their hands were clammier that day. The plants were huge, casting a fuscous tinge on the shored-up house. 125

Mrs Skerritt looked out of the door. 126

"Is this," she said, "I am not yet not yet ready to see." 127

Clay told Marj she must go away, for that day at least, he would send for 128
her, then he took his mother inside.

Mrs Skerritt did not meet Marj again, except in the mirror, in which she 129
saw with something of a shock there is no such thing as permanence.

Shortly after she died of something. They said it was her ticker. 130

And Clay brought Marj to live in the house in which he had been born and 131
lived. They did not go on a honeymoon, because, as Marj said, marriage
should be serious. Clay hoped he would know what to do as they lay in the
bed Mum and Dadda had used. Lost in that strange and lumpy acre Clay
and Marj listened to each other.

But it was good. He continued going to the Customs. Once or twice he 132
pinched the lobe of Marj's ear.

"What's got into you?" she asked. 133

He continued going to the Customs. He brought her a Java sparrow in 134
a cage. It was a kind of love poem.

To which Marj replied: "I wonder if it's gunna scatter its seed on the 135
wall-to-wall. We can always spread a newspaper, though."

And did. 136

Clay went to the Customs. He sat at his own desk. He used his elbows 137
more than before, because his importance had increased.

"Take this letter away, Miss Venables," he said. "There are only two 138
copies. When I expected five. Take it away," he said.

Miss Venables pouted, but took it away. She, like everybody, saw that 139
something had begun to happen. They would watch Mr Skerritt, and wait
for it.

But Marj, she was less expectant. She accepted the houseful of fretwork, 140
the things the mother-in-law had put away—sets of string-coloured doilies
for instance, once she came across a stuffed canary in a cardboard box. She
did not remark, but accepted. Only once she failed to accept. Until Clay
asked:

"What has become of the photo?" 141

"It is in that cupboard," she said. 142

He went and fetched out the wedding group, and stuck it where it had 143
been, on a fretwork table. At least he did not ask why she had put the
photo away, and she was glad, because she would not have known what
to answer. The bits of your husband you would never know were bad
enough, but not to understand yourself was worse.

So Marj stuck to the carpet-sweeper, she was glad of the fluff under the 144
bed, she was glad of the pattern on the lino, the cartons of Crispies that she
bought—so square. Even light is solid when the paths lead inward. So she
listened to the carpet-sweeper.

All this time, she realized, something had been happening to Clay. For 145
one thing his hair had begun to grow. Its long wisps curled like feather

behind his ears. He himself, she saw, was not yet used to the silky daring of his hair, which formerly had pricked to order.

"Level with the lobes of the ears, Mr McGillivray, please," Clay would now explain.   146

McGillivray, who was old by this, and infallibly kind, always refrained from commenting.   147

So did the gentlemen at the Customs—it was far too strange. Even the young ladies, who had been prepared to giggle at first, got the shivers for something they did not understand.   148

Only when the hair had reached as far as Mr Skerritt's shoulders did Mr Archbold send for Clay.   149

"Is it necessary, Mr Skerritt?" his superior asked, who had the additional protection of a private office.   150

Clay replied: "Yes."   151

He stood looking.   152

He was allowed to go away.   153

His wife Marj decided there is nothing to be surprised at. It is the only solution. Even if the fretwork crackled, she would not hear. Even if the hanging basket sprouted hair instead of fern, she would not see. There were the chops she put in front of her husband always so nicely curled on the plate. Weren't there the two sides of life?   154

One evening Clay came up out of the terraced garden, where the snails wound, and the sea smells. He stood for some considerable time in front of his parents' wedding group. The great shoe, or boat, or bridge, had never appeared so structural. Looking back he seemed to remember that this was the occasion of his beginning the poem, or novel, or regurgitation, which occupied him for the rest of his life.   155

Marj was certain that that was the evening he closed the door.   156

She would lie and call: "Aren't you gunna come to bed, Clay?"   157

Or she would stir at the hour when the sheets are greyest, when the air trembles at the withheld threat of aluminium, Marj would ungum her mouth to remark: "But Clay, the alarm hasn't gone off yet!"   158

From now on it seemed as though his body never stayed there long enough to warm the impression it left on the bed. She could hardly complain, though. He made love to her twice a year, at Christmas, and at Easter, though sometimes at Easter they might decide against—there was the Royal Agricultural Show, which is so exhausting.   159

All this is beside the point. It was the sheets of paper which counted, on which Clay wrote, behind the door of that little room which his wife failed to remember, it was soon so long since she had been inside. One of the many things Marj Skerritt learned to respect was another person's privacy.   160

So Clay wrote. At first he occupied himself with objects, the mysterious life which inanimacy contains. For several years in the beginning he was occupied with this.   161

. . . the table standing continues standing its legs so permanent of course you can take an axe and swing it cut into the flesh as Poles do every once in a while then the shriek murder murder but mostly nothing disturbs the maps the childhood journeys on the frozen wave of wooden water no boat whether wood or iron when you come to think satin either ever sails from A to B except in the mind of the passenger so the table standing standing under an electric bulb responds unlikely unless to determination or desperation of a Polish kind . . .

One night Clay wrote: "I have never observed a flowerpot intimately 162 until now its hole is fascinating the little down of green moss it is of greater significance than what is within though you can fill it if you decide to if you concentrate long enough . . .

Up till now he had not turned his attention to human beings, though he 163 had been surrounded by them all his life. In actual fact he did not turn his attention to them now, he was intruded on. And Lova was not all that human, or not at first, a presence rather, or sensation of possession.

That night Clay got the hiccups, he was so excited, or nervous. The 164 reverberations were so metallic he failed to hear his wife Marj, her grey voice: "Aren't you gunna come to bed, Clay?"

Lova was, by comparison, a greenish yellow, of certain fruits, and plant- 165 flesh.

"Lova Lova Lova," he wrote first, to try it out. 166

He liked it so much it surprised him it had not come to him before. He 167 could have sat simply writing the name, but Lova grew more palpable.

. . . her little conical breasts at times ripening into porepores detachable by sleight of hand or windy days yet so elusive fruit and shoes distributed amongst the grass . . .

In the beginning Lova would approach from behind glass, her skin had 168 that faint hothouse moisture which tingles on the down of ferns, her eyes a ferny brown that complemented his own if he had known. But he knew no more than gestures at first, the floating entanglement of hair in mutual agreement, the slight shiver of skin passing over skin. She would ascend and descend the flights of stone steps, inhabiting for a moment the angles of landings of old moss-upholstered stone. The leaves of the monstera deliciosa sieved her at times into a dispersed light. Which he alone knew how to re-assemble. On rare occasions their mouths would almost meet, at the bottom of the garden, where the smell of rotting was and the liquid manure used to stand, which had long since dried up. She was not yet real, and might never be. No. He would make her. But there were the deterrents. The physical discords.

Marj said: "My hands are that chapped I must ask Mr Todd's advice. 169 You can enjoy a chat with a chemist, doctors are most of them too busy pushing you out."

And Lova got the herpes. Clay could not look at her at first. As she sat 170 at her own little table, taking the fifteen varieties of pills, forcing them into her pig's snout, Lova would smile still, but it was sad. And soon the sore had become a scab. He could not bring himself to approach. And breath, besides.

For nights and nights Clay could not write a word. Or to be precise, he wrote over several nights: ". . . a drying and a dying . . ." 171

If he listened, all he could hear was the rustle of Lova's assorted pills, the ruffling of a single sterile date-palm, the sound of Marj turning in the bed. 172

Then it occurred to his panic the shored-up house might break open. It was so rotten, so dry. He could not get too quickly round the table, scattering the brittle sheets of paper. Motion detached itself from his feet in the shape of abrupt, leather slippers. Skittering to reach the door. 173

Clay did not, in fact, because Lova he now saw locking locking locked it, popping the key afterwards down between. 174

Lova laughed. And Clay stood. The little ripples rose up in her throat, perhaps it was the cold key, and spilled over, out of her mouth, her wet mouth. He knew that the private parts of babies tasted as tender as Lova's mouth. 175

He had never tried. But suspected he must. 176

She came to him. 177

"Bum to you!" Lova said. 178

She sat in his lap then, and with his free hand he wrote, the first of many white nights: "At last my ryvita has turned to velveeta life is no longer a toast-rack." 179

"Golly," said Lova, "what it is to be an educated feller! Honest, Clay, it must be a great satisfaction to write, if only to keep one of your hands occupied." 180

She laughed again. When he had his doubts. Does every face wear the same expression unless it is your own? He would have liked to look at the wedding group, to verify, but there were all those stairs between, and darkness. All he could hear was the sound of Marj breaking wind. Marj certainly had said at breakfast: "It is the same. Whatever the manufacturers tell you, that is only to sell the product." 181

But Lova said: "It is different, Clay, as different as cumquats from pomegranates. You are the differentest of all perhaps. I could lap up the cream of your genius." 182

She did, in fact, look at moments like a cat crouched in his lap, but would close at once, and open like a knife. 183

"I would eat you," she repeated, baring her pointed teeth, when he had thought them broad and spaced, as in Mum or Marj. 184

Although he was afraid, he wrote with his free right hand: "I would not trust a razor-blade to any but my own . . ." 185

When Lova looked it over. 186

"Shoot!" she said. "That is what I am!" 187

He forgot about her for a little, for writing down what he had to write.   188

. . . Lova sat in my lap smelling of crushed carrot tops she has taken the frizz out of her hair but cannot make it smell less green I would not trust her further than without meaning to cast aspersions you can't trust even your own thoughts past midnight . . .

"Chip Chip Chip chipped off his finger," Lova said. "Anyway it begins   189
with C."

"Oh dear,"C began to cry. "Oh dear dear dear oh Lova!"   190

"When does D come in?" she asked.   191

"D isn't born," he said, "and pretty sure won't be. As for A, A is in bed.   192
No," he corrected. "A am not."

Suddenly he wished he was.   193

He realised he was eye to eye with Lova their lashes grappling together   194
in gummy agreement but melancholy to overflowing. They were poured into each other.

After that, Clay finished, for the night at least, and experienced the great   195
trauma of his little empty room, for Lova had vanished, and there were only the inkstains on his fingers to show that she had even been there.

There was nothing for it now but to join Marj in the parental bed, where   196
he wondered whether he would ever be able to rise again. He was cold, cold.

Actually Marj turned over and said: "Clay, I had an argument with Mr   197
Tesoriero over the turnips. I told him you couldn't expect the public to buy them flabby."

But Clay slept, and in fact he did not rise, not that morning, the first in   198
many years, when the alarm clock scattered its aluminum trays all over the house.

Clay Skerritt continued going to the Customs. They had got used to him by   199
then, even to his hair, the streaks in it.

He realised it was time he went to McGillivray's again, but some young   200
dago came out, and said:

"Nho! Nho! McGillivray gone. Dead. How many years? Five? Six?   201

So Clay Skerritt went away.   202

It was natural enough that it should have happened to McGillivray. Less   203
natural were the substances. The pretending houses. The asphalt which had lifted up.

Then he saw the pointed heel, caught in the crack, wrenching at it. He   204
saw the figure. He saw. He saw.

When she turned round, she said: 205

"Yes, It's all very well. For you. With square heels. Bum bums."   206

Wrenching at her heel all the while.   207

"But Lova," he said, putting out his hands.   208

She was wearing a big-celled honeycomb sweater.   209

"Oh, yes!" she said.   210
And laughed.   211
"If that's how you feel," he answered.   212
"If that's how I *feel!*"   213
His hands were shaking, and might have caught in the oatmeal wool.   214
"I'm not gunna stand around exchanging words with any long-haired   215
nong in the middle of Military Road. Not on yours!"
"Be reasonable," he begged.   216
"What is reasonable!?" she asked.   217
He could not tell. Nor if she had asked: what is love?   218
"Aren't you going to know me then?" he said.   219
"I know you," she said, sort of flat—two boards could not have come   220
together with greater exactitude.
"And it is time," she said, "to go."   221
Jerking at her stuck heel.   222
"I've come here for something," he remembered. "Was it birdseed?"   223
"Was it my Aunt Fanny!"   224
Then she got her heel free and all the asphalt was crackling up falling   225
around them in scraps of torn black tinkly paper.
If he could have explained that love cannot be explained.   226
All the while ladies were going in and out, strings eating into their   227
fingers together with their rings. One lady had an alsatian, a basket sus-
pended from its teeth, it did not even scent the trouble.
It was Saturday morning. Clay went home.   228
That evening, after they had finished their spaghetti on toast, because   229
they were still paying off the Tecnico, Marj said:
"Clay, I had a dream."   230
"No!" he shouted.   231
Where could he go? There was nowhere now.   232
Except on the Monday there was the Customs and Excise. He could not   233
get there quick enough. To sharpen his pencils. To move the paper-clips to
the other side of the ink-eraser.
When what he was afraid might happen, happened.   234
Lova had followed him to the Customs.   235
The others had not spotted it yet, for it could have been any lady passing   236
the day at the Customs in pursuit of her unlawful goods. Only no lady
would have made so straight for Mr Skerritt's desk, nor would she have
been growing from her big-celled oatmeal sweater quite so direct as Lova
was.
She had those little, pointed, laughing teeth.   237
"Well," she opened, "you didn't reckon on this."   238
She was so certain of herself by now, he was afraid she might jump out   239
of her jumper.
He sat looking down, at the letter from Dooley and Mann, Import   240
Agents, re the Bechstein that got lost.
"Listen, Lova," he advised, "Not in here. It won't help find the piano."   241

"Pianner? A fat lot of pianner! You can't play that one on me." 242

"You may be right," he answered. 243

"Right!" she said. "Even if I wasn't. Even if I was flippin' wrong!" 244

She put her handbag on the desk. 245

"If anyone's gunna play, I'm the one," she said. 246

Sure enough the old black upright slid around the corner from behind 247
Archbold's glassed-in office, followed by the little leather-upholstered
stool, from which the hair was bursting out. Lova seemed satisfied. She
laughed, and when she had sat down, began to dish out the gay sad jazz.
Playing and playing. Her little hands were jumping and frolicking on their
own. The music playing out of every worm hole in the old, sea-changed
piano.

Clay looked up, to see Archbold looking down. Miss Titmuss had taken 248
her personal towel, and was having trouble with her heels as she made her
way towards the toilet.

When Lova got up. She was finished. Or not quite. She began to drum 249
with her bum on the greasy, buckled-up rashers of keys of the salt-cured
old piano.

"There!" she shouted. 250

She came and sat on the corner of his desk. She had never been so 251
elastic. It was her rage of breathing. He was unable to avoid the pulse of
her suspender, winking at him from her thigh.

One or two other of the Customs officials had begun to notice, he ob- 252
served desperately through the side-curtains of his hair.

So he said: "Look here, Lova, a scene at this stage will make it well nigh 253
impossible for me to remain in the Service. And what will we do without
the pension? Marj must be taken into account. I mean to say, it is the
prestige as much as the money. Otherwise, we have learnt to do on tea and
bread."

Lova laughed then. 254

"Ha! *Ha! Ha!*" 255

There is no way of writing it but how it was written on the wall. For it 256
was. It got itself printed up on the wall which ran at right angles to Archbold's office.

Clay sat straight, straight. His adam's apple might not endure it much 257
longer.

"Scenes are so destructive," he said, or begged. 258

So his mum had told him. 259

"If that is what you want," said Lova, "you know I was never one for 260
holding up procedure for the sake of filling in a form."

And she ripped it off the pad from under his nose. Her hands were so 261
naked, and could get a whole lot nakeder. He was afraid he might be
answerable.

"I would never suggest," she shouted, "that the pisspot was standing 262
right end up when it wasn't."

But he had to resist, not so much for personal reasons as for the sake of 263 public decorum, for the honour of the Department. He had to protect the paper-clips.

Because their hands were wrestling, troubling the desk. Him and Lova. 264
At any moment the carton might burst open. At any. It happened quite quickly, breathily, ending in the sigh of scatteration.

"I will leave you for now," she said, getting off the corner of the desk, 265
and pulling down her sweater, which had rucked up.

Almost every one of his colleagues had noticed by this, but all had the 266
decency to avoid passing audible judgment on such a very private situation.

When it was over a little while, Miss Titmuss got down and gathered up 267
the paper-clips, because she was sorry for Mr Skerritt.

He did not wait to thank or explain, but took his hat, treading carefully 268
to by-pass the eyes, and caught the ferry to the other side.

Marj said: "Aren't you early, Clay? Sit on the veranda a while. I'll bring you 269
a cuppa, and a slice of that pound cake, it's still eatable I think."

So he sat on the veranda, where his mother used to sit and complain, 270
and felt the southerly get inside his neckband, and heard the date-palm starting up. Sparrows gathered cautiously.

Marj said: "Clay, if you don't eat up, it'll be tea." 271

You can always disregard, though, and he went inside the room, which 272
he did not even dread. There she was, sitting in the other chair, in the oatmeal sweater. Her back turned. Naturally.

"Lova," he began. 273

Then she came towards him, and he saw that she herself might sink in 274
the waters of time she spread before him cunningly the nets of water smelling of nutmeg over junket the steamy mornings and the rather shivery afternoons.

If he did not resist. 275

She was just about as resistant as water not the tidal kind but a glad 276
upward plume of water rising and falling back as he put his hands gently lapping lapping. She was so gentle.

Marj began to knock on the door. 277

"Tea's getting cold, Clay," she announced. 278

It was, too. That is the way of things. 279

"I made you a nice devilled toast." 280

She went away, but returned, and held her ear to the dry rot. 281

"Clay?" she asked. "Don't you mind?" 282

Marj did not like to listen at doors because of her regard for privacy. 283

"Well," she said, "I never knew you to act like this." 284

It could have been the first time in her life that Marj had opened a door. 285

Then she began to scream. She began to create. It was unlike her. 286

She could not see his face because of all that hair. The hair and the 287
boards between them were keeping it a secret.

"This is something I never bargained for," she cried.   288
    For the blood had spurted out of the leg of the table. Just a little.   289
    And that old shoe. He lay holding a white shoe.   290
    "I never ever saw a shoe!" she moaned. "Of all the junk she put away,   291
just about every bit of her, and canaries and things, never a shoe!"
    As Clay lay.   292
    With that stiff shoe.   293
    "I don't believe it!" Marj cried.   294
    Because everyone knows that what isn't isn't, even when it is.   295

STUDY QUESTIONS

1. Analyze Clay's relationship with his mother. In what ways is she a positive figure? How does she fail him? How does he fail her?
2. What does his mother's explanation of her child's name tell us about her life? How does it affect the child's life? What wider associations does it suggest? Why is it the title of the story?
3. Compare and contrast Marj and Lova. How is Marj like Clay's mother? What aspects of Clay's life and needs do Marj and Lova represent?
4. Discuss the theme of conformity versus nonconformity in this story.
5. Discuss this story as a study of the artist and the risks he or she runs in trying to address the demands of the creative imagination.

NEW GUINEA

◎ KAMA KERPI

Kama Kerpi (b. ?) is a graduate of the University of Papua New Guinea. A dramatist whose Voices on the Raide *was performed by the National Theatre Company, Kerpi is also an activist who works in his native Chimbu region to prevent clan wars.*

In Papua New Guinea, the intrusion of Western influence was also marked by the appearance of Western consumer goods, metamorphosed by the native population as "cargo." Western colonization also resulted in an increased materialism in Papua New Guinea. In "Cargo," Abram refers to this penetration of capitalist patterns of consumption as "madness."

Cargo

1

"Cargo . . . cargo is what our people want. It has thrown everyone into madness," said Abram. "We must act now or never," he added as an afterthought, taking off the bandage around Cain's arm.

2

"It was as if a man who was eating a meal prepared by his wife suddenly jumped up with anger on hearing from his friend that at midday his wife was caught opening her legs to her secret lover. But I cannot understand why the white men are so greedy as to keep the secret to themselves," responded Cain, closing his eyes as Abram pressed his fingers around the boil on his right arm. "We are the proper owners and demand that secret to be torn open. All those endless debates at the men's house has brought us nowhere."

3

"It must be like this boil," said Abram, pressing Cain's boil a little harder. "I mean, the secret of our dead people's cargo."

4

"Someone has got to tear it open." He felt the pain shoot through his arm spasmodically, and he winced, feeling the blood pulsing around the boil. The pain was terrible, and he closed his eyes several times. The desire and frustration to obtain dead people's cargo must be like this boil that was bulging with pus. Maybe to certain people the secret was like a pain in their hearts, growing as their anxieties increased. As these thoughts entered his mind, Cain felt like driving a sharp nail into the centre of the boil to force out all the pus and let in air.

"Last week Bola's brother, returning from a coastal town, claimed that   5 he brought with him the secret of obtaining cargo from our dead people. If what he says is true then it's the holy water and the Bible that is keeping us blind. And to think that the Church has prevented us from acquiring our property. It's a little hard to believe."

"Bullshit with the Church," said Cain as he ran his eyes up and down   6 where new boils were developing on his arm. Maybe all the churches were like those contagious boils, he told himself. "They preach 'thou shall not steal', and yet they steal under our nose," he added.

Cain had never before spoken against the churches. Now that he was   7 beginning to, the ugliness the boil created on his arm must have had some effect. Since the boil had been giving him a lot of physical pain he had begun to be more aware of another type of pain that occurs in the soul—a spiritual pain. But then all pains can be cured, and this suggested that there must be some hope in store.

"They preach the Ten Commandments, yet they soil their hands in   8 things that are not theirs," said Abram. "We have become slaves to their teachings. Our people say when an enemy smiles at you his heart curses you and wishes you ill fate."

Abram, having finished bandaging Cain's arm, averted his eyes to the   9 far ridges where his people lived and farmed. You are all blind, ignorant fools, he told himself. It's a pity they do not realize that it's the Church that's robbing them. The pity he had for them turned around to face him. This created a sense of mission that crept into his heart, and he began to wrestle with it silently. Sure enough, pity had created hope and hope in turn increased his anxieties.

"Abram . . . what can we do?" said Cain.   10

"Just you answer me one question," said Abram so quickly it was as if   11 an idea that had crept into his mind was beginning to leave him. "If a man came at you with a spear intending to kill you, what would you do?" Abram moved closer to Cain's ear and almost whispered, "You would not stand and watch . . . at least I wouldn't."

"I wouldn't either . . . I would fight."   12

"Cain, you have got the point . . . you have got it. You defeat him by   13 simply taking the spear from him. And that's what I have been thinking about. If the Church is using the holy water and the Bible to blind us, we make use of them to defeat it." Abram looked into Cain's face and blinked several times in the noon sun. He looked uneasy; he was planning something, and whatever it was it had to be checked twice if not three times.

"Bola's brother was simply saying that you defeat the Church by its own   14
weapons. Bola must know more, at least the first steps of obtaining cargo."

"Yes, he must. You know his sister died last week. He is playing mar-   15
bles over there. Go and bring him over. He might need some marbles."

Cain went over and brought back Bola.   16

"Do you need some marbles?" said Abram, rattling the marbles in his   17
pockets. "You can have twenty. But before you have them, tell me about
this secret your brother brought with him."

The question had taken Bola by surprise. A look of hate appeared on his   18
face, and deep inside he sneered and wished that they would take a bee-
line to hell. Bola's sister had died not long ago and he was planning to
catch the Reverend Father stealing the cargo. And what his sister gave
belonged to his family. He had just lost a game of marbles and the twenty
marbles in Abram's pocket would help him to get his own back. From his
confused mind a saying began to take shape and then hammer at him. His
father had always said that when a man dances at the first rains of the wet
season he is foolish, because the storms that will be coming will kill him.

"It's a mission. Our people need help in the dark; we must lead the way.   19
We must be the beacon in the night," said Cain with emphasis, when he
realized that Bola was not going to answer their question.

"And we can only do it by finding the secret of obtaining it . . . I mean   20
the cargo," added Abram. He realized that he had to convince Bola, otherwise he had to make guesswork and start from there.

"You know ten pigs await anyone who discovers the secret," said Cain.   21
"That's a lifetime wealth."

"Really? But I do not need pigs. My father has got a lot of them." Bola's   22
tribe and Cain's and Abram's tribe had always been enemies. And Bola had
not forgotten that their young men had killed a close relative of his father.
He gave them a sullen look and went away.

"Greedy bastard. Son of a pig," muttered Abram.   23

"Just think, ten pigs. I will ask my grandfather, who died last year, to   24
help me. He used to like me above my other brothers and sisters. Last
week my father slaughtered a pig near the old man's grave. My father
requested him to watch over my steps."

"That is probably the reason why you scored good marks in your school-   25
work. I used to be better than you before." Abram then looked around to
ensure that no one was about and continued, almost whispering: "A few
days ago my father killed a pig in my grandmother's name, requesting that
she should let my mother bear one last child in her old age; at least a boy
to follow my footsteps in learning white man's knowledge. Our people
have a saying that if you have a brother then in any fight your back is
always protected—of course, you can apply it to anything."

Cain watched a small boy walk towards the bell. The boy lifted up a big   26
object and hit the bell. It was time for class; if they were late a big cane
awaited them. Taking a deep breath he said, "I have got a plan we might

work at. We will talk about it after class. It may take a long time before the secret is in our hands."

"I think my plans are similar to yours. We can defeat them by their own weapons. When we discover the secret we will hand it over to the elders and at the same time claim our ten pigs." 27

"Yeah, we will do that." 28

The two boys walked towards the classroom, privately making great plans to find the secret of obtaining cargo. At times they were carried off into fantasy. 29

The half moon crept languidly from behind some low hills and poured its silver lights over the mission station. It was as if milk was poured on a table. The moonbeams danced on the leaves and the blades of grass like angels celebrating the homecoming of a prodigal son. The corrugated roof of the church reflected a greyish white colour, and in the silent atmosphere it resembled a mammoth statue. The stars twinkled in magnitude like countless Easter candles, while the trees stood in mute silence casting vivid shadows on the lawn. 30

Two dark figures darted across the playground in mortal hurry as if they were the last species making for Noah's Ark. They made for the church and were immediately swallowed up in the dark. Far up at the altar was a glow of light that burnt day and night. It was symbolic of God's presence. They felt secure. 31

"Hold the cross and the Bible. I will go and get some holy water. It's at the back of the altar. I won't be long." Abram's voice trailed off into silence. Giving the cross and the Bible to Cain, he vanished into the darkness. 32

Cain waited with the cross in his left hand and the Bible in his right. A good five minutes must have elapsed. His legs were beginning to pain a little, and the frigid air of the night began to send waves of shiver up and down his body. "What is taking him so long?" he asked himself. He made a firm decision that he would have to go for Abram if he didn't come in the next few minutes. But he warned himself that their job must be fruitful. The darkness seemed to be alive with moving figures. They were beginning to test his courage. "The mission must come to success," he shouted silently to himself, closing his eyes. "It's imperative that the elders have the secret of obtaining our dead people's cargo. We must not fail. Our people have been fooled by the white man. It must come to success," he whispered, impulsively folding his fist. 33

"Cain . . . where are you?" It was Abram's voice. For a moment Cain was taken aback. 34

"I am here. Did you get the holy water?" 35

"Sure I did!" exclaimed Abram, walking towards Cain's voice. "Cain." 36

"What?" 37

"I also got some wine!" 38

"But why wine? You will spoil our plans with . . ." 39

"Hold your tongue. Did they not say blood and water ran down his 40
body while hanging on the cross? I have perfected the plan by bringing in
wine."

"Yes . . . yes, you are right. I am beginning to have illusions of our kin 41
dancing to the beat of the kundus!"

"Well, stop it then. Let's get to work and have your daydreams come 42
true," said Abram.

Far into the night their ears tuned to a monotonous cry of a night bird. 43

"That's the right moment. The dead people are stirring alive in their 44
graves. We must track Reverend Father; otherwise he will elude our
trap." Abram's voice became inaudible as he fiddled in his hip pocket for
a match. He struck one and immediately it burnt, a yellow flame with a
ring of blue at the burning end. Cain tore a page from the Bible and set
it on fire. Immediately the light cast horror figures on the cement wall of
the church. Then they set the Bible down, the cross immediately on top
of it.

"Let's begin the ceremony," whispered Cain, holding up the light. 45

Abram poured a few drops of holy water into the cup of his hand and 46
dripped it around the cross and the Bible. The church had not been swept,
and, as the drops fell, round balls formed a ring around the objects. Then
Abram drank half the wine, making the sign of the cross very slowly. He
passed the bottle to Cain, who had not recovered from mumbling some
prayers. Cain then began imitating Abram, and when he emptied the last
drop of the contents he placed the bottle in front of him and, closing his
eyes, awaited Abram to proceed with the prayers.

"The lord is my shepherd," began Abram, "of whom should I be afraid? 47
If an enemy—ah—ah . . ."

"Encamps against," prompted Cain. 48

". . . Encamps against me, let him tremble and fall. If a friend is deceit- 49
ful, let him grow hairs in his eyes. O Lord, we hear; Cain, son of Koirap,
and me, Abram, son of Sua, request you, in the presence of the darkness
and the silence of the valley, the moon above, and the dark ridges awaiting
dawn, to help us track down Reverend Father. Open our eyes, we pray,
and let the riches pass on to the rightful owners. We seek the guidance of
Mary and all the saints and angels in heaven. In the name of the Father,
Son and the Holy Ghost."

"Amen," they chorused. A smile of satisfaction hovered on their lips. 50

"You hold the cross, and if any devils attack us put the cross in front of 51
you and walk towards them and say, 'Begone, devil.' I will hold the Bible."
As Cain's voice trailed off into silence, they got up and walked to the back
of the church.

Immediately behind the church were the graveyards of both missionar- 52
ies and devout Catholics who demanded before their deaths that they
should be buried near the house of the Lord. It was affirmed that their

spirits would make an agonizing journey to the house of the Lord if they were buried in the tribal graveyards scattered on the hills and the ridges. The graveyard at the back of the church was well kept, with low flowers bubbling in profusion, like drippings on a hot frying pan. A few pine trees grew, with rich green natural needles. In the moonlight, they stood almost terrified, as if awaiting a death sentence. The Reverend Father's house stood parallel to the church with a neat lawn in between. His toilet was in line with his house, and because it was a few yards from the graves they had been suspicious about it. It was thought to be the passageway to the dead people's cargo beneath the graves. Previously, Cain and Abram had inspected the toilet and were convinced that the wooden hole was a passageway to the underworld, and if they followed Reverend Father they were bound to catch him tricking their grandfathers. Then they would explain where the cargo really went.

"We will wait under that coffee tree. It's near the toilet. Now, remember to recite the Hail Mary when your ears track the slightest movement!" They hurried across the lawn, kicking a few dried leaves. Sitting under the coffee tree, they waited tensely as if ready to pounce at their prey. The broad green leaves stole most of the moonlight but provided the best hiding place. And there they waited. The seconds crept into minutes and the minutes into hours. The half moon crept away from behind the *nop* trees. An instinctive fear of failing crept into them, threatening to smash their optimism to shatters. 53

Suddenly their vagrant thoughts were distracted by a door opening and closing. It came from the direction of Reverend Father's house. The beam of a flashlight danced wildly on the lawn and then took its place in front of a figure. For Cain and Abram excitement shot through them, setting their hearts in vibrant tattoo. The fluid language of Reverend Father's movements suggested that he was hurrying on an errand. A smile of satisfaction appeared on their lips. He was hurrying to receive the goods, they told themselves. 54

Cain and Abram immediately held the cross and the Bible in front of them and whispered as many Hail Marys as they could before he got any nearer. 55

"Do not lose sight of him," whispered Cain when he paused after the fifth quick Hail Mary. 56

"Em," grunted Abram with a tinkle of anger for having been interrupted in his prayer. The Reverend Father stood for a brief moment outside the toilet and, after looking around, gave the door a push and walked in. The door let out a groaning sound. The flashlight threw its light, splinters of which escaped through the cracks and cast long golden figures on the lawn. 57

"What do we do? Should we give him a few minutes more? Or go in after him?" 58

"We will give him a few more minutes. Say about two minutes. When we think he is down the toilet we will follow him. We will then tell our kin why their cargo does not reach our hands." 59

"You are right. We will tell them that it's the white man's Bible and holy   60
water that has kept us blind."

"What's that over there?" asked Abram in a startled manner, his hands   61
impulsively pointing at two dark figures crawling on their bellies towards
the back of the toilet.

"Hell, who could they be?" said Cain. His voice was barely audible, as   62
if questioning himself.

"Look! They are peeping in through the cracks!" The last word had not   63
left Abram's mouth when the door was literally thrown open. The two
figures sprinted away as if they had witnessed their dead grandfathers
coming back to life. Meanwhile the Reverend Father flashed the light and
surveyed the vicinity. For a brief moment the light fell on the coffee tree
where Cain and Abram were hiding, and seemed to stop. Cain sweated
profusely, while Abram threw open his lap-lap and urinated from fear.
Fear of being caught crept over their desire to see the mission come to
success. Both grieved but sighed when the Reverend Father hurried away,
buttoning his long trousers, looking over his shoulder as if to check if
anyone was following him.

"It's their fault. They spoiled our plans. Did you see fear on the Rever-   64
end Father's face against the moonlight?" said Cain.

"He hurried away as if he was discovered," replied Abram. "Let us go   65
and find out who spoiled our plans."

Cain and Abram dashed to the back of the church. There they encoun-   66
tered Bola and his friend Mickle. They were sitting trying to get back their
breath after the fast run. Cain came forward and stood over Bola with a
menacing look on his face.

"Why did you spoil our trap . . . you toothless ones?" he rattled as   67
anger and bitterness flooded through him.

Bola was surprised to see Cain and Abram. They must have been after   68
my sister's cargo, he told himself. If they wanted a fight he would give
them one, but for the moment he would control his anger.

"We were after my sister's cargo." He spoke calmly, fighting to control   69
his anger.

"But you spoiled our trap . . . stupid," came back Cain's reply.   70

"You were out to steal my sister's cargo . . . you fat thief."   71

"You cow. Did not my father push you to the ridges during the dark   72
days of tribal warfare? Your father is a weak bull."

A new madness took hold of Bola. An angry look appeared on his face.   73
He stood up. His eyelids narrowed, his molars came together, his fingers
folded and the muscles around his arms tightened. He shook a little. Bola
could not recall anyone calling his father a weak man. And no one dared
to. How could anyone dare call his father a weak man? He was the father
of the seven clans living on the ridge. He was well spoken of, and when he
was at war with another tribe his name would blow with the wind. How
could anyone dare speak false about his father?

"Your father impregnated a pig . . . you are their product," shouted   74
Bola.

This sparked a fight. At first they stood their ground and exchanged a   75
few punches, then they grabbed each other, and as they rolled over and
over on the grass they exchanged abuse. Both called upon the art of throwing each other that they had learned from older men. And at times wild
fists were thrown only to scare the other.

Abram watched Cain. At first he seemed to do well, avoiding Bola's wild   76
blows. But with boils all over his arms he would not last long.

"Let's stop them," said Abram when he realized that Bola was gaining   77
the upper hand. It was some time before they pulled the two apart, and it
was some time before the fighters calmed down from making attempts at
getting each other.

"Listen, we are all after the secret of obtaining our dead people's cargo.   78
Our people say that when a man gets up before the sun to work in the
gardens he will get a lot of work done. Of course, he should shake off
sleep, otherwise he would be a foolish man. I think we have been foolish.
We must have some teamwork." Turning to Bola he said, "How about
some teamwork?"

"We will think about it first," replied Bola grudgingly.   79

They were all embittered by repeated failures. But another adventure   80
awaited them. They must track the Reverend Father stealing their cargo.
And all the wealth flowing into the hands of the white Reverend Father
would arrest their interest. Maybe tomorrow night they would work as a
team.

The glamour of the moonlight on the quiet mission station was enchant-   81
ing and allayed their failure, moving a faint excitement in them. They
would not abandon themselves to despair, because tomorrow was a new
day, and there another adventure awaited them. The moon was high
above, smiling. Nothing changed.

STUDY QUESTIONS

1. Who do Abram and Cain believe hold the secret to obtaining "cargo"
   and how do they propose to discover this secret?
2. Reading the story as a fable on the loss of native culture, how is the
   white Reverend Father implicated in this "theft"?
3. The story portrays a "misunderstanding" of how goods are produced.
   The young characters believe that the "cargo" comes from their "dead
   people" but that white men are keeping the secret for this production
   from them. Discuss Abram and Cain's "misunderstanding" as a critique of first world exploitation of third world resources. How do the
   comic elements complicate this political reading?

ALLEN CURNOW

Allen Curnow (b. 1911), son of a clergyman, studied for the Anglican ministry but decided on a career in journalism instead. He worked for a year in London, visited the United States, then settled down at the University of Auckland to teach English. From his first book of poems, Valley of Decision *(1933), onward, his work has been preoccupied with New Zealand scenes, themes, and history. His poems are often praised for their subtle techniques and vivid images.*

The Skeleton of the Great Moa[1] in the Canterbury Museum, Christchurch

The skeleton of the moa on iron crutches
Broods over no great waste; a private swamp
Was where this tree grew feathers once, that hatches
Its dusty clutch, and guards them from the damp.

interesting failure to adapt on islands,   5
Taller but not more fallen than I, who come
Bone to his bone, peculiarly New Zealand's.
The eyes of children flicker round this tomb

Under the skylights, wonder at the huge egg
Found in a thousand pieces, pieced together   10

---

1. Great Moa: *Large, extinct, flightless bird of New Zealand.*

But with less patience than the bones that dug
In time deep shelter against ocean weather:

Not I, some child, born in a marvellous year,
Will learn the trick of standing upright here.

STUDY QUESTIONS

1. This poem (a SONNET composed of three QUARTRAINS and a concluding COUPLET) begins with an image of the skeleton of the moa, a giant bird once found all over New Zealand and now extinct. In what ways does the comparison between the moa and the narrator work?
2. The narrator is standing among children in the museum. What are his hopes for the younger generation?
3. New Zealand is part of the Antipodes, that is, the side of the world opposite (or upside down) from Europe, specifically England, the colonizing country. With this in mind, explain the multiple meanings implied in the poem's last line.

◎ JANET FRAME

Janet Frame (b. 1924) is a fourth-generation New Zealander well known as a novelist, short story writer, and poet. She trained as a teacher, then spent eight years hospitalized for emotional and mental problems. She traveled in the United Kingdom and Europe before returning to New Zealand, where she is now an acclaimed writer. Frequently her fiction explores conflicts between a woman's sensibility, a yearning for more, and a diminished and unsupportive environment. Her works include a collection of stories, The Lagoon *(1951), and a novel,* Owls Do Cry *(1957).*

The Day of the Sheep

It should not have rained. The clothes should have been slapped warm and dry with wind and sun and the day not have been a leafless cloudy secret hard to understand. It is always nice to understand the coming and going of a day. Tell her, blackbird that pirrup-pirruped and rainwater that trickled down the kitchen window-pane and dirty backyard that oozed mud and housed puddles, tell her though the language be something she cannot construe having no grammar of journeys.

Why is the backyard so small and suffocating and untidy? On the rope 2 clothesline the washing hangs limp and wet, Tom's underpants and the sheets and my best tablecloth. We'll go away from here, Tom and me, we'll go some other place, the country perhaps, he likes the country but he's going on and on to a prize in Tatts and a new home, flat-roofed with blinds down in the front room and a piano with curved legs, though Tom's in the Dye Works just now, bringing home handkerchiefs at the end of each week, from the coats with no names on.

'Isn't it stealing Tom?' 3

'Stealing my foot, I tell you I've worked two years without a holiday.' 4 You see? Tom striving for his rights and getting them even if they turn out to be only a small anonymous pile of men's handkerchiefs, but life is funny and people are funny, laugh and the world laughs with you.

She opens the wash-house door to let the blue water out of the tubs, she 5 forgot all about the blue water, and then of all the surprises in the world there's a sheep in the wash-house, a poor sheep not knowing which way to turn, fat and blundering with the shy anxious look sheep have.

'Shoo Shoo.' 6

Sheep are silly animals they're so scared and stupid, they either stand 7 still and do nothing or else go round and round getting nowhere, when they're in they want out and when they're out they sneak in, they don't stay in places, they get lost in bogs and creeks and down cliffs, if only they stayed where they're put.

'Shoo Shoo.' 8

Scared muddy and heavy the sheep lumbers from the wash-house and 9 then bolts up the path, out the half-open gate on to the street and then round the corner out of sight, with the people stopping to stare and say well I declare for you never see sheep in the street, only people.

It should not have rained, the washing should have been dry and why did 10 the sheep come and where did it come from to here in the middle of the city?

A long time ago there were sheep (she remembers, pulling out the plug 11 so the dirty blue water can gurgle away, what slime I must wash more often why is everything always dirty) sheep, and I walked behind them with bare feet on a hot dusty road, with the warm steamy nobbles of sheep dirt getting crushed between my toes and my Father close by me powerful and careless, and the dogs padding along the spit dribbling from the loose corners of their mouths, Mac and Jock and Rover waiting for my Father to cry Way Back Out, Way Back Out. Tom and me will go some other place I think. Tom and me will get out of here.

She dries her hands on the corner of her sack apron. That's that. A 12 flat-roofed house and beds with shiny covers, and polished fire-tongs, and a picture of moonlight on a lake.

She crosses the backyard, brushing aside the wet clothes to pass. My   13
best tablecloth. If visitors come tonight I am sunk.

But no visitors only Tom bringing cousin Nora, while the rain goes off,   14
she has to catch the six o'clock bus at the end of the road. I must hurry I
must be quick it is terrible to miss something. Cousin Nora widowed
remarried separated and anxious to tell. Cousin Nora living everywhere
and nowhere chained to number fifty Toon Street it is somewhere you
must have somewhere even if you know you haven't got anywhere. And
what about Tom tied up to a little pile of handkerchiefs and the prize that
happens tomorrow, and Nance, look at her, the washing's still out and
wet, she is tired and flurried, bound by the fearful chain of time and the
burning sun and sheep and day that are nowhere.

'But of course Nance I won't have any dinner, you go on dishing up for   15
Tom while I sit here on the sofa.'

'Wait, I'll move those newspapers, excuse the muddle, we seem to be in   16
a fearful muddle.'

'Oh is that today's paper, no it's Tuesday's, just think on Tuesday Peter   17
and I were up in the north island. He wanted me to sell my house you
know, just fancy, he demanded that I sell it and I said not on your life did
you marry me for myself or for my house and he said of course he married
me for myself but would I sell the house, why I said, well you don't need
it now he said, we can live up north, but I do need it I've lived in it nearly
all of my life, it's my home, I live there.'

Cousin Nora, dressed in navy, her fleecy dark hair and long soft wobbly   18
face like a horse.

'Yes I've lived there all my life, so of course I said quite definitely no. Is   19
that boiled bacon, there's nothing I like better, well if you insist, just the
tiniest bit on a plate, over here will do, no no fuss, thank you. Don't you
think I was right about the house? I live there.'

What does Tom think? His mouth busies itself with boiled bacon while   20
his fingers search an envelope for the pink sheet that means Tatts results,
ten thousand pounds first prize, a flat-roofed house and statues in the
garden. No prize but first prize will do, Tom is clever and earnest, the
other fellows have tickets in Tatts, why not I the other fellows take handkerchiefs home and stray coats sometimes why not I and Bill Tent has a
modern house one of those new ones you can never be too interested in
where you live. Tom is go-ahead. In the front bedroom there's an orange
coloured bed-lamp, it's scorched a bit now but it was lovely when it
came, he won it with a question for a radio quiz, his name over the air
and all—

Name the planets and their distance from the sun.   21

Name the planets.   22

Oh the sun is terribly far away but of course there's only been rain   23
today, pirrup-pirruping blackbirds, how it rains and the sheep why I must
tell them about the sheep.

Nora leans forward, 'Nance you are dreaming, what *do* you think about   24
the house?'

'Oh, always let your conscience be your guide.'   25

(Wear wise saws and modern instances like a false skin a Jiminy Cricket   26
overcoat.)

'That's what I say too, your conscience, and that's why we separated,   27
you heard of course?'

Yes Nance knows, from Nora herself as soon as it happened Dear Nance   28
and Tom you'll hardly believe it but Peter and I have decided to go our own
ways, you and Tom are lucky you get on so well together no fuss about
where to live you don't know how lucky you are.

No fuss but lost, look at the house look at the kitchen, and me going   29
backwards and forwards carrying dishes and picking up newspapers and
dirty clothes, muddling backwards and forwards in little irrelevant journeys, but going backwards always, to the time of the sun and the hot dusty
road and a powerful father crying Way Back Out Way Back Out.

'Oh, Oh I must tell you, there was a sheep today in the wash-house.'   30

'A what?'   31

'A sheep. I don't know where he lived but I chased him away.'   32

'Oh I say, really, ha ha, it's a good job we've got somewhere to live, I in   33
my house (even though I had to break with Peter) and you and Tom in
yours.

'We *have* got somewhere to live haven't we, not like a lost sheep ha ha.   34
What's the matter Tom?'

'74898, not a win.'   35

The pink ticket thrust back quickly into the envelope and put on the   36
stand beside the wireless, beside the half-open packet of matches and the
sheaf of bills and the pile of race-books.

'Well, I'm damned, let's turn on the news, it's almost six.'   37

'Oh it's almost six and my bus!'   38

'So it is Nora.'   39

Quick it is terrible to lose something for the something you miss may be   40
something you have looked for all your life, in the north island and the
south island and the number fifty Toon Street.

'Goodbye and thank you for the little eat and you must come and see me   41
sometime and for goodness sake Nance get a perm or one of those cold
waves, your hair's at the end of its tether.'

Here is the news.   42

Quick goodbye then.   43

Why am I small and cramped and helpless why are there newspapers on   44
the floor and why didn't I remember to gather up the dirt, where am I
living that I'm not neat and tidy with a perm. Oh if only the whole of being
were blued and washed and hung out in the far away sun. Nora has
travelled she knows about things, it would be nice to travel if you knew
where you were going and where you would live at the end or do we ever

know, do we ever live where we live, we're always in other places, lost, like sheep, and I cannot understand the leafless cloudy secret and the sun of any day.

STUDY QUESTIONS

1. The story is told from Nance's point of view. Describe Nance's world. How does the rainy day further dramatize the dominant impressions conveyed about her setting?
2. Tatts is a lottery that Nance's husband, Tom, plays. Contrast Tom's present position and his hopes for the future if he wins with a Tatts ticket.
3. How do the differences between Nance's relationship with Tom and Nora's relationship with Peter relate to the story's theme? What is the theme?
4. Discuss the significance of the sheep in the washhouse as a figure from Nance's childhood and as a figure in her present life.

◎ PATRICIA GRACE

Patricia Grace (b. 1937) was born in Wellington. Her first book, Waiariki (1975), was the first collection of short stories published by a Maori woman writer. Her stories treat the intimate familial network of Maori society and portray the conflicts between its traditional communal values and the countervalues of modernization and the European settlers. Her writing, from within this imaginative construction of an indigenous world, views the historical intrusions of white settlement sharply and critically.

And So I Go

O ur son, brother, grandchild, you say you are going away from this place you   1
love, where you are loved. Don't go. We warm you. We give you strength, we
give you love.
These people are yours.
These hills, this soil, this wide stretch of sea.
This quiet place.

This land is mine, this sea, these people. Here I give love and am loved   2
but I must go, this is in me. I go to learn new ways and to make a way for
those who follow because I love.

My elders, brothers and sisters, children of this place, we must go on.   3
This place we love cannot hold us always. The world is large. Not forever
can we stay here warm and quiet to turn the soil and reap the sea and live
our lives. This I have always known. And so I go ahead for those who
come. To stand mid-stream and hold a hand to either side. It is in me. Am
I not at once dark and fair, fair and dark? A mingling. Since our blue-eyed
father held our dark-eyed mother's hand and let her lead him here.

But, our brother, he came, and now his ways are hers out of choice because of   4
love.

And I go because of love. For our mother and her people and for our   5
father. For you and for our children whose mingling will be greater than
our own. I make a way. Learn new ways. So I can take up that which is our
father's and hold it to the light. Then the people of our mother may come
to me and say, 'How is this?' And I will hold the new thing to the light for
them to see. Then take up that which is our mother's and say to those of
our father, 'You see? See there, that is why.'

And brother, what of us. Must we do this too? Must we leave this quiet place at   6
the edge of hills, at the edge of sea and follow you? For the sake of our mother's
people who are our own. And for our father and because we love?

You must choose but if you do not feel it in you, stay here in warmth.   7
Let me do this and do not weep for my going. I have this power in me. I
am full. I ache for this.

Often I have climbed these hills and run about as free as rain. Stood on   8
the highest place and looked down on great long waves looping on to
sand. Where we played, grew strong, learned our body skills. And
learned the ways of summers, storms, and tides. From where we
stepped into the spreading sea to bathe or gather food. I have watched
and felt this ache in me.

I have watched the people. Seen myself there with them living too. Our   9
mother and our blue-eyed father who came here to this gentle place that
gives us life and strength. Watched them work and play, laugh and cry,
and love.

Seen our uncle sleeping. Brother of our mother. Under a tree bright and   10
heavy with sunned fruit. And beside our uncle his newest baby daughter
sleeping too. And his body-sweat ran down and over her head in a new
baptising. I was filled with strength.

And old Granny Roka sits on her step combing her granddaughter's   11
hair, patiently grooming. Plaiting and tying the heavy tangled kelp which
is her pride. Or walk together on the mark of tide, old Granny and the
child, collecting sun-white sticks for the fire. Tying the sticks into bundles
and carrying them on their backs to the little house. Together.

And seen the women walk out over rocks when the tide is low, sub-   12
merging by a hole of rock with clothes ballooning. Surfacing with wine-red
crayfish, snapping tails and clawing air on a still day. And on a special day
the river stones fired for cooking by our father, our cousins, and our uncles
who laugh and sing. Working all as one.

Our little brother's horse walks home with our little one asleep. Resting   13
a head on his pony's neck, breathing in the warm horse stink, knees locked
into its sides. Fast asleep on the tired flesh of horse. And I ache. But not
forever this. And so I go.

And when you go our brother as you say you must will you be warm? Will you   14
know love? Will an old woman kiss your face and cry warm tears because of who you
are? Will children take your hands and say your name? In your new life our brother
will you sing?

The warmth and love I take from here with me and return for their   15
renewal when I can. It is not a place of loving where I go, not the same as
love that we have known.

> No love fire there to warm one's self beside
> No love warmth
> Blood warmth
> Wood and tree warmth
> Skin on skin warmth
> Tear warmth
> Rain warmth
> Earth warmth
> Breath warmth
> Child warmth
> Warmth of sunned stones
> Warmth of sunned water
> Sunned sand
> Sand ripple
> Water ripple
> Ripple sky
> (Sky Earth
> Earth Sky
> And our beginning)

And you ask me shall I sing. I tell you this. The singing will be here   16
within myself. Inside this body. Fluting through these bones. Ringing in
the skies of being. Ribboning in the course of blood to soothe swelled limbs
and ache bruised heart.

You say to us our brother you will sing. But will the songs within be songs of   17
joy? Will they ring? Out in the skies of being as you say? Pipe through bone, caress
flesh wounding? Or will the songs within be ones of sorrow.

> Of warmth dreams
> Love dreams
> Of aching
> And flesh bruising.
> If you listen will it be weeping that you hear?
> Lament of people
> Earth moan
> Water sigh
> Morepork cry of death?

My sisters, brothers, loved ones, I cannot tell. But there will be gladness 18
for me in what I do. I ask no more. Some songs will be of joy and others
hold the moan and sigh, the owl cry and the throb of loneliness.

What will you do then our brother when the singing dirges through your veins, 19
pressing and swelling in your throat and breast, pricking at your mind with its
aching needles of sound?

What should I do but deny its needling and stealing into mind. Its 20
pressing into throat and breast. I will not put a hand of comfort over body
hardenings nor finger blistered veins in soothing. The wail, the lament
shall not have my ear. I will pay the lonely body ache no mind. Thus I go.

I stand before my dark-eyed mother, blue-eyed father, brothers, sisters. 21
My aunts and uncles, and their children and these old ones. All the dark-
eyed, light-eyed minglings of this place.

We gather. We sing and dance together for my going. We laugh and cry. 22
We touch. We mingle tears as blood.

I give you my farewell. 23

Now I stand on a tide-wet rock to farewell you sea. I listen and hear your 24
great heart thud. I hear you cry. Do you too weep for me? Do you reach out
with mottled hands to touch my brow and anoint my tear-wet face with
tears of salt? Do not weep but keep them well. Your great heart beats I
know for such as these. Give them sea, your great sea love. Hold them
gently. Already they are baptised in your name.

> As am I
> And take your renewal where I go
> And your love
> Take your strength
> And deep heart thud
> Your salt kiss
> Your caring.

Now on a crest of hill in sweeping wind. Where I have climbed and run. 25
And loved and walked about. With life brimming full in me as though I
could die of living.

Guardian hill you do not clutch my hand, you do not weep. You know 26
that I must go and give me blessing. You guard with love this quiet place
rocking at the edge of sea . . .

And now at the highest place I stand. And feel a power grip me. And a 27
lung-bursting strength. A trembling in my legs and arms. A heavy ache
weighting down my groin.

And I lie on soil in all my heaviness and trembling. Stretch out my arms 28
on wide Earth Mother and lay my face on hers. Then call out my love and
speak my vow.

And feel release in giving to you earth, and to you sea, to these people. 29

So I go. And behind me the sea-moan and earth-cry, the sweet lament 30
of people. Towards the goddess as she sleeps I go. On with light upon my
face.

STUDY QUESTIONS

1. The story is told in two voices. The first voice (italicized) is that of the
   traditional Maori community. Analyze this voice. What does it suggest
   about traditional Maori attitudes toward the outside world?
2. The second voice is that of the "son, brother, grandchild." What does
   the image "at once dark and fair, fair and dark" suggest of this speaker?
3. What reasons does the second speaker give for leaving his community
   and land?
4. Discuss the story's use of poetic images to express emotional attachments to a place and a people.

WITI IHIMAERA

*Witi Ihimaera (b. 1944) was born in Gisborne and has worked as a journalist
and diplomat. Ihimaera's fiction presents a native view that uses Maori oral
tradition and mythology usually neglected by the pakehas (foreigners, usually,
but not always white). He uses humor, wit, and lightness of tone to create
empathy for his Maori characters and to comment on race relations without
undue moralizing. The following selection is from* Dear Miss Mansfield
(1989).

His First Ball

Just why it was that he, Tuta Wharepapa, should receive the invitation was a mystery to him. Indeed, when it came, in an envelope bearing a very imposing crest, his mother mistook it for something entirely different—notice of a traffic misdemeanour, a summons perhaps, or even worse, an overdue account. She fingered it gingerly, holding it as far away from her body as possible—just in case a pair of hands came out to grab her fortnightly cheque—and said, 'Here, Tuta. It must be a bill.' She thrust it quickly at her son before he could get away and, wriggling her fingers to get rid of the taint, waited for him to open it.

'Hey—' Tuta said as he stared down at the card. His face dropped such a long way that his mother—her name was Coral—became alarmed. Visions of pleading in court on his behalf flashed through her mind. 'Oh, Tuta, how bad is it?' she said as she prepared to defend her son against all-comers. But Tuta remained speechless and Coral had to grab the card from his hands. 'What's this?' she asked. The card was edged with gold:

> The Aide-de-Camp in Waiting
> Is Desired By Their Excellencies

'Oh, Tuta, what have you done?' Coral said. But Tuta was still in a state of shock. Then, 'Read on, Mum,' he said.

> To invite Mr Tuta Wharepapa
> To A Dance At Government House

Coral's voice drifted away into speechlessness like her son's. Then she compressed her lips and jabbed Tuta with an elbow. 'I'm tired of your jokes,' she said. 'It's not a joke, Mum,' Tuta responded. 'I know you, Tuta,' Coral continued. 'True, Mum, honest. One of the boys must be having me on.' Coral looked at Tuta, unconvinced. 'Who'd want to have *you* at their flash party?' she asked. 'Just wait till I get the joker who sent this,' Tuta swore to himself. Then Coral began to laugh. 'You? Go to Government House? You don't even know how to bow!' And she laughed and laughed so much at the idea that Tuta couldn't take it. 'Where are you going, Your Highness?' Coral asked. 'To find out who sent this,' Tuta replied, waving the offending invitation in her face. 'By the time I finish with him—or her'—because he suddenly realised Coral herself might have sent it '—they'll be laughing on the other side of their face.' With that, he strode out of the kitchen. 'Oh, Tuta?' he heard Coral call, all la-di-da, 'If you ore gooing pahst Goverment Howse please convay may regahrds to—' and she burst out laughing again.

Tuta leapt on to his motorbike and, over the rest of the day, roared around the city calling on his mates from the factory. 'It wasn't me, Tuta,'

Crazy-Joe said as he sank a red ball in the billiard saloon, 'but I tell you, man, you'll look great in a suit.' Nor was it Blackjack over at the garage, who said, 'But listen, mate, when you go grab some of those Diplo number plates for me, ay?' And neither was it Des, who moonlighted as Desirée Dawn at the strip club, or Sheree, who worked part time at the pinball parlour. 'You couldn't take a partner, could you?' Desirée Dawn breathed hopefully. 'Nah, you wouldn't be able to fit on my bike,' Tuta said—apart from which he didn't think a six-foot transvestite with a passion for pink boas and slit satin dresses would enjoy it all that much. By the end of the day Tuta was no wiser, and when he arrived at Bigfoot's house and found his mate waiting for him in a tiara, he knew that word was getting around. Then it came to him that perhaps the invitation was real after all. Gloria Simmons would know—she was the boss's secretary and knew some lords.

'Oh,' Mrs Simmons whispered reverently as Tuta handed her the crested 6
envelope. She led Tuta into the sitting-room. 'It looks real,' she said as she held it to the light. Then she opened the envelope and, incredulous, asked '*You* received this?' Tuta nodded. 'You didn't just pick it up on the street,' Mrs Simmons continued, 'and put your name on it?' Offended, Tuta shook his head, saying 'You don't think I want to go, do you?' Mrs Simmons pursed her lips and said, 'Perhaps there's another Tuta Wharepapa, and you got his invitation in error.' And Mrs Simmons's teeth smiled and said, 'In that case, let me ring Government House and let them know.' With that, Mrs Simmons went into another room, where Tuta heard her dialling. Then *her* voice went all la-di-da too as she trilled, 'Ooo, Gahverment Howse? May ay speak to the Aide-de-Camp? Ooo, har do yoo do. So sorry to trouble you but ay am ringing to advayse you—' Tuta rolled his eyes— how come everybody he told about the invitation got infected by some kind of disease! Then he became acutely aware that Mrs Simmons had stopped talking. He heard her gasp. He heard her say in her own lingo, 'You mean to tell me that this is for real? That you people actually sent an invite to a—a—boy who packs batteries in a factory?' She put down the telephone and returned to the sitting-room. She was pale but calm as she said, 'Tuta dear, difficult though this may be, can you remember the woman who came to look at the factory about two months ago?' Tuta knitted his eyebrows. 'Yeah, I think so. That must have been when we opened the new extension.' Mrs Simmons closed her eyes. 'The woman, Tuta. The woman.' Tuta thought again. 'Oh yeah, there *was* a lady, come to think of it, a horsey-looking lady who—' Mrs Simmons interrupted him. 'Tuta, dear, that lady was the wife of the Governor-General.'

Dazed, Tuta said, 'But she didn't say who she was.' And he listened as 7
Mrs Simmons explained that Mrs Governor-General had been very impressed by the workers at the factory and that Tuta was being invited to represent them. 'Of course you will have to go,' Mrs Simmons said. 'One does not say "No" to the Crown.' Then Mrs Simmons got up and telephone Tuta's mother. 'Coral? Gloria here. Listen, about Tuta, you and I

should talk about what is required. What for? Why, when he goes to the ball of course! Now—' *Me? Go to a ball?* Tuta thought. *With all those flash people, all those flash ladies with their crowns and diamonds and emeralds? Not bloody likely—Bigfoot can go, he's already got a tiara, yeah. Not me. They'll have to drag me there. I'm not going. Not me. No fear. No WAY.* But he knew, when he saw the neighbours waiting for him at home that, of course, his mother had already flapped her mouth to everybody. 'Oh yes,' she was telling the neighbours when Tuta walked in, 'it was delivered by special messenger. This dirty big black car came and a man, must have been a flunkey, knocked on the door and—' Then Coral saw Tuta and, 'Oh Tuta,' she cried, opening her arms to him as if she hadn't seen him for days.

After that, of course, there was no turning back. The boss from the factory called to put the hard word on Tuta. Mrs Simmons RSVPeed by telephone and—'Just in case, Tuta dear'—by letter and, once that was done, he had to go. The rest of his mates at the factory got into the act, also, cancelling the airline booking he made to get out of town and, from thereon in, followed him everywhere. 'Giz a break, fellas,' Tuta pleaded as he tried to get out, cajole or bribe himself out of the predicament. But Crazy-Joe only said, 'Lissen, if you don't get there then I'm—' and he drew a finger across his throat, and Blackjack said, 'Hey, man, I know a man who knows a man who can get us a Rolls for the night—' and Bigfoot just handed him the tiara. And boy, did Coral ever turn out to be the walking compendium of What To Do And How To Do It At A Ball. 'Gloria says that we have to take you to a tailor so you can hire a suit. Not just any suit and none of your purple numbers either. A black *conservative* suit. And then we have to get you a bowtie and you have to wear black shoes—so I reckon a paint job on your brown ones will do. You've got a white shirt, thank goodness, and we'll have to get some new socks—calf length so that when you sit down people won't see your hairy legs. Now, what else? Oh yes, I've already made an appointment for you to go to have your hair cut, no buts, Tuta, and the boys are taking you there, so don't think you're going to wriggle out of it. By the time that dance comes around we'll have you decked out like the Prince of Wales—' which was just what Tuta was afraid of.

But that was only the beginning. Not only did his appearance have to be radically altered, but his manners had to be brushed up also—and Mrs Simmons was the first to have a go. 'Tuta dear,' she said when he knocked on her door, 'Do come in. Yes, take your boots off but on THE NIGHT, the shoes stay *on*. Please, come this way. No, Tuta, *after* me, just a few steps behind. Never barge, Tuta and don't shamble along. Be PROUD, Tuta, be HAUGHTY'—and she showed him how to put his nose in the air. Tuta followed her, his nose so high that he almost tripped, into the dining-room. 'Voila!' she said. 'Ay?' Tuta answered. Mrs Simmons then realised that this was going to be very difficult. 'I said, "Ta ra!" ' She had set the table with a beautiful cloth—and it appeared to be laid with thousands of knives, forks and spoons. 'This is what it will be like at the ball,' she explained. 'Oh boy,' Tuta said. 'Now, because I'm a lady you must escort me to my seat,' Mrs Simmons said. 'Huh? Can't you walk there yourself?' Tuta asked. 'Just *do* it,' Mrs Simmons responded dangerously, 'and *don't* push me all the way under the table, Tuta, just to the edge will do—' and then, under her breath '—Patience, Gloria dear, *patienza*.' Once seated, she motioned Tuta to a chair opposite her. 'Gee, thanks,' he said. Mrs Simmons paused, thoughtfully, and said, 'Tuta dear, when in doubt don't say *anything*. Just shut your mouth.' She shivered, but really, the boy would only understand common language, '—and keep it shut.' Then she smiled. 'Now follow every action that I make.' Exaggerating the movements for Tuta's benefit, Mrs Simmons said, 'First, take up the spoon. No, not that one, *that* one. That's for your soup, that's for the second course, that's for the third course, that's for the fourth—' Tuta looked helplessly at her. 'Can't I use the same knives and things all the time?' he said. '*Never*,' Mrs Simmons shivered. 'Well, what's all these courses for?' Tuta objected. 'Why don't they just stick all the kai[1] on the table at once?' Mrs Simmons deigned not to answer. Instead she motioned to the glasses, saying, 'Now *this* is for the white wine, this for red wine, this for champagne and this for cognac.' Tuta sighed, saying 'No beer? Thought as much.' Refusing to hear him, Mrs Simmons proceeded, 'You sip your wine just like you sip the soup. Like *so*,' and she showed him. 'No, Tuta, not too fast. And leave the bowl *on* the table, *don't* put it to your lips. No, *don't* slurp. Oh my goodness. Very GOOD, Tuta! Now wipe your lips with the napkin.' Tuta looked puzzled. 'Ay?' he asked. 'The paper napkin on your lap,' Mrs Simmons said. 'This hanky thing?' Tuta responded. 'Why, Tuta!' Mrs Simmons's teeth said, 'How clever of you to work that out. Shall we proceed to the second course? Good!' Mrs Simmons felt quite sure that Professor Higgins didn't have it *this* bad.

Then, of course, there was the matter of learning how to dance—not hot rock but slow *slow* dancing, holding a girl, 'You know,' Mrs Simmons said, '*together*,' adding, 'and young ladies at the ball are never allowed to decline.' So Tuta made a date with Desirée Dawn after hours at the club. Desirée was just overwhelmed to be asked for advice and told her friends Alexis Dynamite and Chantelle Derrier to help her. 'Lissun, honey,' Desirée said as she cracked her gum. 'No matter what the dance is, there's always a basic rhythm.' Chantelle giggled and said, 'Yeah, very basic.' Ignoring her, Desirée hauled Tuta on to the floor, did a few jeté's and, once she had limbered up, said, 'Now *you* lead,' and 'Oo, honey, I didn't know you were so masterful.' Alexis fluttered her false eyelashes and, 'You two don't need music at *all*,' she whispered. Nevertheless, Alexis ran the tape and the music boomed across the club floor. 'This isn't ball music,' Tuta said as he heard the raunch scream out of the saxes. 'How do *you* know?'

10

---

1. kai: *food, a meal (Maori).*

Chantelle responded. And Tuta had the feeling that he wasn't going to learn how to dance in any way except improperly. 'Lissun,' Desirée said, 'Alexis and I will show you. Move your butt over here, Lexie. Now, Tuta honey, just watch. Can ya hear the rhythum? Well you go *boom* and a *boom* and a *boom boom boom*.' And Alexis screamed and yelled, 'Desirée, he wants to dance with the girl, not *make* her in the middle of the floor.' And Chantelle only made matters worse by laughing, 'Yeah, you stupid slut, you want him to end up in prison like you?' At which Desirée gasped, walked over to Chantelle, peeled off both Chantelle's false eyelashes, said, 'Can you see better? Good,' and lammed her one in the mouth. As he exited, Tuta knew he would have better luck with Sheree at the pinball parlour—she used to be good at roller skating and could even do the splits in mid-air.

So it went on. The fitting at the tailor's was duly accomplished ('Hmmmmnnnn,' the tailor said as he measured Tuta up. 'Your shoulders are too wide, your hips too large, you have shorter legs than you should have but—Hmmmmnnnn'), his hair was trimmed to within an inch of propriety, and he painted his brown shoes black. His lessons continued with Mrs Simmons, Tuta's mother, the workers from the factory—even the boss—all pitching in to assist Tuta in the etiquette required. For instance: 'If you're talking you ask about the weather. This is called polite conversation. You say "Isn't it lovely?" to everything, even if it isn't. You always say "Yes" if you're offered something, even if you don't want it. The man with the medals is *not* the waiter. He is His Excellency. The lady who looks like a horse is not in drag and you should *not* ask if her tiara fell off the same truck as Bigfoot's.'

Then, suddenly it was time for Tuta to go to the ball. 'Yes, Mum,' he said to Coral as she fussed around him with a clothes brush, 'I've got a hanky, I've brushed my teeth three times already, the invite is in my pocket—' And when Tuta stepped out the door the whole world was there—the boss, Mrs Simmons, Crazy-Joe, Blackjack, Bigfoot and others from the factory, Desirée Dawn and the neighbours. 'Don't let us down,' the boss said. 'Not too much food on the fork,' Mrs Simmons instructed. 'The third boom is the one that does it,' Desirée Dawn called. 'Don't forget the Diplo plates,' Blackjack whispered. 'And don't drink too much of the beer,' Coral said. Then, there was the car, a Jaguar festooned with white ribbons and two small dolls on the bonnet. 'It's a ball I'm off to,' Tuta said sarcastically, 'not a wedding.' Blackjack shrugged his shoulders. 'Best I could do, mate, and this beauty was just sitting there outside the church and—' He got in and started the motor. Tuta sat in the back and, suddenly, Bigfoot and Crazy-Joe were in either side. 'The boss's orders,' they said. 'We deliver you to the door or else—' Outside, Tuta saw the boss draw a line across their necks. The car drew away and as it did so, Mrs Simmons gave a small scream. 'Oh my goodness, I forgot to tell Tuta that if Nature calls he should not use the bushes,' she said.

Looking back, Tuta never quite understood how he ever survived that journey. At one point a police car drew level on the motorway, but when they looked over at the Jaguar and saw Tuta he could just imagine their disbelief, Nah. Couldn't possibly . . . Nah. His head was whirling with all the etiquette he had learnt and all the instructions he had to remember. He trembled, squirmed, palpitated and sweated all over the seat. Then he was there, and Blackjack was showing the invitation, and the officer at the gate was looking doubtfully at the wedding decorations, and then 'Proceed ahead, sir,' the officer said. *What a long drive,* Tuta thought. *What a big palace. And look at all those flash people. And they're all going in.* 'Well, mate,' Blackjack said, 'Good luck. Look for us in the car park.' And Crazy-Joe said, 'Hey, give the missus a whirl for me, ay?' and with that, and a squeal of tires (Blackjack was always such a show-off), they were gone. 13

He was alone. Him. Tuta Wharepapa. Standing there. At the entrance way. Inside he heard music and the laughter of the guests. Then someone grabbed his arm and said, 'Come along!' and before he knew it he was inside and being propelled along a long hallway. And the young woman who had grabbed him was suddenly pulled away by her companion, and Tuta was alone again. *Oh boy,* he thought. *Look at this red carpet.* He felt quite sure that the paint was running off his shoes and there there were great big black footmarks all the way to where he was now standing. Then a voice BOOMED ahead, and Tuta saw that there was a line of people in front and they were handing their invitations in to the bouncer. Tuta joined them. The bouncer was very old and very dignified—he looked, though, as if he should have been retired from the job years ago. *Nah,* Tuta thought. *He couldn't be a bouncer. Must be a toff.* The toff looked Tuta up and down and thrust out his white-gloved hand. 'I got an invitation,' Tuta said. 'True. I got one.' The toff read the card and his eyebrows arched. 'Your name?' he BOOMED. 'Tuta.' Couldn't he read? Then the toff turned away in the direction of a huge ballroom that stretched right to the end of the world. The room seemed to be hung with hundreds of chandeliers and *thousands* of people were either dancing or standing around the perimeter. There were steps leading down to the ballroom and, at the bottom, was a man wearing medals and a woman whose tiara wasn't as sparkly as Bigfoot's—*them.* And Tuta felt *sure,* when the Major-Domo—for that was who the toff was—stepped forward and opened his mouth to announce him, that *everybody* must have heard him BOOM— 14

'Your Excellencies, Mr Tutae Tockypocka.' 15

Tuta looked for a hole to disappear into. He tried to backpedal down the hallway but there were people behind him. 'No, you got it wrong,' he said between clenched teeth to the Major-Domo. 'Tutae's a rude word.' But the Major-Domo simply sniffed, handed back the invitation, and motioned Tuta down the stairs. Had *they* heard? In trembling anticipation Tuta approached the Governor-General. 'Mr Horrynotta?' the Governor-General smiled. 'Splendid that you were able to come along. Dear? Here's Mr 16

Tutae.' And in front of him was Mrs Governor-General. 'Mr Forrimoppa, how kind of you to come. May I call you Tutae? Please let me introduce you to Lord Wells.' And Lord Wells, too. 'Mr Mopperuppa, quiet a mouthful, what. Not so with Tutae, what?' *You don't know the half of it,* Tuta thought gloomily. And then Mrs Governor-General just *had* to, didn't she, giggle and pronounce to all and sundry, 'Everybody, you must meet Mr Tutae.' And that's who Tuta became all that evening. 'Have you met Mr Tutae yet? No? Mr Tutae, this is Mr—' And Tuta would either shake hands or do a stiff little bow and look around for that hole in the floor. He once made an attempt to explain what 'tutae' was but heard Mrs Simmons's voice: 'If in doubt, Tuta, *don't.*' So instead he would draw attention away from that word by asking about the weather. 'Do you think it will rain?' he would ask. 'Oh, not inside, Mr Tutae!'—and the word got around that Mr Tutae was such a wit, so funny, so quaint, that he soon found himself exactly where he didn't want to be—at the centre of attention. In desperation, he asked every woman to dance. 'Why, certainly, Mr Tutae!' they said, because ladies never said no. So he danced with them all—a fat lady, a slim lady, a lady whose bones cracked all the time—and, because he was nervous, he went *boom* at every third step, and *that* word got around too. And as the Governor-General waltzed past he shouted, 'Well done, Tutae, jolly good show.'

No matter what he tried to do Tuta could never get away from being at the centre of the crowd or at the centre of attention. Instead of being gratified, however, Tuta became more embarrassed. Everybody seemed to laugh at his every word, even when it wasn't funny, or to accept his way of dancing because it was so *daring.* It seemed as if he could get away with anything. At the same time, Tuta suddenly realised that he was the only Maori there and that perhaps people were mocking him. He wasn't a real person to them, but rather an Entertainment. Even when buffet dinner was served, the crowd still seemed to mock him, pressing in upon him with 'Have some hors-d'oeuvres, Mr Tutae. Some *escalope* of veal, perhaps? You must try the pâté de foie gras! A slice of *jambon*? What about some langouste? Oh, the raspberry gâteau is just divine!' It was as if the crowd knew very well his ignorance of such delicacies and, by referring to them, was putting him down. In desperation Tuta tried some caviar. 'Oh, Mr Tutae, we can see that you just love caviar!' Tuta gave a quiet, almost dangerous, smile. 'Yes,' he said. 'I think it's just divine.'

So it went on. But then, just after the buffet, a Very Important Person arrived and, relieved, Tuta found himself deserted. Interested, he watched as the one who had just arrived became the centre of attention. 'It always happens this way,' a voice said behind Tuta. 'I wouldn't worry about it.' Startled, Tuta turned around and saw a huge fern. 'Before you,' the fern continued, 'it was me.' Then Tuta saw that a young woman was sitting behind the fern. 'I'm not worried,' he said to her, 'I'm glad.' The woman sniffed and said, 'You certainly looked as if you were enjoying it.' Tuta parted the fronds to get a good look at the woman's face—it was a pleasant face, one which could be pretty if it didn't frown so much. 'Shift over,' Tuta said. 'I'm coming to join you.' He sidled around the plant and sat beside her. 'My name is—' he began. 'Yes, I know,' the woman said quickly, 'Mr Tutae.' Tuta shook his head vigorously, '*No*, not Tutae. Tuta.' The woman looked at him curiously and, 'Is there a difference?' she asked. 'You better believe it,' Tuta said. 'Oh—' the woman sniffed. 'I'm Joyce.'

The music started to play again. Joyce squinted her eyes and Tuta sighed, 'Why don't you put on your glasses?' Joyce squealed, 'How did you know?' before popping them on and parting the fronds. 'I'm a sociology student,' Joyce muttered. 'Don't you think people's behaviour is just amazing? I mean ay-*may*zing?' Tuta shrugged his shoulders and wondered if Joyce was looking at something he couldn't see. 'I mean,' Joyce continued, 'look at them out there, just *look* at them. This could be India under the Raj. All this British Imperial graciousness and yet the carpet is being pulled from right beneath their feet.' Puzzled, Tuta tried to see the ball through Joyce's eyes, but failed. 'Ah well,' Joyce sighed. Then she put her hand out to Tuta so that he could shake it, saying 'Goodbye, Mr Tuta.' Tuta looked at her and, 'Are you going?' he asked. 'Oh no,' Joyce said, 'I'm staying here until everybody leaves. But *you* must go out and reclaim attention.' Tuta laughed. 'That new guy's welcome,' he said. 'But don't you want to fulfil their expectations?' Joyce asked. Tuta paused, and 'If that means what I think it means, no,' he said. 'Good,' Joyce responded, 'You are perfectly capable of beating them at their own game. Good luck.'

Then, curious, Tuta asked, 'What did you mean when you said that before me it had been *you*?' Joyce shifted uneasily, took off her glasses and said, 'Well, I'm not a Maori, but I thought it would have been obvious—' *Oh,* Tuta thought, *she's a plain Jane and people have been making fun of her.* 'But that doesn't matter to me,' Tuta said gallantly. 'Really?' Joyce asked. 'I'll prove it,' Tuta said. 'How about having the next dance.' Joyce gasped, 'Are you *sure*?' Taken aback, Tuta said, 'Of course, I'm sure.' And Joyce said, 'But are you *sure* you're sure!' To show her, Tuta stood up and took her hand. Joyce sighed and shook her head. 'Well, don't say I didn't warn you.' Then she stood up . . . and up . . . and UP.

'Oh,' Tuta said as he parted the fronds to look up at Joyce's face. She must have been six feet six at least. He and Joyce regarded each other miserably. Joyce bit her lip. *Well you asked for it,* Tuta thought. 'Come on,' he said, 'let's have a good time.' He reached up, grabbed her waist, put his face against her chest, and they waltzed into the middle of the floor. There, Tuta stood as high on his toes as possible. *Oh, why did I come?* he thought. Then the music ended and he took Joyce back to the fern. 'I'm sorry I'm such a bad dancer,' she apologised. 'I always took the man's part at school.' Tuta smiled at her, 'That's no sweat. Well—' And he was just about to leave her when he suddenly realised that after all he and Joyce were both outsiders really. And it came to him that, bloody hell, if you could not join

19

20

21

them—as if he would really want to do *that*—then, yes, he could beat them if he wanted to. Not by giving in to them, but by being strong enough to stand up to them. Dance, perhaps, but using his own steps. Listen, also, not to the music of the band but to the music in his head. He owed it, after all, to generous but silly wonderful mixed-up Mum, Mrs Simmons, Desirée Dawn, and the boys—Crazy-Joe, Blackjack and Bigfoot—who were out *there* but wanting to know enough to get *in*. But they needed to come in on their own terms—that's what they would have to learn—as the real people they were and not as carbon copies of the people already on the inside. Once they learnt that, *oh, world, watch out, for your walls will come down in a flash, like Jericho.*

'Look,' Tuta said, 'how about another dance!' Joyce looked at him in disbelief. 'You're a sucker for punishment, aren't you!' she muttered. 'Why?' Tuta bowed, mockingly. 'Well, for one thing, it would be just divine.' At that, Joyce let out a peal of laughter. She stood up again. 'Thank you,' Joyce whispered. Then, 'You know, this is my first ball.' And Tuta smiled and 'It's *my* first ball too,' he said. 'From now on, balls like these will never be the same again.' He took her hand and the band began to wail a sweet but *oh-so-mean* saxophone solo as he led her on to the floor. 22

STUDY QUESTIONS

1. What is the initial response of Coral, Tuta's mother, to her son's invitation to the dance at Government House? How does her attitude change and what does the change signify?

2. Mrs Simmons acts as a mediator between Tuta, the working-class Maori character, and Government House, representing the ruling British upper class. What does she perceive as important skills for Tuta to learn to participate in the dance? Do you agree with her?

3. Joyce describes the Governor's ball as like "India under the Raj," that is, as an anachronistic manifestation of British imperialism. Explain how this comparison works.

4. Tuta knows he's an outsider at Government House from the moment he receives the invitation. What else does he learn after the waltz with Joyce? What does this insight suggest in terms of positions of margins and centers?

5. Discuss the use of different registers of English in the story (for example, working class, upper class, standard English) and how they contribute to the construction of character, conflict, and theme.

SAMOA

◎ ALBERT WENDT

*Albert Wendt (b. 1939) was born in Apia, West Samoa, and educated as a
teenager in New Zealand. His return as an adult to Samoa led to his
rethinking of the configuration of native and Westernized cultures in his
society, a configuration that is a source of tension in his writing. As a pioneer
Polynesian writer, his fiction shows his adaptation of English to accommodate
a different cultural world.*

Excerpt from *Pouliuli*

Chapter 1

Early on a drizzly Saturday morning Faleasa Osovae—the seventy-six-
year-old titled head of the Aiga Faleasa, faithful husband of a devoted
Felefele, stern but generous father of seven sons and five obedient daughters, and the most respected alii in the village of Malaelua—woke with a
strange bitter taste in his mouth to find, as he looked out to the rain and his
village, and then at his wife snoring softly beside him in the mosquito net,
and the rest of his aiga (about sixty bodies wrapped in sleeping sheets)
who filled the spacious fale, that everything and everybody that he was
used to and had enjoyed, and that till then had given meaning to his
existence, now filled him with an almost unbearable feeling of revulsion—
yes, that was the only word for it, revulsion. He despised everything he
had been, had become, had achieved: his forty years as a deacon and lay
preacher; his almost unlimited power in the matai council; his large profitable cacao plantation; his title as the highest-ranking matai in Malaelua;
his nationally respected reputation as an orator; his detailed knowledge of
genealogies and history, which was envied by other matai; his utter loyalty
and devotion to his village and aiga and church; his unquestioned repu-

1

tation as a just, honourable, courageous, and humble man of unimpeach-
able integrity; and his perfect health. (In his seventy-six years he had only
been seriously ill once. He still had nearly all his teeth and hair.) Even the
familiar smell of his fale and relatives now repelled him. He sniffed back
the mucus in his nose, caught it at the back of his throat, pulled up the side
of the mosquito net, and spat it out on to the paepae. But the feeling of
nausea surged up from the centre of his chest and he started coughing
loudly, repeatedly; and then he was vomiting uncontrollably, the thick,
half-digested food and bile and stench shooting out of his mouth and over
his sleeping wife who, a few offended seconds later, was awake and slapping him on the back and calling to her daughters to bring a basin. But
when the first bout of painful spewing stopped, Faleasa pushed her away
through the side of the net, which tore with a protesting R-R-RIP-P, and
toppled out on to a group of their sleeping grandchildren who woke up
screaming and woke the whole aiga, who, in turn, scrambled up and
around a now weeping Felefele and a Faleasa who advanced shouting at
them to get out of *his* fale and scattered them with his kicking feet and
flailing fists. And soon they were all through the fale blinds and over the
paepae into neighboring fale and houses which belonged to their aiga and
from which, safe from Faleasa's inexplicable wrath, they observed him
fearfully, unwilling to agree with Elefane, the eldest son, that their up-to-
then-was-always-sane father was now suffering a spell of insanity or that
an aitu had taken possession of him during the night by entering his brain,
lungs, heart, and belly, especially his belly, because no human being could
spew out that unbreathable amount of vomit.

'What are we to do?' Felefele asked. (All the neighboring aiga were   2
awake by then; and most of them were on their paepae and verandas
enjoying Faleasa's performance.)

'We shall never be able to live down this disgrace,' her daughters said.   3

Faleasa ripped all the mosquito nets from the strings that tied them to   4
the rafters and hurled them out of the fale—the paepae was shrouded with
white netting. He then gathered all the pillows, sleeping sheets, and mats
and threw them out as well. Felefele sent some of the girls to bring her
treasured possessions out of the rain but, as they approached, Faleasa
threatened to kill them if they touched anything, so they retreated to
Felefele who, no longer worried about her husband's health but extremely
angry with him, stood up arms akimbo and called to him to stop being
childish and think about how their village would view his senile behavior—
she emphasized the word senile, which angered Faleasa more and made
him grab the large wooden chest in which all their clothes were kept, pull
it clattering across the pebble floor to the front paepae, take out armfuls of
clothes and scatter them across the paepae and grass, all the time exclaim-
ing loudly that his wife and children and relatives were a pack of greedy,
gluttonous, uncouth, uncivilised dogs. When the chest was empty he

rolled it down the paepae; it broke into large pieces. He then sat down cross-legged in the middle of the fale, arms folded across his heaving chest, head held high defiantly, the nausea gone. 'Stay like that for all we care!' Felefele called. Then she ordered their aiga not to pay any attention to their *sick* father but to go about their normal activities as if he wasn't there.

He would remain in this position that whole morning, thought Faleasa, 5 as though saying to everyone that he had the inalienable right to defy them and to own nothing but an empty fale, the defiant breath in his lungs, the pools of rapidly drying vomit and their honest stench; and no one, absolutely no one, was going to take any of them away from him. No one dared—the people of Malaelua went about their normal chores; so did his aiga, but they paused often to observe him. At about ten o'clock, the rain having stopped, Felefele sent Elefane to him with a foodmat laden with his favorite food—faalifu talo, home-made cocoa, and fried pisupo. Elefane didn't even reach the edge of the paepae before an unfatherly stone whispered past his head. He wheeled swiftly and scrambled back to Felefele on his aging forty-five-year-old legs, telling everyone that Faleasa was truly possessed and needed the pastor or a fofo to exorcise the aitu. Felefele sent him to fetch Pastor Filemoni. (It wasn't Christian to get a fofo.)

At noon Faleasa saw Filemoni crossing the road and coming towards 6 him; the pastor's white shirt and lavalava gleamed in the light and distracted Faleasa from Filemoni's smother of flab: Filemoni, only in his early thirties, a recent graduate from Malua Theological College, and Felefele's nephew—which was why, through Faleasa's influence, he had been appointed pastor at Malaelua—was fast achieving obese proportions. Up to this critical morning Faleasa had always been tolerant of Filemoni's inadequacies which were many: for instance, he was extremely lazy and didn't bother to compose inspiring sermons; he was arrogant and from the pulpit chastised everyone, except Faleasa, who offended him; he insisted on receiving large monetary donations for his upkeep at the end of every month; he was a shallow thinker who hid his shallowness behind a mask of glibness, bigotry, and pretensions; his breath stank but he didn't know it because he believed his total body odour to be the sweetest perfume the village of Malaelua had ever breathed; his wife and two children were intolerably spoilt, condescending, disrespectful of the faa-Samoa, an embodiment of the worst characteristics of the town where his wife was born the daughter of a government clerk. But now, as Faleasa watched Filemoni waddling self-consciously (knowing every Malaeluan was observing him) up to his fale, the dizzy spell of nausea started turning inside his head again.

Pompous pile of expensive excrement! Faleasa cursed to himself as 7 Filemoni reached the edge of the paepae, paused, and, standing on the tips of his toes, peered into the fale. Filemoni's eyes lit up when he sighted Faleasa and he hurried up the paepae and sat down opposite Faleasa who stared unwaveringly at him.

'How are you?' Filemoni chose the informal approach (after all Faleasa 8
was his uncle), his nostrils breathing warily because the whole fale stank of
vomit.

'Touch your arse!' Faleasa greeted him. 9

Ignoring his uncle's profane remark—it was the first time he'd heard 10
Faleasa, whom he respected, swearing—Filemoni prattled on about how
unreliable the weather was. 'Touch your arse and smell your own foul
stench!' Faleasa enlarged on his first unique greeting. Again the pastor
ignored it. Faleasa raised his voice, his eyes wild with what Filemoni
thought was madness, and said, 'Touch your arse and smell your own foul
stench because you and your stench deserve each other!' This time Filemoni couldn't ignore it: he, Filemoni Matau, was a Servant of God and the
son of an alii and therefore had his self-respect, pride, status, and courage
to protect. Faleasa was obviously sick, possessed by a vindictive aitu, so
Filemoni gazed forgivingly at him, knowing he had to address the aitu
directly if he wanted to exorcise it.

'Demon, what are you doing inside this good old man?' Filemoni asked 11
the aitu.

Faleasa nearly laughed when he realised what their diagnosis of his 12
ailment was but he decided to play along. Deepening his voice to make it
sound like his mother's who had died years before, he said, 'I am inhabiting my son's body because I want to destroy his goodness.' He saw
Filemoni start to tremble.

'You are his mother?' Filemoni asked. Faleasa nodded his head as if he 13
was now mesmerised by the pastor. 'But why?'

'I can't stand his goodness. As you know, he is the most generous, most 14
compassionate, most honest, most Christian person in Malaelua, and when
he dies he will go to Heaven for sure!'

'Demon, evil disciple of Satan,' declaimed Filemoni, 'I order you, in the 15
sacred name of Jesus, to leave the body of this good servant!'

Faleasa laughed his mother's laugh as though he was completely mad, 16
and watched Filemoni cringe with fright. 'Touch your holy arse!' his
mother, through Faleasa, shouted at Filemoni. 'You've got no power because you're one of the most wicked men in Malaelua, a Pharisee[1]
through and through. Only a truly good man can drive me out, and the
only good man in Malaelua is my son whose carcass I now inhabit!'
Faleasa continued to laugh shrilly, imitating what he thought was a lunatic's laughter. As he laughed he crawled slowly towards Filemoni. He,
after trying frantically to control his fear, jumped up and backed away
from Faleasa, who bared his teeth and neighed like a horse. When
Faleasa splattered a stream of hot vomit on to Filemoni's legs he wheeled
and fled down the paepae and across the malae, not daring to look back

---

1. Pharisee: *A hypocritical or self-righteous person.*

and completely forgetting that all Malaelua were witnessing his cowardly retreat.

Faleasa wiped his mouth, aware that for some unknown reason he could vomit whenever he chose to, and decided that he was really enjoying himself. After Filemoni's failure he knew they would resort to a pagan cure—a fofo. After all, he, Faleasa Osovae, was their leader and was therefore worth saving at any cost, even if it meant using cures which the Church condemned as downright heretical. Being possessed and deranged had definite advantages: he could, with impunity, scare the excrement out of all his worthless kin and village.   17

Hunger tugged at his belly so he yelled for some food. Two of his married daughters, Tina and Palaai, both prodigious breeders, gossips, and relentless schemers who were always after him with their cunning ways to confer matai titles on their worthless husbands, came scrambling into the fale with a foodmat laden with food, a kettle of cocoa, and a basin of water. He tried his best to keep on looking possessed, his eyes glazed with madness, his body stiffly frozen in that defiant posture which was beginning to exact a painful toll on his old muscles, back, and backside. Warily, but still trying to smile, his daughters placed the food in front of him and withdrew to sit at the back posts in readiness to serve him. Still gazing fixedly ahead, Faleasa again used his mother's voice. 'Get out, you scheming whores!' he ordered. When they were out of sight he ate eagerly, quickly. The food tasted delicious.   18

Nothing about his past, he reflected, seemed real, important, vital, necessary—he had shed it all like a useless skin. Yes, he had been reborn; but he realised they would not accept his new self: they needed him to be the thoroughly domesticated, generous, always-willing-to-sacrifice-himself-for-them father, provider, arbitrator, floormat. They had grown accustomed to the taste of his old carcass. Now they would choke on the poison of his new self. He chuckled at the thought.   19

He finished eating, washed his hands in the basin of water, and threw everything out on to the paepae, where the plates, Felefele's best ones, smashed on the stones. Getting his ali—he was the only person in Malaelua who still used one—he lay down and was soon fast asleep. He would need all his physical strength if he was to combat them.   20

When he awoke the smell of vomit was gone, the fale felt clean, and he found he was covered with a fresh sleeping sheet. He jerked up to a sitting position, suspiciously. They had come in and cleaned the fale. Except for the chest he had broken, everything was back in its normal place, arranged, as always, according to Felefele's sanity, as it were. He started to feel trapped, as though Felefele's orderly mind, in which he now realised he had been living for nearly fifty years, was again closing in round him like a smothering womb. He jumped up and shuffled about the fale, placing well-aimed pools of vomit in strategic positions (for instance, over the mattress of the only bed), and rearranging everything according to the   21 chaotic freedom of his rebirth, as it were. He did his best to appear possessed, utterly frightening to his aiga and to Malaelua, while he did the rearranging.

An hour or so later, not that time seemed important to him any more, 22 while he was lying on his back and gazing up into the fale dome, contemplating nothing (he discovered it was extremely healing to contemplate the Void), he heard the sound of brave footsteps coming up the front paepae and into the fale. He didn't bother to look; he knew what the man's profession was. Filemoni, Christ's man, had failed; now they were turning to the Devil. Faleasa felt the man sit down at one of the front posts, felt the man scrutinising him carefully, felt the hesitancy, the tremors of fear, as the man prepared to talk to him. As he felt all this through his pores—he could describe it to himself in no other way—he realised that here was another marvellous quality of his new self. His wrinkled, scarred, thick hide had achieved a new and miraculous sensitivity: he could see with it, feel with it, think with it.

'Go away!' he said, without bothering to look at the fofo. 'I don't need 23 you.'

The man insisted on greeting him formally and then said, 'But you do 24 need this humble person, sir.' From his sound and feel Faleasa gathered that the man would be physically very small, a tight knot of cunning energy about fifty years old; he would be well-skilled in the subtle manipulation of language to trick unwary victims into parting with their possessions such as aitu, money, ietoga, food; his extra-large skull would be covered with a short-cropped bristle of black hair, his nose almost as wide as a pig's snout, his eyes perpetually darting in search of valuables he could take possession of; and his body would be pock-marked with healed sores, the result of malnutrition in childhood.

'Why do I need you?' Faleasa asked, still gazing up into the fale dome. 25

The fofo coughed politely. 'Your concerned aiga have told this humble 26 man that you are ill, sir, and urgently in need of this humble person's type of cure.'

'I am not possessed by an aitu, if that's what you mean by being ill.' 27 Faleasa sat up and faced the fofo for the first time. 'Do I look possessed to you?' The fofo studied him from under knitted brows; then his eyes darted to the vomit and chaos in the fale. But, before he could use it as proof that Faleasa was possessed, Faleasa told him that he had wrecked the fale when his nagging wife had angered him. 'You know what wives can be like,' he said. 'They can be very cruel.' The man nodded eagerly, encouraging him to talk on, but Faleasa wasn't going to have any of that and he wasn't going to waste any more time with this charlatan, so he got up, with the man observing his every move, reached up to the lowest fale rafter for the tobacco tin in which he kept his money, returned and sat down only a yard or so in front of the man, opened the tin, emptied all his money on to the mat, and with slow deliberateness counted every note and coin. 'Thirty dollars and forty-five cents,' he concluded. Then, carefully wrapping the soiled notes round the coins, he reached out, clutched the man's right hand, turned it palm upwards, gazed mercilessly into his eyes, thumped the money on to his palm, closed the man's rough fingers round it, and said: 'If you think I've got an aitu in my guts then you can return all that money to me. But, if you believe what I've said, that I'm as healthy as you are, then you may keep the money as a contribution from this humble old man to help pay your travelling expenses.' The man bowed his head but made no move to return the money. 'Put it in your shirt pocket,' Faleasa suggested. The man's hand obeyed him. 'Now that our small problem has been solved what shall we discuss?'

'This humble person is a poor man with a large hungry aiga, sir,' the   28
man confessed, his head still bowed.

'Who isn't poor?' interrupted Faleasa.   29

'That's why this worthless person has accepted your generous gift, sir,'   30
continued the fofo.

'Don't worry,' Faleasa said, 'your honour and self-respect are still intact.   31
There is no need to feel you have sold them to this worthless old man.' The man smiled. 'Don't go yet. I have gifts for your wife and hungry children as well.' Faleasa went over to the ola in which, while he had been asleep, Felefele had stored all their aiga's clothes, selected the best dresses, lava-lava, and shirts, and piled them into the fofo's willing lap. 'And you don't need to thank this worthless old man for these things,' he said. 'On your way out go to my aiga who got you to visit me and thank them; the clothes belong to them.' The man nodded, mumbled thank you, thank you, and got up to go. 'Would you do one small favour for this worthless old man?' Faleasa asked.

'Anything,' the fofo replied, 'anything, sir!'   32

'When you discuss the case of this helpless old man with his strong aiga   33
tell them that you failed to drive the aitu out of this old man's entrails.' The fofo nodded again and hurried out of the fale.

Faleasa watched him enter the fale in which Felefele and her scheming   34
brood were waiting for him. When they saw he was watching they lowered the fale blinds. Faleasa rested his cunning head on his ali and smiled triumphantly.

That evening after he had bathed in the pool he returned home to find   35
that his fale had been tidied and his aiga were gathered in it ready for their evening lotu. He examined them disdainfully, dressed behind a curtain that Felefele had strung across the side of the fale where he slept, then emerged and commanded them to leave him alone. If they dared send him another insane fofo, he said, he would put fatal curses on all of them. Felefele and some of their daughters and grandchildren started to cry, but he ordered them to get out of *his* fale and said that from then on there would be no more lotu—he didn't believe in that Christian nonsense any more. Elefane started to declaim a speech he had prepared to try to placate

his father but Faleasa told him to shut his hypocritical gob and get out. Felefele accused him of not loving them any more but he only laughed loudly and maniacally, which frightened the children into a shrieking cacophony of tears, and told them to have their ridiculous lotu somewhere else, this fale was his and only his and nobody was to enter it without his permission. They left and he soon heard them having their lotu in the next fale. He got out the large transistor radio which he had bought on his last visit to Apia to sell some cacao beans and turned it up full volume; the blaring sound of guitar music soon drowned out not only his aiga's lotu but the whole neighbourhood's, and he knew that next day the matai council would meet to discuss his behaviour, especially his humiliation of their pastor. He also knew that no matter how irate the council was with him it wouldn't fine him because its members would still be afraid of his power, and fining a madman possessed by an aitu would make them look ridiculous and very unchristian. They would only caution his aiga to keep him under firm control, and say that if he broke any more bylaws they would impose heavy penalties on his aiga—after all, possessed persons weren't responsible for their irresponsibility. Good! he laughed to himself, good!

Because he had spent seventy-six years living like them, *being* them, he 36
could predict their every move, a great advantage in his exhilarating battle for survival as a free man. For example, their next move would be for Filemoni, Felefele, and Elefane to organise his best friends to visit him and try to talk him out of his aitu (and vice versa). Filemoni would lead the delegation because he suffered from delusions of grandeur; and he would be braver than on his first visit because he would have a gang to back him.

When the lotu were over Faleasa switched off the radio and yelled to his 37
aiga to bring him his evening meal and be quick about it. His food was served on tin plates. He'd *solve* that. He ate hungrily, washed his mouth and hands, and then bent every plate, implement, and cup in half and threw them out on to the paepae. From the kitchen fale he heard Felefele's muffled cursing when the women showed her the damaged implements and utensils. He also heard his quick-tempered youngest son, Moaula, who was in his late thirties and married to a sullen woman, exclaim: 'The ungrateful old fool. I should go and knock the insanity out of his head!' (He wouldn't dare of course because assaulting one's parent was taboo.) Moaula was his favourite son; he possessed much courage, a quality sadly lacking in all his other children. 'Don't ever talk about your father that way again!' Faleasa heard Elefane warn Moaula. Faleasa wondered how long it would take before his beloved aiga started warring among themselves. He would play off one faction against the other—a technique he was master of after years of manipulating Malaelua politics.

After five games of patience it dawned on him that this was the first day 38
in his adult life he hadn't said any prayers, hadn't sung any hymns, hadn't read the Bible, hadn't pretended to like his thirty or so snotty-nosed grandchildren, hadn't made decisions that suited everyone but himself, and

hadn't sacrificed a little bit more of himself for the sake of his aiga, village, and church. He whooped piercingly and noticed all his neighbours and aiga gazing in his direction. Some of the elders shook their heads sadly. Alas, such a good man now driven insane by the Devil, he imagined them saying to one another. Fools! he thought.

Moaula's wife, Solimanava, and two of her young daughters entered hesitantly to hang up his mosquito net. He continued listening to the radio and playing patience. They moved round quietly, not daring to attract his attention. He pointed at the centre of the fale and they strung up the net there, spread out his sleeping mats, put his ali at the head of the mats, and crept out of the fale. 39

'Thank you,' he said to Solimanava in his most un-insane voice. She gasped audibly with relief, her sullen face breaking into a grimace of surprise. 'Thank you,' he repeated, 'but tell your stupid husband to copulate some joy and sense into you!' He bared his teeth at her and she almost screamed as she turned and fled, with his best insane laughter chasing her. 40

He put out his hurricane lamp, got under his net, stretched out, with his head on his ali, and gazed up into the dark healing Void (so he called it). Later, with the muffled sound of the surf brushing at his ears, he thought about what would happen the next morning, and enjoyed anticipating it: he would destroy Filemoni, who owed his pastorship to him and had proven utterly unsuited to the position, and maybe *save*, yes, that was the word for it, save some of his closest friends, whom Filemoni would bring with him, from the self-destroying ritual. He especially wanted to save Laaumatua Lemigao, his most precious companion since childhood. 41

It was well into the morning but he remained in his mosquito net. His daughters brought him his morning meal and he ate it inside his net, which further persuaded everyone that he was truly possessed. When his daughters tried to talk to him he behaved as if they were invisible, and they left in tears. He had discovered that silence was another effective weapon he could use against them. So, while he lay in his net, waiting for Filemoni and his cohorts to arrive, he rehearsed how he would use that silence. He injected a look of uncomprehending indifference into his face, his eyes assumed a dead withdrawn look, and a little later he succeeded in manufacturing enough spittle to dribble slowly out of the corners of his mouth. He sat up and practised his new act repeatedly. 42

This was how Filemoni and three of Faleasa's best friends found him. When Felefele saw the party entering Faleasa's fale she sent a daughter to take down his net. She did so with her father sitting there dribbling, and withdrawn into an infuriating silence, which, when she told Felefele and Elefane about it, they interpreted as the final silence of the possessed, the bedevilled. 43

Filemoni and his group of persuaders greeted Faleasa formally, according to custom. No reply, no reaction: just the dead eyes, the slow dribble, 44 the almost imperceptible rocking of the body backwards and forwards, the flies buzzing round it.

'He's got worse,' Filemoni whispered to the others. They nodded and 45 continued to stare at Faleasa who noticed that Laaumatua Lemigao wasn't with them.

'What are we going to do?' Sau, who was in his sixties, asked Filemoni. 46 He only shook his head sadly.

'Yes, what are we going to do?' the other old men, Tupo and Vaelupa, 47 asked.

'It's probably his age that's made his mind go,' said Sau. Tupo and 48 Vaelupa agreed with him but Filemoni disagreed strongly.

'No. When I visited this unfortunate but venerable old man yesterday I 49 clearly heard his dead mother speaking through him. There can be no doubt about that. He is possessed by an evil aitu.' For the next fifteen minutes or so they discussed Faleasa's condition without bothering to whisper any more. From this, Faleasa concluded, his act had convinced them that he couldn't comprehend anything.

'But why his mother's aitu?' Filemoni asked. 'His mother loved him.' 50

'It's probably an aitu pretending to be his mother so we would think 51 twice about exorcising it,' suggested Vaelupa, who, Faleasa remembered, was respected in Malaelua for his logic. Tupo, who was always easily dominated by the other matai but whom Faleasa admired for his warmth and kindness and humility, agreed with Vaelupa but suggested that they shouldn't discuss the matter too loudly as the aitu inside Faleasa might be listening to them.

'Just look at his eyes,' said Sau. 'Does he look as if he's hearing any- 52 thing?' Faleasa almost blinked, unable to believe the lack of concern in Sau's remark, but he was still hopeful that Sau was his friend—fifty years of believing this was difficult to erase from one's heart. Sau erased it with his next remarks: 'We all know, he's always been slightly odd, arrogant, and too dictatorial—mind you, that doesn't mean I disliked him. But that's why this tragedy has happened to him. One can almost say he is being punished by the Almighty for his past.' For a painful minute Faleasa couldn't believe it: Sau had surely always been a friend whom he had trusted. The agony of betrayal almost shattered his act. He felt the nausea returning, born out of the depths of his pain, but he swallowed it back when a few seconds later he admitted to himself that Sau was pretentious, hypocritical excrement like Filemoni, and he didn't need any of them, not even Laaumatua who hadn't bothered to visit him. He was free. They were still trapped in their excreta and stench. Yes, he was free and could do without the ungrateful wretches he had placed in influential positions in Malaelua.

'Yes, he was always a hypocrite,' said Vaelupa. The fat, elephantiasis- 53 ridden thief! Faleasa cursed to himself, remembering how, when Vaelupa had secretly used Malaelua funds and he had found out before the council did, Vaelupa had pleaded with him and he had paid back all the money himself.

'That's not true!' Tupo said. Sau, Vaelupa, and Filemoni ignored his remark. 'That's not true,' Tupo repeated more loudly. They gazed at him as though saying, So what! you're not important, and Tupo looked dejectedly at the floor. The wretches, like his aiga, had used him all these years. What a naive, gullible person he must have been.   54

'As another human being in need of our help we must help him.' Filemoni said.   55

'But how?' Sau asked.   56

'Perhaps we should take him into the Apia hospital and get one of those clever palagi[1] doctors to examine him,' Tupo said after the others had failed to come up with any useful suggestions. Faleasa agreed with Tupo but he saw the others shake their heads and dismiss the suggestion with clicking tongues.   57

'He's not ill physically,' said Filemoni.   58

'Palagi doctors don't know how to cure Samoan illnesses anyway,' Sau added. 'And this is a Samoan illness.'   59

'He's possessed of an evil aitu,' Vaelupa elaborated further. Tupo only looked dejected again.   60

At that point Felefele and a group of women brought them food: chicken, pork, fish, baked taro, and palusami. But no one put any food in front of Faleasa. Filemoni hurried through a short prayer, then they attacked the large piles of food. They ate as though Faleasa was invisible or had assumed the unimportant presence of a fly. Only Tupo glanced at him with concern from time to time.   61

Faleasa waited until they were halfway through their piles of food, then he started to laugh hysterically (or so they believed), with tears streaming from his eyes and saliva drooling out of his mouth. They looked at him, at first with embarrassment and then with sadistic curiosity. He stopped laughing abruptly. A breathless silence fell as he scrutinised each one of them.   62

'They have poisoned you!' he hissed. For a moment they didn't understand. 'There's poison in the food you're eating,' he repeated. Filemoni spat out the food and pushed his foodmat away violently, so did Sau and Vaelupa. Tupo, always the last to realise what was happening, looked at the hunk of taro in his left hand, then again at Faleasa. 'Can you feel the pain yet?' Faleasa asked. 'Feel the poison eating into your greedy stomachs and intestines?'   63

'He's lying,' Felefele said apologetically. 'Please excuse his behaviour; he doesn't know what he's saying.'   64

'Get out!' Faleasa ordered her. She stormed out to the kitchen fale.   65

---

1. palagi: *a Pacific Islands name for a European.*

Turning again to the three frightened men, Faleasa said, 'You're going to die. The poison will eat your insides away—slowly!' Filemoni gasped; a low uncontrollable whimpering issued from Sau's trembling mouth; Vaelupa gargled with some water and spat on to the paepae; and Tupo asked:

'Why did you do it, Faleasa?' 66

Shaking his head slowly, Faleasa said, 'They did!' and pointed at the 67
women of his aiga sitting at the back posts. 'And he did!' and pointed at Filemoni, who protested his innocence with an almost shouted 'No! No! No!' 'Go and die in your own fale!' Faleasa ordered them. 'I don't want you to stink out my fale!' When they refused to leave and Filemoni began to preach to him about behaving like a child, Faleasa hurled handfuls of pebbles from the floor at them.

Tupo got up politely, wished Faleasa well, and left, with most of his 68
honour intact in the eyes of the Malaeluans who had been watching the confrontation. Filemoni, now outraged by a madman's attack on his self-importance, shouted to Faleasa (a helpless madman) to shut his arrogant gob (and immediately lost the little respect the Malaeluans had for him), ordered Faleasa's children to keep their 'insane and violent matai away from human beings' (and immediately turned the whole Aiga Faleasa against him—when Moaula was told about Filemoni's insulting remark he threatened to disembowel, distongue, and dislife Filemoni, cousin or no cousin!). Filemoni realised with horror what his big mouth had just said and what it was going to cost him, and immediately apologised to the whole Aiga Faleasa; but Felefele, standing on the paepae of the kitchen fale, ordered him to please leave their fale, and said, they, his loyal cousins and relatives, didn't want to ever see him again. Faleasa, she shouted, was definitely *not* insane! So Filemoni staggered up and stumbled out of the fale, cursing his mouth for getting him into trouble again. Sau and Vaelupa started to apologise to the Aiga Faleasa on behalf of the pastor but Faleasa scooped up more pebbles and scattered them, like stinging spittle, over the two men. They scrambled to their shaking legs and backed out of the fale, vowing to get the council to fine the Aiga Faleasa because of their disrespectful treatment of Pastor Filemoni and them, two high-ranking alii. Faleasa deserved to be possessed and insane, Sau said to Vaelupa when they were a safe distance from Faleasa's fale.

'But why?' Laaumatua asked. Faleasa had just described to his lifelong 69
friend his plan and his transformation from what he called 'cannibal meat' into a 'free angel'. When Faleasa didn't reply Laaumatua exclaimed, 'It's insane!' realised the implications of his remark, and apologised. It was midnight; they had met secretly in the church.

'But you're right, Laau,' Faleasa said, 'it is an insane plan but I'm con- 70
vinced it's the only *sane* thing I can and must do if I want to remain sane myself.' He paused and then added: 'Perhaps in our insane world in which

terror and violence feed on the heart's sinews, what we call insanity or, rather, those people we brand as insane are really the only sane creatures among us. Who knows. For seventy-six years I lived what I now see as an insane existence. I was easy meat for all the cannibals; and the worst, the most rapacious of all, were my own aiga and village.' Alone in the black midnight silence and stillness of the church they were beings without physical form, mere voices trying to hear each other, like spirits who, with the coming of dawn, would disappear from the earth.

'Why did you have to tell me though? Couldn't you have left me alone, safe in my belief that you'd gone mad?' 71

'I'm not courageous enough to do it alone,' replied Faleasa. 'I need your support, your courage, and our understanding. There are too many cannibals and too few missionaries.' He tried to laugh but couldn't. 72

'I must go,' said Laaumatua. 73

Faleasa reached out and held his arm. 'You will help me, Laau?' he asked. Laaumatua tugged his arm away. 74

They were silent for an awkward space, as the darkness throbbed in their eyes and confined them more tightly in the greater darkness of their individual selves; then Laaumatua said: 'The individual freedom you have discovered and now want to maintain is contrary to the very basis of our way of life. Have you considered that? For over thirty years you, Faleasa, and a few other matai have led our village, and your leadership, as was the ancient practice, has been based firmly on the principle that you exist to serve others, to serve the very people you are now branding as cannibals. A good leader doesn't live for himself but for his people. And you, Faleasa, wanted the leadership.' 75

Faleasa agreed but added: 'If I had my life to live again I would not become a leader. And now I all I want for the remaining years of my life is to be free. . . . Surely I have earned that?' he pleaded. 76

That week an exciting tale of the ignominious defeat of three sane matai and a pastor by a possessed old man circulated through Malaelua and spilt over into the neighbouring villages. The tale, like any other, grew in complexity, size, and inventiveness as it spread from imagination to imagination, but one basic theme consolidated itself: the old man was the hero, the sane matai and pastor were the villains. Only Laaumatua, who had refused to accompany Filemoni and his party to Faleasa's fale and whom Faleasa had got to start circulating the tale, knew who had coined it. 77

STUDY QUESTIONS

1. At the age of seventy-six, Faleasa revolts against his life and his community. What aspects of his life does he reject?

2. How do different members of his family respond to his changed behavior? What do their different responses tell us about their characters?
3. Faleasa is situated in a privileged position in his community. Analyze the social hierarchy that constitutes his community and his position in it.
4. Discuss how the use of the pastor and the fofo to exorcise Faleasa's alleged demons function to SATIRIZE elements of Samoan society.
5. Do you consider the insertion of Samoan words in this story necessary? What is the effect of various local colloquialisms and of these non-English words?

THEMATIC QUESTIONS

1. Motifs of freedom and travel appear in several works from both Australia and New Zealand. Drawing on poems such as David Malouf's "Off the Map," Les Murray's "The Dream of Wearing Shorts Forever," and Patricia Grace's "And So I Go," discuss the different treatment of these themes.

2. Frontier life, the life of the open land, is a literary source for Katharine Susannah Prichard, Xavier Herbert, and Patricia Grace. Compare and contrast the role of frontier and pastoral life as it is portrayed in the selections by these authors.

3. Analyze the words, phrases, and images used to describe the land in the selections from Australia. Compare the impressions created by these diction choices with those from the New Zealand selections.

4. The uneasy and unequal relationship between males and females is a theme that may be found in Elizabeth Jolley's "Mr Parker's Valentine" and Janet Frame's "The Day of the Sheep." Analyze these stories from this perspective, making clear the sources, channels, and results of this unequal relationship.

5. The pain of bigotry, snobbery, and humiliation is experienced by various characters in these selections. Examine Xavier Herbert's "Clothes Make the Man," the excerpt from Colin Johnson's *Dr. Wooreddy's Prescription for Enduring the Ending of the World*, and Witi Ihimaera's "His First Ball" from this point of view, comparing and contrasting the source of bigotry or injury for the victims and the consequences they encounter.

6. Race relationships have been and are a concern for Australian culture. Examine texts such as Judith Wright's "Bora Ring," Xavier Herbert's "Clothes Make the Man," the passage from Johnson's *Dr. Wooreddy's*

Prescription for Enduring the Ending of the World, and Patricia Grace's "And So I Go" for what they tell us about black-white encounters, both past and present.

7. Compare and contrast the literary treatment of white-Aborigine relations with that of white-Maori relations in the stories and poems you have studied.

8. The critique of white colonialism is a major theme in contemporary writing, especially writing produced by indigenous writers. Discuss the criticism of colonial settlement, the domination over native peoples, and the economic exploitation of these people as demonstrated in the work of writers such as Colin Johnson, Patricia Grace, Kama Kerpi, and Albert Wendt.

9. While very different in treatment, Colin Johnson's piece and Allen Curnow's poem "The Skeleton of the Great Moa in the Canterbury Museum, Christchurch," may appear to suggest a parallel vision of evolutionary and colonial history. Discuss the themes developed in these two works, paying special attention to where they diverge in their representations.

10. Compare and contrast Patricia Grace's story "And So I Go" with the passage from Albert Wendt's *Pouliuli.* In what ways are they constructed as an insider's view of indigenous South Pacific societies?

11. The theme of the individual's struggle against social conformity is apparent in the work of Patrick White, Janet Frame, and Albert Wendt. Discuss the different treatments of this theme in these authors' stories.

EUROPE

EUROPE

Introduction

A t the turn of the twentieth century, Europe, one of the small-est continents, actually a peninsula extending from the land-mass Eurasia, appeared to be at the apogee of its power.[1] In spite of linguistic, political, and ethnic fragmentation, this small continent had amassed a concentration of the world's wealth and technology. For a variety of reasons, including its array of natural resources, most significantly coal and iron; its deep harbors; and its secular orientation, Europe had been the first region in the world to industrialize. Consequently, in 1900, the factories of Europe were the workshops for the world's manufactured goods and its great metropolises were the centers of international finance. Indeed, a host of Western European nations, some as tiny as Belgium and Holland, dominated over three fourths of the world's population. Domination was achieved through either direct political control as in the case of colonies in Africa or unequal trade relationships as in the case of the ostensibly independent nations of South America. Because of Europe's wealth, productivity, and worldwide expansion, historians often refer to the period from the seventeenth century, when Europe first began to gain its predominant role, to the twentieth century as the age of European ascendancy. During this time Europe was the hub of an integrated world order that it largely had created for its own

---

1. *The Ural Mountains separate Europe from Asia. The former Soviet Union, the world's largest nation, spans both Europe and Asia. Its most populous territory, about a third of its area, is in Europe.*

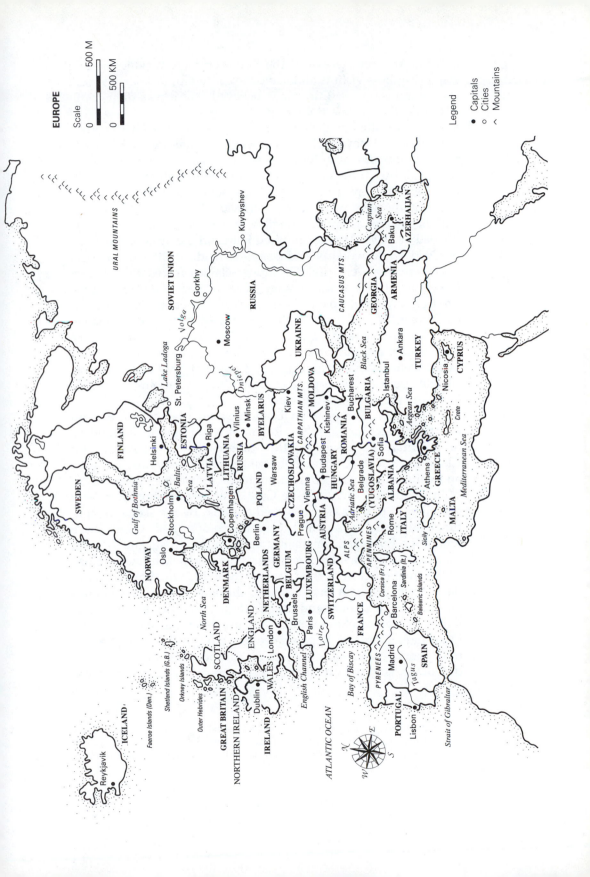

benefit. And on the eve of the two world wars, which would claim 70 million victims and leave the continent, in 1945, a virtual charnel house, most Europeans believed that it was their continent's destiny to rule the world.

What was this civilization which took upon itself the ideology of global power? In many ways Europe was a heterogeneous society primarily composed of nation-states that had waged wars with each other and would continue through the first half of the twentieth century to do so. National consciousness and national animosities were strong. Individuals belligerently identified themselves as French, English, or German. Europe was also divided by class. Aristocrats still dominated the apex of the social pyramid while workers and peasants made up the great base. Class tensions were rife. The upper classes feared the poor as fomentors of class warfare, which actually did take place in Russia, Germany, and Spain. Technology also separated the regions of Europe. The nations of the Northwest were predominately industrial, urban, and wealthy. The peoples of the South and East were largely agrarian and technologically backward. Yet, in spite of the welter of national, class, and regional divisions, it is possible to speak of a European civilization with defining characteristics and a common worldview.

Historically, European civilization evolved between the ninth and twelfth centuries. In its origins, it was primarily a blending of "Germanic" folkways, the Graeco-Roman heritage, and Christian teaching.[1] The religious element was predominant, and early Europeans often thought of themselves as living in "Christendom." The majestic Gothic cathedrals they built were testimonials to their God-centered outlook. By the sixteenth century, however, a significant secularization had taken place within the European sensibility. Renaissance artists and writers, not necessarily forsaking religious themes, took human beings as the chief concern of their art and thought. Whether Leonardo da Vinci or William Shakespeare, the aim of the Renaissance master was to understand and to depict the physical and material, as well as the spiritual and psychological nature of the individual. From the Renaissance on, the individual in the material world became the subject of European discourse and endeavor. In fact, the creation of a human-centered rather than a

---

1. *Certainly other influences shaped European civilization as well. For example, Islamic Spain stimulated the founding of medieval universities, Europeans learned mathematical numerals from India, and Chinese boat-building techniques made possible the sixteenth-century European transoceanic voyages.*

God-centered outlook is one of Europe's chief legacies to world culture.

The secular thrust of European civilization took many forms. Physically it was manifested in the technological advances stemming from the scientific revolution; in capitalism, a uniquely dynamic economic system; in the conquest of other ancient civilizations such as the Indian; and in industrialization and the invention of power-driven machines that multiplied a thousandfold human productive potential. In transforming their way of life from an agrarian to a largely commercial and technological one, Europeans broke with the earlier values of traditional societies. Instead of looking to their ancestors or established authorities for moral validation, Europeans developed values that celebrated rationalism, the certainty of scientific "laws," and material progress.[1] Asserting the ascendancy of their values, Europeans came to believe in the superiority of their own civilization.

Cultural arrogance and the theory of Europe's right to dominate other peoples were the negative correlations of European secularism. A positive correlation was the formulation of a new theory of society. The concern with the human and material world eventually led Europeans to conceive of society not as hierarchically ordered, but as made up of free and autonomous individuals who had specific rights. This concept was first clearly affirmed with the guarantee by the English Parliament of civil and legal liberties in the 1690s, and it became part of the European and world heritage with the French Revolutionaries' Declaration of the Rights of Man and the Citizen in 1789.

A society composed of free individuals with specific civil, social, and political rights, however, was not quickly or easily realized in Europe. Nineteenth-century political thinking as well as political struggles contested the issues of what were the rights of citizens and which groups or classes were members of the political nation. While working-class people marched, petitioned, and in some cases built barricades in order to win suffrage, liberal theorists such as John Stuart Mill warned that the very growth of government negated liberty. On the other hand, socialists like Karl Marx thundered that true freedom lay in the attainment of social and economic equality. And women had to speak and struggle largely by themselves not only for political rights, which

---

1. *This broad generalization needs to be qualified. From the Renaissance on, there was a dissenting view in regard to the benefits of technology and science. From Christopher Marlowe's* Dr. Faustus *to Aldous Huxley's* Brave New World *there is a pessimistic strain of thinking about what scientific knowledge will mean for humanity.*

they would not gain until the twentieth century, but for the right to control property and, most important, for legal authority over their children. Nineteenth-century literature, in turn, addressed the societal significance of the individual. If the subject of Renaissance art had been the nature of humanity, the topic of the great nineteenth-century novels became the individual in relation to society. Writers such as Charles Dickens, Gustave Flaubert, Emile Zola, and Leo Tolstoy depicted beings whose individuality and inner nature became known through a life of social interaction.

The advent of the twentieth century marked a turning point in European history. At the very time Europe appeared to have achieved a hegemony of world power, it was undergoing a multifaceted and pervasive cultural crisis. Certainties held since the Renaissance about human nature and the composition of the universe seemed to be eroding. The social/political theorizing of the nineteenth century already had been indicative of an underlying disquietude which had been greatly intensified by the intellectual upheaval wrought by Darwinist thinking. The publication of Darwin's *The Origin of Species* in 1859 had undermined and cast doubt upon both the Christian cosmogony and the belief in the centrality of human rationalism. After Darwin, Homo sapiens was only a tiny, perhaps even fleeting, part of the instinctual evolutionary process. Now, at the beginning of the twentieth century, atomic physics and the theory of relativity revolutionized the very concept of matter while Freud's explorations of the forces of the unconscious cast further doubt upon human rationalism. In fact, philosophers such as Friedrich Nietzsche and Henri Bergson celebrated the creative, liberating powers of the irrational. The upheaval in perception and cognition was equally profound in literature and art. To some Europeans, in the avant-garde of the arts, reality was no longer open simply to portrayal but needed to be unearthed in an atomized world of multitudinous substructures. The exploration of the elusive, and frequently deceptive, psychological terrain became the province of art. Turning from representational modes of expression, the modernists, whether Pablo Picasso in painting or Marcel Proust, Franz Kafka, or James Joyce in writing, emphasized the constituent elements of their craft—color, shape, light, sound, words—as the agents for perceiving the hidden reality. They, moreover, evolved new techniques for evoking the psychological/emotional terrain. The Symbolists in their writing, for example, projected emotional states upon "symbolic" objects.

The cultural revolution presaged the cataclysmic social and political events of the twentieth century. Economic and political competition led European nation-states into World War I in 1914.

Its conclusion four years later saw a disillusioned, embittered, and exhausted continent. Even the victors, France and England, were indebted to their ally, the United States. World power was beginning its shift away from Europe. The war, moreover, had not solved the issues of militarism and competitiveness. Nationalists throughout Europe, but most specifically in defeated Germany, dreamed about revenge and a new struggle for European hegemony.

World War I also unleashed the class warfare whose specter had haunted the continent throughout the nineteenth century. The ideal of citizens endowed with civil, political, and social rights had been only inconclusively realized. The men of Western Europe had achieved universal suffrage by the twentieth century, though women did not get the vote until after World War I. In Eastern Europe, amid an impoverished population, autocracy ruled. Under the intensified suffering and deprivation caused by World War I, the Russian peasants and workers united and fought a social and political revolution that brought a Communist government to power in 1917. The political revolution corresponded to a cultural ferment that had permeated Russian literary and artistic circles from the beginning of the twentieth century. Grouped in schools, issuing manifestos, writers and poets, whether Symbolists, Futurists, or Acmeists, all had engaged in a provocative questioning of the role of art and of the artist in traditional Russian society. The ferment carried into the 1920s, a fruitful but short-lived period of artistic openness and widespread experimentation in Soviet society. Artists and writers focused on the experience of the Revolution and Civil War, depicted the conflict between the old and the new in Soviet society, and some, such as the Constructivists, argued for the creation of art that would be truly representative of both socialism and modern technology.

The Russian Communist victory, however, polarized the Europe of the interwar period. On the left were those who supported the Communist experiment and urged reforms that would lessen the inequalities of their own societies. On the right were those who not only opposed Marxism, but who came to revoke the whole liberal heritage of the French Revolution. Writers and artists, too, became politically divided, though most agreed on a disdain for the mores and norms of traditional bourgeois culture. Thus the modernists, on the political right and left, continued their experimentation with techniques and forms. Among them, the most radical and innovative were the Surrealists, who created jarring verbal and pictorial associations in order to liberate the individual and social unconscious. On the other hand, writers like the social realists argued for a polemical art of ideas that would help shape a more egalitarian political consciousness.

The worldwide depression that began in 1929 intensified the sense of malaise that permeated European society. In Italy and Germany and then in Spain and Portugal, Fascist parties established totalitarian regimes. The irrational forces that Freud had diagnosed, that the avant-garde had explored, seemed realized in the organized violence and manipulative mass psychology of the Nazi Party. In contrast to the militaristic exuberance of the Fascists, those Europeans believing in the rights of individuals seemed immobilized. Ineffectual reform movements, such as the Popular Front in France, failed to lessen inequalities in society. In the Soviet Union, the Communist experiment had mired by the 1930s into Stalinist totalitarianism with its rigid suppression of artistic freedom.

In 1939, the discontent of European society exploded into World War II. Begun by the Fascist powers, this became the most destructive war of the modern age. It was a truly global war, in which both sides regarded civilians as chief military targets. It was a war in which genocide was devised and implemented as a policy of state and European Jews suffered the Holocaust. It was the war which with the bombings of Hiroshima and Nagasaki initiated the atomic age with its consequent nuclear arms race. Ultimately, Fascism was defeated but at the cost of close to 50 million lives, of whom 42 million were Europeans. The end of the war also was the end of the era of European hegemony. World dominance was not won by one of the traditional European powers, but passed instead to the United States, whose role as a global power came to be challenged by the Soviet Union. The European eclipse from the world stage was further demonstrated by the post–World War II loss of colonies. The anti-Fascist struggle with its emphasis on democratic rights had given great impetus to the independence movements that had been evolving in the colonies throughout the twentieth century. Concomitantly, war exhaustion made it more difficult for the European states to militarily maintain their colonies. Decolonization took two forms. One was the formal granting of independence by the colonial power to the formal colony, as in the case of India. The other was through wars of national liberation, as in the case of Algeria. By the mid-1970s, the age of European empires would come to an end.

In 1945, Europe was a shattered shadow of its former self. Its infrastructure was destroyed; its cities were in ruins; millions of hapless refugees sought shelter and livelihoods. The continent, like Germany, was divided into two spheres of influence, the

American in the West and the Soviet in the East. Although there was a longing throughout the continent that out of the cataclysm would arise a new, less bellicose, more egalitarian Europe, reconstruction was shaped to a significant degree by the exigencies of the cold war. Western Europe developed along capitalist and democratic lines; the nations of Eastern Europe followed a socialist and totalitarian model. The West reindustrialized, lessened the inequalities of its society through welfare legislation, and created the Common Market, the basis for the economic union of the 1990s. Such legislation served to lessen the old antagonism among classes and among nations. The Eastern nations, led by the Soviet Union, industrialized, modernized their agriculture, and, most significantly, raised the educational level of their populations. Until 1989, the Berlin Wall symbolized that there were two Europes, the Western having a higher standard of living and more individual liberty and the Eastern lacking in both freedom and in material goods.

In the initial post–World War II period, "Stalinist" cultural policies were imposed upon all of Eastern Europe. With Stalin's death in 1953, there was a waxing and waning of periods of liberalization and periods of repression. Within these parameters, Eastern European writers attempted to assess the historical/ philosophical meaning of their collective and individual experiences. Experimenting with various forms ranging from the theater of the absurd to the autobiographical narrative, they at times had to make themselves known through illegal typescripts (the Soviet samizdats) and tapescripts. Because of censorship and repression, some prominent writers—Aleksandr Solzhenitsyn in the Soviet Union, Czeslaw Milosz in Poland, Milan Kundera in Czechoslovakia—went into exile and continued to write in the West. Whether in exile or not, Eastern European writers as a whole concerned themselves with exploring in their works the broad questions of individual and social truth and morality.

Political uprisings throughout the postwar period showed that Eastern European populations were as restive as their writers for greater political and cultural freedom. Until the mid-1980s, Soviet troops or the threat of troops was used to quell these uprisings. A similar longing for liberalization on the part of the Soviet populations changed that nation's domestic and foreign policies. Thus, the Soviets did not interfere in the great popular demonstrations that arose throughout Eastern Europe in 1989. Within that year the majority of totalitarian regimes fell and these societies and governments underwent a process of democratization. Likewise, the removal of the Berlin Wall and the reunification of Germany signaled an end to the post–World War II division of the continent. Then, in 1991, the Soviet Union came to an end. Nationalist movements in the various republics led to the dissolution of the political entity that Lenin had created seventy years previously. Although it is too early to assess the future prospects of the newly independent republics, the former Soviet Union clearly is and will remain the dominant force in this area.

Today, the nations of Europe appear to face the possibility of creating a truly common future. There are serious difficulties. Economic problems, political rivalries, the effects of long-term ecological abuse, and ethnic animosities are all obstacles to a unified Europe. Yet with the dissolution of two rigidly separated power blocs, there are grounds for optimism that this European civilization with its common ancestry and common intellectual and artistic achievements will realize a transnational European future.

Twentieth-century literature speaks to the possibility of such a commonality. European literature, though reflective of each nation's heritage, is rooted in two broad literary traditions which are influential in the evolution of the contemporary sensibility. These traditions, the realist and the modernist, including the avant-garde, transcend national and ideological boundaries. They comprise the framework for twentieth-century European literary expression and are the grounding for the contemporary literary and artistic movement known as postmodernism.

The realist tradition, whose basic form is the biographical narrative, reaches back to the very foundations of European literature. The stories of Chaucer, Boccaccio, and Rabelais are its antecedents. Informed by the Renaissance concern with humanity in the secular world, the realist tradition presumes the possibility of a linear and spatial depiction of reality. It is firmly rooted in the view of art as mimetic representation.

The flowering of the realist tradition came in the nineteenth century with the great social novels of Flaubert, Tolstoy, and Dickens. This was the era of the convulsive changes wrought by the eruptive and disruptive growth of capitalism—industrialization, the establishment of a world market, the rise of the bourgeoisie to political power. Throughout the continent, novelists were at one in the belief that the inner being of individuals could be rendered and made comprehensible only in relation to their social and historical conditions. As George Eliot wrote, "It is the habit of my imagination to strive after as full a vision of the medium in which a character moves as of the character itself." Striving to express the dualism of the individual and of social reality, nineteenth-century novelists created the complex paradigm that realists of the twentieth century have followed. The realist paradigm is informed by the vision of human beings as free and autonomous agents in society. Yet the development of their individualities is limited or defined by society through such issues as class, gender, materialist values, and political oppression. The artistic tension of realism resides, then, in the depiction of the problematic nature of the individual as a social being. The underlying supposition is that the reader and author are united in a joint endeavor to comprehend this nature and that the very telling of the tale leads to a process of enlightenment. Eventually, some writers like Emile Zola and George Bernard Shaw came to argue an important transformative role for art. They held that the very telling of the tale could transform reality by enlightening the collective perception. The politically committed writers of the 1930s held a similar view. In our anthology the stories of Maxim Gorky, Natalia Ginzburg, and Frank O'Connor are within this broad realist tradition of the narrative of the problematic hero.

The paradigm of modernism is quite different in that it tends to reject the concepts of mimetic representation and of referentiality. As stated above, the modernist avant-garde originated in the multifarious questioning about the nature of reality at the turn of the twentieth century. Unlike realists, modernist writers such as James Joyce, Franz Kafka, and Virginia Woolf do not presume the existence of a mutually shared, self-evident reality between the reader and writer. Here they are influenced by nonlinear concepts of time and of consciousness. Postulating time as a continuous flow and consciousness as an embodiment of both past and present, modernists are at odds with a narrative depiction of plot and character. In their view reality is obscure. It is obscured by the very simultaneity of experience. It is obscured by the imprisonment of each individual in a private consciousness. It is the task of the writer, whose realm is quite distinct from that of nature, to use the medium of art to decode this hidden reality.

In their view of art as an aesthetically rendered, intellectual construct of decipherment, modernists place great emphasis on the constituent elements of their craft. Whether to defamiliarize the world as in the case of Surrealists or to find a language expressive of subjective consciousness as in the case of Formalists such as Joyce, literary techniques are of utmost importance to these writers. Waging a battle against conventional means of expression as deceptive of the human condition, modernists greatly expanded the domain of writing with, for example, the use of Symbolist imagery and stream-of-consciousness techniques. Significantly, the impetus to modernist writing is a vision of the loneliness and separation of human beings. Progeny of mass industrial society, modernists speak to the anomie of this society.

Their artistic endeavor of decipherment represents the attempt to break through the bonds of isolation. In this sense, modernist writers are the seekers of an elusive coherence and unity in the atomized world of mass society. On the other hand, the modernist emphasis on the aesthetic of artistry has an inherent tendency to exhalt the artwork in itself and to separate it from society. For some modernists the very subject of art has become the aesthetic creation rather than the human individual. In this anthology the stories of Joyce, Kafka, and Woolf represent the modernist vision.

Contemporary writers, the postmodernists, are heirs to the modernists' explorations of the subjectivity of reality. In their work, the postmodernists utilize the artistic techniques and practices formulated by their predecessors. Recognizing the complexity unearthed by the twentieth-century avant-garde, postmodernists carry it further to probe the very subjectivity of the writer as well as of the reader. They extend and deepen the modernist paradigm by their very questioning of the ability of the artist to ever fully succeed in the endeavor of decipherment. To postmodernists the creation of "art" that stands as a "universal truth" outside the bounds of the interior monologue of the writer or reader is illusionary. In their recognition of the subjectivity of the writer/reader, postmodernists place a renewed emphasis on the influence of society/culture upon the individual as upon the work of art. Here, they are clearly akin to the realist tradition, which understands that inner consciousness is shaped by one's social being. The postmodernists living, on the one hand, in the era of decolonization, feminist reappraisal of male domination, and struggles for racial equality, and, on the other hand, in the era of global media and mass consumerism understand that gender, race, class, the condition of domination or subordination, as the reifying discourse of the mass media, all contribute to the bonds of isolation within society and serve to create the subjectivity of the work of art. The project of the postmodernists, then, is the decoding of the social consciousness by inserting a variety of discourses into artistic creation. Thus, they utilize not only modernist techniques but images, motifs, and ideas from contemporary mass culture as well as from non-Western societies. Nor do postmodernists shun the narrative, but view it as a significant means of reinstating historical time for the purpose of deciphering and concretizing social reality. In this anthology the stories of Beckett, Buzzati, Duras, Tolstaya, and Kundera illustrate the varying postmodernist approaches.

Gundega Kazaks

Franz Kafka

Franz Kafka (1883–1924) is a Czech writer who is one of the main figures in the emergence of modernism. Kafka's achievement is that in his novels The Trial *(1925),* The Castle *(1926), and* Amerika *(1927) and in his short fiction, he created the opaque, modernist sensibility. Influenced by Freud, Kafka's writings have a dreamlike quality in that they call forth interpretation but never give a conclusive, irrefutable meaning to the reader. This is because Kafka does not permit the authorial presence as an interpretative guide. Thus, though Kafka uses the narrative framework, the reader is only able to infer the subjective reality of the protagonist who, in turn, reveals the self through unconscious acts, inadvertent slips, or dreams. Kafka's techniques are well demonstrated in ''A Hunger Artist,'' where the protagonist's situation and motivations are not unmasked until his death. This story and the rest of Kafka's short stories are available in English translation in* The Complete Stories *(1988).*

A Hunger Artist

During these last decades the interest in professional fasting has markedly diminished. It used to pay very well to stage such great performances under one's own management, but today that is quite impossible. We live in a different world now. At one time the whole town took a lively interest in the hunger artist; from day to day of his fast the excitement mounted; everybody wanted to see him at least once a day; there were people who bought season tickets for the last few days and sat from morning till night in front of his small barred cage; even in the nighttime there were visiting hours, when the whole effect was heightened by torch flares; on fine days the cage was set out in the open air, and then it was the children's special treat to see the hunger artist; for their elders he was often

1

just a joke that happened to be in fashion, but the children stood open-mouthed, holding each other's hands for greater security, marveling at him as he sat there pallid in black tights, with his ribs sticking out so prominently, not even on a seat but down among straw on the ground, sometimes giving a courteous nod, answering questions with a constrained smile, or perhaps stretching an arm through the bars so that one might feel how thin it was, and then again withdrawing deep into himself, paying no attention to anyone or anything, not even to the all-important striking of the clock that was the only piece of furniture in his cage, but merely staring into vacancy with half-shut eyes, now and then taking a sip from a tiny glass of water to moisten his lips.

Besides casual onlookers there were also relays of permanent watchers 2 selected by the public, usually butchers, strangely enough, and it was their task to watch the hunger artist day and night, three of them at a time, in case he should have some secret recourse to nourishment. This was nothing but a formality, instituted to reassure the masses, for the initiates knew well enough that during his fast the artist would never in any circumstances, not even under forcible compulsion, swallow the smallest morsel of food; the honor of his profession forbade it. Not every watcher, of course, was capable of understanding this, there were often groups deliberately huddled together in a rented corner to play cards with great absorption, obviously intending to give the hunger artist the chance of a little refreshment, which they supposed he could draw from some private hoard. Nothing annoyed the artist more than such watchers; they made him miserable; they made his fast seem unendurable; sometimes he mastered his feebleness sufficiently to sing during their watch for as long as he could keep going, to show them how unjust their suspicions were. But that was of little use; they only wondered at his cleverness in being able to fill his mouth even while singing. Much more to his taste were the watchers who sat close up to the bars, who were not content with the dim night lighting of the hall but focused him in the full glare of the electric pocket torch given them by the impresario. The harsh light did not trouble him at all, in any case he could never sleep properly, and he could always drowse a little, whatever the light, at any hour, even when the hall was thronged with noisy onlookers. He was quite happy at the prospect of spending a sleepless night with such watchers; he was ready to exchange jokes with them, to tell them stories out of his nomadic life, anything at all to keep them awake and demonstrate to them again that he had no eatables in his cage and that he was fasting as not one of them could fast. But his happiest moment was when the morning came and an enormous breakfast was brought them, at his expense, on which they flung themselves with the keen appetite of healthy men after a weary night of wakefulness. Of course there were people who argued that this breakfast was an unfair attempt to bribe the watchers, but that was going rather too far, and when they were invited to take on a night's vigil without a breakfast, merely for the sake of the cause, they made themselves scarce, although they stuck stubbornly to their suspicions.

Such suspicions, anyhow, were a necessary accompaniment to the profession of fasting. No one could possibly watch the hunger artist continuously, day and night, and so no one could produce first-hand evidence that the fast had really been rigorous and continuous; only the artist himself could know that, he was therefore bound to be the sole completely satisfied spectator of his own fast. Yet for other reasons he was never satisfied; it was not perhaps mere fasting that had brought him to such skeleton thinness that many people had regretfully to keep away from his exhibitions, because the sight of him was too much for them, perhaps it was dissatisfaction with himself that had worn him down. For he alone knew, what no other initiate knew, how easy it was to fast. It was the easiest thing in the world. He made no secret of this, yet people did not believe him, at the best they set him down as modest, most of them, however, thought he was out for publicity or else was some kind of cheat who found it easy to fast because he had discovered a way of making it easy, and then had the impudence to admit the fact, more or less. He had to put up with all that, and in the course of time had got used to it, but his inner dissatisfaction always rankled, and never yet, after any term of fasting—this must be granted to his credit—had he left the cage of his own free will. The longest period of fasting was fixed by his impresario at forty days, beyond that term he was not allowed to go, not even in great cities, and there was good reason for it, too. Experience had proved that for about forty days the interest of the public could be stimulated by a steadily increasing pressure of advertisement, but after that the town began to lose interest, sympathetic support began notably to fall off; there were of course local variations as between one town and another or one country and another, but as a general rule forty days marked the limit. So on the fortieth day the flower-bedecked cage was opened, enthusiastic spectators filled the hall, a military band played, two doctors entered the cage to measure the results of the fast, which were announced through a megaphone, and finally two young ladies appeared, blissful at having been selected for the honor, to help the hunger artist down the few steps leading to a small table on which was spread a carefully chosen invalid repast. And at this very moment the artist always turned stubborn. True, he would entrust his bony arms to the outstretched helping hands of the ladies bending over him, but stand up he would not. Why stop fasting at this particular moment, after forty days of it? He had held out for a long time, an illimitably long time; why stop now, when he was in his best fasting form, or rather, not yet quite in his best fasting form? Why should he be cheated of the fame he would get for fasting longer, for being not only the record hunger artist of all time, which presumably he was already, but for beating his own record by a performance beyond human imagination, since he felt that there were no limits to his capacity for fasting? His public pretended to admire him so much, why should it have so little patience with him; if he could endure fasting longer, why shouldn't the public endure it? Besides, he was tired, he was comfortable sitting in the straw, and now he was supposed to lift himself to his full height and go down to a meal the very thought of which gave him a nausea that only the presence of the ladies kept him from betraying, and even that with an effort. And he looked up into the eyes of the ladies who were apparently so friendly and in reality so cruel, and shook his head, which felt too heavy on its strengthless neck. But then there happened yet again what always happened. The impresario came forward, without a word—for the band made speech impossible—lifted his arms in the air above the artist, as if inviting Heaven to look down upon its creature here in the straw, this suffering martyr, which indeed he was, although in quite another sense; grasped him around the emaciated waist, with exaggerated caution, so that the frail condition he was in might be appreciated; and committed him to the care of the blanching ladies, not without secretly giving him a shaking so that his legs and body tottered and swayed. The artist now submitted completely; his head was lolled on his breast as if it had landed there by chance; his body hollowed out; his legs in a spasm of self-preservation clung close to each other at the knees, yet scraped on the ground as if it were not really solid ground, as if they were only trying to find solid ground; and the whole weight of his body, a featherweight after all, relapsed onto one of the ladies who, looking around for help and panting a little—this post of honor was not at all what she had expected it to be—first stretched her neck as far as she could to keep her face at least free from contact with the artist, then finding this impossible, and her more fortunate companion not coming to her aid but merely holding extended in her own trembling hand the little bunch of knucklebones that was the artist's, to the great delight of the spectators burst into tears and had to be replaced by an attendant who had long been stationed in readiness. Then came the food, a little of which the impresario managed to get between the artist's lips, while he sat in a kind of half-fainting trance, to the accompaniment of cheerful patter designed to distract the public's attention from the artist's condition; after that, a toast was drunk to the public, supposedly prompted by a whisper from the artist in the impresario's ear, the band confirmed it with a mighty flourish, the spectators melted away, and no one had any cause to be dissatisfied with the proceedings, no one except the hunger artist himself, he only, as always.

So he lived for many years, with small regular intervals of recuperation, in visible glory, honored by the world, yet in spite of that troubled in spirit, and all the more troubled because no one would take his trouble seriously. What comfort could he possibly need? What more could he possibly wish for? And if some good-natured person, feeling sorry for him, tried to console him by pointing out that his melancholy was probably caused by fasting, it could happen, especially when he had been fasting for some time, that he reacted with an outburst of fury and to the general alarm began to shake the bars of his cage like a wild animal. Yet the impresario had a way of punishing these outbreaks which he rather enjoyed putting into operation. He would apologize publicly for the artist's behavior, which was only to be excused, he admitted, because of the irritability caused by fasting; a condition hardly to be understood by well-fed people; then by natural transition he went on to mention the artist's equally incomprehensible boast that he could fast for much longer than he was doing; he praised the high ambition, the good will, the great self-denial undoubtedly implicit in such a statement; and then quite simply countered it by bringing out photographs, which were also on sale to the public, showing the artist on the fortieth day of a fast lying in bed almost dead from exhaustion. This perversion of the truth, familiar to the artist though it was, always unnerved him afresh and proved too much for him. What was a consequence of the premature ending of his fast was here presented as the cause of it! To fight against this lack of understanding, against a whole world of nonunderstanding, was impossible. Time and again in good faith he stood by the bars listening to the impresario, but as soon as the photographs appeared he always let go and sank with a groan back onto his straw, and the reassured public could once more come close and gaze at him.

A few years later when the witnesses of such scenes called them to   5
mind, they often failed to understand themselves at all. For meanwhile the aforementioned change in public interest had set in; it seemed to happen almost overnight; there may have been profound causes for it, but who was going to bother about that; at any rate the pampered hunger artist suddenly found himself deserted one fine day by the amusement-seekers, who went streaming past him to other more-favored attractions. For the last time the impresario hurried him over half Europe to discover whether the old interest might still survive here and there; all in vain; everywhere, as if by secret agreement, a positive revulsion from professional fasting was in evidence. Of course it could not really have sprung up so suddenly as all that, and many premonitory symptoms which had not been sufficiently remarked or suppressed during the rush and glitter of success now came retrospectively to mind, but it was now too late to take any countermeasures. Fasting would surely come into fashion again at some future date, yet that was no comfort for those living in the present. What, then, was the hunger artist to do? He had been applauded by thousands in his time and could hardly come down to showing himself in a street booth at village fairs, and as for adopting another profession, he was not only too old for that but too fanatically devoted to fasting. So he took leave of the impresario, his partner in an unparalleled career, and hired himself to a large circus; in order to spare his own feelings he avoided reading the conditions of his contract.

A large circus with its enormous traffic in replacing and recruiting men,   6
animals, and apparatus can always find a use for people at any time, even for a hunger artist, provided of course that he does not ask too much, and

in this particular case anyhow it was not only the artist who was taken on but his famous and long-known name as well, indeed considering the peculiar nature of his performance, which was not impaired by advancing age, it could not be objected that here was an artist past his prime, no longer at the height of his professional skill, seeking a refuge in some quiet corner of a circus; on the contrary, the hunger artist averred that he could fast as well as ever, which was entirely credible, he even alleged that if he were allowed to fast as he liked, and this was at once promised him without more ado, he could astound the world by establishing a record never yet achieved, a statement that certainly provoked a smile among the other professionals, since it left out of account the change in public opinion, which the hunger artist in his zeal conveniently forgot.

He had not, however, actually lost his sense of the real situation and took it as a matter of course that he and his cage should be stationed, not in the middle of the ring as a main attraction, but outside, near the animal cages, on a site that was after all easily accessible. Large and gaily painted placards made a frame for the cage and announced what was to be seen inside it. When the public came thronging out in the intervals to see the animals, they could hardly avoid passing the hunger artist's cage and stopping there for a moment, perhaps they might even have stayed longer had not those pressing behind them in the narrow gangway, who did not understand why they should be held up on their way toward the excitements of the menagerie, made it impossible for anyone to stand gazing quietly for any length of time. And that was the reason why the hunger artist, who had of course been looking forward to these visiting hours as the main achievement of his life, began instead to shrink from them. At first he could hardly wait for the intervals; it was exhilarating to watch the crowds come streaming his way, until only too soon—not even the most obstinate self-deception, clung to almost consciously, could hold out against the fact—the conviction was borne in upon him that these people, most of them, to judge from their actions, again and again, without exception, were all on their way to the menagerie. And the first sight of them from the distance remained the best. For when they reached his cage he was at once deafened by the storm of shouting and abuse that arose from the two contending factions, which renewed themselves continuously, of those who wanted to stop and stare at him—he soon began to dislike them more than the others—not out of real interest but only out of obstinate self-assertiveness, and those who wanted to go straight on to the animals. When the first great rush was past, the stragglers came along, and these, whom nothing could have prevented from stopping to look at him as long as they had breath, raced past with long strides, hardly even glancing at him, in their haste to get to the menagerie in time. And all too rarely did it happen that he had a stroke of luck, when some father of a family fetched up before him with his children, pointed a finger at the hunger artist, and explained at length what the phenomenon meant, telling stories of earlier

7

years when he himself had watched similar but much more thrilling performances, and the children, still rather uncomprehending, since neither inside nor outside school had they been sufficiently prepared for this lesson—what did they care about fasting?—yet showed by the brightness of their intent eyes that new and better times might be coming. Perhaps, said the hunger artist to himself many a time, things would be a little better if his cage were set not quite so near the menagerie. That made it too easy for people to make their choice, to say nothing of what he suffered from the stench of the menagerie, the animals' restlessness by night, the carrying past of raw lumps of flesh for the beasts of prey, the roaring at feeding times, which depressed him continually. But he did not dare to lodge a complaint with the management; after all, he had the animals to thank for the troops of people who passed his cage, among whom there might always be one here and there to take an interest in him, and who could tell where they might seclude him if he called attention to his existence and thereby to the fact that, strictly speaking, he was only an impediment on the way to the menagerie.

A small impediment, to be sure, one that grew steadily less. People 8 grew familiar with the strange idea that they could be expected, in times like these, to take an interest in a hunger artist, and with this familiarity the verdict went out against him. He might fast as much as he could, and he did so; but nothing could save him now, people passed him by. Just try to explain to anyone the art of fasting! Anyone who has no feeling for it cannot be made to understand it. The fine placards grew dirty and illegible, they were torn down; the little notice board telling the number of fast days achieved, which at first was changed carefully every day, had long stayed at the same figure, for after the first few weeks even this small task seemed pointless to the staff; and so the artist simply fasted on and on, as he had once dreamed of doing, and it was no trouble to him, just as he had always foretold, but no one counted the days, no one, not even the artist himself, knew what records he was already breaking, and his heart grew heavy. And when once in a while some leisurely passer-by stopped, made merry over the old figure on the board, and spoke of swindling, that was in its way the stupidest lie ever invented by indifference and inborn malice, since it was not the hunger artist who was cheating, he was working honestly, but the world was cheating him of his reward.

Many more days went by, however, and that too came to an end. An 9 overseer's eye fell on the cage one day and he asked the attendants why this perfectly good cage should be left standing there unused with dirty straw inside it; nobody knew, until one man, helped out by the notice board, remembered about the hunger artist. They poked into the straw with sticks and found him in it. "Are you still fasting?" asked the overseer, "when on earth do you mean to stop?" "Forgive me, everybody," whispered the hunger artist; only the observer, who had his ear to the bars, understood him. "Of course," said the overseer, and tapped his forehead with a finger to let the attendants know what state the man was in, "we forgive you." "I always wanted you to admire my fasting," said the hunger artist. "We do admire it," said the overseer, affably. "But you shouldn't admire it," said the hunger artist. "Well then we don't admire it," said the overseer, "but why shouldn't we admire it?" "Because I have to fast, I can't help it," said the hunger artist. "What a fellow you are," said the overseer, "and why can't you help it?" "Because," said the hunger artist, lifting his head a little and speaking, with his lips pursed, as if for a kiss, right into the overseer's ear, so that no syllable might be lost, "because I couldn't find the food I liked. If I had found it, believe me, I should have made no fuss and stuffed myself like you or anyone else." These were his last words, but in his dimming eyes remained the firm though no longer proud persuasion that he was still continuing to fast.

"Well, clear this out now!" said the overseer, and they buried the hunger artist, straw and all. Into the cage they put a young panther. Even the most insensitive felt it refreshing to see this wild creature leaping around the cage that had so long been dreary. The panther was all right. The food he liked was brought him without hesitation by the attendants; he seemed not even to miss his freedom; his noble body, furnished almost to the busting point with all that it needed, seemed to carry freedom around with it too; somewhere in his jaws it seemed to lurk; and the joy of life streamed with such ardent passion from his throat that for the onlookers it was not easy to stand the shock of it. But they braced themselves, crowded around the cage, and did not want ever to move away.

Translated from the German by Willa and Edwin Muir

STUDY QUESTIONS

1. Describe the style of "A Hunger Artist." What is the relationship between the story's style and content?
2. Discuss the different levels of irony in the story.
3. Explain the meaning of the title. Is it possible to see the story as an allegory about the creative artist in society?
4. By what steps does Kafka reveal the hunger artist's deception?
5. What is the significance of the panther?

⑤ Jaroslav Seifert

Jaroslav Seifert (1901–1986) was a leading Czech poet. The son of a poor, religiously devout mother, Seifert experienced the spiritual and aesthetic dimensions of Catholicism in Prague's many baroque churches. At the same time, he was drawn to the popular culture of laboring people and in such early books as The City in Tears *(1920) wrote proletarian poetry advocating revolution. After a trip to Paris, he came under the influence of Apollinaire's work, but by the 1930s he found his mature voice in drawing upon Czech motifs, in depicting moments of everyday life, and in experimenting with the use of colloquial language. From this time on, his poetry explored love in its myriad forms, had a directness of tone, and evoked a balladic quality. These features were particularly evident in his* Helmet of Clay *(1945) and in other poems commemorating the tragic World War II experience of the Czechoslovak people. From the 1950s on, Seifert had some difficulty in publishing his new poetry, which was frequently deemed too subjective by the Communist government. Seifert took a prominent role in Prague Spring, the 1968 movement to democratize Czechoslovak society. In 1984 he won the Nobel Prize for Literature. English translations of his poems are available in* The Selected Poetry of Jaroslav Seifert *(1987).*

Lost Paradise

The Old Jewish Cemetery
is one great bouquet of grey stone
on which time has trodden.
I was drifting among the graves,
thinking of my mother.   5
She used to read the Bible.

The letters in two columns
welled up before her eyes
like blood from a wound.
The lamp was guttering and smoking   10
and Mother put on her glasses.
At times she had to blow it out
and with her hairpin straighten
the glowing wick.

But when she closed her tired eyes   15
she dreamed of Paradise,
before God had garrisoned it
with armed cherubim . . .
Often she fell asleep over the Book
which slipped from her lap.   20

I was still young
when I discovered in the Old Testament
those fascinating verses about love
and eagerly searched for
the passages on incest . . .   25
That time I did not yet suspect
how much tenderness is hidden in the names
of Old Testament women.

Adah is Ornament and Orpah
is a Hind,   30
Naamah is the Pleasant
and Nikol is the Little Brook.
Abigail is the Fount of Exultation.

But if I recall how helplessly I watched
as they dragged off the Jews,   35
even the crying children,
I still shudder with horror
and a chill runs down my spine.

Jemima is the Dove and Tamar
a Palm Tree.   40
Tirzah is Pleasantness
and Zilpah a Raindrop.
My God, how beautiful this is.

We were living in hell
yet no one dared to strike the weapon   45
from the murderers' hands.
As if within our hearts we did not have
a spark of humanity!

The name Jecholiah means
The Lord is Mighty.   50
And yet their frowning God
gazed over the barbed wire
and did not move a finger—

Delilah is the Delicate, Rachel
the Ewe Lamb,   55
Deborah the Bee
and Esther the Bright Star.

I'd just returned from the cemetery
when the June evening with its scents
leaned against the windows.   60
But from the silent distance now and then came thunder
of a future war.
There is no time without murder.

I almost forgot:
Rhoda is the Rose.   65
And this flower perhaps is the only thing
that's left us on earth
from ancient Paradise.

Translated from the Czech by George Gibiam
and Ewald Oses

STUDY QUESTIONS

1. What is the significance of the title? How does Seifert account for the
   loss of paradise? What is the role of the poet's mother in the poem?
   What does she represent?
2. What is the poet's attitude to non-Jews during World War II? Does he
   include himself in the indictment? What effect does his use of Old
   Testament names have?

☺ MILAN KUNDERA

*Milan Kundera (b. 1929) was born in Czechoslovakia into a highly cultured
musical family. In his youth, Kundera experienced Nazi occupation and, as
most Czechs after World War II, initially favored Communism. He later came
to disagree with its totalitarianism and took an important role in the
movement for cultural freedom, the Prague Spring. After its repression,
Kundera was deprived of a means of earning a living and went into permanent
exile in France. In his youth, Kundera was influenced by surrealism and
experimented with poetry. By the end of the 1950s, he turned to writing*

novels and short stories because he felt that fiction was the best means for exploring the crisis of modernity which Kundera viewed as encompassing a recognition of the limits of rationalism and secularism while still upholding these as significant ideals. The protagonists of Kundera's short stories in Laughable Loves *and his novels* The Joke, Life Is Elsewhere, The Book of Laughter and Forgetting, *and* The Unbearable Lightness of Being *wish to obliviate this dilemma. Most frequently through erotic passion, they engage in a collective forgetting, from which Kundera prods them with jokes, irony, and misadventures.*

Edward and God

1

We can advantageously begin Edward's story in his elder brother's little house in the country. His brother was lying on the couch and saying to Edward, "Ask the old hag. Never mind, just go and talk to her. Of course she's a pig, but I believe that even in such creatures a conscience exists. Just because she once did me dirt, now perhaps she'll be glad if you'll allow her to make amends for her past wrongdoings." 1

Edward's brother was still the same, a good-natured guy and a lazy one. Just this way perhaps had he been lolling on the couch in his university attic when, many years ago (Edward was still a little boy then), he had lazed and snored away the day of Stalin's death. The next day he had unsuspectingly gone to the department and caught sight of his fellow student, Miss Chehachkova, standing in ostentatious rigidity in the middle of the hall like a statue of grief. Three times he circled her and then began to roar with laughter. The offended girl denounced her fellow student's laughter as political provocation and Edward's brother had had to leave school and go to work in a village, where since that time he had acquired a little house, a dog, a wife, two children, and even a cottage. 2

In this village house, then, was he now lying on the couch and speaking to Edward. "We used to call her the chastising scourge of the working class. But as a matter of fact this needn't concern you. Today she's an aging female and she was always after young boys, so she'll meet you halfway." 3

Edward was at that time very young. He had just graduated from teachers' college (the course his brother had not completed), and was looking for a position. The next day, following his brother's advice, he knocked on the director's door. Then he saw a tall, bony woman with the greasy black hair of a gypsy, black eyes, and black down under her nose. Her ugliness relieved him of the shyness to which feminine beauty still always reduced him, so that he managed to talk to her in a relaxed manner, amiably, even courteously. The directress was evidently delighted by his approach and 4 several times said with perceptible elation, "We need young people here." She promised to find a place for him.

2

And so Edward became a teacher in a small Czech town. This made him neither happy nor sad. He always tried hard to distinguish between the important and the unimportant, and he put his teaching career into the category of *unimportant*. Not that teaching itself was unimportant; after all, it constituted his livelihood (in this respect, in fact, he was deeply attached to it, because he knew that he would not be able to earn a living any other way). But he considered it unimportant in terms of his true nature. He hadn't selected it. Social demand, his party record, the certificate from high school, entrance examinations had selected it for him. The interlocking conjunction of all these forces eventually dumped him (as a crane drops a sack onto a truck) from secondary school into teachers' college. He didn't want to go there (it was superstitiously stigmatized by his brother's failure), but eventually he acquiesced. He understood, however, that his occupation would be among the fortuitous aspects of his life. It would be attached to him like a false beard—which is something laughable.

If, however, his professional duties were something not important (laughable, in fact), perhaps on the contrary, what he did voluntarily was. In his new place of work Edward soon found a young girl who struck him as beautiful, and he began to pursue her with a seriousness that was almost genuine. Her name was Alice and she was, as he discovered to his sorrow on their first dates, very reserved and virtuous.

Many times during their evening walks he had tried to put his arm around her so that he could touch the region of her right breast from behind, and each time she'd seized his hand and pushed it away. One day when he was repeating this experiment once again and she (once again) was pushing his hand away, she stopped and asked: "Do you believe in God?"

With his sensitive ears Edward caught secret overtones in this question and immediately forgot about the breast.

"Do you?" Alice repeated her question and Edward didn't dare answer. Do not let us condemn him for fearing to be frank; in his new place of work he felt lonely and was too attracted to Alice to risk losing her favor over a single solitary answer.

"And you?" he asked in order to gain time.

"Yes, I do." And once again she urged him to answer her.

Until this time it had never occurred to him to believe in God. He understood, however, that he must not admit this. On the contrary, he saw that he should take advantage of the opportunity and knock together from faith in God a nice Trojan horse, within whose belly, according to the ancient example, he would enter the girl's heart unobserved. Only it wasn't so easy for Edward to say to Alice simply *yes, I believe in God*. He wasn't at all cynical and was ashamed to lie; the vulgar and uncompromising nature of a lie went against the grain with him. If he absolutely had to tell a lie, even so he wanted it to remain as close as possible to the truth. For that reason he replied in an exceptionally thoughtful voice:

"I don't really know, Alice, what I should say to you about this. Certainly I believe in God. But . . ." He paused and Alice glanced up at him in surprise. "But I want to be completely frank with you. May I?" 13

"You must be frank," she said. "Otherwise surely there wouldn't be any sense in our being together." 14

"Really?" 15

"Really," said Alice. 16

"Sometimes I'm bothered by doubts," said Edward in a low voice. "Sometimes I doubt whether He really exists." 17

"But how can you doubt that!" Alice almost shrieked. 18

Edward was silent, and after a moment's reflection a familiar thought struck him: "When I see so much evil around me, I often wonder how it is possible that God would permit it all." 19

This sounded so sad that Alice seized his hand. "Yes, the world is indeed full of evil, I know this only too well. But for just that reason you must believe in God. Without Him all this suffering would be in vain. Nothing would have any meaning. And if that were so, I couldn't live at all." 20

"Perhaps you're right," said Edward thoughtfully, and on Sunday he went to church with her. He dipped his fingers in the font and crossed himself. Then there was the Mass and people sang, and with the others he sang a hymn whose tune was familiar, but to which he didn't know the words. Instead of the prescribed words he chose only various vowels and always started to sing a fraction of a second behind the others, because he only dimly recollected even the tune. Yet the moment he became certain of the tune, he let his voice ring out fully, so that for the first time in his life he realized that he had a beautiful bass. Then they all began to recite the Lord's Prayer and some old ladies knelt. He could not hold back a compelling desire to kneel too on the stone floor. He crossed himself with impressive arm movements and experienced the incredible feeling of being able to do something that he'd never done in his life, neither in the classroom nor on the street, nowhere. He felt magnificently free. 21

When it was all over, Alice looked at him with a radiant expression in her eyes. "Can you still say that you have doubts about Him?" 22

"No." 23

And Alice said, "I would like to teach you to love Him just as I do." 24

They were standing on the broad steps of the church and Edward's soul was full of laughter. Unfortunately, just at that moment the directress was walking by and she saw them. 25

3

This was bad. We must recall (for the sake of those to whom perhaps the   26
historical background of the story is missing) that although it is true people
weren't forbidden to go to church, all the same, churchgoing was not
without a certain danger.

This is not so difficult to understand. Those who had been leading the   27
fight for the revolution were very proud, and their pride went by the name
of: *standing on the correct side of the front lines.* When ten or twelve years have
already passed since the revolution (as had happened approximately at the
time of our story), the front lines begin to melt away, and with them the
correct side. No wonder former adherents of the revolution feel cheated
and are quick to seek *substitute* fronts. Thanks to religion they can (as
aetheists opposing believers) stand again in all their glory on the correct
side and retain that so habitual and precious sense of their own superiority.

But to tell the truth, the substitute front was also useful to others, and   28
it will perhaps not be too premature to disclose that Alice was one of them.
Just as the directress wanted to be on the *correct* side, Alice wanted to be on
the *opposite* side. During the revolution they had nationalized her dad's
business and Alice hated those who had done this to him. But how should
she show her hatred? Perhaps by taking a knife and avenging her father?
But this sort of thing is not the custom in Bohemia. Alice had a better
alternative for expressing her opposition: she began to believe in God.

Thus the Lord came to the aid of both sides (who had already almost lost   29
the living reason for their positions), and, thanks to Him, Edward found
himself between Scylla and Charybdis.

When on Monday morning the directress came up to Edward in the staff   30
room, he felt very insecure. There was no way he could invoke the friendly
atmosphere of their first talk because since that time (whether through
artlessness or carelessness) he had never again engaged in polite conversation with her. The directress therefore had good reason to address him
with a conspicuously cold smile:

"We saw each other yesterday, didn't we?"   31

"Yes, we did," said Edward.   32

The directress went on, "I can't understand how a young man can go to   33
church." Edward shrugged his shoulders in bewilderment and the directress shook her head. "A young man."

"I went to see the baroque interior of the cathedral," said Edward by   34
way of an excuse.

"Ah, so that's it," said the directress ironically, "I didn't know you had   35
such artistic interests."

This conversation wasn't a bit pleasant for Edward. He remembered   36
how his brother had circled his fellow student three times and then roared
with laughter. It seemed to him that family history was repeating itself and
he felt afraid. On Saturday he made his excuses over the telephone to

Alice, saying that he wouldn't be going to church because he had a cold.

"You are a real mollycoddle," Alice rebuked him after Sunday and it seemed to Edward that her words sounded cold. So he began to tell her (enigmatically and vaguely, because he was ashamed to admit his fear and his true reasons) about the wrongs being done him at school, and about the horrible directress who was persecuting him for no reason. He wanted to get her pity and sympathy, but Alice said: 37

"My woman boss, on the contrary, isn't bad at all," and giggling, she began to relate stories about her work. Edward listened to her merry voice and became more and more gloomy. 38

4

Ladies and gentlemen, these were weeks of torment. Edward longed hellishly for Alice. Her body fired him up and yet this very body was utterly inaccessible to him. The settings in which their dates took place were also agonizing. Either they hung about together for an hour or two in the streets after dark or they went to the movies. The banality and the negligible erotic possibilities of these two variants (there weren't any others) prompted Edward to think that perhaps he would achieve more outstanding successes if they could meet in a different environment. Once, with an ingenuous face, he proposed that for the weekend they go to the country and visit his brother, who had a cottage in a wooded valley by a river. He excitedly described the innocent beauties of nature. However, Alice (naive and credulous in every other respect) swiftly saw through him and categorically refused. It wasn't Alice alone who was repulsing him. It was Alice's God Himself (eternally vigilant and wary). 39

This God embodied a single idea (He had no other wishes or concerns): He forbade extramarital sex. He was therefore a rather comical God, but let's not laugh at Alice for that. Of the ten commandments which Moses gave to the people, fully nine didn't trouble her at all; she didn't feel like killing or not honoring her father, or coveting her neighbor's wife. But the one remaining commandment she felt to be not *self-evident*, and therefore a genuine inconvenience and imposition, the famous seventh: *Thou shalt not commit adultery*. If she wanted to put her religious faith into practice somehow, to prove and demonstrate it, she had then to fasten onto this single commandment. She had thereby created for herself from an obscure, diffuse, and abstract God, a God who was quite specific, comprehensible, and concrete: the God of No Fornication. 40

I ask you where in fact does fornication begin? Every woman fixes this boundary for herself according to totally mysterious criteria. Alice quite happily allowed Edward to kiss her, and after many, many attempts she eventually became reconciled to letting him stroke her breasts. However, at the middle of her body, let's say at her navel, she drew a strict and un- 41 compromising line below which lay the area of sacred prohibitions, the area of Moses's denial and of the anger of the Lord.

Edward began to read the Bible and to study basic theological literature. 42 He had decided to fight Alice with her own weapons.

"Alice dear," he then said to her, "if we love God, nothing is forbidden. 43 If we long for something, it's because of His will. Christ wanted nothing but that we should all be ruled by love."

"Yes," said Alice, "but a different love from the one you're thinking of." 44

"There's only one love," said Edward. 45

"That would certainly suit you," she said, "only God set down certain 46 commandments, and we must abide by them."

"Yes, the Old Testament God," said Edward, "but not the Christian 47 God."

"How's that? Surely there's only one God," objected Alice. 48

"Yes," said Edward, "only the Jews of the Old Testament understood 49 him a little differently from the way we do. Before the coming of Christ, men had to abide above all by a specific system of God's commandments and laws. What a man was like inside was not so important. But Christ considered some of these prohibitions and regulations to be external. For Him, the most important thing was what a man is like inside. When a man is true to his own ardent, believing heart, everything he does will be good and pleasing to God. After all, that's why St. Paul said, 'Everything is pure to the man who is pure at heart.' "

"Only I wonder if you are this pure-hearted man." 50

"And St. Augustine," continued Edward, "said, 'Love God and do what 51 it pleases you to do.' Do you understand, Alice? Love God and do what it pleases you to do!"

"Only what pleases you will never please me," she replied, and Edward 52 understood that his theological assault had foundered completely this time, therefore he said:

"You don't like me." 53

"I do," said Alice in a terribly matter-of-fact way. "And that's why I 54 don't want us to do anything that we shouldn't do!"

As we have already mentioned, these were tormenting weeks. And the 55 torment was that much greater because Edward's desire for Alice was not only the desire of a body for a body; on the contrary, the more she refused him her body, the more lonesome and afflicted he became and the more he coveted her heart as well. However, neither her body nor her heart wanted to do anything about it; they were equally cold, equally wrapped up in themselves, and contentedly self-sufficient.

It was precisely this unruffled moderation of hers which exasperated 56 Edward most in his relations with Alice. Although in other respects he was quite a sober young man, he began to long for some extreme action through which he could drive Alice out of her unruffled state. And because it was too risky to provoke her through blasphemy or cynicism (to which by nature he was attracted), he had to go to the opposite (and therefore far more difficult) extreme, which would coincide with Alice's own position but would be so overdone that it would put her to shame. To put it more simply: Edward began to exaggerate his religiousness. He didn't miss a single visit to church (his desire for Alice was greater than his fear of unpleasantness) and once there he behaved with eccentric humility: at every opportunity he knelt, while Alice prayed beside him and crossed herself standing, because she was afraid for her stockings.

One day he criticized her for her lukewarm religiosity. He reminded her   57
of Jesus's words: "Not everyone who says to me 'Lord, Lord' shall enter the kingdom of heaven." He criticized her, saying that her faith was formal, external, shallow. He criticized her for being too pleased with herself. He criticized her for not being aware of anyone except herself.

As he was saying all this (Alice was not prepared for his attack and   58
defended herself feebly), he suddenly caught sight of a cross on the opposite corner of the street, an old, neglected, metal cross with a rusty, iron Christ. He pretentiously slipped his arm out from under Alice's, stopped and (as a protest against her indifferent heart and a sign of his new offensive) crossed himself with stubborn conspicuousness. He did not even really get to see how this affected Alice, because at that moment he spied on the other side of the street the woman janitor who worked at the school. She was looking at him. Edward realized that he was lost.

5

His fears were confirmed when two days later the woman janitor stopped   59
him in the corridor and loudly informed him that he was to present himself the next day at twelve o'clock at the directress's office: "We have something to talk to you about, comrade."

Edward was overcome by anxiety. In the evening he met Alice so that,   60
as usual, they could hang about for an hour or two in the streets, but Edward no longer pursued his religious crusade. He was downcast and longed to confide what had happened to him, but he didn't dare, because he knew that in order to save his unloved (but indispensable) job, he was ready to betray the Lord without hesitation the next morning. For this reason he preferred not to say a word about the inauspicious summons, so he couldn't even get any consolation. The following day he entered the directress's room in a mood of utter dejection.

In the room four judges awaited him: the directress, the woman janitor,   61
one of Edward's colleagues (a tiny man with glasses), and an unknown (gray-haired) gentleman, whom the others called Comrade Inspector. The directress asked Edward to be seated, and told him they had invited him for just a friendly and unofficial talk. For, she said, the manner in which Edward had been conducting himself in his extracurricular life was making

them all uneasy. As she said this she looked at the inspector, who nodded his head in agreement, then at the bespectacled teacher, who had been watching her attentively the whole time. Now, intercepting her glance, he launched into a fluent speech about how we wanted to bring up healthy young people without prejudices and how we had complete responsibility for them because we (the teachers) served as models for them. Precisely for this reason, he said, we could not countenance a religious person within our walls. He developed this thought at length and finally declared that Edward's behavior was a disgrace to the whole school.

Even a few minutes earlier Edward had been convinced that he would 62 deny his recently acquired God and admit that his church attendance and his crossing himself in public were only jokes. Now, however, face to face with the real situation, he felt that he couldn't do it. He could not, after all, say to these four people, so serious and so excited, that they were getting excited about some misunderstanding, some bit of foolishness. He understood that to do that would be to involuntarily mock their earnestness, and he also realized that what they were expecting from him were only quibbles and excuses which they were prepared in advance to reject. He understood (in a flash, there wasn't time for lengthy cogitation) that at that moment the most important thing was for him to appear truthful—more precisely, that his statements should resemble the ideas they had constructed about him. If he was to succeed in correcting these ideas to a certain extent, he would also have to play their game to a certain extent. Therefore he said:

"Comrades, may I be frank?"   63

"Of course," said the directress. "After all, that's why you're here."   64

"And you won't be angry?"   65

"Just talk," said the directress.   66

"Very well, I shall confess to you then. I really do believe in God."   67

He glanced at his judges and it seemed to him that they all exhaled with 68 satisfaction. Only the woman janitor snapped at him. "In this day and age, comrade? In this day and age?"

Edward went on. "I knew that you would get angry if I told the truth.   69 But I don't know how to lie. Don't ask me to lie to you."

The directress said (gently): "No one wants you to lie. It's good that you 70 are telling the truth. Only, please tell me how you, a young man, can believe in God!"

"Today, when we fly to the moon!" The teacher lost his temper.   71

"I can't help it," said Edward. "I don't want to believe in Him. Really, 72 I don't."

"How come you say you don't want to believe, if you do?" The gray-   73 haired gentleman (in an exceedingly kind tone of voice) joined the conversation.

"I don't want to believe, but I do believe." Edward quietly repeated his 74 confession.

The teacher laughed, "But there's a contradiction in that!" 75

"Comrades, I'm telling it the way it is," said Edward. "I know very well 76
that faith in God leads us away from reality. What would socialism come
to if everyone believed that the world was in God's hands? No one would
do anything and everyone would just rely on God."

"Exactly," agreed the directress. 77

"No one has ever yet proved that God exists," stated the teacher with 78
glasses. Edward continued: "The history of mankind is distinguished from
prehistory by the fact that people have taken their fate into their own
hands and do not need God."

"Faith in God leads to fatalism," said the directress. 79

"Faith in God belongs to the Middle Ages," said Edward, and then the 80
directress said something again and the teacher said something and Edward said something and the inspector said something, and they were all
in complete accord, until finally the teacher with glasses exploded, interrupting Edward:

"So why do you cross yourself in the street, when you know all this?" 81

Edward looked at him with an immensely sad expression and then said, 82
"Because I believe in God."

"But there's a contradiction in that!" repeated the teacher joyfully. 83

"Yes," admitted Edward, "there is. There is a contradiction between 84
knowledge and faith. Knowledge is one thing and faith another. I recognize that faith in God will lead us to obscurantism. I recognize that it would
be better if He didn't exist. But when here inside I . . ." he pointed with his
finger to his heart, "feel that He exists . . . You see, comrades, I'm telling
it to you the way it is. It's better that I confess to you, because I don't want
to be a hypocrite. I want you to know what I'm really like," and he hung
his head.

The teacher's brain was no larger, proportionally, than his body. He 85
didn't know that even the strictest revolutionary considers force only a
necessary evil and believes the intrinsic *good* of the revolution lies in re-
education. He, who had become a revolutionary overnight, did not enjoy
too much respect from the directress and did not suspect that at this moment Edward, who had placed himself at his judges' disposal as a difficult
case and yet as an object capable of being remolded, had a thousand times
more value than he. And because he didn't suspect it, he attacked Edward
with severity and declared that people who did not know how to part with
their medieval faith belonged in the Middle Ages and should leave the
modern school.

The directress let him finish his speech then administered her rebuke: "I 86
don't like it when heads roll. This comrade was frank; he told us everything just as it was. We must know how to respect this." Then she turned
to Edward. "The comrades are right, of course, when they say that religious people cannot educate our youth. What do you yourself suggest?"

"I don't know, comrades," said Edward unhappily. 87

"This is what I think," said the inspector. "The struggle between the old 88
and the new goes on not only between classes, but also within each individual man. Just such a struggle is going on inside our comrade here. With
his reason he knows, but feeling pulls him back. We must help our comrade in this struggle, so that reason may triumph."

The directress nodded. Then she said: "I myself will take charge of 89
him."

6

Edward had thus averted the most pressing danger. His fate as a teacher 90
was now in the hands of the directress exclusively, which was entirely to
his satisfaction. He remembered his brother's observation that the directress was always after young men, and with all his vacillating, youthful
self-confidence (now deflated, then exaggerated) he resolved to win the
contest by gaining as a man the favor of his ruler.

When, according to an agreement, he visited her a few days later in her 91
office, he tried to assume a light tone. He used every opportunity to slip an
intimate remark or bit of subtle flattery into the conversation, or to emphasize by way of discreet double-talk his curious position as a man in the
hands of a woman. But he was not to be permitted to choose the tone of the
conversation. The directress spoke to him affably, but with the utmost
restraint. She asked him what he was reading, then she herself named
some books and recommended that he should read them. She evidently
wanted to embark upon the lengthy job to be done on his thinking. Their
short meeting ended with her inviting him to her place.

As a result of the directress's reserve, Edward's self-confidence was 92
deflated again, so he entered her bachelor apartment meekly, with no
intention of conquering her with his masculine charm. She seated him in
an armchair and, assuming a friendly tone, asked him what he felt like
having: some coffee perhaps? He said that he didn't. Some alcohol then?
He was embarrassed: "If you have some cognac . . ." and was immediately
afraid that he had been presumptuous. But the directress replied affably:
"No, I don't have cognac, but I do have a little wine," and she fetched a
half-empty bottle, whose contents were just sufficient to fill two tumblers.

Then she told Edward that he must not look upon her as some inquis- 93
itor; after all, everyone had a complete right to profess what he recognized
as right. Naturally, it is another matter (she added at once) whether he is
then fit or not fit to be a teacher; for that reason, she said, they had had
(although they hadn't been happy about it) to summon Edward and have
a talk with him and they (at least she and the inspector) were very pleased
with the frank manner in which he had spoken to them, and the fact that
he had not denied anything. Then she said she had talked with the inspector about Edward for a very long time and they had decided that they

would summon him for another interview in six months' time and that until then the directress would help his development through her influence. And once again she emphasized that she merely wanted *to help him in a friendly way*, that she was neither an inquisitor nor a policeman. Then she mentioned the teacher who had attacked Edward so sharply, and said, "That man is hiding something himself and so he would be ready to sacrifice others. Also, the woman janitor is letting it be known everywhere that you were insolent, and pig-headedly stuck to your opinions, as she puts it. She's not to be talked out of the view that you should be dismissed from the school. Of course, I don't agree with her, but you cannot startle her so completely again. I wouldn't be happy either if someone who crosses himself public in the street were teaching my children."

Thus the directress showed Edward in a single outpouring of sentences 94 how attractive were the prospects of her mercy, and also how menacing the prospects of her severity. And then to prove that their meeting was genuinely a friendly one, she digressed to other subjects; she talked about books and led him to her bookcase. She raved about Rolland's *Enchanted Soul* and scolded him for not having read it. Then she asked how he was getting on at the school, and after his conventional reply, she herself spoke at length. She said that she was grateful to fate for her position; she liked her work because it was a means for her to educate children and thus be in continuous and real touch with the future, and only the future could, in the end, justify all this suffering, of which she said ("Yes, we must admit it") there was plenty. "If I did not believe that I was living for something more than just my own life, I couldn't perhaps live at all."

These words suddenly sounded very ingenuous and it was not clear 95 whether the directress was trying to confess or to commence the expected ideological polemic about the meaning of life. Edward decided to interpret them in their personal sense and asked her in a low, discreet voice:

"And how about your own life?" 96

"My life?" she repeated after him. 97

"Wouldn't it have been satisfying in itself?" 98

A bitter smile appeared on her face and Edward felt almost sorry for her 99 at that moment. She was pitifully hideous: her black hair cast a shadow over her bony, elongated face and the black down under her nose began to look as conspicuous as a mustache. Suddenly he glimpsed all the sorrow of her life. He perceived her gypsylike features, revealing passion, and he perceived her ugliness, revealing the hopelessness of that passion; he imagined how she had passionately turned into a living statue of grief upon Stalin's death, how she had passionately sat up late at hundreds of thousands of meetings, how she had passionately struggled against poor Jesus. And he understood that all this was only a sad outlet for her desire, which could not flow where she wished it to. Edward was young and his compassion was not used up. He looked at the directress with sympathy. She, however, as if ashamed of having involuntarily fallen silent, now assumed a brisk tone and went on:

"It doesn't depend on that at all, Edward. Anyhow, a man is not in the world only for his own sake. He always lives for something." She looked deeply into his eyes: "However, the question is for what. For something real or for something fictitious? God—that is a beautiful fiction. But the future of the people, Edward, that is reality. And I have lived for reality, I have given up everything for reality." 100

She spoke with such an air of commitment, that Edward did not stop feeling that sudden rush of human sympathy which had awoken in him a short while before. It struck him as stupid that he should be lying to another human being (one fellow creature to another), and it seemed to him that this intimate moment in their conversation offered him the opportunity to cast away finally the unworthy (and after all difficult) pretense of being a believer. 101

"But I quite agree with you," he quickly assured her. "I too prefer reality. Don't take this religion of mine so seriously." 102

He soon learned that a man should never let himself be led astray by a rash fit of emotion. The directress looked at him in surprise and said with perceptible coldness: "Don't pretend. I liked you because you were frank. Now you're pretending to be something that you aren't." 103

No, Edward was not to be permitted to step out of the religious costume in which he had originally clothed himself. He quickly reconciled himself to this and tried hard to correct the bad impression: "No, I didn't mean to be evasive. Of course I believe in God, I would never deny that. I only wanted to say that I also believe in the future of humanity, in progress and all that. After all, if I didn't believe in that, what would my work as a teacher be for? Why should children be born and why should we live at all? And I've come to think that it is also God's will that society continue to advance toward something better. I have thought that a man can believe in God and in communism, that it is possible for them to be combined." 104

"No," the directress smiled with maternal authoritativeness, "it isn't possible for those two things to be combined." 105

"I know," said Edward sadly. "Don't be angry with me." 106

"I'm not angry. You are still a young man and you obstinately stick to what you believe. No one understands you the way I do. After all I was young once too. I know what it's like to be young. And I like your youthfulness. Yes, I rather like you." 107

And now it finally happened. Neither earlier nor later, but now, at precisely the right moment. It is evident that Edward was not the instigator but merely the instrument. When the directress said she rather liked him he replied, not too expressively: 108

"I like you too." 109

"Really?" 110

"Really." 111

"Well I never! I'm an old woman . . ." objected the directress. 112

"That's not true," Edward had to say. 113

"But it is," said the directress. 114

"You're not at all old, that's nonsense," he had to say very resolutely. 115
"You think so?" 116
"It happens that I like you very much." 117
"Don't lie. You know you mustn't lie." 118
"I'm not lying. You're pretty." 119
"Pretty?" The directress made a face to show that she didn't really 120
believe it.

"Yes, pretty," said Edward, and because he was struck by the obvious 121
incredibility of his assertion, he at once took pains to support it: "I'm mad
about black-haired women like you."

"You like black-haired women?" asked the directress. 122
"I'm mad about them," said Edward. 123
"And why haven't you come by all the time that you've been at the 124
school? I had the feeling that you were avoiding me."

"I was ashamed," said Edward. "Everyone would have said that I was 125
sucking up to you. No one would have believed that I was coming to see
you only because I liked you."

"But you must not be ashamed," said the directress. "Now it has *been* 126
decided that you must meet with me from time to time."

She looked into his eyes with her large brown irises (let us admit that in 127
themselves they were beautiful), and just before he left she lightly stroked
his hand, so that this foolish fellow went off with the sprightly feelings of
a winner.

7

Edward was sure that the unpleasant affair had been settled to his advan- 128
tage, and the next Sunday, feeling carefree and impudent, he went to
church with Alice. Not only that, he went full of self-confidence—for (although this arouses in us a compassionate smile) in retrospect, he perceived the events at the directress's apartment as glaring evidence of his
masculine appeal.

In addition, this particular Sunday in church he noticed that Alice was 129
somehow different; as soon as they met she slipped her hand under his
arm and even in church clung to him. Formerly she had behaved modestly
and inconspicuously; now she kept looking around and smilingly greeted
at least ten acquaintances.

This was curious and Edward didn't understand it. 130

Then two days later as they were walking together along the streets after 131
dark, Edward became aware to his amazement that her kisses, once so
unpleasantly matter-of-fact, had become damp, warm, and passionate.
When they stopped for a moment under a street lamp he found that her
eyes were looking amorously at him.

"Let me tell you this, I like you," blurted out Alice and immediately 132 covered his mouth. "No, no, don't say anything; I'm ashamed, I don't want to hear anything."

Again they walked a little way and again they stopped. This time Alice   133
said, "Now I understand everything. I understand why you reproached me for being too comfortable in my faith."

Edward, however, didn't understand anything. So he also didn't say   134
anything. When they'd walked a bit further, Alice said, "And you didn't say anything to me. Why didn't you say anything to me?"

"And what should I have said to you?" asked Edward.   135

"Yes, that's you all over," she said with quiet enthusiasm. "Others   136
would put on airs; but you are silent. But that's exactly why I like you."

Edward began to suspect what she was talking about, but nevertheless   137
he questioned her. "What are you talking about?"

"About what happened to you."   138

"And who told you about it?"   139

"Come on! Everybody knows about it. They summoned you, they   140
threatened you, and you laughed in their faces. You didn't retract anything. Everyone admires you."

"But I didn't tell anyone about it."   141

"Don't be naive. A thing like that gets around. After all, it's no small   142
matter. How often today do you find someone who has a little courage?"

Edward knew that in a small town every event is quickly turned into a   143
legend, but he hadn't suspected that the worthless episodes he'd been involved in, whose significance he'd never overestimated, possessed the stuff of which legends are made. He hadn't sufficiently realized how very useful he was to his fellow countrymen who, as is well-known, do not really like *heroes* (men who struggle and conquer), but rather *martyrs*, for such men soothingly reassure them about their loyal inactivity, and corroborate their view that life provides only two alternatives: to be submissive or to be destroyed. Nobody doubted that Edward would be destroyed, and admiringly and complacently they all passed this on, until now, through Alice, he himself encountered the beautiful image of his own crucifixion. He accepted it cold-bloodedly and said:

"But my not retracting anything was after all a matter of course. Anyone   144
would have done that much."

"Anyone?" blurted out Alice. "Look around you at what they all do!   145
How cowardly they are! They would renounce their own mothers!"

Edward was silent and Alice was silent. They walked along holding   146
hands. Then Alice said in a whisper: "I would do anything for you."

No one had ever said such words to Edward. They were an un-   147
expected gift. Of course, Edward knew that they were an undeserved gift, but he said to himself that if fate withheld from him deserved gifts, he had a complete right to accept these undeserved ones. Therefore he said:

"No one can do anything for me any more."   148

"How's that?" whispered Alice.   149

"They'll drive me from the school and those who speak of me today as   150
a hero won't lift a finger for me. Only one thing is certain. I shall remain
entirely alone."

"You won't," Alice shook her head.   151

"I will," said Edward.   152

"You won't!" Alice almost shrieked.   153

"They've all abandoned me."   154

"I'll never abandon you," said Alice.   155

"You will," said Edward sadly.   156

"No, I won't," said Alice.   157

"No, Alice," said Edward, "you don't like me. You've never liked me."   158

"That's not true," whispered Alice and Edward noticed with satisfaction   159
that her eyes were wet.

"You don't, Alice; a person can feel that sort of thing. You were always   160
cold to me. A woman who loves a man doesn't behave like that. I know
that very well. And now you feel pity for me, because you know they want
to ruin me. But you don't really like me and I don't want you to deceive
yourself about it."

They walked still further, silently, holding hands. Alice cried quietly for   161
a while, then all at once she stopped walking and amid sobs said, "No,
that's not true. You mustn't believe that. That's not true."

"It is," said Edward, and when Alice did not stop crying, he suggested   162
that on Saturday they go to the country. In a beautiful valley by the river
was his brother's cottage, where they could be alone.

Alice's face was wet with tears as she dumbly nodded her assent.   163

8

That was on Tuesday, and when on Thursday he was again invited to   164
the directress's bachelor apartment, he made his way there with gay self-
assurance, for he had absolutely no doubt that his natural charm would
definitively dissolve the church scandal into little more than a cloud of
smoke, a mere nothing. But this is the way life goes: a man imagines that
he is playing his role in a particular play, and does not suspect that in
the meantime they have changed the scenery without his noticing, and
he unknowingly finds himself in the middle of a rather different performance.

He was again seated in the armchair opposite the directress. Between   165
them was a little table and on it a bottle of cognac and two glasses. And this
bottle of cognac was precisely that new prop by which a bright man with
a sober temperament would have immediately recognized that the church
scandal was no longer the matter in question.

But innocent Edward was so intoxicated with himself that at first he 166
didn't realize this at all. He quite gaily took part in the opening conversation (the subject matter of which was vague and general). He drank the
glass that was offered him, and was quite ingenuously bored. After half an
hour or an hour the directress inconspicuously changed to more personal
topics; she talked a lot about herself and from her words there emerged
before Edward the image that she wanted: that of a sensible, middle-aged
woman, not too happy, but reconciled to her lot in a dignified way; a
woman who regretted nothing and even expressed satisfaction that she
was not married, because only in this way, after all, could she fully enjoy
her independence and privacy. This life had provided her with a beautiful
apartment, where she felt happy and where perhaps now Edward was also
not too uncomfortable.

"No, it's really very nice here," said Edward, and he said it glumly, 167
because just at that moment he had stopped feeling good. The bottle
of cognac (which he had inadvertently asked for on his first visit and
which was now hurried to the table with such menacing readiness), the
four walls of the bachelor apartment (creating a space which was becoming ever more constricting and confining), the directress's monologue (focusing on subjects ever more personal), her glance (dangerously
fixed), all this caused *the change of program* to begin finally to get to him.
He understood that he had entered into a situation, the development
of which was irrevocably predetermined. He realized that his livelihood
was jeopardized not by the directress's aversion, but just the contrary,
by his physical aversion to this skinny woman with the down under
her nose, who was urging him to drink. His anxiety made his throat contract.

He listened to the directress and had a drink, but now his anxiety was 168
so strong that the alcohol had no effect on him at all. On the other hand,
after a couple of drinks the directress was already so thoroughly carried
away that she abandoned her usual sobriety, and her words acquired an
exaltation that was almost threatening. "One thing I envy you," she said,
"that you are so young. You cannot know yet what disappointment is,
what disillusion is. You still see the world as full of hope and beauty."

She leaned across the table in Edward's direction and in gloomy silence 169
(with a smile that was rigidly forced) fixed her frightfully large eyes on
him, while he said to himself that if he didn't manage to get a bit drunk,
he'd be in real trouble before the evening was over. To that end he poured
some cognac into his glass and downed it quickly.

And the directress went on: "But I want to see it like that! The way you 170
do!" And then she got up from the armchair, thrust out her chest, and said,
"That I am not a boring woman! That I'm not!" And she walked around the
little table and grabbed Edward by the sleeve. "That I'm not!"

"No," said Edward. 171

"Come, let's dance," she said, and letting go of Edward's arm she skipped over to the radio and turned the dial until she found some dance music. Then she stood over Edward with a smile.

Edward got up, seized the directress, and began to guide her around the room to the rhythm of the music. Every now and then the directress would tenderly lay her head on his shoulder, then suddenly raise it again, to gaze into his eyes, then, after another little while, she would sing along with the melody in a low voice.

Edward felt so out of sorts that several times he stopped dancing to have a drink. He longed for nothing more than to put an end to the discomfort of this interminable trudging around, but also he feared nothing more. For the discomfort of what would follow the dancing seemed to him even more unbearable. And so he continued to guide the lady who was singing to herself around the room and at the same time steadily (and meticulously) observe in himself the influence of the alcohol, which he longed for. When it finally seemed to him that his brain was sufficiently deadened, with his right arm he firmly pressed the directress against his body and put his left hand on her breast.

Yes, he did the very thing that had been frightening him the whole evening. He would have given anything not to have had to do this, but if he did it all the same, then believe me, it was only because he really *had* to. The situation, which he had got into at the very beginning of the evening, was so compelling that, though it was no doubt possible to slow down its course, it was not possible to stop it, so that when Edward put his hand on the directress's breast, he was merely submitting to totally irreversible necessity.

The results of his action exceeded all expectations. As if by magic command, the directress began to writhe in his arms and in no time had placed her hairy upper lip on his mouth. Then she dragged him onto the couch and, wildly writhing and loudly sighing, bit his lip and the tip of his tongue, which hurt Edward a lot. Then she slipped out of his arms, said, "Wait!" and ran off to the bathroom.

Edward licked his finger and found out that his tongue was bleeding slightly. The bite hurt so much that his painstakingly induced intoxication receded, and once again his throat contracted from anxiety at the thought of what awaited him. From the bathroom could be heard a loud running and splashing of water. He picked up the bottle of cognac, put it to his lips, and drank deeply.

But by this time the directress had already appeared in the doorway in a transparent nylon nightgown (thickly decorated with lace over the breasts), and was walking steadily toward Edward. She embraced him. Then she stepped back and reproachfully asked, "Why are you still dressed?"

Edward took off his jacket and, looking at the directress (who had her big eyes fixed on him), he couldn't think of anything but the fact that there

172

173

174

175

176

177

178

179

was the greatest likelihood that his body would sabotage his assiduous will. Wishing therefore to arouse his body somehow or other, he said in an uncertain voice, "Undress completely."

With a violent and enthusiastically obedient movement she flung off her 180 nylon nightie and bared her skinny white body, in the middle of which her thick black bush protruded in gloomy desolation. She came slowly toward him and with terror Edward discovered what he already knew anyway: his body was completely fettered by anxiety.

I know, gentlemen, that in the course of the years you have become 181 accustomed to the occasional insubordination of your own bodies, and that this no longer upsets you at all. But understand, Edward was young then! His body's sabotage threw him into an incredible panic each time and he bore it as an inexpiable disgrace, whether the witness to it was a beautiful face or one as hideous and comical as the directress's. The directress was now only a step away from him, and he, frightened and not knowing what to do, all at once said, he didn't even know how (it was rather the fruit of inspiration than of cunning reflection): "No, no, on Lord, no! No, it is a sin, it would be a sin!" and jumped away.

The directress kept coming toward him muttering in a husky voice: 182 "What sin? There's no sin!"

Edward retreated behind the round table, where they had been sitting a 183 while before: "No, I can't do this, I can't do it."

The directress pushed aside the armchair, standing in her path, and 184 went after Edward, never taking her large brown eyes off him. "There is no sin! There is no sin!"

Edward went around the table, behind him was only the couch and the 185 directress was a mere step away. Now he could no longer escape and perhaps his very desperation advised him at this moment of impasse to command her: "Kneel!"

She stared at him uncomprehendingly, but when he once again re- 186 peated in a firm (though desperate) voice, "Kneel!" she enthusiastically fell to her knees in front of him and embraced his legs.

"Take those hands off," he called her to order. "Clasp them!" 187
Once again she looked at him uncomprehendingly. 188
"Clasp them! Did you hear?" 189
She clasped her hands. 190
"Pray," he commanded. 191
She had her hands clasped and she glanced up at him devotedly. 192
"Pray, so that God may forgive us," he hissed. 193
She had her hands clasped. She was looking up at him with her large 194 eyes and Edward not only obtained an advantageous respite, but looking down at her from above, he began to lose the oppressive feeling that he was mere prey, and he regained his self-assurance. He stepped back, away from her, so that he could survey the whole of her, and once again commanded, "Pray!"

When she remained silent, he yelled: "Aloud!" 195

And the skinny, naked, kneeling woman began to recite: "Our Father, 196
who art in heaven, hallowed be Thy name, Thy kingdom come. . . ."

As she uttered the words of the prayer, she glanced up at him as if he 197
were God Himself. He watched her with growing pleasure. In front of him
was kneeling the directress, being humiliated by a subordinate; in front of
him a naked revolutionary was being humiliated by prayer; in front of him
a praying lady was being humiliated by her nakedness.

This threefold image of degradation intoxicated him and something un- 198
expected suddenly happened: his body revoked its passive resistance. Edward was excited!

As the directress said, "And lead us not into temptation," he quickly 199
threw off all his clothes. When she said, "Amen," he violently lifted her off
the floor and dragged her onto the couch.

9

That was on Thursday, and on Saturday Edward went with Alice to the 200
country to visit his brother, who welcomed them warmly and lent them the
key to the nearby cottage.

The two lovers spent the whole afternoon wandering through the woods 201
and meadows. They kissed and Edward's contented hands found that the
imaginary line, level with her navel which separated the sphere of innocence from that of fornication, didn't count any more. At first he wanted to
verify the so long awaited event verbally, but he became frightened of
doing so and understood that he had to keep silent.

His judgment was quite correct, it seemed. Alice's unexpected turn- 202
about had occurred independently of his many weeks of persuasion,
independently of his argumentation, independently of any *logical* consideration whatsoever. In fact, it was based exclusively upon the news of
Edward's martyrdom, consequently upon a *mistake*, and it had been de-
duced quite *illogically* even from this mistake. Why should Edward's sufferings for his fidelity to his beliefs have as a result Alice's infidelity to
God's law? If Edward had not betrayed God before the fact-finding commission, why should she now betray Him before Edward?

In such a situation any reflection expressed aloud could reveal to Alice 203
the inconsistency of her attitude. So Edward prudently kept silent, which
went unnoticed, because Alice herself kept chattering. She was gay, and
nothing indicated that this turnabout in her soul had been dramatic or
painful.

When it got dark they went back to the cottage, turned on the lights, 204
made the bed, and kissed, whereupon Alice asked Edward to turn off the
lights. However, the light of the stars continued to show through the
window, so Edward had to close the shutters as well upon Alice's request.
Then, in total darkness, Alice undressed and gave herself to him

Edward had been looking forward to this moment for so many weeks, but surprisingly enough, now, when it was actually taking place, he didn't have the feeling that it would be as significant as the length of time he had been waiting for it suggested; it seemed to him so easy and self-evident that during the act of intercourse he was almost not concentrating. Rather, he was vainly trying to drive away the thoughts that were running through his head of those long, futile weeks when Alice had tormented him with her coldness. It all came back to him: the suffering at the school, of which she had been the cause, and, instead of gratitude for her giving of herself to him, he began to feel a certain vindictiveness and anger. It irritated him how easily and remorselessly she was now betraying her God of No Fornication, whom she had once so fanatically worshiped. It irritated him that nothing was able to throw her off balance, no desire, no event, no upset. It irritated him how she experienced everything without inner conflict— self-confidently and easily. And when this irritation threatened to overcome him with its power, he strove to make love to her passionately and furiously so as to force from her some sort of sound, moan, word, or pathetic cry, but he didn't succeed. The girl was quiet and in spite of all his exertions in their love-making, it ended silently and undramatically.

Then she snuggled up against his chest and quickly fell asleep, while Edward lay awake for a long time and realized that he felt no joy at all. He made an effort to imagine Alice (not her physical appearance but, if possible, her being in its entirety) and it occurred to him that he saw her *blurred*.

Let's stop at this word: Alice, as Edward had seen her until this time, was, with all her naiveté, a stable and distinct being. The beautiful simplicity of her looks seemed to accord with the unaffected simplicity of her faith, and her simple fate seemed to be a substantiation of her attitude. Until this time Edward had seen her as solid and coherent; he could laugh at her, he could curse her, he could besiege her with his guile, but he (involuntarily) had to respect her.

Now, however, the unpremeditated snare of false news caused a split in the coherence of her being and it seemed to Edward that her convictions were in fact only something *extraneous* to her fate, and her fate only something extraneous to her body. He saw her as an accidental conjunction of a body, thoughts, and a life's course; an inorganic conjunction, arbitrary and unstable. He visualized Alice (she was breathing deeply on his shoulder) and he saw her body separately from her thoughts. He liked this body but the thoughts struck him as ridiculous, and together they did not form a whole being. He saw her as an ink line spreading on blotting paper, without contours, without shape.

He really liked this body. When Alice got up in the morning, he forced her to remain naked, and, although just yesterday she had stubbornly insisted on closed shutters, for even the dim light of the stars had bothered her, she now altogether forgot her shame. Edward was scrutinizing her (she gaily pranced about, looking for a package of tea and cookies for breakfast), and Alice, when she glanced at him after a moment, noticed that he was lost in thought. She asked him what was the matter. Edward replied that after breakfast he had to go and see his brother.

His brother inquired how he was getting on at the school. Edward 210 replied that on the whole it was fine, and his brother said, "That Chehachkova is a pig, but I forgave her long ago. I forgave her, for she did not know what she was doing. She wanted to harm me, but instead she helped me find a beautiful life. As a farmer I earn more, and contact with Nature protects me from the skepticism to which city-dwellers are prone."

"That woman, as a matter of fact, brought me some happiness too," said 211 Edward, lost in thought, and he told his brother how he had fallen in love with Alice, how he had feigned a belief in God, how they had judged him, how Chehachkova had wanted to re-educate him, and how Alice had finally given herself to him thinking he was a martyr. The only thing he didn't tell was how he had forced the directress to recite the Lord's Prayer, because he saw disapproval in his brother's eyes. He stopped talking and his brother said:

"I may have a great many faults, but one I don't have: I've never dis- 212 simulated and I've said to everyone's face what I thought."

Edward liked his brother and his disapproval hurt, so he made an effort 213 to justify himself and they began to argue. In the end Edward said:

"I know, brother, that you are a straightforward man, and that you 214 pride yourself on it. But put one question to yourself: *why* in fact should one tell the truth? What obliges us to do it? And why do we consider telling the truth a virtue? Imagine that you meet a madman, who claims that he is a fish and that we are all fish. Are you going to argue with him? Are you going to undress in front of him and show him that you don't have fins? Are you going to say to his face what you think? Well, tell me!"

His brother was silent and Edward went on: "If you told him the whole 215 truth and nothing but the truth, only what you really thought, you would enter into a serious conversation with a madman and you yourself would become mad. And it is the same way with the world that surrounds us. If I obstinately told a man the truth to his face, it would mean that I was taking him seriously. And to take something so unimportant seriously means to become less than serious oneself. I, you see, *must* lie, if I don't want to take madmen seriously and become one of them myself."

10

It was Sunday afternoon and the two lovers left for town. They were alone 216 in a compartment (the girl was already gaily chattering away again), and Edward remembered how some time ago he had looked forward to finding in Alice, whom he'd chosen voluntarily, the seriousness of life, which his duties would never provide for him. And with regret he realized (the train idyllically clattered against the joints between the rails) that the love affair he'd experienced with Alice was worthless, made up of chance and errors, without any importance or sense whatsoever. He heard Alice's words, he saw her gestures (she squeezed his hand), and it occurred to him that these were signs devoid of meaning, currency without funds, weights made of paper, and that he couldn't grant them significance any more than God could the prayer of the naked directress. And all of a sudden it seemed to him that, in fact, all the people whom he'd met in his new place of work were only ink lines spreading on blotting paper, beings with interchangeable attitudes, beings without firm substance. But what was worse, what was far worse (it struck him next) was that he himself was only a shadow of all these shadowy people. After all, he had been exhausting his own brain only to adjust to them and imitate them. Yet even if he was inwardly laughing, and thus making an effort to mock them secretly (and so exonerate his accommodation), it didn't alter the case. For even malicious imitation remains imitation, and the shadow that mocks remains a shadow, subordinate, derivative, and wretched, and nothing more.

It was ignominious, horribly ignominious. The train idyllically clattered against the joints between the rails (the girl chattered away) and Edward said: 217

"Alice, are you happy?"   218

"Sure," said Alice.   219

"I'm miserable," said Edward.   220

"What, are you crazy?" said Alice.   221

"We shouldn't have done it. It shouldn't have happened."   222

"What's gotten into you? After all, you're the one who wanted to do it!"   223

"Yes, I wanted to," said Edward, "but that was my greatest mistake, for which God will never forgive me. It was a sin, Alice."   224

"Come on, what's happened to you?" said the girl calmly. "You yourself always used to say that God wants love most of all!"   225

When Edward heard Alice, after the fact, coolly appropriating the theological sophistries with which he had so unsuccessfully taken the field a while ago, fury seized him: "I used to say that to test you. Now I've found out how well you are able to be faithful to God! But a person who is able to betray God is able to betray man a hundred times more easily."   226

Alice found more ready answers, but it would have been better for her if she hadn't, because they only provoked his vindictive rage. Edward went on and on talking (in the end he used the words "disgust" and "physical aversion") until finally he did obtain from this placid and gentle face sobs, tears, and moans.   227

"Goodbye," he told her at the station and left her in tears. Only at home several hours later, when this curious anger had subsided, did it occur to him what he had done. He imagined her body, which had pranced stark   228 naked in front of him that morning, and when he realized that this beautiful body was lost to him because he himself, of his own free will, had driven it away, he inwardly called himself an idiot and had a mind to slap his own face.

But what had happened, had happened, and it was no longer possible to right anything. 229

Though we must truthfully say that even if the idea of the beautiful, rejected body caused Edward a certain amount of grief, he coped with this loss fairly soon. If once the need for physical love had tormented him and reduced him to a state of longing, it was the short-lived need of a recent arrival. Edward no longer suffered from this need. Once a week he visited the directress (habit had relieved his body of its initial anxieties), and he resolved to continue to visit her, until his position at the school was clarified. Besides this, with increasing success he chased all sorts of other women and girls. As a consequence of both, he began to appreciate far more the times when he was alone, and became fond of solitary walks, which he sometimes combined (come, let us turn our attention to this for the last time) with a visit to a church. 230

No, don't be apprehensive, Edward did not begin to believe in God. Our story does not intend to be crowned with the effect of so ostentatious a paradox. But Edward, even if he was almost certain that God did not exist, after all felt happy and nostalgic entertaining the thought of Him. 231

God is essence itself, whereas Edward had never found (and since the incidents with the directress and with Alice, a number of years had passed) anything essential in his love affairs, or in his teaching, or in his thoughts. He was too bright to concede that he saw the essential in the unessential, but he was too weak not to long secretly for the essential. 232

Ah, ladies and gentlemen, a man lives a sad life when he cannot take anything or anyone seriously. 233

And that is why Edward longed for God, for God alone is relieved of the distracting obligation of *appearing* and can merely *be*. For He solely constitutes (He Himself, alone and nonexistent) the essential opposite of his unessential (but so much more existent) world. 234

And so Edward occasionally sits in church and looks thoughtfully at the cupola. Let us take leave of him at just such a time. It is afternoon, the church is quiet and empty. Edward is sitting in a pew tormented with sorrow, because God does not exist. But just at this moment his sorrow is so great that suddenly from its depth emerges the genuine *living* face of God. Look! Yes. Edward is smiling! He is smiling, and his smile is happy . . . 235

Please, keep him in your memory with this smile. 236

Translated from the Czech by Suzanne Rappaport

STUDY QUESTIONS

1. What features of "Edward and God" are unique to Eastern Europe? Which ones are universal?
2. What is Edward's view of society? How does it influence his behavior? What does he mean when he says, "I, you see, *must* lie, if I don't want to take madmen seriously and become one of them myself"?
3. Discuss Edward's involvement with religion. How does it affect his life?
4. How do Edward's relationship with Alice and the directress lead to deeper understanding of the human condition?
5. Discuss the author's use of humor and irony in conveying the meaning of the story.

FRANCE

Colette

Sidonie Gabrielle Colette (1873–1954), known simply as "Colette," was a prolific French novelist, short story writer, dramatist, librettist, and essayist who became the first woman to receive a French state burial. A master craftsperson in all her writing, the dramatic irony in her work is carefully elaborated by the use of symbolic detail and metaphor. Never associated with a particular artistic movement, Colette is regarded as the first truly feminist writer. Drawing inspiration from her own life in the French demimonde, which included three marriages and several lesbian relationships, Colette's literary province is female nature, most notably in its experience of love and sexuality. In her novels such as Chéri *(1920) and* My Mother's House *(1922) as in her short stories—available in English as* The Collected Stories of Colette *(1983)—women are the sexual subjects and it is their point of view that Colette depicts. This portrayal is informed by Colette's pessimistic view of an irreconcilable tension between men and women. The shifting sexual desires that she renders in her fiction are to Colette the clearest proofs of a basic disunity of spirit between male and female.*

The Other Wife

"Table for two? This way, Monsieur, Madame, there is still a table next to the window, if Madame and Monsieur would like a view of the bay." 1

Alice followed the maître d'. 2

"Oh, yes. Come on, Marc, it'll be like having lunch on a boat on the water . . ." 3

Her husband caught her by passing his arm under hers. "We'll be more comfortable over there." 4

"There? In the middle of all those people? I'd much rather . . ." 5

"Alice, please." 6

He tightened his grip in such a meaningful way that she turned around. 7
"What's the matter?"

"Shh . . ." he said softly, looking at her intently, and led her toward the 8
table in the middle.

"What is it, Marc?" 9

"I'll tell you, darling. Let me order lunch first. Would you like the 10
shrimp? Or the eggs in aspic?"

"Whatever you like, you know that." 11

They smiled at one another, wasting the precious time of an overworked 12
maître d', stricken with a kind of nervous dance, who was standing next to
them, perspiring.

"The shrimp," said Marc. "Then the eggs and bacon. And the cold 13
chicken with a romaine salad. *Fromage blanc*? The house specialty? We'll go
with the specialty. Two strong coffees. My chauffeur will be having lunch
also, we'll be leaving again at two o'clock. Some cider? No, I don't trust it
. . . Dry champagne."

He sighed as if he had just moved an armoire, gazed at the colorless 14
midday sea, at the pearly white sky, then at his wife, whom he found
lovely in her little Mercury hat with its large, hanging veil.

"You're looking well, darling. And all this blue water makes your eyes 15
look green, imagine that! And you've put on weight since you've been
traveling . . . It's nice up to a point, but only up to a point!"

Her firm, round breasts rose proudly as she leaned over the table. 16

"Why did you keep me from taking that place next to the window?" 17

Marc Seguy never considered lying. "Because you were about to sit next 18
to someone I know."

"Someone I don't know?" 19

"My ex-wife." 20

She couldn't think of anything to say and opened her blue eyes wider. 21

"So what, darling? It'll happen again. It's not important." 22

The words came back to Alice and she asked, in order, the inevitable 23
questions. "Did she see you? Could she see that you saw her? Will you
point her out to me?"

"Don't look now, please, she must be watching us . . . The lady with 24
brown hair, no hat, she must be staying in this hotel. By herself, behind
those children in red . . ."

"Yes. I see." 25

Hidden behind some broad-brimmed beach hats, Alice was able to look 26
at the woman who, fifteen months ago, had still been her husband's wife.

"Incompatibility," Marc said. "Oh, I mean . . . total incompatibility! We 27
divorced like well-bred people, almost like friends, quietly, quickly. And
then I fell in love with you, and you really wanted to be happy with me.

How lucky we are that our happiness doesn't involve any guilty parties or victims!"

The woman in white, whose smooth, lustrous hair reflected the light 28 from the sea in azure patches, was smoking a cigarette with her eyes half closed. Alice turned back toward her husband, took some shrimp and butter, and ate calmly. After a moment's silence she asked: "Why didn't you ever tell me that she had blue eyes, too?"

"Well, I never thought about it!" 29

He kissed the hand she was extending toward the bread basket and she 30 blushed with pleasure. Dusky and ample, she might have seemed some-what coarse, but the changeable blue of her eyes and her wavy, golden hair made her look like a frail and sentimental blonde. She vowed overwhelm-ing gratitude to her husband. Immodest without knowing it, everything about her bore the overly conspicuous marks of extreme happiness.

They ate and drank heartily, and each thought the other had forgotten 31 the woman in white. Now and then, however, Alice laughed too loudly, and Marc was careful about his posture, holding his shoulders back, his head up. They waited quite a long time for their coffee, in silence. An incandescent river, the straggled reflection of the invisible sun overhead, shifted slowly across the sea and shone with a blinding brilliance.

"She's still there, you know," Alice whispered. 32

"Is she making you uncomfortable? Would you like to have coffee some- 33 where else?"

"No, not at all! She's the one who must be uncomfortable! Besides, she 34 doesn't exactly seem to be having a wild time, if you could see her . . ."

"I don't have to. I know that look of hers." 35

"Oh, was she like that?" 36

He exhaled his cigarette smoke through his nostrils and knitted his 37 eyebrows. "Like that? No. To tell you honestly, she wasn't happy with me."

"Oh, really now!" 38

"The way you indulge me is so charming, darling . . . It's crazy . . . 39 You're an angel . . . You love me . . . I'm so proud when I see those eyes of yours. Yes, those eyes . . . She . . . I just didn't know how to make her happy, that's all. I didn't know how."

"She's just difficult!" 40

Alice fanned herself irritably, and cast brief glances at the woman in 41 white, who was smoking, her head resting against the back of the cane chair, her eyes closed with an air of satisfied lassitude.

Marc shrugged his shoulders modestly. 42

"That's the right word," he admitted. "What can you do? You have to 43 feel sorry for people who are never satisfied. But we're satisfied . . . Aren't we, darling?"

She did not answer. She was looking furtively, and closely, at her hus- 44 band's face, ruddy and regular; at his thick hair, threaded here and there with white silk; at his short, well-cared-for hands; and doubtful for the first time, she asked herself, "What more did she want from him?"

And as they were leaving, while Marc was paying the bill and asking for the chauffeur and about the route, she kept looking, with envy and curiosity, at the woman in white, this dissatisfied, this difficult, this superior . . .   45

Translated from the French by Matthew Ward

STUDY QUESTIONS

1. How does Colette use the reflection of light to create a mood of ambiguity in "The Other Wife"? Find the different instances of light imagery.
2. What is the significance of Marc's ordering the food? Why does the author devote so much of a very short story to food and eating?
3. How does Alice's mood change when Marc says, "I don't have to. I know that look of hers." How had Alice regarded the first wife before this statement? How does she regard her now?
4. What are Alice's feelings for Marc at the beginning of the story? What are they at the end?
5. For what are eyes metaphors?

⊚ ANDRÉ BRETON

André Breton (1896–1966) was a French poet and essayist who was the founder and chief theoretician of Surrealism. Breton began medical studies with the aim of becoming a psychiatrist, but the experience of World War I turned him permanently to literary work with the aim of using his art to create a new vision. In his theoretical essays, the **Manifestos** *(1924, 1930, 1942), Breton postulated that knowledge was incomplete because it previously had relied on rationalism. Art in its power to reveal the subconscious, the realm of desires, dreams, and intuitions, had an important role in expanding human understanding. The project of the surrealist artist was the discovery of the self, both collective and individual. To this end, Breton developed techniques, particularly of automatic writing and free association, by which to capture the spontaneity, the exigency, the very spirit of emotion. "Free Union" was one of Breton's most striking free association poems in which through a succession of unordered images he evoked the urgency of desire. A* *collection of Breton's poetry has been published in English,* Poems of André Breton: A Bilingual Anthology *(1982), as have his major theoretical statements, in* What Is Surrealism? Selected Writings *(1978).*

Free Union

My wife whose hair is a brush fire
Whose thoughts are summer lightning
Whose waist is an hourglass
Whose waist is the waist of an otter caught in the teeth of a
    tiger   5
Whose mouth is a bright cockade with the fragrance of a star of
    the first magnitude
Whose teeth leave prints like the tracks of white mice over
    snow
Whose tongue is made out of amber and polished glass   10
Whose tongue is a stabbed wafer
The tongue of a doll with eyes that open and shut
Whose tongue is incredible stone
My wife whose eyelashes are strokes in the handwriting of a
    child   15
Whose eyebrows are nests of swallows
My wife whose temples are the slate of greenhouse roofs
With steam on the windows
My wife whose shoulders are champagne
Are fountains that curl from the heads of dolphins under the   20
    ice
My wife whose wrists are matches
Whose fingers are raffles holding the ace of hearts
Whose fingers are fresh cut hay
My wife with the armpits of martens and beech fruit   25
And Midsummer Night
That are hedges of privet and nesting places for sea snails
Whose arms are of sea foam and a landlocked sea
And a fusion of wheat and a mill
Whose legs are spindles   30
In the delicate movements of watches and despair
My wife whose calves are sweet with the sap of elders
Whose feet are carved initials
Keyrings and the feet of steeplejacks who drink
My wife whose neck is fine milled barley   35
Whose throat contains the Valley of Gold

And encounters in the bed of the maelstrom
My wife whose breasts are of the night
And are undersea molehills
And crucibles of rubies   40
My wife whose breasts are haunted by the ghosts of
    dew-moistened roses
Whose belly is a fan unfolded in the sunlight
Is a giant talon
My wife with the back of a bird in vertical flight   45
With a back of quicksilver
And bright lights
My wife whose nape is of smooth worn stone and wet chalk
And of a glass slipped through the fingers of someone who has
    just drunk   50
My wife with the thighs of a skiff
That are lustrous and feathered like arrows
Stemmed with the light tailbones of a white peacock
And imperceptible balance
My wife whose rump is sandstone and flax   55
Whose rump is the back of a swan and the spring
My wife with the sex of an iris
A mine and a platypus
With the sex of an alga and old-fashioned candies
My wife with the sex of a mirror   60
My wife with eyes full of tears
With eyes that are purple armor and a magnetized needle
With eyes of savannahs
With eyes full of water to drink in prisons
My wife with eyes that are forests forever under the ax   65
My wife with eyes that are the equal of water and air and earth
    and fire

Translated from the French by David Antin

STUDY   QUESTIONS

1. Discuss Breton's use of imagery in "Free Union" and show how it
   conveys emotional and psychological experience.
2. What is the purpose of the poem? What does it accomplish?

ⓢ ALBERT CAMUS

Albert Camus (1913–1960) was an Algerian-born French writer who was associated with the ideas of existentialism and its call for individual moral commitment. Camus came from an extremely poor working-class family and grew up in hardship, which was intensified by his bouts with tuberculosis. His adulthood, in turn, was imprinted with the growth of Fascism and the struggle against it. During World War II, Camus lived in France and worked with the French Resistance against Nazi occupation. The issue of the French-Algerian War was not as clear-cut for Camus. He condemned the brutality and bitterness of the conflict, but he was not able to take a proindependence position.

From early on in his life, Camus aspired to document and to become involved with the moral issues of his time. To this end, he created a threefold career in literature, theater, and journalism. Most of his works are permeated by a sense of moral distress and a lack of collective ethical values. His protagonists grope in a solitary manner to define their humanity. Algeria, its landscape, its light, its French colonial culture was the setting of many of these works. His novels The Stranger *(1942) and* The Plague *(1947) and several of his short stories are situated there. Yet, except for "The Guest," Camus did not directly concern himself with the issues of colonialism. The Arab figures in his works were always mysterious and largely unknowable to his French protagonists. His writing reflected the divided society that European colonialism created.*

The Guest

The schoolmaster was watching the two men climb towards him. One 1 was on horseback, the other on foot. They had not yet tackled the abrupt rise leading to the schoolhouse built on the hillside. They were toiling onwards, making slow progress in the snow, among the stones, on the vast expanse of the high, deserted plateau. From time to time the horse stumbled. Without hearing anything yet, he could see the breath issuing from the horse's nostrils. One of the men, at least, knew the region. They were following the trail although it had disappeared days ago under a layer of dirty white snow. The schoolmaster calculated that it would take them half an hour to get on to the hill. It was cold; he went back into the school to get a sweater.

He crossed the empty, frigid classroom. On the blackboard the four 2 rivers of France, drawn with dour different coloured chalks, had been flowing towards their estuaries for the past three days. Snow had suddenly fallen in mid-October after eight months of drought without the transition of rain, and the twenty pupils, more or less, who lived in the villages scattered over the plateau had stopped coming. With fair weather they would return. Daru now heated only the single room that was his lodging, adjoining the classroom and giving also on to the plateau to the east. Like the class windows, his window looked to the south too. On that side the school was a few kilometres from the point where the plateau began to slope towards the south. In clear weather could be seen the purple mass of the mountain range where the gap opened on to the desert.

Somewhat warmed, Daru returned to the window from which he had   3 first seen the two men. They were no longer visible. Hence they must have tackled the rise. The sky was not so dark, for the snow had stopped falling during the night. The morning had opened with a dirty light which had scarcely become brighter as the ceiling of clouds lifted. At two in the afternoon it seemed as if the day were merely beginning. But still this was better than those three days when the thick snow was falling amidst unbroken darkness with little gusts of wind that rattled the double door of the classroom. Then Daru had spent long hours in his room, leaving it only to go to the shed and feed the chickens or get some coal. Fortunately the delivery truck from Tadjid, the nearest village to the north, had brought his supplies two days before the blizzard. It would return in forty-eight hours.

Besides, he had enough to resist a siege, for the little room was cluttered   4 with bags of wheat that the administration left as a stock to distribute to those of his pupils whose families had suffered from the drought. Actually they had all been victims because they were all poor. Every day Daru would distribute a ration to the children. They had missed it, he knew, during these bad days. Possibly one of the fathers or big brothers would come this afternoon and he could supply them with grain. It was just a matter of carrying them over to the next harvest. Now shiploads of wheat were arriving from France and the worst was over. But it would be hard to forget that poverty, that army of ragged ghosts wandering in the sunlight, the plateaux burned to a cinder month after month, the earth shrivelled up little by little, literally scorched, every stone bursting into dust under one's foot. The sheep had died then by thousands and even a few men, here and there, sometimes without anyone's knowing.

In contrast with such poverty, he who lived almost like a monk in his   5 remote schoolhouse, none the less satisfied with the little he had and with the rough life, had felt like a lord with his whitewashed walls, his narrow couch, his unpainted shelves, his well, and his weekly provision of water and food. And suddenly this snow, without warning, without the foretaste of rain. This is the way the region was, cruel to live in, even without men—who didn't help matters either. But Daru had been born here. Everywhere else, he felt exiled.

He stepped out on to the terrace in front of the schoolhouse. The two   6 men were now half-way up the slope. He recognized the horseman as

Balducci, the old gendarme he had known for a long time. Balducci was holding on the end of a rope an Arab who was walking behind him with hands bound and head lowered. The gendarme waved a greeting to which Daru did not reply, lost as he was in contemplation of the Arab dressed in a faded blue jellaba, his feet in sandals but covered with socks of heavy raw wool, his head surmounted by a narrow, short *chèche*. They were approaching. Balducci was holding back his horse in order not to hurt the Arab, and the group was advancing slowly.

Within earshot, Balducci shouted: "One hour to do the three kilometres from El Ameur!" Daru did not answer. Short and square in his thick sweater, he watched them climb. Not once had the Arab raised his head. "Hello," said Daru when they got up on to the terrace. "Come in and warm up." Balducci painfully got down from his horse without letting go the rope. From under his bristling moustache he smiled at the schoolmaster. His little dark eyes, deep-set under a tanned forehead, and his mouth surrounded with wrinkles made him look attentive and studious. Daru took the bridle, led the horse to the shed, and came back to the two men, who were now waiting for him in the school. He led them into his room. "I am going to heat up the classroom," he said. "We'll be more comfortable there." When he entered the room again, Balducci was on the couch. He had undone the rope tying him to the Arab, who had squatted near the stove. His hands still bound, the *chèche* pushed back on his head, he was looking towards the window. At first Daru noticed only his huge lips, fat, smooth, almost negroid; yet his nose was straight, his eyes were dark and full of fever. The *chèche* revealed an obstinate forehead and, under the weathered skin now rather discoloured by the cold, the whole face had a restless and rebellious look that struck Daru when the Arab, turning his face towards him, looked him straight in the eyes. "Go into the other room," said the schoolmaster, "and I'll make you some mint tea." "Thanks," Balducci said. "What a nuisance! How I long for retirement." And addressing his prisoner in Arabic: "Come on, you." The Arab got up and, slowly, holding his bound wrists in front of him, went into the classroom.

With the tea, Daru brought a chair. But Balducci was already enthroned 8
on the nearest pupil's desk and the Arab had squatted against the teacher's platform facing the stove, which stood between the desk and the window. When he held out the glass of tea to the prisoner, Daru hesitated at the sight of his bound hands. "He might perhaps be untied." "Certainly," said Balducci. "That was for the journey." He started to get to his feet. But Daru, setting the glass on the floor, had knelt beside the Arab. Without saying anything, the Arab watched him with his feverish eyes. Once his hands were free, he rubbed his swollen wrists against each other, took the glass of tea, and sucked up the burning liquid in swift little sips.

"Good," said Daru. "And where are you headed for?" 9
Balducci withdrew his moustache from the tea. "Here, my boy." 10

"Odd pupils! And you're spending the night?" 11

"No. I'm going back to El Ameur. And you will deliver this fellow to 12
Tinguit. He is expected at police headquarters."

Balducci was looking at Daru with a friendly little smile. 13

"What's this story?" asked the schoolmaster. "Are you pulling my leg?" 14

"No, my boy. Those are the orders." 15

"The orders? I'm not . . ." Daru hesitated, not wanting to hurt the old 16
Corsican. "I mean, that's not my job."

"What! What's the meaning of that? In wartime people do all kinds of 17
jobs."

"Then I'll wait for the declaration of war!" 18

Balducci nodded. 19

"O.K. But the orders exist and they concern you too. Things are brew- 20
ing, it appears. There is talk of a forthcoming revolt. We are mobilized, in
a way."

Daru still had his obstinate look. 21

"Listen, my boy," Balducci said. "I like you and you must understand. 22
There's only a dozen of us at El Ameur to patrol throughout the whole
territory of a small department and I must get back in a hurry. I was told
to hand this man over to you and return without delay. He couldn't be kept
there. His village was beginning to stir; they wanted to take him back. You
must take him to Tinguit tomorrow before the day is over. Twenty kilometres shouldn't worry a husky fellow like you. After that, all will be over.
You'll come back to your pupils and your comfortable life."

Behind the wall the horse could be heard snorting and pawing the earth. 23
Daru was looking out of the window. Decidedly, the weather was clearing
and the light was increasing over the snow plateau. When all the snow was
melted, the sun would take over again and once more would burn the
fields of stone. For days, still, the unchanging sky would shed its dry light
on the solitary expanse where nothing had any connexion with man.

"After all," he said, turning around towards Balducci, "what did he 24
do?" And, before the gendarme had opened his mouth, he asked: "Does
he speak French?"

"No, not a word. We had been looking for him for a month, but they 25
were hiding him. He killed his cousin."

"Is he against us?" 26

"I don't think so. But you can never be sure." 27

"Why did he kill?" 28

"A family squabble, I think. One owed the other grain, it seems. It's not 29
at all clear. In short, he killed his cousin with a billhook. You know, like a
sheep, *kreezk!*"

Balducci made the gesture of drawing a blade across his throat and the 30
Arab, his attention attracted, watched him with a sort of anxiety. Daru felt
a sudden wrath against the man, against all men with their rotten spite,
their tireless hates, their blood lust.

But the kettle was singing on the stove. He served Balducci more tea, 31
hesitated, then served the Arab again, who, a second time, drank avidly.
His raised arms made the jellaba fall open and the schoolmaster saw his
thin, muscular chest.

"Thanks, my boy," Balducci said. "And now, I'm off." 32

He got up and went towards the Arab, taking a small rope from his 33
pocket.

"What are you doing?" Daru asked dryly. 34

Balducci, disconcerted, showed him the rope. 35

"Don't bother." 36

The old gendarme hesitated. "It's up to you. Of course, you are armed?" 37

"I have my shot-gun." 38

"Where?" 39

"In the trunk." 40

"You ought to have it near your bed." 41

"Why? I have nothing to fear." 42

"You're mad. If there's an uprising, no one is safe, we're all in the same 43
boat."

"I'll defend myself. I'll have time to see them coming." 44

Balducci began to laugh, then suddenly the moustache covered the 45
white teeth.

"You'll have time? O.K. That's just what I was saying. You have always 46
been a little cracked. That's why I like you, my son was like that."

At the same time he took out his revolver and put it on the desk. 47

"Keep it; I don't need two weapons from here to El Ameur." 48

The revolver shone against the black paint of the table. When the gen- 49
darme turned towards him, the schoolmaster caught the smell of leather
and horseflesh.

"Listen, Balducci," Daru said suddenly, "every bit of this disgusts me, 50
and most of all your fellow here. But I won't hand him over. Fight, yes, if
I have to. But not that."

The old gendarme stood in front of him and looked at him severely. 51

"You're being a fool," he said slowly. "I don't like it either. You don't 52
get used to putting a rope on a man even after years of it, and you're even
ashamed—yes, ashamed. But you can't let them have their way."

"I won't hand him over," Daru said again. 53

"It's an order, my boy, and I repeat it." 54

"That's right. Repeat to them what I've said to you: I won't hand him 55
over."

Balducci made a visible effort to reflect. He looked at the Arab and at 56
Daru. At last he decided.

"No, I won't tell them anything. If you want to drop us, go ahead; I'll 57
not denounce you. I have an order to deliver the prisoner and I'm doing so.
And now you'll just sign this paper for me."

"There's no need. I'll not deny that you left him with me." 58

"Don't be mean with me. I know you'll tell the truth. You're from here 59
abouts and you are a man. But you must sign, that's the rule."

Daru opened his drawer, took out a little square bottle of purple ink, the 60
red wooden penholder with the "sergeant-major" pen he used for making
models of penmanship, and signed. The gendarme carefully folded the
paper and put it into his wallet. Then he moved towards the door.

"I'll see you off," Daru said. 61

"No," said Balducci. "There's no use being polite. You insulted me." 62

He looked at the Arab, motionless in the same spot, sniffed peevishly, 63
and turned away towards the door. "Good-bye, son," he said. The door
shut behind him. Balducci appeared suddenly outside the window and
then disappeared. His footsteps were muffled by the snow. The horse
stirred on the other side of the wall and several chickens fluttered in fright.
A moment later Balducci reappeared outside the window leading the horse
by the bridle. He walked towards the little rise without turning round and
disappeared from sight with the horse following him. A big stone could be
heard bouncing down. Daru walked back towards the prisoner, who, without stirring, never took his eyes off him. "Wait," the schoolmaster said in
Arabic and went towards the bedroom. As he was going through the door,
he had a second thought, went to the desk, took the revolver, and stuck it
in his pocket. Then, without looking back, he went into his room.

For some time he lay on his couch watching the sky gradually close over, 64
listening to the silence. It was this silence that had seemed painful to him
during the first days here, after the war. He had requested a post in the
little town at the base of the foothills separating the upper plateaux from
the desert. There, rocky walls, green and black to the north, pink and
lavender to the south, marked the frontier of eternal summer. He had been
named to a post farther north, on the plateau itself. In the beginning, the
solitude and the silence had been hard for him on these wastelands peopled only by stones. Occasionally, furrows suggested cultivation, but they
had been dug to uncover a certain kind of stone good for building. The
only ploughing here was to harvest rocks. Elsewhere a thin layer of soil
accumulated in the hollows would be scraped out to enrich paltry village
gardens. This is the way it was: bare rock covered three-quarters of the
region. Towns sprang up, flourished, then disappeared; men came by,
loved one another or fought bitterly, then died. No one in this desert,
neither he nor his guest, mattered. And yet, outside this desert neither of
them, Daru knew, could have really lived.

When he got up, no noise came from the classroom. He was amazed at 65
the unmixed joy he derived from the mere thought that the Arab might
have fled and that he would be alone with no decision to make. But the
prisoner was there. He had merely stretched out between the stove and the
desk. With eyes open, he was staring at the ceiling. In that position, his
thick lips were particularly noticeable, giving him a pouting look. "Come,"
said Daru. The Arab got up and followed him. In the bedroom, the school-

master pointed to a chair near the table under the window. The Arab sat down without taking his eyes off Daru.

"Are you hungry?" 66

"Yes," the prisoner said. 67

Daru set the table for two. He took flour and oil, shaped a cake in a 68
frying-pan, and lighted the little stove that functioned on bottled gas. While the cake was cooking, he went out to the shed to get cheese, eggs, dates, and condensed milk. When the cake was done he set it on the window-sill to cool, heated some condensed milk diluted with water, and beat up the eggs into an omelet. In one of his motions he knocked against the revolver stuck in his right pocket. He set the bowl down, went into the classroom, and put the revolver in his desk drawer. When he came back to the room, night was falling. He put on the light and served the Arab. "Eat," he said. The Arab took a piece of the cake, lifted it eagerly to his mouth, and stopped short.

"And you?" he asked. 69

"After you. I'll eat too." 70

The thick lips opened slightly. The Arab hesitated, then bit into the cake 71
determinedly.

The meal over, the Arab looked at the schoolmaster. "Are you the 72
judge?"

"No, I'm simply keeping you until tomorrow." 73

"Why do you eat with me?" 74

"I'm hungry." 75

The Arab fell silent. Daru got up and went out. He brought back a 76
folding bed from the shed, set it up between the table and the stove, at right angles to his own bed. From a large suitcase which, upright in a corner, served as a shelf for papers, he took two blankets and arranged them on the camp-bed. Then he stopped, felt useless, and sat down on his bed. There was nothing more to do or to get ready. He had to look at this man. He looked at him, therefore, trying to imagine his face bursting with rage. He couldn't do so. He could see nothing but the dark yet shining eyes and the animal mouth.

"Why did you kill him?" he asked in a voice whose hostile tone sur- 77
prised him.

The Arab looked away. 78

"He ran away. I ran after him." 79

He raised his eyes to Daru again and they were full of a sort of woeful 80
interrogation. "Now what will they do to me?"

"Are you afraid?" 81

He stiffened, turning his eyes away. 82

"Are you sorry?" 83

The Arab stared at him open-mouthed. Obviously he did not under- 84
stand. Daru's annoyance was growing. At the same time he felt awkward and self-conscious with his big body wedged between the two beds.

"Lie down there," he said impatiently. "That's your bed."   85
The Arab didn't move. He called to Daru: 86
"Tell me!"   87
The schoolmaster looked at him.   88
"Is the gendarme coming back tomorrow?"   89
"I don't know."   90
"Are you coming with us?"   91
"I don't know. Why?"   92

The prisoner got up and stretched out on top of the blankets, his feet   93
towards the window. The light from the electric bulb shone straight into
his eyes and he closed them at once.

"Why?" Daru repeated, standing beside the bed.   94

The Arab opened his eyes under the blinding light and looked at him,   95
trying not to blink.

"Come with us," he said.   96

In the middle of the night, Daru was still not asleep. He had gone to bed,   97
after undressing completely; he generally slept naked. But when he suddenly realized that he had nothing on, he hesitated. He felt vulnerable and
the temptation came to him to put on his clothes again. Then he shrugged
his shoulders; after all, he wasn't a child and, if need be, he could break his
adversary in two. From his bed he could observe him, lying on his back,
still motionless with his eyes closed under the harsh light. When Daru
turned out the light, the darkness seemed to coagulate all of a sudden.
Little by little, the night came back to life in the window where the starless
sky was stirring gently. The schoolmaster soon made out the body lying at
his feet. The Arab still did not move, but his eyes seemed open. A faint
wind was prowling around the schoolhouse. Perhaps it would drive away
the clouds and the sun would reappear.

During the night the wind increased. The hens fluttered a little and then   98
were silent. The Arab turned over on his side with his back to Daru, who
thought he heard him moan. Then he listened for his guest's breathing,
become heavier and more regular. He listened to that breath so close to him
and mused without being able to go to sleep. In this room where he had
been sleeping alone for a year, this presence bothered him. But it bothered
him also by imposing on him a sort of brotherhood he knew well but
refused to accept in the present circumstances. Men who share the same
rooms, soldiers or prisoners, develop a strange alliance as if, having cast off
their armour with their clothing, they fraternized every evening, over and
above their differences, in the ancient community of dream and fatigue.
But Daru shook himself; he didn't like such musings, and it was essential
to sleep.

A little later, however, when the Arab stirred slightly, the schoolmaster   99
was still not asleep. When the prisoner made a second move, he stiffened,

on the alert. The Arab was lifting himself slowly on his arms with almost the motion of a sleepwalker. Seated upright in bed, he waited motionless without turning his head towards Daru, as if he were listening attentively. Daru did not stir; it had just occurred to him that the revolver was still in the drawer of his desk. It was better to act at once. Yet he continued to observe the prisoner, who, with the same slithery motion, put his feet on the ground, waited again, then began to stand up slowly. Daru was about to call out to him when the Arab began to walk, in a quite natural but extraordinarily silent way. He was heading towards the door at the end of the room that opened into the shed. He lifted the latch with precaution and went out, pushing the door behind him but without shutting it. Daru had not stirred. "He is running away," he merely thought. "Good riddance!" Yet he listened attentively. The hens were not fluttering; the guest must be on the plateau. A faint sound of water reached him, and he didn't know what it was until the Arab again stood framed in the doorway, closed the door carefully, and came back to bed without a sound. Then Daru turned his back on him and fell asleep. Still later he seemed, from the depths of his sleep, to hear furtive steps around the schoolhouse. "I'm dreaming! I'm dreaming!" he repeated to himself. And he went on sleeping.

When he awoke, the sky was clear; the loose window let in a cold, pure air. The Arab was asleep, hunched up under the blankets now, his mouth open, utterly relaxed. But when Daru shook him, he started dreadfully, staring at Daru with wild eyes as if he had never seen him and such a frightened expression that the schoolmaster stepped back. "Don't be afraid. It's me. You must eat." The Arab nodded his head and said yes. Calm had returned to his face, but his expression was vacant and listless.

The coffee was ready. They drank it seated together on the folding bed as they munched their pieces of the cake. Then Daru led the Arab under the shed and showed him the tap where he washed. He went back into the room, folded the blankets and the bed, made his own bed and put the room in order. Then he went through the classroom and out on to the terrace. The sun was already rising in the blue sky; a soft, bright light was bathing the deserted plateau. On the ridge the snow was melting in spots. The stones were about to reappear. Crouched on the edge of the plateau, the schoolmaster looked at the deserted expanse. He thought of Balducci. He had hurt him, for he had sent him off in a way as if he didn't want to be associated with him. He could still hear the gendarme's farewell and, without knowing why, he felt strangely empty and vulnerable. At that moment, from the other side of the schoolhouse, the prisoner coughed. Daru listened to him almost despite himself and then, furious, threw a pebble that whistled through the air before sinking into the snow. That man's stupid crime revolted him, but to hand him over was contrary to honour. Merely thinking of it made him smart with humiliation. And he cursed at one and the same time his own people who had sent him this Arab and the Arab too who had dared to kill and not managed to get away.

Daru got up, walked in a circle on the terrace, waited motionless, and then went back into the schoolhouse.

The Arab, leaning over the cement floor of the shed, was washing his teeth with two fingers. Daru looked at him and said: "Come." He went back into the room ahead of the prisoner. He slipped a hunting-jacket on over his sweater and put on walking-shoes. Standing, he waited until the Arab had put on his *chèche* and sandals. They went into the classroom and the schoolmaster pointed to the exit, saying: "Go ahead." The fellow didn't bulge. "I'm coming," said Daru. The Arab went out. Daru went back into the room and made a package of pieces of rusk, dates, and sugar. In the classroom, before going out, he hesitated a second in front of his desk, then crossed the threshold and locked the door. "That's the way," he said. He started towards the east, followed by the prisoner. But, a short distance from the schoolhouse, he thought he heard a slight sound behind them. He retraced his steps and examined the surroundings of the house; there was no one there. The Arab watched him without seeming to understand. "Come on," said Daru. 102

They walked for an hour and rested beside a sharp peak of limestone. The snow was melting faster and faster and the sun was drinking up the puddles at once, rapidly cleaning the plateau, which gradually dried and vibrated like the air itself. When they resumed walking, the ground rang under their feet. From time to time a bird rent the space in front of them with a joyful cry. Daru breathed in deeply the fresh morning light. He felt a sort of rapture before the vast familiar expanse, now almost entirely yellow under its dome of blue sky. They walked an hour more, descending towards the south. They reached a level height made up of crumbly rocks. From there on, the plateau sloped down, eastward, towards a low plain where there were a few spindly trees and, to the south, towards outcroppings of rock that gave the landscape a chaotic look. 103

Daru surveyed the two directions. There was nothing but the sky on the horizon. Not a man could be seen. He turned towards the Arab, who was looking at him blankly. Daru held out the package to him. "Take it," he said. "There are dates, bread, and sugar. You can hold out for two days. Here are a thousand francs too." The Arab took the package and the money but kept his full hands at chest level as if he didn't know what to do with what was being given him. "Now look," the schoolmaster said as he pointed in the direction of the east, "there's the way to Tinguit. You have a two-hour walk. At Tinguit you'll find the administration and the police. They are expecting you." The Arab looked towards the east, still holding the package and the money against his chest. Daru took his elbow and turned him rather roughly towards the south. At the foot of the height on which they stood could be seen a faint path. "That's the trail across the plateau. In a day's walk from here you'll find pasture lands and the first nomads. They'll take you in and shelter you according to their law." The Arab had now turned towards Daru and a sort of panic was visible in his 104 expression. "Listen," he said. Daru shook his head: "No, be quiet. Now I'm leaving you." He turned his back on him, took two long steps in the direction of the school, looked hesitantly at the motionless Arab, and started off again. For a few minutes he heard nothing but his own step resounding on the cold ground and did not turn his head. A moment later, however, he turned around. The Arab was still there on the edge of the hill, his arms hanging now, and he was looking at the schoolmaster. Daru felt something rise in his throat. But he swore with impatience, waved vaguely, and started off again. He had already gone some distance when he again stopped and looked. There was no longer anyone on the hill.

Daru hesitated. The sun was now rather high in the sky and was be-   105
ginning to beat down on his head. The schoolmaster retraced his steps, at first somewhat uncertainly, then with decision. When he reached the little hill he was bathed in sweat. He climbed it as fast as he could and stopped, out of breath, at the top. The rock-fields to the south stood out sharply against the blue sky, but on the plain to the east a steamy heat was already rising. And in that slight haze, Daru, with heavy heart, made out the Arab walking slowly on the road to prison.

A little later, standing before the window of the classroom, the school-   106
master was watching the clear light bathing the whole surface of the plateau, but he hardly saw it. Behind him on the blackboard, among the winding French rivers, sprawled the clumsily chalked-up words he had just read: "You handed over our brother. You will pay for this." Daru looked at the sky, the plateau, and, beyond, the invisible lands stretching all the way to the sea. In this vast landscape he had loved so much, he was alone.

Translated from the French by Justin O'Brien

STUDY QUESTIONS

1. How does Camus describe nature in "The Guest"? How does this imagery add to the mood of the isolation of each of the three characters?
2. Why does Balducci feel insulted by Daru? Why does he refer to Daru as "son" in leaving?
3. Why doesn't the Arab escape during the night, and why does he choose the road to prison? What similarity is there between his choice and Daru's?
4. How does the author regard Daru? Balducci? The Arab?
5. The story is set at the beginning of the Algerian War for Independence. In what ways is the war relevant to the structure and plot of the story?

🌀 MARGUERITE DURAS

Marguerite Duras (b. 1914) is a French novelist, dramatist, and filmmaker, several of whose novels have been made into films. She was born of a colonial background in present-day Vietnam, where her parents were teachers. In 1932, she moved to Paris and variously studied law, mathematics, and political science until she gravitated to literary work. Although in her youth Duras was a political radical and for a time belonged to the French Communist Party, she now is identified with aesthetic radicalism, particularly through her association with the nouveau roman (new novel) movement. Nouveau roman writers came to prominence in post–World War II France concurrently with socially committed writers like Albert Camus and Jean-Paul Sartre. Unlike their compatriots, nouveau roman writers eschew writing as an expression of significant insight or a depiction of an accurate reality. Rather they see writing as an exploration of vision—that of the writer and that of the reader. Duras in her mature work Moderato Cantabile *(1958),* The Ravishing of Lol Stein *(1966),* The Vice-Consul *(1968), and* Love *(1972) and the screenplay* Hiroshima, mon amour *(1960) renders anecdotes and even stories but expects the engaged reader to decipher creatively a structure or an interlinking of events. This excerpt from* Moderato Cantabile *illustrates Duras's conception of the writer as the observer who describes scenes whose meaning the "reader become artist" has to interpret.*

From *Moderato Cantabile*

"Will you please read what's written above the score?" the lady asked. 1

"Moderato cantabile," said the child. 2

The lady punctuated his reply by striking the keyboard with a pencil. 3
The child remained motionless, his head turned towards his score.

"And what does moderato cantabile mean?" 4

"I don't know." 5

A woman, seated ten feet away, gave a sigh. 6

"Are you quite sure you don't know what moderato cantabile means?" 7
the lady repeated.

The child did not reply. The lady stifled an exasperated groan, and again 8
struck the keyboard with her pencil. The child remained unblinking. The
lady turned.

"Madame Desbaresdes, you have a very stubborn little boy." 9

Anne Desbaresdes sighed again. 10

"You don't have to tell me," she said. 11

The child, motionless, his eyes lowered, was the only one to remember 12
that dusk had just exploded. It made him shiver.

"I told you the last time, I told you the time before that, I've told you a 13
hundred times, are you sure you don't know what it means?"

The child decided not to answer. The lady looked again at the object 14
before her, her rage mounting.

"Here we go again," said Anne Desbaresdes under her breath. 15

"The trouble is," the lady went on, "the trouble is you don't want to say 16
it."

Anne Desbaresdes also looked again at this child, from head to toe, but 17
in a different way from the lady.

"You're going to say it this minute," the lady shouted. 18

The child showed no surprise. He still didn't reply. Then the lady struck 19
the keyboard a third time, so hard that the pencil broke. Right next to the
child's hands. His hands were round and milky, still scarcely formed. They
were clenched and unmoving.

"He's a difficult child," Anne Desbaresdes offered timidly. 20

The child turned his head towards the voice, quickly towards his 21
mother, to make sure of her existence, then resumed his pose as an object,
facing the score. His hands remained clenched.

"I don't care whether he's difficult or not, Madame Desbaresdes," said 22
the lady. "Difficult or not, he has to do as he's told, or suffer the consequences."

In the ensuing silence the sound of the sea came in through the open 23
window. And with it the muffled noise of the town on this spring afternoon.

"For the last time. Are you sure you don't know what it means?" 24

A motorboat was framed in the open window. The child, facing his 25
score, hardly moved—only his mother noticed it—as the motorboat passed
through his blood. The low purr of the motor could be heard throughout
the town. There were only a few pleasure craft. The whole sky was tinted
pink by the last rays of the sun. Outside, on the docks, other children
stopped and looked.

"Are you really sure, for the last time now, are you sure you don't know 26
what it means?"

Again, the motorboat passed by. 27

The lady was taken aback by such stubbornness. Her anger abated, and 28
she so despaired at being so unimportant to this child who, by a single
gesture, she could have made to answer her, that she was suddenly aware
of the sterility of her own existence.

"What a profession, what a profession," she lamented. 29

Anne Desbaresdes made no comment, but tilted her head slightly as if, 30
perhaps, agreeing.

The motorboat had finally passed from the frame of the open window. 31
The sound of the sea arose, boundless, in the child's silence.

"Moderato?"   32

The child opened his fist, moved it, and lightly scratched his calf. His   33
gesture was unconstrained, and perhaps the lady admitted its innocence.

"I don't know," he said, after he had finished scratching himself.   34

The color of the sunset suddenly became so magnificent that it changed   35
the gold of the child's hair.

"It's easy," the woman said a bit more calmly.   36

She blew her nose.   37

"What a child," Anne Desbaresdes said happily, "really, what a child!   38
How in the world did I happen to have such an obstinate . . ."

The lady decided that such pride deserved no comment.   39

"It means," she said to the child, as though admitting defeat, "for the   40
hundredth time, it means moderately and melodiously."

"Moderately and melodiously," the child said mechanically.   41

The lady turned around.   42

"Really. I mean *really*."   43

"Yes, it's terrible," Anne Desbaresdes said, laughing, "stubborn as a   44
goat. It's terrible."

"Begin again," the lady said.   45

The child did not begin again.   46

"I said begin again."   47

The child still did not move. The sound of the sea again filled the silence   48
of his stubbornness. The pink sky exploded in a final burst of color.

"I don't want to learn how to play the piano," the child said.   49

In the street downstairs a woman screamed, a long, drawn-out scream   50
so shrill it overwhelmed the sound of the sea. Then it stopped abruptly.

"What was that?" the child shouted.   51

"Something happened," the lady said.   52

The sound of the sea moved in again. The pink sky began to fade.   53

"No," said Anne Desbaresdes, "it's nothing."   54

She got up and went to the piano.   55

"You're so nervous," the lady said, looking at both of them with a   56
disapproving air.

Anne Desbaresdes took her child by the shoulders, shook him, and   57
almost shouted:

"You've got to learn the piano, you've got to."   58

The child was also trembling, for the same reason, because he was   59
afraid.

"I don't like the piano," he murmured.   60

Scattered shouts followed the first, confirming an already established   61
fact, henceforth reassuring. So the lesson went on.

"You've got to," Anne Desbaresdes insisted.   62

The lady shook her head, disapproving such tenderness. Dusk began to   63
sweep over the sea. And the sky slowly darkened, except for the red in the
west, till that faded as well.

"Why?" the child asked. 64

"Because music, my love . . ." 65

The child took his time, trying to understand, did not understand, but 66
admitted it.

"All right. But who screamed?" 67

"I'm waiting," said the lady. 68

He began to play. The music rose above the murmur of a crowd that was 69
beginning to gather on the dock beneath the window.

"There now, there you are," Anne Desbaresdes said happily, "you see." 70

"When he wants to," the lady said. 71

The child finished the sonatina. The noise from the street grew more 72
insistent, invading the room.

"What's going on?" the child asked again. 73

"Play it again," the lady replied. "And don't forget: moderato cantabile. 74
Think of a lullaby."

"I never sing him songs," Anne Desbaresdes said. "Tonight he's going 75
to ask me for one, and he'll ask me so sweetly I won't be able to refuse."

The lady didn't want to listen. The child began to play Diabelli's sona- 76
tina again.

"B flat," the lady said sharply, "you always forget." 77

The growing clamor of voices of both sexes rose from the dock. Every- 78
one seemed to be saying the same thing, but it was impossible to distinguish the words. The sonatina went innocently along, but this time, in the
middle of it, the lady could take no more.

"Stop." 79

The child stopped. The lady turned to Anne Desbaresdes. 80

"I'm sure something serious has happened." 81

They all went to the window. To their left, some twenty yards from the 82
building, a crowd had already gathered on the dock in front of the café
door. From the neighboring streets people were running up to join the
crowd. Everyone was looking into the café.

"I'm afraid this part of town . . ." the lady said. 83

She turned and took the boy's arm. "Start again, one last time, where 84
you left off."

"What's happened?" 85

"Your sonatina." 86

The child played. He played it at the same tempo as before, and as the 87
end of the lesson approached he gave it the nuances she wanted, moderato
cantabile.

"It upsets me when he does as he's told like that," Anne Desbaresdes 88
said. "I guess I don't know what I want. It's a cross I have to bear."

The child went on playing well. 89

"What a way to bring him up, Madame Desbaresdes," the lady said 90
almost happily.

Then the child stopped. 91

"Why are you stopping?"   92

"I thought . . ."   93

He began playing the sonatina again. The noise of the crowd grew   94
increasingly loud, becoming so powerful, even at that height, that it
drowned out the music.

"Don't forget that B flat in the key," the lady said, "otherwise it would 95
be perfect."

Once again the music crescendoed to its final chord. And the hour was   96
up. The lady announced that the lesson was finished for today.

"You'll have plenty of trouble with that one, I don't mind telling you,"   97
she said.

"I already do. He worries me to death."   98

Anne Desbaresdes bowed her head, her eyes closed in the painful smile   99
of endless childbirth. Below, a welter of shouts and orders proved the
consummation of an unknown incident.

"Tomorrow we'll know it perfectly," the lady said.   100

The child ran to the window.   101

"Some cars are coming," he said.   102

The crowd blocked both sides of the café entrance, and was still grow-   103
ing, but the influx from the neighboring streets had lessened. Still, it was
much larger than one might have suspected. The people moved aside and
made a path for a black van to get through. Three men got out and went
into the café.

"Police," someone said.   104

Anne Desbaresdes asked what had happened.   105

"Someone's been killed. A woman."   106

She left her child in front of Mademoiselle Giraud's door, joined the   107
body of the crowd, and made her way forward till she reached the front
row of silent people looking through the open windows. At the far end of
the café, in the semi-darkness of the back room, a woman was lying motionless on the floor. A man was crouched over her, clutching her shoulders, and saying quietly:

"Darling. My darling."   108

He turned and looked at the crowd; they saw his eyes, which were   109
expressionless, except for the stricken, indelible, inward look of his desire.
The patronne stood calmly near the van and waited.

"I tried to call you three times."   110

"Poor woman," someone said.   111

"Why?" Anne Desbaresdes asked.   112

"No one knows."   113

In his delirium the man threw himself on the inert body. An inspector   114
took him by the arm and pulled him up. He did not resist. It seemed that
all dignity had left him forever. He looked absently at the inspector. The
inspector let go of him, took a notebook and pencil from his pocket, asked
for the man's identity, and waited.

"It's no use. I won't say anything now," the man said.   115

The inspector didn't press the matter, and went over to join his col-   116
leagues who were questioning the patronne at the last table in the back
room.

The man sat down beside the dead woman, stroked her hair and smiled   117
at her. A young man with a camera around his neck dashed up to the café
door and took a picture of the man sitting there smiling. By the glare of the
flash bulb the crowd could see that the woman was still young, and that
blood was coming from her mouth in thin trickles, and that there was
blood on the man's face where he had kissed her. In the crowd, someone
said:

"It's horrible," and turned away.   118

The man lay down again beside his wife's body, but only for a moment.   119
Then, as if he were tired, he got up again.

"Don't let him get away," the patronne shouted.   120

But the man had only got up in order to find a better position, closer   121
to the body. He lay there, seemingly resolute and calm, holding her
tightly in his arms, his face pressed to hers, in the blood flowing from
her mouth.

But the inspectors had finished taking the patronne's testimony and   122
slowly, in single file, walked over to him, an identical air of utter boredom
on their faces.

The child, sitting obediently on Mademoiselle Giraud's front steps, had 123
almost forgotten. He was humming the Diabelli sonatina.

"It was nothing," Anne Desbaresdes said. "Now we must go home."   124

The child followed her. More policemen arrived—too late, for no reason. 125
As they passed the café the man came out, flanked by the inspectors. The
crowd parted silently to let him through.

"He's not the one who screamed," the child said. "He didn't scream."   126

"No, it wasn't he. Don't look."   127

"Why did she . . . ?"   128

"I don't know."   129

The man walked meekly to the van. Then, when he reached it, he   130
shook off the inspectors, and, without a word, ran quickly back towards
the café. But just as he got there the lights went out. He stopped dead,
again followed the inspectors to the van, and got inside. Then, perhaps,
he was crying, but it was already too dark to see anything but his trembling, bloodstained face. If he was crying, it was too dark to see his tears.

"Really," Anne Desbaresdes said as they reached the Boulevard de la Mer, 131
"you might remember it once and for all. Moderato means moderately
slow, and cantabile means melodiously. It's easy."

Translated from the French by Richard Seaver

STUDY QUESTIONS

1. What elements of the traditional story does Duras forgo in "Moderato Cantabile"? What aspects does she retain?
2. How does the author suggest movement or action? What is the sense of time that she creates?
3. What is the relationship of the various characters to each other?
4. Identify the cinematic techniques she employs.
5. What is the meaning of the phrase "moderato cantabile"? What is its significance in the story?

GERMANY

⑥ RAINER MARIA RILKE

Rainer Maria Rilke (1875–1926) is one of the great poets of German literature. For the most part self-taught, he was a key initiator of German modernism. According to the critic James Rolleston, Rilke transformed German poetry from its nineteenth-century aural model to its twentieth-century visual and sculptural model, a change that is clearly evident in Rilke's own poetry from his student verse to such mature works as The Duino Elegies *(1923) and* The Sonnets to Orpheus *(1936). In achieving this transformation, Rilke was influenced by the painting of Paul Cézanne and the sculpture of Auguste Rodin. Rilke came to view language the way a sculptor views stone—as the raw material out of which the artist arduously shapes and constructs the art object or the poem. The significance of the finished poem lay in the moment of acute perception that it generated for both the poet and the reader. Rilke, who loathed the materialism of industrial, urban society, aspired that his poetry in creating moments of lucidity would draw his readers into communion with the spiritual wellsprings of Western civilization.*

The Blind Man. Paris.

Look, where he goes he interrupts the town
—which *is* not where his darkness is—
like a dark crack going through a clear
light-coloured cup. And the reflection

of things is painted on him as on paper;   5
he does not take it in.
Only his feeling stirs as if it caught
the world in little waves:

a silence, a resistance; waiting,
he seems to choose somebody, lifts his hand   10
devotedly and almost festive
as though to give himself in marriage.

Translated from the German by Ruth Speirs

Archaic Torso of Apollo

We cannot know his legendary head
with eyes like ripening fruit. And yet his torso
is still suffused with brilliance from inside,
like a lamp, in which his gaze, now turned to low,

5

gleams in all its power. Otherwise
the curved breast could not dazzle you so, nor could
a smile run through the placid hips and thighs
to that dark center where procreation flared.

Otherwise this stone would seem defaced
beneath the translucent cascade of the shoulders   10
and would not glisten like a wild beast's fur:

would not, from all the borders of itself,
burst like a star: for here there is no place
that does not see you. You must change your life.

Translated from the German by Stephen Mitchell

STUDY QUESTIONS

1. What figures of speech does Rilke use to evoke the situation of the
   blind man in "The Blind Man. Paris."? How do these figurative comparisons impact on the poem as a whole? What does the poet mean by
   "as though to give himself in marriage?"
2. In what ways does the poet create the mood of an urban environment?
   What is his attitude toward this environment? What does he mean by
   line 2, "—which *is* not where his darkness is—"?
3. In "Archaic Torso of Apollo," who is Apollo? What did he represent in
   the ancient world? How does the poet evoke Apollo's mythic significance? How does he convince the reader of its universal meaning?

4. What is the poet saying about the function of art? What does he mean in lines 13–14:

> ". . . for here there is no place
> that does not see you. You must change your life."?

⟲ NELLY SACHS

Nelly Sachs (1891–1970) was one of the most poignant and eloquent poets writing of the Holocaust. Though Sachs wrote poetry prior to World War II, it was the persecution and suffering of the Jewish people that gave her her specific poetic voice. Having escaped with her Jewish mother from Germany to Sweden in 1940, Sachs began writing with a new vision when, as she said, "Death gave me my language." Sachs wrote because poetry was the only means she had of expressing her anguish and sorrow at the Nazis' atrocities. Initially, her verse testified to the horror and despair of the death camps. Her first volume was entitled In the Dwellings of Death *(1947). Eventually, a transcendent spirit came to permeate Sachs's poetry. In volumes such as* And No One Knows Where to Go *(1957) and* Flight and Metamorphosis *(1959), suffering was still attested to, but Sachs linked the fate of Jews with that of humanity in a continual process of death and rebirth. In 1966, she shared the Nobel Prize with S. Y. Agnon.*

Chorus of the Rescued

We, the rescued,
From whose hollow bones death had begun to whittle his
    flutes,
And on whose sinews he had already stroked his bow—
Our bodies continue to lament   5
With their mutilated music.
We, the rescued,
The nooses wound for our necks still dangle
before us in the blue air—
Hourglasses still fill with our dripping blood.   10
We, the rescued,
The worms of fear still feed on us.
Our constellation is buried in dust.
We, the rescued,

Beg you: 15
Show us your sun, but gradually.
Lead us from star to star, step by step.
Be gentle when you teach us to live again.
Lest the song of a bird,
Or a pail being filled at the well,   20
Let our badly sealed pain burst forth again
and carry us away—
We beg you:
Do not show us an angry dog, not yet—
It could be, it could be   25
That we will dissolve into dust—
Dissolve into dust before your eyes.
For what binds our fabric together?

Translated from the German by Michael Roloff

STUDY   QUESTIONS

1. How does Sachs define the situation of Holocaust survivors in "Chorus of the Rescued"? Which images in the poem best evoke their experience?
2. Does the poem offer a reprieve from suffering?

◎ BERTOLT BRECHT

Bertolt Brecht (1898–1956) was a renowned German dramatist, poet, and theatrical director and producer whose creation of epic theater, a drama of loosely knit, episodic scenes, was a major twentieth-century innovation. A youthful participant in Weimar culture, Brecht was fascinated with the relationship of form and matter. A study of Marxism convinced him of the primacy of content in art. From the 1930s on, Brecht held that art should teach the reader/audience to see the human condition within the configuration of social, economic, and historical forces. To fulfill this didactic purpose and to create true art, Brecht developed the innovative techniques of epic theater. Breaking with the notion of theater as an imitation of reality in which the audience emotionally reacts to the protagonists, Brecht in his plays Galileo *(1943),* Mother Courage and Her Children *(1941),* The Good Woman of Setzuan *(1943), and* The Caucasian Chalk Circle *(1948), aimed to* stimulate the spectators' thinking. Using techniques of alienation, such as telling the plot beforehand to break the emotional impact of the scene, and of gestus to keep actors in an objective attitude toward their roles, Brecht from the 1930s on, during his long exile from Fascist Germany, created drama and poetry that approached his audience in a critical manner with the aim of getting his spectators and readers to perceive reality in a new and politically meaningful way.

To Posterity

1

Indeed I live in the dark ages!
A guileless word is an absurdity. A smooth forehead betokens
A hard heart. He who laughs
Has not yet heard
The terrible tidings.   5

Ah, what an age it is
When to speak of trees is almost a crime
For it is a kind of silence about injustice!
And he who walks calmly across the street,
Is he not out of reach of his friends   10
In trouble?

It is true: I earn my living
But, believe me, it is only an accident.
Nothing that I do entitles me to eat my fill.
By chance I was spared. (If my luck leaves me   15
I am lost.)

They tell me: eat and drink. Be glad you have it!
But how can I eat and drink
When my food is snatched from the hungry
And my glass of water belongs to the thirsty?   20
And yet I eat and drink.

I would gladly be wise.
The old books tell us what wisdom is:
Avoid the strife of the world, live out your little time
Fearing no one,   25

Using no violence,
Returning good for evil—
Not fulfillment of desire but forgetfulness
Passes for wisdom.
I can do none of this: 30
Indeed I live in the dark ages!

2

I came to the cities in a time of disorder
When hunger ruled.
I came among men in a time of uprising
And I revolted with them.   35
So the time passed away
Which on earth was given me.

I ate my food between massacres.
The shadow of murder lay upon my sleep.
And when I loved, I loved with indifference.   40
I looked upon nature with impatience.
So the time passed away
Which on earth was given me.

In my time streets led to the quicksand.
Speech betrayed me to the slaughterer.   45
There was little I could do. But without me
The rulers would have been more secure. This was my hope.
So the time passed away
Which on earth was given me.

Men's strength was little. The goal   50
Lay far in the distance,
Easy to see if for me
Scarcely attainable.
So the time passed away
Which on earth was given me.   55

3

You, who shall emerge from the flood
In which we are sinking,
Think—
When you speak of our weaknesses,

Also of the dark time   60
That brought them forth.

For we went, changing our country more often than our shoes,
In the class war, despairing
When there was only injustice and no resistance.

For we knew only too well: 65
Even the hatred of squalor
Makes the brow grow stern.
Even anger against injustice
Makes the voice grow harsh. Alas, we
Who wished to lay the foundations of kindness   70
Could not ourselves be kind.

But you, when at last it comes to pass
That man can help his fellow man,
Do not judge us
Too harshly.   75

Translated from the German by H. R. Hays

STUDY QUESTIONS

1. "To Posterity" is in many ways a summary of Brecht's times. What are
   the historical events he refers to in the poem?
2. What type of world does the author evoke? How is the narrator affected by it? What moral dilemmas does he confront?
3. What are some examples of the poem's use of irony?

⟲ Heinrich Böll

*Heinrich Böll (1917–1985) was a German novelist, poet, and short story
writer who well might be called the conscience of his age for maintaining the
conviction that the artist needs to be concerned with documenting the Fascist
past and with critiquing the materialism of contemporary German society.
Born of a pious, but antiinstitutional Catholic family and unwillingly
conscripted into the German army during World War II, Böll drew his
guiding vision from Christian social teaching and from his revulsion at the*

cruelties and injustices he witnessed under the Nazis. A denunciation of the perversion of human values whether through war, conformity, or materialism is pronounced in all his work from such early collections as Traveller, If You Come to Spa . . . *(1950) and his first novel,* Adam, Where Art Thou? *(1951), to mature novels such as* Group Portrait with Lady *(1971). To avoid lapsing into sentimentality or mere moralism, Böll experimented with techniques. He elaborated complex narrative structures, used multilayered chronology, and effectively offset pathos with satire. At the same time he succeeded in maintaining a lyricism in his writing that gave testimonial to his wish to create an "aesthetic of the humane." "The Balek Scales," with its compassion for the oppressed, illuminates both Böll's moral vision and his experimentation with chronology and narration.*

The Balek Scales

Where my grandfather came from, most of the people lived by working in the flax sheds. For five generations they had been breathing in the dust which rose from the crushed flax stalks, letting themselves be killed off by slow degrees, a race of long-suffering, cheerful people who ate goat cheese, potatoes, and now and then a rabbit; in the evening they would sit at home spinning and knitting; they sang, drank mint tea and were happy. During the day they would carry the flax stalks to the antiquated machines, with no protection from the dust and at the mercy of the heat which came pouring out of the drying kilns. Each cottage contained only one bed, standing against the wall like a closet and reserved for the parents, while the children slept all round the room on benches. In the morning the room would be filled with the odor of thin soup; on Sundays there was stew, and on feast days the children's faces would light up with pleasure as they watched the black acorn coffee turning paler and paler from the milk their smiling mother poured into their coffee mugs. 1

The parents went off early to the flax sheds, the housework was left to the children: they would sweep the room, tidy up, wash the dishes and peel the potatoes, precious pale-yellow fruit whose thin peel had to be produced afterwards to dispel any suspicion of extravagance or carelessness. 2

As soon as the children were out of school they had to go off into the woods and, depending on the season, gather mushrooms and herbs: woodruff and thyme, caraway, mint and foxglove, and in summer, when they had brought in the hay from their meager fields, they gathered hayflowers. A kilo of hayflowers was worth one pfennig, and they were sold by the apothecaries in town for twenty pfennigs a kilo to highly strung ladies. The mushrooms were highly prized: they fetched twenty pfennigs 3 a kilo and were sold in the shops in town for one mark twenty. The children would crawl deep into the green darkness of the forest during the autumn when dampness drove the mushrooms out of the soil, and almost every family had its own places where it gathered mushrooms, places which were handed down in whispers from generation to generation.

The woods belonged to the Baleks, as well as the flax sheds, and in my grandfather's village the Baleks had a chateau, and the wife of the head of the family had a little room next to the dairy where mushrooms, herbs and hayflowers were weighed and paid for. There on the table stood the great Balek scales, an old-fashioned, ornate bronze-gilt contraption, which my grandfather's grandparents had already faced when they were children, their grubby hands holding their little baskets of mushrooms, their paper bags of hayflowers, breathlessly watching the number of weights Frau Balek had to throw on the scale before the swinging pointer came to rest exactly over the black line, that thin line of justice which had to be redrawn every year. Then Frau Balek would take the big book covered in brown leather, write down the weight, and pay out the money, pfennigs or ten-pfennig pieces and very, very occasionally, a mark. And when my grandfather was a child there was a big glass jar of lemon drops standing there, the kind that cost one mark a kilo, and when Frau Balek—whichever one happened to be presiding over the little room—was in a good mood, she would put her hand into this jar and give each child a lemon drop, and the children's faces would light up with pleasure, the way they used to when on feast days their mother poured milk into their coffee mugs, milk that made the coffee turn paler and paler until it was as pale as the flaxen pigtails of the little girls.   4

One of the laws imposed by the Baleks on the village was: no one was permitted to have any scales in the house. The law was so ancient that nobody gave a thought as to when and how it had arisen, and it had to be obeyed, for anyone who broke it was dismissed from the flax sheds, he could not sell his mushrooms or his thyme or his hayflowers, and the power of the Baleks was so far-reaching that no one in the neighboring villages would give him work either, or buy his forest herbs. But since the days when my grandfather's parents had gone out as small children to gather mushrooms and sell them in order that they might season the meat of the rich people of Prague or be baked into game pies, it had never occurred to anyone to break this law: flour could be measured in cups, eggs could be counted, what they had spun could be measured by the yard, and besides, the old-fashioned bronze-gilt, ornate Balek scales did not look as if there was anything wrong with them, and five generations had entrusted the swinging black pointer with what they had gone out as eager children to gather from the woods.   5

True, there were some among these quiet people who flouted the law,   6 poachers bent on making more money in one night than they could earn in a whole month in the flax sheds, but even these people apparently never thought of buying scales or making their own. My grandfather was the first person bold enough to test the justice of the Baleks, the family who lived in the chateau and drove two carriages, who always maintained one boy from the village while he studied theology at the seminary in Prague, the family with whom the priest played taroc every Wednesday, on whom the local reeve, in his carriage emblazoned with the Imperial coat-of-arms, made an annual New Year's Day call and on whom the Emperor conferred a title on the first day of the year 1900.

My grandfather was hard-working and smart: he crawled further into   7
the woods than the children of his clan had crawled before him, he pen-etrated as far as the thicket where, according to legend, Bilgan the Giant was supposed to dwell, guarding a treasure. But my grandfather was not afraid of Bilgan: he worked his way deep into the thicket, even when he was quite little, and brought out great quantities of mushrooms; he even found truffles, for which Frau Balek paid thirty pfennigs a pound. Every-thing my grandfather took to the Baleks he entered on the back of a torn-off calendar page: every pound of mushrooms, every gram of thyme, and on the right-hand side, in his childish handwriting, he entered the amount he received for each item; he scrawled in every pfennig, from the age of seven to the age of twelve, and by the time he was twelve the year 1900 had arrived, and because the Baleks had been raised to the aristocracy by the Emperor, they gave every family in the village a quarter of a pound of real coffee, the Brazilian kind; there was also free beer and tobacco for the men, and at the chateau there was a great banquet; many carriages stood in the avenue of poplars leading from the entrance gates to the chateau.

But the day before the banquet the coffee was distributed in the little   8
room which had housed the Balek scales for almost a hundred years, and the Balek family was now called Balek von Bilgan because, according to legend, Bilgan the Giant used to have a great castle on the site of the present Balek estate.

My grandfather often used to tell me how he went there after school to   9
fetch the coffee for four families: the Cechs, the Weidlers, the Vohlas and his own, the Brüchers. It was the afternoon of New Year's Eve: there were the front rooms to be decorated, the baking to be done, and the families did not want to spare four boys and have each of them go all the way to the chateau to bring back a quarter of a pound of coffee.

And so my grandfather sat on the narrow wooden bench in the little   10
room while Gertrud the maid counted out the wrapped four-ounce pack-ages of coffee, four of them, and he looked at the scales and saw that the pound weight was still lying on the left-hand scale; Frau Balek von Bilgan was busy with preparations for the banquet. And when Gertrud was about to put her hand into the jar with the lemon drops to give my grandfather

one, she discovered it was empty: it was refilled once a year, and held one kilo of the kind that cost a mark.

Gertrud laughed and said: "Wait here while I get the new lot," and my grandfather waited with the four four-ounce packages which had been wrapped and sealed in the factory, facing the scales on which someone had left the pound weight, and my grandfather took the four packages of coffee, put them on the empty scale, and his heart thudded as he watched the black finger of justice come to rest on the left of the black line: the scale with the pound weight stayed down, and the pound of coffee remained up in the air; his heart thudded more than if he had been lying behind a bush in the forest waiting for Bilgan the Giant, and he felt in his pocket for the pebbles he always carried with him so he could use his catapult to shoot the sparrows which pecked away at his mother's cabbage plants—he had to put three, four, five pebbles beside the packages of coffee before the scale with the pound weight rose and the pointer at last came to rest over the black line. My grandfather took the coffee from the scale, wrapped the five pebbles in his kerchief, and when Gertrud came back with the big kilo bag of lemon drops which had to last for another whole year in order to make the children's faces light up with pleasure, when Gertrud let the lemon drops rattle into the glass jar, the pale little fellow was still standing there, and nothing seemed to have changed. My grandfather only took three of the packages, then Gertrud looked in startled surprise at the white-faced child who threw the lemon drop onto the floor, ground it under his heel, and said: "I want to see Frau Balek."

"Balek von Bilgan, if you please," said Gertrud.

"All right, Frau Balek von Bilgan," but Gertrud only laughed at him, and he walked back to the village in the dark, took the Cechs, the Weidlers and the Vohlas their coffee, and said he had to go and see the priest.

Instead he went out into the dark night with his five pebbles in his kerchief. He had to walk a long way before he found someone who had scales, who was permitted to have them; no one in the villages of Blaugau and Bernau had any, he knew that, and he went straight through them till, after two hours' walking, he reached the little town of Dielheim where Honig the apothecary lived. From Honig's house came the smell of fresh pancakes, and Honig's breath, when he opened the door to the half-frozen boy, already smelled of punch, there was a moist cigar between his narrow lips, and he clasped the boy's cold hands firmly for a moment, saying: "What's the matter, has your father's lung got worse?"

"No, I haven't come for medicine, I wanted . . ." My grandfather undid his kerchief, took out the five pebbles, held them out to Honig and said: "I wanted to have these weighed." He glanced anxiously into Honig's face, but when Honig said nothing and did not get angry, or even ask him anything, my grandfather said: "It is the amount that is short of justice," and now, as he went into the warm room, my grandfather realized how wet his feet were. The snow had soaked through his cheap shoes, and in the forest the branches had showered him with snow which was now melting, and he was tired and hungry and suddenly began to cry because he thought of the quantities of mushrooms, the herbs, the flowers, which had been weighed on the scales which were short five pebbles' worth of justice. And when Honig, shaking his head and holding the five pebbles, called his wife, my grandfather thought of the generations of his parents, his grandparents, who had all had to have their mushrooms, their flowers, weighed on the scales, and he was overwhelmed by a great wave of injustice, and began to sob louder than ever, and, without waiting to be asked, he sat down on a chair, ignoring the pancakes, the cup of hot coffee which nice plump Frau Honig put in front of him, and did not stop crying till Honig himself came out from the shop at the back and, rattling the pebbles in his hand, said in a low voice to his wife: "Fifty-five grams, exactly."

My grandfather walked the two hours home through the forest, got a 16 beating at home, said nothing, not a single word, when he was asked about the coffee, spent the whole evening doing sums on the piece of paper on which he had written down everything he had sold to Frau Balek, and when midnight struck, and the cannon could be heard from the chateau, and the whole village rang with shouting and laughter and the noise of rattles, when the family kissed and embraced all round, he said into the New Year silence: "The Baleks owe me eighteen marks and thirty-two pfennigs." And again he thought of all the children there were in the village, of his brother Fritz who had gathered so many mushrooms, of his sister Ludmilla; he thought of the many hundreds of children who had all gathered mushrooms for the Baleks, and herbs and flowers, and this time he did not cry but told his parents and brothers and sisters of his discovery.

When the Baleks von Bilgan went to High Mass on New Year's Day, 17 their new coat-of-arms—a giant crouching under a fir tree—already emblazoned in blue and gold on their carriage, they saw the hard, pale faces of the people all staring at them. They had expected garlands in the village, a song in their honor, cheers and hurrahs, but the village was completely deserted as they drove through it, and in church the pale faces of the people were turned toward them, mute and hostile, and when the priest mounted the pulpit to deliver his New Year's sermon he sensed the chill in those otherwise quiet and peaceful faces, and he stumbled painfully through his sermon and went back to the altar drenched in sweat. And as the Baleks von Bilgan left the church after Mass, they walked through a lane of mute, pale faces. But young Frau Balek von Bilgan stopped in front of the children's pews, sought out my grandfather's face, pale little Franz Brücher, and asked him, right there in the church: "Why didn't you take the coffee for your mother?" And my grandfather stood up and said: "Because you owe me as much money as five kilos of coffee would cost." And he pulled the five pebbles from his pocket, held them out to the young woman and said: "This much, fifty-five grams, is short in every pound of your justice"; and before the woman could say anything the men and women in the church lifted up their voices and sang: "The justice of this earth, O Lord, hath put Thee to death. . . ."

While the Baleks were at church, Wilhelm Vohla, the poacher, had 18 broken into the little room, stolen the scales and the big fat leatherbound book in which had been entered every kilo of mushrooms, every kilo of hayflowers, everything bought by the Baleks in the village, and all afternoon of that New Year's Day the men of the village sat in my great-grandparents' front room and calculated, calculated one tenth of everything that had been bought—but when they had calculated many thousands of talers and had still not come to an end, the reeve's gendarmes arrived, made their way into my great-grandfather's front room, shooting and stabbing as they came, and removed the scales and the book by force. My grandfather's little sister Ludmilla lost her life, a few men were wounded, and one of the gendarmes was stabbed to death by Wilhelm Vohla the poacher.

Our village was not the only one to rebel: Blaugau and Bernau did 19 too, and for almost a week no work was done in the flax sheds. But a great many gendarmes appeared, and the men and women were threatened with prison, and the Baleks forced the priest to display the scales publicly in the school and demonstrate that the finger of justice swung to and fro accurately. And the men and women went back to the flax sheds—but no one went to the school to watch the priest: he stood there all alone, helpless and forlorn with his weights, scales, and packages of coffee.

And the children went back to gathering mushrooms, to gathering 20 thyme, flowers and foxglove, but every Sunday, as soon as the Baleks entered the church, the hymn was struck up: "The justice of this earth, O Lord, hath put Thee to death," until the reeve ordered it proclaimed in every village that the singing of this hymn was forbidden.

My grandfather's parents had to leave the village, and the new grave of 21 their little daughter; they became basket weavers, but did not stay long anywhere because it pained them to see how everywhere the finger of justice swung falsely. They walked along behind their cart, which crept slowly over the country roads, taking their thin goat with them, and passers-by could sometimes hear a voice from the cart singing: "The justice of this earth, O Lord, hath put Thee to death." And those who wanted to listen could hear the tale of the Baleks von Bilgan, whose justice lacked a tenth part. But there were few who listened.

Translated from the German by Leila Venrewitz

STUDY QUESTIONS

1. "The Balek Scales" takes place at the turn of the century. Böll depicts class divisions between peasants and the nobility. What is the nature of the relations between the two groups?
2. How does the narrator's grandfather challenge the Balek family? What effect does this have on the peasant community?
3. What function does Bilgan the Giant have in the story?
4. Explain the significance of the phrase "The justice of this earth, O Lord, hath put Thee to death."

GREAT BRITAIN

⑥ D. H. LAWRENCE

D. H. Lawrence (1885–1930) was an English novelist, short story writer, poet, essayist, and dramatist. His early life in a miner's family is well known from his splendid semiautobiographical novel Sons and Lovers *(1913). Lawrence achieved fame as well as notoriety at an early age. Rebelling against the strictures of Victorianism, believing in the redemptive powers of nature, particularly in its sexual aspects, Lawrence made depiction of emotional expression integral to his art. Hence, the eroticism within his work caused controversy. The controversy, in turn, led Lawrence into permanent exile from England in search of a society in which he would be in closer communion with nature. A search for wholeness, whether symbolized by nature or intimate relationships, is signal in Lawrence's writing. This does not preclude, however, the world of reason or cognition. Lawrence's novels such as* Sons and Lovers, Women in Love *(1920),* The Rainbow *(1915), and* Lady Chatterley's Lover *(1928) and his short stories, collected in* Complete Short Stories of D. H. Lawrence *(1977), masterfully delineate the polarity of instinct and reason and are acutely grounded in psychological truth.*

The Horse Dealer's Daughter

"Well, Mabel, and what are you going to do with yourself?" asked Joe, with foolish flippancy. He felt quite safe himself. Without listening for an answer, he turned aside, worked a grain of tobacco to the tip of his tongue, and spat it out. He did not care about anything, since he felt safe himself.

The three brothers and the sister sat round the desolate breakfast table, attempting some sort of desultory consultation. The morning's post had given the final tap to the family fortunes, and all was over. The dreary dining-room itself, with its heavy mahogany furniture, looked as if it were waiting to be done away with.

1

2

But the consultation amounted to nothing. There was a strange air of 3 ineffectuality about the three men, as they sprawled at table, smoking and reflecting vaguely on their own condition. The girl was alone, a rather short, sullen-looking young woman of twenty-seven. She did not share the same life as her brothers. She would have been good-looking, save for the impressive fixity of her face, "bull-dog," as her brothers called it.

There was a confused tramping of horses' feet outside. The three men all 4 sprawled round in their chairs to watch. Beyond the dark holly bushes that separated the strip of lawn from the high-road, they could see a cavalcade of shire horses swinging out of their own yard, being taken for exercise. This was the last time. These were the last horses that would go through their hands. The young men watched with critical, callous look. They were all frightened at the collapse of their lives, and the sense of disaster in which they were involved left them no inner freedom.

Yet they were three fine, well-set fellows enough. Joe, the eldest, was a 5 man of thirty-three, broad and handsome in a hot, flushed way. His face was red, he twisted his black mustache over a thick finger, his eyes were shallow and restless. He had a sensual way of uncovering his teeth when he laughed, and his bearing was stupid. Now he watched the horses with a glazed look of helplessness in his eyes, a certain stupor of downfall.

The great draft-horses swung past. They were tied head to tail, four of 6 them, and they heaved along to where a lane branched off from the high-road, planting their great hoofs floutingly in the fine black mud, swinging their great rounded haunches sumptuously, and trotting a few sudden steps as they were led into the lane, round the corner. Every movement showed a massive, slumbrous strength, and a stupidity which held them in subjection. The groom at the head looked back, jerking the leading rope. And the cavalcade moved out of sight up the lane, the tail of the last horse, bobbed up tight and stiff, held out taut from the swinging great haunches as they rocked behind the hedges in a motionlike sleep.

Joe watched with glazed hopeless eyes. The horses were almost like his 7 own body to him. He felt he was done for now. Luckily he was engaged to a woman as old as himself, and therefore her father, who was steward of a neighboring estate, would provide him with a job. He would marry and go into harness. His life was over, he would be a subject animal now.

He turned uneasily aside, the retreating steps of the horses echoing in 8 his ears. Then, with foolish restlessness, he reached for the scraps of bacon-rind from the plates, and making a faint whistling sound, flung them to the terrier that lay against the fender. He watched the dog swallow them, and waited till the creature looked into his eyes. Then a faint grin came on his face, and in a high, foolish voice he said:

"You won't get much more bacon, shall you, you little b—?" 9

The dog faintly and dismally wagged its tail, then lowered its haunches, 10 circled round, and lay down again.

There was another helpless silence at the table. Joe sprawled uneasily in 11 his seat, not willing to go till the family conclave was dissolved. Fred Henry, the second brother, was erect, clean-limbed, alert. He had watched the passing of the horses with more *sang-froid*.[1] If he was an animal, like Joe, he was an animal which controls, not one which is controlled. He was master of any horse, and he carried himself with a well-tempered air of mastery. But he was not master of the situations of life. He pushed his coarse brown mustache upwards, off his lip, and glanced irritably at his sister, who sat impassive and inscrutable.

"You'll go and stop with Lucy for a bit, shan't you?" he asked. The girl   12
did not answer.

"I don't see what else you can do," persisted Fred Henry.   13

"Go as a skivvy,"[2] Joe interpolated laconically.   14

The girl did not move a muscle.   15

"If I was her, I should go in for training for a nurse," said Malcolm, the   16
youngest of them all. He was the baby of the family, a young man of twenty-two, with a fresh, jaunty *museau*.[3]

But Mabel did not take any notice of him. They had talked at her and   17
round her for so many years, that she hardly heard them at all.

The marble clock on the mantelpiece softly chimed the half-hour, the   18
dog rose uneasily from the hearth-rug and looked at the party at the breakfast-table. But still they sat on in ineffectual conclave.

"Oh, all right," said Joe suddenly, apropos of nothing. "I'll get a move   19
on."

He pushed back his chair, straddled his knees with a downward jerk, to   20
get them free, in horsey fashion, and went to the fire. Still he did not go out of the room; he was curious to know what the others would do or say. He began to charge his pipe, looking down at the dog and saying in a high, affected voice:

"Going wi' me? Going wi' me are ter? Tha'rt goin' further than tha   21
counts on just now, dost hear?"

The dog faintly wagged its tail, the man stuck out his jaw and covered   22
his pipe with his hands, and puffed intently, losing himself in the tobacco, looking down all the while at the dog with an absent brown eye. The dog looked up at him in mournful distrust. Joe stood with his knees stuck out, in real horsey fashion.

"Have you had a letter from Lucy?" Fred Henry asked of his sister.   23

"Last week," came the neutral reply.   24

"And what does she say?"   25

There was no answer.   26

"Does she *ask* you to go and stop there?" persisted Fred Henry.   27

---

1. Sang-froid: *Coolness, composure.*
2. Skivvy: *Domestic worker.*
3. Museau: *Slang for face.*

"She says I can if I like." 28

"Well, then, you'd better. Tell her you'll come on Monday." 29

This was received in silence. 30

"That's what you'll do then, is it?" said Fred Henry, in some exasper- 31
ation.

But she made no answer. There was a silence of futility and irritation in 32
the room. Malcolm grinned fatuously.

"You'll have to make up your mind between now and next Wednes- 33
day," said Joe loudly, "or else find yourself lodgings on the curbstone."

The face of the young woman darkened, but she sat on immutable. 34

"Here's Jack Fergusson!" exclaimed Malcolm, who was looking aim- 35
lessly out of the window.

"Where?" exclaimed Joe loudly. 36

"Just gone past." 37

"Coming in?" 38

Malcolm craned his neck to see the gate. 39

"Yes," he said. 40

There was a silence. Mabel sat on like one condemned, at the head of the 41
table. Then a whistle was heard from the kitchen. The dog got up and
barked sharply. Joe opened the door and shouted:

"Come on." 42

After a moment a young man entered. He was muffled up in overcoat 43
and a purple woolen scarf, and his tweed cap, which he did not remove,
was pulled down on his head. He was of medium height, his face was
rather long and pale, his eyes looked tired.

"Hello, Jack! Well, Jack!" exclaimed Malcolm and Joe. Fred Henry merely 44
said: "Jack."

"What's doing?" asked the newcomer, evidently addressing Fred 45
Henry.

"Same. We've got to be out by Wednesday. Got a cold?" 46

"I have—got it bad, too." 47

"Why don't you stop in?" 48

"*Me* stop in? When I can't stand on my legs, perhaps I shall have a 49
chance," the young man spoke huskily. He had a slight Scotch accent.

"It's a knock-out, isn't it," said Joe, boisterously, "if a doctor goes round 50
croaking with a cold. Looks bad for the patients, doesn't it?"

The young doctor looked at him slowly. 51

"Anything the matter with *you*, then?" he asked sarcastically. 52

"Not as I know of. Damn your eyes, hope not. Why?" 53

"I thought you were very concerned about the patients, wondered if 54
you might be one yourself."

"Damn it, no, I've never been patient to no flaming doctor, and hope I 55
never shall be," returned Joe.

At this point Mabel rose from the table, and they all seemed to become 56
aware of her existence. She began putting the dishes together. The young

doctor looked at her, but did not address her. He had not greeted her. She went out of the room with the tray, her face impassive and unchanged.

"When are you off then, all of you?" asked the doctor. 57

"I'm catching the eleven-forty," replied Malcolm. "Are you goin' down 58
wi' th' trap.[1] Joe?"

"Yes, I've told you I'm going down wi' th' trap, haven't I?" 59

"We'd better be getting her in then. So long, Jack, if I don't see you 60
before I go," said Malcolm, shaking hands.

He went out, followed by Joe, who seemed to have his tail between his 61
legs.

"Well, this is the devil's own," exclaimed the doctor, when he was left 62
alone with Fred Henry. "Going before Wednesday, are you?"

"That's the orders," replied the other. 63

"Where, to Northampton?" 64

"That's it." 65

"The devil!" exclaimed Fergusson, with quiet chagrin. 66

And there was silence between the two. 67

"All settled up, are you?" asked Fergusson. 68

"About." 69

There was another pause. 70

"Well, I shall miss yer, Freddy, boy," said the young doctor. 71

"And I shall miss thee, Jack," returned the other. 72

"Miss you like hell," mused the doctor. 73

Fred Henry turned aside. There was nothing to say. Mabel came in 74
again, to finish clearing the table.

"What are *you* going to do, then, Miss Pervin?" asked Fergusson. "Go- 75
ing to your sister's, are you?"

Mabel looked at him with her steady, dangerous eyes, that always made 76
him uncomfortable, unsettling his superficial ease.

"No," she said. 77

"Well, what in the name of fortune *are* you going to do? Say what you 78
mean to do," cried Fred Henry, with futile intensity.

But she only averted her head, and continued her work. She folded the 79
white table-cloth, and put on the chenille cloth.

"The sulkiest bitch that ever trod!" muttered her brother. 80

But she finished her task with perfectly impassive face, the young doctor 81
watching her interestedly all the while. Then she went out.

Fred Henry stared after her, clenching his lips, his blue eyes fixing in 82
sharp antagonism, as he made a grimace of sour exasperation.

"You could bray her into bits, and that's all you'd get out of her," he 83
said, in a small, narrowed tone.

The doctor smiled faintly. 84

---

1. Trap: *A light two-wheeled carriage.*

"What's she *going* to do, then?" he asked. 85

"Strike me if *I* know!" returned the other. 86

There was a pause. Then the doctor stirred. 87

"I'll be seeing you tonight, shall I?" he asked to his friend. 88

"Ay—where's it to be? Are we going over to Jessdale?" 89

"I do't know. I've got such a cold on me. I'll come round to the 'Moon 90
and Stars,' anyway."

"Let Lizzie and May miss their night for once, eh?" 91

"That's it—if I feel as I do now." 92

"All's one—" 93

The two young men went through the passage and down to the back 94
door together. The house was large, but it was servantless now, and desolate. At the back was a small bricked houseyard and beyond that a big
square, graveled fine and red, and having stables on two sides. Sloping,
dank, winter-dark fields stretched away on the open sides.

But the stables were empty. Joseph Pervin, the father of the family, had 95
been a man of no education, who had become a fairly large horse dealer.
The stables had been full of horses, there was a great turmoil and come-
and-go of horses and of dealers and grooms. Then the kitchen was full of
servants. But of late things had declined. The old man had married a
second time, to retrieve his fortunes. Now he was dead and everything
was gone to the dogs, there was nothing but debt and threatening.

For months, Mabel had been servantless in the big house, keeping the 96
home together in penury for her ineffectual brothers. She had kept house
for ten years. But previously it was with unstinted means. Then, however
brutal and coarse everything was, the sense of money had kept her proud,
confident. The men might be foul-mouthed, the women in the kitchen
might have bad reputations, her brothers might have illegitimate children.
But so long as there was money, the girl felt herself established, and
brutally proud, reserved.

No company came to the house, save dealers and coarse men. Mabel 97
had no associates of her own sex, after her sister went away. But she did
not mind. She went regularly to church, she attended to her father. And
she lived in the memory of her mother, who had died when she was
fourteen, and whom she had loved. She had loved her father, too, in a
different way, depending upon him, and feeling secure in him, until at the
age of fifty-four he married again. And then she had set hard against him.
Now he had died and left them all hopelessly in debt.

She had suffered badly during the period of poverty. Nothing, however, 98
could shake the curious, sullen, animal pride that dominated each member
of the family. Now, for Mabel, the end had come. Still she would not cast
about her. She would follow her own way just the same. She would always
hold the keys of her own situation. Mindless and persistent, she endured
from day to day. Why should she think? Why should she answer anybody?
It was enough that this was the end, and there was no way out. She need

not pass any more darkly along the main street of the small town, avoiding every eye. She need not demean herself any more, going into the shops and buying the cheapest food. This was at an end. She thought of nobody, not even of herself. Mindless and persistent, she seemed in a sort of ecstasy to be coming nearer to her fulfillment, her own glorification, approaching her dead mother, who was glorified.

In the afternoon she took a little bag, with shears and sponge and a small scrubbing-brush, and went out. It was a gray, wintry day, with saddened, dark green fields and an atmosphere blackened by the smoke of foundries not far off. She went quickly, darkly along the causeway, heeding nobody, through the town to the churchyard. 99

There she always felt secure, as if no one could see her, although as a matter of fact she was exposed to the stare of everyone who passed along under the churchyard wall. Nevertheless, once under the shadow of the great looming church, among the graves, she felt immune from the world, reserved within the thick churchyard wall as in another country. 100

Carefully she clipped the grass from the grave, and arranged the pinky white, small chrysanthemums in the tin cross. When this was done, she took an empty jar from a neighboring grave, brought water, and carefully, most scrupulously sponged the marble headstone and the coping-stone. 101

It gave her sincere satisfaction to do this. She felt in immediate contact with the world of her mother. She took minute pains, went through the park in a state bordering on pure happiness, as if in performing this task she came into a subtle, intimate connection with her mother. For the life she followed here in the world was far less real than the world of death she inherited from her mother. 102

The doctor's house was just by the church. Fergusson, being a mere hired assistant, was slave to the countryside. As he hurried now to attend to the outpatients in the surgery, glancing across the graveyard with his quick eye, he saw the girl at her task at the grave. She seemed so intent and remote, it was like looking into another world. Some mystical element was touching in him. He slowed down as he walked, watching her as if spellbound. 103

She lifted her eyes, feeling him looking. Their eyes met. And each looked again at once, each feeling, in some way, found out by the other. He lifted his cap and passed on down the road. There remained distinct in his consciousness, like a vision, the memory of her face, lifted from the tombstone in the churchyard, and looking at him with slow, large, portentous eyes. It *was* portentous, her face. It seemed to mesmerize him. There was a heavy power in her eyes which laid hold of his whole being, as if he had drunk some powerful drug. He had been feeling weak and done before. Now the life came back into him, he felt delivered from his own fretted, daily self. 104

He finished his duties at the surgery as quickly as might be, hastily filling up the bottles of the waiting people with cheap drugs. Then, in 105 perpetual haste, he set off again to visit several cases in another part of his round, before teatime. At all times he preferred to walk if he could, but particularly when he was not well. He fancied the motion restored him.

The afternoon was falling. It was gray, deadened, and wintry, with a slow, moist, heavy coldness sinking in and deadening all the faculties. But why should he think or notice? He hastily climbed the hill and turned across the dark green fields, following the black cinder-track. In the distance, across a shallow dip in the country, the small town was clustered like smoldering ash, a tower, a spire, a heap of low, raw, extinct houses. And on the nearest fringe of the town, slopping into the dip, was Oldmeadow, the Pervins' house. He could see the stables and the outbuildings distinctly, as they lay towards him on the slope. Well, he would not go there many more times! Another resource would be lost to him, another place gone: the only company he cared for in the alien, ugly little town he was losing. Nothing but work, drudgery, constant hastening from dwelling to dwelling among the colliers and the iron-workers. It wore him out, but at the same time he had a craving for it. It was a stimulant to him to be in the homes of the working people, moving, as it were, through the innermost body of their life. His nerves were excited and gratified. He could come so near, into the very lives of the rough, inarticulate, powerful emotional men and women: He grumbled, he said he hated the hellish hole. But as a matter of fact it excited him, the contact with the rough, strongly-feeling people was a stimulant applied direct to his nerves. 106

Below Oldmeadow, in the green, shallow, soddened hollow of fields, lay a square, deep pond. Roving across the landscape, the doctor's quick eye detected a figure in black passing through the gate of the field, down towards the pond. He looked again. It would be Mabel Pervin. His mind suddenly became alive and attentive. 107

Why was she going down there? He pulled up on the path on the slope above, and stood staring. He could just make sure of the small black figure moving in the hollow of the failing day. He seemed to see her in the midst of such obscurity, that he was like a clairvoyant, seeing rather with the mind's eye than with ordinary sight. Yet he could see her positively enough, whilst he kept his eye attentive. He felt, if he looked away from her, in the thick, ugly falling dusk, he would lose her altogether. 108

He followed her minutely as she moved, direct and intent, like something transmitted rather than stirring in voluntary activity, straight down from the field towards the pond. There she stood on the bank for a moment. She never raised her head. Then she waded slowly into the water. 109

He stood motionless as the small black figure walked slowly and deliberately towards the center of the pond, very slowly, gradually moving deeper into the motionless water, and still moving forward as the water got up to her breast. Then he could see her no more in the dusk of the dead afternoon. 110

"There!" he exclaimed. "Would you believe it?" 111

And he hastened straight down, running over the wet, soddened fields, 112 pushing through the hedges, down into the depression of callous wintry obscurity. It took him several minutes to come to the pond. He stood on the bank, breathing heavily. He could see nothing. His eyes seemed to penetrate the dead water. Yes, perhaps that was the dark shadow of her black clothing beneath the surface of the water.

He slowly ventured into the pond. The bottom was deep, soft clay, he sank in, and the water clasped dead cold round his legs. As he stirred he could smell the cold, rotten clay that fouled up into the water. It was objectionable in his lungs. Still, repelled and yet not heeding, he moved deeper into the pond. The cold water rose over his thighs, over his loins, upon his abdomen. The lower part of his body was all sunk in the hideous cold element. And the bottom was so deeply soft and uncertain, he was afraid of pitching with his mouth underneath. He could not swim, and was afraid. 113

He crouched a little, spreading his hands under the water and moving them round, trying to feel for her. The dead cold pond swayed upon his chest. He moved again, a little deeper, and again, with his hands underneath, he felt all around under the water. And he touched her clothing. But it evaded his fingers. He made a desperate effort to grasp it. 114

And so doing he lost his balance and went under, horribly, suffocating in the foul earthy water, struggling madly for a few moments. At last, after what seemed an eternity, he got his footing, rose again into the air, and looked around. He gasped, and knew he was in the world. Then he looked at the water. She had risen near him. He grasped her clothing, and drawing her nearer, turned to make his way to land again. 115

He went very slowly, carefully, absorbed in the slow progress. He rose higher, climbing out of the pond. The water was now only about his legs; he was thankful, full of relief to be out of the clutches of the pond. He lifted her and staggered on to the bank, out of the horror of wet, gray clay. 116

He laid her down on the bank. She was quite unconscious and running with water. He made the water come from her mouth, he worked to restore her. He did not have to work very long before he could feel the breathing begin again in her; she was breathing naturally. He worked a little longer. He could feel her live beneath his hands; she was coming back. He wiped her face, wrapped her in his overcoat, looked round into the dim, dark gray world, then lifted her and staggered down the bank and across the fields. 117

It seemed an unthinkably long way, and his burden so heavy he felt he would never get to the house. But at last he was in the stable-yard, and then in the house-yard. He opened the door and went into the house. In the kitchen he laid her down on the hearth-rug and called. The house was empty. But the fire was burning in the grate. 118

Then again he kneeled to attend to her. She was breathing regularly, her eyes wide open and as if conscious, but there seemed something missing in her look. She was conscious in herself, but unconscious of her surroundings. 119

He ran upstairs, took blankets from a bed, and put them before the fire 120 to warm. Then he removed her saturated, earthy-smelling clothing, rubbed her dry with a towel, and wrapped her naked in the blankets. Then he went into the dining-room, to look for spirits. There was a little whiskey. He drank a gulp himself, and put some into her mouth.

The effect was instantaneous. She looked full into his face, as if she had been seeing him for some time, and yet had only just become conscious of him. 121

"Dr. Fergusson?" she said. 122

"What?" he answered. 123

He was divesting himself of his coat, intending to find some dry clothing upstairs. He could not bear the smell of the dead, clayey water, and he was mortally afraid for his own health. 124

"What did I do?" she asked. 125

"Walked into the pond," he replied. He had begun to shudder like one sick, and could hardly attend to her. Her eyes remained full on him, he seemed to be going dark in his mind, looking back at her helplessly. The shuddering became quieter in him, his life came back to him, dark and unknowing, but strong again. 126

"Was I out of my mind?" she asked, while her eyes were fixed on him all the time. 127

"Maybe, for the moment," he replied. He felt quiet, because his strength had come back. The strange fretful strain had left him. 128

"Am I out of my mind now?" she asked. 129

"Are you?" he reflected a moment. "No," he answered truthfully, "I don't see that you are." He turned his face aside. He was afraid now, because he felt dazed, and felt dimly that her power was stronger than his, in this issue. And she continued to look at him fixedly all the time. "Can you tell me where I shall find some dry things to put on?" he asked. 130

"Did you dive into the pond for me?" she asked. 131

"No," he answered. "I walked in. But I went in overhead as well." 132

There was silence for a moment. He hesitated. He very much wanted to go upstairs to get into dry clothing. But there was another desire in him. And she seemed to hold him. His will seemed to have gone to sleep, and left him, standing there slack before her. But he felt warm inside himself. He did not shudder at all, though his clothes were sodden on him. 133

"Why did you?" she asked. 134

"Because I didn't want you to do such a foolish thing," he said. 135

"It wasn't foolish," she said, still gazing at him as she lay on the floor, with a sofa cushion under her head. "It was the right thing to do. *I* knew best, then." 136

"I'll go and shift these wet things," he said. But still he had not the power to move out of her presence, until she sent him. It was as if she had the life of his body in her hands, and he could not extricate himself. Or perhaps he did not want to. 137

Suddenly she sat up. Then she became aware of her own immediate 138 condition. She felt the blankets about her, she knew her own limbs. For a moment it seemed as if her reason were going. She looked around, with wild eye, as if seeking something. He stood still with fear. She saw her clothing lying scattered.

"Who undressed me?" she asked, her eyes resting full and inevitable on his face. 139

"I did," he replied, "to bring you round." 140

For some moments she sat and gazed at him, awfully, her lips parted. 141

"Do you love me, then?" she asked. 142

He only stood and stared at her, fascinated. His soul seemed to melt. 143

She shuffled forward on her knees, and put her arms round him, round his legs, as he stood there, pressing her breasts against his knees and thighs, clutching him with strange, convulsive certainty, pressing his thighs against her, drawing him to her face, her throat, as she looked up at him with flaring, humble eyes of transfiguration, triumphant in first possession. 144

"You love me," she murmured, in strange transport, yearning and triumphant and confident. "You love me. I know you love me, I know." 145

And she was passionately kissing his knees, through the wet clothing, passionately and indiscriminately kissing his knees, his legs, as if unaware of everything. 146

He looked down at the tangled wet hair, the wild, bare, animal shoulders. He was amazed, bewildered, and afraid. He had never thought of loving her. He had never wanted to love her. When he rescued her and restored her, he was a doctor, and she was a patient. He had had no single personal thought of her. Nay, this introduction of the personal element was very distasteful to him, a violation of his professional honor. It was horrible to have her there embracing his knees. It was horrible. He revolted from it, violently. And yet—and yet—he had not the power to break away. 147

She looked at him again, with the same supplication of powerful love, and that same transcendent, frightening light of triumph. In view of the delicate flame which seemed to come from her face like a light, he was powerless. And yet he had never intended to love her. He had never intended. And something stubborn in him could not give way. 148

"You love me," she repeated, in a murmur of deep, rhapsodic assurance. "You love me." 149

Her hands were drawing him, drawing him down to her. He was afraid, even a little horrified. For he had, really, no intention of loving her. Yet her hands were drawing him towards her. He put out his hand quickly to steady himself, and grasped her bare shoulder. A flame seemed to burn the hand that grasped her soft shoulder. He had no intention of loving her: his whole will was against his yielding. It was horrible. And yet wonderful was the touch of her shoulders, beautiful the shining of her face. Was she perhaps mad? He had a horror of yielding to her. Yet something in him ached also. 150

He had been staring away at the door, away from her. But his hand   151
remained on her shoulder. She had gone suddenly very still. He looked
down at her. Her eyes were now wide with fear, with doubt, the light was
dying from her face, a shadow of terrible grayness was returning. He could
not bear the touch of her eyes' question upon him, and the look of death
behind the question.

With an inward groan he gave way, and let his heart yield towards her.   152
A sudden gentle smile came on his face. And her eyes, which never left his
face, slowly, slowly filled with tears. He watched the strange water rise in
her eyes, like some slow fountain coming up. And his heart seemed to
burn and melt away in his breast.

He could not bear to look at her any more. He dropped on his knees and   153
caught her head with his arms and pressed her face against his throat. She
was very still. His heart, which seemed to have broken, was burning with
a kind of agony in his breast. And he felt her slow, hot tears wetting his
throat. But he could not move.

He felt the hot tears wet his neck and the hollows of his neck, and he   154
remained motionless, suspended through one of man's eternities. Only
now it had become indispensable to him to have her face pressed close to
him; he could never let her go again. He could never let her head go away
from the close clutch of his arm. He wanted to remain like that for ever,
with his heart hurting him in a pain that was also life to him. Without
knowing, he was looking down on her damp, soft brown hair.

Then, as it were suddenly, he smelt the horrid stagnant smell of that   155
water. And at the same moment she drew away from him and looked at
him. Her eyes were wistful and unfathomable. He was afraid of them, and
he fell to kissing her, not knowing what he was doing. He wanted her eyes
not to have that terrible, wistful, unfathomable look.

When she turned her face to him again, a faint delicate flush was glow-   156
ing, and there was again dawning that terrible shining of joy in her eyes,
which really terrified him, and yet which he now wanted to see, because
he feared the look of doubt still more.

"You love me?" she said, rather faltering.   157

"Yes." The word cost him a painful effort. Not because it wasn't true.   158
But because it was too newly true, the *saying* seemed to tear open again his
newly torn heart. And he hardly wanted it to be true, even now.

She lifted her face to him, and he bent forward and kissed her on the   159
mouth, gently, with the one kiss that is an eternal pledge. And as he kissed
her his heart strained again in his breast. He never intended to love her.
But now it was over. He had crossed over the gulf to her, and all that he
had left behind had shriveled and become void.

After the kiss, her eyes again slowly filled with tears. She sat still, away   160
from him, with her face drooped aside, and her hands folded in her lap.
The tears fell very slowly. There was complete silence. He too sat there
motionless and silent on the hearth-rug. The strange pain of his heart that

was broken seemed to consume him. That he should love her? That this was love! That he should be ripped open in this way! Him, a doctor! How they would all jeer if they knew! It was agony to him to think they might know.

In the curious naked pain of the thought he looked again to her. She was still sitting there drooped into a muse. He saw a tear fall, and his heart flared hot. He saw for the first time that one of her shoulders was quite uncovered, one arm bare, he could see one of her small breasts; dimly, because it had become almost dark in the room.   161

"Why are you crying?" he asked, in an altered voice.   162

She looked up at him, and behind her tears the consciousness of her situation for the first time brought a dark look of shame to her eyes.   163

"I'm not crying, really," she said, watching him, half frightened.   164

He reached his hand, and softly closed it on her bare arm.   165

"I love you! I love you!" he said in a soft, low vibrating voice, unlike himself.   166

She shrank, and dropped her head. The soft, penetrating grip of his hand on her arm distressed her. She looked up at him.   167

"I want to go," she said. "I want to go and get you some dry things."   168

"Why?' he said. "I'm all right."   169

"But I want to go," she said. "And I want you to change your things."   170

He released her arm, and she wrapped herself in the blanket, looking at him rather frightened. And still she did not rise.   171

"Kiss me," she said wistfully.   172

He kissed her, but briefly, half in anger.   173

Then, after a second, she rose nervously, all mixed up in the blanket. He watched her in her confusion as she tried to extricate herself and wrap herself up so that she could walk. He watched her relentlessly, as she knew. And as she went, the blanket trailing, and as he saw a glimpse of her feet and her white leg, he tried to remember her as she was when he had wrapped her in the blanket. But then he didn't want to remember, because she had been nothing to him then, and his nature revolted from remembering her as she was when she was nothing to him.   174

A tumbling, muffled noise from within the dark house startled him. Then he heard her voice: "There are clothes." He rose and went to the foot of the stairs, and gathered up the garments she had thrown down. Then he came back to the fire, to rub himself down and dress. He grinned at his own appearance when he had finished.   175

The fire was sinking, so he put on coal. The house was now quite dark, save for the light of a street-lamp that shone in faintly from beyond the holly trees. He lit the gas with matches he found on the mantelpiece. Then he emptied the pockets of his own clothes, and threw all his wet things in a heap into the scullery. After which he gathered up her sodden clothes, gently, and put them in a separate heap on the copper-top in the scullery.   176

It was six o'clock on the clock. His own watch had stopped. He ought to   177 go back to the surgery. He waited, and still she did not come down. So he went to the foot of the stairs and called:

"I shall have to go." 178

Almost immediately he heard her coming down. She had on her best 179
dress of black voile, and her hair was tidy, but still damp. She looked at
him—and in spite of herself, smiled.

"I don't like you in those clothes," she said. 180

"Do I look a sight?" he answered. 181

They were shy of one another. 182

"I'll make you some tea," she said. 183

"No, I must go." 184

"Must you?" And she looked at him again with the wide, strained, 185
doubtful eyes. And again, from the pain of his breast, he knew how he
loved her. He went and bent to kiss her, gently, passionately, with his
heart's painful kiss.

"And my hair smells so horrible," she murmured in distraction. "And 186
I'm so awful, I'm so awful! Oh, no, I'm too awful." And she broke into
bitter, heartbroken sobbing. "You can't want to love me, I'm horrible."

"Don't be silly, don't be silly," he said, trying to comfort her, kissing 187
her, holding her in his arms. "I want you, I want to marry you, we're going
to be married, quickly, quickly—tomorrow if I can."

But she only sobbed terribly, and cried. 188

"I feel awful. I feel awful. I feel I'm horrible to you." 189

"No, I want you, I want you," was all he answered, blindly, with that 190
terrible intonation which frightened her almost more than her horror lest
he should *not* want her.

S T U D Y   Q U E S T I O N S

1. In "The Horse Dealer's Daughter," what is Mabel's situation within her family? What is her relationship with her brothers? What are her feelings for her mother? For her father?
2. What are Mabel's feelings in the churchyard? What does the author mean when he says, "For the life she followed here in the world was far less real than the world of death she inherited from her mother"?
3. How does the churchyard episode foreshadow Mabel's subsequent relationship with Dr. Fergusson?
4. How does animal imagery function in the story? How does it contrast to the imagery of the pond?
5. How does Lawrence define Mabel? How does he define Dr. Fergusson? What is the author's attitude toward their relationship?

⊚ VIRGINIA WOOLF

Virginia Woolf (1882–1941) was an innovative English novelist and a major literary presence in the first half of the twentieth century. Woolf's father, the critic and essayist Leslie Stephen, was the doyen of the Victorian Age. Woolf, in her turn, spearheaded the cultural rupture with the nineteenth century. She did this in several ways. As a member of the Bloomsbury Group, Woolf called into question and poked fun at traditional values and opinions. As the founder of the Hogarth Press with her husband, Leonard, Woolf published and publicized modernist literature. And, most of all, through her novels and essays Woolf determinedly broke with the model of the narrative novel, which she criticized for simply telling stories about external life. In the essay "Mr. Bennet and Mrs. Brown" (1924), Woolf argued that the real task of literature was the search for the character's inner life, which was formed by the impingement and collusion of numerous emotions, ideas, impressions, and experiences both past and present. The aim of the writer was to unearth and to record these "atoms" that shaped the phenomenon of consciousness. In her novels Jacob's Room *(1922),* Mrs. Dalloway *(1925),* To the Lighthouse *(1927), and* The Waves *(1931) Woolf developed different techniques for "tunneling" and "digging caves" behind a character, caves in which she could establish the immediacy of the past and the significance of the character's relationship to the world of nature, for Woolf held that the interior life was not just a product of the individual's social relations but was in constant flux and correspondence to the forces of the natural world. Woolf's own life, though artistically and intellectually prolific, was troubled by agonizing nervous breakdowns, and in 1941 she committed suicide. Woolf's stories are available in the volume* The Complete Shorter Fiction of Virginia Woolf *(1986).*

The Mark on the Wall

Perhaps it was the middle of January in the present year that I first   1
looked up and saw the mark on the wall. In order to fix a date it is necessary to remember what one saw. So now I think of the fire; the steady film of yellow light upon the page of my book; the three chrysanthemums in the round glass bowl on the mantelpiece. Yes, it must have been the winter time, and we had just finished our tea, for I remember that I was smoking a cigarette when I looked up and saw the mark on the wall for the first time. I looked up through the smoke of my cigarette and my eye lodged for a moment upon the burning coals, and that old fancy of the crimson flag flapping from the castle tower came into my mind, and I thought of the cavalcade of red knights riding up the side of the black rock. Rather to my relief the sight of the mark interrupted the fancy, for it is an

old fancy, an automatic fancy, made as a child perhaps. The mark was a small round mark, black upon the white wall, about six or seven inches above the mantelpiece.

How readily our thoughts swarm upon a new object, lifting it a little 2 way, as ants carry a blade of straw so feverishly, and then leave it. . . . If that mark was made by a nail, it can't have been for a picture, it must have been for a miniature—the miniature of a lady with white powdered curls, powder-dusted cheeks, and lips like red carnations. A fraud of course, for the people who had this house before us would have chosen pictures in that way—an old picture for an old room. That is the sort of people they were—very interesting people, and I think of them so often, in such queer places, because one will never see them again, never know what happened next. They wanted to leave this house because they wanted to change their style of furniture, so he said, and he was in process of saying that in his opinion art should have ideas behind it when we were torn asunder, as one is torn from the old lady about to pour out tea and the young man about to hit the tennis ball in the back garden of the suburban villa as one rushes past in the train.

But for that mark, I'm not sure about it; I don't believe it was made by 3 a nail after all; it's too big, too round, for that. I might get up, but if I got up and looked at it, ten to one I shouldn't be able to say for certain; because once a thing's done, no one ever knows how it happened. Oh! dear me, the mystery of life; the inaccuracy of thought! The ignorance of humanity! To show how very little control of our possessions we have—what an accidental affair this living is after all our civilization—let me just count over a few of the things lost in one lifetime, beginning, for that seems always the most mysterious of losses—what cat would gnaw, what rat would nibble—three pale blue canisters of book-binding tools? Then there were the bird cages, the iron hoops, the steel skates, the Queen Anne coal-scuttle, the bagatelle board, the hand organ—all gone, and jewels, too. Opals and emeralds, they lie about the roots of turnips. What a scraping paring affair it is to be sure! The wonder is that I've any clothes on my back, that I sit surrounded by solid furniture at this moment. Why, if one wants to compare life to anything, one must liken it to being blown through the Tube at fifty miles an hour—landing at the other end without a single hairpin in one's hair! Shot out at the feet of God entirely naked! Tumbling head over heels in the asphodel meadows like brown paper parcels pitched down a shoot in the post office! With one's hair flying back like the tail of a racehorse. Yes, that seems to express the rapidity of life, the perpetual waste and repair; all so casual, all so haphazard. . . .

But after life. The slow pulling down of thick green stalks so that the cup 4 of the flower, as it turns over, deluges one with purple and red light. Why, after all, should one not be born there as one is born here, helpless, speechless, unable to focus one's eyesight, groping at the roots of the grass, at the toes of the Giants? As for saying which are trees, and which are men and women, or whether there are such things, that one won't be in a condition to do for fifty years or so. There will be nothing but spaces of light and dark, intersected by thick stalks, and rather higher up perhaps, rose-shaped blots of an indistinct colour—dim pinks and blues—which will, as time goes on, become more definite, become—I don't know what. . . .

And yet that mark on the wall is not a hole at all. It may even be caused 5 by some round black substance, such as a small rose leaf, left over from the summer, and I, not being a very vigilant housekeeper—look at the dust on the mantelpiece, for example, the dust which, so they say, buried Troy three times over, only fragments of pots utterly refusing annihilation, as one can believe.

The tree outside the window taps very gently on the pane. . . . I want 6 to think quietly, calmly, spaciously, never to be interrupted, never to have to rise from my chair, to slip easily from one thing to another, without any sense of hostility, or obstacle. I want to sink deeper and deeper, away from the surface, with its hard separate facts. To steady myself, let me catch hold of the first idea that passes . . . Shakespeare. . . . Well, he will do as well as another. A man who sat himself solidly in an arm-chair, and looked into the fire, so—A shower of ideas fell perpetually from some very high Heaven down through his mind. He leant his forehead on his hand, and people, looking in through the open door—for this scene is supposed to take place on a summer's evening—But how dull this is, this historical fiction! It doesn't interest me at all. I wish I could hit upon a pleasant track of thought, a track indirectly reflecting credit upon myself, for those are the pleasantest thoughts, and very frequent even in the minds of modest mouse-coloured people, who believe genuinely that they dislike to hear their own praises. They are not thoughts directly praising oneself; that is the beauty of them; they are thoughts like this:

"And then I came into the room. They were discussing botany. I said 7 how I'd seen a flower growing on a dust heap on the site of an old house in Kingsway. The seed, I said, must have been sown in the reign of Charles the First. What flowers grew in the reign of Charles the First?" I asked—(But I don't remember the answer.) Tall flowers with purple tassels to them perhaps. And so it goes on. All the time I'm dressing up the figure of myself in my own mind, lovingly, stealthily, not openly adoring it, for if I did that, I should catch myself out, and stretch my hand at once for a book in self-protection. Indeed, it is curious how instinctively one protects the image of oneself from idolatry or any other handling that could make it ridiculous, or too unlike the original to be believed in any longer. Or is it not so very curious after all? It is a matter of great importance. Suppose the looking-glass smashes, the image disappears, and the romantic figure with the green of forest depths all about it is there no longer, but only that shell of a person which is seen by other people—what an airless, shallow, bald, prominent world it becomes! A world not to be lived in. As we face each other in omnibuses and underground railways we are looking into the mirror; that accounts for the vagueness, the gleam of glassiness, in our eyes. And the novelists in future will realize more and more the importance of these reflections, for of course there is not one reflection but an almost infinite number; those are the depths they will explore, those the phantoms they will pursue, leaving the description of reality more and more out of their stories, taking a knowledge of it for granted, as the Greeks did and Shakespeare perhaps—but these generalizations are very worthless. The military sound of the world is enough. It recalls leading articles, cabinet ministers—a whole class of things indeed which, as a child, one thought the thing itself, the standard thing, the real thing, from which one could not depart save at the risk of nameless damnation. Generalizations bring back somehow Sunday in London, Sunday afternoon walks, Sunday luncheons, and also ways of speaking of the dead, clothes, and habits—like the habit of sitting all together in one room until a certain hour, although nobody liked it. There was a rule for everything. The rule for tablecloths at that particular period was that they should be made of tapestry with little yellow compartments marked upon them, such as you may see in photographs of the carpets in the corridors of the royal palaces. Tablecloths of a different kind were not real tablecloths. How shocking, and yet how wonderful it was to discover that these real things, Sunday luncheons, Sunday walks, country houses, and tablecloths were not entirely real, were indeed half phantoms, and the damnation which visited the disbeliever in them was only a sense of illegitimate freedom. What now takes the place of those things I wonder, those real standard things? Men perhaps, should you be a woman; the masculine point of view which governs our lives, which sets the standard, which establishes Whitaker's Table of Precedency,[1] which has become, I suppose, since the war, half a phantom to many men and women, which soon, one may hope, will be laughed into the dustbin where the phantoms go, the mahogany sideboards and the Landseer prints, Gods and Devils, Hell and so forth, leaving us all with an intoxicating sense of illegitimate freedom—if freedom exists. . . .

In certain lights that mark on the wall seems actually to project from the wall. Nor is it entirely circular. I cannot be sure, but it seems to cast a perceptible shadow, suggesting that if I ran my finger down that strip of the wall it would, at a certain point, mount and descend a small tumulus, a smooth tumulus like those barrows on the South Downs which are, they say, either tombs or camps. Of the two I should prefer them to be tombs, desiring melancholy like most English people, and finding it natural at the end of a walk to think of the bones stretched beneath the turf. . . . There must be some book about it. Some antiquary must have dug up those

---

1. *A table listing the rank order of the British aristocracy and notables in* Whitaker's Almanak *(est. 1868), an annual publication like the* World Almanac *in the United States.*

bones and given them a name. . . . What sort of a man is an antiquary, I wonder? Retired Colonels for the most part, I daresay, leading parties of aged labourers to the top here, examining clods of earth and stone, and getting into correspondence with the neighbouring clergy, which, being opened at breakfast time, gives them a feeling of importance, and the comparison of arrow-heads necessitates cross-country journeys to the country towns, an agreeable necessity both to them and to their elderly wives, who wish to make plum jam or to clean out the study, and have every reason for keeping that great question of the camp or the tomb in perpetual suspension, while the Colonel himself feels agreeably philo-sophic in accumulating evidence on both sides of the question. It is true that he does finally incline to believe in the camp; and, being opposed, indites a pamphlet which he is about to read at the quarterly meeting of the local society when a stroke lays him low, and his last conscious thoughts are not of wife or child, but of the camp and that arrow-head there, which is now in the case at the local museum, together with the foot of a Chinese murderess, a handful of Elizabethan nails, a great many Tudor clay pipes, a piece of Roman pottery, and the wineglass that Nelson drank out of— proving I really don't know what.

No, no, nothing is proved, nothing is known. And if I were to get up at 9 this very moment and ascertain that the mark on the wall is really—what shall we say?—the head of a gigantic old nail, driven in two hundred years ago, which has now, owing to the patient attrition of many generations of housemaids, revealed its head above the coat of paint, and is taking its first view of modern life in the sight of a white-walled fire-lit room, what should I gain?—Knowledge? Matter for further speculation? I can think sitting still as well as standing up. And what is knowledge? What are our learned men save the descendants of witches and hermits who crouched in caves and in woods brewing herbs, interrogating shrew-mice and writing down the language of the stars? And the less we honour them as our superstitions dwindle and our respect for beauty and health of mind increases. . . . Yes, one could imagine a very pleasant world. A quiet, spacious world, with the flowers so red and blue in the open fields. A world without professors or specialists or house-keepers with the profiles of policemen, a world which one could slice with one's thought as a fish slices the water with his fin, grazing the stems of the water-lilies, hanging suspended over nests of white sea eggs. . . . How peaceful it is down here, rooted in the centre of the world and gazing up through the grey waters, and their sudden gleams of light, and their reflections—if it were not for Whitaker's Almanack—if it were not for the Table of Precedency!

I must jump up and see for myself what that mark on the wall really 10 is—a nail, a rose-leaf, a crack in the wood?

Here is nature once more at her old game of self-preservation. This train 11 of thought, she perceives, is threatening mere waste of energy, even some collision with reality, for who will ever be able to lift a finger against

Whitaker's Table of Precedency? The Archbishop of Canterbury is followed by the Lord High Chancellor; the Lord High Chancellor is followed by the Archbishop of York. Everybody follows somebody, such is the philosophy of Whitaker; and the great thing is to know who follows whom. Whitaker knows, and let that, so Nature counsels, comfort you, instead of enraging you; and if you can't be comforted, if you must shatter this hour of peace, think of the mark on the wall.

I understand Nature's game—her prompting to take action as a way of 12 ending any thought that threatens to excite or to pain. Hence, I suppose, comes our slight contempt for men of action—men, we assume, who don't think. Still, there's no harm in putting a full stop to one's disagreeable thoughts by looking at a mark on the wall.

Indeed, now that I have fixed my eyes upon it, I feel that I have grasped 13 a plank in the sea; I feel a satisfying sense of reality which at once turns the two Archbishops and the Lord High Chancellor to the shadows of shades. Here is something definite, something real. Thus, waking from a midnight dream of horror, one hastily turns on the light and lies quiescent, worshipping the chest of drawers, worshipping solidity, worshipping reality, worshipping the impersonal world which is a proof of some existence other than ours. That is what one wants to be sure of. . . . Wood is a pleasant thing to think about. It comes from a tree; and trees grow, and we don't know how they grow. For years and years they grow, without paying any attention to us, in meadows, in forests, and by the side of rivers—all things one likes to think about. The cows swish their tails beneath them on hot afternoons; they paint rivers so green that when a moorhen dives one expects to see its feathers all green when it comes up again. I like to think of the fish balanced against the stream like flags blown out; and of water-beetles slowly raising domes of mud upon the bed of the river. I like to think of the tree itself: first of the close dry sensation of being wood; then the grinding of the storm; then the slow, delicious ooze of sap; I like to think of it, too, on winter's nights standing in the empty field with all leaves close-furled, nothing tender exposed to the iron bullets of the moon, a naked mast upon an earth that goes tumbling, tumbling, all night long. The song of birds must sound very loud and strange in June; and how cold the feet of insects must feel upon it, as they make laborious progresses up the creases of the bark, or sun themselves upon the thin green awning of the leaves, and look straight in front of them with diamond-cut red eyes. . . . One by one the fibres snap beneath the immense cold pressure of the earth, then the last storm comes and, falling, the highest branches drive deep into the ground again. Even so, life isn't done with; there are a million patient, watchful lives still for a tree, all over the world, in bedrooms, in ships, on the pavement, lining rooms, where men and women sit after tea, smoking cigarettes. It is full of peaceful thoughts, happy thoughts, this tree. I should like to take each one separately—but something is getting in the way. . . . Where was I? What has it all been about?

A tree? A river? The Downs? Whitaker's Almanack? The fields of asphodel? I can't remember a thing. Everything's moving, falling, slipping, vanishing. . . . There is a vast upheaval of matter. Someone is standing over me and saying:

"I'm going out to buy a newspaper."   14

"Yes?"   15

"Though it's no good buying newspapers. . . . Nothing ever happens.   16
Curse this war; God damn this war! . . . All the same, I don't see why we should have a snail on our wall."

Ah, the mark on the wall! It was a snail.   17

STUDY QUESTIONS

1. How would you define the main theme of "The Mark on the Wall"? How is "the mark" structurally central to this theme?
2. Find the different metaphors that Woolf uses for memory. What encompasses recollection for Woolf?
3. Find the different metaphors that Woolf uses for thought. From the story decide what Woolf's conception of thought is. How does she incorporate psychology into it?
4. What is the significance of her discussion of "those real standard things"? Of the antiquary?
5. Find the instances of "tunneling" that Woolf uses in regard to the narrator's past and in regard to the narrator's relationship with the natural world.

⟲ W. H. AUDEN

W. H. Auden (1907–1973) was a leading English poet, dramatist, essayist, and librettist. Educated at Oxford, Auden quickly achieved wide acclaim. His early poetry, in its broad social and political concerns, in its references to subject matter from sociology, psychology, biology, and political theory, reflects the intellectual interests of his time. Indeed, Auden has been referred to as the poetic voice of the generation of the 1930s. His poetry articulates a striving to comprehend the individual's position within Western culture which, with the advent of Fascism and of worldwide depression, appeared to have reached a watershed. Thus, Auden's epigrammatic poetry, with its conversational, at times laconic, style is informed by an intense desire to make moral sense of his time. After World War II, Auden's sociopolitical orientation gave way to a spiritual/religious emphasis, and he turned the landscape of his poetry from society to nature. "The Unknown Citizen" and "Musée des Beaux Arts" in their sociopolitical allusions and in their ironic style are illustrative of Auden's prewar writing.

The Unknown Citizen

(To JS/07/M/378
This Marble Monument
Is Erected by the State)

He was found by the Bureau of Statistics to be
One against whom there was no official complaint,
And all the reports on his conduct agree
That, in the modern sense of an old-fashioned word, he was a
    saint,
For in everything he did he served the Greater Community.   5
Except for the War till the day he retired
He worked in a factory and never got fired,
But satisfied his employers, Fudge Motors Inc.
Yet he wasn't a scab or odd in his views,
For his Union reports that he paid his dues,   10
(Our report on his Union shows it was sound)
And our Social Psychology workers found
That he was popular with his mates and liked a drink.
The Press are convinced that he bought a paper every day
And that his reactions to advertisements were normal in every   15
    way.
Policies taken out in his name prove that he was fully insured,
And his Health-card shows he was once in hospital but left it
    cured.
Both Producers Research and High-Grade Living declare   20
He was fully sensible to the advantages of the Instalment Plan
And had everything necessary to the Modern Man,
A phonograph, a radio, a car and a frigidaire.
Our researchers into Public Opinion are content
That he held the proper opinions for the time of year;   25
When there was peace, he was for peace; when there was war,
    he went.
He was married and added five children to the population,
Which our Eugenist says was the right number for a parent of
    his generation,   30

And our teachers report that he never interfered with their
   education.
Was he free? Was he happy? The question is absurd:
Had anything been wrong, we should certainly have heard.   35

Musée des Beaux Arts[1]

About suffering they were never wrong,
The Old Masters: how well they understood
Its human position; how it takes place
While someone else is eating or opening a window or just
   walking dully along;   5
How, when the aged are reverently, passionately waiting
For the miraculous birth, there always must be
Children who did not specially want it to happen, skating
On a pond at the edge of the wood:
They never forgot   10
That even the dreadful martyrdom must run its course
Anyhow in a corner, some untidy spot
Where the dogs go on with their doggy life and the torturer's
   horse
Scratches its innocent behind on a tree.
In Brueghel's *Icarus*,[2] for instance: how everything turns away   15
Quite leisurely from the disaster; the ploughman may
Have heard the splash, the forsaken cry,
But for him it was not an important failure; the sun shone
As it had to on the white legs disappearing into the green
Water; and the expensive delicate ship that must have seen   20
Something amazing, a boy falling out of the sky,
Had somewhere to get to and sailed calmly on.

STUDY QUESTIONS

1. How does "The Unknown Citizen" question modern society?
2. Discuss Auden's use of irony in "The Unknown Citizen". Give examples.

------

1. *Museum of Fine Arts.*

2. **Icarus** *by the Flemish painter Pieter Brueghel (c. 1520–1569) depicts the fall of Icarus, who in
   Greek mythology, had flown too close to the sun on man-made wings of feathers and wax.*

3. What does the speaker in "Musée des Beaux Arts" find revealing about the paintings of the Old Masters? What is their truth?
4. How many examples does the author use in this poem? Discuss each one according to its vision of life.
5. Does painting have advantages in conveying the subtlety of human experience? What attributes are unique to literature?

⊚ SAMUEL SELVON

England has been the site of an emerging and lively black British culture as a result of the massive emigration of South Asians, Caribbeans, and Africans since the 1950s. The rainbow of ethnic and cultural diversity that existed outside of Britain in its empire is now reflected within the country itself. Samuel Selvon (b. 1923) is among the first generation of black British writers. Born in Trinidad of East Indian parents, he attended local schools and served as a radio operator on a British minesweeper during World War II. After the war he returned to Trinidad and worked as a journalist for the Trinidad Guardian *and began writing short stories. In 1950, he emigrated to England, where he lived permanently until 1978. Since then, he has divided his time among England, Canada, and the Caribbean. He has published ten novels, including* A Brighter Sun *(1952),* Lonely Londoners *(1956),* Moses Migrating *(1983), and* The Housing Lark *(1990). He has also published three children's books and several collections of stories, most recently* Foreday Morning *(1990). The setting of his fiction is divided between Trinidad and England. He is best known for the humorous and sensitive way he portrays the life of emigrants in England and his mastery of vernacular speech and West Indian oral traditions. "Come Back to Grenada" exemplifies these talents.*

Come Back to Grenada

E very time when winter come round, George so cold that he have to give up trying to get warm, and he used to sit down by the gas fire in the basement room he had in Bayswater, and think back 'bout them days in Grenada before the war.

Is so it was with him every winter—when the cold hit him so, he long to go back home, but in the summer, when all them white girls have on pretty clothes and coasting in the park, you mad to tell him then 'bout going back home, he want to kill you, he would say that you talking damn foolishness, that Brit'n is he country, and that he never going back to no small island life.

Well sometimes some of the boys used to drop round to have an old talk, especially on a Sunday morning, because George working night in a factory where they making things to clean pot and pan, and any other time but on a Sunday morning he does be sleeping sound, and if anybody mad enough to come and see him during the week, he play as if he didn't hear the bell when they ring it. If they ask him 'bout it afterwards, he say, 'Man, the bell not working properly, I tell the damn landlord 'bout it, but up to now he ain't fix it.' 3

Well Sunday morning is big old talk, George still lying down in bed under the blankets, and the boys making themself at home, some on the ground, some sitting down on the edge of the bed, some standing up. The fellars used to mop George coffee and bread good, so George begin to get up early and make breakfast and put away everything before they come, because some of them real hard, if even they ain't hungry they storing away something for when they go back outside. 4

So it turn out like a joke—the boys saying, 'But a-a, George, you living bad, man. No bread? No coffee? 5

And George warm under the blankets and he belly full up with food, would laugh kiff-kiff as if is a joke in truth, and say, 'No man, I didn't have time to buy my rations yesterday.' 6

As for the gas fire, when old talk going hot and the gas burning low, George used to sit up and reach for he trousers from off the chair where they hanging and fumble in the pocket and say, 'I did forget to get some shillings for the meter. Any of you-all have a shilling?' 7

Then all the boys would begin to put they hand in they pocket and look all about, saying, no, they sorry man, but they ain't have a shilling, they only have two-shilling and sixty-cent piece, what ain't no use as the slot in the meter could only hold shilling. But in the end one of them does always have to shell up one, because George laying down there and he wouldn't budge until one of them find a shilling somewhere: 'Aps! Look I have one, it was right down in the corner of my pocket, I didn't feel it the first time.' 8

And the old talk does always be about home in the West Indies, in Trinidad and Jamaica and Barbados and Grenada, what they used to do, how they used to catch cascadoo in the river with pin and twine, and fly mad bull and play zwill, and pitch marble with byayr and buicken and buttards one, and talaline farts, and how rum so cheap back home, but over here everybody only drinking tea and ale. The old talk coming and going, they talking about all kind of thing, but in the end is always about home in the West Indies, how life was so good. But even though they saying that none of them making the suggestion to go back, as if they shame to say they miss home though they talking about good calaloo and 9 pound plantain lunch on a Sunday, or a breadfruit roast with saltfish, and how down there the sun does be shining all the time.

Is some real characters does come round by George. You might think that when they come England they go change a little bit when they mix up with the English people and them, but is just as if they in a backyard in George Street in Port of Spain, all kind of common laugh and bacchanal talk going on brisk. They does treat Piccadilly Circus like Green Corner, and walked down Oxford Street is if they breezing down Frederick Street, and if they meet you in the road or in a bus or in the tube, is a big shout, 'What happening there, papa?' **10**

And as for how they dress, nobody does mind your business in this London, so the boys cool, no fuss, all kind of second hand jacket and mildew overcoat and old hat with the brim turn up. **11**

It had a fellar name Fatman. Well nobody know how he living, he is a man of mystery, because he ain't have no work, and the way he does get on, the small raise from the National Assistance is not the cause. One day the boys surprise to see Fatman driving motor car. 'Which part you get that, old man?' they ask him. **12**

'I pick it up cheap down by Kensal Rise, man,' he answer them. **13**

Well the second day Fatman get this car he meet up in an accident with a bus and he had to go to court. He come round by George mourning, with a lot of forms he had to full up. Fatman always confuse when he have forms to full up, and in this country you have bags of that to do. He and he wife always arguing, is not that way, no, you put the date in the wrong place, man, why you so stupid, you can't see where it say date of birth in the next line? So Fatman take up the forms and go round by George to full them up. **14**

Then it have another fellar name Gogee, who from Trinidad. Gogee is really a nice fellar, but he like to get on ignorant sometimes. It have a thing with he and another Trinidadian fellar name Scottie what does always make George laugh for so. Scottie is a fellar with a little education, and he well like the English customs and thing, he does be polite and say thanks and he does get up in the bus and the tube to let them women sit down, which is a thing even them Englishmen don't do. And when he dress, you think is some Englishman going to work in the city, with bowler hat and umbrella and brief case. Only thing Scottie face black. **15**

Well Scottie used to organise little fêtes here and there, like dance and party and so on. And everytime he worried if Gogee would turn up, because Gogee like to play rab and make Scottie feel small, though it does only be fun he making. Like one time, Scottie standing up near the door of the dancehall, dressup in black suit and bow tie, saying good evening and how do you do to all the people that coming to the dance. Well you could imagine Gogee bursting through the door in a hot jitterbug suit and bawling out, 'Scottie, you old reprobate! What happening?' **16**

Naturally Scottie feel bad that in front of all these English people Gogee   17
getting on so. 'Listen man,' he plead with Gogee, 'Why don't you behave
and comport yourself properly in front of people and stop behaving like a
ruffian?'

That put Gogee in a real worthless mood, and the more Scottie try to be   18
gentleman, the more Gogee getting on like if he back in Trinidad, and he
meet up with a good friend unexpected at a freeness.

'But how Scottie man, you looking prosperous, things going good with   19
you. I hear you did make bags of money out of that fête you had by King's
Cross last Saturday night. You think you will make a lot tonight? You got
a good band playing tonight?'

And with that Gogee push past Scottie and barge into the dancehall,   20
ignoring the fellar that collecting tickets as if is he self what giving the
dance.

And during the fête, whenever Gogee catch Scottie watching him out of   21
the corner of he eye, he starting to jock waist for so, and fanning with he
jacket, and jumping up as if he at a Carnival slackness in the Queen's Park
Building, only to make Scottie get vex.

Scottie shaking he head and saying he don't know why the boys don't   22
behave like gentlemen for a change, that the English people would say
how they don't know how to get on civilise. But Gogee and the boys high,
they having a royal time, they only getting the band to play calypso and
they dancing left and right.

Whenever Scottie have a fête, he too frighten that the boys rob and   23
cause fight and disgrace, but it never have anything serious, except the
time when a Jamaican fellar bust a coca-cola bottle on Fatman head because
Fatman did dancing too close with he girl.

Poor Scottie, he not a bad sort of fellar really, but the boys like to pick on   24
him so much, because they feel he playing stuckup and talking like Englishman. And now from the time Scottie see them coming through the
door at any fête he giving, he know they not going to pay, and he does tell
them to pass in quick and don't stand up and jam the door. It get so that
all them West Indian hear how Scottie is a gentleman, and you should
know that none of them ever pay at any of Scottie fête.

Then again, the boys might start to give Frederick picong when Scottie   25
beg them to ease up. If Fatman is man of mystery, well Frederick is mystery
father, because he is one Jamaican that you could never contact at all, he
don't stay in one place for long. It must be ain't have nobody who know
this London like he, it ain't have a part that he ain't live in already, and
why you think? Because he don't pay rent no place where he got to live. Is
test like him who muddy the water for a lot of other fellars. When Frederick
get a place what taking coloured people, he tell the landlord that he is
student, and that he does get money from home every two weeks. And he
move in with everything, including an old banjo that he does play when he
walking in the road, or standing up in a queue. Then when the Saturday

come and the landlord come round to collect the rent, no mister Frederick there at all, he out off long time, in the night when it dark and nobody could see.

Next time you hear 'bout Frederick, is because he gone the other side of London to live. One day you hear he living Notting Hill Gate, the next day you hear he move and gone Clapham, a week after that you might bounce him up in Highgate. So he moving from landlord to landlord, owing them one two three weeks rent. Is a good thing London such a big place—by the time Frederick go round by all the places, he go be an old man and still doing the same thing, and still he would have plenty new places to go. 26

And the truth is, he really start up like a student, but he get in a mooch with an English girl, and since that time he forget all about studying and he start to hustle. 27

Well all these episodes coming up in the old talk in George room. Until if George get in a good mood, he might get up and make some tea for the boys, and take a bread and some butter out of the cupboard. 28

They always giving George tone about going back to the West Indies, because George leave an old grandmother back home and she always writing and saying why you don't come back to Grenada, and telling him she would dead soon, that he better come quick. And he have a girlfriend too that he leave behind, the poor girl writing nearly every week, darling dou-dou why you don't come back Grenada and let we married? 29

But is as if London get in George blood, all the big building, all the big light and the big celebration, the trains that does go under the ground, and how nobody minding you business like in a small island. He used to stand up by the Circus and watch all them big advertising light going on and going off, like if is Carnival all the time, and people moving all about in the big life in London, all kind of Rolls-Royce in the road, and them rich people going theatre and ballet. One time Scottie did even encourage him to go to the Royal Albert Hall to hear a fellar play violin, and George put on a clean suit and he went and sit down, but when it was halfway he tell Scottie to come and go. 30

So even though it have times when things hard with him, still he feel as if he can't leave London at all. In the winter, when snow come and it so cold that he have to wear two three pullover even when he sleeping, he does get a feeling to leave, because life hard in the winter, not even a shilling to put in the gas. Them times, he does think a lot 'bout Grenada, how down there the sun shining all the time, you could bathe in the sea everyday. Here it so cold that George does only bathe 'bout once a month, and not only because the weather grim, but it have so much confusion when you want to bathe, you have to clean out this big basin thing that just like a coffin, then you have to put money in the gas to get hot water, and let the water full up in the basin. You does have to sit down in it. You know how sometimes them people in the country back home bathing the children, putting them in a bucket of water? Well is just like that. Well, he have 31 enough money save up, so when is winter the thought does come to him.

But after when the winter gone and birds sing and all the trees begin to 32
put on leaves again, and flowers come and now and then the old sun
shining, George would say he go stay until after the summer.

Every year is the same story, that's why he still in this country. In the 33
beginning George used to shape up by the National Assistance people
every week, but since he get this nightwork he working steady. Them
English people think the boys lazy and goodfornothing and always on the
dole, but George know is only because the white people don't want to give
them work.

One time when he did new in England George get a work in a factory, 34
and all the people in the place say they go strike unless the boss fire
George. It was a big ballad in all the papers, they put it under a big
headline, saying how the colour bar was causing trouble again, and a fellar
come with a camera and wanted to take George photo, but George say no.
Anyway a few days after that the boss call George and tell him that he
worry, but as they cutting down the staff he would have to go. He put it
in a real diplomatic way, so as not to make George feel bad, but he did well
know is only because they didn't want him in the place.

So it not really as easy for the boys as some people think. True, it have 35
some of them what only want to ants on the government, and don't do no
work, only playing billiards and rummy all the time, but the majority of the
boys willing to work if they could hustle a job somewhere.

Them was grim days when George wasn't working. He had to hustle all 36
about, and sometimes nothing but a cup of weak tea to face the cold. He
see real hell to get a place to live, all about landlords and landladies saying
that they sorry, the rooms full up, but in truth is because they don't like
black people.

Sometimes when George did walking down the road minding he own 37
business, some little white child bawl out, 'Mummy, look at that black
man!' And poor George don't know what to do. The child mother scold it
and say, 'You mustn't say that, dear.'

But thing like that happen so much time that George skin come like 38
rubber, and he bounce like a ball from house to house until he feel like if
the vengeance of Moco on him. Then he get the basement room in Bayswater. Is a Pole who own the house, too besides, that's why he get the
room.

Right after that he start up the nightwork and things brighten up a little 39
bit. He eating regular meals and now and then he going to the tailor in
Charing Cross Road and getting fit for a sharp suit, because now he have
money is no more readymade or secondhand for him.

Every Saturday morning, he does go by a continental shop which part 40
have a lot of food to see, like what he accustom to, like red beans and
blackeye peas and rice and saltfish. It even have dasheen and green fig
sometimes. It have a lot of spades does go in that shop to buy, bags of

them, and is joke to see how they does get on just as if they in a Chinaman shop back home. Couple Jamaica woman does stand up and talk while they waiting for message, 'But girl, if I tell you! She did lose the baby, yes . . . halfpound saltfish, please, the dry codfish. Yes, as I was telling you. . . . and two pound rice, and halfpound red beans, no, not that one, that one in the bag in the corner . . .'

This time so, they ain't bothering they head about the other people in the queue at all, they mauvalanging and bursting out in some loud kya-kya laugh like them macoumere in the market in George Street back home.   41

And George can't help thinking how things change a lot since he first come England, how now it have so many spades that you bouncing up with one every corner you turn. All them ships that coming bringing more and more, and all the newspapers writing about how these West Indians coming and like nothing could stop them, and how the Government best hads do something or else plenty trouble would cause in London.   42

And again long time thing like saltfish hard like gold to get. George had was to go in a small shop in Soho what was the only place in London you could get that, but now it have 'bout ten shop with it, because the English shopkeepers like they know the spades like they little fish.   43

Another thing is, George don't know how so many people know him, but every time a shipload of fellars land up in Paddington from the boat train, plenty of them coming round by George, saying that so and so did tell them that George would help them out when they reach in London. He come like godfather, he don't know how to refuse them, all these fellars coming and putting they worries on he shoulders, how they can't find a work, how it so cold, how place hard to get. Well George do what he could to ease the situation for them—he get about four work for some Jamaican in the factory where he is, and in the evening when he get time off, if he in a good mood he go round with them now and then to look for place to live, because by this time George know all them landlord and landlady who don't want no black people in they house.   44

He did have good fun with them Jamaican, they used to come and tell him how they get lose on the tube, how they wanted to go Piccadilly but they find theyself in Shepherd Bush. And George say that they 'fraid to put they money in the bank, that they does keep it in a suitcase under the bed, and count it up every week, and when it have enough they sending for they brother and sister and cousin.   45

Long time George used to feel lonely little bit, but all that finish with since so much West Indian come London. All kind of steel band fête all about in the city, in St. Pancras Hall, down Wimbledon, all down by Pentonville. The boys beating pan in Piccadilly Circus and even jumping up in the road when the Lord Mayor did riding in he coach.   46

So now all those things George does be studying when the idea come in he head to go back Grenada. He study what he would do if he go back in that small island, and he feel that he would never get on if he go back. It   47

have so many things in London that he don't agree with, so much prejudice about the place, so much hustling, things so expensive. And yet every
year when the spring round the corner, is as if it give him a new spirit to
stay.

Then in the summer he putting on jitterbug shirt and walking about,   48
coasting all by Hyde Park in the night, standing up by the corner near
Marble Arch listening to them fellars who does stand up on box and say
what they like and no policeman don't interfere with them, and eyeing any
sharp craft that standing up near, waiting to ask if she would come in the
yard for a cup of tea. He done with English girls now, is only continental
he looking for, French and Norwegian in front.

When he have a night off, is because he dressing up and walking from   49
the Water to Trafalgar Square, watching the night life, thinking how he in
this big country walking about, instead of sitting down on some concrete
bridge over a canal in the West Indies old talking with the boys. Is how you
want him to leave this big life?

Is true sometimes when he think serious he could see that he ain't   50
getting no place in a hurry, that is the same thing he doing everyday. But
still, it don't matter what you do, as long as you living in London, that is
a big thing in itself, that alone have big prestige, he could imagine how the
people back home when they talk about him how they does say that he is
a big shot, that he living in the same place as the Queen. They don't know
how he catching he royal to make a living.

But that was another thing, how London so full up of people that it   51
don't matter what you do, nobody does mind your business. One time a
fellar in a room next to George did dead and nobody know nothing for
'bout a week. The tess stay here all this time, dead, and nobody don't
know nothing even though they living in the same house. That was the
one thing used to frighten George sometimes. . . . how he ain't have no
family to watch over him if he sick, and nobody to turn to in hard times.
But that thought like a drop in the ocean.

And so year after year the same thing happening again and again. He   52
telling he grandmother and this girl in Grenada that yes, he would come
next year, but when next year came he still doing the nightwork in the
factory, he still old talking with the boys on a Sunday morning, he still
coasting all about the streets of London, with no definite place to go, no
definite aim in life.

And it reach a stage now where he get so accustom to the pattern that   53
he can't do anything about it. All he know is that he living in London, and
that he will dead there one day. And that is all. He not worrying he head
about anything else. He not even bothering with the colour bar question
any more. At first he used to get on ignorant when anybody tell him
anything, but now he just smiling like a philosopher when they call him a
black man. He can't even sympathise with them fellars who new and feel
the lash for the first time and come round by him to mourn, like when

landlord slam door in they face, or people leave them standing up in the queue to attend to somebody else. All them things happen to him already, and he pass through all them stages, so now he does only smile when the boys in sorrow.

Even the winter come like nothing now, he laughing to see Englishman 54 stamping foot in the bus queue to keep warm, while he just have he hand in he pocket standing up cool. And he get a lot of English habit now, like talking about the weather, and if anybody say how it cold he used to talk like an old veteran 'bout the winter this country had some years ago. He drinking tea all the time, and reading newspaper in the tube and bus.

In fact, he and Scottie is good friend now, and the other day he buy a 55 bowler hat and an umbrella and they went for a walk in the park, the two of them talking and nodding they head, and saying good evening to all the sharp girls that pass. He even reading *The Times* now . . . whenever he going out, he folding *The Times* so that the name would show and putting it under he arm.

And so as far as he could see, is no more Grenada for him at all. Espe- 56 cially now how so much West Indians hustling up to the old Brit'n, as if things really brown in the islands. And the way he have it figure out, if he stay in the work he have now, he go be able to peel off and spend the summer on the continent. It have a sharp Austrian girl does visit him in the yard . . . she come over here to work as a maidservant for some rich people, and George make contact one night in Baker Street, where she was standing waiting for a bus. Well, she tell him she going back in the summer, and that he must too.

And that is the case. When he think 'bout home it does look so far away 57 that he feel as if he don't belong there no more. And though he does really miss the sun, he make up he mind to write to grandmother and this girl and tell them that they best hads forget all about him, because he staying in this big country until he dead, and he ain't coming back to Grenada unless he win a big football pool, and even then, it would only be for a holiday.

STUDY QUESTIONS

1. In what ways are the central character's ambivalent feelings about living in England expressed in "Come Back to Grenada"? Does he resolve them?
2. On one level the story is about survival. Selvon celebrates the tenacity and inventiveness of West Indian immigrants. Cite examples.
3. What are some of the different personality types in the story?
4. How does the author reveal sympathy for his characters?
5. What are the most amusing incidents in the story?

GREECE

⑥ GEORGE SEFERIS

*George Seferis (1900–1971) was a renowned Greek poet, essayist, and critic
who is regarded as having introduced modernist forms and techniques into
Greek writing. Seferis was born in the Greek city of Smyrna in Asia Minor.
Its destruction in 1922, the dispersal of its population, and the incorporation
of Asia Minor into Turkey became a tragic motif that haunted Seferis all his
life. Economically and socially, Seferis came from an elite background. He
studied law at the Sorbonne and made diplomacy his career. While in France,
Seferis closely read the French Symbolists whose aesthetic views influenced his
early volumes of poetry. The works of T. S. Eliot and Ezra Pound, however,
had a more lasting impact on him. Seferis's publication of* Turning Point
(1931) and Mythhistorema *(1935), with their use of free verse and their
sense of the contemporaneity of the Greek past marked Seferis's modernist
evolution. From that time on, the geographic as well as historical landscape of
Greece formed the terrain of Seferis's poetry, while the vernacular language
of ordinary Greeks became his poetic building blocks. The critic Carmen
Capri-Karka has noted that even the philosophic/ethical principles of his
discourse were situated in a moral law of justice originating with
Anaximander and Aeschylus. In 1963 he became the first Greek to win the
Nobel Prize in Literature. Seferis's poems are available in English in* George
Seferis: Collected Poems 1924–1955 *(1981).*

Tuesday

"I went down to St. James Infirmary."

I got lost in the town.
The gardens are hidden by the hospital of Don Juan Tavera.
Advertisements wrapping up the streets.
Each man walks without knowing
whether he's at a beginning or an end,   5
whether he's going to his mother, his daughter, or his mistress
whether he'll judge or be judged
whether he'll escape, whether he's escaped already;
he doesn't know.
At every corner a gramophone shop   10
in every shop a hundred gramophones
for each gramophone a hundred records
on every record
someone living plays with someone dead.
Take the steel needle and separate them   15
if you can.

Now what poet? Do you remember what poet
tried out the steel needle
on the seams of man's skull?
Do you remember his song that night?   20
I remember that he asked us for an aspirin
his eyes moved inside black rings
he was pale, and two deep wrinkles
bound his forehead. Or was it you
maybe? Or me? Or was it maybe   25
silent Antigone with those shoulders
rounded over her breasts?
I kept her with me ten nights
and each dawn she would weep for her child.
I remember I was looking for a pharmacy. For whom, I don't   30
    know.
They were all closed.

I got lost in the town
no one is going to remove the hospital
full of crippled children gesturing   35
at me or at others following me.
Odors of medicine in the air

turn heavy, fall in love and mesh
with vapors from cars going off
to the country with pre-Raphaelite couples   40
thoroughly blond if somehow a bit evaporated.

In the spring of 1923, Livia Rimini,
the film star, died in her bath;
they found her dead amidst her perfume
and the water was not yet cold.   45
Yet in the movies yesterday
she gazed at me with her useless eyes.

Translated from the Greek by Edmund Keeley

STUDY QUESTIONS

1. In what ways is "Tuesday" modern? How does it define the human
   condition?
2. What is the significance of the following details: streets, advertisements, gramophone, needle, Antigone, pharmacy, crippled children,
   Livia Rimini?

⊚ ODYSSEUS ELYTIS

*Odysseus Elytis (b. 1911) was one of the great figures of the Greek literary
renaissance. Born on Crete, he was educated in Athens, where he studied law.
A reading of Paul Eluard's poetry, however, turned him to poetry and art.
Although Elytis never became a surrealist, Surrealism's techniques and
premises left a revolutionary impact upon him. He believed that Surrealism
gave him insights to unfettering the unconscious as a source of lyric poetry.
For example, Elytis used automatism in stimulating his creative imagination.
On the other hand, Elytis's finished work was highly structured. His first
book of poetry probed states of inner harmony through a celebration of Greek
nature. The experiences of World War II and the Greek Civil War gave to
Elytis's poetry a messianic, redemptive mission, the quest of poetically
reestablishing the Greek spirit. In 1959 he published his highly complex work,
The Axion Esti (1974). Modeled upon the Byzantine mass, it was a lyrical
epic of the nature of Greece and of the spirit of its people. In recent decades,
Elytis has returned to a more personal vision. Volumes such as The Light*

Tree and the Fourteenth Beauty *(1979)*, The Little Mariner *(1980)*, *and* Selected Poems *(1981)* render the poet's epiphanies. One of the foremost innovators in twentieth-century Greek writing, Elytis was awarded the Nobel Prize for Literature in 1979.

Sun the First

So often when I speak of the sun
In my tongue becomes tangled one
Large rose full of red.
But it is not bearable for me to be silent.

I

I don't know anymore the night terrible anonymity of death
In the small turn of my soul a fleet of stars comes to port.
Guard of evening because you shine next to the sky-colored
Little wind of an island that dreams of me
Proclaiming the dawn from its tall boulders   5
My two eyes embrace and sail you with the star
Of my correct heart: I don't know anymore the night.

I don't know anymore the names of a people that deny me
Clearly I read the shells the leaves the stars
Enmity is useless for me on the roads of the sky   10
Unless it is a dream that sees me once again
In tears walking through the sea of deathlessness
Evening under the curve of your golden fire
Night that is only night I do not know her.

II

Body of Summer

Time has gone since the last rain was heard   15
Over the ants and the lizards
Now sky burns without end
Fruit paint their mouth
Earth's pores open slowly slowly
And next to the water that drips syllabically   20
A huge plant looks the sun eye to eye!

Who is it lies on the high beaches
On his back toking silversmoked olive leaves
The cicadas are warmed in his ears
Ants work in his chest   25
Lizards slide in the grass of underarm
And from his feet's kelp a wave lightly passing
Sent by the young siren who sang:

O body of summer nude burnt
Eaten by oil and by salt   30
Body of boulder and shiver of heart
Large windblown of the hair tree-graceful
Basilbreath over the curly pubes
Full of small stars and fir needles
Body deep sailship of the day!   35

Slow rains come rapid hailstorms
Land slinks by whipped in the nails of the snow
That bruises in the depths with savage waves
The hills plunge in the clouds' thick teats

And yet behind it all you smile without care   40
And find again your immortal hour
As the sun on the beaches finds you again
As in your naked health the sun

III

Day shiny shell of the voice you made me by
Naked to walk in my daily Sundays   45
Among the welcome of the shores
Blow the first-known wind
Spread out the greens of tenderness
So that the sun may loll his head
And light the poppies with his lips   50
The poppies that the proud will scythe
To keep no sign on their naked chest
But the blood of defiance that undoes sorrow
Arriving at the memory of freedom.

I spoke the love the health of the rose the ray   55
That alone directly finds the heart
Greece who with certainty steps on the sea
Greece who travels me always
On naked snow-glorious mountains.

I give my hand to justice   60
Transparent fountain source at the peak
My sky is deep and unaltered
What I love is always being born
What I love is beginning always.

IV

Drinking Corinthian sun   65
Reading the marbles
Climbing over arbor seas
Targeting with the fishing spear
A covenant fish that slips
I found the leaves the sun's psalm has by heart   70
The live dry land desire rejoices
To open.

I drink water I cut fruit
I shove my hand in the leafy wind
The lemon trees irrigate the pollen of summer   75
Green birds tear my dreams
I leave in a glance
Eyes wide where the world becomes again
Beautiful from the beginning to the measurement of the heart.

Translated from the Greek by Olga Broumas

STUDY QUESTIONS

1. "Sun the First" is a celebration of the strength and power of the sun.
   The author explores the effects of these attributes in different ways.
   Categorize them, and explain their significance.
2. Can you tell that the poem is Greek or Mediterranean? How?
3. Explain why nature is an important reference for the imagination.

IRELAND

WILLIAM BUTLER YEATS

William Butler Yeats (1865–1939) was a noted Irish poet, dramatist, and essayist whom T. S. Eliot memorialized as "the greatest poet of our time." Yeats was born into the Protestant ascendancy and in his youth became fervently involved in poetry and the Irish cultural revival. He learned Gaelic, studied Irish sagas and folklore, lectured on the Irish past, and helped establish the Abbey Theatre. His devotion to Ireland, though not uncritical of aspects of Irish nationalism, formed one of the main inspirational motifs in his literary work. The nature of County Sligo as well as the feats of the Irish warrior of pagan times Cú Chulainn informed his poetry. As significant an influence on Yeats's poetic imagination was his revulsion at the materialism of urban, technological culture. Reviling its crassness as leading to anarchy and chaos, Yeats sought recourse in myth, the supernatural, spiritualism, and the occult. Yeats's mature poetry evoked a lurking boding of the eventuality of universal destruction. Yeats, however, did not allow his poetry to succumb to his dread of the future, but interwove within it a vivid sense of the joyousness and beauty of life. A consummate craftsman who revised his work, yet at times used the trance for inspiration, Yeats achieved in his writing a rare dramatic tension. He had the ability to palpably render a crucial moment or perception and then to distill its essence into the poetic construct.

Easter 1916[1]

I have met them at close of day
Coming with vivid faces
From counter or desk among grey
Eighteenth-century houses.
I have passed with a nod of the head   5
Or polite meaningless words,
Or have lingered awhile and said
Polite meaningless words,
And thought before I had done
Of a mocking tale or a gibe   10
To please a companion
Around the fire at the club,
Being certain that they and I
But lived where motley is worn:
All changed, changed utterly: 15
A terrible beauty is born.

That woman's days were spent
In ignorant good-will,
Her nights in argument
Until her voice grew shrill.   20
What voice more sweet than hers
When, young and beautiful,
She rode to harriers?
This man had kept a school
And rode our wingèd horse;   25
This other his helper and friend
Was coming into his force;
He might have won fame in the end,
So sensitive his nature seemed,
So daring and sweet his thought.   30
This other man I had dreamed
A drunken, vainglorious lout.
He had done most bitter wrong
To some who are near my heart,
Yet I number him in the song;   35
He, too, has resigned his part

---

1. Date of uprising by a group of Irish nationalists; some are referred to in the second stanza and four are named near the end of the poem.

In the casual comedy;
He, too, has been changed in his turn,
Transformed utterly:
A terrible beauty is born.   40

Hearts with one purpose alone
Through summer and winter seem
Enchanted to a stone
To trouble the living stream.
The horse that comes from the road,   45
The rider, the birds that range
From cloud to tumbling cloud,
Minute by minute they change;
A shadow of cloud on the stream
Changes minute by minute;   50
A horse-hoof slides on the brim,
And a horse plashes within it;
The long-legged moor-hens dive,
And hens to moor-cocks call;
Minute by minute they live: 55
The stone's in the midst of all.

Too long a sacrifice
Can make a stone of the heart.
O when may it suffice?
That is Heaven's part, our part   60
To murmur name upon name,
As a mother names her child
When sleep at last has come
On limbs that had run wild.
What is it but nightfall?   65
No, no, not night but death;
Was it needless death after all?
For England may keep faith
For all that is done and said.
We know their dream; enough   70
To know they dreamed and are dead;
And what if excess of love
Bewildered them til they died?
I write it out in a verse—
MacDonagh and MacBride   75
And Connolly and Pearse
Now and in time to be,
Wherever green is worn,
Are changed, changed utterly:
A terrible beauty is born.   80

STUDY QUESTIONS

1. In "Easter 1916," what is Yeats's attitude to the nationalists before the uprising? What does the poet mean in lines 72–73:

    > "And what if excess of love
    > Bewildered them til they died?"

2. What is the function of the poem's third stanza? To what purposes does the poet use the stone/heart metaphor?
3. How does the recurring line "A terrible beauty is born" (lines 16, 40, and 80) emphasize the dramatic conflict of the poem?

ⓢ JAMES JOYCE

James Joyce (1882–1941) was one of the most influential novelists of the twentieth century. Born in a Catholic family in Dublin, Joyce early on left Catholicism and Ireland to spend his adult life living and writing in continental Europe. Ireland, however, became the fabric of his fiction. If Joyce left Ireland because he found its culture too constricting, he likewise modified the structure of the narrative novel because he found its form inadequate to his literary aim of exploring consciousness. Joyce's innovations first emerged in A Portrait of the Artist as a Young Man *(1916) which he wrote from the point of view of the developing personality of the young protagonist. To give complexity and authorial presence, Joyce intertwined symbolic themes into Stephen Dedalus's growing perceptions of the world and of himself. In its use of internal monologues,* Portrait *was a precursor of Joyce's revolutionary work* Ulysses *(1922). Here Joyce, in effect, created a new novelistic form.* Ulysses *is a tightly constructed mosaic of external and internal monologues. This mosaic renders not only the consciousness of the characters but of a whole city, Dublin, on June 16, 1904.* Ulysses *is equally significant for Joyce's examination of the role of language, in Richard Ellmann's words, as "the product and prompter of unconscious imaginings." Joyce carried this exploration further in* Finnegans Wake *(1939), in which he used multiple voices and linguistic techniques to transform language so that he could evoke the unconscious and the world of dreams. The selection below is from Joyce's early collection of short stories,* Dubliners *(1914). Although it does not demonstrate Joyce's later techniques, in its scrupulously controlled naturalistic style and in its ironic probing of emotions, it does show Joyce's concern with the psyche and his mastery of language.*

Araby

North Richmond Street, being blind, was a quiet street except at the hour when the Christian Brothers' School[1] set the boys free. An uninhabited house of two storeys stood at the blind end, detached from its neighbours in a square ground. The other houses of the street, conscious of decent lives within them, gazed at one another with brown imperturbable faces.

The former tenant of our house, a priest, had died in the back drawing-room. Air, musty from having been long enclosed, hung in all the rooms, and the waste room behind the kitchen was littered with old useless papers. Among these I found a few paper-covered books, the pages of which were curled and damp: *The Abbot*, by Walter Scott, *The Devout Communicant* and *The Memoirs of Vidocq*.[2] I liked the last best because its leaves were yellow. The wild garden behind the house contained a central apple-tree and a few straggling bushes under one of which I found the late tenant's rusty bicycle-pump. He had been a very charitable priest; in his will he had left all his money to institutions and the furniture of his house to his sister.

When the short days of winter came dusk fell before we had well eaten our dinners. When we met in the street the houses had grown sombre. The space of sky above us was the colour of ever-changing violet and towards it the lamps of the street lifted their feeble lanterns. The cold air stung us and we played till our bodies glowed. Our shouts echoed in the silent street. The career of our play brought us through the dark muddy lanes behind the houses where we ran the gauntlet of the rough tribes from the cottages, to the back doors of the dark dripping gardens where odours arose from the ashpits, to the dark odorous stables where a coachman smoothed and combed the horse or shook music from the buckled harness. When we returned to the street light from the kitchen windows had filled the areas. If my uncle was seen turning the corner we hid in the shadow until we had seen him safely housed. Or if Mangan's sister came out on the doorstep to call her brother in to his tea we watched her from our shadow peer up and down the street. We waited to see whether she would remain or go in and, if she remained, we left our shadow and walked up to Mangan's steps resignedly. She was waiting for us, her figure defined by the light from the half-opened door. Her brother always teased her before he obeyed and I stood by the railings looking at her. Her dress swung as

---

1. *A famous Catholic day school in Dublin.*
2. *The Abbot (1820) by Sir Walter Scott (1771–1832) is an historical romance about Mary Queen of Scots; The Devout Communicant (1813) is a Catholic guide to "pious meditations" by Friar Pacificus Baker (1695–1774); The Memoirs of Vidocq (1829) traces the career of François-Jules Vidocq (1775–1857), a French criminal-turned-detective.*

she moved her body and the soft rope of her hair tossed from side to side.

Every morning I lay on the floor in the front parlour watching her door. 4
The blind was pulled down to within an inch of the sash so that I could not
be seen. When she came out on the doorstep my heart leaped. I ran to the
hall, seized my books and followed her. I kept her brown figure always in
my eye and, when we came near the point at which our ways diverged, I
quickened my pace and passed her. This happened morning after morning. I had never spoken to her, except for a few casual words, and yet her
name was like a summons to all my foolish blood.

Her image accompanied me even in places the most hostile to romance. 5
On Saturday evenings when my aunt went marketing I had to go to carry
some of the parcels. We walked through the flaring streets, jostled by
drunken men and bargaining women, amid the curses of labourers, the
shrill litanies of shop-boys who stood on guard by the barrels of pigs'
cheeks, the nasal chanting of street-singers, who sang a *come-all-you*[1] about
O'Donovan Rossa,[2] or a ballad about the troubles in our native land. These
noises converged in a single sensation of life for me: I imagined that I bore
my chalice safely through a throng of foes. Her name sprang to my lips at
moments in strange prayers and praises which I myself did not understand. My eyes were often full of tears (I could not tell why) and at times
a flood from my heart seemed to pour itself out into my bosom. I thought
little of the future. I did not know whether I would ever speak to her or not
or, if I spoke to her, how I could tell her of my confused adoration. But my
body was like a harp and her words and gestures were like fingers running
upon the wires.

One evening I went into the back drawing-room in which the priest had 6
died. It was a dark rainy evening and there was no sound in the house.
Through one of the broken panes I heard the rain impinge upon the earth,
the fine incessant needles of water playing in the sodden beds. Some
distant lamp or lighted window gleamed below me. I was thankful that I
could see so little. All my senses seemed to desire to veil themselves and,
feeling that I was about to slip from them, I pressed the palms of my hands
together until they trembled, murmuring: *"O love! O love!"* many times.

At last she spoke to me. When she addressed the first words to me I was 7
so confused that I did not know what to answer. She asked me was I going
to *Araby*. I forgot whether I answered yes or no. It would be a splendid
bazaar, she said she would love to go.

"And why can't you?" I asked. 8

While she spoke she turned a silver bracelet round and round her wrist. 9
She could not go, she said, because there would be a retreat that week in

---

1. *One of any number of popular street songs on a topical subject beginning "Come all you . . . ."*
2. *Refers to Jeremiah O'Donovan (1831–1915), a leader in Ireland's struggle for independence,
   whose activities earned him the nickname "Dynamite Rossa."*

her convent. Her brother and two other boys were fighting for their caps and I was alone at the railings. She held one of the spikes, bowing her head towards me. The light from the lamp opposite our door caught the white curve of her neck, lit up her hair that rested there and, falling, lit up the hand upon the railing. It fell over one side of her dress and caught the white border of a petticoat, just visible as she stood at ease.

"It's well for you," she said.   10

"If I go," I said, "I will bring you something."   11

What innumerable follies laid waste my waking and sleeping thoughts   12
after that evening! I wished to annihilate the tedious intervening days. I
chafed against the work of school. At night in my bedroom and by day in
the classroom her image came between me and the page I strove to read.
The syllables of the word *Araby* were called to me through the silence in
which my soul luxuriated and cast an Eastern enchantment over me. I
asked for leave to go to the bazaar on Saturday night. My aunt was surprised and hoped it was not some Freemason[1] affair. I answered few questions in class. I watched my master's face pass from amiability to sternness;
he hoped I was not beginning to idle. I could not call my wandering
thoughts together. I had hardly any patience with the serious work of life
which, now that it stood between me and my desire, seemed to me child's
play, ugly monotonous child's play.

On Saturday morning I reminded my uncle that I wished to go to the   13
bazaar in the evening. He was fussing at the hallstand, looking for the
hat-brush, and answered me curtly:

"Yes, boy, I know."   14

As he was in the hall I could not go into the front parlour and lie   15
at the window. I left the house in bad humour and walked slowly towards the school. The air was pitilessly raw and already my heart misgave
me.

When I came home to dinner my uncle had not yet been home. Still it   16
was early. I sat staring at the clock for some time and, when its ticking
began to irritate me, I left the room. I mounted the staircase and gained the
upper part of the house. The high cold empty gloomy rooms liberated me
and I went from room to room singing. From the front window I saw my
companions playing below in the street. Their cries reached me weakened
and indistinct and, leaning my forehead against the cool glass, I looked
over at the dark house where she lived. I may have stood there for an hour,
seeing nothing but the brown-clad figure cast by my imagination, touched
discreetly by the lamplight at the curved neck, at the hand upon the railings and at the border below the dress.

When I came downstairs again I found Mrs. Mercer sitting at the fire.   17
She was an old garrulous woman, a pawnbroker's widow, who collected

---

1. *A Protestant fraternal organization.*

used stamps for some pious purpose. I had to endure the gossip of the tea-table. The meal was prolonged beyond an hour and still my uncle did not come. Mrs. Mercer stood up to go: she was sorry she couldn't wait any longer, but it was after eight o'clock and she did not like to be out late, as the night air was bad for her. When she had gone I began to walk up and down the room, clenching my fists. My aunt said:

"I'm afraid you may put off your bazaar for this night of Our Lord." 18

At nine o'clock I heard my uncle's latchkey in the halldoor. I heard him 19 talking to himself and heard the hallstand rocking when it had received the weight of his overcoat. I could interpret these signs. When he was midway through his dinner I asked him to give me the money to go the bazaar. He had forgotten.

"The people are in bed and after their first sleep now," he said. 20

I did not smile. My aunt said to him energetically: 21

"Can't you give him the money and let him go? You've kept him late 22 enough as it is."

My uncle said he was very sorry he had forgotten. He said he believed 23 in the old saying: "All work and no play makes Jack a dull boy." He asked me where I was going and, when I had told him a second time he asked me did I know *The Arab's Farewell to his Steed*.[1] When I left the kitchen he was about to recite the opening lines of the piece to my aunt.

I held a florin[2] tightly in my hand as I strode down Buckingham Street 24 towards the station. The sight of the streets thronged with buyers and glaring with gas recalled to me the purpose of my journey. I took my seat in a third-class carriage of a deserted train. After an intolerable delay the train moved out of the station slowly. It crept onward among ruinous houses and over the twinkling river. At Westland Row Station a crowd of people pressed to the carriage doors; but the porters moved them back, saying that it was a special train for the bazaar. I remained alone in the bare carriage. In a few minutes the train drew up beside an improvised wooden platform. I passed out on to the road and saw by the lighted dial of a clock that it was ten minutes to ten. In front of me was a large building which displayed the magical name.

I could not find any sixpenny entrance and, fearing that the bazaar 25 would be closed, I passed in quickly through a turnstile, handing a shilling to a weary-looking man. I found myself in a big hall girdled at half its height by a gallery. Nearly all the stalls were closed and the greater part of the hall was in darkness. I recognised a silence like that which pervades a church after a service. I walked into the centre of the bazaar timidly. A few people were gathered about the stalls which were still open. Before a

---

1. *A poem by the English poet-novelist Caroline Norton (1808–1877).*
2. *Two shillings; a shilling was until recently one-twentieth of a British pound.*

curtain, over which the words *Café Chantant*[1] were written in coloured lamps, two men were counting money on a salver. I listened to the fall of the coins.

Remembering with difficulty why I had come I went over to one of the stalls and examined porcelain vases and flowered tea-sets. At the door of the stall a young lady was talking and laughing with two young gentlemen. I remarked their English accents and listened vaguely to their conversation. 26

"O, I never said such a thing!" 27

"O, but you did!" 28

"O, but I didn't!" 29

"Didn't she say that?" 30

"Yes. I heard her." 31

"O, there's a . . . fib!" 32

Observing me the young lady came over and asked me did I wish to buy anything. The tone of her voice was not encouraging; she seemed to have spoken to me out of a sense of duty. I looked humbly at the great jars that stood like eastern guards at either side of the dark entrance to the stall and murmured: 33

"No, thank you." 34

The young lady changed the position of one of the vases and went back to the two young men. They began to talk of the same subject. Once or twice the young lady glanced at me over her shoulder. 35

I lingered before her stall, though I knew my stay was useless, to make my interest in her wares seem the more real. Then I turned away slowly and walked down the middle of the bazaar. I allowed the two pennies to fall against the sixpence in my pocket. I heard a voice call from one end of the gallery that the light was out. The upper part of the hall was now completely dark. 36

Gazing up into the darkness I saw myself as a creature driven and derided by vanity; and my eyes burned with anguish and anger. 37

STUDY QUESTIONS

1. Who is the narrator? How does Joyce use language to show that these events are long past?
2. Who is the other central character in the story?
3. How are the physical setting and day-to-day life described? In what ways do these illumine the boy's emotional extremes?

---

1. *Concert coffee house.*

4. What is the experience that makes the protagonist's eyes burn with "anguish and anger" at the bazaar?
5. How does irony determine our interpretation of the events in the story?

◎ FRANK O'CONNOR

Frank O'Connor (1903–1966), whose real name was Michael O'Donovan, was an Irish short story writer and major cultural figure. Coming from an impoverished, laboring family, O'Connor educated himself to become a writer, translator, university lecturer, and, until he resigned on the issue of censorship, a director of the Abbey Theatre. As a youth, O'Connor fought with the Irish Republican Army and was imprisoned by the British. With Irish independence, his primary interest became writing. O'Connor saw the short story as an art form particularly pertinent to the lives of ordinary people. He believed that it had originated in the telling of folktales and had evolved out of a sense of human loneliness. O'Connor sought to create an oral quality so that his stories would ring with the tone of the human voice. He likewise sought to mitigate the loneliness of ordinary people by depicting their lives and celebrating in his portrayals the resilience of the human spirit. During the 1940s a number of his books, including Dutch Interior *(1940) and* The Common Cord *(1947), were banned by the Irish government. His short fiction has been published as* Collected Stories *(1981).*

The Drunkard

It was a terrible blow to Father when Mr. Dooley on the terrace died. Mr. Dooley was a commercial traveller with two sons in the Dominicans and a car of his own, so socially he was miles ahead of us, but he had no false pride. Mr. Dooley was an intellectual, and, like all intellectuals the thing he loved best was conversation, and in his own limited way Father was a well-read man and could appreciate an intelligent talker. Mr. Dooley was remarkably intelligent. Between business acquaintances and clerical contacts, there was very little he didn't know about what went on in town, and evening after evening he crossed the road to our gate to explain to Father the news behind the news. He had a low, palavering voice and a knowing smile, and Father would listen in astonishment, giving him a conversational lead now and again, and then stump triumphantly in to Mother with his face aglow and ask: "Do you know what Mr. Dooley is after telling me?" Ever since, when somebody has given me some bit of information off the record I have found myself on the point of asking: "Was it Mr. Dooley told you that?"

Till I actually saw him laid out in his brown shroud with the rosary beads entwined between his waxy fingers I did not take the report of his death seriously. Even then I felt there must be a catch and that some summer evening Mr. Dooley must reappear at our gate to give us the lowdown on the next world. But Father was very upset, partly because Mr. Dooley was about one age with himself, a thing that always gives a distinctly personal turn to another man's demise; partly because now he would have no one to tell him what dirty work was behind the latest scene at the Corporation. You could count on your fingers the number of men in Blarney Lane who read the papers as Mr. Dooley did, and none of these would have overlooked the fact that Father was only a laboring man. Even Sullivan, the carpenter, a mere nobody, thought he was a cut above Father. It was certainly a solemn event.

"Half past two to the Curragh," Father said meditatively, putting down the paper.

"But you're not thinking of going to the funeral?" Mother asked in alarm.

" 'Twould be expected," Father said, scenting opposition. "I wouldn't give it to say to them."

"I think," said Mother with suppressed emotion, "it will be as much as anyone will expect if you go to the chapel with him."

("Going to the chapel," of course, was one thing, because the body was removed after work, but going to a funeral meant the loss of a half-day's pay.)

"The people hardly know us," she added.

"God between us and all harm," Father replied with dignity, "we'd be glad if it was our own turn."

To give Father his due, he was always ready to lose a half day for the sake of an old neighbor. It wasn't so much that he liked funerals as that he was a conscientious man who did as he would be done by; and nothing could have consoled him so much for the prospect of his own death as the assurance of a worthy funeral. And, to give Mother her due, it wasn't the half-day's pay she begrudged, badly as we could afford it.

Drink, you see, was Father's great weakness. He could keep steady for months, even for years, at a stretch, and while he did he was as good as gold. He was first up in the morning and brought the mother a cup of tea in bed, stayed at home in the evenings and read the paper; saved money and bought himself a new blue serge suit and bowler hat. He laughed at the folly of men who, week in week out, left their hard-earned money with the publicans; and sometimes, to pass an idle hour, he took pencil and paper and calculated precisely how much he saved each week through being a teetotaller. Being a natural optimist he sometimes continued this calculation through the whole span of his prospective existence and the total was breathtaking. He would die worth hundreds.

If I had only known it, this was a bad sign; a sign he was becoming   12
stuffed up with spiritual pride and imagining himself better than his neighbors. Sooner or later, the spiritual pride grew till it called for some form of celebration. Then he took a drink—not whiskey, of course; nothing like that—just a glass of some harmless drink like lager beer. That was the end of Father. By the time he had taken the first he already realized that he had made a fool of himself, took a second to forget it and a third to forget that he couldn't forget, and at last came home reeling drunk. From this on it was "The Drunkard's Progress," as in the moral prints. Next day he stayed in from work with a sick head while Mother went off to make his excuses at the works, and inside a fortnight he was poor and savage and despondent again. Once he began he drank steadily through everything down to the kitchen clock. Mother and I knew all the phases and dreaded all the dangers. Funerals were one.

"I have to go to Dunphy's to do a half-day's work," said Mother in   13
distress. "Who's to look after Larry?"

"I'll look after Larry," Father said graciously. "The little walk will do   14
him good."

There was no more to be said, though we all knew I didn't need anyone   15
to look after me, and that I could quite well have stayed at home and looked after Sonny, but I was being attached to the party to act as a brake on Father. As a brake I had never achieved anything, but Mother still had great faith in me.

Next day, when I got home from school, Father was there before me and   16
made a cup of tea for both of us. He was very good at tea, but too heavy in the hand for anything else; the way he cut bread was shocking. Afterwards, we went down the hill to the church, Father wearing his best blue serge and a bowler cocked to one side of his head with the least suggestion of the masher. To his great joy he discovered Peter Crowley among the mourners. Peter was another danger signal, as I knew well from certain experiences after Mass on Sunday morning; a mean man, as Mother said, who only went to funerals for the free drinks he could get at them. It turned out that he hadn't even known Mr. Dooley! But Father had a sort of contemptuous regard for him as one of the foolish people who wasted their good money in public-houses when they could be saving it. Very little of his own money Peter Crowley wasted!

It was an excellent funeral from Father's point of view. He had it all well   17
studied before we set off after the hearse in the afternoon sunlight.

"Five carriages!" he exclaimed. "Five carriages and sixteen covered cars!   18

There's one alderman, two councillors and 'tis unknown how many priests. I didn't see a funeral like this from the road since Willie Mack, the publician, died."

"Ah, he was well liked," said Crowley in his husky voice.   19

"My goodness, don't I know that?" snapped Father. "Wasn't the man   20
my best friend? Two nights before he died—only two nights—he was over telling me the goings-on about the housing contract. Them fellows in the Corporation are night and day robbers. But even I never imagined he was as well connected as that."

Father was stepping out like a boy, pleased with everything; the other   21
mourners, and the fine houses along Sunday's Well. I knew the danger signals were there in full force: a sunny day, a fine funeral, and a distinguished company of clerics and public men were bringing out all the natural vanity and flightiness of Father's character. It was with something like genuine pleasure that he saw his old friend lowered into the grave; with the sense of having performed a duty and the pleasant awareness that however much he would miss poor Mr. Dooley in the long summer evenings, it was he and not poor Mr. Dooley who would do the missing.

"We'll be making tracks before they break up," he whispered to Crow-   22
ley as the gravediggers tossed in the first shovelfuls of clay, and away he went, hopping like a goat from grassy hump to hump. The drivers, who were probably in the same state as himself, though without months of abstinence to put an edge on it, looked up hopefully.

"Are they nearly finished, Mick?" bawled one.   23

"All over now bar the last prayers," trumpeted Father in the tone of one   24
who brings news of great rejoicing.

The carriages passed us in a lather of dust several hundred yards from   25
the public-house, and Father, whose feet gave him trouble in hot weather, quickened his pace, looking nervously over his shoulder for any sign of the main body of mourners crossing the hill. In a crowd like that a man might be kept waiting.

When we did reach the pub the carriages were drawn up outside, and   26
solemn men in black ties were cautiously bringing out consolation to mysterious females whose hands reached out modestly from behind the drawn blinds of the coaches. Inside the pub there were only the drivers and a couple of shawly women. I felt if I was to act as a brake at all, this was the time, so I pulled Father by the coattails.

"Dadda, can't we go home now?" I asked.   27

"Two minutes now," he said, beaming affectionately. "Just a bottle of   28
lemonade and we'll go home."

This was a bribe, and I knew it, but I was always a child of weak   29
character. Father ordered lemonade and two pints. I was thirsty and swallowed my drink at once. But that wasn't Father's way. He had long months of abstinence behind him and an eternity of pleasure before. He took out his pipe, blew through it, filled it, and then lit it with loud pops, his eyes

bulging above it. After that he deliberately turned his back on the pint, leaned one elbow on the counter in the attitude of a man who did not know there was a pint behind him, and deliberately brushed the tobacco from his palms. He had settled down for the evening. He was steadily working through all the important funerals he had ever attended. The carriages departed and the minor mourners drifted in till the pub was half full.

"Dadda," I said, pulling his coat again, "can't we go home now?" 30

"Ah, your mother won't be in for a long time yet," he said benevolently 31
enough. "Run out in the road and play, can't you?"

It struck me as very cool, the way grown-ups assumed that you could 32
play all by yourself on a strange road. I began to get bored as I had so often
been bored before. I knew Father was quite capable of lingering there till
nightfall. I knew I might have to bring him home, blind drunk, down
Blarney Lane, with all the old women at their doors, saying: "Mick Delaney
is on it again." I knew that my mother would be half crazy with anxiety;
that next day Father wouldn't go out to work; and before the end of the
week she would be running down to the pawn with the clock under her
shawl. I could never get over the lonesomeness of the kitchen without a
clock.

I was still thirsty. I found if I stood on tiptoe I could just reach Father's 33
glass, and the idea occurred to me that it would be interesting to know
what the contents were like. He had his back to it and wouldn't notice. I
took down the glass and sipped cautiously. It was a terrible disappointment. I was astonished that he could even drink such stuff. It looked as if
he had never tried lemonade.

I should have advised him about lemonade but he was holding forth 34
himself in great style. I heard him say that bands were a great addition to
a funeral. He put his arms in the position of someone holding a rifle in
reverse and hummed a few bars of Chopin's Funeral March. Crowley
nodded reverently. I took a longer drink and began to see that porter might
have its advantages. I felt pleasantly elevated and philosophic. Father
hummed a few bars of the Dead March in *Saul.* It was a nice pub and a very
fine funeral, and I felt sure that poor Mr. Dooley in Heaven must be highly
gratified. At the same time I thought they might have given him a band. As
Father said, bands were a great addition.

But the wonderful thing about porter was the way it made you stand 35
aside, or rather float aloft like a cherub rolling on a cloud, and watch
yourself with your legs crossed, leaning against a bar counter, not worrying about trifles but thinking deep, serious, grown-up thoughts about life
and death. Looking at yourself like that, you couldn't help thinking after a
while how funny you looked, and suddenly you got embarrassed and
wanted to giggle. But by the time I had finished the pint, that phase too
had passed; I found it hard to put back the glass, the counter seemed to
have grown so high. Melancholia was supervening again.

"Well," Father said reverently, reaching behind him for his drink, "God 36 rest the poor man's soul, wherever he is!" He stopped, looked first at the glass, and then at the people round him. "Hello," he said in a fairly good-humored tone, as if he were prepared to consider it a joke, even if it was in bad taste, "who was at this?"

There was silence for a moment while the publican and the old women looked first at Father and then at his glass. 37

"There was no one at it, my good man," one of the women said with an offended air. "Is it robbers you think we are?" 38

"Ah, there's no one here would do a thing like that, Mick," said the publican in a shocked tone. 39

"Well, someone did it," said Father, his smile beginning to wear off. 40

"If they did, they were them that were nearer it," said the woman darkly, giving me a dirty look; and at the same moment the truth began to dawn on Father. I suppose I must have looked a bit starry-eyed. He bent and shook me. 41

"Are you all right, Larry?" he asked in alarm. 42

Peter Crowley looked down at me and grinned. 43

"Could you beat that?" he exclaimed in a husky voice. 44

I could, and without difficulty. I started to get sick. Father jumped back in holy terror that I might spoil his good suit, and hastily opened the back door. 45

"Run! run! run!" he shouted. 46

I saw the sunlit wall outside with the ivy overhanging it, and ran. The intention was good but the performance was exaggerated, because I lurched right into the wall, hurting it badly, as it seemed to me. Being always very polite, I said "Pardon" before the second bout came on me. Father, still concerned for his suit, came up behind and cautiously held me while I got sick. 47

"That's a good boy!" he said encouragingly. "You'll be grand when you get that up." 48

Begor, I was not grand! Grand was the last thing I was. I gave one unmerciful wail out of me as he steered me back to the pub and put me sitting on the bench near the shawlies. They drew themselves up with an offended air, still sore at the suggestion that they had drunk his pint. 49

"God help us!" moaned one, looking pityingly at me, "isn't it the likes of them would be fathers?" 50

"Mick," said the publican in alarm, spraying sawdust on my tracks, "that child isn't supposed to be in here at all. You'd better take him home quick in case a bobby would see him." 51

"Merciful God!" whimpered Father, raising his eyes to Heaven and clapping his hands silently as he only did when distraught, "what misfortune was on me? Or what will his mother say? . . . If women might stop at home and look after their children themselves!" he added in a snarl for the benefit of the shawlies. "Are them carriages all gone, Bill?" 52

"The carriages are finished long ago, Mick," replied the publican. 53

"I'll take him home," Father said despairingly . . . "I'll never bring you out again," he threatened me. "Here," he added, giving me a clean handkerchief from his breast pocket, "put that over your eye."

The blood on the handkerchief was the first indication I got that I was cut, and instantly my temple began to throb and I set up another howl.

"Whisht, whisht, whisht!" Father said testily, steering me out the door. "One'd think you were killed. That's nothing. We'll wash it when we get home."

"Steady now, old scout!" Crowley said, taking the other side of me. "You'll be all right in a minute."

I never met two men who knew less about the effects of drink. The first breath of fresh air and the warmth of the sun made me groggier than ever and I pitched and rolled between wind and tide till Father started to whimper again.

"God Almighty, and the whole road out! What misfortune was on me didn't stop at my work! Can't you walk straight?"

I couldn't. I saw plain enough that, coaxed by the sunlight, every woman old and young in Blarney Lane was leaning over her half-door or sitting on her doorstep. They all stopped gabbling to gape at the strange spectacle of two sober, middle-aged men bringing home a drunken small boy with a cut over his eye. Father, torn between the shamefast desire to get me home as quick as he could, and the neighborly need to explain that it wasn't his fault, finally halted outside Mrs. Roche's. There was a gang of old women outside a door at the opposite side of the road. I didn't like the look of them from the first. They seemed altogether too interested in me. I leaned against the wall of Mrs. Roche's cottage with my hands in my trouser pockets, thinking mournfully of poor Mr. Dooley in his cold grave on the Curragh, who would never walk down the road again, and, with great feeling, I began to sing a favorite song of Father's.

> "Though lost to Mononia and cold in the grave
> He returns to Kincora no more."

"Wisha, the poor child!" Mrs. Roche said. "Haven't he a lovely voice, God bless him!"

That was what I thought myself, so I was the more surprised when Father said "Whisht!" and raised a threatening finger at me. He didn't seem to realize the appropriateness of the song, so I sang louder than ever.

"Whisht, I tell you!" he snapped, and then tried to work up a smile for Mrs. Roche's benefit. "We're nearly home now. I'll carry you the rest of the way."

But, drunk and all as I was, I knew better than to be carried home ignominiously like that.

"Now," I said severely, "can't you leave me alone? I can walk all right. 'Tis only my head. All I want is a rest."

"But you can rest at home in bed," he said viciously, trying to pick me up, and I knew by the flush on his face that he was very vexed. 66

"Ah, Jasus," I said crossly, "what do I want to go home for? Why the hell can't you leave me alone?" 67

For some reason the gang of old women at the other side of the road thought this very funny. They nearly split their sides over it. A gassy fury began to expand in me at the thought that a fellow couldn't have a drop taken without the whole neighborhood coming out to make game of him. 68

"Who are ye laughing at?" I shouted, clenching my fists at them. "I'll make ye laugh at the other side of yeer faces if ye don't let me pass." 69

They seemed to think this funnier still; I had never seen such ill-mannered people. 70

"Go away, ye bloody bitches!" I said. 71

"Whisht, whisht, whisht, I tell you!" snarled Father, abandoning all pretense of amusement and dragging me along behind him by the hand. I was maddened by the women's shrieks of laughter. I was maddened by Father's bullying. I tried to dig in my heels but he was too powerful for me, and I could only see the women by looking back over my shoulder. 72

"Take care or I'll come back and show ye!" I shouted. "I'll teach ye to let decent people pass. Fitter for ye to stop at home and wash yeer dirty faces." 73

" 'Twill be all over the road," whimpered Father. "Never again, never again, not if I lived to be a thousand!" 74

To this day I don't know whether he was forswearing me or the drink. By way of a song suitable to my heroic mood I bawled "The Boys of Wexford," as he dragged me in home. Crowley, knowing he was not safe, made off and Father undressed me and put me to bed. I couldn't sleep because of the whirling in my head. It was very unpleasant, and I got sick again. Father came in with a wet cloth and mopped up after me. I lay in a fever, listening to him chopping sticks to start a fire. After that I heard him lay the table. 75

Suddenly the front door banged open and Mother stormed in with Sonny in her arms, not her usual gentle, timid self, but a wild, raging woman. It was clear that she had heard it all from the neighbors. 76

"Mick Delaney," she cried hysterically, "what did you do to my son?" 77

"Whisht, woman, whisht, whisht!" he hissed, dancing from one foot to the other. "Do you want the whole road to hear?" 78

"Ah," she said with a horrifying laugh, "the road knows all about it by this time. The road knows the way you filled your unfortunate innocent child with drink to make sport for you and that other rotten, filthy brute." 79

"But I gave him no drink," he shouted, aghast at the horrifying interpretation the neighbors had chosen to give his misfortune. "He took it while my back was turned. What the hell do you think I am?" 80

"Ah," she replied bitterly, "everyone knows what you are now. God forgive you, wasting our hard-earned few ha'pence on drink, and bringing up your child to be a drunken corner-boy like yourself." 81

Then she swept into the bedroom and threw herself on her knees by the 82
bed. She moaned when she saw the gash over my eye. In the kitchen
Sonny set up a loud bawl on his own, and a moment later Father appeared
in the bedroom door with his cap over his eyes, wearing an expression of
the most intense self-pity.

"That's a nice way to talk to me after all I went through," he whined. 83
"That's a nice accusation, that I was drinking. Not one drop of drink
crossed my lips the whole day. How could it when he drank it all? I'm the
one that ought to be pitied, with my day ruined on me, and I after being
made a show for the whole road."

But next morning, when he got up and went out quietly to work with his 84
dinner-basket, Mother threw herself on me in the bed and kissed me. It
seemed it was all my doing, and I was being given a holiday till my eye got
better.

"My brave little man!" she said with her eyes shining. "It was God did 85
it you were there. You were his guardian angel."

STUDY QUESTIONS

1. What purpose does the discussion of Father's relationship with Mr.
   Dooley serve in "The Drunkard"? In what other ways does O'Connor
   create a mood of sympathy for Father and his one great flaw?
2. Who is the narrator? Is the story told strictly from his point of view?
3. The mother is a slight participant in events. How does she contribute
   to the story's structure and theme?
4. How would you characterize the level of diction? Does it convey the
   boy's consciousness? Does it convey the mother's? The father's?
5. What is the function of humor in the story? What sense does it give us
   about the author's attitude toward the characters?

⑥ SAMUEL BECKETT

*Samuel Beckett (1906–1989) was an Irish-born novelist, playwright, and poet
whose major works are seminal in the evolution of postmodernism. Beckett's
literary career can be viewed in two phases. Influenced by Joyce and Proust,
the youthful Beckett of the 1930s and early 1940s elaborated themes of human
illusion in a vivid, evocative, and, at times, even luxuriant language. In the
post–World War II period, Beckett, who had lived most of his adult life in
France and had fought in the French Resistance, dramatically changed to
writing in French. Beckett's turning away from English and the new austerity*

of his style were devices to create tension in his work and to keep the artfulness of language from veiling the uncertainty of the human condition. Beckett's postwar trilogy of novels—Molloy (1951), Malone Dies (1951), and The Unnamable (1953)—evoked a consistent mood of anguish about the impossibility of defining one's being. Beckett also has employed comic devices, particularly in his plays, as a means of maintaining aesthetic distance and focusing the audience's attention on the theme of the fragmented self in an unknowable universe. Plays such as Waiting for Godot (1952) and Endgame (1957) won Beckett vast public acclaim in the 1950s and 1960s and inaugurated the postmodernist era. He was awarded the Nobel Prize in Literature in 1969. "As the Story Was Told" is representative of Beckett's creation of the "anonymous" voice struggling to decipher itself through memories and tales that are impossible to reconstitute.

As the Story Was Told

A s the story was told me I never went near the place during sessions. I asked what place and a tent was described at length, a small tent the colour of its surroundings. Wearying of this description I asked what sessions and these in their turn were described, their object, duration, frequency and harrowing nature. I hope I was not more sensitive than the next man, but finally I had to raise my hand. I lay there quite still for a time, then asked where I was while all this was going forward. In a hut, was the answer, a small hut in a grove some two hundred yards away, a distance even the loudest cry could not carry, but must die on the way. This was not so strange as at first sight it sounded when one considered the stoutness of the canvas and the sheltered situation of the hut among the trees. Indeed the tent might have been struck where it stood and moved forward fifty yards or so without inconvenience. Lying there with closed eyes in the silence which followed this information I began to see the hut, though unlike the tent it had not been described to me, but only its situation. It reminded me strongly of a summer-house in which as a child I used to sit quite still for hours on end, on the window-seat, the whole year round. It had the same five log walls, the same coloured glass, the same diminutiveness, being not more than ten feet across and so low of ceiling that the average man could not have held himself erect in it, though of course there was no such difficulty for the child. At the centre, facing the coloured panes, stood a small upright wicker chair with arm-rests, as against the summer-house's window-seat. I sat there very straight and still, with my arms along the rests, looking out at the orange light. It must have been shortly after six, the sessions closing punctually at that hour, for as I watched a hand appeared in the doorway and held out to me a sheet of writing. I took and read it, then tore it in four and put the pieces in the waiting hand to take away. A little later the whole scene disappeared. As the story was told me the man succumbed in the end to his ill-treatment, though quite old enough at the time to die naturally of old age. I lay there a long time quite still—even as a child I was unusually still and more and more so with the passing years—till it must have seemed the story was over. But finally I asked if I knew exactly what the man—I would like to give his name but cannot—what exactly was required of the man, what it was he would not or could not say. No, was the answer, after some little hesitation no, I did not know what the poor man was required to say, in order to be pardoned, but would have recognized it at once, yes, at a glance, if I had seen it.

STUDY QUESTIONS

1. Who is the narrator and what is his situation in "As the Story Was Told"? Does he fully understand his own condition?
2. What is the relationship of the tent, the hut, and the summer-house? Where is the narrator? How long has he been there?
3. What is the relationship of the narrator to the poor man who succumbed?
4. How would you interpret the meaning of the story? Is it possible to know the story? Is it possible to know what the poor man was required to say?

⊚ SEAMUS HEANEY

Seamus Heaney (b. 1939) is a noted Irish poet who was born and raised on a farm in Catholic County Derry in Northern Ireland. He attended university in violence-troubled Belfast and taught there until 1972, when he moved to the Republic of Ireland. Heaney's poetry is steeped in remembrance of the rural life of Northern Ireland. It is a poetry whose roots are deeply familial. Personal memories and feelings inspire its discourse but do not limit its universal pertinence. Heaney's later work reflects his interest in ancient Irish history. Using the Irish bog as symbol of both past and present, Heaney's poetry elicits a spirit of commonality between the living and the dead of the Celtic world. His many books include Death of a Naturalist *(1966),* Field Work *(1979),* The Haw Lantern *(1989), and* Selected Poems *(1990).*

Digging

Between my finger and my thumb
The squat pen rests; snug as a gun.

Under my window, a clean rasping sound
When the spade sinks into gravelly ground;
My father, digging. I look down   5

Till his straining rump among the flowerbeds
Bends low, comes up twenty years away
Stooping in rhythm through potato drills
Where he was digging.

The coarse boot nestled on the lug, the shaft   10
Against the inside knee was levered firmly.
He rooted out tall tops, buried the bright edge deep
To scatter new potatoes that we picked
Loving their cool hardness in our hands.

By God, the old man could handle a spade.   15
Just like his old man.

My grandfather cut more turf in a day
Than any other man on Toner's bog.
Once I carried him milk in a bottle
Corked sloppily with paper. He straightened up   20
To drink it, then fell to right away

Nicking and slicing neatly, heaving sods
Over his shoulder, going down and down
For the good turf. Digging.

The cold smell of potato mould, the squelch and slap   25
Of soggy peat, the curt cuts of an edge
Through living roots awaken in my head.
But I've no spade to follow men like them.

Between my finger and my thumb
The squat pen rests.   30
I'll dig with it.

STUDY QUESTIONS

1. How does Heaney establish a relationship with his father and grand-father in "Digging"?
2. Discuss the double meaning of the title.
3. How does the poet define his role as a writer?

Eugenio Montale

Eugenio Montale (1896–1981) was an Italian poet, essayist, and critic who won the Nobel Prize in Literature in 1975. Montale first prepared for an operatic career, and his early volumes of poetry have a strong musical influence. In taking up poetry, Montale supported himself with translations and journalism—often with great difficulty—when he was victimized for refusing to join the Fascist Party. From its early musical imprint, Montale's poetry underwent a general transformation to a more pictorial orientation. In his later work, he turned to the rugged landscape of the Ligurian coast for poetic symbols. He also came to use a language more evocative of the rugged setting. He argued that the very value of poetry lay in its attempt to express what was beyond the power of mere words. Much of Montale's work represents a quest to comprehend the loneliness, the angst, the very precariousness of the human experience. Some of his poetry, however, is celebratory of life and love. "The Lemon Trees" represents the joyous aspect in his poetic vision. Various collections of his poetry are available in English, including The Storm and Other Things *(1956) and* New Poems *(1976).*

The Lemon Trees

Listen, the poets laureate
Walk only among plants
of unfamiliar name: boxwood, acanthus;
I, for my part, prefer the streets that fade
to grassy ditches where a boy   5
hunting the half-dried puddles
sometimes scoops up a meagre eel;
the little paths that wind along the slopes,
plunge down among the cane-tufts,

and break into the orchards, among trunks of the lemon trees. 10
Better if the jubilee of birds
is quenched, swallowed entirely in the blue:
more clear to the listener murmur of friendly boughs
in air that scarcely moves,
that fills the senses with this odor 15
inseparable from earth,
and rains an unquiet sweetness in the breast.
Here by a miracle is hushed
the war of the diverted passions,
here even to us poor falls our share of riches, 20
and it is the scent of the lemon trees.

See, in these silences
in which things yield and seem
about to betray their ultimate secret,
sometimes one half expects 25
to discover a mistake of Nature,
the dead point of the world, the link which will not hold,
the thread to disentangle which might set us at last
in the midst of a truth.
The eyes cast round, 30
the mind seeks harmonizes disunites
in the perfume that expands
when day most languishes.
Silences in which one sees
in each departing human shadow 35
some dislodged Divinity.
But the illusion wanes and time returns us
to our clamorous cities where the blue appears
only in patches, high up, among the gables.
The rain falls wearying the earth, 40
the winter tedium weighs on the roofs,
the light grows miserly, bitter the soul.
When one day through a half-shut gate,
among the leafage of a court
the yellows of the lemon blaze 45
and the heart's ice melts
and songs
pour into the breast
from golden trumpets of solarity.

Translated from the Italian by Irma Brandeis

1. Discuss Montale's vision of nature in "The Lemon Trees." What is the significance of the lemon trees? How do they provide a contrast with the world of "clamorous cities"?

⑥ DINO BUZZATI

Dino Buzzati (1906–1972) was one of Italy's avant-garde experimentalists. Influenced by Kafka and by modernist theories in general, Buzzati devoted his talents as a writer and painter to creating an art that was critical first of Fascism and then of the commercial nature of contemporary society. Buzzati's fiction employed surrealist techniques to probe ironically the values and edifices of consumerism. He aimed at the same time to write a popular literature that would draw idioms and motifs from mass culture while at the same time avoiding its clichés and stereotypes. Buzzati wanted art to engage the ordinary person and faulted modernism for having severed itself from a broad audience. His books of fiction available in English include Catastrophe and Other Stories *(1982),* Restless Nights *(1983), and* The Siren *(1984).*

The Falling Girl

Marta was nineteen. She looked out over the roof of the skyscraper, and seeing the city below shining in the dusk, she was overcome with dizziness. 1

The skyscraper was silver, supreme and fortunate in that most beautiful and pure evening, as here and there the wind stirred a few fine filaments of cloud against an absolutely incredible blue background. It was in fact the hour when the city is seized by inspiration and whoever is not blind is swept away by it. From that airy height the girl saw the streets and the masses of buildings writhing in the long spasm of sunset; and at the point where the white of the houses ended, the blue of the sea began. Seen from above, the sea looked as if it were rising. And since the veils of the night were advancing from the east, the city became a sweet abyss burning with pulsating lights. Within it were powerful men, and women who were even more powerful, furs and violins, cars glossy as onyx, the neon signs of nightclubs, the entrance halls of darkened mansions, fountains, diamonds, old silent gardens, parties, desires, affairs, and, above all, that 2 consuming sorcery of the evening which provokes dreams of greatness and glory.

Seeing these things, Marta hopelessly leaned out over the railing and let herself go. She felt as if she were hovering in the air, but she was falling. Given the extraordinary height of the skyscraper, the streets and squares down at the bottom were very far away. Who knows how long it would take her to get there. Yet the girl was falling. 3

At that hour the terraces and balconies of the top floors were filled with rich and elegant people who were having cocktails and making silly conversation. They were scattered in crowds, and their talk muffled the music. Marta passed before them and several people looked out to watch her. 4

Flights of that kind (mostly by girls, in fact) were not rare in the skyscraper and they constituted an interesting diversion for the tenants; this was also the reason why the price of those apartments was very high. 5

The sun had not yet completely set and it did its best to illuminate Marta's simple clothing. She wore a modest, inexpensive spring dress bought off the rack. Yet the lyrical light of the sunset exalted it somewhat, making it chic. 6

From the millionaires' balconies, gallant hands were stretched out toward her, offering flowers and cocktails. "Miss, would you like a drink? . . . Gentle butterfly, why not stop a minute with us?" 7

She laughed, hovering, happy (but meanwhile she was falling): "No, thanks, friends. I can't. I'm in a hurry." 8

"Where are you headed?" they ask her. 9

"Ah, don't make me say," Marta answered, waving her hands in a friendly good-bye. 10

A young man, tall, dark, very distinguished, extended an arm to snatch her. She liked him. And yet Marta quickly defended herself: "How dare you, sir?" and she had time to give him a little tap on the nose. 11

The beautiful people, then, were interested in her and that filled her with satisfaction. She felt fascinating, stylish. On the flower-filled terraces, amid the bustle of waiters in white and the bursts of exotic songs, there was talk for a few minutes, perhaps less, of the young woman who was passing by (from top to bottom, on a vertical course). Some thought her pretty, others thought her so-so, everyone found her interesting. 12

"You have your entire life before you," they told her, "why are you in such a hurry? You still have time to rush around and busy yourself. Stop with us for a little while, it's only a modest little party among friends, really, you'll have a good time." 13

She made an attempt to answer but the force of gravity had already quickly carried her to the floor below, then two, three, four floors below; in fact, exactly as you gaily rush around when you are just nineteen years old. 14

Of course, the distance that separated her from the bottom, that is, from 15 street level, was immense. It is true that she began falling just a little while ago, but the street always seemed very far away.

In the meantime, however, the sun had plunged into the sea; one could see it disappear, transformed into a shimmering reddish mushroom. As a result, it no longer emitted its vivifying rays to light up the girl's dress and make her a seductive comet. It was a good thing that the windows and terraces of the skyscraper were almost all illuminated and the bright reflections completely gilded her as she gradually passed by. 16

Now Marta no longer saw just groups of carefree people inside the apartments; at times there were even some businesses where the employees, in black or blue aprons, were sitting at desks in long rows. Several of them were young people as old as or older than she, and weary of the day by now, every once in a while they raised their eyes from their duties and from typewriters. In this way they too saw her, and a few ran to the windows. "Where are you going? Why so fast? Who are you?" they shouted to her. One could divine something akin to envy in their words. 17

"They're waiting for me down there," she answered. "I can't stop. Forgive me." And again she laughed, wavering on her headlong fall, but it wasn't like her previous laughter anymore. The night had craftily fallen and Marta started to feel cold. 18

Meanwhile, looking downward, she saw a bright halo of lights at the entrance of a building. Here long black cars were stopping (from the great distance they looked as small as ants), and men and women were getting out, anxious to go inside. She seemed to make out the sparkling of jewels in that swarm. Above the entrance flags were flying. 19

They were obviously giving a large party, exactly the kind that Marta dreamed of ever since she was a child. Heaven help her if she missed it. Down there opportunity was waiting for her, fate, romance, the true inauguration of her life. Would she arrive in time? 20

She spitefully noticed that another girl was falling about thirty meters above her. She was decidedly prettier than Marta and she wore a rather classy evening gown. For some unknown reason she came down much faster than Marta, so that in a few moments she passed by her and disappeared below, even though Marta was calling her. Without doubt she would get to the party before Marta; perhaps she had a plan all worked out to supplant her. 21

Then she realized that they weren't alone. Along the sides of the skyscraper many other young women were plunging downward, their faces taut with the excitement of the flight, their hands cheerfully waving as if to say: look at us, here we are, entertain us, is not the world ours? 22

It was a contest, then. And she only had a shabby little dress while those other girls were dressed smartly like high-fashion models and some even wrapped luxurious mink stoles tightly around their bare shoulders. So self-assured when she began the leap, Marta now felt a tremor growing 23 inside her; perhaps it was just the cold; but it may have been fear too, the fear of having made an error without remedy.

It seemed to be late at night now. The windows were darkened one after 24 another, the echoes of music became more rare, the offices were empty, young men no longer leaned out from the windowsills extending their hands. What time was it? At the entrance to the building down below— which in the meantime had grown larger, and one could now distinguish all the architectural details—the lights were still burning, but the bustle of cars had stopped. Every now and then, in fact, small groups of people came out of the main floor wearily drawing away. Then the lights of the entrance were also turned off.

Marta felt her heart tightening. Alas, she wouldn't reach the ball in time. 25 Glancing upwards, she saw the pinnacle of the skyscraper in all its cruel power. It was almost completely dark. On the top floors a few windows here and there were still lit. And above the top the first glimmer of dawn was spreading.

In a dining recess on the twenty-eighth floor a man about forty years old 26 was having his morning coffee and reading his newspaper while his wife tidied up the room. A clock on the sideboard indicated 8:45. A shadow suddenly passed before the window.

"Alberto!" the wife shouted. "Did you see that? A woman passed by." 27

"Who was it?" he said without raising his eyes from the newspaper. 28

"An old woman," the wife answered. "A decrepit old woman. She 29 looked frightened."

"It's always like that," the man muttered. "At these low floors only 30 falling old women pass by. You can see beautiful girls from the hundred-and-fiftieth floor up. Those apartments don't cost so much for nothing."

"At least down here there's the advantage," observed the wife, "that 31 you can hear the thud when they touch the ground."

"This time not even that," he said, shaking his head, after he stood 32 listening for a few minutes. Then he had another sip of coffee.

Translated from the Italian by Lawrence Venuti

STUDY QUESTIONS

1. From what point of view is "The Falling Girl" told? Is any other point of view possible?
2. For what is the falling girl a metaphor? How does the author use imagery to communicate the girl's false consciousness?
3. Why does Buzzati have the wife observe, "At least down here there's the advantage . . . that you can hear the thud when they touch ground"?

⟲ NATALIA GINZBURG

Natalia Ginzburg (b. 1916) is one of Italy's foremost writers. Ginzburg is representative of the writer engaged with the history of her society. Coming, on her mother's side, from a cosmopolitan Jewish/socialist background, Ginzburg, like her family, suffered persecution under the Fascists. From World War II on, her writing has been permeated by a sense of the need to chronicle one's time. Significantly for Ginzburg, the story of a protagonist cannot be understood without depicting that individual's public history. Influenced by Hemingway, Ginzburg's style is tight and restrained. Her mature work has intertwined lyrical and ironical qualities so that her quest for the past is muted by a feeling of nostalgia. This is clearly evident in her novelistic family chronicle, Voices in the Evening *(1961), from which "Old Balotta" is taken. Other books in English are* All Our Yesterdays *(1989) and* The Road to the City: Two Novellas *(1990). In 1983, Ginzburg was elected as an independent left candidate to the Italian Parliament.*

Old Balotta

Old De Francisci was known as old Balotta or Little Ball. He was short 1
and stout with a big paunch, as round as round, which overflowed above the waist of his trousers, and he had large drooping moustaches discoloured by the cigars which he chewed and sucked. He began with a workshop hardly as big as 'from here to there', my father relates. He went about on his bicycle with an old haversack in which he put his lunch, and he used to eat it leaning against a wall of the yard, covering his jacket with crumbs and draining the wine from the bottle's neck. That wall is still there, and it is known as old Balotta's wall because in the evening after the day's work he used to stand there with his cap on the back of his head smoking a cigar and chatting with his workmen.

My father says, 'When old Balotta was here certain things did not hap- 2
pen.'

Old Balotta was a Socialist. He always remained one, although after the 3
coming of Fascism he dropped his habit of uttering his thoughts aloud. He became in the end melancholy and sullen. When he got up in the morning he would say to his wife Cecilia,

'What a stink, anyway.' 4

And would add, 5

'I cannot endure it.' 6

Signora Cecilia would say, 7

'You cannot endure the smell from your factory any more?' And he said, 8

'No, I cannot endure it any more.' And again, 9

'I cannot go on with this life.' 10

'It is enough that you are healthy,' said Signora Cecilia. 11

'You,' said old Balotta to his wife, 'are always saying something fresh 12
and original.'

Later he had trouble with his gall-bladder and said to his wife, 13

'Now I haven't even got my health, I cannot go on.' 14

'One goes on until God gives the word,' Signora Cecilia told him. 15

'Pah! God! We *should* have to bring God into it!' 16

He still took up his place against the wall in the yard. The wall and that 17
corner of the yard is all that remains of the old workshop. The rest now is
a building of reinforced concrete, almost as big as the whole village. But he
no longer ate those hunks of bread. The doctor had ordered him a diet of
boiled vegetables which he was obliged to eat at home, sitting up to a table;
and he had also forbidden him his wine, his cigar and the bicycle. They
used to take him to the works in a motor-car.

Old Balotta brought up a boy, a distant relation, who had been left an 18
orphan as a small child, and he had him educated with his own sons. His
name is Fausto, but everyone calls him Purillo; because he always wears a
beret of the kind called *purillo,* drawn down over his ears. When Fascism
came Purillo became a Fascist, and old Balotta said,

'Naturally, because Purillo is like a gold-fly which when it settles settles 19
on dung.'

Old Balotta would be walking up and down the yard of the factory, his 20
hands behind his back, his beret thrust down on the nape of his neck, his
greasy worn scarf about his throat, like a piece of rope, and he would stop
in front of Purillo, who was now working in the factory and say,

'You, Purillo, are distasteful to me. I cannot bear you.' 21

Purillo would grin, curling his small mouth and showing his fine white 22
teeth; he would spread out his arms and say,

'I cannot possibly be to everyone's taste.' 23

'True,' said old Balotta, and he would walk away with his hands behind 24
his back, with his shambling gait, shuffling his shoes as though they were
slippers.

However, when he began to be ill, he named Purillo as manager of the 25
factory.

Signora Cecilia gave herself no peace over this affront to her sons. 26

'Why Purillo?' she asked. 'Why not Mario? Why not Vincenzo?' 27

But old Balotta said, 28

'Don't you push yourself in here. Push yourself into your sauces. Purillo 29
has a good brain. Your sons are not worth a fig. Purillo has a fine brain
even if I cannot bear him.' And he added,

'Only, everything will go to the dogs with this war.' 30

Purillo had always lived with them at La Casetta, as old Balotta's villa 31
was called. He had bought it for a small sum, at the time of the first war.
When he bought it, it had been a peasant's house with a kitchen garden,

orchard and vineyard. Later he enlarged and embellished it with a veranda and balconies, preserving at the same time something of its rustic appearance. So Purillo had always lived with them, until one fine day old Balotta turned him out. Purillo went to live at Le Pietre on the other side of the hill, which old Balotta had bought for his brother and sister, Barba Tommaso and Magna Maria, a house which old Balotta regarded in a way as a place of exile to which he banished his sons at various times when there was too much quarreling. But when he sent Purillo there it was clear that it was final. The evening that he had gone away Signora Cecilia burst into tears at table, not that she had any special affection for Purillo, but she felt not having him any more in the house where she had always had him from a baby. Old Balotta said,

'You won't waste your tears over Purillo, will you? I am eating my supper better without that ugly snout.' 32

Neither Barba Tommaso nor Magna Maria was asked if they were ready to have Purillo with them. But in any case old Balotta never asked either of them for their consent or opinion on any matter. 33

He used to say, 34

'My brother Barba Tommaso, speaking with all respect, is a ninny.' 35

'My sister Magna Maria, speaking with all respect, is a half wit.' 36

Nor, of course, was Purillo asked either if he liked being with Barba Tommaso and Magna Maria. 37

However, Purillo spent very little time with these two old people. He took his meals with them and after dinner brought out a snakeskin case with his initials in gold on it. 38

'Cigarette, Barba Tommaso?' 39

'Cigarette, Magna Maria?' 40

He never troubled himself to say anything else. 41

He pulled his beret over his head and went off to the works. 42

Barba Tommaso and Magna Maria feared and respected him. They did not dare say a word when he hung up a large photograph of himself in the dining-room wearing a black shirt and raising his arm to the salute among some Party officers who had come to visit the works. 43

Barba Tommaso and Magna Maria had never had any definite political opinions. Still they would whisper to one another, 44

'If Balotta comes here one day, what will happen then?' 45

That was in any case an improbable eventuality. Old Balotta never came to Le Pietre. 46

Then the war came. Balotta's sons went on service, but Purillo was not called up because he had some constriction of the throat or chest—and he had had pleurisy as a child and a murmur could still be heard on one side. 47

After the Eighth of September Purillo came one night to wake up Balotta and Signora Cecilia. He told them to dress at once and come away, because the Fascists were intending to come and get them. Balotta protested and 48 said he would not move. He said that everyone in the neighborhood liked him and no one would venture to do anything to him. But Purillo with a face like marble had seized a suitcase and stood there with his hands on his belt saying,

'We mustn't lose time. Put some things in this and let us go.' 49

Thereupon old Balotta got up and began to dress. He fumbled over his 50 braces and buttons with his freckled hands that were covered with white wrinkled skin.

'Where are we going?' he said. 51

'To Cignano.' 52

'To Cignano, to Cignano! And to whose house?' 53

'I am thinking.' 54

Signora Cecilia, in her alarm, wandered round the rooms picking up at 55 random what she found there, some flower vases which she put in a bag, silver spoons and old camisoles.

Purillo got them into a motor-car. He drove without saying a word, with 56 his long beaky nose curving over his black bristling moustache, his little mouth tight shut, his cap drawn over his ears.

'You, Purillo,' said old Balotta, 'are probably saving my life. All the 57 same, you are distasteful to me, and I cannot bear you.'

And Purillo this time said, 58

'I am not bound to be to your taste.' 59

'That is true,' said old Balotta. 60

Purillo always spoke formally to old Balotta, because Balotta had never 61 told him to say *thou*.

At Cignano, Purillo had rented a small apartment for them. They passed 62 the days in the kitchen, where the stove was. Purillo came to see them almost every evening.

The Fascists did actually come to La Casetta and they broke the win- 63 dows and ripped up the chairs with bayonets.

Signora Cecilia died at Cignano. She had struck up a friendship with the 64 landlady, and passed away holding her hand. Old Balotta had gone to find a doctor. When he returned with one his wife was dead.

He just could not believe it, and went on speaking to her and shaking 65 her. He thought she had merely fainted.

Only he and Purillo were at the funeral, and the lady who owned the 66 house. Barba Tommaso and Magna Maria were ill, with fever.

'Funk fever,' said old Balotta. 67

Purillo did not appear there any more. So Balotta was alone, though he 68 seemed to want Purillo. Every minute he was asking the landlady,

'But where has Purillo run off to?' 69

It became known that Purillo had escaped to Switzerland, having been 70 threatened with death either by the Fascists or by the Partisans. The factory remained entirely on the shoulders of an old surveyor, one Borzaghi. But the factory meant nothing any more to old Balotta.

His memory began to fail somewhat. He often fell asleep on a chair in 71
the kitchen with his head bowed. He would wake up with a start and ask
the landlady,

'Where are my children?' 72

He asked her this with a threatening air as though she had got them 73
hidden from him in the store-room cupboard.

'The boys, the grown-up ones, are at the war,' said the landlady. 'Don't 74
you remember that they are at the war? Little Tommasino is at school; and
the girls, Gemmina is in Switzerland and Raffaella is in the mountains with
the Partisans.'

'What a life!' said old Balotta. 75

And then he went to sleep again, bending forward, and starting up from 76
time to time and looking round with his lack-lustre eyes like one who did
not know where he was.

After the Liberation, Magna Maria came to take him away in a car, with 77
the chauffeur. He recognized him, as he was the son of one of his workmen, and embraced him. He held out two flabby fingers to Magna Maria,
looking askance at her.

He said, 78

'You didn't come to Cecilia's funeral.' 79

'I was in quarantine,' said Magna Maria. 80

They took him to La Casetta. Magna Maria had cleared away the broken 81
glass and tidied up the rooms a little with the peasant woman's help. But
there were no mattresses or sheets, no plate or china. Complete devastation existed in the garden, just where once upon a time one saw Signora
Cecilia moving about in the midst of her roses, with her blue apron, her
scissors attached to her belt, and her watering pot in her hand.

Old Balotta went away with Magna Maria to Le Pietre. Barba Tommaso 82
was there just the same as ever, rosy faced in his clean shirt and white
flannel trousers.

Old Balotta came and sat down and suddenly began sobbing into his 83
handkerchief, like a little child.

Magna Maria stroked his head and kept on repeating, 84

'Splendid, splendid. You are splendid. How splendid you are!' 85

Barba Tommaso said, 86

'I was the first to see the Partisans come. I was at the window with my 87
telescope; General Sartorio was there, too. I saw them approaching up the
road. I went to meet them with two bottles of wine, because I guessed they
were thirsty.'

And he said, 88

'At the factory, the Germans have carried off all the machinery. But it 89
does not matter, because now the Americans will give us new machinery.'

Old Balotta said, 90

'You just keep quiet. What a ninny you always are!' 91

'Borzaghi was very brave,' said Magna Maria. 'The Germans arrested 92 him, but he threw himself out of the train as it was going, and fractured his shoulder.'

And she said, 93

'You know that they killed Nebbia?' 94

'Nebbia?' 95

'Why yes. The Fascists took him and killed him, just there at the back, 96 on those rocks there. It was at night and we heard him cry out. And in the morning our woman found his scarf, and his spectacles all broken, and his cap, that fur one which he always wore.'

Old Balotta was looking at the setting sun above the sloping rocks be- 97 hind the house which is for that reason called Le Pietre, and at the clumps of pine trees which cover that side of the hill, and beyond the hills at the mountains with their sharp snowy peaks, and the long blue shadows of the glaciers and a white sugar-loaf summit, known as Lo Scivolo, 'the Slide', where his children used to go on Sundays with their friends.

The following day the major came to invite him to make a speech in 98 honour of the Liberation. They brought him out on the balcony of the town hall and below was a large crowd, the whole piazza was full. There were people also right down the street, they had climbed up the trees and telegraph poles. He recognized faces, some of his workmen, but he felt shy about speaking. He leaned with his hands on the balustrade and said,

'Viva il Socialismo!' 99

Then he remembered Nebbia. He took off his beret and said, 100

'Viva il Nebbia!' 101

Loud applause broke out like the roll of thunder; and he was rather 102 frightened and then suddenly felt very happy.

Then he wanted to speak again, but he did not know what else to say. 103 He gasped and fumbled with his coat collar. They led him from the balcony, because now the mayor was to speak.

While they were on their way home Barba Tommaso said to him, 104

'Nebbia was never a Socialist, he was a Communist.' 105

'No matter,' said old Balotta, 'and you shut up, what a ninny you always 106 are!'

At home again, Magna Maria put him to bed. He was flushed and 107 fevered and had difficulty with his breathing.

He died in the night. 108

In the neighbourhood they said what a tragedy—that old Balotta is 109 dead. Who knows what has become of his children, and the factory is left in Purillo's hands.

They said, 110

'All those children and not one of them here at the moment of his 111 death.'

The day after he died his younger daughter Raffaella appeared, the one 112 who had been in the mountains with the Partisans. She was wearing trousers, a red handkerchief round her neck, and a pistol in a holster.

She was eager for her father to see her with that pistol. She came to Le   113
Pietre and found Magna Maria at the garden gate with black crepe on her
head. Maria began to cry and said,
    'What a tragedy—what a tragedy!'   114
    Then she embraced Raffaella and said,   115
    'How splendid you are! Yes, splendid, splendid!' and added,   116
    'But don't you ever fire that pistol here.'   117

Translated from the Italian by D. M. Low

STUDY QUESTIONS

1. In "Old Balotta," what is the effect of Ginzburg's juxtaposition of the colloquial, slangy conversational style of the characters about whom the story is told with the formal language of third-person narrative?
2. How is old Balotta characterized? Who is Purillo? What is their relationship?
3. Through Balotta's story what do we learn about the Fascist period in Italy? Look for different ways and different levels in which Fascism affected public and personal life.
4. Note the various instances of courage the author mentions. Why does she present them in a matter-of-fact tone?

ITALO CALVINO

Italo Calvino (1923–1985) was an Italian novelist, short story writer, and critic. At the time of his death, Calvino was one of the most cosmopolitan and stylistically versatile of Europe's post–World War II writers. Calvino was born in Cuba, where his parents were agronomists who returned to Italy in the mid-1920s. Fascism and World War II dominated Calvino's physical coming of age while the Resistance and his association with Italian neorealists molded his intellectual maturation. Hence, Calvino's early novels were in the neorealist tradition of social parables, which first focused on the Resistance experience and then on issues of concern to postindustrial society. Calvino's mature imagination, however, encompassed many other modes of writing. In his versatility and in his eclectic sources of inspiration, he could be regarded as the premier postmodernist. For example, Calvino drew upon such diverse sources as Italian folktales (Italian Folktales [1956]), Boccaccio (The Castle of Crossed Destinies [1973]), scientific theories (Cosmicomics [1965]) while he divided If on a Winter's Night a Traveller *(1979) into ten sections, each parodying a different literary style. In all his works, critics have noted Calvino's elegance, craftsmanship, wit, and continual enjoyment in illuminating different aspects of the collective and individual being.*

The Adventure of a Reader

T he coast road ran high above the cape; the sea was below, a sheer drop, and on all sides, as far as the hazy mountainous horizon. The sun was on all sides, too, as if the sky and the sea were two glasses magnifying it. Down below, against the jagged, irregular rocks of the cape, the calm water slapped without making foam. Amedeo Oliva climbed down a steep flight of steps, shouldering his bicycle, which he then left in a shady place, after closing the padlock. He continued down the steps amid spills of dry yellow earth and agaves jutting into the void, and he was already looking around for the most comfortable stretch of rock to lie down. Under his arm he had a rolled-up towel and, inside the towel, his bathing trunks and a book. 1

The cape was a solitary place: only a few groups of bathers dived into the water or took the sun, hidden from one another by the irregular con- formation of the place. Between two boulders that shielded him from view, Amedeo undressed, put on his trunks, and began jumping from the top of one rock to the next. Leaping in this way on his skinny legs, he crossed half the rocky shore, sometimes almost grazing the faces of half-hidden pairs of bathers stretched out on beach towels. Having gone past an outcrop of sandy rock, its surface porous and irregular, he came upon smooth stones, with rounded corners; Amedeo took off his sandals, held them in his hand, and continued running barefoot, with the confidence of someone who can judge distances between rocks and whose soles nothing can hurt. He reached a spot directly above the sea; there was a kind of shelf running around the cliff at the halfway point. There Amedeo stopped. On a flat ledge he arranged his clothes, carefully folded, and set the sandals on them, soles up, so no gust of wind would carry everything off (in reality, only the faintest breath of air was stirring, from the sea; but this precaution was obviously a habit with him). A little bag he was carrying turned into a rubber cushion; he blew into it until it had filled out, then set it down; and below it, at a point slightly sloping from that rocky ledge, he spread out his towel. He flung himself on it supine, and already his hands were opening his book at the marked page. So he lay stretched out on the ledge, in that sun glaring on all sides, his skin dry (his tan was opaque, irregular, as of one who takes the sun without any method but doesn't burn); on the rubber cushion he set his head sheathed in a white canvas cap, moistened (yes, he had also climbed down to a low rock, to dip his cap in the water), immobile except for his eyes (invisible behind his dark glasses), which 2 followed along the black and white lines the horse of Fabrizio del Dongo. Below him opened a little cove of greenish-blue water, transparent almost to the bottom. The rocks, according to their exposure, were bleached white or covered with algae. A little pebble beach was at their foot. Every now and then Amedeo raised his eyes to that broad view, lingered on a glinting of the surface, on the oblique dash of a crab; then he went back, gripped, to the page where Raskolnikov counted the steps that separated him from the old woman's door, or where Lucien de Rubempré, before sticking his head into the noose, gazed at the towers and roofs of the Conciergerie.

For some time Amedeo had tended to reduce his participation in active life to the minimum. Not that he didn't like action: on the contrary, love of action nourished his whole character, all his tastes; and yet, from one year to the next, the yearning to be someone who did things declined, declined, until he wondered if he had ever really harbored that yearning. His interest in action survived, however, in his pleasure in reading; his passion was always the narration of events, the stories, the tangle of human situations— nineteenth-century novels especially, but also memoirs and biographies, and so on down to thrillers and science fiction, which he didn't disdain but which gave him less satisfaction because they were short. Amedeo loved thick tomes, and in tackling them he felt the physical pleasure of under- taking a great task. Weighing them in his hand, thick, closely printed, squat, he would consider with some apprehension the number of pages, the length of the chapters, then venture into them, a bit reluctant at the beginning, without any desire to perform the initial chore of remembering the names, catching the drift of the story; then he would entrust himself to it, running along the lines, crossing the grid of the uniform page, and beyond the leaden print the flame and fire of battle appeared, the cannon- ball that, whistling through the sky, fell at the feet of Prince Andrei, and the shop filled with engravings and statues where Frédéric Moreau, his heart in his mouth, was to meet the Arnoux family. Beyond the surface of the page you entered a world where life was more alive than here on this side: like the surface of the water that separates us from that blue-and- green world, rifts as far as the eye can see, expanses of fine, ribbed sand, creatures half animal and half vegetable.

The sun beat down hard, the rock was burning, and after a while Amedeo felt he was one with the rock. He reached the end of the chapter, closed the book, inserted an advertising coupon to mark his place, took off his canvas cap and his glasses, stood up half dazed, and with broad leaps went down to the far end of the rock, where a group of kids were con- stantly, at all hours, diving in and climbing out. Amedeo stood erect on a shelf over the sea, not too high, a couple of yards above the water; his eyes, still dazzled, contemplated the luminous transparence below him, and all of a sudden he plunged. His dive was always the same: headlong, fairly correct, but with a certain stiffness. The passage from the sunny air to the tepid water would have been almost unnoticeable if it hadn't been abrupt. He didn't surface immediately: he liked to swim underwater, down, down, his belly almost scrapping bottom, as long as his breath held out. He very much enjoyed physical effort, setting himself difficult assignments (for this he came to read his book at the cape, making the climb on his bicycle, pedaling up furiously under the noonday sun). Every time, swimming underwater, he tried to reach a wall of rocks that rose at a certain point from the sandy bed and was covered by a thick patch of sea grasses. He surfaced among those rocks and swam around a bit; he began to do "the Australian crawl" methodically, but expending more energy than necessary; soon, tired of swimming with his face in the water, as if blind, he took to a freer side stroke; sight gave him more satisfaction than movement, and in a little while he gave up the side stroke to drift on his back, moving less and less regularly and steadily, until he stopped altogether, in a deadman's-float. And so he turned and twisted in that sea as in a bed without sides; he would set himself the goal of a sandbar to be reached, or limit the number of strokes, and he couldn't rest until he had carried out that task. For a while he would dawdle lazily, then he would head out to sea, taken by the desire to have nothing around him but sky and water; for a while he would move close to the rocks scattered along the cape, not to overlook any of the possible itineraries of that little archipelago. But as he swam, he realized that the curiosity occupying more and more of his mind was to know the outcome—for example—of the story of Albertine. Would Marcel find her again, or not? He swam furiously or floated idly, but his heart was between the pages of the book left behind on shore. And so, with rapid strokes, he would regain his rock, seek the place for climbing up, and, almost without realizing it, he would be up there again, rubbing the Turkish towel on his back. Sticking the canvas cap on his head once more, he would lie in the sun again, to begin the next chapter.

He was not, however, a hasty, voracious reader. He had reached the age   5
when rereading a book—for the second, third, or fourth time—affords more pleasure than a first reading. And yet he still had many continents to discover. Every summer, the most laborious packing before his departure for the sea involved the heavy suitcase to be filled with books. Following the whims and dictates of the months of city life, each year Amedeo would choose certain famous books to reread and certain authors to essay for the first time. And there, on the rock, he went through them, lingering over sentences, often raising his eyes from the page to ponder, to collect his thoughts. At a certain point, raising his eyes in this way, he saw that on the little pebble beach below, in the cove, a woman had appeared and was lying there.

She was deeply tanned, thin, not very young or particularly beautiful,   6
but nakedness became her (she wore a very tiny "two-piece," rolled up at the edges to get as much sun as she could), and Amedeo's eye was drawn

to her. He realized that as he read he was raising his eyes more and more often from the book to gaze into the air; this air was the air that lay between that woman and himself. Her face (she was stretched out on the sloping shore, on a rubber mattress, and at every flicker of his pupils Amedeo saw her legs, not shapely but harmonious, the excellently smooth belly, the bosom slim in a perhaps not unpleasant way but probably sagging a bit, the shoulders a bit too bony, and then the neck and the arms, and the face masked by the sunglasses and by the brim of the straw hat) was slightly lined, lively, aware, and ironic. Amedeo classified the type: the independent woman, on holiday by herself, who dislikes crowded beaches and prefers the more deserted rocks, and likes to lie there and become black as coal; he evaluated the amount of lazy sensuality and of chronic frustration there was in her; he thought fleetingly of the likelihood of a rapidly consummated fling, measured it against the prospect of a trite conversation, a program for the evening, probable logistic difficulties, the effort of concentration always required to become acquainted, even superficially, with a person; and he went on reading, convinced that this woman couldn't interest him at all.

But he had been lying on that stretch of rock for too long, or else those fleeting thoughts had left a wake of restlessness in him; anyway, he felt an ache, the hardness of the rock under the towel that was his only pallet began to chafe him. He got up to look for another spot where he could stretch out. For a moment, he hesitated between two places that seemed equally comfortable to him: one more distant from the little beach where the tanned lady was lying (actually behind an outcrop of rock that blocked the sight of her), the other closer. The thought of approaching and of then perhaps being led by some unforeseeable circumstance to start a conversation, and thus perforce to interrupt his reading, made him immediately prefer the farther spot; but when he thought it over, it really would look as if, the moment that lady had arrived, he wanted to run off, and this might seem a bit rude; so he picked the closer spot, since his reading absorbed him so much anyway that the view of the lady—not specially beautiful, for that matter—could hardly distract him. He lay on one side, holding the book so that it blocked the sight of her, but it was awkward to keep his arm at that height, and in the end he lowered it. Now, every time he had to start a new line, the same gaze that ran along the lines encountered, just beyond the edge of the page, the legs of the solitary vacationer. She, too, had shifted slightly, looking for a more comfortable position, and the fact that she had raised her knees and crossed her legs precisely in Amedeo's direction allowed him to observe better her proportions, not unattractive. In short, Amedeo (though a shaft of rock was sawing at his hip) couldn't have found a finer position: the pleasure he could derive from the sight of the tanned lady—a marginal pleasure, something extra, but not for that reason to be discarded, since it could be enjoyed with no effort—did not mar the pleasure of reading, but was inserted into its normal process, so that now he was sure he could go on reading without being tempted to look away.

Everything was calm; only the course of his reading flowed on, with the motionless landscape serving as frame; the tanned lady had become a necessary part of this landscape. Amedeo was naturally relying on his own ability to remain absolutely still for a long time, but he hadn't taken into account the woman's restlessness: now she rose, was standing, making her way among the stones toward the water. She had moved—Amedeo understood immediately—to get a closer look at a great medusa that a group of boys were bringing ashore, poking at it with lengths of reed. The tanned lady bent toward the overturned body of the medusa and was questioning the boys; her legs rose from wooden clogs with very high heels, unsuited to those rocks; her body, seen from behind as Amedeo now saw it, was that of a more attractive younger woman than she had first seemed to him. He thought that, for a man seeking a romance, that dialogue between her and the fisher-boys would have been a "classic" opening: approach, also remark on the capture of the medusa, and in that way engage her in conversation. The very thing he wouldn't have done for all the gold in the world! he added to himself, plunging again into his reading. 8

To be sure, this rule of conduct of his also prevented him from satisfying a natural curiosity concerning the medusa, which seemed, as he saw it there, of unusual dimensions, and also of a strange hue between pink and violet. This curiosity about marine animals was in no way a sidetrack, either; it was coherent with the nature of his passion for reading. At that moment, in any case, his concentration on the page he was reading—a long descriptive passage—had been relaxing; in short, it was absurd that to protect himself against the danger of starting a conversation with that woman he should also deny himself spontaneous and quite legitimate impulses such as that of amusing himself for a few minutes by taking a close look at a medusa. He shut his book at the marked page and stood up. His decision couldn't have been more timely: at that same moment the lady moved away from the little group of boys, preparing to return to her mattress. Amedeo realized this as he was approaching and felt the need of immediately saying something in a loud voice. He shouted to the kids, "Watch out! It could be dangerous!" 9

The boys, crouched around the animal, didn't even look up: they continued, with the lengths of reed they held in their hands, to try to raise it and turn it over; but the lady turned abruptly and went back to the shore, with a half-questioning, half-fearful air. "Oh, how frightening! Does it bite?" 10

"It you touch it, it stings," he explained and realized he was heading not toward the medusa but toward the lady, who, for some reason, covered her bosom with her arms in a useless shudder and cast almost furtive glances, first at the supine animal, then at Amedeo. He reassured her, and so, predictably, they started conversing; but it didn't matter, because 11

Amedeo would soon be going back to the book awaiting him: he only wanted to take a glance at the medusa. He led the tanned lady over, to lean into the center of the circle of boys. The lady was now observing with revulsion, her knuckles against her teeth, and at a certain point, as she and he were side by side, their arms came into contact and they delayed a moment before separating them. Amedeo then started talking about medusas. His direct experience wasn't great, but he had read some books by famous fishermen and underwater explorers, so—skipping the smaller fauna—he began promptly talking about the famous manta. The lady listened to him, displaying great interest and interjecting something from time to time, always irrelevantly, the way women will. "You see this red spot on my arm? That wasn't a medusa, was it?" Amedeo touched the spot, just above the elbow, and said no. It was a bit red because she had been leaning on it while lying down.

With that, it was all over. They said good-bye; she went back to her place, and he to his, where he resumed reading. It had been an interval lasting the right amount of time, neither more nor less, a human encounter, not unpleasant (the lady was polite, discreet, unassuming) precisely because it was barely adumbrated. In the book he now found a far fuller and more concrete attachment to reality, where everything had a meaning, an importance, a rhythm. Amedeo felt himself in a perfect situation: the printed page opened true life to him, profound and exciting, and, raising his eyes, he found a pleasant but casual juxtaposition of colors and sensations, an accessory and decorative world that couldn't commit him to anything. The tanned lady, from her mattress, gave him a smile and a wave; he replied also with a smile and a vague gesture, and immediately lowered his eyes. But the lady had said something.   12

"Eh?"   13

"You're reading. Do you read all the time?"   14

"Mmm . . ."   15

"Interesting?"   16

"Yes."   17

"Enjoy yourself!"   18

"Thank you."   19

He mustn't raise his eyes again. At least not until the end of the chapter.   20
He read it in a flash. The lady now had a cigarette in her mouth and motioned to him, as she pointed to it. Amedeo had the impression that for some time she had been trying to attract his attention. "I beg your pardon?"

". . . match. Forgive me. . . ."   21

"Oh, I'm very sorry. I don't smoke. . . ."   22

The chapter was finished. Amedeo rapidly read the first lines of the next   23
one, which he found surprisingly attractive, but to begin the next chapter without anxiety he had to resolve as quickly as possible the matter of the match. "Wait!" He stood up, began leaping among the rocks, half dazed by

the sun, until he found a little group of people smoking. He borrowed a box of matches, ran to the lady, lighted her cigarette, ran back to return the matches; and they said to him, "Keep them, you can keep them." He ran again to the lady to leave the matches with her, and she thanked him; he waited a moment before leaving her, but realized that after this delay he had to say something, and so he said, "You aren't swimming?"

"In a little while," the lady said. "What about you?" 24

"I've already had my swim." 25

"And you're not going to take another dip?" 26

"Yes, I'll read one more chapter, then have a swim again." 27

"Me, too, when I finish my cigarette, I'll dive in." 28

"See you later then." 29

"Later . . ." 30

This kind of appointment restored to Amedeo a calm such as he—now 31 he realized—had not known since the moment he became aware of the solitary lady: now his conscience was no longer oppressed by the thought of having to have any sort of relationship with that lady; everything was postponed to the moment of their swim—a swim he would have taken anyway, even if the lady hadn't been there—and for now he could abandon himself without remorse to the pleasure of reading. So thoroughly that he didn't notice when, at a certain point—before he had reached the end of the chapter—the lady finished her cigarette, stood up, and approached him to invite him to go swimming. He saw the clogs and the straight legs just beyond the book; his eyes moved up; he lowered them again to the page—the sun was dazzling—and read a few lines in haste, looked up again, and heard her say, "Isn't your head about to explode? I'm going to have a dip!" It was nice to stay there, to go on reading and look up every now and then. But since he could no longer put it off, Amedeo did something he never did: he skipped almost half a page, to the conclusion of the chapter, which he read, on the other hand, with great attention, and then he stood up. "Let's go. Shall we dive from the point there?"

After all the talk of diving, the lady cautiously slipped into the water 32 from a ledge on a level with it. Amedeo plunged headlong from a higher rock than usual. It was the hour of the still slow inclining of the sun. The sea was golden. They swam in that gold, somewhat separated: Amedeo at times sank for a few strokes underwater and amused himself by frightening the lady, swimming beneath her. Amused himself, after a fashion: it was kid stuff, of course, but for that matter, what else was there to do, anyway? Swimming with another person was slightly more tiresome than swimming alone, but the difference was minimal. Beyond the gold glints, the water's blue deepened, as if from down below rose an inky darkness. It was useless: nothing equaled the savor of life found in books. Skimming over some bearded rocks in mid-water and leading her, frightened (to help her onto a sandbar, he also clasped her hips and bosom, but his hands, from the immersion, had become almost insensitive, with white, wrinkled pads), Amedeo turned his gaze more and more often toward land, where the colored jacket of his book stood out. There was no other story, no other possible expectation beyond what he had left suspended, between the pages where his bookmark was; all the rest was an empty interval.

However, returning to shore, giving her a hand, drying himself, then 33 each rubbing the other's back, finally created a kind of intimacy, so that Amedeo felt it would have been impolite to go off on his own once more. "Well," he said, "I'll stretch out and read here; I'll go get my book and pillow." And *read:* he had taken care to warn her. She said, "Yes, fine. I'll smoke a cigarette and read *Annabella* a bit myself." She had one of those women's magazines with her, and so both of them could lie and read, each on his own. Her voice struck him like a drop of cold water on the nape of the neck, but she was only saying, "Why do you want to lie there on that hard rock? Come onto the mattress: I'll make room for you." The invitation was polite, the mattress was comfortable, and Amedeo gladly accepted. They lay there, he facing in one direction and she in the other. She didn't say another word, she leafed through those illustrated pages, and Amedeo managed to sink completely into his reading. It was a lingering sunset, when the heat and light hardly decline but remain only barely, sweetly attenuated. The novel Amedeo was reading had reached the point where the darkest secrets of characters and plot are revealed, and you move in a familiar world, and you achieve a kind of parity, an ease between author and reader: you proceed together, and you would like to go on forever.

On the rubber mattress it was possible to make those slight movements 34 necessary to keep the limbs from going to sleep, and one of his legs, in one direction, came to graze a leg of hers, in the other. He didn't mind this, and kept his leg there; and obviously she didn't mind, either, because she also refrained from moving. The sweetness of the contact mingled with the reading and, as far as Amedeo was concerned, made it the more complete; but for the lady it must have been different, because she rose, sat up, and said, "Really . . ."

Amedeo was forced to raise his head from the book. The woman was 35 looking at him, and her eyes were bitter.

"Something wrong?" he asked. 36

"Don't you ever get tired of reading?" she asked. "You could hardly be 37 called good company! Don't you know that, with women, you're supposed to make conversation?" she added; her half smile was perhaps meant only to be ironic, though to Amedeo, who at that moment would have paid anything rather than give up his novel, it seemed downright threatening. What have I got myself into, moving down here? he thought. Now it was clear that with this woman beside him he wouldn't read a line.

I must make her realize she's made a mistake, he thought, that I'm not 38 at all the type for a beach courtship, that I'm the sort it's best not to pay too much attention to. "Conversation," he said, aloud, "what kind of conversation?" and he extended his hand toward her. There, now: if I lay a hand on her, she will surely be insulted by such an unsuitable action, maybe she'll give me a slap and go away. But whether it was his own natural reserve, or there was a different, sweeter yearning that in reality he was pursuing, the caress, instead of being brutal and provocatory, was shy, melancholy, almost entreating: he grazed her throat with his fingers, lifted a little necklace she was wearing, and let it fall. The woman's reply consisted of a movement, first slow, as if resigned and a bit ironic—she lowered her chin to one side, to trap his hand—then rapid, as if in a calculated, aggressive spring: she bit the back of his hand. "Ow!" Amedeo cried. They moved apart.

"Is this how you make conversation?" the lady said. 39

There, Amedeo quickly reasoned, my way of making conversation 40 doesn't suit her, so there won't be any conversing, and now I can read; he had already started a new paragraph. But he was trying to deceive himself: he understood clearly that by now they had gone too far, that between him and the tanned lady a tension had been created that could no longer be interrupted; he also understood that he was the first to wish not to interrupt it, since in any case he wouldn't be able to return to the single tension of his reading, all intimate and interior. He could, on the contrary, try to make this exterior tension follow, so to speak, a course parallel to the other, so that he would not be obliged to renounce either the lady or the book.

Since she had sat up, with her back propped against a rock, he sat beside 41 her, put his arm around her shoulders, keeping his book on his knees. He turned toward her and kissed her. They moved apart, then kissed again. Then he lowered his head toward the book and resumed reading.

As long as he could, he wanted to continue reading. His fear was that he 42 wouldn't be able to finish the novel: the beginning of a summer affair could be considered the end of his calm hours of solitude, for a completely different rhythm would dominate his days of vacation; and obviously, when you are completely lost in reading a book, if you have to interrupt it, then pick it up again some time later, most of the pleasure is lost: you forget so many details, you never manage to become immersed in it as before.

The sun was gradually setting behind the next promontory, and then 43 the next, and the one after that, leaving remnants of color against the light. From the little coves of the cape, all the bathers had gone. Now the two of them were alone. Amedeo had his arm around the woman's shoulders, he was reading, he gave her kisses on the neck and on the ears—which it seemed to him she liked—and every now and then, when she turned, on the mouth; then he resumed reading. Perhaps this time he had found the ideal equilibrium: he could go on like this for a hundred pages or so. But once again it was she who wanted to change the situation. She began to stiffen, almost to reject him, and then said, "It's late. Let's go. I'm going to dress."

This abrupt decision opened up quite different prospects. Amedeo was   44
a bit disoriented, but he didn't stop to weigh the pros and cons. He had
reached a climax in the book, and her dimly heard words, "I'm going to
dress," had, in his mind, immediately been translated into these others:
While she dresses, I'll have time to read a few pages without being disturbed.

But she said, "Hold up the towel, please," addressing him as *tu* for   45
perhaps the first time. "I don't want anyone to see me." The precaution
was useless because the shore by now was deserted, but Amedeo con-
sented amiably, since he could hold up the towel while remaining seated
and so continue to read the book on his knees.

On the other side of the towel, the lady had undone her halter, paying   46
no attention to whether he was looking at her or not. Amedeo didn't know
whether to look at her, pretending to read, or to read, pretending to look
at her. He was interested in the one thing and the other, but looking at her
seemed too indiscreet, while going on reading seemed too indifferent. The
lady did not follow the usual method used by bathers who dress outdoors,
first putting on clothes and then removing the bathing suit underneath
them. No: now that her bosom was bared, she also took off the bottom of
her suit. This was when, for the first time, she turned her face toward him;
and it was a sad face, with a bitter curl to the mouth, and she shook her
head, shook her head and looked at him.

Since it has to happen, it might as well happen immediately, Amedeo   47
thought, diving forward, book in hand, one finger between the pages; but
what he read in that gaze—reproach, commiseration, dejection, as if to say:
Stupid, all right, we'll do it if it has to be done like this, but you don't
understand a thing, any more than the others—or, rather, what he did *not*
read, since he didn't know how to read gazes, but only vaguely sensed,
roused in him a moment of such transport toward the woman that, embracing her and falling onto the mattress with her, he only slightly turned
his head toward the book to make sure it didn't fall into the sea.

It had fallen, instead, right beside the mattress, open, but a few pages   48
had flipped over; and Amedeo, even in the ecstasy of his embraces, tried
to free one hand to put the bookmark at the right page. Nothing is more
irritating when you're eager to resume reading than to have to search
through the book, unable to find your place.

Their lovemaking was a perfect match. It could perhaps have been ex-   49
tended a bit longer: but, then, hadn't everything been lightning-fast in
their encounter?

Dusk was falling. Below, the rocks opened out, sloping, into a little   50
harbor. Now she had gone down there and was halfway into the water.
"Come down: we'll have a last swim. . . ." Amedeo, biting his lip, was
counting how many pages were left till the end.

Translated from the Italian by D. M. Low

STUDY QUESTIONS

1. In "The Adventure of a Reader," why is Amedeo addicted to reading? What does he get from it?
2. Identify the crucial moments where reading becomes a barrier to or substitute for authentic experience.
3. What does Amedeo's obsession reveal about the human condition?
4. Is there a moral to the story?

⊚ Bruno Schulz

*Bruno Schulz (1892–1942) was born and lived in Drogobycz, Poland, where
he was murdered by the Nazis. Like Kafka, who greatly influenced him,
Schulz made his Eastern European homeland the terrain of his short stories.
Schulz was a modernist whose evocative and at times enigmatic writing
conveyed his ironic and sorrowing attitude to the materialist ethos and
technology of contemporary civilization. To Schulz the chimney stacks of
Drogobycz were "the black pipes of a Devil's organ." His twofold attitude is
seen clearly in his comic/tragic creation of "the father," the central character
in* The Street of Crocodiles *(1934) from which "Birds" is taken. His
writings have been published in English as* The Complete Fiction of Bruno
Schulz: The Street of Crocodiles and Sanatorium Under the Sign of the
Hourglass *(1989).*

Birds

Came the yellow days of winter, filled with boredom. The rust-coloured   1
earth was covered with a threadbare, meagre tablecloth of snow full of
holes. There was not enough of it for some of the roofs and so they stood
there, black and brown, shingle and thatch, arks containing the sooty
expanses of attics—coal-black cathedrals, bristling with ribs of rafters,
beams and spars—the dark lungs of winter winds. Each dawn revealed
new chimney stacks and chimney pots which had emerged during the
hours of darkness, blown up by the night winds: the black pipes of a
Devil's organ. The chimney-sweeps could not get rid of the crows which in
the evening covered the branches of the trees around the church with
living black leaves, then took off, fluttering, and came back, each clinging
to its own place on its own branch, only to fly away at dawn in large flocks,
like gusts of soot, flakes of dirt, undulating and fantastic, blackening with

their insistent crowing the musty-yellow streaks of light. The days hardened with cold and boredom like last year's loaves of bread. One began to cut them with blunt knives without appetite, with a lazy indifference.

Father had stopped going out. He banked up the stoves, studied the 2 ever elusive essence of fire, experienced the salty, metallic taste and the smoky smell of wintry flames, the cool caresses of salamanders that licked the shiny soot in the throat of the chimney. He applied himself lovingly at that time to all manner of small repairs in the upper regions of the rooms. At all hours of the day one could see him crouched on top of a ladder, working at something under the ceiling, at the cornices over the tall windows, at the counter-weights and chains of the hanging lamps. Following the custom of house painters, he used a pair of steps as enormous stilts and he felt perfectly happy in that bird's eye perspective close to the sky, leaves and birds painted on the ceiling. He grew more and more remote from practical affairs. When my mother, worried and unhappy about his condition, tried to draw him into a conversation about business, about the payments due at the end of the month, he listened to her absent-mindedly, anxiety showing in his abstracted look. Sometimes he stopped her with a warning gesture of the hand in order to run to a corner of the room, put his ear to a crack in the floor and, by lifting the index finger of both hands, emphasise the gravity of the investigation, and begin to listen intently. At that time we did not yet understand the sad origin of these eccentricities, the deplorable complex which had been maturing in him.

Mother had no influence over him, but he gave a lot of respectful at- 3 tention to Adela. The cleaning of his room was to him a great and important ceremony, of which he always arranged to be a witness, watching all Adela's movements with a mixture of apprehension and pleasurable excitement. He ascribed to all her functions a deeper, symbolic meaning. When, with young firm gestures, the girl pushed a long-handled broom along the floor, father could hardly bear it. Tears would stream from his eyes, silent laughter transformed his face and his body was shaken by spasms of delight. He was ticklish to the point of madness. It was enough for Adela to waggle her fingers at him to imitate tickling, for him to rush through all the rooms in a wild panic, banging the doors after him, to fall at last flat on the bed in the furthest room and wriggle in convulsions of laughter, imagining the tickling which he found irresistible. Because of this, Adela's power over father was almost limitless.

At that time we noticed for the first time father's passionate interest in 4 animals. To begin with, it was the passion of the huntsman and the artist rolled into one. It was almost perhaps a deeper, biological sympathy of one creature for kindred, yet different forms of life, a kind of experimenting in the unexplored regions of existence. Only at a later stage did matters take that uncanny, complicated, essentially sinful and unnatural turn, which it is better not to bring into the light of day.

But it all began with the hatching out of birds' eggs. 5

With a great outlay of effort and money, father imported from Hamburg, 6 or Holland, or from zoological stations in Africa, birds' eggs on which he set enormous broody hens from Belgium. It was a process which fascinated me as well—this hatching out of the chicks, which were real anomalies of shape and colour. It was difficult to anticipate in these monsters with enormous, fantastic beaks which they opened wide immediately after birth, hissing greedily to show the backs of their throats, in these lizards with frail, naked bodies of hunchbacks, the future peacocks, pheasants, grouse or condors. Placed in cotton-wool, in baskets, this dragon brood lifted blind, wall-eyed heads on thin necks, croaking voicelessly from their dumb throats. My father would walk along the shelves, dressed in a green baize apron like a gardener in a hothouse of cacti, and conjure up from noth-ingness these blind bubbles, pulsating with life, these impotent bellies receiving the outside world only in the form of food, these growths on the surface of life, climbing blindfold towards the light. A few weeks' later when these blind buds of matter burst open, the rooms were filled with the bright chatter and scintillating chirruping of its new inhabitants. The birds perched on the curtain pelmets, on the tops of wardrobes; they nestled in the tangle of tin branches and the metal scrolls of the hanging lamps.

While father pored over his large ornithological textbooks and studied 7 their coloured plates, these feathery phantasms seemed to rise from the pages and fill the rooms with colours, with splashes of crimson, strips of sapphire, verdigris and silver. At feeding time they formed a motley, un-dulating bed on the floor, a living carpet which at the intrusion of a stranger would fall apart, scatter into fragments, flutter in the air, and finally settle high under the ceilings. I remember in particular a certain condor, an enormous bird with a featherless neck, its face wrinkled and knobbly. It was an emaciated ascetic, a Buddhist lama, full of imperturbable dignity in its behaviour, guided by the rigid ceremonial of its great species. When it sat facing my father, motionless in the monumental position of ageless Egyptian idols, its eye covered with a whitish cataract which it pulled down sideways over its pupil to shut itself up completely in the contem-plation of its dignified solitude—it seemed, with its stony profile, like an older brother of my father's. Its body and muscles seemed to be made of the same material, it had the same hard, wrinkled skin, the same desic-cated bony face, the same horny deep eye sockets. Even the hands, strong in the joints, my father's long thick hands with their rounded nails, had their counterpart in the condor's claws. I could not resist the impression, when looking at the sleeping condor, that I was in the presence of a mummy—a dried out, shrunken mummy of my father. I believe that even my mother noticed this strange resemblance although we never discussed the subject. It is significant that the condor used my father's chamberpot.

Not content with the hatching out of more and more new specimens, 8 my father arranged the marriages of birds in the attic, he sent out match-makers, he tied up eager attractive brides in the holes and crannies under the roof, and soon the roof of our house, an enormous double-ridged shingle roof, became a real birds' hostel, a Noah's ark to which all kinds of feathery creatures flew from far afield. Long after the liquidation of the birds' paradise, this tradition persisted in the avian world and during the period of spring migration our roof was besieged by whole flocks of cranes, pelicans, peacocks and sundry other birds. However, after a short period of splendour, the whole undertaking took a sorry turn.

It soon became necessary to move my father to two rooms at the top of 9 the house which had served as box rooms. We could hear from there, at dawn, the mixed clangour of birds' voices. The wooden walls of the attic rooms, helped by the resonance of the empty space under the gables, sounded with the roar, the flutterings, the crowing, the gurgling, the mating cries. For a few weeks father was lost to view. He only rarely came down to the flat and, when he did, we noticed that he seemed to have shrunk, to have become smaller and thinner. Occasionally forgetting himself, he would rise from his chair at table, wave his arms as if they were wings, and emit a long-drawn-out bird's call while his eyes misted over. Then, rather embarrassed, he would join us in laughing it off and try to turn the whole incident into a joke.

One day, during spring cleaning, Adela suddenly appeared in father's 10 birds' kingdom. Stopping in the doorway, she wrung her hands at the foetid smell that filled the room, the heaps of droppings covering the floor, the tables and the chairs. Without hesitation, she flung open a window and, with the help of a long broom, she prodded the whole mass of birds into life. A fiendish cloud of feathers and wings arose screaming and Adela, like a furious Maenad protected by the whirlwind of her thyrsus, danced the dance of destruction. My father, waving his arms in panic, tried to lift himself into the air with his feathered flock. Slowly the winged cloud thinned until at last Adela remained on the battlefield, exhausted and out of breath, along with my father who now, adopting a worried hang dog expression, was ready to accept complete defeat.

A moment later, my father came downstairs—a broken man, an exiled 11 king who had lost his throne and his kingdom.

Translated from the Polish by Celina Wieniewska

STUDY QUESTIONS

1. How does Schulz use the imagery of the town in winter to create a backdrop for the father's fantasy in "Birds"? What is this fantasy?
2. What are the attitudes of the other family members toward the father? Do their attitudes change? Does the father change?
3. What is the role of the maid, Adela? What is her power over the father? What is the author's attitude toward her?

4. For what are the birds metaphors?
5. Is it possible to make a comparison between the father in this story and the main character in Kafka's "A Hunger Artist"?

⑥ CZESLAW MILOSZ

Czeslaw Milosz (b. 1911) is a foremost Polish poet, novelist, essayist, and critic who has lived in exile since 1951. Milosz, like most Eastern Europeans, suffered the catastrophes of Fascism, World War II, and Stalinism. As a result, he is a pessimist who recognizes the constant reality of evil but who also argues that the cataclysms of the twentieth century have ended poetry's elitist isolation from the people. Mass suffering has made poetry ever more necessary and has reintegrated its voice into everyday culture. According to Milosz, poetry's lyrical qualities, the songs within it, engage people in reflection on ethical and metaphysical issues. Milosz has made it incumbent upon his own poetry to serve as a witness to the self and to history in a world in which evil is an ever-present contender. His poetry has been published in English in Selected Poems: Revised Collected Poems, 1931–1987 *(1988).*

My Faithful Mother Tongue

Faithful mother tongue,
I have been serving you.
Every night, I used to set before you little bowls of colors
so you could have your birch, your cricket, your finch
as preserved in my memory.   5

This lasted many years.
You were my native land; I lacked any other.
I believed that you would also be a messenger
between me and some good people
even if they were few, twenty, ten   10
or not born, as yet.

Now, I confess my doubt.
There are moments when it seems to me I have squandered my
    life.
For you are a tongue of the debased,   15

of the unreasonable, hating themselves
even more than they hate other nations,
a tongue of informers,
a tongue of the confused,
ill with their own innocence.   20

But without you, who am I?
Only a scholar in a distant country,
a success, without fears and humiliations.
Yes, who am I without you?
Just a philosopher, like everyone else.   25

I understand, this is meant as my education:
the glory of individuality is taken away,

Fortune spreads a red carpet
before the sinner in a morality play
while on the linen backdrop a magic lantern throws   30
images of human and divine torture.

Faithful mother tongue,
perhaps after all it's I who must try to save you.
So I will continue to set before you little bowls of colors
bright and pure if possible,   35
for what is needed in misfortune is a little order and beauty.

S T U D Y   Q U E S T I O N S

1. What is the central theme of "My Faithful Mother Tongue"? What are
   Milosz's feelings about his native land? What is the significance of the
   word "faithful"? How does the poet feel about his exile? What is the
   purpose of his allusion to "a morality play"?
2. Why does the poet refer to poems as "little bowls of color"? How do
   poems bring order?

THE FORMER SOVIET UNION

ᖩ ANNA AKHMATOVA

Anna Akhmatova (1888–1966) was a Russian poet and translator whose works form a significant link between the culture of pre-Revolutionary Russia and that of the Soviet Union. Associated from an early age with the Acmeist poets, who argued for and created a poetry of simplicity, clarity, and precision, by 1917 Akhmatova already had gained wide acclaim with three volumes of love lyrics. After the Revolution, she elected to stay in the Soviet Union for patriotic rather than political reasons. Her post-1917 work rooted itself in Russian national culture as it continued to explore the themes of love, grief, and betrayal. After her volume Anno Domini MCMXXI *(1922), she was not able to publish until World War II, when her great national poems were written and published. After the war, she again was forced into silence. After Stalin's death in 1953, she was gradually rehabilitated. When Akhmatova died, she was mourned as a poet and as a heroic national figure. All of her poetry is available in English translation in the two-volume* Complete Poems of Anna Akhmatova *(1990).*

"I Am Not One of Those Who Left the Land . . ."

I am not one of those who left the land
to the mercy of its enemies.
Their flattery leaves me cold,
my songs are not for them to praise.

But I pity the exile's lot.   5
Like a felon, like a man half-dead,
dark is your path, wanderer;
wormwood infects your foreign bread.

But here, in the murk of conflagration,
where scarcely a friend is left to know,   10
we, the survivors, do not flinch
from anything, not from a single blow.

Surely the reckoning will be made
after the passing of this cloud.
We are the people without tears,   15
straighter than you . . . more proud . . .

Translated from the Russian by Stanley Kunitz

The First Long-Range Artillery
Shell in Leningrad

A rainbow of people rushing around,
And suddenly everything changed completely,
This wasn't a normal city sound,
It came from unfamiliar country.
True, it resembled, like a brother,   5
One peal of thunder or another,
But every natural thunder contains
The moisture of clouds, fresh and high,
And the thirst of fields with drought gone dry,
A harbinger of happy rains,   10
And this was as arid as hell ever got,
And my distracted hearing would not
Believe it, if only because of the wild
Way it started, grew, and caught,
And how indifferently it brought   15
Death to my child.

Translated from the Russian by Lyn Coffin

STUDY QUESTIONS

1. Discuss how "I Am Not One of Those Who Left the Land . . ." is a
   response to exiles who left the Soviet Union after the revolution.
2. What is the poet's prognosis for the future?
3. Why are exiles associated with felons and the half-dead?

4. What is the strength and pride of the survivors?
5. Who is the speaker in "The First Long-Range Artillery Shell in Leningrad"? What is the event that the poem is recounting? What word choice has Akhmatova made so that the poem depicts a collective as well as an individual experience?
6. What are the similarities that the poet draws between thunder and artillery shells? What are the differences? How is the contrast she makes effective in emphasizing the death of the child?

⑥ ISAAC BABEL

Isaac Babel (1894–1941) was born in Odessa, Russia, of Jewish parents. A foremost Soviet modernist, Babel also has the distinction of being the first Jew to enter Russian literature as a Russian writer. Primarily a writer of short fiction, Babel's early stories, collected in Odessa Tales *(1927), center on the cultural values of his urban childhood in a Russia of growing anti-Semitism. World War I and the Bolshevik Revolution, however, were the seminal experiences in Babel's intellectual and artistic development. His mature work elaborates the conflict between imaginative idealism and corporeal reality. Babel's finest volume of short stories,* Red Cavalry *(1926), from which "My First Goose" is taken, is particularly noteworthy for its exemplary craftsmanship. With tight, economical writing, Babel renders in his stories the moment of subjective crisis and the resultant shift in an individual's inner consciousness.*

My First Goose

Savitsky, Commander of the VI Division, rose when he saw me, and I wondered at the beauty of his giant's body. He rose, the purple of his riding breeches and the crimson of his little tilted cap and the decorations stuck on his chest cleaving the hut as a standard cleaves the sky. A smell of scent and the sickly sweet freshness of soap emanated from him. His long legs were like girls sheathed to the neck in shining riding boots.

He smiled at me, struck his riding whip on the table, and drew toward him an order that the Chief of Staff had just finished dictating. It was an order for Ivan Chesnokov to advance on Chugunov-Dobryvodka with the regiment entrusted to him, to make contact with the enemy and destroy the same.

"For which destruction," the Commander began to write, smearing the whole sheet, "I make this same Chesnokov entirely responsible, up to and including the supreme penalty, and will if necessary strike him down on the spot; which you, Chesnokov, who have been working with me at the front for some months now, cannot doubt." 3

The Commander signed the order with a flourish, tossed it to his orderlies and turned upon me gray eyes that danced with merriment. 4

I handed him a paper with my appointment to the Staff of the Division. 5

"Put it down in the Order of the Day," said the Commander. "Put him down for every satisfaction save the front one. Can you read and write?" 6

"Yes, I can read and write," I replied, envying the flower and iron of that youthfulness. "I graduated in law from St. Petersburg University." 7

"Oh, are you one of those grinds?" he laughed. "Specs on your nose, too! What a nasty little object! They've sent you along without making any enquiries; and this is a hot place for specs. Think you'll get on with us?" 8

"I'll get on all right," I answered, and went off to the village with the quartermaster to find a billet for the night. 9

The quartermaster carried my trunk on his shoulder. Before us stretched the village street. The dying sun, round and yellow as a pumpkin, was giving up its roseate ghost to the skies. 10

We went up to a hut painted over with garlands. The quartermaster stopped, and said suddenly, with a guilty smile: 11

"Nuisance with specs. Can't do anything to stop it, either. Not a life for the brainy type here. But you go and mess up a lady, and a good lady too, and you'll have the boy patting you on the back." 12

He hesitated, my little trunk on his shoulder; then he came quite close to me, only to dart away again despairingly and run to the nearest yard. Cossacks were sitting there, shaving one another. 13

"Here, you soldiers," said the quartermaster, setting my little trunk down on the ground. "Comrade Savitsky's orders are that you're to take this chap in your billets, so no nonsense about it, because the chap's been through a lot in the learning line." 14

The quartermaster, purple in the face, left us without looking back. I raised my hand to my cap and saluted the Cossacks. A lad with long straight flaxen hair and the handsome face of the Ryazan Cossacks went over to my little trunk and tossed it out at the gate. Then he turned his back on me and with remarkable skill emitted a series of shameful noises. 15

"To your guns—number double-zero!" an older Cossack shouted at him, and burst out laughing. "Running fire!" 16

His guileless art exhausted, the lad made off. Then, crawling over the ground, I began to gather together the manuscripts and tattered garments that had fallen out of the trunk. I gathered them up and carried them to the other end of the yard. Near the hut, on a brick stove, stood a cauldron in which pork was cooking. The steam that rose from it was like the far-off smoke of home in the village, and it mingled hunger with desperate loneliness in my head. Then I covered my little broken trunk with hay, turning it into a pillow, and lay down on the ground to read in *Pravda* Lenin's speech at the Second Congress of the Comintern. The sun fell upon me from behind the toothed hillocks, the Cossacks trod on my feet, the lad made fun of me untiringly, the beloved lines came toward me along a thorny path and could not reach me. Then I put aside the paper and went out to the landlady, who was spinning on the porch. 17

"Landlady," I said, "I've got to eat." 18

The old woman raised to me the diffused whites of her purblind eyes and lowered them again. 19

"Comrade," she said, after a pause, "what with all this going on, I want to go and hang myself." 20

"Christ!" I muttered, and pushed the old woman in the chest with my fist. "You don't suppose I'm going to go into explanations with you, do you?" 21

And turning around I saw somebody's sword lying within reach. A severe-looking goose was waddling about the yard, inoffensively preening its feathers. I overtook it and pressed it to the ground. Its head cracked beneath my boot, cracked and emptied itself. The white neck lay stretched out in the dung, the wings twitched. 22

Her blind eyes and glasses glistening, the old woman picked up the slaughtered bird, wrapped it in her apron, and started to bear it off toward the kitchen. 23

"Comrade," she said to me, after a while, "I want to go and hang myself." And she closed the door behind her. 24

The Cossacks in the yard were already sitting around their cauldron. They sat motionless, stiff as heathen priests at a sacrifice, and had not looked at the goose. 25

"The lad's all right," one of them said, winking and scooping up the cabbage soup with his spoon. 26

The Cossacks commenced their supper with all the elegance and restraint of peasants who respect one another. And I wiped the sword with sand, went out at the gate, and came in again, depressed. Already the moon hung above the yard like a cheap earring. 27

"Hey, you," suddenly said Surovkov, an older Cossack. "Sit down and feed with us till your goose is done." 28

He produced a spare spoon from his boot and handed it to me. We supped up the cabbage soup they had made, and ate the pork. 29

"What's in the newspaper?" asked the flaxen-haired lad, making room   30
for me.

"Lenin writes in the paper," I said, pulling out *Pravda*. "Lenin writes   31
that there's a shortage of everything."

And loudly, like a triumphant man hard of hearing, I read Lenin's   32
speech out to the Cossacks.

Evening wrapped about me the quickening moisture of its twilight   33
sheets; evening laid a mother's hand upon my burning forehead. I read on
and rejoiced, spying out exultingly the secret curve of Lenin's straight line.

"Truth tickles everyone's nostrils," said Surovkov, when I had come to   34
the end. "The question is, how's it to be pulled from the heap. But he goes
and strikes at it straight off like a hen pecking at a grain!"

This remark about Lenin was made by Surovkov, platoon commander of   35
the Staff Squadron; after which we lay down to sleep in the hayloft. We
slept, all six of us, beneath a wooden roof that let in the stars, warming one
another, our legs intermingled. I dreamed: and in my dreams saw women.
But my heart, stained with bloodshed, grated and brimmed over.

Translated from the Russian by Walter Morison

STUDY QUESTIONS

1. Who is the protagonist and what is his initial reaction to the Commander in "My First Goose"?
2. Why does Babel employ irony throughout the story? Give examples
   and explain their function.
3. What does the goose symbolize? What are the similarities and differences between the protagonist's experiences with the goose and the
   narrator's experience with the bazaar in "Araby"?
4. Is it possible to identify the author's attitude toward the Russian Revolution? Look for indications.

⑥ OSIP MANDELSTAM

*Osip Mandelstam (1891–1938) was a preeminent Russian poet and essayist
who perished in one of Stalin's concentration camps. Mandelstam was born in
a Jewish family in Warsaw, grew up in St. Petersburg, and for several years
in his youth traveled and studied in Western Europe. Upon returning to
Russia in 1911, he helped launch, together with Anna Akhmatova and her*

husband, Nikolai Gumilyov, the Acmeist movement. His first volume of poetry, Stone (1913), is marked by its skill, its multilayered meanings, and its conceptual and imagistic weavings. In this work as in his later verse, Mandelstam evoked the poetic vision as the mediator of intellectual and spiritual consciousness. Highly erudite, his poetry ranged the reference points of Western culture. The complexity of his work was intensified by his almost riddlelike use of words with varied nuances and connotations. From 1928, Mandelstam experienced difficulty with Stalinist orthodoxy. In 1933, as a symbol of free expression, he wrote and recited "The Stalin Epigram," an outspoken satire on Stalin. For this he was sentenced to concentration camps. His poems from this period, which speak of loss and forebodings of death, convey, in the words of Omry Ronen, the "poignant mood of the Siberian convicts' traditional songs." Mandelstam's poems have been widely translated into English, including the volume Selected Poems of Osip Mandelstam (1984).

The Stalin Epigram[1]

Our lives no longer feel ground under them.
At ten paces you can't hear our words.

But whenever there's a snatch of talk
it turns to the Kremlin mountaineer,

the ten thick worms his fingers,
his words like measures of weight, 5

the huge laughing cockroaches on his top lip,
the glitter of his boot-rims.

Ringed with a scum of chicken-necked bosses
he toys with the tributes of half-men.

10

One whistles, another meouws, a third snivels.
He pokes out his finger and he alone goes boom.

He forges decrees in a line like horseshoes,
One for the groin, one the forehead, temple, eye.

---

1. This poem was the occasion of Mandelstam's first arrest when word of it reached the authorities (1934).

He rolls the executions on his tongue like berries.
He wishes he could hug them like big friends from home.   15

Translated from the Russian by Clarence Brown
and W. S. Merwin

Leningrad

I've come back to my city. These are my own old tears,
my own little veins, the swollen glands of my childhood.

So you're back. Open wide. Swallow
the fish-oil from the river lamps of Leningrad.

Open your eyes. Do you know this December day,   5
the egg-yolk with the deadly tar beaten into it?

Petersburg! I don't want to die yet!
You know my telephone numbers.

Petersburg! I've still got the addresses:
I can look up dead voices.   10

I live on back stairs, and the bell,
torn out nerves and all, jangles in my temples.

And I wait till morning for guests that I love,
and rattle the door in its chains.

Translated from the Russian by Clarence Brown
and W. S. Merwin

STUDY QUESTIONS

1. What images does Mandelstam use to voice his disdain for Stalin? For
   Stalin's henchmen? What does the poet imply about Stalin's motivations?
2. What effect has Stalin's terror had on society as a whole? In what ways
   is "The Stalin Epigram" a political act?
3. What is the speaker's attitude toward Leningrad? Later in the poem,

why does he refer to it as Petersburg? What does the use of the two names emphasize?

4. Why does the speaker recall a childhood illness? What relationship does the illness have to his present situation? What does the bell with its "turn out nerves and all" symbolize? How else does the speaker allude to the violence of the Revolution? How does the speaker evoke a mood of fear?

⑥ ANDREY VOZNESENSKY

Andrey Yoznesensky (b. 1933) is a Russian poet who rose to international prominence in the 1960s. Initially, he studied painting and architecture, but he turned to a career in poetry after receiving signal encouragement from Boris Pasternak. The inspiration for Voznesensky's work comes from his pastoral identity with the Russian motherland. Its landscape and its people are the fabric of his poetry. In writing, Voznesensky employs a mixed language in which he intertwines formal diction with colloquial expressions so that his verse has a folklike quality. Critics have referred to Voznesensky's long poems as "lyrical reportage" because of their themes and aural qualities. This term is also apt because of the didactic thrust of some of his work. In the post-Stalinist era, the writing and the public reading of poetry came to have an important sociopolitical function. Voznesensky's poetry, with its multiple meanings and its postulation of moral questions, keenly expresses Soviet society's self-examination. His work, including Antiworlds *(1966),* Voznesensky: Selected Poems *(1966), and* An Arrow in the Wall *(1957), has been widely translated by English-speaking poets.*

Foggy Street

A fogbound suburb, like a fat
Cock-pigeon.
Like anchor-buoys
The militiamen.
    Foggy weather.   5
What century is it? What era?
Everything's shattered, delirious.
The people, as if
    they'd been taken apart.

I roam through the streets 10
Or rather, struggle through cottonwool.
Noses. Small headlights. . . . Vizors. Everything double.
Your galoshes, sir. You've got the right head, I trust?

That is
          the way she is. Soon as her lips leave mine 15
She is at least two, and alive, yet not mine anymore—
A widow: a moment ago
                    she was yours, and now: a stranger.

      I brush past people, lampposts. . . . Venus?
      No, an ice-cream vendor. Friends? 20
      O they are hothouse flowers. . . . And you?

You just stand there, pinching your earlobes,
All alone, in that enormous cape.
      And what is that? A mustache?!
      And hoarfrost in that hairy old ear! 25

Stumble on, fight and live through the fog,
                          and you'll never know
Whose cheek you are touching—Ouch! Murk, murk—
      No one can hear you shout. . . .
      How good it is 30
                when the day
                      breaks clear!

Translated from the Russian by Anselm Hollo

STUDY QUESTIONS

1. In "Foggy Street," what does the fog represent? How does the poet
   define the human condition?
2. Do the last lines of the poem convey a political message?

⑤ Tatyana Tolstaya

Tatyana Tolstaya (b. 1951) is a gifted Russian writer who comes from an illustrious literary family. Her grandfather was Alexsey Tolstoy, an important novelist of the 1920s and 1930s, while the great nineteenth-century novelist Leo Tolstoy was a distant relative. Tolstaya studied philology, has worked as an editor of Oriental literature, and recently has been a visiting lecturer in Russian literature at several American universities. She published her first volume of short stories, On the Golden Porch *(1989), in 1983. The work was widely acclaimed for its effervescent style and its skillful juxtaposition of illusion and reality. Tolstaya has said that she writes about the ordinary individual who meets with the disappointments of life. Her literary interest is in the person "who was not taken to the holiday celebration." Her stories, though dealing with disillusionment, do not leave a sense of bitterness. She has the gift for depicting reality in a life-affirming manner.*

Fire and Dust

Where is she now, that lunatic Svetlana, nicknamed Pipka, about whom some people, with the nonchalance of youth, used to say, "But I mean, is Pipka really human?" and others, exasperated: "Why do you let her in? Keep an eye on your books! She'll walk off with everything!" No, they were wrong: The only things assignable to Pipka's conscience are a light blue Simenon and a white wool sweater with knitted buttons, and it was already darned at the elbow anyway. And to hell with the sweater! Much more valuable things had vanished since that time: Rimma's radiant youth; the childhood of her children; the freshness of her hopes, blue as the morning sky; the secret, joyful trust with which Rimma listened to the voice of the future whispering for her alone—what laurels, flowers, islands, and rainbows had not been promised to her, and where is it all? She didn't begrudge the sweater; Rimma herself had forcibly thrust Svetlana into that little-needed sweater when she threw the insane girl, half dressed as always, out into the raging autumn one cold, branch-lashed Moscow midnight. Rimma, already in her nightgown, shifted impatiently from one foot to the other in the doorway, pressing her shivering legs together; she kept nodding, advancing, showing Svetlana the door, but Svetlana was trying to get something out, to finish what she had to say, with a nervous giggle, a quick shrug of the shoulders, and in her pretty white face black eyes burned like an insane abyss and the wet abyss of her mouth mumbled in a hurried dither—a hideous black mouth, where the stumps of the teeth made you think of old, charred ruins. Rimma advanced, gaining ground inch by inch, and Svetlana talked on and on and on, waving her hands all

1

about as if she were doing exercises—nocturnal, night-owl, unbelievable exercises—and then, demonstrating the enormous size of something—but Rimma wasn't listening—she gestured so expansively that she smashed her knuckles against the wall and in her surprise said nothing for a moment, pressing the salty joints to her lips, which seemed singed by her disconnected pronouncements. That was when the sweater was shoved at her—you'll warm up in the taxi—the door was slammed shut, and Rimma, vexed and laughing, ran to Fedya under the warm blanket. "I barely managed to get rid of her." The children tossed and turned in their sleep. Tomorrow was an early day. "You could have let her spend the night," muttered Fedya through his sleep, through the warmth, and he was very handsome in the red glow of the night-light. Spend the night? Never! And where? In old man Ashkenazi's room? The old man tossed and turned incessantly on his worn-out couch, smoked something thick and smelly, coughed, and in the middle of the night would get up and go to the kitchen for a drink of water from the tap, but all in all it wasn't bad, he wasn't a bother. When guests came he would loan chairs, get out a jar of marinated mushrooms, untangle rats' nests of sticky tinned fruit drops for the children. They would seat him at one end of the table and he would chuckle, swing his legs, which didn't reach the floor, and smoke into his sleeve: "Never mind, you young people, be patient—I'll die soon and the whole apartment will be yours." "May you live to be a hundred, David Danilich," Rimma would reassure him, but still it was pleasant to dream about the time when she would be mistress of an entire apartment, not a communal one, but her own, when she would do major remodeling—cover the preposterous five-cornered kitchen from top to bottom in tile and get a new stove. Fedya would defend his dissertation, the children would go to school—English, music, figure skating. . . . What else could she imagine? A lot of people envied them in advance. But of course it was not tile, not well-rounded children that shone from the wide-open spaces of the future like a rainbow-colored fire, a sparkling arc of wild rapture (and Rimma honestly wished old man Ashkenazi long life—there's time enough for everything); no, something greater, something completely different, important, overwhelming, and grand clamored and glittered up ahead, as though Rimma's ship, sailing along a dark channel through blossoming reeds, were on the verge of coming into the green, happy, raging sea.

In the meantime, life was not quite real, it was life in anticipation, lived out of a suitcase, slipshod, lightweight—a pile of junk in the hallway, midnight guests: Petyunya in his sky-blue tie, the childless Elya and Alyosha, and others; Pipka's nocturnal visits and her outrageous conversations. How hideous Pipka was with those black detoothed stumps—yet lots of people liked her, and often at the end of a festive evening one of the men couldn't be accounted for: Pipka had whisked him away while no one was looking—always in a taxi—to her place in Perlovka. That was where she holed up, renting a cheap little wooden shack with a front yard. At one time Rimma even worried about Fedya—he was flighty and Pipka was crazy and capable of anything. If not for those rotten stumps in her hurried mouth, it might have been worth thinking about not allowing her into the family home. Especially since Fedya often said mysteriously, "If Svetlanka would just keep her mouth shut, you could actually talk to her!" And she was forever trembling, half dressed, or dressed topsy-turvy: crusty stiff children's boots on bare feet in the middle of winter, her hands all chapped.

No one knew where Pipka went, just as no one knew where she actually 3
came from—she had simply shown up and that was that. Her stories were outrageous and confused: It seems she'd wanted to go to drama school and had even been accepted, but in a market she met some pickled-garlic merchants and was gagged and taken off to Baku in a white Volga with no license plates. There they supposedly ravished her, knocked out half her teeth, and abandoned her, naked, on the seashore in a pool of oil. The next morning, she claimed, she was found by a wild mountain man in transit through Baku; he carried her off to his hut high in the mountains and held her there all summer, feeding her melon from a knife through the cracks in his shack, and in the fall he traded her to a visiting ethnographer for a watch with no hands. Still completely naked, she and the ethnographer, who called her Svetka-Pipetka, which is where she got her nickname, holed up in an abandoned watchtower, dating back to Shamil's time, that was covered with rotten Persian rugs—the ethnographer studied their patterns with a magnifying glass. At night eagles defecated on them. "Shoo, shoo, damn you!" Pipka would act it out, racing around the room with an indignant expression, frightening the children. When winter came, the ethnographer left to go higher into the mountains, and at the first snowfall Svetlana descended into a valley where the people calculated time by the lunar calendar and shot at a schoolmarm through the school window, publicly marking the number of casualties with notches on a post in the center of the bazaar. There were more than eight hundred notches; the Regional Department of Public Education couldn't manage—several pedagogical institutes worked exclusively for this valley. There Svetlana had an affair with the local store manager. But she quickly dumped him, finding him insufficiently manly: Instead of sleeping as a Caucasian horseman should, on his back in a *papakha* fur cap with a sword at his side, fiercely displaying his wide, muscular shoulders, the local store manager would curl up, snuffle and whimper in his sleep, shuffling his legs; he explained in his own defense that he dreamed of gunfire. Toward spring Pipka reached Moscow on foot, sleeping in haystacks and avoiding the high roads; several times she was bitten by dogs. For some reason she went through the Ural Mountains. But then geography gave her even more trouble than her private life; she called the Urals the Caucasus, and placed Baku on the Black Sea. Maybe there really was some kind of truth in her nightmarish stories, who knows. Rimma was used to them and hardly listened; she thought her own thoughts, surrendering to her own unhur-

ried daydreams. Almost nobody listened to Pipka anyway—after all, was she really human? Only occasionally some newcomer, enthralled by Pipka's nonsense, by the disgorged fountain of tales, would exclaim in joyous amazement, "Boy, does she ever lay it on! A thousand and one nights!" That was the type Pipka usually carried off to her semifantastic Perlovka, if it actually existed: Was it really possible to believe that Svetlana was employed by the owners to dig troughs around the dahlias and that she ate fish-bone meal along with the chickens? As always, during a simple gathering of friends, amid the noise and chatter and clatter of forks, a dreamy somnolence overtook Rimma, marvelous dream-visions real as life appeared, pink and blue mists, white sails; the roar of the ocean could be heard, far off, beckoning, like the steady roar that issued from the giant shell gracing the sideboard. Rimma loved to close her eyes and put the shell to her ear—from those monstrous, salmon-colored jaws you could hear the call of a faraway country, so far away that a place could no longer be found for it on the globe, and it smoothly ascended, this country, and settled in the sky with all of its lakes, parrots, and crashing coastal breakers. And Rimma also glided in the sky amid pink, feathery clouds— everything promised by life will come to pass. No need to stir, no need to hurry, everything will come all by itself. To slip silently down dark channels . . . to listen to the approaching roar of the ocean . . . Rimma would open her eyes and, smiling, look at her guests through the tobacco smoke and dreams—at lazy, satisfied Fedya, at David Danilich swinging his legs— and slowly return to earth. And it will start with something insignificant . . . it will start bit by bit. . . . She felt the ground with her legs, which were weakened by the flight. Oh, the apartment would have to be first, of course. The old man's room would be the bedroom. Baby-blue curtains. No, white ones. White, silky, fluffy, gathered ones. And a white bed. Sunday morning. In a white peignoir, her hair flowing (time to let her hair grow out, but the peignoir had already been secretly bought, she couldn't resist) . . . Rimma would stroll through the apartment to the kitchen. . . . The aroma of coffee . . . To new acquaintances she would say, "And in this room, where the bedroom is now, an old man used to live. . . . So sweet . . . He wasn't a bother. And after his death we took it over. . . . It's a shame—such a wonderful old man!" Rimma would rock back and forth on her chair, smiling at the still-living old man: "You smoke a lot, David Danilich. You should take care of yourself." The old man only coughed and waved her away, as if to say, Never mind. I'm not long for this place. Why bother?

How lovely it was to float and meander through time—and time meanders through you and melts away behind, and the sound of the sea keeps beckoning; time to take a trip to the South and breathe the sea air, stand on the shore stretching your arms and listening to the wind. . . . How sweetly life melts away—the children, and loving Fedya, and the anticipation of the white bedroom. The guests are envious; well, my dears, go ahead and

4

envy, enormous happiness awaits me up ahead—what kind, I won't say, I myself don't know, but voices whisper, "Just wait, wait!" Petyunya, sitting over there biting his nails, is envious. He doesn't have a wife or an apartment, he's puny, he's ambitious, he wants to be a journalist, he loves bright ties, we should give him ours, the orange one, we don't need it, happiness awaits us. Elya and Alyosha are also envious, they don't have any children, they've gone and gotten a dog, how boring. Old man Ashkenazi sitting there, he's envious of my youth, my white bedroom, my ocean roar; farewell, old man, it will soon be time for you to leave, your eyes shut tight under copper coins. Now Svetlana . . . she envies no one, she has everything, but it's only imaginary, her eyes and her frightful mouth burn like fire—Fedya shouldn't sit so close—her talk is crazy, kingdoms rise and fall by the dozens in her head all in one night. Fedya shouldn't sit so close. Fedya! Come sit over here. She's spinning her yarns and you're all ears?

Life was happy and easy, they laughed at Petyunya, at his passion for ties, said he was destined for a great journalistic future, asked him ahead of time not to put on airs if he traveled overseas; Petyunya was embarrassed, and he wrinkled his mousy little face: What are you talking about, guys, let's hope I make it through the institute! 5

Petyunya was wonderful, but sort of rumpled, and, moreover, he tried to play up to Rimma, though only indirectly, to be sure: He would slice onions for her in the kitchen and hint that he, frankly, had plans for his life. Oh-ho! Rimma laughed. What plans could he have, when such incredible things awaited her! You'd be better off setting your sights on Elya, she'll dump Alyosha anyway. Or else Svetka-Pipetka over there. Pipetka was getting married, Petyunya said. To whom, I'd like to know? 6

It was soon discovered to whom: to old man Ashkenazi. The old man, feeling sorry for Pipka's little feet in their children's boots, for her frozen little hands, distressed about her nighttime taxi expenses, and all in all succumbing to a teary, senile altruism, conceived the idea—behind Rimma's back!—of marrying that vagrant who blazed with a black fire and of registering her, naturally, in the living space promised to Rimma and Fedya. A scene complete with sedatives ensued. "You should be ashamed, shame on you!" cried Rimma, her voice breaking. "But I've got nothing to be ashamed of," answered the old man from the couch, where he lay amid broken springs, his head thrown back to stop the flow of blood from his nose. Rimma applied cold compresses and sat up with him all night. When the old man dozed off, his breathing shallow and irregular, she measured the window in his room. Yes, the white material was the right width. Light blue wallpaper over here. In the morning they made up. Rimma forgave the old man, he cried, she gave him Fedya's shirt and fed him hot pancakes. Svetlana heard something about it and didn't show up for a long time. Then Petyunya also vanished and the guess was that Svetlana had carried him off to Perlovka. Everyone who ended up there disappeared for 7 ages, and when they returned they were not themselves for quite some time.

Petyunya showed up one evening six months later with a vague expression on his face, his trousers covered to the waist in mud. Rimma had trouble getting anything out of him. Yes, he had been there. He helped Pipka with the work. It was a very hard life. Everything was very complicated. He had walked all the way from Perlovka. Why was he covered in mud? Oh, that . . . He and Pipka had wandered around Perlovka with kerosene lanterns all last night, looking for the right house. A Circassian had given birth to a puppy. Yes, that's what happened. Yes, I know— Petyunya pressed his hands to his chest—I know that there aren't any Circassian people in Perlovka. This was the last one. Svetlana says she knows for sure. It's a very good story for the "Only Facts" column of the newspaper. "What's got into you, are you off your rocker too?" asked Rimma, blinking. "Why do you say that? I saw the puppy myself." "And the Circassian?" "They weren't letting anyone in to see him. It was the middle of the night, after all." "Sleep it off," said Rimma. They put Petyunya in the hall with the junk. Rimma fretted, tossing and turning all night, and in the morning she decided that "Circassian" was a dog's name. But at breakfast she couldn't bring herself to increase the lunacy with questions, and, anyway, Petyunya was glum and soon left. 8

Then all of a sudden Svetlana had to move her things from Perlovka to some other place right away—figuring out the geography of it was useless; it had to be by taxi, of course, and for some reason Fedya's help was absolutely essential. Hesitating a bit, Rimma let him go. It was ten in the morning, so it wasn't very likely that anything could . . . He returned at three that night, behaving very strangely. "Where were you?" Rimma was waiting in the hall in her nightgown. "You see, there were a lot of complications. . . . We ended up having to go to Serpukhov, she has twins in the Children's Home there." "What twins?" Rimma shouted. "Tiny ones, about a year old, I think. Siamese. Their heads are joined together. Karina and Angela." "What heads? Are you out of your mind? She's been coming here for ages. Have you ever noticed her having a baby?" No, of course he hadn't noticed her having a baby or anything like that, but they really did go to Serpukhov, and they did drop off a package: frozen hake. That's right, hake for the twins. He himself stood in the cashier's line to pay for the fish. Rimma burst into tears and slammed the door. Fedya remained in the hall, scratching at the door and swearing that he himself didn't understand anything, but that they were called Karina and Angela—of that he was sure. 9

After that Pipka disappeared again for a long while, and the episode was forgotten. But for the first time something in Rimma cracked—she looked around and saw that time kept flowing on, yet the future still hadn't arrived, and Fedya was not so handsome anymore, and the children had picked up bad words on the street, and old man Ashkenazi coughed and 10 lived on, and wrinkles had already crept up to her eyes and mouth, and the junk in the hallway was still just lying there. And the roar of the ocean had grown muffled, and they hadn't gone to the South after all—everything had been put off until the future, which just didn't want to arrive.

Troubled days followed. Rimma lost heart; she kept trying to understand at what point she'd taken the wrong path leading to that far-off, melodious happiness, and often she sat lost in thought; meanwhile, her children were growing up and Fedya sat in front of the television, not wanting to write his dissertation, and outside the window either a cottony blizzard blew or an insipid city sun peeked through summer clouds. Their friends grew old, it became harder for them to get themselves going, Petyunya had completely vanished somewhere, flashy ties went out of fashion, Elya and Alyosha got another unruly dog and there was no one to leave it with evenings. At Rimma's job new coworkers had appeared, big Lucy and little Lucy, but they didn't know about Rimma's plans for happiness and didn't envy her; rather, they envied Kira from the planning department, who had a large, expensive wardrobe, who exchanged hats for books, books for meat, meat for medicine or hard-to-come-by theater tickets, and spoke in an irritated tone of voice to someone on the phone: "But you know perfectly well how much I love jellied tongue."

And one evening, when Fedya was watching television and Rimma was sitting with her head on the table listening to the old man coughing on the other side of the wall, in burst Pipka, all fire and flame, rosy-cheeked, looking younger, as sometimes happens with insane people, and smiling, her blazing mouth full of sparkling white teeth. "Thirty-six!" she shouted from the threshold and banged her fist on the top of the doorway. "Thirty-six what?" said Rimma, lifting her head from the table. "Thirty-six teeth!" said Pipka. And she told the story of how she got a job as a cabin boy on a steamer bound for Japan, and since the steamer was already overstaffed she had to sleep in a cauldron with the meat and rice, and the captain had rendered her honor but the captain's assistant had rent it; and a rich Japanese man fell in love with her on the way and wanted to arrange their marriage by telegraph without delay, but they couldn't find the right Japanese characters and the deal fell apart; and then—while they were washing the meat-and-rice cauldron in some port or other—she was kidnapped by a pirate junk and sold to a rich plantation owner, and she spent a year working on Malaysian hemp plantations, where she was bought by a rich Englishman for an Olympics memorial ruble, which, as everyone knows, is highly prized among Malaysian numismatists. The Englishman carried her off to misty Albion; first, he lost her in the thick mist, but then he found her, and to celebrate he footed the bill for the most expensive and fashionable set of thirty-six teeth, which only a real moneybags could afford. He gave her smoked pony for the road and now she, Pipka, was finally going to Perlovka to get her things. "Open your mouth," said Rimma with hatred. And in Svetlana's readily opened mouth she counted, fighting

11

12

vertigo, all thirty-six—how they fit in there was beyond comprehension, but they were indeed teeth. "I can chew steel wire now. If you want, I'll bite off a bit of the cornice," the monster started to say, and Fedya was watching with great interest, but Rimma began waving her hands: That's all, that's it, it's late, we want to sleep, and she thrust taxi money on her, and pushed her toward the door, and threw her the volume of Simenon. For heaven's sake, take it, read a little tonight, only just leave! And Pipka left, clutching the walls to no avail, and no one ever saw her again. "Fedya, shall we take a trip to the South?" Rimma asked. "Absolutely," Fedya answered readily, as he had done many times over the years. That's all right, then. That means we will go after all. To the South! And she listened to the voice that still faintly whispered something about the future, about happiness, about long, sound sleep in a white bedroom, but the words were already difficult to make out. "Hey, look—it's Petyunya!" said Fedya in surprise. On the television screen, under palm trees, small and sullen, with a microphone in his hands, stood Petyunya, and he was cursing some kind of cocoa plantations, and the black people passing by turned around to look at him, and his huge tie erupted like a pustular African sunrise, but there wasn't a whole lot of happiness to be seen on his face either.

Now Rimma knew that they'd all been tricked, but by whom and when, 13 she couldn't remember. She sorted through it all day by day, searching for a mistake, but didn't find any. Everything was somehow covered with dust. Occasionally—strange to say—she felt like talking it over with Pipka, but Pipka didn't come around anymore.

It was summer again, the heat had arrived, and through the thick dust 14 the voice from the future once again whispered something. Rimma's children were grown, one had married and the other was in the army, the apartment was empty, and she had trouble sleeping at night—the old man coughed incessantly on the other side of the wall. Rimma no longer wanted to turn the old man's room into a bedroom, and she didn't have the white peignoir anymore—moths from the junk in the hall had eaten it, without even looking at what they ate. Arriving at work, Rimma complained to big Lucy and little Lucy that moths were now devouring even German things; little Lucy gasped, holding her palms to her cheeks, and big Lucy grew angry and glum. "If you want to outfit yourselves, girls," said the experienced Kira, breaking away from her telephonic machinations, "I can take you to a place. I have a friend. Her daughter just got back from Bahrain. You can pay later. It's good stuff. Vera Esafovna got seven hundred rubles' worth on Saturday. They lived well over there in Bahrain. Swam in a pool, they want to go again." "Why don't we?" said big Lucy. "Oh, I have so many debts," whispered the little one.

"Quick, quick, girls, we'll take a taxi," said Kira, hurrying them. "We 15 can make it during lunch break." And, feeling like schoolgirls cutting class, they piled into a cab, inundating one another with the smells of perfume and lit cigarettes, and whirled off down hot summer side streets strewn with sunny linden-tree husks and patches of warm shadow; a southerly wind was blowing, and through the gasoline fumes it carried the exultation and brilliance of the far-off South; the blazing blue heavens, the mirrorlike shimmer of vast seas, wild happiness, wild freedom, the madness of hopes coming true. . . . Hopes for what? God only knows! And in the apartment they entered, holding their breath in anticipation of a happy consumer adventure, there was also a warm wind fluttering and billowing the white tulle on the windows and doors, which were opened wide onto a spacious balcony—everything here was spacious, large, free. Rimma felt a little envious of this apartment. A powerful woman—the mistress of the goods for sale—swiftly threw open the secret room. The goods were rumpled, heaped up in television boxes on an ever-rising double bed, and reflected in the mirror of a massive wardrobe. "Dig in," ordered Kira, standing in the doorway. Trembling, the women buried their hands in boxes crammed with silky, velvety, see-through, gold-embroidered stuff; they pulled things out, yanking, getting tangled in ribbons and ruffles; their hands fished things out while their eyes already groped for something else, an alluring bow or frill; inside Rimma a vein twitched rapidly, her ears burned, and her mouth was dry. It was all like a dream. And, as happens in the cruel scenario of dreams, a certain crack in the harmony soon emerged and began to grow, a secret defect, which threatened to resound in catastrophe. These things—what is this anyway?—weren't right, they weren't what they seemed at first. The eye began to distinguish the cheapness of these gaudy, fake gauze skirts hardly fit for a corps de ballet, the pretentiousness of those violet turkey-wattle jabots, and the unfashionable lines of those thick velvet jackets; these were throwaways; we were invited to the leftovers of someone else's feast; others have already rummaged here, have already trampled the ground; someone's greedy hands have already defiled the magical boxes, snatched up and carried off those very things, the real ones that made the heart beat and that particular vein twitch. Rimma fell on other boxes, groped about the disheveled double bed, but neither there, nor there . . . And the things that she grabbed in despair from the piles and held up to herself, anxiously looking in the mirror, were laughably small, short, or ridiculous. Life had gone and the voice of the future was singing for others. The woman, the owner of the goods, sat like Buddha and watched, astute and scornful. "What about this?" Rimma pointed at the clothes hanging on coat hangers along the walls, fluttering in the warm breeze. "Sold. That's sold too." "Is there anything—in my size?" "Go on, give her something," Kira, who was propped up against the wall, said to the woman. Thinking for a moment, the woman pulled out something gray from behind her back, and Rimma, hurriedly undressing, revealing all the secrets of her cheap undergarments to her girlfriends, slithered into the appropriate openings. Adjusting and tugging, she inspected her mercilessly bright reflection. The warm breeze still played about in the sunny room, indifferent to the commerce being conducted.

She didn't exactly understand what she had put on; she gazed miserably at the little black hairs on her white legs, which looked as if they'd gotten soggy or been stored in dark trunks all winter, at her neck, its goosey flesh stretched out in fright, at her flattened hair, her stomach, her wrinkles, the dark circles under her eyes. The dress smelled of other people—others had already tried it on. "Very good. It's you. Take it," pressured Kira, who was the woman's secret confederate. The woman watched, silent and disdainful. "How much?" "Two hundred." Rimma choked, trying to tear off the poisoned clothing. "It's awfully stylish, Rimmochka," said little Lucy guiltily. And to consummate the humiliation, the wind blew open the door to the next room, revealing a heavenly vision: the woman's young, divinely sculpted daughter, suntanned to a nut-colored glow—the one who had come back from Bahrain, who darted out of swimming pools filled with clear blue water—a flash of white garments, blue eyes; the woman got up and shut the door. This sight was not for mortal eyes.

The southerly wind blew the refuse of blossoming lindens into the old   16
entryway, warmed the shabby walls. Little Lucy descended the stairs sideways, hugging the mountain of things she'd chosen, almost crying—once again she'd gotten herself into terrible debt. Big Lucy kept a hostile silence. Rimma walked with her teeth clenched: The summer day had darkened, destiny had teased her and had a laugh. And she already knew that the blouse she'd bought at the last minute in a fit of desperation was junk, last year's leaves, Satan's gold, fated to turn into rotten scraps in the morning, a husk sucked and spit out by the blue-eyed Bahrain houri.

She rode in the saddened, silent taxi and said to herself, Still, I do have   17
Fedya and the children. But the comfort was false, feeble, it was all over, life had shown its empty face, its matted hair and sunken eye sockets. And she imagined the long-desired South, where she'd been dying to go for so many years, as yellowed and dusty, with bunches of prickly dry plants, with spittle and scraps of paper rocking on brackish waves. And at home there was the grimy old communal apartment and the immortal old man, Ashkenazi, and Fedya, whom she knew so well she could scream, and the whole viscous stream of years to come, not yet lived but already known, through which she would have to drag herself as through dust covering a road to the knees, the chest, the neck. And the siren's song, deceitfully whispering sweet words to the stupid swimmer about what wouldn't come to pass, fell silent forever.

No, there were some other events—Kira's hand withered, Petyunya   18
came back for visits and talked at length about the price of oil, Elya and Alyosha buried their dog and got a new one, old man Ashkenazi finally washed his windows with the help of the Dawn Company, but Pipka never showed up again. Some people knew for a fact that she'd married a blind storyteller and had taken off for Australia—to shine with her new white teeth amid the eucalyptus trees and duck-billed platypuses above the coral reefs, but others crossed their hearts and swore that she'd been in a crash

and burned up in a taxi on the Yaroslavl highway one rainy, slippery night, and that the flames could be seen from afar rising in a column to the sky. They also said that the fire couldn't be brought under control, and that when everything had burned out, nothing was found at the site of the accident. Only cinders.

Translated from the Russian by Jamey Gambrell

STUDY QUESTIONS

1. Contrast the characters of Rimma and Pipka in "Fire and Dust." Do they represent two different attitudes toward life? Discuss.
2. Who is the narrator? From what point of view is the story told?
3. How does Tolstaya use exaggeration as a technique?
4. Rimma believes that she is able to will her dreams. What is the author's attitude toward dreams? What is the author's attitude toward youth? What is the significance of the shopping trip? Why does Rimma eventually long to see Pipka?
5. Explain the meaning of the title. Find the different uses of fire and dust imagery in the story.

SPAIN

⑤ FEDERICO GARCÍA LORCA

Federico García Lorca (1898–1936), the Spanish poet, dramatist, and essayist, was born and raised in the Moorish city of Granada. In his short life, García Lorca was a seminal modernist who at the same time was a truly national poet. Multitalented in all the arts, García Lorca studied law before he moved to Madrid and took up a literary life. In the 1920s Madrid was a center for vanguard artists and intellectuals, and there García Lorca was influenced by Cubism, Symbolism, and Surrealism. Assimilating their techniques and practices, García Lorca used them to infuse his poetry with new modes of perception. His artistic greatness lies in his excellent rendering an avant-garde imagery and sensibility while at the same time rooting his work in the motifs and poetic structures of traditional Spanish culture. His volumes of poetry Deep Song *(1931) and* The Gypsy Ballads *(1928) and his elegy* Lament for the Death of a Bullfighter *(1937) are steeped in the ballads and dirges of Spain. Traditional culture is also the basis of García Lorca's poetic theater, particularly his tragedies,* Blood Wedding *(1933),* Yerma *(1934), and* The House of Bernarda Alba *(1936). The physically harsh province of Andalusia with its equally stringent code of honor is the motif, or as some critics have argued, the main protagonist of these plays. In writing poetic theater, García Lorca had both artistic and didactic aims. He wished to return poetry to theater, to turn drama away from realism. He also wanted to bring theater closer to a folk sensibility so that it would become a means of enlightening and politicizing the ordinary people of Spain at a time when the Republic was coming under assault from Fascists. In 1936, García Lorca was captured and murdered by Spanish Fascists. The poem "Lament for Ignacio Sanchez Mejias" is typical of the author's work. The subject matter, the death of a bullfighter, and style, a traditional dirge, are deeply rooted in Spanish folklore.*

Lament for Ignacio Sanchez Mejias

1. *Cogida and Death*

A t five in the afternoon.
It was exactly five in the afternoon.
A boy brought the white sheet
at five in the afternoon.
A frail of lime ready prepared
at five in the afternoon. 5
The rest was death, and death alone
at five in the afternoon.

The wind carried away the cottonwool
at five in the afternoon. 10
And the oxide scattered crystal and nickel
at five in the afternoon.
Now the dove and the leopard wrestle
at five in the afternoon.
And a thigh with a desolate horn 15
at five in the afternoon.
The bass-string struck up
at five in the afternoon.
Arsenic bells and smoke
at five in the afternoon. 20
Groups of silence in the corners
at five in the afternoon.
And the bull alone with a high heart!
At five in the afternoon.
When the sweat of snow was coming 25
at five in the afternoon,
when the bull ring was covered in iodine
at five in the afternoon.
death laid eggs in the wound
at five in the afternoon. 30
At five in the afternoon.
Exactly at five o'clock in the afternoon.

A coffin on wheels is his bed
at five in the afternoon.
Bones and flutes resound in his ears 35
at five in the afternoon.
Now the bull was bellowing through his forehead

at five in the afternoon.
The room was iridescent with agony
at five in the afternoon. 40
In the distance the gangrene now comes
at five in the afternoon.
Horn of the lily through green groins
at five in the afternoon.
The wounds were burning like suns 45
at five in the afternoon,
and the crowd was breaking the windows
at five in the afternoon.
At five in the afternoon.
Ah, that fatal five in the afternoon! 50
It was five by all the clocks!
It was five in the shade of the afternoon!

2. *The Spilled Blood*

I will not see it!

Tell the moon to come
for I do not want to see the blood 55
of Ignacio on the sand.

I will not see it!

The moon wide open.
Horse of still clouds,
and the grey bull ring of dreams 60
with willows in the barreras.

I will not see it!

Let my memory kindle!
Warn the jasmines
of such minute whiteness! 65

I will not see it!

The cow of the ancient world
passed her sad tongue
over a snout of blood
spilled on the sand, 70
and the bulls of Guisando,
partly death and partly stone,
bellowed like two centuries

sated with treading the earth.
No.   75
I do not want to see it!
I will not see it!

Ignacio goes up the tiers
with all his death on his shoulders.
He sought for the dawn   80
but the dawn was no more.
He seeks for his confident profile
and the dream bewilders him.
He sought for his beautiful body
and encountered his opened blood.   85
I will not see it!
I do not want to hear it spurt
each time with less strength:
that spurt that illuminates
the tiers of seats, and spills   90
over the corduroy and the leather
of a thirsty multitude.
Who shouts that I should come near!
Do not ask me to see it!

His eyes did not close   95
when he saw the horns near,
but the terrible mothers
lifted their heads.
And across the ranches,
an air of secret voices rose,   100
shouting to celestial bulls,
herdsmen of pale mist.
There was no prince in Seville
who could compare with him,
nor sword like his sword   105
nor heart so true.
Like a river of lions
was his marvellous strength,
and like a marble torso
his firm drawn moderation.   110
The air of Andalusian Rome
gilded his head
where his smile was a spikenard
of wit and intelligence.
What a great torero in the ring!   115

What a good peasant in the sierra!
How gentle with the sheaves!
How hard with the spurs!
How tender with the dew!
How dazzling in the fiesta! 120
How tremendous with the final
banderillas of darkness!

But now he sleeps without end.
Now the moss and the grass
open with sure fingers 125
the flower of his skull.
And now his blood comes out singing;
singing along marshes and meadows,
sliding on frozen horns,
faltering soulless in the mist, 130
stumbling over a thousand hoofs
like a long, dark, sad tongue,
to form a pool of agony
close to the starry Guadalquivir.
Oh, white wall of Spain! 135
Oh, black bull of sorrow!
Oh, hard blood of Ignacio!
Oh, nightingale of his veins!
No.
I will not see it! 140
No chalice can contain it,
no swallows can drink it,
no frost of light can cool it,
nor song nor deluge of white lilies,
no glass can cover it with silver. 145
No.
I will not see it!

3. *The Laid Out Body*

Stone is a forehead where dreams grieve
without curving waters and frozen cypresses.
Stone is a shoulder on which to bear Time 150
with trees formed of tears and ribbons and planets.

I have seen grey showers move towards the waves
raising their tender riddled arms,
to avoid being caught by the lying stone
which loosens their limbs without soaking the blood. 155

For stone gathers seed and clouds,
skeleton larks and wolves of penumbra:
but yields not sounds nor crystals nor fire,
only bull rings and bull rings and more bull rings without
   walls.

Now, Ignacio the well born lies on the stone.   160
All is finished. What is happening? Contemplate his face:
death has covered him with pale sulphur
and has placed on him the head of a dark minotaur.

All is finished. The rain penetrates his mouth.
The air, as if mad, leaves his sunken chest,   165
and Love, soaked through with tears of snow,
warms itself on the peak of the herd.

What are they saying? A stenching silence settles down.
We are here with a body laid out which fades away,
with a pure shape which had nightingales   170
and we see it being filled with depthless holes.

Who creases the shroud? What he says is not true!
Nobody sings here, nobody weeps in the corner,
nobody pricks the spurs, nor terrifies the serpent.
Here I want nothing else but the round eyes   175
to see this body without a chance of rest.

Here I want to see those men of hard voice.
Those that break horses and dominate rivers;
those men of sonorous skeleton who sing
with a mouth full of sun and flint.   180

Here I want to see them. Before the stone.
Before this body with broken reins.
I want to know from them the way out
for this captain strapped down by death.

I want them to show me a lament like a river   185
which will have sweet mists and deep shores,
to take the body of Ignacio where it loses itself
without hearing the double panting of the bulls.

Loses itself in the round bull ring of the moon
which feigns in its youth a sad quiet bull: 190
loses itself in the night without song of fishes
and in the white thicket of frozen smoke.

I don't want them to cover his face with handkerchiefs
that he may get used to the death he carries.

Go, Ignacio; feel not the hot bellowing.   195
Sleep, fly, rest: even the sea dies!

4. *Absent Soul*

The bull does not know you, nor the fig tree,
nor the horses, nor the ants in your own house.
The child and the afternoon do not know you
because you have died for ever.   200

The back of the stone does not know you,
nor the black satin in which you crumble.
Your silent memory does not know you
because you have died for ever.

The autumn will come with small white snails,   205
misty grapes and with clustered hills,
but no one will look into your eyes
because you have died for ever.

Because you have died for ever,
like all the dead of the Earth,   210
like all the dead who are forgotten
in a heap of lifeless dogs.

Nobody knows you. No. But I sing of you.
For posterity I sing of your profile and grace.
Of the signal maturity of your understanding.   215
Of your appetite for death and the taste of its mouth.
Of the sadness of your once valiant gaiety.

It will be a long time, if ever, before there is born
an Andalusian so true, so rich in adventure.

I sing of his elegance with words that groan,   220
and I remember a sad breeze through the olive trees.

Translated from the Spanish by
Stephen Spender and J. L. Gili

STUDY QUESTIONS

1. How does the poem lament the death of Ignacio Sanchez? Why is it divided into four sections? What is each one's focus?
2. How does the poem portray bullfighters?
3. What is the poet's view of death? Is transcendence possible?

SWEDEN

⑤ Margareta Ekström

Margareta Ekström (b. 1930) is a significant Swedish poet, novelist, and short story writer. Born into a literary family, Ekström studied sociology, psychology, and religion, as well as literary history. Since 1960 she has worked as a critic and writer. Unfortunately, as with many Scandinavian writers, little of her work has been translated into English. Her collection of short stories Death's Midwives *(1985) speaks to her sensitive rendering of female characters, often children and elderly women. Ekström is especially interested in how mortality limits but does not define human experience. Her characters are often situated, to quote Ekström, on that "razor-fine edge between buzz and silence, struggle and immobility." Her short story collection* The Day I Began My Studies in Philosophy and Other Stories *was published in English translation in 1989.*

Death's Midwives

When she lost her hair she finally began to cry. It fell out in tufts; her hands were full of it. Bewildered, she passed her hand over her head and felt its familiar shape. Her ears resisted, they bent resiliently. Her forehead felt damp, her nose more pointed. I'm going bald, she thought. And then she began to cry. 1

She was now sixty-four years old, and she calculated that she hadn't cried for twenty years. Not like this, she thought when she finally sat up in bed and turned the tear-drenched pillow over to the cool side. This wasn't angry crying, it was crying that came from deepest exhaustion, crying that originated from the deepest roots of sorrow. Her whole body took part, and it left her thinner and weaker, frail and broken. Anything could happen to her now. She was defenseless. She had been shaken by forces stronger than those she herself used to call upon when angry, upset or occasionally hysterical. 2

After a short nap she looked up at the grayish-yellow ceiling. There was   3
a crack that looked like the Gulf of Finland. A damp spot represented
Leningrad. She had just returned from a trip and she was about forty. The
museums had unwound their corridors and shown her their paintings. She
was only forty then, and what was hard and painful in her stomach was,
of course, the child. Turning her head now, she saw the view she had also
seen then: the candy-pink high-rises and, beyond, the park with the blooming chestnuts, the green clouds of elm foliage, the yellow maple blossoms.
It was all so distinct that she thought she could smell them. But she had
already been deprived of fragrances a long time ago. Something was growing and pressing: would she perhaps give birth through the ear?

The walls were silent, and they listened. She had asked to be spared   4
from a painting with two red tulips in a ceramic jug and a black book lying
coquettishly askew in its bottom right corner. Sometimes she searched for
the hole where the hook had been. She could see it very well after making
the effort to find her glasses. It had become a nail on which to hang her
thoughts. As long as I can see the hole, she thought . . . And then she
imagined how she would in her most difficult hour fix that black dot with
her eyes until she was engulfed by the millimeter-sized tunnel and finally
enclosed by the wall. Like so many other struggling bodies who with one
weak and trembling sigh had been devoured by those walls.

"Isn't there some tonic I can use for my hair?" she wondered when the   5
day-nurse came. But unfortunately the nurse didn't join in the game at
once, hesitating for an awful moment while smiles of pity, surprise and
almost reproach passed over her familiar rosy face. The girl was too young.
Wouldn't she be scared, later, when the time came?

Finally, she collected her wits and said: "Why, of course, Mrs. Malm. I   6
can ask the doctor if you'd like."

"No, thank you, I can do it myself," she said tiredly. Her playfulness   7
was over. First so many lies, then these ice-cold showers of truth, truth and
more truth. She couldn't stand them anymore. It was too late anyway to
become conditioned.

She hadn't touched herself for a long time. She remembered fruitless   8
rubbings and ticklings, hour-long work-ups without even an echo of pleasure. Just a stubborn effort to make something happen to cause the dry lips
to become damp, to feel a smile in her middle.

Now she thought of her vagina as an empty inkwell, forgotten in an   9
uninhabited summer cottage. A pen dipping into it would splay and squeak
and slide against the shiny walls and the rust-colored residue in the corners.

In moments of fright she would sometimes wind a strand of her thin-   10
ning hair around her index finger and bite the knuckles of the other hand,
as she had done when a child. By the white or inflamed red marks she
could then, the next day, read the depth of her dread.

"It's all part of the picture," the spunky midwife had said, while press-   11 ing her stomach. It was her standing expression: it's part of the picture. Part of the picture, as well, were the swollen varicose veins, the heartburn, the water breaking too early, the unbearable pain, and finally the struggling little boy, held up by one foot, screaming and dangling, with vernix, umbilical cord and the little red sex. Part of the picture was also laughter and tears of joy and, alongside her, the newly bathed infant who with shiny eyes captured her for life.

She had felt more like someone being born than someone giving birth. 12 She had been enclosed in the tunnel, there was no way back. When the pain pressed its utmost and she doubled up like a jackknife, and her urine sprayed all over the starched hospital gown, and the paper basin it was destined for was crushed in a hand which no longer obeyed her, then she had looked at the window. Five stories. One jump.

Now she lay in the other wing, on the same floor. But the thought of 13 crossing the room and trying to see if she was strong enough to unlatch the window nauseated her. She wanted to save her strength. She wanted to continue. Despite the pain. And her mind laughed at this illogic, this instinct of self-preservation which was self-devastating, and her laughter turned into a grimace. There was little room for the intellect in this sorrowful business. Just as little as the other time when he was to be pressed out, caught and cut free in order finally to be able to look at her.

By means of many ingenious small movements and stratagems, she was 14 able to get hold of her purse and to take out her diary. After the entry "K.S.," which was the name of the hospital, six weeks ago, there was nothing but empty pages. She had kept good notes before, but now it seemed completely unnecessary. In one pocket she had put the farewell letter to her son. She took it out sometimes to read it. It made her smile because it was for him, but actually she should perhaps cry since she would probably never see him again. She would change a word, add something, some sort of nonsense, something that would make him laugh. She remembered the interminable love letters to his father, the joy of writing them and reading them again and again before mailing them. The joy of awareness and of self-expression. The feeling that all was crystal-clear between them, that nothing needed to be searched for, suspected or interpreted from looks or gestures. Then, after that total, overwhelming effort, there had been a slow downhill slope, a dilution, a growing indifference which attacked both of them like a mutual consumption. By then, their son was eighteen years old, and they found no reason to pretend. They drifted apart and both forgot their love. She tried to remember how it had felt, but could only evoke the certainty of their friendship, possibly respect, and their independence from each other, which was just as complete as if they had been born in different centuries. It wasn't indifference. They kept in touch. They cared. But it was no longer necessary.

The nurses came and went. The nuisance of the rounds was diminished 15 to the bare essentials. Mostly, she was left in peace. Sometimes she asked for sleeping pills and got them, but never many at a time. They overestimated her desire to take a shortcut.

Some of the nurse's aides were talkative. They would tell her of neighbors who didn't take off their clogs in the house, of foreigners who bought the wrong things at the supermarket, of children who complained about their mothers working. She listened, her head supported by two pillows, and tried to smile. A girl whose name was Brita lent her a turquoise chiffon scarf to cover her hair. "That looks good on you!" she beamed. But it didn't make her want to take out her mirror from the pocket of her purse. 16

When she was pregnant she had also been transformed into an inert being without exterior. Everything took place inside her, in her veins, in her womb, her head. She had closed her eyes to keep out the outside world and she had mumbled to the midwife: "Excuse me for closing my eyes, it seems so impolite." But she had wanted to concentrate on what was happening inside her body, and on the child struggling in the narrow tunnel. 17

Suddenly the oxygen mask had been pressed against her mouth. Someone had raised her head and said, "Take a deep breath, take a deep breath! Deeper still!" 18

And when she protested—no, no, she didn't want any help—they had answered that it wasn't for her sake, but for the child's. But this time they had fooled her. She had taken deep breaths thinking about the child, but they had only wheeled her into the intensive care unit, where she woke up with needles and tubes. Naturally, she thought, deep inside I knew that it wasn't for the sake of the child now—not now—he's more than twenty years old and needs neither my oxygen nor my blood. Still, out of sheer obedience, she had taken those deep breaths. 19

She leafed through the diary backwards. There. That's when it was. She made a mark with her thumbnail. That's when she breathed out of sheer obedience. Otherwise she wouldn't be here now, and her thumbnail would have been like ashes that had annoyingly fallen on a white sheet someone living near the south cemetery had hung up to dry. Not much had happened after that. She had been taken back to her room, and the lab results had become worse and worse. She knew this because she felt a tiredness that was deeper than any she had experienced in her life. A dullness, an indifference. "I'm turning to stone," she thought. "Molecules move more slowly, form different patterns. Nothing can move me. That jump through the window is an impossibility, and soon my thinking will stop as well." 20

She read a little in *Memoirs of Hadrian* and wondered whether Marguerite Yourcenar was still alive or, if not, what her death had been like. When she was younger, she had been curious about death. She had never seen a relation die. Nor any death by accident. Perhaps the blood-covered man in the cigar store on Tegner Avenue was dying, but she had had her little boy outside in the car, and had hurried off to protect him from the sight, and herself from his difficult questions. 21

She knew nothing of what lay ahead—just as little as she had known 22 about childbirth when she was here before. A record with advice about relaxing was the only thing a friend had had time to give her on that day before she was hospitalized. Breathe deeply. Relax. Don't be so tense. Let your limbs go limp and loose. Perhaps she should listen to it again now?

She remembered the storm waves of her contractions. How, like at the seashore, you could see them from afar, as they mercilessly came closer. She had made herself dull, heavy and indifferent, allowed the pain to wash through her as though through someone else. And she had felt how it had "worked," how everything had opened up, how the child had come closer to his life. Never before had she been so close to death. Not her own, not a personal death. But so near the border between life and death. She had thought, quite clearly: "Now I know more about death than I did before," and all the while she had been lying there creating life. 23

The midwives had come and gone. Some went to lunch. Others worked part time. And a nurse's aide had told her about her children's new teacher. About how much fun it was to watch the children relate to each other. It isn't really fun until you have two. She had thought about what it would be like to have two men. She'd had two once, and until the complications it had been lots of fun. Unusually much fun. But she hadn't been especially interested in how they related to each other. 24

Otherwise, she didn't think about her body more than she had to, right now. She was happy when she could urinate without a catheter. But her mouth was dry. The damp washcloth dabbing her lips was a pleasure, as was the sip of orange juice which she could wash around in her mouth and then spit out obediently. "It's like being a wine-taster," she had tried to tell the consulting physician, but her tongue wouldn't co-operate, so she had to remain silent. Why tell jokes? Was it so important for her to make a good impression? So courageous on her deathbed. "You have no idea how witty she was despite knowing she didn't have long to live!" 25

"I can tell this isn't your first baby, Ma'am," the nurse who shaved her pubic hair had flattered her that night in the basement where she had also had her enema and the blood tests. It was her first baby, and she had felt proud of being so composed and reasonable, so cooperative. 26

But wouldn't she have moaned and screamed if she had given birth lying alone in a ditch? And now, were she to lie on an Alpine slope, the victim of a plane crash with only space and death ahead . . . how would she behave? What would be her facial expression, what screams and curses would she address to the grass, the stones and the distant clouds? 27

They are arranged like iron filings over the earth, the smoke-gray clouds. Each of them is filled with so many microscopic iron particles that they are forced to submit to the earth's magnetic pattern. She remembers the creation myth which she had read in its scientific version, and she remembers her great joy about these poetic facts. Maybe the earth changes its rolling rhythm when all the trees in the northern hemisphere suddenly get leaves and so offer increased resistance to the wind? And perhaps the rolling 28 speed increases again in the fall when the branches stick up naked into the sky?

This was better than Isis and Osiris, better than Ask and Embla and Ygdrasil—or were they all equally distant from the truth, the same story in different versions? 29

When she was still actively alive she used to complain about each day that passed without new knowledge, new ideas. Now she wondered dully what it had all been for. It was dullness, rather than anguish. A disgusting lethargy. Even what she could manage became impossible, the very desire was cut off at the roots. She tried to remember the child, the child's father. The two bodies she had loved most. Straight shoulders, angular joints, firm jaws, looks that warmed her and gave her light. But it seemed unreal. Less real than the brown medicine bottle and the small iridescent medicine cups that one could stack in long flexible chains to rattle when there was nothing to listen to on the radio. 30

How long would this go on? And death, a relief? Can nothingness relieve? Relief from what? 31

"I have lived a good life, better than almost any I have heard of, and better than I could have hoped when I was your age," she had written in the letter. But between the lines he could perhaps read that no matter how good it had been, now in retrospect it all seemed horribly unnecessary, and so his life was unnecessary, as were the copulation which had created his little body, the labor pains and her pushing him out to life, air and his own breathing. 32

No, not that. To have borne him, to have succeeded in getting him out whole, that could never feel unnecessary. There was the limit to her skepticism, and she was a common she-fox, a natural female bear, an entirely genuine cat mother. The baby was in her belly and had to come out. The baby had to be licked. The baby needed milk, and tenderness and warmth, and to lie as close to her as though still inside the darkness of her belly. This was beyond what was necessary or unnecessary. It simply was. And she cherished this idea and held onto it. Sometimes she took out his picture—in it he was twelve years old, ephebically beautiful and mischievous—she would hold it for a long time in her hand and hoped to die that way. 33

She was in the tunnel, and there was no going back. But she wasn't put on a high iron bed, nor was she restrained, and no one listened with a stethoscope to her stomach and then said comfortingly: "I'll stay here now until it's over." 34

Until it's over. Then she would be two people. She had never imagined dying in childbirth. The baby kicked and wanted to come out. She had protected it for nine whole months and she wouldn't let it down during the last nine hours. And yet she had never been so close to death, since it was across that border the child had to go in order to live. 35

Now it was her turn. And she asked the girl Brita how long her shift was. "Until six, as usual," she said. "See you tomorrow morning!" 36

Tomorrow morning? No, oh no, would it take that long? But her body 37
wanted it to take that long, and preferably a little longer.

Now, as then, flowers arrived from friends. Flowers from the child's 38
father. They glowed with all their colors and withered. She herself glowed
with fever and withered at the same time. She and the flowers were alike:
cut off from their natural root systems, nourished with cold fluids which
were pumped directly into the circulatory system. She saw the tulips: their
stems full of water, they stretched, despite knowing that they would die.
The lilac leaves didn't bother to pretend. But the five-pointed little flowers
with their drop of sweet nectar in the middle bloomed one by one, and she
asked a cleaning woman to give her some—yes, to pick them off, so that
she could suck the little stems as she had done in the summer, long ago.
She would have liked to ask the consulting physician to whistle with a lilac
leaf between his thumbs, but probably he didn't know how and he was
embarrassed enough as it was. And she was embarrassed herself. Confused and ashamed. How would she manage her death?

With the baby, newly bathed and dressed, in her arms, she had felt 39
ashamed too. She had made an ironical face at his father and said: "This is
like an ad for baby powder!" She had been wheeled through interminable
corridors, and the little one slept in its white cocoon in her arms, his
wrinkled cheek so close that she couldn't keep from caressing it. It was all
so new. And her breasts which had lain so flat in their bra cups and rested
in young men's hands, now they were suddenly to become troughs for the
little pig who slurped and ate. She had loved nursing him and would most
likely have kept on for a year if the DDT scare hadn't become so acute that
mothers were warned about nursing.

I'll fall asleep, she was thinking. And when I wake up it'll be over. 40
Nothing is working any longer. Even the pain has almost stopped. The
pain has died before me. Just like my sense of smell, my hearing, my sight.
I have been left behind, I am the last in my own funeral procession.

Then the older night nurse had sat down close to her bed, and had taken 41
her hand, saying: "I'll stay until . . ."

That's what it was like. Some midwives left before life came. Others 42
stayed to keep watch. I'll stay now until you die, one body says to another.
And one of them will get up, straighten her hair and go home to clean her
house, do her shopping, have intercourse, weed the garden, borrow books
at the library, and go through the envelopes of grocery receipts, while the
other will remain. Dead still. All alone.

Then she began to talk. With her thin voice she tried to explain and 43
disentangle. Like a child, she begged for better grades, for a longer vacation.

But the heavy-set woman in her forties took out her knitting and the 44
lamp shone on her brown hair where a few white strands gleamed.

She tried to read by the pale glow of the night light. 45

"Even water is an enjoyment, and now in my illness I must partake of 46 it sparingly. Yet even when I struggle with death, when they will mix it with the last of the bitter medicine, I will make an effort to savor its freshness on my lips."

But the book fell, and she was too tired to think about it. A harsh light fell on her closed lids. Someone pulled off the turquoise scarf, she whimpered as if in her sleep. *Memoirs of Hadrian*, a hard cultured voice said, and she understood that they were putting away her belongings. She was to suffer through the last of the contractions completely naked and almost bald. 47

"A hand to hold when you die," his drunken voice echoed. He was nineteen and newly graduated, the same as she. They had been hugging and drinking on the couch in her dormitory room and in her honor he had executed a death-defying balancing act outside her window. 48

No, no hand to hold. She hadn't wanted the child's father when the little one came. I'd rather be alone with the pains. You can come afterwards and share in the pleasure. No, no, no, it isn't for your sake, it's for mine. I'm the one who has to go through it. I want to be alone! 49

The bed was so wet suddenly. But when she said: "My water!" the stupid aide just came with a glass of water. She grasped for words, for memories, for signs which would be understood. It all was so new for her. She felt bewildered and uncivilized. A bitter satisfaction went through her: today had brought new knowledge, new ideas. 50

"There, there, take it easy!" And a broad, warm hand patted her cheek, stroked the back of her hand. 51

Just as before, she was their lawful prey. She remembered unknown women who patted her big, hard, pregnant belly. She had reminded them of something wonderful. What was the knitting woman beside her thinking about, now that she had come to the armhole? 52

"Is he all right?" 53

"Sure, just take it easy, you're doing fine. You're four fingers now. You're dilating just fine." A friendly Finn had his finger deep inside her and gave her a report from the life on the other side of birth. 54

She had hoped that he would remember and send her stocks and snapdragons. But instead the flowers had come from her colleagues at the university. What did they have to do with her giving birth? 55

Nosegay. Buttercup. Fleetfoot. Happy lark. Mother's little Oedipussycat. And she had promised they would marry soon, as soon as he got a little bit bigger. And at three months he fell asleep on top of her in a wide bouncing bed in England, she also fell asleep and dreamed that he was inside her, but only with his tiny little penis, and it was a sweet, happy union, very far from incest and pornography. And yet, she hadn't been able to tell anyone about it. 56

The queer knitting woman stuck her needles into her, one after the other, purl one, knit one, and the knit one's had barbs. She turned slowly to her side, but there were new tubes that got in the way. A voice echoed 57

688   EUROPE • SWEDEN

in a loudspeaker and footsteps ran. Footsteps ran away with young bodies, away from her immobility.

At last she worked herself to the surface, she had dived too deeply from the cliff into the black water. Her mother and father smiled at her in their blue bathing robes and the rock smelled like sunshine and tanned skin. Her whole body shivered, and she had blue gooseflesh. They had to rub her warm, but she continued to shiver. 58

Then, she was suddenly sitting in a back yard. The book on her lap was *Memoirs of Hadrian*. An oak spread its greenery over her like a parasol. Through an open window she heard his voice. It prattled and babbled, it expounded and explained. And he couldn't say "s." She made an effort to stretch her neck and look up. The sun shone in through the window. The chestnuts on the horizon bowed to an imperceptible breeze. Their scent did not reach her. The knitting woman had fallen asleep. The light hit the shiny intravenous bottle, which reflected blindingly. 59

All she saw was the sunshine bouncing against the nursery window, and his voice babbled on, and when she made an effort to somehow see his face the sun struck her with its double-edged axe. 60

Like the whirling of balls of fluff and music on a cotton piano. Whispering and shuffling, moving and covering. Tubing disconnected, clothing removed, before the stiffness makes it more difficult. Like a shadow play, this whole thousand-headed hospital which is slowly sinking into the darkness of a new day, while a ray of light is laughing in the window and a child talks and talks about life. 61

Translated from the Swedish
by Eva Claeson

STUDY QUESTIONS

1. Describe the imagery of "Death's Midwives." In what ways are the images interrelated? How are the images of birth and death sequenced?
2. What does the character come to understand about the meaning of her own life and death?
3. Loneliness and communion are the two polarities of human experience that Ekström explores in the story. Find instances of how the author juxtaposes these conditions.
4. In what ways does the author transform the conclusion of the story into the sense of a new beginning?

SWITZERLAND

🌀 FRIEDRICH DURRENMATT

Friedrich Durrenmatt (1921–1990) is an internationally renowned dramatist whose tragic-comic approach to theater has been instrumental in shaping the themes of contemporary drama. The son of a Protestant pastor, Durrenmatt was born in a small town near Bern, Switzerland. Although Durrenmatt's religious background initially drew him to the ideas of Søren Kierkegaard, in later life he came to call himself "an uprooted Protestant." Durrenmatt studied philosophy and literature at the University of Zurich, where he was continually tormented by a sense of guilt at being sheltered from Fascism. World War II became for him the decisive event of the twentieth century and left him with an irredeemable sense of spiritual despair. Durrenmatt elaborated his pessimism about humankind into dramatic theory. According to him, tragedy as an art form could no longer convey the suffering and horror of the twentieth century. Neither could realistic art, which, Durrenmatt argued, obscured the paradoxical nature of humanity. Theater had to create a contrived and artificial counterreality, which, with its use of the grotesque and comic, would reveal humanity's debasement. To convey the "fall of man," Durrenmatt in plays like The Visit *(1962) and* The Physicists *(1964) created a drama of two-dimensional figures whose exaggerated characteristics personify the loss of spiritual values. In* The Visit, *the bizarre Claire Zachanassian, the richest woman in the world, is the dehumanized product of the very power that she has gained. Durrenmatt's great achievement as a playwright lies in that through the use of the grotesque and the absurd he is able to reinstate a moral vision into his pessimistic dramas.*

The Visit

CHARACTERS

(In order of appearance)

HOFBAUER (FIRST MAN)	SECOND GRANDCHILD
HELMESBERGER (SECOND MAN)	MIKE
WECHSLER (THIRD MAN)	MAX
VOGEL (FOURTH MAN)	FIRST BLIND MAN
PAINTER	SECOND BLIND MAN
STATION MASTER	ATHLETE
BURGOMASTER	FRAU BURGOMASTER
TEACHER	FRAU SCHILL
PASTOR	DAUGHTER
ANTON SCHILL	SON
CLAIRE ZACHANASSIAN	DOCTOR NÜSSLIN
CONDUCTOR	FRAU BLOCK (FIRST WOMAN)
PEDRO CABRAL	TRUCK DRIVER
BOBBY	REPORTER
POLICEMAN	TOWNSMAN
FIRST GRANDCHILD	

The action of the play takes place in and around the little town of Güllen, somewhere in Europe.

There are three acts.

ACT ONE

A railway-crossing bell starts ringing. Then is heard the distant sound of a locomotive whistle. The curtain rises.

The scene represents, in the simplest possible manner, a little town somewhere in Central Europe. The time is the present. The town is shabby and ruined, as if the plague had passed there. Its name, Güllen, is inscribed on the shabby signboard which adorns the façade of the railway station. This edifice is summarily indicated by a length of rusty iron paling, a platform parallel to the proscenium, beyond which one imagines the rails to be, and a baggage truck standing by a wall on which a torn timetable, marked "Fahrplan," is affixed by three nails. In the station wall is a door with a sign: "Eintritt Verboten."[1] This leads to the STATION MASTER's office.

---

1. *No Entrance.*

Left of the station is a little house of gray stucco, formerly whitewashed. It has a tile roof, badly in need of repair. Some shreds of travel posters still adhere to the windowless walls. A shingle hanging over the entrance, left, reads: "Männer."[1] On the other side of the shingle reads: "Damen."[2] Along the wall of the little house there is a wooden bench, backless, on which four men are lounging cheerlessly, shabbily dressed, with cracked shoes. A fifth man is busied with paintpot and brush. He is kneeling on the ground, painting a strip of canvas with the words: "Welcome, Clara."

The warning signal rings uninterruptedly. The sound of the approaching train comes closer and closer. The STATION MASTER *issues from his office, advances to the center of the platform and salutes.*

The train is heard thundering past in a direction parallel to the footlights, and is lost in the distance. The men on the bench follow its passing with a slow movement of their heads, from left to right.

FIRST MAN: The "Emperor." Hamburg-Naples.
SECOND MAN: Then comes the "Diplomat."
THIRD MAN: Then the "Banker."
FOURTH MAN: And at eleven twenty-seven the "Flying Dutchman." Venice-Stockholm.
FIRST MAN: Our only pleasure—watching trains.

(The station bell rings again. The STATION MASTER *comes out of his office and salutes another train. The men follow its course right to left)*

FOURTH MAN: Once upon a time the "Emperor" and the "Flying Dutchman" used to stop here in Güllen. So did the "Diplomat," the "Banker," and the "Silver Comet."
SECOND MAN: Now it's only the local from Kaffigen and the twelve-forty from Kalberstadt.
THIRD MAN: The fact is, we're ruined.
FIRST MAN: What with the Wagonworks shut down . . .
SECOND MAN: The Foundry finished . . .
FOURTH MAN: The Golden Eagle Pencil Factory all washed up . . .
FIRST MAN: It's life on the dole.
SECOND MAN: Did you say life?
THIRD MAN: We're rotting.
FIRST MAN: Starving.
SECOND MAN: Crumbling.
FOURTH MAN: The whole damn town.

(The station bell rings)

THIRD MAN: Once we were a center of industry.
PAINTER: A cradle of culture.

---

1. *Men.*
2. *Ladies.*

FOURTH MAN: One of the best little towns in the country.

FIRST MAN: In the world.

SECOND MAN: Here Goethe slept.

FOURTH MAN: Brahms composed a quartet.

THIRD MAN: Here Berthold Schwarz invented gunpowder.[1]

PAINTER: And I once got first prize at the Dresden Exhibition of Contemporary Art. What am I doing now? Painting signs.

(The station bell rings. The STATION MASTER comes out. He throws away a cigarette butt. The men scramble for it)

FIRST MAN: Well, anyway, Madame Zachanassian will help us.

FOURTH MAN: If she comes . . .

THIRD MAN: If she comes.

SECOND MAN: Last week she was in France. She gave them a hospital.

FIRST MAN: In Rome she founded a free public nursery.

THIRD MAN: In Leuthenau, a bird sanctuary.

PAINTER: They say she got Picasso to design her car.

FIRST MAN: Where does she get all that money?

SECOND MAN: An oil company, a shipping line, three banks and five railways—

FOURTH MAN: And the biggest string of geisha houses in Japan.

(From the direction of the town come the BURGOMASTER, the PASTOR, the TEACHER and ANTON SCHILL. The BURGOMASTER, the TEACHER and SCHILL are men in their fifties. The PASTOR is ten years younger. All four are dressed shabbily and are sad-looking. The BURGOMASTER looks official. SCHILL is tall and handsome, but graying and worn; nevertheless a man of considerable charm and presence. He walks directly to the little house and disappears into it)

PAINTER: Any news, Burgomaster? Is she coming?

    ALL: Yes, is she coming?

BURGOMASTER: She's coming. The telegram has been confirmed. Our distinguished guest will arrive on the twelve-forty from Kalberstadt. Everyone must be ready.

TEACHER: The mixed choir is ready. So is the children's chorus.

BURGOMASTER: And the church bell, Pastor?

PASTOR: The church bell will ring. As soon as the new bell ropes are fitted. The man is working on them now.

BURGOMASTER: The town band will be drawn up in the market place and the Athletic Association will form a human pyramid in her honor—the top man will hold the wreath with her initials. Then lunch at the Golden Apostle. I shall say a few words.

TEACHER: Of course.

---

1. *Berthold Schwarz was a German monk who lived in the fourteenth century. The invention of gunpowder has been attributed to him and to many others.*

BURGOMASTER: I had thought of illuminating the town hall and the cathedral, but we can't afford the lamps.

PAINTER: Burgomaster—what do you think of this?

(*He shows the banner*)

BURGOMASTER: (*Calls*) Schill! Schill!

TEACHER: Schill!

(SCHILL *comes out of the little house*)

SCHILL: Yes, right away. Right away.

BURGOMASTER: This is more in your line. What do you think of this?

SCHILL: (*Looks at the sign*) No, no, no. That certainly won't do, Burgomaster. It's much too intimate. It shouldn't read: "Welcome, Clara." It should read: "Welcome, Madame . . ."

TEACHER: Zachanassian.

BURGOMASTER: Zachanassian.

SCHILL: Zachanassian.

PAINTER: But she's Clara to us.

FIRST MAN: Clara Wäscher.

SECOND MAN: Born here.

THIRD MAN: Her father was a carpenter. He built this.

(*All turn and stare at the little house*)

SCHILL: All the same . . .

PAINTER: If I . . .

BURGOMASTER: No, no, no. He's right. You'll have to change it.

PAINTER: Oh, well, I'll tell you what I'll do. I'll leave this and I'll put "Welcome, Madame Zachanassian" on the other side. Then if things go well, we can always turn it around.

BURGOMASTER: Good idea. (*To* SCHILL) Yes?

SCHILL: Well, anyway, it's safer. Everything depends on the first impression.

(*The train bell is heard. Two clangs. The* PAINTER *turns the banner over and goes to work*)

FIRST MAN: Hear that? The "Flying Dutchman" has just passed through Leuthenau.

FOURTH MAN: Eleven twenty.

BURGOMASTER: Gentlemen, you know that the millionairess is our only hope.

PASTOR: Under God.

BURGOMASTER: Under God. Naturally. Schill, we depend entirely on you.

SCHILL: Yes, I know. You keep telling me.

BURGOMASTER: After all, you're the only one who really knew her.

SCHILL: Yes, I knew her.

PASTOR: You were really quite close to one another, I hear, in those days.

SCHILL: Close? Yes, we were close, there's no denying it. We were in love. I was young—good-looking, so they said—and Clara—you know, I can still see her in the great barn coming toward me—like a light out of the darkness. And in the Konradsweil Forest she'd come running to meet me—barefooted—her beautiful red hair streaming behind her. Like a witch. I was in love with her, all right. But you know how it is when you're twenty.

PASTOR: What happened?

SCHILL: *(Shrugs)* Life came between us.

BURGOMASTER: You must give me some points about her for my speech.

(He takes out his notebook)

SCHILL: I think I can help you there.

TEACHER: Well, I've gone through the school records. And the young lady's marks were, I'm afraid to say, absolutely dreadful. Even in deportment. The only subject in which she was even remotely passable was natural history.

BURGOMASTER: Good in natural history. That's fine. Give me a pencil.

(He makes a note)

SCHILL: She was an outdoor girl. Wild. Once, I remember, they arrested a tramp, and she threw stones at the policeman. She hated injustice passionately.

BURGOMASTER: Strong sense of justice. Excellent.

SCHILL: And generous . . .

ALL: Generous?

SCHILL: Generous to a fault. Whatever little she had, she shared—so good-hearted. I remember once she stole a bag of potatoes to give to a poor widow.

BURGOMASTER: *(Writing in notebook)* Wonderful generosity—

TEACHER: Generosity.

BURGOMASTER: That, gentlemen, is something I must not fail to make a point of.

SCHILL: And such a sense of humor. I remember once when the oldest man in town fell and broke his leg, she said, "Oh, dear, now they'll have to shoot him."

BURGOMASTER: Well, I've got enough. The rest, my friend, is up to you.

(He puts the notebook away)

SCHILL: Yes, I know, but it's not so easy. After all, to part a woman like that from her millions—

BURGOMASTER: Exactly. Millions. We have to think in big terms here.

TEACHER: If she's thinking of buying us off with a nursery school—

ALL: Nursery school!

PASTOR: Don't accept.

TEACHER: Hold out.

SCHILL: I'm not so sure that I can do it. You know, she may have forgotten me completely.

BURGOMASTER: *(He exchanges a look with the* TEACHER *and the* PASTOR*)* Schill, for many years you have been our most popular citizen. The most respected and the best loved.

SCHILL: Why, thank you . . .

BURGOMASTER: And therefore I must tell you—last week I sounded out the political opposition, and they agreed. In the spring you will be elected to succeed me as Burgomaster. By unanimous vote.

(The others clap their hands in approval)

SCHILL: But, my dear Burgomaster—!

BURGOMASTER: It's true.

TEACHER: I'm a witness. I was at the meeting.

SCHILL: This is—naturally, I'm terribly flattered— It's a completely unexpected honor.

BURGOMASTER: You deserve it.

SCHILL: Burgomaster! Well, well—! *(Briskly)* Gentlemen, to business. The first chance I get, of course, I shall discuss our miserable position with Clara.

TEACHER: But tactfully, tactfully—

SCHILL: What do you take me for? We must feel our way. Everything must be correct. Psychologically correct. For example, here at the railway station, a single blunder, one false note, could be disastrous.

BURGOMASTER: He's absolutely right. The first impression colors all the rest. Madame Zachanassian sets foot on her native soil for the first time in many years. She sees our love and she sees our misery. She remembers her youth, her friends. The tears well up into her eyes. Her childhood companions throng about her. I will naturally not present myself like this, but in my black coat with my top hat. Next to me, my wife. Before me, my two grandchildren all in white, with roses. My God, if it only comes off as I see it! If only it comes off. *(The station bell begins ringing)* Oh, my God! Quick! We must get dressed.

FIRST MAN: It's not her train. It's only the "Flying Dutchman."

PASTOR: *(Calmly)* We have still two hours before she arrives.

SCHILL: For God's sake, don't let's lose our heads. We still have a full two hours.

BURGOMASTER: Who's losing their heads? *(To* FIRST *and* SECOND MAN*) When her train comes, you two, Helmesberger and Vogel, will hold up the banner with "Welcome Madame Zachanassian." The rest will applaud.*

THIRD MAN: Bravo!

(He applauds)

BURGOMASTER: But, please, one thing—no wild cheering like last year with the government relief committee. It made no impression at all and we still haven't received any loan. What we need is a feeling of genuine sincerity. That's how we greet with full hearts our beloved sister who has been away from us so long. Be sincerely moved, my friends, that's the secret; be sincere. Remember you're not dealing with a child. Next a few brief words from me. Then the church bell will start pealing—

PASTOR: If he can fix the ropes in time.

(The station bell rings)

BURGOMASTER: —Then the mixed choir moves in. And then—

TEACHER: We'll form a line down here.

BURGOMASTER: Then the rest of us will form in two lines leading from the station—

(He is interrupted by the thunder of the approaching train. The men crane their heads to see it pass. The STATION MASTER advances to the platform and salutes. There is a sudden shriek of air brakes. The train screams to a stop. The four men jump up in consternation)

PAINTER: But the "Flying Dutchman" never stops!

FIRST MAN: It's stopping.

SECOND MAN: In Güllen!

THIRD MAN: In the poorest—

FIRST MAN: The dreariest—

SECOND MAN: The lousiest—

FOURTH MAN: The most God-forsaken hole between Venice and Stockholm.

STATION MASTER: It cannot stop!

(The train noises stop. There is only the panting of the engine)

PAINTER: It's stopped!

(The STATION MASTER runs out)

OFFSTAGE VOICES: What's happened? Is there an accident?

(A hubbub of offstage voices, as if the passengers on the invisible train were alighting)

CLAIRE: *(Offstage)* Is this Güllen?

CONDUCTOR: *(Offstage)* Here, here, what's going on?

CLAIRE: *(Offstage)* Who the hell are you?

CONDUCTOR: *(Offstage)* But you pulled the emergency cord, madame!

CLAIRE: *(Offstage)* I always pull the emergency cord.

STATION MASTER: *(Offstage)* I must ask you what's going on here.

CLAIRE: *(Offstage)* And who the hell are you?

STATION MASTER: *(Offstage)* I'm the Station Master, madame, and I must ask you—

CLAIRE: *(Enters)* No!

(From the right CLAIRE ZACHANASSIAN *appears. She is an extraordinary woman. She is in her fifties, red-haired, remarkably dressed, with a face as impassive as that of an ancient idol, beautiful still, and with a singular grace of movement and manner. She is simple and unaffected, yet she has the haughtiness of a world power. The entire effect is striking to the point of the unbelievable. Behind her comes her fiancé,* PEDRO CABRAL, *tall, young, very handsome, and completely equipped for fishing, with creel and net, and with a rod case in his hand. An excited* CONDUCTOR *follows)*

CONDUCTOR: But, madame, I must insist! You have stopped "The Flying Dutchman." I must have an explanation.

CLAIRE: Nonsense. Pedro.

PEDRO: Yes, my love?

CLAIRE: This is Güllen. Nothing has changed. I recognize it all. There's the forest of Konradsweil. There's a brook in it full of trout, where you can fish. And there's the roof of the great barn. Ha! God! What a miserable blot on the map.

(She crosses the stage and goes off with PEDRO*)*

SCHILL: My God! Clara!

TEACHER: Claire Zachanassian!

ALL: Claire Zachanassian!

BURGOMASTER: And the town band? The town band! Where is it?

TEACHER: The mixed choir? The mixed choir!

PASTOR: The church bell! The church bell!

BURGOMASTER: *(To the* FIRST MAN*)* Quick! My dress coat. My top hat. My grandchildren. Run! Run! *(*FIRST MAN *runs off. The* BURGOMASTER *shouts after him)* And don't forget my wife!

(General panic. The THIRD MAN *and* FOURTH MAN *hold up the banner, on which only part of the name has been painted: "Welcome Mad—"* CLAIRE *and* PEDRO *re-enter, right)*

CONDUCTOR: *(Mastering himself with an effort)*

MADAME. The train is waiting. The entire international railway schedule has been disrupted. I await your explanation.

CLAIRE: You're a very foolish man. I wish to visit this town. Did you expect me to jump off a moving train?

CONDUCTOR: *(Stupefied)* You stopped the "Flying Dutchman" because you wished to visit the town?

CLAIRE: Naturally.

CONDUCTOR: *(Inarticulate)* Madame!

STATION MASTER: Madame, if you wished to visit the town, the twelve forty from Kalberstadt was entirely at your service. Arrival in Güllen, one seventeen.

CLAIRE: The local that stops at Loken, Beisenbach, and Leuthenau? Do you expect me to waste three-quarters of an hour chugging dismally through this wilderness?

CONDUCTOR: Madame, you shall pay for this!

CLAIRE: Bobby, give him a thousand marks.

(BOBBY, *her butler, a man in his seventies, wearing dark glasses, opens his wallet. The townspeople gasp*)

CONDUCTOR: *(Taking the money in amazement)* But, madame!

CLAIRE: And three thousand for the Railway Widows' Relief Fund.

CONDUCTOR: *(With the money in his hands)* But we have no such fund, madame.

CLAIRE: Now you have.

(*The* BURGOMASTER *pushes his way forward*)

BURGOMASTER: *(He whispers to the* CONDUCTOR *and* TEACHER*)* The lady is Madame Claire Zachanassian!

CONDUCTOR: Claire Zachanassian? Oh, my God! But that's naturally quite different. Needless to say, we would have stopped the train if we'd had the slightest idea. *(He hands the money back to* BOBBY*)* Here, please. I couldn't dream of it. Four thousand. My God!

CLAIRE: Keep it. Don't fuss.

CONDUCTOR: Would you like the train to wait, madame, while you visit the town? The administration will be delighted. The cathedral porch. The town hall—

CLAIRE: You may take the train away. I don't need it any more.

STATION MASTER: All aboard!

(*He puts his whistle to his lips.* PEDRO *stops him*)

PEDRO: But the press, my angel. They don't know anything about this. They're still in the dining car.

CLAIRE: Let them stay there. I don't want the press in Güllen at the moment. Later they will come by themselves. *(To* STATION MASTER*)* And now what are you waiting for?

STATION MASTER: All aboard!

(*The* STATION MASTER *blows a long blast on his whistle. The train leaves. Meanwhile, the* FIRST MAN *has brought the* BURGOMASTER'*s dress coat and top hat. The* BURGOMASTER *puts on the coat, then advances slowly and solemnly*)

CONDUCTOR: I trust madame will not speak of this to the administration. It was a pure misunderstanding.

(*He salutes and runs for the train as it starts moving*)

BURGOMASTER: *(Bows)* Gracious lady, as Burgomaster of the town of Güllen, I have the honor—

(The rest of the speech is lost in the roar of the departing train. He continues speaking and gesturing, and at last bows amid applause as the train noises end)

CLAIRE: Thank you, Mr. Burgomaster.

(She glances at the beaming faces, and lastly at SCHILL, *whom she does not recognize. She turns upstage)*

SCHILL: Clara!
CLAIRE: *(Turns and stares)* Anton?
SCHILL: Yes. It's good that you've come back.
CLAIRE: Yes. I've waited for this moment. All my life. Ever since I left Güllen.
SCHILL: *(A little embarrassed)* That is very kind of you to say, Clara.
CLAIRE: And have you thought about me?
SCHILL: Naturally. Always. You know that.
CLAIRE: Those were happy times we spent together.
SCHILL: Unforgettable.

(He smiles reassuringly at the BURGOMASTER*)*

CLAIRE: Call me by the name you used to call me.
SCHILL: *(Whispers)* My kitten.
CLAIRE: What?
SCHILL: *(Louder)* My kitten.
CLAIRE: And what else?
SCHILL: Little witch.
CLAIRE: I used to call you my black panther. You're gray now, and soft.
SCHILL: But you are still the same, little witch.
CLAIRE: I am the same? *(She laughs)* Oh, no, my black panther, I am not at all the same.
SCHILL: *(Gallantly)* In my eyes you are. I see no difference.
CLAIRE: Would you like to meet my fiancé? Pedro Cabral. He owns an enormous plantation in Brazil.
SCHILL: A pleasure.
CLAIRE: We're to be married soon.
SCHILL: Congratulations.
CLAIRE: He will be my eighth husband *(*PEDRO *stands by himself downstage, right)* Pedro, come here and show your face. Come along, darling—come here! Don't sulk. Say hello.
PEDRO: Hello.
CLAIRE: A man of few words! Isn't he charming? A diplomat. He's interested only in fishing. Isn't he handsome, in his Latin way? You'd swear he was a Brazilian. But he's not—he's a Greek. His father was a White Russian. We were betrothed by a Bulgarian priest. We plan to be married in a few days here in the cathedral.
BURGOMASTER: Here in the cathedral? What an honor for us!

CLAIRE: No. It was my dream, when I was seventeen, to be married in Güllen cathedral. The dreams of youth are sacred, don't you think so, Anton?

SCHILL: Yes, of course.

CLAIRE: Yes, of course. I think so, too. Now I would like to look at the town. (*The mixed choir arrives, breathless, wearing ordinary clothes with green sashes*) What's all this? Go away. (*She laughs*) Ha! Ha! Ha!

TEACHER: Dear lady—(*He steps forward, having put on a sash also*) Dear lady, as Rector of the high school and a devotee of that noble muse, Music, I take pleasure in presenting the Güllen mixed choir.

CLAIRE: How do you do?

TEACHER: Who will sing for you an ancient folk song of the region, with specially amended words—if you will deign to listen.

CLAIRE: Very well. Fire away.

(*The* TEACHER *blows a pitch pipe. The mixed choir begins to sing the ancient folk song with the amended words. Just then the station bell starts ringing. The song is drowned in the roar of the passing express. The* STATION MASTER *salutes. When the train has passed, there is applause*)

BURGOMASTER: The church bell! The church bell! Where's the church bell?

(*The* PASTOR *shrugs helplessly*)

CLAIRE: Thank you, Professor. They sang beautifully. The big little blond bass—no, not that one—the one with the big Adam's apple—was most impressive. (*The* TEACHER *bows. The* POLICEMAN *pushes his way professionally through the mixed choir and comes to attention in front of* CLAIRE ZACHANASSIAN) Now, who are you?

POLICEMAN: (*Clicks heels*) Police Chief Schultz. At your service.

CLAIRE: (*She looks him up and down*) I have no need of you at the moment. But I think there will be work for you by and by. Tell me, do you know how to close an eye from time to time?

POLICEMAN: How else could I get along in my profession?

CLAIRE: You might practice closing both.

SCHILL: (*Laughs*) What a sense of humor, eh?

BURGOMASTER: (*Puts on the top hat*) Permit me to present my grandchildren, gracious lady. Hermine and Adolphine. There's only my wife still to come.

(*He wipes the perspiration from his brow, and replaces the hat. The little girls present the roses with elaborate curtsies*)

CLAIRE: Thank you, my dears. Congratulations, Burgomaster. Extraordinary children.

(*She plants the roses in* PEDRO'S *arms. The* BURGOMASTER *secretly passes his top hat to the* PASTOR, *who puts it on*)

BURGOMASTER: Our pastor, madame.

(*The* PASTOR *takes off the hat and bows*)

CLAIRE: Ah. The pastor. How do you do? Do you give consolation to the dying?

PASTOR: (*A bit puzzled*) That is part of my ministry, yes.

CLAIRE: And to those who are condemned to death?

PASTOR: Capital punishment has been abolished in this country, madame.

CLAIRE: I see. Well, it could be restored, I suppose.

(*The* PASTOR *hands back the hat. He shrugs his shoulders in confusion*)

SCHILL: (*Laughs*) What an original sense of humor!

(*All laugh, a little blankly*)

CLAIRE: Well, I can't sit here all day—I should like to see the town.

(*The* BURGOMASTER *offers his arm*)

BURGOMASTER: May I have the honor, gracious lady?

CLAIRE: Thank you, but these legs are not what they were. This one was broken in five places.

SCHILL: (*Full of concern*) My kitten!

CLAIRE: When my airplane bumped into a mountain in Afghanistan. All the others were killed. Even the pilot. But as you see, I survived. I don't fly any more.

SCHILL: But you're as strong as ever now.

CLAIRE: Stronger.

BURGOMASTER: Never fear, gracious lady. The town doctor has a car.

CLAIRE: I never ride in motors.

BURGOMASTER: You never ride in motors?

CLAIRE: Not since my Ferrari crashed in Hong Kong.

SCHILL: But how do you travel, then, little witch? On a broom?

CLAIRE: Mike—Max! (*She claps her hands. Two huge bodyguards come in, left, carrying a sedan chair. She sits in it*) I travel this way—a bit anti-quated, of course. But perfectly safe. Ha! Ha! Aren't they magnificent? Mike and Max. I bought them in America. They were in jail, condemned to the chair. I had them pardoned. Now they're condemned to my chair. I paid fifty thousand dollars apiece for them. You couldn't get them now for twice the sum. The sedan chair comes from the Louvre. I fancied it so much that the President of France gave it to me. The French are so impulsive, don't you think so, Anton? Go!

(*Mike and Max start to carry her off*)

BURGOMASTER: You wish to visit the cathedral? And the old town hall?

CLAIRE: No. The great barn. And the forest of Konradsweil. I wish to go with Anton and visit our old haunts once again.

THE PASTOR: Very touching.

CLAIRE: *(To the butler)* Will you send my luggage and the coffin to the Golden Apostle?

BURGOMASTER: The coffin?

CLAIRE: Yes. I brought one with me. Go!

TEACHER: Hip-hip—

ALL: Hurrah! Hip-hip, hurrah! Hurrah!

(They bear off in the direction of the town. The TOWNSPEOPLE burst into cheers. The church bell rings)

BURGOMASTER: Ah, thank God—the bell at last.

(The POLICEMAN is about to follow the others, when the two BLIND MEN appear. They are not young, yet they seem childish—a strange effect. Though they are of different height and features, they are dressed exactly alike, and so create the effect of being twins. They walk slowly, feeling their way. Their voices, when they speak, are curiously high and flutelike, and they have a curious trick of repetition of phrases)

FIRST BLIND MAN: We're in—

BOTH BLIND MEN: Güllen.

FIRST BLIND MAN: We breathe—

SECOND BLIND MAN: We breathe—

BOTH BLIND MEN: We breathe the air, the air of Güllen.

POLICEMAN: *(Startled)* Who are you?

FIRST BLIND MAN: We belong to the lady.

SECOND BLIND MAN: We belong to the lady. She calls us—

FIRST BLIND MAN: Kobby.

SECOND BLIND MAN: And Lobby.

POLICEMAN: Madame Zachanassian is staying at the Golden Apostle.

FIRST BLIND MAN: We're blind.

SECOND BLIND MAN: We're blind.

POLICEMAN: Blind? Come along with me, then. I'll take you there.

FIRST BLIND MAN: Thank you, Mr. Policeman.

SECOND BLIND MAN: Thanks very much.

POLICEMAN: Hey! How do you know I'm a policeman, if you're blind?

BOTH BLIND MEN: By your voice. By your voice.

FIRST BLIND MAN: All policemen sound the same.

POLICEMAN: You've had a lot to do with the police, have you, little men?

FIRST BLIND MAN: Men he calls us!

BOTH BLIND MEN: Men!

POLICEMAN: What are you then?

BOTH BLIND MEN: You'll see. You'll see.

(The POLICEMAN claps his hands suddenly. The BLIND MEN turn sharply toward the sound. The POLICEMAN is convinced they are blind)

POLICEMAN: What's your trade?
BOTH BLIND MEN: We have no trade.
SECOND BLIND MAN: We play music.
FIRST BLIND MAN: We sing.
SECOND BLIND MAN: We amuse the lady.
FIRST BLIND MAN: We look after the beast.
SECOND BLIND MAN: We feed it.
FIRST BLIND MAN: We stroke it.
SECOND BLIND MAN: We take it for walks.
POLICEMAN: What beast?
BOTH BLIND MEN: You'll see—you'll see.
SECOND BLIND MAN: We give it raw meat.
FIRST BLIND MAN: And she gives us chicken and wine.
SECOND BLIND MAN: Every day—
BOTH BLIND MEN: Every day.
POLICEMAN: Rich people have strange tastes.
BOTH BLIND MEN: Strange tastes—strange tastes.

(The POLICEMAN puts on his helmet)

POLICEMAN: Come along, I'll take you to the lady.

(The two BLIND MEN turn and walk off)

BOTH BLIND MEN: We know the way—we know the way.

(The station and the little house vanish. A sign representing the Golden Apostle descends. The scene dissolves into the interior of the inn. The Golden Apostle is seen to be in the last stages of decay. The walls are cracked and moldering, and the plaster is falling from the ancient lath. A table represents the café of the inn. The BURGOMASTER and the TEACHER sit at this table, drinking a glass together. A procession of TOWNSPEOPLE, carrying many pieces of luggage, passes. Then comes a coffin, and, last, a large box covered with a canvas. They cross the stage from right to left)

BURGOMASTER: Trunks. Suitcases. Boxes. (He looks up apprehensively at the ceiling) The floor will never bear the weight. (As the large covered box is carried in, he peers under the canvas, then draws back) Good God!
TEACHER: Why, what's in it?
BURGOMASTER: A live panther. (They laugh. The BURGOMASTER lifts his glass solemnly) Your health, Professor. Let's hope she puts the Foundry back on its feet.
TEACHER: (Lifts his glass) And the Wagonworks.
BURGOMASTER: And the Golden Eagle Pencil Factory. Once that starts moving, everything else will go. Prosit.[1]

---

1. Your health.

(They touch glasses and drink)

TEACHER: What does she need a panther for?

BURGOMASTER: Don't ask me. The whole thing is too much for me. The Pastor had to go home and lie down.

TEACHER: *(Sets down his glass)* If you want to know the truth, she frightens me.

BURGOMASTER: *(Nods gravely)* She's a strange one.

TEACHER: You understand, Burgomaster, a man who for twenty-two years has been correcting the Latin compositions of the students of Güllen is not unaccustomed to surprises. I have seen things to make one's hair stand on end. But when this woman suddenly appeared on the platform, a shudder tore through me. It was as though out of the clear sky all at once a fury descended upon us, beating its black wings—

(The POLICEMAN comes in. He mops his face)

POLICEMAN: Ah! Now the old place is livening up a bit!

BURGOMASTER: Ah, Schultz, come and join us.

POLICEMAN: Thank you. *(He calls)* Beer!

BURGOMASTER: Well, what's the news from the front?

POLICEMAN: I'm just back from Schiller's barn. My God! What a scene! She had us all tiptoeing around in the straw as if we were in church. Nobody dared to speak above a whisper. And the way she carried on! I was so embarrassed I let them go to the forest by themselves.

BURGOMASTER: Does the fiancé go with them?

POLICEMAN: With his fishing rod and his landing net. In full marching order. *(He calls again)* Beer!

BURGOMASTER: That will be her seventh husband.

TEACHER: Her eighth.

BURGOMASTER: But what does she expect to find in the Konradsweil forest?

POLICEMAN: The same thing she expected to find in the old barn, I suppose. The—the—

TEACHER: The ashes of her youthful love.

POLICEMAN: Exactly.

TEACHER: It's poetry.

POLICEMAN: Poetry.

TEACHER: Sheer poetry! It makes one think of Shakespeare, of Wagner. Of Romeo and Juliet.

(The SECOND MAN comes in as a waiter. The POLICEMAN is served his beer)

BURGOMASTER: Yes, you're right. *(Solemnly)* Gentlemen, I would like to propose a toast. To our great and good friend, Anton Schill, who is even now working on our behalf.

POLICEMAN: Yes! He's really working.

BURGOMASTER: Gentlemen, to the best-loved citizen of this town. My successor, Anton Schill!

(They raise their glasses. At this point an unearthly scream is heard. It is the black panther howling offstage. The sign of the Golden Apostle rises out of sight. The lights go down. The inn vanishes. Only the wooden bench, on which the four men were lounging in the opening scene, is left on the stage, downstage right. The procession comes on upstage. The two bodyguards carry in CLAIRE's sedan chair. Next to it walks SCHILL. PEDRO walks behind, with his fishing rod. Last come the two BLIND MEN and the butler. CLAIRE alights)

CLAIRE: Stop! Take my chair off somewhere else. I'm tired of looking at you. *(The bodyguards and the sedan chair go off)* Pedro darling, your brook is just a little further along down that path. Listen. You can hear it from here. Bobby, take him and show him where it is.

BOTH BLIND MEN: We'll show him the way—we'll show him the way.

(They go off, left. PEDRO follows. BOBBY walks off, right)

CLAIRE: Look, Anton. Our tree. There's the heart you carved in the bark long ago.

SCHILL: Yes. It's still there.

CLAIRE: How it has grown! The trunk is black and wrinkled. Why, its limbs are twice what they were. Some of them have died.

SCHILL: It's aged. But it's there.

CLAIRE: Like everything else. *(She crosses, examining other trees)* Oh, how tall they are. How long it is since I walked here, barefoot over the pine needles and the damp leaves! Look, Anton. A fawn.

SCHILL: Yes, a fawn. It's the season.

CLAIRE: I thought everything would be changed. But it's all just as we left it. This is the seat we sat on years ago. Under these branches you kissed me. And over there under the hawthorn, where the moss is soft and green, we would lie in each other's arms. It is all as it used to be. Only we have changed.

SCHILL: Not so much, little witch. I remember the first night we spent together, you ran away and I chased you till I was quite breathless—

CLAIRE: Yes.

SCHILL: Then I was angry and I was going home, when suddenly I heard you call and I looked up, and there you were sitting in a tree, laughing down at me.

CLAIRE: No. It was in the great barn. I was in the hayloft.

SCHILL: Were you?

CLAIRE: Yes. What else do you remember?

SCHILL: I remember the morning we went swimming by the waterfall, and afterwards we were lying together on the big rock in the sun, when suddenly we heard footsteps and we just had time to snatch up our clothes and run behind the bushes when the old pastor appeared and scolded you for not being in school.

CLAIRE: No. It was the schoolmaster who found us. It was Sunday and I was supposed to be in church.

SCHILL: Really?

CLAIRE: Yes. Tell me more.

SCHILL: I remember the time your father beat you, and you showed me the cuts on your back, and I swore I'd kill him. And the next day I dropped a tile from a roof top and split his head open.

CLAIRE: You missed him.

SCHILL: No!

CLAIRE: You hit old Mr. Reiner.

SCHILL: Did I?

CLAIRE: Yes. I was seventeen. And you were not yet twenty. You were so handsome. You were the best-looking boy in town.

(The two BLIND MEN begin playing mandolin music offstage, very softly)

SCHILL: And you were the prettiest girl.

CLAIRE: We were made for each other.

SCHILL: So we were.

CLAIRE: But you married Mathilde Blumhard and her store, and I married old Zachanassian and his oil wells. He found me in a whorehouse in Hamburg. It was my hair that entangled him, the old golden beetle.

SCHILL: Clara!

CLAIRE: *(She claps her hands)* Bobby! A cigar.

(BOBBY appears with a leather case. He selects a cigar, puts it in a holder, lights it, and presents it to CLAIRE)

SCHILL: My kitten smokes cigars!

CLAIRE: Yes. I adore them. Would you care for one?

SCHILL: Yes, please. I've never smoked one of those.

CLAIRE: It's a taste I acquired from old Zachanassian. Among other things. He was a real connoisseur.

SCHILL: We used to sit on this bench once, you and I, and smoke cigarettes. Do you remember?

CLAIRE: Yes. I remember.

SCHILL: The cigarettes I bought from Mathilde.

CLAIRE: No. She gave them to you for nothing.

SCHILL: Clara—don't be angry with me for marrying Mathilde.

CLAIRE: She had money.

SCHILL: But what a lucky thing for you that I did!

CLAIRE: Oh?

SCHILL: You were so young, so beautiful. You deserved a far better fate than to settle in this wretched town without any future.

CLAIRE: Yes?

SCHILL: If you had stayed in Güllen and married me, your life would have been wasted, like mine.

CLAIRE: Oh?

SCHILL: Look at me. A wretched shopkeeper in a bankrupt town!

CLAIRE: But you have your family.

SCHILL: My family! Never for a moment do they let me forget my failure, my poverty.

CLAIRE: Mathilde has not made you happy?

SCHILL: *(Shrugs)* What does it matter?

CLAIRE: And the children?

SCHILL: *(Shakes his head)* They're so completely materialistic. You know, they have no interest whatever in higher things.

CLAIRE: How sad for you.

(A moment's pause, during which only the faint tinkling of the music is heard)

SCHILL: Yes. You know, since you went away my life has passed by like a stupid dream. I've hardly once been out of this town. A trip to a lake years ago. It rained all the time. And once five days in Berlin. That's all.

CLAIRE: The world is much the same everywhere.

SCHILL: At least you've seen it.

CLAIRE: Yes. I've seen it.

SCHILL: You've lived in it.

CLAIRE: I've lived in it. The world and I have been on very intimate terms.

SCHILL: Now that you've come back, perhaps things will change.

CLAIRE: Naturally. I certainly won't leave my native town in this condition.

SCHILL: It will take millions to put us on our feet again.

CLAIRE: I have millions.

SCHILL: One, two, three.

CLAIRE: Why not?

SCHILL: You mean—you will help us?

CLAIRE: Yes.

(A woodpecker is heard in the distance)

SCHILL: I knew it—I knew it. I told them you were generous. I told them you were good. Oh, my kitten, my kitten.

(He takes her hand. She turns her head away and listens)

CLAIRE: Listen! A woodpecker.

SCHILL: It's all just the way it was in the days when we were young and full of courage. The sun high above the pines. White clouds, piling up on one another. And the cry of the cuckoo in the distance. And the wind rustling the leaves, like the sound of surf on a beach. Just as it was years ago. If only we could roll back time and be together always.

CLAIRE: Is that your wish?

SCHILL: Yes. You left me, but you never left my heart. (*He raises her hand to his lips*) The same soft little hand.

CLAIRE: No, not quite the same. It was crushed in the plane accident. But they mended it. They mend everything nowadays.

SCHILL: Crushed? You wouldn't know it. See, another fawn.

CLAIRE: The old wood is alive with memories.

(PEDRO *appears, right, with a fish in his hand*)

PEDRO: See what I've caught, darling. See? A pike. Over two kilos.

(*The* BLIND MEN *appear onstage*)

BOTH BLIND MEN: (*Clapping their hands*) A pike! A pike! Hurrah! Hurrah!

(*As the* BLIND MEN *clap their hands,* CLAIRE *and* SCHILL *exit, and the scene dissolves. The clapping of hands is taken up on all sides. The townspeople wheel in the walls of the café. A brass band strikes up a march tune. The door of the Golden Apostle descends. The townspeople bring in tables and set them with ragged tablecloths, cracked china, and glassware. There is a table in the center, upstage, flanked by two tables perpendicular to it, right and left. The* PASTOR *and the* BURGOMASTER *come in.* SCHILL *enters. Other townspeople filter in, left and right. One, the* ATHLETE, *is in gymnastic costume. The applause continues*)

BURGOMASTER: She's coming! (CLAIRE *enters upstage, center, followed by* BOBBY) The applause is meant for you, gracious lady.

CLAIRE: The band deserves it more than I. They blow from the heart. And the human pyramid was beautiful. You, show me your muscles. (*The* ATHLETE *kneels before her*) Superb. Wonderful arms, powerful hands. Have you ever strangled a man with them?

ATHLETE: Strangled?

CLAIRE: Yes. It's perfectly simple. A little pressure in the proper place, and the rest goes by itself. As in politics.

(*The* BURGOMASTER'S *wife comes up, simpering*)

BURGOMASTER: (*Presents her*) Permit me to present my wife, Madame Zachanassian.

CLAIRE: Annette Dummermuth. The head of our class.

BURGOMASTER: (*He presents another sour-looking woman*) Frau Schill.

CLAIRE: Mathilde Blumhard. I remember the way you used to follow Anton with your eyes, from behind the shop door. You've grown a little thin and dry, my poor Mathilde.

SCHILL: My daughter, Ottilie.

CLAIRE: Your daughter . . .

SCHILL: My son, Karl.

CLAIRE: Your son. Two of them!

(The town Doctor comes in, right. He is a man of fifty, strong and stocky, with bristly black hair, a mustache, and a saber cut on his cheek. He is wearing an old cutaway)

Doctor: Well, well, my old Mercedes got me here in time after all!
Burgomaster: Dr. Nüsslin, the town physician. Madame Zachanassian.
Doctor: Deeply honored, madame.

(He kisses her hand. Claire studies him)

Claire: It is you who signs the death certificates?
Doctor: Death certificates?
Claire: When someone dies.
Doctor: Why certainly. That is one of my duties.
Claire: And when the heart dies, what do you put down? Heart failure?
Schill: *(Laughing)* What a golden sense of humor!
Doctor: Bit grim, wouldn't you say?
Schill: *(Whispers)* Not at all, not at all. She's promised us a million.
Burgomaster: *(Turns his head)* What?
Schill: A million!
All: *(Whisper)* A million!

(Claire turns toward them)

Claire: Burgomaster.
Burgomaster: Yes?
Claire: I'm hungry. *(The girls and the waiter fill glasses and bring food. There is a general stir. All take their places at the tables)* Are you going to make a speech?

(The Burgomaster bows. Claire sits next to the Burgomaster. The Burgomaster rises, tapping his knife on his glass. He is radiant with good will. All applaud)

Burgomaster: Gracious lady and friends. Gracious lady, it is now many years since you first left your native town of Güllen, which was founded by the Elector Hasso and which nestles in the green slope between the forest of Konradsweil and the beautiful valley of Pückenried. Much has taken place in this time, much that is evil.
Teacher: That's true.
Burgomaster: The world is not what it was; it has become harsh and bitter, and we too have had our share of harshness and bitterness. But in all this time, dear lady, we have never forgotten our little Clara. *(Applause)* Many years ago you brightened the town with your pretty face as a child, and now once again you brighten it with your presence. *(Polite applause)* We haven't forgotten you, and we haven't forgotten your family. Your mother, beautiful and robust even in her old age—*(He looks for his notes on the*

table)—although unfortunately taken from us in the bloom of her youth by an infirmity of the lungs. Your respected father, Siegfried Wäscher, the builder, an example of whose work next to our railway station is often visited—(SCHILL *covers his face)*—that is to say, admired—a lasting monument of local design and local workmanship. And you, gracious lady, whom we remember as a golden-haired—(*He looks at her)*—little red-headed sprite romping about our peaceful streets—on your way to school—which of us does not treasure your memory? (*He pokes nervously at his notebook)* We well remember your scholarly attainments—

TEACHER: Yes.

BURGOMASTER: Natural history . . . Extraordinary sense of justice . . . And, above all, your supreme generosity. (*Great applause)* We shall never forget how you once spent the whole of your little savings to buy a sack of potatoes for a poor starving widow who was in need of food. Gracious lady, ladies and gentlemen, today our little Clara has become the world-famous Claire Zachanassian who has founded hospitals, soup kitchens, charitable institutes, art projects, libraries, nurseries, and schools, and now that she has at last once more returned to the town of her birth, sadly fallen as it is, I say in the name of all her loving friends who have sorely missed her: Long live our Clara!

ALL: Long live our Clara!

(Cheers. Music. Fanfare. Applause. CLAIRE rises)

CLAIRE: Mr. Burgomaster. Fellow townsmen. I am greatly moved by the nature of your welcome and the disinterested joy which you have manifested on the occasion of my visit to my native town. I was not quite the child the Burgomaster described in his gracious address . . .

BURGOMASTER: Too modest, madame.

CLAIRE: In school I was beaten—

TEACHER: Not by me.

CLAIRE: And the sack of potatoes which I presented to Widow Boll, I stole with the help of Anton Schill, not to save the old trull from starvation, but so that for once I might sleep with Anton in a real bed instead of under the trees of the forest. (*The townspeople look grave, embarrassed)* Nevertheless, I shall try to deserve your good opinion. In memory of the seventeen years I spent among you, I am prepared to hand over as a gift to the town of Güllen the sum of one billion marks. Five hundred million to the town, and five hundred million to be divided per capita among the citizens.

(There is a moment of dead silence)

BURGOMASTER: A billion marks?
CLAIRE: On one condition.

(Suddenly a movement of uncontrollable joy breaks out. People jump on chairs, dance about, yell excitedly. The ATHLETE turns handsprings in front of the speaker's table)

SCHILL: Oh, Clara, you astonishing, incredible, magnificent woman! What a heart! What a gesture! Oh—my little witch!

(He kisses her hand)

BURGOMASTER: *(Holds up his arms for order)* Quiet! Quiet, please! On one condition, the gracious lady said. Now, madame, may we know what that condition is?
CLAIRE: I will tell you. In exchange for my billion marks, I want justice.

(Silence)

BURGOMASTER: Justice, madame?
CLAIRE: I wish to buy justice.
BURGOMASTER: But justice cannot be bought, madame.
CLAIRE: Everything can be bought.
BURGOMASTER: I don't understand at all.
CLAIRE: Bobby, step forward.

(The butler goes to the center of the stage. He takes off his dark glasses and turns his face with a solemn air)

BOBBY: Does anyone here present recognize me?
FRAU SCHILL: Hofer! Hofer!
ALL: Who? What's that?
TEACHER: Not Chief Magistrate Hofer?
BOBBY: Exactly. Chief Magistrate Hofer. When Madame Zachanassian was a girl, I was presiding judge at the criminal court of Güllen. I served there until twenty-five years ago, when Madame Zachanassian offered me the opportunity of entering her service as butler. I accepted. You may consider it a strange employment for a member of the magistracy, but the salary—

(CLAIRE bangs the mallet on the table)

CLAIRE: Come to the point.
BOBBY: You have heard Madame Zachanassian's offer. She will give you a billion marks—when you have undone the injustice that she suffered at your hands here in Güllen as a girl.

(All murmur)

BURGOMASTER: Injustice at our hands? Impossible!
BOBBY: Anton Schill . . .

SCHILL: Yes?
BOBBY: Kindly stand.

(SCHILL *rises. He smiles, as if puzzled. He shrugs*)

SCHILL: Yes?
BOBBY: In those days, a bastardy case was tried before me. Madame Claire Zachanassian, at that time called Clara Wäscher, charged you with being the father of her illegitimate child. (*Silence*) You denied the charge. And produced two witnesses in your support.
SCHILL: That's ancient history. An absurd business. We were children. Who remembers?
CLAIRE: Where are the blind men?
BOTH BLIND MEN: Here we are. Here we are.

(MIKE *and* MAX *push them forward*)

BOBBY: You recognize these men, Anton Schill?
SCHILL: I never saw them before in my life. What are they?
BOTH BLIND MEN: We've changed. We've changed.
BOBBY: What were your names in your former life?
FIRST BLIND MAN: I was Jacob Hueblein. Jacob Hueblein.
SECOND BLIND MAN: I was Ludwig Sparr. Ludwig Sparr.
BOBBY: (*To* SCHILL) Well?
SCHILL: These names mean nothing to me.
BOBBY: Jacob Hueblein and Ludwig Sparr, do you recognize the defendant?
FIRST BLIND MAN: We're blind.
SECOND BLIND MAN: We're blind.
SCHILL: Ha-ha-ha!
BOBBY: By his voice?
BOTH BLIND MEN: By his voice. By his voice.
BOBBY: At that trial, I was the judge. And you?
BOTH BLIND MEN: We were the witnesses.
BOBBY: And what did you testify on that occasion?
FIRST BLIND MAN: That we had slept with Clara Wäscher.
SECOND BLIND MAN: Both of us. Many times.
BOBBY: And was it true?
FIRST BLIND MAN: No.
SECOND BLIND MAN: We swore falsely.
BOBBY: And why did you swear falsely?
FIRST BLIND MAN: Anton Schill bribed us.
SECOND BLIND MAN: He bribed us.
BOBBY: With what?
BOTH BLIND MEN: With a bottle of schnapps.

BOBBY: And now tell the people what happened to you. *(They hesitate and whimper)* Speak!

FIRST BLIND MAN: *(In a low voice)* She tracked us down.

BOBBY: Madame Zachanassian tracked them down. Jacob Hueblein was found in Canada. Ludwig Sparr in Australia. And when she found you, what did she do to you?

SECOND BLIND MAN: She handed us over to Mike and Max.

BOBBY: And what did Mike and Max do to you?

FIRST BLIND MAN: They made us what you see.

(The BLIND MEN cover their faces. MIKE and MAX push them off)

BOBBY: And there you have it. We are all present in Güllen once again. The plaintiff. The defendant. The two false witnesses. The judge. Many years have passed. Does the plaintiff have anything further to add?

CLAIRE: There is nothing to add.

BOBBY: And the defendant?

SCHILL: Why are you doing this? It was all dead and buried.

BOBBY: What happened to the child that was born?

CLAIRE: *(In a low voice)* It lived a year.

BOBBY: And what happened to you?

CLAIRE: I became a whore.

BOBBY: Why?

CLAIRE: The judgment of the court left me no alternative. No one would trust me. No one would give me work.

BOBBY: So. And now, what is the nature of the reparation you demand?

CLAIRE: I want the life of Anton Schill.

(FRAU SCHILL springs to ANTON's side. She puts her arms around him. The children rush to him. He breaks away)

FRAU SCHILL: Anton! No! No!

SCHILL: No— No— She's joking. That happened long ago. That's all forgotten.

CLAIRE: Nothing is forgotten. Neither the mornings in the forest, nor the nights in the great barn, nor the bedroom in the cottage, nor your treachery at the end. You said this morning that you wished that time might be rolled back. Very well—I have rolled it back. And now it is I who will buy justice. You bought it with a bottle of schnapps. I am willing to pay one billion marks.

(The BURGOMASTER stands up, very pale and dignified)

BURGOMASTER: Madame Zachanassian, we are not in the jungle. We are in Europe. We may be poor, but we are not heathens. In the name of the town of Güllen, I decline your offer. In the name of humanity. We shall never accept.

(All applaud wildly. The applause turns into a sinister rhythmic beat. As CLAIRE *rises, it dies away. She looks at the crowd, then at the* BURGOMASTER)

CLAIRE: Thank you, Burgomaster. *(She stares at him a long moment)* I can
 wait.

(She turns and walks off)

Curtain

ACT TWO

*The façade of the Golden Apostle, with a balcony on which chairs and a table are set out. To the right of the inn is a sign which reads: "*ANTON SCHILL, HANDLUNG.*"[1] Under the sign the shop is represented by a broken counter. Behind the counter are some shelves with tobacco, cigarettes, and liquor bottles. There are two milk cans. The shop door is imaginary, but each entrance is indicated by a doorbell with a tinny sound.*

It is early morning.

SCHILL *is sweeping the shop. The* SON *has a pan and brush and also sweeps. The* DAUGHTER *is dusting. They are singing "The Happy Wanderer."*

SCHILL: Karl—

*(*KARL *crosses with a dustpan.* SCHILL *sweeps dust into the pan. The doorbell rings. The* THIRD MAN *appears, carrying a crate of eggs)*

THIRD MAN: 'Morning.
 SCHILL: Ah, good morning, Wechsler.
THIRD MAN: Twelve dozen eggs, medium brown. Right?
 SCHILL: Take them, Karl. *(The* SON *puts the crate in a corner)* Did they
   deliver the milk yet?
   SON: Before you came down.
THIRD MAN: Eggs are going up again, Herr Schill. First of the month.

(He gives SCHILL *a slip to sign)*

 SCHILL: What? Again? And who's going to buy them?
THIRD MAN: Fifty pfennig a dozen.
 SCHILL: I'll have to cancel my order, that's all.
THIRD MAN: That's up to you, Herr Schill.

*(*SCHILL *signs the slip)*

---

 1. *"Anton Schill, Merchandise."*

SCHILL: There's nothing else to do. *(He hands back the slip)* And how's the family?

THIRD MAN: Oh, scraping along. Maybe now things will get better.

SCHILL: Maybe.

THIRD MAN: *(Going)* 'Morning.

SCHILL: Close the door. Don't let the flies in. *(The children resume their singing)* Now, listen to me, children. I have a little piece of good news for you. I didn't mean to speak of it yet awhile, but well, why not? Who do you suppose is going to be the next Burgomaster? Eh? *(They look up at him)* Yes, in spite of everything. It's settled. It's official. What an honor for the family, eh? Especially at a time like this. To say nothing of the salary and the rest of it.

SON: Burgomaster!

SCHILL: Burgomaster. *(The SON shakes him warmly by the hand. The DAUGHTER kisses him)* You see, you don't have to be entirely ashamed of your father. *(Silence)* Is your mother coming down to breakfast soon?

DAUGHTER: Mother's tired. She going to stay upstairs.

SCHILL: You have a good mother, at least. There you are lucky. Oh, well, if she wants to rest, let her rest. We'll have breakfast together, the three of us. I'll fry some eggs and open a tin of the American ham. This morning we're going to breakfast like kings.

SON: I'd like to, only—I can't.

SCHILL: You've got to eat, you know.

SON: I've got to run down to the station. One of the laborers is sick. They said they could use me.

SCHILL: You want to work on the rails in all this heat? That's no work for a son of mine.

SON: Look, Father, we can use the money.

SCHILL: Well, if you feel you have to.

(The son goes to the door. The DAUGHTER moves toward SCHILL)

DAUGHTER: I'm sorry, Father. I have to go too.

SCHILL: You too? And where is the young lady going, if I may be so bold?

DAUGHTER: There may be something for me at the employment agency.

SCHILL: Employment agency?

DAUGHTER: It's important to get there early.

SCHILL: All right. I'll have something nice for you when you get home.

SON and DAUGHTER: *(Salute)* Good day, Burgomaster.

(The SON and DAUGHTER go out. The FIRST MAN comes into SCHILL's shop. Mandolin and guitar music are heard offstage)

SCHILL: Good morning, Hofbauer.

FIRST MAN: Cigarettes. *(SCHILL takes a pack from the shelf)* Not those. I'll have the green today.

SCHILL: They cost more.

FIRST MAN: Put it in the book.

SCHILL: What?

FIRST MAN: Charge it.

SCHILL: Well, all right, I'll make an exception this time—seeing it's you, Hofbauer.

(SCHILL *writes in his cash book*)

FIRST MAN: (*Opening the pack of cigarettes*) Who's that playing out there?

SCHILL: The two blind men.

FIRST MAN: They play well.

SCHILL: To hell with them.

FIRST MAN: They make you nervous? (SCHILL *shrugs. The* FIRST MAN *lights a cigarette*) She's getting ready for the wedding, I hear.

SCHILL: Yes. So they say.

(*Enter the* FIRST *and* SECOND WOMAN. *They cross to the counter*)

FIRST MAN: Good morning, good morning.

SECOND MAN: Good morning.

FIRST MAN: Good morning.

SCHILL: Good morning, ladies.

FIRST WOMAN: Good morning, Herr Schill.

SECOND WOMAN: Good morning.

FIRST WOMAN: Milk please, Herr Schill.

SCHILL: Milk.

SECOND WOMAN: And milk for me too.

SCHILL: A liter of milk each. Right away.

FIRST WOMAN: Whole milk, please, Herr Schill.

SCHILL: Whole milk?

SECOND WOMAN: Yes. Whole milk, please.

SCHILL: Whole milk, I can only give you half a liter each of whole milk.

FIRST WOMAN: All right.

SCHILL: Half a liter of whole milk here, and half a liter of whole milk here. There you are.

FIRST WOMAN: And butter please, a quarter kilo.

SCHILL: Butter, I haven't any butter. I can give you some very nice lard?

FIRST WOMAN: No. Butter.

SCHILL: Goose fat? (*The* FIRST WOMAN *shakes her head*) Chicken fat?

FIRST WOMAN: Butter.

SCHILL: Butter. Now, wait a minute, though. I have a tin of imported butter here somewhere. Ah. There you are. No, sorry, she asked first, but I can order some for you from Kalberstadt tomorrow.

SECOND WOMAN: And white bread.

SCHILL: White bread.

(He takes a loaf and a knife)

SECOND WOMAN: The whole loaf.
 SCHILL: But a whole loaf would cost . . .
SECOND WOMAN: Charge it.
 SCHILL: Charge it?
FIRST WOMAN: And a package of milk chocolate.
 SCHILL: Package of milk chocolate—right away.
SECOND WOMAN: One for me, too, Herr Schill.
 SCHILL: And a package of milk chocolate for you, too.
FIRST WOMAN: We'll eat it here, if you don't mind.
 SCHILL: Yes, please do.
SECOND WOMAN: It's so cool at the back of the shop.
 SCHILL: Charge it?
WOMEN: Of course.
 SCHILL: All for one, one for all.

(The SECOND MAN enters)

SECOND MAN: Good morning.
THE TWO WOMEN: Good morning.
 SCHILL: Good morning, Helmesberger.
SECOND MAN: It's going to be a hot day.
 SCHILL: Phew!
SECOND MAN: How's business?
 SCHILL: Fabulous. For a while no one came, and now all of a sudden I'm running a luxury trade.
SECOND MAN: Good!
 SCHILL: Oh, I'll never forget the way you all stood by me at the Golden Apostle in spite of your need, in spite of everything. That was the finest hour of my life.
FIRST MAN: We're not heathens, you know.
SECOND MAN: We're behind you, my boy; the whole town's behind you.
FIRST MAN: As firm as a rock.
FIRST WOMAN: *(Munching her chocolate)* As firm as a rock, Herr Schill.
BOTH WOMEN: As firm as a rock.
SECOND MAN: There's no denying it—you're the most popular man in town.
FIRST MAN: The most important.
SECOND MAN: And in the spring, God willing, you will be our Burgomaster.
FIRST MAN: Sure as a gun.
 ALL: Sure as a gun.

(Enter PEDRO with fishing equipment and a fish in his landing net)

 PEDRO: Would you please weigh my fish for me?

SCHILL: *(Weighs it)* Two kilos.

PEDRO: Is that all?

SCHILL: Two kilos exactly.

PEDRO: Two kilos!

(He gives SCHILL *a tip and exits)*

SECOND WOMAN: The fiancé.

FIRST WOMAN: They're to be married this week. It will be a tremendous wedding.

SECOND WOMAN: I saw his picture in the paper.

FIRST WOMAN: *(Sighs)* Ah, what a man!

SECOND MAN: Give me a bottle of schnapps.

SCHILL: The usual?

SECOND MAN: No, cognac.

SCHILL: Cognac? But cognac costs twenty-two marks fifty.

SECOND MAN: We all have to splurge a little now and again—

SCHILL: Here you are. Three Star.

SECOND MAN: And a package of pipe tobacco.

SCHILL: Black or blond?

SECOND MAN: English.

SCHILL: English! But that makes twenty-three marks eighty.

SECOND MAN: Chalk it up.

SCHILL: Now, look. I'll make an exception this week. Only, you will have to pay me the moment your unemployment check comes in. I don't want to be kept waiting. *(Suddenly)* Helmesberger, are those new shoes you're wearing?

SECOND MAN: Yes, what about it?

SCHILL: You too, Hofbauer. Yellow shoes! Brand new!

FIRST MAN: So?

SCHILL: *(To the woman)* And you. You all have new shoes! New shoes!

FIRST WOMAN: A person can't walk around forever in the same old shoes.

SECOND WOMAN: Shoes wear out.

SCHILL: And the money. Where does the money come from?

FIRST WOMAN: We got them on credit, Herr Schill.

SECOND WOMAN: On credit.

SCHILL: On credit? And where all of a sudden do you get credit?

SECOND MAN: Everybody gives credit now.

FIRST WOMAN: You gave us credit yourself.

SCHILL: And what are you going to pay with? Eh? *(They are all silent.* SCHILL *advances upon them threateningly)* With what? Eh? With what? With what?

(Suddenly he understands. He takes his apron off quickly, flings it on the counter, gets his jacket, and walks off with an air of determination. Now the shop sign vanishes. The shelves are pushed off. The lights go up on the balcony of the Golden Apostle, and the balcony unit

itself moves forward into the optical center. CLAIRE *and* BOBBY *step out on the balcony.* CLAIRE *sits down.* BOBBY *serves coffee)*

CLAIRE: A lovely autumn morning. A silver haze on the streets and a violet sky above. Count Holk would have liked this. Remember him, Bobby? My third husband?

BOBBY: Yes, madame.

CLAIRE: Horrible man!

BOBBY: Yes, madame.

CLAIRE: Where is Monsieur Pedro? Is he up yet?

BOBBY: Yes, madame. He's fishing.

CLAIRE: Already? What a singular passion!

*(*PEDRO *comes in with the fish)*

PEDRO: Good morning, my love.

CLAIRE: Pedro! There you are.

PEDRO: Look, my darling. Four kilos!

CLAIRE: A jewel! I'll have it grilled for your lunch. Give it to Bobby.

PEDRO: Ah—it is so wonderful here! I like your little town.

CLAIRE: Oh, do you?

PEDRO: Yes. These people, they are all so—what is the word?

CLAIRE: Simple, honest, hard-working, decent.

PEDRO: But, my angel, you are a mind reader. That's just what I was going to say—however did you guess?

CLAIRE: I know them.

PEDRO: Yet when we arrived it was all so dirty, so—what is the word?

CLAIRE: Shabby.

PEDRO: Exactly. But now everywhere you go, you see them busy as bees, cleaning their streets—

CLAIRE: Repairing their houses, sweeping—dusting—hanging new curtains in the windows—singing as they work.

PEDRO: But you astonishing, wonderful woman! You can't see all that from here.

CLAIRE: I know them. And in their gardens—I am sure that in their gardens they are manuring the soil for the spring.

PEDRO: My angel, you know everything. This morning on my way fishing I said to myself, look at them all manuring their gardens. It is extraordinary—and it's all because of you. Your return has given them a new—what is the word?

CLAIRE: Lease on life?

PEDRO: Precisely.

CLAIRE: The town was dying, it's true. But a town doesn't have to die. I think they realize that now. People die, not towns! *(*BOBBY *appears)* A cigar.

(The lights fade on the balcony, which moves back upstage. Somewhat to the right, a sign descends. It reads: "Polizei." The POLICEMAN *pushes a desk under it. This, with the bench, becomes the police station. He places a bottle of beer and a glass on the desk, and goes to hang up his coat offstage. The telephone rings)*

POLICEMAN: Schultz speaking. Yes, we have a couple of rooms for the night. No, not for rent. This is not the hotel. This is the Güllen police station.

(He laughs and hangs up. SCHILL *comes in. He is evidently nervous)*

SCHILL: Schultz.
POLICEMAN: Hello, Schill. Come in. Sit down. Beer?
SCHILL: Please.

(He drinks thirstily)

POLICEMAN: What can I do for you?
SCHILL: I want you to arrest Madame Zachanassian.
POLICEMAN: Eh?
SCHILL: I said I want you to arrest Madame Zachanassian.
POLICEMAN: What the hell are you talking about?
SCHILL: I ask you to arrest this woman at once.
POLICEMAN: What offense has the lady committed?
SCHILL: You know perfectly well. She offered a billion marks—
POLICEMAN: And you want her arrested for that?

(He pours beer into his glass)

SCHILL: Schultz! It's your duty.
SCHULTZ: Extraordinary! Extraordinary idea!

(He drinks his beer)

SCHILL: I'm speaking to you as your next Burgomaster.
POLICEMAN: Schill, that's true. The lady offered us a billion marks. But that doesn't entitle us to take police action against her.
SCHILL: Why not?
POLICEMAN: In order to be arrested, a person must first commit a crime.
SCHILL: Incitement to murder.
POLICEMAN: Incitement to murder is a crime. I agree.
SCHILL: Well?
POLICEMAN: And such a proposal—if serious—constitutes an assault.
SCHILL: That's what I mean.
POLICEMAN: But her offer can't be serious.
SCHILL: Why?
POLICEMAN: The price is too high. In a case like yours, one pays a thousand marks, at the most two thousand. But not a billion! That's

ridiculous. And even if she meant it, that would only prove she was out of her mind. And that's not a matter for the police.

SCHILL: Whether she's out of her mind or not, the danger to me is the same. That's obvious.

POLICEMAN: Look, Schill, you show us where anyone threatens your life in any way—say, for instance, a man points a gun at you—and we'll be there in a flash.

SCHILL: *(Gets up)* So I'm to wait till someone points a gun at me?

POLICEMAN: Pull yourself together, Schill. We're all for you in this town.

SCHILL: I wish I could believe it.

POLICEMAN: You don't believer it?

SCHILL: No. No, I don't. All of a sudden my customers are buying white bread, whole milk, butter, imported tobacco. What does it mean?

POLICEMAN: It means business is picking up.

SCHILL: Helmesberger lives on the dole; he hasn't earned anything in five years. Today he bought French cognac.

POLICEMAN: I'll have to try your cognac one of these days.

SCHILL: And shoes. They all have new shoes.

POLICEMAN: And what have you got against new shoes? I'm wearing a new pair myself.

(He holds out his foot)

SCHILL: You too?

POLICEMAN: Why not?

(He pours out the rest of his beer)

SCHILL: Is that Pilsen you're drinking now?

POLICEMAN: It's the only thing.

SCHILL: You used to drink the local beer.

POLICEMAN: Hogwash.

(Radio music is heard offstage)

SCHILL: Listen. You hear?

POLICEMAN: "The Merry Widow." Yes.

SCHILL: No. It's a radio.

POLICEMAN: That's Bergholzer's radio.

SCHILL: Bergholzer!

POLICEMAN: You're right. He should close his window when he plays it. I'll make a note to speak to him.

(He makes a note in his notebook)

SCHILL: And how can Bergholzer pay for a radio?

POLICEMAN: That's his business.

SCHILL: And you, Schultz, with your new shoes and your imported beer—how are you going to pay for them?

POLICEMAN: That's my business. (*His telephone rings. He picks it up*) Police Station, Güllen. What? What? Where? Where? How? Right, we'll deal with it.

(*He hangs up*)

SCHILL: (*He speaks during the* POLICEMAN'S *telephone conversation*) Schultz, listen. No. Schultz, please—listen to me. Don't you see they're all . . . Listen, please. Look, Schultz. They're all running up debts. And out of these debts comes this sudden prosperity. And out of this prosperity comes the absolute need to kill me.

POLICEMAN: (*Putting on his jacket*) You're imagining things.

SCHILL: All she has to do is to sit on her balcony and wait.

POLICEMAN: Don't be a child.

SCHILL: You're all waiting.

POLICEMAN: (*Snaps a loaded clip into the magazine of a rifle*) Look, Schill, you can relax. The police are here for your protection. They know their job. Let anyone, any time, make the slightest threat to your life, and all you have to do is let us know. We'll do the rest . . . Now, don't worry.

SCHILL: No, I won't.

POLICEMAN: And don't upset yourself. All right?

SCHILL: Yes. I won't. (*Then suddenly, in a low tone*) You have a new gold tooth in your mouth!

POLICEMAN: What are you talking about?

SCHILL: (*Taking the* POLICEMAN'S *head in his hands, and forcing his lips open*) A brand new, shining gold tooth.

POLICEMAN: (*Breaks away and involuntarily levels the gun at* SCHILL) Are you crazy? Look, I've no time to waste. Madame Zachanassian's panther's broken loose.

SCHILL: Panther?

POLICEMAN: Yes, it's at large. I've got to hunt it down.

SCHILL: You're not hunting a panther and you know it. It's me you're hunting!

(*The* POLICEMAN *clicks on the safety and lowers the gun*)

POLICEMAN: Schill! Take my advice. Go home. Lock the door. Keep out of everyone's way. That way you'll be safe. Cheer up! Good times are just around the corner!

(*The lights dim in this area and light up on the balcony.* PEDRO *is lounging in a chair.* CLAIRE *is smoking*)

PEDRO: Oh, this little town oppresses me.

CLAIRE: Oh, does it? So you've changed your mind?

PEDRO: It is true, I find it charming, delightful—

CLAIRE: Picturesque.

PEDRO: Yes. After all, it's the place where you were born. But it is too quiet for me. Too provincial. Too much like all small towns everywhere. These people—look at them. They fear nothing, they desire nothing, they strive for nothing. They have everything they want. They are asleep.

CLAIRE: Perhaps one day they will come to life again.

PEDRO: My God—do I have to wait for that?

CLAIRE: Yes, you do. Why don't you go back to your fishing?

PEDRO: I think I will.

(PEDRO *turns to go*)

CLAIRE: Pedro.

PEDRO: Yes, my love?

CLAIRE: Telephone the president of Hambro's Bank.[1] Ask him to transfer a billion marks to my current account.

PEDRO: A billion? Yes, my love.

(*He goes. The lights fade on the balcony. A sign is flown in. It reads: "Rathaus."[2] The* THIRD MAN *crosses the stage, right to left, wheeling a new television set on a hand truck. The counter of* SCHILL's *shop is transformed into the* BURGOMASTER's *office. The* BURGOMASTER *comes in. He takes a revolver from his pocket, examines it and sets it down on the desk. He sits down and starts writing.* SCHILL *knocks*)

BURGOMASTER: Come in.

SCHILL: I must have a word with you, Burgomaster.

BURGOMASTER: Ah, Schill. Sit down, my friend.

SCHILL: Man to man. As your successor.

BURGOMASTER: But of course. Naturally.

(SCHILL *remains standing. He looks at the revolver*)

SCHILL: Is that a gun?

BURGOMASTER: Madame Zachanassian's black panther's broken loose. It's been seen near the cathedral. It's as well to be prepared.

SCHILL: Oh, yes. Of course.

BURGOMASTER: I've sent out a call for all able-bodied men with firearms. The streets have been cleared. The children have been kept in school. We don't want any accidents.

SCHILL: (*Suspiciously*) You're making quite a thing of it.

---

1. *One of the principal banks of England.*
2. *"City Hall."*

BURGOMASTER: *(Shrugs)* Naturally. A panther is a dangerous beast. Well? What's on your mind? Speak out. We're old friends.

SCHILL: That's a good cigar you're smoking, Burgomaster.

BURGOMASTER: Yes. Havana.

SCHILL: You used to smoke something else.

BURGOMASTER: Fortuna.

SCHILL: Cheaper.

BURGOMASTER: Too strong.

SCHILL: A new tie? Silk?

BURGOMASTER: Yes. Do you like it?

SCHILL: And have you also bought new shoes?

BURGOMASTER: *(Brings his feet out from under the desk)* Why, yes. I ordered a new pair from Kalberstadt. Extraordinary! However did you guess?

SCHILL: That's why I'm here.

(The THIRD MAN knocks)

BURGOMASTER: Come in.

THIRD MAN: The new typewriter, sir.

BURGOMASTER: Put it on the table. *(The THIRD MAN sets it down and goes)* What's the matter with you? My dear fellow, aren't you well?

SCHILL: It's you who don't seem well, Burgomaster.

BURGOMASTER: What do you mean?

SCHILL: You look pale.

BURGOMASTER: I?

SCHILL: Your hands are trembling. *(The BURGOMASTER involuntarily hides his hands)* Are you frightened?

BURGOMASTER: What have I to be afraid of?

SCHILL: Perhaps this sudden prosperity alarms you.

BURGOMASTER: Is prosperity a crime?

SCHILL: That depends on how you pay for it.

BURGOMASTER: You'll have to forgive me, Schill, but I really haven't the slightest idea what you're talking about. Am I supposed to feel like a criminal every time I order a new typewriter?

SCHILL: Do you?

BURGOMASTER: Well, I hope you haven't come here to talk about a new typewriter. Now, what was it you wanted?

SCHILL: I have come to claim the protection of the authorities.

BURGOMASTER: Ei! Against whom?

SCHILL: You know against whom.

BURGOMASTER: You don't trust us?

SCHILL: The woman has put a price on my head.

BURGOMASTER: If you don't feel safe, why don't you go to the police?

SCHILL: I have just come from the police.

BURGOMASTER: And?

SCHILL: The chief has a new gold tooth in his mouth.

BURGOMASTER: A new—? Oh, Schill, really! You're forgetting. This is Güllen, the town of humane traditions. Goethe slept here. Brahms composed a quartet. You must have faith in us. This is a law-abiding community.

SCHILL: Then arrest this woman who wants to have me killed.

BURGOMASTER: Look here, Schill. God knows the lady has every right to be angry with you. What you did there wasn't very pretty. You forced two decent lads to perjure themselves and had a young girl thrown out on the streets.

SCHILL: That young girl owns half the world.

(A moment's silence)

BURGOMASTER: Very well, then, we'll speak frankly.

SCHILL: That's why I'm here.

BURGOMASTER: Man to man, just as you said. *(He clears his throat)* Now— after what you did, you have no moral right to say a word against this lady. And I advise you not to try. Also—I regret to have to tell you this—there is no longer any question of your being elected Burgomaster.

SCHILL: Is that official?

BURGOMASTER: Official.

SCHILL: I see.

BURGOMASTER: The man who is chosen to exercise the high post of Burgomaster must have, obviously, certain moral qualifications. Qualifications which, unhappily, you no longer possess. Naturally, you may count on the esteem and friendship of the town, just as before. That goes without saying. The best thing will be to spread the mantle of silence over the whole miserable business.

SCHILL: So I'm to remain silent while they arrange my murder?

(The BURGOMASTER gets up)

BURGOMASTER: *(Suddenly noble)* Now, who is arranging your murder? Give me the names and I will investigate the case at once. Unrelentingly. Well? The names?

SCHILL: You.

BURGOMASTER: I resent this. Do you think we want to kill you for money?

SCHILL: No. You don't want to kill me. But you want to have me killed.

(The lights go down. The stage is filled with men prowling about with rifles, as if they were stalking a quarry. In the interval the POLICEMAN's bench and the BURGOMASTER's desk are shifted somewhat, so that they will compose the setting for the sacristy. The stage empties. The lights come up on the balcony. CLAIRE appears)

CLAIRE: Bobby, what's going on here? What are all these man doing with guns? Whom are they hunting?

BOBBY: The black panther has escaped, madame.

CLAIRE: Who let him out?

BOBBY: Kobby and Lobby, madame.

CLAIRE: How excited they are! There may be shooting?

BOBBY: It is possible, madame.

(The lights fade on the balcony. The sacristan comes in. He arranges the set, and puts the altar cloth on the altar. Then SCHILL comes on. He is looking for the PASTOR. The PASTOR enters, left. He is wearing his gown and carrying a rifle)

SCHILL: Sorry to disturb you, Pastor.

PASTOR: God's house is open to all. *(He sees that SCHILL is staring at the gun)* Oh, the gun? That's because of the panther. It's best to be prepared.

SCHILL: Pastor, help me.

PASTOR: Of course. Sit down. *(He puts the rifle on the bench)* What's the trouble?

SCHILL: *(Sits on the bench)* I'm frightened.

PASTOR: Frightened? Of what?

SCHILL: Of everyone. They're hunting me down like a beast.

PASTOR: Have no fear of man, Schill. Fear God. Fear not the death of the body. Fear the death of the soul. Zip up my gown behind, Sacristan.

SCHILL: I'm afraid, Pastor.

PASTOR: Put your trust in heaven, my friend.

SCHILL: You see, I'm not well. I shake. I have such pains around the heart. I sweat.

PASTOR: I know. You're passing through a profound psychic experience.

SCHILL: I'm going through hell.

PASTOR: The hell you are going through exists only within yourself. Many years ago you betrayed a girl shamefully, for money. Now you think that we shall sell you just as you sold her. No, my friend, you are projecting your guilt upon others. It's quite natural. But remember, the root of our torment lies always within ourselves, in our hearts, in our sins. When you have understood this, you can conquer the fears that oppress you; you have weapons with which to destroy them.

SCHILL: Siemethofer has bought a new washing machine.

PASTOR: Don't worry about the washing machine. Worry about your immortal soul.

SCHILL: Stockers has a television set.

PASTOR: There is also great comfort in prayer. Sacristan, the bands. *(SCHILL crosses to the altar and kneels. The sacristan ties on the PASTOR's bands)* Examine your conscience, Schill. Repent. Otherwise your fears will consume you. Believe me, this is the only way. We have no other. *(The church bell begins to peal. SCHILL seems relieved)*

Now I must leave you. I have a baptism. You may stay as long as you like. Sacristan, the Bible, Liturgy, and Psalter. The child is beginning to cry. I can hear it from here. It is frightened. Let us make haste to give it the only security which this world affords.

SCHILL: A new bell?

PASTOR: Yes. Its tone is marvelous, don't you think? Full. Sonorous.

SCHILL: *(Steps back in horror)* A new bell! You too, Pastor? You too?

(The PASTOR *clasps his hands in horror. Then he takes* SCHILL *into his arms)*

PASTOR: Oh, God, God forgive me. We are poor, weak things, all of us. Do not tempt us further into the hell in which you are burning. Go, Schill, my friend, go my brother, go while there is time.

(The PASTOR *goes.* SCHILL *picks up the rifle with a gesture of desperation. He goes out with it. As the lights fade, men appear with guns. Two shots are fired in the darkness. The lights come up on the balcony, which moves forward)*

CLAIRE: Bobby! What was that shooting? Have they caught the panther?

BOBBY: He is dead, madame.

CLAIRE: There were two shots.

BOBBY: The panther is dead, madame.

CLAIRE: I loved him. *(Waves* BOBBY *away)* I shall miss him.

(The TEACHER *comes in with two little girls, singing. They stop under the balcony)*

TEACHER: Gracious lady, be so good as to accept our heartfelt condolences. Your beautiful panther is no more. Believe me, we are deeply pained that so tragic an event should mar your visit here. But what could we do? The panther was savage, a beast. To him our human laws could not apply. There was no other way—(SCHILL *appears with the gun. He looks dangerous. The girls run off, frightened. The* TEACHER *follows the girls)* Children—children—children!

CLAIRE: Anton, why are you frightening the children?

(He works the bolt, loading the chamber, and raises the gun slowly)

SCHILL: Go away, Claire—I warn you. Go away.

CLAIRE: How strange it is, Anton! How clearly it comes back to me! The day we saw one another for the first time, do you remember? I was on a balcony then. It was a day like today, a day in autumn without a breath of wind, warm as it is now—only lately I am always cold. You stood down there and stared at me without moving. I was embarrassed. I didn't know what to do. I wanted to go back into the darkness of the room, where it was safe, but I couldn't. You stared up at me darkly, almost angrily, as if you wished to hurt me, but your eyes were full of passion. (SCHILL *begins to lower the rifle involuntarily)* Then, I don't know why, I left the balcony and I came down and stood in the street beside you.

You didn't greet me, you didn't say a word, but you took my hand and we walked together out of town into the fields, and behind us came Kobby and Lobby, like two dogs, sniveling and giggling and snarling. Suddenly you picked up a stone and hurled it at them, and they ran yelping back into the town, and we were alone. (SCHILL *has lowered the rifle completely. He moves forward toward her, as close as he can come*) That was the beginning, and everything else had to follow. There is no escape.

(*She goes in and closes the shutters.* SCHILL *stands immobile. The* TEACHER *tiptoes in. He stares at* SCHILL, *who doesn't see him. Then he beckons to the children*)

TEACHER: Come children, sing. Sing.

(*They begin singing. He creeps behind* SCHILL *and snatches away the rifle.* SCHILL *turns sharply. The* PASTOR *comes in*)

PASTOR: Go, Schill—go!

(SCHILL *goes out. The children continue singing, moving across the stage and off. The Golden Apostle vanishes. The crossing bell is heard. The scene dissolves into the railway-station setting, as in Act One. But there are certain changes. The timetable marked "Fahrplan" is now new, the frame freshly painted. There is a new travel poster on the station wall. It has a yellow sun and the words: "Reist in den Süden."*[1] *On the other side of the Fahrplan is another poster with the words: "Die Passionsspiele Oberammergau."*[2] *The sound of passing trains covers the scene change.* SCHILL *appears with an old valise in his hand, dressed in a shabby trench coat, his hat on his head. He looks about with a furtive air, walking slowly to the platform. Slowly, as if by chance, the townspeople enter, from all sides.* SCHILL *hesitates, stops*)

BURGOMASTER: (*From upstage, center*) Good evening, Schill.
SCHILL: Good evening.
POLICEMAN: Good evening.
SCHILL: Good evening.
PAINTER: (*Enters*) Good evening.
SCHILL: Good evening.
DOCTOR: Good evening.
SCHILL: Good evening.
BURGOMASTER: So you're taking a little trip?
SCHILL: Yes. A little trip.
POLICEMAN: May one ask where to?
SCHILL: I don't know.
PAINTER: Don't know?

---

1. *"Travel in the South."*
2. *"The Oberammergau Passion Play,"* portraying the suffering and death of Jesus, is performed in the south German village every ten years.

SCHILL: To Kalberstadt.

BURGOMASTER: *(With disbelief, pointing to the valise)* Kalberstadt?

SCHILL: After that—somewhere else.

PAINTER: Ah. After that somewhere else.

(The FOURTH MAN *walks in)*

SCHILL: I thought maybe Australia.

BURGOMASTER: Australia!

ALL: Australia!

SCHILL: I'll raise the money somehow.

BURGOMASTER: But why Australia?

POLICEMAN: What would you be doing in Australia?

SCHILL: One can't always live in the same town, year in, year out.

PAINTER: But Australia—

DOCTOR: It's a risky trip for a man of your age.

BURGOMASTER: One of the lady's little men ran off to Australia . . .

ALL: Yes.

POLICEMAN: You'll be much safer here.

PAINTER: Much!

*(*SCHILL *looks about him in anguish, like a beast at bay)*

SCHILL: *(Low voice)* I wrote a letter to the administration at Kaffigen.

BURGOMASTER: Yes? And?

(They are all intent on the answer)

SCHILL: They didn't answer.

(All laugh)

DOCTOR: Do you mean to say you don't trust old friends? That's not very
flattering, you know.

BURGOMASTER: No one's going to do you any harm here.

DOCTOR: No harm here.

SCHILL: They didn't answer because our postmaster held up my letter.

PAINTER: Our postmaster? What an idea.

BURGOMASTER: The postmaster is a member of the town council.

POLICEMAN: A man of the utmost integrity.

DOCTOR: He doesn't hold up letters. What an idea! *(The crossing bell starts
ringing)*

STATION MASTER: *(Announces)* Local to Kalberstadt!

*(The townspeople all cross down to see the train arrive. Then they turn, with their backs to
the audience, in a line across the stage.* SCHILL *cannot get through to reach the train)*

SCHILL: *(In a low voice)* What are you all doing here? What do you want of
me?

BURGOMASTER: We don't like to see you go.

DOCTOR: We've come to see you off.

(*The sound of the approaching train grows louder*)

SCHILL: I didn't ask you to come.
POLICEMAN: But we have come.
DOCTOR: As old friends.
   ALL: As old friends.

(*The* STATION MASTER *holds up his paddle. The train stops with a screech of brakes. We hear the engine panting offstage*)

VOICE: (*Offstage*) Güllen!
BURGOMASTER: A pleasant journey.
DOCTOR: And long life!
PAINTER: And good luck in Australia!
   ALL: Yes, good luck in Australia.

(*They press around him jovially. He stands motionless and pale*)

SCHILL: Why are you crowding me?
POLICEMAN: What's the matter now?

(*The* STATION MASTER *blows a long blast on his whistle*)

SCHILL: Give me room.
DOCTOR: But you have plenty of room.

(*They all move away from him*)

POLICEMAN: Better get aboard, Schill.
SCHILL: I see. I see. One of you is going to push me under the wheels.
POLICEMAN: Oh, nonsense. Go on, get aboard.
SCHILL: Get away from me, all of you.
BURGOMASTER: I don't know what you want. Just get on the train.
SCHILL: No. One of you will push me under.
DOCTOR: You're being ridiculous. Now, go on, get on the train.
SCHILL: Why are you all so near me?
DOCTOR: The man's gone mad.
STATION MASTER: 'Board!

(*He blows his whistle. The engine bell clangs. The train starts*)

BURGOMASTER: Get aboard man. Quick.

(*The following speeches are spoken all together until the train noises fade away*)

DOCTOR: The train's starting.
   ALL: Get aboard, man. Get aboard. The train's starting.
SCHILL: If I try to get aboard, one of you will hold me back.
   ALL: No, no.
BURGOMASTER: Get on the train.

SCHILL: *(In terror, crouches against the wall of the* STATION MASTER's *office)* No—no—no. No. *(He falls on his knees. The others crowd around him. He cowers on the ground, abjectly. The train sounds fade away)* Oh, no—no—don't push me, don't push me!

POLICEMAN: There. It's gone off without you.

(Slowly they leave him. He raises himself up to a sitting position, still trembling. A TRUCK DRIVER *enters with an empty can)*

TRUCK DRIVER: Do you know where I can get some water? My truck's boiling over. *(*SCHILL *points to the station office)* Thanks. *(He enters the office, gets the water and comes out. By this time,* SCHILL *is erect)* Missed your train?

SCHILL: Yes.

TRUCK DRIVER: To Kalberstadt?

SCHILL: Yes.

TRUCK DRIVER: Well, come with me. I'm going that way.

SCHILL: This is my town. This is my home. *(With strange new dignity)* No, thank you. I've changed my mind. I'm staying.

TRUCK DRIVER: *(Shrugs)* All right.

(He goes out. SCHILL *picks up his bag, looks right and left, and slowly walks off)*

Curtain

ACT THREE

Music is heard. Then the curtain rises on the interior of the old barn, a dim, cavernous structure. Bars of light fall across the shadowy forms, shafts of sunlight from the holes and cracks in the walls and roof. Overhead hang old rags, decaying sacks, great cobwebs. Extreme left is a ladder leading to the loft. Near it, an old haycart. Left, CLAIRE ZACHANASSIAN *is sitting in her gilded sedan chair, motionless, in her magnificent bridal gown and veil. Near the chair stands an old keg.*

BOBBY: *(Comes in, treading carefully)* The doctor and the teacher from the high school to see you, madame.

CLAIRE: *(Impassive)* Show them in.

*(*BOBBY *ushers them in as if they were entering a hall of state. The two grope their way through the litter. At last they find the lady, and bow. They are both well dressed in new clothes, but are very dusty)*

BOBBY: Dr. Nüsslin and Professor Müller.

DOCTOR: Madame.

CLAIRE: You look dusty, gentlemen.

DOCTOR: *(Dusts himself off vigorously)* Oh, forgive us. We had to climb over an old carriage.

TEACHER: Our respects.

DOCTOR: A fabulous wedding.

TEACHER: Beautiful occasion.

CLAIRE: It's stifling here. But I love this old barn. The smell of hay and old straw and axle grease—it is the scent of my youth. Sit down. All this rubbish—the haycart, the old carriage, the cask, even the pitchfork—it was all here when I was a girl.

TEACHER: Remarkable place.

(He mops his brow)

CLAIRE: I thought the pastor's text was very appropriate. The lesson a trifle long.

TEACHER: I Corinthians 13.[1]

CLAIRE: Your choristers sang beautifully, Professor.

TEACHER: Bach. From the *St. Matthew Passion*.

DOCTOR: Güllen has never seen such magnificence! The flowers! The jewels! And the people.

TEACHER: The theatrical world, the world of finance, the world of art, the world of science . . .

CLAIRE: All these worlds are now back in their Cadillacs, speeding toward the capital for the wedding reception. But I'm sure you didn't come here to talk about them.

DOCTOR: Dear lady, we should not intrude on your valuable time. Your husband must be waiting impatiently.

CLAIRE: No, no, I've packed him off to Brazil.

DOCTOR: To Brazil, madame?

CLAIRE: Yes. For his honeymoon.

TEACHER *and* DOCTOR: Oh! But your wedding guests?

CLAIRE: I've planned a delightful dinner for them. They'll never miss me. Now what was it you wished to talk about?

TEACHER: About Anton Schill, madame.

CLAIRE: Is he dead?

TEACHER: Madame, we may be poor. But we have our principles.

CLAIRE: I see. Then what do you want?

TEACHER: *(He mops his brow again)* The fact is, madame, in anticipation of your well-known munificence, that is, feeling that you would give the town some sort of gift, we have all been buying things. Necessities . . .

DOCTOR: With money we don't have.

(The TEACHER blows his nose)

---

1. See I Corinthians 13:13: "But now abideth faith, hope, love, these three; and the greatest of these is love."

CLAIRE: You've run into debt?

DOCTOR: Up to here.

CLAIRE: In spite of your principles?

TEACHER: We're human, madame.

CLAIRE: I see.

TEACHER: We have been poor for a long time. A long, long time.

DOCTOR: *(He rises)* The question is, how are we going to pay?

CLAIRE: You already know.

TEACHER: *(Courageously)* I beg you, Madame Zachanassian, put yourself in our position for a moment. For twenty-two years I've been cudgeling my brains to plant a few seeds of knowledge in this wilderness. And all this time, my gallant colleague, Dr. Nüsslin, has been rattling around in his ancient Mercedes, from patient to patient, trying to keep these wretches alive. Why? Why have we spent our lives in this miserable hole? For money? Hardly. The pay is ridiculous.

DOCTOR: And yet, the professor here has declined an offer to head the high school in Kalberstadt.

TEACHER: And Dr. Nüsslin has refused an important post at the University of Erlangen. Madame, the simple fact is, we love our town. We were born here. It is our life.

DOCTOR: That's true.

TEACHER: What has kept us going all these years is the hope that one day the community will prosper again as it did in the days when we were young.

CLAIRE: Good.

TEACHER: Madame, there is no reason for our poverty. We suffer here from a mysterious blight. We have factories. They stand idle. There is oil in the valley of Pückenried.

DOCTOR: There is copper under the Konradsweil Forest. There is power in our streams, in our waterfalls.

TEACHER: We are not poor, madame. If we had credit, if we had confidence, the factories would open, orders and commissions would pour in. And our economy would bloom together with our cultural life. We would become once again like the towns around us, healthy and prosperous.

DOCTOR: If the Wagonworks were put on its feet again—

TEACHER: The Foundry.

DOCTOR: The Golden Eagle Pencil Factory.

TEACHER: Buy these plants, madame. Put them in operation once more, and I swear to you, Güllen will flourish and it will bless you. We don't need a billion marks. Ten million, properly invested, would give us back our life, and incidentally return to the investor an excellent dividend. Save us, madame. Save us, and we will not only bless you, we will make money for you.

CLAIRE: I don't need money.

DOCTOR: Madame, we are not asking for charity. This is business.

CLAIRE: It's a good idea . . .

DOCTOR: Dear lady! I knew you wouldn't let us down.

CLAIRE: But it's out of the question. I cannot buy the Wagonworks. I already own them.

DOCTOR: The Wagonworks?

TEACHER: And the Foundry?

CLAIRE: And the Foundry.

DOCTOR: And the Golden Eagle Pencil Factory?

CLAIRE: Everything. The valley of Pückenried with its oil, the forest of Konradsweil with its ore, the barn, the town, the streets, the houses, the shops, everything. I had my agents buy up this rubbish over the years, bit by bit, piece by piece, until I had it all. Your hopes were an illusion, your vision empty, your self-sacrifice a stupidity, your whole life completely senseless.

TEACHER: Then the mysterious blight—

CLAIRE: The mysterious blight was I.

DOCTOR: But this is monstrous!

CLAIRE: Monstrous. I was seventeen when I left this town. It was winter. I was dressed in a sailor suit and my red braids hung down my back. I was in my seventh month. As I walked down the street to the station, the boys whistled after me, and someone threw something. I sat freezing in my seat in the Hamburg Express. But before the roof of the great barn was lost behind the trees, I had made up my mind that one day I would come back . . .

TEACHER: But, madame—

CLAIRE: *(She smiles)* And now I have. *(She claps her hands)* Mike. Max. Take me back to the Golden Apostle. I've been here long enough.

(MIKE and MAX start to pick up the sedan chair. The TEACHER pushes MIKE away.)

TEACHER: Madame. One moment. Please. I see it all now. I had thought of you as an avenging fury, a Medea, a Clytemnestra—but I was wrong. You are a warm-hearted woman who has suffered a terrible injustice, and now you have returned and taught us an unforgettable lesson. You have stripped us bare. But now that we stand before you naked, I know you will set aside these thoughts of vengeance. If we made you suffer, you too have put us through the fire. Have mercy, madame.

CLAIRE: When I have had justice. Mike!

(She signals to MIKE and MAX to pick up the sedan chair. They cross the stage. The TEACHER bars the way)

TEACHER: But, madame, one injustice cannot cure another. What good will it do to force us into crime? Horror succeeds horror, shame is piled on shame. It settles nothing.

CLAIRE: It settles everything.

(They move upstage toward the exit. The TEACHER follows)

TEACHER: Madame, this lesson you have taught us will never be forgotten. We will hand it down from father to son. It will be a monument more lasting than any vengeance. Whatever we have been, in the future we shall be better because of you. You have pushed us to the extreme. Now forgive us. Show us the way to a better life. Have pity, madame—pity. That is the highest justice.

(The sedan chair stops)

CLAIRE: The highest justice has no pity. It is bright and pure and clear. The world made me into a whore; now I make the world into a brothel. Those who wish to go down, may go down. Those who wish to dance with me, may dance with me. *(To her porters)* Go.

(She is carried off. The lights black out. Downstage, right, appears SCHILL's shop. It has a new sign, a new counter. The doorbell, when it rings, has an impressive sound. FRAU SCHILL stands behind the counter in a new dress. The FIRST MAN enters, left. He is dressed as a prosperous butcher, a few bloodstains on his snowy apron, a gold watch chain across his open vest)

FIRST MAN: What a wedding! I'll swear the whole town was there. Cigarettes.

FRAU SCHILL: Clara is entitled to a little happiness after all. I'm happy for her. Green or white?

FIRST MAN: Turkish. The bridesmaids! Dancers and opera singers. And the dresses! Down to here.

FRAU SCHILL: It's the fashion nowadays.

FIRST MAN: Reporters! Photographers! From all over the world! *(In a low voice)* They will be here any minute.

FRAU SCHILL: What have reporters to do with us? We are simple people, Herr Hofbauer. There is nothing for them here.

FIRST MAN: They're questioning everybody. They're asking everything. *(The FIRST MAN lights a cigarette. He looks up at the ceiling)* Footsteps.

FRAU SCHILL: He's pacing the room. Up and down. Day and night.

FIRST MAN: Haven't seen him all week.

FRAU SCHILL: He never goes out.

FIRST MAN: It's his conscience. That was pretty mean, the way he treated poor Madame Zachanassian.

FRAU SCHILL: That's true. I feel very badly about it myself.

FIRST MAN: To ruin a young girl like that— God doesn't forgive it. *(FRAU SCHILL nods solemnly with pursed lips. The butcher gives her a level*

glance) Look, I hope he'll have sense enough to keep his mouth
shut in front of the reporters.

FRAU SCHILL: I certainly hope so.

FIRST MAN: You know his character.

FRAU SCHILL: Only too well, Herr Hofbauer.

FIRST MAN: If he tries to throw dirt at our Clara and tell a lot of lies, how
she tried to get us to kill him, which anyway she never meant—

FRAU SCHILL: Of course not.

FIRST MAN: —Then we'll really have to do something! And not because of
the money— (He spits) But out of ordinary human decency. God
knows Madame Zachanassian has suffered enough through him
already.

FRAU SCHILL: She has indeed.

(The TEACHER comes in. He is not quite sober)

TEACHER: (Looks about the shop) Has the press been here yet?

FIRST MAN: No.

TEACHER: It's not my custom, as you know, Frau Schill—but I wonder if I
could have a strong alcoholic drink?

FRAU SCHILL: It's an honor to serve you, Herr Professor. I have a good
Steinhäger.[1] Would you like to try a glass?

TEACHER: A very small glass.

(FRAU SCHILL serves bottle and glass. The TEACHER tosses off a glass)

FRAU SCHILL: Your hand is shaking, Herr Professor.

TEACHER: To tell the truth, I have been drinking a little already.

FRAU SCHILL: Have another glass. It will do you good. (He accepts another
glass)

TEACHER: Is that he up there, walking?

FRAU SCHILL: Up and down. Up and down.

FIRST MAN: It's God punishing him.

(The PAINTER comes in with the SON and the DAUGHTER)

PAINTER: Careful! A reporter just asked us the way to this shop.

FIRST MAN: I hope you didn't tell him.

PAINTER: I told him we were strangers here.

(They all laugh. The door opens. The SECOND MAN darts into the shop)

SECOND MAN: Look out, everybody! The press! They are across the street
in your shop, Hofbauer.

FIRST MAN: My boy will know how to deal with them.

SECOND MAN: Make sure Schill doesn't come down, Hofbauer.

---

1. A kind of gin.

FIRST MAN: Leave that to me.

(They group themselves about the shop)

TEACHER: Listen to me, all of you. When the reporters come I'm going to speak to them. I'm going to make a statement. A statement to the world on behalf of myself as Rector of Güllen High School and on behalf of you all, for all your sakes.

PAINTER: What are you going to say?

TEACHER: I shall tell the truth about Claire Zachanassian.

FRAU SCHILL: You're drunk, Herr Professor; you should be ashamed of yourself.

TEACHER: I should be ashamed? You should all be ashamed!

SON: Shut your trap. You're drunk.

DAUGHTER: Please, Professor—

TEACHER: Girl, you disappoint me. It is your place to speak. But you are silent and you force your old teacher to raise his voice. I am going to speak the truth. It is my duty and I am not afraid. The world may not wish to listen, but no one can silence me. I'm not going to wait—I'm going over to Hofbauer's shop now.

ALL: No, you're not. Stop him. Stop him.

(They all spring at the TEACHER. *He defends himself. At this moment,* SCHILL *appears through the door upstage. In contrast to the others, he is dressed shabbily in an old black jacket, his best)*

SCHILL: What's going on in my shop? *(The townsmen let go of the* TEACHER *and turn to stare at* SCHILL) *What's the trouble, Professor?*

TEACHER: Schill, I am speaking out at last! I am going to tell the press everything.

SCHILL: Be quiet, Professor.

TEACHER: What did you say?

SCHILL: Be quiet.

TEACHER: You want me to be quiet?

SCHILL: Please.

TEACHER: But, Schill, if I keep quiet, if you miss this opportunity—they're over in Hofbauer's shop now . . .

SCHILL: Please.

TEACHER: As you wish. If you too are on their side, I have no more to say.

(The doorbell jingles. A REPORTER *comes in)*

REPORTER: Is Anton Schill here? *(Moves to* SCHILL) *Are you Herr Schill?*

SCHILL: What?

REPORTER: Herr Schill.

SCHILL: Er—no. Herr Schill's gone to Kalberstadt for the day.

REPORTER: Oh, thank you. Good day.

(He goes out)

PAINTER: *(Mops his brow)* Whew! Close shave.

(He follows the REPORTER *out)*

SECOND MAN: *(Walking up to* SCHILL*)* That was pretty smart of you to keep your mouth shut. You know what to expect if you don't.

(He goes)

FIRST MAN: Give me a Havana. *(*SCHILL *serves him)* Charge it. You bastard!

(He goes. SCHILL *opens his account book)*

FRAU SCHILL: Come along, children—

*(*FRAU SCHILL, *the* SON *and the* DAUGHTER *go off, upstage)*

TEACHER: They're going to kill you. I've known it all along, and you too, you must have known it. The need is too strong, the temptation too great. And now perhaps I too will join against you. I belong to them and, like them, I can feel myself hardening into something that is not human—not beautiful.

SCHILL: It can't be helped.

TEACHER: Pull yourself together, man. Speak to the reporters; you've no time to lose.

*(*SCHILL *looks up from his account book)*

SCHILL: No. I'm not going to fight any more.

TEACHER: Are you so frightened that you don't dare open your mouth?

SCHILL: I made Claire what she is, I made myself what I am. What should I do? Should I pretend that I'm innocent?

TEACHER: No, you can't. You are as guilty as hell.

SCHILL: Yes.

TEACHER: You are a bastard.

SCHILL: Yes.

TEACHER: But that does not justify your murder. *(*SCHILL *looks at him)* I wish I could believe that for what they're doing—for what they're going to do—they will suffer for the rest of their lives. But it's not true. In a little while they will have justified everything and forgotten everything.

SCHILL: Of course.

TEACHER: Your name will never again be mentioned in this town. That's how it will be.

SCHILL: I don't hold it against you.

TEACHER: But I do. I will hold it against myself all my life. That's why—

(The doorbell jingles. The BURGOMASTER *comes in. The* TEACHER *stares at him, then goes out without another word)*

BURGOMASTER: Good afternoon, Schill. Don't let me disturb you. I've just dropped in for a moment.

SCHILL: I'm just finishing my accounts for the week. *(A moment's pause)*

BURGOMASTER: The town council meets tonight. At the Golden Apostle. In the auditorium.

SCHILL: I'll be there.

BURGOMASTER: The whole town will be there. Your case will be discussed and final action taken. You've put us in a pretty tight spot, you know.

SCHILL: Yes. I'm sorry.

BURGOMASTER: The lady's offer will be rejected.

SCHILL: Possibly.

BURGOMASTER: Of course, I may be wrong.

SCHILL: Of course.

BURGOMASTER: In that case—are you prepared to accept the judgment of the town? The meeting will be covered by the press, you know.

SCHILL: By the press?

BURGOMASTER: Yes, and the radio and the newsreel. It's a very ticklish situation. Not only for you—believe me, it's even worse for us. What with the wedding, and all the publicity, we've become famous. All of a sudden our ancient democratic institutions have become of interest to the world.

SCHILL: Are you going to make the lady's condition public?

BURGOMASTER: No, no, of course not. Not directly. We will have to put the matter to a vote—that is unavoidable. But only those involved will understand.

SCHILL: I see.

BURGOMASTER: As far as the press is concerned, you are simply the intermediary between us and Madame Zachanassian. I have whitewashed you completely.

SCHILL: That is very generous of you.

BURGOMASTER: Frankly, it's not for your sake, but for the sake of your family. They are honest and decent people.

SCHILL: Oh—

BURGOMASTER: So far we've all played fair. You've kept your mouth shut and so have we. Now can we continue to depend on you? Because if you have any idea of opening your mouth at tonight's meeting, there won't be any meeting.

SCHILL: I'm glad to hear an open threat at last.

BURGOMASTER: We are not threatening you. You are threatening us. If you speak, you force us to act—in advance.

SCHILL: That won't be necessary.

BURGOMASTER: So if the town decides against you?

SCHILL: I will accept their decision.

BURGOMASTER: Good. *(A moment's pause)* I'm delighted to see there is still a spark of decency left in you. But—wouldn't it be better if we didn't have to call a meeting at all? (*He pauses. He takes a gun from his pocket and puts it on the counter*) I've brought you this.

SCHILL: Thank you.

BURGOMASTER: It's loaded.

SCHILL: I don't need a gun.

BURGOMASTER: (*He clears his throat*) You see? We could tell the lady that we had condemned you in secret session and you had anticipated our decision. I've lost a lot of sleep getting to this point, believe me.

SCHILL: I believe you.

BURGOMASTER: Frankly, in your place, I myself would prefer to take the path of honor. Get it over with, once and for all. Don't you agree? For the sake of your friends! For the sake of our children, your own children—you have a daughter, a son—Schill, you know our need, our misery.

SCHILL: You've put me through hell, you and your town. You were my friends, you smiled and reassured me. But day by day I saw you change—your shoes, your ties, your suits—your hearts. If you had been honest with me then, perhaps I would feel differently toward you now. I might even use that gun you brought me. For the sake of my friends. But now I have conquered my fear. Alone. It was hard, but it's done. And now you will have to judge me. And I will accept your judgment. For me that will be justice. How it will be for you, I don't know. (*He turns away*) You may kill me if you like. I won't complain, I won't protest, I won't defend myself. But I won't do your job for you either.

BURGOMASTER: (*Takes up his gun*) There it is. You've had your chance and you won't take it. Too bad. (*He takes out a cigarette*) I suppose it's more than we can expect of a man like you. (SCHILL *lights the* BURGOMASTER's *cigarette*) Good day.

SCHILL: Good day. (*The* BURGOMASTER *goes.* FRAU SCHILL *comes in, dressed in a fur coat. The* DAUGHTER *is in a new red dress. The* SON *has a new sports jacket*) What a beautiful coat, Mathilde!

FRAU SCHILL: Real fur. You like it?

SCHILL: Should I? What a lovely dress, Ottilie!

DAUGHTER: *C'est très chic, n'est-ce pas?*[1]

SCHILL: What?

FRAU SCHILL: Ottilie is taking a course in French.

SCHILL: Very useful. Karl—whose automobile is that out there at the curb?

SON: Oh, it's only an Opel. They're not expensive.

SCHILL: You bought yourself a car?

---

1. *It's very smart, isn't it?*

SON: On credit. Easiest thing in the world.
FRAU SCHILL: Everyone's buying on credit now, Anton. These fears of
yours are ridiculous. You'll see. Clara has a good heart. She only
means to teach you a lesson.
DAUGHTER: She means to teach you a lesson, that's all.
SON: It's high time you got the point, Father.
SCHILL: I get the point. *(The church bells start ringing)* Listen. The bells of
Güllen. Do you hear?
SON: Yes, we have four bells now. It sounds quite good.
DAUGHTER: Just like Gray's Elegy.
SCHILL: What?
FRAU SCHILL: Ottilie is taking a course in English literature.
SCHILL: Congratulations! It's Sunday. I should very much like to take a
ride in your car. Our car.
SON: You want to ride in the car?
SCHILL: Why not? I want to ride through Konradsweil Forest. I want to
see the town where I've lived all my life.
FRAU SCHILL: I don't think that will look very nice for any of us.
SCHILL: No—perhaps not. Well, I'll go for a walk by myself.
FRAU SCHILL: Then take us to Kalberstadt, Karl, and we'll go to a cinema.
SCHILL: A cinema? It's a good idea.
FRAU SCHILL: See you soon, Anton.
SCHILL: Good-bye, Ottilie. Good-bye, Karl, Good-bye, Mathilde.
FAMILY: Good-bye.

(They go out)

SCHILL: Good-bye. *(The shop sign flies off. The lights black out. They come up
at once on the forest scene)* Autumn. Even the forest has turned to
gold.

(SCHILL wanders down to the bench in the forest. He sits. CLAIRE's voice is heard)

CLAIRE: *(Offstage)* Stop. Wait here. *(CLAIRE comes in. She gazes slowly up at
the trees, kicks at some leaves. Then she walks slowly down center. She
stops before a tree, glances up the trunk)* Bark-borers. The old tree is
dying.

(She catches sight of SCHILL)

SCHILL: Clara.
CLAIRE: How pleasant to see you here. I was visiting my forest. May I sit
by you?
SCHILL: Oh, yes. Please do. *(She sits next to him)* I've just been saying
good-bye to my family. They've gone to the cinema. Karl has
bought himself a car.
CLAIRE: How nice.

SCHILL: Ottilie is taking French lessons. And a course in English litera-
ture.
CLAIRE: You see? They're beginning to take an interest in higher things.
SCHILL: Listen. A finch. You hear?
CLAIRE: Yes. It's a finch. And a cuckoo in the distance. Would you like
some music?
SCHILL: Oh, yes. That would be very nice.
CLAIRE: Anything special?
SCHILL: "Deep in the Forest."
CLAIRE: Your favorite song. They know it.

(She raises her hand. Offstage, the mandolin and guitar play the tune softly)

SCHILL: We had a child?
CLAIRE: Yes.
SCHILL: Boy or girl?
CLAIRE: Girl.
SCHILL: What name did you give her?
CLAIRE: I called her Genevieve.
SCHILL: That's a very pretty name.
CLAIRE: Yes.
SCHILL: What was she like?
CLAIRE: I saw her only once. When she was born. Then they took her
away from me.
SCHILL: Her eyes?
CLAIRE: They weren't open yet.
CLAIRE: And her hair?
CLAIRE: Black, I think. It's usually black at first.
SCHILL: Yes, of course. Where did she die, Clara?
CLAIRE: In some family. I've forgotten their name. Meningitis, they said.
The officials wrote me a letter.
SCHILL: Oh, I'm so very sorry, Clara.
CLAIRE: I've told you about our child. Now tell me about myself.
SCHILL: About yourself?
CLAIRE: Yes. How I was when I was seventeen in the days when you
loved me.
SCHILL: I remember one day you waited for me in the great barn. I had to
look all over the place for you. At last I found you lying in the
haycart with nothing on and a long straw between your lips . . .
CLAIRE: Yes. I was pretty in those days.
SCHILL: You were beautiful, Clara.
CLAIRE: You were strong. The time you fought with those two railway
men who were following me, I wiped the blood from your face
with my red petticoat. *(The music ends)* They've stopped.
SCHILL: Tell them to play "Thoughts of Home."
CLAIRE: They know that too.

(The music plays)

SCHILL: Here we are, Clara, sitting together in our forest for the last time. The town council meets tonight. They will condemn me to death, and one of them will kill me. I don't know who and I don't know where. Clara, I only know that in a little while a useless life will come to an end.

(He bows his head on her bosom. She takes him in her arms)

CLAIRE: *(Tenderly)* I shall take you in your coffin to Capri. You will have your tomb in the park of my villa, where I can see you from my bedroom window. White marble and onyx in a grove of green cypress. With a beautiful view of the Mediterranean.

SCHILL: I've always wanted to see it.

CLAIRE: Your love for me died years ago, Anton. But my love for you would not die. It turned into something strong, like the hidden roots of the forest; something evil, like white mushrooms that grow unseen in the darkness. And slowly it reached out for your life. Now I have you. You are mine. Alone. At last and forever, a peaceful ghost in a silent house.

(The music ends)

SCHILL: The song is over.

CLAIRE: Adieu, Anton.

(CLAIRE kisses ANTON, a long kiss. Then she rises)

SCHILL: Adieu.

(She goes. SCHILL remains sitting on the bench. A row of lamps descends from the flies. The townsmen come in from both sides, each bearing his chair. A table and chairs are set upstage, center. On both sides sit the townspeople. The POLICEMAN, in a new uniform, sits on the bench behind SCHILL. All the townsmen are in new Sunday clothes. Around them are technicians of all sorts, with lights, cameras, and other equipment. The townswomen are absent. They do not vote. The BURGOMASTER takes his place at the table, center. The DOCTOR and the PASTOR sit at the same table, at his right, and the TEACHER in his academic gown, at his left)

BURGOMASTER: *(At a sign from the radio technician, he pounds the floor with his wand of office)* Fellow citizens of Güllen, I call this meeting to order. The agenda: there is only one matter before us. I have the honor to announce officially that Madame Claire Zachanassian, daughter of our beloved citizen, the famous architect Siegfried Wäscher, has decided to make a gift to the town of one billion marks. Five hundred million to the town, five hundred million to be divided per capita among the citizens. After certain necessary preliminaries, a vote will be taken, and you, as citizens of Güllen, will signify your will by a show of hands. Has anyone any objection to this mode of procedure? The pastor? *(Silence)* The police? *(Silence)* The town health official? *(Silence)* The Rector of Güllen High School? *(Silence)* The political opposition? *(Silence)* I shall then proceed to the vote—*(The* TEACHER *rises. The* BURGOMASTER *turns in surprise and irritation)* You wish to speak?

TEACHER: Yes.

BURGOMASTER: Very well.

(He takes his seat. The TEACHER *advances. The movie camera starts running)*

TEACHER: Fellow townsmen. *(The photographer flashes a bulb in his face)* Fellow townsmen. We all know that by means of this gift, Madame Claire Zachanassian intends to attain a certain object. What is this object? To enrich the town of her youth, yes. But more than that, she desires by means of this gift to re-establish justice among us. This desire expressed by our benefactress raises an all-important question. Is it true that our community harbors in its soul such a burden of guilt?

BURGOMASTER: Yes! True!

SECOND MAN: Crimes are concealed among us.

THIRD MAN: *(He jumps up)* Sins!

FOURTH MAN: *(He jumps up also)* Perjuries.

PAINTER: Justice!

TOWNSMEN: Justice! Justice!

TEACHER: Citizens of Güllen, this, then, is the simple fact of the case. We have participated in an injustice. I thoroughly recognize the material advantages which this gift opens to us—I do not overlook the fact that it is poverty which is the root of all this bitterness and evil. Nevertheless, there is no question here of money.

TOWNSMEN: No! No!

TEACHER: Here there is no question of our prosperity as a community, or our well-being as individuals— The question is—must be— whether or not we wish to live according to the principles of justice, those principles for which our forefathers lived and fought and for which they died, those principles which form the soul of our Western culture.

TOWNSMEN: Hear! Hear!

(Applause)

TEACHER: *(Desperately, realizing that he is fighting a losing battle, and on the verge of hysteria)* Wealth has meaning only when benevolence comes of it, but only he who hungers for grace will receive grace. Do you feel this hunger, my fellow citizens, this hunger of the spirit, or do you feel only that other profane hunger, the hunger of the body? That is the question which I, as Rector of your high school, now propound to you. Only if you can no longer tolerate the presence of evil among you, only if you can in no circumstances endure a world in which injustice exists, are you worthy to receive Madame Zachanassian's billion and fulfill the condition bound up with this gift. If not—(*Wild applause. He gestures desperately for silence*) If not, then God have mercy on us!

(*The townsmen crowd around him, ambiguously, in a mood somewhat between threat and congratulation. He takes his seat, utterly crushed, exhausted by his effort. The* BURGOMASTER *advances and takes charge once again. Order is restored*)

BURGOMASTER: Anton Schill—(*The* POLICEMAN *gives* SCHILL *a shove.* SCHILL *gets up*) Anton Schill, it is through you that this gift is offered to the town. Are you willing that this offer should be accepted?

(SCHILL *mumbles something*)

RADIO REPORTER: (*Steps to his side*) You'll have to speak up a little, Herr Schill.

SCHILL: Yes.

BURGOMASTER: Will you respect our decision in the matter before us?

SCHILL: I will respect your decision.

BURGOMASTER: Then I proceed to the vote. All those who are in accord with the terms on which this gift is offered will signify the same by raising their right hands. (*After a moment, the* POLICEMAN *raises his hand. Then one by one the others. Last of all, very slowly, the* TEACHER) All against? The offer is accepted. I now solemnly call upon you, fellow townsmen, to declare in the face of all the world that you take this action, not out of love for worldly gain . . .

TOWNSMEN: (*In chorus*) Not out of love for worldly gain . . .

BURGOMASTER: But out of love for the right.

TOWNSMEN: But out of love for the right.

BURGOMASTER: (*Holds up his hand, as if taking an oath*) We join together, now, as brothers . . .

TOWNSMEN: (*Hold up their hands*) We join together, now, as brothers . . .

BURGOMASTER: To purify our town of guilt . . .

TOWNSMEN: To purify our town of guilt . . .

BURGOMASTER: And to reaffirm our faith . . .

TOWNSMEN: And to reaffirm our faith . . .

BURGOMASTER: In the eternal power of justice.

TOWNSMEN: In the eternal power of justice.

(*The lights go off suddenly*)

SCHILL: (*A scream*) Oh, God!

VOICE: I'm sorry, Herr Burgomaster. We seem to have blown a fuse. (*The lights go on*) Ah—there we are. Would you mind doing that last bit again?

BURGOMASTER: Again?

THE CAMERAMAN: *(Walks forward)* Yes, for the newsreel.

BURGOMASTER: Oh, the newsreel. Certainly.

THE CAMERAMAN: Ready now? Right.

BURGOMASTER: And to reaffirm our faith . . .

TOWNSMEN: And to reaffirm our faith . . .

BURGOMASTER: In the eternal power of justice.

TOWNSMEN: In the eternal power of justice.

THE CAMERAMAN: *(To his assistant)* It was better before, when he screamed "Oh, God."

(The assistant shrugs)

BURGOMASTER: Fellow citizens of Güllen, I declare this meeting adjourned. The ladies and gentlemen of the press will find refreshments served downstairs, with the compliments of the town council. The exits lead directly to the restaurant.

THE CAMERAMAN: Thank you.

(The newsmen go off with alacrity. The townsmen remain on the stage. SCHILL gets up)

POLICEMAN: *(Pushes SCHILL down)* Sit down.

SCHILL: Is it to be now?

POLICEMAN: Naturally, now.

SCHILL: I thought it might be best to have it at my house.

POLICEMAN: It will be here.

BURGOMASTER: Lower the lights. *(The lights dim)* Are they all gone?

VOICE: All gone.

BURGOMASTER: The gallery?

SECOND VOICE: Empty.

BURGOMASTER: Lock the doors.

THE VOICE: Locked here.

SECOND VOICE: Locked here.

BURGOMASTER: Form a lane. *(The men form a lane. At the end stands the ATHLETE in elegant white slacks, a red scarf around his singlet)* Pastor. Will you be so good?

(The PASTOR walks slowly to SCHILL)

PASTOR: Anton Schill, your heavy hour has come.

SCHILL: May I have a cigarette?

PASTOR: Cigarette, Burgomaster.

BURGOMASTER: Of course. With pleasure. And a good one.

(He gives his case to the PASTOR, who offers it to SCHILL. The POLICEMAN lights the cigarette. The PASTOR returns the case)

PASTOR: In the words of the prophet Amos—

SCHILL: Please—

(He shakes his head)

PASTOR: You're no longer afraid?
SCHILL: No. I'm not afraid.
PASTOR: I will pray for you.
SCHILL: Pray for us all.

(The PASTOR bows his head)

BURGOMASTER: Anton Schill, stand up!

(SCHILL hesitates)

POLICEMAN: Stand up, you swine!
BURGOMASTER: Schultz, please.
POLICEMAN: I'm sorry. I was carried away. *(SCHILL gives the cigarette to the POLICEMAN. Then he walks slowly to the center of the stage and turns his back on the audience)* Enter the lane.

(SCHILL hesitates a moment. He goes slowly into the lane of silent men. The ATHLETE stares at him from the opposite end. SCHILL looks in turn at the hard faces of those who surround him, and sinks slowly to his knees. The lane contracts silently into a knot as the men close in and crouch over. Complete silence. The knot of men pulls back slowly, coming downstage. Then it opens. Only the DOCTOR is left in the center of the stage, kneeling by the corpse, over which the TEACHER's gown has been spread. The DOCTOR rises and takes off his stethoscope)

PASTOR: Is it all over?
DOCTOR: Heart failure.
BURGOMASTER: Died of joy.
    ALL: Died of joy.

(The townsmen turn their backs on the corpse and at once light cigarettes. A cloud of smoke rises over them. From the left comes CLAIRE ZACHANASSIAN, dressed in black, followed by BOBBY. She sees the corpse. Then she walks slowly to center stage and looks down at the body of SCHILL)

CLAIRE: Uncover him. *(BOBBY uncovers SCHILL's face. She stares at it a long moment. She sighs)* Cover his face.

(BOBBY covers it. CLAIRE goes out, up center. BOBBY takes the check from his wallet, holds it out peremptorily to the BURGOMASTER, who walks over from the knot of silent men. He holds out his hand for the check. The lights fade. At once the warning bell is heard, and the scene dissolves into the setting of the railway station. The gradual transformation of the shabby town into a thing of elegance and beauty is now accomplished. The railway station glitters with neon lights and is surrounded with garlands, bright posters, and flags. The townsfolk, men and women, now in brand new clothes, form themselves into a group in front of the station. The sound of the approaching train grows louder. The train stops)

STATION MASTER: Güllen-Rome Express. All aboard, please. *(The church*

*bells start pealing. Men appear with trunks and boxes, a procession
which duplicates that of the lady's arrival, but in inverse order. Then
come the* Two Blind Men, *then* Bobby, *and* Mike *and* Max *carrying
the coffin. Lastly* Claire. *She is dressed in modish black. Her head is
high, her face as impassive as that of an ancient idol. The procession
crosses the stage and goes off. The people bow in silence as the coffin
passes. When* Claire *and her retinue have boarded the train, the* Station Master *blows a long blast)* 'Bo—ard!

*(He holds up his paddle. The train starts and moves off slowly, picking up speed. The crowd
turns slowly, gazing after the departing train in complete silence. The train sounds fade)*

The curtain falls slowly

STUDY QUESTIONS

1. Chart the important events in Claire Zachanassian's life.
2. Explain why Anton Schill becomes a victim of greed. Does he atone for his past sins?
3. How does the town rationalize its actions?
4. What moral issues does the play confront?
5. Does the play offer any hope for the future? Explain.
6. To what extent is the play's exaggerated and unrealistic style effective in conveying the author's message?

THEMATIC QUESTIONS

1. One of the great legacies of European civilization is that of individual self-worth. One of the central themes of European literature, however, is that of society's obstruction of individual self-fulfillment. Compare and contrast how this theme is articulated by various writers: Böll, Ginzburg, Kundera, Tolstaya, Yeats.

2. Europeans have created a largely secular, urban, and, in many ways, materialistic civilization. Drawing upon the writing of Auden, Buzzati, Lawrence, Montale, Rilke, and Schulz, analyze how these writers view this civilization. Do they lament a severance with nature? Do they postulate a disjuncture in human experience? Do they posit that the role of the artist is to mediate this disjuncture?

3. A major development in modern European literature has been a distancing between the author and his characters. Analyze how the stories of Woolf, Duras, Beckett, Buzzati, and Breton no longer present a reality solely defined by the author, but offer a series of images which the reader needs to creatively interpret.

4. A significant issue in modern European discourse is the problematic nature of human relations. Analyze this dilemma in the various selections and assess what, in each case, are the limitations and obstacles to meaningful human interaction.

5. The works of García Lorca, Ekström, Colette, Duras, Breton, in particular, focus on gender- and sex-related issues. Compare and contrast how each author makes gender differences crucial to the dramatic structure of the piece of writing.

6. Böll, Joyce, Kundera, O'Connor, Tolstaya, among others, deal with the disillusion of youthful visions. How does each author depict the process of disenchantment and to what does he/she attribute it?

7. A major issue in twentieth-century European literature has been the question of the role of art, and the artist, in society. How do writers like

Brecht, Calvino, Heaney, Milosz, and Rilke approach and elaborate this topic?

8. The works by Sachs and Seifert render the experience of the Holocaust. Consider the way in which each of these writers presents the Holocaust. Babel, García Lorca, Mandelstam, Akhmatova likewise concern themselves with the effects of human violence. Compare and contrast their works to the Holocaust writers.

9. Many European writers have taken political positions in regard to Fascism, the Russian Revolution, totalitarianism, and nationalism. Identify which works raise political concerns and in what manner. Does a political point of view dominate any of them?

LATIN AMERICA AND THE CARIBBEAN

LATIN AMERICA AND THE CARIBBEAN

Introduction

The term Latin America usually refers to those countries in South, Central, and North America where Spanish and Portuguese are spoken. The Dutch-, French-, and English-speaking countries of South America as well as the islands of the Caribbean sometimes are included. Bounded by the Atlantic and Pacific oceans, the Caribbean is synonymous with the West Indies. It designates the clusters of islands that separate the Gulf of Mexico and the Caribbean Sea from the Atlantic Ocean. Located south of Florida, these islands extend as far as South America.

Geographically and culturally this region is diverse. Latin America has snow-covered mountain ranges, arid deserts, humid jungles, grass-covered plains, and rainy coastal forests. Much of the land consists of high mountain ranges, such as the Andes, followed by plains drained by the Amazon, Orinoco, and Paraná rivers. The natural resources of the region are substantial, although unevenly distributed. There is an abundance of metals and minerals—for example, copper in Chile, gold in Brazil—while important reserves of petroleum exist in Venezuela, Argentina, Colombia, and Mexico. Extensive forests cover large tracts of land. Export crops such as coffee, sugar, bananas, and cotton are cultivated in many areas. Livestock production and fishing are important commercial activities in many countries as well (only Paraguay and Bolivia lack a coastline).

Rio Grande

MEXICO

Gulf of Mexico

BAHAMAS

ATLANTIC OCEAN

Havana

CUBA

DOMINICAN REPUBLIC

Guadalajara

Mexico City

JAMAICA

PUERTO RICO (U.S.)

BELIZE

HONDURAS

HAITI

ANTIGUA AND *Barbuda (Ant.)*

Guadeloupe (Fr.)

GUATEMALA

Caribbean Sea

Martinique (Fr.)

EL SALVADOR

NICARAGUA

BARBADOS

Managua

Panama City

Caracas

GRENADA

TRINIDAD AND TOBAGO

COSTA RICA

PANAMA

VENEZUELA

SURINAME

Medellín

GUYANA

FRENCH GUYANA (FR.)

Bogotá

COLOMBIA

Equator

Quito

ECUADOR

Manaus

Galapagos Islands (Ecuador)

Madeira River

Amazon River

Bélem

ANDES MOUNTAINS

BRAZIL

PERU

Lima

BOLIVIA

Lake Titicaca

La Paz

Brasília

Sucre

PACIFIC OCEAN

PARAGUAY

Rio de Janeiro

São Paulo

Río Paraná

Asunción

CHILE

ARGENTINA

URUGUAY

Santiago

Montevideo

Buenos Aires

Río de la Plata

N
W   E
S

FALKLAND ISLANDS
(MALVINAS) (U.K.)

Cape Horn

LATIN AMERICA AND THE CARIBBEAN

Scale

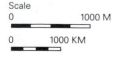

0   1000 M

0   1000 KM

Legend

● Capitals
○ Cities
^ Mountains

Because of a history of economic dependence and unequal exchange with Europe and the United States, Latin America has been slow to industrialize. It has had difficulty breaking out of the exploitative trade relationship of exporting raw materials and importing manufactured goods. Where industrialization has taken place, it has been uneven and concentrated in certain areas. The most industrialized nations in Latin America are Mexico, Argentina, and Brazil, followed by Venezuela, Colombia, Peru, and Chile. Few of these countries are self-sufficient in manufacturing goods, and they are plagued by continuing economic and fiscal problems.

The islands of the Caribbean were formed by volcanic activity millions of years ago. With mountainous regions, fertile valleys, and tropical plains, they are known for the production of sugar, coffee, spices, and tropical fruits. The coastal seas are rich in marine life. Except for Trinidad, Jamaica, and Cuba, however, there are limited mineral resources, and only Trinidad has petroleum deposits. The economies of the islands are geared to the export of agricultural products and, for those who have them, mineral commodities. Manufacturing is limited, though there has been some industrial development in Puerto Rico, Jamaica, Trinidad, and Martinique with varying degrees of success. Tourism has become increasingly a major source of income for most island economies. In spite of attempts to develop regional autonomy through political organization and cooperative economic efforts, the Caribbean, like Latin America, has not been able to free itself completely from its dependency on Europe and North America.

The population of Latin America and the Caribbean is a complex mosaic of diverse races and cultures. The amalgam of four ethnic groups—Native American, European, African, and Asian—varies from country to country depending on each specific history. For example, the racial composition and cultural dynamic in Mexico, Ecuador, Bolivia, and Peru, where Native Americans survived Spanish subjugation and a mestizo culture emerged, are different from the West Indies, where Native Americans were annihilated and African slaves provided the nexus for a hybrid culture. Racially, Argentina, Uruguay, and Chile have a relatively homogeneous population of European descent, while Brazil and Guyana have heterogeneous ones.

The Catholic Church attempted to create a unified Christian culture throughout the area and in many respects was successful. The church provided education and a sense of religious identity, as well as the parameters for a common worldview. It failed, however, to alleviate social disparity. Hence, Latin America and Caribbean societies have been affected in important ways by the nature of the power relations among different ethnic groups and by the social and economic status accorded to them. In most countries, class divisions still reflect the racial hierarchies established after European conquest. In others, the correlation is less obvious. What remains constant throughout the region is the legacy of past class relations. Even in the more industrialized nations, class divisions are pronounced and correspond to harsh socioeconomic and political inequities. Power remains in the hands of the privileged. Poverty is rampant, and there are enormous discrepancies between the living standard of the upper and middle classes and the rest of society, who comprise the impoverished majority.

The history of Latin America and of the Caribbean is important to understanding the region. Before the voyages of discovery during the late fifteenth century, the New World was inhabited by diverse Native American populations with societies that ranged from the simple to the complex. The highly developed civilizations of the Inca, Maya, and Aztec were systematically destroyed by the conquering Europeans. With superior weaponry, conquistadors such as Hernán Cortés and Francisco Pizarro slaughtered countless numbers of people in their search for gold and precious metals. The plunder from these expeditions, and the riches derived from subsequent forced labor in mines and plantations, established the distorted economic pattern that continues to this day. For centuries, the wealth, labor power, and consumer needs of the region have been dictated or influenced by foreign powers to their own advantages.

Historically, Europe's economic development and prosperity have been nourished by its colonies. Until they achieved independence in the nineteenth century, most Latin American countries were organized politically according to the absolutist rule of Spain and Portugal. As a result, the colonies were rife with bureaucratic mismanagement, corruption, and greed. Gradually, the more advanced European countries, England and France, began to plan a significant role commercially. Slaves from Africa were brought by these countries to the New World in increasing numbers, and they became a primary source of labor in Brazil and the Caribbean, where the native populations had been exterminated. With the development of a cash-crop agriculture for export, the region was further integrated into the economies of the metropolitan centers, and a local planter and mercantile class emerged. Eventually, this class came into conflict with the policies of colonial rule and led the struggle for independence. In Brazil there was a bloodless transition. In the rest of Latin America revolutionary wars under the adept leadership of Simón

Bolívar and José de San Martín won independence. Afterward Latin America fragmented into separate nation states that assumed ostensibly republican forms of government. In reality, during much of the nineteenth-century power struggles among local caudillos (strongmen) dominated political life.

As a result, there was little economic growth. This situation began to change toward the end of the century. With the industrialization of Europe and the United States and the expansion of the international capitalist economy, Latin America became globally important again as a source of raw materials and as a market for manufactured goods. During the first decades of the twentieth century, foreign capital once again flooded into the region to develop local import/export economies. These changes had significant effects on traditional social and political structures. The middle and working classes expanded, developed their own organizations, and challenged the dominance of political ruling elites. The middle and working classes also provided a market for local manufacturing enterprises. It was the growth of these classes that sparked a nationalist response to foreign interests, which in turn further challenged the prevailing sociopolitical structures. The Mexican Revolution of 1910 exemplified this process. It likewise foreshadowed the emerging power of the peasantry as a force for social change. Coinciding with these developments, the United States began its policy of military intervention in the Caribbean and Central America to protect its financial interests. The political ramifications of U.S. intervention are still evident today, whether in recent policy toward Central America or in the periodic "anti-Yanqui" mood that sweeps Central America.

From the 1930s on, a number of important changes occurred. A worldwide depression cut Latin America off from foreign investment. As prices of export goods plummeted, Latin American governments had to intervene in their economies. Multiclass populist coalitions became important political forces and pluralistic political party systems began to take hold. World War II generated significant economic growth in Brazil, Mexico, and Argentina as well as in some of the less-developed countries. A post–World War II demand for Latin American exports financed some industrialization, and as a result social diversification accelerated. The expectations that increased with industrialization and the expansion of trade were, however, short-lived. By the 1960s large-scale unemployment and poverty persisted, social and political conflicts increased, and new authoritarian regimes emerged, often led by the military. Authoritarianism, in turn, spawned protest movements ranging from terroristic guerrilla activities to the peace and social justice work done by proponents of liberation theology. Ultimately, despite the progress that has taken place over the past few decades, the dilemma of the region stems from its continued dependence on market-oriented economic policies geared to international trade. This dependence has limited autonomous development and made it difficult to resolve the region's social and economic problems. The situation is even more dire in those countries that have not undergone some significant industrialization and social diversification. Socioeconomic and political conditions, which remain much as they were at the turn of the century, are marked by extreme differences between the "haves and the have-nots." Repressive, military-backed governments maintain the status quo. Even where there is democracy, political stability is often precarious, given the enormity of the socioeconomic problem.

The historical trajectory of the Caribbean, as indicated previously, resembles that of the rest of Latin America in terms of the broad social, economic, and political patterns. The West Indian islands, like the mainland, were colonized by European powers and incorporated into their commercial spheres of interest. Both regions share a violent history from the conquest of the indigenous populations to the institutionalization of slavery and subsequent oppression by authoritarian governments. There is also a similarity with regard to the social significance of race and ethnicity. The Caribbean, as much of Latin America, has been a victim of U.S. military intervention. There are important differences between the two regions as well. The English-speaking islands did not gain independence until the 1960s, and Puerto Rico and Martinique are still governed by the U.S. and France, respectively. The colonial plantation economy has had a more lasting effect on the region than in some parts of Latin America. As a result, social and economic development has been restricted despite the initial changes that came about with independence. Apart from these comparisons, it is important to note that the Caribbean has influenced Latin America politically, first with the Haitian Revolution of 1791 and more recently through the Cuban revolution of 1959. Both revolutions, despite their limitations and failures, established a tradition of resistance to foreign domination and authoritarian rule. Both revolutions have served to inspire liberation movements in Latin America in their struggle for social and economic justice.

Latin American and Caribbean literature has achieved an important reputation worldwide. During the past twenty years especially, work by leading writers has been translated into many languages. Whereas previously Latin American and Caribbean literature was inspired by European and North American writing, in recent years the process has been reversed. It is to Latin American and Caribbean writers that others turn for stylistic techniques as well as for artistic and moral vision. In ways that have eluded many of their contemporaries, Latin American writers have managed to depict the complexity of modern life, their turbulent history, and the hybrid culture of their region within the context of a modernist sensibility.

Twentieth-century writing from Latin America and the Caribbean did not emerge in a vacuum. Following the European conquest, Native American literature that consisted of lyric poetry, prayers, and ritual drama was researched and collected by friars and priests. Their compilations became sources to which a future generation of writers would turn for an understanding of the religious beliefs and social mores of pre-Colombian peoples. Similarly, historical and travel narratives written by the clergy and military gave testimony to the conquest and destruction of Native American culture, recorded the legends and fantasies of conquistadors, and described the marvels of the New World. Early colonial literature ignored much of the region's cultural heritage and was largely derivative of European masters. But with time writers began to recognize the value of exploring their own experiences as well as their own environment. Indeed, their writing helped develop a political and intellectual consciousness for emancipation. On the eve of independence, a new literature that was intent on creating a national culture and associated with social and political reform emerged.

During this period throughout Latin America, the historical novel became an important instrument for expressing a national identity. Novelists took the opportunity to attack the evils of colonial rule, to celebrate the deeds of the national heroes, and to bring to light repressed subjects, such as the plight of Native Americans. For example, in Cuba where the struggle for independence from Spain lasted until the end of the nineteenth century, the antislavery novel became an important vehicle for expressing the nationalist cause for freedom. The writings of José Martí went so far as to call for the artistic creation of an original culture in which the indigenous and Hispanic elements would be synthesized.

The Mexican revolution (1910–1917), with its egalitarian principles and commitment to social transformation, had a profound impact on literature and the arts in Latin America and the Caribbean. The muralists Diego Rivera, David Siqueiros, and José Clemente Orozco created a socially committed art that was at the same time deeply nationalistic and innovative in its use of pre-Colombian motifs. The novelists Mariano Azuela and Martín Luis

Guzmán confronted the social and political challenges of the Mexican revolution. Yet it was the later experimental fiction of Miguel Angel Asturias and Carlos Fuentes that did justice to the creative spirit of the Mexican muralists. Asturias and Fuentes dispensed with conventional realism and turned to myth and legend to reconstruct the cultural and historical experience of their region. Their writing had a vast influence throughout Latin America.

Similarly, the American occupation of Haiti (1915–1934) generated a nationalist response among artists and intellectuals. Throughout the West Indies, there was a renewed interest in the African influences on society. Jacques Rouman (Haiti), Nicolás Guillén (Cuba), and Aimé Césaire (Martinique) became the leading proponents of Afro-Caribbean culture, as did Derek Walcott (St. Lucia), and Earl Lovelace (Trinidad) in the late 1950s, '60s, and '70s. The artistic endeavors of the later generation of writers coincided with the independence struggle in the English-speaking islands. Their discourse expressed the search for an authentic national identity. In Brazil, a similar process can be seen in the novels of Jorge Amado. Today, the search for a national identity remains a chief concern of writers and intellectuals throughout Latin America, where a hybrid culture persists.

Twentieth-century Latin American and Caribbean literature is distinguished by its artistic sophistication. Ironically, Latin American and Caribbean writers were able to forge a unique and authentic national literature only after they had appropriated modern European and North American artistic innovations and adapted them to their own cultural needs. First romanticism, naturalism, and realism provided local artists with techniques and methodologies for delineating the social and historical contours of Latin American and Caribbean life. These, however, proved to be too limiting for capturing the complexity of experience in the region. It was the European avant-garde that liberated the vision of Latin American and Caribbean writers from prior literary constraints. Surrealism, expressionism, and the stream-of-consciousness techniques of James Joyce and William Faulkner inspired artists to explore through dream, myth, legend, and the unconscious the colorful and vibrant world of the continent. Several generations of writers utilized and modified the new techniques. The most prominent are Jorge Luis Borges (Argentina), Alejo Carpentier (Cuba), Miguel Asturias (Guatemala), Ernesto Sábato (Argentina), Mario Vargas Llosa (Peru), Gabriel García Márquez (Colombia), as well as Julio Cortázar (Argentina), Wilson Harris (Guyana), Carlos Fuentes (Mexico), Manuel Puig (Argentina), Guillermo Cabrera Infante (Cuba), Clarice Lispector (Brazil), and Isabel Allende (Chile). Although these writers have different concerns in their fiction, they share a common belief that literature should not conform to preconceived formulas or ideas. For them freedom of the imagination is a creative weapon against the confining bureaucracy and brutal injustice that characterizes their societies. For Alejo Carpentier and Gabriel García Márquez "magical realism," the term most often associated with this literary phenomenon, allows the artist to blend myth and history, fantasy and reality, the individual and the collective, the traditional and the modern, and the civilized and the barbarous in ways that truly reflect the enormous diversity and depth of human experience. Not all writers in the region are so ambitious. Most try to mix experimental techniques with more conventional ones. This is especially true in countries that are undergoing social and political crises or are in the first stages of developing a national identity. Under these circumstances, writers often want clarity and simplicity in order to reach a wider audience. Therefore, they are drawn to realism. Similarly, Latin American and Caribbean poets have tended to modify avant-garde styles to voice directly their social and political concerns. This is well illustrated in Aimé Césaire's long poem *Return to My Native Land* and in the works of César Vallejo (Peru) and Pablo Neruda (Chile). What drives all of this literature irrespective of literary techniques is the attempt to achieve an authentic vision that is unique to the various nations in this part of the world.

Norman A. Spencer

ANTIGUA

 ## JAMAICA KINCAID

Jamaica Kincaid (b. 1949) is an exciting new voice in Caribbean literature. Born in St. John's, Antigua, she spent her early childhood on the island but emigrated to the United States to further her education. After completing college, she worked as a free-lance writer, publishing articles and short stories in The New Yorker, Rolling Stone, Ms., *and the* Paris Review. *Since 1976, she has been a staff writer for* The New Yorker. *Publication of the collection of stories* At the Bottom of the River *(1983), where "Girl" was published, brought her instant success, winning the Morton Dauwen Zabel Award from the American Academy and Institute of Arts and Letters.* Annie John *(1985) and* A Small Place *(1988) followed. In "Girl" Kincaid draws on local folk idioms and speech patterns to capture the flavor and texture of her childhood experience with female family members.*

Girl

Wash the white clothes on Monday and put them on the stone heap; wash the color clothes on Tuesday and put them on the clothesline to dry; don't walk barehead in the hot sun; cook pumpkin fritters in very hot sweet oil; soak your little cloths right after you take them off; when buying cotton to make yourself a nice blouse, be sure that it doesn't have gum on it, because that way it won't hold up well after a wash; soak salt fish overnight before you cook it; is it true that you sing benna in Sunday school?; always eat your food in such a way that it won't turn someone else's stomach; on Sundays try to walk like a lady and not like the slut you are so bent on becoming; don't sing benna in Sunday school; you mustn't speak to wharf-rat boys, not even to give directions; don't eat fruits on the street—flies will follow you; *but I don't sing benna on Sundays at all and never in Sunday school;* this is how to sew on a button; this is how to make a buttonhole for the button you have just sewed on; this is how to hem a dress when you see the hem coming down and so to prevent yourself from looking like the slut I know you are so bent on becoming; this is how you iron your father's khaki shirt so that it doesn't have a crease; this is how you iron your father's khaki pants so that they don't have a crease; this is how you grow okra—far from the house, because okra tree harbors red ants; when you are growing dasheen,[1] make sure it gets plenty of water or else it makes your throat itch when you are eating it; this is how you sweep a corner; this is how you sweep a whole house; this is how you sweep a yard; this is how you smile to someone you don't like too much; this is how you smile to someone you don't like at all; this is how you smile to someone you like completely; this is how you set a table for tea; this is how you set a table for dinner; this is how you set a table for dinner with an important guest; this is how you set a table for lunch; this is how you set a table for breakfast; this is how to behave in the presence of men who don't know you very well, and this way they won't recognize immediately the slut I have warned you against becoming; be sure to wash every day, even if it is with your own spit; don't squat down to play marbles—you are not a boy, you know; don't pick people's flowers—you might catch something; don't throw stones at blackbirds, because it might not be a blackbird at all; this is how to make a bread pudding; this is how to make doukona; this is how to make pepper pot; this is how to make a good medicine for a cold; this is how to make a good medicine to throw away a child before it even becomes a child; this is how to catch a fish; this is how to throw back a fish you don't like; and that way something bad won't fall on you; this is how to bully a man; this is how a man bullies you; this is how to love a man, and if this doesn't work there are other ways, and if they don't work don't feel too bad about giving up; this is how to spit up in the air if you feel like it, and this is how to move quick so that it doesn't fall on you; this is how to make ends meet; always squeeze bread to make sure it's fresh; *but what if the baker won't let me feel the bread?*; you mean to say that after all you are really going to be the kind of woman who the baker won't let near the bread?

STUDY QUESTIONS

1. What do you learn about the author's childhood in "Girl"? What is the nature of her relationship with older family members?
2. How are female children in the story prepared for the real world?
3. What are the author's feelings about her childhood?

---

1. Dasheen: *A root which is a staple food of the tropics.*

ARGENTINA

 JORGE LUIS BORGES

Jorge Luis Borges (1899–1986) is considered one of Latin America's most important twentieth-century writers. The metaphysical themes, fantastic plots, and stylistic experiments of his fiction has influenced writers all over the world. Born in Buenos Aires, Borges' upbringing was cosmopolitan. He spoke several languages and was well versed in European literature. As a young man, he lived in Switzerland and Spain, where he was introduced to the latest literary innovations and artistic movements. Borges began his career as a poet influenced by the European avant-garde but soon concentrated on the essay and short story. In contrast to the social realism of his contemporaries, he viewed his stories not as artistic representations of the real world but as literary recreations of the cultural labyrinth fabricated throughout history. In his imaginary world, certainties cease to exist. Beneath outward appearances there exist endless contradictions. Any search for meaning and transcendence becomes futile.

Borges' writing can be categorized by three distinct phases: his early phase of nationalism, his retreat into universalism, and his return to his roots. While the cosmopolitan nature of his writing can be viewed as a denial of regional culture, it is also responsible for bringing international recognition to Latin American literature and making it possible for writers to explore the rich and complex historical legacy of the continent, a transition that occurred in his own writing. In "The Intruder," he adopts a more conventional, realistic storytelling technique and anchors its subject in the Latin machismo cult.

Among Borges' many books to appear in English, the best known are The Adelph and Other Stories, 1933–1969 *(1970) and* Labyrnths: Selected Short Stories and Other Writings *(1962).*

The Intruder

. . . passing the love of women.
2 Samuel 1:26

P eople say (but this is unlikely) that the story was first told by Eduardo, 1
the younger of the Nelsons, at the wake of his elder brother Cristián,
who died in his sleep sometime back in the nineties out in the district of
Morón. The fact is that someone got it from someone else during the course
of that drawn-out and now dim night, between one sip of maté and the
next, and told it to Santiago Dabove, from whom I heard it. Years later, in
Turdera, where the story had taken place, I heard it again. The second and
more elaborate version closely followed the one Santiago told, with the
usual minor variations and discrepancies. I set down the story now because I see in it, if I'm not mistaken, a brief and tragic mirror of the
character of those hard-bitten men living on the edge of Buenos Aires
before the turn of the century. I hope to do this in a straightforward way,
but I see in advance that I shall give in to the writer's temptation of emphasizing or adding certain details.

In Turdera, where they lived, they were called the Nilsens. The priest 2
there told me that his predecessor remembered having seen in the house of
these people—somewhat in amazement—a worn Bible with a dark binding
and black-letter type; on the back flyleaf he caught a glimpse of names and
dates written in by hand. It was the only book in the house—the roaming
chronicle of the Nilsens, lost as one day all things will be lost. The rambling
old house, which no longer stands, was of unplastered brick; through the
arched entranceway you could make out a patio paved with red tiles and
beyond it a second one of hard-packed earth. Few people, at any rate, ever
set foot inside; the Nilsens kept to themselves. In their almost bare rooms
they slept on cots. Their extravagances were horses, silver-trimmed riding
gear, the short-bladed dagger, and getting dressed up on Saturday nights,
when they blew their money freely and got themselves into boozy brawls.
They were both tall, I know, and wore their red hair long. Denmark or Ireland, which they probably never heard of, ran in the blood of these two
Argentine brothers. The neighborhood feared the Redheads; it is likely that
one of them, at least, had killed his man. Once, shoulder to shoulder, they
tangled with the police. It is said that the younger brother was in a fight with
Juan Iberra in which he didn't do too badly, and that, according to those in
the know, is saying something. They were drovers, teamsters, horse
thieves, and, once in a while, professional gamblers. They had a reputation
for stinginess, except when drink and cardplaying turned them into spend-
ers. Of their relatives or where they themselves came from, nothing is
known. They owned a cart and a yoke of oxen.

Their physical makeup differed from that of the rest of the toughs who 3
gave the Costa Brava its unsavory reputation. This, and a lot that we don't
know, helps us understand the close ties between them. To fall out with
one of them was to reckon with two enemies.

The Nilsens liked carousing with women, but up until then their amo- 4
rous escapades had always been carried out in darkened passageways or in
whorehouses. There was no end of talk, then, when Cristián brought
Juliana Burgos to live with him. Admittedly, in this way he gained a servant, but it is also true that he took to squandering on her the most hideous
junk jewelry and showing her off at parties. At those dingy parties held in
tenements, where suggestive dance steps were strictly forbidden and
where, at that time, partners still danced with a good six inches of light
showing between them. Juliana was a dark girl and her eyes had a slight
slant to them; all anyone had to do was look at her and she'd break into a
smile. For a poor neighborhood, where drudgery and neglect wear women
out, she was not bad-looking.

In the beginning, Eduardo went places with them. Later, at one point, 5
he set out on a journey north to Arrecifes on some business or other,
returning home with a girl he had picked up along the way. But after a few
days he threw her out. He turned more sullen; he took to drinking alone
at the corner saloon and kept completely to himself. He had fallen in love
with Cristián's woman. The whole neighborhood, which may have realized it before he did, maliciously and cheerfully looked forward to the
enmity about to break out between the two brothers.

Late one night, on coming home from the corner, Eduardo saw Cris- 6
tián's horse, a big bay, tied to the hitching post. Inside the patio, dressed
in his Sunday best, his older brother was waiting for him. The woman
shuttled in and out serving maté. Cristián said to Eduardo, "I'm on my
way over to Farfas' place, where they're throwing a party. Juliana stays
here with you; if you want her, use her."

His tone was half commanding, half friendly. Eduardo stood there a 7
while staring at him, not knowing what to do. Cristián got up, said
goodbye—to his brother, not to Juliana, who was no more than an object—
mounted his horse, and rode off at a jog, casually.

From that night on they shared her. Nobody will ever know the details 8
of this strange partnership which outraged even the Costa Brava's sense of
decency. The arrangement went well for several weeks, but it could not
last. Between them the brothers never mentioned her name, not even to
call her, but they kept looking for, and finding, reasons to be at odds. They
argued over the sale of some hides, but what they were really arguing
about was something else. Cristián took to raising his voice, while Eduardo
kept silent. Without knowing it, they were watching each other. In tough
neighborhoods a man never admits to anyone—not even to himself—that
a woman matters beyond lust and possession, but the two brothers were
in love. This, in some way, made them feel ashamed.

One afternoon, in the square in Lomas, Eduardo ran into Juan Iberra, who congratulated him on this beauty he'd got hold of. It was then, I believe, that Eduardo let him have it. Nobody—not to *his* face—was going to poke fun at Cristián.

The woman attended both men's wants with an animal submission, but she was unable to keep hidden a certain preference, probably for the younger man, who had not refused sharing her but who had not proposed it either.

One day, they ordered Juliana to bring two chairs out into the first patio and then not show her face for a while because they had things to talk over. Expecting a long session between them, she lay down for a nap, but before very long they woke her up. She was to fill a sack with all her belongings, including her glass-bead rosary and the tiny crucifix her mother had left her. Without any explanation, they lifted her onto the oxcart and set out on a long, tiresome, and silent journey. It had rained; the roads were heavy with mud and it was nearly daybreak before they reached Morón. There they sold her to the woman who ran the whorehouse. The terms had already been agreed to; Cristián pocketed the money and later on split it with his brother.

Back in Turdera, the Nilsens, up till then trapped in the web (which was also a routine) of this monstrous love affair, tried to take up their old life of men among men. They went back to cardplaying, to cockfights, to their Saturday night binges. At times, perhaps, they felt they were saved, but they often indulged—each on his own—in unaccountable or only too accountable absences. A little before the year was out, the younger brother said he had business in the city. Immediately, Cristián went off to Morón; at the hitching post of the whorehouse he recognized Eduardo's piebald. Cristián walked in; there was his brother, sure enough, waiting his turn. It is said that Cristián told him, "If we go on this way, we'll wear out the horses. We'd be better off keeping her close at hand."

He spoke with the owner of the place, drew a handful of coins out of his money belt, and they took the girl away. Juliana rode with Cristián. Eduardo dug his spurs into his horse, not wanting to see them together.

They went back to what has already been told. Their solution had ended in failure, for the two had fallen into cheating. Cain was on the loose here, but the affection between the Nilsens was great—who knows what hard times and what dangers they may have faced together!—and they preferred taking their feelings out on others. On strangers, on the dogs, on Juliana, who had set this wedge between them.

The month of March was coming to a close and there was no sign of the heat's letting up. One Sunday (on Sundays people go to bed early), Eduardo, on his way home from the corner saloon, saw that Cristián was yoking the oxen. Cristián said to him, "Come on. We have to leave some hides off at Pardo's place. I've already loaded them; let's make the best of the night air."

Pardo's warehouse lay, I believe, farther south; they took the old cattle trail, then turned down a side road. As night fell, the countryside seemed wider and wider. 16

They skirted a growth of tall reeds; Cristián threw down the cigar he had just lit and said evenly, "Let's get busy, brother. In a while the buzzards will take over. This afternoon I killed her. Let her stay here with all her trinkets, she won't cause us any more harm." 17

They threw their arms around each other, on the verge of tears. One more link bound them now—the woman they had cruelly sacrificed and their common need to forget her. 18

Translated from the Spanish by
Norman Thomas Di Giovanni

STUDY QUESTIONS

1. What are characteristics of the Nilsen brothers in "The Intruder"?
2. Explain the brothers' obsession with Juliana. Why is she killed? How does her death affect the brothers' relationship with each other?
3. How does the story define male/female roles?
4. What was the author's purpose in writing the story?

JULIO CORTÁZAR

Julio Cortázar (1914–1984), a seminal literary figure during the 1960s, was one of Latin America's most influential writers. His accomplishment lies in his synthesis of Joyce and Surrealism and in his attempt to achieve a revolution in consciousness. Cortázar was born in Brussels to Argentine parents. When he was four, he moved with his family to Buenos Aires, where he attended the university and began his career as a writer. He published his first stories in one of Argentina's leading literary journals, but they went almost unnoticed. In 1952, Cortázar emigrated to France to escape the censorship and political repression of Perón. Settling in Paris, he worked as a free-lance translator for UNESCO, continued to write, and became an outspoken supporter of the Cuban and Nicaraguan revolutions.

Cortázar's breakthrough as a writer came with the publication of the novel Hopscotch in 1963. Experimental in form and in its use of language, it sets out to assault bourgeois sensibilities in its celebration of the erotic, the spontaneous, and the improvisational world of jazz. Set in Paris and Buenos

Aires, the work rejects the rationalism of European civilization and posits instead a return to the natural, authentic world of the senses, where perception emerges free of restraint. The ironic playful approach to reality that characterizes Hopscotch is carried over in Cortázar's stories and other novels. His subtle narratives challenge logic and convention by making the fantastic a part of everyday life. In the novel A Manual for Manuel (1973), Cortázar confronts the political reality of Latin America by incorporating the horror of torture into a bizarre tale of fact and fiction. Similarly, in the story "House Taken Over" the mysterious and the unusual evoke history and raise questions about its meaning.

House Taken Over

We liked the house because, apart from its being old and spacious (in a day when old houses go down for a profitable auction of their construction materials), it kept the memories of great-grandparents, our paternal grandfather, our parents and the whole of childhood. 1

Irene and I got used to staying in the house by ourselves, which was crazy, eight people could have lived in that place and not have gotten in each other's way. We rose at seven in the morning and got the cleaning done, and about eleven I left Irene to finish off whatever rooms and went to the kitchen. We lunched at noon precisely; then there was nothing left to do but a few dirty plates. It was pleasant to take lunch and commune with the great hollow, silent house, and it was enough for us just to keep it clean. We ended up thinking, at times, that that was what had kept us from marrying. Irene turned down two suitors for no particular reason, and María Esther went and died on me before we could manage to get engaged. We were easing into our forties with the unvoiced concept that the quiet, simple marriage of sister and brother was the indispensable end to a line established in this house by our grandparents. We would die here someday, obscure and distant cousins would inherit the place, have it torn down, sell the bricks and get rich on the building plot; or more justly and better yet, we would topple it ourselves before it was too late. 2

Irene never bothered anyone. Once the morning housework was fin-ished, she spent the rest of the day on the sofa in her bedroom, knitting. I couldn't tell you why she knitted so much; I think women knit when they discover that it's a fat excuse to do nothing at all. But Irene was not like that, she always knitted necessities, sweaters for winter, socks for me, handy morning robes and bedjackets for herself. Sometimes she would do a jacket, then unravel it the next moment because there was something that didn't please her; it was pleasant to see a pile of tangled wool in her knitting basket fighting a losing battle for a few hours to retain its shape. 3

Saturdays I went downtown to buy wool; Irene had faith in my good taste, was pleased with the colors and never a skein had to be returned. I took advantage of these trips to make the rounds of the bookstores, uselessly asking if they had anything new in French literature. Nothing worthwhile had arrived in Argentina since 1939.

But it's the house I want to talk about, the house and Irene, I'm not very 4 important. I wonder what Irene would have done without her knitting. One can reread a book, but once a pullover is finished you can't do it over again, it's some kind of disgrace. One day I found that the drawer at the bottom of the chiffonier, replete with mothballs, was filled with shawls, white, green, lilac. Stacked amid a great smell of camphor—it was like a shop; I didn't have the nerve to ask her what she planned to do with them. We didn't have to earn our living, there was plenty coming in from the farms each month, even piling up. But Irene was only interested in the knitting and showed a wonderful dexterity, and for me the hours slipped away watching her, her hands like silver sea-urchins, needles flashing, and one or two knitting baskets on the floor, the balls of yarn jumping about. It was lovely.

How not to remember the layout of that house. The dining room, a living 5 room with tapestries, the library and three large bedrooms in the section most recessed, the one that faced toward Rodríguez Peña. Only a corridor with its massive oak door separated that part from the front wing, where there was a bath, the kitchen, our bedrooms and the hall. One entered the house through a vestibule with enameled tiles, and a wrought-iron grated door opened onto the living room. You had to come in through the vestibule and open the gate to go into the living room; the doors to our bedrooms were on either side of this, and opposite it was the corridor leading to the back section; going down the passage, one swung open the oak door beyond which was the other part of the house; or just before the door, one could turn to the left and go down a narrower passageway which led to the kitchen and the bath. When the door was open, you became aware of the size of the house; when it was closed you had the impression of an apartment, like the ones they build today, with barely enough room to move around in. Irene and I always lived in this part of the house and hardly ever went beyond the oak door except to do the cleaning. Incredible how much dust collected on the furniture. It may be Buenos Aires is a clean city, but she owes it to her population and nothing else. There's too much dust in the air, the slightest breeze and it's back on the marble console tops and in the diamond patterns of the tooled-leather desk set. It's a lot of work to get it off with a feather duster; the motes rise and hang in the air, and settle again a minute later on the pianos and the furniture.

I'll always have a clear memory of it because it happened so simply and 6 without fuss. Irene was knitting in her bedroom, it was eight at night, and

I suddenly decided to put the water up for *mate*.[1] I went down the corridor as far as the oak door, which was ajar, then turned into the hall toward the kitchen, when I heard something in the library or the dining room. The sound came through muted and indistinct, a chair being knocked over onto the carpet or the muffled buzzing of a conversation. At the same time or a second later, I heard it at the end of the passage which led from those two rooms toward the door. I hurled myself against the door before it was too late and shut it, leaned on it with the weight of my body; luckily, the key was on our side; moreover, I ran the great bolt into place, just to be safe.

I went down to the kitchen, heated the kettle, and when I got back with the tray of *mate*, I told Irene: 7

"I had to shut the door to the passage. They've taken over the back part."   8

She let her knitting fall and looked at me with her tired, serious eyes.   9

"You're sure?"   10

I nodded.   11

"In that case," she said, picking up her needles again, "we'll have to live on this side."   12

I sipped at the *mate* very carefully, but she took her time starting her work again. I remember it was a grey vest she was knitting. I liked that vest.   13

The first few days were painful, since we'd both left so many things in the part that had been taken over. My collection of French literature, for example, was still in the library. Irene had left several folios of stationery and a pair of slippers that she used a lot in the winter. I missed my briar pipe, and Irene, I think, regretted the loss of an ancient bottle of Hesperidin. It happened repeatedly (but only in the first few days) that we would close some drawer or cabinet and look at one another sadly.   14

"It's not here."   15

One thing more among the many lost on the other side of the house.   16

But there were advantages, too. The cleaning was so much simplified that, even when we got up late, nine thirty for instance, by eleven we were sitting around with our arms folded. Irene got into the habit of coming to the kitchen with me to help get lunch. We thought about it and decided on this: while I prepared the lunch, Irene would cook up dishes that could be eaten cold in the evening. We were happy with the arrangement because it was always such a bother to have to leave our bedrooms in the evening and start to cook. Now we made do with the table in Irene's room and platters of cold supper.   17

Since it left her more time for knitting, Irene was content. I was a little   18

---

1. Mate: *An infusion of the leaves of a Brazilian holly used as a beverage in South America.*

lost without my books, but so as not to inflict myself on my sister, I set about reordering papa's stamp collection; that killed some time. We amused ourselves sufficiently, each with his own thing, almost always getting together in Irene's bedroom, which was the more comfortable. Every once in a while, Irene might say:

"Look at this pattern I just figured out, doesn't it look like a clover?"   19

After a bit it was I, pushing a small square of paper in front of her so that   20
she could see the excellence of some stamp or another from Eupen-et-Malmédy. We were fine, and little by little we stopped thinking. You can live without thinking.

(Whenever Irene talked in her sleep, I woke up immediately and stayed   21
awake. I never could get used to this voice from a statue or a parrot, a voice that came out of the dreams, not from a throat. Irene said that in my sleep I flailed about enormously and shook the blankets off. We had the living room between us, but at night you could hear everything in the house. We heard each other breathing, coughing, could even feel each other reaching for the light switch when, as happened frequently, neither of us could fall asleep.

Aside from our nocturnal rumblings, everything was quiet in the house.   22
During the day there were the household sounds, the metallic click of knitting needles, the rustle of stamp-album pages turning. The oak door was massive, I think I said that. In the kitchen or the bath, which adjoined the part that was taken over, we managed to talk loudly, or Irene sang lullabies. In a kitchen there's always too much noise, the plates and glasses, for there to be interruptions from other sounds. We seldom allowed ourselves silence there, but when we went back to our rooms or to the living room, then the house grew quiet, half-lit, we ended by stepping around more slowly so as not to disturb one another. I think it was because of this that I woke up irremediably and at once when Irene began to talk in her sleep.)

Except for the consequences, it's nearly a matter of repeating the same   23
scene over again. I was thirsty that night, and before we went to sleep, I told Irene that I was going to the kitchen for a glass of water. From the door of the bedroom (she was knitting) I heard the noise in the kitchen; if not the kitchen, then the bath, the passage off at that angle dulled the sound. Irene noticed how brusquely I had paused, and came up beside me without a word. We stood listening to the noises, growing more and more sure that they were on our side of the oak door, if not the kitchen then the bath, or in the hall itself at the turn, almost next to us.

We didn't wait to look at one another. I took Irene's arm and forced her   24
to run with me to the wrought-iron door, not waiting to look back. You could hear the noises, still muffled but louder, just behind us. I slammed the grating and we stopped in the vestibule. Now there was nothing to be heard.

"They've taken over our section," Irene said. The knitting had reeled off 25
from her hands and the yarn ran back toward the door and disappeared
under it. When she saw that the balls of yarn were on the other side, she
dropped the knitting without looking at it.

"Did you have time to bring anything?" I asked hopelessly. 26

"No, nothing." 27

We had what we had on. I remembered fifteen thousand pesos in the 28
wardrobe in my bedroom. Too late now.

I still had my wrist watch on and saw that it was 11 P.M. I took Irene 29
around the waist (I think she was crying) and that was how we went into
the street. Before we left, I felt terrible; I locked the front door up tight and
tossed the key down the sewer. It wouldn't do to have some poor devil
decide to go in and rob the house, at that hour and with the house taken
over.

Translated from the Spanish by Paul Blackburn

STUDY QUESTIONS

1. Discuss the relationship between the narrator and his sister in "House
   Taken Over." What does it represent?
2. Describe the house and explain its history. Why is it taken over by
   noises? What do they symbolize?
3. Why do the brother and sister acquiesce at the end of the story?
4. What is the meaning of the story? Can there be different interpretations?

 # LUISA VALENZUELA

*Luisa Valenzuela (b. 1938) is one of the few Latin American women writers
who is well known in the United States. Several of her novels and short story
collections have been translated into English—The Lizard's Tail (1983),
Other Weapons (1986), He Who Searches (1987), and Open Door
(1989)—and she has received several literary awards and fellowships.
Valenzuela was born in Buenos Aires and grew up in an intellectual
environment. Her mother was Luisa Mercedes Levinson, a respected Argentine
author. She graduated from the University of Buenos Aires, then embarked on
a career as an editor and free-lance journalist for local newspapers and
magazines. Valenzuela has traveled extensively and has lived in France,*

Mexico, and the United States. Over the past twenty years, she has been a member of the faculty of Columbia University and New York University.

Valenzuela's fiction challenges the prevailing social, political, and religious institutions in Latin America and pays particular attention to male/female relations, marriage, and sexual taboos. Her critique posits the possibility for change through mutual understanding and collective action. The story "I'm Your Horse in the Night" documents the experience of the political underground in Latin America.

I'm Your Horse in the Night

The doorbell rang: three short rings and one long one. That was the signal, and I got up, annoyed and a little frightened; it could be them, and then again, maybe not; at these ungodly hours of the night it could be a trap. I opened the door expecting anything except him, face to face, at last.   1

He came in quickly and locked the door behind him before embracing me. So much in character, so cautious, first and foremost checking his—our—rear guard. Then he took me in his arms without saying a word, not even holding me too tight but letting all the emotions of our new encounter overflow, telling me so much by merely holding me in his arms and kissing me slowly. I think he never had much faith in words, and there he was, as silent as ever, sending me messages in the form of caresses.   2

We finally stepped back to look at one another from head to foot, not eye to eye, out of focus. And I was able to say Hello showing scarcely any surprise despite all those months when I had no idea where he could have been, and I was able to say   3

> I thought you were fighting up north
> I thought you'd been caught
> I thought you were in hiding
> I thought you'd been tortured and killed
> I thought you were theorizing about the revolution in another country

Just one of many ways to tell him I'd been thinking of him, I hadn't stopped thinking of him or felt as if I'd been betrayed. And there he was, always so goddamn cautious, so much the master of his actions.   4

"Quiet, Chiquita. You're much better off not knowing what I've been up to."   5

Then he pulled out his treasures, potential clues that at the time eluded me: a bottle of cachaça and a Gal Costa record. What had he been up to in Brazil? What was he planning to do next? What had brought him back, risking his life, knowing they were after him? Then I stopped asking myself   6 questions (quiet, Chiquita, he'd say). Come here, Chiquita, he was saying, and I chose to let myself sink into the joy of having him back again, trying not to worry. What would happen to us tomorrow, and the days that followed?

Cachaça's a good drink. It goes down and up and down all the right 7
tracks, and then stops to warm up the corners that need it most. Gal Costa's voice is hot, she envelops us in its sound and half-dancing, half-floating, we reach the bed. We lie down and keep on staring deep into each other's eyes, continue caressing each other without allowing ourselves to give in to the pure senses just yet. We continue recognizing, rediscovering each other.

Beto, I say, looking at him. I know that isn't his real name, but it's the 8
only one I can call him out loud. He replies:

"We'll make it someday, Chiquita, but let's not talk now." 9

It's better that way. Better if he doesn't start talking about how we'll 10
make it someday and ruin the wonder of what we're about to attain right now, the two of us, all alone.

"A noite eu so teu cavalo," Gal Costa suddenly sings from the record 11
player.

"I'm your horse in the night," I translate slowly. And so as to bind him 12
to a spell and stop him from thinking about other things:

"It's a saint's song, like in the *macumba*. Someone who's in a trance says 13
she's the horse of the spirit who's riding her, she's his mount."

"Chiquita, you're always getting carried away with esoteric meanings 14
and witchcraft. You know perfectly well that she isn't talking about spirits. If you're my horse in the night it's because I ride you, like this, see? . . . Like this . . . That's all."

It was so long, so deep and so insistent, so charged with affection that 15
we ended up exhausted. I feel asleep with him still on top of me.

I'm your horse in the night. 16

The goddamn phone pulled me out in waves from a deep well. Making an 17
enormous effort to wake up, I walked over to the receiver, thinking it could be Beto, sure, who was no longer by my side, sure, following his inveterate habit of running away while I'm asleep without a word about where he's gone. To protect me, he says.

From the other end of the line, a voice I thought belonged to 18
Andrés—the one we call Andrés—began to tell me:

"They found Beto dead, floating down the river near the other bank. It 19
looks as if they threw him alive out of a chopper. He's all bloated and decomposed after six days in the water, but I'm almost sure it's him."

"No, it can't be Beto," I shouted carelessly. Suddenly the voice no 20
longer sounded like Andrés: it felt foreign, impersonal.

"You think so?" 21

"Who is this?" Only then did I think to ask. But that very moment they 22
hung up.

Ten, fifteen minutes? How long must I have stayed there staring at the 23
phone like an idiot until the police arrived? I didn't expect them. But, then
again, how could I not? Their hands feeling me, their voices insulting and
threatening, the house searched, turned inside out. But I already knew. So
what did I care if they broke every breakable object and tore apart my
dresser?

They wouldn't find a thing. My only real possession was a dream and 24
they can't deprive me of my dreams just like that. My dream the night
before, when Beto was there with me and we loved each other. I'd dreamed
it, dreamed every bit of it, I was deeply convinced that I'd dreamed it all in
the richest detail, even in full color. And dreams are none of the cops'
business.

They wanted reality, tangible facts, the kind I couldn't even begin to 25
give them.

Where is he, you saw him, he was here with you, where did he go? 26
Speak up, or you'll be sorry. Let's hear you sing, bitch, we know he came
to see you, where is he, where is he holed up? He's in the city, come on,
spill it, we know he came to get you.

I haven't heard a word from him in months. He abandoned me, I haven't 27
heard from him in months. He ran away, went underground. What do I
know, he ran off with someone else, he's in another country. What do I
know, he abandoned me, I hate him, I know nothing.

(Go ahead, burn me with your cigarettes, kick me all you wish, threaten, 28
go ahead, stick a mouse in me so it'll eat my insides out, pull my nails out,
do as you please. Would I make something up for that? Would I tell you he
was here when a thousand years ago he left me forever?)

I'm not about to tell them my dreams. Why should they care? I haven't 29
seen that so-called Beto in more than six months, and I loved him. The man
simply vanished. I only run into him in my dreams, and they're bad dreams
that often become nightmares.

Beto, you know now, if it's true that they killed you, or wherever you may 30
be, Beto, I'm your horse in the night and you can inhabit me whenever you
wish, even if I'm behind bars. Beto, now that I'm in jail I know that I
dreamed you that night; it was just a dream. And if by some wild chance
there's a Gal Costa record and a half-empty bottle of cachaça in my house,
I hope they'll forgive me: I will them out of existence.

Translated from the Spanish by Delorah Bonner

STUDY QUESTIONS

1. Explain the setting of "I'm Your Horse in the Night." Who is Beto, and what is his relationship to the narrator? What is remarkable about their encounter?
2. Why do the police visit the narrator? How does she respond?
3. What is the significance of the dream?

Carlos Drummond de Andrade

Carlos Drummond de Andrade (1902–1987) is Brazil's most widely read modernist poet. He is the great popular voice in modern Latin American poetry with themes on the individual, family, love, friends, and society. Through an unassuming lyric style, he made his poetry accessible to the general reading public without sacrificing literary goals. Born in the state of Minas Gerais, he grew up on a ranch, studied to be a pharmacist, worked as a journalist and editor of modernist literary journals, and was for most of his life a socially committed public servant working in Rio de Janeiro in various government agencies. Like many writers of his generation, he was devoted to the cause of socialism.

Andrade began writing somber, introspective poems that reflected a sense of pessimism and despair about the human condition. Eventually, he was able to transcend solitude, alienation, and bitterness by identifying intellectually with other suffering human beings who were struggling to end injustice and oppression. In 1945, Andrade published one of his most important and successful books, The People's Rose, *in which he condemned the baseness of modern life while at the same time conveying a spirit of hope and optimism. "Death in a Plane" appeared in this collection and is typical of the poetry that contemplates the human condition.*

Death in a Plane

I awaken for death.
I shave, dress, put on my shoes.
It is my last day: a day
not broken by one premonition.
Everything happens as usual.   5
I head for the street. I am going to die.

I shall not die now. A whole day
unfolds before me.
What a long day it is! And in the street
what a lot of steps I take! And what a lot of things   10
have accumulated in time! Without paying much attention
I keep on going. So many faces
crowded into a notebook!

I visit the bank. What good
is the money, if a few hours later   15
the police come and take it
from the hole that was my chest?
But I don't see myself wounded and bloody.
I am clean, spotless, bright, summery.
Nevertheless, I walk toward death.   20
I walk into offices, into mirrors
into hands that are offered, into eyes
that are nearsighted, into mouths that smile or simply talk.
I do not say goodbye, I know nothing, I am not afraid:
death hides   25
its breath and its strategy.

I lunch. What for? I eat a fish in a sauce of gold and cream.
It is my last fish on my last
fork. The mouth distinguishes, chooses, decides,
swallows. Music passes through the sweets, a shiver   30
from a violin or the wind, I don't know. It isn't death.
It is the sun. The crowded trolleys. Work.
I am in a great city and I am a man
in a cogwheel. I am in a rush. I am going to die.
I ask the slow ones to clear a path for me. I don't look   35
at the cafés rattling with coffee cups and conversation.
I don't look at the shaded wall of the old hospital.
Nor at the posters. I am in a rush. I buy a paper. It's a rush
even if it means death!

The day already come around to its midpoint does not tell me   40
that I too have begun to come to an end. I am tired.
I want to sleep, but the preparations. The telephone.
The bills. The letters. I do a thousand things
that will create another thousand, here, there, in the United
   States.   45
I'll do anything. I make dates
that I shall never keep, I utter words in vain
I lie, saying: "Until tomorrow." But tomorrow won't be.

I decline with the afternoon, my head aches, I defend myself,
hand myself a pill: at least   50
the water drowns what hurts,
the fly, the buzzing . . . but nothing I will die from: death
   cheats,
cheats like a soccer player,
chooses like a cashier,   55
carefully, among illnesses and disasters.

Still it isn't death, it is the shadow
over tired buildings, the interval between
two races. Heavy business slows down,
engineers, executives, laborers, are finishing up.   60
But cabdrivers, waiters, and a thousand other
nighttime workers are getting started. The city
changes hands.

I go home. Again I clean up.
So my hair will be neat   65
and my nails not bring to mind the rebellious child of long ago.
The clothes without dust. The plastic suitcase.
I lock up my room. I lock up my life.
The elevator locks me up. I am calm.

For the last time I look at the city.   70
I can still turn back, put off death,
not take that car. Not go.
I can turn and say: "Friends,
I forgot a paper, there's no trip."
Then go to the casino, read a book.   75

But I take the car. I point out the place
where something is waiting. The field. Searchlights.
I pass by marble, glass, chrome.
I climb some steps. I bend. I enter
death's interior.   80

Death arranges seats to make the wait
more comfortable. Here one meets
those who are going to die and do not know it.
Newspapers, coffee, chewing gum, cotton for the ear,
small services daintily surround   85

our strapped-in bodies.
We are going to die, it is not only
my single and limited death,
twenty of us will be destroyed,
twenty of us will die, 90
twenty of us will be smashed to bits, and right now.

Or almost now. First the private,
personal, silent death of the individual.
I die secretly and without pain,
to live only as a piece of twenty, 95
and in me incorporate all the pieces
of those who are silently dying as I am.
All of us are one in twenty, a bouquet
of vigorous breaths about to be blown apart.

And we hang, 100
coldly we hang over the loves
and business of the country.
Toy streets disappear,
lights dim, hills dissolve,
there is only a mattress of clouds, 105
only a cold oxygen tube grazes my ears,
a tube that is sealed: and inside
the illumined and lukewarm body we live
in comfort and solitude, quiet and nothingness.

So smooth in the night is this machine and so easily does it cut 110
through increasingly larger blocks of air
that I live
my final moment and it's as if
I had been living for years
before and after today 115
a continuous and indomitable life
where there were no pauses, lapses, dreams.

I am twenty in the machine
that purrs softly
between starry pictures and the remote breaths of earth, 120
I feel at home thousands of meters high,
neither bird, nor myth,
I take stock of my powers,
and I fly without mystery,
a body flying, holding onto pockets, watches, nails, 125
tied to the earth by memory and muscular habit,
flesh soon to explode.

Oh, whiteness, serenity under the violence
of death without previous notice,
careful despite the unavoidable closeness   130
of atmospheric danger,
a shattering blast of air, splinter of wind
on the neck, lightning
flash burst crack
broken we tumble   135
straight down I fall and am turned into news.

Translated from the Portuguese by Mark Strand

STUDY QUESTIONS

1. In what way does the poet's contemplation of the airplane crash in "Death in a Plane" pose philosophical questions about the meaning of life and death?
2. How do the simple language and the description of everyday events contribute to the poem's meaning?

ADELIA PRADO

Adelia Prado (b. 1935) is one of Brazil's best-known contemporary poets. Educated in philosophy and religion, she is presently a minister for culture in her hometown, Divinopolis, in the state of Minas Gerais. To date, she has published four volumes of poetry and three works of fiction. There is a growing interest in her work in the United States. Translations of her poems have appeared in numerous journals, and a collection of her poems is being prepared for her English-speaking audience.

Prado's poetry is deeply philosophical. Through its conversational language and juxtaposition of details and experiences from the ordinary world, it probes what it means to be human. "Denouement" is typical in this respect. Through various reversals of perspective, it celebrates the vitality and mystery of life.

Denouement

I have great admiration for ships
and for certain people's handwriting which I attempt to imitate.
Of my entire family, I'm the only one who has seen the ocean.
I describe it over and over, they say "hmm"
and continue circling the chicken-coop with wire.   5
I tell about the spume, and the wearisome size of the waters,
they don't remember there's such a place as Kenya,
they'd never guess I'm thinking of Tanzania.
Eagerly they show me the lot: this is where the kitchen will be,
that's where we'll put in a garden.   10
So what do I do with the coast?
It was a pretty afternoon the day I planted myself in the window,
    between uncles,
and saw the man with his fly open,
the trellis angry with roses.   15
Hours and hours we talked unconsciously in Portuguese
as if it were the only language in the world.
Faith or no, I ask where are my people who are gone;
because I'm human, I zealously cover the pan of leftover sauce.
How could we know how to live a better life than this,   20
when even weeping it feels so good to be together?
Suffering belongs to no language.
I suffered and I suffer both in Minas Gerais and at the edge of
    the ocean.
I stand in awe of being alive. Oh, moon over the backlands,   25
oh, forests I don't need to see to get lost in,
oh, great cities and states of Brazil that I love as if I had
    invented them.
Being Brazilian places me in a way I find moving
and this, which without sinning I can call fate,   30
gives my desire a rest.
Taken all at once, it's far too intelligible, I can't take it.
Night! Make yourself useful and cover me with sleep.
Me and the thought of death just can't get used to each other.
I'll tremble with fear until the end.   35
And meanwhile everything is so small.
Compared to my heart's desire
the sea is a drop.

Translated from the Portuguese by Ellen Watson

STUDY QUESTIONS

1. What philosophical issues does "Denouement" confront? How does the poet define her experience? What is her predicament?
2. What function do nature and the ordinary details of life have in the poem?
3. What is the meaning of the two last lines? How do they put into perspective the experience that is evoked in the rest of the poem?

 ## CLARICE LISPECTOR

Clarice Lispector (1925–1977) was born while her parents were emigrating from the Ukraine to Brazil. Initially settling in Recife, she eventually moved to Rio de Janeiro, where she grew up and resided most of her life. Before turning to writing full-time, Lispector studied law and worked as a journalist and editor. Later she married a Brazilian diplomat and lived abroad for a number of years. Up to her death, she was active in the most innovative and experimental literary circles of her time. Lispector is considered one of Brazil's most important and influential novelists and short story writers. Experimenting with form and stressing the philosophic and psychological, she aimed at revealing the universal human condition in its local circumstances. Her work departed significantly from the regional and sociologically oriented literature that preceded it, and in this respect it has much in common with the fiction of Borges and Cortázar. Lispector is also known for her exploration of female subjectivity. Her portrayal of women as isolated and entrapped in a private world of frustration and rage was considered revolutionary for its time. She first came to prominence in 1961 with the publication of the novel The Apple in the Dark, *a symbolic exploration of the birth and abandonment of human consciousness. This was followed by several novels and collections of stories. Her best-known work is the novel* The Hour of the Star *(1978), which was made into a successful film. Set in São Paulo, it tells the story of a half-literate typist from the country who turns to Hollywood films and radio commercials for spiritual sustenance. "The Body" is from one of Lispector's most recent collections of stories. It is, in part, a departure from the subtle and mysterious fiction of her previous work. Complex and philosophical, it is overtly erotic and humorous in its exploration of human relations.*

The Body

X avier was a fierce, full-blooded man. Very strong, this guy. Loved the
tango. Went to see *The Last Tango in Paris* and got terribly excited. He
didn't understand the film: he thought it was a sex movie. He didn't realize
it was the story of a desperate man.

The night he saw *The Last Tango in Paris* the three of them went to bed
together: Xavier, Carmen, and Beatrice. Everyone knew that Xavier was a
bigamist, living with two women.

Every night it was one of them. Sometimes twice a night. The extra one
would remain watching. Neither was jealous of the other.

Beatrice ate anything that didn't move: she was fat and dumpy. Carmen
was tall and thin.

The night of the last tango in Paris was memorable for the three of them.
By dawn they were exhausted. But Carmen got up in the morning, prepared a great breakfast—with heaping spoonfuls of thick condensed milk—
and brought it to Beatrice and Xavier. She was groggy with sleep and had
to take a cold shower to snap back into shape.

That day—Sunday—they dined at three in the afternoon. Beatrice, the
fat one, cooked. Xavier drank French wine. And ate a whole fried chicken
by himself. The two women ate the other chicken. The chickens were filled
with a stuffing made of raisins and prunes, nice and moist.

At six o'clock the three of them went to church. They seemed a bolero.
Ravel's bolero.

That night they stayed home watching television and eating. Nothing
happened that night: they all three were very tired.

And so it went, day after day.

Xavier worked hard to support the two women and himself, to provide
big spreads. And once in a while he would cheat on both of them with a
first-rate prostitute. But he didn't say anything about this at home because
he was no fool.

Days, months, years went by. Nobody died. Xavier was forty-seven.
Carmen thirty-nine. And Beatrice had already turned fifty.

Life was good to them. Sometimes Carmen and Beatrice would go out in
order to buy sexy nightgowns. And to buy perfume. Carmen was the more
elegant. Beatrice, with her overflowing flesh, would pick out bikini panties
and a bra too small for her enormous breasts.

One day Xavier got home quite late at night; the two were desperate. If
they had only known that he had been with his prostitute! The three were
in truth four, like the Three Musketeers.

Xavier arrived with a bottomless hunger. And opened a bottle of champagne. He was full of energy. He spoke excitedly with the two of them,
telling them that the pharmaceutical business which he owned was doing

well financially. And he proposed that they go, the three of them, to Montevideo, to stay in a luxury hotel.

In a great hurry-scurry, the three suit cases were packed. 15

Carmen took all of her complicated make-up. Beatrice went out and 16 bought a miniskirt. They went by plane. They sat down in a row of three seats: he between the two women.

In Montevideo they bought anything they felt like. Even a sewing ma- 17 chine for Beatrice and a typewriter which Carmen wanted so as to be able to learn how to type. Actually she didn't need anything, poor nothing that she was. She kept a diary: she noted down on the pages of a thick, red-bound notebook the dates on which Xavier asked for her. She gave the diary to Beatrice to read.

In Montevideo they bought a book of recipes. Only it was in French, 18 and they understood nothing. The ingredients looked more like dirty words.

Then they bought a recipe book in Spanish. And they did the best they 19 could with the sauces and the soups. They learned to make "rosbif." Xavier gained seven pounds and his bull-like strength increased.

Sometimes the two women would stretch out on the bed. The day was 20 long. And, although they were not homosexuals, they excited each other and made love. Sad love.

One day they told Xavier about it. 21

Xavier trembled. And wanted the two of them to make love in front of 22 him that night. But, ordered up like this, it all ended in nothing. The two women cried, and Xavier became furious.

For three days he didn't say a word to them. 23

But, during this period, and without any request, the two women went 24 to bed together and succeeded.

The three didn't go to the theater. They preferred television. Or eating 25 out.

Xavier had bad table manners: he would pick up food with his hands 26 and make a lot of noise chewing, besides eating with his mouth open. Carmen, who was more genteel, would feel revolted and ashamed. But Beatrice was totally shameless, even walking around the house stark naked.

No one knows how it began. But it began. 27

One day Xavier came home from work with traces of lipstick on his 28 shirt. He couldn't deny that he had been with his favorite prostitute. Carmen and Beatrice each grabbed a piece of wood, and they chased Xavier all over the house. He ran like a madman, shouting, "Forgive me, forgive me, forgive me!"

The two women, tired out, finally give up chasing him. 29

At three in the morning Xavier wanted to have a woman. He called 30 Beatrice because she was less vindictive. Beatrice, soft and tired, gave herself to the desires of the man who seemed a superman.

But the following day they told him that they wouldn't cook for him anymore. That he'd better work it out with his third woman. 31

Both of them cried from time to time, and Beatrice made a potato salad for the two of them. 32

That afternoon they went to the movies. They ate out and didn't come home until midnight. They found Xavier beaten, sad, and hungry. He tried to explain: "It's just that sometimes I want to do it during the daytime!" 33

"Well then," said Carmen, "why don't you come home then?" 34

He promised he would. And he cried. When he cried, Carmen and Beatrice felt heartbroken. That night the two women made love in front of him, and he ate out his heart with envy. 35

How did the desire for revenge begin? The two women drew closer all the time and began to despise him. 36

He did not keep his promise but sought out the prostitute. She really turned him on because she used a lot of dirty language. And called him a son-of-a-bitch. He took it all. 37

Until there came a certain day. 38

Or better, a night. Xavier was sleeping placidly, like the good citizen he was. The two women were sitting together at a table, pensive. Each one thought of her lost childhood. And of death. Carmen said: 39

"One day the three of us will die." 40

Beatrice answered: 41

"And for what?" 42

They had to wait patiently for the day on which they would close their eyes forever. And Xavier? What should be done with Xavier? He looked like a sleeping child. 43

"Are we going to wait for him to die a natural death?" asked Beatrice. 44

Carmen thought, thought and said: 45

"I think we ought to figure something out, the two of us." 46

"What kind of thing?" 47

"I don't know yet." 48

"But we have to decide." 49

"You can leave it to me, I know what to do." 50

And nothing was done, nothing at all. In a little while it would be dawn, and nothing had happened. Carmen made good strong coffee for the two of them. And they ate chocolates until they were nauseous. And nothing, nothing at all. 51

They turned on the portable radio and listened to some poignant Schubert. It was pure piano. Carmen said: 52

"It has to be today." 53

Carmen led and Beatrice obeyed. It was a special night: full of stars which looked at them sparkling and tranquil. What silence. But what silence! The two went up close to Xavier to see if it would inspire them. Xavier snorted. Carmen felt really inspired. 54

She said to Beatrice: 55
"There are two butcher knives in the kitchen." 56
"So what?" 57
"So there are two of us, and we've got two knives." 58
"So what?" 59
"So, you ass, we two have arms and can do what we have to do. God 60
directs us."
"Wouldn't it be better not to mention God at this moment?" 61
"Do you want me to talk about the Devil? No, I speak of God who is the 62
master of all. Of space and time."
Then they went to the kitchen. The two butcher knives were newly 63
sharpened, of fine, polished steel. Would they have the strength?
They would, yes. 64
They were armed. The bedroom was dark. They struck blindly, stabbing 65
at the bedclothes. It was a cold night. Then they finally were able to make
out the sleeping body of Xavier.
Xavier's rich blood spread across the bed and dripped down onto the 66
floor—a lavish waste. Carmen and Beatrice sat down next to the dining-
room table, under the yellow light of the naked bulb, exhausted. To kill
requires strength. Human strength. Divine strength. The two were sweaty,
silent, knocked out. If it had been possible, they wouldn't have killed their
great love.
And now? Now they had to get rid of the body. The body was large. The 67
body was heavy.
So the two women went into the garden and, armed with two shovels, 68
dug a grave in the ground.
And, in the dark of the night, they carried the corpse out into the 69
garden. It was difficult because Xavier dead seemed to weigh more than
when he was alive, since his spirit had left him. As they carried him, they
groaned from exhaustion and grief. Beatrice cried.
They put the huge corpse in the grave, covered it with the humid and 70
fragrant earth of the garden, earth good for planting. Then they went back
into the house, made some more coffee, and pulled themselves together
a bit.
Beatrice, great romantic that she was—having filled her life with comic- 71
book romances about crossed or lost love—Beatrice had the idea of planting roses in that fertile soil.
So they went out again to the garden, took a stem of red roses, and 72
planted it on the sepulcher of the lamented Xavier. Day was dawning. The
garden gathered dew. The dew was a blessing on the murder. Such were
their thoughts, seated on the white bench that was out there.
The days passed. The two women bought black dresses. And scarcely 73
ate. When night came sadness fell over them. They no longer felt like
cooking. In a rage, Carmen, the hotheaded one, tore up the book of recipes

in French. She kept the one in Spanish: you never know when you might need it again.

Beatrice took over the cooking. They both ate and drank in silence. The stalk of red roses seemed to have taken hold. Good planter's hands, good prosperous earth. Everything was working out. 74

And so the story would have ended. 75

But it so happened that Xavier's secretary found his boss's long absence strange. There were important papers to be signed. Since Xavier's house had no telephone, he went there himself. The house seemed bathed in "mala suerte," evil fortune. The two women told him that Xavier had gone on a trip, that he had gone to Montevideo. The secretary didn't much believe them, but behaved as if he swallowed the story. 76

The following week the secretary went to the police. With the police you don't play games. At first they didn't want to believe his story. But, in the face of the secretary's insistence, they lazily decided to order the polygamist's house searched. All in vain: no trace of Xavier. 77

Then Carmen spoke: 78

"Xavier is in the garden." 79

"In the garden? Doing what?" 80

"Only God knows." 81

"But we didn't see anything or anybody." 82

They went out to the garden: Carmen, Beatrice, the secretary named Albert, two policemen, and two other men whose identities are unknown. Seven people. Then Beatrice, without a tear in her eye, showed them the flowering grave. Three men opened the grave, ruining the stalk of roses, which suffered this human brutality for no reason at all. 83

And they saw Xavier. He was horrible, deformed, already half eaten away by worms, with his eyes open. 84

"And now?" said one of the policemen. 85

"And now we arrest the two women." 86

"But," said Carmen, "let us be in the same cell." 87

"Look," said one of the policemen, right in front of the astonished secretary, "it's best to pretend that nothing at all happened, otherwise there will be lots of noise, lots of paper work, lots of gossip." 88

"You two," said the other policeman, "pack your bags and go and live in Montevideo. And don't bother us anymore." 89

The two women said thank you very much. 90

And Xavier didn't say anything. For, in fact, he had nothing to say. 91

Translated from the Portuguese by Alexis Levitin

STUDY QUESTIONS

1. What philosophical issues does "The Body" raise about the human condition?
2. In what ways does the story's title reflect its subject? How is sexuality portrayed?
3. What is the author's view of her characters? How does she use irony and humor?
4. What does the attitude of the police reveal about society?

CHILE

 PABLO NERUDA

Pablo Neruda (1904–1973) is considered one of the great poets of the twentieth century, one whose subjects ranged from the personal and erotic to the historical and political. He is best known as a literary spokesman for the aspirations of the common people of the Third World. Born Ricardo Eliezer Neftali Reyes y Basoalto in Parral, Chile, he took a pseudonym because his father, a railway worker, did not want him to be a poet. Neruda began writing when he was a student at the University of Chile. During this period, he joined with Bohemian poets who were promoting free love, anarchism, and experimental poetry. In 1927, he began a long career as a diplomat. Initially posted to Burma, Ceylon, and Singapore, he underwent significant changes as a person and writer. Exposed to the harsh realities of imperialism and reading widely in French and English poetry, he adopted via Rimbaud and Whitman the concept of poet as seer. Returning to Chile in 1932, he published the first part of his collection of poetry Residence on Earth, *which revolutionized Hispanic verse with its dazzling combination of symbolism and surrealism. By the late 1930s Neruda was a committed leftist, and increasingly his poetry depicted sociopolitical themes. During the 1940s he joined the Communist Party, was elected to the Chilean senate, and was forced to flee his country as a political exile. He returned to Chile in 1953. After a trip to Peru, where he visited the ancient Inca ruins of Machu Picchu, he wrote one of his most successful collections of poems,* The General Song *(1968). Following the tradition of celebrating the grandeur of Latin America's land and history, Neruda included a sobering portrait of the continent's harsh sociopolitical and economic reality and paid tribute to the emerging consciousness of the downtrodden, who were positioning themselves for liberation. To the end of his life, Neruda remained an optimist. He continued writing politically committed poetry, but he also wrote simple, humorous verse about everyday living. In 1971 he won the Nobel Prize in Literature. He died in 1973 just after his close friend, President Salvador Allende, was overthrown by the Chilean military. "The United Fruit Co." and "Poet's Obligation" are typical of Neruda's socially conscious poetry.*

The United Fruit Co.

When the trumpets had sounded and all
    was in readiness on the face of the earth,
Jehovah divided his universe:
Anaconda, Ford Motors,
Coca-Cola Inc., and similar entities: 5
the most succulent item of all,
The United Fruit Company Incorporated
reserved for itself: the heartland
and coasts of my country,
the delectable waist of America.   10
They rechristened their properties:
the "Banana Republics"—
and over the languishing dead,
the uneasy repose of the heroes
who harried that greatness,   15
their flags and their freedoms,
they established an *opéra bouffe*:
they ravished all enterprise,
awarded the laurels like Caesars,
unleashed all the covetous, and contrived   20
the tyrannical Reign of the Flies—
Trujillo the fly, and Tacho the fly,
the flies called Carias, Martinez,
Ubico—all of them flies, flies
dank with the blood of their marmalade   25
vassalage, flies buzzing drunkenly
on the populous middens:
the fly-circus fly and the scholarly
kind, case-hardened in tyranny.
Then in the bloody domain of the flies   30
The United Fruit Company Incorporated
sailed off with a booty of coffee and fruits
brimming its cargo boats, gliding
like trays with the spoils
of our drowning dominions.   35
And all the while, somewhere in the sugary
hells of our seaports,
smothered by gases, an Indian
fell in the morning:
a body spun off, an anonymous   40
chattel, some numeral tumbling,

a branch with its death running out of it
in the vat of the carrion, fruit laden and foul.

Translated from the Spanish by Ben Belitt

Poet's Obligation

To whoever is not listening to the sea
this Friday morning, to whoever is cooped up
in house or office, factory or woman
or street or mine or harsh prison cell:
to him I come, and, without speaking or looking,   5
I arrive and open the door of his prison,
and a vibration starts up, vague and insistent,
a great fragment of thunder sets in motion
the rumble of the planet and the foam,
the raucous rivers of the ocean flood,   10
the star vibrates swiftly in its corona,
and the sea is beating, dying and continuing.

So, drawn on by my destiny,
I ceaselessly must listen to and keep
the sea's lamenting in my awareness,   15
I must feel the crash of the hard water
and gather it up in a perpetual cup
so that, wherever those in prison may be,
wherever they suffer the autumn's castigation,
I may be there with an errant wave,   20
I may move, passing through windows,
and hearing me, eyes will glance upward
saying 'How can I reach the sea?'
And I shall broadcast, saying nothing,
the starry echoes of the wave,   25
a breaking up of foam and of quicksand,
a rustling of salt withdrawing,
the grey cry of sea-birds on the coast.

So, through me, freedom and the sea
will make their answer to the shuttered heart.   30

Translated from the Spanish by Alastair Reid

1. How and to what effect is religious and insect imagery used in "The United Fruit Co."?
2. Where in "The United Fruit Co." is irony used?
3. How does the poet define the role of the United Fruit Co.?
4. How does the author view the poet's responsibility in "Poet's Obligation"?
5. Discuss the use of nature imagery in "Poet's Obligation."

 ISABEL ALLENDE

Isabel Allende (b. 1942) is one of Latin America's leading writers. Born in Peru of Chilean diplomats, she has lived in several countries in Latin America and currently resides in the San Francisco Bay area. She has worked for the United Nations Food and Agriculture Organization and was for many years a journalist. She only began to write fiction in the early 1980s. Since then, her novels, The House of the Spirits, Of Love and Shadows, *and* Eva Luna, *have become international best-sellers. Influenced by the "magic realism" of an older generation of writers, Allende's lyric voice skillfully mingles the personal and the political.*

Phantom Palace

When five centuries earlier the bold renegades from Spain with their bone-weary horses and armor candescent beneath an American sun stepped upon the shores of Quinaroa, Indians had been living and dying in that same place for several thousand years. The conquistadors announced with heralds and banners the "discovery" of a new land, declared it a possession of a remote emperor, set in place the first cross, and named the place San Jerónimo, a name unpronounceable to the natives. The Indians observed these arrogant ceremonies with some amazement, but the news had already reached them of the bearded warriors who advanced across the world with their thunder of iron and powder; they had heard that wherever these men went they sowed sorrow and that no known people had been capable of opposing them: all armies had succumbed before that handful of centaurs. These Indians were an ancient tribe, so poor that not even the most befeathered chieftain had bothered to exact taxes from them, and so meek that they had never been recruited for war. They had lived in peace since the dawn of time and were not eager to change their habits because of some crude strangers. Soon, nevertheless, they comprehended the magnitude of the enemy and they understood the futility of attempting to ignore them; their presence was overpowering, like a heavy stone bound to every back. In the years that followed, the Indians who had not died in slavery or as a result of the different tortures improvised to entrench the new gods, or as victims of unknown illnesses, scattered deep into the jungle and gradually lost even the name of their people. Always in hiding, like shadows among the foliage, they survived for centuries, speaking in whispers and mobilizing by night. They came to be so skillful in the art of dissimulation that history did not record them, and today there is no evidence of their passage through time. Books do not mention them, but the *campesinos* who live in the region say they have heard them in the forest, and every time the belly of a young unmarried woman begins to grow round and they cannot point to the seducer, they attribute the baby to the spirit of a lustful Indian. People of that place are proud of carrying a few drops of the blood of those invisible beings mingled with the torrential flow from English pirates, Spanish soldiers, African slaves, adventurers in search of El Dorado, and, later, whatever immigrant stumbled onto these shores with his pack on his back and his head filled with dreams.

Europe consumed more coffee, cocoa, and bananas than we as a nation could produce, but all that demand was no bonanza for us; we continued to be as poor as ever. Events took a sudden turn when a black man digging a well along the coast drove his pick deep into the ground and a stream of petroleum spurted over his face. Toward the end of the Great War there was a widely held notion that ours was a prosperous country, when in truth most of the inhabitants still squished mud between their toes. The fact was that gold flowed only into the coffers of El Benefactor and his retinue, but there was hope that someday a little would spill over for the people. Two decades passed under this democratic totalitarianism, as the President for Life called his government, during which any hint of subversion would have been crushed in the name of his greater glory. In the capital there were signs of progress: motorcars, movie houses, ice cream parlors, a hippodrome, and a theater that presented spectaculars from New York and Paris. Every day dozens of ships moored in the port, some carrying away petroleum and others bringing in new products, but the rest of the country drowsed in a centuries-long stupor. 2

One day the people of San Jerónimo awakened from their siesta to the deafening pounding that presaged the arrival of the steam engine. The railroad tracks would unite the capital with this small settlement chosen by El Benefactor as the site for his Summer Palace, which was to be constructed in the style of European royalty—no matter that no one knew how 3 to distinguish summer from winter, since both were lived under nature's hot, humid breath. The sole reason for erecting such a monumental work on this precise spot was that a certain Belgian naturalist had affirmed that if there was any truth to the myth of the Earthly Paradise, this landscape of incomparable beauty would have been the location. According to his observations the forest harbored more than a thousand varieties of brightly colored birds and numerous species of wild orchids, from the *Brassia*, which is as large as a hat, to the tiny *Pleurothallis*, visible only under a magnifying glass.

The idea of the Palace had originated with some Italian builders who   4
had called on His Excellency bearing plans for a hodgepodge of a villa, a labyrinth of countless columns, wide colonnades, curving staircases, arches, domes and capitals, salons, kitchens, bedchambers, and more than thirty baths decorated with gold and silver faucets. The railroad was the first stage in the enterprise, indispensable for transporting tons of materials and hundreds of workmen to this remote corner of the world, in addition to the supervisors and craftsmen brought from Italy. The task of putting together that jigsaw puzzle lasted four years: flora and fauna were transmuted in the process, and the cost was equivalent to that of all the warships of the nation's fleet, but it was paid for punctually with the dark mineral that flowed from the earth, and on the anniversary of the Glorious Ascent to Power the ribbon was cut to inaugurate the Summer Palace. For the occasion the locomotive of the train was draped in the colors of the flag, and the freight cars were replaced by parlor cars upholstered in plush and English leather; the formally attired guests included members of the oldest aristocracy who, although they detested the cold-blooded Andean who had usurped the government, did not dare refuse his invitation.

El Benefactor was a crude man with the comportment of a peon; he   5
bathed in cold water and slept on a mat on the floor with his boots on and his pistol within arm's reach; he lived on roast meat and maize, and drank nothing but water and coffee. His black cigars were his one luxury; he considered anything else a vice befitting degenerates or homosexuals— including alcohol, which he disapproved of and rarely offered at his table. With time, nevertheless, he was forced to accept a few refinements, because he understood the need to impress diplomats and other eminent visitors if they were not to carry the report abroad that he was a barbarian. He did not have a wife to mend his Spartan ways. He believed that love was a dangerous weakness. He was convinced that all women, except his own mother, were potentially perverse and that the most prudent way to treat them was to keep them at arm's length. He had always said that a man asleep in an amorous embrace was as vulnerable as a premature baby; he demanded, therefore, that his generals sleep in the barracks and limit their family life to sporadic visits. No woman had ever spent the night in his bed or could boast of anything more than a hasty encounter. No

woman, in fact, ever made a lasting impression until Marcia Lieberman entered his life.

The celebration for the inauguration of the Summer Palace was a stellar 6 event in the annals of El Benefactor's government. For two days and two nights alternating orchestras played the most current dance tunes and an army of chefs prepared an unending banquet. The most beautiful mulatto women in the Caribbean, dressed in sumptuous gowns created for the occasion, whirled through salons with officers who had never fought in a battle but whose chests were covered with medals. There was every sort of diversion: singers imported from Havana and New Orleans, flamenco dancers, magicians, jugglers and trapeze artists, card games and dominoes, and even a rabbit hunt. Servants released the rabbits from their cages, and the guests pursued the scampering pack with finely bred greyhounds; the chase came to an end when one wit blasted all the black-necked swans gliding across the lake. Some guests passed out in their chairs, drunk with dancing and liquor, while others jumped fully clothed into the swimming pool or drifted off in pairs to the bedchambers. El Benefactor did not want to know the details. After greeting his guests with a brief speech, and beginning the dancing with the most aristocratic lady present, he had returned to the capital without a farewell. Parties put him in a bad humor. On the third day the train made the return journey, carrying home the enervated *bons vivants*. The Summer Palace was left in a calamitous state: the baths were dunghills, the curtains were dripping with urine, the furniture was gutted, and the plants drooped in their flower-pots. It took the servants a week to clean up the ravages of that hurricane.

The Palace was never again the scene of a bacchanal. Occasionally El 7 Benefactor went there to get away from the pressures of his duties, but his repose lasted no more than three or four days, for fear that a conspiracy might be hatched in his absence. The government required eternal vigilance if power was not to slip through his fingers. The only people left in all that enormous edifice were the personnel entrusted with its maintenance. When the clatter of the construction equipment and the train had stilled, and the echoes of the inaugural festivities died down, the region was once again calm, and the orchids flowered and birds rebuilt their nests. The inhabitants of San Jerónimo returned to their habitual occupations and almost succeeded in forgetting the presence of the Summer Palace. That was when the invisible Indians slowly returned to occupy their territory.

The first signs were so subtle that no one paid attention to them; foot- 8 steps and whispers, fleeting silhouettes among the columns, the print of a hand on the clean surface of a table. Gradually food began to disappear from the kitchens, and bottles from the wine cellars; in the morning, some beds seemed to have been slept in. The servants blamed one another but never raised their voices because no one wanted the officer of the guard to take the matter into his hands. It was impossible to watch the entire expanse of that house, and while they were searching one room they would hear sighs in the adjoining one; but when they opened that door they would find only a curtain fluttering, as if someone had just stepped through it. The rumor spread that the Palace was under a spell, and soon the fear spread even to the soldiers, who stopped walking their night rounds and limited themselves to standing motionless at their post, eyes on the surrounding landscape, weapons at the ready. The frightened servants stopped going down to the cellars and, as a precaution, locked many of the rooms. They confined their activities to the kitchen and slept in one wing of the building. The remainder of the mansion was left unguarded, in the possession of the incorporeal Indians who had divided the rooms with invisible lines and taken up residence there like mischievous spirits. They had survived the passage of history, adapting to changes when they were inevitable, and when necessary taking refuge in a dimension of their own. In the rooms of the Palace they at last found refuge; there they noiselessly made love, gave birth without celebration, and died without tears. They learned so thoroughly all the twists and turns of that marble maze that they were able to exist comfortably in the same space with the guards and servants, never so much as brushing against them, as if they existed in a different time.

Ambassador Lieberman debarked in the port with his wife and a full cargo 9 of personal belongings. He had traveled with his dogs, all his furniture, his library, his collection of opera recordings, and every imaginable variety of sports equipment, including a sailboat. From the moment his new destination had been announced, he had detested that country. He had left his post as Vice Consul in Vienna motivated by the ambition to obtain an ambassadorship, even if it meant South America, a bizarre continent for which he had not an ounce of sympathy. Marcia, his wife, took the appointment with better humor. She was prepared to follow her husband throughout his diplomatic pilgrimage—even though each day she felt more remote from him and had little interest in his mundane affairs—because she was allowed a great deal of freedom. She had only to fulfill certain minimal wifely requirements, and the remainder of her time was her own. In fact, her husband was so immersed in his work and his sports that he was scarcely aware of her existence; he noticed her only when she was not there. Lieberman's wife was an indispensable complement to his career; she lent brilliance to his social life and efficiently managed his complicated domestic staff. He thought of her as a loyal partner, but he had never been even slightly curious about her feelings. Marcia consulted maps and an encyclopedia to learn the particulars of that distant nation, and began studying Spanish. During the two weeks of the Atlantic crossing she read books by the famous Belgian naturalist and, even before arriving, was enamored of that heat-bathed geography. As she was a rather withdrawn woman, she was happier in her garden than in the salons where she had to accompany her husband, and she concluded that in the new post she would have fewer social demands and could devote herself to reading, painting, and exploring nature.

Lieberman's first act was to install fans in every room of his residence. 10 Immediately thereafter he presented his credentials to the government authorities. When El Benefactor received him in his office, the couple had been in the city only a few days, but the gossip that the Ambassador's wife was a beautiful woman had already reached the caudillo's ears. For reasons of protocol he invited them to dinner, although he found the diplomat's arrogance and garrulity insufferable. On the appointed night Marcia Lieberman entered the Reception Hall on her husband's arm and, for the first time in a long lifetime, a woman caused El Benefactor to gasp for breath. He had seen more lithe figures, and faces more beautiful, but never such grace. She awakened memories of past conquests, fueling a heat in his blood that he had not felt in many years. He kept his distance that evening, observing the Ambassador's wife surreptitiously, seduced by the curve of her throat, the shadow in her eyes, the movement of her hands, the solemnity of her bearing. Perhaps it crossed his mind that he was more than forty years older than she and that any scandal would have repercussions far beyond the national boundaries, but that did not discourage him; on the contrary, it added an irresistible ingredient to his nascent passion.

Marcia Lieberman felt the man's eyes fastened on her like an indecent 11 caress, and she was aware of the danger, but she did not have the strength to escape. At one moment she thought of telling her husband they should leave, but instead remained seated, hoping the old man would approach her and at the same time ready to flee if he did. She could not imagine why she was trembling. She had no illusions about her host; the signs of age were obvious from where she was sitting: the wrinkled and blemished skin, the dried-up body, the hesitant walk. She could imagine his stale odor and knew intuitively that his hands were claws beneath the white kid gloves. But the dictator's eyes, clouded by age and the exercise of so much cruelty, still held a gleam of power that held her frozen in her chair.

El Benefactor did not know how to pay court to a woman; until that 12 moment he had never had need to do so. That fact acted in his favor, for had he harassed Marcia with a Lothario's gallantries she would have found him repulsive and would have retreated with scorn. Instead she could not refuse him when a few days later he knocked at her door, dressed in civilian clothes and without his guards, looking like a dreary great-grandfather, to tell her that he had not touched a woman for ten years and that he was past temptations of that sort but, with all respect, he was asking her to accompany him that afternoon to a private place where he could rest his head in her queenly lap and tell her how the world had been when he was still a fine figure of a macho and she had not yet been born.

"And my husband?" Marcia managed to ask in a whisper-thin voice. 13

"Your husband does not exist, my child. Now only you and I exist," the President for Life replied as he led her to his black Packard. 14

Marcia did not return home, and before the month was out Ambassador Lieberman returned to his country. He had left no stone unturned in searching for his wife, refusing at first to accept what was no secret, but when the evidence of the abduction became impossible to ignore, Lieberman had asked for an audience with the Chief of State and demanded the return of his wife. The interpreter tried to soften his words in translation, but the President captured the tone and seized the excuse to rid himself once and for all of that imprudent husband. He declared that Lieberman had stained the honor of the nation with his absurd and unfounded accusations and gave him three days to leave the country. He offered him the option of withdrawing without a scandal, to protect the dignity of the country he represented, since it was to no one's interest to break diplomatic ties and obstruct the free movement of the oil tankers. At the end of the interview, with the expression of an injured father, he added that he could understand the Ambassador's dilemma and told him not to worry, because in his absence, he, El Benefactor, would continue the search for his wife. As proof of his good intents he called the Chief of Police and issued instructions in the Ambassador's presence. If at any moment Lieberman had thought of refusing to leave without Marcia, a second thought must have made clear to him that he was risking a bullet in the brain, so he packed his belongings and left the country before the three days were up. 15

Love had taken El Benefactor by surprise at an age when he no longer remembered the heart's impatience. This cataclysm rocked his senses and thrust him back into adolescence, but not sufficiently to dull his vulpine cunning. He realized that his was a passion of sensuality, and he could not imagine that Marcia returned his emotions. He did not know why she had followed him that afternoon, but his reason indicated that it was not for love, and, as he knew nothing about women, he supposed that she had allowed herself to be seduced out of a taste for adventure, or greed for power. In fact, she had fallen prey to compassion. When the old man embraced her, anxiously, his eyes watering with humiliation because his manhood did not respond as it once had, she undertook, patiently and with good will, to restore his pride. And thus after several attempts the poor man succeeded in passing through the gates and lingering a few brief instants in the proffered warm gardens, collapsing immediately thereafter with his heart filled with foam. 16

"Stay with me," El Benefactor begged, as soon as he had recovered from fear of succumbing upon her. 17

And Marcia had stayed, because she was moved by the aged caudillo's loneliness, and because the alternative of returning to her husband seemed less interesting than the challenge of slipping past the iron fence this man had lived behind for eighty years. 18

El Benefactor kept Marcia hidden on one of his estates, where he visited   19
her daily. He never stayed the night with her. Their time together was
spent in leisurely caresses and conversation. In her halting Spanish she
told him about her travels and the books she had read; he listened, not
understanding much, content simply with the cadence of her voice. In turn
he told her stories of his childhood in the arid lands of the Andes, and of
his life as a soldier; but if she formulated some question he immediately
threw up his defenses, observing her from the corner of his eyes as if she
were the enemy. Marcia could not fail to note this implacable stoniness and
realized that his habit of distrust was much stronger than his need to yield
to tenderness, and so, after a few weeks, she resigned herself to defeat.
Once she had renounced any hope of winning him over with love, she lost
interest in him and longed to escape the walls that sequestered her. But it
was too late. El Benefactor needed her by his side because she was the
closest thing to a companion he had known; her husband had returned to
Europe and she had nowhere to turn in this land; and even her name was
fading from memory. The dictator perceived the change in her and his
mistrust intensified, but that did not cause him to stop loving her. To
console her for the confinement to which she was now condemned—her
appearance outside would have confirmed Lieberman's accusations and
shot international relations to hell—he provided her with all the things she
loved: music, books, animals. Marcia passed the hours in a world of her
own, every day more detached from reality. When she stopped encouraging him, El Benefactor found it impossible to embrace her, and their meetings resolved into peaceful evenings of cookies and hot chocolate. In his
desire to please her, El Benefactor invited her one day to go with him to the
Summer Palace, so she could see the paradise of the Belgian naturalist she
had read so much about.

The train had not been used since the inaugural celebration ten years   20
before and was so rusted that they had to make the trip by automobile,
escorted by a caravan of guards; a crew of servants had left a week before,
taking everything needed to restore the Palace to its original luxury. The
road was no more than a trail defended by chain gangs against encroaching
vegetation. In some stretches they had to use machetes to clear the ferns,
and oxen to haul the cars from the mud, but none of that diminished
Marcia's enthusiasm. She was dazzled by the landscape. She endured the
humid heat and the mosquitoes as if she did not feel them, absorbed by a
nature that seemed to welcome her in its embrace. She had the impression
that she had been there before, perhaps in dreams or in another life, that
she belonged there, that until that moment she had been a stranger in the
world, and that her instinct had dictated every step she had taken, including that of leaving her husband's house to follow a trembling old man, for
the sole purpose of leading her here. Even before she saw the Summer
Palace, she knew that it would be her last home. When the edifice finally
rose out of the foliage, encircled by palm trees and shimmering in the sun,

Marcia breathed a deep sigh of relief, like a shipwrecked sailor when he sees home port.

Despite the frantic preparations that had been made to receive them, the mansion still seemed to be under a spell. The Roman-style structure, conceived as the center of a geometric park and grand avenues, was sunk in the riot of a gluttonous jungle growth. The torrid climate had changed the color of the building materials, covering them with a premature patina; nothing was visible of the swimming pool and gardens. The greyhounds had long ago broken their leashes and were running loose, a ferocious, starving pack that greeted the newcomers with a chorus of barking. Birds had nested in the capitals of the columns and covered the reliefs with droppings. On every side were signs of disorder. The Summer Palace had been transformed into a living creature defenseless against the green invasion that had surrounded and overrun it. Marcia leapt from the automobile and ran to the enormous doors where the servants awaited, oppressed by the heat of the dog days. One by one she explored all the rooms, the great salons decorated with crystal chandeliers that hung from the ceilings like constellations and French furniture whose tapestry upholstery was now home to lizards, bedchambers where bed canopies were blanched by intense sunlight, baths where moss had grown in the seams of the marble. Marcia ever stopped smiling; she had the face of a woman recovering what was rightfully hers.

When El Benefactor saw Marcia so happy, a touch of the old vigor returned to warm his creaking bones, and he could embrace her as he had in their first meetings. Distractedly, she acceded. The week they had planned to spend there lengthened into two, because El Benefactor had seldom enjoyed himself so much. The fatigue accumulated in his years as tyrant disappeared, and several of his old man's ailments abated. He strolled with Marcia around the grounds, pointing out the many species of orchids climbing the treetrunks or hanging like grapes from the highest branches, the clouds of white butterflies that covered the ground, and the birds with iridescent feathers that filled the air with their song. He frolicked with her like a young lover, he fed her bits of the delicious flesh of wild mangoes, with his own hands he bathed her in herbal infusions, and he made her laugh by serenading her beneath her window. It had been years since he had been away from the capital, except for brief flights to provinces where his presence was required to put down some insurrection and to renew the people's belief that his authority was not to be questioned. This unexpected vacation had put him in a fine frame of mind; life suddenly seemed more fun, and he had the fantasy that with this beautiful woman beside him he could govern forever. One night he unintentionally fell asleep in her arms. He awoke in the early morning, terrified, with the clear sensation of having betrayed himself. He sprang out of bed, sweating, his heart galloping, and observed Marcia lying there, a white odalisque in repose, her copper hair spilling across her face. He informed his guards that he was returning to the city. He was not surprised when Marcia gave no sign of going with him. Perhaps in his heart he preferred it that way, since he understood that she represented his most dangerous weakness, that she was the only person who could make him forget his power.

El Benefactor returned to the capital without Marcia. He left behind a 23
half-dozen soldiers to guard the property and a few employees to serve her, and he promised he would maintain the road so that she could receive his gifts, provisions, mail, and newspapers and magazines. He assured her that he would visit her often, as often as his duties as Chief of State permitted, but when he said goodbye they both knew they would never meet again. El Benefactor's caravan disappeared into the ferns and for a moment silence fell over the Summer Palace. Marcia felt truly free for the first time in her life. She removed the hairpins holding her hair in a bun, and shook out her long hair. The guards unbuttoned their jackets and put aside their weapons, while the servants went off to hang their hammocks in the coolest corners they could find.

For two weeks the Indians had observed the visitors from the shadows. 24
Undeceived by Marcia Lieberman's fair skin and marvelous curly hair, they recognized her as one of their own but they had not dared materialize in her presence because of the habit of centuries of clandestinity. After the departure of the old man and his retinue, they returned stealthily to oc-cupy the space where they had lived for generations. Marcia knew intu-itively that she was never alone, that wherever she went a thousand eyes followed her, that she moved in a ferment of constant murmuring, warm breathing, and rhythmic pulsing, but she was not afraid; just the oppo-site, she felt protected by friendly spirits. She became used to petty an-noyances: one of her dresses disappeared for several days, then one morning was back in a basket at the foot of her bed; someone devoured her dinner before she entered the dining room; her watercolors and books were stolen, but also she found freshly cut orchids on her table, and some evenings her bath waited with mint leaves floating in the cool water; she heard ghostly notes from pianos in the empty salons, the panting of lovers in the armoires, the voices of children in the attics. The servants had no explanation for those disturbances and she stopped ask-ing, because she imagined they themselves were part of the benevolent conspiracy. One night she crouched among the curtains with a flashlight, and when she felt the thudding of feet on the marble, switched on the beam. She thought she saw shadowy, naked forms that for an instant gazed at her mildly and then vanished. She called in Spanish, but no one answered. She realized she would need enormous patience to uncover those mysteries, but it did not matter because she had the rest of her life before her.

* * *

A few years later the nation was jolted by the news that the dictatorship 25
had come to an end for a most surprising reason: El Benefactor had died.
He was a man in his dotage, a sack of skin and bones that for months had
been decaying in life, and yet very few people imagined that he was mortal. No one remembered a time before him; he had been in power so many
decades that people had become accustomed to thinking of him as an
inescapable evil, like the climate. The echoes of the funeral were slow to
reach the Summer Palace. By then most of the guards and servants, bored
with waiting for replacements that never came, had deserted their posts.
Marcia listened to the news without emotion. In fact, she had to make an
effort to remember her past, what had happened beyond the jungle, and
the hawk-eyed old man who had changed the course of her destiny. She
realized that with the death of the tyrant the reasons for her remaining
hidden had evaporated; she could return to civilization, where now, surely,
no one was concerned with the scandal of her kidnapping. She quickly
discarded that idea, however, because there was nothing outside the snarl
of the surrounding jungle that interested her. Her life passed peacefully
among the Indians; she was absorbed in the greenness, clothed only in a
tunic, her hair cut short, her body adorned with tattoos and feathers. She
was utterly happy.

A generation later, when democracy had been established in the nation 26
and nothing remained of the long history of dictators but a few pages in
scholarly books, someone remembered the marble villa and proposed that
they restore it and found an Academy of Art. The Congress of the Republic
sent a commission to draft a report, but their automobiles were not up to
the grueling trip, and when finally they reached San Jerónimo no one could
tell them where the Summer Palace was. They tried to follow the railroad
tracks, but the rails had been ripped from the ties and the jungle had
erased all traces. Then the Congress sent a detachment of explorers and a
pair of military engineers who flew over the area in a helicopter; the vegetation was so thick that not even they could find the site. Details about the
Palace were misplaced in people's memories and the municipal archives;
the notion of its existence became gossip for old women; reports were
swallowed up in the bureaucracy and, since the nation had more urgent
problems, the project of the Academy of Art was tabled.

Now a highway has been constructed that links San Jerónimo to the rest 27
of the country. Travelers say that sometimes after a storm, when the air is
damp and charged with electricity, a white marble palace suddenly rises up
beside the road, hovers for a few brief moments in the air, like a mirage,
and then noiselessly disappears.

Translated from the Spanish by Margaret Sayers Peden

STUDY QUESTIONS

1. How does "Phantom Palace" conform to the definition of "magic realism" provided in the introduction?
2. What is the author's political vision? What is her view of the historical legacy of Europe's conquest of Indians?
3. Why is Marcia attracted to El Benefactor? What does she represent in the novel?

COLOMBIA

 ## GABRIEL GARCÍA MÁRQUEZ

Gabriel García Márquez (b. 1928) is Latin America's most acclaimed and widely known writer, the first international best-seller in Latin America's history. Along with Cuba's Alejo Carpentier and Guatemala's Miguel Angel Asturias, he is one of the leading practitioners of "magic realism"—the exotic and phantasmagorical style that derives from the juxtaposition of diverse cultures and the interplay of myth, history, and human consciousness.

Born in Aracataca, Colombia, García Márquez spent the early years of his life in the home of his grandparents, where he was exposed to the legends, myths, and superstitions of the region. Later he studied law at the University of Bogotá and worked as a journalist in Colombia, the United States, and Europe. During most of the 1960s he lived in Mexico and wrote film scripts. From 1967 through 1975, he resided in Spain, and recently he has divided his time between Bogotá and Mexico City. Like many Latin American intellectuals, he supported the Allende government in Chile and the Cuban and Nicaraguan revolutions.

García Márquez has written several novels and volumes of short stories, but his reputation rests on One Hundred Years of Solitude *(1967), a novel that has been praised as a literary masterpiece and one of the great novels of the twentieth century. Through an overlapping of the real and the fantastic, history and myth, García Márquez explores the intimate relationship between the sociopolitical structure of his country and the behavior of its inhabitants. Similarly, "Big Mama's Funeral" uses myth, fantasy, and exaggeration to portray the death and funeral of a remarkable ninety-two-year-old matriarch.*

Big Mama's Funeral

This is, for all the world's unbelievers, the true account of Big Mama, absolute sovereign of the Kingdom of Macondo, who lived for ninety-   1 two years, and died in the odor of sanctity one Tuesday last September, and whose funeral was attended by the Pope.

Now that the nation, which was shaken to its vitals, has recovered its balance; now that the bagpipers of San Jacinto, the smugglers of Guajira, the rice planters of Sinú, the prostitutes of Caucamayal, the wizards of Sierpe, and the banana workers of Aracataca have folded up their tents to recover from the exhausting vigil and have regained their serenity, and the President of the Republic and his Ministers and all those who represented the public and supernatural powers on the most magnificent funeral occasion recorded in the annals of history have regained control of their estates; now that the Holy Pontiff has risen up to Heaven in body and soul; and now that it is impossible to walk around in Macondo because of the empty bottles, the cigarette butts, the gnawed bones, the cans and rags and excrement that the crowd which came to the burial left behind; now is the time to lean a stool against the front door and relate from the beginning the details of this national commotion, before the historians have a chance to get at it.

Fourteen weeks ago, after endless nights of poultices, mustard plasters, and leeches, and weak with the delirium of her death agony, Big Mama ordered them to seat her in her old rattan rocker so she could express her last wishes. It was the only thing she needed to do before she died. That morning, with the intervention of Father Anthony Isabel, she had put the affairs of her soul in order, and now she needed only to put her worldly affairs in order with her nine nieces and nephews, her sole heirs, who were standing around her bed. The priest, talking to himself and on the verge of his hundredth birthday, stayed in the room. Ten men had been needed to take him up to Big Mama's bedroom, and it was decided that he should stay there so they should not have to take him down and then take him up again at the last minute.

Nicanor, the eldest nephew, gigantic and savage, dressed in khaki and spurred boots, with a .38-caliber long-barreled revolver holstered under his shirt, went to look for the notary. The enormous two-story mansion, fragrant from molasses and oregano, with its dark apartments crammed with chests and the odds and ends of four generations turned to dust, had become paralyzed since the week before, in expectation of that moment. In the long central hall, with hooks on the walls where in another time butchered pigs had been hung and deer were slaughtered on sleepy August Sundays, the peons were sleeping on farm equipment and bags of salt, awaiting the order to saddle the mules to spread the bad news to the four corners of the huge hacienda. The rest of the family was in the living room. The women were limp, exhausted by the inheritance proceedings and lack of sleep; they kept a strict mourning which was the culmination of countless accumulated mournings. Big Mama's matriarchal rigidity had surrounded her fortune and her name with a sacramental fence, within which uncles married the daughters of their nieces, and the cousins married their aunts, and brothers their sisters-in-law, until an intricate mesh of consanguinity was formed, which turned procreation into a vicious circle. Only Magdalena, the youngest of the nieces, managed to escape it. Terrified by hallucinations, she made Father Anthony Isabel exorcise her, shaved her head, and renounced the glories and vanities of the world in the novitiate of the Mission District.

On the margin of the official family, and in exercise of the *jus primae* 5 *noctis*, the males had fertilized ranches, byways, and settlements with an entire bastard line, which circulated among the servants without surnames, as godchildren, employees, favorites, and protégés of Big Mama.

The imminence of her death stirred the exhausting expectation. The 6 dying woman's voice, accustomed to homage and obedience, was no louder than a bass organ pipe in the closed room, but it echoed in the most far-flung corners of the hacienda. No one was indifferent to this death. During this century, Big Mama had been Macondo's center of gravity, as had her brothers, her parents, and the parents of her parents in the past, in a dominance which covered two centuries. The town was founded on her surname. No one knew the origin, or the limits or the real value of her estate, but everyone was used to believing that Big Mama was the owner of the waters, running and still, of rain and drought, and of the district's roads, telegraph poles, leap years, and heat waves, and that she had furthermore a hereditary right over life and property. When she sat on her balcony in the cool afternoon air, with all the weight of her belly and authority squeezed into her old rattan rocker, she seemed, in truth, infinitely rich and powerful, the richest and most powerful matron in the world.

It had not occurred to anyone to think that Big Mama was mortal, except 7 the members of her tribe, and Big Mama herself, prodded by the senile premonitions of Father Anthony Isabel. But she believed that she would live more than a hundred years, as did her maternal grandmother, who in the War of 1885 confronted a patrol of Colonel Aureliano Buendía's, barricaded in the kitchen of the hacienda. Only in April of this year did Big Mama realize that God would not grant her the privilege of personally liquidating, in an open skirmish, a horde of Federalist Masons.

During the first week of pain, the family doctor maintained her with 8 mustard plasters and woolen stockings. He was a hereditary doctor, a graduate of Montpellier, hostile by philosophical conviction to the progress of his science, whom Big Mama had accorded the lifetime privilege of preventing the establishment in Macondo of any other doctors. At one time he covered the town on horseback, visiting the doleful, sick people at dusk, and Nature had accorded him the privilege of being the father of many another's children. But arthritis kept him stiff-jointed in bed, and he ended up attending to his patients without calling on them, by means of suppositions, messengers, and errands. Summoned by Big Mama, he crossed the plaza in his pajamas, leaning on two canes, and he installed himself in the sick woman's bedroom. Only when he realized that Big Mama was dying did he order a chest with porcelain jars labeled in Latin brought, and for three weeks he besmeared the dying woman inside and out with all sorts of academic salves, magnificent stimulants, and masterful suppositories. Then he applied bloated toads to the site of her pain, and leeches to her kidneys, until the early morning of that day when he had to face the dilemma of either having her bled by the barber or exorcised by Father Anthony Isabel.

Nicanor sent for the priest. His ten best men carried him from the parish 9
house to Big Mama's bedroom, seated on a creaking willow rocker, under the mildewed canopy reserved for great occasions. The little bell of the Viaticum in the warm September dawn was the first notification to the inhabitants of Macondo. When the sun rose, the little plaza in front of Big Mama's house looked like a country fair.

It was like a memory of another era. Until she was seventy, Big Mama 10
used to celebrate her birthday with the most prolonged and tumultuous carnivals within memory. Demijohns of rum were placed at the townspeople's disposal, cattle were sacrificed in the public plaza, and a band installed on top of a table played for three days without stopping. Under the dusty almond trees, where, in the first week of the century, Colonel Aureliano Buendía's troops had camped, stalls were set up which sold banana liquor, rolls, blood puddings, chopped fried meat, meat pies, sausage, yucca breads, crullers, buns, corn breads, puff paste, *longanizas*,[1] tripes, coconut nougats, rum toddies, along with all sorts of trifles, gewgaws, trinkets, and knicknacks, and cockfights and lottery tickets. In the midst of the confusion of the agitated mob, prints and scapularies with Big Mama's likeness were sold.

The festivities used to begin two days before and end on the day of her 11
birthday, with the thunder of fireworks and a family dance at Big Mama's house. The carefully chosen guests and the legitimate members of the family, generously attended by the bastard line, danced to the beat of the old pianola which was equipped with the rolls most in style. Big Mama presided over the party from the rear of the hall in an easy chair with linen pillows, imparting discreet instructions with her right hand, adorned with rings on all her fingers. On that night the coming year's marriages were arranged, at times in complicity with the lovers, but almost always counseled by her own inspiration. To finish off the jubilation, Big Mama went out to the balcony, which was decorated with diadems and Japanese lanterns, and threw coins to the crowd.

That tradition had been interrupted, in part because of the successive 12
mournings of the family and in part because of the political instability of the last few years. The new generations only heard stories of those splen-

---

1. longaniza: *a kind of long sausage.*

did celebrations. They never managed to see Big Mama at High Mass, fanned by some functionary of the Civil Authority, enjoying the privilege of not kneeling, even at the moment of the elevation, so as not to ruin her Dutch-flounced skirt and her starched cambric petticoats. The old people remembered, like a hallucination out of their youth, the two hundred yards of matting which were laid down from the manorial house to the main altar the afternoon on which Maria del Rosario Castañeda y Montero attended her father's funeral and returned along the matted street endowed with a new and radiant dignity, turned into Big Mama at the age of twenty-two. That medieval vision belonged then not only to the family's past but also the nation's past. Ever more indistinct and remote, hardly visible on her balcony, stifled by the geraniums on hot afternoons, Big Mama was melting into her own legend. Her authority was exercised through Nicanor. The tacit promise existed, formulated by tradition, that the day Big Mama sealed her will the heirs would declare three nights of public merrymaking. But at the same time it was known that she had decided not to express her last wishes until a few hours before dying, and no one thought seriously about the possibility that Big Mama was mortal. Only this morning, awakened by the tinkling of the Viaticum, did the inhabitants of Macondo become convinced not only that Big Mama was mortal but also that she was dying.

Her hour had come. Seeing her in her linen bed, bedaubed with aloes up to her ears, under the dust-laden canopy of Oriental crêpe, one could hardly make out any life in the thin respiration of her matriarchal breasts. Big Mama, who until she was fifty rejected the most passionate suitors, and who was well enough endowed by Nature to suckle her whole issue all by herself, was dying a virgin and childless. At the moment of extreme unction, Father Anthony Isabel had to ask for help in order to apply the oils to the palms of her hands, for since the beginning of her death throes Big Mama had had her fists closed. The attendance of the nieces was useless. In the struggle, for the first time in a week, the dying woman pressed against her chest the hand bejeweled with precious stones and fixed her colorless look on the nieces, saying, "Highway robbers." Then she saw Father Anthony Isabel in his liturgical habit and the acolyte with the sacramental implements, and with calm conviction she murmured, "I am dying." Then she took off the ring with the great diamond and gave it to Magdalena, the novice, to whom it belonged since she was the youngest heir. That was the end of a tradition: Magdalena had renounced her inheritance in favor of the Church.

At dawn Big Mama asked to be left alone with Nicanor to impart her last instructions. For half an hour, in perfect command of her faculties, she asked about the conduct of her affairs. She gave special instructions about the disposition of her body, and finally concerned herself with the wake. "You have to keep your eyes open," she said. "Keep everything of value under lock and key, because many people come to wakes only to steal." A

13

14

moment later, alone with the priest, she made an extravagant confession, sincere and detailed, and later on took Communion in the presence of her nieces and nephews. It was then that she asked them to seat her in her rattan rocker so that she could express her last wishes.

Nicanor had prepared, on twenty-four folios written in a very clear hand, a scrupulous account of her possessions. Breathing calmly, with the doctor and Father Anthony Isabel as witnesses, Big Mama dictated to the notary the list of her property, the supreme and unique source of her grandeur and authority. Reduced to its true proportions, the real estate was limited to three districts, awarded by Royal Decree at the founding of the Colony; with the passage of time, by dint of intricate marriages of convenience, they had accumulated under the control of Big Mama. In that unworked territory, without definite borders, which comprised five townships and in which not one single grain had ever been sown at the expense of the proprietors, three hundred and fifty-two families lived as tenant farmers. Every year, on the eve of her name day, Big Mama exercised the only act of control which prevented the lands from reverting to the state: the collection of rent. Seated on the back porch of her house, she personally received the payment for the right to live on her lands, as for more than a century her ancestors had received it from the ancestors of the tenants. When the three-day collection was over, the patio was crammed with pigs, turkeys, and chickens, and with the tithes and first fruits of the land which were deposited there as gifts. In reality, that was the only harvest the family ever collected from a territory which had been dead since its beginnings, and which was calculated on first examination at a hundred thousand hectares. But historical circumstances had brought it about that within those boundaries the six towns of Macondo district should grow and prosper, even the county seat, so that no person who lived in a house had any property rights other than those which pertained to the house itself, since the land belonged to Big Mama, and the rent was paid to her, just as the government had to pay her for the use the citizens made of the streets.

On the outskirts of the settlements, a number of animals, never counted and even less looked after, roamed, branded on the hindquarters with the shape of a padlock. This hereditary brand, which more out of disorder than out of quantity had become familiar in distant districts where the scattered cattle, dying of thirst, strayed in summer, was one of the most solid supports of the legend. For reasons which no one had bothered to explain, the extensive stables of the house had progressively emptied since the last civil war, and lately sugar-cane presses, milking parlors, and a rice mill had been installed in them.

Aside from the items enumerated, she mentioned in her will the existence of three containers of gold coins buried somewhere in the house during the War of Independence, which had not been found after periodic and laborious excavations. Along with the right to continue the exploitation of the rented land, and to receive the tithes and first fruits and all sorts of extraordinary donations, the heirs received a chart kept up from generation to generation, and perfected by each generation, which facilitated the finding of the buried treasure.

Big Mama needed three hours to enumerate her earthly possessions. In 18 the stifling bedroom, the voice of the dying woman seemed to dignify in its place each thing named. When she affixed her trembling signature, and the witnesses affixed theirs below, a secret tremor shook the hearts of the crowds which were beginning to gather in front of the house, in the shade of the dusty almond trees of the plaza.

The only thing lacking then was the detailed listing of her immaterial 19 possessions. Making a supreme effort—the same kind that her forebears made before they died to assure the dominance of their line—Big Mama raised herself up on her monumental buttocks, and in a domineering and sincere voice, lost in her memories, dictated to the notary this list of her invisible estate:

The wealth of the subsoil, the territorial waters, the colors of the flag, 20 national sovereignty, the traditional parties, the rights of man, civil rights, the nation's leadership, the right of appeal, Congressional hearings, letters of recommendation, historical records, free elections, beauty queens, transcendental speeches, huge demonstrations, distinguished young ladies, proper gentlemen, punctilious military men, His Illustrious Eminence, the Supreme Court, goods whose importation was forbidden, liberal ladies, the meat problem, the purity of the language, setting a good example, the free but responsible press, the Athens of South America, public opinion, the lessons of democracy, Christian morality, the shortage of foreign exchange, the right of asylum, the Communist menace, the ship of state, the high cost of living, republican traditions, the underprivileged classes, statements of political support.

She didn't manage to finish. The laborious enumeration cut off her last 21 breath. Drowning in the pandemonium of abstract formulas which for two centuries had constituted the moral justification of the family's power, Big Mama emitted a loud belch and expired.

That afternoon the inhabitants of the distant and somber capital saw the 22 picture of a twenty-year-old woman on the first page of the extra editions, and thought that it was a new beauty queen. Big Mama lived again the momentary youth of her photograph, enlarged to four columns and with needed retouching, her abundant hair caught up atop her skull with an ivory comb and a diadem on her lace collar. That image, captured by a street photographer who passed through Macondo at the beginning of the century, and kept in the newspaper's morgue for many years in the section of unidentified persons, was destined to endure in the memory of future generations. In the dilapidated buses, in the elevators at the Ministries, and in the dismal tearooms hung with pale decorations, people whispered with veneration and respect about the dead personage in her sultry, malarial region, whose name was unknown in the rest of the country a few hours before—before it had been sanctified by the printed word. A fine drizzle covered the passers-by with misgiving and mist. All the church bells tolled for the dead. The President of the Republic, taken by surprise by the news when on his way to the commencement exercises for the new cadets, suggested to the War Minister, in a note in his own hand on the back of the telegram, that he conclude his speech with a minute of silent homage to Big Mama.

The social order had been brushed by death. The President of the Re- 23 public himself, who was affected by urban feelings as if they reached him through a purifying filter, managed to perceive from his car in a momentary but to a certain extent brutal vision the silent consternation of the city. Only a few low cafés remained open; the Metropolitan Cathedral was readied for nine days of funeral rites. At the National Capitol, where the beggars wrapped in newspapers slept in the shelter of the Doric columns and the silent statues of dead Presidents, the lights of Congress were lit. When the President entered his office, moved by the vision of the capital in mourning, his Ministers were waiting for him dressed in funereal garb, standing, paler and more solemn than usual.

The events of that night and the following ones would later be identified 24 as a historic lesson. Not only because of the Christian spirit which inspired the most lofty personages of public power, but also because of the abnegation with which dissimilar interests and conflicting judgments were conciliated in the common goal of burying the illustrious body. For many years Big Mama had guaranteed the social peace and political harmony of her empire, by virtue of the three trunks full of forged electoral certificates which formed part of her secret estate. The men in her service, her protégés and tenants, elder and younger, exercised not only their own rights of suffrage but also those of electors dead for a century. She exercised the priority of traditional power over transitory authority, the predominance of class over the common people, the transcendence of divine wisdom over human improvisation. In times of peace, her dominant will approved and disapproved canonries, benefices, and sinecures, and watched over the welfare of her associates, even if she had to resort to clandestine maneuvers or election fraud in order to obtain it. In troubled times, Big Mama contributed secretly for weapons for her partisans, but came to the aid of her victims in public. That patriotic zeal guaranteed the highest honors for her.

The President of the Republic had not needed to consult with his ad- 25 visers in order to weigh the gravity of his responsibility. Between the Palace reception hall and the little paved patio which had served the viceroys as a *cochère*,[1] there was an interior garden of dark cypresses where a Portuguese monk had hanged himself out of love in the last days of the

---

1. cochère: *carriage entrance.*

Colony. Despite his noisy coterie of bemedaled officials, the President could not suppress a slight tremor of uncertainty when he passed that spot after dusk. But that night his trembling had the strength of a premonition. Then the full awareness of his historical destiny dawned on him, and he decreed nine days of national mourning, and posthumous honors for Big Mama at the rank befitting a heroine who had died for the fatherland on the field of battle. As he expressed it in the dramatic address which he delivered that morning to his compatriots over the national radio and television network, the Nation's Leader trusted that the funeral rites for Big Mama would set a new example for the world.

Such a noble aim was to collide nevertheless with certain grave incon- 26 veniences. The judicial structure of the country, built by remote ancestors of Big Mama, was not prepared for events such as those which began to occur. Wise Doctors of Law, certified alchemists of the statutes, plunged into hermeneutics and syllogisms in search of the formula which would permit the President of the Republic to attend the funeral. The upper strata of politics, the clergy, the financiers lived through entire days of alarm. In the vast semicircle of Congress, rarefied by a century of abstract legislation, amid oil paintings of National Heroes and busts of Greek thinkers, the vocation of Big Mama reached unheard-of proportions, while her body filled with bubbles in the harsh Macondo September. For the first time, people spoke of her and conceived of her without her rattan rocker, her afternoon stupors, and her mustard plasters, and they saw her ageless and pure, distilled by legend.

Interminable hours were filled with words, words, words, which re- 27 sounded throughout the Republic, made prestigious by the spokesmen of the printed word. Until, endowed with a sense of reality in that assembly of aseptic lawgivers, the historic blahblahblah was interrupted by the reminder that Big Mama's corpse awaited their decision at 104° in the shade. No one batted an eye in the face of that eruption of common sense in the pure atmosphere of the written law. Orders were issued to embalm the cadaver, while formulas were adduced, viewpoints were reconciled, or constitutional amendments were made to permit the President to attend the burial.

So much had been said that the discussions crossed the borders, tra- 28 versed the ocean, and blew like an omen through the pontifical apartments at Castel Gandolfo. Recovered from the drowsiness of the torpid days of August, the Supreme Pontiff was at the window watching the lake where the divers were searching for the head of a decapitated young girl. For the last few weeks, the evening newspapers had been concerned with nothing else, and the Supreme Pontiff could not be indifferent to an enigma located such a short distance from his summer residence. But that evening, in an unforeseen substitution, the newspapers changed the photographs of the possible victims for that of one single twenty-year-old woman, marked off with black margins. "Big Mama," exclaimed the Supreme Pontiff, recognizing instantly the hazy daguerreotype which many years before had been offered to him on the occasion of his ascent to the Throne of Saint Peter. "Big Mama," exclaimed in chorus the members of the College of Cardinals in their private apartments, and for the third time in twenty centuries there was an hour of confusion, chagrin, and bustle in the limitless empire of Christendom, until the Supreme Pontiff was installed in his long black limousine en route to Big Mama's fantastic and far-off funeral.

The shining peach orchards were left behind, the Via Appia Antica with   29
warm movie stars tanning on terraces without as yet having heard any news of the commotion, and then the somber promontory of Castel Sant' Angelo on the edge of the Tiber. At dusk the resonant pealing of St. Peter's Basilica mingled with the cracked tinklings of Macondo. Inside his stifling tent across the tangled reeds and the silent bogs which marked the boundary between the Roman Empire and the ranches of Big Mama, the Supreme Pontiff heard the uproar of the monkeys agitated all night long by the passing of the crowds. On his nocturnal itinerary, the canoe had been filled with bags of yucca, stalks of green bananas, and crates of chickens, and with men and women who abandoned their customary pursuits to try their luck at selling things at Big Mama's funeral. His Holiness suffered that night, for the first time in the history of the Church, from the fever of insomnia and the torment of the mosquitoes. But the marvelous dawn over the Great Old Woman's domains, the primeval vision of the balsam apple and the iguana, erased from his memory the suffering of his trip and compensated him for his sacrifice.

Nicanor had been awakened by three knocks at the door which an-   30
nounced the imminent arrival of His Holiness. Death had taken possession of the house. Inspired by successive and urgent Presidential addresses, by the feverish controversies which had been silenced but continued to be heard by means of conventional symbols, men and congregations the world over dropped everything and with their presence filled the dark hallways, the jammed passageways, the stifling attics; and those who arrived later climbed up on the low walls around the church, the palisades, vantage points, timberwork, and parapets, where they accommodated themselves as best they could. In the central hall, Big Mama's cadaver lay mummifying while it waited for the momentous decisions contained in a quivering mound of telegrams. Weakened by their weeping, the nine nephews sat the wake beside the body in an ecstasy of reciprocal surveillance.

And still the universe was to prolong the waiting for many more days.   31
In the city-council hall, fitted out with four leather stools, a jug of purified water, and a burdock hammock, the Supreme Pontiff suffered from a perspiring insomnia, diverting himself by reading memorials and administrative orders in the lengthy, stifling nights. During the day, he distributed

Italian candy to the children who approached to see him through the window, and lunched beneath the hibiscus arbor with Father Anthony Isabel, and occasionally with Nicanor. Thus he lived for interminable weeks and months which were protracted by the waiting and the heat, until the day Father Pastrana appeared with his drummer in the middle of the plaza and read the proclamation of the decision. It was declared that Public Order was disturbed, ratatatat, and that the President of the Republic, ratatatat, had in his power the extraordinary prerogatives, ratatatat, which permitted him to attend Big Mama's funeral, ratatatat, tatatat, tatat, tatat.

The great day had arrived. In the streets crowded with carts, hawkers of 32 fried foods, and lottery stalls, and men with snakes wrapped around their necks who peddled a balm which would definitively cure erysipelas and guarantee eternal life; in the mottled little plaza where the crowds had set up their tents and unrolled their sleeping mats, dapper archers cleared the Authorities' way. There they were, awaiting the supreme moment: the washerwomen of San Jorge, the pearl fishers from Cabo de la Vela, the fishermen from Ciénaga, the shrimp fishermen from Tasajera, the sorcerers from Mojajana, the salt miners from Manaure, the accordionists from Valledupar, the fine horsemen of Ayapel, the ragtag musicians from San Pelayo, the cock breeders from La Cueva, the improvisers from Sábanas de Bolívar, the dandies from Rebolo, the oarsmen of the Magdalena, the shysters from Monpox, in addition to those enumerated at the beginning of this chronicle, and many others. Even the veterans of Colonel Aureliano Buendía's camp—the Duke of Marlborough at their head, with the pomp of his furs and tiger's claws and teeth—overcame their centenarian hatred of Big Mama and those of her line and came to the funeral to ask the President of the Republic for the payment of their veterans' pensions which they had been waiting for for sixty years.

A little before eleven the delirious crowd which was sweltering in the 33 sun, held back by an imperturbable élite force of warriors decked out in embellished jackets and filigreed morions, emitted a powerful roar of jubilation. Dignified, solemn in their cutaways and top hats, the President of the Republic and his Ministers, the delegations from Parliament, the Supreme Court, the Council of State, the traditional parties and clergy, and representatives of Banking, Commerce, and Industry made their appearance around the corner of the telegraph office. Bald and chubby, the old and ailing President of the Republic paraded before the astonished eyes of the crowds who had seen him inaugurated without knowing who he was and who only now could give a true account of his existence. Among the archbishops enfeebled by the gravity of their ministry, and the military men with robust chests armored with medals, the Leader of the Nation exuded the unmistakable air of power.

In the second rank, in a serene array of mourning crêpe, paraded the 34 national queens of all things that have been or ever will be. Stripped of their earthly splendor for the first time, they marched by, preceded by the universal queen: the soybean queen, the green-squash queen, the banana queen, the meal yucca queen, the guava queen, the coconut queen, the kidney-bean queen, the 255-mile-long-string-of-iguana-eggs queen, and all the others who are omitted so as not to make this account interminable.

In her coffin draped in purple, separated from reality by eight copper 35
turnbuckles, Big Mama was at that moment too absorbed in her formaldehyde eternity to realize the magnitude of her grandeur. All the splendor which she had dreamed of on the balcony of her house during her heat-induced insomnia was fulfilled by those forty-eight glorious hours during which all the symbols of the age paid homage to her memory. The Supreme Pontiff himself, whom she in her delirium imagined floating above the gardens of the Vatican in a resplendent carriage, conquered the heat with a plaited palm fan, and honored with his Supreme Dignity the greatest funeral in the world.

Dazzled by the show of power, the common people did not discern the 36
covetous bustling which occurred on the rooftree of the house when agreement was imposed on the town grandees' wrangling and the catafalque was taken into the street on the shoulders of the grandest of them all. No one saw the vigilant shadow of the buzzards which followed the cortege through the sweltering little streets of Macondo, nor did they notice that as the grandees passed they left a pestilential train of garbage in the street. No one noticed that the nephews, godchildren, servants, and protégés of Big Mama closed the doors as soon as the body was taken out, and dismantled the doors, pulled the nails out of the planks, and dug up the foundations to divide up the house. The only thing which was not missed by anyone amid the noise of that funeral was the thunderous sigh of relief which the crowd let loose when fourteen days of supplications, exaltations, and dithyrambs were over, and the tomb was sealed with a lead plinth. Some of those present were sufficiently aware as to understand that they were witnessing the birth of a new era. Now the Supreme Pontiff could ascend to Heaven in body and soul, his mission on earth fulfilled, and the President of the Republic could sit down and govern according to his good judgment, and the queens of all things that have been or ever will be could marry and be happy and conceive and give birth to many sons, and the common people could set up their tents where they damn well pleased in the limitless domains of Big Mama, because the only one who could oppose them and had sufficient power to do so had begun to rot beneath a lead plinth. The only thing left then was for someone to lean a stool against the doorway to tell this story, lesson and example for future generations, so that not one of the world's disbelievers would be left who did not know the story of Big Mama, because tomorrow, Wednesday, the garbage men will come and will sweep up the garbage from her funeral, forever and ever.

STUDY QUESTIONS

1. Discuss "Big Mama's Funeral" as a historical parable. How does the author use the story as a means of unveiling the feudalistic power structure and social relations of Latin America's recent past?
2. What does Big Mama represent? Describe her personality traits, family relations, and social ties.
3. What is the purpose of the President of the Republic and the Supreme Pontiff?
4. Discuss García Márquez's use of exaggeration and the fantastic.

C U B A

NICOLÁS GUILLÉN

Nicolás Guillén (1902–1989), internationally acclaimed black poet and folklorist, was born in Camagüey, Cuba. The son of a newspaper editor who was killed by the government, he experienced poverty in his youth but managed to complete secondary school and went on to study law in Havana. Subsequently, he became a journalist, magazine editor, and a founder of a research center for the study of Afro-Caribbean culture. He began writing in the 1920s under the influence of European modernists who were in rebellion against Western tradition. Later, his interest in Cuban folklore and music provided a foundation for his poetry. His first major work, Sound Themes, *appeared in 1930 and was hailed as a major effort to bring Afro-Cuban culture into the mainstream of Cuban literature. Using a popular Cuban musical form, the* son, *he explored the socioeconomic and psychological factors that guide the lives of Afro-Caribbean people. In later volumes, he expanded his themes to include a wider range of subjects and a broader historical perspective. Guillén's volumes that have been translated into English include* The Great Zoo and Other Poems *(1967, tr.) and* Tengo *(1964, tr.).*

He remained throughout his career a poet and prophet of the common people. Seeing into their wounds and suffering, he offered the solution of hope and revolt. From the beginning, Guillén viewed his role as an artist as inseparable from his commitments as a political activist. In the 1930s, he became a member of the Cuban Communist Party and a spokesman for left-wing causes, which resulted in periods of exile and extensive travel abroad. After Fidel Castro came to power in 1959, Guillén actively supported the Cuban revolution and held positions in the government. "Can You?" and "Ballad of the Two Grandfathers" typify his concerns with politics and culture.

Can You?

for Lumir Civrny, in Prague

Can you sell me the air that passes through your fingers
and hits your face and undoes your hair?
Maybe you could sell me five dollars' worth of wind,
or more, perhaps sell me a cyclone?
Maybe you would sell me   5
the thin air, the air
(not all of it) that sweeps
into your garden blossom on blossom
into your garden for the birds,
ten dollars of pure air.   10

    The air it turns and passes
    with butterfly-like spins.
    No one owns it, no one.

Can you sell me some sky,
the sky that's blue at times,   15
or gray again at times,
a small part of your sky,
the one you bought—you think—with all the trees
of your orchard, as one who buys the ceiling with the house?
Can you sell me a dollar's worth   20
of sky, two miles
of sky, a fragment of your sky,
whatever piece you can?

    The sky is in the clouds.
    The clouds are high, they pass.   25
    No one owns them, no one.

Can you sell me some rain, the water
that has given you your tears and wets your tongue?
Can you sell me a dollar's worth of water
from the spring, a pregnant cloud,   30
as soft and graceful as a lamb,
or even water fallen on the mountain,
or water gathered in the ponds
abandoned to the dogs,
or one league of the sea, a lake perhaps,   35
a hundred dollars' worth of lake?

The water falls, it runs.
The water runs, it passes.
No one holds it, no one.

Can you sell me some land, the deep night   40
of the roots, the teeth of
dinosaurs and the scattered lime
of distant skeletons?
Can you sell me long since buried jungles, birds now extinct,
fish fossilized, the sulphur   45
of volcanoes, a thousand million years
rising in spiral? Can you
sell me some land, can you
sell me some land, can you?

The land that's yours is mine.   50
The feet of all walk on it.
No one owns it, no one.

Translated from the Spanish by Robert Márquez

Ballad of the Two Grandfathers

S hadows which only I see,
I'm watched by my two grandfathers.
A bone-point lance,
a drum of hide and wood:
my black grandfather.   5
A ruff on a broad neck,
a warrior's gray armament:
my white grandfather.

Africa's humid jungles
with thick and muted gongs . . .   10
"I'm dying!"
(My black grandfather says).
Waters dark with alligators,
mornings green with coconuts . . .
"I'm tired!"   15
(My white grandfather says).
Oh sails of a bitter wind,
galleon burning for gold . . .

"I'm dying"
(My black grandfather says).
Oh coasts with virgin necks
deceived with beads of glass . . . !
"I'm tired!"
(My white grandfather says).
Oh pure and burnished sun,
imprisoned in the tropic's ring;
Oh clear and rounded moon
above the sleep of monkeys!

So many ships, so many ships!
So many Blacks, so many Blacks!
So much resplendent cane!
How harsh the trader's whip!
A rock of tears and blood,
of veins and eyes half-open,
of empty dawns
and plantation sunsets,
and a great voice, a strong voice,
splitting the silence.
So many ships, so many ships,
so many Blacks!

Shadows which only I see,
I'm watched by my two grandfathers.

Don Federico yells at me
and Taita Facundo is silent;
both dreaming in the night
and walking, walking.
I bring them together.
                    "Federico!
Facundo!" They embrace. They sigh,
they raise their sturdy heads;
both of equal size,
beneath the high stars;
both of equal size,
a Black longing, a White longing,
both of equal size,
they scream, dream, weep, sing.
They dream, weep, sing.
They weep, sing.
Sing!

Translated from the Spanish by Robert Márquez
and David Arthur McMurray

STUDY QUESTIONS

1. Discuss "Can You?" as an attack on materialism and a critique of the rules of the marketplace.
2. Which images in "Can You?" evoke freedom and beauty? How do they convey the poem's meaning?
3. Discuss the difference between the two grandfathers in "Ballad of the Two Grandfathers." How do their historical roles differ?
4. How does the poet reconcile the differences between the two grandfathers?
5. Discuss the broad historical and cultural implications of "Ballad of the Two Grandfathers."

EL SALVADOR

MANLIO ARGUETA

Manlio Argueta (b. 1936) is a politically committed writer who brought international attention to the Salvadoran struggle against social and political repression. Born in San Miguel, El Salvador, he was active during the mid-1950s in a literary circle that opposed the ruling military dictatorship. The group's political involvement resulted in persecution, imprisonment, death, and exile. Argueta was forced to flee to Costa Rica, where he is now director of the Costa Rican Institute, which is engaged in political and cultural issues concerning Central America.

Argueta has published three volumes of poetry and four novels and has won several international writing awards. His most famous novels are One Day of Life *(1983), which documents the life of a typical peasant family caught in the terror and violence of present-day El Salvador, and* Cuzcatlán: Where the Southern Sea Beats *(1987), which re-creates the history of a Salvadoran community and its relation to the land and nature, its near feudal poverty, and its perseverance in the face of brutal military oppression. "Microbus to San Salvador," a self-contained section from* Cuzcatlán, *reveals the strength and determination of Salvadorans who have chosen to challenge injustice and create new lives for themselves. It is also a telling story documenting the changing roles of men and women.*

Microbus to San Salvador

My alias is Beatriz. Ticha is my nickname. Age: twenty-four. Peasant 1
background. Currently living in San Miguel, though I travel frequently to San Salvador; sometimes, but not that often, I get off the bus
near San Vicente to visit my two sons, who are living with my parents
outside Apastepeque, near the lagoon.

Favorite pastime: reflection. Or daydreaming, some people call it. 2

Element of nature which is special to me: *metate*. It's a precious stone, 3
made from the lava of volcanoes; my parents, grandparents, and great-grandparents all made a living from it. They made grinding stones. For grinding corn. We peasants grind corn using the strength of our arms. On a *metate* base shaped like a small washtub, using a pestle, also made of *metate*, we mash corn that has been cooked in water and ashes. The ashes help to soften it. After a few pounds of the pestle, which is also called the handstone, the corn becomes a spongy white dough, which has a pleasant feel and a very agreeable taste. That's what we peasants live on. We form the dough into a tortilla by kneading it with our fingers and palms, then we put it over the fire on a *comal*, or clay griddle. The tortilla is our bread. It is life.

No peasant home is without a grindstone. I used to help my parents 4
make grindstones. That's why *metate* is my favorite stone. The flower I prefer is mignonette.

I wonder where we would be without corn. Nowhere. We eat tortillas 5
with salt our whole life. We *campesinos*, peasants. I grew up on them. We live and love on them. Sometimes there are beans. We also eat leaves, a lot of leaves; flowers of all kinds; the top shoot of certain plants, especially pines; and herbs, quite a few herbs. Also, we run across small game every now and then: *garrobo* lizards, iguanas, rabbits, coati, *pacas*; or *tacuacines*, which are large rodents that are very good to eat, seeing as nobody eats their chickens anymore.

But we like tortillas with salt best of all. There wouldn't be a meal 6
without them. Anyway, that's all we need to fill us up. Because, of course, that's all there is.

To us, life is a miracle of God. 7

Living is something else: keeping your body free of disease, not dying 8
from rickets or diarrhea; or starvation. Over half the small children in a given family die from these causes.

Maybe that's why we always want big families. It's a kind of defense to 9
keep the race alive. Besides, the more hands a family has, the better its chances to earn its daily bread.

We must also survive. That's something else again. 10

They're after us. The authorities haven't been able to even look at a 11
peasant since 1932 without being filled with rage. Now, half a century later, things have gotten out of control. There are no jails. If you fall into the hands of the law, you're dead. They say our country is too small for the amount of people who live here. People who say that have studied abroad, or they're foreigners who support the authorities. The government says it too. They claim there are too many of us, that's what the problem is. They teach that in the military academy. The advisers teach it. I don't know how they rationalize it, but from time to time they shout: You're a plague, you poor people are a curse from God. People were happy before Cuzcatlán got populated. You've been multiplying like the fish and loaves. It's time to wipe out poverty. They say it in a way that makes it sound pretty.

However, we live by the strength of our hands and produce the wealth 12
that those who are well-off possess. The rich used to be happy. Not anymore. It's our fault. That's how a lot of professional soldiers—those who
have studied in military schools both here and abroad—put it. Because the
advisers are the same way.

The advisers don't know anything about us. That's the problem. They 13
come to our country in big airplanes. They tour the countryside in their
helicopters. They wear dark glasses so they can't see our light. They drive
bulletproof Cherokees. They don't speak Spanish. How are they going to
understand us like that?

They are happy. We survive. 14

They're after us. They murder us. The most common cause of death for 15
someone like me is decapitation. Dismemberment. Just as the conquistadors did five hundred years ago. They use to threaten you with jail. Every
estate, every hacienda, had its own jail. Whenever a person didn't want to
work for the *patrón*, the owner of the estate, he was jailed as a vagrant and
a troublemaker. There's still a law against vagrants and troublemakers, but
it no longer applies. Now they apply a swift death instead. If the advisers
knew our history, would they still treat us the same? I don't know. Besides,
our history is sad and boring. Maybe they're not interested in hearing
about it. We're interested, though, because it gives us strength. It teaches
us to survive.

We've learned how to survive. That's why I use an alias. 16

I have two sons. I will never have a big family. I don't live with them right 17
now. They live with my parents in a hamlet near Apastepeque. And my
grandmother lived just a few miles from there, north of the lagoon. For a
long time, before I was born, my grandparents lived on the south shore,
but it was flooded and they were forced to move. They planted annatto
trees and beans on a little parcel there, together with their children and
Grandma's father, Emiliano. For a while they made a living making grindstones and selling things like cottage cheese and *conserva de leche*, or milk
pudding. Recently, they decided to abandon the grindstone trade. People
weren't buying them anymore. Since the stones lasted for many, many
years, longer than a lifetime, people stopped buying them. Everybody
already had one. My family sold them. They've had them in their huts
since my great-great-grandfather's time, and they treat them like jewels.
That was a problem, so we had to give up the trade: the stones lasted
forever.

I always got along well with my grandmother. She died a few months 18
ago. She was sixty. It's her name I use as my alias. She's a symbol for me.
You wouldn't think that with the age difference and the distance between
us I would take her name. But it's symbolic. Her name was Beatriz.

Besides our ages, there were other differences between us. She never 19
left her hamlet; never cared for cities. I did, because one day I decided to

leave the zone of Apastepeque; in essence, I was following in the footsteps of my older sister Antonia. It was actually my father's aunt who got us to leave home; she took us to work with her in a cooperative in Chalate. This aunt was my godmother. "You must come with me," she said, "so you can have a better life." And so you can survive.

I was forced to take the children to live with my parents when my *compañero*, their father, died. I realized it would be impossible to take care of them. They went back to the place of my birth. I don't know what will become of them.

When my *compa* was alive, we took turns looking after the kids. I worked in the Social Improvement Textile Factory, which was run by the government in San Miguel before they turned it into a garrison. Now you can't even use that street to get to the train station if you want to go to Colonia Belén. At night I had plenty of time to study the principles of nursing—we called it first aid—which was a course given by the trade union. And my *compa* was involved in his own affairs, though I was never quite sure what they were. I did know that he hadn't worked in the factory for over two years because they fired him for being a union member. We got along all right, living and surviving. He went under an assumed name like me.

When the factory became a garrison, we were all laid off. No severance pay, nothing. The union helped out a lot, though, because we decided to keep it going even though the factory no longer existed, so we went to San Salvador to the Ministry of Labor to see if they wouldn't give us at least enough to live on for a month.

That was our excuse to stay organized. Because once they fire you, forget it. You could drop dead asking for handouts. So we didn't press too hard, but we did have an excuse to get together and go to San Salvador to meet with other trade unions. And that's how I got so deeply involved in the struggle. I had some previous experience from the cooperatives in Chalate, which was good because it helped me learn what it means to defend your rights.

Once they killed my *compañero*, things changed. I couldn't keep on living in San Miguel with my children. My reputation as a union member and the wife of a slain worker was a direct threat. I explained the situation to my parents and they understood. So did my grandmother. The little ones could live in both places. It was barely an hour's walk between them.

Together we'll fight the war.

If I hadn't been organized, I would have wound up dead like thousands of other people. The vast majority of the forty thousand people killed in the last three years are innocent. It's part of the extermination plan.

I don't include myself among the innocent. I try and fight back, so that's why I use an assumed name and do other things. We're at war. If I hadn't left the hamlet, I wouldn't really have known what was going on. I would have been a victim. Thanks to my father's aunt, we're advancing and seeing life in a different way. Both my sister Antonia and I. We both went to Chalate. We worked in a cooperative there; but to get organized we went to San Miguel. Fleeing practically.

That woman was very advanced. I never would have guessed. My father's aunt. 28

You never know when you'll get caught by the authorities. They're strong. Maybe stronger than we are because they don't have to hide or use assumed names. We have to, in order to survive. 29

We do have one big advantage: we've organized ourselves. That's where we excel. And in conscience, too. 30

Sometimes I think this whole life is a dream. 31

After being away for a few years, I have to go back to Chalate for a couple of days, they have asked me to identify someone whose name doesn't even deserve to be mentioned. We'd like to be forgiving. We're an emotional people, maybe because of the life we lead. They show us only their cruel side to arouse our feelings. They think if they take their rage out on us, our contempt will turn to hate, and then they'll have an excuse to exterminate us. That's been the authorities' policy for the last three years. If we speak out, they kill us. If we're suspected of speaking out, they disappear us. And if we keep our mouths shut, they think we're hiding something. So they kill us for that, too. We used to have a right to remain silent, at least. Now they make us talk so we don't keep our hatred to ourselves. Then they have another excuse to kill us. "Everything that moves in the zone is suspicious," the military chief has told the pilots who drop bombs from their airplanes. We even have to be careful about the way we look at people. We have to choke back the tears for our dead. If we mourn them, that makes us their accomplices. So we get killed. The key is to learn how to hide your emotions. That's very characteristic of this war. We're not even allowed to cry. 32

So I don't know what will happen when I meet Corporal Martínez, prisoner of the guerrillas in Chalate. I have to give testimony on him. That's where I'm going, to Chalate. It's a difficult situation. Though they say people are at their best when things get tough. 33

I've always enjoyed reflection. I think of it as a way to live two lives. Especially now that the authorities show no mercy and use us as targets for their new weapons, which we've never seen before. 34

I'd rather forget Corporal Martínez. And think about my *compañero* instead, about the last time we traveled together on this same microbus. He really gives me strength and confidence. He was like a brother. I liked it that way. We lived through a lot of hard times and a lot of separations. One time he was gone for six months. Without a word. But I knew nothing would happen to him. Because he was working for our survival. 35

The last time I saw him we were together on the bus. 36

To tell the truth, it's very sad being alone with nothing but a shadow or 37 the thought of him suddenly appearing with the same old smile and greeting, carrying a couple of oranges in a plastic bag.

I was just thinking—not about the last time I saw him but about the time he disappeared for six months. We didn't have any children yet. It's harder to be alone when you don't have children. 38

Always waiting for him to appear. I got far in my first-aid studies. Without a husband or kids around I had time to spare. Each night when I came back to our room at the hostel, I hoped he would be there to surprise me—sitting quietly on one of our two stools, like all the times before, waiting to pick me up and hug me, and then we'd squeeze each other tight, never wanting to let go, and we'd walk together still clinging to one another. Then I'd stand on his feet and he'd spin me around the room. Both of us laughing wildly. We could stay that way for a long time. 39

But he wouldn't be there. And I'd be filled with sadness. Those were six desperate months. Now, to think we'll never be together again. Not me or his two children. Separated for the rest of our lives. 40

It took a lot out of me to give my kids to my parents; but they understood. My *compañero* was dead, and there was no way I could keep them in my room and take care of them—I was working both at the factory and for the union. 41

The day he was killed, we were traveling on the bus together. He was only going as far as San Vicente, and I was going all the way to San Salvador, because we were on two separate assignments. 42

It was just a mile or two to the San Vicente stop, where he would get off and continue on foot into the city—there was a mile and a half to go on the highway when the microbus was pulled over by a patrol. There were over a hundred *guardias* hidden on a side road with "Mazinger" trucks. 43

It's an awful experience running into them. You never know what they'll do next. They told the driver to pull over. We thought they would search us. I made a mental note of the contents of my purse. I had my identification card, a picture I took in Barrios Park, San Miguel, with my two kids, a couple of centavos, and all the other odds and ends you carry around for goodness knows what reason. I felt better. 44

My *compa* and I were sitting together without saying a word. Like total strangers. When the patrol surprised us like that, coming around the bend, we thought they'd open fire and people got nervous. My *compa* took my hand and surreptitiously slipped it around his waist. This surprised me. But then I realized what he was doing, because I felt a metallic object beneath his shirt. I squeezed his hand for several seconds to let him know I didn't want him to shoot it and get killed. What could he do, anyway? He let go of my hand when he knew I'd found the weapon. Clutching his hand for those few seconds made me feel like they would never end. Life walks right up and slaps you, just like that. Standing on his feet, whirling around the room, holding on to each other. For dear life, so nothing would break us apart. 45

We have a humble home. A single room with a hallway leading out to a   46
patio surrounded by other run-down rooms—communal toilets right there
in the middle of the patio, which is how you can tell it's a *mesón,* a hostel.
Our room is big enough to fit a bed, a pinewood table, and two stools. On
the table there's an instant-coffee container filled with some crepe paper
flowers: a vase. There's also a closet which we bought with our savings
after our first year in San Miguel. The closet is divided in half. On one side
there are a few shelves, and on the other there's a pole for hanging dresses
and shirts; below, there are two drawers to which my *compañero* added
false bottoms for storing sensitive documents. Hanging from a nail on the
wall is a print of a little boy with curly hair holding a globe in his left hand;
his right is near his heart giving the sign of benediction; there's a halo over
his head and a slight smile on his face; a white tunic hangs from one of his
shoulders; the other is bare. He is *El Salvador del Mundo,* the Savior of the
World. Between the curly haired boy and the cardboard backing that holds
him in the wooden frame there is another, hidden print of Monsignor
Romero.

We keep it hidden in order not to cause problems with the authorities;   47
it could cost us a disappearance into one of their subterranean jails.

The hallway leading to the patio is divided by a newspaper-covered   48
partition, and that's where we keep a kerosene stove.

We lived in that room for almost six years. Both our kids were born   49
there. Mesón Las Flores, San Miguel.

We were happy at the *mesón.* Despite the fact my *compañero* occasionally   50
had to leave for long periods of time on union business. But I knew he'd
come back sooner or later, even if he'd been gone for months. He'd always
come back at night, knocking three times with a long pause between each
knock. I opened the door and he stood there, not coming in; he just looked
at me, hunting me down with his eyes and his smile. I, the nervous doe.
Whenever we got together again, we played this happy game for the first
few seconds. Then he came in, took my head in one hand, and closed the
door with the other. We never took our eyes off one another. We never
stopped smiling. And the minute the door was shut, we'd leap into each
other's arms.

We were lucky to have a room on the street. It was better for catching   51
the breezes that blew through the open door. It's hot in San Miguel. So
nobody closes doors facing the street. That way everybody knows everybody else, because no one can hide behind four walls.

We were happy there. And scared sometimes, because we weren't na-   52
tives and it took a while to adjust to the way people did things: you had to
let your neighbors know everything you were doing that day—where are
you going, where have you been, what did you do there, can I help you,
let me come along, I'll join you, what's your name, would you like a piece

of sweetbread, may I borrow a pinch of salt. In other words, all the things that make you feel a part of the community—making contact, talking in doorways, on the street, at the corner. People think you're strange if you keep to yourself. People like us who were involved in union activities after work had to tell our neighbors at the *mesón* that we'd be late, but we'd be back by such and such a time. And then I had to explain my *compañero's* long absences. Naturally we were always making things up.

But from another point of view, it's an advantage, it's not so hard to be   53 alone. In fact, you're never alone. You just have to get used to it. You get to know people and you realize they don't mean to pry, they just want to help. In spite of the difficulties, we liked San Miguel. We were happy as long as we could be together. The long separations didn't matter. They made us feel that much closer. It was a terrible blow. If it wasn't for our two sons, I would never have gotten over his death. And that wouldn't have been good, because it would have affected my work and my prospects.

Translated from the Spanish by Clark Hansen

STUDY QUESTIONS

1. To what extent does "Microbus to San Salvador" challenge the conventional view of male/female relations in Latin America? How does the author convey the changing role of women?
2. How has the narrator's involvement in the liberation struggle changed her life?
3. In what ways does the story break down stereotypes of the poor and disenfranchised?
4. What accounts for the story's suspense and tension?

MARTINIQUE

 # Aimé Césaire

Aimé Césaire (b. 1913) is one of the world's leading black intellectuals. He is a renowned poet, playwright, and essayist as well as one of his island's most active cultural and political figures. Born in Basse-Pointe, Martinique, Césaire grew up in a family of modest means. He distinguished himself early as a brilliant student, winning scholarships to attend the Lycée Schoelcher in Fort-de-France and the prestigious Lycée Louis-le-Grand in Paris. He went on to earn advanced degrees at L'Ecole Normale Superieure, France's highest institution of learning in the liberal arts. While living abroad, Césaire became active in left-wing politics and was a founder of negritude, an influential literary and intellectual movement that attacked colonialism and celebrated the culture of Africa and Africa's diaspora. During this period, he wrote his famous prose poem Return to My Native Land *(1947), which denounces racial injustice and champions liberation for the oppressed. In this work and in subsequent volumes of poetry, Césaire was influenced by surrealism. Employing experimental literary techniques, he explored the unconscious and attempted to uncover a black identity that had been repressed and denied by colonialism. He continued this project in his plays and essays, but in these efforts he made a more thorough analysis of the social and political aspects of life under colonial rule.*

Apart from his role as a literary intellectual, Césaire has made important contributions as a politician. After he returned to Martinique, he joined the French Communist Party and at different times was elected to the National Assembly in Paris and mayor of Fort-de-France. During the 1950s, Césaire became disillusioned with the party's paternalistic attitude toward its overseas sections and its failure to condemn Stalinism. After the Hungarian rebellion of 1956, he resigned and formed a new political organization. Césaire continues to be active in politics and remains committed to black culture issues. "Out of Alien Days" illustrates Césaire's use of imagery and expresses his political vision.

Out of Alien Days

my people

when
out of alien days
on reknotted shoulders will you sprout a head really your own
and your word   5

the notice dispatched to the traitors
to the masters
the restituted bread the washed earth
the given earth

when   10
when will you cease to be the dark toy
in the carnival of others
or in another's field
the obsolete scarecrow?

tomorrow   15
when is tomorrow my people
the mercenary rout
once the feast is over

instead the redness of the east in the balisier's heart

people of interrupted foul sleep   20
people of reclimbed abysses
people of tamed nightmares
nocturnal people lovers of the fury of thunder
a higher sweeter broader tomorrow

and the torrential swell of lands   25
under the salubrious plow of the storm

Translated from the French by Clayton Eshleman and
Annette Smith

STUDY QUESTIONS

1. In "Out of Alien Days," what does the author mean by "alien days," "traitors/to the masters," and "the obsolete scarecrow"?
2. What does Césaire call for in "Out of Alien Days" when he invokes "the fury of thunder" and the "plow of the storm"?

MEXICO

Octavio Paz

*Octavio Paz (b. 1914), a poet, essayist, and 1990 Nobel Prize winner, is one
of the great literary intellectuals of Latin America. Deeply rooted in Hispanic
culture and at home with European tradition, he turned to existentialism and
surrealism in his search for an authentic Latin American identity. The time he
spent living in Asia contributed further to the development of a pluralistic
perspective for understanding human experience. By the 1960s he turned to
indigenous Native American traditions in search of a remedy to the cultural
fragmentation of Latin America.*

*Born on the outskirts of Mexico City, Paz developed a commitment to
social causes at an early age. His grandfather was one of the first novelists to
plead the cause of Indians, and his father, a lawyer, represented the rebel
leader Emiliano Zapata in the United States during the Mexican revolution.
As a student at the University of Mexico, Paz became active in left-wing
writers' organizations and traveled to Spain during the Spanish Civil War.
Afterward, he visited the United States on a Guggenheim Fellowship and on
his return to Mexico entered the diplomatic service. Over the years, he held
several high government positions. Paz began publishing his poetry as a
student and later edited a number of important literary and intellectual
journals. His mature poetry is a blend of symbolism and surrealism and an
attempt to bridge the gap between the personal and the general, the individual
and society. His concern with this problem led to* The Labyrinth of Solitude
*(1950), in which he traced Mexico's national identity to the conquest of the
continent. Most of his poetry is available in English in* The Collected
Poems, 1957–1987 *(1987). The prose poem "Obsidian Butterfly" is typical of
Paz's effort to retrieve and give meaning to the indigenous culture of his
region. Here he pays tribute to the Indian goddess Itzpapálotl, who has been
incorporated into the religious cult of the Virgin of Guadalupe.*

Obsidian Butterfly[1]

They killed my brothers, my children, my uncles. On the banks of Lake   1
Texcoco I began to weep. Whirlwinds of saltpeter rose from Peñon hill,
gently picked me up, and left me in the courtyard of the Cathedral. I made
myself so small and gray that many mistook me for a pile of dust. Yes I,
mother of flint and star, I, bearer of the ray, am now but a blue feather that
a bird loses in the brambles. Once, I would dance, my breasts high and
turning, turning, turning until I became still, and then I would sprout
leaves, flowers, fruit. The eagle throbbed in my belly. I was the mountain
that creates you as it dreams, the house of fire, the primordial pot where
man is cooked and becomes man. In the night of the decapitated words my
sister and I, hand in hand, leapt and sang around the I, the only standing
tower in the razed alphabet. I still remember my songs:

> *Light, headless light*
> *Golden-throated light*
> *Sings in the thicket green*

They told us: the straight path never leads to winter. And now my   2
hands tremble, the words are caught in my throat. Give me a chair and a
little sun.

In other times, every hour was born from the vapor of my breath,   3
danced a while on the point of my dagger, and disappeared through the
shining door of my hand mirror. I was the tattooed noon and naked midnight, the little jade insect that sings in the grass at dawn, and the clay
nightingale that summons the dead. I bathed in the sun's waterfall, I
bathed in myself, soaked in my own splendor. I was the flint that rips the
storm clouds of night and opens the doors of the showers. I planted gardens of fire, gardens of blood, in the Southern sky. Its coral branches still
graze the foreheads of lovers. There love is the meeting of two meteors in
the middle of space, and not this obstinacy of rocks rubbing each other to
ignite a sparking kiss.

Each night is an eyelid the thorns never stop piercing. And the day   4
never ends, never stops counting itself, broken into copper coins. I am
tired of so many stone beads scattered in the dust. I am tired of this
unfinished solitaire. Lucky the mother scorpion who devours her young.
Lucky the spider. Lucky the snake that sheds its skin. Lucky the water that
drinks itself. When will these images stop devouring me? When will I stop
falling in those empty eyes?

---

1. Obsidian butterfly: *Itzpapálotl, goddess sometimes confused with Teteoinan, our mother, and
Tonatzin. All of these female divinities were fused in the cult which, since the 16th century, has
worshiped the Virgin of Guadalupe.*

I am alone and fallen, grain of corn pulled from the ear of time. Sow me   5
among the battle dead. I will be born in the captain's eye. Rain down on
me, give me sun. My body, plowed by your body, will turn into a field
where one is sown and a hundred reaped. Wait for me on the other side of
the year: you will meet me like a lightning flash stretched to the edge of
autumn. Touch my grass breasts. Kiss my belly, sacrificial stone. In my
navel the whirlwind grows calm: I am the fixed center that moves the
dance. Burn, fall into me: I am the pit of living lime that cures the bones of
their afflictions. Die in my lips. Rise from my eyes. Images gush from my
body: drink in these waters and remember what you forgot at birth. I am
the wound that does not heal, the small solar stone: if you strike me, the
world will go up in flames.

Take my necklace of tears. I wait for you on this side of time where light   6
has inaugurated a joyous reign: the covenant of the enemy twins, water,
that escapes between our fingers, and ice, petrified like a king in his pride.
There you will open my body to read the inscription of your fate.

Translated from the Spanish by Eliot Weinberger

STUDY QUESTIONS

1. What is the goddess's condition in "Obsidian Butterfly"? Identify and
   discuss the imagery that reveals her past splendor.
2. How does the poem confront Mexican history?

 # ROSARIO CASTELLANOS

*Rosario Castellanos (1915–1974) is considered one of Latin America's foremost
women writers. A poet, novelist, short story writer, and essayist, she was a
leading feminist and defender of Native American culture. Born in Mexico
City, she studied philosophy at the University of Mexico, went on to do
postgraduate work in Spain, and was employed at different times by the
Indian Institutes in Chiapas and Mexico City. She was a distinguished
journalist who wrote regularly on the role of Mexican women for local
newspapers and magazines; in addition, she published several volumes of
poetry, two novels about the Tzotzil Indians, three volumes of short stories,
and four volumes of essays.* Meditation on the Threshold: A Bilingual
Anthology of Poetry *and* A Rosario Castellanos Reader *appeared in
English in 1988.*

Castellanos's poetry dwells on such themes as love, destiny, loneliness,

*and death, while her fiction covers a wide range, from a focus on Native
American and mestizo life to the depiction of a declining landed aristocracy.
In much of her work, Castellanos explores the difficulty of being a woman in a
patriarchal society. In "Death of the Tiger," she confronts the fate of Indians
under Spanish colonial rule.*

Death of the Tiger

1 The Bolometic tribe consisted of families of the same blood. Their protecting spirit, their *waigel*, was the tiger, whose name they were entitled
to bear because of their courage and their daring.

2 After immemorial pilgrimages (fleeing from the coast, from the sea and
its suicidal temptation), the men of this race finally established themselves
in the mountainous region of Chiapas, in a plateau rich in pastures, woods
and water. There prosperity made them lift their heads up high, and filled
their hearts with haughtiness and greed. Frequently the Bolometic would
come down from the mountains to feed on the possessions of the neighbouring tribes.

3 With the arrival of the white men, known as *caxlanes*, the belligerent and
fiery Bolometic leapt into battle with such force that they dashed themselves against the invading iron and crumbled to pieces. Worse than vanquished, aghast, the Bolometic felt for the first time in their own flesh the
rigours of defeat. They were stripped of their belongings, thrown into jail,
forced into slavery. Those who managed to escape (their newly acquired
poverty inspired them, made them invisible to their enemies' fury) sought
refuge at the foot of the hills. There they stopped to look back and see what
the calamity had left them, and there they began a precarious life in which
the memory of past greatness slowly vanished, and history became a dying
fire that no one was capable of rekindling.

4 From time to time, a few of the bravest men would climb down to the
neighbouring settlements and trade in their harvest; they would also visit
the sanctuaries, praying to the Higher Powers that They cease tormenting
their *waigel*, their tiger, whom the shaman could hear, roaring and
wounded, high above in the thicket. The Bolometic were generous in their
offerings, and yet their prayers were not answered. Their tiger was yet to
receive many more wounds.

5 The *caxlanes'* greed cannot be stifled either by force or with gifts. It sleeps
not. It watches, wide awake, within the white men, within their children,
within their children's children. And the *caxlanes* march on, never sleeping,
trampling the earth with the iron hoofs of their horses, casting around their
hawk's eyes, nervously clicking their whips.

6 The Bolometic saw the advancing threat but did not run, as before, to lift

the weapons they no longer had the courage to wield. They drew together, trembling with fear, to discuss their own conduct, as if they were about to appear before a demanding and merciless tribunal. They would not defend themselves: how could they? They had forgotten the art of war and had not learnt that of arguing. They would humble themselves. But the white man's heart is made of stuff that does not grow soft with prayers. And mercy is a fine plum on a captain's helmet, but does not dust the sand that dries the clerk's legal documents.

"In this speaking paper all truth is set. And the truth is that all this land, 7
with its hillsides good for the sowing of corn, with its pine forests to be felled for logs and fire-wood, with its rivers good for mills, is the property of Don Diego Mijangos y Orantes, who has proven direct lineage from that other Don Diego Mijangos, conquistador, and from the later Mijangos, respectable slave traders. Therefore you, Sebastian Gomez Escopeta, and you, Lorenzo Perez Diezmo, and you, Juan Dominguez Ventana, or whatever your name is, you're not wanted here, you're taking up room that doesn't belong to you, and that is a crime punished by the law. Off with you, you good-for-nothings. Away."

Centuries of submission had deformed that race. Quickly they lowered 8
their faces in obeisance; meekly they turned their backs to run. The women went ahead, carrying the children and a few necessary utensils. The elderly men followed on slow feet. And further back, protecting the exodus, the men.

Hard days, with no goal in sight. Leaving one place because it was 9
unfriendly, and another not to fight over it with its owners. Provisions and vittles were scarce. Those whom hunger bit more cruelly than others dared to sneak out at night, near the maize fields, and under cover of darkness would steal a few ripe stalks of grain, a few edible leaves. But the dogs would sniff out the strangers and bark their warning. The guards would arrive whirling their machetes and making such a racket that the intruders would flee, panic-stricken. But they would carry on their quest, starving, in hiding, the long hair bedraggled and the clothes in shreds.

Misery ravaged the tribe, badly protected from the harsh weather. The 10
cold breathed upon them its lethal breath and shrouded them in a whitish, thick fog. First the children, who died without understanding why, their little fists tightly clenched as if trying to cling onto the last wisp of heat. Then the old people, huddled next to the campfire ashes, without uttering a single moan. The women hid themselves to die, with a last display of modesty, as in the happy old days they had hidden themselves to give birth.

These were the ones who stayed behind, those who would never see 11
their new homeland. They finally set up camp on a high terrace, so high that it cut in two the white man's cold breath, a land swept by hostile winds, poor, scorned even by the vilest weeds and creepers, the earth showing its barren entrails through the deep cracks. The brackish water lay far away.

A few stole pregnant ewes and herded them in secret. The women set   12
up a loom, waiting for the first shearing. Others ploughed the land, the
inflexible, avaricious land. The rest set off on long journeys to pray for
divine benevolence in sanctuaries set aside for holy worship.

But times were grim and hunger was on the rampage, going from house   13
to house, knocking at every door with its bony hand.

The men, after meeting in council, decided to leave. The women fore-   14
went the last mouthful so as not to hand them an empty basket. And at the
crossroads they said their farewells.

On and on. The Bolometic never rested, even at night. Their torches   15
could be seen snaking down the blackness of the hills.

Now, in Ciudad Real men no longer live according to their whims or   16
their needs. In the planning of this city of white men, of *caxlanes*, what
ruled was the intelligence. The streets cross each other in geometrical
patterns. The houses are of one and the same height, of one and the
same style. A few display on their facades a coat of arms, because their
owners are the descendants of those warriors—conquistadores, the first
colonisers—whose deeds still ring with an heroic peal in certain family
names: Marin, De la Tovilla, Mazariegos.

During the colonial centuries and the first decades of independence,   17
Ciudad Real was the provincial seat of government. It boasted the opu-
lence and abundance of commerce, it became the beacon of culture. But in
the years to come, only one high function still kept its seat in Ciudad Real:
the bishopric.

Now the city's splendour was a thing of the past. Decay gnawed at its   18
very innards. Men with neither temerity nor vision, full of their own importance, deep in the contemplation of the past, gave up the political
sceptre, let go the reins of commerce, closed the book of intellectual endeavours. Surrounded by a tight ring of Indian communities, all silently
hostile, Ciudad Real always maintained with them a one-sided relationship. The systematic plunder was answered by a latent grumbling that a
few times exploded into bloody uprisings. And each time Ciudad Real
seemed less capable of stifling these by itself. Neighbouring towns—
Comitan, Tuxtla, Chiapa de Corzo—came to its aid. Towards them flew the
wealth, fame, command. Ciudad Real became nothing but a presumptuous
and empty shell, a scarecrow that only scared the Indian soul, stubbornly
attached to fear.

The Bolometic crossed the first streets amid the silent disapproval of the   19
passersby who, with squeamish gestures, avoided brushing that offensive
misery.

The Indians examined the spectacle before their eyes with curiosity,   20
insistence, and lack of understanding. The massive walls of the *caxlanes'*
temples weighed upon them almost as if they were obliged to carry that
weight on their shoulders. The exquisite beauty of the ornaments—certain
iron railings, the detailed carving of some of the stones—awoke in the

Bolometic the desire to destroy them. They laughed at the sudden appearance of an object whose purpose they could not guess: fans, porcelain figures, lace clothing. They remained in ecstasy in front of a photographer's samples: postcards in which a melancholy lady appeared, meditating next to a broken column, while in the distant horizon sunk the also melancholy sun.

And people? How did the Bolometic see the people? They did not recognize the pettiness of these little men, short, plump, red-cheeked, the lees of a full-blooded, intrepid race. In front of their eyes they only saw the lightning which, in the past, had struck them down. And through the ugliness and decadence, the superstitious soul of the defeated could still make out the mysterious sign of the omnipotent *caxlan* god.

The women of Ciudad Real, the *coletas*, shuffled along the streets with small reticent steps, like doves; the eyes lowered, the cheeks blushing under the rough stroke of the wind. Silence and mourning went with them. And when they spoke, they spoke with that moss-like voice which puts tiny children to sleep, comforts the sick, helps the dying. The voice of those who watch the men go by from behind a windowpane.

The marketplace attracted the foreigners with its bustle. Here was the throne of plenty. Here was corn which stuffed the granaries with its yellow gold; here were red-blooded beasts, slaughtered, hanging from enormous hooks. The mellow fruits, delicious: peaches with their skins of eternal youth; bananas, strong and sturdy; the apple that, at times, tastes like the blade of a knife. And coffee, fragrant from a distance. And sweet preserves, baroque, christened with faraway tribal names: *tartaritas, africanas*. And bread with which God greets man every morning.

This was what the Bolometic saw, and they saw it with an amazement that was not touched with greed, that destroyed any thoughts of greed. With religious amazement.

The policeman in charge of watching over the marketplace was strolling aimlessly along the stalls, humming a song, waving away, here and there, a stray fly. But when he noticed the presence of the bunch of ragged loafers—he was accustomed to seeing them on their own, not in a group and with a leader—he automatically became suspicious. He gripped tight onto his stick, ready to swing it at the first attempt to steal, or to break that long and nebulous article of the law which he had never read but in whose existence he believed: causing public disturbances. But the Bolometic's intentions seemed to be peaceful. They had left the marketplace and were now looking for an empty spot among the pews of the Church of La Merced. On their haunches, the Indians patiently began to pick off their fleas and eat them. The policeman watched them from afar, please because contempt was on his side.

A gentleman who kept hovering around the Bolometic decided at last that he would speak to them. Fat, bald, full of forced merriment, he said to them in their own tongue:

"So, you there. Are you looking for work?" 27

The Bolometic looked at each other quickly and in panic. Each one left 28
upon the other the responsibility of answering. Finally, the one who looked
the most venerable—he was the most respected of the group because of his
age and because he had once before been to Ciudad Real—asked:

"Can you find us work? Are you a 'collector'?" 29

"Exactly, my good fellow. And known to be fair and honest. My name 30
is Juvencio Ortiz."

"Ah yes. Don Juvencio." 31

The comment was less an echo of his fame than a sign of good manners. 32
Silence spread upon them like a stain. Don Juvencio drummed his fingers
on the curve of his stomach, at the height of the waistcoat button where the
watch chain should have hung. Remembering that he did not yet own a
watch chain made him dig his spurs into the conversation.

"Well, then? Do we have a deal?" 33

But the Indians were in no hurry. There is never any hurry to fall into a 34
trap.

"We came down from our lands. There's not much there, sir. The crops 35
won't give."

"Exactly my point. Let's go to the office and sort out the details." 36

Don Juvencio began to walk, certain that the Indians would follow. 37
Hypnotized by his assurance, the Indians went after him.

What Don Juvencio so pompously called his "office" was a dirty circular 38
room on one of the streets off the marketplace. The furniture consisted of
two wooden tables—more than once the splinters of their badly smoothed
top had torn the sleeves of the only suits Don Juvencio and his associate
possessed—a shelf full of papers, and two chairs of unsteady legs. On one
of them, perched with the provisional attitude of a bird, was Don Juvencio's associate: a large profile, protected by a green plastic visor. He croaked
as the visitors appeared before him.

"What good things are you bringing us, Don Juvencio?" 39

"Whatever I could get hold of, my dear friend. Competition is tough. 40
'Collectors' with fewer merits than mine—and I have a lawyer's degree,
given by the Law School of Ciudad Real—and less experienced than myself, steal our clients away."

"They use other methods. You've never made use of drink, for instance. 41
A drunk Indian never notices what he does or what he agrees to do. But
skimping on drink . . ."

"Not at all. But taking advantage of these poor souls when they are 42
unconscious is, as His Illustrious Don Manuel Oropeza would say, a des-
picable thing to do."

Don Juvencio's associate showed his teeth in a wicked little smile. 43

"Well, your morals make our fortune. You were the one who said that 44
everything might be lacking in this world, but there would always be
Indians to spare. So we'll see. The farms that have put us in charge

of their management run the risk of losing their crops for want of workers."

"Wise men change opinions, my dear partner. I also used to say. . . .   45
But anyway, no need to complain. Here they are."

Don Juvencio made a wide gesture with his arm, like a magician un-   46
veiling his bag of tricks. But his associate's admiration remained un-
daunted.

"These?"   47

Don Juvencio saw himself obliged to change his tone of voice.   48

"These! Don't use that tone of voice with me. . . . What's wrong with   49
them?"

Don Juvencio's associate shrugged his shoulders.   50

"They've got vultures pecking at their back, that's what's wrong. They'll   51
never endure the climate on the coast. And you, who are so particular. . . ."

Don Juvencio drew close to his associate, lifting a finger in mock anger.   52

"You. . . . No wonder they call you a Jonah! Just remember, dear friend,   53
the saying about minding one's own business. Is it our responsibility
whether these Indians stand up or not to the climate? Our only obligation
is to see that they arrive alive at the farm. What happens afterwards is none
of our business."

And to avoid further discussion he moved towards the shelf and took   54
out a pile of papers. After handing them over to his associate, Don Juvencio turned towards the Bolometic and ordered:

"Come on now, get in line. One by one, go up to this gentleman's desk   55
and answer his questions. No lies, because the gentleman is a sorcerer and
can hurt you badly. You know why he wears that visor? So as not to burn
you with his eyes."

The Bolometic listened with ever-growing anguish. How would they be   56
able to keep on hiding their true name?

They waited. But they knew it was useless.   57

And this is how the Bolometic placed the name of their *waigel*, the   58
wounded tiger, under the will and command of those ink-stained hands.

"Pablo Gomez Bolom."   59

"Daniel Hernandez Bolom."   60

"Jose Dominguez Bolom."   61

Don Juvencio's associate drilled the Indians with useless suspicion. As   62
usual, he thought, they were making fun of him. Afterwards, when they
escaped from the farms without paying their debts, no one would be able
to find them, because the place they said they came from did not exist, and
the names they gave as theirs were false.

But no, in the name of the Holy Virgin of Caridad, enough! Don Juven-   63
cio's associate banged his fist on the table, furious. His knowledge of the
Indian tongue was not enough to allow him to argue. Grumbling, all he
said was:

"Bolom! I'll give you 'bolom'! Let's see the next one." 64

As soon as they had finished the associate let Don Juvencio know. 65

"Forty. What farm shall we send them to?" 66

"We'll service Don Federico Werner once and for all. He's the most 67
urgent. Write down 'Coffee Plantation El Suspiro.' In Tapachuela."

As he wrote, his eyes protected by the green visor, Don Juvencio's 68
associate insisted:

"Forty's not enough." 69

"Not enough? Forty Indians to pick the coffee beans on one farm? Worse 70
is nothing. Not enough?"

"The forty won't reach the farm. They won't last the journey." 71

And Don Juvencio's associate turned the page, satisfied he was right. 72

With the advance money they had received, the Bolometic began their 73
journey. Gradually, they left behind the wilderness of the hills and were
shrouded in a sad, gritty breeze that broke into their misery. They could
smell in the breeze sweet things. And they felt restless, like dogs on the
trace of an unknown prey.

The height, leaving them so abruptly, shattered their eardrums. They 74
were in pain, they bled from their ears. When the Bolometic reached the
sea, they thought that its immense fury was mute.

The only presence that never left them was the cold, unwilling to aban- 75
don the bodies it had always held in its grip. Every day, at the same time,
even when the tropical sun hit the grey stones, the cold would uncoil like
a repulsive snake and slither over the Bolometic's bodies, stiffening their
jaws, their arms and legs, with a terrible trembling. After that, the Bolometic would feel faint, shrunk, as if little by little the cold were shrivelling
them in order to better fit in their awaiting tomb.

Those who survived that long journey were never able to return. The 76
debts would form a cage, link after link, chaining them to their new master.
In the eardrum scars there echoed, more and more faintly, the voices of
their women, calling them, and of their children, dying out.

The tiger in the hills was never heard of again. 77

Translated from the Spanish by Alberto Manguel

STUDY QUESTIONS

1. How does the title reflect the story's subject?
2. In what way is the story a chronicle of Indian life? How does it account
   for the demise of Native America?
3. Why are traditional storytelling devices appropriate for the story?

NICARAGUA

 ## SERGIO RAMÍREZ

Sergio Ramírez (b. 1942) is Nicaragua's leading fiction writer. Born in Masatepe, Nicaragua, he studied law and served for many years in Costa Rica at the Secretary General of the Council of Central American Universities. As a leading opponent of the Somoza dictatorship and an active member of the Sandinista National Liberation Front, he was forced to live in exile, in Europe, for several years. When the Sandinistas came to power in 1979, he became vice president of his country. He has published three collections of stories and two novels and is best known for his epic novel, To Bury Our Fathers *(1985), in which he uses popular legend, historical reminiscences, and a lively cast of characters to offer a panoramic view of Nicaragua during the Somoza era when the country was on the brink of revolution. "Charles Atlas Also Dies" is typical of the author's use of irony and humor to convey human vulnerability. It is also representative of Ramírez's interest in confronting the contradictions of Latin American culture and in exploring the psychological ramifications of imperialism.*

Charles Atlas Also Dies

Charles Atlas swears that sand story is true.
Edwin Pope, Sports Editor,
The Miami Herald

H ow well I remember Captain Hatfield USMC on the day he came   1
down to the quayside at Bluefields to see me off on the boat to New York. He gave me his parting words of advice, and lent me his English cashmere coat: it must be cold up there, he said. He came with me to the gangway and then, after I had clambered into the launch, gave me a long

handshake. As I rode out to the steamer, which stood well off the coast, I saw him for the last time, a lean, bent figure in army boots and fatigues, waving me good-bye with his cap. I say for the last time because three days later he was killed in a Sandinista attack on Puerto Cabezas, where he was garrison commander.

Captain Hatfield USMC was a good friend. He taught me to speak English with his Cortina method records, played for me every night in the barracks at San Fernando on the wind-up gramophone. It was he who introduced me to American cigarettes. But above all, I remember him for one thing: he enrolled me in the Charles Atlas correspondence course, and later helped me get to New York to see the great man in person. 2

It was in San Fernando, a small town up in the Segovias Mountains, that I first met Captain Hatfield USMC. That was back in 1926: I was a telegraph operator, and he arrived in command of the first column of Marines, with the task of forcing General Sandino and his followers down from Mount Chipote, where they had holed up. It was me who transmitted his messages to Sandino and received the replies. Our close friendship, though, started from the day he gave me a list of the inhabitants of San Fernando and asked me to mark all those I thought might be involved with the rebels or had relatives among them. The next day they were all marched off, tied up, to Ocotal, where the Americans had their regional headquarters. That night, to show his gratitude, he gave me a packet of Camels (which were completely unknown in Nicaragua in those days) and a magazine with pin-up photos. It was there I read the ad that changed my whole life, transforming me from a weakling into a new man: 3

THE 97-POUND WEAKLING
WHO MADE HIMSELF THE WORLD'S
MOST PERFECTLY DEVELOPED MAN

Ever since I was a child, I had suffered from being puny. I can remember how once when I was strolling around the square in San Fernando after Mass with my girlfriend Ethel—I was 15 at the time—two big hefty guys walked past us, laughing at me. One of them turned back and kicked sand in my face. When Ethel asked me, "Why did you let them do that?" all I could find to reply was: "First of all, he was a big bastard; and second, I couldn't see a thing for the sand in my eyes." 4

I asked Captain Hatfield USMC for help in applying for the course advertised in the magazine, and he wrote on my behalf to Charles Atlas in New York, at 115 East 23rd Street, to ask for the illustrated brochure. Almost a year later—San Fernando is in the midst of the mountains, where the heaviest fighting was going on—I received the manila envelope containing several colored folders and a letter signed by Charles Atlas himself. "The Complete Dynamic Tension Course, the summit in body-building. Simply tell me where on your body you'd like muscles of steel. Are you fat and flabby? Limp and listless? Do you tire easily and lack energy? Do you 5 stay in your shell and let others walk off with the prettiest girls, the best jobs, etc? Give me just seven days and I'll prove that I can turn you too into a real man, full of health, of confidence in yourself and your own strength."

Mr. Atlas also said in his letter that this course would cost a total of thirty dollars. That kind of money was far beyond my means, so again I turned to Captain Hatfield USMC, who presented me with another list of local people, almost all of whom I marked for him. The money was soon sent off, and within the year I had received the complete course of 14 lessons with their 42 exercises. Captain Hatfield took personal charge of me. The exercises took only 15 minutes a day. "Dynamic Tension is a completely natural system. It requires no mechanical apparatus that might strain the heart or other vital organs. You need no pills, special diet, or other tricks. All you need are a few minutes of your spare time each day—and you'll really enjoy it!" 6

But since I had more spare time than I knew what to do with, I could dedicate myself wholeheartedly to the exercises for three hours rather than fifteen minutes every day. At night I was studying English with Captain Hatfield. After only a month, my progress was astonishing. My shoulders had broadened, my waist had slimmed down, and my legs had firmed up. Scarcely four years after that big bully had kicked sand in my eyes, I was a different man. One day, Ethel showed me a photo of the mythological god Atlas in a magazine. "Look," she said, "he's just like you." Then I knew I was on the right track and would one day fulfill my dreams. 7

Four months later, my English was good enough for me to be able to write and thank Mr. Atlas myself: "Everything is OK." I was a new man with biceps of steel, and capable of a feat like the one I performed in the capital, Managua, the day that Captain Hatfield USMC took me there to give a public demonstration of my strength. Dressed in a tiger-skin leotard, I pulled a Pacific Railway car full of chorus girls for a distance of two hundred yards. President Moncada himself, together with the special American envoy Mr. Hanna and Colonel Friedmann, the commander of the Marines in Nicaragua, all came to see me. 8

Doubtless it was this achievement, which was reported in all the newspapers, that made it easier for Captain Hatfield to forward the application I had made when the two of us left San Fernando: a trip to the United States to meet Charles Atlas in person. Captain Hatfield's superiors in Managua made a formal request to Washington, and just over a year later this was approved. The news appeared in the papers at the time; more precisely, in *La Noticia* for September 18, 1931, I was photographed standing next to the US cultural attaché, a certain Mr. Fox, this being almost certainly the first cultural exchange between our two countries, although they became so common afterwards. The caption read: "Leaving for a tour of physical culture centers in the United States, where he will also meet outstanding personalities from the world of athletics." 9

So it was that, following a peaceful crossing with a short call at the port 10 of Veracruz, we arrived in New York on November 23, 1931. I must confess that, as the ship berthed, a feeling of great desolation overwhelmed me, despite all the warnings Captain Hatfield USMC had given me. From books, photographs, and maps, I had formed a precise image of New York City—but it was a static one. This was torn to shreds by the frenetic movement of animate and inanimate objects around me, and I was plunged into a terrifying fantasy full of invisible trains, a sky blackened by countless chimneys, a stench of soot and sewage, the scream of distant sirens, and a constant rumbling from the earth beneath my feet.

I was met by someone from the State Department, who took care of 11 immigration and drove me to my hotel—the Hotel Lexington to be exact—a huge brick building on 48th Street. He told me everything had been arranged for me to see Mr. Atlas the following morning. I was to be picked up at my hotel and taken to the offices of Charles Atlas, Inc., where everything would be explained to me. With that we said good-bye, as he had to return to Washington the same evening.

It was cold in New York, so I went to bed early, full of an understand- 12 able excitement now that I was reaching my journey's end and seeing my greatest ambition fulfilled. I looked out at the infinity of lights from skyscraper windows that sparkled through the fog. Somewhere out there, I thought, behind one of those windows, is Charles Atlas. He's reading, having dinner, sleeping, or talking to someone. Or perhaps he's doing the nightly exercises—numbers 23 and 24 in the handbook (flexing the neck and wrists). Maybe he has a smile on his fresh, cheerful face beneath hair greying at the temples. Or perhaps he is still busy replying to the thousands of letters he receives every day, and sending off the packages with the handbooks. One thing suddenly occurred to me: I couldn't imagine Charles Atlas with clothes on. I always thought of him in his swimming trunks, with his muscles flexed, but found it impossible to picture him in a suit or hat. I rummaged in my suitcase till I found the signed photograph he had sent me on completion of the course. There he stood, hands cupped behind his head, body slightly arched and his pectoral muscles effortlessly tensed, his legs together, and one shoulder tilted higher than the other. It was beyond me to try and imagine such a body clothed, and the idea was still turning in my mind as I fell asleep.

By five in the morning I was already awake. I carried out exercises 1 and 13 2 (how thrilling to be doing them in New York for the very first time) and imagined that Charles Atlas was probably performing the same ones right at that moment. I took my shower and dressed as slowly as possible, killing time, but by seven o'clock I was downstairs in the hotel lobby waiting to be picked up as instructed. Although Charles Atlas did not exactly specify it, I never ate breakfast anyway.

At nine o'clock sharp the man from Charles Atlas, Inc., arrived. Waiting 14 for us outside was a black limousine with gold trim on its windows and grey velvet curtains. The escort did not open his mouth once during the whole trip, nor did the chauffeur so much as glance around. We drove for half an hour along streets lined with the same brick buildings, row upon row of windows, and always the dull daylight between the skyscrapers as though it was about to rain. The black car finally pulled up in front of the eagerly awaited number 115 on East 23rd Street. It was a depressing street full of warehouses and wholesale depositories. I remember that across from Charles Atlas, Inc., was an umbrella factory and a small park of dusty, withered trees. All the buildings seemed to have their windows boarded up.

To reach the front entrance of Charles Atlas, Inc., we climbed some   15
stone steps up to a small terrace, where a life-sized statue of the mytho-logical god Atlas was carrying the world on his shoulders. The inscription read: *Mens sana in corpore sano.* We went in through a squeaky revolving door of polished glass set in black enamelled frames. The walls of the lobby were covered with huge blow-ups of all the photographs of Charles Atlas I knew so well. What a thrill to recognize each of them in turn: particularly the one in the center, which showed him, a harness around his neck, pulling ten automobiles while a shower of ticker-tape fell about him. Magnificent!

I was shown into the office of Mr. William Rideout, Jr., the general   16
manager of Charles Atlas, Inc. Within a few moments I was joined by a middle-aged man with a gaunt face and eyes sunk deep into dark sockets. He held out a pale hand, on which a mass of blue veins stood out, then sat down behind a small, square desk. He switched on a lamp behind him, though to me this hardly seemed necessary, as the window let in enough light already.

The offices were rather shabby. The desk was littered with piles of letters   17
identical to the one I had received at the start of the course. The wall in front of me was dominated by an enormous photograph (one I had never seen before) of Charles Atlas proudly showing off his pectoral muscles. Mr. Rideout asked me to take a seat, then began to speak without so much as looking up at me. He kept staring at a paperweight on the desk, and had his hands crossed in front of him. It was plain from his expression that he found it a great effort to talk. I was trying so hard to follow his dull monotonous voice that it wasn't until he paused to wipe the corners of his mouth that I notice something my nervousness had prevented me from seeing before: his clenched hands and lowered head could only mean exercise 18 of the Dynamic Tension System. I must admit I was so moved I came close to tears.

"I welcome you most cordially," Mr. Rideout Jr. had begun, "and I hope   18
you have an enjoyable stay in New York. I'm sorry not to be able to talk proper Spanish with you as I should have wished, but I only speak *un poquito.*" As he said this, he measured out a tiny gap between the thumb and first finger of his right hand, then burst out laughing for the first and only time, as though he had said something tremendously funny.

Mr. Rideout Jr. then beamed at me condescendingly while he straightened his tie. "I am the general manager of Charles Atlas, Inc., and it is a great pleasure for my company to receive you as an official guest of the US State Department. We will do all we can to make your stay here with us a pleasant one." He again dabbed at his lips with the handkerchief, then launched into a longer speech, which gave me the opportunity to observe his aged secretary as she turned down the Venetian blind on the street window, throwing the room into semi-darkness. Its whole appearance changed in an instant, and new objects came to the fore, as if Charles Atlas had suddenly shifted his pose in the many photographs displayed on the walls. 19

"I'm delighted that you should have come from so far away to meet Charles Atlas, and must confess that this is the first time anything of the kind has happened in the entire history of the company," Mr. Rideout Jr. was saying. "As in any commercial enterprise, we keep to ourselves certain matters which, should they become public knowledge, would only harm our interests. For that reason I must ask you to swear a solemn oath of silence concerning what I am about to tell you." 20

He repeated the same warning several times, speaking calmly and evenly now. I swallowed and nodded my agreement. 21

"Swear out loud," he said. 22

"I swear," I managed to get out. 23

Although by now we were completely alone in the room, and the only sound was the hum of the radiator, Mr. Rideout Jr. looked all around him before he spoke. 24

"Charles Atlas doesn't exist," he whispered, leaning over towards me. Then he dropped back into his seat, and stared at me with a grave expression on his face. "I know this must come as a great shock to you, but it's the truth. We invented our product in the last century, and Charles Atlas is a trademark like any other, like the cod fisherman on the Scott's emulsion box or the clean-shaven face on Gillette razor-blades. It's simply what we sell." 25

During our long talks after the English classes back in San Fernando, Captain Hatfield USMC had often warned me about this kind of situation: never drop your guard. Be like a boxer—don't be taken by surprise. Stand up for yourself. Don't let them fool you. 26

"Very well," I said, rising to my feet, "I shall have to inform Washington of this." 27

"What's that?" Mr. Rideout Jr. exclaimed, also getting to his feet. 28

"Yes, that's right, I'll have to tell Washington about this setback." (Washington is a magic word, Captain Hatfield USMC had taught me. Use it when you're in a tight spot, and if by any chance that doesn't work, hit them with the other, the State Department: that's a knockout.) 29

"I beg you to believe me. I'm telling you the truth," Mr. Rideout said, but with a faltering voice. 30

"I'd like to cable the State Department." 31

"I swear I'm not lying to you . . ." were his parting words as he backed 32
his way out of the room, closing a narrow door behind him. I was left all
on my own in the gloom. If I were to believe Captain Hatfield, the trembling in my legs must be caused by passing underground trains.

It was late afternoon before Mr. Rideout Jr. appeared again. Hammer 33
away, keep hammering at them, I could hear Captain Hatfield USMC
advising me.

"I will never believe that Charles Atlas doesn't exist," I said before he 34
had a chance to speak. He crumpled into his chair.

"All right, you win," he conceded, with a wave of his hand. "The firm 35
has agreed for you to meet Mr. Atlas."

I smiled and thanked him with a satisfied nod. Be kind and polite once 36
you know you've won, another of Captain Hatfield USMC's recommendations.

"But you must promise to adhere strictly to the following conditions. 37
The State Department has been consulted, and they have approved the
document that you are to sign. You must undertake to leave the country
after seeing Mr. Atlas. A passage has been booked for you on the *Vermont*,
which sails at midnight. You must also refrain from making any public or
private comment on your meeting, and from relating anything that may
happen, or your personal impressions, to anyone at all. It is only on these
conditions that the board has given its approval."

The aging secretary came in again and handed Mr. Rideout a sheet of 38
paper. He pushed it over to me. "Sign here," he said peremptorily.

Without another word, I signed where he was pointing. Once you've 39
got what you want, sign any damn thing apart from your death sentence:
Captain Hatfield USMC.

Mr. Rideout Jr. took the document, folded it carefully, and put it in the 40
middle drawer of the desk. Even as he was doing so, I felt myself being
lifted from the chair. I looked round and saw two huge muscle-bound men
dressed in black, with identical shaven heads and scowls. No doubt their
bodies too had been developed thanks to the rigors of the Dynamic Tension System.

"These gentlemen will go with you. Follow their instructions to the 41
letter." At that, Mr. Rideout Jr. disappeared once more through the narrow
door, without so much as a farewell handshake.

The two men, without ever loosening their grip, led me out into a long 42
corridor, which eventually brought us to a wooden staircase. They barked
at me to go down first: by the bottom, I was in complete darkness. One of
them pushed past me and knocked on a door. It was opened from the far
side by a third man who was the mirror image of my two. We stepped out
onto a small concrete landing-stage. I couldn't say for certain where we
were, because the fog had come swirling down again, but I'm pretty certain
it was the river front, for they led me over to a tugboat, which set off at a

snail's pace into the mist. The stench from the refuse barges it was pulling reached us even up in the prow.

Night had fallen by the time we disembarked and continued our way on foot along an alley lined with stacks of empty bottle crates. We pushed our way through circles of black children playing marbles by the light of gas lamps and finally emerged into a square where tufts of withered grass alternated with dirty strips of trampled ice left from a snowfall. In front of us were the backs of four or five dark buildings with their tangled web of fire escapes. The hum of distant traffic and the wail of trains miles away came and went on the smoke-filled air. 43

Renewed pressure on my arms directed me to one side of the square, and we entered the courtyard of a grim edifice that turned out to be a church, whose dank, acrid-smelling walls were covered in bas-reliefs of angels, flowers and saints. By the light of a match that one of my companions struck to find the door knocker, I managed to read the name on a bronze plaque: Abyssinian Baptist Church. As the booming echoes of the knocker faded in the icy night, the door was opened by another guard, also huge, muscle-bound and tough-looking. 44

We walked up the main nave to the high altar, then I was pushed towards a door on the left. I was filled with sadness and exhaustion. I felt so unsure of what might happen next that I almost regretted having provoked the situation I now found myself in. Again though, Captain Hatfield USMC's voice raised my spirits: once you're on your way, my boy, never look back. 45

An old woman in a starched white uniform stood waiting for me. My two friends finally let go of me, and positioned themselves on either side of the door. "You've got precisely half an hour," one of them growled. The aged nurse led the way along a dazzlingly white corridor. Ceiling, walls, all the doors we passed, even the floor tiles were white, while the fluorescent strips only added to this pure, empty light. 46

The old woman hobbled slowly to a double door at the end of the corridor. One side was open, but the view inside was blocked by a folding screen. With a trembling hand she gestured for me to go in, then vanished. I knocked gently three times, but nobody seemed to have heard the timid rap of my knuckles on the blistered layers of paint that had been daubed repeatedly on the door. 47

My heart was in my mouth as I knocked once more, determined that if there was no answer this time I would turn back. But suddenly a tall, ungainly nurse with thinning, bleached hair who was also dressed in dazzling white appeared from behind the screen. She gave me a broad, relaxed smile that revealed her perfect horse teeth. 48

"Come in," she said. "Mr. Atlas is expecting you." 49

The room was bathed in the same artificial whiteness, the same empty light in which millions of tiny dust particles floated. All the objects in the room were white too: the chairs and a medical trolley piled with cotton 50 wool, gauze, bottles and surgical instruments. The walls were bare, apart from a painting that showed the white naked body of a beautiful young woman stretched out on a table while an ancient surgeon held up the heart he had just cut from her. There were bed pans on the floor, and the windows were covered with blinds that during the day must filter out nearly all the light.

At the back of the room on a raised platform was a high, jointed bed with a complicated system of levers and springs. I tiptoed slowly towards it, then stopped halfway, almost overcome by the smell of disinfectant. I looked around for one of the white chairs to sit on, but the nurse, who was already beside the bed, beckoned me, smiling, to come forward. 51

On the bed lay the unmoving apparition of a giant, muscular body, its head buried somewhere among the pillows. When the nurse leaned over to whisper something, the body stirred with difficulty and came upright. Two of the pillows fell to the floor, but as I started to pick them up, she stopped me with her hand. 52

"Welcome," said a voice that echoed strangely as though through an antiquated megaphone. It brought a lump to my throat—I wished with all my heart I hadn't started this. 53

"Thank you, thank you so much for your visit," the voice was now saying. "Believe me, I really appreciate it," the words came bubbling out, as though the voice were drowning in a sea of thick saliva. Then there was silence, and the huge body fell back onto the pillows. 54

I cannot describe my grief. I would have preferred a thousand times to have believed that Charles Atlas was an invention, that he had never existed, than to have to confront the reality that *this* was he. He spoke from behind a gauze mask, but I glimpsed that a metal plate had been screwed in to replace his lower jaw. 55

"Cancer of the jaw," he gasped, "spreading now to the vital organs. Until I was 95, I had an iron constitution. Now that I'm over a hundred, I can't complain. I've never smoked, and never drunk more than an occasional glass of champagne at Christmas or New Year. I never had any illness worse than a common cold, and the doctor was always telling me, until just recently, that I could have children if I wanted to. When in 1843 I won the title of the world's most perfectly developed man . . . in Chicago . . . I remember . . ." but at this point his voice trailed off in a series of pitiful wheezes, and he remained silent for some time. 56

"It was 1843 when I discovered the Dynamic Tension System and set up the correspondence courses, on the advice of a sculptress, Miss Ethel Whitney, who I used to pose for as a model." 57

Then Charles Atlas lifted his enormous arms from under the sheets. He flexed his biceps and cupped his hands behind his head. In doing so he dislodged the bed covers so that I caught sight of his torso, still identical to the photos, apart from the white fuzz on his chest. It must have cost him a great effort, because he began to moan, and the nurse rushed 58 to his side. She pulled the sheets back up, and adjusted the plate on his jaw.

"I was 14 years old when I left Italy with my mother," he went on. "I had no idea then that I was going to make a fortune with my courses. I was born in Calabria in 1827. My real name is Angelo Siciliano; my father had come to New York a year earlier and we followed him. One day when I was at Coney Island with my girl friend, a big bully kicked sand in my face, so I . . ." 59

"Exactly the same happened to me, that's why . . ." I tried to explain, but he kept on as though he were completely oblivious to my presence. 60

". . . began to do exercises. My body developed tremendously. One day my girlfriend pointed to a statue of the mythological god Atlas on a hotel roof and said to me: Look, you are just like that statue." 61

"Listen," I put in, "that statue . . ." It was no use. His voice swept on like a muddy river, brushing aside everything in its path. 62

"I stared up at the statue and thought to myself: you're not going to get ahead with a name like yours, people here are too prejudiced. Why not call yourself Atlas? And I also changed Angelino for Charles. Then came my days of glory. I can remember when I pulled a railcar full of chorus girls for two hundred yards . . ." 63

"Good God," I cried out, "exactly the same as . . ." but his voice, precise and eternal, ploughed on. 64

"Have you seen the statue of Alexander Hamilton outside the Treasury building in Washington? Well, that's me." He again raised his arms and made as though he were hauling a heavy weight, a railcar full of chorus girls perhaps. This time the pain must have been even more intense, because he groaned at length and fell prone on the bed. After a long while, he started to speak again, but by now all I wanted to do was leave. 65

"I remember Calabria," he said, squirming in the bed. The nurse tried to calm him, then went over to the trolley to make up some drops for him. ". . . Calabria, and my mother singing, her face ruddy from the flames of the oven." He gurgled something I couldn't follow, the sound of his voice echoing through the room in a series of agonised croaks. "A song . . ." 66

I had lost all notion of what was going on, when suddenly the insistent buzzing of a bell brought me back to myself. It resounded all down the corridors before bouncing back to its point of departure in the room, and I finally realized it came from the nurse tugging at a bell cord above the bed, while Charles Atlas lay sprawled naked on his back on the floor, spattered with blood, the metal plate dangling from his jaw. 67

All at once the room was filled with footsteps, voices, and shadows. I felt myself being lifted bodily from the chair by the same strong arms that had guided me there. In the jumble of images and sounds as I was being dragged from the room I heard the nurse cry out: "My God, the strain was too much for him; he couldn't resist that last pose!" and saw several men lifting the body onto a stretcher and hurrying it out. 68

Now, in old age as I write these lines, I still find it hard to believe that 69
Charles Atlas isn't alive. I wouldn't have the heart to disillusion all the
youngsters who write to him every day asking about his course, still under
the spell of his colossal figure, his smiling, confident face, as he holds a
trophy or hauls a railcar full of chorus girls, a hundred laughing, crushed
girls waving their flowery bonnets through the windows, and in the incredulous crowds thronging the pavements to watch, a hand raises a hat to
the sky.

I left New York the same night. I was weighed down with sorrow and 70
remorse, convinced I was guilty in some way, if only of having witnessed
such a tragedy. Back in Nicaragua, with Captain Hatfield USMC dead and
the war over, I tried my hand at various things: working in a circus, as a
weightlifter, then as a bodyguard. My physique isn't what it once was.
Thanks to the Dynamic Tension System, though, I could still have children. If I wanted to.

Translated from the Spanish
by Nick Caistor

STUDY QUESTIONS

1. Discuss the narrator's relationship with the marine captain in "Charles
   Atlas Also Dies." Why does he become a collaborator? Why does the
   U.S. government reward him?
2. What does Charles Atlas represent?
3. After he returns from New York is the narrator still captivated by the
   Charles Atlas myth? What is revealing about the story's last sentence?
4. Discuss the author's use of irony and humor.

PERU

César Vallejo

César Vallejo (1892–1938), one of Latin America's most important and original poets, was the youngest of a large mestizo family in a small village in Santiago de Chuco, Peru. Both grandfathers were Spanish priests; both grandmothers were their native concubines. This colonial legacy was to influence Vallejo's writing, and throughout his life he took pride in his Native American ancestry. As a young man, Vallejo went to Lima to study medicine but transferred to the University of Trujillo, where he earned a degree in literature. When he began to write poetry, Peru was governed by a military-backed dictatorship. In response, Vallejo was drawn to Marxism and as a writer embraced the rebellious spirit of the European avant-garde. He radically transformed Spanish verse into a vehicle capable of expressing the subtlety and complexity of Latin American experience. His first volume of poetry introduced indigenous themes in popular speech patterns and turned Native America into a symbol of humanity's inability to realize its potential because of injustice and oppression. For political reasons, Vallejo was forced to emigrate to Paris, where he eked out a meager existence writing for Peruvian newspapers. Living in exile, he became a spokesman for left-wing causes, joined the Communist Party, and supported the Republican partisans of the Spanish Civil War. His experience as a cosmopolitan expatriot and political activist did not overshadow his poetry. During the latter part of his life, he continued to write about his memories of Peru, and his political poetry remained subtle, linked to the dilemmas of the human condition. "A Man Passes with a Loaf of Bread on His Shoulder" is typical of his concern with the plight of the disadvantaged. Among his many volumes of poetry to appear in English are The Complete Posthumous Poetry *(1979),* Selected Poems of César Vallejo *(1981), and* The Black Heralds *(1990).*

A Man Passes with a Loaf of Bread on His Shoulder . . .

A man passes with a loaf of bread on his shoulder.
Am I going thereafter to write about him, my double?

Another sits down, scratches himself, removes a louse from his
    armpit, kills it.
What good would it do to talk about psychoanalysis?   5

Another has attacked my chest with a club in his hand.
Shall I then discuss Socrates with the doctor?

A lame man gives his arm to a little boy.
After that, am I going to read André Breton?

A man shivers with cold, coughs, spits up blood.   10
Will it ever be fitting to allude to my inner soul?

Another scratches in the mud for husks and bones.
How then can I write about infinity?

A mason falls from the roof, dies before breakfast.
How then can I launch a new metaphor or rhythm?   15

A storekeeper cheats a customer of one gram.
How then can I talk about the Fourth Dimension?

A banker falsifies his accounts.
What tears are then left for the theater?

A cripple sleeps with one foot on his shoulder.   20
Shall I later on talk about Picasso, of all people?

Someone sobs at the side of a grave.
How can I consider my admission to the academy?

A man cleans his rifle in the kitchen.
What good would it do to talk more about it?   25

Someone walks by counting his fingers.
How can I think of the *not-me* without crying aloud?

Translated from the Spanish by Lillian Lowenfels
and Nan Braymer

1. Discuss how the poet confronts the problem of the relationship between literature and human suffering. What questions does he raise?
2. What examples does the poet use to illustrate the conflict between the concerns of art and the demands of everyday living?

 # MARIO VARGAS LLOSA

Mario Vargas Llosa (b. 1936) is among the most successful of the new Latin American novelists who came to prominence during the 1960s. Like Argentina's Cortázar and Colombia's Márquez, he was influenced by the European avant-garde and the stream-of-consciousness techniques of Joyce and Faulkner. Unlike many of his contemporaries, he incorporates these innovations into a fictional framework. His novels are meticulously crafted with strong characterization and plot development, and expand the basic themes of Latin American literature—the abuse of power, corruption, and social oppression.

Vargas Llosa was born in Arequipa, Peru, attended the University of San Marcos, and did graduate work at the University of Madrid. For many years he lived in exile in Europe and, like most intellectuals of his generation, supported left-wing causes. Since his return to Peru, he has become more conservative. His reputation as a writer began with his first novel, The Time of the Hero *(1963), which turned a national military academy into a microcosm for Peruvian society and was the basis for a scathing condemnation of violence and corruption.* The Green House *(1966) is Vargas Llosa's most complex work and considered to be his masterpiece. Set in two locations, a provincial city and the Amazon wilderness, the novel interweaves myth and fantasy in an exploration of a divided Peru rife with internal tensions. "Sunday, Sunday" is a conventionally written story that centers on the life of upper-middle-class youth.*

Sunday, Sunday

H e held his breath for an instant, dug his fingernails into the palms of   1
his hands and said very quickly: "I'm in love with you." He saw her
blush suddenly, as if someone had slapped her cheeks, which were radi-

antly pale and very smooth. Terrified, he felt his confusion rising in him, petrifying his tongue. He wanted to run away, to put an end to it: in the gloomy winter morning there rose up from deep inside him the weakness that always discouraged him at decisive moments. A few minutes before, in the midst of the lively, smiling crowd strolling in Miraflores' Central Park, Miguel was still repeating to himself: "Right now. When we get to Pardo Avenue, I'll get up the nerve. Oh, Rubén, if you knew how much I hate you!" And still earlier at church, seeking out Flora, he had glimpsed her at the base of a column and, opening a path with his elbows without begging pardon of the women he was pushing aside, succeeded in getting close to her. Saying hello in a low voice, he repeated to himself, stubbornly, as he had that dawn lying in his bed, watching day break: "There's no other way. I've got to do it today. In the morning. You'll pay for this yet, Rubén." And the night before, he had cried for the first time in many years when he realized how that dirty trick was being planned. People were staying in the park and Pardo Avenue was deserted. They walked down the tree-lined promenade under the tall, densely crowned rubber trees. I've got to get a move on, Miguel thought, if I'm not going to foul myself up. Out of the corner of his eye he looked around him: there was no one about; he could try. Slowly, he stretched out his left hand until it touched hers; the contact made him aware that he was sweating. He begged for some miracle to happen, for that humiliation to be over. What do I say to her now? he thought. What do I say to her now? She had pulled back her hand and he was feeling forsaken and silly. All his brilliant lines, feverishly rehearsed the night before, had dissolved like soap bubbles.

"Flora," he stammered, "I've waited a long time for this moment. Ever   2
since I met you, you're all I think about. I'm in love for the first time, believe me. I've never known a girl like you."

Once again a compacted white space in his brain—a void. The pressure   3
could not get any higher: his skin gave way like rubber and his fingernails struck bone. Still, he went on talking with difficulty, pausing, overcoming his embarrassed stammer, trying to describe an impulsive, consuming passion until he found with relief that they had reached the first circle on Pardo Avenue, and then he fell silent. Flora lived between the second and third trees past the oval. They stopped and looked at each other: Flora was still red, and being flustered had filled her eyes with a moist brightness. Despairing, Miguel told himself that she had never looked more beautiful: a blue ribbon held her hair back and he could see the start of her neck as well as her ears, two tiny, perfect question marks.

"Look, Miguel," Flora said; her voice was gentle, full of music, steady.   4
"I can't answer you right now. But my mother doesn't want me to go with boys till I finish school."

"Flora, all mothers say the same thing," Miguel insisted. "How's she   5
going to find out? We'll see each other whenever you say, even if it's only on Sundays."

"I'll give you an answer but first I've got to think it over," Flora said, lowering her eyes. And after several seconds she added: "Excuse me, but I have to go now; it's getting late."   6

Miguel felt a deep weariness, a feeling that spread throughout his entire body and relaxed him.   7

"You're not mad at me, Flora?" he asked humbly.   8

"Don't be silly," she replied animatedly. "I'm not mad."   9

"I'll wait as long as you want," Miguel said. "But we'll keep on seeing each other, won't we? We'll go to the movies this afternoon, okay?"   10

"I can't this afternoon," she said softly. "Martha's asked me over to her house."   11

A hot, violent flush ran through him and he felt wounded, stunned at this answer, which he had been expecting and which now seemed cruel to him. What Melanés had insidiously whispered into his ear Saturday afternoon was right. Martha would leave them alone; it was the usual trick. Later Rubén would tell the gang how he and his sister had planned the situation, the place and the time. As payment for her services, Martha would have demanded the right to spy from behind the curtain. Anger suddenly drenched his hands.   12

"Don't be like that, Flora. Let's go to the matinee like we said. I won't talk to you about this, I promise."   13

"I can't, really," Flora said. "I've got to go to Martha's. She stopped by my house to ask me yesterday. But later I'll go to Salazar Park with her."   14

He did not see any hope even in those last words. A little later he was gazing at the spot where the frail, angelic figure had disappeared under the majestic arch of the rubber trees along the avenue. It was possible to compete with a mere adversary, not with Rubén. He recalled the names of girls invited by Martha, other Sunday afternoons. Now he was unable to do anything; he was defeated. Then, once more, there came to mind that image which saved him every time he experienced frustration: out of a distant background of clouds puffed up with black smoke, at the head of a company of cadets from the naval academy, he approached a reviewing stand set up in the park; illustrious men in formal attire with top hats in hand, and ladies with glittering jewels were applauding him. A crowd, in which the faces of his friends and enemies stood out, packed the sidewalks and watched him in wonder, whispering his name. Dressed in blue, a full cape flowing from his shoulders, Miguel led the march, looking toward the horizon. His sword was raised, his head described a half circle in the air; there at the center of the reviewing stand was Flora, smiling. He saw Rubén off in one corner, in tatters and ashamed, and confined himself to a brief, disdainful glance as he marched on, disappearing amid hurrahs.   15

Like steam wiped off a mirror, the image vanished. He was at the door of his house; he hated everyone, he hated himself. He entered and went straight up to his room, throwing himself face down on the bed. In the cool darkness, the girl's face appeared between his eyes and their lids—"I love   16 you, Flora," he said out loud—and then Rubén with his insolent jaw and hostile smile: the faces were alongside each other; they came closer. Rubén's eyes twisted in order to look at him mockingly while his mouth approached Flora.

He jumped up from the bed. The closet mirror showed him an ashen face with dark circles under the eyes. "He won't see her," he decided. "He won't do this to me; I won't let him play that dirty trick on me." 17

Pardo Avenue was still deserted. Stepping up his pace without pausing, he walked to the intersection at Grau Avenue. He hesitated there. He felt cold: he had left his jacket in his room and just his shirt was not enough to protect him from the wind blowing off the sea and tangling itself with a soft murmuring in the dense branches of the rubber trees. The dreaded image of Flora and Rubén together gave him courage and he continued walking. From the doorway of the bar next to the Montecarlo movie house, he saw them at their usual table, lords of the corner formed by the rear and left-hand walls. Francisco, Melanés, Tobias, the Brain—they all noticed him and after a moment's surprise turned toward Rubén, their faces wicked and excited. He recovered his poise immediately: in front of men he certainly did know how to behave. 18

"Hello!" he said to them, drawing near. "What's new?" 19

"Sit down," said the Brain, pushing a chair toward him. "What miracle's brought you here?" 20

"You haven't been around here for ages," Francisco said. 21

"I felt like seeing you," Miguel answered pleasantly. "I knew you'd be here. What's so surprising? Or aren't I one of the Hawks anymore?" 22

He took a seat between Melanés and Tobias. Rubén was across from him. 23

"Cuncho!" shouted the Brain. "Bring another glass. One that's not too greasy." 24

Cuncho brought the glass and the Brain filled it with beer. Miguel said, "To the Hawks," and drank. 25

"You might as well drink the glass while you're at it," Francisco said. "You sure are thirsty!" 26

"I bet you went to one o'clock mass," said Melanés, winking in satisfaction as he always did when he was starting some mischief. "Right?" 27

"I did," Miguel said, unruffled. "But just to see a chick, nothing else." 28

He looked at Rubén with defiant eyes but Rubén did not let on; he was drumming his fingers on the table and whistling very softly, with the point of his tongue between his teeth, Pérez Prado's "The Popoff Girl." 29

"Great!" applauded Melanés. "Okay, Don Juan. Tell us, which chick?" 30

"That's a secret." 31

"There are no secrets between Hawks," Tobias reminded him. "You forget already? C'mon, who was it?" 32

"What's it to you?" Miguel asked. 33

"A lot," Tobias said. "Got to know who you're going around with to know who you are." 34

"You lost that round," Melanés said to Miguel. "One to nothing." 35

"I'll bet I can guess who it is," Francisco said. "You guys don't know?" 36

"I do already," Tobias said. 37

"Me too," said Melanés. He turned to Rubén with very innocent eyes and voice. "And you, brother, can you guess who it is?" 38

"No," said Rubén coldly. "And I don't care." 39

"My stomach's on fire," said the Brain. "Nobody's going to get a beer?" 40

Melanés drew a pathetic finger across his throat. "I have not money, darling," he said in English. 41

"I'll buy a bottle," announced Tobias with a solemn gesture. "Let's see who follows my example. We've got to put out the fire in this booby." 42

"Cuncho, bring half a dozen bottles of Cristal," said Miguel. 43

There were shouts of joy, exclamations. 44

"You're a real Hawk," Francisco declared. 45

"A friendly son of a bitch," added Melanés. "Yeah, a real super Hawk." 46

Cuncho brought the beers. They drank. They listened to Melanés telling dirty, crude, wild, hot stories and Tobias and Francisco started up a heavy discussion about soccer. The Brain told an anecdote. He was on his way from Lima to Miraflores by bus. The other passengers got off at Arequipa Avenue. At the top of Javier Prado, Tomasso, the White Whale, got on— that albino who's six feet four and still in grammar school, lives in Quebrada, you with me? Pretending to be really interested in the bus, he started asking the driver questions, leaning over the seat in front of him while he was slowly slitting the upholstery on the back of the seat with his knife. 47

"He was doing it because I was there," asserted the Brain. "He wanted to show off." 48

"He's a mental retard," said Francisco. "You do things like that when you're ten. They're not funny at his age." 49

"What happened afterwards is funny." The Brain laughed. " 'Listen, driver, can't you see that whale's destroying your bus?' " 50

"What?" yelled the driver, screeching to a stop. His ears burning, his eyes popping out, Tomasso the White Whale was forcing the door open. 51

"With his knife," the Brain said. "Look how he's left the seat." 52

At last the White Whale managed to get out. He started running down Arequipa Avenue. The driver ran after him, shouting, "Catch that bastard!" 53

"Did he catch him?" Melanés asked. 54

"Don't know. I beat it. And I stole the ignition key as a souvenir. Here it is." 55

He took a small, silver-plated key out of his pocket and tossed it onto the table. The bottles were empty. Rubén looked at his watch and stood up. 56

"I'm going," he said. "See you later." 57

"Don't go," said Miguel. "I'm rich today. I'll buy us all lunch." 58

A flurry of slaps landed on his back; the Hawks thanked him loudly, 59
they sang his praises.

"I can't," Rubén said. "I've got things to do." 60

"Go on, get going, boy," Tobias said. "And give Martha my regards." 61

"We'll be thinking of you all the time, brother," Melanés said. 62

"No," Miguel yelled out. "I'm inviting everybody or nobody. If Rubén 63
goes, that's it."

"Now you've heard it, Hawk Rubén," Francisco said. "You've got to 64
stay."

"You've got to stay," Melanés said. "No two ways about it." 65

"I'm going," Rubén said. 66

"Trouble is, you're drunk," said Miguel. "You're going because you're 67
scared of looking silly in front of us, that's the trouble."

"How many times have I carried you home dead drunk?" asked Rubén. 68
"How many times have I helped you up the railing so your father wouldn't
catch you? I can hold ten times as much as you."

"You used to," Miguel said. "Now it's rough. Want to see?" 69

"With pleasure," Rubén answered. "We'll meet tonight, right here?" 70

"No, right now." Miguel turned toward the others, spreading his arms 71
wide. "Hawks, I'm making a challenge."

Delighted, he proved that the old formula still had the same force as 72
before. In the midst of the happy commotion he had stirred up, he saw
Rubén sit down, pale.

"Cuncho!" Tobias shouted. "The menu. And two swimming pools of 73
beer. A Hawk has just made a challenge."

They ordered steak with spiced onions and a dozen beers. Tobias lined 74
up three bottles for each of the competitors and the rest for the others.
They ate, scarcely speaking. Miguel took a drink after each mouthful and
tried to look lively, but his fear of not being able to hold enough beer
mounted in proportion to the sour taste at the back of his throat. They
finished off the six bottles long after Cuncho had removed the plates.

"You order," Miguel said to Rubén. 75

"Three more each." 76

After the first glass of the new round, Miguel heard a buzzing in his 77
ears; his head was a slow-spinning roulette wheel and everything was
whirling.

"I've got to take a piss," he said. "I'm going to the bathroom." 78

The Hawks laughed. 79

"Give up?" Rubén asked. 80

"I'm going to take a piss," Miguel shouted. "If you want to, order 81
more."

In the bathroom he vomited. Then he washed his face over and over, 82
trying to erase all the telltale signs. His watch said four-thirty. Despite his

heavy sickness, he felt happy. Now Rubén was powerless. He went back to their table.

"Cheers," Rubén said, raising his glass. 83

He's furious, Miguel thought. But I've fixed him now. 84

"Smells like a dead body," Melanés said. "Somebody's dying on us 85
around here."

"I'm fresh as a daisy," Miguel asserted, trying to hold back his dizziness 86
and nausea.

"Cheers," Rubén repeated. 87

When they had finished the last beer, his stomach felt like lead; the 88
voices of the others reached his ears as a confused mixture of sounds. A
hand suddenly appeared under his eyes; it was white with long fingers; it
caught him by the chin; it forced him to raise his head; Rubén's face had
gotten larger. He was funny-looking, so rumpled and mad.

"Give up, snot-nose?" 89

Miguel stood up suddenly and shoved Rubén, but before the show 90
could go on, the Brain stepped in.

"Hawks never fight," he said, forcing them to sit down. "You two are 91
drunk. It's over. Let's vote."

Against their will, Melanés, Francisco and Tobias agreed to a tie. 92

"I'd won already," Rubén said. "This one can't even talk. Look at him." 93

As a matter of act, Miguel's eyes were glassy, his mouth hung open and 94
a thread of saliva dribbled off his tongue.

"Shut up," said the Brain. "We wouldn't call you any champion at beer 95
drinking."

"You're no beer-drinking champion," Melanés emphasized. "You're 96
just a champion at swimming, the wizard of the pools."

"You better shut up," Rubén said. "Can't you see your envy's eating 97
you alive?"

"Long live the Esther Williams of Miraflores!" shouted Melanés. 98

"An old codger like you and you don't even know how to swim," said 99
Rubén. "You want me to give you some lessons?"

"We know already, champ," the Brain said. "You won a swimming 100
championship. And all the chicks are dying over you. You're a regular little
champion."

"He's no champion of anything," Miguel said with difficulty. "He's just 101
a phony."

"You're keeling over," Rubén answered. "Want me to take you home, 102
girlie?"

"I'm not drunk," Miguel protested. "And you're just a phony." 103

"You're pissed because I'm going to go steady with Flora," Rubén said. 104
"You're dying of jealousy. Think I don't understand things?"

"Just a phony," Miguel said. "You won because your father's union 105
president; everybody knows he pulled a fast one, and you only won on
account of that."

"At least I swim better than you," Rubén said. "You don't even know how to surf." 106

"You don't swim better than anybody," Miguel said. "Any girl can leave you behind." 107

"Any girl," said Melanés. "Even Miguel, who's a mother." 108

"Pardon me while I laugh," Rubén said. 109

"You're pardoned, your Highness," Tobias said. 110

"You're getting at me because it's winter," Rubén said. "If it wasn't, I'd challenge you all to go to the beach to see who's so cocksure in the water." 111

"You won the championship on account of your father," Miguel said. "You're just a phony. When you want to swim with me, just let me know—don't be so timid. At the beach, at Terraces, wherever you want." 112

"At the beach," Rubén said. "Right now." 113

"You're just a phony," Miguel said. 114

Rubén's face suddenly lit up and in addition to being spiteful, his eyes became arrogant again. 115

"I'll bet you on who's in the water first," he said. 116

"Just a phony," said Miguel. 117

"If you win," Rubén said, "I promise you I'll lay off Flora. And if I win, you can go peddle your wares someplace else." 118

"Who do you think you are?" Miguel stammered. "Asshole, just who do you think you are?" 119

"Listen, Hawks," Rubén said, spreading his arms, "I'm making a challenge." 120

"Miguel's in no shape now," the Brain said. "Why don't you two flip a coin for Flora?" 121

"And why're you butting in?" Miguel said. "I accept. Let's go to the beach." 122

"You're both crazy," Francisco said. "I'm not going down to the beach in this cold. Make another bet." 123

"He's accepted," Rubén said. "Let's go." 124

"When a Hawk challenges somebody, we all bite our tongues," Melanés said. "Let's go to the beach. And if they don't have the guts to go into the water, we throw them in." 125

"Those two are smashed," insisted the Brain. "The challenge doesn't hold." 126

"Shut up, Brain," Miguel roared. "I'm a big boy now. I don't need you to take care of me." 127

"Okay," said the Brain, shrugging his shoulders. "Screw you, then." 128

They left. Outside a quiet gray atmosphere was waiting for them. Miguel breathed in deeply; he felt better. Francisco, Melanés and Rubén walked in front; behind them, Miguel and the Brain. There were pedestrians on Grau Avenue, mostly maids on their day off in gaudy dresses. Ashen men with thick, lanky hair preyed around them and looked them over greedily. The 129 women laughed, showing their gold teeth. The Hawks did not pay any attention to them. They walked on with long strides as the excitement mounted in them.

"Better now?" asked the Brain. 130

"Yeah," answered Miguel. "The air's done me good." 131

They turned the corner at Pardo Avenue. They marched in a line, spread 132 out like a squadron under the rubber trees of the promenade, over the flagstones heaved up at intervals by the enormous roots that sometimes pushed through the surface like grappling hooks. Going down the cross-town street, they passed two girls. Rubén bowed ceremoniously.

"Hi, Rubén," they sang in duet. 133

Tobias imitated them in falsetto: "Hi, Rubén, you prince." 134

The crosstown street ends at a forking brook: on one side winds the 135 embankment, paved and shiny; on the other a slope that goes around the hill and reaches the sea. It is known as the "bathhouse path"; its pavement is worn smooth and shiny from automobile tires and the feet of swimmers from many, many summers.

"Let's warm up, champs," Melanés shouted, breaking into a sprint. The 136 others followed his example.

They ran against the wind and light fog rising off the beach, caught up 137 in an exciting whirlwind: through their ears, mouths and noses the air penetrated to their lungs and a sensation of relief and well-being spread through their bodies as the drop became steeper, and at one point their feet no longer obeyed anything but a mysterious force coming from the depths of the earth. Their arms like propellers, a salty taste on their tongues, the Hawks descended the slope at a full run until they reached the circular platform suspended over the bathhouse. Some fifty yards offshore, the sea vanished in a thick cloud that seemed about to charge the cliffs, those high, dark breakwaters jutting up around the entire bay.

"Let's go back," said Francisco. "I'm cold." 138

At the edge of the platform is a railing, stained in places by moss. An 139 opening marks the top of the nearly vertical stairway leading down to the beach. From up there the Hawks looked down on a short ribbon of open water at their feet and the strange, bubbling surface where the fog was blending with the foam off the waves.

"I'll go back if this guy gives up," Rubén said. 140

"Who's talking about giving up?" responded Miguel. "Who the hell do 141 you think you are?"

Rubén went down the stairway three steps at a time, unbuttoning his 142 shirt as he descended.

"Rubén!" shouted the Brain. "Are you nuts? Come back!" 143

But Miguel and the others were also going down and the Brain followed 144 them.

From the balcony of the long, wide building that nestles against the hill 145 and houses the dressing rooms, down to the curving edge of the sea, there is a slope of gray stone where people sun themselves during the summer. From morning to dusk the small beach boils with excitement. Now the water covered the slope and there were no brightly colored umbrellas or lithe girls with tanned bodies, no reverberating, melodramatic screams from children and women when a wave succeeded in splashing them before it retreated, dragging murmuring stones and round pebbles. Not even a strip of beach could be seen, since the tide came in as far as the space bounded by the dark columns holding the building up in the air. Where the undertow began, the wooden steps and cement supports, decorated by stalactites and algae, were barely visible.

"You can't see the surf," said Rubén. "How're we going to do this?"   146

They were in the left-hand gallery, in the women's section; their faces   147
were serious.

"Wait till tomorrow," the Brain said. "By noon it'll be clear. Then we'll   148
be able to check on you."

"Since we're here, let's do it now," Melanés said. "They can check on   149
themselves."

"Okay with me," Rubén said. "And you?"   150

"Me too," Miguel said.   151

When they had stripped, Tobias joked about the blue veins scaling   152
Miguel's smooth stomach. They went down. Licked incessantly by the water for months on end, the wooden steps were smooth and slippery. Holding on to the iron railing so as not to fall, Miguel felt a shivering mount from the soles of his feet up to his brain. He thought that in one way the fog and the cold favored him: winning now did not depend on skill so much as on endurance, and Rubén's skin was purplish too, puckered in millions of tiny goose bumps. One step below, Rubén's athletic body bent over: tense, he was waiting for the ebb of the undertow and the arrival of the next wave, which came in noiselessly, airily, casting a spray of foamy droplets before it. When the crest of the wave was six feet from the step, Rubén plunged in: with his arms out like spears and his hair on end from the momentum of his leap, his body cut straight through the air and he fell without bending, without lowering his head or tucking his legs in; he bounced in the foam, scarcely went under, and immediately taking advantage of the tide, he glided out into the water, his arms surfacing and sinking in the midst of a frantic bubbling and his feet tracing a precise, rapid wake. Miguel in turn climbed down one more step and waited for the next wave. He knew that the water was shallow there and that he should hurl himself like a plank, hard and rigid, without moving a muscle, or he would crash into the rocks. He closed his eyes and jumped and he did not hit bottom, but his body was whipped from forehead to knees and he felt a fierce stinging as he swam with all his might in order to restore to his limbs the warmth that the water had suddenly snatched from them. He was in that strange section of the sea near the shore at Miraflores where the undertow and the waves meet and there are whirlpools and crosscurrents,

and the summer months were so far in the past that Miguel had forgotten how to clear it without stress. He did not recall that you had to relax your body and yield, allowing yourself to be carried submissively in the drift, to stroke only when you rose on a wave and were at the crest in that smooth water flowing with the foam and floating on top of the currents. He did not recall that it is better to endure patiently and with some cunning that first contact with the exasperating sea along the shore that tugs at your limbs and hurls streams of water in your mouth and eyes, better to offer no resistance, to be a cork, to take in air only when a wave approaches, to go under—scarcely if they broke far out and without force or to the very bottom if the crest was nearby—to grab hold of some rock and, always on the alert, to wait out the deafening thunder of its passing, to push off in a single movement and to continue advancing, furtively, by hand strokes, until finding a new obstacle, and then going limp, not fighting the whirlpools, to swirl deliberately in the sluggish eddy and to escape suddenly, at the right moment, with a single stroke. Then a calm surface unexpectedly appears, disturbed only by harmless ripples; the water is clear, smooth, and in some spots the murky underwater rocks are visible.

After crossing the rough water, Miguel paused, exhausted, and took in air. He saw Rubén not far off, looking at him. His hair fell over his forehead in bangs; his teeth were clenched.   153

"Do we go on?"   154

"We go on."   155

After a few minutes of swimming, Miguel felt the cold, which had momentarily disappeared, invade him again, and he speeded up his kicking because it was in his legs, above all in his calves, that the water affected him most, numbing them first and hardening them later. He swam with his face in the water and every time his right arm came out, he turned his head to exhale the breath he had held in and to take in another supply, with which he scarcely submerged his forehead and chin once again so as not to slow his own motion and, on the contrary, to slice the water like a prow and to make his sliding through it easier. With each stroke, out of one eye he could see Rubén, swimming smoothly on the surface, effortlessly, kicking up no foam now, with the grace and ease of a gliding seagull. Miguel tried to forget Rubén and the sea and the surf (which must still be far out, since the water was clear, calm and crossed only by newly formed waves). He wanted to remember only Flora's face, the down on her arms which on sunny days glimmered like a little forest of golden threads, but he could not prevent the girl's image from being replaced by another— misty, usurping, deafening—which fell over Flora and concealed her; the image of a mountain of furious water, not exactly the surf (which he had reached once, two summers ago, and whose waves were violent with green and murky foam because at that spot, more or less, the rocks came to an end, giving rise to the mud that the waves churned to the surface and mixed with nests of algae and jellyfish, staining the sea) but rather a real   156 ocean tormented by internal cataclysms whipping up monstrous waves that could have encompassed an entire ship and capsized it with surprising quickness, hurling into the air passengers, launches, masts, sails, buoys, sailors, portholes and flags.

He stopped swimming, his body sinking until it was vertical; he lifted his head and saw Rubén moving off. He thought of calling to him on any pretext, of saying to him, for example, "Why don't we rest for a minute?" but he did not do it. All the cold in his body seemed concentrated in his calves; he could feel his stiffened muscles, his taut skin, his accelerated heart. He moved his feet feverishly. He was at the center of a circle of dark water, walled in by the fog. He tried to catch sight of the beach or the shadow of the cliffs when the mist let up, but that vague gauze which dissolved as he cut through was not transparent. He saw only a small, greenish-black patch and a cover of clouds level with the water. Then he felt afraid. He was suddenly struck by the memory of the beer he had drunk and thought: I guess that's weakened me. In an instant it seemed as if his legs and arms had disappeared. He decided to turn back, but after a few strokes in the direction of the beach, he made an about-face and swam as gently as he could. "I won't reach the shore alone," he said to himself. "It's better to be close to Rubén; if I wear out, I'll tell him he beat me but let's go back." Now he was swimming wildly, his head up, swallowing water, flailing the sea with stiff arms, his gaze fixed on the imperturbable form ahead of him. 157

The movement and effort brought his legs back to life; his body regained some of its heat, the distance separating him from Rubén had decreased and that made him feel calmer. He overtook him a little later; he stretched out an arm and grabbed one of his feet. Rubén stopped instantly. His eyes were bright red and his mouth was open. 158

"I think we've gotten turned around," Miguel said. "Seems to me we're swimming parallel to the beach." 159

His teeth were chattering but his voice was steady. Rubén looked all around. Miguel watched him, tense. 160

"You can't see the beach anymore," Rubén said. 161

"You couldn't for some time," Miguel said. "There's a lot of fog." 162

"We're not turned around," Rubén said. "Look. Now you can see the surf." 163

As a matter of fact, some small waves were approaching them, with a fringe of foam that dissolved and suddenly re-formed. They looked at each other in silence. 164

"We're already out near the surf, then," Miguel said finally. 165

"Yeah. We swam fast." 166

"I've never seen so much fog." 167

"You very tired?" Rubén asked. 168

"Me? You crazy? Let's get going." 169

He immediately regretted saying that, but it was already too late. Rubén   170
had said, "Okay, let's get going."

He succeeded in counting up to twenty strokes before telling himself he   171
could not go on: he was hardly advancing; his right leg was half paralyzed
by the cold, his arms felt clumsy and heavy. Panting, he yelled, "Rubén!"
Rubén kept on swimming. "Rubén, Rubén!" He turned toward the beach
and started to swim, to splash about, really, in desperation; and suddenly
he was begging God to save him: he would be good in the future, he would
obey his parents, he would not miss Sunday mass, and then he recalled
having confessed to the Hawks that he only went to church "to see a chick"
and he was sure as a knife stab that God was going to punish him by
drowning him in those troubled waters he lashed so frantically, waters
beneath which an atrocious death awaited him, and afterwards, perhaps,
hell. Then, like an echo, there sprang to his mind a certain old saying
sometimes uttered by Father Alberto in religion class, something about
divine mercy knowing no bounds, and while he was flailing the sea with
his arms—his legs hung like dead weights—with his lips moving, he
begged God to be good to him, he was so young, and he swore he would
go to the seminary if he was saved, but a second later, scared, he corrected
himself, and promised that instead of becoming a priest he would make
sacrifices and other things, he would give alms, and at that point he realized how hesitating and bargaining at such a critical moment could be fatal
and then he heard Rubén's maddened shouts, very nearby, and he turned
his head and saw him, about ten yards away, his face half sunk in the
water, waving an arm, pleading: "Miguel, brother, come over here, I'm
drowning, don't go away!"

He remained motionless, puzzled, and suddenly it was as though   172
Rubén's desperation banished his own; he felt himself recovering his courage, felt the stiffness in his legs lessening.

"I've got a stomach cramp," Rubén shrieked. "I can't go any farther,   173
Miguel. Save me, for God's sake. Don't leave me, brother."

He floated toward Rubén and was on the point of swimming up to him   174
when he recalled that drowning people always manage to grab hold of
their rescuers like pincers and take them down; and he swam off, but the
cries terrified him and he sensed that if Rubén drowned, he would not be
able to reach the beach either, and he turned back. Two yards from Rubén,
who was quite white and shriveled, sinking and surfacing, he shouted:
"Don't move, Rubén. I'm going to pull you but don't try to grab me; if you
grab me we'll sink, Rubén. You're going to stay still, brother. I'm going to
pull you by the head; don't touch me." He kept at a safe distance and
stretched out a hand until he reached Rubén's hair. He began to swim with
his free arm, trying with all his strength to assist with his legs. The movement was slow, very laborious. It sapped all his power and he was hardly
aware of Rubén, complaining monotonously, suddenly letting out terrible

screams—"I'm going to die, Miguel, save me"—or retching in spasms. He was exhausted when he stopped. With one hand he held Rubén up, with the other he traced circles on the surface. He breathed deeply through his mouth. Rubén's face was contracted in pain, his lips folded back in a strange grimace.

"Brother," murmured Miguel, "we've only got a little way to go. Try. Rubén, answer me. Yell. Don't stay like that." 175

He slapped him hard and Rubén opened his eyes; he moved his head weakly. 176

"Yell, brother," Miguel repeated. "Try to stretch. I'm going to rub your stomach. We've only got a little way to go; don't give up." 177

His hand searched under the water, found a hard knot that began at Rubén's navel and took up a large part of his belly. He went over it many times, first slowly, then hard, and Rubén shouted, "I don't want to die, Miguel, save me!" 178

He started swimming again, dragging Rubén by the chin this time. Whenever a wave overtook them, Rubén choked; Miguel yelled at him to spit. And he kept on swimming, without stopping for a moment, closing his eyes at times, excited because a kind of confidence had sprung up in his heart, a warm, proud, stimulating feeling that protected him against the cold and the fatigue. A rock grazed one of his legs and he screamed and hurried on. A moment later he was able to stand up and pass his arms around Rubén. Holding him pressed up against himself, feeling his head leaning on one of his shoulders, he rested for a long while. Then he helped Rubén to stretch out on his back and, supporting him with his forearm, forced him to stretch his knees; he massaged his stomach until the knot began to loosen. Rubén was not shouting anymore; he was doing everything to stretch out completely and was rubbing himself with both his hands. 179

"Are you better?" 180

"Yeah, brother, I'm okay now. Let's get out." 181

An inexpressible joy filled them as they made their way over rocks, heads bent against the undertow, not feeling the sea urchins. Soon they saw the sharp edges of the cliffs, the bathhouse, and finally, close to shore, the Hawks standing on the women's balcony, looking for them. 182

"Hey!" Rubén said. 183

"Yeah?" 184

"Don't say anything to them. Please don't tell them I called out. We've always been very close friends, Miguel. Don't do that to me." 185

"You really think I'm that kind of louse?" Miguel said. "Don't worry. I won't say anything." 186

They climbed out, shivering. They sat down on the steps in the midst of an uproar from the Hawks. 187

"We were about to send our sympathy to your families," Tobias said. 188

"You've been in for more than an hour," the Brain said. "C'mon, how did it turn out?" 189

Speaking calmly while he dried his body with his undershirt, Rubén   190
explained: "Nothing to tell. We went out to the surf and came back. That's
how we Hawks are. Miguel beat me. Just barely, by a hand. Of course, if
it'd been in a swimming pool, he'd have made a fool of himself."

Slaps of congratulation rained down on Miguel, who had dressed with-   191
out drying off.

"You're getting to be a man," Melanés told him.   192

Miguel did not answer. Smiling, he thought how that same night he   193
would go to Salazar Park. All Miraflores would soon know, thanks to
Melanés, that he had won the heroic contest and Flora would be waiting
for him with glowing eyes. A gold future was opening before him.

Translated from the Spanish by Gregory Kolovakos
and Ronald Christ

STUDY QUESTIONS

1. Explain the rivalry between Miguel and Rubén in "Sunday, Sunday."
   Why is their behavior immature?
2. What is Flora's role? How do social conventions restrict her life?
3. Discuss the story as an initiation rite. What does Miguel learn from the
   swimming contest with Rubén? Does he achieve adulthood?
4. How is honor shown as an important value?

PUERTO RICO

 ## Rosario Ferré

Rosario Ferré (b. 1942) was born in Ponce, Puerto Rico. She grew up in a traditional upper-class family and was educated on the island and in the United States. Ferré is one of Puerto Rico's best-known and innovative writers. She began her career as a founder and editor of the journal Zona de carga y descarga *(Loading and Unloading Zone), which promoted Puerto Rican culture and social reform. She went on to publish short stories, a novel, essays, and children's books. Several of her books have appeared in English including* Maldito Amor *(1988),* Sonatinas *(1989), and* Sweet Diamond Dust *(1989). The primary focus of her work is the plight of contemporary Puerto Rican women caught in a superficial and materialistic world. "Mercedes Benz 220 SL" explores this theme while unveiling class divisions and the social attitudes of the rich.*

Mercedes Benz 220 SL

The Mercedes is fantastic, Mom, don't you think so, look how it fields the curves and sticks to the asphalt *vrroom* powerful the steering wheel responds to the touch of my fingertips through pigskin gloves they were a present from you so I could take the car out on its first spin, so my hands wouldn't slip over the grooves of the wheel that turn right and left at the slightest pressure from my fingers, the crossed lances on the hood flash chrome every-which-way see the passersby in the rain looking at us Mom what a car, it feels like a tank the mudguards up ahead rolling rhinoceros my family's always had big cars, Mom, the first Rolls Royce in San Juan was theirs, big as hope and poor as black we've got to show them who runs this country, Mom, we've got too many people living on this island, crowded together like monkeys they like to smell each other's sweat, rub each other like bedbugs, that's what they like, a riot, how amusing, Mom, 1

I never thought of our overpopulation problem that way before, that man's coming our way, Dad, he's right in front of us, careful, you'll hit him, a man was walking with his back to the car along the shoulder of the road, pressing with his thumb the golden disc of the horn that shone in the center of the elegant beige leather steering wheel, I love the touch of this wheel, squeezing the golden disc, it sounds just like the first trumpet in Das Reingold, Mom, but the man doesn't hear, doesn't get off the road until the last minute when he leapt sideways, the mudguards spared his head by an inch, he fell flat on his face in the ditch, I'll pick you off next time, you long-tailed monkey, next time you'll drop out of the trees, you're frightened, Mom, you're white as a sheet, it's because I'm thinking of the patrol car, Dad, it's for your sake, the hell with patrol cars, Mom, it's incredible that you should worry about them now, you still don't know who your husband is, this car is like a fortress, wherever we go it'll put us in the right, that's what I bought it for, Mom, what nonsense, do you think I work from eight to eight just to put fat on my ass, in this country power is the only thing that counts, Mom, don't you forget it.

He floored the pedal and shot off in a straight line, at least there's no   2
traffic at this hour, Sunday morning is the best time to drive on this island's roads, the woman silently rubs the last beads of her rosary, I'm going to put the seat back to see if I can sleep a little, Dad, it's still dark and I'm a bit sleepy, these seats are really sexy, Mom, slipping his hand over the short, grey pile that yields to his fingertips, dolled up in your three hundred dollar alligator shoes and your nine carat emerald cut diamond ring, when I bought it you said it looked like an ice rink and I wanted to laugh, Mom, that's a good one, a ring as big as a skating rink, how you love to squander money, the stores and the church have me in the poor house, but I don't complain, Mom, it's fine with me, you're every inch a lady and I couldn't manage without you.

He took his hand from the steering wheel and reached into the darkness   3
to caress the forehead of the woman who slept at his side, I love you Dad, I said when I felt his hand on my face as I prayed again to the Holy Mother, you're like a little boy with a new toy, the truth is you work too hard, poor dear, you deserve a reward, it's not right to kill yourself working, only sometimes you make me suffer so with your lack of consideration like right now don't go so fast, Dad, the road is wet, the car could skid, you never pay attention, you never listen, it's just as if I were talking to myself, rubbing my arms because suddenly I feel cold, the trees shoot out from the sides forming a tunnel that is gobbling us up narrow-and-dark up ahead, wide-and-falling-on-us behind, we must be doing ninety, please, Dad, God forgive us and the Virgin protect us the wipers won't go fast enough to clear the huge raindrops, it's always been like this, since we got married twenty years ago he buys me everything, he's a good provider, but always the same deafness, I'm always at his side and always alone, eating alone, sleeping alone, once I looked at myself in the mirror, I opened my mouth,

touched my palate with my finger to see if any sound came out, testing, one, two, three, my mouth formed the words for things, wood and hair, eye and lip, checking, the flow of breath, testing, one two three, but nothing came out, it was clogged up in there as if the opening were too small or the words too large, edges painfully jammed into the gums. I forced the words upward from the back of my throat but to no avail, it felt like I was touching a mute hole, I put my finger in deeper every time and then I looked at myself in the mirror and thought I was going crazy. Then my son was born and I could speak again.

She lay back in the seat and watched his profile outlined in darkness. 4 The dashboard lights lit up his heavy features, his childlike smile. She closed her eyes and crossed her arms over her chest to rub her shoulders. And now she was alone again, because her son had left home after many angry disputes with his father. He said the business made him want to vomit, he was fed up with Dad's threatening to disinherit him, one morning I found a note on his bed don't look for me I'll come see you on Sundays. Of course we searched but he was always changing addresses until at last Dad got tired of shelling out money for private detectives and let him go to hell, he said, I'm not going to work my hide off just to waste thousands of dollars on detectives tracking out the likes of a prima donna who doesn't give a damn about money, raise crows and they'll pick out your eyes I've always said, and I wept but it was no use because deep down I knew Dad was right. Look at that road ahead of us, Mom, it's all ours, if it weren't six o'clock Sunday morning it'd be packed full of cars, one on top of the other like monkeys, that's what they're like, the stink of apes, the stench of chimps, smooth, so smooth, the gas pedal to the floor, these Germans make cars as if they were tanks, Mom, no matter what it knocks off the steel body won't even dent, if it hits you it means a one-way ticket to kingdom come.

Standing before the kitchen sink, the girl picked up the cup from which 5 she had just drunk coffee, and slid her finger over the blue roses of the porcelain. She turned on the hot water tap, squeezed the plastic bottle and let three sluggish drops fall. She watched them slide slowly down the cup. The liquid, a raw green, reminded her of her fear, but when she let the water fill the cup it dissolved harmlessly in suds, spilling over the edge. She wiped the cup and dried it, feeling the glaze squeak clean under her fingertips, and then put it, still warm, on the table. She dried her reddened hands on her skirt and looked out through the kitchen window at the patio. In the grey light of dawn, the plants nodded at her under the rain as if they were wanderers that had lost their way. A mist was rising from the wet earth and the smell reminded her of when she was a child and used to bury things nobody wanted in the garden: a comb with missing teeth; a plastic swan with a ribbon around its neck, "Fernando and María, Happiness Always," that her mother had brought back as a keepsake from a wedding; a half-used lipstick; a thimble. I always enjoyed burying things nobody wanted so only I knew where they were. When it rains hard like now I remember it clearly, I see myself breathing the smell of the clods of earth that crumble between my fingers. Then when I went out for a spell in the garden, I'd walk over the buried things that only I knew were there. Now I stand over the little comb, I'd say to myself in a low voice, now I'm stepping over the wings of the swan, now over my old Easter bonnet, as if the power to remember every detail of the hidden objects somehow made me different from everyone else.

She left the kitchen sink and looked around at the half-furnished room.   6
She had nothing to do so she began to pull out the bureau's half empty drawers. She opened the almost empty closet and rattled the wire hangers together. It didn't bother her at all to have so few belongings; on the contrary, she welcomed the peace that an empty room brings. They usually sat on the floor at dinner and ate on a straw tatami which she kept scrupulously clean. In the mornings, before six o'clock, they would both do their zen meditation together, sitting in lotus position with pistil straight backs and warbling like birds the mantra's sacred words. Then a soft ray of light fell on her hand and made her think of him. She realized she couldn't picture his face away from this place; he was part of the room itself, of the books, orderly, aligned on the table, of the little gas stove, of the faded bedspread covering the thin mattress which lay on the floor, of the bronze fish mobile that tinkled to the comforting beat of the rain against the window. Then she heard his knock on the door, ran to meet him and embraced him. Should you go today she asked, because look how it's raining, you're drenched. Yes; I agreed to go every Sunday.

If you go early we'll have Sunday to ourselves, I tell him. You should   7
come with me, Mom has never met you and perhaps she'd come to like you, Dad might even forgive us both. No, it's better they don't meet me, let's leave it for now, I'll go with you as far as the house, as usual, and then I'll go. She looked out the window again, everything's so dark and still, the rain makes it seem like nighttime. Sunday mornings always seem endless, people sleep forever behind closed doors. It's as though they grew roots under their sheets, or as if they lay with ears pressed against the windows, listening to the dry rasp of sunlight as it slowly climbs the walls.

The woman sat up in the car seat and tried to make out the silhouette of   8
houses through the raindrops that spread a thick, transparent skin down the windshield. As they neared their own street she gave a sigh of relief, feeling the end of her travail near. She put away her rosary, shut her handbag and let her body relax little by little, anticipating the moment when they would slow down, her hand on the handle to open the door, the car before their house at last. She saw him first, the dark figure zigzagging in the half-light of dawn trying to get out of the way of the car but trapped by the side of the building, it all happened in a fraction of a second. He came out of nowhere, his body swept by the curtain of rain which smothered everything. The mudguard hit with a thud and all of a

sudden he was stuck to the hood, how awful, Dad, please stop, I told you we were going too fast, I begged you a hundred times, the body splayed across the hood, you have to get out and do something, Dad, you have to get out, shut up, for God's sake, you're driving me crazy, sitting side by side unable to think, looking at the rain that kept on falling as if nothing had happened, as if it wanted to rinse out the blood from the platinum surface, the grotesque shadow sprawled over the chrome trim like a mashed-up doll.

The low voice began again its endless string of swear words, crowded   9
together like monkeys the better to smell the stink, the better to rut the stench, you can't even drive out at dawn on Sunday morning on this island without there being that thing crushed on top of the car, wiping the windshield from the inside as though nothing had happened, after all the world goes on perfectly ordered on this side of the glass, sitting comfortably on the grey pile, eyes glued to the windshield, telling himself that it was all right, nothing had happened which couldn't be fixed, his hand on the latch but unable to open the door.

The girl approached the car in the downpour, hair plastered to her face.   10
She paused before the lighted headlights, useless now in the early morning light. They watched her from behind the windshield slide the body over the hood, struggling to support his weight against hers. Then she let the boy down slowly over the side, before stretching him out on the pavement. I lowered the window halfway and the rain splashed on my face, my mouth filled with water, what's going on, I screamed, what should we do, Dad, he lowered his window an inch and peered out, shut up you idiot, the whole neighborhood will hear you, that woman has taken charge of him now, she's sat him on the ground with his head on her lap, we'd better go, I'll leave her our name and address, how can we leave, Dad, the man is hurt, we can't leave him lying on the road in this downpour, don't argue with me, you're hysterical, we're not going to put him in the car and stain the new upholstery with all that blood. And so Dad scribbled something on a piece of paper lowered his window an inch more to put out his hand and let go of the note so that it fluttered to the side of the road.

He started the engine and backed up, the screeching tires began bearing   11
down on the asphalt. Mom caressed the grey pile gently, as if trying to appease it. The upholstery, of course, how stupid of me not to think of it, so new, so soft, so alien to anything as disagreeable as a smear of blood, and she curled up in her bucket seat and began to pray. Thank you, oh God, for the protection, for the security, for the wonderful armor of a car around us, God forgive us and the Virgin protect us, one can't live without money, calming down little by little as they drove closer to home. She wiped her forehead, a nightmare, maybe it never happened, exhausted, anxious to lower herself into a hot tub, not to think about anything but the peaceful white ceiling over her room.

It had been raining all through lunchtime when the doorbell rang. I   12 opened the door and recognized her immediately, she held the crumpled piece of paper in her hand. It fell apart as I tried to read it, "Contact us if we can be of help," next to the address of our house. She opened the door and I showed her the note. She turned white, as I knew she would when she saw me. Please wait here, Miss, I'll be right back. She half-closed the door and went in. My hands were in a sweat, Dad, I dried them on my skirt as I went to find you. I looked for you all over the house but you'd already left for the office. My husband's not here, Miss, can I be of help, please come in. I walked over the doorstep, let my feet sink in the carpet and saw the stairway you had talked to me so much about, the handrail you used to slide down as a child as you burst through the door of the patio, the panes of glass in the living room window were blue and pink, just as you'd told me. Have a seat, Miss, please sit down. No Ma'am I'm not going to stay long. I looked out through the blue pane and saw you sitting next to the fountain in the garden, it's not fair, it's just not fair to see you all tinted in blue in the middle of the patio, playing a different game now where I can't reach you, where I can't be with you, swaying blue on the other side of the pane of glass, the water flowing hard and blue against your hands, your white face on my lap bleeding, stained by the rain that now gushes out of me too and I can't stop it, what's the matter, Miss, why, you're crying.

Are you the young lady who was with the stranger that awful night, I   13
asked her, my hand trembling on the goosedown pillow as I leaned curiously towards her. I wasn't sure it had really happened, it seemed like a nightmare, tell me, how is the boy, I've been so concerned about him. I felt terribly guilty for not having gotten out of the car to help you, for not having shared the unpleasantness, that's why my husband left that piece of paper with you, so you could get in touch with us and wouldn't think we were just common hit-and-runs. I'm sorry that at the moment my husband wasn't much help, he was so upset by the whole thing I almost had to take him to the hospital later he was in such a state. He's a good man, Miss, I love him very much, and he suffers from terribly high blood pressure, I was afraid he'd have a heart attack that night. But it's different now, I'm sure we can help that poor boy Miss, were there hospital bills, were there drug expenses, we'll pay for everything, I assure you. Only I'm curious to know why it took you so long to reach us, to get in contact with us, why didn't you come to see us the very next day, you'd have found friends to help you out, to take the boy to the best specialists, believe me, Miss, we want to help.

Thank you Ma'am, but I didn't come here to talk about that. Then the   14
accident wasn't serious, what a relief, Miss, thank God. My friend is dead, Ma'am, I wanted you to know that. He was buried two weeks ago; I took care of the arrangements myself. A simple coffin, a simple grave. There was no funeral that you may call as such; only a few friends and myself. He had no family. That's all. But it was my duty to tell you. The boy is dead

and buried. Good-bye, Ma'am. You mean you're leaving, don't you want to explain what happened, Miss, please wait until my husband returns, I'm sure he'll want to give you something, at least help out with some of the expenses of the burial, you can't leave like this without even telling us his name, Miss, we'd like to know that poor boy's name.

A few days later the girl stood once again in front of the kitchen window 15 and turned on the hot water tap. It was Sunday, so she didn't have to go to work. She could spend the whole day thinking, remembering about things. She squeezed the plastic bottle and let three drops of green liquid fall on her empty coffee cup. She watched the blue rose of the porcelain disappear under the soapsuds that rose to the edge. She knew that today the woman would wait again all day for her son, to no avail. She could almost see her leaning out the front door for the hundredth time, looking down the empty street at the short row of houses as the sun rose in the sky, making the walls seem more solid and heavily shadowed. She put her hand in the water and carefully rinsed out the cup and saucer. She could almost hear her say, I mustn't worry, this Sunday is like any other Sunday, he's just later than usual. For a while the girl went on looking through the window at the lush garden. The woman left the doorway and sat on the edge of her bed. There's no reason to get upset, he'll come next week if he doesn't come today, she said to herself out loud, as her eyes wandered to the bedspread. She patted the silk coverlet tenderly and thought of the expense of keeping a nice house. I just bought this coverlet a year ago and it already looks worn, there's no end to what a house will require, the redecorating is endless. After all, I made the right decision not to leave Dad, he keeps doing foolish things to scare me, like driving a hundred miles an hour down a highway, but it's not that he doesn't love me, it's just his way. All my friends envy me my husband because he's such a financial success, and this year, God willing, we'll make our usual trip to Europe. In Madrid I'll buy a Loewe suede coat for a bargain; and in Paris I'll visit Michel Swiss on the Rue de la Paix and Dior and Guerlain on the Place de la Victoire. And in addition to all that, I have him and he has me and we'll grow old together and never be alone. Young people want to be free and at the same time feel loved but they won't pay the price, life is hard, it's not a bowl of cherries, no, those who think life is a bowl of cherries have it all wrong. The girl opened the kitchen door and went out into the garden. She felt the ground with her feet and crouched down, burying her hands in the wet earth. She then began to reconstruct the memory of his face, his hands, his arms. She felt at peace. Now she was sure no one would ever discover where he had been buried.

Isn't it a splendid Sunday morning to go for a ride in our Mercedes, 16 Mom, we haven't done this for a while and I just had it specially waxed. I had new hubcaps put on it and now it's sexier than ever, it shines in the dark like a chromium rhinoceros, just look at that highway up ahead, empty of cars and leading to kingdom come, it's just waiting for us, Mom, in this country there are so many people on the road you can't go for a ride any more except at dawn on Sundays, that's the only time one can put one's head out the door and breathe. Now we can plan our trip to Europe in peace, Mom, tell me where you want to go.

First I have to tell you something, Dad, the strangest thing happened yesterday afternoon, a girl came to the house, she had a piece of paper in her hand, the very one you scribbled our address on under the rain the day that man threw himself under our car, it was definitely the same, I'm sure of it, I recognized your handwriting. You can't imagine what a time I had; she didn't complain, she didn't say more than ten words. She stood in the middle of the room and just stared at me for what must have been like fifteen minutes, until I began to think she was out of her mind. This girl wants something, I told myself. But I couldn't say anything, I just stood there in the middle of the room and stared back at her, begging all the saints to make you come back early from the office so you'd deal with her and let her know she couldn't blackmail us, that sort of thing doesn't go over with us because we have all the right friends in the right places. Still, I tried to be as civil to her as possible and kept asking her about the fellow, I was truly concerned and tried to learn all I could about the accident to see how we could help when the wretch cuts me short and tells me in an angry voice, the boy is dead, Ma'am. I buried him, just like that and nothing else, the boy is dead, I buried him, as if it were the most natural thing in the world to bury the dead yourself. I was struck absolutely dumb, unable to say a word. I felt as if a corkscrew or something were twisting into my left side and then was pulling hard. I had to sit down on the sofa I felt so faint. She went on looking at me without a word for I don't know how long, and all I could do was sit there with that terrible pain in my chest.

But thank God I finally came to. I sat up on the sofa and told myself you're a fool, Mom, if you're going to let yourself be upset by what a stranger tells you. Life is always tragic and if you put it into your mind to save humanity you're sunk, give away what you have and you'll end up begging, we must all stand up and bear our cross. And just then I realized what the wretch was saying. That you had run over the fellow and killed him, that you were totally to blame. I flew at her in a rage how dare you, you insolent wimp, you know me, Dad, I may complain and grumble, gripe and fume, but when I see you under fire I turn into a fiend. I could already see her coming at you with a charge of first-degree murder and a million dollar lawsuit, my God, this world is full of swine. Your friend threw himself under the car, I was there, I saw it, I screamed back at her. I'll testify in any court and swear on any Bible to that fact. And I was still talking, setting things straight for her, when she turned her back on me and began walking towards the door and all I could do was stand there, watch her open it calmly and step out, with my mouth open and the words stuck in my throat. And then I sat down on the sofa with that thing twisting into my chest and thought I was going to die.

Don't let it bother you, Mom, you should have told me about it sooner, 19
I would have made inquiries last night. If she shows up again at the house
you mustn't open the door, if I'm not in tell the maid you can't talk to her,
she can come see me at the office, I'll know how to deal with her. Forget
about it for now, Mom, just look at the Mercedes go, watch it glide along
the empty road purring like a car, its fenders shining in the dark like a
chromium rhinoceros' . . .

Translated from the Spanish by Rosario Ferré

STUDY QUESTIONS

1. What is the Mercedes' importance in "Mercedes Benz 200 SL"? To
   what extent does it embody the values of the rich? Why is it referred to
   as a "chromium rhinoceros"?
2. Discuss the father's social attitudes. How would you characterize the
   mother's situation?
3. How do the mysteries surrounding the son and the hit-and-run create
   suspense?
4. What is remarkable about the girl's behavior?

ST. LUCIA

 # DEREK WALCOTT

Derek Walcott (b. 1930) is considered one of the finest poets writing in English. He is also one of the Caribbean's most acclaimed playwrights and theater directors. Born in Castries, St. Lucia, to a West Indian mother and an English father, Walcott attended local schools and graduated from the University of the West Indies at Jamaica. After completing his education, he first earned his living as a teacher and a journalist. In 1959, he founded the Trinidad Theatre Workshop, which he directed until 1977. Since then he has divided his time between the United States and the Caribbean.

Walcott has received numerous honors and awards for his literary accomplishments. His plays have been performed throughout the English-speaking Caribbean and in England, Canada, and the United States. His best-known play, Dream on Monkey Mountain *(1967), was filmed for television, and its production by the Negro Ensemble of New York won the prestigious Obie award. He has published many books of poetry, including* Collected Poems 1948–1984 *(1986).*

Walcott's strength as a writer is his ability to use creatively the rich traditions of Creole culture. This is in evidence in his well-known poem "The Spoiler's Return," which draws heavily on vernacular speech and Trinidad's popular calypso and carnival traditions. In the poem, he assumes the persona of "The Moghby Spoiler," a calypsonian popular in Trinidad in the 1940s and '50s, who Walcott imagines returning from the dead to view postcolonial society. Walcott is thus able to confront the sociopolitical conflicts of the Caribbean as they affect the lives and struggles of ordinary people and to provide testimony to the vitality and strength of Caribbean culture.

The Spoiler's Return

For Earl Lovelace

I sit high on this bridge in Laventille,
watching that city where I left no will
but my own conscience and rum-eaten wit,
and limers passing see me where I sit,
ghost in brown gabardine, bones in a sack,   5
and bawl: "Ay, Spoiler, boy! When you come back?"
And those who bold don't feel they out of place
to peel my limeskin back, and see a face
with eyes as cold as a dead macajuel,
and if they still can talk, I answer: "Hell."   10
I have a room there where I keep a crown,
and Satan send me to check out this town.
Down there, that Hot Boy have a stereo
where, whole day, he does blast my caiso;
I beg him two weeks' leave and he send me   15
back up, not as no bedbug or no flea,
but in this limeskin hat and floccy suit,
to sing what I did always sing: the truth.
Tell Desperadoes when you reach the hill,
I decompose, but I composing still: 20

I going to bite them young ladies, partner,
like a hot dog or a hamburger
and if you thin, don't be in a fright
is only big fat women I going to bite.

The shark, racing the shadow of the shark   25
across clear coral rocks, does make them dark—
that is my premonition of the scene
of what passing over this Caribbean.
Is crab climbing crab-back, in a crab-quarrel,
and going round and round in the same barrel,   30
is sharks with shirt-jacs, sharks with well-pressed fins,
ripping we small-fry off with razor grins;
nothing ain't change but colour and attire,
so back me up, Old Brigade of Satire,
back me up, Martial, Juvenal, and Pope   35
to hang theirself I giving plenty rope),
join Spoiler' chorus, sing the song with me,
Lord Rochester, who praised the nimble flea:

Were I, who to my cost already am
One of those strange, prodigious creatures, Man,   40
A spirit free, to choose for my own share,
What case of flesh and blood I pleased to wear,
I hope when I die, after burial,
To come back as an insect or animal.

I see these islands and I feel to bawl,   45
"area of darkness" with V. S. Nightfall.

Lock off your tears, you casting pearls of grief
on a duck's back, a waxen dasheen leaf,
the slime crab's carapace is waterproof
and those with hearing aids turn off the truth,   50
and their dark glasses let you criticize
your own presumptuous image in their eyes.
Behind dark glasses is just hollow skull,
and black still poor, though black is beautiful.
So, crown and mitre me Bedbug the First—   55
the gift of mockery with which I'm cursed
is just a insect biting Fame behind,
a vermin swimming in a glass of wine,
that, dipped out with a finger, bound to bite
its saving host, ungrateful parasite,   60
whose sting, between the cleft arse and its seat,
reminds Authority man is just meat,
a moralist as mordant as the louse
that the good husband brings from the whorehouse,
the flea whose itch to make all Power wince,   65
will crash a fête, even at his life's expense,
and these pile up in lime pits by the heap,
daily, that our deliverers may sleep.
All those who promise free and just debate,
then blow up radicals to save the state,   70
who allow, in democracy's defence,
a parliament of spiked heads on a fence,
all you go bawl out, "Spoils, things ain't so bad."
This ain't the Dark Age, is just Trinidad,
is human nature, Spoiler, after all,   75
it ain't big genocide, is just bohbohl;
safe and conservative, 'fraid to take side,
they say that Rodney commit suicide,
is the same voices that, in the slave ship,
smile at their brothers, "Boy, is just the whip,"   80
I free and easy, you see me have chain?

A little censorship can't cause no pain,
a little graft can't rot the human mind,
what sweet in goat-mouth sour in his behind.
So I sing with Attila, I sing with Commander,   85
what right in Guyana, right in Uganda.
The time could come, it can't be very long,
when they will jail calypso for picong,
for first comes television, then the press,
all in the name of Civic Righteousness;   90
it has been done before, all Power has
made the sky shit and maggots of the stars,
over these Romans lying on their backs,
the hookers swaying their enormous sacks,
until all language stinks, and the truth lies,   95
a mass for maggots and a fête for flies;
and, for a spineless thing, rumour can twist
into a style the local journalist—
as bland as a green coconut, his manner
routinely tart, his sources the Savannah   100
and all pretensions to a native art
reduced to giggles at the coconut cart,
where heads with reputations, in one slice,
are brought to earth, when they ain't eating nice;
and as for local Art, so it does go,   105
the audience have more talent than the show.

Is Carnival, straight Carnival that's all,
the beat is base, the melody bohbohl,
all Port of Spain is a twelve-thirty show,
some playing Kojak, some Fidel Castro,   110
some Rastamen, but, with or without locks,
to Spoiler is the same old khaki socks,
all Frederick Street stinking like a closed drain,
Hell is a city much like Port of Spain,
what the rain rots, the sun ripens some more,   115
all in due process and within the law,
as, like a sailor on a spending spree,
we blow our oil-bloated economy
on projects from here to eternity,
and Lord, the sunlit streets break Spoiler's heart,   120
to have natural gas and not to give a fart,
to see them line up, pitch-oil tin in hand:
each independent, oil-forsaken island,
like jeering at some scrunter with the blues,
while you lend him some need-a-half-sole shoes,   125

some begging bold as brass, some coming meeker,
but from Jamaica to poor Dominica
we make them know they begging, every loan
we send them is like blood squeezed out of stone,
and giving gives us back the right to laugh   130
that we couldn't see we own black people starve,
and, more we give, more we congratulate
we-self on our own self-sufficient state.
In all them project, all them Five-Year Plan,
what happen to the Brotherhood of Man?   135
Around the time I dead it wasn't so,
we sang the Commonwealth of caiso,
we was in chains, but chains made us unite,
now who have, good for them, and who blight, blight;
my bread is bitterness, my wine is gall,   140
my chorus is the same: "I want to fall."
Oh, wheel of industry, check out your cogs!
Between the knee-high trash and khaki dogs
Arnold's Phoenician trader reach this far,
selling you half-dead batteries for your car;   145
the children of Tagore, in funeral shroud,
curry favour and chicken from the crowd;
as for the Creoles, check their house, and look,
you bust your brain before you find a book,
when Spoiler see all this, ain't he must bawl,   150
"area of darkness," with V. S. Nightfall?
Corbeaux like cardinals line the La Basse
in ecumenical patience while you pass
the Beetham Highway—Guard corruption's stench,
you bald, black justices of the High Bench—   155
and beyond them the firelit mangrove swamps,
ibises practising for postage stamps,
Lord, let me take a tax South again
and hear, drumming across Caroni Plain,
the tabla in the Indian half hour   160
when twilight fills the mud huts of the poor,
to hear the tattered flags of drying corn
rattle a sky from which all the gods gone,
their bleached flags of distress waving to me
from shacks, adrift like rafts on a green sea,   165
"Things ain't go change, they ain't go change at all,"
to my old chorus: "Lord, I want to bawl."
The poor still poor, whatever arse they catch.
Look south from Laventille, and you can watch
the torn brown patches of the Central Plain   170

slowly restitched by needles of the rain,
and the frayed earth, crisscrossed like old bagasse,
spring to a cushiony quilt of emerald grass,
and who does sew and sow and patch the land?
The Indian. And whose villages turn sand?   175
The fishermen doomed to stitching the huge net
of the torn foam from Point to La Fillette.
One thing with hell, at least it organize
in soaring circles, when any man dies
he must pass through them first, that is the style,   180
Jesus was down here for a little while,
cadaverous Dante, big-guts Rabelais,
all of them wave to Spoiler on their way.
Catch us in Satan tent, next carnival:
Lord Rochester, Quevedo, Juvenal,   185
Maestro, Martial, Pope, Dryden, Swift, Lord Byron,
the lords of irony, the Duke of Iron,
hotly contending for the monarchy
in couplets or the old re-minor key,
all those who gave earth's pompous carnival   190
fatigue, and groaned "O God, I feel to fall!"
all those whose anger for the poor on earth
made them weep with a laughter beyond mirth,
names wide as oceans when compared with mine
salted my songs, and gave me their high sign.   195
All you excuse me, Spoiler was in town;
you pass him straight, so now he gone back down.

STUDY QUESTIONS

1. What do you learn about Spoiler? What does he discover on his return? How has society changed?
2. How does the poem define the role of the artist? When does art come into conflict with society? What is the author's view of popular culture?
3. Interpret the ending of the poem.

TRINIDAD

◢ EARL LOVELACE

Earl Lovelace (b. 1935) has become over the last two decades one of the leading lights of a new wave of West Indian writing. He has won recognition as an outstanding novelist and short story writer as well as a reputation as a promising playwright. Lovelace was born in a small village in Trinidad, spent his childhood in the neighboring island of Tobago, and returned to Trinidad to complete his secondary school education. Except for the time spent in the United States studying at Johns Hopkins University, he has lived and worked on the island as a teacher, agricultural officer, forest ranger, journalist, and, more recently, as writer in residence at the University of the West Indies. To date, he has published four novels, a collection of plays, and a selection of short stories. His work covers a wide range of subjects from problematic issues concerning culture and identity to the conflicts surrounding race, gender, and class. The Dragon Can't Dance *(1990) placed Lovelace in the forefront of West Indian writing. Grounded in the rich traditions of popular Creole culture, the work offers a liberating critique of colonial and neocolonial oppression that envisions the possibility of its transcendence. "Shoemaker Arnold" reveals the author's sensitivity to the lives and struggles of common people.*

Shoemaker Arnold

S hoemaker Arnold stood at the doorway of his little shoemaker shop, hands on hips, his body stiffened in that proprietorial and undefeated stubbornness, announcing, not without some satisfaction, that if in his life he had not been triumphant, neither had the world defeated him. It would be hard, though, to imagine how he could be defeated, since he exuded such a hard tough unrelenting cantankerousness, gave off such a sense of readiness for confrontation, that if Trouble had to pick someone to clash

1

with, Shoemaker Arnold would not be the one. To him, the world was his shoemaker shop. There he was master and anyone entering would have to surrender not only to his opinion on shoes and leather and shoemaker apprentices, but to his views on politics, women, religion, flying objects, or any of the myriad subjects he decided to discourse upon, so that over the years he had arrived at a position where none of the villagers bothered to dispute him, and to any who dared maintain a view contrary to the one he was affirming, he was quick to point out, 'This place is mine. Here, I do as I please. I say what I want. Who don't like it, the door is open.'

His wife had herself taken that advice many years earlier, and had moved not only out of his house but out of the village, taking with her their three children, leaving him with his opinions, an increasing taste for alcohol, and the tedium of having to prepare his own meals. It is possible that he would have liked to take one of the village girls to live with him, but he was too proud to accept that he had even that need, and he would look at the girls go by outside his shop, hiding, behind his dissatisfied scowl a fine, appraising, if not lecherous, eye; but if one of them happened to look in, he would snarl at her, 'What you want here?' So that between him and the village girls there existed this teasing challenging relationship of antagonism and desire, the girls themselves walking with greater flourish and style when they went past his shoemaker shop, swinging their backsides and cutting their eyes, and he, scowling, dissatisfied.

With the young men of the village his relationship was no better. As far as he was concerned none of them wanted to work and he had no intention of letting them use his shoemaker shop as a place to loiter. Over the years he had taken on numerous apprentices, keeping them for a month or two and sometimes for just a single day, then getting rid of them; and it was not until Norbert came to work with him that he had had what could be considered regular help.

Norbert, however, was no boy. He was a drifter, a rum drinker, and exactly that sort of person that one did not expect Arnold to tolerate for more than five minutes. Norbert teased the girls, was chummy with the loiterers, gambled, drank too much, and, anytime the spirit moved him, would up and take off and not return for as much as a month. Arnold always accepted him back. Of course he quarrelled, he complained, but the villagers who heard him were firm in their reply: 'Man, you like it. You like Norbert going and coming when he please, doing what he want. You like it.'

More than his leavings, Norbert would steal Arnold's money, sell a pair of shoes, lose a side of shoes, charge people and pocket the money, not charge some people at all, and do every other form of wickedness to be imagined in the circumstances. It must have been that because Norbert was so indisputably in the wrong that it moved Arnold to exhibit one of his rare qualities, compassion. It was as if Arnold needed Norbert as the means through which to declare not only to the world, but to declare to himself, that he had such a quality; to prove to himself that he was not the cantankerous person people made him out to be. So, on those occasions when he welcomed back the everlasting prodigal, Arnold, forgiving and compassionate, would be imbued with the idea of his own goodness, and he would feel that in the world, truly, there was not a more generous soul than he.

Today was one such day. Two weeks before Christmas, Norbert had left 6 to go for a piece of ice over by the rumshop a few yards away. He had returned the day before. 'Yes,' thought Arnold, 'look at me, I not vex.' Arnold was glad for the help, for he had work that people had already paid advances on and would be coming in to collect before New Year's day. That was one thing he appreciated about Norbert. Norbert was faithful, but Norbert had to get serious about the right things. He was faithful in too many frivolous things. He was faithful to the girl who dropped in and wanted a dress, to a friend who wanted a nip. A friend would pass in a truck and say, 'Norbert, we going San Fernando.' Norbert would put down the shoes he was repairing, jump on the truck without a change of underwear even, and go. It wasn't rum. It was some craziness, something inside him that just took hold of him. Sometimes, a week later he would return, grimy, stale, thin, as if he had just hitch-hiked around the world in a coal bin, slip into the shop, sit down and go back to work as if nothing out of the way had happened. And he could work when he was working. Norbert could work. Any shop in Port of Spain would be glad to have him. Faithful worker. Look at that! This week when most tradesmen had already closed up for Christmas there was Norbert working like a machine to get people's shoes ready. Appreciation. It shows appreciation. People don't have appreciation again, but Norbert had appreciation. Is how you treat people, he thought. You have to understand them. Look how cool he here working in my shoemaker shop this big Old Year's day when all over the island people feteing.

At the door he was watching two girls going down the street, nice, 7 young, with the spirit of rain and breezes about them. Then his eyes picked up a donkey cart approaching slowly from the direction of the Main Road which led to Sangre Grande, and he stood there in front his shoemaker shop, his lips pulled back and looked at the cart come up and go past. Old Man Moses, the charcoal burner, sat dozing in the front, his chin on his chest, and the reins in his lap. To the back sat a small boy with a cap on and a ragged shirt, his eyes alert, his feet hanging over the sides of the cart, one hand resting on a small brown and white dog sitting next to him.

Place dead, he thought, seeing the girls returning; and, looking up at the 8 sky, he saw the dark clouds and that it was going to rain and he looked at the cart. 'Moses going up in the bush. Rain going to soak his tail,' he said. And as if suddenly irritated by that thought, he said, 'You mean Moses aint have no family he could spend New Year's by,' his tone drumming up his outrage. 'Why his family can't take him in and let him eat and drink and be merry for the New Year instead of going up in the bush for rain to soak his tail? That is how we living in this world,' he said, seating himself on the workbench and reaching for the shoe to be repaired. 'That is how we living. Like beast.'

'Maybe he want to go up in the bush,' Norbert said. 'Maybe he going to attend his coal pit, to watch it that the coals don't burn up and turn powder.' 9

'Like blasted beast,' Arnold said. 'Beast,' as if he had not heard Norbert. 10

But afterwards, after he had begun to work, had gotten into the rhythm of sewing and cutting and pounding leather, and had begun the soft firm waxing of the twine, the sense of the approaching New Year hit him and he thought of the girls and the rain, and he thought of his own life and his loneliness and his drinking and of the world and of people, people without families, on pavements and in orphanages and those on park benches below trees. 'The world have to check up on itself,' he said. 'The world have to check up. . . . And you, Norbert, you have to check up on yourself,' he said broaching for the first time the matter of Norbert's leaving two weeks before Christmas and returning only yesterday. 'I not against you. You know I not against you. I talk because I know what life is. I talk because I know about time. Time is all we have, boy. Time. . . . A Time to live and a time to die. You hear what I say, Norbert?' 11

'What you say?' 12

'I say, it have a time to live and a time to die. . . . You think we living?' 13

Norbert leaned his head back a little, and for a few moments he seemed to be gazing into space, thinking, concentrating. 14

'We dying,' he said, 'we dying no arse.' 15

'You damn right. Rum killing us. Rum. Not bombs or Cancer or something sensible. Rum. You feel rum should kill you?' 16

Norbert drew the twine out of the stitch and smiled. 17

'But in this place, rum must kill you. What else here could kill a man? What else to do but drink and waste and die. That is why I talk. People don't understand me when I talk; but that is why I talk.' 18

Norbert threaded the twine through the stitch with his smile and in one hand he held the shoe and with the other he drew out the twine: 'We dying no arse!' as if he had hit on some truth to be treasured now. 'We dying . . . no arse.' 19

'That is why I talk, I want us . . . you to check up, to put a little oil in your lamp, to put a little water in your wine.' 20

Norbert laughed. He was thinking with glee, even as he said it, 'We dying no arse, all o'we, everybody. Ha ha ha ha,' and he took up his hammer and started to pound in the leather over the stitch 'Ha ha ha ha ha!' 21

Arnold had finished the shoe he was repairing and he saw now the pile of shoes in the shoemaker shop. 'One day I going to sell out all the shoes that people leave here. They hurry hurry for you to repair them. You use 22 leather, twine, nails, time. You use time, and a year later, the shoes still here watching you. Going to sell out every blasted one of them this New Year.'

'All o'we, every one of us,' Norbert chimed.   23

'That is why this shoemaker shop always like a junk heap.'   24

'Let us send for a nip of rum, nuh,' Norbert said, and as Arnold looked   25
at him, 'I will buy. This is Old Year's, man.'

'Rum?' Arnold paused. 'How old you is, boy?'   26

'Twenty-nine.'   27

'Twenty-nine! You making joke. You mean I twenty-one years older   28
than you? We dying in truth. Norbert, we dying. Boy, life really mash you
up.' And he threw down the shoe he was going to repair.

'We have three more shoes that people coming for this evening,' Nor-   29
bert said, cautioning. 'Corbie shoes, Synto shoes and Willie Paul sandals.'

Arnold leaned and picked up the shoe again. 'Life aint treat you good at   30
all. I is twenty-one years older than you? Norbert, you have to check up,'
he said. 'Listen, man, you getting me frighten. When I see young fellars
like you in his condition I does get frighten. . . . Listen. Norbert, tell me
something! I looking mash up like you? Eh? Tell me the truth. I looking
mash up like you?'

Norbert said, 'We dying no arse, all o'we everybody.'   31

'No. Serious. Tell me, I looking mash up like you?'   32

'Look, somebody by the door,' Norbert said.   33

'What you want?' Arnold snapped. It was one of the village girls, a   34
plump one with a bit of her hair plastered down over her forehead making
her look like a fat pony.

'You don't have to shout at me, you know. I come for Synto shoes.'   35

'Well, I don't want no loitering by the door. Come inside and siddown   36
and wait. I now finishing it.' He saw her turn to look outside and she said
something to somebody. 'Somebody there with you?'

'She don't want to come in.'   37

'Let her come in too. I don't want no loitering by the door. This is a   38
business place.' He called out, 'Come in. What you hanging back for?'

The girl who came in was the one that reminded him of rain and moss   39
and leaves. He tried to look away from her, but he couldn't. And she too
was looking at him.

'You 'fraid me?' And he didn't know how his voice sounded, though at   40
that moment he thought he wanted it to sound tough.

'A little,' she said.   41

'Siddown,' he said, and Norbert's eyes nearly popped open. What was   42
he seeing? Arnold was getting up and taking the chair from the corner,
dusting it too. 'Sit down. The shoes will finish just now.'

She watched him work on the shoe and the whole shoemaker shop was   43
big like all space and filled with breathlessness and rain and moss and
green leaves.

'You is Synto daughter?'   44
'Niece,' she said.   45

And when he was finished repairing the shoes, he looked around for a   46
paper bag in which to put them, because he saw that she had not come
with any bag herself. 'When you coming for shoes you must bring something to wrap it in. You can't go about with shoes in your hand just so.'

'Yes,' she said. 'Yes.' Quickly as if wanting to please him.   47

He found some old newspaper he was saving to read when he had time   48
and he folded the shoes in it and wrapped it with twine and he gave it to
her and she took it and she said 'thank you' with that funny little face and
that voice that made something inside him ache and she left, leaving the
breathlessness in the shoemaker shop and the scent of moss and aloes and
leaves and it was like if all his work was finished. And when he caught his
breath he pushed his hand in his pocket and brought out money and said
to Norbert, 'Go and buy a nip.' And they drank the nip, the two of them,
and he asked Norbert, 'Where you went when you went for the ice?' And
he wasn't really listening for no answer, for he had just then understood
how Norbert could, how a man could, leave and go off. He had just
understood how he could leave everything and go just so.

'You had a good time?' Though those weren't the right words. A good   49
time! People didn't leave for a good time. It was for something more. It was
out of something deeper, a call, something that was awakened in the
blood, the mind. 'You know what I mean?'

'Yes,' Norbert said, kinda sadly, soft, and frightened for Arnold but not   50
wanting to show it.

Arnold said, 'I dying too.' And then he stood up and said sort of sud-   51
den, 'This place need some pictures. And we must keep paper bags like in
a real "establishment",' and with that same smile he said, 'Look at that, eh.
That girl say she 'fraid me a little. Yes, I suppose that is correct. A little. Not
that she 'fraid me. She 'fraid me a little.'

When they closed the shop that evening they both went up Tapana   52
Trace by Britto. Britto was waiting for them.

'Ah,' he said, 'Man reach. Since before Christmas I drinking and I can't   53
get drunk. It aint have man to drink rum with again. But I see man now.'

They went inside and Britto cleared the table and put three bottles of   54
rum on it, one before each one of them, a mug of water and a glass each,
and they began to drink.

Half an hour later the *parang* band came in and they sang an *aguanaldo*   55
and a *joropo* and they drank and Norbert started to sing with them the nice
festive Spanish music that made Arnold wish he could cry. And then it was
night and the *parang* band was still there and Britto wife family came in and
a couple of Britto friends and the women started dancing with the little
children and then Josephine, Britto neighbour, held on to Arnold and
pulled him onto the floor to dance, and he tried to dance a little and then
he sat down and they took down the gas lamp and pumped it and Britto's

wife brought out the portion of *lappe* that she had been cooking on a wood fire in the yard and they ate and drank and with the music and the children and the women, everything, the whole thing was real sweet. It was real sweet. And Norbert, more drunk than sober, sitting in a corner chatting down Clemencia sister picked up another bottle of rum, broke the seal and about to put it to his lips, caught Arnold's eye and hesitated, then he put it to his lips again. He said, 'Let me dead.' And Arnold sat and thought about this girl, the one that filled the world with breathlessness and the scent of aloes and leaves and moss and he felt if she was sitting there beside him he would be glad to dead too.

STUDY QUESTIONS

1. What are Shoemaker Arnold's personality traits at the story's beginning? Describe his situation.
2. Who is Norbert? What is his philosophy of life?
3. Discuss Shoemaker Arnold's relationship with Norbert. How does Norbert influence Shoemaker Arnold's behavior?
4. Discuss the ending.

 V. S. NAIPAUL

V. S. Naipaul (b. 1932), the most prolific writer from the West Indies, occupies an important place in contemporary literature as an interpreter of colonial and postcolonial experience. East Indian by descent, he was born and grew up in Trinidad. At age eighteen he emigrated to England and attended Oxford University. Upon graduation, he worked as a radio broadcaster for the BBC and wrote book reviews for The New Statesman. *After a few years, he gave up regular employment and devoted all of his energies to writing and traveling. Journeying back and forth between England and the Caribbean, Latin America, India, Africa, and the United States, Naipaul developed a global consciousness that became the underlying foundation of much of his journalism and fiction. Over time his reputation as a writer grew, and increasingly he assumed the role of interpreter of the Third World for the West, although this role and his artistic vision have been contested. Naipaul is universally recognized as a major literary talent, and there is a consensus that his early novels* A House for Mr. Biswas *(1961) and* The Mimic Men *(1967) have made a significant contribution to an understanding of the human predicament in colonial and postcolonial societies. The growing cynicism,*

desolation, and nihilism of his later books and the fact that he saves his fiercest invective for the postcolonial governments and regimes of emerging Third World nations has raised serious questions. For many, he is merely confirming preexisting stereotypes and senselessly distorting the genuine attempts of non-Western societies to achieve self-sufficiency and decency. For others, his value lies in the unveiling of disturbing truths and the challenge that comes from his provocative revelations. The autobiographical story ''The Pyrotechnicist'' looks back at a colonial society that distorted the individual's quest for a meaningful existence. At the same time, it celebrates the energy and effort of those who struggle for recognition despite social deprivation.

The Pyrotechnicist

A stranger could drive through Miguel Street and just say 'Slum!' because he could see no more. But we, who lived there, saw our street as a world, where everybody was quite different from everybody else. Man-man was mad; George was stupid; Big Foot was a bully; Hat was an adventurer; Popo was a philosopher; and Morgan was our comedian. 1

Or that was how we looked upon him. But, looking back now after so many years, I think he deserved a lot more respect than we gave him. It was his own fault, of course. He was one of those men who deliberately set out to clown and wasn't happy unless people were laughing at him, and he was always thinking of new crazinesses which he hoped would amuse us. He was the sort of man who, having once created a laugh by sticking the match in his mouth and trying to light it with his cigarette, having once done that, does it over and over again. 2

Hat used to say, 'Is a damn nuisance, having that man trying to be funny all the time, when all of us well know that he not so happy at all.' 3

I felt that sometimes Morgan knew his jokes were not coming off, and that made him so miserable that we all felt unkind and nasty. 4

Morgan was the first artist I ever met in my life. He spent nearly all his time, even when he was playing the fool, thinking about beauty. Morgan made fireworks. He loved fireworks, and he was full of theories about fireworks. Something about the Cosmic Dance or the Dance of Life. But this was the sort of talk that went clean over our heads in Miguel Street. And when Morgan saw this, he would begin using even bigger words. Just for the joke. One of the big words I learnt from Morgan is the title of this sketch. 5

But very few people in Trinidad used Morgan's fireworks. All the big fêtes in the island passed—Races, Carnival, Discovery Day, the Indian Centenary—and while the rest of the island was going crazy with rum and music and pretty women by the sea, Morgan was just going crazy with rage. 6

Morgan used to go to the Savannah and watch the fireworks of his 7
rivals, and hear the cheers of the crowd as the fireworks spattered and
spangled the sky. He would come in a great temper and beat all his children. He had ten of them. His wife was too big for him to beat.

Hat would say, 'We better send for the fire-brigade.' 8

And for the next two or three hours Morgan would prowl in a stupid 9
sort of way around his back-yard, letting off fireworks so crazily that we
used to hear his wife shouting, 'Morgan, stop playing the ass. You make
ten children and you have a wife, and you can't afford to go and dead
now.'

Morgan would roar like a bull and beat on the galvanized-iron fence. 10

He would shout, 'Everybody want to beat me. Everybody.' 11

Hat said, 'You know we hearing the real Morgan now.' 12

These fits of craziness made Morgan a real terror. When the fits were on 13
him, he had the idea that Bhakcu, the mechanical genius who was my
uncle, was always ready to beat him, and at about eleven o'clock in the
evenings, the idea just seemed to explode in his head.

He would beat on the fence and shout, 'Bhakcu, you fat-belly good-for- 14
nothing son-of-a-bitch, come out and fight like a man.'

Bhakcu would keep on reading the *Ramayana*, in his doleful singing 15
voice; lying flat on his belly on his bed.

Bhakcu was a big man, and Morgan was a very small man, with the 16
smallest hands and the thinnest wrists in Miguel Street.

Mrs Bhakcu would say, 'Morgan, why you don't shut up and go to 17
sleep?'

Mrs Morgan would reply, 'Hey, you thin-foot woman! You better leave 18
my husband alone, you hear. Why you don't look after your own?'

Mrs Bhakcu would say, 'You better mind your mouth. Otherwise I come 19
up and turn your face with one slap, you hear.'

Mrs Bhakcu was four feet high, three feet wide, and three feet deep. Mrs 20
Morgan was a little over six foot tall and built like a weight-lifter.

Mrs Morgan said, 'Why you don't get your big-belly husband to go and 21
fix some more motor-car, and stop reading that damn stupid sing-song he
always sing-songing?'

By this time Morgan would be on the pavement with us, laughing in a 22
funny sort of way, saying, 'Hear them women and them!' He would drink
some rum from a hip-flask and say, 'Just watch and see. You know the
calypso?

> The more they try to do me bad
> Is the better I live in Trinidad

Time so next year, I go have the King of England and the King of America 23
paying me millions to make fireworks for them. The most beautiful fireworks anybody ever see.

And Hat or somebody else would ask, 'You go make the fireworks for them?' 24

Morgan would say, 'Make *what*? Make nothing. By this time so next year, I go have the King of England the King of America paying me millions to make fireworks for them. The most beautiful fireworks anybody ever see.' 25

And, in the meantime, in the back of the yard, Mrs Bhakcu was saying, '*He* have big belly. But what yours have? I don't know what yours going to sit on next year this time, you hear.' 26

And next morning Morgan was as straight and sober as ever, talking about his experiments. 27

This Morgan was more like a bird than a man. It was not only that he was as thin as a match-stick. He had a long neck that could swivel like a bird's. His eyes were bright and restless. And when he spoke it was in a pecking sort of way, as though he was not throwing out words, but picking up corn. He walked with a quick, tripping step, looking back over his shoulder at somebody following who wasn't there. 28

Hat said, 'You know how he get so? Is his wife, you know. He fraid she too bad. Spanish woman, you know. Full of blood and fire.' 29

Boyee said, 'You suppose that is why he want to make fireworks so?' 30

Hat said, 'People funny like hell. You never know with them.' 31

But Morgan used to make a joke of even his appearance, flinging out his arms and feet when he knew people were looking at him. 32

Morgan also made fun of his wife and his ten children. 'Is a miracle to me,' he said, 'that a man like me have ten children. I don't know how I manage it.' 33

Edward said, 'How you sure is your children?' 34

Morgan laughed, and said, 'I have my doubts.' 35

Hat didn't like Morgan. He said, 'Is hard to say. But it have something about him I can't really take. I always feel he overdoing everything. I always feel the man lying about everything. I feel that he even lying to hisself.' 36

I don't think any of us understood what Hat meant. Morgan was becoming a little too troublesome, and it was hard for all of us to begin smiling as soon as we saw him, which was what he wanted. 37

Still his firework experiments continued; and every now and then we heard an explosion from Morgan's house, and we saw the puffs of coloured smoke. This was one of the standing amusements of the street. 38

But as time went by and Morgan found that no one was willing to buy his fireworks, he began to make fun even of his fireworks. He was not content with the laughter of the street when there was an explosion in his house. 39

Hat said, 'When a man start laughing at something he fight for all the 40 time, you don't know whether to laugh or cry.' And Hat decided that Morgan was just a fool.

I suppose it was because of Hat that we decided not to laugh at Morgan any more. 41

Hat said, 'It go make him stop playing the fool.' 42

But it didn't. 43

Morgan grew wilder than ever, and began challenging Bhakcu to fight about two or three times a week. He began beating his children more than ever. 44

And he made one last attempt to make us laugh. 45

I heard about it from Chris, Morgan's fourth son. We were in the café at the corner of Miguel Street. 46

Chris said, 'Is a crime to talk to you now, you know.' 47

I said, 'Don't tell me. Is the old man again?' 48

Chris nodded and he showed me a sheet of paper, headed CRIME AND PUNISHMENT. 49

Chris said with pride, 'Look at it.' 50

It was a long list, with entries like this: 51

For fighting	i) at home	Five strokes
	ii) in the street	Seven strokes
	iii) at school	Eight strokes

Chris looked at me and said in a very worried way, 'It funny like hell, eh? This sort of thing make blows a joke.' 52

I said yes, and asked, 'But you say is a crime to talk to me. Where it is?' 53

Chris showed me: 54

| For talking to street rabs | Four strokes |
| For playing with street rabs | Eight strokes |

I said, 'But your father don't mind talking to us. What wrong if you talk to us?' 55

Chris said, 'But this ain't nothing at all. You must come on Sunday and see what happen.' 56

I could see that Chris was pleased as anything. 57

About six of us went that Sunday. Morgan was there to meet us and he took us into his drawing room. Then he disappeared. There were many chairs and benches as though there was going to be a concert. Morgan's eldest son was standing at a little table in the corner. 58

Suddenly this boy said, 'Stand!' 59

We all stood up, and Morgan appeared, smiling all round. 60

I asked Hat, 'Why he smiling so?' 61

Hat said, 'That is how the magistrates and them does smile when they come in court.' 62

Morgan's eldest son shouted, 'Andrew Morgan!' 63

Andrew Morgan came and stood before his father. 64

The eldest boy read very loudly, 'Andrew Morgan, you are charged with   65
stoning the tamarind tree in Miss Dorothy's yard; you are charged with
ripping off three buttons for the purpose of purchasing some marbles; you
are charged with fighting Dorothy Morgan; you are charged with stealing
two *tolums* and three sugar-cakes. Do you plead guilty or not guilty?'

Andrew said, 'Guilty.'   66

Morgan, scribbling on a sheet of paper, looked up.   67

'Have you anything to say?'   68

Andrew said, 'I sorry, sir.'   69

Morgan said, 'We will let the sentences run concurrently. Twelve   70
strokes.'

One by one, the Morgan children were judged and sentenced. Even the   71
eldest boy had to receive some punishment.

Morgan then rose and said, 'These sentences will be carried out this   72
afternoon.'

He smiled all round, and left the room.   73

The joke misfired completely.   74

Hat said, 'Nah, nah, man, you can't make fun of your own self and your   75
own children that way, and invite all the street to see. Nah, it ain't right.'

I felt the joke was somehow terrible and frightening.   76

And when Morgan came out on the pavement that evening, his face   77
fixed in a smile, he got none of the laughter he had expected. Nobody ran
up to him and clapped him on the back, saying, 'But this man Morgan
really mad, you hear. You hear how he beating his children these
days . . . ?' No one said anything like that. No one said anything to him.

It was easy to see he was shattered.   78

Morgan got really drunk that night and challenged everybody to fight.   79
He even challenged me.

Mrs Morgan had padlocked the front gate, so Morgan could only run   80
about in his yard. He was as mad as a mad bull, bellowing and butting at
the fence. He kept saying over and over again, 'You people think I not a
man, eh? My father had eight children. I is his son. I have ten. I better than
all of you put together.'

Hat said, 'He soon go start crying and then he go sleep.'   81

But I spent a lot of time that night before going to sleep thinking about   82
Morgan, feeling sorry for him because of that little devil he had inside him.
For that was what I thought was wrong with him. I fancied that inside him
was a red, grinning devil pricking Morgan with his fork.

Mrs Morgan and the children went to the country.   83

Morgan no longer came out to the pavement, seeking our company. He   84
was busy with his experiments. There were a series of minor explosions
and lots of smoke.

Apart from that, peace reigned in our end of Miguel Street.   85

I wondered what Morgan was doing and thinking in all that solitude.   86

The following Sunday it rained heavily, and everyone was forced to go   87
to bed early. The street was wet and glistening, and by eleven there was no
noise save for the patter of the rain on the corrugated-iron roofs.

A short, sharp shout cracked through the street, and got us up.   88

I could hear windows being flung open, and I heard people saying,   89
'What happen? What happen?'

'Is Morgan. Is Morgan. Something happening by Morgan.'   90

I was already out in the street and in front of Morgan's house. I never   91
slept in pyjamas. I wasn't in that class.

The first thing I saw in the darkness of Morgan's yard was the figure of   92
a woman hurrying away from the house to the back gate that opened on to
the sewage trace between Miguel Street and Alfonso Street.

It was drizzling now, not very hard, and in no time at all quite a crowd   93
had joined me.

It was all a bit mysterious—the shout, the woman disappearing, the   94
dark house.

Then we heard Mrs Morgan shouting, 'Teresa Blake, Teresa Blake, what   95
you doing with my man?' It was a cry of great pain.

Mrs Bhakcu was at my side. 'I always know about this Teresa, but I keep   96
my mouth shut.'

Bhakcu said, 'Yes, you know everything, like your mother.'   97

A light came on in the house.   98

Then it went off again.   99

We heard Mrs Morgan saying, 'Why you fraid the light so for? Ain't you   100
is man? Put the light on, let we see the great big man you is.'

The light went on; then off again.   101

We heard Morgan's voice, but it was so low we couldn't make out what   102
he was saying.

Mrs Morgan said, 'Yes, hero.' And the light came on again.   103

We heard Morgan mumbling again.   104

Mrs Morgan said, 'No, hero.'   105

The light went off; then it went on.   106

Mrs Morgan was saying, 'Leave the light on. Come, let we show the big   107
big hero to the people in the street. Come, let we show them what man
really make like. You is not a anti-man, you is real man. You ain't only
make ten children with me, you going to make more with somebody else.'

We heard Morgan's voice, a fluting unhappy thing.   108

Mrs Morgan said, 'But what you fraid now for? Ain't you is the funny   109
man? The clown? Come, let them see the clown and the big man you is. Let
them see what man really make like.'

Morgan was wailing by this time, and trying to talk.   110

Mrs Morgan was saying, 'If you try to put that light off, I break up your   111
little thin tail like a match-stick here, you hear.'

Then the front door was flung open, and we saw.   112

Mrs Morgan was holding up Morgan by his waist. He was practically   113
naked, and he looked so thin, he was like a boy with an old man's face. He
wasn't looking at us, but at Mrs Morgan's face, and he was squirming in
her grasp, trying to get away. But Mrs Morgan was a strong woman.

Mrs Morgan was looking not at us, but at the man in her arm.   114

She was saying, 'But this is the big man I have, eh? So this is the man   115
I married and slaving all my life for?' And then she began laughing, in a
croaking, nasty way.

She looked at us for a moment, and said, 'Well, laugh now. He don't   116
mind. He always want people to laugh at him.'

And the sight was so comic, the thin man held up so easily by the fat   117
woman, that we did laugh. It was the sort of laugh that begins gently and
then builds up into a bellowing belly laugh.

For the first time since he came to Miguel Street, Morgan was really   118
being laughed at by the people.

And it broke him completely.   119

All the next day we waited for him to come out to the pavement, to   120
congratulate him with our laughter. But we didn't see him.

Hat said, 'When I was little, my mother used to tell me, "Boy, you   121
laughing all day. I bet you, you go cry tonight." '

That night my sleep was again disturbed. By shouts and sirens.   122

I looked through the window and saw a red sky and red smoke.   123

Morgan's house was on fire.   124

And what a fire! Photographers from the papers were climbing up into   125
other people's houses to get their pictures, and people were looking at
them and not at the fire. Next morning there was a first-class picture with
me part of the crowd in the top right-hand corner.

But what a fire it was! It was the most beautiful fire in Port of Spain since   126
1933 when the Treasury (of all places) burnt down, and the calypsonian
sang:

> It was a glorious and a beautiful scenery
> Was the burning of the Treasury.

What really made the fire beautiful was Morgan's fireworks going off.   127
Then for the first time everybody saw the astonishing splendour of Morgan's fireworks. People who used to scoff at Morgan felt a little silly. I have
travelled in many countries since, but I have seen nothing to beat the
fireworks show in Morgan's house that night.

But Morgan made no more fireworks.   128

Hat said, 'When I was a little boy, my mother used to say, "If a man   129
want something, and he want it really bad, he does get it, but when he get
it he don't like it." '

Both of Morgan's ambitions were fulfilled. People laughed at him, and   130 they still do. And he made the most beautiful fireworks in the world. But as Hat said, when a man gets something he wants badly, he doesn't like it.

As we expected, the thing came out in court. Morgan was charged with arson. The newspaper people had a lot of fun with Morgan, within the libel laws. One headline I remember: PYROTECHNICIST ALLEGED PYROMANIAC. 131

But I was glad, though, that Morgan got off. 132

They said Morgan went to Venezuela. They said he went mad. They said he became a jockey in Colombia. They said all sorts of things, but the people of Miguel Street were always romancers. 133

STUDY QUESTIONS

1. What does the author in "The Pyrotechnicist" find exciting about the world he grew up in? Does he break down stereotypes about the poor and marginalized or does he further them?
2. What is remarkable about Morgan? Why is making fireworks so important to him? What accounts for his fits of craziness and terror? Why is he defeated after the explosion in his house?
3. How does the community view Morgan? Does its attitude toward him change?

THEMATIC QUESTIONS

1. The European conquest and its effect on Native American life is an important theme in Latin American literature. Discuss how it is portrayed in the selections by Castellanos, Paz, and Allende.
2. Using the selections by Ramírez and Ferré, discuss how Latin American writers use the United States as a literary theme.
3. How do Borges and Vargas Llosa portray male identity? Discuss the differences and similarities in their treatment.
4. Discuss how García Márquez and Allende use magic realism as a literary technique for revealing social and historical reality.
5. The stories by V. S. Naipaul and Earl Lovelace depict lives of the marginal and the disadvantaged. Discuss their social vision.
6. An important theme in Caribbean literature is the search for cultural identity. Explain how it is treated in the selections by Guillén, Walcott, and Kincaid.
7. In what ways do "I'm Your Horse in the Night" and "Microbus to San Salvador" confront the terror of right-wing totalitarian governments?
8. How does the politically engaged poetry of Neruda, Vallejo, and Guillén reflect a common vision? Discuss and cite examples.
9. In what ways is Isabel Allende's "Phantom Palace" similar to Julio Cortázar's "House Taken Over"? How do they differ?
10. Discuss how Carlos Drummond de Andrade and Clarice Lispector portray the human condition in modern society.

NORTH AMERICA

NORTH AMERICA

Introduction

Geographically speaking, North America is composed of three nations: the United States of America, Canada, and Mexico. However, Mexico's linguistic and cultural ties with the rest of Latin America suggest its inclusion in that section; "North America" here will indicate only Canada and the United States. Indeed, these two countries alone cover a landmass of over three and a half million square miles and almost four million square miles, respectively. Canada shares a border of 5,500 miles with the United States. To the south, the United States has a shorter border with its only other land neighbor, Mexico.

The United States is the fourth largest country in the world, and the fourth most populous, with about 250 million people. Its size, regional diversity, and natural resources, encompassing a landmass from the Atlantic to the Pacific oceans and from the Gulf of Mexico to the Bering Straits, and its long political stability have made the country one of the most powerful nations in the history of the world. Its economic and military strength has also resulted in the influence and dispersion of U.S. political and cultural ideologies throughout the globe. Yet the country is unevenly developed, and even within local regions striking differences in living standards exist.

Since the Civil War (1861–1865), the United States has remained a fairly stable union of states; in the twentieth century, five more states joined the union, including Hawaii and Alaska in 1959, to make a total of fifty. Throughout the twentieth century, beginning especially with the Spanish-American War (1898), in which it acquired Cuba and the Philippines, the United States has moved

NORTH AMERICA

Scale

0   500 M

0   500 KM

Legend

● Capitals
○ Cities
∧ Mountains

from an isolationist position to an international leadership role in world affairs. A post–World War II period of economic expansion resulted in confidence, prosperity, and, some critics say, cultural stagnation in the fifties. Although not faced with an immediate military threat, the United States was engaged in an ideological struggle that pitted its democratic capitalist system against the totalitarian Communist system of the Soviet Union, its rival for world dominance. The ideological conflict, known as the Cold War, drew the United States into military engagements in Asia—in Korea in the 1950s and Vietnam in the 1960s.

The 1960s are generally remembered for the civil unrest created by dissension over the U.S. military conflict in Vietnam. A small Southeast Asian country, Vietnam had been fighting a war of national liberation, led by Communists, against the French in the 1950s, when the U.S. government under President John F. Kennedy entered the conflict. Arguing that the West should intervene to prevent the country from being overtaken by the Communists, the U.S. government quickly escalated troop levels. By the time the United States withdrew its forces in 1973, 58,000 U.S. soldiers had been killed.

The Civil Rights movement also added to the ferment of the sixties. Protests against segregation laws and other forms of race discrimination in the 1950s and '60s headed by African American leaders such as Martin Luther King, Jr., and Malcolm X led to legislation removing overt racial discrimination in U.S. society. The African American struggle for full human rights was picked up by other minorities and by women in the 1970s, resulting in a contemporary cultural sensitivity to issues of diversity and pluralism.

The 1970s, however, were also years of severe economic problems, arising in part from an increase in oil prices that produced deficits and international trade imbalance. The U.S. industrial machine was also beginning to slow down even as it faced increasing competition from nations such as Japan and Germany.

United States literature in the twentieth century is an extremely complex and contradictory set of phenomena reflecting the increasing commodification of books, a growing literate and middle-class audience willing to be tutored by elitist gatekeepers, and the evolution of subgroups that advanced counterhegemonic expressions, techniques, and materials. The mass marketing of popular literature, as in westerns, thrillers, harlequin romances, and horror tales, is highly developed for a consumer market. Middle-class-approved reading was reinforced by the establishment of book clubs and franchised bookstores that followed the middle class move to the suburbs from the 1950s onward. The questioning of authority, of social conventions and standards, as seen in the civil rights, free speech, and feminist movements, resulted in, among other things, a rethinking of the canon of U.S. literature.

Generally, this revisionism has led to modifications in the predominantly white and male representation in traditional U.S. literary curricula to include more writing by women and by ethnic citizens. Canon revision follows a shift in position in critical readings, from a valuation of literature as aesthetic and universal to one that reads it as based on material circumstances, historically contextualized, and embedded in ideological positionings.

Twentieth-century United States literature, therefore, is marked by ferment exhibited in shifts and innovations in techniques, styles, and genres, incorporation of themes and materials once thought nonliterary, and the appearance of regional and ethnic and gender-identified writings that interrogate the notion of mainstream, masculine, and European-dominant cultures, features that are often thought of as elements of modernism.

The early part of the twentieth century (1910–1945) saw the assertion of the individual in a struggle against forms of social authority. This modernistic theme often went together with narrative strategies associated with realism, an earlier method of fiction that emphasized literature as imitation, creating simulacra that approximate to the observable physical and sensate world. Later writers such as John Cheever and John Updike, even as they portrayed characters at odds with their social surroundings, employed realism to achieve their effects and themes. Much contemporary United States and Canadian literature is still written within the traditions of realism.

We think of the contemporary United States as being in a period after the energies of modernism seem to have been spent, after the idealism of the post–World War II era foundered on the disillusionment of U.S. military misadventures in Asia in the fifties and sixties. In literary studies, the term "postmodern" signifies a rejection of the privileged position of literary texts, including the position of the author as a stable and knowable subject undergirding social constructs of identity. The postmodernist emphasis on indeterminate discourses, forms of writing without clearly marked structures that help guide readers' responses and interpretations, is sometimes set up in opposition to the contemporary claims of ethnic and feminist writers who articulate race and gender identity politics in their work. The overt political themes and community portrayals in the poems of Carolyn Forché and Rita Dove, for example, assume an urgent presence of the subject and of determined relations to sociopolitical realities that a postmodernist sensibility would question. On the other hand, the postmodernist emphasis on incongruity, inconsistency, and instability of narrative positions can be read as approximate or sympathetic to many stylistic features of postcolonial writing that, coming from multicultural impacted societies, exhibited hybrid expressive features such as acute shifts in style and registers, forms of conjunctions that show gaps, breaks, or idiosyncratic seams, and the grafting of different, sometimes contradictory, traditions and forms together.

The majority of the writers in this anthology are contemporary. A few of the major figures of modern U.S. literature are represented, for they embody the traditions from which contemporary writers still draw. Thus, Wallace Stevens, William Carlos Williams, Elizabeth Bishop, and Langston Hughes are included. Wallace Stevens's rigorous aestheticism still forms one pole of U.S. poetics that later poets such as James Wright, despite their differences, ground themselves in. Williams's emphasis on the quotidian, elevation of the unpoetic, and appeal to an American mobility in scansion are still influential precepts in contemporary U.S. poetry. Elizabeth Bishop's metrical explorations parallel her treatment of human relations and conditions; a feminist before her time, Bishop rejected heterosexual constraints while observing the strictest tact in her poems. And Langston Hughes's use of African-American images, themes, and rhythms opened the way for a flowering of African-American voices.

Contemporary U.S. literature is especially provocative in its range and variety of ethnic and gendered bodies of writing. Native American, African-American, Chicano American, and Asian American writers are among the most interesting authors publishing today. They introduce themes, concerns, and narrative styles that are new to mainstream U.S. literature. Leslie Silko rewrites tribal myths and tells the story of the only nonimmigrant Americans in the nation as they have to negotiate the conflicts of cultures that form their historical conditions. Maxine Hong Kingston reimagines the American experience of Chinese immigrants in order to claim America for the Chinese Americans. African Americans such as James Baldwin and August Wilson write of the complex sociopolitical situations of African Americans before and after the civil rights movement, lives in which human dignity and desire must accommodate and are compromised by material reality: poverty, economic exploitation, physical necessity.

Rich in natural resources such as timber and various minerals, Canada is composed of ten provinces and two territories. It is bounded by three oceans, the Arctic on the north, the Pacific on the west, and the Atlantic on the east. The United States on the south (and northwest) is its only land neighbor.

Canada is often overshadowed by its richer, noisier neighbor. While it is larger in size than the United States, it has approximately one tenth of the U.S. population, 80 percent of whom live within 100 miles of the U.S. border. Proximity to the United States, a historically unequal political relation to Britain and France across the Atlantic, and the vast uninhabited tracts of the interior and north are among the factors put forward by critics to explain the relative quietism of Canadian culture up to the second half of the twentieth century.

Although Canada was largely settled by loyalists who moved north after the peace settlement in 1783 and America declared its independence from Britain, the two nations have usually cooperated with each other in trade and foreign affairs. Generally, Canada, which also has a majority of English speakers made up of immigrants who have displaced Native American peoples, is seen as sharing similar Anglo-European values and concerns with the United States.

But like the United States, Canada is undergoing tremendous social and political change. French Canadians (the French were the first to settle Canada in large numbers in the seventeenth and eighteenth centuries) make up 27 percent of the population, and their push for cultural and linguistic nationalism in the province of Quebec may yet break Canada up into a number of autonomous provinces; at any rate, it puts into question the Anglo domination of Canadian nationalism and the economy.

Canadian writers work hard to set up a distinct identity from the United States, based on the specific and local features of Canadian history and experience. Unlike the United States, which rapidly settled the Midwest and whose colonizing energies were only halted at the edge of the Pacific Ocean (Hawaii, Micronesia, Guam, and the Philippines, however, are examples of U.S. colonial expansion across the Pacific), Canadians chiefly settled along the two coasts and on the southern border. The theme of empty space, of a wilderness interior, is a continuous motif in Canadian literature. Thus, although three quarters of the population are urban dwellers, Canadian writers draw strongly on images of nature and retain their sense of human isolation before a vast physical and natural force.

Contemporary Canadian authors also distinguish themselves from the Anglo-dominant culture. Michel Tremblay, for example, situates himself as a working-class French Quebecois; even in translation, his prose maintains the vivid idioms and color of his original French dialect. Mordecai Richler and Irving Layton explore Jewish-Canadian milieus, while Joy Kogawa's poems and fictions remind us of the strong historical presence of Asians in Canadian history and culture. As Canada changes its immigration policies, from a European-biased quota, to welcome Asians, Caribbeans, and Africans, so too its literature reflects and is transformed by these different presences. Some of the shock of contemporary multiculturalism, the difficulty that an Anglo-based population faces in coming to terms with seemingly radically alien customs, can be read in Margaret Atwood's sensitive yet satirical story, "Dancing Girls."

Atwood also represents a global phenomenon that is as strong in Canada as elsewhere, that is, the emergence of writers concerned with women's ways of looking at experience. Generally described as feminist writers, authors such as Atwood give us examples of imaginations that deliberately set out to construct experience as gendered, that is, as particular to one sex. We can argue that whereas in the past much literature was read as presenting "universals," we know now that these universals of ideas and types should more appropriately be seen as coming from the experience of males and were drawn from societies in which chiefly men held power. The rise and development of the British novel was closely related to the emergence of women as authors. From Jane Austen onward, the novel as a genre was able to accommodate the growing pressure of British women to imagine their places in society. But it is only in the later half of the twentieth century that numbers of women from many different countries began to speak as their own subjects and with deliberate consciousness of their writing as women's writing. Atwood is only one representative of such women's writing in this anthology. (See the Thematic Table of Contents, under "The Woman Question.")

Although sharing close material and historical and cultural features with the United States, Canadian writers write from very different traditions. More closely tied to Britain and France, they display stylistic, linguistic, and thematic concerns that are clearly not in the vein of "American" exuberance, avant-gardism, and experimentalism. Even in their formulation of cultural marginalism, many Canadian writers' works appeal to traditions that are continuous with the traditions of continental European literary communities. At the same time, while influenced by literary movements in the United States, they attempt to delineate experiences that are specific to Canadian cultural circumstances.

Shirley Geok-lin Lim

CANADA

Irving Layton

Irving Layton (b. 1912) emigrated from Romania with his Russian-Jewish family to Canada in 1913. The author and editor of some fifty books of poetry and fiction, Layton is a major figure in Canadian literature. His many awards include the Governor General's Medal for A Red Carpet for the Sun *(1959). Layton is a controversial poet and a harsh critic of traditional Anglo-Saxon Canadian culture. His own writing has been criticized as uneven in achievement and excessive in its social attitudes. His best poems, many of which are included in* The Collected Poems of Irving Layton *(1977), are inventive in the treatment of their themes, confident in tone, complex in structure, and elegant in diction and style.*

Berry Picking

S ilently my wife walks on the still wet furze
Now darkgreen the leaves are full of metaphors
Now lit up is each tiny lamp of blueberry.
The white nails of rain have dropped and the sun is free.

And whether she bends or straightens to each bush   5
To find the children's laughter among the leaves
Her quiet hands seem to make the quiet summer hush—
Berries or children, patient she is with these.

I only vex and perplex her; madness, rage
Are endearing perhaps put down upon the page;   10
Even silence daylong and sullen can then
Enamour as restraint or classic discipline.

So I envy the berries she puts in her mouth,
The red and succulent juice that stains her lips;
I shall never taste that good to her, nor will they   15
Displease her with a thousand barbarous jests.

How they lie easily for her hand to take,
Part of the unoffending world that is hers;
Here beyond complexity she stands and stares
And leans her marvellous head as if for answers.   20

No more the easy soul my childish craft deceives
Nor the simpler one for whom yes is always yes;
No, now her voice comes to me from a far way off
Though her lips are redder than the raspberries.

STUDY QUESTIONS

1. How does "Berry Picking" construct the difference between the wife's
   relationship with the natural world—summer, berries, children—and
   her relationship with the husband?
2. Why does the speaker envy the berries that the wife puts in her mouth?
   What multiple associations does the image of eating berries suggest?
3. What does the concluding stanza say about the husband's attitude
   toward his wife and the marriage?

✳ ANNE HÉBERT

*Anne Hébert (b. 1916) is considered Canada's most important French-speaking
poet of the twentieth century. Born in Quebec, she has divided her adult life
between France and Canada and has received many of the major literary prizes
of both countries. A noted playwright and fiction writer as well as poet, she
frequently draws on themes from her Catholic childhood. She first gained
attention for poems that explore the tension between the aesthetic and the
mystical to frame either a tragic or celebratory vision. A critical attitude
toward French and Quebecois culture underlies her use of violent images and
strong, haunting symbols. She frequently uses elements of the Gothic
tradition, such as the grotesque and bizarre, to represent the violence
embedded in patriarchal societies.*

The Thin Girl

I am a thin girl
And I have lovely bones.

I take care of them
And pity them strangely.

I polish them endlessly   5
Like old metals.

Jewels and flowers
Are out of season.

One day I'll seize my lover
To make myself a silver reliquary.   10

I'll hang myself
In his absent heart's place.

Who is this
Cold and unexpected guest in you, filled space?

You walk,   15
You stir,
Each of your gestures
A frightful ornament in a bezel[1] of death.

I receive your trembling
Like a gift.   20

And sometimes,
In your breast, fixed,
I half open
My watery eyes:

Bizarre and childish dreams   25
Stir
Like green water.

---

1. *A slanting surface or bevel; the upper, faceted portion of a cut gem.*

1. Reading "The Thin Girl" as a portrayal of the eating disorder known as anorexia nervosa, discuss the speaker's attitudes toward her physical self (her "lovely bones").
2. The poem constructs a relationship between the persona of the thin girl and a "Cold and unexpected guest." What does the poem suggest about the presence of this other, this "you"?
3. The poem speaks of a lover with an "absent heart," opening up a number of other allusions to absences, such as out-of-season jewels and flowers. How can this dwelling on absence be a source of "Bizarre and childish dreams"?

❇ MORDECAI RICHLER

Mordecai Richler (b. 1923) has been called "an exile twice over"—a Jew in Canada and (for much of his life) a Canadian in London. Despite Richler's time abroad, his writing is deeply grounded in the Montreal Jewish community, where he was born and in which he spent his formative years. His fiction celebrates that nearly vanished milieu in sharply observed and often hilarious detail. Richler is best known for his novel The Apprenticeship of Duddy Kravitz *(1959), which was adapted to become the most successful Canadian movie made up to that time. His most recent novel is* Solomon Gursky Was Here *(1990).*

The Summer My Grandmother Was Supposed to Die

D r Katzman discovered the gangrene on one of his monthly visits. 'She won't last a month,' he said.   1

He said the same the second month, the third and the fourth, and now she lay dying in the heat of the back bedroom.   2

'God in heaven,' my mother said, 'what's she holding on for?'   3

The summer my grandmother was supposed to die we did not chip in with the Greenbaums to take a cottage in the Laurentians. My grandmother, already bed-ridden for seven years, could not be moved again. The doctor came twice a week. The only thing was to stay in the city and   4 wait for her to die or, as my mother said, pass away. It was a hot summer, her bedroom was just behind the kitchen, and when we sat down to eat we could smell her. The dressings on my grandmother's left leg had to be changed several times a day and, according to Dr Katzman, any day might be her last in this world. 'It's in the hands of the Almighty,' he said.

'It won't be long now,' my father said, 'and she'll be better off, if you   5
know what I mean?'

A nurse came every day from the Royal Victorian Order. She arrived   6
punctually at noon and at five to twelve I'd join the rest of the boys under the outside staircase to peek up her dress as she climbed to our second-storey flat. Miss Bailey favoured absolutely beguiling pink panties, edged with lace, and that was better than waiting under the stairs for Cousin Bessie, for instance, who wore enormous cotton bloomers, rain or shine.

I was sent out to play as often as possible, because my mother felt it was   7
not good for me to see somebody dying. Usually, I would just roam the scorched streets. There was Duddy, Gas sometimes, Hershey, Stan, Arty and me.

'Before your grandmaw kicks off,' Duddy said, 'she's going to roll her   8
eyes and gurgle. That's what they call the death-rattle.'

'Aw, you know everything. *Putz.*'   9

'I read it, you jerk,' Duddy said, whacking me one, 'in Perry Mason.'   10

Home again I would usually find my mother sour and spent. Sometimes   11
she wept.

'She's dying by inches,' she said to my father one stifling night, 'and   12
none of them ever come to see her. Oh, such children,' she added, going on to curse them vehemently in Yiddish.

'They're not behaving right. It's certainly not according to Hoyle,' my   13
father said.

Dr Katzman continued to be astonished. 'It must be will-power alone   14
that keeps her going,' he said. 'That, and your excellent care.'

'It's not my mother any more in the back room, Doctor. It's an animal.   15
I want her to die.'

'Hush. You don't mean it. You're tired.' Dr Katzman dug into his black   16
bag and produced pills for her to take. 'Your wife's a remarkable woman,' he told my father.

'You don't so say,' my father replied, embarrassed.   17

'A born nurse.'   18

My sister and I used to lie awake talking about our grandmother. 'After   19
she dies,' I said, 'her hair will go on growing for another twenty-four hours.'

'Says who?'   20

'Duddy Kravitz. Do you think Uncle Lou will come from New York for   21
the funeral?'

'I suppose so.'   22

'Boy, that means another fiver for me. Even more for you.'   23

'You shouldn't say things like that or her ghost will come back to haunt   24
you.'

'Well, I'll be able to go to her funeral anyway. I'm not too young any   25
more.'

I was only six years old when my grandfather died, and so I wasn't allowed   26
to go to his funeral.

I have one imperishable memory of my grandfather. Once he called me   27
into his study, set me down on his lap, and made a drawing of a horse for
me. On the horse he drew a rider. While I watched and giggled he gave the
rider a beard and the fur-trimmed round hat of a rabbi, a *straimel*, just like
he wore.

My grandfather had been a Zaddik, one of the Righteous, and I've been   28
assured that to study Talmud with him had been an illuminating experience. I wasn't allowed to go to his funeral, but years later I was shown the
telegrams of condolence that had come from Eire and Poland and even
Japan. My grandfather had written many books: a translation of the Book
of Splendour (the Zohar) into modern Hebrew, some twenty years work,
and lots of slender volumes of sermons, hasidic tales, and rabbinical com-
mentaries. His books had been published in Warsaw and later in New
York.

'At the funeral,' my mother said, 'they had to have six motorcycle po-   29
licemen to control the crowds. It was such a heat that twelve women
fainted—and I'm *not* counting Mrs Waxman from upstairs. With her, you
know, *anything* to fall into a man's arms. Even Pinsky's. And did I tell you
that there was even a French Canadian priest there?'

'Aw, you're kidding me.'   30

'The priest was some *knacker*. A bishop maybe. He used to study with   31
the *zeyda*. The *zeyda* was a real personality, you know. Spiritual and
worldly-wise at the same time. Such personalities they don't make any
more. Today rabbis and peanuts come in the same size.'

But, according to my father, the *zeyda* (his father-in-law) hadn't been as   32
celebrated as all that. 'There are things I could say,' he told me. 'There was
another side to him.'

My grandfather had sprung from generations and generations of rabbis,   33
his youngest son was a rabbi, but none of his grandchildren would be one.
My Cousin Jerry was already a militant socialist. I once heard him say,
'When the men at the kosher bakeries went out on strike the *zeyda* spoke
up against them on the streets and in the *shuls*.[1] It was of no consequence
to him that the men were grossly underpaid. His superstitious followers
had to have bread. Grandpappy,' Jerry said, 'was a prize reactionary.'

---

1. Shul: *A Jewish religious school.*

A week after my grandfather died my grandmother suffered a stroke. 34
Her right side was completely paralysed. She couldn't speak. At first it's
true, she could manage a coherent word or two and move her right hand
enough to write her name in Hebrew. Her name was Malka. But her
condition soon began to deteriorate.

My grandmother had six children and seven step-children, for my 35
grandfather had been married before. His first wife had died in the old
country. Two years later he had married my grandmother, the only daughter of the most affluent man in the *shtetl*,[1] and their marriage had been a
singularly happy one. My grandmother had been a beautiful girl. She had
also been a shrewd, resourceful, and patient wife. Qualities, I fear, indispensable to life with a Zaddik. For the synagogue paid my grandfather no
stipulated salary and much of the money he picked up here and there he
had habitually distributed among rabbinical students, needy immigrants
and widows. A vice, for such it was to his impecunious family, which
made him as unreliable a provider as a drinker. To carry the analogy
further, my grandmother had to make hurried, surreptitious trips to the
pawnbroker with her jewellery. Not all of it to be redeemed, either. But her
children had been looked after. The youngest, her favourite, was a rabbi in
Boston, the oldest was the actor-manager of a Yiddish theatre in New York,
and another was a lawyer. One daughter lived in Montreal, two in Toronto. My mother was the youngest daughter and when my grandmother
had her stroke there was a family conclave and it was decided that my
mother would take care of her. This was my father's fault. All the other
husbands spoke up—they protested hotly that their wives had too much
work—they could never manage it—but my father detested quarrels and so
he was silent. And my grandmother came to stay with us.

Her bedroom, the back bedroom, had actually been promised to me for 36
my seventh birthday, but now I had to go on sharing a room with my
sister. So naturally I was resentful when each morning before I left for
school my mother insisted that I go in and kiss my grandmother goodbye.

'Bouyo-bouyo,' was the only sound my grandmother could make. 37

During those first hopeful months—'Twenty years ago who would have 38
thought there'd be a cure for diabetes?' my father asked. 'Where there's
life, you know'—my grandmother would smile and try to speak, her eyes
charged with effort; and I wondered if she knew that I was waiting for her
room.

Even later there were times when she pressed my hand urgently to her 39
bosom with her surprisingly strong left arm. But as her illness dragged on
and on she became a condition in the house, something beyond hope or
reproach, like the leaky ice-box, there was less recognition and more ritual
in those kisses. I came to dread her room. A clutter of sticky medicine

---

1. Shtetl: *Yiddish word for the Jewish communities in Eastern Europe.*

bottles and the cracked toilet chair beside the bed; glazed but imploring eyes and a feeble smile, the wet smack of her crooked lips against my cheeks. I flinched from her touch. And after two years, I protested to my mother, 'What's the use of telling her I'm going here or I'm going there? She doesn't even recognize me any more.'

'Don't be fresh. She's your grandmother.' 40

My uncle who was in the theatre in New York sent money regularly to 41
help support my grandmother and, for the first few months, so did the other children. But once the initial and sustaining excitement had passed the children seldom came to our house any more. Anxious weekly visits— 'And how is she today, poor lamb?'—quickly dwindled to a dutiful monthly looking in, then a semi-annual visit, and these always on the way to somewhere.

When the children did come my mother was severe with them. 'I have 42
to lift her on that chair three times a day maybe. And what makes you think I always catch her in time? Sometimes I have to change her linen twice a day. That's a job I'd like to see your wife do,' she said to my uncle, the rabbi.

'We could send her to the Old People's Home.' 43

'Now there's an idea,' my father said. 44

'Not so long as I'm alive.' My mother shot my father a scalding look, 45
'Say something, Sam.'

'Quarrelling will get us nowhere. It only creates bad feelings.' 46

Meanwhile, Dr Katzman came once a month. 'It's astonishing,' he would 47
say each time. 'She's as strong as a horse.'

'Some life for a person,' my father said. 'She can't speak—she doesn't 48
recognize anybody—what is there for her?'

The doctor was a cultivated man; he spoke often for women's clubs, 49
sometimes on Yiddish literature and other times, his rubicund face hot with menace, the voice taking on a doomsday tone, on the cancer threat. 'Who are we to judge?' he asked.

Every evening, during the first few months of my grandmother's ill- 50
ness, my mother would read her a story by Sholem Aleichem. 'Tonight she smiled,' my mother would report defiantly. 'She understood. I can tell.'

Bright afternoons my mother would lift the old lady into a wheelchair 51
and put her out in the sun and once a week she gave her a manicure. Somebody always had to stay in the house in case my grandmother called. Often, during the night, she would begin to wail unaccountably and my mother would get up and rock her mother in her arms for hours. But in the fourth year of my grandmother's illness the strain began to tell. Besides looking after my grandmother, my mother had to keep house for a husband and two children. She became scornful of my father and began to find fault with my sister and me. My father started to spend his evenings playing pinochle at Tansky's Cigar & Soda. Weekends he took me to visit

his brothers and sisters. Wherever my father went people had little snippets of advice for him.

'Sam, you might as well be a bachelor. One of the other children should take the old lady for a while. You're just going to have to put your foot down for once.'   52

'Yeah, in your face, maybe.'   53

My Cousin Libby, who was at McGill,[1] said, 'This could have a very damaging effect on the development of your children. These are their formative years, Uncle Samuel, and the omnipresence of death in the house . . .'   54

'What you need is a boy friend,' my father said. '*And how.*'   55

After supper my mother took to falling asleep in her chair, even in the middle of Lux Radio Theatre. One minute she would be sewing a patch in my breeches or making a list of girls to call for a bingo party, proceeds for the Talmud Torah, and the next she would be snoring. Then, inevitably, there came the morning she just couldn't get out of bed and Dr Katzman had to come round a week before his regular visit. 'Well, well, this won't do, will it?'   56

Dr Katzman led my father into the kitchen. 'Your wife's got a gallstone condition,' he said.   57

My grandmother's children met again, this time without my mother, and decided to put the old lady in the Jewish Old People's Home on Esplanade Street. While my mother slept an ambulance came to take my grandmother away.   58

'It's for the best,' Dr Katzman said, but my father was in the back room when my grandmother held on tenaciously to the bedpost, not wanting to be moved by the two men in white.   59

'Easy does it, granny,' the younger man said.   60

Afterwards my father did not go in to see my mother. He went out for a walk.   61

When my mother got out of bed two weeks later her cheeks had regained their normal pinkish hue; for the first time in months, she actually joked with me. She became increasingly curious about how I was doing in school and whether or not I shined my shoes regularly. She began to cook special dishes for my father again and resumed old friendships with the girls on the parochial school board. Not only did my father's temper improve, but he stopped going to Tansky's every night and began to come home early from work. But my grandmother's name was seldom mentioned. Until one evening, after I'd had a fight with my sister, I said, 'Why can't I move into the back bedroom now?'   62

My father glared at me. 'Big-mouth.'   63

'It's empty, isn't it?'   64

---

1. McGill: *A private university in Montreal, Canada's most prestigious.*

The next afternoon my mother put on her best dress and coat and new   65
spring hat.

'Don't go looking for trouble,' my father said.   66

'It's been a month. Maybe they're not treating her right.'   67

'They're experts.'   68

'Did you think I was never going to visit her? I'm not inhuman, you   69
know.'

'Alright, go.' But after she had gone my father stood by the window and   70
said, 'I was born lucky, and that's it.'

I sat on the outside stoop watching the cars go by. My father waited on   71
the balcony above, cracking peanuts. It was six o'clock, maybe later, when
the ambulance slowed down and rocked to a stop right in front of our
house. 'I knew it,' my father said. 'I was born with all the luck.'

My mother got out first, her eyes red and swollen, and hurried upstairs   72
to make my grandmother's bed.

'You'll get sick again,' my father said.   73

'I'm sorry, Sam, but what could I do? From the moment she saw me she   74
cried and cried. It was terrible.'

'They're recognized experts there. They know how to take care of her   75
better than you do.'

'Experts? Expert murderers you mean. She's got bedsores, Sam. Those   76
dirty little Irish nurses they don't change her linen often enough they hate
her. She must have lost twenty pounds in there.'

'Another month and you'll be flat on your back again. I'll write you a   77
guarantee, if you want.'

My father became a regular at Tansky's again and, once more, I had to   78
go in and kiss my grandmother in the morning. Amazingly, she had begun
to look like a man. Little hairs had sprouted on her chin, she had grown a
spiky grey moustache, and she was practically bald.

Yet again my uncles and aunts sent five dollar bills, though erratically,   79
to help pay for my grandmother's support. Elderly people, former followers of my grandfather, came to inquire about the old lady's health. They sat
in the back bedroom with her, leaning on their canes, talking to themselves
and rocking to and fro. 'The Holy Shakers,' my father called them. I
avoided the seamed, shrunken old men because they always wanted to
pinch my cheeks or trick me with a dash of snuff and laugh when I sneezed.
When the visit with my grandmother was over the old people would
unfailingly sit in the kitchen with my mother for another hour, watching
her make *lokshen*, slurping lemon tea out of a saucer. They would recall the
sayings and books and charitable deeds of the late Zaddik.

'At the funeral,' my mother never wearied of telling them, 'they had to   80
have six motorcycle policemen to control the crowds.'

In the next two years there was no significant change in my grandmoth-   81
er's condition, though fatigue, ill-temper, and even morbidity enveloped
my mother again. She fought with her brothers and sisters and once, after

a particularly bitter quarrel, I found her sitting with her head in her hands. 'If, God forbid, I had a stroke,' she said, 'would you send me to the Old People's Home?'

'Of course not.' 82

'I hope that never in my life do I have to count on my children for 83 anything.'

The seventh summer of my grandmother's illness she was supposed to die 84 and we did not know from day to day when it would happen. I was often sent out to eat at an aunt's or at my other grandmother's house. I was hardly ever at home. In those days they let boys into the left-field bleachers of Delormier Downs free during the week and Duddy, Gas sometimes, Hershey, Stan, Arty and me spent many an afternoon at the ball park. The Montreal Royals, kingpin of the Dodger farm system, had a marvellous club at the time. There was Jackie Robinson, Roy Campanella, Lou Ortiz, Red Durrett, Honest John Gabbard, and Kermit Kitman. Kitman was our hero. It used to give us a charge to watch that crafty little Jew, one of ours, running around out there with all those tall dumb southern crackers. 'Hey, Kitman,' we would yell, 'Hey, shmo-head, if your father knew you played ball on *shabus*—' Kitman, alas, was all field and no hit. He never made the majors. 'There goes Kermit Kitman,' we would holler, after he had gone down swinging again, 'the first Jewish strike-out king of the International League.' This we promptly followed up by bellowing choice imprecations in Yiddish.

It was after one of these games, on a Friday afternoon, that I came home 85 to find a crowd gathered in front of our house.

'That's the grandson,' somebody said. 86

A knot of old people stood staring at our front door from across the 87 street. A taxi pulled up and my aunt hurried out, hiding her face in her hands.

'After so many years,' a woman said. 88

'And probably next year they'll discover a cure. Isn't that always the 89 case?'

The flat was clotted. Uncles and aunts from my father's side of the 90 family, strangers, Dr Katzman, neighbours, were all milling around and talking in hushed voices. My father was in the kitchen, getting out the apricot brandy. 'Your grandmother's dead,' he said.

'Where's Maw?' 91

'In the bedroom with . . . You'd better not go in.' 92

'I want to see her.' 93

My mother wore a black shawl and glared down at a knot of handker- 94 chief clutched in a fist that had been cracked by washing soda. 'Don't come in here,' she said.

Several bearded round-shouldered men in shiny black coats surrounded 95 the bed. I couldn't see my grandmother.

'Your grandmother's dead.'   96
'Daddy told me.'   97
'Go wash your face and comb your hair.'   98
'Yes.'   99
'You'll have to get your own supper.'   100
'Sure.'   101
'One minute. The *baba*[1] left some jewellery. The necklace is for Rifka and   102
the ring is for your wife.'
'Who's getting married?'   103
'Better go and wash your face. Remember behind the ears, please.'   104

Telegrams were sent, the obligatory long distance calls were made, and   105
all through the evening relatives and neighbours and old followers of the
Zaddik poured into the house. Finally, the man from the funeral parlour
arrived.

'There goes the only Jewish businessman in town,' Segal said, 'who   106
wishes all his customers were German.'
'This is no time for jokes.'   107
'Listen, life goes on.'   108

My Cousin Jerry had begun to affect a cigarette holder. 'Soon the reli-   109
gious mumbo-jumbo starts,' he said to me.
'Wha'?'   110
'Everybody is going to be sickeningly sentimental.'   111

The next day was the sabbath and so, according to law, my grandmother   112
couldn't be buried until Sunday. She would have to lie on the floor all
night. Two grizzly women in white came to move and wash the body and
a professional mourner arrived to sit up and pray for her. 'I don't trust his
face,' my mother said. 'He'll fall asleep.'
'He won't fall asleep.'   113
'You watch him, Sam.'   114
'A fat lot of good prayers will do her now. Alright! Okay! I'll watch him.'   115

My father was in a fury with Segal.   116
'The way he goes after the apricot brandy you'd think he never saw a   117
bottle in his life before.'

Rifka and I were sent to bed, but we couldn't sleep. My aunt was   118
sobbing over the body in the living room; there was the old man praying,
coughing and spitting into his handkerchief whenever he woke; and the
hushed voices and whimpering from the kitchen, where my father and
mother sat. Rifka allowed me a few drags off her cigarette.

'Well, *pisherke*, this is our last night together. Tomorrow you can take   119
over the back room.'
'Are you crazy?'   120

---

1. Baba: *Affectionate word for "grandmother."*

'You always wanted it for yourself, didn't you?' 121

'She died in there, but.' 122

'So?' 123

'I couldn't sleep in there now.' 124

'Good night and happy dreams.' 125

'Hey, let's talk some more.' 126

'Did you know,' Rifka said, 'that when they hang a man the last thing 127
that happens is that he has an orgasm?'

'A wha'?' 128

'Skip it. I forgot you were still in kindergarten.' 129

'Kiss my Royal Canadian—' 130

'At the funeral, they're going to open the coffin and throw dirt in her 131
face. It's supposed to be earth from Eretz.[1] They open it and you're going
to have to look.'

'Says you.' 132

A little while after the lights had been turned out Rifka approached my 133
bed, her head covered with a sheet and her arms raised high. 'Bouyo-
bouyo. Who's that sleeping in my bed? Woo-woo.'

My uncle who was in the theatre and my aunt from Toronto came to the 134
funeral. My uncle, the rabbi, was there too.

'As long as she was alive,' my mother said, 'he couldn't even send her 135
five dollars a month. I don't want him in the house, Sam. I can't bear the
sight of him.'

'You're upset,' Dr Katzman said, 'and you don't know what you're 136
saying.'

'Maybe you'd better give her a sedative,' the rabbi said. 137

'Sam will you speak up for once, please.' 138

Flushed, eyes heated, my father stepped up to the rabbi. 'I'll tell you this 139
straight to your face, Israel,' he said. 'You've gone down in my estimation.'

The rabbi smiled a little. 140

'Year by year,' my father continued, his face burning a brighter red, 141
'your stock has gone down with me.'

My mother began to weep and she was led unwillingly to a bed. While 142
my father tried his utmost to comfort her, as he muttered consoling things,
Dr Katzman plunged a needle into her arm. 'There we are,' he said.

I went to sit on the stoop outside with Duddy. My uncle, the rabbi, and 143
Dr Katzman stepped into the sun to light cigarettes.

'I know exactly how you feel,' Dr Katzman said. 'There's been a death 144
in the family and the world seems indifferent to your loss. Your heart is
broken and yet it's a splendid summer day . . . a day made for love and
laughter . . . and that must seem very cruel to you.'

---

1. Eretz: *Israel.*

The rabbi nodded; he sighed.   145

'Actually,' Dr Katzman said, 'it's remarkable that she held out for so   146
long.'

'Remarkable?' the rabbi said. 'It's written that if a man has been married   147
twice he will spend as much time with his first wife in heaven as he did on
earth. My father, may he rest in peace, was married to his first wife for
seven years and my mother, may she rest in peace, has managed to keep
alive for seven years. Today in heaven she will be able to join my father,
may he rest in peace.'

Dr Katzman shook his head. 'It's amazing,' he said. He told my uncle   148
that he was writing a book based on his experiences as a healer. 'The
mysteries of the human heart.'

'Yes.'   149

'Astonishing.'   150

My father hurried outside. 'Dr Katzman, please. It's my wife. Maybe the   151
injection wasn't strong enough. She just doesn't stop crying. It's like a tap.
Can you come in, please?'

'Excuse me,' Dr Katzman said to my uncle.   152

'Of course.' My uncle turned to Duddy and me. 'Well, boys,' he said,   153
'what would you like to be when you grow up?'

STUDY QUESTIONS

1. "The Summer My Grandmother Was Supposed to Die" begins with
   the summer the grandmother has gangrene and ends with her death
   four months later, but it actually spans seven years. What are the
   familial and communal bonds that motivate the daughter to nurse her
   mother through seven years of illness?
2. What consequences does the grandmother's presence have on the narrator's family?
3. The rabbi, the youngest child of the sick woman, comes from Boston to
   attend his mother's funeral. How does the narrator's mother's rejection of his presence in her house function as a criticism—of him personally or of the community he represents?
4. How does humor function in the story as a strategy for moral and
   social satire?

✺ JOY KOGAWA

Joy Kogawa (b. 1935) was born in Vancouver, British Columbia, on Canada's west coast, of Japanese ancestry. A poet and fiction writer, her first novel, Obasan (1981), has received numerous awards. Obasan uses the historical and autobiographical narratives of the Japanese Canadians on the west coast during the Second World War who, like Japanese Americans in the United States, were relocated by force from their homes, separated from their families, and settled in harsh areas in the Canadian interior. Kogawa's style is poetic and stylistically innovative, using symbols, imagery, and repeated motifs to explore the forging of the Japanese Canadian identity.

Excerpt from *Obasan*

There are only two letters in the grey cardboard folder. The first is a brief 1 and emotionless statement that Grandma Kato, her niece's daughter, and my mother are the only ones in the immediate family to have survived. The second letter is an outpouring.

I remember Grandma Kato as thin and tough, not given to melodrama 2 or overstatement of any kind. She was unbreakable. I felt she could endure all things and would survive any catastrophe. But I did not then understand what catastrophes were possible in human affairs.

Here, the ordinary Granton rain slides down wet and clean along the 3 glass leaving a trail on the window like the Japanese writing on the thin blue-lined paper—straight down like a bead curtain of asterisks. The rain she describes is black, oily, thick, and strange.

"In the heat of the August sun," Grandma writes, "however much the 4 effort to forget, there is no forgetfulness. As in a dream, I can still see the maggots crawling in the sockets of my niece's eyes. Her strong intelligent young son helped me move a bonsai tree that very morning. There is no forgetfulness."

When Nakayama-sensei reaches the end of the page, he stops reading 5 and folds the letter as if he has decided to read no more. Aunt Emily begins to speak quietly, telling of a final letter from the Canadian missionary, Miss Best.

How often, I am wondering, did Grandma and Mother waken in those 6 years with the unthinkable memories alive in their minds, the visible evidence of horror written on their skin, in their blood, carved in every mirror they passed, felt in every step they took. As a child I was told only that Mother and Grandma Kato were safe in Tokyo, visiting Grandma Kato's ailing mother.

"Someday, surely, they will return," Obasan used to say. 7

The two letters that reached us in Vancouver before all communication 8
ceased due to the war told us that Mother and Grandma Kato had arrived
safely in Japan and were staying with Grandma Kato's sister and her husband in their home near the Tokyo Gas Company. My great-grandmother
was then seventy-nine and was not expected to live to be eighty but,
happily, she had become so well that she had returned home from the
hospital and was even able on occasion to leave the house.

Nakayama-sensei opens the letter again and holds it, reading silently. 9
Then looking over to Stephen, he says, "It is better to speak, is it not?"

"They're dead now," Stephen says. 10

Sensei nods. 11

"Please read, Sensei," I whisper. 12

"Yes," Aunt Emily says. "They should know." 13

Sensei starts again at the beginning. The letter is dated simply 1949. It 14
was sent, Sensei says, from somewhere in Nagasaki. There was no return
address.

"Though it was a time of war," Grandma writes, "what happiness that 15
January, 1945, to hear from my niece Setsuko, in Nagasaki." Setsuko's
second child was due to be born within the month. In February, just as
American air raids in Tokyo were intensifying, Mother went to help her
cousin in Nagasaki. The baby was born three days after she arrived. Early
in March, air raids and alarms were constant day and night in Tokyo. In
spite of all the dangers of travel, Grandma Kato went to Nagasaki to be
with my mother and to help with the care of the new baby. The last day she
spent with her mother and sister in Tokyo, she said they sat on the tatami
and talked, remembering their childhood and the days they went chestnut-
picking together. They parted with laughter. The following night,
Grandma Kato's sister, their mother and her sister's husband died in the
B-29 bombings of March 9, 1945.

From this point on, Grandma's letter becomes increasingly chaotic, the 16
details interspersed without chronological consistency. She and my
mother, she writes, were unable to talk of all the things that happened. The
horror would surely die sooner, they felt, if they refused to speak. But the
silence and the constancy of the nightmare had become unbearable for
Grandma and she hoped that by sharing them with her husband, she could
be helped to extricate herself from the grip of the past.

"If these matters are sent away in this letter, perhaps they will depart a 17
little from our souls," she writes. "For the burden of these words, forgive
me."

Mother, for her part, continued her vigil of silence. She spoke with no 18
one about her torment. She specifically requested that Stephen and I be
spared the truth.

In all my high-school days, until we heard from Sensei that her grave 19
had been found in Tokyo, I pictured her trapped in Japan by government

regulations, or by an ailing grandmother. The letters I sent to the address in Tokyo were never answered or returned. I could not know that she and Grandma Kato had gone to Nagasaki to stay with Setsuko, her husband who was a dentist, and their two children, four-year-old Tomio and the new baby, Chieko.

The baby, Grandma writes, looked so much like me that she and my 20 mother marvelled and often caught themselves calling her Naomi. With her widow's peak, her fat cheeks and pointed chin, she had a heart-shaped face like mine. Tomio, however, was not like Stephen at all. He was a sturdy child, extremely healthy and athletic, with a strong will like his father. He was fascinated by his new baby sister, sitting and watching her for hours as she slept or nursed. He made dolls for her. He helped to dress her. He loved to hold her in the bath, feeling her fingers holding his fingers tightly. He rocked her to sleep in his arms.

The weather was hot and humid that morning of August 9. The air-raid 21 alerts had ended. Tomio and some neighbourhood children had gone to the irrigation ditch to play and cool off as they sometimes did.

Shortly after eleven o'clock, Grandma Kato was preparing to make 22 lunch. The baby was strapped to her back. She was bending over a bucket of water beside a large earthenware storage bin when a child in the street was heard shouting, "Look at the parachute!" A few seconds later, there was a sudden white flash, brighter than a bolt of lightning. She had no idea what could have exploded. It was as if the entire sky were swallowed up. A moment later she was hurled sideways by a blast. She had a sensation of floating tranquilly in a cool whiteness high above the earth. When she regained consciousness, she was slumped forward in a sitting position in the water bin. She gradually became aware of the moisture, an intolerable heat, blood, a mountain of debris and her niece's weak voice sounding at first distant, calling the names of her children. Then she could hear the other sounds—the far-away shouting. Around her, a thick dust made breathing difficult. Chieko was still strapped to her back, but made no sound. She was alive but unconscious.

It took Grandma a long time to claw her way out of the wreckage. When 23 she emerged, it was into an eerie twilight formed of heavy dust and smoke that blotted out the sun. What she saw was incomprehensible. Almost all the buildings were flattened or in flames for as far as she could see. The landmarks were gone. Tall columns of fire rose through the haze and everywhere the dying and the wounded crawled, fled, stumbled like ghosts among the ruins. Voices screamed, calling the names of children, fathers, mothers, calling for help, calling for water.

Beneath some wreckage, she saw first the broken arm, then the writhing 24 body of her niece, her head bent back, her hair singed, both her eye sockets blown out. In a weak and delirious voice, she was calling Tomio. Grandma Kato touched her niece's leg and the skin peeled off and stuck to the palm of her hand.

It isn't clear from the letter but at some point she came across Tomio, his 25 legs pumping steadily up and down as he stood in one spot not knowing where to go. She gathered him in her arms. He was remarkably intact, his skin unburned.

She had no idea where Mother was, but with the two children, she be- 26 gan making her way towards the air-raid shelter. All around her people one after another collapsed and died, crying for water. One old man no longer able to keep moving lay on the ground holding up a dead baby and crying, "Save the children. Leave the old." No one took the dead child from his outstretched hands. Men, women, in many cases indistinguishable by sex, hairless, half-clothed, hobbled past. Skin hung from their bodies like tattered rags. One man held his bowels in with the stump of one hand. A child whom Grandma Kato recognized lay on the ground asking for help. She stopped and told him she would return as soon as she could. A woman she knew was begging for someone to help her lift the burning beam beneath which her children were trapped. The woman's children were friends of Tomio's. Grandma was loath to walk past, but with the two children, she could do no more and kept going. At no point does Grandma Kato mention the injuries she herself must have sustained.

Nearing the shelter, Grandma could see through the greyness that the 27 entrance was clogged with dead bodies. She remembered then that her niece's father-in-law lived on a farm on the hillside, and she began making her way back through the burning city towards the river she would have to cross. The water, red with blood, was a raft of corpses. Farther upstream, the bridge was twisted like noodles. Eventually she came to a spot where she was able to cross and, still carrying the two children, Grandma Kato made her way up the hillside.

After wandering for some time, she found a wooden water pipe drib- 28 bling a steady stream. She held Tomio's mouth to it and allowed him to drink as much as he wished though she had heard that too much water was not good. She unstrapped the still unconscious baby from her back. Exhausted, she drank from the pipe, and gathering the two children in her arms, she looked out at the burning city and lapsed into a sleep so deep she believed she was unconscious.

When she awakened, she was in the home of her niece's relatives and 29 the baby was being fed barley water. The little boy was nowhere.

Almost immediately, Grandma set off to look for the child. Next day she 30 returned to the area of her niece's home and every day thereafter she looked for Mother and the lost boy, checking the lists of the dead, looking over the unclaimed corpses. She discovered that her niece's husband was among the dead.

One evening when she had given up the search for the day, she sat 31 down beside a naked woman she'd seen earlier who was aimlessly chipping wood to make a pyre on which to cremate a dead baby. The woman was utterly disfigured. Her nose and one cheek were almost gone. Great wounds and pustules covered her entire face and body. She was completely bald. She sat in a cloud of flies and maggots wriggled among her wounds. As Grandma watched her, the woman gave her a vacant gaze, then let out a cry. It was my mother.

The little boy was never found. Mother was taken to a hospital and   32
was expected to die, but she survived. During one night she vomited yellow fluid and passed a great deal of blood. For a long time—Grandma does not say how long—Mother wore bandages on her face. When they were removed, Mother felt her face with her fingers, then asked for a cloth mask. Thereafter she would not take off her mask from morning to night.

"At this moment," Grandma writes, "we are preparing to visit Chieko-   33
chan in the hospital." Chieko, four years old in 1949, waited daily for their visit, standing in the hospital corridor, tubes from her wrist attached to a bottle that was hung above her. A small bald-headed girl. She was dying of leukemia.

"There may not be many more days," Grandma concludes.   34

After this, what could have happened? Did they leave the relatives in   35
Nagasaki? Where and how did they survive?

When Sensei is finished reading, he folds and unfolds the letter, nod-   36
ding his head slowly.

I put my hands around the teapot, feeling its round warmth against my   37
palms. My skin feels hungry for warmth, for flesh. Grandma mentioned in her letter that she saw one woman cradling a hot-water bottle as if it were a baby.

Sensei places the letter back in the cardboard folder and closes it with   38
the short red string around the tab.

"That there is brokenness," he says quietly. "That this world is broken-   39
ness. But within brokenness is the unbreakable name. How the whole earth groans till Love returns."

I stand up abruptly and leave the room, going into the kitchen for some   40
more hot water. When I return, Sensei is sitting with his face in his hands.

Stephen is staring at the floor, his body hunched forward motionless.   41
He glances up at me then looks away swiftly. I sit on a stool beside him and try to concentrate on what is being said. I can hear Aunt Emily telling us about Mother's grave. Then Nakayama-sensei stands and begins to say the Lord's Prayer under his breath. "And forgive us our trespasses—forgive us our trespasses—" he repeats, sighing deeply, "as we forgive others. . . ." He lifts his head, looking upwards. "We are powerless to forgive unless we first are forgiven. It is a high calling my friends—the calling to forgive. But no person, no people is innocent. Therefore we must forgive one another."

I am not thinking of forgiveness. The sound of Sensei's voice grows as   42
indistinct as the hum of distant traffic. Gradually the room grows still and

it is as if I am back with Uncle again, listening and listening to the silent earth and the silent sky as I have done all my life.

I close my eyes.   43

Mother. I am listening. Assist me to hear you.   44

STUDY QUESTIONS

1. The daughter tells the story of her missing mother through a combination of memory and the grandmother's letter, dated 1949. What happened to Grandma Kato and the mother, both Canadian citizens, after they left Canada to visit Grandma Kato's sick mother in Japan?
2. What are the possible reasons for the two women's decision never to return to Canada and for the mother's injunction against telling her children what had happened to her?
3. Nakayama-sensei, the pastor, reads the letter that finally breaks this silence; he speaks for love and prays for forgiveness. What does the statement "[N]o people is innocent. Therefore we must forgive one another" mean in the context of the historical narrative of World War II?
4. The grandmother's letter focuses chiefly on women and children and shows them not as perpetrators of violence but as victims of violence. What social and political criticism is suggested in this focus?

❋ MARGARET ATWOOD

Margaret Atwood (b. 1939) was born in Ottawa, Ontario. She grew up in Quebec and Ontario and studied under the literary critic Northrop Frye at the University of Toronto. The author of numerous novels, books of poetry, short stories, and essays, Atwood elucidates themes that have resonance for the Canadian identity—the importance of geography, of pioneering and survival. She is an equally significant literary figure in the United States, where much of her work—especially the early novel Surfacing *(1972) and* The Handmaid's Tale *(1985)—has found its warmest reception from feminist readers. Her books of poetry include* Selected Poems, 1965–1975 *(1987) and* Selected Poems II, Poems Selected and New, 1976–1986 *(1987). Her most recent short story collection is* Bluebeard's Egg and Other Stories *(1983).*

Dancing Girls

The first sign of the new man was the knock on the door. It was the landlady, knocking not at Ann's door, as she'd thought, but on the other door, the one east of the bathroom. Knock, knock, knock; then a pause, soft footsteps, the sound of unlocking. Ann, who had been reading a book on canals, put it down and lit herself a cigarette. It wasn't that she tried to overhear: in this house you couldn't help it.

"Hi!" Mrs. Nolan's voice loud, overly friendly. "I was wondering, my kids would love to see your native costume. You think you could put it on, like, and come down?"

A soft voice, unintelligible.

"Gee, that's great! We'd sure appreciate it!"

Closing and locking, Mrs. Nolan slip-slopping along the hall in, Ann knew, her mauve terry-cloth scuffies and flowered housecoat, down the stairs, hollering at her two boys. "You get into this room right now!" Her voice came up through Ann's hot air register as if the grate were a PA system. *It isn't those kids who want to see him*, she thought. *It's her.* She put out the cigarette, reserving the other half for later, and opened her book again. What costume? Which land, this time?

Unlocking, opening, soft feet down the hall. They sounded bare. Ann closed the book and opened her own door. A white robe, the back of a brown head, moving with a certain stealth or caution toward the stairs. Ann went into the bathroom and turned on the light. They would share it; the person in that room always shared her bathroom. She hoped he would be better than the man before, who always seemed to forget his razor and would knock on the door while Ann was having a bath. You wouldn't have to worry about getting raped or anything in this house though, that was one good thing. Mrs. Nolan was better than any burglar alarm, and she was always there.

That one had been from France, studying Cinema. Before him there had been a girl, from Turkey, studying Comparative Literature. Lelah, or that was how it was pronounced. Ann used to find her beautiful long auburn hairs in the washbasin fairly regularly; she'd run her thumb and index finger along them, enviously, before discarding them. She had to keep her own hair chopped off at ear level, as it was brittle and broke easily. Lelah also had a gold tooth, right at the front on the outside where it showed when she smiled. Curiously, Ann was envious of this tooth as well. It and the hair and the turquoise-studded earrings Lelah wore gave her a gypsy look, a wise look that Ann, with her beige eyebrows and delicate mouth, knew she would never be able to develop, no matter how wise she got. She herself went in for "classics," tailored skirts and Shetland sweaters; it was the only look she could carry off. But she and Lelah had been friends, smoking cigarettes in each other's rooms, commiserating with each other about the difficulties of their courses and the loudness of Mrs. Nolan's voice. So Ann was familiar with that room; she knew what it looked like inside and how much it cost. It was no luxury suite, certainly, and she wasn't surprised at the high rate of turnover. It had an even more direct pipeline to the sounds of the Nolan family than hers had. Lelah had left because she couldn't stand the noise.

The room was smaller and cheaper than her room, though painted the 8 same depressing shade of green. Unlike hers, it did not have its own tiny refrigerator, sink and stove; you had to use the kitchen at the front of the house, which had been staked out much earlier by a small enclave of mathematicians, two men and one woman, from Hong Kong. Whoever took that room either had to eat out all the time or run the gamut of their conversation, which even when not in Chinese was so rarefied as to be unintelligible. And you could never find any space in the refrigerator, it was always full of mushrooms. This from Lelah; Ann herself never had to deal with them since she could cook in her own room. She could see them, though, as she went in and out. At mealtimes they usually sat quietly at the kitchen table, discussing surds, she assumed. Ann suspected that what Lelah had really resented about them was not the mushrooms: they simply made her feel stupid.

Every morning, before she left for classes, Ann checked the bathroom 9 for signs of the new man—hairs, cosmetics—but there was nothing. She hardly ever heard him; sometimes there was that soft, barefooted pacing, the click of his lock, but there were no radio noises, no coughs, no conversations. For the first couple of weeks, apart from that one glimpse of a tall, billowing figure, she didn't even see him. He didn't appear to use the kitchen, where the mathematicians continued their mysteries undisturbed; or if he did, he cooked while no one else was there. Ann would have forgotten about him completely if it hadn't been for Mrs. Nolan.

"He's real nice, not like some you get," she said to Ann in her piercing 10 whisper. Although she shouted at her husband, when he was home, and especially at her children, she always whispered when she was talking to Ann, a hoarse, avid whisper, as if they shared disreputable secrets. Ann was standing in front of her door with the room key in her hand, her usual location during these confidences. Mrs. Nolan knew Ann's routine. It wasn't difficult for her to pretend to be cleaning the bathroom, to pop out and waylay Ann, Ajax and rag in hand, whenever she felt she had something to tell her. She was a short, barrel-shaped woman: the top of her head came only to Ann's nose, so she had to look up at Ann, which at these moments made her seem oddly childlike.

"He's from one of them Arabian countries. Though I thought they wore 11 turbans, or not turbans, those white things, like. He just has this funny hat, sort of like the Shriners. He don't look much like an Arab to me. He's got these tattoo marks on his face. . . . But he's real nice."

Ann stood, her umbrella dripping onto the floor, waiting for Mrs. Nolan 12 to finish. She never had to say anything much; it wasn't expected. "You think you could get me the rent on Wednesday?" Mrs. Nolan asked. Three days early; the real point of the conversation, probably. Still, as Mrs. Nolan had said back in September, she didn't have much of anyone to talk to. Her husband was away much of the time and her children escaped outdoors whenever they could. She never went out herself except to shop, and for Mass on Sundays.

"I'm glad it was you took the room," she'd said to Ann. "I can talk to 13 you. You're not, like, foreign. Not like most of them. It was his idea, getting this big house to rent out. Not that he has to do the work or put up with them. You never know what they'll do."

Ann wanted to point out to her that she was indeed foreign, that she 14 was just as foreign as any of the others, but she knew Mrs. Nolan would not understand. It would be like that fiasco in October. *Wear your native costume.* She had responded to the invitation out of a sense of duty, as well as one of irony. Wait till they get a load of my native costume, she'd thought, contemplating snowshoes and a parka but actually putting on her good blue wool suit. There was only one thing *native costume* reminded her of: the cover picture on the Missionary Sunday School paper they'd once handed out, which showed children from all the countries of the world dancing in a circle around a smiling white-faced Jesus in a bedsheet. That, and the poem in the *Golden Windows Reader*:

> Little Indian, Sioux or Cree,
> Oh, don't you wish that you were me?

The awful thing, as she told Lelah later, was that she was the only one 15 who'd gone. "She had all this food ready, and not a single other person was there. She was really upset, and I was so embarrassed for her. It was some Friends of Foreign Students thing, just for women: students and the wives of students. She obviously didn't think I was foreign enough, and she couldn't figure out why no one else came." Neither could Ann, who had stayed far too long and had eaten platefuls of crackers and cheese she didn't want in order to soothe her hostess' thwarted sense of hospitality. The woman, who had tastefully-streaked ash-blonde hair and a livingroom filled with polished and satiny traditional surfaces, had alternately urged her to eat and stared at the door, as if expecting a parade of foreigners in their native costumes to come trooping gratefully through it.

Lelah smiled, showing her wise tooth. "Don't they know any better 16 than to throw those things at night?" she said. "Those men aren't going to let their wives go out by themselves at night. And the single ones are afraid to walk on the streets alone, I know I am."

"I'm not," Ann said, "as long as you stay on the main ones, where it's 17 lighted."

"Then you're a fool," Lelah said. "Don't you know there was a girl 18 murdered three blocks from here? Left her bathroom window unlocked. Some man climbed through the window and cut her throat."

"I always carry my umbrella," Ann said. Of course there were certain places where you just didn't go. Scollay Square, for instance, where the prostitutes hung out and you might get followed, or worse. She tried to explain to Lelah that she wasn't used to this, to any of this, that in Toronto you could walk all over the city, well, almost anywhere, and never have any trouble. She went on to say that no one here seemed to understand that she wasn't like them, she came from a different country, it wasn't the same; but Lelah was quickly bored by this. She had to get back to Tolstoy, she said, putting out her cigarette in her unfinished cup of instant coffee. (*Not strong enough for her, I suppose,* Ann thought.) 19

"You shouldn't worry," she said. "You're well off. At least your family doesn't almost disown you for doing what you want to do." Lelah's father kept writing her letters, urging her to return to Turkey, where the family had decided on the perfect husband for her. Lelah had stalled them for one year, and maybe she could stall them for one more, but that would be her limit. She couldn't possibly finish her thesis in that time. 20

Ann hadn't seen much of her since she'd moved out. You lost sight of people quickly here, in the ever-shifting population of hopeful and despairing transients. 21

No one wrote her letters urging her to come home, no one had picked out the perfect husband for her. On the contrary. She could imagine her mother's defeated look, the greying and sinking of her face, if she were suddenly to announce that she was going to quit school, trade in her ambitions for fate, and get married. Even her father wouldn't like it. *Finish what you start,* he'd say, *I didn't and look what happened to me.* The bungalow at the top of Avenue Road, beside a gas station, with the roar of the expressway always there, like the sea, and fumes blighting the Chinese elm hedge her mother had planted to conceal the pumps. Both her brothers had dropped out of high school; they weren't the good students Ann had been. One worked in a print shop now and had a wife; the other had drifted to Vancouver, and no one knew what he did. She remembered her first real boyfriend, beefy, easygoing Bill Decker, with his two-tone car that kept losing the muffler. They'd spent a lot of time parked on side streets, rubbing against each other through all those layers of clothes. But even in that sensual mist, the cocoon of breath and skin they'd spun around each other, those phone conversations that existed as a form of touch, she'd known this was not something she could get too involved in. He was probably flabby by now, settled. She'd had relationships with men since then, but she had treated them the same way. *Circumspect.* 22

Not that Mrs. Nolan's back room was any step up. Out one window there was a view of the funeral home next door; out the other was the yard, which the Nolan kids had scraped clean of grass and which was now a bog of half-frozen mud. Their dog, a mongrelized German Shepherd, was kept 23 tied there, where the kids alternately hugged and tormented it. ("Jimmy! Donny! Now you leave that dog alone!" "Don't do that, he's filthy! Look at you!" Ann covering her ears, reading about underground malls.) She'd tried to fix the room up, she'd hung a Madras spread as a curtain in front of the cooking area, she'd put up several prints, Braque still-lifes of guitars and soothing Cubist fruit, and she was growing herbs on her windowsill; she needed surroundings that at least tried not to be ugly. But none of these things helped much. At night she wore earplugs. She hadn't known about the scarcity of good rooms, hadn't realized that the whole area was a student slum, that the rents would be so high, the available places so dismal. Next year would be different; she'd get here early and have the pick of the crop. Mrs. Nolan's was definitely a leftover. You could do much better for the money; you could even have a whole apartment, if you were willing to live in the real slum that spread in narrow streets of three-storey frame houses, fading mustard yellow and soot grey, nearer the river. Though Ann didn't think she was quite up to that. Something in one of the good old houses, on a quiet back street, with a little stained glass, would be more like it. Her friend Jetske had a place like that.

But she was doing what she wanted, no doubt of that. In high school 24 she had planned to be an architect, but while finishing the preliminary courses at university she had realized that the buildings she wanted to design were either impossible—who could afford them?—or futile. They would be lost, smothered, ruined by all the other buildings jammed inharmoniously around them. This was why she had decided to go into Urban Design, and she had come here because this school was the best. Or rumoured to be the best. By the time she finished, she intended to be so well-qualified, so armoured with qualifications, that no one back home would dare turn her down for the job she coveted. She wanted to rearrange Toronto. Toronto would do for a start.

She wasn't yet too certain of the specific details. What she saw were 25 spaces, beautiful green spaces, with water flowing through them, and trees. Not big golf-course lawns, though; something more winding, something with sudden turns, private niches, surprising vistas. And no formal flower beds. The houses, or whatever they were, set unobtrusively among the trees, the cars kept . . . where? And where would people shop, and who would live in these places? This was the problem: she could see the vistas, the trees and the streams or canals, quite clearly, but she could never visualize the people. Her green spaces were always empty.

She didn't see her next-door neighbour again until February. She was 26 coming back from the small local supermarket where she bought the food for her cheap, carefully balanced meals. He was leaning in the doorway of what, at home, she would have called a vestibule, smoking a cigarette and staring out at the rain, through the glass panes at the side of the front door.

He should have moved a little to give Ann room to put down her umbrella, but he didn't. He didn't even look at her. She squeezed in, shook her deflated umbrella and checked her mail box, which didn't have a key. There weren't usually any letters in it, and today was no exception. He was wearing a white shirt that was too big for him and some greenish trousers. His feet were not bare, in fact he was wearing a pair of prosaic brown shoes. He did have tattoo marks, though, or rather scars, a set of them running across each cheek. It was the first time she had seen him from the front. He seemed a little shorter than he had when she'd glimpsed him heading towards the stairs, but perhaps it was because he had no hat on. He was curved so listlessly against the doorframe, it was almost as if he had no bones.

There was nothing to see through the front of Mrs. Nolan's door except the traffic, sizzling by the way it did every day. He was depressed, it must be that. This weather would depress anyone. Ann sympathized with his loneliness, but she did not wish to become involved in it, implicated by it. She had enough trouble dealing with her own. She smiled at him, though since he wasn't looking at her this smile was lost. She went past him and up the stairs. 27

As she fumbled in her purse for her key, Mrs. Nolan stumped out of the bathroom. "You see him?" she whispered. 28

"Who?" Ann said. 29

"*Him.*" Mrs. Nolan jerked her thumb. "Standing down there, by the door. He does that a lot. He's bothering me, like. I don't have such good nerves." 30

"He's not doing anything," Ann said. 31

"That's what I mean," Mrs. Nolan whispered ominously. "He never does nothing. Far as I can tell, he never goes out much. All he does is borrow my vacuum cleaner." 32

"Your vacuum cleaner?" Ann said, startled into responding. 33

"That's what I said." Mrs. Nolan had a rubber plunger which she was fingering. "And there's more of them. They come in the other night, up to his room. Two more, with the same marks and everything, on their faces. It's like some kind of, like, a religion or something. And he never gave the vacuum cleaner back till the next day." 34

"Does he pay the rent?" Ann said, trying to switch the conversation to practical matters. Mrs. Nolan was letting her imagination get out of control. 35

"Regular," Mrs. Nolan said. "Except I don't like the way he comes down, so quiet like, right into my house. With Fred away so much." 36

"I wouldn't worry," Ann said in what she hoped was a soothing voice. "He seems perfectly nice." 37

"It's always that kind," Mrs. Nolan said. 38

Ann cooked her dinner, a chicken breast, some peas, a digestive biscuit. Then she washed her hair in the bathroom and put it up in rollers. She had 39 to do that, to give it body. With her head encased in the plastic hood of her portable dryer she sat at her table, drinking instant coffee, smoking her usual half cigarette, and attempting to read a book about Roman aqueducts, from which she hoped to get some novel ideas for her current project. (An aqueduct, going right through the middle of the obligatory shopping centre? Would anyone care?) Her mind kept flicking, though, to the problem of the man next door. Ann did not often try to think about what it would be like to be a man. But this particular man . . . Who was he, and what was happening to him? He must be a student, everyone here was a student. And he would be intelligent, that went without saying. Probably on scholarship. Everyone here in the graduate school was on scholarship, except the real Americans, who sometimes weren't. Or rather, the women were, but some of the men were still avoiding the draft, though President Johnson had announced he was going to do away with all that. She herself would never have made it this far without scholarships; her parents could not have afforded it.

So he was here on scholarship, studying something practical, no doubt, nuclear physics or the construction of dams, and, like herself and the other foreigners, he was expected to go away again as soon as he'd learned what he'd come for. But he never went out of the house; he stood at the front door and watched the brutish flow of cars, the winter rain, while those back in his own country, the ones that had sent him, were confidently expecting him to return some day, crammed with knowledge, ready to solve their lives. . . . *He's lost his nerve*, Ann thought. *He'll fail.* It was too late in the year for him ever to catch up. Such failures, such paralyses, were fairly common here, especially among the foreigners. He was far from home, from the language he shared, the wearers of his native costume; he was in exile, he was drowning. What did he do, alone by himself in his room at night?

Ann switched her hair dryer to COOL and wrenched her mind back to aqueducts. She could see he was drowning but there was nothing she could do. Unless you were good at it you shouldn't even try, she was wise enough to know that. All you could do for the drowning was to make sure you were not one of them.

The aqueduct, now. It would be made of natural brick, an earthy red; it would have low arches, in the shade of which there would be ferns and, perhaps, some delphiniums, in varying tones of blue. She must learn more about plants. Before entering the shopping complex (trust him to assign a shopping complex; before that he had demanded a public housing project), it would flow through her green space, in which, she could now see, there were people walking. Children? *But not children like Mrs. Nolan's.* They would turn her grass to mud, they'd nail things to her trees, their mangy dogs would shit on her ferns, they'd throw bottles and pop cans into her aqueduct. . . . And Mrs. Nolan herself, and her Noah's Ark of seedy, brilliant foreigners, where would she put them? For the houses of the Mrs.

Nolans of this world would have to go; that was one of the axioms of Urban Design. She could convert them to small offices, or single-floor apartments; some shrubs and hanging plants and a new coat of paint would do wonders. But she knew this was temporizing. Around her green space, she could see, there was now a high wire fence. Inside it were trees, flowers and grass, outside the dirty snow, the endless rain, the grunting cars and the half-frozen mud of Mrs. Nolan's drab backyard. That was what *exclusive* meant, it meant that some people were excluded. Her parents stood in the rain outside the fence, watching with dreary pride while she strolled about in the eternal sunlight. Their one success.

Stop it, she commanded herself. *They want me to be doing this.* She unwound her hair and brushed it out. Three hours from now, she knew, it would be limp as ever because of the damp. 43

The next day, she tried to raise her new theoretical problem with her friend Jetske. Jetske was in Urban Design, too. She was from Holland, and could remember running through the devastated streets as a child, begging small change, first from the Germans, later from the American soldiers, who were always good for a chocolate bar or two. 44

"You learn how to take care of yourself," she'd said. "It didn't seem hard at the time, but when you are a child, nothing is that hard. We were all the same, nobody had anything." Because of this background, which was more exotic and cruel than anything Ann herself had experienced (what was a gas pump compared to the Nazis?), Ann respected her opinions. She liked her also because she was the only person she'd met here who seemed to know where Canada was. There were a lot of Canadian soldiers buried in Holland. This provided Ann with at least a shadowy identity, which she felt she needed. She didn't have a native costume, but at least she had some heroic dead bodies with which she was connected, however remotely. 45

"The trouble with what we're doing . . . ," she said to Jetske, as they walked towards the library under Ann's umbrella. "I mean, you can rebuild one part, but what do you do about the rest?" 46

"Of the city?" Jetske said. 47

"No," Ann said slowly. "I guess I mean of the world." 48

Jetske laughed. She had what Ann now thought of as Dutch teeth, even and white, with quite a lot of gum showing above them and below the lip. "I didn't know you were a socialist," she said. Her cheeks were pink and healthy, like a cheese ad. 49

"I'm not," Ann said. "But I thought we were supposed to be thinking in total patterns." 50

Jetske laughed again. "Did you know," she said, "that in some countries you have to get official permission to move from one town to another?" 51

Ann didn't like this idea at all. "It controls the population flow," Jetske said. "You can't really have Urban Design without that, you know." 52

"I think that's awful," Ann said. 53

"Of course you do," Jetske said, as close to bitterness as she ever got. 54
"You've never had to do it. Over here you are soft in the belly, you think
you can always have everything. You think there is freedom of choice. The
whole world will come to it. You will see." She began teasing Ann again
about her plastic headscarf. Jetske never wore anything on her head.

Ann designed her shopping complex, putting in a skylight and banks of 55
indoor plants, leaving out the aqueduct. She got an A.

In the third week of March, Ann went with Jetske and some of the 56
others to a Buckminster Fuller lecture. Afterwards they all went to the pub
on the corner of the Square for a couple of beers. Ann left with Jetske about
eleven o'clock and walked a couple of blocks with her before Jetske turned
off towards her lovely old house with the stained glass. Ann continued by
herself, warily, keeping to the lighted streets. She carried her purse under
her elbow and held her furled umbrella at the ready. For once it wasn't
raining.

When she got back to the house and started to climb the stairs, it struck 57
her that something was different. Upstairs, she knew. Absolutely, something was out of line. There was curious music coming from the room next
door, a high flute rising over drums, thumping noises, the sound of voices.
The man next door was throwing a party, it seemed. *Good for him*, Ann
thought. He might as well do something. She settled down for an hour's
reading.

But the noises were getting louder. From the bathroom came the sound 58
of retching. There was going to be trouble. Ann checked her door to make
sure it was locked, got out the bottle of sherry she kept in the cupboard
next to the oven, and poured herself a drink. Then she turned out the light
and sat with her back against the door, drinking her sherry in the faint blue
light from the funeral home next door. There was no point in going to bed:
even with her earplugs in, she could never sleep.

The music and thumpings got louder. After a while there was a banging 59
on the floor, then some shouting, which came quite clearly through Ann's
hot-air register. "I'm calling the police! You hear? I'm calling the police!
You get them out of here and get out yourself!" The music switched off, the
door opened, and there was a clattering down the stairs. Then more
footsteps—Ann couldn't tell whether they were going up or down—and
more shouting. The front door banged and the shouts continued on down
the street. Ann undressed and put on her nightgown, still without turning
on the light, and crept into the bathroom. The bathtub was full of vomit.

This time Mrs. Nolan didn't even wait for Ann to get back from classes. She 60
waylaid her in the morning as she was coming out of her room. Mrs. Nolan
was holding a can of Drano and had dark circles under her eyes. Somehow
this made her look younger. *She's probably not much older than I am*, Ann
thought. Until now she had considered her middle-aged.

"I guess you saw the mess in there," she whispered.   61

"Yes, I did," Ann said.   62

"I guess you heard all that last night." She paused.   63

"What happened?" Ann asked. In fact she really wanted to know.   64

"He had some dancing girls in there! Three dancing girls, and two other   65
men, in that little room! I thought the ceiling was gonna come right down
on our heads!"

"I did hear something like dancing," Ann said.   66

"Dancing! They was jumping, it sounded like they jumped right off the   67
bed onto the floor. The plaster was coming off. Fred wasn't home, he's not
home yet. I was afraid for the kids. Like, with those tattoos, who knows
what they was working themselves up to?" Her sibilant voice hinted of
ritual murders, young Jimmy and runny-nosed Donny sacrificed to some
obscure god.

"What did you do?" Ann asked.   68

"I called the police. Well, the dancing girls, as soon as they heard I was   69
calling the police, they got out of here, I can tell you. Put on their coats and
was down the stairs and out the door like nothing. You can bet they didn't
want no trouble with the police. But not the others, they don't seem to
know what police means."

She paused again, and Ann asked, "Did they come?"   70

"Who?"   71

"The police."   72

"Well, you know around here it always takes the police a while to get   73
there, unless there's some right outside. I know that, it's not the first time
I've had to call them. So who knows what they would've done in the
meantime? I could hear them coming downstairs, like, so I just grabs the
broom and I chased them out. I chased them all the way down the street."

Ann saw that she thought she had done something very brave, which   74
meant that in fact she had. She really believed that the man next door and
his friends were dangerous, that they were a threat to her children. She
had chased them single-handedly, yelling with fear and defiance. But he
had only been throwing a party.

"Heavens," she said weakly.   75

"You can say that again," said Mrs. Nolan. "I went in there this morn-   76
ing, to get his things and put them out front where he could get them
without me having to see him. I don't have such good nerves, I didn't sleep
at all, even after they was gone. Fred is just gonna have to stop driving
nights, I can't take it. But you know? He didn't have no things in there. Not
one. Just an old empty suitcase?"

"What about his native costume?" Ann said.   77

"He had it on," Mrs. Nolan said. "He just went running down the street   78
in it, like some kind of a loony. And you know what else I found in there?
In one corner, there was this pile of empty bottles. Liquor. He must've
been drinking like a fish for months, and never threw out the bottles. And

in another corner, there was this pile of burnt matches. He could've burnt the house down, throwing them on the floor like that. But the worst thing was, you know all the times he borrowed my vacuum cleaner?"

"Yes," Ann said. 79

"Well, he never threw away the dirt. There it all was, in the other corner 80 of the room. He must've just emptied it out and left it there. I don't get it." Mrs. Nolan, by now, was puzzled rather than angry.

"Well," Ann said. "That certainly is strange." 81

"Strange?" Mrs. Nolan said. "I'll tell you it's strange. He always paid 82 the rent though, right on time. Never a day late. Why would he put the dirt in a corner like that, when he could've put it out in a bag like everyone else? It's not like he didn't know. I told him real clear which were the garbage days, when he moved in."

Ann said she was going to be late for class if she didn't hurry. At the 83 front door she tucked her hair under her plastic scarf. Today it was just a drizzle, not heavy enough for the umbrella. She started off, walking quickly along beside the double line of traffic.

She wondered where he had gone, chased down the street by Mrs. 84 Nolan in her scuffies and flowered housecoat, shouting and flailing at him with a broom. She must have been at least as terrifying a spectacle to him as he was to her, and just as inexplicable. Why would this woman, this fat crazy woman, wish to burst in upon a scene of harmless hospitality, banging and raving? He and his friends could easily have overpowered her, but they would not even have thought about doing that. They would have been too frightened. What unspoken taboo had they violated? What would these cold, mad people do next?

Anyway, he did have some friends. They would take care of him, at 85 least for the time being. Which was a relief, she guessed. But what she really felt was a childish regret that she had not seen the dancing girls. If she had known they were there, she might even have risked opening her door. She knew they were not real dancing girls, they were probably just some whores from Scollay Square. Mrs. Nolan had called them that as a euphemism, or perhaps because of an unconscious association with the word *Arabian*, the vaguely Arabian country. She never had found out what it was. Nevertheless, she wished she had seen them. Jetske would find all of this quite amusing, especially the image of her backed against the door, drinking sherry in the dark. It would have been better if she'd had the courage to look.

She began to think about her green space, as she often did during this 86 walk. The green, perfect space of the future. She knew by now that it was cancelled in advance, that it would never come into being, that it was already too late. Once she was qualified, she would return to plan tasteful mixes of residential units and shopping complexes, with a lot of underground malls and arcades to protect people from the snow. But she could allow herself to see it one last time.

The fence was gone now, and the green stretched out endlessly, fields
and trees and flowing water, as far as she could see. In the distance,
beneath the arches of the aqueduct, a herd of animals, deer or something,
was grazing. (She must learn more about animals.) Groups of people were
walking happily among the trees, holding hands, not just in twos but in
threes, fours, fives. The man from next door was there, in his native
costume, and the mathematicians, they were all in their native costumes.
Beside the stream a man was playing the flute; and around him, in long
flowered robes and mauve scuffies, their auburn hair floating around their
healthy pink faces, smiling their Dutch smiles, the dancing girls were
sedately dancing.

Owl Song

I am the heart of a murdered woman
who took the wrong way home
who was strangled in a vacant lot and not buried
who was shot with care beneath a tree
who was mutilated by a crisp knife.   5
There are many of us.

I grew feathers and tore my way out of her;
I am shaped like a feathered heart.
My mouth is a chisel, my hands
the crimes done by hands.   10

I sit in the forest talking of death
which is monotonous:
though there are many ways of dying
there is only one death song,
the colour of mist: 15
it says Why Why

I do not want revenge, I do not want expiation,
I only want to ask someone
how I was lost,
how I was lost   20

I am the lost heart of a murderer
who has not yet killed,
who does not yet know he wishes
to kill; who is still the same
as the others   25

I am looking for him,
he will have answers for me,
he will watch his step, he will be
cautious and violent, my claws
will grow through his hands   30
and become claws, he will not be caught.

STUDY QUESTIONS

1. In "Dancing Girls," what is the relationship between Ann and Mrs. Nolan, her landlady? Why does Mrs. Nolan choose to confide in her?

2. In what ways are Ann and Lelah different, and what does Ann's response to these differences say about her character?

3. Although Ann is studying Urban Design, she is unable to "vizualize the people" who would live in her rearranged city of Toronto. What are the possible intentions of meaning behind this represented "gap" in the character's imagination?

4. Trace the progress of Mrs. Nolan's unhappiness with her "foreign" tenant. How would you reinterpret the incidents that disturbed her in a different cultural context so that they appear innocent rather than dangerous?

5. Do you read Ann's final vision of multicultural harmony as an actual ideal to work for? How does the adjective "sedately" in the final sentence comment on Ann's character and on the fate of the "foreigner" Mrs. Nolan chases out of the house?

6. The first stanza of "Owl Song" enumerates a number of violent scenes. What is the effect of this clausal development?

7. By the fifth stanza, the image of the murdered woman's heart has been transformed to "the lost heart of a murderer." How is the poem's theme to be drawn from the relation between these two images?

8. The poem says, "I do not want revenge, I do not want expiation / I only want to ask someone / how I was lost." Does the poem achieve its stated function of questioning male violence against women without rousing a vengeful or guilty response? Should our response be restrained in these ways?

MICHEL TREMBLAY

Michel Tremblay (b. 1942) uses a Montreal working-class French idiom in his work. He is a prolific playwright whose plays have received international acclaim. After 1975, he moved from drama to writing novels. His work contains autobiographical elements, a strong critique of the institution of the family, and a major focus on the marginality of the working-class French Quebecois. His novel The Fat Woman Next Door Is Pregnant *(English translation, 1981), from which the narrative that follows is excerpted, must be read not simply as Canadian literature but also in the context of a distinctly French Quebecois culture and history, which includes a history of political and economic oppression.*

Excerpt from *The Fat Woman Next Door Is Pregnant*

Edouard and Thérèse had got up at the same time. Their rooms faced each other, so they'd found themselves nose to nose when they opened their doors. "You're up early, mon oncle Edouard. And today's Saturday!" "When you gotta go, little girl, it doesn't matter what day it is." They both ran to the bathroom at the very back of the house, past the dining room and the kitchen. Thérèse got there first, but yielded her place to her mother's brother. Marcel, Thérèse's brother, who was so small, despite his four years, that people thought he was barely two and a half or three, heard them running and when Thérèse and Edouard passed him, he lisped a shy good morning, but the two runners didn't hear him. Marcel slept in the dining room, in a bed disguised as a sofa in the daytime. It was far too big for him and he hated it. Marcel witnessed all the comings and goings in the house—and God knows, there were lots. When his uncle Gabriel, who worked nights, came home around two in the morning, Marcel would wave at him. But Gabriel, preoccupied, tired, head drooping, rarely looked in the baby's direction. He would hurry into his own bedroom which opened off the dining room, where the fat pregnant woman, his wife, was waiting for him. When Albertine, Marcel and Thérèse's mother, got up at night to make some tea to calm her nerves, Marcel would slip out of bed and follow her into the kitchen. She would take him in her arms as she waited for the water to boil—and Marcel inevitably would fall asleep, his head resting against his mother's plump shoulder. Albertine would rock her youngest child as she stared at the tea kettle. Sometimes, she fell asleep on her feet, leaning against the stove, waking with a start just as Marcel was about to fall, or the water began to boil over on the coal stove making

1

an unpleasant sputtering sound. And when old Victoire, the mother of Edouard, Gabriel and Albertine, got up every night to go to the bathroom, Marcel would huddle in a corner of his bed and close his eyes. Marcel was afraid of Victoire. Not that she was mean or nasty. But a strange sickness in her left leg made her limp, made her suffer dreadfully and made her irritable. And so, she was often impatient with her grandchildren. Victoire passed Marcel's bed like a shadow and slipped through the kitchen, then into the back room where she began to produce sounds that would have made Richard or Philippe, the sons of Gabriel and the fat woman, laugh, but which literally terrified the little boy. When she was finished, she would let out a sort of long moan and vigorously pull the chain. The sucking sound of the water flushing drove Marcel almost crazy with fear, because he knew it meant the old woman was about to limp past his bed again. Would she jump into his bed, jump on him with both feet as his cousin Philippe, four years his elder and already a smooth talker and storyteller, had promised? Would she beat him, kill him, eat him up? But Victoire walked past without giving him a thought. Marcel went back to sleep, trembling. "You been in there a long time, mon oncle. Let me make peepee, then you can go back." Edouard came grumbling out of the bathroom. Immediately, Marcel shot across the dining room and kitchen and threw himself into the arms of his uncle, who tossed him up to the ceiling, as the child shouted and laughed. "What do you want for breakfast, Marcel? Eggs? Two dozen? And bacon? Two pounds? And toast? Two whole loaves of bread? Coffee? Two coffeepots?" Thérèse shouted from the bathroom. "You're going to wake up the whole house!" "Shut up and piss!" "You know very well he doesn't eat any of that stuff anyway . . ." "If he doesn't eat any of that stuff, it's because you don't give it to him! I'm sick and tired of seeing him eat pabulum . . ." "He doesn't eat it because it doesn't agree with him." "That's your mother's bright idea, Thérèse, that it doesn't agree with him . . ." Thérèse came out of the bathroom, tying her pajama cord. "You can go in now." "Will you start the coffee in the meanwhile, my pretty little chickie?" Edouard rushed into the bathroom as Thérèse bent over her little brother. "Did you make peepee?" "No." "Do you have to go?" "Yeth." Thérèse picked Marcel up and took him to the edge of the kitchen sink. "Go on, or it'll be too late . . ." Pink with pleasure, Marcel took out his little penis and bent his head over the sink. "Do you always look at yourself like that when you make peepee?" "Yeth." "Why?" "'Cause I like to." "Dirty!" "Diddy? Why, diddy?" "You'll find out soon enough!" Thérèse was eleven. The same age as Richard, the elder son of the fat woman and Gabriel. Thérèse and Richard had been born two days apart: Thérèse on October 31, and Richard, two days later, on November 2. Thérèse was a clown, merry, always making faces, like a Hallowe'en party, while Richard was serious, sad, pale and tedious as the Mass for the dead. But they were inseparable, Thérèse, having fun as naturally as breathing, Richard, being glum no matter what he did. "You're going to wake up my father with your fooling around and we'll get hell again!" Richard was standing in the kitchen doorway, tall for his age, his ears sticking out, his eyes puffy. "Your father usually gets up on Saturday, Coco, so we can make as much noise as we want." "But you don't have to start at eight o'clock in the morning!" "I see, now you're starting, eh?" Thérèse put her brother down, went over to her cousin and kissed him on the neck. Richard wiped the kiss away with his hand. "Breakfast ready?" Thérèse gave him a withering look. "No, I've only had time to make noise!" Edouard came out of the bathroom just then. "Thérèse, go and dress your brother. And Richard, go somewhere else and sulk. I'm making the breakfast this morning!" The kitchen was vacated in two seconds flat and Edouard got down to work. He took one of the fat woman's aprons (he himself was rather corpulent, thank you), tied it neatly at the back, then opened the door of the icebox.

Richard shared a double room at the front of the house with Victoire, his grandmother, and his uncle Edouard. He slept in a folding bed under the archway. Every night, he went to a dark corner and pulled out the iron bed which was folded in two, with blankets and sheets hanging out of it, and began to struggle with two hooks that were too tight and refused to budge. Of course, the hooks would let go all at once, the bed would unfold and the slack, worn-out springs would clatter and twang. And every morning, Richard had to fold up the bed again, sweating bullets, and puffing and wheezing. The hooks would refuse to go into their spaces, the feet wouldn't fold, the thin mattress was suddenly too thick—and as his grandmother, who didn't even seem to be enjoying herself, looked on placidly, the boy, dishevelled, red and out of breath, would finally close up his bed. As he pushed the heap of iron into its corner, Richard would curse the fate that had condemned him to leave his parents' room and end up here, in this hole, that reeked of his grandmother's medicines and his uncle Edouard's cologne—Yardley Lotus. That morning, while his grandmother was still asleep, her mouth wide open, as if she were uttering a final cry of despair, Richard didn't tackle his bed. For lack of anything better to do, he turned his head towards the old woman. He could see her face between two bars of the brass bed. In the five years he'd been sleeping in the same room with her, Richard had spent an incalculable number of hours watching his grandmother die. In fact, every time he examined her in her sleep, grumbling, scarcely breathing, mouth open to reveal bare white gums as sharp as knives, Richard expected to see her expire. She was an exhausted flickering candle, a dismantled gasping clock, a motor at the end of the road, a dog grown too old, a servant who had finished serving and was dying of boredom, a useless old woman, a beaten human being, his grandmother. If she wanted to do anything in the house, her daughter-in-law, the fat woman, or her daughter, Albertine, very attentively would anticipate her intentions: "You just rest . . . you've done enough work in your life . . . sit down, Momma, your leg . . ." The old woman would lay down the dishcloth or the wooden spoon, swallowing so she wouldn't explode. Richard had often seen his grandmother weep with rage, leaning against the window in her room that looked out on the outside staircase. He'd even heard her curse the two women, cast impotent spells on them; he'd seen her stick out her tongue and pretend to be kicking them. From morning to night, she wandered from her bedroom to the dining room, from the dining room to her bedroom, a superfluous object of attention in this house where everyone and everything had assigned tasks or at least some use—except for her. She would have liked to take out the garbage, make supper, wash the fat woman, soak the curtains in the bathtub, wallop Philippe or Thérèse or Richard or Marcel, but wallop someone; instead, though, she invariably ended up in front of the radio, her ear pressed against Donalda's confidences or fat Georgiana's mercurial moods. In the very middle of a snore, Victoire opened her glassy eyes and her hand removed a white lock from her forehead. Richard immediately looked away. "What time is it?" Richard didn't answer. "What time is it? I know you aren't asleep, Coco. You're all dressed!" "Eight o'clock, Mémère. A little after." Victoire cleared her throat, took a small handkerchief from under her pillow and spat. Copiously. Richard shut his eyes. Victoire sat up with some difficulty and looked at her grandson. "Will you stop spying on me, for Heaven's sake!" Richard quickly turned his head towards his grandmother. "No." Long silence. Victoire, who was very short-sighted, couldn't see her grandson. But she could feel him looking at her. She could always feel him looking at her. It was the same look that had just drawn her from her sleep. "Someday when you're asleep, Mémère's going to get up and come and wring your little neck. Like a chicken." "No. You love me too much." The woman smiled. "You think so?" "Yes." In turn, Richard smiled. "I like it better when you're awake." "Me too!"

Dragging Marcel behind her, Thérèse burst into the other double room, the one that included the bedroom of her mother, Albertine, and the living room where she and her cousin Philippe had been sleeping for several years. Thérèse and Philippe shared the same sofa in a cavalcade of laughing, slapping, jumping, tickling and ill-concealed modesty. Misunderstood modesty, too. Philippe was only eight, but already he knew where to fumble and how to avoid slaps by assuming an innocent or a guileless attitude. Thérèse and Philippe's sofa was a constant source of amused murmuring, an oasis of gaiety in the midst of the desert of extinguished passions and unappeased desires that inhabited the four corners of the house. Albertine slept at the back of the double room, in a sort of boat, black in colour and black in mien, that her husband, Paul, now off at war, thank God, had brought from the wilds of his native Laurentians as a wedding present twelve years earlier. Albertine had always hated that rancid-smelling box where the worst experiences of her life had caught her by surprise when she was scarcely more than an adolescent, when she was ignorant and pure beyond common measure. She had been, and was still, subjected to this bed as to some inevitable catastrophe that might occur long after it has been announced and then go on to mark and direct an entire lifetime. The whole existence of this rather fat but very beautiful woman was contained between the painted planks, on the worn-out mattress, in the thin, frayed linen sheets: disillusion at the small amount of pleasure—when she had been promised paradise—could be read there just beneath the surface. Albertine had just awakened when her children rushed past the door like a whirlwind. Immediately, she sat up in bed, her head bristling with rag curlers, arms bare, in a pale pink cotton nightdress. "How come you're tearing the house apart so early in the morning? Isn't the baby dressed yet? Did he eat? Did he wet the bed again?" Thérèse looked at her mother with a broad smile, as Marcel hid behind her. She spoke softly, as though she were awakening her mother after a very peaceful night. "Bonjour, Momma. How are you this morning? Sleep all right?" Visibly disconcerted, Albertine stared at her daughter, taken aback, her arm still raised accusingly, but not so sure of herself now. "Bon, okay. I get it." She threw back the covers and swung her legs out of the bed. "Bring in the baby." Thérèse picked up her brother and brought him to their mother. Amazed to see her suddenly so gentle, Marcel looked at her as though he'd never seen her before: he was torn between a desire to cry, brought on by Albertine's anger, and a need to snuggle in her arms, because he loved her beyond reason—even beyond his fear. Sensing the baby's hesitation, Albertine decided to smile. Marcel opened his eyes wide, eyes that were wild with happiness, and began to laugh uncontrollably, so that his stomach quivered and his shoulders shook. "There's one you don't even have to tickle!" Albertine tossed Marcel onto his back on the bed. "Good thing I've got you!" Thérèse, who couldn't explain the mixture of delight and jealousy that stirred inside her, moved away from the enormous bed from which Marcel's laughter burst out in bubbles of joy. Thérèse and Albertine had had a serious conversation the night before. Or rather, Thérèse had tried to talk with her mother the night before. Wild with fear, but with her mind made up, she had come right out and asked her mother to stop shouting all the time when Marcel was around. The only answer the little girl received was a slap behind the ear, but all the same, she sensed that she'd made her point. And here was the proof. Seeing her mother smile and play with Marcel when she woke up, stroking the soles of his feet and nibbling at him, was a rare and brand new experience, too new, perhaps, for Thérèse to be able to relish it completely. And she knew very well that, in any case, her brother would be the only one to benefit from it. Hadn't she done it all for him? So as not to see him shift from laughter to tears whenever Albertine's frustrations exploded in rude words and hysterical cries? Her mother hadn't frightened her for a long time now and her abrupt changes of mood left Thérèse indifferent; no, not completely—her mother's changes of mood were beginning to awaken in her a brand new feeling that she didn't understand yet, but which filled her with a doleful joy that was ill-defined, almost unhealthy: contempt. She couldn't name this feeling, but she knew instinctively that she must bury it deep inside her, behind barricaded doors, in that place where you are alone, always alone, to savour the cold dish that leaves a sickly sweet taste in the mouth. Thérèse sat on the edge of the sofa. Philippe was pretending to be asleep. Thérèse lifted the covers, lay down beside her cousin and huddled against the little boy's plump, soft body. She pressed her mouth against her cousin's ear: "If you sleep so much, your little thing won't get stiff!" Philippe laughed so loud everyone in the house was startled.

"The bay isn't an open bay. It doesn't open onto the ocean. No . . . it's an 4 enclosed bay. When you look straight ahead, you don't see the open sea. The two arms of the bay close in . . . they practically touch. If you want to get there by boat, you have to go in between those two closed arms. It's the calmest bay in the world because the waves from the open sea don't come to the beach. The waves are still. Always. And in behind you, there's the mountains. So high, the clouds get stuck on them and never come out to the bay. It never rains on the bay in the winter because the mountains hold back the clouds. It's never ever rained in the winter." Arms folded over her enormous bosom, head against the back of the chair that she hadn't left for almost two months now, the fat woman spoke in a soft, even voice, without intonation. The intonation was in her eyes. Her eyes saw the bay, the waves, the rocks, sensed the clouds clinging to the mountains, like angel's hair on the branches of a Christmas tree. When the vision was too beautiful, the fat woman's eyes filled with tears and she let them fall to her chin, to her neck. "I could sit in the water, just on the edge of the shore and feel myself sinking into the sand. Because when you sit in the sand on the edge of the water, the waves hollow out a hole underneath you. I'd put on a housedress with every colour of the rainbow in it and people would point to me and say: 'See how happy that fat woman is!' I'd lie on my back at the edge of the water and the waves would come and spread their foam around my head. The whole month of January. The whole month of February. The whole month of March. We wouldn't hear a word about the war and we wouldn't know who'd died or disappeared or been maimed for life. You'd read *Notre-Dame de Paris* or *Eugénie Grandet* out loud, and when the waves weren't filling my ears, I'd listen. . . . I'd stay there, pinned down by the sun, and fondled by the ocean. And I could have as many babies as I wanted!" Lulled by the sound of his wife's voice, Gabriel had been asleep for several minutes. He began to snore, gently, as though not to disturb the fat woman. She looked at him for a few seconds, then went on with her story, as though he were still awake. "At noon, you'd go and pick pine-apples and coconuts. We'd eat under the palm trees, laughing and kissing. All the children I'd had would be at our feet, all the time, and we'd love it!" The bedroom door opened and Albertine, carrying a basin, burst in. "Sleep well?" "Not a wink." "Do you have to . . . ?" "Of course." Albertine slipped the basin between the fat woman's legs. "It gets more and more complicated. Seems like you're getting fatter and fatter." "I *am* getting fatter, it's normal. . . . I've got another two months." "If you hadn't de-cided to have a baby at your age . . ." "Now, don't start that again, Bar-tine!" Marcel had followed his mother into the bedroom, but he didn't dare come up to the armchair. "Allô, Marcel. . . . I heard you crying last night. Did you have a bad dream?" The little boy scampered off like a frightened squirrel. "The coffee smells good." "I'll bring you some in a while, but I don't know how good it'll be. Edouard's making it!" The fat woman smiled. "Edouard! Edouard, doing us the honour of lifting a finger in the house? Now I've heard everything!" Albertine took the basin from between the fat woman's legs. "I'll come and change you after breakfast. You must be sweltering in here . . ." The fat woman frowned. "You're so nice this morning, Bartine." "I'll explain everything . . ." Albertine walked away from the armchair. "Wake up my husband. He has to eat." Albertine bent over her brother and gave him a gentle push. Gabriel opened his eyes. Albertine withdrew without a word, closing the door behind her. "Sorry. I feel asleep while you were talking. I had a hard day yesterday . . ." "Doesn't matter. Anyway, I think I dream more for myself than for you." "No. I like listening to you. It's as if we were there." "Go and eat." Gabriel got up and kissed his wife on her forehead. Her forehead was damp with sweat. "Want to try and get up this morning?" "You know very well I'm not supposed to." When the door had closed behind her husband, the fat woman turned to the window of their bedroom. She could see the shed at the end of the wooden gallery, part of the third floor of the house and a scrap of blue sky the size of a handkerchief. The rebellion she'd kept inside her for so long, that she'd managed to subdue at the bottom of her belly—a wild animal that refused to be tamed, which she had nourished with dreams and lies—suddenly awoke in her throat and the fat woman opened her mouth to scream. But a single word came out, like an admission of defeat or an accusation: "Acapulco!"

STUDY QUESTIONS

1. The house in "The Fat Woman Next Door Is Pregnant" contains three generations—the grandmother, her three children, a daughter-in-law, and four grandchildren. How does Marcel, the youngest member, re-spond to some of the members of this extended family?

2. Analyze Thérèse's relationship with Marcel, her younger brother, and their mother, Albertine. Why does she feel "delight and jealousy" as Albertine plays with Marcel?
3. Gabriel's wife—the outsider in the family—is pregnant and restricted to her bed. How does she negotiate her position in this self-enclosed and busy household?
4. The extended family (grandparents, aunts, uncles, cousins) is sometimes idealized as offering more community, nurturing, and stability than is possible in a nuclear family (father, mother, children). In what ways does this narrative support or contradict such an interpretation?

 MICHAEL ONDAATJE

Michael Ondaatje (b. 1943) was born in Sri Lanka and immigrated to Canada in 1962. A prolific short story writer and novelist, he has also won the Governor General's Award for Literature for two books: The Collected Works of Billy the Kid *(1970) and* There's a Trick with a Knife I'm Learning to Do: Poems, 1962–1978 *(1979). The latter book, like his most recent novel,* In the Skin of a Lion *(1987), incorporates materials drawn from his Sri Lankan background. Ondaatje's work explores the character of relations and roles—such as father and son or male and female—that have lost their traditional meanings and ordered constructions.*

Letters & Other Worlds

"for there was no more darkness for him and, no doubt like Adam before the fall, he could see in the dark"

M y father's body was a globe of fear
His body was a town we never knew
He hid that he had been where we were going
His letters were a room he seldom lived in
In them the logic of his love could grow   5

My father's body was a town of fear
He was the only witness to its fear dance
He hid where he had been that we might lose him
His letters were a room his body scared

He came to death with his mind drowning.   10
On the last day he enclosed himself
in a room with two bottles of gin, later
fell the length of his body
so that brain blood moved
to new compartments   15
that never knew the wash of fluid
and he died in minutes of a new equilibrium.

His early life was a terrifying comedy
and my mother divorced him again and again.
he would rush into tunnels magnetized   20
by the white eye of trains
and once, gaining instant fame,
managed to stop a Perahara[1] in Ceylon
—the whole procession of elephants dancers
local dignitaries—by falling   25
dead drunk onto the street.

As a semi-official, and semi-white at that,
the act was seen as a crucial
turningpoint in the Home Rule Movement
and led to Ceylon's independence in 1948.   30

(My mother had done her share too—
her driving so bad
she was stoned by villagers
whenever her car was recognized)

For 14 years of marriage   35
each of them claimed he or she
was the injured party.
Once on the Colombo[2] docks
saying goodbye to a recently married couple
my father, jealous   40
at my mother's articulate emotion,
dove into the waters of the harbour
and swam after the ship waving farewell.
My mother pretending no affiliation
mingled with the crowd back to the hotel.   45

---

1. Perahara (or Anuradhapura Perahara): *A religious festival held each year in Ceylon (Sri Lanka) to mark the birth of an important Hindu god, Vishnu.*

2. Colombo: *The capital of Sri Lanka (Ceylon), also its principal port.*

Once again he made the papers
though this time my mother
with a note to the editor
corrected the report—saying he was drunk
rather than broken hearted at the parting of friends. 50
The married couple received both editions
of *The Ceylon Times* when their ship reached Aden.[1]

And then in his last years
he was the silent drinker,
the man who once a week 55
disappeared into his room with bottles
and stayed there until he was drunk
and until he was sober.

There speeches, head dreams, apologies,
the gentle letters, were composed. 60
With the clarity of architects
he would write of the row of blue flowers
his new wife had planted,
the plans for electricity in the house,
how my half-sister fell near a snake 65
and it had awakened and not touched her.
Letters in a clear hand of the most complete empathy
his heart widening and widening and widening
to all manner of change in his children and friends
while he himself edged 70
into the terrible acute hatred
of his own privacy
till he balanced and fell
the length of his body
the blood screaming in 75
the empty reservoir of bones
the blood searching in his head without metaphor

STUDY QUESTIONS

1. In "Letters & Other Worlds" the poet distinguishes between the father's
   body and his writing (letters). Contrast the character of the father as it
   appears in his letters with his character as it is seen in his actions.

---

1. Aden: *The main port city of Yemen.*

2. The poem contains, among other things, an ironic narration of the father's alcoholic acts. How are the public misinterpretations of these actions related to the assertions of his character expressed in the first two stanzas?
3. The early stanzas claim that the father concealed his fears and had a character unknown to others. How do the images used in the poem make known this mystery of the father's self? Does the poem succeed in this attempt?

UNITED STATES

✺ WALLACE STEVENS

Wallace Stevens (1879–1955), addressing the loss of faith in divine and absolute authority in the twentieth century, sought another truth in the imagination and in external reality. He constructed this "Supreme Fiction" as an act of the mind "finding what will suffice." His Collected Poems *(1954), for which he won the Pulitzer Prize, appeared when he was seventy-five and demonstrates his lifelong concerns and themes, among them meditations on near metaphysical issues on the nature of beauty, mind, poetry, and the human longing for transcendence. His complex poetry, weaving abstract thought and sensuous details, has remained an important influence on U.S. poets.*

Of Modern Poetry

The poem of the mind in the act of finding
What will suffice. It has not always had
To find: the scene was set; it repeated what
Was in the script.
                    Then the theatre was changed   5
To something else. Its past was a souvenir.
It has to be living, to learn the speech of the place.
It has to face the men of the time and to meet
The women of the time. It has to think about war
And it has to find what will suffice. It has   10
To construct a new stage. It has to be on that stage
And, like an insatiable actor, slowly and
With meditation, speak words that in the ear,
In the delicatest ear of the mind, repeat,
Exactly, that which it wants to hear, at the sound   15

Of which, an invisible audience listens,
Not to the play, but to itself, expressed
In an emotion as of two people, as of two
Emotions becoming one. The actor is
A metaphysician in the dark, twanging   20
An instrument, twanging a wiry string that gives
Sounds passing through sudden rightnesses, wholly
Containing the mind, below which it cannot descend,
Beyond which it has no will to rise.
                          It must   25
Be the finding of a satisfaction, and may
Be of a man skating, a woman dancing, a woman
Combing. The poem of the act of the mind.

No Possum, No Sop, No Taters

He is not here, the old sun,
    As absent as if we were asleep.

The field is frozen. The leaves are dry.
    Bad is final in this light.

In this bleak air the broken stalks   5
    Have arms without hands. They have trunks

Without legs or, for that, without heads.
    They have heads in which a captive cry

Is merely the moving of a tongue.
    Snow sparkles like eyesight falling to earth,   10

Like seeing fallen brightly away.
    The leaves hop, scraping on the ground.

It is deep January. The sky is hard.
    The stalks are firmly rooted in ice.

It is in this solitude, a syllable,   15
    Out of these gawky flitterings,

Intones its single emptiness,
    The savagest hollow of winter-sound.

It is here, in this bad, that we reach
The last purity of the knowledge of good.   20

The crow looks rusty as he rises up.
Bright is the malice in his eye . . .

One joins him there for company,
But at a distance, in another tree.

STUDY QUESTIONS

1. According to "Of Modern Poetry," what is the major difference between traditional and modern poetry?
2. The poem is itself the subject of the poem, that is, it is self-reflexive.
   According to "Of Modern Poetry," who is its audience? Discuss the
   relationship between poem (speaker) and audience. What is suggested
   in the image of "two emotions becoming one"?
3. "Of Modern Poetry" is not concerned with traditional forms of poetry
   such as narrative and lyric but with "[T]he poem of the act of the
   mind." Analyze how the modern poem can be read as an "actor" and
   "A metaphysician in the dark."
4. "No Possum, No Sop, No Taters" describes a winter scene. What
   emotional impressions dominate this scene?
5. Discuss the changing point of view in the poem from "we" to "one."
   What is achieved by the use of the impersonal "one" in the final
   stanza?
6. What kinds of philosophical position on the relationship between good
   and evil is implied in the relationship between "the last purity of the
   knowledge of good" and "this bad"? How do the poem's winter images function in relation to this position?

❉ EZRA POUND

*Ezra Pound (1885–1972) was a highly controversial cultural figure and a key
exponent of modernism in all the arts. He acted as an editor and a mentor to
many of the most influential twentieth-century writers in the United States
and Britain, including T. S. Eliot, James Joyce, William Carlos Williams,
H.D., and Marianne Moore. He is best known for his* Cantos, *a long
experimental poem composed of esoteric European literary allusions meshed*

with his wide and idiosyncratic interests in economics, Chinese culture, and politics, among other things. Pound was a founder of the Imagist movement, which advocated pictorial precision and minimal linguistic embellishment. "In a Station of the Metro" has come to be known as the exemplary Imagist poem. Born and raised in Idaho, Pound spent much of his adult life in Europe and took up the cause of Fascism in Italy during World War II. After the war he was charged with treason and was committed as mentally unsound to St. Elizabeth's Hospital in Washington, D.C.

In a Station of the Metro[1]

The apparition of these faces in the crowd;
Petals on a wet, black bough.

The River-Merchant's Wife:
A Letter

While my hair was still cut straight across my forehead[2]
I played about the front gate, pulling flowers.
You came by on bamboo stilts, playing horse,
You walked about my seat, playing with blue plums.
And we went on living in the village of Chokan.   5
Two small people, without dislike or suspicion.

At fourteen I married My Lord you.
I never laughed, being bashful.
Lowering my head, I looked at the wall.
Called to, a thousand times, I never looked back.   10

At fifteen I stopped scowling,
I desired my dust to be mingled with yours
Forever and forever and forever.
Why should I climb the look out?

---

1. Metro: *The Paris subway.*
2. *A figural way of saying "When I was a child."*

At sixteen you departed, 15
You went into far Ku-to-en, by the river of swirling eddies,
And you have been gone five months.
The monkeys make sorrowful noise overhead.

You dragged your feet when you went out.
By the gate now, the moss is grown, the different mosses, 20
Too deep to clear them away!
The leaves fall early this autumn, in wind.
The paired butterflies are already yellow with August
Over the grass in the West garden;
They hurt me. I grow older. 25
If you are coming down through the narrows of the river
    Kiang,
Please let me know beforehand,
And I will come out to meet you
                As far as Cho-fū-Sa.[1] 30

                                    By Rihaku[2]

STUDY   QUESTIONS

1. What kinds of impressions and emotions are suggested in "In a Station
   of the Metro" through the juxtaposition of the crowded urban scene
   with the sensuous image drawn from nature?
2. "The River-Merchant's Wife: A Letter" is based on a loose translation
   of a poem by the eighth-century Chinese poet, Li Po. How does Pound
   use different cultural materials to demonstrate some features of the
   modern sensibility? How do this poem's style and form illustrate
   William Carlos Williams's famous dictum, "No ideas/but in things"?
3. What is the dramatic situation that the speaker constructs for us in
   "The River-Merchant's Wife"? How is the speaker's character also revealed in the process?
4. Analyze images of time in "The River-Merchant's Wife" and discuss
   their significance in the poem's emotional effects.

---

1. *Ch'ang-feng-sha, several hundred miles up river from Chokan.*
2. Rihaku: *The Japanese name of Li Po (701–762), from whose original Chinese poem Pound made
   this loose translation.*

WILLIAM CARLOS WILLIAMS

*William Carlos Williams (1883–1963) is a major influence in contemporary
American poetry. Departing from conservative and traditional poetic forms,
Williams experimented with colloquial American speech, free verse, and the
flexible line, among other stylistic features. Influenced by the modernist
movement in Europe, Williams wrote on subjects usually held to be unpoetical
and insisted on the significance of the everyday and the seemingly ordinary.
Williams's insistence on "the concrete particular" and on (American) place
and occasion as the field for poetry is a significant counter to the classicist and
elitist practitioners such as T. S. Eliot and Ezra Pound, who looked to
European tradition for their inspiration.*

A Sort of Song

L et the snake wait under
  his weed
and the writing
be of words, slow and quick, sharp
to strike, quiet to wait,   5
sleepless.

—through metaphor to reconcile
the people and the stones.
Compose. (No ideas
but in things) Invent!   10
Saxifrage is my flower that splits
the rocks.

STUDY QUESTIONS

1. Discuss how writing is like the figure of "the snake . . . under his
   weed."
2. Define the term "metaphor" and discuss how "A Sort of Song" illustrates its theme, "through metaphor to reconcile/the people and the
   stones."
3. Williams's line "No ideas/but in things" has been often taken as the
   rallying cry for modernist poetry. To your mind, how revolutionary is
   this position, which disestablishes abstractions and privileges the concrete, today?

❀ LANGSTON HUGHES

Langston Hughes (1902–1967) was born in Missouri and began his literary career during the Harlem Renaissance in the early 1920s. The best-known African American writer of his time, he continued to write and publish for over forty years, serving as a model for such writers as Gwendolyn Brooks and Alice Walker. His poems and stories treat themes of social realism with equal measures of anger and humor, incorporating his knowledge of African American history and folk culture and using the rhythms and idioms of blues and jazz. Hughes was enormously prolific, writing, editing, and translating dozens of books in all genres.

Railroad Avenue

Dusk dark
   On Railroad Avenue.
Lights in the fish joints,
Lights in the pool rooms.
A box-car some train   5
Has forgotten
In the middle of the
Block.
A player piano,
A victrola.   10
    942
    Was the number.

A boy
Lounging on a corner.
A passing girl   15
With purple powdered skin.
    Laughter
    Suddenly
    Like a taut drum.
    Laughter   20
    Suddenly
    Neither truth nor lie.
    Laughter
Hardening the dusk dark evening.
    Laughter   25
Shaking the lights in the fish joints,

Rolling white balls in the pool rooms,
And leaving untouched the box-car
Some train has forgotten.

The Negro Speaks of Rivers

I 've known rivers:
I've known rivers ancient as the world and older than the
    flow of human blood in human veins.

My soul has grown deep like the rivers.

I bathed in the Euphrates when dawns were young.   5
I built my hut near the Congo and it lulled me to sleep.
I looked upon the Nile and raised the pyramids above it.
I heard the singing of the Mississippi when Abe Lincoln
      went down to New Orleans, and I've seen its muddy
      bosom turn all golden in the sunset.   10

I've known rivers:
Ancient, dusky rivers.

My soul has grown deep like the rivers.

STUDY QUESTIONS

1. "Railroad Avenue" can be read as a description of an urban setting, one whose details convey emotional and thematic content. What are the differences between the details presented in the first and second stanzas? How, and as a result of what action, has the scene changed?
2. What kinds of suggestions are carried in the various metaphors for laughter in stanza two? What do these metaphors suggest about the intention behind the laughter? What is meant by the assertion that such laughter is "Neither truth nor lie"?
3. "The Negro Speaks of Rivers" was written when African Americans were identified as Negros. The term is no longer in popular use, as it is associated with a period in U.S. history when legislation enforced racial segregation and inequality. With this context in mind, what is suggested in the lines "I've known rivers ancient as the world. . . . /My soul has grown deep like the rivers"?

4. What are the various civilizations enumerated in "The Negro Speaks of Rivers," and what is achieved by this cultural encompassment?

✦ Elizabeth Bishop

Elizabeth Bishop (1911–1979) was born in Massachusetts, but spent much of her adult life abroad, especially in Brazil. At the age of four she was separated from her mother, who was institutionalized for mental problems, and raised by an aunt in Nova Scotia. She began publishing poems in 1935 and gradually established her reputation with each book. In 1956, she won the Pulitzer Prize for Poetry. In 1969 her Complete Poems *won the National Book Award. Bishop's life, travels, and years of voluntary exile made her sympathetic to experiences of marginality. Her poems are notable for a distinctive complex voice and for their uncompromising attitudes toward difficult human concerns.*

The Man-Moth[1]

Here, above
cracks in the buildings are filled with battered moonlight.
The whole shadow of Man is only as big as his hat.
It lies at his feet like a circle for a doll to stand on,
and he makes an inverted pin, the point magnetized to the   5
    moon.
He does not see the moon; he observes only her vast
    properties,
feeling the queer light on his hands, neither warm nor cold,
of a temperature impossible to record in thermometers.   10

        But when the Man-Moth
pays his rare, although occasional, visits to the surface,
the moon looks rather different to him. He emerges
from an opening under the edge of one of the sidewalks
and nervously begins to scale the faces of the buildings.   15
He thinks the moon is a small hole at the top of the sky,

---

1. *Newspaper misprint for "mammoth."*

proving the sky quite useless for protection.
He trembles, but must investigate as high as he can climb.

      Up the façades,
his shadow dragging like a photographer's cloth behind him,   20
he climbs fearfully, thinking that this time he will manage
to push his small head through that round clean opening
and be forced through, as from a tube, in black scrolls on the
    light.
(Man, standing below him, has no such illusions.)   25
But what the Man-Moth fears most he must do, although
he fails, of course, and falls back scared but quite unhurt.

      Then he returns
to the pale subways of cement he calls his home. He flits,
he flutters, and cannot get aboard the silent trains   30
fast enough to suit him. The doors close swiftly.
The Man-Moth always seats himself facing the wrong way
and the train starts at once at its full, terrible speed,
without a shift in gears or a gradation of any sort.
He cannot tell the rate at which he travels backwards.   35

      Each night he must
be carried through artificial tunnels and dream recurrent
    dreams.
Just as the ties recur beneath his train, these underlie
his rushing brain. He does not dare look out the window,   40
for the third rail, the unbroken draught of poison,
runs there beside him. He regards it as a disease
he has inherited the susceptibility to. He has to keep
his hands in his pockets, as others must wear mufflers.

      If you catch him,   45
hold up a flashlight to his eye. It's all dark pupil,
an entire night itself, whose haired horizon tightens
as he stares back, and closes up the eye. Then from the lids
one tear, his only possession, like the bee's sting, slips.
Slyly he palms it, and if you're not paying attention   50
he'll swallow it. However, if you watch, he'll hand it over,
cool as from underground springs and pure enough to drink.

STUDY QUESTIONS

1. From the description offered in "The Man-Moth," what inferences are we to make of the Man-Moth's environment and character?
2. How is the creature the poet calls the Man-Moth different from "Man"?
3. The poem contains many metaphors that cluster to suggest certain attitudes about human existence. What are some of these metaphors, and what do they reveal about the poet's attitudes?
4. The Man-Moth is not intended as a realistic character. What are the elements of fantasy that result in the portrayal of this figure?

JAMES BALDWIN

James Baldwin (1924–1987) wrote plays, poems, novels, and short stories, but it is his essays that have had the greatest impact on American literature and society. Born in Harlem, Baldwin lived in Paris for many years to escape the destructive race politics of the United States, and much of his writing, including the early novel Giovanni's Room *(1956), is set in France. But he was an active witness to the oppression of African Americans; his passionate and intelligent prose delineates the values that fueled the civil rights movement of the sixties and explores the dilemma of African American characters caught in an often hostile culture.*

The Rockpile

Across the street from their house, in an empty lot between two houses, stood the rockpile. It was a strange place to find a mass of natural rock jutting out of the ground; and someone, probably Aunt Florence, had once told them that the rock was there and could not be taken away because without it the subway cars underground would fly apart, killing all the people. This, touching on some natural mystery concerning the surface and the center of the earth, was far too intriguing an explanation to be challenged, and it invested the rockpile, moreover, with such mysterious importance that Roy felt it to be his right, not to say his duty, to play there. 1

Other boys were to be seen there each afternoon after school and all day Saturday and Sunday. They fought on the rockpile. Sure footed, dangerous, and reckless, they rushed each other and grappled on the heights, 2 sometimes disappearing down the other side in a confusion of dust and screams and upended, flying feet. "It's a wonder they don't kill themselves," their mother said, watching sometimes from the fire escape. "You children stay away from there, you hear me?" Though she said "children," she was looking at Roy, where he sat beside John on the fire escape."The good Lord knows," she continued, "I don't want you to come home bleeding like a hog every day the Lord sends." Roy shifted impatiently, and continued to stare at the street, as though in this gazing he might somehow acquire wings. John said nothing. He had not really been spoken to: he was afraid of the rockpile and of the boys who played there.

Each Saturday morning John and Roy sat on the fire escape and watched   3
the forbidden street below. Sometimes their mother sat in the room behind them, sewing, or dressing their younger sister, or nursing the baby, Paul. The sun fell across them and across the fire escape with a high, benevolent indifference; below them, men and women, and boys and girls, sinners all, loitered; sometimes one of the church-members passed and saw them and waved. Then, for the moment that they waved decorously back, they were intimidated. They watched the saint, man or women, until he or she had disappeared from sight. The passage of one of the redeemed made them consider, however vacantly, the wickedness of the street, their own latent wickedness in sitting where they sat; and made them think of their father, who came home early on Saturdays and who would soon be turning this corner and entering the dark hall below them.

But until he came to end their freedom, they sat, watching and longing   4
above the street. At the end of the street nearest their house was the bridge which spanned the Harlem River and led to a city called the Bronx; which was where Aunt Florence lived. Nevertheless, when they saw her coming, she did not come from the bridge, but from the opposite end of the street. This, weakly, to their minds, she explained by saying that she had taken the subway, not wishing to walk, and that, besides, she did not live in *that* section of the Bronx. Knowing that the Bronx was across the river, they did not believe this story ever, but, adopting toward her their father's attitude, assumed that she had just left some sinful place which she dared not name, as, for example, a movie palace.

In the summertime boys swam in the river, diving off the wooden dock,   5
or wading in from the garbage-heavy bank. Once a boy, whose name was Richard, drowned in the river. His mother had not known where he was; she had even come to their house, to ask if he was there. Then, in the evening, at six o'clock, they had heard from the street a woman screaming and wailing; and they ran to the windows and looked out. Down the street came the woman, Richard's mother, screaming, her face raised to the sky and tears running down her face. A woman walked beside her, trying to make her quiet and trying to hold her up. Behind them walked a man, Richard's father, with Richard's body in his arms. There were two white policemen walking in the gutter, who did not seem to know what should

be done. Richard's father and Richard were wet, and Richard's body lay across his father's arms like a cotton baby. The woman's screaming filled all the street; cars slowed down and the people in the cars stared; people opened their windows and looked out and came rushing out of doors to stand in the gutter, watching. Then the small procession disappeared within the house which stood beside the rockpile. Then, *"Lord, Lord, Lord!"* cried Elizabeth, their mother, and slammed the window down.

One Saturday, an hour before his father would be coming home, Roy 6 was wounded on the rockpile and brought screaming upstairs. He and John had been sitting on the fire escape and their mother had gone into the kitchen to sip tea with Sister McCandless. By and by Roy became bored and sat beside John in restless silence; and John began drawing into his schoolbook a newspaper advertisement which featured a new electric locomotive. Some friends of Roy passed beneath the fire escape and called him. Roy began to fidget, yelling down to them through the bars. Then a silence fell. John looked up. Roy stood looking at him.

"I'm going downstairs," he said. 7

"You better stay where you is, boy. You know Mama don't want you 8 going downstairs."

"I be right *back*. She won't even know I'm gone, less you run and tell 9 her."

"I ain't *got* to tell her. What's going to stop her from coming in here and 10 looking out the window?"

"She's talking," Roy said. He started into the house. 11

"But Daddy's going to be home soon!" 12

"I be back before *that*. What you all the time got to be so *scared* for?" He 13 was already in the house and he now turned, leaning on the windowsill, to swear impatiently, "I be back in *five* minutes."

John watched him sourly as he carefully unlocked the door and disap- 14 peared. In a moment he saw him on the sidewalk with his friends. He did not dare to go and tell his mother that Roy had left the fire escape because he had practically promised not to. He started to shout, *Remember, you said five minutes!* but one of Roy's friends was looking up at the fire escape. John looked down at his schoolbook: he became engrossed again in the problem of the locomotive.

When he looked up again he did not know how much time had passed, 15 but now there was a gang fight on the rockpile. Dozens of boys fought each other in the harsh sun: clambering up the rocks and battling hand to hand, scuffed shoes sliding on the slippery rock; filling the bright air with curses and jubilant cries. They filled the air, too, with flying weapons: stones, sticks, tin cans, garbage, whatever could be picked up and thrown. John watched in a kind of absent amazement—until he remembered that Roy was still downstairs, and that he was one of the boys on the rockpile. Then he was afraid; he could not see his brother among the figures in the sun; and he stood up, leaning over the fire-escape railing. Then Roy appeared from the other side of the rocks; John saw that his shirt was torn; he was laughing. He moved until he stood at the very top of the rockpile. Then, something, an empty tin can, flew out of the air and hit him in the forehead, just above the eye. Immediately, one side of Roy's face ran with blood, he fell and rolled on his face down the rocks. Then for a moment there was no movement at all, no sound, the sun, arrested, lay on the street and the sidewalk and the arrested boys. Then someone screamed or shouted; boys began to run away, down the street, toward the bridge. The figure on the ground, having caught its breath and felt its own blood, began to shout. John cried, "Mama! Mama!" and ran inside.

"Don't fret, don't fret," panted Sister McCandless as they rushed down 16
the dark, narrow, swaying stairs, "don't fret. Ain't a boy been born don't get his knocks every now and again. *Lord!*" they hurried into the sun. A man had picked Roy up and now walked slowly toward them. One or two boys sat silent on their stoops; at either end of the street here was a group of boys watching. "He ain't hurt bad," the man said, "Wouldn't be making this kind of noise if he was hurt real bad."

Elizabeth, trembling, reached out to take Roy, but Sister McCandless, 17
bigger, calmer, took him from the man and threw him over her shoulder as she once might have handled a sack of cotton. "God bless you," she said to the man, "God bless you, son." Roy was still screaming. Elizabeth stood behind Sister McCandless to stare at his bloody face.

"It's just a flesh wound," the man kept saying, "just broke the skin, 18
that's all." They were moving across the sidewalk, toward the house. John, not now afraid of the staring boys, looked toward the corner to see if his father was yet in sight.

Upstairs, they hushed Roy's crying. They bathed the blood away, to 19
find, just above the left eyebrow, the jagged, superficial scar. "Lord, have mercy,' murmured Elizabeth, "another inch and it would've been his eye." And she looked with apprehension toward the clock. "Ain't it the truth," said Sister McCandless, busy with bandages and iodine.

"When did he go downstairs?" his mother asked at last. 20

Sister McCandless now sat fanning herself in the easy chair, at the head 21
of the sofa where Roy lay, bound and silent. She paused for a moment to look sharply at John. John stood near the window, holding the newspaper advertisement and the drawing he had done.

"We was sitting on the fire escape," he said. "Some boys he knew called 22
him."

"When?" 23

"He said he'd be back in five minutes." 24

"Why didn't you tell me he was downstairs?" 25

He looked at his hands, clasping his notebook, and did not answer. 26

"Boy," said Sister McCandless, "you hear your mother a-talking to 27
you?"

He looked at his mother. He repeated: 28

"He said he'd be back in five minutes."   29

"He said he'd be back in five minutes," said Sister McCandless with   30
scorn, "don't look to me like that's no right answer. You's the man of the
house, you supposed to look after your baby brothers and sisters—you
ain't supposed to let them run off and get half-killed. But I expect," she
added, rising from the chair, dropping the cardboard fan, "your Daddy'll
make you tell the truth. Your Ma's way too soft with you."

He did not look at her, but at the fan where it lay in the dark red,   31
depressed seat where she had been. The fan advertised a pomade for the
hair and showed a brown woman and her baby, both with glistening hair,
smiling happily at each other.

"Honey," said Sister McCandless, "I got to be moving along. Maybe I   32
drop in later tonight. I don't reckon you going to be at Tarry Service
tonight?"

Tarry Service was the prayer meeting held every Saturday night at   33
church to strengthen believers and prepare the church for the coming of
the Holy Ghost on Sunday.

"I don't reckon," said Elizabeth. She stood up; she and Sister McCan-   34
dless kissed each other on the cheek. "But you be sure to remember me in
your prayers."

"I surely will do that." She paused, with her hand on the door knob,   35
and looked down at Roy and laughed. "Poor little man," she said, "reckon
he'll be content to sit on the fire escape *now*."

Elizabeth laughed with her. "It sure ought to be a lesson to him. You   36
don't reckon," she asked nervously, still smiling, "he going to keep that
scar, do you?"

"Lord, no," said Sister McCandless, "ain't nothing but a scratch. I de-   37
clare, Sister Grimes, you worse than a child. Another couple of weeks and
you won't be able to *see* no scar. No, you go about your housework, honey,
and thank the Lord it weren't no worse." She opened the door; they heard
the sound of feet on the stairs. "I expect that's the Reverend," said Sister
McCandless, placidly, "I *bet* he going to raise cain."

"Maybe it's Florence," Elizabeth said. "Sometimes she get here about   38
this time." They stood in the doorway, staring, while the steps reached the
landing below and began again climbing to their floor. "No," said Elizabeth then, "that ain't her walk. That's Gabriel."

"Well, I'll just go on," said Sister McCandless, "and kind of prepare his   39
mind." She pressed Elizabeth's hand as she spoke and started into the hall,
leaving the door behind her slightly ajar. Elizabeth turned slowly back into
the room. Roy did not open his eyes, or move; but she knew that he was
not sleeping; he wished to delay until the last possible moment any contact
with his father. John put his newspaper and his notebook on the table and
stood, leaning on the table, staring at her.

"It wasn't my fault," he said. "I couldn't stop him from going down-   40
stairs."

"No," she said, "you ain't got nothing to worry about. You just tell your 41
Daddy the truth."

He looked directly at her, and she turned to the window, staring into the 42
street. What was Sister McCandless saying? Then from her bedroom she
heard Delilah's thin wail and she turned, frowning, looking toward the
bedroom and toward the still open door. She knew that John was watching
her. Delilah continued to wail, she thought, angrily, *Now that girl's getting
too big for that*, but she feared that Delilah would awaken Paul and she
hurried into the bedroom. She tried to soothe Delilah back to sleep. Then
she heard the front door open and close—too loud, Delilah raised her
voice, with an exasperated sigh Elizabeth picked the child up. Her child
and Gabriel's, her children and Gabriel's: Roy, Delilah, Paul. Only John
was nameless and a stranger, living, unalterable testimony to his mother's
days of sin.

"What happened?" Gabriel demanded. He stood, enormous, in the cen- 43
ter of the room, his black lunchbox dangling from his hand, staring at the
sofa where Roy lay. John stood just before him, it seemed to her astonished
vision just below him, beneath his fist, his heavy shoe. The child stared at
the man in fascination and terror—when a girl down home she had seen
rabbits stand so paralyzed before the barking dog. She hurried past Gabriel
to the sofa, feeling the weight of Delilah in her arms like the weight of a
shield, and stood over Roy, saying:

"Now, ain't a thing to get upset about, Gabriel. This boy sneaked down- 44
stairs while I had my back turned and got hisself hurt a little. He's alright
now."

Roy, as though in confirmation, now opened his eyes and looked gravely 45
at his father. Gabriel dropped his lunchbox with a clatter and knelt by the
sofa.

"How you feel, son? Tell your Daddy what happened?" 46

Roy opened his mouth to speak and then, relapsing into panic, began to 47
cry. His father held him by the shoulder.

"You don't want to cry. You's Daddy's little man. Tell your Daddy what 48
happened."

"He went downstairs," said Elizabeth, "where he didn't have no busi- 49
ness to be, and got to fighting with them bad boys playing on the rockpile.
That's what happened and it's a mercy it weren't nothing worse."

He looked up at her. "Can't you let this boy answer me for hisself?" 50

Ignoring this, she went on, more gently: "He got cut on the forehead, 51
but it ain't nothing to worry about."

"You call a doctor? How you know it ain't nothing to worry about?" 52

"Is you got money to be throwing away on doctors? No, I ain't called no 53
doctor. Ain't nothing wrong with my eyes that I can't tell whether he's hurt
or not. He got a fright more'n anything else, and you ought to pray God it
teaches him a lesson."

"You got a lot to say *now*," he said, "but I'll have *me* something to say 54 in a minute. I'll be wanting to know when all this happened, what you was doing with your eyes *then*." He turned back to Roy, who had lain quietly sobbing eyes wide open and body held rigid: and who now, at his father's touch, remembered the height, the sharp, sliding rock beneath his feet, the sun, the explosion of the sun, his plunge into darkness and his salty blood; and recoiled, beginning to scream, as his father touched his forehead. "Hold still, hold still," crooned his father, shaking, "hold still. Don't cry. Daddy ain't going to hurt you, he just wants to see this bandage, see what they've done to his little man." But Roy continued to scream and would not be still and Gabriel dared not lift the bandage for fear of hurting him more. And he looked at Elizabeth in fury: "Can't you put that child down and help me with this boy? John, take your baby sister from your mother—don't look like neither of you got good sense."

John took Delilah and sat down with her in the easy chair. His mother bent over Roy, and held him still, while his father, carefully—but still Roy screamed—lifted the bandage and stared at the wound. Roy's sobs began to lessen. Gabriel readjusted the bandage. "You see," said Elizabeth, finally, "he ain't nowhere near dead." 55

"It sure ain't your fault that he ain't dead." He and Elizabeth considered each other for a moment in silence. "He came mightly close to losing an eye. Course, his eyes ain't as big as your'n, so I reckon you don't think it matters so much." At this her face hardened; he smiled. "Lord, have mercy," he said, "you think you ever going to learn to do right? Where was you when all this happened? Who let him go downstairs?" 56

"Ain't nobody let him go downstairs, he just went. He got a head just like his father, it got to be broken before it'll bow. I was in the kitchen." 57

"Where was Johnnie?" 58

"He was in here." 59

"Where?" 60

"He was on the fire escape." 61

"Didn't he know Roy was downstairs?" 62

"I reckon." 63

"What you mean, you reckon? He ain't got your big eyes for nothing, does he?" He looked over at John. "Boy, you see your brother go downstairs?" 64

"Gabriel, ain't no sense in trying to blame Johnnie. You know right well if you have trouble making Roy behave, he ain't going to listen to his brother. He don't hardly listen to me." 65

"How come you didn't tell your mother Roy was downstairs?" 66

John said nothing, staring at the blanket which covered Delilah. 67

"Boy, you hear me? You want me to take a strap to you?" 68

"No, you ain't," she said. "You ain't going to take no strap to this boy, not today you ain't. Ain't a soul to blame for Roy's lying up there now but you—you because you done spoiled him so that he thinks he can do just anything and get away with it. I'm here to tell you that ain't no way to raise 69 no child. You don't pray to the Lord to help you do better than you been doing, you going to live to shed bitter tears that the Lord didn't take his soul today." And she was trembling. She moved, unseeing, toward John and took Delilah from his arms. She looked back at Gabriel, who had risen, who stood near the sofa, staring at her. And she found in his face not fury alone, which would not have surprised her; but hatred so deep as to become insupportable in its lack of personality. His eyes were struck alive, unmoving, blind with malevolence—she felt, like the pull of the earth at her feet, his longing to witness her perdition. Again, as though it might be propitiation, she moved the child in her arms. And at this his eyes changed, he looked at Elizabeth, the mother of his children, the helpmeet given by the Lord. Then her eyes clouded; she moved to leave the room; her foot struck the lunchbox lying on the floor.

"John," she said, "pick up your father's lunchbox like a good boy." 70

She heard, behind her, his scrambling movement as he left the easy 71
chair, the scrape and jangle of the lunchbox as he picked it up, bending his dark head near the toe of his father's heavy shoe.

STUDY QUESTIONS

1. How do the two brothers respond to the attractions of the street below their apartment in "The Rockpile"? How do their different responses tell us about their differences in character?

2. Why is the street "forbidden" to the children? Is it only the mother who forbids it?

3. Unlike the others, who are Gabriel and Elizabeth's children, John is presented as "nameless and a stranger, living, unalterable testimony to his mother's days in sin." How does this position explain the tensions in Gabriel's relationship with John?

4. Analyze the duality in Gabriel's perceptions of Elizabeth—one as with deep "hatred" and as "the helpmeet given by the Lord." How does Gabriel's ambivalence toward Elizabeth result in her need to protect John?

5. What is the significance suggested in the story's major symbols, for example, the symbol of the rockpile and of the father's shoes?

✳ FLANNERY O'CONNOR

*Flannery O'Connor (1925–1964) spent her entire life in and around the town of Milledgeville, Georgia. A devout Catholic, she gave life to characters whose religious impulses are often inseparably joined to cruelty, passion, and humor. O'Connor, who suffered from the debilitating and incurable disease of lupus, peopled many stories with the physically, mentally, and spiritually compromised, yet her mastery of comedy and the ironic twist effectively safeguarded her work from any shred of sentimentality. Often compared to William Faulkner, whose many novels critiqued the social and psychological consequences of slavery and the Civil War, O'Connor herself wrote two novels—*Wise Blood *(1952) and* The Violent Bear It Away *(1960). Her short fiction is collected in* The Complete Stories *(1971).*

The Life You Save May Be Your Own

T he old woman and her daughter were sitting on their porch when Mr. 1 Shiftlet came up their road for the first time. The old woman slid to the edge of her chair and leaned forward, shading her eyes from the piercing sunset with her hand. The daughter could not see far in front of her and continued to play with her fingers. Although the old woman lived in this desolate spot with only her daughter and she had never seen Mr. Shiftlet before, she could tell, even from a distance, that he was a tramp and no one to be afraid of. His left coat sleeve was folded up to show there was only half an arm in it and his gaunt figure listed slightly to the side as if the breeze were pushing him. He had on a black town suit and a brown felt hat that was turned up in the front and down in the back and he carried a tin tool box by a handle. He came on, at an amble, up her road, his face turned toward the sun which appeared to be balancing itself on the peak of a small mountain.

The old woman didn't change her position until he was almost into her 2 yard; then she rose with one hand fisted on her hip. The daughter, a large girl in a short blue organdy dress, saw him all at once and jumped up and began to stamp and point and make excited speechless sounds.

Mr. Shiftlet stopped just inside the yard and set his box on the ground 3 and tipped his hat at her as if she were not in the least afflicted; then he turned toward the old woman and swung the hat all the way off. He had long black slick hair that hung flat from a part in the middle to beyond the tips of his ears on either side. His face descended in forehead for more than half its length and ended suddenly with his features just balanced over a jutting steel-trap jaw. He seemed to be a young man but he had a look of composed dissatisfaction as if he understood life thoroughly.

"Good evening," the old woman said. She was about the size of a cedar fence post and she had a man's gray hat pulled down low over her head.   4

The tramp stood looking at her and didn't answer. He turned his back and faced the sunset. He swung both his whole and his short arm up slowly so that they indicated an expanse of sky and his figure formed a crooked cross. The old woman watched him with her arms folded across her chest as if she were the owner of the sun, and the daughter watched, her head thrust forward and her fat helpless hands hanging at the wrists. She had long pink-gold hair and eyes as blue as a peacock's neck.   5

He held the pose for almost fifty seconds and then he picked up his box and came on to the porch and dropped down on the bottom step. "Lady," he said in a firm nasal voice, "I'd give a fortune to live where I could see me a sun do that every evening."   6

"Does it every evening," the old woman said and sat back down. The daughter sat down too and watched him with a cautious sly look as if he were a bird that had come up very close. He leaned to one side, rooting in his pants pocket, and in a second he brought out a package of chewing gum and offered her a piece. She took it and unpeeled it and began to chew without taking her eyes off him. He offered the old woman a piece but she only raised her upper lip to indicate she had no teeth.   7

Mr. Shiftlet's pale sharp glance had already passed over everything in the yard—the pump near the corner of the house and the big fig tree that three or four chickens were preparing to roost in—and had moved to a shed where he saw the square rusted back of an automobile. "You ladies drive?" he asked.   8

"That car ain't run in fifteen year," the old woman said. "The day my husband died, it quit running."   9

"Nothing is like it used to be, lady," he said. "The world is almost rotten."   10

"That's right," the old woman said. "You from around here?"   11

"Name Tom T. Shiftlet," he murmured, looking at the tires.   12

"I'm pleased to meet you," the old woman said. "Name Lucynell Crater and daughter Lucynell Crater. What you doing around here, Mr. Shiftlet?"   13

He judged the car to be about a 1928 or '29 Ford. "Lady," he said, and turned and gave her his full attention, "lemme tell you something. There's one of these doctors in Atlanta that's taken a knife and cut the human heart—the human heart," he repeated, leaning forward, "out of a man's chest and held it in his hand," and he held his hand out, palm up, as if it were slightly weighted with the human heart, "and studied it like it was a day-old chicken, and lady," he said, allowing a long significant pause in which his head slid forward and his clay-colored eyes brightened, "he don't know no more about it than you or me."   14

"That's right," the old woman said.   15

"Why, if he was to take a knife and cut into every corner of it, he still   16
wouldn't know no more than you or me. What you want to bet?"

"Nothing," the old woman said wisely. "Where you come from, Mr.   17
Shiftlet?"

He didn't answer. He reached into his pocket and brought out a sack of   18
tobacco and a package of cigarette papers and rolled himself a cigarette,
expertly with one hand, and attached it in a hanging position to his upper
lip. Then he took a box of wooden matches from his pocket and struck
one on his shoe. He held the burning match as if he were studying the
mystery of flame while it traveled dangerously toward his skin. The
daughter began to make loud noises and to point to his hand and shake
her finger at him, but when the flame was just touching him, he leaned
down with his hand cupped over it as if he were going to set fire to his
nose and lit the cigarette.

He flipped away the dead match and blew a stream of gray into the   19
evening. A sly look came over his face. "Lady," he said, "nowadays,
people'll do anything anyways. I can tell you my name is Tom T. Shiftlet
and I come from Tarwater, Tennessee, but you never have seen me before:
how you know I ain't lying? How you know my name ain't Aaron Sparks,
lady, and I come from Singleberry, Georgia, or how you know it's not
George Speeds and I come from Lucy, Alabama, or how you know I ain't
Thompson Bright from Toolafalls, Mississippi?"

"I don't know nothing about you," the old woman muttered, irked.   20

"Lady," he said, "people don't care how they lie. Maybe the best I can   21
tell you is, I'm a man; but listen lady," he said and paused and made his
tone more ominous still, "what is a man?"

The old woman began to gum a seed. "What you carry in that tin box,   22
Mr. Shiftlet?" she asked.

"Tools," he said, put back. "I'm a carpenter."   23

"Well, if you come out here to work, I'll be able to feed you and give you   24
a place to sleep but I can't pay. I'll tell you that before you begin," she said.

There was no answer at once and no particular expression on his face.   25
He leaned back against the two-by-four that helped support the porch roof.
"Lady," he said slowly, "there's some men that some things mean more
to them than money." The old woman rocked without comment and the
daughter watched the trigger that moved up and down in his neck. He
told the old woman then that all most people were interested in was
money, but he asked what a man was made for. He asked her if a man
was made for money, or what. He asked her what she thought she was
made for but she didn't answer, she only sat rocking and wondered if a
one-armed man could put a new roof on her garden house. He asked a
lot of questions that she didn't answer. He told her that he was twenty-
eight years old and had lived a varied life. He had been a gospel singer,
a foreman on the railroad, an assistant in an undertaking parlor, and he
come over the radio for three months with Uncle Roy and his Red Creek

Wranglers. He said he had fought and bled in the Arm Service of his country and visited every foreign land and that everywhere he had seen people that didn't care if they did a thing one way or another. He said he hadn't been raised that away.

A fat yellow moon appeared in the branches of the fig tree as if it were 26 going to roost there with the chickens. He said that a man had to escape to the country to see the whole world and that he wished he lived in a desolate place like this where he could see the sun go down every evening like God made it to do.

"Are you married or are you single?" the old woman asked. 27

There was a long silence. "Lady," he asked finally, "where would you 28 find you an innocent woman today? I wouldn't have any of this trash I could just pick up."

The daughter was leaning very far down, hanging her head almost 29 between her knees, watching him through a triangular door she had made in her overturned hair; and she suddenly fell in a heap on the floor and began to whimper. Mr. Shiftlet straightened her out and helped her get back in the chair.

"Is she your baby girl?" he asked. 30

"My only," the old woman said, "and she's the sweetest girl in the 31 world. I would give her up for nothing on earth. She's smart too. She can sweep the floor, cook, wash, feed the chickens, and hoe. I wouldn't give her up for a casket of jewels."

"No," he said kindly, "don't ever let any man take her away from you." 32

"Any man come after her," the old woman said, " 'll have to stay around 33 the place."

Mr. Shiftlet's eye in the darkness was focused on part of the automobile 34 bumper that glittered in the distance. "Lady," he said, jerking his short arm up as if he could point with it to her house and yard and pump, "there ain't a broken thing on this plantation that I couldn't fix for you, one-arm jackleg or not. I'm a man," he said with a sullen dignity, "even if I ain't a whole one. I got," he said, tapping his knuckles on the floor to emphasize the immensity of what he was going to say, "a moral intelligence!" and his face pierced out of the darkness into a shaft of doorlight and he stared at her as if he were astonished himself at this impossible truth.

The old woman was not impressed with the phrase. "I told you you 35 could hang around and work for food," she said, "if you don't mind sleeping in that car yonder."

"Why listen, lady," he said with a grin of delight, "the monks of old 36 slept in their coffins!"

"They wasn't as advanced as we are," the old woman said. 37

The next morning he began on the roof of the garden house while Lucy- 38 nell, the daughter, sat on a rock and watched him work. He had not been around a week before the change he had made in the place was apparent. He had patched the front and back steps, built a new hog pen, restored a fence, and taught Lucynell, who was completely deaf and had never said a word in her life, to say the word "bird." The big rosy-faced girl followed him everywhere, saying "Burrttddt ddbirrttdt," and clapping her hands. The old woman watched from a distance, secretly pleased. She was ravenous for a son-in-law.

Mr. Shiftlet slept on the hard narrow back seat of the car with his feet out the side window. He had his razor and a can of water on a crate that served him as a bedside table and he put a piece of mirror against the back glass and kept his coat neatly on a hanger that he hung over one of the windows. 39

In the evenings he sat on the steps and talked while the old woman and Lucynell rocked violently in their chairs on either side of him. The old woman's three mountains were black against the dark blue sky and were visited off and on by various planets and by the moon after it had left the chickens. Mr. Shiftlet pointed out that the reason he had improved this plantation was because he had taken a personal interest in it. He said he was even going to make the automobile run. 40

He had raised the hood and studied the mechanism and he said he could tell that the car had been built in the days when cars were really built. You take now, he said, one man puts in one bolt and another man puts in another bolt and another man puts in another bolt so that it's a man for a bolt. That's why you have to pay so much for a car: you're paying all those men. Now if you didn't have to pay but one man, you could get you a cheaper car and one that had had a personal interest taken in it, and it would be a better car. The old woman agreed with him that this was so. 41

Mr. Shiftlet said that the trouble with the world was that nobody cared, or stopped and took any trouble. He said he never would have been able to teach Lucynell to say a word if he hadn't cared and stopped long enough. 42

"Teach her to say something else," the old woman said. 43

"What you want her to say next?" Mr. Shiftlet asked. 44

The old woman's smile was broad and toothless and suggestive. "Teach her to say 'sugarpie,' " she said. 45

Mr. Shiftlet already knew what was on her mind. 46

The next day he began to tinker with the automobile and that evening he told her that if she would buy a fan belt, he would be able to make the car run. 47

The old woman said she would give him the money. "You see that girl yonder?" she asked, pointing to Lucynell who was sitting on the floor a foot away, watching him, her eyes blue in the dark. "If it was ever a man wanted to take her away, I would say, 'No man on earth is going to take that sweet girl of mine away from me!' but if he was to say, 'Lady, I don't want to take her away, I want her right here,' I would say, 'Mister, I don't blame you none. I wouldn't pass up a chance to live in a permanent place and get the sweetest girl in the world myself. You ain't no fool,' I would say." 48

"How old is she?" Mr. Shiftlet asked casually. 49

"Fifteen, sixteen," the old woman said. The girl was nearly thirty but 50
because of her innocence it was impossible to guess.

"It would be a good idea to paint it, too," Mr. Shiftlet remarked. "You 51
don't want it to rust out."

"We'll see about that later," the old woman said. 52

The next day he walked into town and returned with the parts he needed 53
and a can of gasoline. Late in the afternoon, terrible noises issued from the
shed and the old woman rushed out of the house, thinking Lucynell was
somewhere having a fit. Lucynell was sitting on a chicken crate, stamping
her feet and screaming, "Burrddttt! bddurrddtttt!' but her fuss was
drowned out by the car. With a volley of blasts it emerged from the shed,
moving in a fierce and stately way. Mr. Shiftlet was in the driver's seat,
sitting very erect. He had an expression of serious modesty on his face as
if he had just raised the dead.

That night, rocking on the porch, the old woman began her business at 54
once. "You want you an innocent woman, don't you?" she asked sympathetically. "You don't want none of this trash."

"No'm, I don't," Mr. Shiftlet said. 55

"One that can't talk," she continued, "can't sass you back or use foul 56
language. That's the kind for you to have. Right there," and she pointed to
Lucynell sitting cross-legged in her chair, holding both her feet in her
hands.

"That's right," he admitted. "She wouldn't give me any trouble." 57

"Saturday," the old woman said, "you and her and me can drive into 58
town and get married."

Mr. Shiftlet eased his position on the steps. 59

"I can't get married right now," he said. "Everything you want to do 60
takes money and I ain't got any."

"What you need with money?" she asked. 61

"It takes money," he said. "Some people'll do anything anyhow these 62
days, but the way I think, I wouldn't marry no woman that I couldn't take
on a trip like she was somebody. I mean take her to a hotel and treat her.
I wouldn't marry the Duchesser Windsor," he said firmly, "unless I could
take her to a hotel and giver something good to eat.

"I was raised thataway and there ain't a thing I can do about it. My old 63
mother taught me how to do."

"Lucynell don't even know what a hotel is," the old woman muttered. 64
"Listen here, Mr. Shiftlet," she said, sliding forward in her chair, "you'd
be getting a permanent house and a deep well and the most innocent girl
in the world. You don't need no money. Lemme tell you something: there
ain't any place in the world for a poor disabled friendless drifting man."

The ugly words settled in Mr. Shiftlet's head like a group of buzzards in 65
the top of a tree. He didn't answer at once. He rolled himself a cigarette

and lit it and then he said in an even voice, "Lady, a man is divided into two parts, body and spirit."

The old woman clamped her gums together. 66

"A body and a spirit," he repeated. "The body, lady, is like a house: it 67 don't go anywhere; but the spirit, lady, is like a automobile: always on the move, always . . ."

"Listen, Mr. Shiftlet," she said, "my well never goes dry and my house 68 is always warm in the winter and there's no mortgage on a thing about this place. You can go to the courthouse and see for yourself. And yonder under that shed is a fine automobile." She laid the bait carefully. "You can have it painted by Saturday. I'll pay for the paint."

In the darkness, Mr. Shiftlet's smile stretched like a weary snake waking 69 up by a fire. After a second he recalled himself and said, "I'm only saying a man's spirit means more to him than anything else. I would have to take my wife off for the week end without no regards at all for cost. I got to follow where my spirit says to go."

"I'll give you fifteen dollars for a week-end trip," the old woman said in 70 a crabbed voice. "That's the best I can do."

"That wouldn't hardly pay for more than the gas and the hotel," he 71 said. "It wouldn't feed her."

"Seventeen-fifty," the old woman said. "That's all I got so it isn't any 72 use you trying to milk me. You can take a lunch."

Mr. Shiftlet was deeply hurt by the word "milk." He didn't doubt that 73 she had more money sewed up in her mattress but he had already told her he was not interested in her money. "I'll make that do," he said and rose and walked off without treating with her further.

On Saturday the three of them drove into town in the car that the paint 74 had barely dried on and Mr. Shiftlet and Lucynell were married in the Ordinary's office while the old woman witnessed. As they came out of the courthouse, Mr. Shiftlet began twisting his neck in his collar. He looked morose and bitter as if he had been insulted while someone held him. "That didn't satisfy me none," he said. "That was just something a woman in an office did, nothing but paper work and blood tests. What do they know about my blood? If they was to take my heart and cut it out," he said, "they wouldn't know a thing about me. It didn't satisfy me at all."

"It satisfied the law," the old woman said sharply. 75

"The law," Mr. Shiftlet said and spit. "It's the law that don't satisfy 76 me."

He had painted the car dark green with a yellow band around it just 77 under the windows. The three of them climbed in the front seat and the old woman said, "Don't Lucynell look pretty? Looks like a baby doll." Lucynell was dressed up in a white dress that her mother had uprooted from a trunk and there was a Panama hat on her head with a bunch of red wooden cherries on the brim. Every now and then her placid expression was changed by a sly isolated little thought like a shoot of green in the desert. "You got a prize!" the old woman said.

Mr. Shiftlet didn't even look at her. 78

They drove back to the house to let the old woman off and pick up the 79 lunch. When they were ready to leave, she stood staring in the window of the car, with her fingers clenched around the glass. Tears began to seep sideways out of her eyes and run along the dirty creases in her face. "I ain't never been parted with her for two days before," she said.

Mr. Shiftlet started the motor. 80

"And I wouldn't let no man have her but you because I seen you would 81 do right. Good-by, Sugarbaby," she said, clutching at the sleeve of the white dress. Lucynell looked straight at her and didn't seem to see her there at all. Mr. Shiftlet eased the car forward so that she had to move her hands.

The early afternoon was clear and open and surrounded by pale blue 82 sky. Although the car would go only thirty miles an hour, Mr. Shiftlet imagined a terrific climb and dip and swerve that went entirely to his head so that he forgot his morning bitterness. He had always wanted an automobile but he had never been able to afford one before. He drove very fast because he wanted to make Mobile by nightfall.

Occasionally he stopped his thoughts long enough to look at Lucynell in 83 the seat beside him. She had eaten the lunch as soon as they were out of the yard and now she was pulling the cherries off the hat one by one and throwing them out the window. He became depressed in spite of the car. He had driven about a hundred miles when he decided that she must be hungry again and at the next small town they came to, he stopped in front of an aluminum-painted eating place called The Hot Spot and took her in and ordered her a plate of ham and grits. The ride had made her sleepy and as soon as she got up on the stool, she rested her head on the counter and shut her eyes. There was no one in The Hot Spot but Mr. Shiftlet and the boy behind the counter, a pale youth with a greasy rag hung over his shoulder. Before he could dish up the food, she was snoring gently.

"Give it to her when she wakes up," Mr. Shiftlet said. "I'll pay for it 84 now."

The boy bent over her and stared at the long pink-gold hair and the 85 half-shut sleeping eyes. Then he looked up and stared at Mr. Shiftlet. "She looks like an angel of Gawd," he murmured.

"Hitch-hiker," Mr. Shiftlet explained. "I can't wait. I got to make Tus- 86 caloosa."

The boy bent over again and very carefully touched his finger to a strand 87 of the golden hair and Mr. Shiftlet left.

He was more depressed than ever as he drove on by himself. The late 88 afternoon had grown hot and sultry and the country had flattened out. Deep in the sky a storm was preparing very slowly and without thunder as if it meant to drain every drop of air from the earth before it broke. There were times when Mr. Shiftlet preferred not to be alone. He felt too that a man with a car had a responsibility to others and he kept his eye out for a hitchhiker. Occasionally he saw a sign that warned: "Drive carefully. The life you save may be your own."

The narrow road dropped off on either side into dry fields and here and 89 there a shack or a filling station stood in a clearing. The sun began to set directly in front of the automobile. It was a reddening ball that through his windshield was slightly flat on the bottom and top. He saw a boy in overalls and a gray hat standing on the edge of the road and he slowed the car down and stopped in front of him. The boy didn't have his hand raised to thumb the ride, he was only standing there, but he had a small cardboard suitcase and his hat was set on his head in a way to indicate that he had left somewhere for good. "Son," Mr. Shiftlet said, "I see you want a ride."

The boy didn't say he did or he didn't but he opened the door of the car 90 and got in, and Mr. Shiftlet started driving again. The child held the suitcase on his lap and folded his arms on top of it. He turned his head and looked out the window away from Mr. Shiftlet. Mr. Shiftlet felt oppressed. "Son," he said after a minute, "I got the best old mother in the world so I reckon you only got the second best."

The boy gave him a quick dark glance and then turned his face back out 91 the window.

"It's nothing so sweet," Mr. Shiftlet continued, "as a boy's mother. She 92 taught him his first prayers at her knee, she give him love when no other would, she told him what was right and what wasn't, and she seen that he done the right thing. Son," he said, "I never rued a day in my life like the one I rued when I left that old mother of mine."

The boy shifted in his seat but he didn't look at Mr. Shiftlet. He unfolded 93 his arms and put one hand on the door handle.

"My mother was a angel of Gawd," Mr. Shiftlet said in a very strained 94 voice. "He took her from heaven and giver to me and I left her." His eyes were instantly clouded over with a mist of tears. The car was barely moving.

The boy turned angrily in the seat. "You go to the devil!" he cried. "My 95 old woman is a flea bag and yours is a stinking pole cat!" and with that he flung the door open and jumped out with his suitcase into the ditch.

Mr. Shiftlet was so shocked that for about a hundred feet he drove along 96 slowly with the door still open. A cloud, the exact color of the boy's hat and shaped like a turnip, had descended over the sun, and another, worse looking, crouched behind the car. Mr. Shiftlet felt that the rottenness of the world was about to engulf him. He raised his arm and let it fall again to his breast. "Oh Lord!" he prayed. "Break forth and wash the slime from this earth!"

The turnip continued slowly to descend. After a few minutes there was 97 a guffawing peal of thunder from behind and fantastic raindrops, like tin-can tops, crashed over the rear of Mr. Shiftlet's car. Very quickly he stepped on the gas and with his stump sticking out the window he raced the galloping shower into Mobile.

1. What does Mr. Shiftlet do to gain the trust of the old woman and her daughter in "The Life You Save May Be Your Own"?
2. Is Shiftlet really "a poor disabled friendless drifting man"? How and why does Shiftlet respond to the old woman's description of him?
3. Why does the old woman want Shiftlet for her son-in-law? Why does Shiftlet agree to marry the daughter?
4. How is Shiftlet's view of the world and of the times related to the period in U.S. history in which the story is set?
5. What kind of criticism of Southern morality is suggested in the story's images (for example, Shiftlet's arms forming a crooked cross, the daughter as an angel of God), plot, and character development?

❉ ALLEN GINSBERG

Allen Ginsberg (b. 1926) is a powerful and innovative poet whose literary accomplishments have sometimes been overshadowed by his outrageous public persona. A leading figure in the Beat movement of the 1950s, the Hippie movement of the 1960s, and the Gay Rights movement of the 1970s, Ginsberg describes himself as a "Jewish Buddhist" who has foresworn drugs for meditation but remains a critic of the establishment. Like the two poets who have most deeply influenced him—the English visionary William Blake and the seminal American Walt Whitman—Ginsberg's work advocates a radical transformation of society to include the traditionally outcast and marginalized. His long poem Howl *(1956) spoke for a generation in a way that only T. S. Eliot's* The Waste Land *had thirty-four years earlier.*

A Supermarket in California

What thoughts I have of you tonight, Walt Whitman, for I walked 1 down the sidestreets under the trees with a headache self-conscious looking at the full moon.

In my hungry fatigue, and shopping for images, I went into the neon 2 fruit supermarket, dreaming of your enumerations!

What peaches and what penumbras! Whole families shopping at night! 3

Aisles full of husbands! Wives in the avocados, babies in the tomatoes!—and you, García Lorca, what were you doing down by the watermelons?

I saw you, Walt Whitman, childless, lonely old grubber, poking among the meats in the refrigerator and eyeing the grocery boys.   4

I heard you asking questions of each: Who killed the pork chops? What price bananas? Are you my Angel?   5

I wandered in and out of the brilliant stacks of cans following you, and followed in my imagination by the store detective.   6

We strode down the open corridors together in our solitary fancy tasting artichokes, possessing every frozen delicacy, and never passing the cashier.   7

Where are we going, Walt Whitman? The doors close in an hour. Which way does your beard point tonight?   8

(I touch your book and dream of our odyssey in the supermarket and feel absurd.)   9

Will we walk all night through solitary streets? The trees add shade to shade, lights out in the houses, we'll both be lonely.   10

Will we stroll dreaming of the lost America of love past blue automobiles in driveways, home to our silent cottage?   11

Ah, dear father, graybeard, lonely old courage-teacher, what America did you have when Charon[1] quit poling his ferry and you got out on a smoking bank and stood watching the boat disappear on the black waters of Lethe?   12

STUDY QUESTIONS

1. What attributes of American society does the supermarket in California symbolize? How is the speaker's position as an outsider in this society suggested through this scene of shopping in the supermarket?
2. "A Supermarket in California," addressed to Walt Whitman, uses the figure of this famous nineteenth-century poet as a symbolic companion for the speaker. How does Whitman's homosexuality figure in identifying some of the poem's major themes?
3. The "myth" of America as a cornucopia of fruitfulness—"the neon fruit supermarket"—is juxtaposed in the final sentence with the Greek myth of the Underworld. What critique of American culture is suggested in this juxtaposition?

---

1. Charon: *In Greek mythology, he was the ferryman who brought people from the land of the living across the Lethe, or river of forgetfulness (see end of poem), to the land of the dead.*

FRANK O'HARA

*Born in Baltimore, Maryland, and educated at Harvard, Frank O'Hara
(1926–1966) was associated with a group of artists and writers known as the
New York School. O'Hara himself worked as an assistant curator at the
Museum of Modern Art in New York, and his poetry demonstrates a clear
affinity with the visual arts. His early death from a car accident and the
quality of "camp" (that is, a combination of the whimsical, inconsequential,
witty, and delightful) in his poetry have added to his mystique. His poems,
however, stand on their own. His reputation was established with the
posthumous publication of* The Collected Poems of Frank O'Hara *(1971).
His poems, expressing personal emotions, impressions, and variations, have
the persuasiveness of immediacy. Often colloquial and witty, they evade form
and avoid easy intellectual statements.*

Why I Am Not a Painter

I am not a painter, I am a poet.
Why? I think I would rather be
a painter, but I am not. Well,

For instance, Mike Goldberg
is starting a painting   I drop in.   5
"Sit down and have a drink" he
says. I drink; we drink. I look
up. "You have SARDINES in it."
"Yes, it needed something there."
"Oh." I go and the days go by   10
and I drop in again. The painting
is going on, and I go, and the days
go by. I drop in. The painting is
finished. "Where's SARDINES?"
All that's left is just   15
letters, "It was too much," Mike says.

But me? One day I am thinking of
a color: orange. I write a line
about orange. Pretty soon it is a
whole page or words, not lines.   20
Then another page. There should be
so much more, not of orange, of

words, of how terrible orange is
and life. Days go by. It is even in
prose, I am a real poet. My poem
is finished and I haven't mentioned
orange yet. It's twelve poems, I call
it ORANGES. And one day in a gallery
I see Mike's painting, called SARDINES.

25

STUDY QUESTIONS

1. According to "Why I Am Not a Painter," how does a painting like that
   by Mike Goldberg evolve? Are the explanations the painter gives for
   why he does what he does rational?
2. The poem's title suggests that painting and poetry are different art
   forms. Does the poet support this suggestion? In what ways are painting a picture and writing a poem different and in what ways similar?
3. The poem works through humor and irony. Analyze the effects of lines
   such as "[the poem] is even in /prose, I am a real poet."

❉ JAMES WRIGHT

*James Wright (1927–1980) was born in the steel-mill town of Martins Ferry,
Ohio, and wrote of both the rural and industrial decay of his early
environment. His work shows a willingness to experiment, moving from
traditional form to images and the rhythms of spoken speech. Wright was
moved by aspects of human suffering and by natural beauty, and he
incorporated this dichotomous vision in his poems. Wright received many
major prizes and fellowships, including the 1972 Pulitzer Prize for* Collected
Poems. *In 1990, ten years after his premature death,* Above the River: The
Complete Poems *was published.*

Lying in a Hammock at William Duffy's Farm in Pine Island, Minnesota

Over my head, I see the bronze butterfly,
    Asleep on the black trunk,
Blowing like a leaf in green shadow.
Down the ravine behind the empty house,
The cowbells follow one another   5
Into the distances of the afternoon.
To my right,
In a field of sunlight between two pines,
The droppings of last year's horses
Blaze up into golden stones.   10
I lean back, as the evening darkens and comes on.
A chicken hawk floats over, looking for home.
I have wasted my life.

To the Muse

It is all right. All they do
Is go in by dividing
One rib from another. I wouldn't
Lie to you. It hurts
Like nothing I know. All they do   5
Is burn their way in with a wire.
It forks in and out a little like a tongue
Of that frightened garter snake we caught
At Cloverfield, you and me, Jenny
So long ago.   10

I would lie to you
If I could.
But the only way I can get you to come up
Out of the suckhole, the south face
Of the Powhatan pit, is to tell you   15
What you know:

You come up after dark, you poise alone
With me on the shore.
I lead you back to this world.

Three lady doctors in Wheeling open   20
Their offices at night.
I don't have to call them, they are always there.
But they only have to put the knife once
Under your breast.
Then they hang their contraption.   25
And you bear it.

It's awkward a while. Still, it lets you
Walk about on tiptoe if you don't
Jiggle the needle.
It might stab your heart, you see.   30
The blade hangs in your lung and the tube
Keeps it draining.
That way they only have to stab you
Once. Oh Jenny,
I wish to God I had made this world, this scurvy   35
And disastrous place. I
Didn't, I can't bear it
Either, I don't blame you, sleeping down there
Face down in the unbelievable silk of spring,
Muse of black sand,   40
Alone.

I don't blame you, I know
The place where you lie.
I admit everything. But look at me.
How can I live without you?   45
Come up to me, love,
Out of the river, or I will
Come down to you.

STUDY   QUESTIONS

1. "Lying in a Hammock at William Duffy's Farm in Pine Island, Minnesota" begins with a series of precisely located images. Analyze them
   for their sensory quality, and discuss what they have in common.
2. Discuss the meanings of the last line, "I have wasted my life." In what

ways are the previous images related to that statement, and in what ways does the statement comment on or change the meanings of these images?

3. In "To the Muse," what images suggest that Jenny, while addressed in the present tense, is actually a fantasy (the Muse) drawn from a dead figure?

4. The poem, drawing on the Greek myths of the three Fates, offers a modern version in the image of the three lady doctors. Analyze the medical/surgical imagery in the poem. What attitudes does it suggest?

5. The poem is a complex and, in many ways, indeterminate utterance. Discuss the elements of indeterminacy in the final stanza and the various, sometimes ambivalent or contradictory, meanings that can be constructed out of this stanza.

❋ ADRIENNE RICH

Adrienne Rich (b. 1929) is a prominent feminist poet whose work demonstrates the changes in women's writing in response to cultural challenges made by women in the later half of the twentieth century. Born in Baltimore, Maryland, to a well-to-do family, she was educated at Radcliffe and won the Yale Series of Younger Poets Award at age twenty-two. Rich gave up her early concern with stanzaic form and rhythm, and her later poems grew more experimental. She traces her intellectual development in a book of essays and speeches, On Lies, Secrets, and Silence *(1979), but it is her poetry that most persuasively reconfigures the positions of woman as wife, mother, daughter, lesbian, and female subject. Some of her best-known books are* Diving into the Wreck: Poems, 1971–1972 *(1973),* The Fact of a Doorframe: Poems Selected and New, 1950–1984 *(1984), and* Your Native Land, Your Life *(1986).*

Diving into the Wreck

First having read the book of myths,
    and loaded the camera,
and checked the edge of the knife-blade,
I put on
the body-armor of black rubber   5
the absurd flippers

the grave and awkward mask.
I am having to do this
not like Cousteau with his
assiduous team   10
aboard the sun-flooded schooner
but here alone.

There is a ladder.
The ladder is always there
hanging innocently   15
close to the side of the schooner.
We know what it is for,
we who have used it.
Otherwise
it is a piece of maritime floss   20
some sundry equipment.

I go down.
Rung after rung and still
the oxygen immerses me
the blue light   25
the clear atoms
of our human air.
I go down.
My flippers cripple me,
I crawl like an insect down the ladder   30
and there is no one
to tell me when the ocean
will begin.

First the air is blue and then
it is bluer and then green and then   35
black I am blacking out and yet
my mask is powerful
it pumps my blood with power
the sea is another story
the sea is not a question of power   40
I have to lean alone
to turn my body without force
in the deep element.

And now: it is easy to forget
what I came for   45
among so many who have always
lived here

swaying their crenellated[1] fans
between the reefs
and besides
you breathe differently down here.

I came to explore the wreck.
The words are purposes.
The words are maps.
I came to see the damage that was done
and the treasures that prevail.
I stroke the beam of my lamp
slowly along the flank
of something more permanent
than fish or weed

the thing I came for:
the wreck and not the story of the wreck
the thing itself and not the myth
the drowned face[2] always staring
toward the sun
the evidence of damage
worn by salt and sway into this threadbare beauty
the ribs of the disaster
curving their assertion
among the tentative haunters.

This is the place.
And I am here, the mermaid whose dark hair
streams black, the merman in his armored body.
We circle silently
about the wreck
we dive into the hold
I am she: I am he

whose drowned face sleeps with open eyes
whose breasts still bear the stress
whose silver, copper, vermeil[3] cargo lies
obscurely inside barrels

50

55

60

65

70

75

80

---

1. *With repeated indentations.*
2. *That of the ornamental female figurehead which formed the prow of old sailing ships.*
3. *Gilded silver, bronze, or copper.*

half-wedged and left to rot
we are the half-destroyed instruments
that once held to a course
the water-eaten log   85
the fouled compass

We are, I am, you are
by cowardice or courage
the one who find our way
back to this scene   90
carrying a knife, a camera
a book of myths
in which
our names do not appear.

To a Poet

I ce splits   under the metal
shovel   another day
hazed light off fogged panes
cruelty of winter   landlocked   your life
wrapped round you   in your twenties   5
an old bathrobe   dragged down
with milkstains   tearstains   dust

Scraping eggcrust from the child's
dried dish   skimming the skin
from cooled milk   wringing diapers   10
Language floats at the vanishing-point
incarnate   breathes the fluorescent bulb
primary   states the scarred grain of the floor
and on the ceiling in torn plaster laughs   *imago*

  and I have fears that you will cease to be   15
  before your pen has glean'd your teeming brain

for you are not a suicide
but no-one calls this murder
Small mouths, needy, suck you: *This is love*

I write this   not for you   20
who fight to write your own

words   fighting up the falls
but for another woman   dumb
with loneliness   dust   seeping plastic bags
with children   in a house   25
where language floats and spins
abortion   in
the bowl

STUDY QUESTIONS

1. The metaphor of diving (as moving downward into an alien and dangerous element) into the unconscious is central to "Diving into the Wreck." Discuss the various extensions to this metaphor—sea, wreck, treasure, mermaid, merman—and how they work metaphorically to deepen the poem's themes.
2. What are the differences implied between "the wreck and not the story of the wreck /the thing itself and not the myth"? What is "the thing" the speaker is looking for?
3. Analyze the speaker's claim that she is both the mermaid and the merman: "I am she: I am he." What kinds of gender notions are being implied here?
4. "To a Poet" alludes to Sylvia Plath, whose brilliant and intense poems are often said to be related to the psychological problems that led her to kill herself. The poem seems to disagree ironically with this interpretation: "for you are not a suicide /but no-one calls this murder/Small mouths, needy, suck you." In what ways could Plath's suicide be interpreted as a murder?
5. How does "To a Poet" present a woman's domestic life?
6. What is the *"abortion"* that "To a Poet" refers to? What does the poet fear for herself?

✳ GARY SNYDER

Gary Snyder (b. 1930) was born in San Francisco and studied Oriental Languages at the University of California, Berkeley. His poems show the influence of Zen Buddhism, which he studied for almost six years in a monastery in Kyoto, Japan. Snyder is often seen as a contemporary Thoreau, whose simplicity yields multiple meanings. His poems come from an ecological sensibility. Written in free form, often spare in diction and using imagistic techniques, the poems demonstrate a consciousness of values found in ritual, nature, and the family. His collection Turtle Island *(1974) received the Pulitzer Prize.*

Axe Handles

One afternoon the last week in April
Showing Kai[1] how to throw a hatchet
One-half turn and it sticks in a stump.
He recalls the hatchet-head
Without a handle, in the shop   5
And go gets it, and wants it for his own.
A broken-off axe handle behind the door
Is long enough for a hatchet,
We cut it to length and take it
With the hatchet head   10
And working hatchet, to the wood block.
There I begin to shape the old handle
With the hatchet, and the phrase
First learned from Ezra Pound
Rings in my ears!   15
"When making an axe handle the pattern is not far off."
And I say this to Kai
"Look: We'll shape the handle
By checking the handle
Of the axe we cut with—"   20
And he sees. And I hear it again:
It's in Lu Ji's *Wen Fu*, fourth century
A.D. "Essay on Literature"—in the
Preface: "In making the handle
Of an axe   25
By cutting wood with an axe
The model is indeed near at hand."
My teacher Shih-hsiang Chen
Translated that and taught it years ago
And I see: Pound was an axe,   30
Chen was an axe, I am an axe
And my son a handle, soon
To be shaping again, model
And tool, craft of culture,
How we go on.   35

---

1. *Snyder's son.*

STUDY QUESTIONS

1. "Axe Handles" begins with a scene of the father and son cutting a handle for a hatchet. What does this scene tell us about the father-son relationship?
2. Discuss the significance of the phrase from the modernist poet Ezra Pound that the father remembers.
3. Shaping an axe handle is physical work. Writing a poem is mental work. What concept of culture is implied in the poem's encompassment of both physical and intellectual labor?
4. Analyze the metaphorization of Pound, Chen, and the father as axes and the son as "a handle." How are these metaphors related to the poem's theme?

Sylvia Plath

Sylvia Plath (1932–1963) achieved great acclaim for her autobiographical novel, The Bell Jar *(1963), but is best known for her emotionally raw yet technically accomplished poems. Plath is exemplary of what is known as the "confessional" poets—others include Anne Sexton, Robert Lowell, and John Berryman—who took the often tragic events of their own lives as their poetic subject matter. In Plath's case, those experiences included the death of her father when she was eight, her struggle against depression and suicidal tendencies, an unhappy marriage to the British poet Ted Hughes, and difficulty reconciling her duties as a mother with her drive as a writer. "Lady Lazarus" was written after an operation for appendicitis, ten years after Plath, then a college student, had tried to kill herself. "Morning Song" concerns the birth of her daughter. Best known for her confessional mode, Plath's exquisitely rendered landscape poems are often overlooked.*

Plath wrote almost all the poems in her posthumous collection, Ariel *(1966), in the last five months before she killed herself. In these poems, particular experiences are transformed into psychological and poetic significance, creating a world of interior violence and extreme emotion.*

Lady Lazarus

I have done it again.
One year in every ten
I manage it——

A sort of walking miracle, my skin
Bright as a Nazi lampshade,   5
My right foot

My paperweight,
My face a featureless, fine
Jew linen.

Peel off the napkin   10
O my enemy.
Do I terrify?——

The nose, the eye pits, the full set of teeth?
The sour breath
Will vanish in a day.   15

Soon, soon the flesh
The grave cave ate will be
At home on me

And I a smiling woman.
I am only thirty.   20
And like the cat I have nine times to die.

This is Number Three.
What a trash
To annihilate each decade.

What a million filaments.   25
The peanut-crunching crowd
Shoves in to see

Them unwrap me hand and foot——
The bit strip tease.
Gentlemen, ladies   30

These are my hands
My knees.
I may be skin and bone,

Nevertheless, I am the same, identical woman.
The first time it happened I was ten.   35
It was an accident.

The second time I meant
To last it out and not come back at all.
I rocked shut

As a seashell.   40
They had to call and call
And pick the worms off me like sticky pearls.

Dying
Is an art, like everything else.
I do it exceptionally well.   45

I do it so it feels like hell.
I do it so it feels real.
I guess you could say I've a call.

It's easy enough to do it in a cell.
It's easy enough to do it and stay put.   50
It's the theatrical

Comeback in broad day
To the same place, the same face, the same brute
Amused shout:

"A miracle!"   55
That knocks me out.
There is a charge

For the eyeing of my scars, there is a charge
For the hearing of my heart——
It really goes.   60

And there is a charge, a very large charge
For a word or a touch
Or a bit of blood

Or a piece of my hair or my clothes.
So, so, Herr Doktor.   65
So, Herr Enemy.

I am your opus,
I am your valuable,
The pure gold baby

That melts to a shriek.   70
I turn and burn.
Do not think I underestimate your great concern.

Ash, ash—
You poke and stir.
Flesh, bone, there is nothing there——   75

A cake of soap,
A wedding ring,
A gold filling.

Herr God, Herr Lucifer
Beware   80
Beware.

Out of the ash
I rise with my red hair
And I eat men like air.

Morning Song

Love set you going like a fat gold watch.
The midwife slapped your footsoles, and your bald cry
Took its place among the elements.

Our voices echo, magnifying your arrival. New statue.
In a drafty museum, your nakedness   5
Shadows our safety. We stand round blankly as walls.

I'm no more your mother
Than the cloud that distils a mirror to reflect its own slow
Effacement at the wind's hand.

All night your moth-breath   10
Flickers among the flat pink roses. I wake to listen:
A far sea moves in my ear.

One cry, and I stumble from bed, cow-heavy and floral
In my Victorian nightgown
Your mouth opens clean as a cat's. The window square   15

Whitens and swallows its dull stars. And now you try
Your handful of notes;
The clear vowels rise like balloons.

STUDY QUESTIONS

1. In "Lady Lazarus," what kinds of attitudes toward men are conveyed in the speaker's address to the doctor who treated her?
2. The doctor as a figure of authority in "Lady Lazarus" is linked with other male authority figures. Who are the others, and what is the feeling of the speaker toward these figures?
3. "Lady Lazarus" plays grimly with a number of allusions. Discuss how it uses the New Testament story of Lazarus and the history of the Holocaust during World War II to suggest the speaker's emotional and psychological condition.
4. "Morning Song" begins with an image of time, "a fat gold watch." Discuss how the poem is organized along a time line. What ideas and emotions are suggested through this time line?
5. List the various metaphors and similes that the narrator/mother applies to her baby. What maternal qualities are expressed through these figures of speech?
6. The poem subtly contrasts the newborn family member and the adults. Elaborate on some of the differences suggested in the second and third stanzas.

✳ RAYMOND CARVER

Raymond Carver (1938–1988), the son of a sawmill worker and a waitress, was born in the Pacific Northwest and spent most of his life there. In spare, precise language his stories depict a working- and lower-class America whose inhabitants struggle with money, alcohol, love, and loneliness. It was a world with which he was all too familiar. He once recounted that for some time his study consisted of the backseat of his car, where he would write before going on duty as a hospital janitor. What John Updike's fiction does for the upper middle class, Carver's does for the working poor, examining marital and familial relations to reveal inner disquietude. In the last decade of his life he achieved considerable literary success, winning a MacArthur "genius" grant and seeing his style widely imitated. Carver was respected for his poetry as well as his fiction, and just before his death he published a final volume in each genre: Where I'm Calling From: New and Selected Stories and New Path to the Waterfall: Poems.

Cathedral

This blind man, an old friend of my wife's, he was on his way to spend the night. His wife had died. So he was visiting the dead wife's relatives in Connecticut. He called my wife from his in-laws'. Arrangements were made. He would come by train, a five-hour trip, and my wife would meet him at the station. She hadn't seen him since she worked for him one summer in Seattle ten years ago. But she and the blind man had kept in touch. They made tapes and mailed them back and forth. I wasn't enthusiastic about his visit. He was no one I knew. And his being blind bothered me. My idea of blindness came from the movies. In the movies, the blind moved slowly and never laughed. Sometimes they were led by seeing-eye dogs. A blind man in my house was not something I looked forward to. 1

That summer in Seattle she had needed a job. She didn't have any money. The man she was going to marry at the end of the summer was in officers' training school. He didn't have any money, either. But she was in love with the guy, and he was in love with her, etc. She'd seen something in the paper: HELP WANTED—*Reading to Blind Man*, and a telephone number. She phoned and went over, was hired on the spot. She'd worked with this blind man all summer. She read stuff to him, case studies, reports, that sort of thing. She helped him organize his little office in the county social-service department. They'd become good friends, my wife and the blind man. How do I know those things? She told me. And she told me something else. On her last day in the office, the blind man asked if he could touch her face. She agreed to this. She told me he touched his fingers to every part of her face, her nose—even her neck! She never forgot it. She even tried to write a poem about it. She was always trying to write a poem. She wrote a poem or two every year, usually after something really important had happened to her. 2

When we first started going out together, she showed me the poem. In the poem, she recalled his fingers and the way they had moved around over her face. In the poem, she talked about what she had felt at the time, about what went through her mind when the blind man touched her nose and lips. I remember I didn't think much of the poem. Of course, I didn't 3 tell her that. Maybe I just don't understand poetry. I admit it's not the first thing I reach for when I pick up something to read.

Anyway, this man who'd first enjoyed her favors, the officer-to-be, he'd been her childhood sweetheart. So okay. I'm saying that at the end of the summer she let the blind man run his hands over her face, said goodbye to him, married her childhood, etc., who was now a commissioned officer, and she moved away from Seattle. But they'd kept in touch, she and the blind man. She made the first contact after a year or so. She called him up one night from an Air Force base in Alabama. She wanted to talk. They talked. He asked her to send him a tape and tell him about her life. She did this. She sent the tape. On the tape, she told the blind man about her husband and about their life together in the military. She told the blind man that she loved her husband but she didn't like it where they lived and she didn't like it that he was a part of the military-industrial thing. She told the blind man she'd written a poem and he was in it. She told him that she was writing a poem about what it was like to be an Air Force officer's wife. The poem wasn't finished yet. She was still writing it. The blind man made a tape. He sent her the tape. She made a tape. This went on for years. My wife's officer was posted to one base and then another. She sent tapes from Moody AFB, McGuire, McConnell, and finally Travis, near Sacramento, where one night she got to feeling lonely and cut off from people she kept losing in that moving-around life. She got to feeling she couldn't go it another step. She went in and swallowed all the pills and capsules in the medicine chest and washed them down with a bottle of gin. Then she got into a hot bath and passed out.

But instead of dying, she got sick. She threw up. Her officer—why should he have a name? he was the childhood sweetheart, and what more does he want?—came home from somewhere, found her, and called the ambulance. In time, she put it all on a tape and sent the tape to the blind man. Over the years, she put all kinds of stuff on tapes and sent the tapes off lickety-split. Next to writing a poem every year, I think it was her chief means of recreation. On one tape, she told the blind man she'd decided to live away from her officer for a time. On another tape, she told him about her divorce. She and I began going out, and of course she told her blind man about it. She told him everything, or so it seemed to me. Once she asked me if I'd like to hear the latest tape from the blind man. This was a year ago. I was on the tape, she said. So I said, okay, I'd listen to it. I got us drinks and we settled down in the living room. We made ready to listen. First she inserted the tape into the player and adjusted a couple of dials. Then she pushed a lever. The tape squeaked and someone began to talk in this loud voice. She lowered the volume. After a few minutes of harmless chitchat, I heard my own name in the mouth of this stranger, this blind man I didn't even know! And then this: "From all you've said about him, I can only conclude—" But we were interrupted, a knock at the door,

4

5

something, and we didn't ever get back to the tape. Maybe it was just as well. I'd heard all I wanted to.

Now this same blind man was coming to sleep in my house. 6

"Maybe I could take him bowling," I said to my wife. She was at the 7 draining board doing scalloped potatoes. She put down the knife she was using and turned around.

"If you love me," she said, "you can do this for me. If you don't love me, 8 okay. But if you had a friend, any friend, and the friend came to visit, I'd make him feel comfortable." She wiped her hands with the dish towel.

"I don't have any blind friends," I said. 9

"You don't have *any* friends," she said. "Period. Besides," she said, 10 "goddamn it, his wife's just died! Don't you understand that? The man's lost his wife!"

I didn't answer. She'd told me a little about the blind man's wife. Her 11 name was Beulah. Beulah! That's a name for a colored woman.

"Was his wife a Negro?" I asked. 12

"Are you crazy?" my wife said. "Have you just flipped or something?" 13 She picked up a potato. I saw it hit the floor, then roll under the stove. "What's wrong with you?" she said. "Are you drunk?"

"I'm just asking," I said. 14

Right then my wife filled me in with more detail than I cared to know. 15 I made a drink and sat at the kitchen table to listen. Pieces of the story began to fall into place.

Beulah had gone to work for the blind man the summer after my wife 16 had stopped working for him. Pretty soon Beulah and the blind man had themselves a church wedding. It was a little wedding—who'd want to go to such a wedding in the first place?—just the two of them, plus the minister and the minister's wife. But it was a church wedding just the same. It was what Beulah had wanted, he'd said. But even then Beulah must have been carrying the cancer in her glands. After they had been inseparable for eight years—my wife's word, *inseparable*—Beulah's health went into a rapid decline. She died in a Seattle hospital room, the blind man sitting beside the bed and holding on to her hand. They'd married, lived and worked together, slept together—had sex, sure—and then the blind man had to bury her. All this without his having ever seen what the goddamned woman looked like. It was beyond my understanding. Hearing this, I felt sorry for the blind man for a little bit. And then I found myself thinking what a pitiful life this woman must have led. Imagine a woman who could never see herself as she was seen in the eyes of her loved one. A woman who could go on day after day and never receive the smallest compliment from her beloved. A woman whose husband could never read the expression on her face, be it misery or something better. Someone who could wear makeup or not—what difference to him? She could, if she wanted, wear green eye-shadow around one eye, a straight pin in her nostril, yellow slacks and purple shoes, no matter. And then to slip off into death, the blind man's hand on her hand, his blind eyes streaming tears—I'm imagining now—her last thought maybe this: that he never even knew what she looked like, and she on an express to the grave. Robert was left with a small insurance policy and half of a twenty-peso Mexican coin. The other half of the coin went into the box with her. Pathetic.

So when the time rolled around, my wife went to the depot to pick him up. With nothing to do but wait—sure, I blamed him for that—I was having a drink and watching the TV when I heard the car pull into the drive. I got up from the sofa with my drink and went to the window to have a look. 17

I saw my wife laughing as she parked the car. I saw her get out of the car and shut the door. She was still wearing a smile. Just amazing. She went around to the other side of the car to where the blind man was already starting to get out. This blind man, feature this, he was wearing a full beard! A beard on a blind man! Too much, I say. The blind man reached into the back seat and dragged out a suitcase. My wife took his arm, shut the car door, and, talking all the way, moved him down the drive and then up the steps to the front porch. I turned off the TV. I finished my drink, rinsed the glass, dried my hands. Then I went to the door. 18

My wife said, "I want you to meet Robert. Robert, this is my husband. I've told you all about him." She was beaming. She had this blind man by his coat sleeve. 19

The blind man let go of his suitcase and up came his hand. 20

I took it. He squeezed hard, held my hand, and then he let it go. 21

"I feel like we've already met," he boomed. 22

"Likewise," I said. I didn't know what else to say. Then I said, "Welcome. I've heard a lot about you." We began to move then, a little group, from the porch into the living room, my wife guiding him by the arm. The blind man was carrying his suitcase in his other hand. My wife said things like, "To your left here, Robert. That's right. Now watch it, there's a chair. That's it. Sit down right here. This is the sofa. We just bought this sofa two weeks ago." 23

I started to say something about the old sofa. I'd liked that old sofa. But I didn't say anything. Then I wanted to say something else, small-talk, about the scenic ride along the Hudson. How going *to* New York, you should sit on the right-hand side of the train, and coming *from* New York, the left-hand side. 24

"Did you have a good train ride?" I said. "Which side of the train did you sit on, by the way?" 25

"What a question, which side!" my wife said. "What's it matter which side?" she said. 26

"I just asked," I said. 27

"Right side," the blind man said. "I hadn't been on a train in nearly 28 forty years. Not since I was a kid. With my folks. That's been a long time. I'd nearly forgotten the sensation. I have winter in my beard now," he said. "So I've been told, anyway. Do I look distinguished, my dear?" the blind man said to my wife.

"You look distinguished, Robert," she said. "Robert," she said. "Robert, it's just so good to see you." 29

My wife finally took her eyes off the blind man and looked at me. I had the feeling she didn't like what she saw. I shrugged. 30

I've never met, or personally known, anyone who was blind. This blind man was late forties, a heavy-set, balding man with stooped shoulders, as if he carried a great weight there. He wore brown slacks, brown shoes, a light-brown shirt, a tie, a sports coat. Spiffy. He also had this full beard. But he didn't use a cane and he didn't wear dark glasses. I'd always thought dark glasses were a must for the blind. Fact was, I wished he had a pair. At first glance, his eyes looked like anyone else's eyes. But it you looked close, there was something different about them. Too much white in the iris, for one thing, and the pupils seemed to move around in the sockets without his knowing it or being able to stop it. Creepy. As I stared at his face, I saw the left pupil turn in toward his nose while the other side made an effort to keep in one place. But it was only an effort, for that eye was on the roam without his knowing it or wanting it to be. 31

I said, "Let me get you a drink. What's your pleasure? We have a little of everything. It's one of our pastimes." 32

"Bub, I'm a Scotch man myself," he said fast enough in this big voice. 33

"Right," I said. Bub! "Sure you are. I knew it." 34

He let his fingers touch his suitcase, which was sitting alongside the sofa. He was taking his bearings. I didn't blame him for that. 35

"I'll move that up to your room," my wife said. 36

"No, that's fine," the blind man said loudly. "It can go up when I go up." 37

"A little water with the Scotch?" I said. 38

"Very little," he said. 39

"I knew it," I said. 40

He said, "Just a tad. The Irish actor, Barry Fitzgerald? I'm like that fellow. When I drink water, Fitzgerald said, I drink water. When I drink whiskey, I drink whiskey." My wife laughed. The blind man brought his hand up under his beard. He lifted his beard slowly and let it drop. 41

I did the drinks, three big glasses of Scotch with a splash of water in each. Then we made ourselves comfortable and talked about Robert's travels. First the long flight from the West Coast to Connecticut, we covered that. Then from Connecticut up here by train. We had another drink concerning that leg of the trip. 42

I remembered having read somewhere that the blind didn't smoke because, as speculation had it, they couldn't see the smoke they exhaled. I thought I knew that much and that much only about blind people. But this 43 blind man smoked his cigarette down to the nubbin and then lit another one. This blind man filled his ashtray and my wife emptied it.

When we sat down at the table for dinner, we had another drink. My wife heaped Robert's plate with cube steak, scalloped potatoes, green beans. I buttered him up two slices of bread. I said, "Here's bread and butter for you." I swallowed some of my drink. "Now let us pray," I said, and the blind man lowered his head. My wife looked at me, her mouth agape. "Pray the phone won't ring and the food doesn't get cold," I said. 44

We dug in. We ate everything there was to eat on the table. We ate like there was no tomorrow. We didn't talk. We ate. We scarfed. We grazed that table. We were into serious eating. The blind man had right away located his foods, he knew just where everything was on his plate. I watched with admiration as he used his knife and fork on the meat. He'd cut two pieces of meat, fork the meat into his mouth, and then go all out for the scalloped potatoes, the beans next, and then he'd tear off a hunk of buttered bread and eat that. He'd follow this up with a big drink of milk. It didn't seem to bother him to use his fingers once in a while, either. 45

We finished everything, including half a strawberry pie. For a few moments, we sat as if stunned. Sweat beaded on our faces. Finally, we got up from the table and left the dirty plates. We didn't look back. We took ourselves into the living room and sank into our places again. Robert and my wife sat on the sofa. I took the big chair. We had us two or three more drinks while they talked about the major things that had come to pass for them in the past ten years. For the most part, I just listened. Now and then I joined in. I didn't want him to think I'd left the room, and I didn't want her to think I was feeling left out. They talked of things that had happened to them—to them!—these past ten years. I waited in vain to hear my name on my wife's sweet lips. "And then my dear husband came into my life"— something like that. But I heard nothing of the sort. More talk of Robert. Robert had done a little of everything, it seemed, a regular blind jack-of-all-trades. But most recently he and his wife had had an Amway distributorship, from which, I gathered, they'd earned their living, such as it was. The blind man was also a ham radio operator. He talked in his loud voice about conversations he'd had with fellow operators in Guam, in the Philippines, in Alaska, and even in Tahiti. He said he'd have a lot of friends there if he ever wanted to go visit those places. From time to time, he'd turn his blind face toward me, put his hand under his beard, ask me something. How long had I been in my present position? (Three years.) Did I like my work? (I didn't.) Was I going to stay with it? (What were the options?) Finally, when I thought he was beginning to run down, I got up and turned on the TV. 46

My wife looked at me with irritation. She was heading toward a boil. Then she looked at the blind man and said, "Robert, do you have a TV?" 47

The blind man said, "My dear, I have two TVs. I have a color set and a black-and-white thing, an old relic. It's funny, but if I turn the TV on, and 48

I'm always turning it on, I turn on the color set. It's funny, don't you think?"

I didn't know what to say to that. I had absolutely nothing to say to that. 49
No opinion. So I watched the news program and tried to listen to what the announcer was saying.

"This is a color TV," the blind man said. "Don't ask me how, but I can 50
tell."

"We traded up a while ago," I said. 51

The blind man had another taste of his drink. He lifted his beard, sniffed 52
it, and let it fall. He leaned forward on the sofa. He positioned his ashtray on the coffee table, then put the lighter to his cigarette. He leaned back on the sofa and crossed his legs at the ankles.

My wife covered her mouth, and then she yawned. She stretched. She 53
said, "I think I'll go upstairs and put on my robe. I think I'll change into something else. Robert, you make yourself comfortable," she said.

"I'm comfortable," the blind man said. 54

"I want you to feel comfortable in this house," she said. 55

"I am comfortable," the blind man said. 56

After she'd left the room, he and I listened to the weather report and then 57
to the sports roundup. By that time, she'd been gone so long I didn't know if she was going to come back. I thought she might have gone to bed. I wished she'd come back downstairs. I didn't want to be left alone with a blind man. I asked him if he wanted another drink, and he said sure. Then I asked if he wanted to smoke some dope with me. I said I'd just rolled a number. I hadn't, but I planned to do so in about two shakes.

"I'll try some with you," he said. 58

"Damn right," I said. "That's the stuff." 59

I got our drinks and sat down on the sofa with him. Then I rolled us two 60
fat numbers. I lit one and passed it. I brought it to his fingers. He took it and inhaled.

"Hold it as long as you can," I said. I could tell he didn't know the first 61
thing.

My wife came back downstairs wearing her pink robe and her pink 62
slippers.

"What do I smell?" she said. 63

"We thought we'd have us some cannabis," I said. 64

My wife gave me a savage look. Then she looked at the blind man and 65
said, "Robert, I didn't know you smoked."

He said, "I do now, my dear. There's a first time for everything. But I 66
don't feel anything yet."

"This stuff is pretty mellow," I said. "This stuff is mild. It's dope you can 67
reason with," I said. "It doesn't mess you up."

"Not much it doesn't, bub," he said, and laughed. 68

My wife sat on the sofa between the blind man and me. I passed her the 69
number. She took it and toked and then passed it back to me. "Which way
is this going?" she said. Then she said, "I shouldn't be smoking this. I can
hardly keep my eyes open as it is. That dinner did me in. I shouldn't have
eaten so much."

"It was the strawberry pie," the blind man said. "That's what did it," he 70
said, and he laughed his big laugh. Then he shook his head.

"There's more strawberry pie," I said. 71

"Do you want some more, Robert?" my wife said. 72

"Maybe in a little while," he said. 73

We gave our attention to the TV. My wife yawned again. She said, 74
"Your bed is made up when you feel like going to bed, Robert. I know you
must have had a long day. When you're ready to go to bed, say so." She
pulled his arm. "Robert?"

He came to and said, "I've had a real nice time. This beats tapes, doesn't 75
it?"

I said, "Coming at you," and I put the number between his fingers. He 76
inhaled, held the smoke, and then let it go. It was like he'd been doing it
since he was nine years old.

"Thanks, bub," he said. "But I think this is all for me. I think I'm begin- 77
ning to feel it," he said. He held the burning roach out for my wife.

"Same here," she said. "Ditto. Me, too." She took the roach and passed 78
it to me. "I may just sit here for a while between you two guys with my
eyes closed. But don't let me bother you, okay? Either one of you. If it
bothers you, say so. Otherwise, I may just sit here with my eyes closed
until you're ready to go to bed," she said. "Your bed's made up, Robert,
when you're ready. It's right next to our room at the top of the stairs. We'll
show you up when you're ready. You wake me up now, you guys, if I fall
asleep." She said that and then she closed her eyes and went to sleep.

The news program ended. I got up and changed the channel. I sat back 79
down on the sofa. I wished my wife hadn't pooped out. Her head lay
across the back of the sofa, her mouth open. She'd turned so that her robe
had slipped away from her legs, exposing a juicy thigh. I reached to draw
her robe back over her, and it was then that I glanced at the blind man.
What the hell! I flipped the robe open again.

"You say when you want some strawberry pie," I said. 80

"I will," he said. 81

I said, "Are you tired? Do you want me to take you up to your bed? Are 82
you ready to hit the hay?"

"Not yet," he said. "No, I'll stay up with you, bub. If that's all right. I'll 83
stay up until you're ready to turn in. We haven't had a chance to talk.
Know what I mean? I feel like me and her monopolized the evening." He
lifted his beard and he let it fall. He picked up his cigarettes and his lighter.

"That's all right," I said. Then I said, "I'm glad for the company." 84

And I guess I was. Every night I smoked dope and stayed up as long as 85

I could before I fell asleep. My wife and I hardly ever went to bed at the same time. When I did go to sleep, I had these dreams. Sometimes I'd wake up from one of them, my heart going crazy.

Something about the church and the Middle Ages was on the TV. Not your run-of-the-mill TV fare. I wanted to watch something else. I turned to the other channels. But there was nothing on them, either. So I turned back to the first channel and apologized. 86

"Bub, it's all right," the blind man said. "It's fine with me. Whatever you want to watch is okay. I'm always learning something. Learning never ends. It won't hurt me to learn something tonight. I got ears," he said. 87

We didn't say anything for a time. He was leaning forward with his head turned at me, his right ear aimed in the direction of the set. Very disconcerting. Now and then his eyelids drooped and then they snapped open again. Now and then he put his fingers into his beard and tugged, like he was thinking about something he was hearing on the television. 88

On the screen, a group of men wearing cowls was being set upon and tormented by men dressed in skeleton costumes and men dressed as devils. The men dressed as devils wore devil masks, horns, and long tails. This pageant was part of a procession. The Englishman who was narrating the thing said it took place in Spain once a year. I tried to explain to the blind man what was happening. 89

"Skeletons," he said. "I know about skeletons," he said, and he nodded. 90

The TV showed this one cathedral. Then there was a long, slow look at another one. Finally, the picture switched to the famous one in Paris, with its flying buttresses and its spires reaching up to the clouds. The camera pulled away to show the whole of the cathedral rising above the skyline. 91

There were times when the Englishman who was telling the thing would shut up, would simply let the camera move around over the cathedrals. Or else the camera would tour the countryside, men in fields walking behind oxen. I waited as long as I could. Then I felt I had to say something. I said, "They're showing the outside of this cathedral now. Gargoyles. Little statues carved to look like monsters. Now I guess they're in Italy. Yeah, they're in Italy. There's paintings on the walls of this one church." 92

"Are those fresco paintings, bub?" he asked, and he sipped from his drink. 93

I reached for my glass. But it was empty. I tried to remember what I could remember. "You're asking me are those frescoes?" I said. "That's a good question. I don't know." 94

The camera moved to a cathedral outside Lisbon. The differences in the Portuguese cathedral compared with the French and Italian were not that great. But they were there. Mostly the interior stuff. Then something occurred to me, and I said, "Something has occurred to me. Do you have any 95 idea what a cathedral is? What they look like, that is? Do you follow me? If somebody says cathedral to you, do you have any notion what they're talking about? Do you know the difference between that and a Baptist church, say?"

He let the smoke dribble from his mouth. "I know they took hundreds 96
of workers fifty or a hundred years to build," he said. "I just heard the man say that, of course. I know generations of the same families worked on a cathedral. I heard him say that, too. The men who began their life's work on them, they never lived to see the completion of their work. In that wise, bub, they're no different from the rest of us, right?" He laughed. Then his eyelids drooped again. His head nodded. He seemed to be snoozing. Maybe he was imagining himself in Portugal. The TV was showing another cathedral now. This one was in Germany. The Englishman's voice droned on. "Cathedrals," the blind man said. He sat up and rolled his head back and forth. "If you want the truth, bub, that's about all I know. What I just said. What I heard him say. But maybe you could describe one to me? I wish you'd do that. If you want to know, I really don't have a good idea."

I stared hard at the shot of the cathedral on the TV. How could I even 97
begin to describe it? But say my life depended on it. Say my life was being threatened by an insane guy who said I had to do it or else.

I stared some more at the cathedral before the picture flipped off into the 98
countryside. There was no use. I turned to the blind man and said, "To begin with, they're very tall." I was looking around the room for clues. "They reach way up. Up and up. Toward the sky. They're so big, some of them, they have to have these supports. To help hold them up, so to speak. These supports are called buttresses. They remind me of viaducts, for some reason. But maybe you don't know viaducts, either? Sometimes the cathedrals have devils and such carved into the front. Sometimes lords and ladies. Don't ask me why this is," I said.

He was nodding. The whole upper part of his body seemed to be mov- 99
ing back and forth.

"I'm not doing so good, am I?" I said. 100

He stopped nodding and leaned forward on the edge of the sofa. As he 101
listened to me, he was running his fingers through his beard. I wasn't getting through to him, I could see that. But he waited for me to go on just the same. He nodded, like he was trying to encourage me. I tried to think what else to say. "They're really big," I said. "They're massive. They're built of stone. Marble, too, sometimes. In those olden days, when they built cathedrals, men wanted to be close to God. In those olden days, God was an important part of everyone's life. You could tell this from their cathedral-building. I'm sorry," I said, "but it looks like that's the best I can do for you. I'm just no good at it."

"That's all right, bub," the blind man said. "Hey, listen. I hope you 102
don't mind my asking you. Can I ask you something? Let me ask you a simple question, yes or no. I'm just curious and there's no offense. You're

my host. But let me ask if you are in any way religious? You don't mind my asking?"

I shook my head. He couldn't see that, though. A wink is the same as 103
a nod to a blind man. "I guess I don't believe in it. In anything. Sometimes it's hard. You know what I'm saying?"

"Sure, I do," he said. 104

"Right," I said. 105

The Englishman was still holding forth. My wife sighed in her sleep. She 106
drew a long breath and went on with her sleeping.

"You'll have to forgive me," I said. "But I can't tell you what a cathedral 107
looks like. It just isn't in me to do it. I can't do any more than I've done."

The blind man sat very still, his head down, as he listened to me. 108

I said, "The truth is, cathedrals don't mean anything special to me. 109
Nothing. Cathedrals. They're something to look at on late-night TV. That's all they are."

It was then that the blind man cleared his throat. He brought something 110
up. He took a handkerchief from his back pocket. Then he said, "I get it, bub. It's okay. It happens. Don't worry about it," he said. "Hey, listen to me. Will you do me a favor? I got an idea. Why don't you find us some heavy paper? And a pen. We'll do something. We'll draw one together. Get us a pen and some heavy paper. Go on, bub, get the stuff," he said.

So I went upstairs. My legs felt like they didn't have much strength in 111
them. They felt like they did after I'd done some running. In my wife's room, I looked around. I found some ballpoints in a little basket on her table. And then I tried to think where to look for the kind of paper he was talking about.

Downstairs, in the kitchen, I found a shopping bag with onion skins in 112
the bottom of the bag. I emptied the bag and shook it. I brought it into the living room and sat down with it near his legs. I moved some things, smoothed the wrinkles from the bag, spread it out on the coffee table.

The blind man got down from the sofa and sat next to me on the carpet. 113

He ran his fingers over the paper. He went up and down the sides of the 114
paper. The edges, even the edges. He fingered the corners.

"All right," he said. "All right, let's do her." 115

He found my hand, the hand with the pen. He closed his hand over my 116
hand. "Go ahead, bub, draw," he said. "Draw. You'll see. I'll follow along with you. It'll be okay. Just begin now like I'm telling you. You'll see. Draw," the blind man said.

So I began. First I drew a box that looked like a house. It could have been 117
the house I lived in. Then I put a roof on it. At either end of the roof, I drew spires. Crazy.

"Swell," he said. "Terrific. You're doing fine," he said. "Never thought 118
anything like this could happen in your lifetime, did you, bub? Well, it's a strange life, we all know that. Go on now. Keep it up."

I put in windows with arches. I drew flying buttresses. I hung great 119 doors. I couldn't stop. The TV station went off the air. I put down the pen and closed and opened my fingers. The blind man felt around over the paper. He moved the tips of his fingers over the paper, all over what I had drawn, and he nodded.

"Doing fine," the blind man said. 120

I took up the pen again, and he found my hand. I kept at it. I'm no artist. 121 But I kept drawing just the same.

My wife opened up her eyes and gazed at us. She sat up on the sofa, her 122 robe hanging open. She said, "What are you doing? Tell me, I want to know."

I didn't answer her. 123

The blind man said, "We're drawing a cathedral. Me and him are work- 124 ing on it. Press hard," he said to me. "That's right. That's good," he said. "Sure. You got it, bub. I can tell. You didn't think you could. But you can, can't you? You're cooking with gas now. You know what I'm saying? We're going to really have us something here in a minute. How's the old arm?" he said. "Put some people in there now. What's a cathedral without people?"

My wife said, "What's going on? Robert, what are you doing? What's 125 going on?"

"It's all right," he said to her. "Close your eyes now," the blind man 126 said to me.

I did it. I closed them just like he said. 127

"Are they closed?" he said. "Don't fudge." 128

"They're closed," I said. 129

"Keep them that way," he said. He said, "Don't stop now. Draw." 130

So we kept on with it. His fingers rode my fingers as my hand went over 131 the paper. It was like nothing else in my life up to now.

Then he said, "I think that's it. I think you got it," he said. "Take a look. 132 What do you think?"

But I had my eyes closed. I thought I'd keep them that way for a little 133 longer. I thought it was something I ought to do.

"Well?" he said. "Are you looking?" 134

My eyes were still closed. I was in my house. I knew that. But I didn't 135 feel like I was inside anything.

"It's really something," I said. 136

STUDY QUESTIONS

1. How would you characterize the relationship between the narrator's wife and the blind man in "Cathedral"? How is that relationship different from the one she has with her husband? Which relationship does the story suggest is more satisfactory?

2. What is the husband's response to the blind man's visit? What preconceptions does he have about blind people?
3. The story opens with the narrator's emotional distance from the blind man. How does this emotional distance change? What takes its place?
4. How does the symbol of the cathedral help us understand the story's theme?

MAXINE HONG KINGSTON

Maxine Hong Kingston (b. 1940) was born in Stockton, California, of immigrant Chinese American parents. Before establishing herself as a writer, Kingston taught in high schools in California and Hawaii. The Woman Warrior: Memoirs of a Girlhood Among Ghosts (1976), her first book, is a semiautobiographical collection of stories that has received enormous attention for its blending of Chinese and American cultural materials and for its feminist challenge to both Asian and American patriarchal attitudes. The material for China Men (1980), from which "The Grandfather of the Sierra Nevada Mountains" is excerpted, was originally part of the first book, but because of organization problems, it became a second book of memoirs.

The Grandfather of the Sierra Nevada Mountains

Excerpt from *China Men*

Slow as usual, Ah Goong arrived in the spring; the work had begun in January 1863. The demon that hired him pointed up and up, east above the hills of poppies. His first job was to fell a redwood, which was thick enough to divide into three or four beams. His tree's many branches spread out, each limb like a little tree. He circled the tree. How to attack it? No side looked like the side made to be cut, nor did any ground seem the place for it to fall. He axed for almost a day the side he'd decided would hit the ground. Halfway through, imitating the other lumberjacks, he struck the other side of the tree, above the cut, until he had to run away. The tree swayed and slowly dived to earth, creaking and screeching like a green animal. He was so awed, he forgot what he was supposed to yell. Hardly any branches broke; the tree sprang, bounced, pushed at the ground with its arms. The limbs did not wilt and fold; they were a small forest, which

1

he chopped. The trunk lay like a long red torso; sap ran from its cuts like crying blind eyes. At last it stopped fighting. He set the log across saw-horses to be cured over smoke and in the sun.

He joined a team of men who did not ax one another as they took 2 alternate hits. They blew up the stumps with gunpowder. "It was like uprooting a tooth," Ah Goong said. They also packed gunpowder at the roots of a whole tree. Not at the same time as the bang but before that, the tree rose from the ground. It stood, then plunged with a tearing of veins and muscles. It was big enough to carve a house into. The men measured themselves against the upturned white roots, which looked like claws, a sun with claws. A hundred men stood on the trunk. They lifted a wagon on it and took a photograph. The demons also had their photograph taken.

Because these mountains were made out of gold, Ah Goong rushed over 3. to the root hole to look for gold veins and ore. He selected the shiniest rocks to be assayed later in San Francisco. When he drank from the streams and saw a flash, he dived in like a duck; only sometimes did it turn out to be the sun or the water. The very dirt winked with specks.

He made a dollar a day salary. The lucky men gambled, but he was not 4 good at remembering game rules. The work so far was endurable. "I could take it," he said.

The days were sunny and blue, the wind exhilarating, the heights god- 5 like. At night the stars were diamonds, crystals, silver, snow, ice. He had never seen diamonds. He had never seen snow and ice. As spring turned into summer, and he lay under that sky, he saw the order in the stars. He recognized constellations from China. There—not a cloud but the Silver River, and there, on either side of it—Altair and Vega, the Spinning Girl and the Cowboy, far, far apart. He felt his heart breaking of loneliness at so much blue-black space between star and star. The railroad he was build-ing would not lead him to his family. He jumped out of his bedroll. "Look! Look!" Other China Men jumped awake. An accident? An avalanche? Injun demons? "The stars," he said. "The stars are here." "Another China Man gone out of his mind," men grumbled. "A sleepwalker." "Go to sleep, sleepwalker." "There. And there," said Ah Goong, two hands point-ing. "The Spinning Girl and the Cowboy. Don't you see them?" "Home-sick China Man," said the China Men and pulled their blankets over their heads. "Didn't you know they were here? I could have told you they were here. Same as in China. Same moon. Why not same stars?" "Nah. Those are American stars."

Pretending that a little girl was listening, he told himself the story about 6 the Spinning Girl and the Cowboy: A long time ago they had visited earth, where they met, fell in love, and married. Instead of growing used to each other, they remained enchanted their entire lifetimes and beyond. They were too happy. They wanted to be doves or two branches of the same tree. When they returned to live in the sky, they were so engrossed in each other that they neglected their work. The Queen of the Sky scratched a river between them with one stroke of her silver hairpin—the river a galaxy in width. The lovers suffered, but she did devote her time to spinning now, and he herded his cow. The King of the Sky took pity on them and ordered that once a year, they be allowed to meet. On the seventh day of the seventh month (which is not the same as July 7), magpies form a bridge for them to cross to each other. The lovers are together for one night of the year. On their parting, the Spinner cries the heavy summer rains.

Ah Goong's discovery of the two stars gave him something to look forward to besides meals and tea breaks. Every night he located Altair and Vega and gauged how much closer they had come since the night before. During the day he watched the magpies, big black and white birds with round bodies like balls with wings; they were a welcome sight, a promise of meetings. He had found two familiars in the wilderness: magpies and stars. On the meeting day, he did not see any magpies nor hear their chattering jaybird cries. Some black and white birds flew overhead, but they may have been American crows or late magpies on their way. Some men laughed at him, but he was not the only China Man to collect water in pots, bottles, and canteens that day. The water would stay fresh forever and cure anything. In ancient days the tutelary gods of the mountains sprinkled corpses with this water and brought them to life. That night, no women to light candles, burn incense, cook special food, Grandfather watched for the convergence and bowed. He saw the two little stars next to Vega—the couple's children. And bridging the Silver River, surely those were black flapping wings of magpies and translucent-winged angels and faeries. Toward morning, he was awakened by rain, and pulled his blankets into his tent. 7

The next day, the fantailed orange-beaked magpies returned. Altair and Vega were beginning their journeys apart, another year of spinning and herding. Ah Goong had to find something else to look forward to. The Spinning Girl and the Cowboy met and parted six times before the railroad was finished. 8

When cliffs, sheer drops under impossible overhangs, ended the road, the workers filled the ravines or built bridges over them. They climbed above the site for tunnel or bridge and lowered one another down in wicker baskets made stronger by lucky words they had painted on all four sides. Ah Goong got to be a basketman because he was thin and light. Some basketmen were fifteen-year-old boys. He rode the basket barefoot, so his boots, the kind to stomp snakes with, would not break through the bottom. The basket swung and twirled, and he saw the world sweep underneath him; it was fun in a way, a cold new feeling of doing what had never been done before. Suspended in the quiet sky, he thought all kinds of crazy thoughts, that if a man didn't want to live any more, he could just cut the ropes or, easier, tilt the basket, dip, and never have to worry again. He could spread his arms and the air would momentarily hold him before he fell past the buzzards, hawks, and eagles, and landed impaled on the tip 9 of a sequoia. This high and he didn't see any gods, no Cowboy, no Spin-ner. He knelt in the basket though he was not bumping his head against the sky. Through the wickerwork, slivers of depths darted like needles, nothing between him and air but thin rattan. Gusts of wind spun the light basket. "Aiya," said Ah Goong. Winds came up under the basket, bounc-ing it. Neighboring baskets swung together and parted. He and the man next to him looked at each other's faces. They laughed. They might as well have gone to Malaysia to collect bird nests. Those who had done high work there said it had been worse; the birds screamed and scratched at them. Swinging near the cliff, Ah Goong stood up and grabbed it by a twig. He dug holes, then inserted the gunpowder and fuses. He worked neither too fast nor too slow, keeping even with the others. The basketmen signaled one another to light the fuses. He struck match after match and dropped the burnt matches over the sides. At last his fuse caught; he waved, and the men above pulled hand over hand hauling him up, pulleys creaking. The scaffolds stood like a row of gibbets. Gallows trees along a ridge. "Hurry, hurry," he said. Some impatient men clambered up their ropes. Ah Goong ran up the ledge road they'd cleared and watched the explo-sions, which banged almost synchronously, echoes booming like war. He moved his scaffold to the next section of cliff and went down in the basket again, with bags of dirt, and set the next charge.

This time two men were blown up. One knocked out or killed by the explosion fell silently, the other screaming, his arms and legs struggling. A desire shot out of Ah Goong for an arm long enough to reach down and catch them. Much time passed as they fell like plummets. The shreds of baskets and a cowboy hat skimmed and tacked. The winds that pushed birds off course and against mountains did not carry men. Ah Goong also wished that the conscious man would fall faster and get it over with. His hands gripped the ropes, and it was difficult to let go and get on with the work. "It can't happen twice in a row," the basketmen said the next trip down. "Our chances are very good. The trip after an accident is probably the safest one." They raced to their favorite basket, checked and double-checked the four ropes, yanked the strands, tested the pulleys, oiled them, reminded the pulleymen about the signals, and entered the sky again. 10

Another time, Ah Goong had been lowered to the bottom of a ravine, which had to be cleared for the base of a trestle, when a man fell, and he saw his face. He had not died of shock before hitting bottom. His hands were grabbing at air. His stomach and groin must have felt the fall all the way down. At night Ah Goong woke up falling, though he slept on the ground, and heard other men call out in their sleep. No warm women tweaked their ears and hugged them. "It was only a falling dream," he reassured himself. 11

Across a valley, a chain of men working on the next mountain, men like ants changing the face of the world, fell, but it was very far away. Godlike, 12 he watched men whose faces he could not see and whose screams he did not hear roll and bounce and slide like a handful of sprinkled gravel.

After a fall, the buzzards circled the spot and reminded the workers for days that a man was dead down there. The men threw piles of rocks and branches to cover bodies from sight. 13

The mountainface reshaped, they drove supports for a bridge. Since hammering was less dangerous than the blowing up, the men played a little; they rode the baskets swooping in wide arcs; they twisted the ropes and let them unwind like tops. "Look at me," said Ah Goong, pulled open his pants, and pissed overboard, the wind scattering the drops. "I'm a waterfall," he said. He had sent a part of himself hurtling. On rare wind-less days he watched his piss fall in a continuous stream from himself almost to the bottom of the valley. 14

One beautiful day, dangling in the sun above a new valley, not the desire to urinate but sexual desire clutched him so hard he bent over in the basket. He curled up, overcome by beauty and fear, which shot to his penis. He tried to rub himself calm. Suddenly he stood up tall and squirted out into space. "I am fucking the world," he said. The world's vagina was big, big as the sky, big as a valley. He grew a habit: whenever he was lowered in the basket, his blood rushed to his penis, and he fucked the world. 15

Then it was autumn, and the wind blew so fiercely, the men had to postpone the basketwork. Clouds moved in several directions at once. Men pointed at dust devils, which turned their mouths crooked. There was ceaseless motion; clothes kept moving; hair moved, sleeves puffed out. Nothing stayed still long enough for Ah Goong to figure it out. The wind sucked the breath out of his mouth and blew thoughts from his brains. The food convoys from San Francisco brought tents to replace the ones that whipped away. The baskets from China, which the men saved for high work, carried cowboy jackets, long underwear, Levi pants, boots, ear-muffs, leather gloves, flannel shirts, coats. They stewed rabbit fur and deerskin into linings. They tied the wide brims of their cowboy hats over their ears with mufflers. And still the wind made confusing howls into ears, and it was hard to think. 16

STUDY QUESTIONS

1. This passage from *China Men* is an imagined biography of a first-generation Chinese American man, a worker on the Central Pacific Rail-road. How do descriptions of his work counter the usual stereotypes of Chinese American males as passive, submissive, and desexualized?
2. How does the myth of the Spinning Girl and the Cowboy figure Ah Goong's feelings about his separation from his wife and family in China?

3. What aspects of style give the impression that the passage is based on historical information? What aspects of style give the impression of fiction—that is, of imaginative writing? What difference does it make if you read it as biography instead of fiction?

❋ AUGUST WILSON

August Wilson (b. 1945), born in Pittsburgh, is a dramatist and published poet. Influenced by writers such as Langston Hughes and Ralph Ellison, Wilson writes on African American communities, culture, and history, creating complex characters whose actions are historically embedded and dramatically convincing. His plays include Ma Rainey's Black Bottom *(1984),* Fences *(1986),* Joe Turner's Come and Gone *(1986),* The Piano Lesson, *which won the 1990 Pulitzer Prize for Drama, and* Two Trains Running *(1990). Many critics praise his use of language, especially the eloquent use of dialect.*

Joe Turner's Come and Gone

CHARACTERS

SETH HOLLY, owner of the boardinghouse
BERTHA HOLLY, his wife
BYNUM WALKER, a rootworker
RUTHERFORD SELIG, a peddler
JEREMY FURLOW, a resident
HERALD LOOMIS, a resident
ZONIA LOOMIS, his daughter
MATTIE CAMPBELL, a resident
REUBEN SCOTT, boy who lives next door
MOLLY CUNNINGHAM, a resident
MARTHA LOOMIS, Herald Loomis's wife

SETTING

August, 1911. A boardinghouse in Pittsburgh. At right is a kitchen. Two doors open off the kitchen. One leads to the outhouse and Seth's workshop. The other to Seth's and Bertha's bedroom. At left is a parlor. The front door opens into the parlor, which gives access to the stairs leading to the upstairs rooms.

There is a small outside playing area.

It is August in Pittsburgh, 1911. The sun falls out of heaven like a stone. The fires of the steel mill rage with a combined sense of industry and progress. Barges loaded with coal and iron ore trudge up the river to the mill towns that dot the Monongahela and return with fresh, hard, gleaming steel. The city flexes its muscles. Men throw countless bridges across the rivers, lay roads, and carve tunnels through the hills spouting with houses.

From the deep and the near South the sons and daughters of newly freed African slaves wander into the city. Isolated, cut off from memory, having forgotten the names of the gods and only guessing at their faces, they arrive dazed and stunned, their hearts kicking in their chests, with a song worth singing. They arrive carrying Bibles and guitars, their pockets lined with dust and fresh hope, marked men and women seeking to scrape from the narrow, crooked cobbles and the fiery blasts of the coke furnace a way of bludgeoning and shaping the malleable parts of themselves into a new identity as free men of definite and sincere worth.

Foreigners in a strange land, they carry as part and parcel of their baggage a long line of separation and dispersement which informs their sensibilities and marks their conduct as they search for ways to reconnect, to reassemble, to give clear and luminous meaning to the song which is both a wail and a whelp of joy.

ACT ONE

Scene One

The lights come up on the kitchen. BERTHA *busies herself with breakfast preparations.* SETH *stands looking out the window at* BYNUM *in the yard.* SETH *is in his early fifties. Born of Northern free parents, a skilled craftsman, and owner of the boardinghouse, he has a stability that none of the other characters have.* BERTHA *is five years his junior. Married for over twenty-five years, she has learned how to negotiate around* SETH'S *apparent orneriness.*

SETH: (*at the window, laughing.*) If that ain't the damndest thing I seen. Look here, Bertha.

BERTHA: I done seen Bynum out there with them pigeons before.

SETH: Naw . . . Naw . . . look at this. That pigeon flopped out of Bynum's hand and he about to have a fit.

(BERTHA *crosses over to the window.*)

He down there on his hands and knees behind that bush looking all over for that pigeon and it on the other side of the yard. See it over there?

BERTHA: Come on and get your breakfast and leave that man alone.

SETH: Look at him . . . he still looking. He ain't seen it yet. All that old mumbo jumbo nonsense. I don't know why I put up with it.

BERTHA: You don't say nothing when he bless the house.

SETH: I just go along with that 'cause of you. You around here sprinkling salt all over the place . . . got pennies lined up across the threshold . . . all that heebie-jeebie stuff. I just put up with that 'cause of you. I don't pay that kind of stuff no mind. And you going down there to the church and wanna come home and sprinkle salt all over the place.

BERTHA: It don't hurt none. I can't say if it help . . . but it don't hurt none.

SETH: Look at him. He done found that pigeon and now he's talking to it.

BERTHA: Theses biscuits be ready in a minute.

SETH: He done drew a big circle with that stick and now he's dancing around. I know he'd better not . . .

(SETH *bolts from the window and rushes to the back door.*)

Hey, Bynum! Don't be hopping around stepping in my vegetables. Hey, Bynum . . . Watch where you stepping!

BERTHA: Seth, leave that man alone.

SETH: (*coming back into the house.*) I don't care how much he be dancing around . . . just don't be stepping in my vegetables. Man got my garden all messed up now . . . planting them weeds out there . . . burying them pigeons and whatnot.

BERTHA: Bynum don't bother nobody. He ain't even thinking about your vegetables.

SETH: I know he ain't! That's why he out there stepping on them.

BERTHA: What Mr. Johnson say down there?

SETH: I told him if I had the tools I could go out here and find me four or five fellows and open up my own shop instead of working for Mr. Olowski. Get me four or five fellows and teach them how to make pots and pans. One man making ten pots is five men making fifty. He told me he'd think about it.

BERTHA: Well, maybe he'll come to see it your way.

SETH: He wanted me to sign over the house to him. You know what I thought of that idea.

BERTHA: He'll come to see you're right.

SETH: I'm going up and talk to Sam Green. There's more than one way to skin a cat. I'm going up and talk to him. See if he got more sense than Mr. Johnson. I can't get nowhere working for Mr. Olowski and selling Selig five or six pots on the side. I'm going up and see Sam Green. See if he loan me the money.

(SETH *crosses back to the window.*)

Now he got that cup. He done killed that pigeon and now he's putting its blood in that little cup. I believe he drink that blood.

BERTHA: Seth Holly, what is wrong with you this morning? Come on and get your breakfast so you can go to bed. You know Bynum don't be drinking no pigeon blood.

SETH: I don't know what he do.

BERTHA: Well, watch him, then. He's gonna dig a little hole and bury that pigeon. Then he's gonna pray over that blood . . . pour it on top . . . mark out his circle and come on into the house.

SETH: That's what he doing . . . he pouring that blood on top.

BERTHA: When they gonna put you back working daytime? Told me two months ago he was gonna put you back working daytime.

SETH: That's what Mr. Olowski told me. I got to wait till he say when. He tell me what to do. I don't tell him. Drive me crazy to speculate on the man's wishes when he don't know what he want to do himself.

BERTHA: Well, I wish he go ahead and put you back working daytime. This working all hours of the night don't make no sense.

SETH: It don't make no sense for that boy to run out of here and get drunk so they lock him up either.

BERTHA: Who? Who they got locked up for being drunk?

SETH: That boy that's staying upstairs . . . Jeremy. I stopped down there on Logan Street on my way home from work and one of the fellows told me about it. Say he seen it when they arrested him.

BERTHA: I was wondering why I ain't seen him this morning.

SETH: You know I don't put up with that. I told him when he came . . .

(BYNUM *enters from the yard carrying some plants. He is a short, round man in his early sixties. A conjure man, or rootworker, he gives the impression of always being in control of everything. Nothing ever bothers him. He seems to be lost in a world of his own making and to swallow any adversity or interference with his grand design.*)

What you doing bringing them weeds in my house? Out there stepping on my vegetables and now wanna carry them weeds in my house.

BYNUM: Morning, Seth. Morning, Sister Bertha.

SETH: Messing up my garden growing them things out there. I ought to go out there and pull up all them weeds.

BERTHA: Some gal was by here to see you this morning, Bynum. You was out there in the yard . . . I told her to come back later.

BYNUM: (*To* SETH.) You look sick. What's the matter, you ain't eating right?

SETH: What if I was sick? You ain't getting near me with none of that stuff.

(BERTHA *sets a plate of biscuits on the table.*)

BYNUM: My . . . my . . . Bertha, your biscuits getting fatter and fatter.

(BYNUM *takes a biscuit and begins to eat.*)

Where Jeremy? I don't see him around this morning. He usually be around riffing and raffing on Saturday morning.

SETH: I know where he at. I know just where he at. They got him down there in the jail. Getting drunk and acting a fool. He down there where he belong with all that foolishness.

BYNUM: Mr. Piney's boys got him, huh? They ain't gonna do nothing but hold on to him for a little while. He's gonna be back here hungrier than a mule directly.

SETH: I don't go for all that carrying on and such. This is a respectable house. I don't have no drunkards or fools around here.

BYNUM: That boy got a lot of country in him. He ain't been up here but two weeks. It's gonna take a while before he can work that country out of him.

SETH: These niggers coming up here with that old backward country style of living. It's hard enough now without all that ignorant kind of acting. Ever since slavery got over with there ain't been nothing but foolish-acting niggers. Word get out they need men to work in the mill and put in these roads . . . and niggers drop everything and head North looking for freedom. They don't know the white fellows looking too. White fellows coming from all over the world. White fellow come over and in six months got more than what I got. But these niggers keep on coming. Walking . . . riding . . . carrying their Bibles. That boy done carried a guitar all the way from North Carolina. What he gonna find out? What he gonna do with that guitar? This the city.

(*There is a knock on the door.*)

Niggers coming up here from the backwoods . . . coming up here from the country carrying Bibles and guitars looking for freedom. They got a rude awakening.

(SETH *goes to answer the door.* RUTHERFORD SELIG *enters. About* SETH's *age, he is a thin white man with greasy hair. A peddler, he supplies* SETH *with the raw materials to make pots and pans which he then peddles door to door in the mill towns along the river. He keeps a list of his customers as they move about and is known in the various communities as the People Finder. He carries squares of sheet metal under his arm.*)

Ho! Forgot you was coming today. Come on in.

BYNUM: If it ain't Rutherford Selig . . . the People Finder himself.

SELIG: What say there, Bynum?

BYNUM: I say about my shiny man. You got to tell me something. I done give you my dollar . . . I'm looking to get a report.

SELIG: I got eight here, Seth.

SETH: (*Taking the sheet metal.*) What is this? What you giving me here? What I'm gonna do with this?

SELIG: I need some dustpans. Everybody asking me about dustpans.

SETH: Gonna cost you fifteen cents apiece. And ten cents to put a handle on them.

SELIG: I'll give you twenty cents apiece with the handles.

SETH: Alright. But I ain't gonna give you but fifteen cents for the sheet metal.

SELIG: It's twenty-five cents apiece for the metal. That's what we agreed on.

SETH: This low-grade sheet metal. They ain't worth but a dime. I'm doing you a favor giving you fifteen cents. You know this metal ain't worth no twenty-five cents. Don't come talking that twenty-five cent stuff to me over no low-grade sheet metal.

SELIG: Alright, fifteen cents apiece. Just make me some dustpans out of them.

(SETH *exits with the sheet metal out the back door.*)

BERTHA: Sit on down there, Selig. Get you a cup of coffee and a biscuit.

BYNUM: Where you coming from this time?

SELIG: I been upriver. All along the Monongahela. Past Rankin and all up around Little Washington.

BYNUM: Did you find anybody?

SELIG: I found Sadie Jackson up in Braddock. Her mother's staying down there in Scotchbottom say she hadn't heard from her and she didn't know where she was at. I found her up in Braddock on Enoch Street. She bought a frying pan from me.

BYNUM: You around here finding everybody how come you ain't found my shiny man?

SELIG: The only shiny man I saw was the Nigras working on the road gang with the sweat glistening on them.

BYNUM: Naw, you'd be able to tell this fellow. He shine like new money.

SELIG: Well, I done told you I can't find nobody without a name.

BERTHA: Here go one of these hot biscuits, Selig.

BYNUM: This fellow don't have no name. I call him John 'cause it was up around Johnstown where I seen him. I ain't even so sure he's one special fellow. That shine could pass on to anybody. He could be anybody shining.

SELIG: Well, what's he look like beside being shiny? There's lots of shiny Nigras.

BYNUM: He's just a man I seen out on the road. He ain't had no special look. Just a man walking toward me on the road. He come up and ask me which way the road went. I told him everything I knew about the road, where it went and all, and he asked me did I have anything to eat 'cause he was hungry. Say he ain't had nothing to eat in three days. Well, I never be out there on the road without a piece of fried meat. Or an orange or an apple. So I give this fellow an orange. He take and eat that orange and told me to come and go along the road a little ways with him, that he had something he wanted to show me. He had a look about him made me wanna go with him, see what he gonna show me.

We walked on a bit and it's getting kind of far from where I met him when it come up on me all of a sudden, we wasn't going the way he had come from, we was going back my way. Since he said he ain't knew nothing about the road, I asked him about this. He say he had a voice inside him telling him which way to go and if I come and go along with him he was gonna show me the Secret of Life. Quite naturally I followed him. A fellow that's gonna show you the Secret of Life ain't to be taken lightly. We get near this bend in the road . . .

(SETH *enters with an assortment of pots.*)

SETH: I got six here, Selig.

SELIG: Wait a minute, Seth. Bynum's telling me about the secret of life. Go ahead, Bynum. I wanna hear this.

(SETH *sets the pots down and exits out the back.*)

BYNUM: We get near this bend in the road and he told me to hold out my hands. Then he rubbed them together with his and I looked down and see they got blood on them. Told me to take and rub it all over me . . . say that was a way of cleaning myself. Then we went around the bend in that road. Got around that bend and it seem like all of a sudden we ain't in the same place. Turn around that bend and everything look like it was twice as big as it was. The trees and everything bigger than life! Sparrows big as eagles! I turned around to look at this fellow and he had this light coming out of him. I had to cover up my eyes to keep from being blinded. He shining like new money with that light. He shined until all the light seemed like it seeped out of him and then he was gone and I was by myself in this strange place where everything was bigger than life.

I wandered around there looking for that road, trying to find my way back from this big place . . . and I looked over and seen my daddy standing there. He was the same size he always was, except for his hands and his mouth. He had a great big old mouth that look like it took up his whole face and his hands were as big as hams. Look like they was too big to carry around. My daddy called me to him. Said he had been thinking about me and it grieved him to see me in the world carrying other people's songs and not having one of my own. Told me he was gonna show me how to find my song. Then he carried me further into this big place until we come to this ocean. Then he showed me something

I ain't got words to tell you. But if you stand to witness it, you done seen something there. I stayed in that place awhile and my daddy taught me the meaning of this thing that I had seen and showed me how to find my song. I asked him about the shiny man and he told me he was the One Who Goes Before and Shows the Way. Said there was lots of shiny men and if I ever saw one again before I died then I would know that my song had been accepted and worked its full power in the world and I could lay down and die a happy man. A man who done left his mark on life. On the way people cling to each other out of the truth they find in themselves. Then he showed me how to get back to the road. I came out to where everything was its own size and I had my song. I had the Binding Song. I choose that song because that's what I seen most when I was traveling . . . people walking away and leaving one another. So I takes the power of my song and binds them together.

(SETH *enters from the yard carrying cabbages and tomatoes.*)

Been binding people ever since. That's why they call me Bynum. Just like glue I sticks people together.

SETH: Maybe they ain't supposed to be stuck sometimes. You ever think of that?

BYNUM: Oh, I don't do it lightly. It cost me a piece of myself every time I do. I'm a Binder of What Clings. You got to find out if they cling first. You can't bind what don't cling.

SELIG: Well, how is that the Secret of Life? I thought you said he was gonna show you the secret of life. That's what I'm waiting to find out.

BYNUM: Oh, he showed me alright. But you still got to figure it out. Can't nobody figure it out for you. You got to come to it on your own. That's why I'm looking for the shiny man.

SELIG: Well, I'll keep my eye out for him. What you got there, Seth?

SETH: Here go some cabbage and tomatoes. I got some green beans coming in real nice. I'm gonna take and start me a grapevine out there next year. Butera says he gonna give me a piece of his vine and I'm gonna start that out there.

SELIG: How many of them pots you got?

SETH: I got six. That's six dollars minus eight on top of fifteen for the sheet metal come to a dollar twenty out the six dollars leave me four dollars and eighty cents.

SELIG: (*Counting out the money.*) There's four dollars . . . and . . . eighty cents.

SETH: How many of them dustpans you want?

SELIG: As many as you can make out them sheets.

SETH: You can use that many? I get to cutting on them sheets figuring how to make dustpans . . . ain't no telling how many I'm liable to come up with.

SELIG: I can use them and you can make me some more next time.

SETH: Alright, I'm gonna hold you to that, now.

SELIG: Thanks for the biscuit, Bertha.

BERTHA: You know you welcome anytime, Selig.

SETH: Which way you heading?

SELIG: Going down to Wheeling. All through West Virginia there. I'll be back Saturday. They putting in new roads down that way. Makes traveling easier.

SETH: That's what I hear. All up around here too. Got a fellow staying here working on that road by the Brady Street Bridge.

SELIG: Yeah, it's gonna make traveling real nice. Thanks for the cabbage, Seth. I'll see you on Saturday.

(SELIG *exits.*)

SETH: (*To* Bynum.) Why you wanna start all that nonsense talk with that man? All that shiny man nonsense.

BYNUM: You know it ain't no nonsense. Bertha know it ain't no nonsense. I don't know if Selig know or not.

BERTHA: Seth, when you get to making them dustpans make me a coffee-pot.

SETH: What's the matter with your coffee? Ain't nothing wrong with your coffee. Don't she make some good coffee, Bynum?

BYNUM: I ain't worried about the coffee. I know she makes some good biscuits.

SETH: I ain't studying no coffeepot, woman. You heard me tell the man I was gonna cut as many dustpans as them sheets will make . . . and all of a sudden you want a coffeepot.

BERTHA: Man, hush up and go on and make me that coffeepot.

(JEREMY *enters the front door. About twenty-five, he gives the impression that he has the world in his hand, that he can meet life's challenges head on. He smiles a lot. He is a proficient guitar player, though his spirit has yet to be molded into song.*)

BYNUM: I hear Mr. Piney's boys had you.

JEREMY: Fined me two dollars for nothing! Ain't done nothing.

SETH: I told you when you come on here everybody know my house. Know these is respectable quarters. I don't put up with no foolishness. Everybody know Seth Holly keep a good house. Was my daddy's house. This house been a decent house for a long time.

JEREMY: I ain't done nothing, Mr. Seth. I stopped by the Workmen's Club and got me a bottle. Me and Roper Lee from Alabama. Had us a half pint. We was fixing to cut that half in two when they came up on us. Asked us if we was working. We told them we was putting

in the road over yonder and that it was our payday. They
snatched hold of us to get that two dollars. Me and Roper Lee
ain't even had a chance to take a drink when they grabbed us.

SETH: I don't go for all that kind of carrying on.

BERTHA: Leave the boy alone, Seth. You know the police do that. Figure
there's too many people out on the street they take some of them
off. You know that.

SETH: I ain't gonna have folks talking.

BERTHA: Ain't nobody talking nothing. That's all in your head. You want
some grits and biscuits, Jeremy?

JEREMY: Thank you, Miss Bertha. They didn't give us a thing to eat last
night. I'll take one of them big bowls if you don't mind.

(*There is a knock at the door.* SETH *goes to answer it. Enter* HERALD LOOMIS *and his
eleven-year-old daughter,* ZONIA. HERALD LOOMIS *is thirty-two years old. He is at times
possessed. A man driven not by the hellhounds that seemingly bay at his heels, but by his
search for a world that speaks to something about himself. He is unable to harmonize the
forces that swirl around him, and seeks to recreate the world into one that contains his image.
He wears a hat and a long wool coat.*)

LOOMIS: Me and my daughter looking for a place to stay, mister. You got
a sign say you got rooms.

(SETH *stares at* LOOMIS, *sizing him up.*)

Mister, if you ain't got no rooms we can go somewhere else.

SETH: How long you plan on staying?

LOOMIS: Don't know. Two weeks or more maybe.

SETH: It's two dollars a week for the room. We serve meals twice a day.
It's two dollars for room and board. Pay up in advance.

(LOOMIS *reaches into his pocket.*)

It's a dollar extra for the girl.

LOOMIS: The girl sleep in the same room.

SETH: Well, do she eat off the same plate? We serve meals twice a day.
That's a dollar extra for food.

LOOMIS: Ain't got no extra dollar. I was planning on asking your missus if
she could help out with the cooking and cleaning and whatnot.

SETH: Her helping out don't put no food on the table. I need that dollar
to buy some food.

LOOMIS: I'll give you fifty cents extra. She don't eat much.

SETH: Okay . . . but fifty cents don't buy but half a portion.

BERTHA: Seth, she can help me out. Let her help me out. I can use some
help.

SETH: Well, that's two dollars a week. Pay up in advance. Saturday to
Saturday. You wanna stay on then it's two more come Saturday.

(LOOMIS *pays* SETH *the money.*)

BERTHA: My name's Bertha. This my husband, Seth. You got Bynum and Jeremy over there.

LOOMIS: Ain't nobody else live here?

BERTHA: They the only ones live here now. People come and go. They the only ones here now. You want a cup of coffee and a biscuit?

LOOMIS: We done ate this morning.

BYNUM: Where you coming from, Mister . . . I didn't get your name.

LOOMIS: Name's Herald Loomis. This my daughter, Zonia.

BYNUM: Where you coming from?

LOOMIS: Come from all over. Whicheverway the road take us that's the way we go.

JEREMY: If you looking for a job, I'm working putting in that road down there by the bridge. They can't get enough mens. Always looking to take somebody on.

LOOMIS: I'm looking for a woman named Martha Loomis. That's my wife. Got married legal with the papers and all.

SETH: I don't know nobody named Loomis. I know some Marthas but I don't know no Loomis.

BYNUM: You got to see Rutherford Selig if you wanna find somebody. Selig's the People Finder. Rutherford Selig's a first-class People Finder.

JEREMY: What she look like? Maybe I seen her.

LOOMIS: She a brownskin woman. Got long pretty hair. About five feet from the ground.

JEREMY: I don't know. I might have seen her.

BYNUM: You got to see Rutherford Selig. You give him one dollar to get her name on his list . . . and after she get her name on his list Rutherford Selig will go right on out there and find her. I got him looking for somebody for me.

LOOMIS: You say he find people. How you find him?

BYNUM: You just missed him. He's gone downriver now. You got to wait till Saturday. He's gone downriver with his pots and pans. He come to see Seth on Saturdays. You got to wait till then.

SETH: Come on, I'll show you to your room.

(SETH, LOOMIS, and ZONIA *exit up the stairs.*)

JEREMY: Miss Bertha, I'll take that biscuit you was gonna give that fellow, if you don't mind. Say, Mr. Bynum, they got somebody like that around here sure enough? Somebody that find people?

BYNUM: Rutherford Selig. He go around selling pots and pans and every house he come to he write down the name and address of whoever lives there. So if you looking for somebody, quite naturally you go and see him . . . 'cause he's the only one who know where everybody live at.

JEREMY: I ought to have him look for this old gal I used to know. It be nice to see her again.

BERTHA: (*Giving* JEREMY *a biscuit.*) Jeremy, today's the day for you to pull them sheets off the bed and set them outside your door. I'll set you out some clean ones.

BYNUM: Mr. Piney's boys done ruined your good time last night, Jeremy . . . what you planning for tonight?

JEREMY: They got me scared to go out, Mr. Bynum. They might grab me again.

BYNUM: You ought to take your guitar and go down to Seefus. Seefus got a gambling place down there on Wylie Avenue. You ought to take your guitar and go down there. They got guitar contest down there.

JEREMY: I don't play no contest, Mr. Bynum. Had one of them white fellows cure me of that. I ain't been nowhere near a contest since.

BYNUM: White fellow beat you playing guitar?

JEREMY: Naw, he ain't beat me. I was sitting at home just fixing to sit down and eat when somebody come up to my house and got me. Told me there's a white fellow say he was gonna give a prize to the best guitar player he could find. I take up my guitar and go down there and somebody had gone up and got Bobo Smith and brought him down there. Him and another fellow called Hooter. Old Hooter couldn't play no guitar, he do more hollering than playing, but Bobo could go at it awhile.

This fellow standing there say he the one that was gonna give the prize and me and Bobo started playing for him. Bobo play something and then I'd try to play something better than what he played. Old Hooter, he just holler and bang at the guitar. Man was the worst guitar player I ever seen. So me and Bobo played and after a while I seen where he was getting the attention of this white fellow. He'd play something and while he was playing it he be slapping on the side of the guitar, and that made it sound like he was playing more than he was. So I started doing it too. White fellow ain't knew no difference. He ain't knew as much about guitar playing as Hooter did. After we play awhile, the white fellow called us to him and said he couldn't make up his mind, say all three of us was the best guitar player and we'd have to split the prize between us. Then he give us twenty-five cents. That's eight cents apiece and a penny on the side. That cured me of playing contest to this day.

BYNUM: Seefus ain't like that. Seefus give a whole dollar and a drink of whiskey.

JEREMY: What night they be down there?

BYNUM: Be down there every night. Music don't know no certain night.

BERTHA: You go down to Seefus with them people and you liable to end up in a raid and go to jail sure enough. I don't know why Bynum tell you that.

BYNUM: That's where the music at. That's where the people at. The people down there making music and enjoying themselves. Some things is worth taking the chance going to jail about.

BERTHA: Jeremy ain't got no business going down there.

JEREMY: They got some women down there, Mr. Bynum?

BYNUM: Oh, they got women down there, sure. They got women everywhere. Women be where the men is so they can find each other.

JEREMY: Some of them old gals come out there where we be putting in that road. Hanging around there trying to snatch somebody.

BYNUM: How come some of them ain't snatched hold of you?

JEREMY: I don't want them kind. Them desperate kind. Ain't nothing worse than a desperate woman. Tell them you gonna leave them and they get to crying and carrying on. That just make you want to get away quicker. They get to cutting up your clothes and things trying to keep you staying. Desperate women ain't nothing but trouble for a man.

(SETH *enters from the stairs.*)

SETH: Something ain't setting right with that fellow.

BERTHA: What's wrong with him? What he say?

SETH: I take him up there and try to talk to him and he ain't for no talking. Say he been traveling . . . coming over from Ohio. Say he a deacon in the church. Say he looking for Martha Pentecost. Talking about that's his wife.

BERTHA: How you know it's the same Martha? Could be talking about anybody. Lots of people named Martha.

SETH: You see that little girl? I didn't hook it up till he said it, but that little girl look just like her. Ask Bynum. (*To* BYNUM.) Bynum. Don't that little girl look just like Martha Pentecost?

BERTHA: I still say he could be talking about anybody.

SETH: The way he described her wasn't no doubt about who he was talking about. Described her right down to her toes.

BERTHA: What did you tell him?

SETH: I ain't told him nothing. The way that fellow look I wasn't gonna tell him nothing. I don't know what he looking for her for.

BERTHA: What else he have to say?

SETH: I told you he wasn't for no talking. I told him where the outhouse was and to keep that gal off the front porch and out of my garden. He asked if you'd mind setting a hot tub for the gal and that was about the gist of it.

BERTHA: Well, I wouldn't let it worry me if I was you. Come on get your sleep.

BYNUM: He says he looking for Martha and he a deacon in the church.

SETH: That's what he say. Do he look like a deacon to you?

BERTHA: He might be, you don't know. Bynum ain't got no special say on whether he a deacon or not.

SETH: Well, if he the deacon I'd sure like to see the preacher.

BERTHA: Come on get your sleep. Jeremy, don't forget to set them sheets outside the door like I told you.

(BERTHA *exits into the bedroom.*)

SETH: Something ain't setting right with that fellow, Bynum. He's one of them mean-looking niggers look like he done killed somebody gambling over a quarter.

BYNUM: He ain't no gambler. Gamblers wear nice shoes. This fellow got on clodhoppers. He been out there walking up and down them roads.

(ZONIA *enters from the stairs and looks around.*)

BYNUM: You looking for the back door, sugar? There it is. You can go out there and play. It's alright.

SETH: (*Showing her the door.*) You can go out there and play. Just don't get in my garden. And don't go messing around in my workshed.

(SETH *exits into the bedroom. There is a knock on the door.*)

JEREMY: Somebody at the door.

(JEREMY *goes to answer the door. Enter* MATTIE CAMPBELL. *She is a young woman of twenty-six whose attractiveness is hidden under the weight and concerns of a dissatisfied life. She is a woman in an honest search for love and companionship. She has suffered many defeats in her search, and though not always uncompromising, still believes in the possibility of love.*)

MATTIE: I'm looking for a man named Bynum. Lady told me to come back later.

JEREMY: Sure, he here. Mr. Bynum, somebody here to see you.

BYNUM: Come to see me, huh?

MATTIE: Are you the man they call Bynum? The man folks say can fix things?

BYNUM: Depend on what need fixing. I can't make no promises. But I got a powerful song in some matters.

MATTIE: Can you fix it so my man come back to me?

BYNUM: Come on in . . . have a sit down.

MATTIE: You got to help me. I don't know what else to do.

BYNUM: Depend on how all the circumstances of the thing come together. How all the pieces fit.

MATTIE: I done everything I knowed how to do. You got to make him come back to me.

BYNUM: It ain't nothing to make somebody come back. I can fix it so he can't stand to be away from you. I got my roots and powders, I can fix it so wherever he's at this thing will come up on him and he won't be able to sleep for seeing your face. Won't be able to eat for thinking of you.

MATTIE: That's what I want. Make him come back.

BYNUM: The roots is a powerful thing. I can fix it so one day he'll walk out his front door . . . won't be thinking of nothing. He won't know what it is. All he knows is that a powerful dissatisfaction done set in his bones and can't nothing he do make him feel satisfied. He'll set his foot down on the road and the wind in the trees be talking to him and everywhere he step on the road, that road'll give back your name and something will pull him right up to your doorstep. Now, I can do that. I can take my roots and fix that easy. But maybe he ain't supposed to come back. And if he ain't supposed to come back . . . then he'll be in your bed one morning and it'll come up on him that he's in the wrong place. That he's lost outside of time from his place that he's supposed to be in. Then both of you be lost and trapped outside of life and ain't no way for you to get back into it. 'Cause you lost from yourselves and where the places come together, where you're supposed to be alive, your heart kicking in your chest with a song worth singing.

MATTIE: Make him come back to me. Make his feet say my name on the road. I don't care what happens. Make him come back.

BYNUM: What's your man's name?

MATTIE: He go by Jack Carper. He was born in Alabama then he come to West Texas and find me and we come here. Been here three years before he left. Say I had a curse prayer on me and he started walking down the road and ain't never come back. Somebody told me, say you can fix things like that.

BYNUM: He just got up one day, set his feet on the road, and walked away?

MATTIE: You got to make him come back, mister.

BYNUM: Did he say goodbye?

MATTIE: Ain't said nothing. Just started walking. I could see where he disappeared. Didn't look back. Just keep walking. Can't you fix it so he come back? I ain't got no curse prayer on me. I know I ain't.

BYNUM: What made him say you had a curse prayer on you?

MATTIE: 'Cause the babies died. Me and Jack had two babies. Two little babies that ain't lived two months before they died. He say it's because somebody cursed me not to have babies.

BYNUM: He ain't bound to you if the babies died. Look like somebody trying to keep you from being bound up and he's gone on back to whoever it is 'cause he's already bound up to her. Ain't nothing to be done. Somebody else done got a powerful hand in it and ain't nothing to be done to break it. You got to let him go find where he's supposed to be in the world.

MATTIE: Jack done gone off and you telling me to forget about him. All my life I been looking for somebody to stop and stay with me. I done already got too many things to forget about. I take Jack Carper's hand and it feel so rough and strong. Seem like he's the strongest man in the world the way he hold me. Like he's bigger than the whole world and can't nothing bad get to me. Even when he act mean sometimes he still make everything seem okay with the world. Like there's part of it that belongs just to you. Now you telling me to forget about him?

BYNUM: Jack Carper gone off to where he belong. There's somebody searching for your doorstep right now. Ain't no need you fretting over Jack Carper. Right now he's a strong thought in your mind. But every time you catch yourself frettin over Jack Carper you push that thought away. You push it out your mind and that thought will get weaker and weaker till you wake up one morning and you won't even be able to call him up on your mind.

(BYNUM *gives her a small cloth packet.*)

Take this and sleep with it under your pillow and it'll bring good luck to you. Draw it to you like a magnet. It won't be long before you forget all about Jack Carper.

MATTIE: How much . . . do I owe you?

BYNUM: Whatever you got there . . . that'll be alright.

(MATTIE *hands* BYNUM *two quarters. She crosses to the door.*)

You sleep with that under your pillow and you'll be alright.

(MATTIE *opens the door to exit and* JEREMY *crosses over to her.* BYNUM *overhears the first part of their conversation, then exits out the back.*)

JEREMY: I overheard what you told Mr. Bynum. Had me an old gal did that to me. Woke up one morning and she was gone. Just took off to parts unknown. I woke up that morning and the only thing I could do was look around for my shoes. I woke up and got out of there. Found my shoes and took off. That's the only thing I could think of to do.

MATTIE: She ain't said nothing?

JEREMY: I just looked around for my shoes and got out of there.

MATTIE: Jack ain't said nothing either. He just walked off.

JEREMY: Some mens do that. Womens too. I ain't gone off looking for her. I just let her go. Figure she had a time to come to herself. Wasn't no use of me standing in the way. Where you from?

MATTIE: Texas. I was born in Georgia but I went to Texas with my mama. She dead now. Was picking peaches and fell dead away. I come up here with Jack Carper.

JEREMY: I'm from North Carolina. Down around Raleigh where they got all that tobacco. Been up here about two weeks. I likes it fine except I still got to find me a woman. You got a nice look to you. Look like you have mens standing in your door. Is you got mens standing in your door to get a look at you?

MATTIE: I ain't got nobody since Jack left.

JEREMY: A woman like you need a man. Maybe you let me be your man. I got a nice way with the women. That's what they tell me.

MATTIE: I don't know. Maybe Jack's coming back.

JEREMY: I'll be your man till he come. A woman can't be by her lonesome. Let me be your man till he come.

MATTIE: I just can't go through life piecing myself out to different mens. I need a man who wants to stay with me.

JEREMY: I can't say what's gonna happen. Maybe I'll be the man. I don't know. You wanna go along the road a little ways with me?

MATTIE: I don't know. Seem like life say it's gonna be one thing and end up being another. I'm tired of going from man to man.

JEREMY: Life is like you got to take a chance. Everybody got to take a chance. Can't nobody say what's gonna be. Come on . . . take a chance with me and see what the year bring. Maybe you let me come and see you. Where you staying?

MATTIE: I got me a room up on Bedford. Me and Jack had a room together.

JEREMY: What's the address? I'll come by and get you tonight and we can go down to Seefus. I'm going down there and play my guitar.

MATTIE: You play guitar?

JEREMY: I play guitar like I'm born to it.

MATTIE: I live at 1727 Bedford Avenue. I'm gonna find out if you can play guitar like you say.

JEREMY: I plays it, sugar, and that ain't all I do. I got a ten-pound hammer and I knows how to drive it down. Good god . . . you ought to hear my hammer ring!

MATTIE: Go on with that kind of talk, now. If you gonna come by and get me I got to get home and straighten up for you.

JEREMY: I'll be by at eight o'clock. How's eight o'clock? I'm gonna make you forget all about Jack Carper.

MATTIE: Go on, now. I got to get home and fix up for you.

JEREMY: Eight o'clock, sugar.

(*The lights go down in the parlor and come up on the yard outside.* ZONIA *is singing and playing a game.*)

ZONIA: I went downtown
To get my grip
I came back home
Just a pullin' the skiff

I went upstairs
To make my bed
I made a mistake
And I bumped my head
Just a pullin' the skiff

I went downstairs
To milk the cow
I made a mistake
And I milked the sow
Just a pullin' the skiff

Tomorrow, tomorrow
Tomorrow never comes
The marrow the marrow
The marrow in the bone.

(REUBEN *enters.*)

REUBEN: Hi.
ZONIA: Hi.
REUBEN: What's your name?
ZONIA: Zonia.
REUBEN: What kind of name is that?
ZONIA: It's what my daddy named me.
REUBEN: My name's Reuben. You staying in Mr. Seth's house?
ZONIA: Yeah.
REUBEN: That your daddy I seen you with this morning?
ZONIA: I don't know. Who you see me with?
REUBEN: I saw you with some man had on a great big old coat. And you was walking up to Mr. Seth's house. Had on a hat too.
ZONIA: Yeah, that's my daddy.
REUBEN: You like Mr. Seth?
ZONIA: I ain't see him much.
REUBEN: My grandpap say he a great big old windbag. How come you living in Mr. Seth's house? Don't you have no house?
ZONIA: We going to find my mother.
REUBEN: Where she at?
ZONIA: I don't know. We got to find her. We just go all over.
REUBEN: Why you got to find her? What happened to her?
ZONIA: She ran away.
REUBEN: Why she run away?
ZONIA: I don't know. My daddy say some man named Joe Turner did something bad to him once and that made her run away.
REUBEN: Maybe she coming back and you don't have to go looking for her.
ZONIA: We ain't there no more.

REUBEN: She could have come back when you wasn't there.

ZONIA: My daddy said she ran off and left us so we going looking for her.

REUBEN: What he gonna do when he find her?

ZONIA: He didn't say. He just say he got to find her.

REUBEN: Your daddy say how long you staying in Mr. Seth's house?

ZONIA: He don't say much. But we never stay too long nowhere. He say we got to keep moving till we find her.

REUBEN: Ain't no kids hardly live around here. I had me a friend but he died. He was the best friend I ever had. Me and Eugene used to keep secrets. I still got his pigeons. He told me to let them go when he died. He say, "Reuben, promise me when I die you'll let my pigeons go." But I keep them to remember him by. I ain't never gonna let them go. Even when I get to be grown up. I'm just always gonna have Eugene's pigeons.

(Pause.)

Mr. Bynum a conjure man. My grandpap scared of him. He don't like me to come over here too much. I'm scared of him too. My grandpap told me not to let him get close enough to where he can reach out his hand and touch me.

ZONIA: He don't seem scary to me.

REUBEN: He buys pigeons from me . . . and if you get up early in the morning you can see him out in the yard doing something with them pigeons. My grandpap say he kill them. I sold him one yesterday. I don't know what he do with it. I just hope he don't spook me up.

ZONIA: Why you sell him pigeons if he's gonna spook you up?

REUBEN: I just do like Eugene do. He used to sell Mr. Bynum pigeons. That's how he got to collecting them to sell to Mr. Bynum. Sometime he give me a nickel and sometime he give me a whole dime.

(Loomis enters from the house.)

LOOMIS: Zonia!

ZONIA: Sir?

LOOMIS: What you doing?

ZONIA: Nothing.

LOOMIS: You stay around this house, you hear? I don't want you wandering off nowhere.

ZONIA: I ain't wandering off nowhere.

LOOMIS: Miss Bertha set that hot tub and you getting a good scrubbing. Get scrubbed up good. You ain't been scrubbing.

ZONIA: I been scrubbing.

LOOMIS: Look at you. You growing too fast. Your bones getting bigger everyday. I don't want you getting grown on me. Don't you get grown on me too soon. We gonna find your mamma. She around here somewhere. I can smell her. You stay on around this house now. Don't you go nowhere.

ZONIA: Yes, sir.

(LOOMIS *exits into the house.*)

REUBEN: Wow, your daddy's scary!

ZONIA: He is not! I don't know what you talking about.

REUBEN: He got them mean-looking eyes!

ZONIA: My daddy ain't got no mean-looking eyes!

REUBEN: Aw, girl, I was just messing with you. You wanna go see Eugene's pigeons? Got a great big coop out the back of my house. Come on, I'll show you.

(REUBEN *and* ZONIA *exit as the lights go down.*)

Scene Two

It is Saturday morning, one week later. The lights come up on the kitchen. BERTHA *is at the stove preparing breakfast while* SETH *sits at the table.*

SETH: Something ain't right about that fellow. I been watching him all week. Something ain't right, I'm telling you.

BERTHA: Seth Holly, why don't you hush up about that man this morning?

SETH: I don't like the way he stare at everybody. Don't look at you natural like. He just be staring at you. Like he trying to figure out something about you. Did you see him when he come back in here?

BERTHA: That man ain't thinking about you.

SETH: He don't work nowhere. Just go out and come back. Go out and come back.

BERTHA: As long as you get your boarding money it ain't your cause about what he do. He don't bother nobody.

SETH: Just go out and come back. Going around asking everybody about Martha. Like Henry Allen seen him down at the church last night.

BERTHA: The man's allowed to go to church if he want. He say he a deacon. Ain't nobody wrong about him going to church.

SETH: I ain't talking about him going to church. I'm talking about him hanging around *outside* the church.

BERTHA: Henry Allen say that?

SETH: Say he be standing around outside the church. Like he be watching it.

BERTHA: What on earth he wanna be watching the church for, I wonder?

SETH: That's what I'm trying to figure out. Looks like he fixing to rob it.

BERTHA: Seth, now do he look like the kind that would rob the church?

SETH: I ain't saying that. I ain't saying how he look. It's how he do. Anybody liable to do anything as far as I'm concerned. I ain't never thought about how no church robbers look . . . but now that you mention it, I don't see where they look no different than how he look.

BERTHA: Herald Loomis ain't the kind of man who would rob no church.

SETH: I ain't even so sure that's his name.

BERTHA: Why the man got to lie about his name?

SETH: Anybody can tell anybody anything about what their name is. That's what you call him . . . Herald Loomis. His name is liable to be anything.

BERTHA: Well, until he tell me different that's what I'm gonna call him. You just getting yourself all worked up about the man for nothing.

SETH: Talking about Loomis: Martha's name wasn't no Loomis nothing. Martha's name is Pentecost.

BERTHA: How you so sure that's her right name? Maybe she changed it.

SETH: Martha's a good Christian woman. This fellow here look like he owe the devil a day's work and he's trying to figure out how he gonna pay him. Martha ain't had a speck of distrust about her the whole time she was living here. They moved the church out there to Rankin and I was sorry to see her go.

BERTHA: That's why he be hanging around the church. He looking for her.

SETH: If he looking for her, why don't he go inside and ask? What he doing hanging around outside the church acting sneaky like?

(BYNUM *enters from the yard.*)

BYNUM: Morning, Seth. Morning, Sister Bertha.

(BYNUM *continues through the kitchen and exits up the stairs.*)

BERTHA: That's who you should be asking the questions. He been out there in that yard all morning. He was out there before the sun come up. He didn't even come in for breakfast. I don't know what he's doing. He had three of them pigeons line up out there. He dance around till he get tired. He sit down awhile then get up and dance some more. He come through here a little while ago looking like he was mad at the world.

SETH: I don't pay Bynum no mind. He don't spook me up with all that stuff.

BERTHA: That's how Martha come to be living here. She come to see Bynum. She come to see him when she first left from down South.

SETH: Martha was living here before Bynum. She ain't come on here when she first left from down there. She come on here after she went back to get her little girl. That's when she come on here.

BERTHA: Well, where was Bynum? He was here when she came.

SETH: Bynum ain't come till after her. That boy Hiram was staying up there in Bynum's room.

BERTHA: Well, how long Bynum been here?

SETH: Bynum ain't been here no longer than three years. That's what I'm trying to tell you. Martha was staying up there and sewing and cleaning for Doc Goldblum when Bynum came. This the longest he ever been in one place.

BERTHA: How you know how long the man been in one place?

SETH: I know Bynum. Bynum ain't no mystery to me. I done seen a hundred niggers like him. He's one of them fellows never could stay in one place. He was wandering all around the country till he got old and settled here. The only thing different about Bynum is he bring all this heebie-jeebie stuff with him.

BERTHA: I still say he was staying here when she came. That's why she came . . . to see him.

SETH: You can say what you want. I know the facts of it. She come on here four years ago all heartbroken 'cause she couldn't find her little girl. And Bynum wasn't nowhere around. She got mixed up in that old heebie-jeebie nonsense with him after he came.

BERTHA: Well, if she came on before Bynum I don't know where she stayed. 'Cause she stayed up there in Hiram's room. Hiram couldn't get along with Bynum and left out of here owing you two dollars. Now, I know you ain't forgot about that!

SETH: Sure did! You know Hiram ain't paid me that two dollars yet. So that's why he be ducking and hiding when he see me down on Logan Street. You right. Martha did come on after Bynum. I forgot that's why Hiram left.

BERTHA: Him and Bynum never could see eye to eye. They always rubbed each other the wrong way. Hiram got to thinking that Bynum was trying to put a fix on him and he moved out. Martha came to see Bynum and ended up taking Hiram's room. Now, I know what I'm taking about. She stayed on here three years till they moved the church.

SETH: She out there in Rankin now. I know where she at. I know where they moved the church to. She right out there in Rankin in that place used to be shoe store. Used to be Wolf's shoe store. They moved to a bigger place and they put that church in there. I know where she at. I know just where she at.

BERTHA: Why don't you tell the man? You see he looking for her.

SETH: I ain't gonna tell that man where that woman is! What I wanna do that for? I don't know nothing about that man. I don't know why he looking for her. He might wanna do her a harm. I ain't gonna carry that on my hands. He looking for her, he gonna have to find her for himself. I ain't gonna help him. Now, if he had come and presented himself as a gentleman—the way Martha Pentecost's husband would have done—then I would have told him. But I ain't gonna tell this old wild-eyed mean-looking nigger nothing!

BERTHA: Well, why don't you get a ride with Selig and go up there and tell her where he is? See if she wanna see him. If that's her little girl . . . you say Martha was looking for her.

SETH: You know me, Bertha. I don't get mixed up in nobody's business.

(BYNUM *enters from the stairs.*)

BYNUM: Morning, Seth. Morning, Bertha. Can I still get some breakfast? Mr. Loomis been down here this morning?

SETH: He done gone out and come back. He up there now. Left out of here early this morning wearing that coat. Hot as it is, the man wanna walk around wearing a big old heavy coat. He come back in here paid me for another week, sat down there waiting on Selig. Got tired of waiting and went on back upstairs.

BYNUM: Where's the little girl?

SETH: She out there in the front. Had to chase her and that Reuben off the front porch. She out there somewhere.

BYNUM: Look like if Martha was around here he would have found her by now. My guess is she ain't in the city.

SETH: She ain't! I know where she at. I know just where she at. But I ain't gonna tell him. Not the way he look.

BERTHA: Here go your coffee, Bynum.

BYNUM: He says he gonna get Selig to find her for him.

SETH: Selig can't find her. He talk all that . . . but unless he get lucky and knock on her door he can't find her. That's the only way he find anybody. He got to get lucky. But I know just where she at.

BERTHA: Here go some biscuits, Bynum.

BYNUM: What else you got over there, Sister Bertha? You got some grits and gravy over there? I could go for some of that this morning.

BERTHA: (*Sets a bowl on the table.*) Seth, come on and help me turn this mattress over. Come on.

SETH: Something ain't right with that fellow, Bynum. I don't like the way he stare at everybody.

BYNUM: Mr. Loomis alright, Seth. He just a man got something on his mind. He just got a straightforward mind, that's all.

SETH: What's that fellow that they had around here? Moses, that's Moses Houser. Man went crazy and jumped off the Brady Street Bridge. I told you when I seen him something wasn't right about him. And I'm telling you about this fellow now.

(*There is a knock on the door.* SETH *goes to answer it. Enter* RUTHERFORD SELIG.)

Ho! Come on in, Selig.

BYNUM: If it ain't the People Finder himself.

SELIG: Bynum, before you start . . . I ain't seen no shiny man now.

BYNUM: Who said anything about that? I ain't said nothing about that. I just called you a first-class People Finder.

SELIG: How many dustpans you get out of that sheet metal, Seth?

SETH: You walked by them on your way in. They sitting out there on the porch. Got twenty-eight. Got four out of each sheet and made Bertha a coffeepot out the other one. They a little small but they got nice handles.

SELIG: That was twenty cents apiece, right? That's what we agreed on.

SETH: That's five dollars and sixty cents. Twenty on top of twenty-eight. How many sheets you bring me?

SELIG: I got eight out there. That's a dollar twenty makes me owe you. . . .

SETH: Four dollars and forty cents.

SELIG: (*Paying him.*) Go on and make me some dustpans. I can use all you can make.

(LOOMIS *enters from the stairs.*)

LOOMIS: I been watching for you. He say you find people.

BYNUM: Mr. Loomis here wants you to find his wife.

LOOMIS: He say you find people. Find her for me.

SELIG: Well, let see here . . . find somebody, is it?

(SELIG *rummages through his pockets. He has several notebooks and he is searching for the right one.*)

Alright now . . . what's the name?

LOOMIS: Martha Loomis. She my wife. Got married legal with the paper and all.

SELIG: (*Writing.*) Martha . . . Loomis. How tall is she?

LOOMIS: She five feet from the ground.

SELIG: Five feet . . . tall. Young or old?

LOOMIS: She a young woman. Got long pretty hair.

SELIG: Young . . . long . . . pretty . . . hair. Where did you last see her?

LOOMIS: Tennessee. Nearby Memphis.

SELIG: When was that?

LOOMIS: Nineteen hundred and one.

SELIG: Nineteen . . . hundred and one. I'll tell you, mister . . . you better off without them. Now you take me . . . old Rutherford Selig could tell you a thing or two about these women. I ain't met one yet I could understand. Now, you take Sally out there. That's all a man needs is a good horse. I say giddup and she go. Say whoa and she stop. I feed her some oats and she carry me wherever I want to go. Ain't had a speck of trouble out of her since I had her. Now, I been married. A long time ago down in Kentucky. I got up one morning and I saw this look on my wife's face. Like way down deep inside her she was wishing I was dead. I walked around that morning and every time I looked at her she had that look on her face. It seem like she knew I could see it on her. Every time I looked at her I got smaller and smaller. Well, I wasn't gonna stay around there and just shrink away. I walked out on the porch and closed the door behind me. When I closed the door she locked it. I went out and bought me a horse. And I ain't been without one since! Martha Loomis, huh? Well, now I'll do the best I can do. That's one dollar.

LOOMIS: (*Holding out dollar suspiciously.*) How you find her?

SELIG: Well now, it ain't no easy job like you think. You can't just go out there and find them like that. There's a lot of little tricks to it. It's not an easy job keeping up with you Nigras the way you move about so. Now you take this woman you looking for . . . this Martha Loomis. She could be anywhere. Time I find her, if you don't keep your eye on her, she'll be gone off someplace else. You'll be thinking she over here and she'll be over there. But like I say there's a lot of little tricks to it.

LOOMIS: You say you find her.

SELIG: I can't promise anything but we been finders in my family for a long time. Bringers and finders. My great-granddaddy used to bring Nigras across the ocean on ships. That's wasn't no easy job either. Sometimes the winds would blow so hard you'd think the hand of God was set against the sails. But it set him well in pay and he settled in this new land and found him a wife of good Christian charity with a mind for kids and the like and well . . . here I am, Rutherford Selig. You're in good hands, mister. Me and my daddy have found plenty Nigras. My daddy, rest his soul, used to find runaway slaves for the plantation bosses. He was the best there was at it. Jonas B. Selig. Had him a reputation stretched clean across the country. After Abraham Lincoln give you all Nigras your freedom papers and with you all looking all over for each other . . . we started finding Nigras for Nigras. Of course, it don't pay as much. But the People Finding business ain't so bad.

LOOMIS: (*Hands him the dollar.*) Find her. Martha Loomis. Find her for me.

SELIG: Like I say, I can't promise you anything. I'm going back upriver, and if she's around in them parts I'll find her for you. But I can't promise you anything.

LOOMIS: When you coming back?

SELIG: I'll be back on Saturday. I come and see Seth to pick up my order on Saturday.

BYNUM: You going upriver, huh? You going up around my way. I used to go all up through there. Blawknox . . . Clairton. Used to go up to Rankin and take that first righthand road. I wore many a pair of shoes out walking around that way. You'd have thought I was a missionary spreading the gospel the way I wandered all around them parts.

SELIG: Okay, Bynum. See you on Saturday.

SETH: Here, let me walk out with you. Help you with them dustpans.

(SETH and SELIG exit out the back. BERTHA enters from the stairs carrying a bundle of sheets.)

BYNUM: Herald Loomis got the People Finder looking for Martha.

BERTHA: You can call him a People Finder if you want to. I know Rutherford Selig carries people away too. He done carried a whole bunch of them away from here. Folks plan on leaving plan by Selig's timing. They wait till he get ready to go, then they hitch a ride on his wagon. Then he charge folks a dollar to tell them where he took them. Now, that's the truth of Rutherford Selig. This old People Finding business is for the birds. He ain't never found nobody he ain't took away. Herald Loomis, you just wasted your dollar.

(BERTHA exits into the bedroom.)

LOOMIS: He say he find her. He say he find her by Saturday. I'm gonna wait till Saturday.

(The lights fade to black.)

Scene Three

It is Sunday morning, the next day. The lights come up on the kitchen. SETH sits talking to BYNUM. The breakfast dishes have been   eared away.

SETH: They can't see that. Neither one of them can see that. Now, how much sense it take to see that? All you got to do is be able to count. One man making ten pots is five men making fifty pots. But they can't see that. Asked where I'm gonna get my five men. Hell, I can teach anybody how to make a pot. I can teach you. I can take you out there and get you started right now. Inside of two weeks you'd know ow to make a pot. All you got to do is want to do it. I can get five men. I ain't worried about getting no five men.

BERTHA: (Calls from the bedroom.) Seth. Come on and get ready now. Reverend Gates ain't gonna be holding up his sermon 'cause you sitting out there talking.

SETH: Now, you take the boy, Jeremy. What he gonna do after he put in that road? He can't do nothing but go put in another one somewhere. Now, if he let me show him how to make some pots and pans . . . then he'd have something can't nobody take away from him. After a while he could get his own tools and go off somewhere and make his own pots and pans. Find him somebody to sell them to. Now, Selig can't make no pots and pans. He can sell them but he can't make them. I get me five men with some tools and we'd make him so many pots and pans he'd have to open up a store somewhere. But they can't see that. Neither Mr. Cohen nor Sam Green.

BERTHA: (*Calls from the bedroom.*) Seth . . . time be wasting. Best be getting on.

SETH: I'm coming, woman! (*To* BYNUM.) Want me to sign over the house to borrow five hundred dollars. I ain't that big a fool. That's all I got. Sign it over to them and then I won't have nothing.

(JEREMY *enters waving a dollar and carrying his guitar.*)

JEREMY: Look here, Mr. Bynum . . . won me another dollar last night down at Seefus! Me and that Mattie Campbell went down there again and I played contest. Ain't no guitar players down there. Wasn't even no contest. Say, Mr. Seth, I asked Mattie Campbell if she wanna come by and have Sunday dinner with us. Get some fried chicken.

SETH: It's gonna cost you twenty-five cents.

JEREMY: That's alright. I got a whole dollar here. Say Mr. Seth . . . me and Mattie Campbell talked it over last night and she gonna move in with me. If that's alright with you.

SETH: Your business is your business . . . but it's gonna cost her a dollar a week for her board. I can't be feeding nobody for free.

JEREMY: Oh, she know that, Mr. Seth. That's what I told her, say she'd have to pay for her meals.

SETH: You say you got a whole dollar there . . . turn loose that twenty-five cents.

JEREMY: Suppose she move in today, then that make seventy-five cents more, so I'll give you the whole dollar for her now till she gets here.

(SETH *pockets the money and exits into the bedroom.*)

BYNUM: So you and that Mattie Campbell gonna take up together?

JEREMY: I told her she don't need to be by her lonesome, Mr. Bynum. Don't make no sense for both of us to be by our lonesome. So she gonna move in with me.

BYNUM: Sometimes you got to be where you supposed to be. Sometimes you can get all mixed up in life and come to the wrong place.

JEREMY: That's just what I told her, Mr. Bynum. It don't make no sense for her to be all mixed up and lonesome. May as well come here and be with me. She a fine woman too. Got them long legs. Knows how to treat a fellow too. Treat you like you wanna be treated.

BYNUM: You just can't look at it like that. You got to look at the whole thing. Now, you take a fellow go out there, grab hold to a woman and think he got something 'cause she sweet and soft to the touch. Alright. Touching's part of life. It's in the world like everything else. Touching's nice. It feels good. But you can lay your hand upside a horse or a cat, and that feels good too. What's the difference? When you grab hold to a woman, you got something there. You got a whole world there. You got a way of life kicking up under your hand. That woman can take and make you feel like something. I ain't just talking about in the way of jumping off into bed together and rolling around with each other. Anybody can do that. When you grab hold to that woman and look at the whole thing and see what you got . . . why, she can take and make something out of you. Your mother was a woman. That's enough right there to show you what a woman is. Enough to show you what she can do. She made something out of you. Taught you converse, and all about how to take care of yourself, how to see where you at and where you going tomorrow, how to look out to see what's coming in the way of eating, and what to do with yourself when you get lonesome. That's a mighty thing she did. But you can't look at a woman to jump off into bed with her. That's a foolish thing to ignore a woman like that.

JEREMY: Oh, I ain't ignoring her, Mr. Bynum. It's hard to ignore a woman got legs like she got.

BYNUM: Alright. Let's try it this way. Now, you take a ship. Be out there on the water traveling about. You out there on that ship sailing to and from. And then you see some land. Just like you see a woman walking down the street. You see that land and it don't look like nothing but a line out there on the horizon. That's all it is when you first see it. A line that cross your path out there on the horizon. Now, a smart man know when he see that land, it ain't just a line setting out there. He know that if you got off the water to go take a good look . . . why, there's a whole world right there. A whole world with everything imaginable under the sun. Anything you can think of you can find on that land. Same with a woman. A woman is everything a man need. To a smart man she water and berries. And that's all a man need. That's all he need to live on. You give me some water and berries and if there ain't nothing else I can live a hundred years. See, you just like a man looking at the horizon from a ship. You just seeing a part of it. But it's a blessing when you learn to look at a woman and see in maybe just a few strands of her hair, the way her cheek curves . . . to see in that everything there is out of life to be gotten. It's a blessing to see that. You know you done right and proud by your mother to see that. But you got to learn it. My telling you ain't gonna mean nothing. You got to learn how to come to your own time and place with a woman.

JEREMY: What about your woman, Mr. Bynum? I know you done had some woman.

BYNUM: Oh, I got them in memory time. That lasts longer than any of them ever stayed with me.

JEREMY: I had me an old gal one time . . .

(There is a knock on the door. JEREMY *goes to answer it. Enter* MOLLY CUNNINGHAM. *She is about twenty-six, the kind of woman that "could break in on a dollar anywhere she goes." She carries a small cardboard suitcase, and wears a colorful dress of the fashion of the day.* JEREMY's *heart jumps out of his chest when he sees her.)*

MOLLY: You got any rooms here? I'm looking for a room.

JEREMY: Yeah . . . Mr. Seth got rooms. Sure . . . wait till I get Mr. Seth. *(Calls.)* Mr. Seth! Somebody here to see you! *(To Molly.)* Yeah, Mr. Seth got some rooms. Got one right next to me. This a nice place to stay, too. My name's Jeremy. What's yours?

*(*SETH *enters dressed in his Sunday clothes.)*

SETH: Ho!

JEREMY: This here woman looking for a place to stay. She say you got any rooms.

MOLLY: Mister, you got any rooms? I seen your sign say you got rooms.

SETH: How long you plan to staying?

MOLLY: I ain't gonna be here long. I ain't looking for no home or nothing. I'd be in Cincinnati if I hadn't missed my train.

SETH: Rooms cost two dollars a week.

MOLLY: Two dollars!

SETH: That includes meals. We serve two meals a day. That's breakfast and dinner.

MOLLY: I hope it ain't on the third floor.

SETH: That's the only one I got. Third floor to the left. That's pay up in advance week to week.

MOLLY: *(Going into her bosom.)* I'm gonna pay you for one week. My name's Molly. Molly Cunningham.

SETH: I'm Seth Holly. My wife's name is Bertha. She do the cooking and taking care of around here. She got sheets on the bed. Towels twenty-five cents a week extra if you ain't got none. You get breakfast and dinner. We got fried chicken on Sundays.

MOLLY: That sounds good. Here's two dollars and twenty-five cents. Look here, Mister . . . ?

SETH: Holly, Seth Holly.

MOLLY: Look here, Mr. Holly. I forgot to tell you. I likes me some company from time to time. I don't like being by myself.

SETH: Your business is your business. I don't meddle in nobody's business. But this is a respectable house. I don't have no riffraff around here. And I don't have no women hauling no men up to their rooms to be making their living. As long as we understand each other then we'll be alright with each other.

MOLLY: Where's the outhouse?

SETH: Straight through the door over yonder.

MOLLY: I get my own key to the front door?

SETH: Everybody get their own key. If you come in late just don't be making no whole lot of noise and carrying on. Don't allow no fussing and fighting around here.

MOLLY: You ain't got to worry about that, mister. Which way you say that outhouse was again?

SETH: Straight through that door over yonder.

(MOLLY *exits out the back door.* JEREMY *crosses to watch her.*)

JEREMY: Mr. Bynum, you know what? I think I know what you was talking about now.

(*The lights go down on the scene.*)

Scene Four

The lights come up on the kitchen. It is later the same evening. MATTIE *and all the residents of the house, except* LOOMIS, *sit around the table. They have finished eating and most of the dishes have been cleared.*

MOLLY: That sure was some good chicken.

JEREMY: That's what I'm talking about. Miss Bertha, you sure can fry some chicken. I thought my mama could fry some chicken. But she can't do half as good as you.

SETH: I know it. That's why I married her. She don't know that, though. She think I married her for something else.

BERTHA: I ain't studying you, Seth. Did you get your things moved in alright, Mattie?

MATTIE: I ain't had that much. Jeremy helped me with what I did have.

BERTHA: You'll get to know your way around here. If you have any questions about anything just ask me. You and Molly both. I get along with everybody. You'll find I ain't no trouble to get along with.

MATTIE: You need some help with the dishes?

BERTHA: I got me a helper. Ain't I, Zonia? Got me a good helper.

ZONIA: Yes, ma'am.

SETH: Look at Bynum sitting over there with his belly all poked out. Ain't saying nothing. Sitting over there half asleep. Ho, Bynum!

BERTHA: If Bynum ain't saying nothing what you wanna start him up for?

SETH: Ho, Bynum!

BYNUM: What you hollering at me for? I ain't doing nothing.

SETH: Come on, we gonna Juba.

BYNUM: You know me, I'm always ready to Juba.

SETH: Well, come on, then.

(SETH *pulls a harmonica and blows a few notes.*)

Come on there, Jeremy. Where's your guitar? Go get your guitar. Bynum says he's ready to Juba.

JEREMY: Don't need no guitar to Juba. Ain't you never Juba without a guitar?

(JEREMY *begins to drum on the table.*)

SETH: It ain't that. I ain't never Juba with one! Figured to try it and see how it worked.

BYNUM: (*Drumming on the table.*) You don't need no guitar. Look at Molly sitting over there. She don't know we Juba on Sunday. We gonna show you something tonight. You and Mattie Campbell both. Ain't that right, Seth?

SETH: You said it! Come on, Bertha, leave them dishes be for a while. We gonna Juba.

BYNUM: Alright. Let's Juba down!

(*The Juba is reminiscent of the Ring Shouts of the African slaves. It is a call and response dance.* BYNUM *sits at the table and drums. He calls the dance as others clap hands, shuffle, and stomp around the table. It should be as African as possible, with the performers working themselves up into a near frenzy. The words can be improvised, but should include some mention of the Holy Ghost. In the middle of the dance* HERALD LOOMIS *enters.*)

LOOMIS: (*In a rage.*) Stop it! Stop!

(*They stop and turn to look at him.*)

You all sitting up here singing about the Holy Ghost. What's so holy about the Holy Ghost? You singing and singing. You think the Holy Ghost coming? You singing for the Holy Ghost to come? What he gonna do, huh? He gonna come with tongues of fire to burn up your woolly heads? You gonna tie onto the Holy Ghost and get burned up? What you got then? Why God got to be so big? Why he got to be bigger than me? How much big is there? How much big do you want?

(LOOMIS *starts to unzip his pants.*)

SETH: Nigger, you crazy!

LOOMIS: How much big you want?

SETH: You done plumb lost your mind!

(LOOMIS *begins to speak in tongues and dance around the kitchen.* SETH *starts after him.*)

BERTHA: Leave him alone, Seth. He ain't in his right mind.

LOOMIS: (*Stops suddenly.*) You all don't know nothing about me. You don't know what I done seen. Herald Loomis done seen some things he ain't got words to tell you.

(LOOMIS *starts to walk out the front door and is thrown back and collapses, terrorstricken by his vision.* BYNUM *crawls to him.*)

BYNUM: What you done seen, Herald Loomis?

LOOMIS: I done seen bones rise up out the water. Rise up and walk across the water. Bones walking on top of the water.

BYNUM: Tell me about them bones, Herald Loomis. Tell me what you seen.

LOOMIS: I come to this place . . . to this water that was bigger than the whole world. And I looked out . . . and I seen them bones rise up out the water. Rise up and begin to walk on top of it.

BYNUM: Wasn't nothing but bones and they walking on top of the water.

LOOMIS: Walking without sinking down. Walking on top of the water.

BYNUM: Just marching in a line.

LOOMIS: A whole heap of them. They come up out the water and started marching.

BYNUM: Wasn't nothing but bones and they walking on top of the water.

LOOMIS: One after the other. They just come up out the water and start to walking.

BYNUM: They walking on the water without sinking down. They just walking and walking. And then . . . what happened, Herald Loomis?

LOOMIS: They just walking across the water.

BYNUM: What happened, Herald Loomis? What happened to the bones?

LOOMIS: They just walking across the water . . . and then . . . they sunk down.

BYNUM: The bones sunk into the water. They all sunk down.

LOOMIS: All at one time! They just all fell in the water at one time.

BYNUM: Sunk down like anybody else.

LOOMIS: When they sink down they made a big splash and this here wave come up . . .

BYNUM: A big wave, Herald Loomis. A big wave washed over the land.

LOOMIS: It washed them out of the water and up on the land. Only . . . only . . .

BYNUM: Only they ain't bones no more.

LOOMIS: They got flesh on them! Just like you and me!

BYNUM: Everywhere you look the waves is washing them up on the land right on top of one another.

LOOMIS: They black. Just like you and me. Ain't no difference.

BYNUM: Then what happened, Herald Loomis?

LOOMIS: They ain't moved or nothing. They just laying there.

BYNUM: You just laying there. What you waiting on, Herald Loomis?

LOOMIS: I'm laying there . . . waiting.

BYNUM: What you waiting on, Herald Loomis?

LOOMIS: I'm waiting on the breath to get into my body.

BYNUM: The breath coming into you, Herald Loomis. What you gonna do now?

LOOMIS: The wind's blowing the breath into my body. I can feel it. I'm starting to breathe again.

BYNUM: What you gonna do, Herald Loomis?

LOOMIS: I'm gonna stand up. I got to stand up. I can't lay here no more. All the breath coming into my body and I got to stand up.

BYNUM: Everybody's standing up at the same time.

LOOMIS: The ground's starting to shake. There's a great shaking. The world's busting half in two. The sky's splitting open. I got to stand up.

(LOOMIS *attempts to stand up.*)

My legs . . . my legs won't stand up!

BYNUM: Everybody's standing and walking toward the road. What you gonna do, Herald Loomis?

LOOMIS: My legs won't stand up.

BYNUM: They shaking hands and saying goodbye to each other and walking every whichaway down the road.

LOOMIS: I got to stand up!

BYNUM: They walking around here now. Mens. Just like you and me. Come right up out the water.

LOOMIS: Got to stand up.

BYNUM: They walking, Herald Loomis. They walking around here now.

LOOMIS: I got to stand up. Get up on the road.

BYNUM: Come on, Herald Loomis.

(LOOMIS *tries to stand up.*)

LOOMIS: My legs won't stand up! My legs won't stand up!

(LOOMIS *collapses on the floor as the lights go down to black.*)

ACT TWO

Scene One

The lights come up on the kitchen. BERTHA *busies herself with breakfast preparations.* SETH *sits at the table.*

SETH: I don't care what his problem is! He's leaving here!

BERTHA: You can't put the man out and he got that little girl. Where they gonna go then?

SETH: I don't care where he go. Let him go back where he was before he come here. I ain't asked him to come here. I knew when I first looked at him something wasn't right with him. Dragging that little girl around with him. Looking like he be sleeping in the woods somewhere. I knew all along he wasn't right.

BERTHA: A fellow get a little drunk he's liable to say or do anything. He ain't done no big harm.

SETH: I just don't have all that carrying on in my house. When he come down here I'm gonna tell him. He got to leave here. My daddy wouldn't stand for it and I ain't gonna stand for it either.

BERTHA: Well, if you put him out you have to put Bynum out too. Bynum right there with him.

SETH: If it wasn't for Bynum ain't no telling what would have happened. Bynum talked to that fellow just as nice and calmed him down. If he wasn't here ain't no telling what would have happened. Bynum ain't done nothing but talk to him and kept him calm. Man acting all crazy with that foolishness. Naw, he's leaving here.

BERTHA: What you gonna tell him? How you gonna tell him to leave?

SETH: I'm gonna tell him straight out. Keep it nice and simple. Mister, you got to leave here!

(MOLLY *enters from the stairs.*)

MOLLY: Morning.

BERTHA: Did you sleep alright in that bed?

MOLLY: Tired as I was I could have slept anywhere. It's a real nice room, though. This is a nice place.

SETH: I'm sorry you had to put up with all that carrying on last night.

MOLLY: It don't bother me none. I done seen that kind of stuff before.

SETH: You won't have to see it around here no more.

(BYNUM *is heard singing offstage.*)

I don't put up with all that stuff. When that fellow come down here I'm gonna tell him.

BYNUM: (*singing*)
Soon my work will all be done
Soon my work will all be done
Soon my work will all be done

I'm going to see the king.

BYNUM: (*Enters.*) Morning, Seth. Morning, Sister Bertha. I see we got Molly Cunningham down here at breakfast.

SETH: Bynum, I wanna thank you for talking to that fellow last night and calming him down. If you hadn. been here ain't no telling what might have happened.

BYNUM: Mr. Loomis alright, Seth. He just got a little excited.

SETH: Well, he can get excited somewhere else 'cause he leaving here.

(MATTIE *enters from the stairs.*)

BYNUM: Well, there's Mattie Campbell.

MATTIE: Good morning.

BERTHA: Sit on down there, Mattie. I got some biscuits be ready in a minute. The coffee's hot.

MATTIE: Jeremy gone already?

BYNUM: Yeah, he leave out of here early. He got to be there when the sun came up. Most working men got to be there when the sun come up. Everybody but Seth. Seth work at night. Mr. Olowski so busy in his shop he got fellows working at night.

(LOOMIS *enters from the stairs.*)

SETH: Mr. Loomis, now . . . I don't want no trouble. I keeps me a respectable house here. I don't have no carrying on like what went on last night. This has been a respectable house for a long time. I'm gonna have to ask you to leave.

LOOMIS: You got my two dollars. That two dollars say we stay till Saturday.

(LOOMIS *and* SETH *glare at each other.*)

SETH: Alright. Fair enough. You stay till Saturday. But come Saturday you got to leave here.

LOOMIS: (*Continues to glare at* SETH. *He goes to the door and calls.*) Zonia. You stay around this house, you hear? Don't you go anywhere.

(LOOMIS *exits out the front door.*)

SETH: I knew it when I first seen him. I knew something wasn't right with him.

BERTHA: Seth, leave the people alone to eat their breakfast. They don't want to hear that. Go on out there and make some pots and pans. That's the only time you satisfied is when you out there. Go on out there and make some pots and pans and leave them people alone.

SETH: I ain't bothering anybody. I'm just stating the facts. I told you, Bynum.

(BERTHA *shoos* SETH *out the back door and exits into the bedroom.*)

MOLLY: (*To* BYNUM.) You one of them voo-doo people?

BYNUM: I got a power to bind folks if that what you talking about.

MOLLY: I thought so. The way you talked to that man when he started all that spooky stuff. What you say you had the power to do to people? You ain't the cause of him acting like that, is you?

BYNUM: I binds them together. Sometimes I help them find each other.

MOLLY: How do you do that?

BYNUM: With a song. My daddy taught me how to do it.

MOLLY: That's what they say. Most folks be what they daddy is. I wouldn't want to be like my daddy. Nothing ever set right with him. He tried to make the world over. Carry it around with him everywhere he go. I don't want to be like that. I just take life as it come. I don't be trying to make it over.

(Pause.)

Your daddy used to do that too, huh? Make people stay together?

BYNUM: My daddy used to heal people. He had the Healing Song. I got the Binding Song.

MOLLY: My mama used to believe in all that stuff. If she got sick she would have gone and saw your daddy. As long as he didn't make her drink nothing. She wouldn't drink nothing nobody give her. She was always afraid somebody was gonna poison her. How your daddy heal people?

BYNUM: With a song. He healed people by singing over them. I seen him do it. He sung over this little white girl when she was sick. They made a big to-do about it. They carried the girl's bed out in the yard and had all her kinfolk standing around. The little girl laying up there in the bed. Doctors standing around can't do nothing to help her. And they had my daddy come up and sing his song. It didn't sound no different than any other song. It was just somebody singing. But the song was its own thing and it come out and took upon this little girl with its power and it healed her.

MOLLY: That's sure something else. I don't understand that kind of thing. I guess if the doctor couldn't make me well I'd try it. But otherwise I don't wanna be bothered with that kind of thing. It's too spooky.

BYNUM: Well, let me get on out here and get to work.

(BYNUM gets up and heads out the back door.)

MOLLY: I ain't meant to offend you or nothing. What's your name . . . Bynum? I ain't meant to say nothing to make you feel bad now.

(BYNUM exits out the back door.)

(to MATTIE.) I hope he don't feel bad. He's a nice man. I don't wanna hurt nobody's feelings or nothing.

MATTIE: I got to go on up to Doc Goldblum's and finish this ironing.

MOLLY: Now, that's something I don't never wanna do. Iron no clothes. Especially somebody else's. That's what I believe killed my mama. Always ironing and working, doing somebody else's work. Not Molly Cunningham.

MATTIE: It's the only job I got. I got to make it someway to fend for myself.

MOLLY: I thought Jeremy was your man. Ain't he working?

MATTIE: We just be keeping company till maybe Jack come back.

MOLLY: I don't trust none of these men. Jack or nobody else. These men liable to do anything. They wait just until they get one woman tied and locked up with them . . . then they look around to see if they can get another one. Molly don't pay them no mind. One's just as good as the other if you ask me. I ain't never met one that meant nobody no good. You got any babies?

MATTIE: I had two for my man, Jack Carper. But they both died.

MOLLY: That be the best. These men make all these babies, then run off and leave you to take care of them. Talking about they wanna see what's on the other side of the hill. I make sure I don't get no babies. My mama taught me how to do that.

MATTIE: Don't make me no mind. That be nice to be a mother.

MOLLY: Yeah? Well, you go on, then. Molly Cunningham ain't gonna be tied down with no babies. Had me a man one time who I thought had some love in him. Come home one day and he was packing his trunk. Told me the time come when even the best of friends must part. Say he was gonna send me a Special Delivery some old day. I watched him out the window when he carried that trunk out and down to the train station. Said if he was gonna send me a Special Delivery I wasn't gonna be there to get it. I done found out the harder you try to hold onto them, the easier it is for some gal to pull them away. Molly done learned that. That's why I don't trust nobody but the good Lord above, and I don't love nobody but my mama.

MATTIE: I got to get on. Doc Goldblum gonna be waiting.

(MATTIE *exits out the front door.* SETH *enters from his workshop with his apron, gloves, goggles, etc. He carries a bucket and crosses to the sink for water.*)

SETH: Everybody gone but you, huh?

MOLLY: That little shack out there by the outhouse . . . that's where you make them pots and pans and stuff?

SETH: Yeah, that's my workshed. I go out there . . . take these hands and make something out of nothing. Take that metal and bend and twist it whatever way I want. My daddy taught me that. He used to make pots and pans. That's how I learned it.

MOLLY: I never knew nobody made no pots and pans. My uncle used to shoe horses.

(JEREMY *enters at the front door.*)

SETH: I thought you was working? Ain't you working today?

JEREMY: Naw, they fired me. White fellow come by told me to give him fifty cents if I wanted to keep working. Going around to all the colored making them give him fifty cents to keep hold to their jobs. Them other fellows, they was giving it to him. I kept hold to mine and they fired me.

SETH: Boy, what kind of sense that make? What kind of sense it make to get fired from a job where you making eight dollars a week and all it cost you is fifty cents. That's seven dollars and fifty cents profit! This way you ain't got nothing.

JEREMY: It didn't make no sense to me. I don't make but eight dollars. Why I got to give him fifty cents of it? He go around to all the colored and he got ten dollars extra. That's more than I make for a whole week.

SETH: I see you gonna learn the hard way. You just looking at the facts of it. See, right now, without the job, you ain't got nothing. What you gonna do when you can't keep a roof over your head? Right now, come Saturday, unless you come up with another two dollars, you gonna be out there in the streets. Down up under one of them bridges trying to put some food in your belly and wishing you had given that fellow that fifty cents.

JEREMY: Don't make me no difference. There's a big road out there. I can get my guitar and always find me another place to stay. I ain't planning on staying in one place for too long noway.

SETH: We gonna see if you feel like that come Saturday!

(SETH *exits out the back.* JEREMY *sees* MOLLY.)

JEREMY: Molly Cunningham. How you doing today, sugar?

MOLLY: You can go on back down there tomorrow and go back to work if you want. They won't even know who you is. Won't even know it's you. I had me a fellow did that one time. They just went ahead and signed him up like they never seen him before.

JEREMY: I'm tired of working anyway. I'm glad they fired me. You sure look pretty today.

MOLLY: Don't come telling me all that pretty stuff. Beauty wanna come in and sit down at your table asking to be fed. I ain't hardly got enough for me.

JEREMY: You know you pretty. Ain't no sense in you saying nothing about that. Why don't you come on and go away with me?

MOLLY: You tied up with that Mattie Campbell. Now you talking about running away with me.

JEREMY: I was just keeping her company 'cause she lonely. You ain't the lonely kind. You the kind that know what she want and how to get it. I need a woman like you to travel around with. Don't you wanna travel around and look at some places with Jeremy? With a woman like you beside him, a man can make it nice in the world.

MOLLY: Molly can make it nice by herself too. Molly don't need nobody leave her cold in hand. The world rough enough as it is.

JEREMY: We can make it better together. I got my guitar and I can play. Won me another dollar last night playing guitar. We can go around and I can play at the dances and we can just enjoy life. You can make it by yourself alright, I agrees with that. A woman like you can make it anywhere she go. But you can make it better if you got a man to protect you.

MOLLY: What places you wanna go around and look at?

JEREMY: All of them! I don't want to miss nothing. I wanna go everywhere and do everything there is to be got out of life. With a woman like you it's like having water and berries. A man got everything he need.

MOLLY: You got to be doing more than playing that guitar. A dollar a day ain't hardly what Molly got in mind.

JEREMY: I gambles real good. I got a hand for it.

MOLLY: Molly don't work. And Molly ain't up for sale.

JEREMY: Sure, baby. You ain't got to work with Jeremy.

MOLLY: There's one more thing.

JEREMY: What's that, sugar?

MOLLY: Molly ain't going South.

(*The lights go down on the scene.*)

Scene Two

The lights come up on the parlor. SETH *and* BYNUM *sit playing a game of dominoes.* BYNUM *sings to himself.*

BYNUM: (*Singing.*)
    They tell me Joe Turner's come and gone
    Ohhh Lordy
    They tell me Joe Turner's come and gone
    Ohhh Lordy
    Got my man and gone

    Come with forty links of chain
    Ohhh Lordy
    Come with forty links of chain
    Ohhhh Lordy
    Got my man and gone

SETH: Come on and play if you gonna play.

BYNUM: I'm gonna play. Soon as I figure out what to do.

SETH: You can't figure out if you wanna play or you wanna sing.

BYNUM: Well sir, I'm gonna do a little of both.

(*Playing.*)

    There. What you gonna do now?

(*Singing.*)

They tell me Joe Turner's come and gone
Ohhh Lordy
They tell me Joe Turner's come and gone
Ohhh Lordy

SETH: Why don't you hush up that noise.

BYNUM: That's a song the women sing down around Memphis. The woman down there made up that song. I picked it up down there about fifteen years ago.

(LOOMIS *enters from the front door.*)

BYNUM: Evening, Mr. Loomis.

SETH: Today's Monday, Mr. Loomis. Come Saturday your time is up. We done ate already. My wife roasted up some yams. She got your plate sitting in there on the table. (*To* Bynum.) Whose play is it?

BYNUM: Ain't you keeping up with the game? I thought you was a domino player. I just played so it got to be your turn.

(LOOMIS *goes into the kitchen, where a plate of yams is covered and set on the table. He sits down and begins to eat with his hands.*)

SETH: (*Plays.*) Twenty! Give me twenty! You didn't know I had that ace five. You was trying to play around that. You didn't know I had that lying there for you.

BYNUM: You ain't done nothing. I let you have that to get mine.

SETH: Come on and play. You ain't doing nothing but talking. I got a hundred and forty points to your eighty. You ain't doing nothing but talking. Come on and play.

BYNUM: (*Singing.*)
They tell me Joe Turner's come and gone
Ohhh Lordy
They tell me Joe Turner's come and gone
Ohhh Lordy
Got my man and gone

He come with forty links of chain
Ohhh Lordy

LOOMIS: Why you singing that song? Why you singing about Joe Turner?

BYNUM: I'm just singing to entertain myself.

SETH: You trying to distract me. That's what you trying to do.

BYNUM: (*Singing.*)
Come with forty links of chain
Ohhh Lordy
Come with forty links of chain
Ohhh Lordy

LOOMIS: I don't like you singing that song, mister!

SETH: Now, I ain't gonna have no more disturbance around here, Herald Loomis. You start any more disturbance and you leavin' here, Saturday or no Saturday.

BYNUM: The man ain't causing no disturbance, Seth. He just say he don't like the song.

SETH: Well, we all friendly folk. All neighborly like. Don't have no squabbling around here. Don't have no disturbance. You gonna have to take that someplace else.

BYNUM: He just say he don't like the song. I done sung a whole lot of songs people don't like. I respect everybody. He here in the house too. If he don't like the song, I'll sing something else. I know lots of songs. You got "I Belong to the Band," "Don't You Leave Me Here." You got "Praying on the Old Campground," "Keep Your Lamp Trimmed and Burning" . . . I know lots of songs.

(*Sings.*)

> Boys, I'll be so glad when payday come
> Captain, Captain, when payday comes
> Gonna catch that Illinois Central
> Going to Kankakee

SETH: Why don't you hush up that hollering and come on and play dominoes.

BYNUM: You ever been to Johnstown, Herald Loomis? You look like a fellow I seen around there.

LOOMIS: I don't know no place with that name.

BYNUM: That's around where I seen my shiny man. See, you looking for this woman. I'm looking for a shiny man. Seem like everybody looking for something.

SETH: I'm looking for you to come and play these dominoes. That's what I'm looking for.

BYNUM: You a farming man, Herald Loomis? You look like you done some farming.

LOOMIS: Same as everybody. I done farmed some, yeah.

BYNUM: I used to work at farming . . . picking cotton. I reckon everybody done picked some cotton.

SETH: I ain't! I ain't never picked no cotton. I was born up here in the North. My daddy was a freedman. I ain't never even seen no cotton!

BYNUM: Mr. Loomis done picked some cotton. Ain't you, Herald Loomis? You done picked a bunch of cotton.

LOOMIS: How you know so much about me? How you know what I done? How much cotton I picked?

BYNUM: I can tell from looking at you. My daddy taught me how to do that. Say when you look at a fellow, if you taught yourself to look for it, you can see his song written on him. Tell you what kind of man he is in the world. Now, I can look at you, Mr. Loomis, and see you a man who done forgot his song. Forgot how to sing it. A fellow forget that and he forget who he is. Forget how he's supposed to mark down life. Now, I used to travel all up and down this road and that . . . looking here and there. Searching. Just like you, Mr. Loomis. I didn't know what I was searching for. The only thing I knew was something was keeping me dissatisfied. Something wasn't making my heart smooth and easy. Then one day my daddy gave me a song. That song had a weight to it that was hard to handle. That song was hard to carry. I fought against it. Didn't want to accept that song. I tried to find my daddy to give him back the song. But I found out it wasn't his song. It was my song. It had come from way deep inside me. I looked long back in memory and gathered up pieces and snatches of things to make that song. I was making it up out of myself. And that song helped me on the road. Made it smooth to where my footsteps didn't bite back at me. All the time that song getting bigger and bigger. That song growing with each step of the road. It got so I used all of myself up in the making of that song. Then I was the song in search of itself. That song rattling in my throat and I'm looking for it. See, Mr. Loomis, when a man forgets his song he goes off in search of it . . . till he find out he's got it with him all the time. That's why I can tell you one of Joe Turner's niggers. 'Cause you forgot how to sing your song.

LOOMIS: You lie! How you see that? I got a mark on me? Joe Turner done marked me to where you can see it? You telling me I'm a marked man. What kind of mark you got on you?

(BYNUM *begins singing.*)

BYNUM: They tell me Joe Turner's come and gone
Ohhh Lordy
They tell me Joe Turner's come and gone
Ohhh Lordy
Got my man and gone

LOOMIS: Had a whole mess of men he catched. Just go out hunting regular like you go out hunting possum. He catch you and go home to his wife and family. Ain't thought about you going home to yours. Joe Turner catched me when my little girl was just born. Wasn't nothing but a little baby sucking on her mama's titty when he catched me. Joe Turner catched me in nineteen hundred and one. Kept me seven years until nineteen hundred and eight. Kept everybody seven years. He'd go out hunting and bring back forty men at a time. And keep them seven years.

I was walking down this road in this little town outside of Memphis. Come up on these fellows gambling. I was a deacon in the Abundant Life Church. I stopped to preach to these fellows to see if maybe I could turn some of them from their sinning when Joe Turner, brother of the Governor of the great sovereign state of Tennessee, swooped down on us and grabbed everybody there. Kept us all seven years.

My wife Martha gone from me after Joe Turner catched me. Got out from under Joe Turner on his birthday. Me and forty other men put in our seven years and he let us go on his birthday. I made it back to Henry Thompson's place where me and Martha was sharecropping and Martha's gone. She taken my little girl and left her with her mama and took off North. We been looking for her ever since. That's been going on four years now we been looking. That's the only thing I know to do. I just wanna see her face so I can get me a starting place in the world. The world got to start somewhere. That's what I been looking for. I been wandering a long time in somebody else's world. When I find my wife that be the making of my own.

BYNUM: Joe Turner tell why he caught you? You ever asked him that?

LOOMIS: I ain't never seen Joe Turner. Seen him to where I could touch him. I asked one of them fellows one time why he catch niggers. Asked him what I got he want? Why don't he keep on to himself? Why he got to catch me going down the road by my lonesome? He told me I was worthless. Worthless is something you throw away. Something you don't bother with. I ain't seen him throw me away. Wouldn't even let me stay away when I was by my lonesome. I ain't tried to catch him when he going down the road. So I must got something he want. What I got?

SETH: He just want you to do his work for him. That's all.

LOOMIS: I can look at him and see where he big and strong enough to do his own work. So it can't be that. He must want something he ain't got.

BYNUM: That ain't hard to figure out. What he wanted was your song. He wanted to have that song to be his. He thought by catching you he could learn that song. Every nigger he caught he's looking for the one he can learn that song from. Now he's got you bound up to where you can't sing your own song. Couldn't sing it them seven years 'cause you was afraid he would snatch it from under you. But you still got it. You just forgot how to sing it.

LOOMIS: (*To Bynum.*) I know who you are. You one of them bones people.

(*The lights go down to black.*)

Scene Three

The lights come up on the kitchen. It is the following morning. MATTIE *and* BYNUM *sit at the table.* BERTHA *busies herself at the stove.*

BYNUM: Good luck don't know no special time to come. You sleep with that up under your pillow and good luck can't help but come to you. Sometimes it come and go and you don't even know it's been there.

BERTHA: Bynum, why don't you leave that gal alone? She don't wanna be hearing all that. Why don't you go on and get out the way and leave her alone?

BYNUM: (*Getting up.*) Alright, alright. But you mark what I'm saying. It'll draw it to you just like a magnet.

(BYNUM *exits up the stairs and* LOOMIS *enters.*)

BERTHA: I got some grits here, Mr. Loomis.

(BERTHA *sets a bowl on the table.*)

If I was you, Mattie, I wouldn't go getting all tied up with Bynum in that stuff. That kind of stuff, even if it do work for a while, it don't last. That just get people more mixed up than they is already. And I wouldn't waste my time fretting over Jeremy either. I seen it coming. I seen it when she first come here. She that kind of woman run off with the first man got a dollar to spend on her. Jeremy just young. He don't know what he getting into. That gal don't mean him no good. She's just using him to keep from being by herself. That's the worst use of a man you can have. You ought to be glad to wash him out of your hair. I done seen all kind of men. I done seen them come and go through here. Jeremy ain't had enough to him for you. You need a man who's got some understanding and who willing to work with that understanding to come to the best he can. You got your time coming. You just tries too hard and can't understand why it don't work for you. Trying to figure it out don't do nothing but give you a troubled mind. Don't no man want a woman with a troubled mind.

You get all that trouble off your mind and just when it look like you ain't never gonna find what you want . . . you look up and it's standing right there. That's how I met my Seth. You gonna look up one day and find everything you want standing right in front of you. Been twenty-seven years now since that happened to me. But life ain't no happy-go-lucky time where everything be just like you want it. You got your time coming. You watch what Bertha's saying.

(SETH *enters.*)

SETH: Ho!
BERTHA: What you doing come in here so late?

SETH: I was standing down there on Logan Street talking with the fellows. Henry Allen tried to sell me that old piece of horse he got.

(*He sees* LOOMIS.)

Today's Tuesday, Mr. Loomis.

BERTHA: (*Pulling him toward the bedroom.*) Come on in here and leave that man alone to eat his breakfast.

SETH: I ain't bothering nobody. I'm just reminding him what day it is.

(SETH *and* BERTHA *exit into the bedroom.*)

LOOMIS: That dress got a color to it.

MATTIE: Did you really see them things like you said? Them people come up out the ocean?

LOOMIS: It happened just like that, yeah.

MATTIE: I hope you find your wife. It be good for your little girl for you to find her.

LOOMIS: Got to find her for myself. Find my starting place in the world. Find me a world I can fit in.

MATTIE: I ain't never found no place for me to fit. Seem like all I do is start over. It ain't nothing to find no starting place in the world. You just start from where you find yourself.

LOOMIS: Got to find my wife. That be my starting place.

MATTIE: What if you don't find her? What you gonna do then if you don't find her?

LOOMIS: She out there somewhere. Ain't no such thing as not finding her.

MATTIE: How she got lost from you? Jack just walked away from me.

LOOMIS: Joe Turner split us up. Joe Turner turned the world upside down. He bound me on to him for seven years.

MATTIE: I hope you find her. It be good for you to find her.

LOOMIS: I been watching you. I been watching you watch me.

MATTIE: I was just trying to figure out if you seen things like you said.

LOOMIS: (*Getting up.*) Come here and let me touch you. I been watching you. You a full woman. A man needs a full woman. Come on and be with me.

MATTIE: I ain't got enough for you. You'd use me up too fast.

LOOMIS: Herald Loomis got a mind seem like you a part of it since I first seen you. It's been a long time since I seen a full woman. I can smell you from here. I know you got Herald Loomis on your mind, can't keep him apart from it. Come on and be with Herald Loomis.

(LOOMIS *has crossed to* MATTIE. *He touches her awkwardly, gently, tenderly. Inside he howls like a lost wolf pup whose hunger is deep. He goes to touch her but finds he cannot.*)

I done forgot how to touch.

(*The lights fade to black.*)

Scene Four

It is early the next morning. The lights come up on ZONIA *and* REUBEN *in the yard.*

REUBEN: Something spooky going on around here. Last night Mr. Bynum was out in the yard singing and talking to the wind . . . and the wind it just be talking back to him. Did you hear it?

ZONIA: I heard it. I was scared to get up and look. I thought it was a storm.

REUBEN: That wasn't no storm. That was Mr. Bynum. First he say something . . . and the wind it say back to him.

ZONIA: I heard it. Was you scared? I was scared.

REUBEN: And then this morning . . . I seen Miss Mabel!

ZONIA: Who Miss Mabel?

REUBEN: Mr. Seth's mother. He got her picture hanging up in the house. She been dead.

ZONIA: How you seen her if she been dead?

REUBEN: Zonia . . . if I tell you something you promise you won't tell anybody?

ZONIA: I promise.

REUBEN: It was early this morning . . . I went out to the coop to feed the pigeons. I was down on the ground like this to open up the door to the coop . . . when all of a sudden I seen some feets in front of me. I looked up . . . and there was Miss Mabel standing there.

ZONIA: Reuben, you better stop telling that! You ain't seen nobody!

REUBEN: Naw, it's the truth. I swear! I seen her just like I see you. Look . . . you can see where she hit me with her cane.

ZONIA: Hit you? What she hit you for?

REUBEN: She says, "Didn't you promise Eugene something?" Then she hit me with her cane. She say, "Let them pigeons go." Then she hit me again. That's what made them marks.

ZONIA: Jeez man . . . get away from me. You done see a haunt!

REUBEN: Shhhh. You promised, Zonia!

ZONIA: You sure it wasn't Miss Bertha come over there and hit you with her hoe?

REUBEN: It was no Miss Bertha. I told you it was Miss Mabel. She was standing right there by the coop. She had this light coming out of her and then she just melted away.

ZONIA: What she had on?

REUBEN: A white dress. Ain't even had no shoes or nothing. Just had on that white dress and them big hands . . . and that cane she hit me with.

ZONIA: How you reckon she knew about the pigeons? You reckon Eugene told her?

REUBEN: I don't know. I sure ain't asked her none. She say Eugene was waiting on them pigeons. Say he couldn't go back home till I let them go. I couldn't get the door to the coop open fast enough.

ZONIA: Maybe she an angel? From the way you say she look with that white dress. Maybe she an angel.

REUBEN: Mean as she was . . . how she gonna be an angel? She used to chase us out her yard and frown up and look evil all the time.

ZONIA: That don't mean she can't be no angel 'cause of how she looked and 'cause she wouldn't let no kids play in her yard. It go by if you got any spots on your heart and if you pray and go to church.

REUBEN: What about she hit me with her cane? An angel wouldn't hit me with her cane.

ZONIA: I don't know. She might. I still say she was an angel.

REUBEN: You reckon Eugene the one who sent old Miss Mabel?

ZONIA: Why he send her? Why he don't come himself?

REUBEN: Figured if he send her maybe that'll make me listen. 'Cause she old.

ZONIA: What you think it feel like?

REUBEN: What?

ZONIA: Being dead.

REUBEN: Like being sleep only you don't know nothing and can't move no more.

ZONIA: If Miss Mabel can come back . . . then maybe Eugene can come back too.

REUBEN: We can go down to the hideout like we used to! He could come back everyday! It be just like he ain't dead.

ZONIA: Maybe that ain't right for him to come back. Feel kinda funny to be playing games with a haunt.

REUBEN: Yeah . . . what if everybody came back? What if Miss Mabel came back just like she ain't dead? Where you and your daddy gonna sleep then?

ZONIA: Maybe they go back at night and don't need no place to sleep.

REUBEN: It still don't seem right. I'm sure gonna miss Eugene. He's the bestest friend anybody ever had.

ZONIA: My daddy say if you miss somebody too much it can kill you. Say he missed me till it liked to killed him.

REUBEN: What if your mama's already dead and all the time you looking for her?

ZONIA: Naw, she ain't dead. My daddy say he can smell her.

REUBEN: You can't smell nobody that ain't here. Maybe he smelling old Miss Bertha. Maybe Miss Bertha your mama?

ZONIA: Naw, she ain't. My mamma got long pretty hair and she five feet from the ground!

REUBEN: Your daddy say when you leaving?

(ZONIA *doesn't respond.*)

Maybe you gonna stay in Mr. Seth's house and don't go looking for your mama no more.

ZONIA: He say we got to leave on Saturday.

REUBEN: Dag! You just only been here for a little while. Don't seem like nothing ever stay the same.

ZONIA: He say he got to find her. Find him a place in the world.

REUBEN: He could find him a place in Mr. Seth's house.

ZONIA: It don't look like we never gonna find her.

REUBEN: Maybe he find her by Saturday then you don't have to go.

ZONIA: I don't know.

REUBEN: You look like a spider!

ZONIA: I ain't no spider!

REUBEN: Got them long skinny arms and legs. You look like one of them Black Widows.

ZONIA: I ain't no Black Widow nothing! My name is Zonia!

REUBEN: That's what I'm gonna call you . . . Spider.

ZONIA: You can call me that, but I don't have to answer.

REUBEN: You know what? I think maybe I be your husband when I grow up.

ZONIA: How you know?

REUBEN: I ask my grandpap how you know and he say when the moon falls into a girl's eyes that how you know.

ZONIA: Did it fall into my eyes?

REUBEN: Not that I can tell. Maybe I ain't old enough. Maybe you ain't old enough.

ZONIA: So there! I don't know why you telling me that lie!

REUBEN: That don't mean nothing 'cause I can't see it. I know it's there. Just the way you look at me sometimes look like the moon might have been in your eyes.

ZONIA: That don't mean nothing if you can't see it. You supposed to see it.

REUBEN: Shucks, I see it good enough for me. You ever let anybody kiss you?

ZONIA: Just my daddy. He kiss me on the cheek.

REUBEN: It's better on the lips. Can I kiss you on the lips?

ZONIA: I don't know. You ever kiss anybody before?

REUBEN: I had a cousin let me kiss her on the lips one time. Can I kiss you?

ZONIA: Okay.

(REUBEN *kisses her and lays his head against her chest.*)

What you doing?

REUBEN: Listening. Your heart singing!

ZONIA: It is not.

REUBEN: Just beating like a drum. Let's kiss again.

(*They kiss again.*)

> Now you mine, Spider. You my girl, okay?

ZONIA: Okay.

REUBEN: When I get grown, I come looking for you.

ZONIA: Okay.

(*The lights fade to black.*)

Scene Five

The lights come up on the kitchen. It is Saturday. BYNUM, LOOMIS, *and* ZONIA *sit at the table.* BERTHA *prepares breakfast.* ZONIA *has on a white dress.*

BYNUM: With all this rain we been having he might have ran into some washed-out roads. If that wagon got stuck in the mud he's liable to be still upriver somewhere. If he's upriver then he ain't coming until tomorrow.

LOOMIS: Today's Saturday. He say he be here on Saturday.

BERTHA: Zonia, you gonna eat your breakfast this morning.

ZONIA: Yes, ma'am.

BERTHA: I don't know how you expect to get any bigger if you don't eat. I ain't never seen a child that didn't eat. You about as skinny as a bean pole.

(*Pause.*)

> Mr. Loomis, there's a place down on Wylie. Zeke Mayweather got a house down there. You ought to see if he got any rooms.

(LOOMIS *doesn't respond.*)

> Well, you're welcome to some breakfast before you move on.

(MATTIE *enters from the stairs.*)

MATTIE: Good morning.

BERTHA: Morning, Mattie. Sit on down there and get you some breakfast.

BYNUM: Well, Mattie Campbell, you been sleeping with that up under your pillow like I told you?

BERTHA: Bynum, I done told you to leave that gal alone with all that stuff. You around here meddling in other people's lives. She don't want to hear all that. You ain't doing nothing but confusing her with that stuff.

MATTIE: (*To* LOOMIS.) You all fixing to move on?

LOOMIS: Today's Saturday. I'm paid up till Saturday.

MATTIE: Where you going to?

LOOMIS: Gonna find my wife.

MATTIE: You going off to another city?

LOOMIS: We gonna see where the road take us. Ain't no telling where we
wind up.
MATTIE: Eleven years is a long time. Your wife . . . she might have taken
up with someone else. People do that when they get lost from
each other.
LOOMIS: Zonia. Come on, we gonna find your mama.

(LOOMIS *and* ZONIA *cross to the door.*)

MATTIE: (*To* ZONIA.) Zonia, Mattie got a ribbon here match your dress.
Want Mattie to fix your hair with her ribbon?

(ZONIA *nods.* MATTIE *ties the ribbon in her hair.*)

There . . . it got a color just like your dress. (*To* LOOMIS.) I hope
you find her. I hope you be happy.
LOOMIS: A man looking for a woman be lucky to find you. You a good
woman, Mattie. Keep a good heart.

(LOOMIS *and* ZONIA *exit.*)

BERTHA: I been watching that man for two weeks . . . and that's the closest
I come to seeing him act civilized. I don't know what's between
you all, Mattie . . . but the only thing that man needs is somebody to make him laugh. That's all you need in the world is love
and laughter. That's all anybody needs. To have love in one hand
and laughter in the other.

(BERTHA *moves about the kitchen as though blessing it and chasing away the huge sadness
that seems to envelop it. It is a dance and demonstration of her own magic, her own remedy
that is centuries old and to which she is connected by the muscles of her heart and the blood's
memory.*)

You hear me, Mattie? I'm talking about laughing. The kind of
laugh that comes from way deep inside. To just stand and laugh
and let life flow right through you. Just laugh to let yourself know
you're alive.

(*She begins to laugh. It is a near-hysterical laughter that is a celebration of life, both its pain
and its blessing.* MATTIE *and* BYNUM *join in the laughter.* SETH *enters from the front door.*)

SETH: Well, I see you all having fun.

(SETH *begins to laugh with them.*)

That Loomis fellow standing up there on the corner watching the
house. He standing right up there on Manila Street.
BERTHA: Don't you get started on him. The man done left out of here and
that's the last I wanna hear of it. You about to drive me crazy with
that man.

SETH: I just say he standing up there on the corner. Acting sneaky like he always do. He can stand up there all he want. As long as he don't come back in here.

(There is a knock on the door. SETH goes to answer it. Enter MARTHA LOOMIS [Pentecost]. She is a young woman about twenty-eight. She is dressed as befitting a member of an Evangelist church. RUTHERFORD SELIG follows.)

SETH: Look here, Bertha. It's Martha Pentecost. Come on in, Martha. Who that with you? Oh . . . that's Selig. Come on in, Selig.

BERTHA: Come on in, Martha. It's sure good to see you.

BYNUM: Rutherford Selig, you a sure enough first-class People Finder!

SELIG: She was right out there in Rankin. You take that first right-hand road . . . right there at that church on Wooster Street. I started to go right past and something told me to stop at the church and see if they needed any dustpans.

SETH: Don't she look good, Bertha.

BERTHA: Look all nice and healthy.

MARTHA: Mr. Bynum . . . Selig told me my little girl was here.

SETH: There's some fellow around here say he your husband. Say his name is Loomis. Say you his wife.

MARTHA: Is my little girl with him?

SETH: Yeah, he got a little girl with him. I wasn't gonna tell him where you was. Not the way this fellow look. So he got Selig to find you.

MARTHA: Where they at? They upstairs?

SETH: He was standing right up there on Manila Street. I had to ask him to leave 'cause of how he was carrying on. He come in here one night—

(The door opens and LOOMIS and ZONIA enter. MARTHA and LOOMIS stare at each other.)

LOOMIS: Hello, Martha.

MARTHA: Herald . . . Zonia?

LOOMIS: You ain't waited for me, Martha. I got out the place looking to see your face. Seven years I waited to see your face.

MARTHA: Herald, I been looking for you. I wasn't but two months behind you when you went to my mama's and got Zonia. I been looking for you ever since.

LOOMIS: Joe Turner let me loose and I felt all turned around inside. I just wanted to see your face to know that the world was still there. Make sure everything still in its place so I could reconnect myself together. I got there and you was gone, Martha.

MARTHA: Herald . . .

LOOMIS: Left my little girl motherless in the world.

MARTHA: I didn't leave her motherless, Herald. Reverend Toliver wanted to move the church up North 'cause of all the trouble the colored folks was having down there. Nobody knew what was gonna happen traveling them roads. We didn't even know if we was gonna make it up here or not. I left her with my mama so she be safe. That was better than dragging her out on the road having to duck and hide from people. Wasn't no telling what was gonna happen to us. I didn't leave her motherless in the world. I been looking for you.

LOOMIS: I come up on Henry Thompson's place after seven years of living in hell, and all I'm looking to do is see your face.

MARTHA: Herald, I didn't know if you was ever coming back. They told me Joe Turner had you and my whole world split half in two. My whole life shattered. It was like I had poured it in a cracked jar and it all leaked out the bottom. When it go like that there ain't nothing you can do to put it back together. You talking about Henry Thompson's place like I'm still gonna be working the land by myself. How I'm gonna do that? You wasn't gone but two months and Henry Thompson kicked me off his land and I ain't had no place to go but to my mama's. I stayed and waited there for five years before I woke up one morning and decided that you was dead. Even if you weren't, you was dead to me. I wasn't gonna carry you with me no more. So I killed you in my heart. I buried you. I mourned you. And then I picked up what was left and went on to make life without you. I was a young woman with life at my beckon. I couldn't drag you behind me like a sack of cotton.

LOOMIS: I just been waiting to look on your face to say my goodbye. That goodbye got so big at times, seem like it was gonna swallow me up. Like Jonah in the whale's belly I sat up in that goodbye for three years. That goodbye kept me out on the road searching. Not looking on women in their houses. It kept me bound up to the road. All the time that goodbye swelling up in my chest till I'm about to bust. Now that I see your face I can say my goodbye and make my own world.

(LOOMIS *takes* ZONIA's *hand and presents her to* MARTHA.)

Martha . . . here go your daughter. I tried to take care of her. See that she had something to eat. See that she was out of the elements. Whatever I know I tried to teach her. Now she need to learn from her mother whatever you got to teach her. That way she won't be no one-sided person.

(LOOMIS *stoops to* ZONIA.)

Zonia, you go live with your mama. She a good woman. You go on with her and listen to her good. You my daughter and I love you like a daughter. I hope to see you again in the world somewhere. I'll never forget you.

ZONIA: (*Throws her arms around* LOOMIS *in a panic.*) I won't get no bigger! My bones won't get no bigger! They won't! I promise! Take me with you till we keep searching and never finding. I won't get no bigger! I promise!

LOOMIS: Go on and do what I told you now.

MARTHA: (*Goes to* ZONIA *and comforts her.*) It's alright, baby. Mama's here. Mama's here. Don't worry. Don't cry.

(MARTHA *turns to* BYNUM.)

Mr. Bynum, I don't know how to thank you. God bless you.

LOOMIS: It was you! All the time it was you that bind me up! You bound me to the road!

BYNUM: I ain't bind you, Herald Loomis. You can't bind what don't cling.

LOOMIS: Everywhere I go people wanna bind me up. Joe Turner wanna bind me up! Reverend Toliver wanna bind me up. You wanna bind me up. Everybody wanna bind me up. Well, Joe Turner's come and gone and Herald Loomis ain't for no binding. I ain't gonna let nobody bind me up!

(LOOMIS *pulls out a knife.*)

BYNUM: It wasn't you, Herald Loomis. I ain't bound you. I bound the little girl to her mother. That's who I bound. You binding yourself. You bound onto your song. All you got to do is stand up and sing it, Herald Loomis. It's right there kicking at your throat. All you got to do is sing it. Then you be free.

MARTHA: Herald . . . look at yourself! Standing there with a knife in your hand. You done gone over to the devil. Come on . . . put down the knife. You got to look to Jesus. Even if you done fell away from the church you can be saved again. The Bible say, "The Lord is my shepherd I shall not want. He maketh me to lie down in green pastures. He leads me beside the still water. He restoreth my soul. He leads me in the path of righteousness for His name's sake. Even though I walk through the shadow of death—"

LOOMIS: That's just where I be walking!

MARTHA: "I shall fear no evil. For Thou art with me. Thy rod and thy staff, they comfort me."

LOOMIS: You can't tell me nothing about no valleys. I done been all across the valleys and the hills and the mountains and the oceans.

MARTHA: "Thou preparest a table for me in the presence of my enemies."

LOOMIS: And all I seen was a bunch of niggers dazed out of their woolly heads. And Mr. Jesus Christ standing there in the middle of them, grinning.

MARTHA: "Thou anointest my head with oil, my cup runneth over."

LOOMIS: He grin that big old grin . . . and niggers wallowing at his feet.

MARTHA: "Surely goodness and mercy shall follow me all the days of my life, and I shall dwell in the house of the Lord forever."

LOOMIS: Great big old white man . . . your Mr. Jesus Christ. Standing there with a whip in one hand and tote board in another, and them niggers swimming in a sea of cotton. And he counting. He tallying up the cotton. "Well, Jeremiah . . . what's the matter, you ain't picked but two hundred pounds of cotton today? Got to put you on half rations." And Jeremiah go back and lay up there on his half rations and talk about what a nice man Mr. Jesus Christ is 'cause he give him salvation after he die. Something wrong here. Something don't fit right!

MARTHA: You got to open your heart and have faith, Herald. This world is just a trial for the next. Jesus offers you salvation.

LOOMIS: I been wading in the water. I been walking all over the River Jordan. But what it get me, huh? I done been baptized with the blood of the lamb and the fire of the Holy Ghost. But what I got, huh? I got salvation? My enemies all around me picking the flesh from my bones. I'm choking on my own blood and all you got to give me is salvation?

MARTHA: You got to be clean, Herald. You got to be washed with the blood of the lamb.

LOOMIS: Blood make you clean? You clean with blood?

MARTHA: Jesus bled for you. He's the Lamb of God who takest away the sins of the world.

LOOMIS: I don't need nobody to bleed for me! I can bleed for myself.

MARTHA: You got to be something, Herald. You just can't be alive. Life don't mean nothing unless it got a meaning.

LOOMIS: What kind of meaning you got? What kind of clean you got, woman? You want blood? Blood make you clean? You clean with blood?

(LOOMIS *slashes himself across the chest. He rubs the blood over his face and comes to a realization.*)

I'm standing! I'm standing. My legs stood up! I'm standing now!

(*Having found his song, the song of self-sufficiency, fully resurrected, cleansed, and given breath, free from any encumbrance other than the workings of his own heart and the bonds of the flesh, having accepted the responsibility for his own presence in the world, he is free to soar above the environs that weighed and pushed his spirit into terrifying contractions.*)

Goodbye, Martha.

(LOOMIS *turns and exits, the knife still in his hands.* MATTIE *looks about the room and rushes out after him.*)

BYNUM: Herald Loomis, you shining! You shining like new money!

(*The lights go down to* BLACK.)

STUDY QUESTIONS

1. The play is set in 1911 in the northern steel town of Pittsburgh. Explain the historical context for the unfolding drama. How does a history of the African-American diaspora from the Southern slave states to the free North states explain characters such as Seth, Jeremy, and Loomis?

2. Although Joe Turner does not appear onstage, his presence dominates the drama, just as his name dominates the title. What aspect of American history and culture does he represent? Discuss Turner's function in the delineation and development of Herald Loomis's character.

3. Rutherford Selig is the only non-African character actually present in the play. How does his role support the portrayal of the drama's socioeconomic world? How is he different from a white character like Joe Turner?

4. Describe the women, Bertha, Mattie, Molly, and Martha. What range of characteristics do they represent? Analyze their relationships with men, and discuss what these constructions of male-female relations suggest about the dramatist's views on gender difference.

5. A current of mysticism runs through the play. Analyze Bynum's role as a shaman figure and the Juba scene in Act One, Scene Four. What do these nonrational elements contribute to the dramatic effect and to our understanding of African-American culture?

6. The play is, among other things, a story of a quest, Loomis's quest for his missing wife, Martha. Discuss the play's conclusion. With the quest completed, what does the play suggest will happen to Loomis?

7. Discuss the use of dialect and singing in the play. Select a monologue, for example, Bynum's speech in Act One, Scene One, or Loomis's speech in Act Two, Scene Two, and analyze the idioms, images, and rhythms that give that passage poetic power.

✳ LESLIE MARMON SILKO

Leslie Marmon Silko (b. 1948) is best known for her novel, Ceremony *(1977), which narrates the struggle of a half Laguna, half Anglo protagonist to adjust to the culture of his New Mexico reservation. Like N. Scott Momaday, Silko uses Native American mythology to express ethnic communal consciousness. In "Coyote Holds a Full House in His Hand," she retells a Laguna fable that uses the trickster figure traditional to tribal folklore. Silko's direct style charges the fable with renewed contemporary significance.*

Coyote Holds a Full House in His Hand

He wasn't getting any place with Mrs. Sekakaku, he could see that. She   1
was warming up leftover chili beans for lunch and when her niece
came over they left him alone on the red plastic sofa and talked at the
kitchen table. Aunt Mamie was still sick that's what her niece was telling
her and they were all so worried because the doctors at Keams Canyon said
they'd tried everything already and old man Ko'ite had come over from
Oraibi and still Aunt Mamie was having dizzy spells and couldn't get out
of bed. He was looking at the same *Life* magazine he'd already looked at
before and it didn't have any pictures of high school girls twirling batons
or plane crashes or anything he wanted to look at more than twice, but he
didn't want to listen to them because then he'd know just what kind of
gossip Mrs. Sekakaku found more important than him and his visit. He set
the magazine down on his lap and traced his finger over the horse head
embossed on the plastic cushion. It was always like that. When he didn't
expect it, it always came to him, but when he wanted something to happen, like with Mrs. Sekakaku, then it shied away. Mrs. Sekakaku's letters
had made the corner of the trading post where the mailboxes were smell
like the perfume counter at Woolworth's. The Mexican woman with the fat
arms was the postmaster and ran the trading post. She didn't approve of
perfumed letters and she used to pretend the letters weren't there even
when he could smell them and see their pastel edges sticking out of the pile
in the general delivery slot.

The Mexican woman thought Pueblo men were great lovers—he knew   2
this because he heard her say so to another Mexican woman one day while
he was finishing his strawberry soda on the other side of the dry goods
section. In the summer he spent a good number of hours there watching
her because she wore sleeveless blouses that revealed her fat upper arms,
full and round, and the tender underarm creases curving to her breasts.
They had not noticed he was still there leaning on the counter behind a pile
of overalls; ". . . the size of a horse" was all that he had heard, but he knew
what she was talking about. They were all like that, those Mexican women.
That was all they talked about when they were alone. "As big as a
horse"—he knew that much Spanish and more too, but she had never
treated him nice, not even when he brought her the heart-shaped box of
candy, carried it on the bus all the way from Albuquerque. He didn't think
it was being older than her because she was over thirty herself—it was
because she didn't approve of men who drank. That was the last thing he
did before he left town; he did it because he had to, because liquor was
illegal on the reservation. So the last thing he did was have a few drinks to
carry home with him the same way other people stocked up on lamb

nipples or extra matches. She must have smelled it on his breath when he handed her the candy because she didn't say anything and she left the box under the counter by the old newspapers and balls of string. The cellophane was never opened and the fine gray dust that covered everything in the store finally settled on the pink satin bow. The postmaster was jealous of the letters that were coming, but she was the one who had sent him into the arms of Mrs. Sekakaku.

In her last two letters Mrs. Sekakaku had been hinting around for him to come to see her at Bean Dance time. This was after Christmas when he had sent a big poinsettia plant all the way to the Second Mesa on the mail bus. Up until then she had never answered the part in his letters where he said he wished he could see the beautiful Hopi mesas with snow on them. But that had been the first time a potted plant ever rode into Hopi on the mail bus and Mrs. Sekakaku finally realized the kind of man he was. All along that had been the trouble at Laguna, nobody understood just what kind of man he was. They thought he was sort of good for nothing, he knew that, but for a long time he kept telling himself to keep on trying and trying. But it seemed like people would never forget the time the whole village was called out to clean up for feast day and he sent his mother to tell them he was sick with liver trouble. He was still hurt because they didn't understand that with liver trouble you can walk around and sometimes even ride the bus to Albuquerque. Everyone was jealous of him and they didn't stop to think how much it meant to his mother to have someone living with her in her old age. All they could talk about was the big C.O.D. that came to the post office in his name and she cashed her pension check to pay for it. But she was the one who told him, "Sonny Boy, if you want that jacket, you go ahead and order it." It was made out of brown vinyl resembling leather and he still wore it whenever he went to town. Even on the day she had the last stroke his two older brothers had been telling her to quit paying his bills for him and to make him get out and live on his own. But she always stood up for him in front of the others even if she did complain privately at times to her nieces who then scolded him about the bills from the record club and the correspondence school. He always knew he could be a lawyer—he had listened to the lawyers in the courtrooms of the Federal Building on those hot summer afternoons when he needed a cool place to sit while he waited for the bus to Laguna. He listened and he knew he could be a lawyer because he was so good at making up stories to justify why things happened the way they did. He thought correspondence school would be different from Indian school which had given him stomach aches and made him run away all through his seventh grade year. Right after that he had cut his foot pretty bad chopping wood for his older brother's wife, the one who kept brushing her arm across his shoulders whenever she poured coffee at the supper table. The foot had taken so long to heal that his mother agreed he shouldn't go back to Indian School or chop wood anymore. A few months after that they were all swimming at

3

the river and he hurt his back in a dive off the old wooden bridge so it was no wonder he couldn't do the same work as the other young men.

When Mildred told him she was marrying that Hopi, he didn't try to stop 4
her although she stood there for a long time like she was waiting for him to say something. He liked things the way they were down along the river after dark. Her mother and aunts owned so many fields they expected a husband to hoe and he had already promised his mother he wouldn't leave her alone in her old age. He thought it would be easier this way but after Mildred's wedding, people who had seen him and Mildred together started joking about how he had lost out to a Hopi.

    Hopi men were famous for their fast hands and the way they could go 5
on all night. Some of the jokes hinted that he was as lazy at lovemaking as he was with his shovel during Spring ditch cleaning and that he took his girl friends to the deep sand along the river so he could lie on the bottom while they worked on top. But later on, some of the older men took him aside and told him not to feel bad about Mildred and told him about women they'd lost to Hopis when they were all working on the railroad together in Winslow. Women believe those stories about Hopi men, they told him, because women like the sound of those stories, and they don't care if it's the Hopi men who are making up the stories in the first place. So when he finally found himself riding the Greyhound bus into Winslow on his way to see Mrs. Sekakaku and the Bean Dance he got to thinking about those stories about Hopi men. It had been years since Mildred had married that Hopi and her aunts and her mother kept the man working in their fields all year round. Even Laguna people said "poor thing" whenever they saw that Hopi man walking past with a shovel on his shoulder. So he knew he wasn't going because of that—he was going because of Mrs. Sekakaku's letters and because it was lonely living in a place where no one appreciates you even when you keep try-ing and trying. At Hopi he could get a fresh start; he could tell people about himself while they looked at the photos in the plastic pages of his wallet.

    He waited for the mail bus and drank a cup of coffee in the café across 6
the street from the pink stucco motel with a cowboy on its neon sign. He had a feeling something in his life was about to change because of this trip, but he didn't know if it would be good for him or bad. Sometimes he was able to look at what he was doing and to see himself clearly two or three weeks into the future. But this time when he looked, he only saw himself getting off the bus on the sandy shoulder of the highway below Second Mesa. He stared up at the Hopi town on the sandrock and thought that probably he would get married.

*   *   *

The last hundred feet up the wagon trail seemed the greatest distance to   7
him and he felt an unaccustomed tightness in his lungs. He knew it wasn't
old age—it was something else—something that wanted him to work for it.
A short distance past the outside toilets at the edge of the mesa top he got
his breath back and their familiar thick odor reassured him. He saw that
one of the old toilets had tipped over and rolled down the side of the mesa
to the piles of stove ashes, broken bottles and corn shucks on the slope
below. He'd get along all right. Like a lot of people, at one time he believed
Hopi magic could outdo all the other Pueblos but now he saw that it was
all the same from time to time and place to place. When Hopi men got tired
of telling stories about all-nighters in Winslow motels then probably the old
men brought it around to magic and how they rigged the Navajo tribal
elections one year just by hiding some little painted sticks over near Window Rock. Whatever it was he had come for, he was ready.

He checked his reflection in the window glass of Mrs. Sekakaku's front   8
door before he knocked. Gray hair made him look dignified, that is what
she had written after he sent her the photographs. He believed in photographs to show people as you were telling them about yourself and the
things you'd done and the places you'd been. He always carried a pocket
camera and asked people passing by to snap one of him outside the fancy
bars and restaurants in the Heights where he walked after he had a few
drinks in the Indian bars downtown. He didn't tell her he'd never been
inside those places, that he didn't think Indians were welcome there. Behind him he could hear a dog barking. It sounded like a small dog but it
also sounded very upset and little dogs were the first ones to bite. So he
turned and at first he thought it was a big rat crawling out the door of Mrs.
Sekakaku's bread oven but it was a small gray wire-haired dog that
wouldn't step out any further. Only lonely widows let their dogs sleep in
the bread oven although they always pretend otherwise and scold the dogs
whenever relatives or guests come. It must have known it was about to be
replaced because is almost choked on its own barking. "Not much longer
little doggy," he was saying softly while he knocked on the door. He was
beginning to wonder if she had forgotten he was coming and he could feel
his confidence lose its footing just a little. She walked up from behind
while he was knocking—something he always dreaded because it made the
person knocking look so foolish—knocking and waiting while the one you
wanted wasn't inside the house at all but was standing right behind you.
The way the little dog was barking probably all the neighbors had seen him
and were laughing. He managed to smile and would have shaken hands
but she was bending over petting the little dog running around and around
her ankles. "I hope you haven't been waiting too long! My poor Aunt
Mamie had one of her dizzy spells and I was over helping." She was still
looking down at the dog while she said this and he noticed she wasn't

wearing her perfume. At first he thought his understanding of the English language must be failing, that really she had only invited him over to the Bean Dance, that he had misread her letters when she said that a big house like hers was lonely and that she did not like walking alone in the evenings from the water faucet outside the village. Maybe all this had only meant she was afraid a bunch of Navajos might jump out from the shadows of the mesa rocks to take turns on top of her. But when she warmed up the leftover chili beans and went on talking to her niece about the dizzy spells he began to suspect what was going on. She was one of those kinds of women who wore Evening in Paris to Laguna feast and sprinkled it on letters but back at Hopi she pretended she was somebody else. She had lured his letters and snapshots and the big poinsettia plant to show off to her sisters and aunts, and now his visit so she could pretend he had come uninvited, overcome with desire for her. He should have seen it all along, but the first time he met her at Laguna feast a gust of wind had shown him the little roll of fat above her garter and left him dreaming of a plunge deep into the crease at the edge of the silk stocking. The old auntie and the dizzy spells gave her the perfect excuse and a story to protect her respectability. It was only 2:30 but already she was folding a flannel nightgown while she talked to her niece. And here he had been imagining the night together the whole bus ride from Laguna—fingering the creases and folds and the little rolls while she squeezed him with both hands. Their night together had suddenly lifted off and up like a butterfly moving away from him, and the breathlessness he had felt coming up the mesa returned. He was feeling bitter—if that's all it took then he'd find a way to get that old woman out of bed. He said it without thinking—the words just found his mouth and he said "excuse me ladies," straightening his belt buckle as he walked across the room, "but it sounds to me like your poor auntie is in bad shape." Mrs. Sekakaku's niece looked at him for the first time all afternoon. "Is he a medicine man?" she asked her aunt and for an instant he could see Mrs. Sekakaku hesitate and he knew he had to say "Yes, it's something I don't usually mention myself. Too many of those guys just talk about it to attract women. But this is a serious case." It was sounding so good that he was afraid he would start thinking about the space between the cheeks of the niece's ass and be unable to go on. But the next thing he said was they had a cure they did at Laguna for dizzy spells like Aunt Mamie was having. He could feel a momentum somewhere inside himself—it wasn't hope, because he knew Mrs. Sekakaku had tricked him—but whatever it was it was going for broke. He imagined the feel of grabbing hold of the tops of the niece's thighs which were almost as fat and would feel almost as good as the tops of Mrs. Sekakaku's thighs. "There would be no charge. This is something I want to do especially for you." That was all it took because these Hopi ladies were like all the other Pueblo women he ever knew, always worrying about saving money, and nothing made them enemies for longer than selling them the melon or mutton leg they felt they should get for free as a love gift. Because all of them, even the thin ones and the old ones, believed he was after them. "Oh, that would be so kind of you! We are so worried about her!" "Well, not so fast," he said even though his heart was racing. "It won't work unless everything is just so. All her clanswomen must come to her house but there can't be any men there, not even outside." He paused. He knew exactly what to say. "This is very important. Otherwise the cure won't work." Mrs. Sekakaku let out her breath suddenly and tightened her lips and he knew that any men or boys not in the kivas preparing for Bean Dance would be sent far away from Aunt Mamie's house. He looked over at the big loaf of fresh oven bread the niece had brought when she came; they hadn't offered him any before, but now after she served him a big bowl of chili beans she cut him a thick slice. It was all coming back to him now about how good medicine men get treated and he wasn't surprised at himself anymore. Once he got started he knew just how it should go. It was getting it started that gave him trouble sometimes. Mrs. Sekakaku and her niece hurried out to contact all the women of the Snow Clan to bring them to Aunt Mamie's for the cure. There were so many of them sitting in rows facing the sickbed—on folding chairs and little canvas stools they'd brought just like they did for a kiva ceremony or a summer dance. He had never stopped to think how many Snow Clan women there might be, and as he walked across the room he wondered if he should have made some kind of age limit. Some of the women sitting there were pretty old and bony but then there were all these little girls—one squatted down in front of him to play jacks and he could see the creases and dimples of her legs below her panties. The initiated girls and the women sat serious and quiet with the ceremonial presence the Hopis are famous for. Their eyes were full of the power the clanswomen shared whenever they gathered together. He saw it clearly and he never doubted its strength. Whatever he took, he'd have to run with it, but the women would prevail as they always had.

He sat on the floor by the fireplace and asked them to line up. He reached into the cold white juniper ashes and took a handful and told the woman standing in front of him to raise her skirt above her knees. The ashes were slippery and carried his hands up and around each curve each fold each roll of flesh on her thighs. He reached high but his fingers never strayed above the edge of the panty leg. They stepped in front of him one after the other and he worked painstakingly with each one—the silvery white ashes billowing up like clouds above skin dusted like early snow on brown hills, and he lost all track of time. He closed his eyes so he could feel them better—the folds of skin and flesh above the knee, little crevices and creases like a hawk feels canyons and arroyos while he is soaring. Some thighs he gripped as if they were something wild and fleet like antelope and rabbits, and the women never flinched or hesitated because they believed the recovery of their clansister depended on them. The dimple and pucker at the edge of the garter and silk stocking brought him back, and he gave special attention to Mrs. Sekakaku, the last one before Aunt Mamie. He traced the ledges and slopes with all his fingers pressing in the ashes. He was out of breath and he knew he could not stand up to get to Aunt Mamie's bed so he bowed his head and pretended he was praying. "I feel better already. I'm not dizzy," the old woman said, not letting anyone help her out of bed or walk with her to the fireplace. He rubbed her thighs as carefully as he had rubbed the others, and he could tell by the feel she'd probably live a long time.

The sun was low in the sky and the bus would be stopping for the outgoing   10
mail pretty soon. He was quitting while he was ahead, while the Hopi men were still in the kivas for Bean Dance. He graciously declined any payment but the women insisted they wanted to do something so he unzipped his jacket pocket and brought out his little pocket camera and a flash cube. As many as they could stood with him in front of the fireplace and someone snapped the picture. By the time he left Aunt Mamie's house he had two shopping bags full of pies and piki bread.

Mrs. Sekakaku was acting very different now—when they got back to   11
her house she kicked the little gray dog and blocked up the oven door with an orange crate. But he told her he had to get back to Laguna right away because he had something important to tell the old men. It was something they'd been trying and trying to do for a long time. At sundown the mail bus pulled onto the highway below Second Mesa but he was tasting one of the pumpkin pies and forgot to look back. He set aside a fine-looking cherry pie to give to the postmaster. Now that they were even again with the Hopi men maybe this Laguna luck would hold out a little while longer.

STUDY QUESTIONS

1. The main character is unnamed, but the story's title suggests a parallel between him and Coyote, a fabled trickster figure in Native American myths. Discuss what we learn of the main character through flashbacks involving his relationship with his mother and his girlfriend, Mildred.
2. This unnamed male is a Pueblo Indian from Laguna. Why is he taking the mail bus to a Hopi town? What is he hoping will happen there?
3. How does the man interpret the differences between Mrs. Sekakaku's presentation of self in her letters to him and her presentation of self when he appears at her door?
4. What does his deception of pretending to be a medicine man gain him? Does the story critique this deception as a negative act?

# CAROLYN FORCHÉ

Carolyn Forché (b. 1950) was born in Detroit. The poet's first book,
Gathering the Tribes (1976), won the Yale Younger Poets Award. Her
second book, The Country Between Us *(1981), achieved critical acclaim and*
wide popularity for its treatment of political oppression in El Salvador, where
Forché had worked gathering information on human rights abuses for Amnesty
International. Forché's poems portray the events in the lives of the disaffiliated
and alien so as to make them disturbingly part of all our experiences.

The Colonel

What you have heard is true. I was in his house. His wife carried a tray of coffee and sugar. His daughter filed her nails, his son went out for the night. There were daily papers, pet dogs, a pistol on the cushion beside him. The moon swung bare on its black cord over the house. On the television was a cop show. It was in English. Broken bottles were embedded in the walls around the house to scoop the kneecaps from a man's legs or cut his hands to lace. On the windows there were gratings like those in liquor stores. We had dinner, rack of lamb, good wine, a gold bell was on the table for calling the maid. The maid brought green mangoes, salt, a type of bread. I was asked how I enjoyed the country. There was a brief commercial in Spanish. His wife took everything away. There was some talk then of how difficult it had become to govern. The parrot said hello on the terrace. The colonel told it to shut up, and pushed himself from the table. My friend said to me with his eyes: say nothing. The colonel returned with a sack used to bring groceries home. He spilled many human ears on the table. They were like dried peach halves. There is no other way to say this. He took one of them in his hands, shook it in our faces, dropped it into a water glass. It came alive there. I am tired of fooling around he said. As for the rights of anyone, tell your people they can go fuck themselves. He swept the ears to the floor with his arm and held the last of his wine in the air. Something for your poetry, no? he said. Some of the ears on the floor caught this scrap of his voice. Some of the ears on the floor were pressed to the ground.

STUDY QUESTIONS

1. "The Colonel" has no line breaks, rhymes, or discernible patterns of stress. Why would you categorize it as a poem? Or would you?

2. What is the colonel's purpose in acting the way he did, and what is the narrator's purpose in telling us about the colonel?
3. The poem succeeds partly through the technique of contrast. What elements are contrasted, and what are the effects of those contrasts on your responses?

✳ RITA DOVE

Rita Dove (b. 1952) was born in Akron, Ohio. She attended Miami University, spent a year studying in Germany on a Fulbright fellowship, received an M.F.A. from the University of Iowa, and is now a professor of English at the University of Virginia.

Perhaps the most notable aspect of Dove's writing is her use of historical material. In The Yellow House on the Corner *(1980) and* Museum *(1983), historical events and personages were the subjects of individual poems or short sequences. But in her Pulitzer Prize–winning* Thomas and Beulah *(1986) that approach came to full flower. The entire volume consists of linked poems paying homage to the experiences of her grandparents, who went north during one of the great waves of African American migration. "Wingfoot Lake" interweaves the projected thoughts, fears, and memories of Dove's widowed grandmother, who is on a company picnic with her daughters. The past seeps through the poem's lines as though between floorboards, and the otherwise unconnected references in the poem run together as elements of the grandmother's life.*

Wingfoot Lake

(Independence Day, 1964)

On her 36th birthday, Thomas had shown her
  her first swimming pool. It had been
his favorite color, exactly—just
so much of it, the swimmers' white arms jutting
into the chevrons of high society.   5
She had rolled up her window
and told him to drive on, fast.

Now this *act of mercy*: four daughters
dragging her to their husbands' company picnic,

white families on one side and them   10
on the other, unpacking the same
squeeze bottles of Heinz, the same
waxy beef patties and Salem potato chip bags.
So he was dead for the first time
on Fourth of July—ten years ago   15

had been harder, waiting for something to happen,
and ten years before that, the girls
like young horses eyeing the track.
Last August she stood alone for hours
in front of the T.V. set   20
as a crow's wing moved slowly through
the white streets of government.
That brave swimming

scared her, like Joanna saying
Mother, we're Afro-Americans now!   25
What did she know about Africa?
Were there lakes like this one
with a rowboat pushed under the pier?
Or Thomas' Great Mississippi
with its sullen silks? (There was   30
the Nile but the Nile belonged

to God.) Where she came from
was the past, 12 miles into town
where nobody had locked their back door,
and Goodyear hadn't begun to dream of a park   35
under the company symbol, a white foot
sprouting two small wings.

STUDY QUESTIONS

1. What is the significance of the date given below the title? What other
   references to time are provided in the poem? How is time or history
   necessary to the poem's meaning?
2. What is the mother's response to the daughter's claim of an African
   American ("*Afro-American*") identity? What might be the reasons for
   her response?
3. What kinds of meanings are associated with the motif of the wing and
   foot in the poem?

JOHN EDGAR WIDEMAN

John Edgar Wideman (b. 1941) is one of several African American writers who began writing in the social ferment of the 1960s. His work shows an interest in experimentation, and his complex style distinguishes him from the Black Arts Movement, which promulgated a black political base to literature. His use of stream-of-consciousness, allusive techniques, and multiple points of view permit fresh constructions of African American cultural identity. With his third novel, The Lynchers *(1973), Wideman entered more fully into explorations of race and history. His most recent books are* Reuben *(1987),* Fever: Twelve Stories *(1989), and* Philadelphia Fire *(1990).*

Presents

I *stood on the bank . . .*   1
    Oh yes, she said. Oh yes and I did not know what she was yessing any   2
more than I know how her voice, her yes reaches from wherever she is to
wherever I am now, except it's like the ships seen from the bank of Jordan
in that song sailing on, sailing on from there to here quietly as a dream.

    Big Mama. Big Mama. Doubling her not because she is not real enough   3
once but because her life takes up so much space. I stare at her afraid to
look away. Scared she'll be gone if I do. Scared I'll be gone.

    Baby, you listen to your Big Mama now. Listen cause I ain't got nothing   4
but mouth and time and hardly none that left.

    He is saucer-eyed. Awkward. A big, nappy head.   5

    She pats each nap and each awakes. A multitude stirring as she passes   6
her old hand once in the air over the crown of his skull.

    Love Jesus and love yourself and love those who love you, sugar. Those   7
who don't love you don't love theyselves and shame on them. Nobody but
Jesus can save their sorry souls.

    She purses her lips. Her tongue pushes that hard-as-the-world bitter   8
lemon into one cheek. She sucks on it. All the sour of it smears her old lips.
She is Big Mama. No bones in her body. Even now, even this Christmas so
close to death the bones cannot claim her. Nothing will crack or snap or
buckle in her. In her lap he will curl and sleep and always find soft room
to snuggle deeper. To fall. To sleep.

    He remembers being big enough to crawl alone under her bed and little   9
enough, little sweet doodlebug, you come on over here gimme some sugar,
to sit upright and his head just grazes the beehive network of springs.
Hiding under her bed and playing with the dust and light he raises and the
tasseled knots of fringed chenille bedspread. Bed so high so you had to

climb up on it. Mind you don't roll off, boy. He did not think *throne* but he knew her bed was raised high to be a special place, to be his Big Mama's bed.

So when she kneels beside the bed he hears the sigh of the room rushing 10 together again over her head, sigh as the fist of her heart, the apron pocket of her chest empties and fills, the grunt and wheeze of his Big Mama dropping to one knee and lifts the spread and her arm disappears as if she's fishing for him under there. Come out, you little doodlebug rascal. I know you hiding in there. Boogeyman get you you don't come from under there. Her arm sweeps and he can see her fingers under the edge of the bed, inside the cave, though he is outside now and it's like being two places at once, hiding and looking for his ownself, watching her old hand, the fingers hooked, beckoning. C'mon out, you monkey you, sweeping a half inch off the floor, precisely at the level of the unfailing, fringed spread hanging off the side of the bed.

What she drags forth this Christmas Eve afternoon as he watches her 11 kneeling beside the bed is wrapped in a blanket. Not him this time, but something covered with a sheet and swaddled in a woolly blanket. Shape-less. Then Big Mama digs into folds and flaps, uncovers woman curves, the taut shaft. There are long strings and a hole in the center. Gently as she goes she cannot help accidents that trick stirrings from the instrument. A bowl of jelly quivering. Perhaps all it needs is the play of her breath as she bends over it, serious and quiet as a child undressing a doll. Or the air all by its ownself is enough to agitate the strings when Big Mama finally has it laid bare across her bed.

The story as he's preached it so many times since is simple. A seven- 12 year-old boy makes his grandmother a song. He intends to sing it for her Christmas Day but Christmas Eve afternoon she calls him into her bed-room and kneels and pulls a guitar wrapped in rags and blankets from under her bed. He is mesmerized and happy. He hugs his Big Mama and can't help telling her about the love song he's made up for her Christmas present. She says you better sing it for me now, baby, and he does and she smiles the whole time he sings. Then she lays out the sad tale of his life as a man. He'll rise in the world, sing for kings and queens but his gift for music will also drag him down to the depths of hell. She tells it gently, he is only a boy, with her eyes fixed on the ceiling and they fill up with tears. Oh yes. Oh yes, yes. Yes, Jesus. The life he must lead a secret pouring out of her. Emptying her. Already she's paying for the good and evil in him. Yes. Yes. She's quiet then. Still. They sit together on the side of her high bed till it's dark outside the window. He can't see snow but smells it, hears how silently it falls. She asks him, sing my song one more time. His little Christmas gift song because he loves to sing and make rhymes and loves his Big Mama and the grace of sweet Jesus is heavy in this season of his birth. By the next morning his Big Mama is dead. The others come for Christmas Day, discover her. He's been awake since dawn, learning to pick out her song quietly on his new guitar. His mother and the rest of them bust in, stomp their snowy shoes in the hallway and Merry Christmas and where's Big Mama? They find her dead in bed and he's been playing ever since. Everything she prophesied right on the money, honey. To this very day. He's been up and he's been down and that's the way she told him it would be all the days of his life. Amen.

Each time in the middle of the story he thinks he won't ever need to tell it again. Scooted up under the skirt of Big Mama's bed. His mother comes over to visit and she fusses at him. You're too big a boy to be hiding go seek under Mama's bed. Don't let him play under there, Mama. Don't baby him. Time he started growing up.   13

His mother visits and takes a bath in Big Mama's iron tub. He sees her bare feet and bare ankles, her bare butt as he holds his breath and quiet as a spider slides to the edge and peeks up through the fringy spread. He lifts the covering to see better. Inch by inch. Quiet as snow. She has a big, round behind with hairs at the bottom. He thinks of watermelons and can't eat that fruit without guilt ever after. He watches her as she stands in front of the mirror of his grandmother's chiffonier. His heart beats fast as it can. He's afraid she'll hear it, afraid she'll turn quickly and find his eye peeking up from under the covers at her. But when she does turn, it's slowly, slowly so he hears the rub of her bare heel on the linoleum where the rug doesn't stretch to where she's standing. He drops the window of his hiding place. He's spared a vision of the front of her. Titties. Pussycat between her legs. Just ankles and bare feet till she finished and wrapped in one Big Mama's housecoats and asking for him in the other room.   14

You been in here all this time? You been hiding under there while I was dressing? Why didn't you say something, boy?   15

The story has more skins than an onion. And like an onion it can cause a grown man to cry when he starts to peeling it.   16

Or else it can go quick. Big Mama said, That's the most beautiful song in the world. Thank you, precious. Thank you and thank Jesus for bringing such a sweet boy to this old woman.   17

Will you teach me how to play?   18

Your old grandmama don't know nothing bout such things. She's tired besides. You learn your ownself. Just beat on it like a drum till something come out sound good to you.   19

The music's in the box like the sword in the stone. Beat it. Pound it. Chisel away. Then one day it gon sound good. Gon slide loose easy as it slided in. Then it's smooth as butter. Then it sings God's praise. Oh yes. Oh yes.   20

She gave him the guitar in Jesus' name. Amened it. Prayed over it with him that Christmas Eve afternoon how many years ago. Well, let's see. I was seven then and I'm an old man now so that's how long it's been, that's how many times I've preached the story.   21

My grandmother believed in raising a joyful noise unto the Lord. Tam-   22 bourines and foot stomping and gut-bucket piano rolls and drums and shouts and yes if you could find one a mean guitar rocking like the ark in heavy seas till it gets good to everybody past the point of foot patting and finger popping in your chair past that till the whole congregation out they seats dancing in the air.

Something born that day and something died. His fate cooked up for him like a mess of black-eyed peas and ham hocks and he's been eating at the table of it ever since. Lean days and fat days. 23

Where did she find a guitar? Who'd played the instrument before it was his? Could it ever be his if other fingers had plucked the strings, run up and down the long neck? Grease and sweat ground into its wood, its metal strings. When he was at last alone with the gift she'd given him and told him not to play till Christmas, he'd peered into the hole in its belly. Held it by its fat hips and shook it to hear if anybody'd left money in there. If the right sound won't come out plucking it, there was always the meaty palm of his hand to knock sense in it. 24

How long did he hide in the church before he carried his box out on the street corner? How long for the Lord, how many licks for the Devil? How long before you couldn't tell one from the other? Him the last to know. Always. 25

A boy wonder. An evil hot blood Buddy Bolden Willie the Lion Robert Johnson wild man boy playing the fool and playing the cowboy fool shit out that thang, man. Yes. Oh yes. 26

And one day Praise God I said, Huh uh. No more. Thank you Jesus and broke it over my knee and cried cause I'd lost my Big Mama. 27

Atlantic City. Niggers pulling rickshaws up and down the Boardwalk. Naw. If I'm lying, I'm flying. They did, boy. Yes they did. Drugging white folks around behind them in these big carts. Like in China, man. Or wherever they keep them things. Saw that shit on the Boardwalk in Atlantic City, U.S. of A. Yeah. And niggers happy to be doing it. Collecting fabulous tips, they say. Hauling peckerwoods around. Not me. See, I knew better. I'd seen the world. Had me a gig in one those little splib clubs on Arctic Avenue. Enough to keep me in whiskey. Didn't need no pad. It was summer. Sleep on the beach. Or sleep with one the ladies dig my playing. A real bed, a shower every few days to scald the sand out my asshole. Living the life, partner. Till I woke up one morning in the gutter. Stone gutter, man. Like a dead rat. Head busted.Vomit all on my clothes. In broad daylight I'm lolling in the gutter, man. Said, Huh uh. No indeed. These the bonds of hell. Done fell clean off the ladder and I'm down in the pit. The goddamn gutter floor of the pit's bottom. I'm lost. Don't a living soul give one dime fuck about me and I don't neither. 28

That's when I hollered, Get me up from here, Big Mama. You said I'd rise and I did. You prophesied I'd fall and here I am. Now reach down and help me up. Gimme your soft silk purse old woman's hand and lift this crusty burden off the street. Take me back to your bosom. Rise and fall, you 29 said. Well, I can't fall no further so carry me on up again. Please. Please. Big Mama. Reach down off the high side of your bed and bring me back.

Her fingers hooked like a eagle's beak. Holding a cloak of feathers fash- 30
ioned from wings of fallen angels. Where you find this, Big Mama? How'm I spozed to play this thing? Beat it, you say. Pound it like a drum. Just step out in the air with it round your shoulders. Let the air take you and fly you on home. Squeeze it till it sound like you need it to sound. Good. Giant steps ain't nothing if they ain't falling up and falling down and carrying you far from this place to another.

Sailing. To meet me in the morning. On Jordan one day. Singing, Yes. 31
Oh yes.

I stood on the bank . . . 32

And my neck ached like I'd been lynched. Like I'd been laid out for dead 33
and hard rock was my pillow and cold ground my bed.

Hard rock my pillow and help me today, Lord. Help me tell it. I scram- 34
ble to my feet and shook the sooty graveclothes and sand and scales and dust and feathers and morning blood off my shoulders. Skinny as a scare-crow. Funky as toejam. My mouth dry and my eyes scored by rusty razors, my tongue like a turtle forgot how to poke his head out his shell. Scram-bled to my aching feet and there it was spread out over me the city of my dreams, Philadelphia all misbegotten and burnt crisp and sour sour at the roots as all my bad teefs.

Play it, son. 35

Bucka do. Bucka do little dee. 36

Black as sugar burnt to the bottom of the pan. And Big Mama told me. 37
She said, Squeeze it to the last drop.

A simple story. Easy to tell to a stranger at the bar who will buy you a 38
drink. Young boy and old woman. Christmastime. Reading each other's minds. Exchanging gifts of song. His fortune told. The brief, bright time of his music. How far it took him, how quickly gone. The candle flaring up, guttering, gone. He'd told it many times. Risen. Fallen. Up. Down. Rubs his crusty eyes and peers into a honey-colored room with no walls, feet scurry past his head, busy going every which way, sandals and brogans and sneakers and shiny Stacy-Adamses and pitter-pat of high-stepper high heels on the pavement as he lifts his head and goes over the whole busi-ness again, trying to settle once and for all who he must be and why it always ends this way his head on the hard rock of curbstone, the ships sailing on, sailing on.

The river is brass or blood or mud depending on the day, the season, the 39
hour. Big Mama is where she is. He is here. Her voice plain as day in his ear. He wishes someone would pat him on his head and say everything's gon be all right.

1. "Presents" is told through at least two points of view—the point of view of the first-person main character and the point of view of a third person. Contrast the different prose styles that characterize and distinguish these points of view.
2. Analyze the young boy's feelings for his grandmother, Big Mama.
3. Discuss the multiple meanings associated with the grandmother's present of the guitar. In return, what present does the boy give to his grandmother?
4. If we think of song or music as a gift, how has this gift (musical talent) affected the main character's life?

❖ SABINE ULIBARRÍ

Sabine Ulibarrí (b. 1919) was born in Sante Fe, New Mexico, and he has taught at the University of New Mexico since 1947. He has published numerous volumes of essays, criticism, and short stories written in Spanish and translated into English, including Tierra Amarilla *(1971),* Mi abuela fumaba puros (My Grandma Smoked Cigars) *(1977), and* El Condor and Other Stories *(1989). Ulibarrí comes from a long established Spanish-speaking community with roots in Spanish and Mexican culture. His fiction recreates this geographical region and is populated with characters who are the descendants of the Spaniards and Mexicans who have inhabited the Southwestern territory for centuries, long before the English colonists settled Virginia or Massachusetts.*

My Grandma Smoked Cigars

The way I've heard it, my grandfather was quite a guy. There are many   1
stories about him. Some respectable, others not quite. One of the latter goes as follows. That returning from Tierra Amarilla to Las Nutrias, after cups and cards, sometimes on his buggy with its spirited trotters, sometimes on his *criollo* horse, he would take off his hat, hang it on a fence post, pull out his six-gun and address himself to the stiff gentleman of his own invention.

"Tell me, who is the richest man in all these parts?"   2

Silence. 3

"Well then, take this." 4

A shot. Splinters flew out of the post or a hole appeared in the hat. 5

"Who's the toughest man around here?" 6

Silence. 7

"Well then, take this." 8

The same thing happened. He was a good shot. More questions of the 9
same kind, punctuated with shots. When the sassy post learned his lesson
and gave my grandfather the answers he wanted to hear, the ritual ended,
and he went on his way, singing or humming some sentimental song of the
period. The shooting was heard back in the town without it bothering
anyone. Someone was sure to say with a smile, "There's don Prudencio
doing his thing."

Of course my grandfather had other sides (the plural is intended) that 10
are not relevant to this narrative. He was a civic, social and political
figure and a family man twice over. What I want to do now is stress the
fact that my relative was a real character: quarrelsome, daring and prank-
ish.

He died in a mysterious way, or perhaps even shameful. I've never been 11
able to find out exactly what streetcar my distinguished antecedent took to
the other world. Maybe that wooden gentleman with his hat pulled over
his eyes, the one who suffered the insults of the hidalgo of Las Nutrias,
gave him a woody and mortal whack. An hidalgo he was—and a father of
more than four.

I never knew him. When I showed up in this world to present my 12
Turriaga credentials, he had already turned his in. I imagine that wherever
he is he's making violent and passionate love to the ladies who went to
heaven—or hell, depending . . . That is if my grandmother hasn't caught
up with him in those worlds beyond the grave.

I don't think he and my grandmother had an idyllic marriage in the 13
manner of sentimental novels where everything is sweetness, softness and
tenderness. Those are luxuries, perhaps decadences, that didn't belong in
that violent world, frequently hostile, of Río Arriba County at the end of
the past century. Furthermore, the strong personalities of both would have
prevented it. I do believe they were very happy. Their love was a passion
that didn't have time to become a habit or just friendship. They loved each
other with mutual respect and fear, something between admiration and
fury, something between tenderness and toughness. Both were children of
their land and their times. There was so much to do. Carve a life from an
unfriendly frontier. Raise their rebellious and ferocious cubs. Their life was
an affectionate and passionate sentimental war.

I say all of this as a preamble in order to enter into my subject: my 14
grandmother. I have so many and so gratifying memories of her. But the
first one of all is a portrait that hangs in a place of honor in the parlor of my
memory.

She had her moments in which she caressed her solitude. She would go off by herself, and everyone knew it was best to leave her alone. 15

She always dressed in black. A blouse of lace and batiste up front. A skirt down to her ankles. All silk. A cotton apron. High shoes. Her hair parted in the middle and combed straight back, smooth and tight, with a round and hard bun in the back. I never saw her hair loose. 16

She was strong. As strong as only she could be. Through the years, in so many situations, small and big tragedies, accidents and problems, I never saw her bend or fold. Fundamentally, she was serious and formal. So a smile, a compliment or a caress from her were coins of gold that were appreciated and saved as souvenirs forever. Coins she never wasted. 17

The ranch was big business. The family was large and problematic. She ran her empire with a sure and firm hand. Never was there any doubt about where her affairs were going nor who held the reins. 18

That first memory: the portrait. I can see her at this moment as if she were before my eyes. A black silhouette on a blue background. Straight, tall and slender. The wind of the hill cleaving her clothes to her body up front, outlining her forms, one by one. Her skirt and her shawl flapping in the wind behind her. Her eyes fixed I don't know where. Her thoughts fixed on I don't know what. An animated statue. A petrified soul. 19

My grandfather smoked cigars. The cigar was the symbol and the badge of the feudal lord, the *patrón*. When on occasion he would give a cigar to the foreman or to one of the hands on impulse or as a reward for a task well done, the transfiguration of those fellows was something to see. To suck on the tobacco was to drink from the fountains of power. The cigar gave you class. 20

They say that when my grandfather died my grandmother would light cigars and place them on ashtrays all over the house. The aroma of the tobacco filled the house. This gave the widow the illusion that her husband was still around. A sentimentalism and romanticism difficult to imagine before. 21

As time went on, and after lighting many a cigar, a liking for the cigars seemed to sneak up on her. She began to smoke the cigars. At nightfall, every day, after dinner, when the tasks of the day were done, she would lock herself in her room, sit in her rocker and light her cigar. 22

She would spend a long time there. The rest of us remained in the living room playing the family role as if nothing were amiss. No one ever dared interrupt her arbitrary and sacred solitude. No one ever mentioned her unusual custom. 23

The cigar that had once been a symbol of authority had now become an instrument of love. I am convinced that in the solitude and in the silence, with the smell and taste of the tobacco, there in the smoke, my grandmother established some kind of mystical communication with my grandfather. I think that there, all alone, that idyllic marriage, full of tenderness, 24 softness and sweetness was attained, not possible while he lived. It was enough to see the soft and transfigured face of the grandmother when she returned to us from her strange communion, to see the affection and gentleness with which she treated us kids.

Right there, and in those conditions, the decisions were made, the positions were taken that ran the business, that directed the family. There in the light or in the shade of an old love, now an eternal love, the spiritual strength was forged that kept my grandmother straight, tall and slender, a throbbing woman of stone, facing the winds and storms of her full life. 25

When my parents married they built their home next to the old family house. I grew up on the windy hill in the center of the valley of Las Nutrias, with pine trees on all the horizons, with the stream full of beaver, trout and suckers, the sagebrush full of rabbits and coyotes, stock everywhere, squirrels and owls in the barn. 26

I grew up alongside my grandmother and far away from her, between tender love and reverent fear. 27

When I was eight years old, it was decided in the family that we should move to Tierra Amarilla so that my brothers and I could attend school. The furrows the tears left on my face still burn, and I still remember their salty taste the day we left my straight, tall and slender grandmother, waving her handkerchief, with the wind on her face on the hill in the center of the valley. 28

In Tierra Amarilla I was antisocial. Having grown up alone, I didn't know how to play with other children. I played with my dogs instead. In spite of this I did all right in school, and one day I was fifteen years old, more or less adapted to my circumstances. 29

One winter day we got ready to go to Las Nutrias. All with a great deal of anticipation. To visit my grandmother was always an event. The family would go with me in the car. My father with the sleigh and the hired hands. It was a matter of cutting fence posts. 30

We sang all the way. That is until we had to leave the highway. There was a lot of snow. The highway had been cleared, but the little road to Las Nutrias hadn't. 31

I put chains on the car, and we set out across the white sea. Now we were quiet and apprehensive. We soon got stuck. After a lot of shoveling and much pushing we continued, only to get stuck again farther on, again and again. 32

We were all exhausted and cold, and the day was drifting away. Finally we climbed the hill and came out of the pine grove from where we could see my grandmother's house. We got stuck again. This time there was no way of pulling the car out. My mother and the children continued on foot, opening their way through two and a half feet of soft snow. My brother Roberto pulled my sister Carmen on a small sled. It was getting dark. A trip of nine miles had taken us all day. 33

Juan Maes, the foreman, quickly came with a team of horses and pulled me home. 34

I had barely come in and was warming up. My mother had brought me 35 dry clothes, when we saw the lights of a car in the pine grove. We saw it approach slowly, hesitating from time to time. It was easier now; the road was now open.

It was my uncle Juan Antonio. The moment he came in we all knew he 36 had bad news. There was a frightening silence. No one said a word. Everyone silent and stiff like wooden figures in a grotesque scene.

My mother broke the silence with a heartbreaking "Alejandro!" 37

My uncle nodded. 38

"What happened?" It was my grandmother. 39

"Alejandro. An accident." 40

"What happened?" 41

"An accidental shot. He was cleaning a rifle. The gun went off." 42

"How is he?" 43

"Not good, but he'll pull through." 44

We all knew he was lying, that my father was dead. We could see it in 45 his face. My mother was crying desperately, on the verge of becoming hysterical. We put our arms around her, crying. My uncle with his hat in his hands not knowing what to do. Another man had come with him. No one had noticed him.

That is when my grandmother went into action. Not a single tear. Her 46 voice steady. Her eyes two flashing spears. She took complete control of the situation.

She went into a holy fury against my father. She called him ungrateful, 47 shameless, unworthy. An inexhaustible torrent of insults. A royal rage. In the meantime she took my mother in her arms and rocked her and caressed her like a baby. My mother submitted and settled down slowly. We did too. My grandmother who always spoke so little did not stop talking that night.

I didn't understand then. I felt a violent resentment. I wanted to defend 48 my father. I didn't because no one ever dared to talk back to my grandmother. Much less me. The truth is that she understood many things.

My mother was on the verge of madness. Something had to be done. 49

My grandmother created a situation, so violent and dramatic, that it 50 forced us all, my mother especially, to fix our attention on her and shift it away from the other situation until we could get used to the tragedy little by little. She didn't stop talking in order not to allow a single aperture through which despair might slip in. Talking, talking, between abuse and lullaby, she managed that my mother, in her vulnerable state, fall asleep in the wee hours of the morning. As she had done so many times in the past, my grandmother had dominated the harsh reality in which she lived.

She understood something else. That my father didn't fire a rifle acci- 51 dentally. The trouble we had to bury him on sacred ground confirmed the infallible instinct of the lady and mistress of Las Nutrias. Everything confirmed the talent and substance of the mother of the Turriaga clan.

The years went by. I was now a professor. One day we returned to visit 52
the grandmother. We were very happy. I've said it before, visiting her was
an event. Things had changed a great deal. With the death of my father,
my grandmother got rid of all the stock. The ranch hands disappeared with
the stock. Rubel and his family were the only ones who remained to look
after her.

When we left the highway and took the little used and much abused 53
road full of the accustomed ruts, the old memories took possession of us.
Suddenly we saw a column of black smoke rising beyond the hill. My sister
shouted.

"Grandma's house!" 54
"Don't be silly. They must be burning weeds, or sage brush, or trash." 55
I said this but apprehension gripped me. I stepped hard on the gas.

When we came out of the pine grove, we saw that only ruins remained 56
of the house of the grandmother. I drove like a madman. We found her
surrounded by the few things that were saved. Surrounded also by neighbors of all the ranches in the region who rushed to help when they saw the
smoke.

I don't know what I expected but it did not surprise me to find her 57
directing all the activities, giving orders. No tears, no whimpers, no laments.

"God gives and God takes away, my son. Blessed be His Holy Name." 58
I did lament. The crystal chandeliers, wrecked. The magnificent sets of 59
tables and washstands with marble tops. The big basins and water jars in
every bedroom, destroyed. The furniture brought from Kansas, turned to
ashes. The bedspreads of lace, crochet, embroidery. The portraits, the
pictures, the memories of a family.

Irony of ironies. There was a jar of holy water on the window sill in the 60
attic. The rays of the sun, shining through the water, converted into a
magnifying glass. The heat and the fire concentrated on a single spot and
set on fire some old papers there. And all of the saints, the relics, the
shrines, the altar to the Santo Niño de Atocha, the palms of Palm Sunday,
all burned up. All of the celestial security went up in smoke.

That night we gathered in what had been our old home. My grand- 61
mother seemed smaller to me, a little subdued, even a little docile: "Whatever you say, my son." This saddened me.

After supper my grandmother disappeared. I looked for her apprehen- 62
sively. I found her where I could very well have suspected. At the top of
the hill. Profiled by the moon. The wind in her face. Her skirt flapping in
the wind. I saw her grow. And she was what she had always been: straight,
tall and slender.

I saw the ash of her cigar light up. She was with my grandfather, the 63
wicked one, the bold one, the quarrelsome one. Now the decisions would

be made, the positions would be taken. She was regaining her spiritual strength. Tomorrow would be another day, but my grandmother would continue being the same one. And I was happy.

STUDY QUESTIONS

1. The story begins with a brief portrait of the grandfather. What aspects of the grandfather's character help to explain the grandmother's development after his death?
2. What does the cigar symbolize? What can be inferred from the changing symbolism of the cigar?
3. What incidents testify to the grandmother's strength?
4. What does the conclusion suggest of the narrator's attitude toward his grandmother, and how does he see their relationship?

❖ AMIRI BARAKA (LEROI JONES)

Amiri Baraka (LeRoi Jones) is a multi-talented poet, dramatist, essayist, novelist, and political activist who significantly changed the course of African American literary culture. A central figure of the 1960s Black Arts Movement, he was a prime influence on the poets and playwrights of his time and has continued to provide artistic and philosophic direction for a new generation of black artists and intellectuals in the United States, England, the Caribbean, and Africa. In important ways, he continues the legacy of the Harlem Renaissance and the Negritude Movement. Like Langston Hughes, Aimé Césaire and Nicholás Guillén, he has committed himself to fashioning a modern literature rooted in the cultural and historical experience of the African diaspora.

Baraka was born in Newark, New Jersey in 1934. After attending Rutgers and Howard universities, he served in the United States Air Force. In the late 1950s and early 1960s, he lived in Greenwich Village in New York City and became one of the leading figures in the bohemian arts scene there. During this period, he edited avant garde literary journals, visited Castro's Cuba, and became famous with the production of his play Dutchman, *which won an Obie Award. After the assassination of Malcolm X, Baraka declared himself a black cultural nationalist, organized the Black Arts Repertory Theatre-School in Harlem, and returned to Newark where he assumed a leadership role in the black liberation movement. By the mid 1970s, he became a Third World marxist supporting left-wing causes in Africa, Asia, and Latin America.*

Baraka has been the recipient of numerous grants and awards. He has written over thirteen volumes of poetry, twenty plays, three jazz operas, a novel, a collection of stories, and seven nonfiction works. He has taught at San Francisco State University and is now Director of the African Studies Program at the State University of New York at Stony Brook. The poem that follows represents a distinct phase in Baraka's literary career. "Real Song Is a Dangerous Number" is a recent poem that expresses Baraka's deep roots in African American culture.

Real Song Is a Dangerous Number

(For Amina, Nina, Grachian, Abdul, and Akida, December)

I am Johnny Ace
accidental suicide
from Russian roulette, maybe my name
is Sam Cooke, dead in a room by an unknown   5
hand. I could be Otis Redding, airplane sunk
at the dock of the bay. You might know me as
Teddy Pendergrass, smashed ½ flat, they say with
a queen, cripple now, but off the scene.
Marvin Gaye, my old man took me   10
away. Bob Marley was my name
in jam down, cancer shot up through
my toe. *Redemption Song* to be heard
no more. If I was white, they'd call me
Lennon, blasted flat by a crazy man.   15
Don't make no deal, you get kill. Yr voice
too strong, yr charisma too long. The rhythm
of yr image, hotter than napalm. But I cd be
a poet name Larry Neal (or Henry Dumas)
for the very same reason I cd also get kill.

STUDY QUESTIONS

1. What does the title of the poem suggest? Why is it appropriate for the poem?
2. How does the poem define the predicament of the artist? Who are the artists mentioned in the poem? What is their cultural significance?

THEMATIC QUESTIONS

1. Discuss images and motifs of violence and loss in Atwood's "Owl Song" and Joy Kogawa's excerpt from her novel *Obasan*. What does each piece suggest about the condition of contemporary human experience?

2. Mordecai Richler's short story "The Summer My Grandmother Was Supposed to Die" and Michael Ondaatje's poem "Letters and Other Worlds" construct an ethnically differentiated world through the events surrounding the death of a family member. Describe these ethnic cultures as they are represented through action, conflict, and character.

3. Family and community are both privileged and criticized in "The Summer My Grandmother Was Supposed to Die" and Michel Tremblay's passage from his novel *The Fat Woman Next Door Is Pregnant*. Analyze these conflicting attitudes and discuss the verbal strategies—e.g., humor, irony—that hold these divergent views together.

4. Margaret Atwood's "Dancing Girls" presents a complex view on mainstream Canadians' fear of the foreign. Discuss the theme, noting the tension between the domestic and the wild, the cooked and the raw, the familiar and the bizarre, which are polarities that undergird much of Canadian writing. Discuss these polarities as they undergird the images and ideas in Atwood's story and in poems such as Irving Layton's "Berry Picking" and Ann Hébert's "The Thin Girl."

5. Wallace Stevens's "No Possum, No Sop, No Taters" is a very different poem from Elizabeth Bishop's "The Man-Moth." Yet both can be read as modernistic in their attitudes, ironic self-consciousness, and strategic use of fantasy. Expand on the elements of modernism that characterize these poems.

6. Analyze the tone of William Carlos Williams's "A Sort of Song." How is this tone related to poems by later poets such as Frank O'Hara, Gary Snyder, and James Wright? Are their poems more similar or more dissimilar in style and voice?

7. Raymond Carver's short story "Cathedral" and Irving Layton's poem "Berry Picking" both deal with marriages. Analyze the husband-wife relationships in these selections, and discuss the attitudes toward and critiques of marriage.

8. Both Maxine Hong Kingston and Joy Kogawa attempt to construct North American/Asian narratives that make "visible" neglected aspects of their community history. Discuss the kinds of "heroism" displayed in the excerpts from Maxine Hong Kingston's *China Men* and Joy Kogawa's *Obasan*, and analyze the relationship between the heroic and these community histories.

9. Compare Langston Hughes's poems with Rita Dove's "Wingfoot Lake." How do they differ in their constructions of African-American history and society? How are they similar?

10. Both James Baldwin's "The Rockpile" and John Edgar Wideman's "Presents" have young African-American boys as their central characters, yet the stories are very different in their representations of childhood. Discuss these differences in terms of the patriarchal and matriarchal organizations constructed in the two narratives.

11. Discuss the use of traditional literary elements such as the trickster figure in Leslie Marmon Silko's "Coyote Holds a Full House in His Hand" and the healer in August Wilson's *Joe Turner's Come and Gone*. What is achieved by the use of such traditional materials?

12. The theme of violence or incipient violence runs through much of contemporary American literature. Discuss how this theme is encapsulated through images, plot development, and characterization in selected poems, stories, and/or plays, for example, "The Rockpile," "Lady Lazarus," "The Colonel," and *Joe Turner's Come and Gone*.

13. Compare and contrast Sylvia Plath's "Morning Song" with Adrienne Rich's "To a Poet." Both poems speak of a woman's role as a mother. What motifs in the Plath poem are picked up and developed more fully in Rich's poem?

14. A major theme in American literature is that of sexuality. Contrast the different lessons on female sexuality represented in Anne Hébert's "The Thin Girl," Margaret Atwood's "Owl Song," and Adrienne Rich's "Diving into the Wreck." Which representation of women do you find more challenging? Explain your response.

15. Analyze the effects of point of view in constructing notions of male-female power relations in "The Rockpile," "Cathedral," and "The Life You Save May Be Your Own."

A   NOTE   ON   FICTION

For further explanation of capitalized terms, refer to the Glossary of Literary Terms, pp. 1125–1141.

Storytelling is an activity that crosses cultures. Australian aborigines, African tribal peoples, the metropolitan sophisticates of Europe and North America, and the postcolonial societies of South America and Asia share an interest in narrative as pleasure and as instruction.

Although gathered from around the world, the stories selected for this anthology are products of twentieth-century technology. Even stories written from largely oral societies such as those by the Nigerian Chinua Achebe and the Ghanaian Ama Ata Aidoo are removed from an oral origin, and we receive them as published printed works. Many of these stories are also received through translation from their original language.

What is immediately apparent is the impression of differences created within a commonality of elements in these stories produced from widely different linguistic, racial, and cultural groups. Even stories from countries apparently familiar and akin to the United States may be culturally divergent, as, for example, the excerpt from Canadian Michel Tremblay's *The Fat Woman Next Door is Pregnant*. Tremblay's work, which is grounded in French Quebecois working-class society, is distinguished by linguistic, regional, and class differences from mainstream white middle-class United States fiction.

In fact, stories from the contemporary United States indicate how fiction exhibits the weight of difference; although written by white writers, the stories by Flannery O'Connor and Raymond Carver are vastly different from each other in theme and style. The differences demonstrate the individualistic and idiosyncratic emphasis of the art form and help explain how differences of race, gender, and class affect the achievements of other writers such as James Baldwin, Maxine Hong Kingston, Leslie Marmon Silko, and John Edgar Wideman, writers within the same national tradition. It is understandable, therefore, that some readers may feel initially overwhelmed by differences in stories from dissimilar cultures—for example, the narrative written by Albert Wendt, a Samoan writer, or the stories of Argentinean experimental writer Jorge Luis Borges, or the Italian modernist Italo Calvino. Individual national histories, diverse language traditions, and local developments form the contexts that shape our reception and interpretation of the stories. For example, the sardonic humor of Milan Kundera's "Edward and God" rises from the ideological quarrel between Communism and Christianity that post-Second-World-War Czechoslovakia experienced under the influence of the Soviet Union. Whatever we can bring to bear on the political and social background will help us understand Kundera's complex story with greater sensitivity and insight.

At the same time, stories generally possess CHARACTERS, agents or objects of action, whether human or nonhuman, as in gods and animals. They also contain PLOTS, series of actions that are often chronologically organized or causally connected. Some plots are conventionally structured. In Yukio Mishima's "Patriotism," for example, the story's introduction leads to a series of complications as the lieutenant and his young bride take on a course of action resulting from the defeat of the military coup. The story's climax occurs with their mutual suicide and concludes with a resolution of issues raised during the narrative. Patricia Grace's "And So I Go" is not conventionally plotted, as it is composed less of action than of lyrical passages that weave themes of the Maori homeland, dislocation, and assimilation into mainstream New Zealand society. Contemporary stories often experiment with TIME-SHIFTS, organizing actions not so much chronologically as by their significance in illuminating motivations and character. Compare, for example, the straightforward arrangement of cause and effect in D. H. Lawrence's "The Horse Dealer's Daughter" and the recursive, backtracking sequence of events in John Edgar Wideman's "Presents." Both are deeply psychological narratives, but the second makes you work harder to figure out what the major childhood influences on the central character are and why he is the way he is. That is, the second story imitates the process of understanding the psychological mysteries of a human being.

These stories convey feelings and provoke thought, as they often express the storyteller's views and values. Readers understand the complex unity of ideas and emotions that compose the effects of a story as the THEME. We understand the theme or message by integrating our understanding of the characters, the plot, and the various major devices the authors have used to get their stories across.

Character, plot, and theme are present in all the stories in this anthology. But they are present in widely differing contexts. In order to appreciate many of the ALLUSIONS or references to literary, cultural, and sociohistorical persons, events, and ideas that writers use to give density and significance to their stories, we have to understand something of the historical and cultural context in which the story is embedded. For example, many of the stories from Latin America have to be read against the political context of the sixteenth-century Spanish conquest of the indigenous peoples, of protest against centuries of colonialism and present economic stagnation and poverty. Rosario Castellanos's "Death of the Tiger," for instance, making use of both political realism and MAGIC REALISM, provides an imagined history of the native tribal people dispossessed by the Spanish conquest of Mexico. Similarly, the stories from Africa and the

Middle East are written against a backdrop of decolonization, as in Mahmoud Darwish's "Identity Card." The social turmoil that decolonization brings with it is represented in many stories from ex-colonial nations, including interrogations of traditional male-female power relations, as in Indonesian Pramoedya Ananta Toer's "Inem" and unequal race relations, for example, in New Zealander Witi Ihimaera's "His First Ball."

Although we can "understand" most stories without a knowledge of their background, this understanding is usually limited. Also, there is a danger that lack of sensitivity to the differences in societies from which the stories come and that they address will lead not merely to diminished understanding but to active misunderstanding and to rejection and prejudice. In this anthology, the introductions to the continents and the headnotes for selections attempt to provide geographical, historical, and local information that will help you locate the stories in a more specific culture.

There is a comfort in staying with what we know, in remaining centered in our own cultures. But reading these stories shows us that we can best appreciate elements of our culture when we see them against other cultures. While the stories are grounded in local histories and mores, they also demonstrate that their originating culture is not a static and ready-made phenomenon. All the stories deal with CONFLICT of one kind or another: conflict between men and women, between peoples of unequal status and different races and classes, between parents and children, between different values and needs. Thus, as expressions of groups of people's values, customs, and ways of living, these stories show culture as constantly evolving in response to changing conditions and to human desires.

Nor are the cultures expressed in these stories' closed worlds. As the peoples of the world interact more and more with each other, as technology makes contact inevitable and isolation impossible, societies respond to the impact of other cultures. Sometimes the impact of different cultures is negative, resulting, for instance, in the loss of indigenous languages and values in the wake of nationalism and modernization, movements introduced by Western nations. The excerpt from *Dr. Wooreddy's Prescription for Surviving the Ending of the World* by Colin Johnson (also known as Mudrooroo Nyoongah) vividly represents—through the physical and social disintegration of the indigenous character, Wooreddy—the destruction of the world of the original populations of Australia through the colonialist invasion of the white settlers. Sometimes the effect of meeting other cultures is less obvious, as in an increasing emphasis for tolerance or individual freedom and the costs of these values. In Mori Yōko's "Spring Storm," Natsuo's success as an actress leads to the end of her marriage. Her husband, Yusuke, is able to acknowledge his jealousy by referring to an analogous relationship between the famous Scandinavian actress Ingrid Bergman and her husband, Roberto Rossellini, indicating the cross-cultural nature of gender dominant-subordinate roles. Many of the stories in this anthology reflect and express these cross-cultural forces.

We can discuss a number of different themes in some stories, especially stories using strategies that complicate interpretation. Some of these complicating strategies are POINT OF VIEW, IRONY, NARRATION, TIME-SHIFTS, ALLEGORY, and even verbal resources such as FIGURATIVE LANGUAGE and ALLUSIONS. POINT OF VIEW indicates the position from which the story is told. The storyteller often chooses to tell the story using the resources of a character different from himself or herself. The OMNISCIENT narrator allows the story to be told absolutely from all angles but can strain credulity and weaken the impression of realism. A LIMITED POINT OF VIEW, whether through a FIRST-PERSON ("I") NARRATOR, as in Sergio Ramírez's "Charles Atlas Also Dies," or a THIRD-PERSON NARRATOR ("he" or "she"—characters who may be either central or peripheral to the narrative action), leads to a greater sense of psychological realism and is more popular with twentieth-century writers. Ghassan Kanafani's story of Palestinian exile seen through the eyes of a young child receives much of its poignancy through the emerging subtext of the narrator's loss of innocence. The use of a limited point of view often leads to situational or dramatic IRONY, when the reader becomes aware of motives or actions of which the narrator or major characters are ignorant. In Pramoedya Ananta Toer's "Inem," for example, the young boy's assertion of his mother's "respectability" is ironically contrasted to the sexual and social abuse of eight-year-old Inem, which the mother condones. VERBAL IRONY is a favorite rhetorical device to enrich and deepen the interest of characters and of actions.

Sometimes stories take on ALLEGORICAL significance when their plots and characters deliberately suggest an import beyond the local, specific, and idiosyncratic. The death of the old man in Elizabeth Jolley's "Mr Parker's Valentine" gestures toward a criticism of the history of aggressive British immigration in Australia and its repercussions on an older settler society. Stories from societies under political stress and change, such as Amos Oz's "Nomad and Viper" or Ngugi wa Thiong'o's "The Return," often reverberate with extranarrative national reference. Or some writers such as Franz Kafka and Samuel Beckett set out to push narrative language to uses that overshoot the bounds of REALISM and suggest allegorical meanings, that is, meaning arrived at through correspondence with ideas outside of the realistic mode.

The interplay of plot, character, point of view, irony, and other narrative strategies and linguistic devices results in a pervasive TONE that distinguishes the style of one storyteller from another. Students of fiction should become familiar with the major literary terms, as they enable us to understand at a deeper level how stories are put together and how they function to evoke and express thought and feeling. The Glossary of Literary Terms in this anthology, therefore, is an essential tool for discussing and writing about fiction.

S.L.

A NOTE ON POETRY

For further explanation of the capitalized terms, refer to the Glossary of Literary Terms, pp. 1125–1141.

Many American readers prefer prose to poetry; in fact, books of poetry form a very small proportion of the publishing market. These readers usually complain that poetry is inaccessible; it is obscure or demands too much work to understand. Some people dislike poems for being too personal or subjective.

But poems come in all forms. Many poems are simple and straightforward. For example, Ezra Pound's two-line poem, "In a Station of the Metro," suggests the natural beauty of urban populations in its unexpected comparison of faces in a crowd to petals on a branch. Of course, the poem's very simplicity results in multiplying emotional associations and ideas for the reader.

Other poems—for example, William Butler Yeats's "Easter, 1916"—treat public events that are historically significant. Yeats's poem commemorates the sacrifices of Nationalist Irish revolutionaries who revolted against British rule in Dublin on Easter Monday 1916. Three hundred people were killed during the unsuccessful insurrection and sixteen ringleaders executed. The poem is both political and personal; it provides a dramatically and emotionally charged interpretation of personalities and events and memorializes them as representative of Irish nationalist culture. Yet it refrains from idealizing violence in the cause of simpleminded patriotism, weighing the "terrible beauty" of political idealism against the human costs: "Too long a sacrifice/Can make a stone of the heart."

Many poems are subjective utterances, coming from autobiographical circumstances, for example, Irving Layton's poem on his relationship with his wife, "Berry Picking," or Amrita Pritam's self-portrait, "Amrita Pritam." Others, such as W. H. Auden's "Musée des Beaux Arts," Adrienne Rich's "Diving into the Wreck," and Pablo Neruda's "The United Fruit Company," weave compelling ideas or images with emotion to arrive at an original or profound view of aspects of human experience.

A poem can be on any SUBJECT, ranging from the conventionally poetic, as in poems on love, birth, death, and other momentous topics, to the mundane and unexpected. Sylvia Plath's "Morning Song" celebrates the birth of her child, Federico García Lorca's "Lament for Ignacio Sanchez Mejias" mourns the death of the Andalusian bull-fighter, and Nissim Ezekiel's "Goodbye Party for Miss Pushpa T. S." makes fun of middle-class Indian social values. All are valid and worthwhile subjects.

No matter what the subject is, successful poems compose THEMES; they construct ideas and emotions that can be read as integrating a statement or expression of human experience. The theme of Plath's poem is motherhood and the ambiguous nature of that bond; of Lorca's poem, the tragic heroism of Hispanic culture; of Ezekiel's poem, the Indian middle class and its stuffy attitudes and pretensions. Some poems have less overt, more abstract or complicated themes that need to be carefully teased out. Rainer Maria Rilke's "Archaic Torso of Apollo" plays with philosophical ideas surrounding the emotional origin of art to arrive at the perception that art is radically transformative: "You must change your life."

Readers often disagree in their reading of these themes, depending on their INTERPRETATION of the poem's words. For example, the distinction between "country" and "people" (the two terms are sometimes read as synonymous) is a significant part of the theme in Sigaporean poet Lee, Tzu Pheng's "My country and my people." In finding identity with her people, the speaker is able to commit herself to a new postcolonial national identity. Differences in opinion on the meaning of a passage or even on the quality of the poem do not imply that there is only one correct way of understanding a poem or that every interpretation is correct. Rather, these disagreements indicate that the effect of poems depends a great deal on their DICTION or word choice. Poems contain AMBIGUOUS diction that is often deliberately multilayered in meaning. Compressed and dense associations of meaning, some of which are contradictory or PARADOXICAL, are a major quality of the language of poetry. George Seferis's poem "Tuesday" deliberately plays upon the random and indeterminate quality of twentieth-century life. The image of Livia Rimini, an actress who died in 1923 but whose figure continues to appear in movies, becomes a metaphor for the irrationality of technological post-war culture in which "someone living plays with someone dead," in which the past and present are intrinsically and tragically intertwined.

While poems generally depend for their effect on diction, poems from different nations and societies call upon different cultural traditions and linguistic conventions.

Poetry from Western countries has its roots in Greco-Roman epics, lyrics, and satires and also in Judeo-Christian literature. These poetic forms and a body of IMAGES and ALLUSIONS are common to many European literatures and are also found in poems from African, Asian, and South American postcolonial countries that have been influenced by Western education. The LYRIC expresses a subjective mood or condition, to elevate emotion. Eugenio Montale's lyrical celebration of Mediterranean landscape, "The Lemon Trees," speaks also to the relationship between the natural world and humans, a relation in which humans, oppressed in "our clamorous cities," may still feel the influence "of the lemon blaze" to inspire them to the transcendence of "songs." In contrast, SATIRE criticizes characteristics of human experience, through mockery, irony, humor, and other rhetorical devices. Ouologuem Yambo's "When Black Men's Teeth Speak Out" satirizes the white colonizers' stereotypes of Africans, exposing their fears of African "savagery" as a means of dehumanizing and controlling the African colonies.

In the Western tradition, some conventions have been privileged over time. Up to the twentieth century, poems were usually arranged according to a FORM or pattern that involved an interplay of elements of RHYTHM, RHYME, repetition, and set numbers of lines. Among the most popular of these forms are the SONNET, a fourteen-line poem (for instance, Rainer Maria Rilke's "Archaic Torso of Apollo" and Allen Curnow's "The Skeleton of the Great Moa"), and the ODE. The modernists, however, rejected the observance of strict forms, and by the 1920's, FREE VERSE became accepted and is now the most popular form in the West.

In non-Western countries, other traditions prevailed. In Japan, for example, poets used traditional forms that depended on syllabic and line count, such as the HAIKU. Post-World-War-Two poets, however, turned to free verse, as they moved away from the formal constriction of these ancient forms. In many African countries where literature was chiefly ORAL, poems were chants or songs committed to communal memory and performed in connection with public events such as weddings, harvests, or certain tribal rituals. Ghanaian poet Kofi Awoonor preserves the declamatory quality of oral poetry in his poem "Night of My Blood." Using repetitions of lines, single words, and images, the poem constructs a communal speaker through the use of the first-person plural, while the syntactical arrangement of ideas into short sentences and phrases permits a mnemonic simplicity that is a feature of oral poetry. However, by the twentieth century, the literature produced in countries such as China, India, Japan, Nigeria, and South Africa showed the influence of Western forms. Japanese and Chinese poets began to write in free verse; some African writers, writing in English, used the conventions of English PROSODY. But this cross-cultural connection works both ways. American poets, for example, have also adapted the haiku for their use and are returning to the oral tradition of performance poetry in order to reach a larger audience, as seen in the work of Allen Ginsberg. Ezra Pound turned to Chinese poetry as an influence for his imagistic manifesto.

Some elements are common in the way language works across cultures. Among them are IMAGES, FIGURES OF SPEECH, and SYMBOLS. Images, while generally visual in nature, also appeal to our senses; they arouse vivid mental and sensory pictures that move us at a level beyond the rational. Figures of speech are language devices that work intellectually and emotionally. For example, the SIMILE and the METAPHOR work by means of noting correspondence and relation between a TENOR and a VEHICLE that are unlike each other. The articulation of similarity can be witty and can uncover something unexpected or insightful. METONYMY, where a part stands for the whole, and SYNEDOCHE, where the whole stands for a part, are examples of figures of speech that work through intellectual recognition and compression. Poetry, like all forms of literature, uses SYMBOLISM to convey meanings in a richly suggestive, nonlogical manner. SYMBOLS are figures or images that take on accumulated, multilayered, sometimes divergent meanings, drawn from the writer's private associations and tapping the readers' and public body of meanings and understandings.

Whatever the particular configuration of form, language, and theme, the vividness, beauty of sound and form, and wit or nobility of emotion and thought of successful poems resonate in our memories.

S.L.

A NOTE ON DRAMA

For further explanation of the capitalized terms, refer to the Glossary of Literary Terms, pp. 1125–1141.

The major difference between drama and fiction or poetry is that drama is performed. Plays come from a tradition of public performance; they are visual, visible, a shared and communal experience in which we, the audience, are immersed in a spectacle enacted live before us.

The Western drama claims its origins in Greek culture, from the plays produced by Athenian dramatists written about the sixth century B.C. These dramas, composed as TRAGEDY or COMEDY, were presented as part of the civic and religious rituals that defined Athenian society. Later, philosophers such as Aristotole analyzed the various conventions of these dramatic forms, which continue to shape the composition of plays to this present day.

Playwrights from every era experiment with and change the major conventions of drama. The PLOT, as the organization of action, was traditionally conceived as a sequence of important moments arranged chronologically, with an introduction, series of complications intensifying the conflict, a CLIMAX clinching the fate of the central characters, a RESOLUTION, and a DENOUEMENT that concludes and summarizes the issues. This triangular shape still operates in many modern plays. Friedrich Duerrenmatt's play *The Visit*, for example, gets much of its power from the suspenseful yet inevitable development of the classic plot structure. The play is composed of three acts. The first act introduces the major characters and dramatic situation. The townspeople of Güllen are preparing for a visit from Claire Zachanassian, an immensely wealthy woman who had grown up in Güllen and who, they hope, will serve as benefactress to their economic troubles. She consents to give them one billion marks on the condition that they execute a fellow citizen who had wronged her when she was seventeen. The second act picks up on the town's initial rejection of her offer to show the citizens' ambivalence and their gradual moral corruption. The final act completes this revenge story and moral tragedy. Anton Schill is murdered, a sacrificial scapegoat for the town's original act of injustice, and the town becomes financially revitalized. The second act, therefore, provides the complications, with Schill's attempts to save himself and to escape the town. The third act contains the climax, when the townspeople and Schill debate his execution, and a denouement, when he is murdered by the male citizens of Güllen. The play's resolution shows the two objectives achieved: Claire Zachanassian leaves with Schill's body in a coffin, and the community of Güllen is economically revitalized.

The traditional plot is less obvious in some contemporary plays. Within the two acts of August Wilson's *Joe Turner's Come and Gone* is the solution to the mystery of the stranger Loomis and his missing wife. But that resolution is not achieved through a central climatic scene. Instead, the plot is looser. It does not concentrate on an individual hero and his or her fate. Instead, its open structure permits a more relaxed inclusion of other important characters (such as the boarding house owner, Seth Holly, and Bynum Walker, the roof worker) and thus a broader dramatization of the African-American community and its history of immigration from the South to the Northern states of the United States.

CHARACTERS were traditionally conceived as either tragic or comic figures, appealing to high tragedy or low comedy. Many dramatists have broken away from this convention, introducing both tragic and comic characters in the same play or even mixing up these elements of nobility and farce in the same character. Duerrenmatt's *The Visit* is relentlessly tragic in conception, but Alu and Makuri in Soyinka's *The Swamp Dwellers* begin as comic characters in a play that is both satirical and tragic in its criticism of the corruption in traditional Nigerian society and of the social disintegration caused by urbanization.

We understand characters through their actions and motivations, but we understand actions as the consequence of character. Many plays function on this level of psychological REALISM, with internal consistency between action and character producing a believable plot. Many contemporary plays, however, ignore consistency and construct elements of SURREALISM and the ABSURD to work on our imaginations. In Kobo Abe's *The Man Who Turned into a Stick,* major characters are non-realistic. The central action—a man's death, perhaps a suicide, in which he is transformed into a stick and is so catalogued by a man and a woman from Hell—is clearly a FANTASY; but the play's theme, its criticism of the mass conformity of twentieth-century urban existence, carries a philosophical message that is meaningful, especially in the context of Japanese values that elevate the social group over the individual person.

While plays from non-Western cultures call on other literary traditions than those of Greek drama, they are usually related in origin to public, communal, and religious rituals. The Japanese theatrical tradition of NOH plays makes greater use of elaborate costumes, masks, rituals, music, and mime than the Western tradition of realistic drama. But much contemporary drama, both Eastern and Western, has been affected cross-culturally; Irish playwright William Butler Yeats was influenced by the Noh tradition, while many dramatists from Asia, Africa, and South America have learned from Greek, Shakespearean, and Western experimental theater.

Wole Soyinka, a Nigerian writer, was educated in English literature. His play *The Swamp Dwellers* criticizes the political corruption of his society through its portrayal of Nigerian folk beliefs, Islamic practices, and familial and communal relations. These "local" materials are deepened by their cross-cultural use of such figures as the Serpent, the blind man, and the twin brothers, figures that possess symbolic meaning in many African and Anglo-European cultures.

We recognize in Soyinka's play common elements of plot and character development, yet we also understand that the play refers specifically to Nigerian social and political circumstances. The Kadiye, or religious leader, who exploits the villagers' gullibility to enrich himself is an indigenous character, just as the blind man who prefers not to depend on the religious charity of the Muslim population to support him is an indigenous character. But their contrasting relations to Igwezu, the disillusioned homecoming son, teaches us across cultures to reject the corrupt exploiter and to look for the faithful "bondsman." Soyinka's literary achievement allows readers to appreciate the different culture in which the play is grounded and to discover a common human experience that makes that culture accessible.

The performative, public, and diversified aspects of drama, whether produced in Africa, the United States, or elsewhere, have made it a persuasive and appealing form. It has been able to use the lyric possibilities of poetry, the resources of spectacle and music, and the narrative structures of fiction to keep audiences in their seats and entertained for centuries and across cultures.

S.L.

THE OTHER GENRE:
A NOTE ON TRANSLATION

Technologies such as mass media and communications, air travel, and international corporate methods of production make it inevitable that we begin to relate to our environment and to each other in a global manner. Contacts with people from other nations lead us to an increased effort to understand their cultures and values. As language and literature are among the chief vehicles and repositories of culture, there is a greater need for translation.

Translation occurs even when the language used is the same. For example, English-speaking societies such as those in Australia and New Zealand have a different vocabulary, specific to their particular environments and cultural histories. The word "bush," signifying the outback or wilderness of the Australian continent, is the site for multiple significances, positive and negative, and is related to a history that includes the aboriginal peoples as well as colonial settlement. Readers have to undertake that kind of cultural translation whenever they approach English-language works from different countries.

Translation becomes more problematic when the work is in a language very different from English. Many of the selections in this anthology are from languages with venerable histories and rich literary traditions. Some of the allusive qualities are lost in translation, as are the effects of sounds, rhythms, even syntactic arrangements. When reading translations, we must keep in mind that while they may provide us with the meaning and some of the sense of style of the work, they in no way reproduce the original in all its oral, aural, and even signifying character.

Most readers of this anthology, however, will read the translations of works written in languages other than English as if they were English-language texts. The effect of good translations is that of smooth, clear communication that manages to capture the idiosyncratic style and the meaning of the particular work. A good translator is usually supposed to be invisible and works instead to make the text or the author visible. Translation, therefore, is a demanding art that serves at least two masters, the original work and the audience for the translation. Some critics and translators are now asserting that translation as a separate art also serves the creative goals of the translator.

Translators have usually been unprivileged in the literary world. They have sometimes gone unnamed or unrecognized. As the art of translation has become more noticed recently, we are beginning to pay more attention to how the translated piece has its own integrity. It is obvious that a translation is neither the original text transformed intact into English or a work written originally in English. Instead, it is receiving critical attention as a third product in which the translator's struggle with the original text becomes an important element as creative achievement.

Reading the translations in this anthology, we may validly ask what was omitted or erased from the original in the translator's attempt to achieve fluency and coherence. If we know the original language, we can undertake to answer this question. Or we can find another translation of the same text to investigate how the translators' different purposes or positions in relation to their roles and to the values of language affected their translation and therefore our understanding of the original work.

Being aware of the "barrier" that translations inevitably raises even as it allows us access to another language story or poem reminds us that literature is not a "transparent" product that offers us easy, simple, and clear insights into human behavior. Instead, translation reminds us that the meaning we make out of language is unstable and opaque, that is, dense and, frequently, indeterminate.

WRITING ABOUT
LITERATURE

Writing about literature is an important enterprise. Like reading, it results in an act of engagement and participation in literary experience. It offers you the opportunity to confront that experience and to explore its broader context. Through the writing process, you are challenged to look at literature in artistic terms as well as in relation to the intellectual ideas and cultural milieu that helped form it. Writing about literature requires, therefore, familiarity with the terminology that describes literary works (plot, characterization, point of view) as well as a basic understanding of the social and historical background of the literature under discussion. If you choose to employ a theoretical or interdisciplinary approach (feminist, psychoanalytical, cultural materialist), you should become familiar with the fundamental tenets of that methodology and learn to apply it. For most writing assignments for this book, it will be sufficient to examine literature according to aesthetic criteria or in relation to its subject matter and thematic concerns.

There are a variety of ways to write about literature. The types of assignments required of you can be classified in four categories: *analysis, explication, evaluation,* and *comparison and contrast.* These approaches offer you the opportunity to clarify, explain, and evaluate your experiences of a given literary work. The first two are related types of interpretative writing. Both examine literary works to understand better their meaning and effect. *Analysis* involves looking at the various elements of a literary text in relation to its overall structure. A focus on images or characterization, for example, can provide insights into the significance and artistry of a given work. Similarly, *explication,* a line-by-line or word-by-word examination of a complex passage, affords you the challenge of unfolding the layers of meaning of a poem, play, or short story. Writing assignments that require you to *evaluate* literature entail interpretation of the meaning and significance of themes and subject matter. They also may involve exploration of the broader social and cultural values implicit in literary works. *Comparison and contrast* examines the similarity and differences between elements within the same work or in relation to comparable features in different works. The possibilities are numerous. You may be asked to discuss characters within a single story or from different sources. You might be required to look at the ways writers approach the same subject or treat similar thematic concerns. Finally, literary assignments that correspond to any of the above categories usually incorporate elements from one of the others. For example, analysis and evaluation often employ comparison and contrast techniques. It is important to remember that these approaches are merely organizing tools for examining literature. Writing assignments are meant to help you discover the subtlety and complexity of a poem, play, or story.

Choosing a topic is the first step in writing about literature. Frequently, instructors will assign a specific topic or provide a list of topics from which to choose, along with guidelines about the length and general format of the paper. Other times you will be left on your own to choose a subject and organize your papers. When this is the case, it is important to know beforehand how long the paper needs to be. This information is important, for the length will often determine which subjects might be appropriate for the assignment. Three pages might be adequate for a discussion of women's oppression in Bessie Head's "The Collector of Treasures," but to compare and contrast her view of traditional African society with Wole Soyinka's in *The Swamp Dwellers* would probably take at least five pages. Research papers that incorporate information and ideas from secondary sources—biography, literary criticism, cultural history—will be longer and entail a more extensive treatment of their subject than routine assignments. Whatever the length, successful completion of a literary paper will require a careful rereading of primary texts and a following through of the basic organizing procedures for formal writing: taking notes, developing arguments, making outlines, writing drafts, and revising.

Equally important to writing literary papers is finding and assessing outside information on a selected topic. This process is integral to writing research papers, but it is also useful preparation for routine writing assignments. Some background information is a prerequisite for understanding most selections from *One World of Literature*. Interpretation of Albert Camus's "The Guest" or Nadine Gordimer's "A Soldier's Embrace" will require some knowledge of African history. Likewise, Lu Xün's stories should be read and analyzed within the context of the social and cultural upheavals that were occurring in China during the early twentieth century. Reference librarians can usually help you locate this type of information and find the secondary sources that discuss the literature and authors under consideration. These materials are listed in a variety of sources, including card catalogues, computer data bases, encyclopedias, bibliographies, and indexes to periodicals. If they are not available at your college library, they can be ordered on interlibrary loan from other libraries. The bibliography for *One World of Literature* offers a list of secondary sources organized by geographical region. You should also consult the following:

Jahn, Janheinz. *A Bibliography of Neo-African Literature from Africa, America and the Caribbean*. London: André Deutsch, 1965.

MLA International Bibliography of Books and Articles on Modern Language and Literature. New York: MLA, 1921–.

Oxford History of English Literature, The. 12 vols. Oxford, Eng.: Oxford University Press, 1945–, in progress.

Penguin Companion to World Literature, The. 4 vols. New York: McGraw-Hill, 1969–71.

Schweik, Robert C., and Riesner, Dieter. *Reference Sources in English and American Literature: An Annotated Bibliography.* New York: Norton, 1977.

While collecting research materials, it is important to evaluate them for their quality and reliability. You can accomplish this by comparing articles and relying on those that document and support their findings with references to primary and secondary materials. You might want to consult materials that present different points of view. When writing about Russian literature, it would be useful to have an understanding of the debates surrounding the Russian Revolution. Similarly, a discussion of Sergio Ramírez's "Charles Atlas Also Dies" or Pablo Neruda's "The United Fruit Co." will require some knowledge of the conflicting views of U.S. foreign policy, and an evaluation of D. H. Lawrence's fiction should take into account the different interpretations of his work. Ideas and information from secondary sources help you develop and sharpen your arguments. Documenting supporting materials gives evidence that you have made a genuine effort in coming to terms with your subject.

N.S.

DOCUMENTATION

Documentation is a method of acknowledging the sources of information and ideas that you use in your paper. It is also a way to indicate the research that you have done on your subject. As a rule, you should give credit to your sources whenever you quote, paraphrase, or summarize. Equally important, you need to acknowledge the origins of the ideas you have incorporated into your paper. Failure to give credit to your sources is to commit plagiarism, to steal the intellectual property of others. Documentation should be viewed as an opportunity to show your ability to synthesize information and arrive at opinions after a careful consideration of diverse perspectives.

The style of documentation recommended for students of literature is the one devised by the Modern Languages Association (MLA). This method entails three procedures: the preparation of parenthetical references in the text, a list of works cited, and explanatory notes. There is, in addition, an alternative MLA style in which note numbers are used and paired with footnotes or endnotes followed by a bibliography.

PARENTHETICAL REFERENCES IN THE TEXT

MLA documentation uses references inserted in parentheses within the text that refer to a list of works cited at the end of the paper. Most often a reference consists of the author's last name and a page number.

Salman Rushdie writes novels to explore postcolonial responsibility (Brennan 27).

In cases where you use more than one source by the same author, you should include a shortened title in the parenthetical reference.

Popular humor and traditional storytelling techniques are employed by Egyptian writers to criticize the Arab world's economic and cultural dependency on the West (Harlow, "Arab Challenge" 117).

When the author's name or the title of the work is mentioned in the text, only a page reference is necessary.

Wole Soyinka argues in *Myth, Literature and the African World* that African writers reinterpret history and contemporary reality for the purpose of racial self-retrieval (105).

There is different punctuation for paraphrases and summaries, direct quotations incorporated into the text, and quotations set off from the text.

Paraphrases and summaries:

Despite his conservative politics and elitist aesthetic values, Yeats remains a great national poet who articulates the experience, aspirations and vision of a people suffering under colonial domination (Said 69).

Direct quotations incorporated into the text:

As Mary Layoun reveals, culture is "one of the areas of struggle for power over society, for the dominance and continuation of certain values, ideas, or ideologies against the challenge of other values, ideas, or ideologies" (59).

According to Raymond Williams, a distinguishing characteristic of Modernism and avant-garde movements is a "rejection of the existing social order and its culture" and a "recourse to a simpler art: either the primitive or exotic, as in the interest in African and Chinese objects and forms, or the folk or popular elements of their native cultures" (59).

Abiola Irele explains that Senghor's doctrine of African socialism is "an ideal in which the spiritual values of traditional Africa are integrated into the process of modernization through new forms of social and political organization and technological progress . . ." (79).

Quotations set off from the text:

. . . this mutual recognition of the power and the seriousness of literature on the part of both writers and dictatorships accounts for the historical phenomenon that the risk of persecution and the writer's commitment frequently increase in direct ratio to each other. (Feuerwerker 75)

EXAMPLES OF FORMATS MOST COMMONLY USED FOR PARENTHETICAL REFERENCES

A work by two or three authors:

When E. M. Foster's *A Passage to India* appeared in 1924, it was the first serious novel of empire by an English writer and the first to mention the possibility of eventual self-government (White and Couzens 5).

An African aesthetic must be grounded in an African sensibility, and the incontestably uncontaminated reservoir of African sensibility is the African oral tradition (Chinweizu, Jemie, and Madubuike 296).

A work by more than three authors:

Beginning with Lu Xün, Chinese short story writers frequently write of modern intellectuals like themselves, who, while wishing to accomplish something important for their country, soon became aware of their individual limitations and the magnitude of the reactionary forces with which they have to contend (Hsia et al. 16).

A work with volume and page number:

The works of Joyce, Proust and Kafka are no longer psychological novels in the sense that the great novels of the nineteenth century were (Hauser 4: 238).

THE WORKS CITED LIST

Parenthetical references refer to a Works Cited list that identifies all the sources that you have used in your paper. This list should appear at the end of your paper as a separate section continuing the page-number sequence of the previous pages. It should be arranged alphabetically according to the last name of each author or the first word of the title—excluding the articles *a, an,* or *and*—if the author is unknown. If you wish to name all the works you have consulted in writing your paper, you should use the title Works Consulted.

Single author:

Martin, Gerald. *Journeys through the Labyrinth: Latin American Fiction in the Twentieth Century.* London: Verso, 1989.

Two or three authors:

First, Ruth, and Ann Scott. *Olive Schreiner.* New York: Schocken, 1980.

More than three authors:

Rubin, Louis D., Jr., et al. *The History of Southern Literature.* Baton Rouge: Louisiana State UP, 1985.

Two or more works by the same author:

Cudjoe, Selwyn. *V. S. Naipaul.* Amherst: U of Massachusetts P, 1988.

———. *Resistance and Caribbean Literature.* Athens: Ohio UP, 1980.

An edited book:

Kaplan, E. Ann, ed. *Postmodernism and Its Discontents.* London: Verso, 1988.

A book with a volume number:

Bigsby, C. W. E., ed. *The Black American Writer.* 2 vols. Baltimore: Penguin, 1969. Vol. 2.

A short story in an anthology:

Mahfouz, Naguib. "The Conjourer Made Off with the Dish." *Egyptian Short Stories.* Ed. Denys Johnson-Davies. Washington, DC: Three Continents Press, 1990. 61–67.

A poem in an anthology:

> Blok, Alexander. "The Twelve." *An Anthology of Russian Literature in the Soviet Period from Gorki to Pasternak.* Ed. Bernard Guilbert Guerney. New York: Random House, 1960. 16–27.

A play in an anthology:

> Mayakovsky, Vladimir. *The Bedbug. Russian Literature of the Twenties.* Ed. Carl R. Proffer et al. Ann Arbor: Ardis, 1987. 467–502.

An article in an anthology:

> Clingman, Stephen. "Writing in a Fractured Society: The Case of Nadine Gordimer." *Literature and Society in South Africa.* Ed. Landeg White and Tim Couzens. New York: Longman, 1984.

More than one article from an anthology:

Cite complete information for anthology, and list individual selections separately in alphabetical order with author, title, editor's last name, and the page numbers for the selection.

> Goldman, Merle, ed. *Modern Chinese Literature in the May Fourth Era.* Cambridge, MA: Harvard UP, 1977.

> Vogel, Ezra F. "The Unlikely Heroes: The Social Role of May Fourth Writers." Goldman, 145–159.

A translation:

> Infante, G. Cabrera. *Three Trapped Tigers.* Trans. Donald Gardner and Suzanne Jill Levine. New York: Harper & Row, 1971.

An article in a journal:

> Raskin, Jonah. "Imperialism: Conrad's Heart of Darkness." *Journal of Contemporary History* 2, no. 2 (1967): 109–127.

An article in a magazine:

> "Voices from the Avant Garde." *Down Beat* 6 Sept. 1964: (+ indicates that the article appears on pages that are not continuous.)

An article in a daily newspaper:

> Wright, Robin. "Achebe Writes about Developing Nigeria the Way Faulkner Did about the South." *Christian Science Monitor* 26 Dec. 1974: 9.

An interview:

> Baraka, Amiri. Interview. *Amiri Baraka/LeRoi Jones: The Quest for a Populist Modernism.* With Werner Sollars. New York: Columbia UP, 1978. 247–62.

A lecture or talk:

Jameson, Fredric. "On Literary and Cultural Import—Substitution in the Third World: The Case of the Testimonio." Morgan Lecture, Dickinson College. Carlisle, PA. 11 Apr. 1986.

EXPLANATORY NOTES

Explanatory notes with superscript numbers are used to cite several sources at the same time and to provide discussion or explanation that you do not want to include in the body of your paper. They give you the opportunity to comment on your sources and to clarify your arguments. The Explanatory Notes section should appear at the end of your paper before the Works Cited page and should follow the numbering sequence of the previous pages.

To Cite Several Sources

In the paper:

Black British culture is an important subject of research in England today.[2]

In the note:

[2] Brennen 5–11; Gilroy 173–219; Hall 236–52; Sivanandan 3–50.

For Explanation

In the paper:

The first two novels of Ayi Kwei Armah are set in Ghana during the early 1960's when Kwame Nkrumah was in power.[3]

In the note:

[3] See Davidson for a balanced view of the historical background to this period. Armah's portrayal of the independence movement coincides in many ways with Davidson's, though there is a significant difference in their views of the post independence period. Davidson is much more understanding of the problems that Nkrumah had to face when he became head of state.

EXAMPLE OF WORKS CITED

Barlow, Tani E. Introduction. *I Myself Am a Woman: Selected Writings of Ding Ling.* By Ding Ling. Boston: Beacon, 1989. 1–45.

Bjorge, Gary J. "Sophia's Diary: An Introduction." *Tamkang Review* 5. 1 (1974): 97–100.

Dolezelová-Velingerová, Milena. "The Origins of Modern Chinese Literature." Goldman, 17–35.

Feuerwerker, Yi-tsi. "The Changing Relationship between Literature and Life: Aspects of the Writer's Role in Ding Ling." Goldman, 281–307.

———. *Ding Ling's Fiction: Ideology and Narrative in Modern Chinese Literature.* Cambridge, MA: Harvard UP, 1982.

———. "Women as Writers in the 1920's and 1930's." *Women in Chinese Society* Ed. Margery Wolf and Roxanne Witke. Stanford: Stanford UP, 1975. 143–168.

Fitzgerald, C. P. *The Birth of Communist China.* Baltimore: Penguin, 1964.

Goldman, Merle. *Literary Dissent in Communist China.* Cambridge, MA: Harvard UP, 1967.

———, ed. *Modern Chinese Literature in the May Fourth Era.* Cambridge, MA: Harvard UP, 1977.

Kristeva, Julia. *About Chinese Women,* New York: Urzin, 1977.

Lee, Leo Ou-fan. *The Romantic Generation of Chinese Writers.* Cambridge, MA: Harvard UP, 1973.

Ling, Ding. *I Myself Am a Woman: Selected Writings of Ding Ling.* Boston: Beacon, 1984.

Snow, Helen Foster. *Women in Modern China.* The Hague: Mouton, 1967.

Spence, Jonathan D. *The Gate of Heavenly Peace: The Chinese and Their Revolution, 1895–1980.* New York: Viking, 1981.

ALTERNATE MLA STYLE: NOTE NUMBERS COMBINED WITH FOOTNOTES/ENDNOTES

Note numbers:

Raised note numbers follow in consecutive order the quotation or information being cited.

At the beginning of *Notebook on the Return to My Native Land,* Aimé Césaire confronts the destitute population of his birthplace: "a clamouring crowd . . . deaf to its own cry of hunger and misery, revolt and hatred."[1]

If you include several quotations from the same text, use parenthetical citations after the first note. This will reduce the number of footnotes or endnotes.

Toward the end of the poem, Césaire is revitalized and envisions a new destiny for his people: "And now suddenly strength and life attack me like a bull . . . veins and veinlets throng with new blood, the fire hoarded in volcanoes, and the gigantic seismic pulse beats the measure of a living body within my blaze" (84).

Footnotes/endnotes:

Raised notes in the body of the paper correspond to footnotes or end-notes. Footnotes should appear at the bottom of the page of the reference four spaces below the last line of the text. Endnotes should be listed in a section at the end of the paper. As a rule, footnotes or endnotes should be supplemented and followed by a bibliography which lists research sources in alphabetical order in the same manner as a Works Cited or Works Consulted section.

Example of Endnotes

[1] Gerald Martin, "On Magical and Social Realism in García Márquez," *Gabriel García Márquez: New Readings.* Ed. Bernard McGuirk and Richard Cardwell (Cambridge: Cambridge UP, 1987) 95–113.

[2] Jean Franco, *The Modern Culture of Latin America: Society and the Artist* (Harmondsworth, Eng.: Penguin, 1970) 20–35.

[3] Edward Galeano, *Open Veins of Latin America* (New York: Monthly Review, 1973) 225–35.

[4] Franco 135

[5] The Sandinista revolution like the Mexican and Cuban revolutions which preceded it became a source of literary inspiration.

[6] John S. Brushwood, "Reality and Imagination in the Novels of García Márquez," *Latin American Literary Review* 13. 25 (1985): 9–14.

GLOSSARY OF
LITERARY TERMS

absurdism A philosophy associated with twentieth-century avant-garde theater, emphasizing irrational elements and human isolation. Time is fluid, characters unfixed, and plot indeterminate. The basis for existentialism.

allegory A representation by which persons, actions, or abstract concepts also stand for some other meaning than themselves. Strict allegories possess one-to-one correspondence, but many contemporary narratives are open to allegorical interpretation.

alliteration Repetition of initial sounds in two or more words of lines of poetry or prose, for ornamental and unifying effect.

allusion A reference to person, event, or situation often familiar to, sometimes remote from, the reader, to add knowledge and other dimensions of feeling to the statement.

ambiguity Uncertainty of meaning that can multiply interpretations, resulting in significant complexity, often leading to obscurity or confusion.

antagonist The character set in opposition to the protagonist or main character in a story or drama, giving rise to *conflict*.

apostrophe A figure of speech in which an absent person or a personified concept is addressed directly.

archetype An image or symbol that functions as a primary source of or merging place for unconscious and subconscious meanings shared collectively by groups of people with common histories and backgrounds.

atmosphere The pervasive mood or tone of a story, usually suggested through description or staging of setting, as in a play; often resulting from choice of language. [See *tone*.]

autobiography A self-narrative tending to introspection, offering intimate revelations of the author. Much contemporary literature exploits autobiographical materials as authors attempt to create greater psychological realism by lessening distance between themselves and their readers.

avant-garde From the French, experimental styles of writing that show innovation in subjects and techniques and often criticize established conventions.

Bildungsroman From the German, a narrative on the early life and psychological, moral, and social development of a major character. Literally, "novel of education."

bourgeois From the French, referring to a member of the middle class. Often used for characters and concepts guided by money and property values. Sometimes used to criticize a conventional or unrefined character.

canon A criterion or standard of measurement; more commonly, referring to the generally approved list of great works of literature or accepted list of an author's work.

catharsis From Aristotle, a term signifying the purgation of feelings and spiritual relief gained at the end of a tragedy.

character The sum total of features that compose a person or animal. May refer to moral and ethical attributes, also to persons in stories, novels, plays, and poems. The central character is also known as the main character or protagonist; the opposing character is the antagonist. Characters who have smaller roles are minor characters.

chorus From Greek tragedy, an uninvolved agent or agents who provide commentary on the main action of a narrative.

class A contemporary tool of literary analysis that takes into account the material conditions of the production of texts and the expression of class character and struggle in these texts.

climax The turning point in a narrative, noted for its intensity and accompanying resolution.

collage Inserting and combining disparate styles and literary forms to create a fresh composition.

collective unconscious A Jungian term arguing that racially inherited images and ideas persist in individual consciousness and unconscious motivations are therefore collectively shared as well as personal.

comedy Amusing literature often using farcical elements; although associated with light and humorous effects, it can sometimes be satirical and serious in intention.

complication A difficult situation, often unexpectedly changing the course of a plot, developing conflict, resulting in more complex characterization, and leading to the climax.

conceit An extended metaphor or image that depends on surprising and fanciful analogy, sometimes remarkable and useful, sometimes overly artificial and strained.

conclusion The closing part of a plot that usually establishes a resolution of earlier conflicts.

concreteness The quality of verisimilitude achieved when writers provide particular sensory details that make thoughts and emotions tangible.

confession(al) Related to writing that discloses apparently autobiographical, intimate, and psychological revelations; a frankness, openness, and daring in self-exposure.

conflict The opposition between characters or forces that structures a plot. Conflict may be physical, as in human against natural forces; or social, between characters; or internal and psychological, within the same person.

connotation Different meanings, either communal or private in nature, associated with a word and not usually given in the dictionary. Compare denotation.

convention A characteristic of a literary genre that has remained unchallenged for a long time and become a fixed expectation.

crisis A structural element in a plot that takes place when opposing forces come together decisively and a significant turning point occurs that leads to a climax.

criticism The process that evaluates strengths and weaknesses and judges the worth of a work.

denotation The exact or literal meaning of a word as given in a dictionary.

denouement From the French, meaning "unraveling" of a plot, following the climax.

dialect A distinctive variation of a language caused by regional, class, and social differences. Dialect is used in dialogue to contrast and express differences in education, class, and social background among characters.

diction Selection of words and patterns of sounds indicating the level of choices that result in a characteristic style.

didacticism That which takes on a moralistic tenor and adopts specific causes. Didactic works may become preachy, political, or propagandistic in effect.

digression A passage that strays from the main theme or plot. Sometimes digressions weaken the narrative pace, but usually they add variety and interest.

documentation The providing of evidence drawn from various documents; citation of authority to support statements. In papers, footnotes and bibliography are major forms of documentation.

dramatic monologue A literary form in which a speaker addresses a silent auditor and reveals a dramatic situation and his own character traits.

dramatic poetry Poems that use dramatic forms such as the monologue to dramatize conflict and character.

economy Concision and precision in use of words.

elegy A poem mourning for the dead.

elision The omission of vowels, consonants, or entire syllables in pronunciation or of entire passages.

emblem A figure, design, or symbol representing an object.

enjambment The result that occurs when a thought or phrase straddles two lines of poetry, continuing past the end of one line to the next.

epic Usually refers to a long narrative poem with elevated language and heroic elements.

epiphany In literature, a sudden intuition presenting a moment of revelation for the character, coined by James Joyce in this context.

episodic A work composed of related but loosely connected stories or scenes.

erotic Referring to sexually suggestive elements in language or to themes dealing with physical passion.

ethnic The condition of belonging to a group of people who are different from other groups because of different cultural practices, language backgrounds, economic or social behavior. These differences are said to have given rise to distinctive bodies of literature, as in African American or Native American literatures. Ethnicity as primordial difference has also resulted in conflict and state oppression, as between the Tamils and Singhalese in Sri Lanka.

etymology The discipline that studies word derivations and histories of particular words.

euphemism The substitution of mild or indirect words for stronger language that may offend.

exegesis Interpretation of difficult passages.

experimental Used to describe writing that replaces conventional forms and language with innovative techniques, sometimes resulting in difficulty and obscurity, but often effective in evoking fresh responses and treating new subjects.

explication An explanation of a literary work; critical analysis based on close reading.

exposition A discourse that defines, interprets, and explains.

Expressionism A term given to the experimental works from Germany (1910–c.1922); often used as a general term to characterize common features; e.g., a sense of crisis, violence, disturbance, urgency; a critical vision of urban and industrial societies taking various forms as nostalgia, comic pessimism, and irrationalism.

fable A simple, short narrative intended to teach moral truths.

fallacy A misleading idea or argument; incorrect reasoning.

fantasy A literary work in which action occurs in an unreal world; having deliberately unreal characters; displaying bizarre and exaggerated elements of imagination.

feminism A method of intellectual and practical analysis that places the perceptions and rights of women first in order to correct a history of male or patriarchal bias. Feminist theories attempt to understand representation from a woman's position, seek to undermine objectivist interpretations that omit gender-charged content, and explain women's writing strategies as specific to their condition of oppression and resistance.

fetishism A displacement of psychic and emotional energy from its original target into a secondary object, as in the centuries-old practice in China of fetishizing the smallness of women's feet that led to the custom of foot binding.

fiction An imagined or invented narrative, intended to entertain and instruct. Usually applied to short stories and novels, although dramas and poems also contain elements of fiction.

figurative language Language that exploits figures of speech, usually making use of correspondence and recognition of likeness. Metaphors and similes build up on recognition of similarities between two otherwise unlike objects; metonymy names a part for the whole, as in using the flag to represent the nation. A synedoche uses the whole to stand for the part, as in John Doe to represent the American people.

first-person narrator The person who tells a story from his or her point of view. The first-person narrator can be the main character or an intimately involved character or a distant yet sympathetic observer.

flashback A narrative technique that moves the action to a time prior to the preceding passage.

folklore Stories, beliefs, and practices associated for a long period of time with a particular group of people; often orally transmitted material, but increasingly preserved in writing.

folktale A narrative that is orally communicated and preserved as part of a people's tradition.

foreshadowing Verbal and dramatic clues that prepare us for future action.

form The structure of a literary work, including its overt arrangement and style. Sometimes thought of as an external scheme that organizes the subject matter, the most successful forms of literature demonstrate a close integration of the pattern of the work and its content.

free verse Poetry that does not follow a regular form but uses such elements as speech patterns and other clues of grammar, emphasis, breath pauses to decide line breaks.

Freudian Referring to the concepts of Sigmund Freud (1856–1939), one of the most influential thinkers of the twentieth century. Among his most important concepts that have received general acceptance in the Western world are the ideas of the unconscious and subconscious mind, the nature of childhood sexuality, and the interpretation of dreams. His ideas have had medical impact on the treatment of psychosis, neurosis, and anxiety and have influenced the themes of many modern writers.

gender The interpretations and explanations of male and female identities and roles in societies; used as a tool for analyzing themes and styles in literature and for reading texts as vehicles of expression of gender.

genre A category or type of literary expression, usually referring to the major "families" of fiction, poetry, and drama, but also used for subcategories such as the short story, novella, novel, autobiography, and essay.

Gestalt From the German for "shape" or "form," a holistic unit, implying a word that is more than the sum of its parts and not capable of being divided from the sum of its parts.

Gothic A term used for a form of late eighteenth- and nineteenth-century novel that has grotesque action, an atmosphere of decadence and turmoil, and a decayed setting. A classic example of Gothic fiction is Mary Shelley's *Frankenstein*. Used today to describe literature with these characteristics.

haiku A traditional Japanese poetic form, composed of three lines divided into seventeen syllables (5, 7, 5). American poets adapted the form for imagistic effects, as in Ezra Pound's "In a Station of the Metro,"

in which the title forms an intrinsic part of the poem.

heuristic Describing any activity that leads to and results in discovering further knowledge for oneself. Most literature is heuristic in that it enables the reader to search out meanings to questions about existence and society.

hubris A concept in Greek tragedy signifying excessive pride or insolence giving rise to a tragic flaw that results in the downfall of the protagonist.

hyperbole The use of exaggeration for effect.

iambic The most common metrical foot in the English language, composed of two syllables, with the first syllable unaccented and the second accented.

icon A representation, usually visual, of a concept or figure; often referring to figures of religious importance.

idiom A special style of speaking or a special expression in a language that has no equivalent in another language; by analogy, signifying something unique or distinctive.

image A vivid mental picture or visualization, often suggested by figures of speech. A fundamental component of literature of the imagination.

imagery The body or group of images found in any one work; language that describes, presenting ideas, actions, and characters in visual ways.

in medias res A Latin term meaning "in the middle of matters"; the device of opening a narrative not at the beginning of the actions but somewhere into the plot.

innuendo The implication of a meaning without directly stating it; a suggestion.

intentional fallacy The mistake of evaluating a literary work in relation to the writer's purpose. Guiding one's interpretation by the expressed or inferred intention of the writer.

interpretation The explanation of a literary passage or work, to understand its meaning through an analysis of its strategies, structure, and language; e.g., to explicate a story's theme through a discussion of its actions and characters.

intimate observer A point of view that uses someone other than the major characters as the narrator (whether first- or third-person); a point of view that is detached yet involved.

invocation The act of calling upon a person, deity, or spirit for help or inspiration; a convention by which the poet addresses a muse or spirit for direction.

irony A technique of posing an attitude or significance that counters or opposes the explicit or stated one. A figure of speech in which one thing is said but the opposite is implied.

Jungian Referring to the concepts of Carl Gustav Jung (1875–1961), chiefly the concept of the collective unconscious that states that a reservoir of common images and associations exist as racial memory for groups of people and also among humans across national boundaries and cultures.

kabuki A popular Japanese theatrical form with stylized acting, music, dance, and elaborate makeup and costumes, in which actors are mimes and lines are spoken by onstage narrators.

lacuna A break or gap; a missing part of a manuscript; in the plural, lacunae, pertaining to obliterations from fading or tears.

lament An expression of sorrow and grief, indicating mourning.

legend A traditional story passed down through generations and accepted by the general population as true; related to myths and sometimes used for any fictitious tale concerning actual people and places.

lesbian Derived from Lesbos, a Greek island in the Aegean Sea, where the islanders were noted for sensual and erotic activities and literature. Refers to female homosexuals.

libido A term used by Freudian psychologists to refer to instinctual drives and desires, usually suggesting a sexual nature.

limited point of view The use of a narrator, whether first-person or third-person, whose restrictions or unreliability is clearly suggested, for purposes of psychological verisimilitude, humor, complexity, or irony.

linear Referring to a straight line, usually used to describe a plot or sequence of actions that follows chronological order.

literal Signifying exact or denotative sense of words; opposed to figurative meanings.

local color The kind of writing that provides particulars of speech, manners, and customs of a local geographical region; involved with verisimilitude of details about regional provinces and dialects.

localism A word, phrase, or usage used and understood in a specific region but not elsewhere.

logic The science of clear reasoning; the process of arriving at correct deductions or constructing reasoned arguments.

logocentric Used to describe the style of discourse that is based on logical argument; implying constructions of ideas proceeding by hierarchical, binary, or dichotomous structures.

lyric Having the qualities of music; subjective poetry expressing emotions and interior states of being; possessing spontaneity and expressiveness.

magic realism A style of writing that emerged as a tradition among Latin American writers, using a combination of fantastic and bizarre elements and sociopolitical history to construct both a celebration and a criticism of their homelands.

Marxist Holding an ideological position associated with the teachings of Karl Marx (1818–1883), who expounded a theory of society that emphasizes the material conditions of ideology and a critique of capitalism and the functions of the state and who argued for an understanding of history as a struggle between classes that eventually leads to the emergence of a classless society.

melodrama An action of elaborate yet oversimplified nature whose effects are sentimental and sensational.

memoir An autobiographical record of events associated with a person or time, based on the author's recollections.

metaphor An imaginative application of an object, person, or idea to an unlikely object, person, or idea; a figure of speech in which analogy or correspondence functions to make vivid or to suggest a fresh aspect or relation. A central device for literature that makes visible hitherto unseen qualities.

metaphysical Relating to a condition in which the physical or material world is infused with mental or spiritual significance; where the somatic and the semantic meet.

meter A measure of patterned stressed and unstressed syllables in lines of poetry. Meter may be composed of fixed patterns or measures or variable measures or a combination of the two. The most common metrical measures in the English language are the iambic (unstressed followed by stressed syllable), trochaic (stressed followed by unstressed syllable), anapestic (two unstressed syllables followed by a stressed syllable), and dactylic (a stressed syllable followed by two unstressed syllables). These units of measurement are called feet. The number of feet in a line dictate the name of the metrical pattern; thus, a pentameter is composed of five feet. Much contemporary poetry observes no regular pattern but is composed of variable feet, a style known as free verse.

metonymy   The use of a part of an object or person to refer to a larger whole; a figure of speech that reduces in order to magnify and intensify meaning.

mimesis, mimetic   Referring to a theory of literature as an imitative art that mirrors the world and its society; dependent on verisimilitude for its effects.

Modernism   A term used to cover a number of positions, sometimes contradictory, said to characterize a period before and after World War I (1890–1930) and used to describe a group of literary works that reflect, express, and constitute such positions; e.g., signifying a criticism or rejection of traditional and conventional modes of thinking and behavior; a questioning of forms of authority; preferring the complex, difficult, and obscure to the simple and straightforward; questioning social values, institutions, and systems; placing the functional before the ornamental or formal; taking into account the different, technical, individual, idiosyncratic, and eccentric.

montage   A term derived from cinematic techniques; a rapid sequence of images and actions that coalesce to create a united impression.

motif   A theme, image, or idea that recurs in a work and that unifies it.

motivation   Causes, either psychological or dramatic, that are imputed to characters and plot to explain or justify their actions.

mysticism   A mode of being that claims to be directly connected to spiritual forces or a higher being; sometimes meaning beyond logical or rational thought.

myth   A traditional story to explain phenomena, but using nonscientific and nonrational narrative that often involves spiritual or superhuman beings; fictitious although sometimes assigned an allegorical truth and in the past passed down orally in a community.

mythopoesis   The literary invention of myths.

narration   Discourse aimed at relating a sequence of events; encompassing simple stories to sophisticated forms in which narrative strategies such as point of view, chronological sequence, dramatic voices, and shifting registers of style are exploited to make the telling of the story as significant as the story itself. Point of view may be first-person (told through an "I"), third-person ("he" or "she" narrator) or omniscient author and may be limited point of view, intimate, or distant narrator.

narrator The person who "tells" the story to the reader or "speaks" to the reader in the poem; not to be confused with the author of the work, the narrator often functions as a character in the work or is presented as unreliable or treated ironically.

New Criticism A school of critical interpretation associated with critics such as I. A. Richards, Yvor Winters, and Kenneth Burke. It emphasized a detailed analysis of the language of a literary work to uncover its layers of meaning; a preference for close textual analysis, and a deliberate downplaying of contextual gloss, i.e., social and historical context.

Noh A form of Japanese drama that grew out of ritual dances in the fourteenth century and settled into a stylized presentation of relatively fixed stories, involving masks, elaborate costumes, chanting, and dancing.

novel A prose narrative—usually long—in which characters are engaged in actions that conventionally display elements of conflict, crisis, and resolution. Besides characters and plot, the novel often is engaged in drawing up settings and conveying themes.

novella A short novel of under one hundred pages, although possessing all the elements of the longer form. [See *novel*.]

ode A poetic term derived from the Greek, consisting of three movements; the irregular ode, more common today, is usually used to describe a lyric poem that has serious intentions.

Oedipus A well-known mythical character in ancient Greek tragedy who was abandoned at birth after a soothsayer predicted he would grow up to kill his father and marry his mother. After Oedipus discovers his horrible sin, he blinds himself and is left to wander with his daughter Antigone as his guide. Freud rejuvenated this myth by using it as a figure to explain infantile male sexuality.

omniscience Absolute understanding of action and motivation displayed by narrators functioning as omniscient authors. A favored narrative method before the twentieth century that has been displaced by the desire for psychological, i.e., limited or uncertain understanding, verisimilitude.

orality, the oral tradition The quality of spoken language; the dependence on the spoken word for transmission of stories as folktales, legends, and myths from one generation to another. With the development of the printing press and other media technology and with the spread of literacy, few communities rely on the oral tradition to preserve their stories. But certain groups still display features of an oral tradition carried over into the printed page, as in the marked degree of orality in African American poetry and the folk elements in Native American literature.

oxymoron The combination of two words or ideas that contradict each other to produce the witty effect of a paradox, as in "loud silence" or "impoverishing affluence."

pantheism A doctrine of religious beliefs that holds a divinity in suffusing the universe; an integration of god with the created world.

parable An allegorical story that aims at conveying a religious lesson or truth.

paradox A statement that says two contradictory things with the effect less of absurdity as of revealing some insight; sometimes implying a self-contradiction indicating falsehood.

parody A gross imitation of something or some person for humorous or mocking purposes; to ridicule by travesty of the original.

pastoral A literary work, usually a poem, that offers a depiction of a rustic world; the use of shepherds as a motif to express an idealized longed-for simplicity; a

convention that sets forward nature and rural activities as an ideal.

pathos The effect of drawing out emotions of pity and compassion in response to the portrayal of suffering.

peripety, peripeteia An unexpected twist in the actions; a reversal in the position of the character.

persona An agent in a drama or a character in a poem or story; distinguished from the author, in referring to the created personality.

plot The organization of a series of actions or events, usually moving through conflicts to a climax and resolution. The arrangement often implies causality and achieves certain affects.

poetics A study of poetry, metrical arrangements, or criticism of poetry.

point of view The position from which the narrative is related; the selection of such position as to affect the arrangement of the narrative, its tone, and final effect. The point of view may be personal or impersonal. The writer may adopt an author-participant position that gives rise to intimacy and revelation of feelings. Or the writer may adopt an author-observant point of view that simulates detachment and distance. The author-omniscient position allows the writer unrestricted reporting as the all-knowing observer.

postmodernism A term used to refer to a group of positions said to characterize an opposition or reaction to Modernism, sometimes also referring to a period in the late twentieth century; features of postmodernist work, sometimes contradictory, include a self-consciousness or playfulness about its own project; a criticism of the elitism implicit in Modernist work; a rejection of or suspicion of coherence or the united subject; and an openness to difference.

pragmatism A school of philosophy associated with certain American thinkers such as C. S. Peirce, William James, and John Dewey that relates meaning to its practical consequences. Pragmatism as redefined by contemporary theorists like Richard Rorty focuses significance on more than idealist notions and takes materialist constructs as part of the discourse of ideationality.

primary source A source of direct and immediate importance; referring to the person with direct information, or the text being studied, or a contemporary interview or conversation.

primitivism A belief that earlier societies possess qualities superior to contemporary culture; that notion of the noble savage who exhibits natural goodness in contrast to the corruption of present humanity.

profile An outline; a kind of biographical sketch that also uses character analysis.

prolepsis A figure of speech that presents an action in the future as already past; or a strategy in argument that anticipates and rebuts an opponent's criticism.

proletarian Referring to the class of society that has no capital or property, the laboring or working class. In literature, used to describe works that portray the struggles of working-class characters.

prosody The forms of metrical arrangement in poetry, specifically the organization of poems into lines with patterns of rhythm or accented syllables in which the sounds and pronunciations of words are important. [See *rhythm*.]

protagonist The main or central character of a novel, short story, or play, although not necessarily a hero.

prototype The model that illustrates representative qualities of a class; similar to an archetype.

provincialism A limited experience of life, with restricted knowledge, or referring to expressions specific to a region.

psyche The force or principle that motivates a character's behavior; or the spiritual or mental force of a human.

psychological Referring to the interior workings of human behavior; focusing on mental and subconscious motivations that affect external action.

race An identification of groups of people by their physical differences, leading to perceived differences in cultures. Used as an analytic tool for the interpretation of texts where racial differences are constructed as positive, negative, or mixed portrayals.

realism A depiction concerned with verisimilitude; a school of writing that contains detailed descriptions of everyday life, usually of middle-class society and treats the ordinary as significant.

resolution Events that follow upon the climax in a plot; or a resolve; plan.

rhetoric The rules and techniques concerning the oral and written use of language; according to Aristotle, the means of organizing content in order to arrive at truth. Today, taken to mean the knowledge of language as literary use, methods of achieving effective communication.

rhyme Similar quality of sound in words; when accented vowels and succeeding sounds are identical; (e.g., The rain in Spain stays mainly on the plain.) Rhyme in poetry is mnemonic, gives pleasure, adds to the unity of the work, supports stanza arrangement, and suggests multiplying meanings. It is sometimes funny.

rhythm In poetry, repetition of accent combined with similar number of syllables. In prose, it is marked by sentence lengths and structures and balanced sentences.

roman à clef From the French, literally "novel with a key." Fiction that uses actual persons and actions.

romance A fanciful narrative with heroic and passionate actions and vivid and supernatural representations.

Romanticism A European movement that emphasized the primacy of the imagination over reason, privileged the artist and individual over society, focused on mystery, the supernatural, and the strange instead of the common and everyday, and shifted the center of perception from the objective to the subjective position.

satire A technique using irony, sarcasm, or mockery that combines humor and wit with a criticism of human folly. Involves moral judgment and a didactic purpose.

scene The place for an action or a situation; a section of a play or a single set of actions that leads to an effect or point.

secondary source Ideas and opinions that are not direct or first hand; information on a work or writer gathered by another person.

semantics The science of the meanings of words; the study of the relations between words and mental and physical responses to them.

semiotics The science of signs; how meaning is coded and understood by humans through all forms of external communication, including gesture, costume, photographs, paintings, music, and shelter.

sentimentalism The effect produced when a writer concentrates to an exaggerated degree on emotional elements and responses; seen in the past as only a negative quality, it is now more positively accepted as a narrative strategy that achieves a morally persuasive end.

setting The place or period in which an action occurs. May include scenery, props, atmosphere, historical significance.

simile A figure of speech that compares two unlike things to reveal a hidden aspect in the subject of comparison.

similitude Resemblance, similarity.

society Organized groups of humans sharing sets of values and customs of living.

soliloquy A speech by a character who is alone, intended to be heard by the audience (or reader) and revealing intimate information.

sonnet A fourteen-line poem, often in iambic pentameter [see *rhythm*]. Derived from the Italian sonnet with its strict division into eight and six lines, the English sonnet is made up of three quatrains and a couplet. The stanza and rhyme arrangements in a sonnet frequently correspond to its development of thought.

spectacle Something visual that is impressive and memorable; a display that magnifies action.

stereotype A characterization drawn not from direct knowledge or acquaintance but from gross generalizations based on gender, class, ethnic, race, marital and other categories. The use of stereotypes usu-

ally indicates conscious or unconscious prejudice or uncritical acceptance of general cultural norms and assumptions. Many writers deliberately evoke stereotypes in order to critique them and to present more complexity in their characters.

stream of consciousness A narrative technique that presents a character's internal thoughts and condition as if they were occurring in the spontaneous, random, and chaotic manner of everyday experience.

subject The topic or focus of the literary work, what it is specifically about, which may include also what it generally means.

subjectivity The expression of personal feeling and experience; focusing upon self; writing in which the private and individual are paramount.

subplot A minor or secondary sequence of actions that may contrast with or emphasize the main plot.

supernatural The realm of being beyond what is known and explainable; concerning the divine or occult.

surrealism A school of writing that focuses on what is beyond reality, beyond the rational, ordinary experience of humans. Influenced by Freudian psychology to depict subconscious or nonrational experiences, as in dreams or random events.

symbol A word, phrase, or expression having complex meanings and values, more than in the literal or denotative sense; representing more or other than itself.

symbolism The deliberate use of symbols as an important means of communicating, ordering, and multiplying the meanings in a literary work; an interlocking and interlayered texture in which various symbols relate together to produce meaning.

synecdoche A kind of metaphor in which a specific or part of a thing is used to represent the whole, or the whole is used to represent a part; e.g., the pen to represent the art of literature.

syntax The arrangement of grammatical parts in a sentence for correctness and for special effects of emphasis and rhythm.

tenor A term used to mean that part of a *simile* or *metaphor* that is being referred to by direct or indirect correspondence in the use of the *image* or *vehicle*; e.g., in William Blake's line, "O rose thou art sick," the rose is the *vehicle* that carries the *tenor*, that is, the corresponding reference to woman or human sexuality. [See *vehicle*.]

tension The relationship between the written text and its suggested significance or between opposed sets of values and meanings or characters in a work that gives rise to interest and form.

textual Referring to the actual written aspects of a work.

theme The conceptual meanings that emerge in a reading of a literary work; the *theme* does not signify the work's stated *subject*, e.g., a man window-shopping in a supermarket in Ginsberg's "A Supermarket in California." Rather, it is composed of the general significances that can be concluded from the work's position on the subject; i.e., a passionate and sympathetic presentation of the isolation of the single/writer/homosexual individual in a familial/consumerist/ heterosexual society. Themes express opinions and values, and criticize or support specific types of human behavior, relationships, and institutions.

third-person narration/point of view When the story is told by an author with all the characters referred to in the third-person pronoun. Sometimes the point of view in the story is attributed to a third-person character, whether a major or minor character, producing the effect of a limited point-of-view for purposes of psychological realism, complexity, humor, or irony. [See *limited point of view*.]

time shift A technique that ignores linear chronological order and moves the narrative forward or backward to different periods for purposes of achieving complexity or suggesting thematic concerns.

tone The stance taken in a piece of writing toward its subject, usually discernible in the choice of language; as in "mocking," "harsh," or "tender." This stance is demonstrable as pervasive in a work, or limited to individual words or passages.

tradition   A coherent and definable group of literary practices, beliefs, and skills that has evolved through a particular period or exhibited itself in a historical moment; e.g., the traditions of British Renaissance drama or the tradition of magic realism in twentieth-century Latin American fiction.

tragedy   The dramatization of conflict, often between an individual and given laws of divine or human society, resulting in the destruction of that individual. The tragic hero, usually male, transgresses the expressed limitations through some fearful action resulting from an error or weakness in his character. [See *tragic flaw*.]

tragic flaw   The principle character weakness that results in the protagonist's downfall.

transitory   Describing the temporal quality of a thing or experience; the theme of transitoriness of any human condition has been popular in many cultures and ages.

trope   Any literary device in which words are used to signify something other than their literal meaning.

type   A family or class of writing, such as the novel or poem; a character with certain qualities and attributes that represent a class of such characters; e.g., Cleopatra as a type of seductive woman.

understatement   A—sometimes humorous—form of speech in which something is deliberately presented as less immediate, important, or striking than it is.

universality   The idea of a quality or qualities that are comprehensively true for every human in every society; appeal that is unrestricted in time and space, but is meaningful everywhere. This theory of literary effects is currently being questioned as race, class, and gender point to differences rather than to universality in literary response.

utopia(n)   The portrayal of an ideal world; visionary representations of society in which evils and injustices are absent. Often used for satirical effect, or reversed into representations of dystopias, societies in which evils and horrors are foregrounded.

vehicle   The image that carries or to which is attached the explicit or implied corresponding meaning or *tenor*. [See *tenor*.]

verbal irony   The use of language that contains or suggests a discrepancy between what is expected or known and what is revealed. [See *irony*.]

verisimilitude   Appearance or resemblance of truth; using techniques of realism to persuade readers to accept the manifest sense and truthfulness of the work.

vers libre   French for free verse; poetry that does not follow regular or patterned measure and stanzas, but is characterized by irregularity and experimentation of form.

voice The distinctive tone, style, perceptions, and diction of a work, either attributed to the author or exploited by the author to strengthen depiction of characters.

BIBLIOGRAPHY

GENERAL

Ames, Roy. *Third World Film Making and the West.* Berkeley: U of California P, 1987.

Ashcroft, Bill, Gareth Griffiths, and Helen Tiffin. *The Empire Writes Back: Theory and Practice in Post-Colonial Literatures.* New York: Routledge, 1989.

Barraclough, Geoffrey. *An Introduction to Contemporary History.* Harmondsworth, Eng. Penguin, 1972.

Berman, Marshall. *All That Is Solid Melts into Air: The Experience of Modernity.* London: Verso, 1983.

Connor, Steven. *Postmodernist Culture.* Oxford: Blackwell, 1989.

Eagleton, Terry. *Literary Theory: An Introduction.* Minneapolis: U of Minnesota P, 1983.

Grossberg, Lawrence, Cary Nelson, and Paula A. Treichler, eds. *Cultural Studies.* London: Routledge, 1992.

Hall, Stuart, et al., eds. *Culture, Media, Language.* London: Hutchison, 1984.

Huyssen, Andreas. *After the Great Divide: Modernism, Mass Culture and Postmodernism.* Bloomington: Indiana UP, 1986.

Kaplan, E. Ann, ed. *Postmodernism and Its Discontents.* London: Verso, 1988.

King, Bruce, ed. *Literatures of the World in English.* London: Routledge, 1974.

Moi, Toril. *Sexual/Textual Politics: Feminist Literary Theory.* London: Routledge, 1985.

Weightman, John. *The Concept of the Avant-Garde: Explorations in Modernism.* La Salle, IL: Library Press, 1973.

Williams, Raymond. *The Politics of Modernism.* London: Verso, 1989.

Wohl, Robert. *The Generation of 1914.* Cambridge, MA: Harvard UP, 1979.

Worsley, Peter. *The Three Worlds: Culture and World Development.* Chicago: U of Chicago P, 1984.

AFRICA AND THE MIDDLE EAST

Africa

Amuta, Chidi. *The Theory of African Literature*. London: Zed Books, 1989.

Barnett, Ursula A. *A Vision of Order: A Study of Black South African Literature in English*. Amherst: U of Massachusetts P, 1983.

Blair, Dorothy S. *African Literature in French*. Cambridge, Eng.: Cambridge UP, 1976.

Brench, A. C. *The Novelists' Inheritance in Black Africa*. New York: Oxford UP, 1967.

Burness, Donald. *Six Writers from Angola, Mozambique and Cape Verde*. Washington, DC: Three Continents, 1977.

Carter, Gwendolyn M., and Patrick O'Meara, eds. *African Independence: The First Twenty-five Years*. Bloomington: Indiana UP, 1985.

Chinweizu. *The West and the Rest of Us: White Predators, Black Slaves and the African Elite*. New York: Vintage, 1975.

Clingman, Stephen. *History from the Inside: The Novels of Nadine Gordimer*. Winchester, MA: Unwin Hyman, 1986.

Coplan, David B. *In Township Tonight! South Africa's Black City Music and Theatre*. London: Longman, 1985.

Crowder, Michael, ed. *The Cambridge History of Africa*. Vol. 8. Cambridge, Eng.: Cambridge UP, 1984.

Davidson, Basil. *Let Freedom Come: Africa in Modern History*. Boston: Little, Brown, 1978.

Davies, Carol Boyce, and Anne Adams Grace, eds. *Ngambika: Studies of Women in African Literature*. Trenton, NJ: Africa World, 1986.

Fanon, Frantz. *The Wretched of the Earth*. New York: Grove, 1968.

Gates, Henry L., Jr., ed. *In the House of Osubgo: Critical Essays on Wole Soyinka*. New York: Oxford UP, 1989.

Gerhart, Gail. *Black Power in South Africa: The Evolution of an Ideology*. Los Angles: U of California P, 1979.

Goodwin, K. L. *Understanding African Poetry: A Study of Ten Poets*. London: Heinemann, 1982.

Gray, Stephen. *Southern African Literature: An Introduction*. London: Rex Collins, 1979.

Hamilton, Russell. *Voices from an Empire: A History of Afro-Portuguese Literature.* Minneapolis: U of Minnesota P, 1975.

Irele, Abiola. *The African Experience in Literature and Ideology.* London: Heinemann, 1981.

JanMohamed, Abdul R. *Manichean Aesthetics: The Politics of Literature in Colonial Africa.* Amherst: U of Massachusetts P, 1983.

Jones, Eldred Durosimi. *The Writing of Wole Soyinka.* London: Heinemann, 1975.

Kavanaagh, Robert. *Theatre and Cultural Struggle in South Africa.* London: Zed Books, 1975.

Kesteloot, Lilyan. *Black Writers in French: A Literary History of Negritude.* Philadelphia: Temple UP, 1975.

Maugham-Brown, David. *Land, Freedom and Fiction: History and Ideology in Kenya.* London: Zed Books, 1985.

Mazrui, Ali M. *The African Condition.* London: Heinemann, 1980.

Mbiti, John S. *African Religions and Philosophy.* New York: Anchor, 1970.

Miller, Christopher L. *Theories of Africans: Francophone Literature and Anthropology in Africa.* Chicago: U of Chicago P, 1991.

Moore, Gerald. *Twelve African Writers.* Bloomington: Indiana UP, 1980.

Mphahlele, Ezekiel. *The African Image.* London: Faber, 1974.

Ngara, Emanuel. *Art and Ideology in the African Novel.* London: Heinemann, 1985.

Ngugi wa Thiong'o. *Decolonising the Mind: The Politics of Language in African Literature.* London: Heinemann, 1986.

Nkosi, Lewis. *Tasks and Masks: Themes and Styles in African Literature.* London: Longman, 1981.

Rodney, Walter. *How Europe Underdeveloped Africa.* Washington, DC: Howard UP, 1981.

Soyinka, Wole. *Myth, Literature and the African World.* Cambridge, Eng.: Cambridge UP, 1976.

Vaillant, Janet G. *Black, French, and African: A Life of Léopold Sédar Senghor.* Cambridge, MA: Harvard UP, 1990.

Watts, Jane. *Black Writers from South Africa.* New York: St. Martin's, 1989.

Wauthier, Claude. *The Literature and Thought of Modern Africa.* Washington, DC: Three Continents, 1979.

Middle East

Allen, Roger. *The Arab Novel: A Historical and Critical Introduction.* Syracuse, NY: Syracuse UP, 1982.

Abramson, Glenda. *The Writing of Yehuda Amichai: A Thematic Approach.* Albany: SUNY Press, 1989.

———. *The Blackwell Companion to Jewish Culture.* New York: Blackwell Reference, 1989.

———. *The Great Transition: The Recovery of the Lost Centers of Modern Hebrew.* Totowa, NJ: Rowman Allanheld, 1985.

Badawi, M. M. "Commitment in Contemporary Arabic Literature." *Journal of Arabic Literature* 1 (1970): 145–61.

———. "The Lamp of Umm Hashim: The Egyptian Intellectual Between East and West." *Journal of World History* 14 (1972): 858–79.

———. *A Critical Introduction to Modern Arabic Poetry.* Cambridge, Eng.: Cambridge UP, 1975.

———. *Modern Arabic Drama in Egypt.* Cambridge, Eng.: Cambridge UP, 1987.

Berque, Jacques. *Cultural Expression in Arab Society Today.* Austin: U of Texas P, 1978.

Boullata, Issa J., ed. *Critical Perspectives on Modern Arabic Literature.* Washington, DC: Three Continents, 1980.

Draz, Ceza Kassem. "In Quest of New Narrative Forms: Irony in the Works of Four Egyptian Writers." *Journal of Arabic Literature* 12.

Fernea, Elizabeth, ed. *Women and Family in the Middle East: New Voices of Change.* Austin: U of Texas P, 1985.

Hamalian, L. and J. D. Yohannan, eds. *New Writing from the Middle East.* New York: NAL, 1978.

Harlow, Barbara. *Resistance Literature.* New York: Methuen, 1987.

Haywood, John. *Modern Arabic Literature: 1800–1970.* London: Lund Humphries, 1971.

Hourani, Albert. *Europe and the Middle East.* Berkeley: U of California P, 1980.

———. *A History of the Arab Peoples.* Cambridge, MA: Harvard UP, 1991.

Jabra, Jabra I. "Modern Arabic Literature and the West." *Journal of Arabic Literature* 2 (1971): 76–91.

Jad, Ali B. *Form and Technique in the Egyptian Novel 1912–1971.* London: Ithaca Press, 1983.

Kilpatrick, Hilary. *The Modern Egyptian Novel*. London: Ithaca Press, 1974.

Laqueur, Walter. *A History of Zionism*. New York: Holt, 1972.

Laroui, Abdallah. *The Crisis of the Arab Intellectual*. Berkeley: U of California P, 1976.

Lyoun, Mary N. *Travels of a Genre: The Modern Novel and Ideology*. Princeton, NJ: Princeton UP, 1990.

Moosa, Matti. *The Origins of Modern Arabic Fiction*. Washington, DC: Three Continents, 1983.

Ostle, R. C., ed. *Studies in Modern Arabic Literature*. London: Aris & Phillips, 1975.

Rabinovich, Isaiah. *Major Trends in Modern Hebrew Fiction*. Chicago: U of Chicago P, 1968.

Said, Edward. *Orientalism*. New York: Vintage, 1979.

———. *The Question of Palestine*. New York: New York Times Books, 1980.

Shohat, Ella. *Israeli Cinema: East/West and the Politics of Representation*. Austin: U Texas P, 1989.

Siddiq, Muhamad. *Man Is a Cause: Political Consciousness and the Fiction of Ghassan Kanafani*. Seattle: U of Washington P, 1984.

Yudkin, Leon I. *Jewish Writing and Identity in the Twentieth Century*. New York: St. Martin's, 1982.

———. *Modern Hebrew Literature in English Translation*. New York: M. Wiener, 1987.

ASIA

China

Anderson, Marston. *The Limits of Realism: Chinese Fiction in the Revolutionary Period*. Berkeley: U of California P, 1990.

Bianco, Lucien. *Origins of the Chinese Revolution: 1915–1949*. Stanford, CA: Stanford UP, 1971.

Chen, Yu-shih. *Realism and Allegory in the Early Fiction of Mao Tun*. Bloomington: Indiana UP, 1986.

Feuerwerker, Yi-tsi Mei. *Ding Ling's Fiction*. Cambridge, MA: Harvard UP, 1982.

Fitzgerald, C. P. *The Birth of Communist China*. Harmondsworth, Eng.: Penguin, 1964.

Goldman, Merle, ed. *Modern Chinese Literature in the May Fourth Era*. Cambridge, MA: Harvard UP, 1982.

Hsia, C. T. *A History of Modern Chinese Fiction*. New Haven, CT: Yale UP, 1971.

Kinkley, Jeffrey C., ed. *After Mao: Chinese Literature and Society: 1978–1981*. Cambridge, MA: Harvard UP, 1985.

Kristeva, Julia. *About Chinese Women*. New York: Urizen, 1977.

Lee, Leo Ou-fan. *The Romantic Generation of Modern Chinese Writers*. Cambridge, MA: Harvard UP, 1973.

———, ed. *Lu Xün and His Legacy*. Berkeley: U of California P, 1985.

———. *Voices from the Iron House: A Study of Lu Xün*. Bloomington: Indiana UP, 1987.

Lee, Yee. *The New Realism: Writings from China After the Cultural Revolution*. New York: Hippocrene, 1985.

Pickowicz, Paul G. *Marxist Literary Thought in China: The Influence of Ch' u Ch' iu-Pai*. Berkeley: U of California P, 1981.

Spence, Jonathan D. *The Gate of Heavenly Peace: The Chinese and Their Revolution, 1895–1980*. New York: Viking, 1981.

———. *The Search for Modern China*. New York: Norton, 1990.

Tse-tsung, Chow. *The May Fourth Movement: Intellectual Revolution in Modern China*. Stanford, CA: Stanford UP, 1967.

India

de Souza, A. *Women in Contemporary India and South Asia*. 2nd ed. Columbia, MO: South Asia Books, 1981.

Erikson, Erik. *Gandhi's Truth: On the Origins of Militant Nonviolence*. New York: Norton, 1969.

George, K. M., ed. *Comparative Indian Literature*. 2 vols. Trichur and Madras, India: Kerala Sahitya Akademi and Macmillan, 1986.

Harrex, S. C. *The Fire and the Offering: The Modern Indian Novel in English*. Calcutta: Writers Workshop, 1977.

Iyengar, K. R. Srinivasa. *Indian Writing in English*. Bombay: Asia Publishing House, 1962.

Jussawalla, Adil. *Family Quarrels: Toward a Criticism of Indian Writing in English*. Bern, Switz.: Peter Lang, 1985.

Moon, Penderal. *Gandhi and Modern India*. New York: Norton, 1969.

Mukherjee, Meenakshi. *The Twice-Born Fiction*. London: Heinemann, 1971.

———. *Realism and Reality: The Novel and Society in India*. New York: Oxford UP, 1985.

Naik, M. K. *A History of Indian Writing in English*. New Delhi: Sahitya Akademi, 1981.

Narasimhaiah, C. D., and C. N. Srinath, eds. *A Common Poetic for Indian Literatures*. Mysore, India: Dhvanyaloka Publications, 1981.

Viswanathan, Gauri. *Masks of Conquest: Literary Study and British Rule in India*. New York: Columbia UP, 1989.

Wolpert, Stanley. *A New History of India*. 3rd ed. New York: Oxford UP, 1989.

Japan

Duus, Peter. *The Rise of Modern Japan*. Boston: Houghton, 1976.

Keene, Donald. *Dawn to the West: Japanese Literature of the Modern Era*. New York: Holt, 1984.

———. *The Pleasures of Japanese Literature*. New York: Columbia UP, 1988.

Miyoshi, Masao. *Accomplices of Silence: The Modern Japanese Novel*. Berkeley: U of California P, 1988.

Reischauer, Edwin O. *Japan: The Story of a Nation*. 4th ed. New York: McGraw, 1989.

Rimer, Thomas J. *Modern Japanese Fiction and Its Tradition*. Princeton, NJ: Princeton UP 1976.

Ueda, Makota. *Modern Japanese Writers and the Nature of Literature*. Stanford, CA: Stanford UP, 1976.

Vietnam

Yeager, Jack A. *The Vietnamese Novel in French: A Literary Response to Colonialism*. Hanover, NH and London: Published for the University of New Hampshire by University Press of New England, 1987.

AUSTRALIA AND OCEANIA

Australia

Dixon, Miriam. *The Real Matilda: Women and Identity in Australia 1788–1975*. Harmondsworth, Eng., Penguin, 1976.

Docker, John. *Australian Cultural Elites*. Sydney: Angus & Robertson, 1974.

Ferrier, Carole, ed. *Gender, Politics and Fiction: Twentieth-Century Australian Women's Novels*. St. Lucia: U of Queensland P, 1985.

Goodwin, Ken. *A History of Australian Literature*. London: Macmillan, 1986.

Healy, J. J. *The Treatment of the Aborigine in Australian Literature*. St. Lucia: U of Queensland P, 1978.

Hergenhan, L., ed. *The Penguin New Literary History of Australia*. Ringwood, Victoria, Austral.: Penguin, 1988.

Hughes, Robert. *The Fatal Shore*. New York: Knopf, 1986.

Kramer, L., ed. *The Oxford History of Australian Literature*. Melbourne: Oxford UP, 1981.

Moore, Tom Inglis. *Social Patterns in Australian Literature*. Sydney: Angus & Robertson, 1971.

Schoemaker, Adam. *Black Words White Page: Aboriginal Literature, 1929–1988*. St. Lucia: U of Queensland P, 1989.

Turner, Graeme. *National Fictions: Literature, Film and the Construction of Australian Narrative*. Sydney: Allen & Unwin, 1986.

White, Richard. *Inventing Australia: Images and Identity*. Sydney: Allen & Unwin, 1981.

Wilkes, G. A. *The Stockyard and the Croquet Lawn*. Melbourne: Edward Arnold, 1981.

Oceania

Subramani. *The Indo-Fijian Experience*. St. Lucia: U of Queensland P, 1979.

———. *South Pacific Literature: From Myth to Fabulation*. Suva, Fiji: U of South Pacific P, 1985.

New Zealand

Curnow, Wystan. *Essays on New Zealand Literature*. Auckland: Heinemann, 1973.

Stead, C. K. *In a Glass Case: Essays on New Zealand Literature*. Auckland: Oxford UP/Auckland, UP, 1979.

EUROPE

General

Anderson, Perry. *Considerations on Western Marxism*. London: Verso, 1976.

———. *In the Tracks of Historical Materialism*. London: Verso, 1983.

Barker, Francis, ed. *Europe and Its Others*. Colchester, Eng.: U of Essex, 1985.

Esslin, Martin. *The Theatre of the Absurd*. New York: Anchor, 1962.

Goldman, Lucien. *Toward a Sociology of the Novel. New York: Routledge, 1986.*

Hobsbawm, Eric. *The Age of Empire: 1875–1914*. New York: Pantheon, 1987.

Hughes, H. Stuart. *Sophisticated Rebels: The Political Culture of European Dissent, 1968–1987*. Cambridge, MA: Harvard UP, 1988.

Kiernan, V. G. *The Lords of Human Kind: European Attitudes Towards the Outside World in the Age of Imperialism*. Harmondsworth, Eng.: Penguin, 1972.

McHale, Brian. *Postmodernist Fiction*. New York: Methuen, 1987.

Austria, Czechoslovakia, and Germany

Banerjee, Maria Nemcova. *Terminal Paradox: The Novels of Milan Kundera*. New York: Grove, 1990.

Bosmajian, Hamida. *Contemporary German Literature and the Shadow of Nazism*. Iowa City: U of Iowa P, 1979.

Demetz, Peter. *From Kafka and Dada to Brecht and Beyond*. Madison: U of Wisconsin P, 1982.

Esslin, Martin. *Brecht: The Man and His Work*. Garden City, NY: Anchor, 1971.

Gay, Peter. *Weimar Culture*. New York: Harper, 1968.

Heller, Erich. *Franz Kafka*. New York: Viking, 1974.

Schorske, Carl E. *Fin-De-Siecle Vienna: Politics and Culture*. New York: Random, 1980.

France

Becker, Lucille Frackman. *Twentieth-Century French Novelists*. Boston: G. K. Hall, 1989.

Brée, Germaine. *Twentieth-Century French Literature*. Chicago: U of Chicago P, 1983.

———. *Women Writers in France*. New Brunswick, NJ: Rutgers UP, 1973.

Hollier, Denis, and R. Howard Bloch, eds. *A New History of French Literature*. Cambridge, MA: Harvard UP, 1989.

Hughes, S. Stuart. *The Obstructed Path: French Social Thought in the Years of Desperations, 1930–1960*. New York: 1968.

O'Brien, Justin. *Contemporary French Literature*. New Brunswick, NJ: Rutgers UP, 1971.

Picon, Caetan. *Contemporary French Literature: 1945 and After*. New York: Ungar, 1974.

Great Britain and Ireland

Bell, Quentin. *Virginia Woolf: A Biography*. New York: Harcourt, 1972.

Bradbury, Malcolm. *The Social Context of Modern English Literature*. New York: Schocken, 1971.

Burgess, Anthony. *The Novel Now: A Guide to Contemporary Fiction*. New York: Pegasus, 1970.

Ellmann, Richard. *James Joyce*. New York: Oxford UP, 1982.

———. *Four Dubliners: Oscar Wilde, William Butler Yeats, James Joyce, Samuel Beckett*. New York: Braziller, 1988.

Ford, Boris, ed. *The New Pelican Guide to English Literature: The Present*. Vol. 8. London: Penguin, 1983.

Fussell, Paul. *The Great War and Modern Memory*. New York: Oxford UP, 1975.

Gilroy, Paul. *"There Ain't No Black in the Union Jack": The Cultural Politics of Race and Nation*. London: Hutchinson, 1987.

Hewison, Robert. *In Anger: British Culture in the Cold War, 1945–1960*. New York: Oxford UP, 1981.

Marcus, Jane. *Art and Anger: Reading Like a Woman*. Columbus: Ohio State UP, 1988.

Raskin, Jonah. *The Mythology of Imperialism: Rudyard Kipling, Joseph Conrad, E. M. Forster, D. H. Lawrence and Joyce Cary*. New York: Random, 1971.

Said, Edward W. "Yeats and Decolonization," in *Nationalism, Colonialism and Literature*. Ed. Terry Eagleton, Fredric Jameson, and Edward W. Said. Minneapolis: U of Minnesota P, 1990.

Williams, Raymond. *The Country and the City*. New York: Oxford UP, 1973.

Italy and Spain

Caesar, Michael, and Peter Hainsworth, eds. *Writers and Society in Contemporary Italy*. New York: St. Martin's, 1984.

Honig, Edwin. *García Lorca*. New York: New Directions, 1963.

Poland and the former Soviet Union

Brown, Edward. *Major Soviet Writers*. New York: Oxford UP, 1973.

Davie, Donald. *Slavic Excursions: Essays on Russian and Polish Literature*. Chicago: U of Chicago P, 1990.

Haraszti, Miklos. *The Velvet Prison: Artists Under State Socialism*. Trans. Katalin and Stephen Landesmann. New York: Basic, 1987.

Hayward, Max. *Writers in Russia: 1917–1978*. New York: Harcourt, 1983.

Milosz, Czeslaw. *The Captive Mind*. New York: Random, 1981.

Slonin, Marc. *Soviet Russian Literature: Writers and Problems: 1917–1977*. New York: Oxford UP, 1977.

Scandinavia

Rossel, Sven H. *A History of Scandinavian Literature: 1870–1980*. Minneapolis: U of Minnesota P, 1982.

LATIN AMERICA AND THE CARRIBEAN

The Caribbean

Arnold, James A. *Modernism and Negritude: The Poetry and Poetics of Aimé Césaire*. Cambridge, MA: Harvard UP, 1981.

Baugh, Edward, ed. *Critics on Caribbean Literature*. London: Allen and Unwin, 1978.

Brown, L. W. *West Indian Poetry*. Boston: Twayne, 1981.

Cardenal, Ernesto. *In Cuba*. New York: New Directions, 1974.

Cartey, Wilfred G. *Black Images*. New York: Teachers College Press, 1970.

Césaire, Aimé. *Discourse on Colonialism*. New York: Monthly Review Press, 1972.

Coulthard, G. R. *Race and Colour in Caribbean Literature*. New York: Oxford UP, 1962.

Cudjoe, Selwyn R. *V. S. Naipaul*. Amherst: U of Massachusetts P, 1988.

———. *Resistance and Caribbean Literature*. Athens: Ohio UP, 1980.

Dash, Michael J. *Literature and Ideology in Haiti: 1915–1961*. London: Macmillan, 1981.

Ellis, Keith. *Cuba's Nicolás Guillén: Poetry and Ideology*. Toronto: U of Toronto P, 1983.

Fanon, Frantz. *Black Skin, White Masks*. New York: Grove, 1968.

Gilkes, Michael. *The West Indian Novel*. Boston: Twayne, 1981.

James, Louis. *The Islands in Between: Essays on West Indian Literature*. London: Oxford UP, 1978.

Knight, Franklin. *The Caribbean: The Genesis of a Fragmented Nationalism*. New York: Oxford UP, 1968.

King, Bruce, ed. *West Indian Literature*. London: Macmillan, 1979.

Lamming, George. *The Pleasures of Exile*. London: Allison & Busby, 1984.

Lewis, Gordon K. *The Growth of the Modern West Indies*. New York: Monthly Review Press, 1969.

Menton, S. *Prose Fiction and the Cuban Revolution*. Austin: U of Texas P, 1975.

Omotoso, Kole. *The Theatrical into Theatre: A Study of the Drama and Theatre of the English-speaking Caribbean*. London: New Beacon Books, 1982.

Ramchand, Kenneth. *The West Indian Novel and Its Background*. London: Faber, 1970.

Salkey, Andrew. *Havana Journal*. New York: Penguin, 1971.

———. *Georgetown Journal*. London: New Beacon Books, 1972.

Sander, Reinhard W. *The Trinidad Awakening: West Indian Literature of the Nineteen-Thirties*. Westport, CT: Greenwood, 1988.

Sartre, Jean-Paul. "Black Orpheus," in *The Black American Writer*. Edited by C. W. E. Bigsby. Vol. 2. Baltimore: Penguin, 1969.

Souza, R. *Major Cuban Novelists: Tradition and Innovation*. Columbia: U of Missouri P, 1976.

Taylor, Patrick. *The Narrative of Liberation: Perspectives on Afro-Caribbean Literature, Popular Culture and Politics*. Ithaca, NY: Cornell UP, 1989.

Warner, Keith Q. *The Trinidad Calypso: A Study of the Calypso as Oral Literature*. London: Heinemann, 1983.

Williams, Eric. *From Columbus to Castro: The History of the Caribbean, 1492–1969*. London: André Deutsch, 1970.

Zavala, Iris, and Rafael Rodriquez, ed. *The Intellectual Roots of Independence: An Anthology of Puerto Rican Political Essays*. New York: Monthly Review Press, 1980.

Latin America

Ambursley, Fitzroy, and Robin Cohen, eds. *Crisis in the Caribbean*. New York: Monthly Review Press, 1983.

Bacarisse, Salvador, ed. *Contemporary Latin American Fiction*. Edinburgh, Scotland: Scottish Academy Press, 1986.

Bethell, L., ed. *Cambridge History of Latin America*. Vol. 4. Cambridge, Eng., Cambridge UP, 1986.

Brotherston, Gordon. *The Emergence of the Latin American Novel*. Cambridge, Eng.: Cambridge UP, 1977.

Brushwood, John. *The Spanish American Novel: A Twentieth Century Survey*. Austin: U of Texas P, 1975.

Chevigny, Bell Gale, and Gari Laguardia, eds. *Reinventing the Americas: Comparative Studies of Literature of the United States and Spanish America*. Cambridge, Eng.: Cambridge UP, 1979.

Coutinho, Afranio. *An Introduction to Literature in Brazil*. New York: Columbia, UP, 1969.

Donoso, José. *The Boom in Spanish American Literature*. New York: Columbia UP, 1977.

Dorfman, Ariel. *Some Write to the Future: Essays on Contemporary Latin American Fiction*. Durham, NC: Duke UP, 1991.

Foster, David W. *Studies in the Contemporary Spanish American Short Story*. Columbia: U of Missouri P, 1979.

Franco, Jean. "From Modernization to Resistance: Latin American Literature 1959–76." *Latin American Perspectives* 16 (1978): 77–97.

———. *The Modern Culture of Latin America: Society and the Artist*. Harmondsworth, Eng.: Penguin, 1970.

———. *Plotting Women: Gender and Representation in Mexico*. New York: Columbia UP, 1989.

Galeano, Edward. *Open Veins of Latin America: Five Centuries of the Pillage of a Continent*. New York: Monthly Review Press, 1973.

Gallagher, David. *Modern Latin American Literature*. New York: Oxford UP, 1974.

Jackson, Richard L. *The Black Image in Latin American Literature*. Albuquerque: U of New Mexico P, 1976.

Katra, William H. *"Contorno": Literary Engagement in Post-Peronist Argentina*. London: Associated University Presses, 1988.

King, John, ed. *Modern Latin American Fiction: A Survey*. London: Faber, 1987.

La Feber, Walter. *Inevitable Revolutions: The United States in Central America.* New York: Norton, 1984.

Magnarelli, S. *The Lost Rib: Female Character in the Spanish American Novel.* London: Associated University Presses, 1985.

Marotti, Giorgio. *Black Character in the Brazilian Novel.* Los Angeles: UCLA CAAS, 1987.

Martin, Gerald. *Journeys Through the Labyrinth: Latin American Fiction in the Twentieth Century.* London: Verso, 1989.

McGuik, B., and R. Cardwell, eds. *Gabriel García Márquez: New Readings.* Cambridge, Eng.: Cambridge UP, 1987.

Meyer, Doris. *Lives on the Line: The Testimony of Contemporary Latin American Authors.* Berkeley: U of California P, 1988.

Miller, Beth. *Women in Hispanic Literature: Icons and Fallen Idols.* Berkeley: U of California P, 1983.

Patai, D. *Myth and Ideology in Contemporary Brazilian Fiction.* London: Associated University Presses, 1983.

Pescatello, Anne, ed. *Female and Male in Latin America.* Pittsburgh: U of Pittsburgh P, 1973.

Skidmore, Thomas E., and Peter H. Smith, *Modern Latin America.* 2d ed. New York: Oxford UP, 1989.

Valis, Noel, and Carol Maier, eds. *In the Feminine Mode: Essays on Hispanic Women Writers.* Lewisburg, PA: Bucknell UP, 1988.

NORTH AMERICA

Canada

Atwood, Margaret. *Survival: A Thematic Guide to Canadian Literature.* Toronto: Anansi, 1972.

Blodgett, E. D. *Configuration: Essays on the Canadian Literatures.* Ontario: ECW Press, 1982.

Davey, Frank. *Surviving the Paraphrase: Eleven Essays on Canadian Literature.* Winnipeg: Turnstone, 1983.

Dorsinville, Max. *Caliban Without Prospero.* Erin, ON, Porcepic Books, 1974.

Frye, Northrop. *The Bush Garden.* Toronto: Anansi, 1972.

New, W. H. *A History of Canadian Literature.* London and Toronto: Macmillan, 1989.

Monkman, Leslie. *A Native Heritage: Images of the Indian in English Canadian Literature.* Toronto: U of Toronto P, 1981.

United States

Altieri, Charles. *Self and Sensibility in Contemporary American Poetry.* Cambridge, Eng.: Cambridge UP, 1984.

Baker, Houston A., Jr., ed. *Three American Literatures: Essays in Chicano, Native American and Asian American Literature.* New York: MLA, 1982.

———. *Blues, Ideology and Afro-American Literature: A Vernacular Theory.* Chicago: U of Chicago P, 1989.

Baker, Houston A., Jr., and Patricia Redmond, eds. *Afro-American Literary Study in the 1990's.* Chicago: U of Chicago P, 1989.

Boelhower, William. *Through a Glass Darkly: Ethnic Semiosis in American Literature.* New York: Oxford UP, 1986.

Bloom, Alexander. *Prodigal Sons: The New York Intellectuals and Their World.* New York: Oxford UP, 1986.

Cruse, Harold. *The Crisis of the Negro Intellectual.* New York: Morrow, 1963.

Dearborn, Mary. *Pocahontas' Daughters: Gender and Ethnicity in American Literature.* New York: Oxford UP, 1986.

Fabré, Geneviève. *Drumbeats, Masks and Metaphor: Contemporary Afro-American Theatre.* Cambridge, MA: Harvard UP, 1983.

———, ed. *European Perspectives on Hispanic Literature in the U.S.* Houston: Arte Publico Press, 1983.

Fiedler, Leslie. *Love and Death in the American Novel.* New York: Stein & Day, 1960.

Gates, Henry L., Jr. *The Signifying Monkey: A Theory of African American Literary Criticism.* New York: Oxford UP, 1988.

———, ed. *Reading Black, Reading Feminist: A Literary Critical Anthology.* New York: NAL, 1990.

Gilbert, James Burkhart. *Writers and Partisans: A History of Literary Radicalism in America.* New York: Wiley, 1968.

Guttman, Allen. *The Jewish Writer in America.* New York: Oxford UP, 1971.

Hassan, Ihab Habib. *Contemporary American Literature: An Introduction, 1945–1972.* New York: Ungar, 1973.

Hooks, Bell. *Yearning: Race, Gender and Cultural Politics.* Boston: South End Press, 1990.

Howe, Irving. *World of Our Fathers.* New York: Harcourt, 1976.

Huggins, Nathan. *Harlem Renaissance*. New York: Oxford UP, 1971.

Johnson, Charles. *Being and Race: Black Writing Since 1970*. Bloomington: Indiana UP, 1988.

Jones, LeRoi. *Blues People*. New York: Morrow, 1963.

Kazin, Alfred. *Bright Book of Life: American Novelists and Storytellers from Hemingway to Mailer*. Boston: Little, 1973.

Kenner, Hugh. *The Pound Era*. Berkeley: U of California P, 1971.

Kiernan, V. G. *America, The New Imperialism: From White Settlement to World Hegemony*. London: Zed Press, 1978.

Kim, Elaine H. *Asian American Literature: An Introduction to the Writings and Their Social Context*. Philadelphia: Temple UP, 1982.

Lasch, Christopher. *The New Radicalism in America, 1889–1963: The Intellectual as Social Type*. New York: Knopf, 1965.

Leitch, Vincent B. *American Literary Criticism: From the Thirties to the Eighties*. New York: Columbia UP, 1988.

Lim, Shirley Geok-lin Lim, ed. *Approaches to Teaching Kingston's The Woman Warrior*. New York: MLA, 1992.

Lincoln, Kenneth. *Native American Renaissance*. Berkeley: U of California P, 1982.

Malin, Irving. *Contemporary American-Jewish Literature: Critical Essays*. Bloomington: Indiana UP, 1973.

Pinsky, R. *The Situation of Poetry: Contemporary Poetry and Its Traditions*. Princeton: Princeton UP, 1971.

Pryse, Marjorie, and Hortense Spillers, eds. *Conjuring: Black Women Writers and Literary Tradition*. Bloomington: Indiana UP, 1985.

Rubin, Louis D., Jr., et al. *The History of Southern Literature*. Baton Rouge: Louisiana State UP, 1985.

Ruoff, A. LaVonne Brown. *American Indian Literatures*. New York: MLA, 1990.

Ruoff, A. LaVonne Brown, and Ward, Jerry W., eds. *Redefining American Literary History*. New York: MLA, 1990.

Susman, Warren I. *Culture as History: The Transformation of American Society*. New York: Pantheon, 1985.

Tanner, Tony. *City of Words: American Fiction, 1950–1970*. New York: Harper, 1971.

Tytell, John. *Naked Angels: The Lives and Literature of the Beat Generation*. New York: McGraw, 1976.

Wallace, Michele. *Invisibility Blues: From Pop to Theory*. London: Verso, 1990.

ACKNOWLEDGMENTS

AFRICA AND THE MIDDLE EAST

Abu-Khalid, Fawziyya. By permission of Kamal Boullata and © Kamal Boullata; published in *Women from the Fertile Crescent*. Three Continents Press, Washington, D.C., 1978.

Achebe, Chinua. "Civil Peace", from GIRLS AT WAR AND OTHER STORIES by Chinua Achebe. Copyright © 1972, 1986 by Chinua Achebe. Used by permission of Doubleday, a division of Bantam Doubleday Dell Publishing Group, Inc.

Aidoo, Ama Ata. From NO SWEETNESS HERE by Ama Ata Aidoo. Reprinted with permission.

Amichai, Yehuda. "Jerusalem" by Yehuda Amichai. From THE SELECTED POETRY OF YEHUDA AMICHAI, edited and translated by Chana Bloch and Stephen Mitchell. English translation copyright © 1968 by Chana Bloch and Stephen Mitchell. Reprinted by permission of HarperCollins Publishers.

Amichai, Yehuda. "Sort of an Apocalypse" by Yehuda Amichai. From THE SELECTED POETRY OF YEHUDA AMICHAI, edited and translated by Chana Bloch and Stephen Mitchell. English translation copyright © 1968 by Chana Bloch and Stephen Mitchell. Reprinted by permission of HarperCollins Publishers.

Awoonor, Kofi. Excerpt from NIGHT OF MY BLOOD. Copyright © 1971 by Kofi Awoonor.

Cronin, Jeremy. Jeremy Cronin "A Person Is a Person Because of Other People," TriQuarterly. Reprinted by Permission.

Darwish, Mahmoud. "Identity Card," by Mahmoud Darwish, from THE MUSIC OF HUMAN FLESH, translated by Denys-Johnson Davies, 1980.

Dib, Mohammed. © Editions du Seuil, 1966.

El Saadawi, Nawal. Reprinted by permission of Methuen London.

Essop, Ahmed. "The Hajji" from *Hajji Musa and the Hindu Fire-Walker* (Readers International, 1988) copyright © 1988 Ahmed Essop. Reprinted by permission.

Gordimer, Nadine. "A Soldier's Embrace", copyright © 1975 by Nadine Gordimer. from A SOLDIER'S EMBRACE by Nadine Gordimer. Used by permission of Viking Penguin, a division of Penguin Books USA Inc.

Head, Bessie. © The Bessie Head Estate, from THE COLLECTOR OF TREASURES,

Heinemann Educational Books, African Writers Series, London 1977. Permission granted by John Johnson Ltd., London.

Hikmet, Nazim. "About Your Hands and Lies" by Nazim Hikmet from *The Epic of Sheik Bedreddin and Other Poems* by Hikmet, translated by Randy Blasing and Mutlu Konuk. Copyright © 1977 by Randy Blasing and Mutlu Konuk. Reprinted by permission of PERSEA BOOKS, INC.

Idriss, Yussef. © Copyright Three Continents Press 1990, 1901 Pennsylvania Ave., N.W., Washington DC 20006, in translation by Denys-Johnson Davies.

Kanafani, Ghassan. By permission of Three Continents Press, and © Ghassan Kanafani, Washington D.C., U.S.A., 1983; *Men in the Sun*.

Mahfouz, Naguib. Naguib Mahfouz, "The Happy Man." Reprinted by permission.

Matshoba, Mututzeli. From CALL ME NOT A MAN: THE STORIES OF MUTUT-ZELI MATSHOBA, by Mututzeli Matshoba. Reprinted with permission of Longman Group U.K.

Ngugi wa Thiong'o. Reprinted with permission of Ngugi wa Thiong'o: *Secret Lives* (Heinemann Educational Books, Portsmouth, NH, and Heinemann Educational Books Oxford, 1975).

Oz, Amos. "Nomad and Viper, from *Where the Jackals Howl and Other Stories* by Amos Oz and translated by Nicholas de Lange, copyright © 1980, 1976 by Amos Oz and Am Oved Publishers, Ltd., English translation, copyright © 1973 by Amos Oz, reprinted by permission of Harcourt Brace Jovanovich, Inc.

Qabula, Alfred Temba. From Alfred Temba Qabula. Reprinted by permission of TriQuarterly.

Sepamla, Sipho. Reprinted by permission of TriQuarterly.

Soyinka, Wole. © Oxford University Press 1964. Reprinted from *Collected Plays 1* by Wole Soyinka (1973) by permission of Oxford University Press.

Yambo, Ouologuem. From "Nouvelle Somme de Poeme Noire," 1966. Reprinted by permission of Presence Africaine.

Senghor, Léopold Sédar. © Oxford University Press 1964. Reprinted from Léopold Sédar Senghor: *Selected Poems* translated by John Reed and Clive Wake (1964) by permission of Oxford University Press.

ASIA

by Longman Publishing Group. Reprinted with permission from Longman Publishing Group.

Qing, Ai. Reprinted by permission of Ai Qing.

Rin, Ishigaki. From THE LONGMAN ANTHOLOGY OF WORLD LITERATURE BY WOMEN: 1875–1975 by Marian Arkin and Barbara Shollar. Copyright © 1989 by Longman Publishing Group. Reprinted with permission from Longman Publishing Group.

Taku, Miki. Reprinted from THE POETRY OF POSTWAR JAPAN edited by Kijime Hajime by permission of the University of Iowa Press. Copyright 1975 by University of Iowa Press.

Toer, Pramoeyda Ananta. From Promoedya Ananta Toer, SIX INDONESIAN SHORT STORIES by Rufus S. Handon, 1968.

Xiaoni, Wang. "Dark Night on a Southbound Train," by Wang Xiaoni, from RED AZALEA: Chinese Poetry Since the Cultural Revolution, edited by Edward Morin. Reprinted by permission of University of Hawaii Press.

Xue, Can. From *Dialogues in Paradise*, translated by Ronald J. Janssen and Jian Zhang. Reprinted by permission of the publisher, Northwestern University Press.

Xün, Lu. From *Selected Stories of Lu Xün*, translated by Hsien-yi and Gladys Yang. Copyright © 1972. Reprinted by permission of Foreign Languages Press.

Yōko, Mori. From *The Mother of Dreams*. Published by Kodansha International Ltd. © 1989. Reprinted by permission. All rights reserved.

AUSTRALIA

Curnow, Allen. From Allen Curnow, *Allen Cumow; Selected Poems 1940–1989*. Copyright © 1990 by Allen Cumow. Reproduced by permission of Penguin Books Ltd., London.

Dawe, Bruce. From *Beyond the Subdivisions*, by Bruce Dawe. Reprinted by permission of Longman Cheshire Pty Limited.

Frame, Janet. "The Day of the Sheep" from: You are now Entering the Human Heart, by Janet Frame. Copyright © 1983, by Janet Frame. Reprinted by permission of Brandt & Brandt Literary Agents, Inc.

Grace, Patricia. Reprinted from WAIARIKI AND OTHER STORIES, first published by Longman Paul Limited, 1975.

Herbert, Xavier. "Clothes Make a Man" by Xavier Herbert from CAPRICORNIA. ©

Robyn Pill 1938. Reprinted by permission of Collins/Angus & Robertson Publishers.

Itihmaera, Witi. Reprinted by permission of Penguin Books (N.Z.) Limited.

Elizabeth Jolley. "Mr Parker's Valentine", from STORIES: ELIZABETH JOLLEY by Elizabeth Jolley. Copyright © 1976, 1979, 1984 by Elizabeth Jolley. Used by permission of Viking Penguin, a division of Penguin Books USA Inc.

Kerpi, Kama. "Cargo," by Kama Kerpi, from *Kovave* 5, No. 1, June 1975. Reprinted by permission of Jacaranda Wiley, Ltd.

Malouf, David. "Off the Map," from *Neighbors in a Thicket* z/e, © 1974. Reprinted by permission of University of Queensland Press.

Murray, Les. From THE DAYLIGHT MOON. Copyright © 1988 by Les Murray. Reprinted by permission of PERSEA BOOKS, INC.

Prichard, Katharine. "The Cooboo" by Katharine Susannah Prichard courtesy to copyright holder R. P. Throssell c/o Curtis Brown (Aust) Pty Ltd., Sidney.

Slessor, Kenneth. "South Country" by Kenneth Slessor from SELECTED POEMS. © Paul Slessor. Reprinted with permission of CollinsAngus & Robertson.

Wendt, Albert. From *Pouliui* by Albert Wendt. Copyright © 1980. Reprinted by permission of University of Hawaii Press.

White, Patrick. From THE BURNT ONES, by Patrick White. Copyright—Patrick White Estate; first published by Eyre & Spottiswoode 1964. Reprinted by permission of Penguin Books Australia, Ltd.

Wright, Judith. "Bora Ring" by Judith Wright from COLLECTED POEMS. © Judith Wright, 1971. Reprinted by permission of Collins/Angus & Robertson Publishers.

EUROPE

Akhmatova, Anna. "The First Long-Range Artillery Shell in Leningrad" is reprinted from ANNA AKHMATOVA, Poems, Selected and Translated by Lyn Coffin, by permission of W. W. Norton & Company, Inc. Copyright © 1983 by Lyn Coffin.

Akhmatova, Anna. From *POEMS OF AKHMATOVA* Selected, translated and introduced by Stanley Kunitz with Max Hayward. Copyright © 1972 by Stanley Kunitz and Max Hayward. By permission of Little, Brown and Company.

Auden, W. H. From COLLECTED POEMS by W. H. Auden, edit., E. Mendelson. Copyright 1940 and renewed 1968 by W. H. Auden. Reprinted by permission of Random House, Inc. and Faber and Faber Ltd.

Babel, Isaac. Reprinted by permission of S. G. Phillips, Inc. from THE COLLECTED STORIES OF ISAAC BABEL. Copyright © 1955 by S. G. Phillips, Inc.

Beckett, Samuel. 'As The Story Was Told' by Samuel Beckett from *Collected Shorter Prose 1945–80* by Samuel Beckett. Copyright © 1973, 1984 by Samuel Beckett. Reproduced by permission of The Beckett Estate and Calder Publications Limited, London.

Böll, Heinrich. From *Heinrich Böll: 18 Stories,* translated by Leila Vennewitz. Copyright 1966. Reprinted by permission of Joan Daves Agency.

Böll, Heinrich. Reprinted by permission of the translator.

Brecht, Bertolt. ''To Posterity'' from *Selected Poems,* copyright 1947 by Bertolt Brecht and H. R. Hays and renewed 1975 by Stefan S. Brecht and H. R. Hays, reprinted by permission of Harcourt Brace Jovanovich, Inc.

Breton, André. From André Breton, *Claire de Terre.* Copyright © 1966 by Editions GALLIMARD. Reprinted by permission of Editions GALLIMARD.

Broumas, Olga. ''Sun The First'' from *What I Love* by Odysseas Elytis. English translation copyrighted © 1986 by Olga Broumas. Used by permission of Copper Canyon Press, P.O. Box 271, Port Townshend, WA 98368.

Buzzati, Dino. Ms. Almerina Buzzati c/o Agenzia Letteraria Internazionale srl, Via F. lli Gabba 3, Milano.

Calvino, Italo. ''The Adventure of a Reader'' from *Difficult Loves* by Italo Calvino, copyright 1949 by Giulio Einaudi editore, Torino; copyright © 1958 by Guilio Einaudi editore. s.p.a., Torino, English translation copyright © 1984 by Harcourt Brace Jovanovich, Inc., reprinted by permission of Harcourt Brace Jovanovich, Inc., reprinted by permission of Harcourt Brace Jovanovich. Reprinted by permission of the estate ofr Italo Calvino.

Camus, Albert. From EXILE AND THE KINGDOM by Albert Camus, trans., J. O'Brien. Copyright © 1957, 1958 by Alfred A. Knopf, Inc. Reprinted by permission of the publisher.

Colette. ''The Other Wife'' from THE COLLECTED STORIES OF COLETTE by Colette, edited by Robert Phelps. Translation copyright © 1983 by Farrar Straus & Giroux, Inc.

Duerrenmatt, Friedrich. From THE VISIT by Friedrich Duerrenmatt, and trans. by Maurice Valency, as an unpublished work entitled ''The Old Lady's Visit,'' adapted by Maurice Valency from DER BESUCH DER ALTEN DAME, by Friedrich Deurrenmatt. Copyright © 1958 by Maurice Valency. Reprinted by permission of Random House, Inc.

Duras, Marguerite. From MODERATO CANTABILE by Marguerite Duras, translated by Richard Seaver. English translation copyright © 1960, 1988 by Grove Press, Inc. Used by permission of Grove Press, Inc.

Ekström, Margareta. Translation copyright © 1985 by Eva Claeson. Reprinted from *Death's Midwives* by permission of Ontario Review Press.

Ginzburg, Natalia. From Natalia Ginzburg, *Voices in the Evening*, translated by D. M. Low. Copyright 1963. Reprinted by permission of Carcanet Press Limited.

Heaney, Seamus. "Digging" from SELECTED POEMS 1966–1987, by Seamus Heaney. Copyright © 1990 by Seamus Heaney.

Joyce, James. "Araby", from DUBLINERS by James Joyce. Copyright 1916 by B. W. Heubsch. Definitive text Copyright © 1967 by the Estate of James Joyce. Used by permission of Viking Penguin, a division of Penguin Books USA Inc.

Kafka, Franz. From FRANZ KAFKA: THE COMPLETE STORIES by Franz Kafka, edited by Nahum N. Glatzer. Copyright 1946, 1947, 1948, 1949, 1954, © 1958, 1971 by Schocken Books Inc. Reprinted by permission of Schocken Books, published by Pantheon Books, a division of Random House, Inc.

Kundera, Milan. From LAUGHABLE LOVES by Milan Kundera, trans., S. Rappaport. Text Copyright © 1974 by Alfred A. Knopf, Inc. Reprinted by permission of the publishers.

Lawrence, D. H. The Horse-Dealer's Daughter", copyright 1922 by Thomas B. Seltzer, Inc., renewed 1950 by Frieda Lawrence, from COMPLETE SHORT STORIES OF D. H. LAWRENCE by D. H. Lawrence. Used by permission of Viking Penguin, a division of Penguin Books USA Inc.

Federico Garcia Lorca. Federico Garcia Lorca: *The Selected Poems of Federico Garcia Lorca*. Copyright © 1955 by New Directions Publishing Corporation. Reprinted by permission of New Directions Publishing Corporation.

Mandelstam, Osip. Reprinted with permission of Atheneum Publishers, an imprint of Macmillan Publishing Company, from OSIP MANDELSTAM: SELECTED POEMS, translated by Clarence Brown and W. S. Merwin. Copyright © 1973 by Clarence Brown and W. S. Merwin.

Montale, Eugenio. Eugenio Montale: *Selected Poems*. Copyright © 1965 by New Directions Publishing Corporation. Reprinted by permission of New Directions Publishing Corporation.

O'Connor, Frank. From COLLECTED STORIES by Frank O'Connor. Copyright 1951 by Frank O'Connor. Reprinted by permission of Alfred A. Knopf, Inc. Originally appeared in "The New Yorker."

Rilke, Rainer Maria. "Archaic Torso of Apollo" from SELECTED POEMS by Rainer Maria Rilke, edit. & trans., S. Mitchell. Copyright © 1982 by Stephen Mitchell. Reprinted by permission of Random House, Inc.

Rilke, Rainer Maria. "The Blind Man, Paris" from *Selected Works Vol. II.* Copyright © by The Hogarth Press. Reprinted by permission of New Directions Publishing Corporation.

Sachs, Nellie. "Chorus of the Rescued" from O THE CHIMNEYS by Nellie Sachs. Copyright © 1967 by Farrar, Straus & Giroux, Inc. Reprinted by permission of Farrar, Straus & Giroux, Inc.

Schulz, Bruno. Copyright © 1989 by Ella Podstolski-Schulz. Reprinted by permission from Walker and Company.

Seferis, George. Keeley, Edmund and Sherrard, Philip, trans., eds., *George Seferis: Collected Poems, 1924–1955.* Copyright © 1967 by Princeton University Press. Reprinted by permission, "TUESDAY".

Seifert, Jaroslav. From *The Selected Poetry of Jaroslav Seifert* translated by Ewald Osers. Copyright 1986. Reprinted by permission of DILIA.

Selvon, Samuel. From "Come Back to Grenada," by Samuel Selvon, *Foreday Morning: Selected Prose 1946–1986.* Copyright 1989. Reprinted by permission of the author.

Tolstaya, Tatiana. From ON THE GOLDEN PORCH by Tatiana Tolstaya, trans., A. Bouis. Copyright © 1989 by Tatiana Tolstaya. Reprinted by permission of Alfred A. Knopf, Inc.

Voznesensky, Andres. "Foggy Street" from SELECTED POEMS OF ANDRES VOZNESENSKY, translated by Anselm Hollo. Copyright © 1964 by Grove Press, Inc. Used by permission of Grove Press, Inc.

Woolf, Virginia. "The Mark on the Wall" from *A Haunted House and Other Stories* by Virginia Woolf, copyright 1944 and renewed 1972 by Harcourt Brace Jovanovich, Inc., reprinted by permission of the publisher.

Yeats, William Butler. Reprinted with permission of Macmillan Publishing Company from THE POEMS OF W. B. YEATS: A NEW EDITION, edited by Richard J. Finneran. Copyright 1924 by Macmillan Publishing Company, renewed 1952 by Bertha Georgie Yeats.

LATIN AMERICA

Allende, Isabel. "Phantom Palace" from *The Stories of Eva Luna* by Isabel Allende. Copyright 1989 Isabel Allende. Reprinted with the permission of Lester & Orpen Dennys Publishers Ltd. c/o Key Porter Books Limited.

Allende, Isabel. Reprinted with the permission of Atheneum Publishers, an imprint of Macmillan Publishing Company, from THE STORIES OF EVA LUNA by Isabel Allende, translated from the Spanish by Margaret Sayers Peck Copyright © 1989 by Isabel Allende. English translation copyright © 1991 by Macmillan Publishing Company.

Argueta, Manlio. From CUZCATLAN by Manlio Argueta, trans., C. Hansen.

Translation Copyright © 1987 Clark Hansen. Reprinted by permission of Random House, Inc.

Borges, Jorge Luis. "The Intruder", from THE ALEPH AND OTHER STORIES by Jorge Luis Borges, translated by Norman Thomas di Giovanni, Translation copyright © 1968, 1969, 1970 by Emece Editores, S.A. and Norman Thomas di Giovanni. Used by permission of the publisher, Dutton, an imprint of New American Library, a division of Penguin Books USA Inc.

Castellanos, Rosario. Rosario Castellanos' story "Death of the Tiger" copyright © 1960. Translation copyright © 1985 by Alberto Manguel from the anthology OTHER FIRES: Stories from the Women of Latin America pages 207–217, originally published by Lester & Orpen Dennys, Canada and by Clarkson N. Potter in the USA.

Castellanos, Rosario. From OTHER FIRES: SHORT FICTION BY LATIN AMERICAN WOMEN edited by Alberto Manguel. Translation copyright © 1986 by Alberto Manguel. Reprinted by permission of Clarkson N. Potter, Inc., a division of Crown Publishers, Inc.

Césaire, Aimé. From *Aime Cesaire; Collected Poetry*, translated and edited by Clayton Eshleman and Annette Smith. Copyright © 1983 by The Regents of the University of California. Reprinted by permission of University of California Press.

Césaire, Aimé. "The Wheel," by *Aimé Césaire: Collected Poetry*, translated and edited by Clayton Eshleman and Annette Smith. Copyright © 1983 by The Regents of the University of California. Reprinted by permission of The University of California Press.

Cortázar, Julio. From END OF THE GAME AND OTHER STORIES by Julio Cortazar, trans., P. Blackburn. Copyright © 1963, 1967 by Random House, Inc. Reprinted by permission of Pantheon Books, a Division of Random House, Inc.

de Andrade Drummon. From TRAVELLING IN THE FAMILY: SELECTED POEMS by Carlos Drummond De Andrade. Copyright © 1986 by Carlos Drummond de Andrade and Thomas Colchie. Reprinted by permission of Random House, Inc.

Ferré, Rosario. Reprinted from THE YOUNGEST DOLL, by Rosario Ferré, by permission of University of Nebraska Press. Copyright © 1991 by the University of Nebraska Press.

Guillén, Nicolás Reprinted from MAN-MAKING WORDS: SELECTED POEMS OF NICOLAS GUILLEN, transl., annot., with an Introduction by Robert Marquez and David Arthur McMurray (University of Massachusetts Press, 1972), copyright © 1972 by Robert Marquez and David Arthur McMurray.

Guillén, Nicolás. Copyright © 1972 by Robert Marquez. Reprinted by permission of Monthly Review Foundation.

Kincaid, Jamaica. "Girl" from AT THE BOTTOM OF THE RIVER by Jamaica Kincaid. Copyright © 1978, 1983 by Jamaica Kincaid.

Lispector, Clarice. Clarice Lispector: *Soulstorm*. Copyright © 1974 by Clarice Lispector. Reprinted by permission of New Directions Publishing Corporation.

Llosa, Mario Vargas. "On Sunday" from THE CUBS AND OTHER STORIES by Mario Vargas Llosa. Translation copyright © 1979 by Harper & Row Publishers, Inc.

Lovelace, Earl. Copyright Earl Lovelace 1982. Reproduced by permission of Curtis Brown, London, Ltd on behalf of Earl Lovelace.

Márquez, Gabriel García. "Big Mama's Funeral" from COLLECTED STORIES by Gabriel García Márquez. English translation copyright © 1968 by Harper & Row, Publishers, Inc. Reprinted by permission of HarperCollins Publishers.

Naipaul, V. S. From MIGUEL STREET by V. S. Naipaul. Copyright © 1959 by V. S. Naipaul. Used by permission with Viking Penguin, a division of Penguin Books USA Inc, and with permission of Wylie, Aitken & Stone.

Neruda, Pablo. "The United Fruit Co." by Pablo Neruda, translated by Ben Belitt, from FIVE DECADES: POEMS 1925–1970. English translation copyright © 1961 by Ben Belitt. Used by permission of Grove Press, Inc.

Neruda, Pablo. "Poet's Obligation" from *Selected Poems* edited by Nathaniel Tarn, translated by Alastair Reid. Copyright © 1990. Reprinted by permission of Random Century Group, on behalf of the Estate of Pablo Neruda.

Paz, Octavio. Octavio Paz: *Eagle or Sun?* Copyright © 1979 by Octavio Paz and Eliot Weinberger. Reprinted by permission of New Directions Publishing Corporation.

Ramírez, Sergio. "Charles Atlas Also Dies" frim *Stories,* by Sergio Ramírez. English language translation copyright © 1986 by Readers International Inc. Reprinted by permission.

Valenzuela, Luisa. "I'm Your Horse in the Night," by Luisa Valenzuela, from OTHER WEAPONS, translated by Deborah Bon. Reprinted by permission of Ediciones del Norte.

Vallejo, César. From *Modern Poetry from Spain and Latin America.* Copyright 1964. Reprinted by permission of Corinth Books.

Walcott, Derek. "The Spoiler's Return" from COLLECTED POEMS by Derek Walcott. Copyright © 1986 by Derek Walcott.

NORTH AMERICA

Atwood, Margaret. "Dancing Girls." Reprinted by permission of Margaret Atwood, © 1982, O. W. Toad Ltd., available in Bantam books edition.

Atwood, Margaret. From *Dancing Girls and Other Stories* by Margaret Atwood. Used by permission of the Canadian Publishers, McClelland & Stewart, Toronto, Ont.

Atwood, Margaret. "Owl Song" from SELECTED POEMS 1965–1975 by Margaret Atwood. Copyright © 1976 by Margaret Atwood. Reprinted by permission of Houghton Mifflin Company. All rights reserved.

Atwood, Margaret. From *Selected Poems 1966–1984*, copyright © Margaret Atwood 1990. Reprinted by permission of Oxford University Press Canada.

Baldwin, James. "The Rockpile," from GOING TO MEET THE MAN by James Baldwin. Copyright. Used by permission of Doubleday, a division of Bantam Doubleday Dell Publishing Group, Inc.

Bishop, Elizabeth. "The Man-Moth" from THE COMPLETE POEMS 1927–1979 by Elizabeth Bishop. Copyright © 1979, 1983 by Alice Helen Methfessel.

Baraka, Amiri. From *The Music: Reflections on Jazz and Blues*. Published by William Morrow. Used by permission.

Carver, Raymond. From CATHEDRAL by Raymond Carver. Copyright © 1983 by Raymond Carver. Reprinted by permission of Alfred A. Knopf, Inc.

Dove, Rita. Reprinted from *Thomas and Beulah*. By permission of Carnegie Mellon University Press 1986 By Rita Dove.

Forché, Carolyn. "The Colonel" from THE COUNTRY BETWEEN US by Carolyn Forché. Copyright © by Carolyn Forché. Reprinted by permission of HarperCollins Publishers.

Ginsberg, Allen. "A Supermarket in California" from COLLECTED POEMS 1947–1980 by Allen Ginsberg. Copyright © 1955 by Allen Ginsberg. Reprinted by permission of HarperCollins Publishers.

Hughes, Langston. From SELECTED POEMS by Langston Hughes. Copyright 1927 by Alfred A. Knopf, Inc. and renewed 1955 by Langston Hughes. Reprinted by permission of the publisher.

Hughes, Langston. From SELECTED POEMS by Langston Hughes. Copyright © 1959 by Langston Hughes. Reprinted by permission of Alfred A. Knopf, Inc.

Hébert, Anne. ANNE HEBERT. "The Thin Girl," copyright © 1987 from ANNE HEBERT: SELECTED POEMS translated by A. Poulin Jr. Reprinted with the permission of BOA Editions. Ltd., 92 Park Ave. Brockport, NY 14420.

Kingston, Maxine Hong. From CHINA MEN by Maxine Hong Kingston, Copyright © 1980 by Maxine Hong Kingston. Reprinted by permission of Alfred A. Knopf, Inc.

Kogawa, Joy. From OBASAN by Joy Kogawa. Copyright © 1982 by Joy Kogawa. Reprinted by permission of David R. Godine, Publisher.

Layton, Irving. From *Collected Poems of Irving Layton* by Irving Layton. Used by permission of the Canadian Publishers, McClelland & Stewart, Toronto.

O'Connor, Flannery. "The Life You Save May Be Your Own" from *A Good Man is Hard to Find*. Copyright 1955. Reprinted by permission of Harcourt Brace Jovanovich.

O'Connor, Frank. From Frank O'Connor, *Collected Stories*. Copyright 1981. Originally appeared in The New Yorker. Reprinted by permission of Joan Daves Agency.

O'Hara, Frank. From COLLECTED POEMS by Frank O'Hara. Copyright © 1958 by Maureen Granville-Smith, Administratrion of the Estate of Frank O'Hara. Reprinted by permission of Alfred A. Knopf, Inc.

Ondaatje, Michael. Reprinted by permission of Michael Ondaatje. From THE CINNAMON PEELER: Selected Poems, by Michael Ondaatje. Copyright © 1989.

Plath, Sylvia. "Lady Lazarus" by Sylvia Plath. Copyright © 1963 by Ted Hughes. From THE COLLECTED POEMS OF SYLVIA PLATH, edited by Ted Hughes. Reprinted by permission of HarperCollins Publishers and Faber and Faber Ltd.

Plath, Sylvia. "Morning Song" by Sylvia Plath. Copyright © 1961 by Ted Hughes. From THE COLLECTED POEMS OF SYLVIA PLATH, edited by Ted Hughes. Reprinted by permission of HarperCollins Publishers and Faber and Faber Ltd.

Pound, Ezra. Ezra Pound: *Personae*. Copyright 1926 by Ezra Pound. Reprinted by permission of New Directions Publishing Corporation.

Rich, Adrienne. "Diving into the Wreck" is reprinted from THE FACT OF A DOORFRAME, Poems Selected and New, 1950–1984, by Adrienne Rich, by permission of W. W. Norton & Company, Inc. Copyright © 1984 by Adrienne Rich. Copyright © 1975, 1978 by W. W. Norton & Company, Inc. Copyright © 1981 by Adrienne Rich.

Rich, Adrienne. "To a Poet" is reprinted from THE DREAM OF A COMMON LANGUAGE, Poems 1974–1977, by Adrienne Rich, by permission of W. W. Norton & Company, Inc. Copyright © 1978 by W. W. Norton & Company, Inc.

Richler, Mordecai. From *The Street* by Mordecai Richler. Used by permission of the Canadian Publishers, McClelland & Stewart, Toronto.

Richler, Mordecai. Reprinted by permission of International Creative Management, Inc. Copyright © 1975 by Mordecai Richler.

Silko, Leslie Marmon. Copyright © 1981 by Leslie Marmon Silko. Reprinted from STORYTELLER by Leslie Marmon Silko, published by Seaver Books, New York, New York.

Snyder, Gary. Excerpted from AXE HANDLES, copyright © 1983 by Gary Snyder. Published by North Point Press and reprinted by permission.

Stevens, Wallace. From COLLECTED POEMS by Wallace Stevens. Copyright 1942 by Wallace Stevens and renewed 1977 Holly Stevens. Reprinted by permission of Alfred A. Knopf, Inc.

Stevens, Wallace. From COLLECTED POEMS by Wallace Stevens. Copyright 1947 by Wallace Stevens. Reprinted by permission of Alfred A. Knopf, Inc.

Tremblay, Michel. From THE FAT WOMAN NEXT DOOR IS PREGNANT © 1981 Michel Tremblay, Talon Books Ltd., Vancouver, B.C. Canada.

Ulibarri. From MY GRANDMA SMOKED CIGARS AND OTHER STORIES OF TIERRA AMARILLA. Copyright © 1977 by Sabine R. Ulibarri. Reprinted by permission of the author.

Wideman, John Edgar. From FEVER: TWELVE STORIES by John Edgar Wideman. Copyright © 1989 by John Edgar Wideman. Reprinted by permission of Henry Holt and Company, Inc.

Williams, William Carlos. William Carlos Williams: *The Collected Poems of William Carlos Williams, 1939–1962, vol. II.* Copyright 1944 by William Carlos Williams. Reprinted by permission of New Directions Publishing Corporation.

Wilson, August. From JOE TURNER'S COME AND GONE by August Wilson. Copyright © 1988 by August Wilson. Used by permission of New American Library, a division of Penguin Books USA Inc.

Wright, James. "Lying in a Hammock at William Duffy's Farm in Pine Island, Minnesota," by James Wright. Reprinted from *Above the River; The Complete Poems of James Wright* © 1990 by Anne Wright. By permission of University Press of New England.

Wright, James. "To the Muse" by James Wright. Reprinted from *Above the River; The Complete Poems of James Wright* © 1990 by Anne Wright. By permission of University Press of New England.

INDEX

Maghrib. *See* Middle East/Maghrib
Magical realism, 762
Mahabharata, 198
Mahfouz, Naguib, 14, 46–47
Malay-Polynesians, 378
Malaysia, 192, 196; colonization of, 194, 195; national canon of, 199; selected literature from, 359
Malcolm X, 908
Mali, Europe and, 4; selected literature from, 97–99
Malouf, David, 374, 378, 413
Manchuria, 195
Mandela, Nelson, 6
Mandelstam, Osip, 657–658
Manhire, Bill, 379
Man-Moth, The (Bishop), 965–966
Man Passes with a Loaf of Bread on His Shoulder, A (Vallejo), 858
Mansfield, Katherine, 379
Man Who Turned into a Stick (Death), The (Abe), 344–357
Manyōshū, 197
Maori writers, 378–379
Mao Zedong, 195, 197
Mark on the Wall, The (Woolf), 576–582
Márquez, Gabriel García, 761, 762, 807
Martí, José, 760
Martinique, 756; colonization of, 759; literary trends in, 761; selected literature from, 834
Marx, Karl, 480
Matshikiza, Todd, 8
Matshoba, Mtutuzeli, 179
Maupassant, Guy de, 198
May Fourth Movement (1919), 197
Meiji Restoration, 197
Melanesia, 378
Mercedes Benz 220 SL (Ferré), 874–882
Mesopotamia, 81
Mexican Revolution (1910–1917), 758, 760
Mexico, 754, 756; literary trends in, 761; selected literature from, 837–845
Microbus to San Salvador (Argueta), 825–832
Micronesia, colonization of, 378, 911

Middle East/Maghrib, Europe and, 10; geography of, 9; literary trends in, 13–14; *See also individual countries*
Migrants (Dawe), 378, 396
Migrant's Lament—A Song (Qabula), 174–176
Mill, John Stuart, 481
Milosz, Czeslaw, 485, 650
Mimetic representation, art as, 486, 487
Mishima, Yukio, 196, 316
Moderato Cantabile (Duras), 541–546
Modernism, 482, 486, 487–488, 907. *See also* Postmodernism
Modern Love Letter, A (Saadawi), 60–65
Modern Secrets (Lim), 359
Modisane, Bloke, 8
Montale, Eugenio, 622
Morning Song (Plath), 999–1000
Morocco, 14
Mother's Inheritance (Abu-Khalid), 143–144
Mphahlele, Ezekiel, 8
Mr Parker's Valentine (Jolley), 405–413
Multiculturalism, 912
Murray, Les A., 376, 378, 397
Musée des Beaux Arts (Auden), 584
My Country and My People (Pheng), 361–362
My Faithful Mother Tongue (Milosz), 650–651
My First Goose (Babel), 654–657
My Grandma Smoked Cigars (Ulibarrí), 1088–1094
My Old Home (Xün), 201–208

Naema—Whereabouts Unknown (Dib), 15–24
Nagasaki, 484
Naipaul, V. S., 895–896
Nakasa, Nat, 8
Narayan, R. K., 199, 239
Narogin, Murdrooroo. *See* Johnson, Colin
Nasserism, 11
Nationalism, Arab, 10–11, 14; European, 482; Latin American, 761; Soviet, 485–486

South Korea, 192, 196

Soviet Union, The Former, 12; dissolution of, 485–486; literary trends in, 485; political revolution in, 483; selected literature from, 652–672; Stalinist totalitarianism in, 484; United States and, 484, 908

Soviet Writers' Congress (1932), 197

Soweto uprising, 8

Soyinka, Wole, 7, 100

Spain, 484; colonization by, 758; selected literature from, 674–679

Spanish-American War (1898), 906

Spoiler's Return, The (Walcott), 884–888

Spring Storm (Yōko), 337–343

Sri Lanka, 192, 194

Stalin, Joseph, 484, 485, 486

Stalin Epigram, The (Mandelstam), 658–659

Stead, C. K., 379

Stevens, Wallace, 910, 957

St. Lucia, literary trends in, 761; selected literature from, 884–888

Stow, Randolph, 374

Stream-of-consciousness techniques, 487, 761

Suez Canal, 9

Suffrage, 483

Summer My Grandmother Was Supposed to Die, The (Richler), 916–926

Sunday, Sunday (Llosa), 859–873

Sun the First (Elytis), 597–599

Supermarket in California, A (Ginsberg), 984–985

Surrealism, 483, 487, 761

Swamp Dwellers, The (Soyinka), 103–130

Sweden, selected literature from, 681–689

Switzerland, selected literature from, 691–749

Symbolists, 482, 483, 487

Taiwan, 192, 194, 195

Taku, Miki, 336

Tao de Ching, 197

Terra Australis Incognito, 374

Thailand, 192, 196

The Bulletin (newspaper), 377

Themba, Can, 8

Thin Girl, The (Hébert), 915

To a Poet (Rich), 993–994

Toer, Pramoedya Ananta, 196, 288

Tolstaya, Tatyana, 662

Tolstoy, Leo, 482, 486, 488

To Posterity (Brecht), 552–554

Totalitarianism, 484

To the Islands (Stow), 376

To the Muse (Wright), 988–989

Tourmaline (Stow), 374

To Whom It May Concern (Sepamla), 172–173

Trade, international, 194, 195, 756, 758, 908

Tremblay, Michel, 911, 946

Trinidad, 756; literary trends in, 761; selected literature from, 889–903

Tuesday (Seferis), 595–596

Tunisia, 10

Ulibarrí, Sabine, 1088

United Arab Emirates, 9

United Fruit Co., The (Neruda), 793–794

United Kingdom. *See* Great Britain

United States, Canada and, 910; Central America and, 758; colonization by, 194, 378, 759, 911; geography of, 906, 907 (map); Iraq and, 12; literary trends in, 908–910; Korea and, 195–196, 908; selected literature from, 957–1094; Soviet Union and, 484, 908; Vietnam and, 195, 196, 908

Unknown Citizen, The (Auden), 583–584

Updike, John, 909

Uruguay, 756

U.S.S.R. *See* Soviet Union, The Former

Valenzuela, Luisa, 774–775

Vallejo, César, 762, 857

Venezuela, 754

Vietnam, 192, 199; colonization of, 194; national canon of, 199; selected literature from, 364–369; United States and, 195, 196, 908

Visit, The (Durrenmatt), 691–749